GAYELLOW PAGES™
THE NATIONAL EDITION
USA and CANADA
1995-6, #21

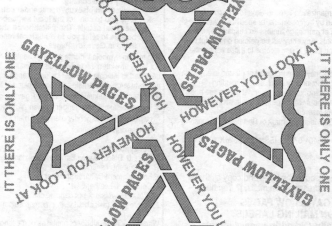

IT THERE IS ONLY ONE

GAYELLOW PAGES™
INFORMING THE LESBIAN, GAY, BISEXUAL & TRANSGENDER COMMUNITY SINCE 1973
Other guides may call themselves the "gay" Yellow Pages,
but there's only one GAYELLOW PAGES

USA/CANADA EDITION
Number 21, 1995/1996

Editor & Publisher
Typesetting & Data Processing
FRANCES GREEN

Advertising Director
Book Sales
HOWARD SMITH

Advertising Sales
MARGE BARTON
(212) 666-6992

Gayellow Pages is published by Renaissance House, PO Box 533 Village Station, New York, NY 10014-0533

Phone (212) 674-0120   Fax (212) 420-1126

No business or organization listed in Gayellow Pages is necessarily owned by homosexuals, or specifically welcomes their participation or patronage, unless so indicated by the appropriate symbols. Any entry will be deleted on receipt of reliable information that it is unwelcome to those concerned.

© 1995   ISBN 1-885404-07-7   ISSN 0363-826X

Planning to go through the book and copy all those names and addresses for a mailing? You need
GAYELLOW PAGES
ON MAILING LABELS
Updated daily. Old addresses eliminated.
New addresses added.
Cost averages 10 cents per label
and we will BUY BACK any that
bounce within sixty days of
your purchase for the price
of a first class stamp!
Send fax number or a self-addressed stamped envelope for details:
PO Box 533 Village Station, New York, NY 10014-0533
(212) 674-0120 Fax (212) 420-1126

To be listed in
GAYELLOW PAGES
please send a stamped self-
addressed envelope to:
Renaissance House, Box 533 Village
Station, New York, NY 10014-0533

The symbols below, preceding the name, indicate a positive response from the business or organization concerned.

★ A not-for-profit enterprise (regardless of tax status) primarily serving lesbian/gay/bisexual/transgender people, although others may be welcome.

☆ A not-for-profit enterprise (regardless of tax status) welcoming though not primarily serving lesbian/gay/bisexual/transgender people.

● A business, wishing to be listed as wholly or partly lesbian/gay/bisexual/transgender owned, welcoming primarily lesbian/gay/bisexual/transgender patronage

○ A business, not wishing to be listed as wholly or partly lesbian/gay/bisexual/transgender owned, but welcoming primarily lesbian/gay/bisexual/transgender patronage

Any entry which does not have one of the above symbols is believed to welcome gay/lesbian/bisexual/transgender patronage, but no direct response had been received at time of publication.

☎ **CALL FOR LOCAL INFORMATION: since businesses open and close, or may change policy of welcoming gay/lesbian/bisexual/transgender patronage, we urge you to contact the local switchboard for the latest details. The switchboard should also be able to refer you to other local resources not listed in Gayellow Pages.**

The margin symbols indicate primary clientele. They do not imply any intention of illegal discrimination. They are designed to indicate the most inclusive range: more narrowly targeted clientele may be indicated in the text.
⚥ gay/lesbian/bisexual/transgender   ⚤ gay/nongay
⚥ lesbian/bisexual/transgender women   ♀ all women
⚥ gay/bisexual/transgender men   ♂ all men
T transsexual/transgender

Other symbols
B Bar *D* Disco; Dance Bar (samesex dancing ok)
R Restaurant *f* snack-style food
E Entertainment/Cabaret/Showbar
C Country *L* Leather/Levi
W Western *d* samesex dancing ok
P Private Club (ask about visitor memberships)

Wheelchair Accessibility of premises or meeting place:
&& Accessible premises and lavatory
(&&) Accessible premises with assistance; accessible lavatory
& Accessible premises; lavatory not known to be accessible
(&) Accessible premises with assistance
(?&) Call ahead for details: places of meetings or activities vary, or special arrangements available.

Paid advertisers' entries appear in bold type. Bold type may also be purchased without display advertising, and, at the publisher's discretion, may be used by way of thanks to information contributors. Comments "in quotes" are made by the entrant: they are not editorial evaluations.

If your business or organization is not yet listed in GAYELLOW PAGES, please send a stamped self-addressed business-size envelope to PO Box 533 Village Station, New York, NY 10014-0533. THERE IS NO CHARGE FOR A BASIC LISTING.

Alice Paul Printers & Mail
Service 216-631-8646 p.373
Alice Reports pub. by Alice B.
Toklas Lesbian & Democratic
Club p.184
Alkire, Britt 303-339-9144
p.193
All About Books 908-247-8744
p.310
All Continent Tours
212-861-5325 p.357
All Destinations Travel, Inc.
714-528-9100 p.158
All God's Children
Community Church
804-499-7096 p.433
All Iowa AIDS Benefit
515-244-0156 p.247
All Points Travel Service
312-525-4700 p.242
All Provincetown Sales &
Rentals 508-487-9000 p.279
All Star Moving & Storage
212-254-2638 p.344
All The Queens Women
718-380-2210 p.349
All Travel 310-312-3368 p.169
All Travel, Inc. 704-853-1111
p.365
All Your Dreams Fulfilled
p.138
All-Ways Travel 203-951-4388
p.200
Allante Personnel Agency
212-229-0600 p.335
Alleghany CA see Grass
Valley p.161
Allegheny College Alumni
Caucus for Gay, Lesbian &
Bisexual Concerns
216-371-0709 p.132
Allegheny College see:
Committee In Support Of Gay,
Lesbian, Bisexual People p.390
Visions—AC p.398
Allegre 608-258-9918 p.443
Allegro 410-837-3906 p.263
ALLEGRO: Alliance of
Lesbian & Gay Religious
Organizations 502-473-1458
p.253
Allen Wells Center for
Pychotherapy & Healing
201-539-0301 p.309
Allentown PA see Lehigh
Valley Area p.389-390
Alley Bar 216-394-9483 p.378
Alley Club 702-333-2808 p.300
ALLGO Pasa pub. by Austin
Latino/a Lesbian & Gay
Organization, Inc p.410
ALLGO see:
Austin Latino/a Lesbian & Gay
Organization, Inc
ALLGO-PASA pub. by ALLGO/
Informe-SIDA p.124
ALLGO/Infor me-SIDA
512-472-2001 p.124
ALLGO/Informe-SIDA
512-472-2001 p.124
The Alliance pub. by Inland
Northwest Gay People's
Association p.237
603-842-4522 p.302
608-348-5596 p.446 p.407
Alliance for Bisexual Lesbian
& Gay Students & Allies
(ABLGSA) 812-231-3724
p.247

Alliance for Bisexual, Lesbian
& Gay Strength, Western
Michigan University
616-387-2134 p.284
Alliance for Justice
507-625-7532 p.286
Alliance For Lesbian & Gay
Religious Organization
(Allegro) 502-581-1829 p.253
Alliance for Sexual Diversity
207-874-6956 p.261
Alliance gaie
Laval-Laurentides
514-334-8218 p.119
Alliance News pub. by
Greater Boston Lesbian & Gay
Political Alliance p.272, 414
Alliance of Cache Valley
(GLA-CV), Gay/Lesbian
801-752-1129 p.423
Alliance of Lesbian & Gay
Organizations of Western
Virginia (ALGO) p.428
Alliance of Lesbian, Gay, &
Bisexual Students, Georgia
State University
404-605-7681 p.232
Alliance of Lesbian-Bi-Gay
Students (ALBGS)
517-353-9795 p.285
Alliance of Massachusetts
Asian Lesbians & Gay Men
p.272
Alliance Ski Club p.309
Allies Blvd Bookstore
Downtown 607-724-8659
p.319
Allies Blvd Bookstore East
607-724-9749 p.319
Alligator News & Books
305-294-4004 p.218
Allison, Judith S., M.Ed, MSH
904-733-3310 p.216
Allison, Lynn, DC
518-884-9395 p.361
Allmen, Rev. Robert J., MS,
M.Div. 516-723-2012 p.356
Allmen, Robert J., MS, M.Div.
516-723-0348 p.332
Alobar Books & Music
407-841-3050 p.223
ALP Horizons—Graphic
Design Services
718-275-8868 p.340
Alpert, Michelle, DO
212-675-9343 p.340
Alpha Omega Chapter-Tri Ess
p.376
Alpha Premium Viatical
Services 800-6060-911 p.304
Alpine Frontrunners
403-234-8973 p.104
ALPS Newsletter pub. by
Associated Lesbians of Puget
Sound p.438
ALPS see:
Associated Lesbians of Puget
Sound
ALSO (Alternative Lifestyles
Support Org), Plymouth
State College 603-535-2796
p.303
Alta Plaza 415-922-1444 p.182
Alta's Bed & Breakfast
907-457-0246 p.151
Altadena CA see Los
Angeles Area p.137, 169
Altamonte Springs FL see
Orlando p.223
Alternate Card Shop
212-645-8966 p.339

Alternate Current p.238
Alternate Trails pub. by
Alaska Women of the
Wilderness p.150
The Alternate Universe pub.
by Alternate Universe
Gaylaxians p.318
Alternate Woman
504-369-6976 p.137
Alternating Currents
513-961-8900 p.371
Alternative 941-277-7002 p.214
p.185
Alternative Approach
Counseling &
Psychotherapy Center
201-736-8785 p.309
Alternative Auto Care
614-294-0580 p.374
Alternative Broadcasting
Service 713-526-3425 p.417
Alternative Connection
503-236-3055 p.385
*Alternative Lifestyles
Directory* 508-999-0078 p.135
615-588-2995 p.405
Alternative Lifestyle Support
Organization (A.L.S.O)
804-855-5212 p.430
Alternative Lifestyles
716-395-5546 p.319
Alternative Lifestyles Union
412-738-2930 p.398
Alternative Modalities pub.
by Alternative
Modalities—GLB PT's p.129
Alternative Modalities—GLB
PT's p.129
Alternative Resources of the
Triad 910-274-2100 p.366
910-748-0031 p.369
Alternative Tours & Travel
504-949-5815 p.258
Alternative Travel
617-246-7480 p.280
Alternative Travels
412-263-2930 p.398
Alternative Video Shop
914-658-3875 p.359
Alternative Youth Club/Tri
State Area 203-975-9139
p.199
Alternatives pub. by National
Lesbian & Gay Journalists
Association p.130
419-522-0044 p.377
518-792-9441 p.361
804-381-6100 p.432
Alternatives Pride & Video
Store 305-463-6006 p.213
Alternatives, College of
William & Mary 804-221-3309
p.433
Altland's Ranch 717-225-4479
p.400
Altman, Norman 212-551-1032
p.342
Altman, Norman D.
203-454-2519 p.203
Alton IL see St Louis Area
p.294, 296
Alton Metro 618-465-8687
p.294
Alumnae/i see:
Allegheny College Alumni
Caucus for Gay, Lesbian &
Bisexual Concerns p.132
Bucknell GALABI p.132
Columbia Bisexual, Gay &
Lesbian Alumni/ae (BiGALA)
p.350

Connecticut College B.G.A.L.A.
(Alumnae/i) p.133
Dartmouth Gay & Lesbian
Alums p.133
Duke GALA p.208
Lesbian & Gay Alumnae/i
Vassar College (LAGA-VC)
p.133
Network of Gay & Lesbian
Alumni/Ae Associations/
NetGALA p.133
Oberlin Lesbian, Gay &
Bisexual Alumni p.133
Principia Gay & Lesbian Alumni
Group p.133, 296
Purdue Lesbian, Bi & Gay
Alumni Group p.133, 321
Queens College (Charlotte, NC)
GALA (Alumni/ae) p.133
Rice University Gay & Lesbian
Alumni Association p.133, 419
University of Southern
California Lambda Alumni
Association p.133
William & Mary GALA (Gay &
Lesbian Alumni/ae) p.133
Yale GALA (Alumnae/i) p.133
Yale GALA/DC p.133, 208
Always On Sunday
201-783-7699 p.309
Always Your Choice
212-677-1777 p.325
Alyson Publications
617-542-5679 p.139
Am Chofshi 207-833-6004
p.259
Am Segulah 800-734-8524
p.200
Am Tikva 617-493-3105 p.273
Am-Vets Club 406-728-3137
p.297
Amarillo Lesbian/Gay Alliance
806-373-5725 p.410
Amazon Autumn 908-354-9052
p.127
Amazon Bookstore
612-338-6560 p.287
Amazon Country, WXPN-FM
(88.5) 215-898-6677 p.392
Amazon Earthworks
503-392-3900 p.146
Amazon Movers 212-343-9415
p.344
Ambiance Bed & Breakfast
613-563-0421 p.114
Ambush 804-498-4301 p.432
AMbush Magazine
504-522-8049 p.253, 258
Ambush/Melody Club
904-376-3772 p.215
Amelia Earhart p.302
American Baptists Concerned
510-465-8652 p.140
American Bear 502-894-8573
p.138
American Civil Liberties
Union chapters USA
212-944-9800 p.128
AR State/County Resources
501-374-2660 p.155
CA State/County Resources
213-977-9500 p.158
CA State/County Resources
415-621-2488 p.157
FL Fort Lauderdale
305-920-7715 p.214
FL Miami Area 305-576-2336
p.221
FL Tampa Bay Area
813-221-1423 p.228

CT Hartford 203-296-9229 p.200
DC Washington Area 202-387-4516 p.209
DC Washington Area 202-861-0017 p.140
FL Fort Lauderdale 305-463-4528 p.214
FL Palm Beach Area 305-744-1591 p.225
FL Tampa Bay Area 813-238-2868 p.229
GA Atlanta 404-409-0203 p.232
HI Oahu 808-536-5536 p.236
IN Fort Wayne 219-484-6492 p.245
IN Indianapolis p.246
KY Louisville 502-473-1458 p.253
LA Baton Rouge 504-383-6010 p.254
MA Boston Area 617-423-9558 p.273
MB Winnipeg 204-284-5208 p.110
MD Baltimore Area 410-325-1519 p.264
ME Portland p.262
MI Detroit 313-563-0892 p.283
MI Grand Rapids 616-454-9779 p.284
MI Lansing p.285
MN Minneapolis/St Paul Area 612-827-3103 p.290
MO St Louis Area 314-997-9897 p.296
NC Triangle Area 919-836-8793 p.368
NJ Maplewood 201-761-7321 p.309
NJ New Brunswick 908-254-7942 p.310
NM State/County Resources 505-898-3343 p.314
NY Albany & Capital Area 518-436-8546 p.319
NY Buffalo 716-833-8995 p.320
NY New York City Area 212-627-6488 p.356
NY New York City Area 212-818-1309 p.356
NY New York City Area 516-781-6225 p.356
NY New York City Area 718-769-3447 p.356
NY State/County Resources 516-781-5942 p.317
NY Utica 315-738-0599 p.362
OH Cincinnati 513-557-2111 p.371
OH Cleveland 216-531-4469 p.374
OH Dayton 513-277-7706 p.376
OH Toledo 419-242-9057 p.378
ON London 519-686-7709 p.114
ON Ottawa/Hull Area 613-746-7279 p.102, 115
ON Toronto 416-763-2300 p.117
OR Portland 503-295-4868 p.385
OR Salem 503-363-0006 p.386
PA Harrisburg p.389
PA Philadelphia Area 215-546-2093 p.396
PA Pittsburgh Area 412-362-4334 p.398
PA State/County Resources 717-829-1341 p.387

QC Montréal 514-937-6576 p.120
RI Providence 401-727-2657 p.402
SK Regina 306-569-3666 p.121
SK Saskatoon 306-382-3669 p.121
TX Austin 512-467-7908 p.411
TX Dallas/Fort Worth Area 214-521-5342 p.415
TX Dallas/Fort Worth Area 817-283-8588 p.415
TX Houston Area 713-880-2872 p.419
VA Arlington 703-912-1662 p.428
VA Norfolk 804-625-5337 p.430
VT Burlington 802-863-1377 p.426
WA Seattle 206-325-7314 p.439
WI Milwaukee 414-444-7177 p.446
Dignity Journal pub. by Dignity Canada Dignité p.102, 115
Dignity Prison Ministry p.132
Dignity/Integrity (Catholic/ Episcopalian) chapters
AZ Phoenix 602-258-2556 p.154
NY Poughkeepsie/Kingston Area 914-724-3209 p.359
NY Rochester Area 716-262-2170 p.360
OK Oklahoma City 405-636-4388 p.379
OK Tulsa 918-298-4648 p.380
WI Madison 608-836-8886 p.444
Dignity/Lafayette p.246
Dignity/Nassau News pub. by Dignity/Nassau p.356
Dignity/USA Journal pub. by Dignity USA p.140
Dillard OR see Roseburg p.125, 385
Dillon CO see Keystone p.196
Dimensions 806-797-9647 p.409, 420
Dimmick Inn 717-296-4021 p.390
Dinah p.369
Dincher, Kevin P., MA, MFCC 716-881-2278 p.320
Diogenes pub. by Boston Professional Alliance, Inc. p.272
Diplomat Health Club 419-255-3700 p.378 616-452-3754 p.284
Direct Aid 612-429-9792 p.287
The Directory Long Beach 310-434-7129 p.163
Directory of Gay & Lesbian Community Publications in the United States & Canada p.135
Directory of Lesbian & Gay Scholarship pub. by Center for Lesbian & Gay Studies p.132, 350
DiRocco's Tall Pines Inn 508-649-9134 p.280
Dirty 718-858-4303 p.353
Dirty Duck Tavern 503-224-8446 p.383
Disability Publications see:
Able-Together p.138
Disability Rag p.130, 252
The Disability Rag & Resource p.136
Dykes, Disability & Stuff p.130, 137

Hikan: The Capable Woman p.274
Hikané: The Capable Woman p.130, 137
It's Okay! p.101
Disability Rag p.130, 252
The Disability Rag & Resource p.136
Disability see:
Disability Rag p.130, 252
Dykes, Disability & Stuff p.130
Hikan: The Capable Woman p.274
Hikané: The Capable Woman p.130
Disabled In Action of Metropolitan New York p.346
Education in a Disabled Gay Environment, Inc (E.D.G.E.) p.346
Rainbow Bridge Organization p.241
Westchester Disabled On The Move p.346
Disabled In Action of Metropolitan New York 718-261-3737 p.346
Disciples of Christ chapters
IN Indianapolis 317-353-1491 p.246
Disciples of Christ see:
Religious Organizations & Publications
Disco Book Store 614-274-9716 p.374
Discovery 210-722-9032 p.420
Discovery III 501-664-4784 p.157
Discreet Boutique 204-947-1307 p.110
Discreet Photographers 718-381-8304 p.326
Distributors/Wholesalers p.101, 127
District 305-764-1111 p.213
District 202 612-871-5559 p.289
District Council 37 Lesbian & Gay Issues Committee 212-815-7575 p.346
Ditson's Pink Triangle News 716-845-6971 p.320
Diva's 306-665-0100 p.121
Divas 418-693-1179 p.118
Diversionary Theatre 619-574-1060 p.180
Diversions Video Bar & Grill 616-451-3800 p.283
Diversions Video Bar & Grill ◆ advertisement p.283
Diversity 208-336-3870 p.236 817-766-2264 p.422
Diversity of Pride 215-351-5315 p.395
Divine Lake Resort 705-385-1212 p.115
Division Of AIDS Services, Human Resources Administration 212-645-7070 p.326
Dix Hills Travel 516-673-6333 p.357
Dixie Belle Complexx 816-471-2424 p.293
Dixie Erotic Book & Video 305-661-5888 p.220
Dixmont ME see Bangor p.259
DJ Mark Productions 210-805-0500 p.421
DJ's 512-476-3611 p.410 817-927-7321 p.412

Dmitri's Guesthouse 619-238-5547 p.177
DNCB Now! 415-954-8896 p.181
Doanleigh Wallagh Inn 816-753-2667 p.292
Doc's Yacht Kare Enterprise 908-324-2177 p.311
Dock 513-241-5623 p.371
Dodds Book Shop 310-438-9948 p.162
Doe Farm p.446
Does Your Mother Know 415-864-3160 p.184
Dog's Best Friend 718-335-0110 p.351
Dog's Place / Dog Grooming 914-636-2020 p.351
Dog-O-Rama 212-353-9186 p.351
Dolce, Tony 201-963-8196 p.342
Doll & Penny's Cafe 604-685-3417 p.108
Dolores Park Inn 415-621-0482 p.181
Dolores Street Baptist Church 415-861-2641 p.186
Dolphin 310-318-3339 p.166
Dolphin Democratic Club 305-763-1530 p.214
Dolphin Travel 305-566-6539 p.214
Domestic Violence see:
Sanctuary for Families p.347
Don Ling's Removal Tattoos 800-247-6817 p.146
Don Ling's Removal Tattoos ◆ advertisement p.146
Don Williams Plumbing & Builder 602-242-5682 p.153
Don't Panic! 212-989-7888 p.332 305-531-7223 p.220 310-652-3668 p.167 415-553-8989 p.183 508-487-1280 p.279
Don't Panic! Designs 310-915-1682 p.144
Don't Tell Mama 212-757-0788 p.328
Donahue & Grolman 617-859-8966 p.272
Donnie's Cafe 75 518-436-0378 p.318
Donnie's Place 412-682-9869 p.396
Donnie's/Cocktails 305-294-5620 p.218
Doorways 314-454-9599 p.294
Doran, Linda, MA, RN, CS 203-536-8804 p.200
Dorchester Gay & Lesbian Alliance (GALA) 617-825-3737 p.272
Dorchester MA see Boston Area p.272-273
Dotson, Samuel, MD 202-543-2664 p.207
Dottie's True Blue Cafe 415-885-2767 p.182
Double Header 206-464-9918 p.436
Double Header Bar & Dance Club 610-277-1070 p.391
Douglas County AIDS Council 503-440-2761 p.385
Douglas County Gay Archives 503-679-9703 p.125, 385
Douglas Dunes Resort 616-857-1401 p.285

Florida AIDS Legal Defense & Education Fund 904-877-6048 p.209

Florida Atlantic University see: Lambda United/LGBA p.212

Florida Gold Coast Chapter GLB Vets 305-782-1095 p.214

Florida HIV/AIDS Hotline 800-FLA-AIDS p.209

Florida International University see: NOW FIU Chapter p.221 Stonewall Student Union p.222

Florida Liberty Alliance 904-877-9303 p.210

Florida Roundup 305-463-0040 p.209

Florida State University see: Lesbian/Gay/Bisexual Student Union, Florida State University p.226

Florida Sunshine Athletic Association 305-754-1923 p.210

Florida Travel Connection Magazine 813-288-0121 p.210

Florists (see also Gardening) p.153, 162, 194, 221, 225, 228, 261, 282, 295, 311, 314, 338, 393, 432

Flowers & Flowers 305-534-1633 p.221

Flowers By Martha Lee 505-256-3518 p.314

Floyd's 310-433-9251 p.162

Fluorescent Igloo 713-524-7342 p.418

Flushing Gays & Lesbians in Recovery 212-683-3900 p.325

Flushing NY see New York City Area p.325, 342-343, 347-350, 356

Fly Creek NY see Cooperstown p.320

Focus 617-876-4488 p.271

Focused Counseling Services, Inc. 609-228-8910 p.306

FocusPoint 612-874-9000 p.289

Fodor's Travel 206-328-5385 p.439

Foggy City Dancers 415-905-4546 p.185

Foggy City Newsletter pub. by Foggy City Dancers p.185

Folderol II 914-726-3822 p.330

Foley, Brian E., Public Accountant 610-434-9852 p.389

Foley, Lyn, MSW, ACSW 603-224-5600 p.302

Folly Beach SC see Charleston p.403

Folsom Gulch 415-495-6402 p.183

Fondation d'Aide Directe-SIDA p.119

Fontana, Larry, MD 212-420-1303 p.340

Fontanella, Robert, CSW 212-741-2739 p.334

Fonville, T. W., MD 212-674-1020 p.340

Food & Friends 202-488-8278 p.205

Food Bar 212-243-2020 p.328

Food For Thought Books 413-253-5432 p.268

Food Outreach, Inc. 314-367-4461 p.294

Food Specialties, Catering (see also Party/Event Services) p.114, 127, 194, 257, 261, 268, 314, 338, 437

Foodery 613-728-3918 p.114

Foosh Productions, Inc. 512-444-9300 p.127

Foot Fraternity 216-449-4114 p.132

FootLoose 504-524-7654 p.256

Footloose Cafe 303-722-3430 p.193

Footnotes pub. by Footprints In Time p.389

Footprints In Time 610-376-1510 p.389

For A Song 603-436-0583 p.303

Forbidden Fruit 512-478-8358 p.145, 410

Fordham University see: Lesbian & Gay Support Group, Fordham University p.349

Foreign Languages see: Lesbian & Gay Foreign Language Club p.349

Foremost Travel 312-346-6643 p.242

Forest Hill MD see Baltimore Area p.264

Forest Hills NY see New York City Area p.330, 335

Forest Park IL see Chicago p.240

Forestville CA see Russian River p.175

Forever Green 516-226-9357 p.327

Forex Travel 617-482-2900 p.273

Fort Collins Travel 970-482-5555 p.196

Fort Hood Area Chapter GLACT 512-932-2718 p.420

Fort Lauderdale Frontrunners 305-566-8413 p.214

Fort Video & News 910-868-9905 p.365

Fort Wayne Gay/Lesbian Resource Center & Archives 219-744-1199 p.245

Fort Worth TX see Dallas/Fort Worth Area p.412-415

Forum For Equality p.258

Forumo pub. by Ligo de Samseksamaj Geesperantistoj (LSG) p.101

Forward Foundation 210-791-0606 p.420

The Forward Look pub. by Joy of Life Metropolitan Community Church p.242

Forward March pub. by Florida Gold Coast Chapter GLB Vets p.214

Foster's 602-263-8313 p.152

Fotografia 212-966-0498 p.326

Fotografia Graphics 212-966-0498 p.340

Foundry 513-461-5200 p.376

The Fountain 305-791-6929 p.214

Fountain City Yacht Club 706-322-8682 p.232

Fountain Square News 513-421-4049 p.371

Fountainview News 713-781-7793 p.418

Four Bays 508-487-0859 p.276

Four Bays Guest House 508-487-0859 p.276

Four Seasons / The Out Back 504-832-0659 p.256

Four Sixty Three Beacon Street Guest House 617-536-1302 p.269

Four Sixty Three Beacon Street Guest House ◆ advertisement p.269

Four Star Video Heaven 608-255-1994 p.444

Fourteen Fifty East/Flash 708-397-4564 p.243

Fourteen Twelve Thalia: A Bed & Breakfast 504-522-0453 p.255

Fourteen Twelve Thalia: A Bed & Breakfast ◆ advertisement p.255

Fourth Street Bookmart 813-821-8824 p.228

Fourth Tuesday 404-662-4353 p.231

Fox 913-384-0369 p.293

Fox & The Hound Bed & Breakfast of New Hope 215-862-5082 p.390

Fox & The Hound Bed & Breakfast of New Hope ◆ advertisement p.391

Fox Studio p.145

Fox Tales pub. by Fox Valley Gay Association p.241

Fox Valley AIDS Project 414-733-2068 p.442

Fox Valley Gay Association 708-392-6882 p.241

Fox's Den 810-787-8821 p.283

Foxes Lounge 505-255-3060 p.314

FPT The Preferred Way in Gay Travel 800-624-0207 p.141, 307

FPT The Preferred Way in Gay Travel ◆ advertisement p.141

Fraas, Linda E. 603-225-0477 p.302

Frameline 415-7 03-8650 p.127 415-703-8650 p.127

Framingham MA see p.273-274

Framingham Regional Alliance of Gay & Lesbian Youth (FRAGLY) 508-655-7183 p.274

Framingham State College GLAF (Gays, Lesbians & Friends) p.273

Framingham State College see: Framingham State College GLAF (Gays, Lesbians & Friends) p.273

Fran's Place 508-595-8961 p.274

Franchino, Charles A., DC 212-673-4331 p.340

Franco's Norma Jean Bar 408-633-2090 p.170

Frank's 318-235-9217 p.254

Frank's Place 203-443-8883 p.201

Frankel Travel 212-714-1700 p.357

Frankel, Bryan, Esq 516-581-1111 p.342

Frankel, Susan I., CSW, BCD 212-866-5756 p.334

Franklin Park IL see Chicago p.240

Franklin Park NJ see New Brunswick p.310

Franklin Sq NY see New York City Area p.351

Frankly Scarlett/Choo Choo's Pub 904-664-2966 p.215

Frankly Scarlett/Choo Choo's Pub ◆ advertisement p.215

Fraser, Gregory 416-924-0600 p.117

Frat House 714-373-FRAT p.170

Fraternity 416-340-1950 p.117

Fraternity House 202-223-4917 p.206

Freddy's Feed & Read 406-549-2127 p.297

Fredericksburg Area HIV/AIDS Support Services, Inc. 703-371-7532 p.429

Frederickson & Associates 612-646-8373 p.288

Fredericton Lesbians & Gays (FLAG) 506-457-2156 p.111

Frederiksted, St Croix VI see St Croix p.427

The Free Press 614-221-2792 p.375

Free State Justice Campaign 410-837-7282 p.262

Freedom Alliance of UMBC 410-455-1901 p.264

Freedom Company 602-252-9493 p.153

Freedom Day Committee 206-292-1035 p.438

Freedom Socialist Newspaper 206-722-2453 p.136

Freely Speaking Toastmasters 206-937-9369 p.438

Freeport NY see New York City Area p.333, 347

Freewheelers Bicycle Shop & Personal Fitness Center 716-473-3724 p.360

Fremont CA see East Bay Area p.160

Fremont Men 510-713-2455 p.160

Fremont Place Book Company 206-547-5970 p.436

Fremont Public Association 206-634-2222 p.436

French Quarter 415-252-7769 p.182 907-276-9049 p.150

French Quarter Reservation Service 504-523-1426 p.255

French see: Cercle français lesgay p.348

Frenchmen 504-948-2166 p.255

Frenchy's Sex Shop 415-776-5940 p.183

Frequency Feminist 416-595-1477 p.116

Fresh Fruit 612-341-3144 p.287

Fresh Fruit Records 800-IS-FRUIT p.134

Fresh Fruit Records ◆ advertisement p.135

Fresh Men p.138

Fresh Pond Travel of Sudbury 508-443-5141 p.273

Fresh Start Bed & Breakfast 902-453-6616 p.112

frican also see Black

GPA News pub. by National Gay Pilots' Association p.130
Grabowski, Robert, RCSW, ACSW 718-261-1346 p.335
Grace and Lace Letter 601-982-2276 p.133, 290
Grace Covenant Fellowship 610-740-0247 p.390
Grace Fellowship 504-944-9836 p.258
Grace Gospel Chapel 206-784-8495 p.439
Graduate 520-622-9233 p.154
Graduate Gay & Lesbian Alliance 716-645-3063 p.320
Graffiti 304-342-4412 p.441
Graffiti Online 404-972-9709 p.126
Graham, Lorna 212-749-6043 p.334
Graham, Sally, Ph.D. 212-807-0543 p.332, 334
Graham, Sharon 315-445-9633 p.361
Gram's Place Bed/Breakfast Guesthouse 813-221-0596 p.226
Grand American Restaurant & Bar 414-731-0164 p.442
Grand Canyon Men's Chorale 602-340-7640 p.153
Grand Central 909-889-5204 p.177
Grand Central Stationery 305-467-2998 p.214
Grand Opening! 617-731-2626 p.271
Grand Palace 304-342-9532 p.441
Grand Rapids AIDS Resource Center 616-459-9177 p.283
Grandis, Edward S., Esq 202-234-8950 p.207
Granite City IL **see St Louis Area** p.294
Granny's Place 313-699-8862 p.281
Granville, Bernard 212-580-9724 p.342
Granville, Bernard ◆ advertisement p.342
Grapevine pub. by Camp Sister Spirit p.123, 290, 356
Grapevine Books 702-786-4869 p.300
Graphic Arts Studio 718-624-4680 p.340
Graphic Impressions 201-484-6116 p.135, 310
Graphics A La Carte 412-243-3341 p.397
Grapik Art Productions p.184
Grass Roots 503-754-7668 p.381
Grayscale Graphics & Design 201-864-3539 p.352
Great American Yankee Freedom Band of Los Angeles 213-734-3472 p.169
Great Expectations Travel Services 716-244-8430 p.360
Great Lakes Bears 312-509-5135 p.241
Great Lakes Counseling 216-992-5995 p.370
Great Lakes Harley Riders p.442
Great Lakes Men's Chorus 810-399-SING p.283
Great Neck NY **see New York City Area** p.357

Great Northern Books 360-733-1650 p.433
Great Outdoors chapters AZ Tucson 520-325-7607 p.155
CA Long Beach p.163
CA Los Angeles Area 818-763-4496 p.168
CA Los Angeles Area p.168
CA San Bernardino/Riverside/ Pomona Area 909-888-7993 p.177
CA San Diego Area 619-557-0168 p.180
FL Miami Area 305-667-2222 p.221
Great Outdoors Santa Barbara 805-564-3646 p.189
Great Ways Travel, Inc. 419-536-8000 p.378
Greater Boston Business Council 617-236-GBBC p.272
Greater Boston Lesbian & Gay Political Alliance 617-338-4297 p.272
Greater Cincinnati AIDS Consortium 513-558-4259 p.371
Greater Cincinnati Gay/ Lesbian Center 513-651-0040 p.371
Greater Cincinnati Gay/ Lesbian Coalition 513-557-2904 p.371
Greater Cincinnati Sports Association 513-751-2513 p.371
Greater Halifax Pride Guide p.112
Greater Kansas City Gay & Lesbian Outdoor Club p.293
Greater Milwaukee Maritime Association 414-475-6800 p.446
Greater New York Gender Alliance 212-765-3561 p.350
Greater Philadelphia Lavender Pages 215-247-1018 p.395
Greater Philadelphia Professional Network (GPPN) 215-336-9676 p.394
Greater Roundtable of Women Professionals 610-789-4938 p.394
Greater San Diego Business Association 619-296-4543 p.179
Greater Santa Barbara Community Association 805-568-3995 p.189
Greater Seattle Business Association 206-443-GSBA p.438
Greater Springfield Gay Nudists p.268
Greater Utica Lambda Fellowship p.362
Greek see: Petalouthas p.347
Greeley Bears 970-352-3399 p.196
Greeley Gay, Lesbian, & Bisexual Alliance (GOLBA) 970-351-2869 p.196
Green & Yellow TV 800-821-5456 p.287
Green Bay WI **see Fox Valley** p.442
Green Door 610-865-5855 p.389 915-858-3174 p.416

Green Gables Bed & Breakfast 503-265-9141 p.382
Green Gables Bookstore 503-265-9141 p.382
Green Lantern 202-638-5133 p.206
Green Rose B&B 604-537-9927 p.106
Green Walrus Screenworks 702-242-0220 p.299
Green's Market & Deli 303-778-8117 p.194
Greenbaum, Richard 212-799-2983 p.343
Greenberg, Elizabeth, DC 212-627-2660 p.340
Greenberg, Michael C., Esq. 215-238-9518 p.394
Greenbush 608-257-BUSH p.443
Greene, Peter, MD, PC 202-399-8135 p.207
Greenhope Farm 802-533-7772 p.426
Greenport NY **see New York City Area** p.325
Greensburg PA **see Pittsburgh Area** p.396
Greenspan, Bernard, DO, PA 201-796-9336 p.307
Greenspon, Scheff & Washington, PC 313-963-1921 p.282
Greenville OH **see Dayton** p.376
Greenwell, Susan 904-434-8511 p.225
The Greenwich Village Press 718-768-2048 p.353
Greenwood Hollow Ridge Bed & Breakfast 501-253-5283 p.156
Greenwood IN **see Indianapolis** p.246
Greetings 212-242-0424 p.340
Greetings From Key West 305-294-1733 p.146, 219
Greg's Ball Room 408-286-4388 p.187
Grenadier Motor Inn 207-646-3432 p.260
Grey Fox Pub 314-772-2150 p.294
Grey Oaks Bed & Breakfast 717-829-7097 p.400
Grey-Knowles Flowers Ltd. 212-LE2-7661 p.338
Greybeard's of London 202-296-0502 p.209
Grid 216-623-0113 p.372
Grid ◆ advertisement p.372
Griffin, David Lindsey, CSW, CAC 212-582-1881 p.334
Griffins MC p.203
Grim's Manor Bed & Breakfast 610-683-7089 p.389
Grinnell see: Stonewall Resource Center p.249
Grooming Services p.159, 192, 194, 221, 225, 257, 259, 274, 318, 340, 360, 384, 390, 397, 420, 422-423, 428, 430, 437
Ground Zero 302-227-8041 p.204 719-635-6086 p.191
Ground Zero Newsletter pub. by Ground Zero, Inc p.191
Group p.195
Groupe Gaie de L'Université Laval 514-649-9478 p.120

GROW, A Community Service 910-675-9222 p.368
Growing American Youth 314-533-5322 p.296
Growler Newsletter pub. by MnBear p.288
Grownups 215-862-9304 p.391
Grunberg Haus Bed & Breakfast 802-244-7726 p.427
Grunberg, Ricki D. 608-275-7003 p.444
Grundmann, Maryann, PhD, LCSW 303-278-4392 p.193
Grundmann, Maryann, PhD, LMSW 303-278-4392 p.196
Gualala Books 707-884-4255 p.161
GUARD (Gays United To Attack Repression & Discrimination) 305-570-5791 p.214
Guelph Gay, Lesbian & Bisexual Equality 519-836-4550 p.113
Guerneville CA **see Russian River** p.135, 174-175
Guest House 412-321-4427 p.396
Guest House Deja Vu 800-867-7316 p.255
Guest House Deja Vu ◆ advertisement p.256
Guesthouse 304-897-5707 p.441
The Guide 617-266-8557 p.135
Guide Gai du Quebec 514-523-9463 p.118
Guild House Campus Ministry 313-662-5189 p.281
Gulf Coast Community News pub. by West Florida Pride Committee p.225
Gulf Gayzette pub. by Greater Utica Lambda Fellowship p.362
Gulfport FL **see Tampa Bay Area** p.227
Gull Walk Inn 508-487-9027 p.276
Gulliver's Travel 908-636-1120 p.313
Gunderson Travel, Inc. 310-657-3944 p.170
Guston, Debra E. 201-447-6660 p.307
Gutierrez, Frank, M.D. 305-771-2120 p.214
Guttman Breast Diagnostic Institute 212-463-8733 p.340
Guys 'n' Dolls Hair Stylists & Tanning Salon 904-457-6092 p.225
Guys Magazine 201-836-9177 p.138
GW Miami Beach 305-534-4763 p.220
GYM see: Gay Youth Milwaukee
Gynergy Books 902-566-5750 p.102
H 303-722-5965 p.195
H. E. Entertainment 219-432-7027 p.134
H. G. Rooster's 813-346-3000 p.226
H.E.L.P. 201-305-7638 p.313
H.E.R.O.E.S. 515-280-6422 p.248
H.G. Roosters 407-832-9119 p.224
H.I.T. Crowd p.440

Islandia NY see New York City Area p.340, 342
Islip NY see New York City Area p.342
ISMIR Events Calendar pub. by International Sexual Minorities Information Resource p.135
Isn't That Special 405-690-5294 p.379
ISO Club 800-IN-SO-JO p.128
ISR Court de Dallas 214-521-8446 p.414
Israel, Laurie, Esq 617-277-3774 p.272
istvan, john emery, ACSW, CISW 203-268-8858 p.202
It's 'Bout Time 520-882-3053 p.154
It's My Pleasure 503-236-0505 p.384
It's Okay! p.101
It's Your Pleasure 616-639-7348 p.285
Italia Bella/Club 5878 703-532-5878 p.428
Ithaca Gay Lesbian Activities Board (IGLAB) p.322
Ithaca Lesbian, Gay & Bisexual Task Force 607-277-4614 p.322
IUPUI Advocate 317-274-8206 p.246
IUSB Women's Center 219-237-4494 p.247
Ivy House Bed & Breakfast 413-549-7554 p.267
Ivy's Resaurant & Bar 415-626-3930 p.182
IXE (Indiana Crossdressers Society) 317-876-5635 p.244
IYG Reachout pub. by Indianapolis Youth Group p.246
J&R Book & Video 305-262-6570 p.221
J-Wag's Lounge 901-725-1909 p.406
J. August's Cafe 908-545-4646 p.310
J. Bette Travel 718-241-3872 p.357
J. Critchley Massage Studio 508-487-3684 p.279
J. Miles Clothing 305-462-2710 p.213
J.B.'s Bar & Grill 519-258-5706 p.118
J.R. Brian's 310-371-7859 p.166
J.R.'s Bar & Grill 713-521-2519 p.417
Jack's Construction Site 601-362-3108 p.291
Jackhammer 415-252-0290 p.182
Jacks Of Color 212-222-9794 p.348
Jackson GALA 307-733-5349 p.448
Jackson Heights NY see New York City Area p.326, 330, 335, 338, 342, 349
Jacksonville Area Sexual Minority Youth Network (JASMYN) 904-565-1668 p.217
Jacksonville Beach FL see Jacksonville p.216-217
Jacksonville NY see Ithaca p.321
Jacobs, Mindy, Ph.D. 202-543-0303 p.206

Jacobson & Macaulay 608-255-5001 p.444
Jacques 617-426-8902 p.270
Jade & Queenie 800-352-1058 p.134
Jade Pagoda 206-322-5900 p.436
Jaded Entertainment Emporium 601-371-0478 p.291
Jag Hair 703-256-8383 p.428
Jaguar 415-863-4777 p.143, 183
Jaguar
♦ advertisement p.183
Jamaica NY see New York City Area p.325-326
Jamaica Plain MA see Boston Area p.131, 138, 270, 273
Jamelos Properties 505-988-3399 p.316
James Madison University see:
Harmony p.429
James White Review 612-339-8317 p.138
James, Frederick, DC 212-473-2273 p.340
Jamie's Sports Bar 816-471-2080 p.293
Jammin' Jo's 916-457-7888 p.175
Jane Addams Book Shop 217-356-2555 p.238
Janes Veterinary Clinic 202-543-6699 p.209
Jarratt, Kent D., ACSW 212-674-7370 p.334, 342
JASMYN see:
Jacksonville Area Sexual Minority Youth Network
Java Java Cafe 713-880-5282 p.417
Java's/Za's 414-435-5476 p.442
Jay Critchley/Massage Studio 508-487-3684 p.279
Jay's B & B 517-496-2498 p.285
Jazi's 412-323-2721 p.396
JC's Fun One Lounge 602-939-0528 p.152
JCHRA Newsletter pub. by Josephine County Human Rights Alliance p.382
Jean, Paula J., PhD 804-329-3940 p.431
Jefferson Banner pub. by Rogue Valley Parents, Families & Friends of Gays p.381
Jefferson House 305-534-5247 p.219
Jeffery Pub 312-363-8555 p.239
Jehovah's Witnesses see:
Common Bond p.374
Jellybean 503-222-5888 p.384
Jenkins House Bed & Breakfast Inn 508-355-6444 p.269
Jerry & David's Travel 619-233-5199 p.180
Jerry's Adult Bookstore 206-272-4700 p.440
Jersey Pride 908-651-7743 p.304
Jeselsohn, Paul, Esq 212-477-2400 p.343
Jessie's After Dark 513-223-2582 p.376

Jesters 606-252-6510 p.252
Jeunesse Lambda/Lambda Youth 514-528-7535 p.120
Jewel Travel 215-546-8747 p.396
Jewel's 213-734-8849 p.165
Jewelry p.148, 160, 223, 279, 288, 309, 342, 394, 418
Jewelry Etc 407-699-0680 p.223
Jewish Comm Aids Task Force 303-321-3399 p.193
Jewish Gaily Forward pub. by Congregation Sha'ar Zahav p.186
Jewish Lesbian Daughters Of Holocast Survivors p.131
Jewish Lesbian Daughters of Holocaust Survivors 608-256-8883 p.132
Jewish see:
Religious Organizations & Publications
Adath Rayoot, Jewish Gays of Central Maryland p.264
Am Chofshi p.259
Am'Segulah p.200
Am Tikva p.273
B'Nai Shalom p.253
Baleboosteh p.382
Bet Mishpachah/Gay & Lesbian Synagogue p.209
Bet Tikvah p.398
Beth Am, The People's Temple p.356
Beth Chayim Chadashim p.169
Beth Rachameem Synagogue p.229
Chevrat 'Or p.173
Chevrei Tikva p.373
Chutzpah p.110
Congregation Berith Sholom p.319
Congregation Bet Haverim p.232
Congregation Beth Ahavah p.396
Congregation Beth El Binah p.415
Congregation Beth Simchat Torah p.356
Congregation Etz Chaim p.222
Congregation Keshet Shalom p.117
Congregation Kol Ami p.169
Congregation Kol Simcha p.171
Congregation Or Chadash p.242
Congregation Sha'ar Zahav p.186
Congregation Tikvah Chadasah p.439
Congregation Yeladim Shel Yisrael p.225
G & L Jewish Group p.376
Jewish Lesbian Daughters of Holocaust Survivors p.132
Jewish Support Group p.246
L'Cha Dodi of the JCRB/AJC p.293
Lesbian & Gay Jews/Shabbat p.368
Mishpachat Alizim p.420
Mishpachat Am p.154
Mishpachat Am Echad p.411
Nayim p.360
New Jersey Lesbian & Gay Havurah p.304
New Jewish Agenda p.238
Rodfei Shalom Fellowship p.214
Simcha p.283
Spinoza p.244

Stephen Wise Free Synagogue - Lesbian & Gay Concerns Group p.356
Tikvat Shalom p.195
World Congress Of Gay & Lesbian Jewish Organizations p.141
Yachad p.180
Yakhdav p.120
Jewish Support Group 317-251-5413 p.246
Jezebel Productions 212-463-0578 p.127
Jiles, Jan 206-627-0214 p.440
Jimmy's 317-638-9039 p.246
JJ's Club Phoenix 216-621-1752 p.372
JJ's Pub 310-837-7443 p.164
JNL Commercial Cleaning 516-462-2643 p.342
JO Clubs see:
Black Jack p.160
Jacks Of Color p.348
LA/OC Jacks p.168, 171
T.O.M. p.360
Vancouver Jacks p.108
Jo Dee's 414-634-9804 p.446
Joan's Place 919-942-5621 p.367
Joanna Hopkinson Movers 201-434-5309 p.344
Jock 212-647-0222 p.138
Joe L's Uptown Bar 212-567-8555 p.328
Joe's Fleur de Lys Cafe & Bar 606-252-7946 p.251
Joesphine's 416-962-6255 p.116
Joey's 601-435-5639 p.291
John Domrose Foundation for Personal Rights p.377
John Jay College see:
Lambda Lesbian & Gay Student Association p.350
John L's 214-520-2525 p.412
Johnny MC's 602-266-0875 p.152
Johnny's Village Inn 305-522-5931 p.213
Johns Hopkins University see:
Bisexual, Gay & Lesbian Alliance at JHU p.264
Johnson, Howard P. 801-466-9151 p.423
Johnson, James E., MD 615-781-2170 p.408
Joint at Black Forest Inn 417-882-6755 p.296
Joly's Two 213-665-6810 p.165
Jon Sims Center for the Performing Arts 415-554-0402 p.185
Jonathan Michaels Cafe 203-248-8808 p.201
Jones Pond Campground 716-567-8100 p.319
Jones, Linda, CSW, ACSW 212-982-9232 p.334
Joq's Tavern 503-287-4210 p.383
Joq's Tavern
♦ advertisement p.383
Joseph's 508-599-9483 p.274
Joseph-Beth Booksellers 606-273-2911 p.252
Josephine County Human Rights Alliance 503-479-0633 p.382
Josie's Cabaret 415-861-7933 p.182

Old Town Bed & Breakfast
312-440-9268 p.238
Old Town Medical Center/
Immune Care of Key West
305-296-4868 p.219
Old Village Inn 207-646-7088
p.261
Old Wives' Tales 503-238-0470
p.383
Old Wives' Tales: Women's
Visions & Books
800-821-4675 p.144, 183
Olde Chester County Brunch
Bunch p.395
Olde Niagara House
716-285-9408 p.358
Older Lesbian Energy p.272
Older Wiser Lesbians (OWLS)
704-376-4745 p.365
Oldsmar FL see Tampa Bay
Area p.228
Oleen's 704-373-9604 p.364
OLGAD: The Organization of
Lesbian & Gay Architects &
Designers 212-475-7652
p.326, 346
Olin Business School see:
Gay & Lesbian Olin Business
School Alliance (GLOBAL)
p.296
The Olive Branch pub. by
AIDS Center at Hope House
p.307
Olivia Records 510-655-0364
p.134
Olivia Travel, Inc.
510-655-0364 p.141
OLOC Reporter pub. by Old
Lesbians Organizing for
Change p.419
OLOG see:
Old Lesbians Organizing for
Change
Olsen, Kirk S. 909-315-8207
p.158
Oly 208-342-1371 p.236
Olympia AIDS Task Force
360-352-2375 p.434
Olympians p.438
Olympic Steam Bath
Downtown 503-227-5718
p.384
Olympic Yacht Club p.438
Omaha Frontrunners/Walkers
402-496-3658 p.298
Omaha Players Club
402-451-7987 p.298
OMEGA (Older Mature & Gay
Action/Advocacy)
716-223-2748 p.360
Omni Adult Bookstore
305-584-6825 p.213
On A Positive Note pub. by
People With AIDS Coalition of
Palm Beach p.224
On Our Backs 415-546-0384
p.138
On Our Way pub. by Women's
Center p.273
On The Beach Resort
809-772-1205 p.427
On The Beach Resort
◆ advertisement p.427
On The Boulevard
818-356-9304 p.174
On The Move: A Mobile
Bookstore 813-223-9171
p.228
On The Waterfront
305-635-5500 p.220

On The Wilde Side
516-435-0005 p.317
On Track pub. by Lesbian
Community Project p.384
On Wings of Leather,
Northwind 604-253-1258
p.101
Once Upon A Time
309-828-3998 p.237
Ondercin, Joseph, PA-C
215-790-6030 p.393
One If By Land 212-228-0822
p.328
ONE in Long Beach
310-434-4455 p.163
One Potato 212-691-6260 p.328
One Saloon 305-296-8118
p.218
One Sky Books 306-652-1571
p.121
One Voice 704-548-0771 p.365
One Voice Mixed Chorus
612-344-9663 p.289
ONE, Inc. 213-735-5252 p.168
One-Four-Four Bed &
Breakfast 410-268-8053 p.262
One-In-Teen Youth Services
615-297-0008 p.408
One-O-Six Off Broadway
210-820-0906 p.421
One-Three-Two North Main
516-324-2246 p.323
Oneida Camp & Lodge
717-465-7011 p.391
Oneletter pub. by ONE, Inc.
p.168
Only With Love 515-282-7158
p.248
Onondaga Community
College see:
Gay & Lesbian & All Student
Association p.361
Onyx Images p.298
Oostburg WI see Milwaukee
p.446
Opa Locka FL see Miami Area
p.221
Open Arms of Minnesota
612-827-2624 p.287
Open Classroom pub. by
American Federation of
Teachers National Gay &
Lesbian Caucus p.129
Open Classroom: News of
Lesbian/Gay Educators
pub. by Gays & Lesbians
United for Education p.129
The Open Closet pub. by
Affirmation Seattle p.433
Open Door Chapel
219-744-1199 p.245
Open Doors: Ohio
University's Gay, Lesbian, &
Bisexual Student Union
614-594-2385 p.370
Open Hand Chicago
312-665-1000 p.239
Open Hands 312-736-5526
p.136, 140, 242
Open Line 515-233-5000 p.248
Open Mind Group (AA) p.319
Open Road Riders of
Chicagoland 708-795-1803
p.241
Open Sky B&B 800-244-3475
p.316
Opera Society Under
Development p.109
Ophthalmologists &
Optometrists p.167, 346

Optimal Moving, Inc.
718-693-3838 p.344
Options Magazine p.136
Opus I 404-634-6478 p.231
Orange CA see Orange
County p.170-171
Orange County Blade
714-494-4898 p.171
Orange County Business &
Professional Association
714-494-0215 p.171
Orca Swim Club 206-325-3604
p.438
Oregon Gay & Lesbian Law
Association 503-229-3988
p.380
Oregon House 503-547-3329
p.386
Oregon Sexual Minority Youth
Network (OSMYN)
503-228-5976 p.381
Oregon State University see:
Lesbian, Gay & Bisexual
Alliance, Oregon State
University p.382
Oregon Women's Land Trust
(OWL) Farm p.381
Org. of Hawaii Arts 'n
Athletics-OHANA
808-926-6157 p.233
Organization for Gay
Awareness 201-746-6196
p.304
Organization for Lesbian &
Gay Student Rights at The
Catholic University of
America (OLGSR)
202-635-5291 p.208
Organization of Gay &
Lesbian Students p.118
Organization of Hawaii Arts
'n' Athletics (OHANA)
808-926-6157 p.233
Organizations/Resources:
Bisexual Focus p.129, 153,
162, 184, 189, 208, 216, 258,
272, 288, 315, 346, 373, 375,
378, 380, 394, 407, 414, 424,
431, 433, 437, 444-445
Organizations/Resources:
Business & Professional
p.101, 103, 108, 110, 114, 117,
129-130, 149-150, 153, 158,
162, 167, 171, 173, 175, 177,
179, 184, 187-189, 191, 194,
197, 200, 208, 210, 212, 214,
219, 221, 223, 228, 230, 241,
246, 249, 253, 259, 262, 264,
266, 268, 272, 279, 282, 288,
295, 298, 300, 304, 315, 317,
346, 359-361, 363-364,
366-367, 369, 371, 375, 380,
387, 390, 394, 397, 403, 410,
414, 418, 421, 428, 430-431,
433, 437-439, 444
Organizations/Resources:
Disability p.130, 241, 252, 274,
346
Organizations/Resources:
Education, Anti-Defamation,
Anti-Violence, Self-Defense
p.110, 130, 168, 184, 191, 194,
208, 210, 233, 235, 241, 251,
261, 268, 272, 282, 286, 288,
293, 346-361, 365, 375, 380,
384, 414, 416, 418, 422,
424-425, 432, 438

Organizations/Resources:
Ethnic, Multicultural p.101,
108, 110-111, 117, 130-131,
158, 160, 168, 179, 184, 187,
194, 208, 214, 221, 228, 231,
241, 252, 264, 272, 282, 288,
293, 295, 298, 300, 310,
320-321, 347, 364-366, 368,
373, 375, 378, 384, 394, 397,
407, 409-410, 414, 418, 421,
425, 431, 438, 445
Organizations/Resources:
Family p.101, 103-104, 108,
110, 115, 117, 131, 150, 153,
155, 160-161, 163, 168,
170-171, 174, 176, 179, 184,
187, 189, 194, 197-198,
200-203, 208, 214, 216, 221,
223-224, 231, 233, 237, 241,
245-248, 250, 252-254, 258,
260-262, 264-265, 268, 272,
281-284, 286, 288, 290, 293,
295, 298, 300-301, 304-305,
320, 347, 359-360, 364-366,
368-371, 373, 376-377,
379-382, 384, 387-388, 390,
394, 397, 400-401, 403-405,
407, 414, 416, 418, 420, 422,
424-426, 432, 438-439, 442, 444
Organizations/Resources:
General, Multipurpose, Pride
p.104-106, 108-109, 111,
113-115, 120-121, 131, 148,
150-153, 155, 160, 163, 168,
171, 177, 179, 184, 187,
189-191, 196-197, 201, 204,
214, 216, 219, 224-226, 233,
235-237, 241, 244-245,
248-252, 254, 258-261,
264-266, 268, 272, 274, 280,
282, 284, 286-288, 290-291,
293-298, 300, 304, 307,
309-310, 312, 316-317, 320,
322, 347-348, 358, 360-362,
364-365, 368-369, 371, 373,
375, 378-382, 384, 387-390,
395, 397-398, 400-401,
403-404, 406-410, 414, 416,
418, 420, 422-423, 425,
428-430, 432, 434, 438, 440,
442, 444-447
Organizations/Resources:
Media (see also Publications)
p.131
Organizations/Resources:
Military/Veterans p.131, 153,
158, 170, 214, 261-262, 348,
369, 384, 419, 435
Organizations/Resources:
Political/Legislative p.101,
104, 106, 110-113, 115, 121,
131-132, 150, 153, 155-156,
158, 160-161, 163, 168, 171,
173, 176, 179, 184-185,
187-189, 191, 194, 197, 208,
210, 214, 216, 221-222,
224-225, 228, 230, 233,
235-238, 241, 244, 250-253,
258-259, 262, 264, 267-268,
272, 281, 284, 288, 290-293,
295-301, 304, 307, 314-315,
317, 348, 359-360, 363,
365-366, 369, 371, 373,
375-376, 378, 380-382, 384,
387-388, 390, 395, 397-399,
401, 407-410, 414, 419,
422-424, 426, 428-430,
432-435, 438, 440, 444, 446
Organizations/Resources:
Prisoner Resources p.132

Park 405-528-4690 p.379
703-342-0946 p.432
Park Ave Travel 716-256-3080
p.360
Park Avenue Bookstore
716-271-6120 p.359
Park Brompton Hotel
312-404-3499 p.238
Park Central Counseling
602-274-0327 p.153
Park Crest Funeral Home
619-260-1280 p.179
Park Manor Suites
619-291-0999 p.178
Park Motel 210-826-3245 p.421
Park Place p.216
Park Pub 904-434-3441 p.225
Park Sportsman's Bar
410-727-8935 p.263
Parker, Richard, DDS
505-982-9222 p.316
Parkleigh 716-244-4842 p.360
Parkway Books & Video
707-437-9969 p.190
Parlee Plus 516-587-8669
p.353
Parliament House Motor Inn
407-425-7571 p.222
Parsonage 415-552-2909 p.186
Partners 208-331-3551 p.236
305-921-9893 p.216
Partners Dance Bar
417-781-9313 p.292
Partners In Growth &
Recovery 802-865-2403 p.425
Partners Task Force for Gay &
Lesbian Couples
206-935-1206 p.132
Partners Travel 604-687-3837
p.109
Partners Western Lounge
417-781-6453 p.292
Party House 714-534-9996
p.171
Party/Event Services (see
also Food Specialties,
Catering) p.134, 242
Pasco AIDS Support
Community Organization
(PASCO) 800-486-8784 p.209
Pass-A-Grill Beach FL see
Tampa Bay Area p.226
Passages 501-442-5845 p.156
Passages Counseling Center
516-698-9222 p.334
Passages Psychological
Services 317-251-1110 p.246
Passion Flower 510-601-7750
p.145, 160
Passion Fruits: Gay &
Lesbian Vegetarians of L.A.
818-282-0753 p.168
Passionflower 904-435-1090
p.225
Passport pub. by International
Wavelength, Inc p.128
Passport Executive Travel
202-337-7718 p.209
Passport Ticket Travel
707-838-1557 p.189
Passport To Leisure
415-621-8300 p.186
Past Time 713-529-9669 p.417
Patch 708-891-9854 p.239
Patchogue NY see New York
City Area p.325, 347, 357
Pater Noster Houses
614-870-6460 p.374
Paths Untrodden Book
Service 212-661-5997 p.144

Paths Untrodden Book
Service
◆ advertisement p.142
Patsy Comer's Antiques &
Jewelry 818-345-1631 p.142,
164
Patti, Vincent-John, ACSW
212-475-3623 p.335
Pavilion Mall Booksellers
216-831-5035 p.372
PAWS see:
Pets Are Wonderful Support
Paz Y Liberacion p.418
PBD Disco 210-682-8019 p.420
PBLU see:
Positive Black Lesbians United
PCAN see:
Pacific Canadian Association
of Nudists
Peace & Justice Store
802-863-8326 p.425
Peace Corps see: Lesbian,
Gay & Bisexual Returned
Peace Corps Volunteers
p.132
Peace Gay Association
403-539-3325 p.105
Peace Resource Center p.248
Peachie's Court 717-326-3611
p.400
Peacock Printing
201-481-9497 p.310
Peanut Gallery & Lounge
417-865-1266 p.296
Pearce, M. Jane 916-452-3883
p.176
Pearl Garden 404-659-4055
p.231
Pearl Street 508-487-2210
p.147
Pearl, Alan, MD 212-724-5188
p.335
Pearls 802-863-2343 p.425
Pearls Booksellers
310-438-8875 p.162
Pearson, Bret 612-673-9482
p.288
Peck, Janet F., M.S.
203-537-3977 p.198
Pecs 619-296-0889 p.178
Peekskill NY see New York
City Area p.326
Peep World Underground
212-643-8907 p.338
Peer Listening Line
617-267-2535 p.273
Peer Support Group (GLBCA)
p.243
Peer Support Program
303-831-6268 p.195
Pegasus 210-299-4222 p.421
212-888-4702 p.328
412-281-2131 p.397
919-782-2481 p.367
Pegasus Travel 606-268-4337
p.252
Pegasus Unusual Books
208-232-6493 p.237
PEI Phoneline 902-566-9733
p.118
Pelham NY see New York
City Area p.349
PEN Magazine 515-265-3214
p.247
Pence WI see Hurley p.443
Pendragons Of Birmingham
p.148
Pendulum 415-863-4441 p.182

Penguin Place: Gay/Lesbian
Community Center of
Philadelphia 215-732-2220
p.392
Peninsula AIDS Foundation
804-591-0971 p.428
Penn GALA p.395
Penn State ABOUT FACE
717-865-3327 p.399
Penn Women's Center
215-898-8611 p.396
Penn Yan NY see Rochester
Area p.360
Pennsmen p.388
Pennsylvania Council for
Sexual Minorities
412-624-5046 p.387
Pennsylvania State University
see:
Lesbian, Gay & Bisexual
Student Alliance, Penn State
University p.399
State College Frontrunners
p.399
Pennyfeather's 212-242-9567
p.328
Pension San Francisco
Tourist Hotel 415-864-1271
p.181
Penthouse Club 713-522-0745
p.417
Penthouse Lounge
719-597-3314 p.192
People for Lesbian, Gay
Bisexual Concerns,
University of Illinois,
Urbana-Champaign
217-384-8040 p.238
People Like Us Books
312-248-6363 p.240
People Like Us Books
◆ advertisement p.239
People Living With Illness
603-778-3011 p.301
People of Color Against AIDS
Network 206-322-7061 p.125
509-624-4314 p.439
People of Color Caucus
512-473-8335 p.409
People of Color Publications
see:
Colorlife! Magazine p.130, 136,
347
Venus p.230
People Of Color see:
Gay, Bisexual, Lesbians of Color
p.321
Jacks Of Color p.348
Kitchen Table: Women of Color
Press p.139
La Lucha p.364
Lesbian & Gay People of Color
Steering Committee p.347
Lesbian Women of Color
(LWOC) p.431
Lesbians of Colour p.117
Men of Color AIDS Prevention
Program (MOCA) p.326
Men Of Color Motivational
Group p.282
National Institute for Women of
Color (NIWC) p.125
People of Color Against AIDS
Network p.125, 439
People of Color Caucus p.409
Womyn of Color of GLCCB
p.264
People United for More
Practical Solutions (PUMPS,
Inc) 617-765-2598 p.272

People With AIDS Coalition
410-625-1677 p.263
People With AIDS Coalition
Houston, Inc. 713-522-2674
p.417
People With AIDS Coalition of
Long Island 516-225-5797
p.325
People With AIDS Coalition of
Palm Beach 407-655-3322
p.224
People With AIDS Coalition of
Tucson (PACT) 520-770-1710
p.154
People With HIV/AIDS
Support Group 919-286-4107
p.367
People's Books 414-962-0575
p.445
Peoria City County Health
Dept. 309-679-6028 p.243
Peper Productions p.127
Pepper's News Stand
304-267-6846 p.441
Peppermint Tours
904-589-6885 p.141
Peppers by Frank Powell
404-872-4000 p.231
Peralandra Books & Music
503-485-4848 p.382
Perceptions 306-244-1930
p.101, 103, 109, 120
Perez Video & Books
619-321-5597 p.172
Performing Arts:
Entertainment, Music,
Recording, Theater, etc.
p.104, 109-110, 115, 118, 121,
134, 148, 150, 153, 158, 163,
169, 176, 180, 185-187, 195,
197, 201, 209-210, 214-216,
229, 232, 236, 242, 249, 253,
258, 264, 283, 289, 296, 299,
304, 335, 350-351, 360, 362,
365, 371, 373, 375-376, 381,
385, 389-390, 395, 398, 407,
411, 414, 419, 421-423, 426,
437, 439-440, 442, 444, 446
Perlswig, Ellis A., MD
203-777-1876 p.201
Perrin & Treggett Booksellers
201-328-8811 p.144, 306
Perrin & Treggett Booksellers
◆ advertisement p.307
Perrine Book & Video
305-233-3913 p.221
Persad Center 412-441-9786
p.396-397
Persona Video 415-775-6143
p.127
Personal Maui 808-572-1589
p.234
Personal Psychic
900-656-4000 p.126
Personal Psychic
◆ advertisement p.125
Personally Speaking
316-269-0913 p.250
Persons With AIDS Society of
British Columbia
604-893-2250 p.105
The Perspective pub. by S.E.
Alaska Gay/Lesbian Alliance
p.151
Pet Nanny 310-431-2233 p.163
Pet's Central 808-848-1688
p.236
The Petal & the Thorn pub.
by The Black Rose p.208
Petalouthas 718-891-3842
p.347

Senior Citizens
also see Prime Timers
Senior Citizens see:
Crones p.426
G Forty Plus Club p.185
GEMS p.200
GLEAM (Gay & Lesbian Elders Active In Minnesota) p.288
GLOW p.306
Information for Older Gay People p.298
Kaleidoscope p.268
LOAF (Lesbians Over Age 50) p.419
Metropolitan Retired Gays/ Lesbians p.208
Old Lesbians Organizing for Change (OLOG) p.419
Older Lesbian Energy p.272
Older Wiser Lesbians (OWLS) p.365
OMEGA (Older Mature & Gay Action/Advocacy) p.360
Prime Of Life Club p.386
Retired GALA of NOVA p.428
SAGE of the Palm Beaches p.225
SAGE/Milwaukee p.446
SAGE/Ottawa p.115
SAGE/Vermont p.424
Seniors & Sunshine p.225
Slightly Older Lesbians p.195, 371
Society for Senior Gay & Lesbian Citizens p.168
Stevens-Gregg Foundation p.153
Seniors & Sunshine 407-588-0774 p.225
Serendib Video 212-229-1316 p.338
Serendipty's 518-584-6077 p.361
Serenity 513-274-1616 p.376
SeroNorth pub. by AIDS Yukon Alliance p.121
Servicemembers Legal Defense Network 202-328-3244 p.131
Setauket NY see New York City Area p.335
Seventh Ave Gifts & Video 212-741-1161 p.338
Seventh Avenue Tobacco 212-242-5067 p.338
Seventh Day Adventist see: Religious Organizations & Publications
Seventy Bradford Street Guest House 508-487-4966 p.277
Severance, Scott 315-446-2867 p.362
Sex & Love Addicts Anonymous 412-441-0956 p.396
Sex Addicts Anonymous 612-871-1520 p.287
713-869-4902 p.124
Sex World Book & Video 612-672-0556 p.288
Sexual Assault Support Services 603-436-4107 p.303
Sexual Compulsives Anonymous 404-239-8048 p.230
Sexual Health Enlightenment (SHE) pub. by Sapphex Learn p.209
Sexual Minority Archives 413-584-7616 p.126, 267

Sexual Minority Student Alliance, Virginia Commonwealth University 804-367-6509 p.432
Sexual Minority Youth Assistance League (SMYAL) 202-546-5940 p.133, 209
Sexual Orientation Civil Rights PAC 513-278-GAYS p.376
Sexuality Information & Education Council of the US (SIECUS) 212-819-9770 p.130
SF Frontrunners Footprint pub. by San Francisco FrontRunners p.185
SHADES 201-485-5689 p.310
716-896-1770 p.320
Shades of Grey Leather 214-521-GREY p.413
Shades of Lavender 718-499-0352 p.332
Shades of The Village 212-255-7767 p.332
Shadow Box 314-429-7309 p.128, 295
Shadowplay BBS 206-706-0992 p.433
Shafer-Baillie Mansion 206-322-4654 p.436
Shaggy Horse 604-688-2923 p.108
Shahan's Saloon 404-523-1535 p.231
Shakespeare & Co 212-529-1330 p.331
Shakti Cove Cottages 360-665-4000 p.434
Shamakami p.130, 138, 184, 186
Shame On The Moon 619-324-5515 p.172
Shamrock Bar 608-255-5029 p.443
Shamrock Lounge 304-327-9570 p.441
Shandon Club 803-771-0339 p.403
Shannon, Joseph W., Ph.D. 614-297-0422 p.375
Shanti Foundation/Tucson 520-622-7107 p.154
Shanti of Juneau 907-463-5665 p.151
Shanti Project 415-864-CARE p.182
Shanti/Seattle 206-322-0279 p.436
Shapiro, Jonathan, PsyD 518-462-6139 p.318
Sharp A's 813-327-4897 p.227
Shaw, Nanette, Ph.D. 212-505-7869 p.335
Shaw, Nanette, PhD 212-505-7869 p.335
Shawnee Mission KS see Kansas City Area p.293-294
Shear Dimensions Hair Studio 610-435-2224 p.390
Shear Envy 806-799-7771 p.420
Sheboygan Antiques 414-452-6757 p.447
Shelix p.268
Shell, John, Ph.D. 303-377-6169 p.194
Shellcraft Shop 908-775-1930 p.305

Shepherd Wellness Community, Church of the Good Shepherd 412-421-8747 p.396
Sherlock's Home p.447
Sherman Oaks CA see Los Angeles Area p.140, 144, 166-167
Sherman, Patricia, MFCC 209-529-9080 p.170
415-968-0897 p.187
Shernoff, Michael, CSW, ACSW 212-675-9563 p.335
Shields-Marley Studios 501-372-6148 p.157
Shinder's Readmore Bookstore 612-333-3628 p.287
Shipley Grill Restaurant 302-652-7797 p.204
ShireMax Inn 508-487-1233 p.277
Shirley NY see New York City Area p.141, 356
Shirley's 804-625-1400 p.430
Shocking Gray 800-788-4729 p.147
The Shofar pub. by Congregation Beth Ahavah p.396
Shooters 513-381-9900 p.371
Shooterz 619-574-0744 p.178
Shore Cafe 207-646-6365 p.261
Shore Inn at Rehoboth 302-227-8487 p.204
Shoreham NY see New York City Area p.147, 350
Short, Doug 513-848-4663 p.376
Shoush, Julie 714-964-7990 p.169
Shouts Bar 702-829-7667 p.300
Shouts Bar & Grill 415-369-9651 p.174
Show Palace 212-944-7867 p.338
Show Palace
◆ advertisement p.339
Shreter, Stephanie, Esq 609-424-2244 p.306
Sibylline of Books 415-626-1245 p.144
SIDAahora pub. by PWA Coalition of New York, Inc p.326
SIDAmerica pub. by Panos Institute p.125
Side 2 Bar 214-528-2026 p.412
Side Kicks 816-931-1430 p.293
Side Saddle Cafe 515-280-7723 p.248
Side Saddle Saloon 319-362-2226 p.248
Side Street 305-525-2007 p.213
Side Traxx Nite Club 616-935-1666 p.285
Sideout 808-822-0082 p.234
Sidestreet Cafe 216-453-8055 p.370
Sidetrack, The Video Bar 312-477-9189 p.240
Sidney's Newsstand 504-524-6872 p.257
SIECUS Reports pub. by Sexuality Information & Education Council of the US p.130
SIECUS see: Sexuality Information & Education Council of the US
Sierra AIDS Council 209-533-2873 p.189

Sierra Club G.L.S./Bay Chapter p.160
Sierra Investments 520-325-7607 p.155
Sierra Pacific Productions 800-828-4336 p.145
SierraWood Guest House 916-577-6073 p.190
Sign of Rainbow p.373
Sign Of The Owl 207-338-4669 p.260
Significant Other Records 212-366-9078 p.134
Signs of Pride 803-862-6944 p.147
Silent Harvest Ministries 214-520-6655 p.140
Silent Partners 915-949-9041 p.421
Silhouette p.398
Silhouette Piano Bar 613-594-0233 p.114
Silhouettes 519-252-0887 p.118
Silicon Valley Gay Men's Chorus 408-275-6344 p.187
Silkwood Books 716-473-8110 p.359
Silver Anchor Enterprises, Inc. 813-788-0147 p.147
Silver Chord Bookstore 904-453-6652 p.225
Silver Dollar 501-663-9886 p.157
Silver Dollar Saloon 210-227-2623 p.421
Silver Dolphins LLC p.412
Silver Fox 310-439-6343 p.162
408-255-3673 p.186
Silver Foxx 208-234-2477 p.237
Silver Lake 302-226-2115 p.204
Silver Lake
◆ advertisement p.203
Silver Lining 516-354-9641 p.327
Silver News 301-779-1024 p.266
Silver Owls 419-242-9057 p.378
Silver Shadows Lodge 916-541-3575 p.190
Silver Star Saloon 918-834-4234 p.380
Silverado 503-224-4493 p.383
Silverlake Lounge 213-663-9636 p.166
Silverman, Philip J., Ph.D. 202-822-0078 p.207
Silverstein Langer Lipner & Newburgh 212-302-5100 p.343
Silverstein, Charles, Ph.D. 212-799-8574 p.335
Simcha 810-353-8025 p.283
Simenowitz, Steven H 516-232-3117 p.342
Simon Fraser University see: GALA Simon Fraser University p.109
Simon Says 513-381-8196 p.371
Simon, Emily 503-241-1553 p.384
Simon, Liz, BCSW 504-899-6024 p.257
Simonton Court Historic Inn & Cottages 305-294-6386 p.218
Simply Equal 405-945-2908 p.379
Simply Equal/OKC 405-521-9696 p.379

South Hadley MA **see** Amherst/Berkshire/ Northampton Area p.268

South Jersey AIDS Alliance 609-347-8799 p.305

South Laguna Beach CA **see** Orange County p.171

South Miami FL **see Miami Area** p.221

South Missippi Aids Task Force 601-435-1234 p.291

South Ogden UT **see Ogden** p.423

South Pasadena CA **see** Pasadena p.174

South Peace AIDS Council 403-538-3388 p.105

South Plains AIDS Resource Center 806-796-7068 p.420

South Portland ME **see** Portland p.261

Southampton NY **see New** York City Area p.324, 331

Southeast Cinema, Inc. 713-451-5470 p.418

Southeast Counseling Services 614-444-0800 p.374

Southeast Gay Rodeo Association 404-760-8126 p.232

Southeast Texas Legal Clinic 713-523-7852 p.418

Southeast Wisconsin AIDS Project 414-657-6644 p.442

Southeastern Arts, Media, & Education Project, Inc (SAME) 404-609-9590 p.232

Southeastern Connecticut AIDS Project 203-447-0884 p.201

Southern Appalachian Lesbian & Gay Alliance (SALGA) 704-645-5908 p.364

Southern Bears, Inc. 404-908-3381 p.231

Southern California Physicians for Human Rights 714-499-4855 p.158

Southern California Women for Understanding/Inland Chapter 909-422-3760 p.177

Southern California Women for Understanding/ Ventura—Santa Barbara 805-644-9564 p.189

Southern Center for Law and Justice 704-567-5530 p.364

Southern Colorado AIDS Project 719-578-9092 p.192

Southern Connecticut State University see: LBG Prism p.201

Southern Country South Florida 305-977-7589 p.214

Southern Exposure Guide 305-294-6303 p.219

Southern Gay Dreams 404-523-3471 p.231

Southern Heritage 910-251-9501 p.368

Southern Illinois University see: Gay & Lesbian Association of Students at SIU-E p.243 Gays, Lesbians, Bisexuals & Friends p.237

Southern Maryland Social Group p.266

Southern New England Friendship Softball League p.197

Southern Nights 407-898-0424 p.223

Southern Oregon State College see: Gay/Lesbian Alliance at Southern Oregon State College p.381

Southern Secrets 615-648-0365 p.406

Southern Shootout 205-595-6315 p.148

Southern Tier AIDS Program 607-798-1706 p.317

Southern Voice 404-876-1819 p.230, 232

Southfield MI **see Detroit** p.126, 282-283

Southpaw Saloon 305-758-9362 p.220

Southside AIDS Venture 804-799-5190 p.429

Southwest Aids Committee 915-772-3494 p.444

Southwest Florida Gay & Lesbian Chorus 941-432-9225 p.215 941-458-1382 p.215

Southwest Harbor ME **see** Bar Harbor p.259

Southwest Louisiana AIDS Council 318-439-5145 p.255

Southwest Men At Large 602-730-8171 p.151

Southwest Veterans Association 602-755-2928 p.153

Spa on Maitland 416-925-1571 p.117

Spadola, Madeline, Psy.D., CADAC 617-636-5725 p.271

Spag's 206-322-3232 p.436

Spankee's Club 214-739-4760 p.412

Spanky's 206-938-3400 p.437

Sparks 210-653-9941 p.421 502-587-8566 p.252

Spartacus Books 604-688-6138 p.108

Spartacus Enterprises 800-666-2604 p.145, 384

Spartacus Enterprises ◆ advertisement p.384

Spartan Motorcycle Club 703-370-5280 p.208

Spartans Wrestling Club 215-546-0735 p.395

Speakeasy's 413-746-0203 p.268

Speaker's Bureau 303-831-6268 p.194

Speaker's Project To End Discrimination 303-333-8388 p.194

Speakers Bureau 704-332-3834 p.365

Spearhead p.117

Specialty Travel 516-289-5070 p.357

Spectrum 319-354-1703 p.249 404-875-8980 p.231 415-457-1115 p.176 718-238-8213 p.327

Spectrum Mini-Storage 800-LOCK-SAF p.344

Speedway Adult Books & Videos 520-795-7467 p.155

Spencer Recovery Center 818-358-3662 p.124

The Sphincterian Quarterly p.144

Sphincterian Quarterly pub. by American Sphincter Society p.144

Spike 212-243-9688 p.329 213-656-9343 p.165

Spike ◆ advertisement p.329

Spinoza 812-333-7973 p.244

Spinsterhaven mar k p.123

Spinsters Ink 612-727-3119 p.139

The Spirit pub. by AIDS Pastoral Care Network p.238

Spirit Crossroads 212-505-0426 p.346

Spirit International Travel Club 800-873-4784 p.290

Spirit Journeys 505-351-4004 p.316

Spirit of the Lakes Ecumenical Community Church (UCC) 612-724-2313 p.290

Spirit of the Rivers Ecumenical Community Church 614-470-0816 p.376

Spirit Wings pub. by Metropolitan Community Church of the Spirit p.389

Spirited Women pub. by SisterSpirit p.385

Spiritworks pub. by Pink Triangle Christian Fellowship p.320

Spivey, Clayton Elizabeth, L.Ac. 410-799-5883 p.265

Splash! 214-522-9283 p.412

Splash 302-227-1927 p.204 302-227-9179 p.204 313-582-0639 p.282

Splash Bar 212-691-0073 p.329

Spokane AIDS Network 509-326-6070 p.439

Spokane Arcade 509-747-1621 p.439

Spokane County Health District AIDS Program 509-324-1542 p.439

Sport also see Rodeo

Sport see: *Pacelines* p.132, 272 Apollo: Friends In Sports Club p.104 Atlanta Venture Sports p.232 Boyer Ski Instruction p.423 Calgary Camp 181 Association p.104 Doc's Yacht Kare Enterprise p.311 English Bay Water Polo Club p.109 Equipe-Montréal 94 p.119 Federation Of Gay Games p.132, 438 Freewheelers Bicycle Shop & Personal Fitness Center p.360 GAMMA p.446 Gay Games p.132 Gotham Sports Association p.349 Greater Cincinnati Sports Association p.371 Group p.195 Hawk, I'm Your Sister p.316 Horn, Jeff D. p.224 Island Triathlon & Bike p.233 Lambda Rollerskating Club p.419

Lavender Menace Women's Sports p.216 Lavender Winds Kite Club p.160 London Sports Alliance p.114 Magic City Athletic Association p.148 Maui Surfing School p.234 Metropolitan Sports Association p.241 North American Gay Amateur Athletic Alliance (NAAGA) p.395 Oak Lawn Ski Club p.414 Organization of Hawaii Arts 'n' Athletics (OHANA) p.233 Pittsburgh Gay Games Delegation p.398 Rainbow Adventures, Sailing Charters p.221 Sailing Affairs p.132 Southern Shootout p.148 Team Austin/Gay Games p.411 TEAM Connecticut Pride p.197 TEAM Houston p.419 Team Philadelphia p.395 TEAM Seattle p.438 TEAM St Louis p.296 Team/Equipe Ottawa p.115 Time Out p.115 TREAT (Three Rivers Eastern Area Tournament) p.398 Velvet Spikers p.390 Windy City Athletic Association p.241 Women Together In Sports p.241

Sport/Fitness Publications see: *Home Team* p.136 *Pacelines* p.132, 136, 272 *Women's Sports & Fitness* p.192

Sporter's 617-742-4084 p.270

Sporters 603-668-9014 p.302

Sports Leisure Travel 916-361-2051 p.176

Sportsman 317-742-6321 p.246

Sportsman Athletic Club 207-784-2251 p.260

Spotlight 213-467-2425 p.165

Spouse/Ex-spouse Support: Gay Married Men's Support Group p.360 PFLAG of Southwestern Connecticut p.197

Spread the Word pub. by Poconos Action Lambda Society p.387

Spring Grove PA **see York** p.400

Spring Street Books 212-219-3033 p.331

Spring Valley CA **see San Diego Area** p.180

Spring Valley Guest Ranch 306-295-4124 p.120

Springfield Area Lesbian Outreach (SALO) 217-528-SALO p.244

Springfield Book & Video 413-781-6833 p.268

Springfield Center NY **see Cooperstown** p.320

Springfield MA **see Amherst/ Berkshire/Northampton Area** p.267-269

Springfield Technical College GLBA 413-781-7822 p.269

Springhill Farm 614-659-2364 p.374

Spruce Street Video 215-985-2955 p.396
SPublications, Literary & Bookselling see: *Feminist Bookstore News* p.137
Spur Productions 212-727-8850 p.357
Spurlock, William Marcus, MD 318-222-8300 p.258
Spurs 513-621-BOOT p.371
Spurs Saloon 619-321-1233 p.172
Square One 305-296-4300 p.218
Squares Across the Border 604-540-4091 p.109
Squiggy's 607-722-2299 p.319
SRO 619-232-1886 p.178
SSGLC see: Society for Senior Gay & Lesbian Citizens, Inc./Project Rainbow
St Ann's Cafe & Deli 504-529-4421 p.257
St Ann's Church of Morrisania - Gay & Lesbian Ministry 718-585-6325 p.356
St Catharines ON **see Niagara Region** p.101, 114
St Cloud MN **see Minneapolis/ St Paul Area** p.288-289
St Cloud State University see: Lesbian, Gay, Bisexual & Transgender Resource Center p.289
Lesbian/Gay/Bisexual/ Transgender Resource Center (LGBTRC) p.289
St Gabriel Community Church (I.C.C.C) 903-581-6923 p.422
St John's Episcopal Church 213-747-6285 p.169
St John's University see: 10% Group p.289
St Joseph County Health Dept, County-City Bldg 219-284-9725 p.247
The St Louis Agapian pub. by Agape Church of St Louis p.296
St Louis Effort for AIDS (EFA) 314-367-2382 p.294
St Marks Women's Health Collective 212-228-7482 p.341
St Matthew's Evangelical Lutheran Church 818-762-2909 p.169
St Maur—Bookseller 209-464-3550 p.144
St Paul MN **see Minneapolis/ St Paul Area** p.126, 287-290
St Paul's United Methodist Church 303-832-4929 p.195
St Petersburg Beach FL **see Tampa Bay Area** p.226
St Petersburg FL **see Tampa Bay Area** p.226-229
St Stephen's Community Church 601-939-7181 p.291
St Thomas VI **see St Thomas** p.427
St. Aelred's Gazette pub. by Integrity of the Sierra p.176
St. Christophe Bed & Breakfast 514-527-7836 p.119
St. Louis Guesthouse 314-773-1016 p.294
St. Marc Spa 416-927-0210 p.117
Sta Travel 213-934-8722 p.170
Stables 417-862-6363 p.296

Stacey's Professional Bookstore 415-421-4687 p.183
Stade B&B 514-254-1250 p.119
Stadium Book & Video 305-623-8933 p.221
Stadtlander's Pharmacy 800-238-7828 p.147
Stadtlanders Pharmacy Wellness Center 212-807-8798 p.352
Stag 703-982-1668 p.432
Stage Door 513-223-7418 p.376 716-886-9323 p.319
Stage Left: An American Café 908-828-4444 p.310
Stagecoach Saloon & Restaurant 410-547-0107 p.263
Stagecoach Saloon & Restaurant
♦ advertisement p.263
Stages 716-232-5070 p.359
Stained Glass see: Crafts
Stained Glass: Cory Glass Works p.271
Stallion 210-734-7977 p.421 310-422-5997 p.162
Stallions 717-232-3060 p.388
Stamford Health Department: AIDS Program 203-967-AIDS p.201
Stamos & Associates 208-338-9668 p.236
Stamps see: Gay & Lesbian History Stamp Club p.132
Stand-Up Harlem 212-926-4072 p.326
Standing Committee for Lesbian, Gay, & Bisexual Awareness, American College Personnel Association p.133
Stanford CA **see Palo Alto** p.173-174
Stanford Inn 218-724-3044 p.286
Stanford Lesbian/Gay & Bisexual Community Center 415-725-4222 p.173
Stanford Lesbian/Gay/ Bisexual Community Center 415-725-4222 p.174
Stanley VA **see Luray** p.429
Stanley's 305-523-9769 p.213
Star Magazine 619-324-4957 p.173
Star Sapphire 212-688-4710 p.329
Stardust Book Emporium 912-236-1441 p.233
Starfish Restaurant 305-673-1717 p.220
Stark, Kelly 901-521-9996 p.407
Starky's 503-230-7980 p.383
Starr Easton Hall 613-283-7479 p.113
Stars 212-647-0222 p.139 401-861-2600 p.402
Stars M.C. 518-436-4917 p.318
Starsearch Video 901-276-2727 p.407
Starz Bar & Restaurant 219-288-7827 p.247
State Bar 810-767-7050 p.283
State College Frontrunners 814-234-8523 p.399

State Farm Insurance: Tony Richards 303-830-0333 p.194
State of Man p.147
State Street Arcade 608-251-4540 p.444
State Street Bookstore 716-263-9919 p.359
State University of New York see:
Alternative Lifestyles p.319
B-GLAD (Bisexual, Gay, Lesbian Alliance for Diversity) p.321
Gay & Lesbian Alliance SUC-Oswego p.358
Gay/Lesbian/Bisexual Union SUNY Purchase p.350
GOAL: Gay Organization for Alternative Lifestyles p.358
Graduate Gay & Lesbian Alliance p.320
Lavender Wimmin Radio Show p.331
Lesbian, Gay & Bisexual Alliance p.349
Lesbian, Gay & Bisexual Alliance at Plattsburgh p.358
Lesbian, Gay, Bisexual Alliance p.320
Lesbian/Gay/Bisexual Alliance SUNY Albany (LGBA) p.318
Lesbian/Gay/Bisexual Association at SUNY Potsdam p.358
Lesbian/Gay/Bisexual Union (LGBU) SUNY-Binghamton p.319
Staten Island AIDS Task Force 718-981-3366 p.326
Staten Island NY **see New York City Area** p.324, 326, 330, 335, 341, 349-350, 352
Station 2 414-383-5755 p.445
Station House 219-962-1017 p.247
Statisticians see: Gay & Lesbian Statisticians' Caucus p.129
Status of Women Action Group 604-383-7322 p.106
Stay 'N Home Pet Sitting 602-547-0575 p.153
STD Clinic 219-449-7504 p.245 305-797-6900 p.214 513-352-3138 p.371 816-474-4901 p.293
STD Clinic, Dept of Health & Human Services 907-343-4611 p.150
STD Clinic, Duval County Public Health Unit 904-633-3620 p.216
Ste-Foy QC **see Québec** p.120
Ste-Thérèse QC **see Montréal** p.119
Steam 415-243-3232 p.139
Steam
♦ advertisement p.122
Steam Works 604-383-6623 p.106 819-283-8431 p.114
Steamworks 510-845-8992 p.160 809-725-4993 p.401
Steel City Centurions & Bears 205-664-0609 p.150
Steel City Softball League p.398
Stefanick, Gary F., DC 212-243-3080 p.341
Stein, Virginia Kramer, MA 908-722-6343 p.312

Steinhorn, Audrey 212-877-5486 p.335 914-452-0374 p.358
Steinmetz, Weinberg & Moats 202-861-0077 p.207
Steketee Office Services 805-653-0271 p.188
Stella's 212-997-4041 p.329
Stephen Nevitt Florist 305-757-8383 p.221
Stephen Wise Free Synagogue - Lesbian & Gay Concerns Group 212-877-4050 p.356
Stepping Stone, Hillcrest Community Recovery Service 619-295-3995 p.178
Stepping Stone: Central Residential Recovery Services 619-584-4010 p.178
Stepping Stones, The Artifactory 415-583-9685 p.173
Sterling Travel 615-399-3626 p.408
Steubenville News 614-282-5842 p.377
Steve Cobb's Haberdashery 212-473-6844 p.332
Steve Farmer Defense Fund p.437
Steve's Broadway News 206-324-7323 p.437
Steve's Gym 702-323-8770 p.300
Steven Baratz Photography 415-647-0247 p.147, 182
Stevens Travel Management 212-696-4300 p.357
Stevens, Lynne, CSW, BCD 212-222-9563 p.335
Stevens-Gregg Foundation 602-241-1604 p.153
Stewart, Charles L. 214-521-3804 p.414
Stewart, Geoffrey S. 212-255-3137 p.343
Stewart, Karen L. 502-589-2986 p.252
Stewart, Lynne F. 212-243-3196 p.343
Stewart-Cole Travel 800-688-3013 p.189
Stick, Stone & Bone 212-807-7024 p.342
Stiletts 319-234-6752 p.249
Stingers Lounge & Grill 313-892-1765 p.282
Stockbridge Ramsdell Bed & Breakfast 914-561-3462 p.358
Stoler, David, DC 617-731-3306 p.272
Stone Pillar B & B 704-295-4141 p.364
Stone Ridge NY **see Poughkeepsie/Kingston Area** p.358
Stone Wall Bed & Breakfast 207-925-1080 p.260
Stone Walls pub. by Island Lesbian & Gay Association p.274
Stone, Judith Ellen, Esq 516-623-0897 p.342
Stonehouse 613-821-3822 p.113
Stonewall 212-463-0950 p.329 813-891-7098 p.229
Stonewall 25, Inc. 212-439-1031 p.131

Tracks 202-488-3320 p.206 813-247-2711 p.228

Trade Trax pub. by Tradeswomen Inc p.130

Trade Wind 914-352-4134 p.361

Trade Winds Inn 508-487-0138 p.277

Trader Tom's Fantasy Depot 305-524-4759 p.213

Trader Tom's of North America, Inc. 305-763-4630 p.213

Tradeswoman Magazine pub. by Tradeswomen Inc p.130

Tradeswomen 510- 649-6160 p.130 510-649-6160 p.130

Tradewinds II 614-461-4110 p.374

Tradewinds Motel & Suites 916-544-6459 p.190

Trading Post 306-653-1769 p.121

Trail Books 305-262-4776 p.221

Trail Marker pub. by Desert Adventures p.153

Tramps 401-421-8688 p.402 405-528-9080 p.379

Tran Sexuals & Genders of America 317-259-1427 p.246

Trans Allegheny Books 304-346-0551 p.441

Transfer 415-861-7499 p.183

Transformation pub. by Women's Project p.157

Transgender Publications see: Cross-Talk p.133

Grace and Lace Letter p.133, 290

He-She Directory p.133

International Transcript/CDS p.395

The Transie Times p.117

TransSisters: The Journal of Transsexual Feminism p.133

Transgender see: Lee's Mardi Gras Boutique p.133, 350

Reluctant Press p.133

Vernon's Specialties/Erotic Variations p.133

Villains p.185

Transgenderists Independence (TGIC) 518-436-4513 p.318

The Transie Times p.117

Transpitt 412-224-6015 p.398

Transportation: Limousine, Taxi, Etc. p.222, 236, 274, 279, 320, 357

Transsexuals In Prison p.133

TransSisters: The Journal of Transsexual Feminism 816-753-7816 p.133

Transsupport p.261

Trapp 801-531-8727 p.423

Travel & Tourist Services (see also Accommodation) p.102, 104, 109, 115, 117, 120, 141-142, 150, 154-155, 158-163, 169-171, 173-174, 176, 180, 186, 189-190, 192, 195-196, 199-200, 203, 209, 212, 214-215, 219, 222, 229, 232, 234, 236, 242-244, 246-247, 250, 252, 254, 258, 262, 265-267, 269, 273, 280, 283-285, 290, 296, 300, 306-307, 311-317, 319-320, 357-358, 360-362, 365-366, 368, 372, 374, 376, 378-379, 381-382, 385, 387-388, 396, 398, 402, 406, 408, 411, 415, 420, 427-428, 431, 439-440, 444, 446-447

Travel About 612-377-8955 p.290

Travel Address-Galaxsea 209-432-9095 p.161

Travel Affair 404-977-6824 p.232

Travel Agents International 503-223-1100 p.385 800-928-0809 p.439

Travel Central 301-587-4000 p.266

Travel Club 812-743-2919 p.141

The Travel Company of Minnesota 518-433-9000 p.319 612-379-9000 p.290

Travel Concepts 401-453-6000 p.402

Travel Corner 503-649-9867 p.381

Travel Experience On Call 408-464-8035 p.189

Travel Friends 214-891-8833 p.415

Travel Lab 213-660-9811 p.170

Travel Masters of NY 516-766-0707 p.357

The Travel People 212-675-6566 p.357

Travel Place 216-734-1886 p.374 509-624-7434 p.440

Travel Professionals Associations see: International Gay Travel Association p.129 Triangle Network p.150

Travel Registry, Inc. 609-921-6900 p.312

Travel Solutions 206-281-7202 p.439

Travel Source 316-342-2854 p.250 813-725-9557 p.229

Travel Tammaro 718-805-0907 p.357

Travel Travel 808-596-0336 p.236

Travel Trends 415-558-6922 p.186

Travel With Hal 714-537-1553 p.171

Travel Wizard 800-934-TRIP p.141, 267, 280

Traveler's Rest 312-262-4225 p.240

Travelodge at the Zoo 619-296-2101 p.178

Travelodge Hotel - Stadium 215-755-6500 p.391

TravelPlex 615-321-3321 p.408

TravelPlex East 614-337-3155 p.376

Travelstar 203-227-7233 p.203

Travlur Lounge & Motel 815-964-7005 p.243

Trax 403-245-8477 p.103 415-864-4213 p.183 602-254-0231 p.152

Trax V 416-963-5196 p.116

Traxx 803-256-1084 p.403

Treasure Box Video & News 910-373-9849 p.366

Treasure Chest 207-772-2225 p.261

Treasure Chest II 207-873-7411 p.262

Treasure Island FL see Tampa Bay Area p.226

TREAT (Three Rivers Eastern Area Tournament) p.398

Treatment Issues pub. by Gay Men's Health Crisis p.124, 326

Treetop Bar 305-294-4737 p.218

Trellis Foundation 702-747-2849 p.300

Tremont Lounge 614-445-9365 p.374

Trends/Garage Disco 614-461-0076 p.374

Trestle 214-826-9988 p.412

Trexx 315-474-6408 p.361

Tri-Cities Chaplaincy/ Tri-Cities Cares 509-783-0873 p.434

TRI-PAC 412-661-3244 p.398

Tri-State AIDS Task Force 304-522-4357 p.440

Tri-State Alliance 812-474-4853 p.245

Tri-State Gay Rodeo Association 513-581-2512 p.244, 251, 369

Tri-State Newsletter pub. by Tri-State Alliance p.245

Triad Business & Professional Guild 910-274-2100 p.366

Triad Health Project 910-275-1654 p.365

The Triangle pub. by Gay/ Lesbian Community Services of Central Florida p.223 414-383-9412 p.445

Triangle Area Gay Scientists 919-929-4997 p.367

Triangle Area Lesbian Feminists 919-688-4398 p.368

Triangle Club 202-659-8641 p.205 206-587-6924 p.438

Triangle Coalition 314-882-4427 p.292

Triangle Coalition Political Action Committee 314-882-4427 p.291

Triangle Community Center 203-853-0600 p.196

Triangle Computer Consultants 615-228-9579 p.408

Triangle Express Productions 310-491-1046 p.162

Triangle Foundation 313-537-3323 p.282

Triangle Inn 505-455-3375 p.316

Triangle Interests 215-487-3736 p.395

Triangle Journal News 901-454-1411 p.407

Triangle Lesbian & Gay Alliance 919-929-4053 p.368

Triangle Network 907-389-2528 p.150

Triangle Palms Guest House 407-799-2221 p.212

Triangle Pointe 706-867-6029 p.232

Triangle Rising pub. by Arkansas Gay & Lesbian Task Force p.155

Triangle Scuba Dive Club 508-881-5019 p.269

Triangle Service Recovery Center p.430

Triangle Services Center 804-497-0814 p.430

Triangle Squares 416-960-5458 p.117

Triangle Therapy 804-591-8735 p.430

Triangle Traders 520-795-7345 p.147

Triangle Travel 212-608-1000 p.357

Triangle World & The Leather Palace 616-373-4005 p.284

Triangles 301-694-8933 p.265

Triangles Cafe 203-798-6996 p.199

Triangular Communications 800-972-9122 p.141, 305

Triangular Communications ◆ advertisement p.125

Triantafillou & Guerin, P.C. 617-577-1505 p.272

Trib's Waystation 610-869-9067 p.400

Triborough Triangles p.269

Tricks 304-232-1267 p.441

Trident Intl. DC 301-297-7539 p.208

Trident Knights 803-769-2094 p.403

Trigo 310-652-9263 p.165

Trigon: Lesbian, Gay & Bisexual Coalition 814-898-7050 p.388

Trikone Magazine pub. by Trikone: Gay & Lesbian South Asians p.131

Trikone: Gay & Lesbian South Asians 408-270-8776 p.131

Trinity College see: Eros p.200

Trinity Dallas Aquatics p.414

Trinity Episcopal Church 415-775-1117 p.186

Trinity Lutheran Church 502-587-8395 p.253

Trio 715-392-5373 p.447

Trio Travel And Imports 414-384-8746 p.446

Triple A Video p.358

Triple Lei 808-874-8645 p.234

Triple Lei ◆ advertisement p.235

Trips Unlimited 314-361-1176 p.296 404-872-8747 p.232

Trips Unlimited, Inc. 504-927-7191 p.254

Trivia: A Journal of Ideas p.138

Trixx Adult Cinema & Bookstore 915-532-6171 p.416

Trooper's 334-433-7436 p.149

Tropical Inn 305-294-9977 p.218

Tropicales 514-521-7708 p.119

Tropicana Motor Hotel Adult Bookstore 520-622-2289 p.155

Troubador Lounge 216-788-4379 p.378

United Leatherfolk of Connecticut p.197
United Lesbians Of African Heritage (ULOAH) 213-960-5051 p.168
United Pride 206-467-6267 p.147
United Services, Inc. 203-774-2020 p.199
United Teachers of Dade Gay & Lesbian Caucus 305-854-0220 p.221
United Theological Seminary Lesbian & Gay Caucus 612-633-8703 p.289
United Theological Seminary see:
United Theological Seminary Lesbian & Gay Caucus p.289
United Voice pub. by United Gays & Lesbians of Wyoming p.447
Unity 516-924-3640 p.350
Unity Fellowship Church 213-936-4948 p.169
Unity Pride Coalition of Ventura County 805-650-9546 p.189
Universal Grill 212-989-5621 p.330
Universal News Agency 213-467-3850 p.166
Universal/Carlson Travel 305-525-5000 p.214
Université du Québec see: Association des Lesbiennes et Gais de l'Université du Québec à Montréal (ALGYQUAM) p.119
Université Laval see: Alliance gaie Laval-Laurentides p.119
Groupe Gaie de L'Université Laval p.120
University Bi & Transgender Community 612-626-2344 p.289
University Bookstore 319-335-3179 p.249
University Center Bookstore 406-243-4921 p.297
University Club 904-378-6814 p.215
University Lesbian, Gay, Bisexual Alliance p.286
University Lesbians 612-625-1611 p.289
University of Alabama see: Auburn Gay & Lesbian Association (AGALA) p.148
Gay/Lesbian/Bisexual Alliance, University of Alabama (GLBA) p.150
UAB G/L Student Union p.148
University of Alberta see: Gays & Lesbians on Campus (GALOC) p.104
University of Arizona see: USUA Bisexual Gay & Lesbian Association p.155
University of Brandon see: Brandon University Gay Association (BUGA) p.110
University of British Columbia see: Gays, Lesbians & Bisexuals of UBC (GLBUBC) p.109
University of Calgary see: Gay, Lesbian & Bisexual Academics, Students & Staff (GLASS) p.104

University of California see: Bisexuals, Gays, Lesbians at Davis (BGLAD) p.159
Boalt Hall/UC Berkeley School of Law Lesbian Gay Bisexual Caucus p.160
Delta Lambda Phi Fraternity, University of California, Davis p.159
GALA: UCLA p.168
Lesbian/Gay/Bisexual Alliance p.189
Lesbian/Gay/Bisexual Organization, University of California, San Diego p.180
Multicultural Bisexual/Gay/Lesbian Alliance (MBLGA) p.160
UC Irvine GLBSU p.171
Union of Lesbians, Gays & Bisexuals p.177
University of California/Los Angeles see: Lesbian/Gay Health & Health Policy Foundation p.128, 157
University of Chicago Gay & Lesbian Alliance 312-702-9734 p.241
University of Chicago see: University of Chicago Gay & Lesbian Alliance p.241
University of Cincinnati Office of Women's Programs & Services 513-556-4401 p.372
University of Cincinnati see: U.C. Alliance of Lesbian, Gay & Bisexual People p.371
University of Cincinnati Office of Women's Programs & Services p.372
University of Connecticut see: Bisexual, Gay & Lesbian Association p.202
University of Delaware see: Lesbian/Gay/Bisexual Student Union at the University of Delaware p.203
University of Florida see: Lesbian, Gay & Bisexual Student Union of the University of Florida p.216
University of Hartford see: Gay & Lesbian Alliance, University of Hartford p.200
University of Hartford Women's Center 203-768-5275 p.200
University of Houston see: Delta Lambda Phi—University of Houston p.419
GLOBAL: the Gay, Lesbian & Bisexual Alliance at UH p.419
University of Illinois see: People for Lesbian, Gay Bisexual Concerns, University of Illinois, Urbana-Champaign p.238
PRIDE at UIC/Spectrum p.241
University of Iowa Lesbian, Gay & Bisexual Staff & Faculty Association 319-335-1125 p.249
University of Iowa see: Spectrum p.249
University of Kansas see: LesBiGay Services of Kansas p.250
University of Kentucky see: UK Lambda p.252

University of Louisville see: GLOBAL (Gay Lesbian or Bisexual Alliance) p.253
University of Maryland see: Freedom Alliance of UMBC p.264
Lesbian, Gay & Bisexual Alliance, University of Maryland p.265
University of Massachusetts see: Everywoman's Center p.269
Lesbian, Bisexual, Gay Alliance (LBGA) p.269
Lesbian, Gay & Bisexual Center p.273
Program for Gay/Lesbian & Bisexual Concerns p.269
University of Miami see: GLBC/University of Miami p.221
University of Michigan see: Lesbian & Gay Bisexual Programs Office p.281
University of Minnesota Lesbian/Gay Law Students Association 612-625-1000 p.289
University of Minnesota see: Matrices p.137
Blue Light Special p.290
Delta Lambda Phi Fraternity/University of Minnesota p.289
E-Quality p.290
Gay, Lesbian, Bisexual, Transgender Programs Office p.289
Safe Haven Program p.290
University Bi & Transgender Community p.289
University Lesbians p.289
University of Minnesota Lesbian/Gay Law Students Association p.289
University of Missouri see: Triangle Coalition p.292
University of Montana Women's Center 406-243-4153 p.297
University of Nevada see: Delta Lambda Phi Fraternity, University of Nevada at Las Vegas p.300
University of New Brunswick see: Gay & Lesbian Alliance of UNB/UST p.111
University of New Hampshire see: Alliance p.302
University of New Mexico see: Lesbian, Bisexual & Gay Alliance p.315
University Lesbian, Gay, Bisexual Alliance p.286
University of New Mexico Women's Center 505-277-3716 p.315
University of New Orleans see: Gay & Lesbian Alliance at the University of New Orleans p.258
University of North Carolina see: Gay & Lesbian Student Association p.366
University of North Dakota see: Gay Men's Support Group p.298
UND G&L Coalition p.369

University of North Texas see: Courage: The Lesbian/Gay/Bisexual Student Organization of UNT p.416
University of Northern Colorado see: Greeley Gay, Lesbian, & Bisexual Alliance (GOLBA) p.196
University of Northern Iowa Gay/Lesbian Outreach (UNIGLOW) 319-273-2676 p.250
University of Northern Iowa see: University of Northern Iowa Gay/Lesbian Outreach (UNIGLOW) p.250
University of Oragon see: Lesbian, Gay, Bisexual Alliance p.382
University of Pennsylvania see: Lesbian, Gay & Bisexual Alliance at Penn p.395
Penn GALA p.395
University of Pitt-Bradford BiGALA 814-362-7654 p.387
University of Pittsburgh see: Bisexual, Gay & Lesbian Alliance at Pitt p.132
Gay & Lesbian Law Caucus at University of Pittsburgh School of Law p.398
Pitt AIDS Center for Treatment (PACT) p.396
Pitt Men's Study p.396
Pitt Treatment Evaluation Unit (PTEV) p.396
University of Rhode Island see: URI Gay/Lesbian/ Bisexual Association p.401
University of Rochester see: Gay, Lesbian, Bisexual & Friends Association (GLBFA) University of Rochester p.360
University of Saskatchewan see: Gays & Lesbians at University of Saskatchewan p.121
University of South Alabama see: Gay, Lesbian, Bisexual Alliance, University of South Alabama p.149
University of South Florida Gay/Lesbian/Bisexual Coalition 813-974-GAYS p.229
University of South Florida see: University of South Florida Gay/Lesbian/Bisexual Coalition p.229
University of Southern California Lambda Alumni Association 213-740-5440 p.133
University of Southern California see: University of Southern California Lambda Alumni Association p.133
University of Southern Maine see: Alliance for Sexual Diversity p.261
University of Texas see: Gay/Lesbian Association of UTA p.414

Very Video 510-881-0185 p.160
Very Video
◆ advertisement p.161
Veterans C.A.R.E.
310-529-6969 p.158
Veterans C.A.R.E. Aware
pub. by Veterans C.A.R.E.
p.158
Veterans C.A.R.E., Inc:
Northern California
707-829-5393 p.158
Veterans for Human Rights
503-223-1373 p.384
Veterinarians p.209, 294, 296,
306, 357, 359, 407
VGA Gayzette pub. by Valley
Gay Alliance p.268
Viatical see:
Insurance Benefits
Vibrations p.401
VICE 212-727-2787 p.137, 353
Vicious Rumors 702-896-1993
p.299
Victor, Hope R., Ph.D.
215-925-0330 p.392
Victor/Victoria's 615-244-7256
p.408
Victoria BC see Vancouver
Island Area p.106-107
Victoria Oaks Inn
303-355-1818 p.192
Victoria Oaks Inn
◆ advertisement p.193
Victoria PWA Society
604-383-7494 p.106
Victoria Travel 513-871-1100
p.372
Victoria's Restaurant
403-244-9991 p.103
Victory! p.251 p.137
VIDA see:
Volunteers In Direct Aid
Video and Stuff 818-761-3162
p.167
Video Book & News
203-573-1116 p.202
Video Central 518-463-4153
p.319
Video Channel 716-442-1140
p.360
Video Emporium 201-361-9440
p.306
Video Exchange 802-244-7004
p.427
Video Fantasies 909-782-8056
p.177
Video Horizons 714-499-4519
p.171
Video Lab 617-493-3105 p.273
Video Max 803-449-3265 p.404
Video Novelty 516-736-3643
p.336
Video Plus 717-334-7038 p.388
Video Rental & Preview Center
714-534-9922 p.171
Video Sales. Rentals.
Services (see also Erotica)
p.109, 160, 163, 195, 200, 242,
273, 294, 311, 315, 319,
357-360, 368, 376, 385, 388,
396, 407, 411, 415, 444
Video Specialties
619-745-6697 p.179
Video Stop 214-747-4722 p.413
Video Variety 716-856-8936
p.320
Video Westport 816-561-6397
p.294
Video X-Press 803-771-0504
p.403
Videoland 214-358-6559 p.413

Vidéomag Plus 514-871-1653
p.119
Videomatica 60 4-734-0411
p.102 604-734-0411 p.102,
109
Videotique 303-861-7465 p.195
Vieux Carre 205-534-5970
p.149
Vieux Carre Rentals
504-525-3983 p.256
View on the Hill 913-371-9370
p.292
Viitala, Ann C., Esq
612-337-9518 p.288
Villa 401-596-1054 p.402
Villa 619-328-7211 p.171
904-248-2020 p.212
Villa Bed & Breakfast
914-337-7050 p.324
Villa Toscana Guest House
312-404-2643 p.238
Village Apothecary
212-807-7566 p.352
Village Army & Navy Store
212-242-6655 p.332
Village Bed & Breakfast
212-387-9117 p.324
Village Book & News
716-887-5027 p.320
Village Clinic 204-453-0045
p.110
Village Green Bookstore
215-230-7610 p.391
716-425-7950 p.321
716-442-1151 p.359
716-723-1600 p.359
716-827-5895 p.320
716-884-1200 p.320
Village Green Realty
914-679-2255 p.362
Village Green Realty
◆ advertisement p.362
Village Inn 707-865-2304 p.174
Village Station 214-526-0690
p.412
Village Travel 217-875-5640
p.243
Villains 415-626-5939 p.185
The Vine pub. by Passion
Flower p.145, 160
Vineyard Haven MA see
Martha's Vineyard Area
p.134, 274
Vinson, Joyce, CSW
516-689-9456 p.335
Vintage Noir 810-543-8733
p.282
Vintage Views pub. by Victoria
Prime Timers p.106
Virago! p.138
Virago 803-256-9090 p.403
Virginia Commonwealth
University see:
Sexual Minority Student
Alliance, Virginia
Commonwealth University
p.432
Virginia Partisans Gay &
Lesbian Democratic Club
703-671-7023 p.428
Virginia Tech see:
Lesbian, Gay & Bisexual
Alliance at Virginia Tech p.428
Virginians for Justice News
pub. by Virginians for Justice
p.428
Virginians for Justice
800-258-7842 p.428
Visart Video 919-382-0650
p.368 919-929-4584 p.368
919-929-7634 p.368

919-932-1945 p.368 p.368
Visibility Project 914-338-5087
p.359
Vision Magazine pub. by King
of Peace Metropolitan
Community Church p.229
Vision Travel 305-444-8484
p.222
Visions 216-566-0060 p.372
312-539-5229 p.240
404-248-9712 p.231
702-786-5455 p.300
Visions & Dreams
316-942-6333 p.251
Visions—AC 412-237-2675
p.398
Vista CA see San Diego Area
p.179-180
Vista Grande Villa Private
Resort/Atrium Hotel
619-322-2404 p.172
Visual Video 212-620-7862
p.338
Visual Voice 800-655-2321
p.147, 244
Vita Mfg 516-563-2553 p.342
Vital Video 212-627-5700 p.338
Vitaletti, Robert, PhD
303-628-5425 p.194
VIVA, Lesbian & Gay Latino
Artists 310-301-8035 p.169
VLC see:
Vancouver Lesbian Connection
Voces de Ambiente p.288
Voice pub. by PFLAG of
Southwestern Connecticut
p.197
Voice and Vision Productions
p.127
Voice Magazine 619-281-8511
p.158, 180
The Voice of Integrity pub. by
Integrity, Inc p.140
Voice of the Turtle pub. by
American Baptists Concerned
p.140
Voices pub. by Brotherrs p.241
Voices of Kentuckiana, Inc.
502-327-4099 p.253
Volare Inn 616-857-4269 p.285
Volleyball see:
Gay Volleyball p.225
Vancouver Gay Volleyball
Association p.109
Vermont Gay Volleyball (VGV)
p.424
Volume 716-885-4580 p.320
Volumes of Pleasure
Bookshop 805-528-5565
p.188
The Volunteer pub. by Gay
Men's Health Crisis p.124, 313,
326
Volunteers In Direct Aid (VIDA)
602-279-VIDA p.152
Vortex 312-975-6622 p.240
Voters for Civil Liberties
p.304
Voyages Exception-L
514-521-2155 p.120
Vrhel, Keith, MD 619-296-0224
p.179
Vuk's 414-672-6900 p.445
Vulcan Steam & Sauna
619-238-1980 p.179
W.E. Mauger Estate B&B
505-242-8755 p.314
W.O.M.Y.N.'s Association
506-457-2156 p.111
Wages Due Lesbians
415-626-4114 p.185

Wagner, Dick, MSW, ACSW
314-965-1942 p.295
Waikiki AA Studios
808-595-7533 p.235
Waikiki Vacation Condos
808-946-9371 p.235
Wainscott NY see New York
City Area p.323, 327
Waitkevicz, Joan, MD
212-645-4790 p.341
Wake County Dept of Health
919-250-3950 p.367
Waking Owl 801-582-7323
p.423
Walden Books 808-922-4154
p.235
Waldo-Knox AIDS Coalition
207-338-1427 p.258
Waldorf Cafe 215-985-1836
p.392
Waldorf Towers Hotel
305-531-7684 p.219
WALE 990 AM 401-521-0990
p.401
Walker's Point Cafe
414-384-7999 p.445
Walker, Sylvia, MSW, LCSW
908-561-6073 p.311
Walking With Integrity pub.
by Integrity/Baltimore p.265
Wall Street 614-464-2800 p.374
Wall Street Lunch Club
212-289-1741 p.344
Wall Street Sauna
212-233-8900 p.342
Wallace, Timothy R., Ph.D.
203-233-6229 p.199
Walls By Cento 216-721-4649
p.372
Walnut CA see Los Angeles
Area p.170
Walnut Creek CA see East
Bay Area p.159
Walsh, Eileen M., MS
914-855-5306 p.358
Walter, Daniel, Psy.D.
804-424-0100 p.433
Waltham MA see Boston Area
p.133, 271, 273
Walton Way Station/
Reflections 706-733-2603
p.232
Walton, Lori, PA-C
215-790-6030 p.394
Wantagh NY see New York
City Area p.325, 327, 353
Wappingers Falls NY see
Poughkeepsie/Kingston Area
p.358
Ward's Computer Consulting
Service 941-278-2893 p.215
Ward, Robin 800-693-2027
p.274
Ware MA see Amherst/
Berkshire/Northampton Area
p.267
Warehouse 201-945-7034
p.307
Warehouse 29 910-333-9333
p.366
Warehouse Bar & Grill
416-465-3687 p.116
Warm Sands Villas
619-323-3005 p.172
Warm Sands Villas
◆ advertisement p.173
Warren County Pride
201-442-0600 p.307
Warren OH see Youngstown
p.378
Warsaw 305-531-4555 p.220

Canada National Resources

Accommodation: Reservations & Exchanges (see also Travel)

♀ • (?ፘ) Canadian Accommodation Network, National PO Box 42-A, Stn M, Montréal, QC H1V 3L6 514-254-1250; call first for Resources Fax

♂ • Home Suite Hom, PO Box 762 Succ. C, Montréal, QC H2L 4L6 212-995-3138; 800-429-4983 US & Canada "Travel & accommodation network for those offering or seeking hospitality & lodging exchange, private B&B, & low cost rentals."

AIDS/HIV Support, Education, Advocacy, Publications

♀ ☆ (?ፘ) Atlantic First Nations AIDS Task Force, PO Box 961, Sydney, NS B1P 6J4 902-539-4107 Fax 902-564-2137 Pub *Atlantic Standard*.

♂ ☆ ᛚ Canadian AIDS Society, 100 Sparks St #400, Ottawa, ON K1P 5B7 613-230-3580 Fax 613-563-4998 Mon-Fri 8.30am-5.30pm.

♀ ☆ Prostitutes Safer Sex Project, Box 1143 Stn F, Toronto, ON M4Y 2T8 416-964-0150

Archives/Libraries/History Projects

♂ • Archives Gaies du Quebec, CP 395 Succ Place du Parc, Montréal, QC H2W 2N9

♀ ★ ᛚᛚ Canadian Lesbian & Gay Archives, PO Box 639 Stn A, Toronto, ON M5W 1G2 416-777-2755 Fax 416-251-8285 Pub *Lesbian & Gay Archivist*.

♀ ☆ (ᛚᛚ) Canadian Women's Movement Archives/Archives canadiénnes du mouvement des femmes, 65 University, Ottawa, ON K1N 9A5 613-564-8129

Crafts Galleries, Supplies (see also Art)

♀ ○ Prairie Leathercraft, 224 2nd Ave S, Saskatoon, SK S7K 1K9 306-934-1684 "Leather, beads, craft supplies."

Distributors/Wholesalers

♀ ☆ Zed Distributors, 93 King St W, Kitchener, ON N2G 1A7 519-570-2196

Legal Services & Resources

♂ ★ Lesbian & Gay Immigration Task Force (LEGIT), mail to LEGIT, PO Box 384, Vancouver, BC V6C 2N2 604-877-7768; 604-856-2453 Pub *LEGIT News*.

Meeting/Contact Services & Publications, Talklines: Men Only

♂ • Gaymates, PO Box 3043, Saskatoon, SK S7K 3S9 306-652-3399 "National penpal/contact club."

Meeting/Contact Services, Publications, Talklines: Women Only

♀ • LYNX, PO Box 4759 Stn E, Ottawa, ON K1S 5H9 "Lesbian correspondence club."

Organizations/Resources: Business & Professional

♂ ★ ᛚᛚ Gazebo Connection, 810 West Broadway #382, Vancouver, BC V5Z 4C9 604-438-5442 Pub *Gazebo Connections*.

Organizations/Resources: Ethnic, Multicultural

♂ ★ Polish Gay & Lesbian Group (PGLG) of Canada, Manulife PO Box 19533, 55 Bloor St West, Toronto, ON M4W 1B0 416-767-9857 Pub *Nasza Bialo-Rozowa (Our White & Pink)*... "Mutual support group for people who are Polish or of Polish descent, campaigning for human rights in Canada & Poland. Chapters in Toronto, London ()ntarion) & Montreal. Call for details."

Organizations/Resources: Family

♂ ☆ Children of Lesbians & Gays Everywhere (COLAGE), Box 187 Stn F, Toronto, ON M4Y 2L5 (in USA 3023 N. Clark, Box121, Chicago, IL 60657)

Organizations/Resources: Political/Legislative

♂ ★ (?ፘ) EGALE (Equality for Gays & Lesbians Everywhere), Arts Court, 2 Daly, Ottawa, ON K1N 6E2 613-230-1043 Fax 613-237-6651

Organizations/Resources: Social, Recreational & Support Groups (see also Sport/Dance/Outdoor)

♂ ★ Ligo de Samseksamaj Geesperantistoj (LSG), PO Box 31017 Market Sq, Kitchener, ON N2H 6M0 519-576-5946 Pub *Forumo*. "Advances the Esperanto language for use in gay interethnic communication."

♂ ★ Rural Gay Men's Group, PO Box 1404, Port Hardy, BC V0N 2P0 604-949-8793

Organizations/Resources: Transgender & Transgender Publications

T ☆ GenderServe, PO Box 57551, Hamilton, ON L8P 4X3 Pub *GenderServe Newsletter*. 'Counseling, education & research.'

Publications: Female & Male Readership

♂ ★ *Angles*, 1170 Bute St, Vancouver, BC V6E 1Z6 604-688-0265 "The magazine of Vancouver's Gay, Lesbian & Bisexual Communities."

♂ ○ *Boudoir Noir*, Box 5, Stn F, Toronto, ON M4Y 2L4 416-591-2387 Fax 416-591-1572 boudoir@the-wire.com

♂ ☆ *It's Okay!*, Phoenix Counsel Inc 1 Springbank Dr, St Catharines, ON L2S 2K1 "International, consumer-written, self-help quarterly on sexuality, sex, self-esteen & disability."

♂ ★ *On Wings of Leather*, Northwind, PO Box 2253, Vancouver, BC V6B 3W2 604-253-1258 "Wiccan, pagan-related, faerie-related material with emphasis on leather, S/M, bondage."

♂ ★ *Perceptions*, PO Box 8581, Saskatoon, SK S7K 6K7 306-244-1930 A Gay/Lesbian Newsmagazine of the Prairies.

♂ ★ *SageNet*, PO Box 2102, Stn D, Ottawa, ON K1P 5W3 613-746-7279 Fax 613-746-0353

♂ ★ *Wayves*, PO Box 34090 Scotia Sq, Halifax, NS B3K 3S1 902-423-6999 wayves@fox.nstn.ca "Covering Atlantic Canada."

♂ ★ *Xtra Magazine*, 491 Church St, Toronto, ON M4Y 2C6 416-925-6665

If you can't find the
NAME, PLACE, SUBJECT, PUBLICATION
please check the index
(then let us know if we missed it!)

Publications: Female Readership

♀ ☆ *Fireweed: A Feminist Quarterly*, PO Box 279 Stn B, Toronto, ON M5T 2W2 416-504-1339

♀ ☆ (♿) *Healthsharing: A Canadian Women's Health Quarterly*, 14 Skey Lane, Toronto, ON M6J 3S4

♀ ☆♿ *Kinesis*, 301-1720 Grant St, Vancouver, BC V5L 2Y6 604-255-5499 "News about women that's not in the dailies."

♀ ☆♿ *Resources for Feminist Research/Documentation sur la recherche féministe*, OISE, 252 Bloor St W., Toronto, ON M5S 1V6

♂ • *sorority*, **PO Box 57, 1172 Bay St, Toronto, ON M5S 2B4 "Quarterly magazine, published by, for & about gay women."**
✦ *sorority advertisement page 103*

♀ • ♿ *The Womanist*, 41 York St, 3rd flr, Ottawa, ON K1N 5S7 613-562-4081

Publishers/Publishing-related Services

♀ • Gynergy Books, PO Box 2023, Charlottetown, PE C1A 7N7 902-566-5750 Fax 902-566-4473 "Lesbian & feminist fiction & nonfiction."

♂ • ★ Queer Press, PO Box 485 Stn P, Toronto, ON M5S 2T1 416-516-3363

♀ ☆♿ Women's Press, 517 College St #233, Toronto, ON M6G 4A2 416-921-2425 Fax 416-921-4428

Religious Organizations & Publications

♂ • ★ Affirm (United Church), PO Box 62032 Arbutus RPO, Vancouver, BC V6J 1Z1 604-737-1723 Pub *Consensus*. "United Church of Canada."

♂ • ★ Brethren/Mennonite Council for Lesbian & Gay Concerns in Eastern Canada, PO Box 43015 Eastwood Sq, Kitchener, ON N2H 6S9

♂ ☆ Canadian Unitarians for Lesbian, Gay & Bisexual Concerns, c/o 188 Eglinton Ave E #706, Toronto, ON M4P 2X7 416-489-4121

♂ • ★ Council on Homosexuality & Religion, PO Box 1912, Winnipeg, MB R3C 3R2 204-772-8215 Fax 204-478-1160

♂ • ★ Dignity Canada Dignité, PO Box 2102 Stn D, Ottawa, ON K1P 5W8 613-746-7279 Fax 613-746-0353 dignity@web.apc.org Pub *Dignity Journal*.

♂ • ★ Seventh-Day Adventist Kinship Canada, PO Box 82578, 5 Pts Mall Postal Outlet, Oshawa, ON L1G 7W7 905-432-2867 Pub *Connection*.

Travel & Tourist Services (see also Accommodation)

♂ • GAYROUTE: Tour-Gay-Canada, mail to T-G-C, Box 1036, Stn C, Montréal, QC H2L 4V3 "Information & service network for travelers to Canada; self-addressed envelope & $2 (no stamps or coins) for costs & details."

♂ • ★ Lesbian & Gay Hospitality Exchange International, PO Box 612 Stn C, Montréal, QC H2L 4K5 Fax 514-523-1599 "International membership network for exchange of hospitality when traveling."

♂ • Maritime Rainbow Connection, 2016 Oxford St, Halifax, NS B3L 2T2 902-422-2380 "Promoting Gay/Lesbian travel to the Maritime provinces."

MAIL ORDER: Books

♂ • Glad Day Bookshop, 598A Yonge St, Toronto, ON M4Y 1Z3 416-961-4161 Fax 416-961-1624

♂ • ♿ L'Androgyne Bookstore, 3636 Boul St Laurent, Montréal, QC H2X 2V4 514-842-4765 2 free catalogs: Gay; Lesbian/Feminist.

♂ • Little Sister's Book & Art Emporium, 1221 Thurlow St, Vancouver, BC V6E 1X4 604-669-1753; 800-567-1662; Fax 604-685-0252

♂ ○ ♿ Mystic Bookshop, 616 Dundas St, London, ON N5W 2Y8 519-673-5440 "New Age, Occult, Queer Culture, Literature, etc."

♀ ☆ Vancouver Women's Books, 315 Cambie St, Vancouver, BC V6B 2N4 604-684-0523; 800-610-6222 BC, AB, Yukon & NWT

♀ • Woman to Womon Books, 12404 114th Ave #106, Edmonton, AB T5M 3M5 403-454-8031

♂ • Womansline Books, 711 Richmond St, London, ON N6A 3H1 519-679-3416

MAIL ORDER: Erotica (Printed, Visual, Equipment)

♂ ○ (♿) Northbound Leather Ltd, 19 St Nicholas St, Toronto, ON M4Y 1W5 416-972-1037 Fax 416-975-1337 "Leather, rubber, B&D toys, etc."

♂ • S.H.H. Services, 291 Adsum Dr, Winnipeg, MB R2P 0V9 204-694-3164 Fax 204-697-1849 "Sexual aids, books, etc."

MAIL ORDER: Gifts, Cards, Pride & Promotional Items

♂ • Out of the Closet, PO Box 8581, Saskatoon, SK S7K 2M8 / 241 2nd Ave S, 3rd flr 306-665-1224

MAIL ORDER: Video (see also Film & Video)

♂ • ♿ Videomatica, 1855 W 4th Ave, Vancouver, BC V6J 1M4 604-734-0411; 604-734-5752 mail order; (800) 665-1469 (Canada) "Rental & sales; Gay/Lesbian-themed catalog available."

Alberta

Province/County Resources

Organizations/Resources: Sport/Dance/Outdoor

♀ ★ Alberta Rockies Gay Rodeo Association, PO Box 23064 Connaught Postal Outlet, Calgary, AB T2S 3B1 403-531-8140

♂ ★ Motorcycle Men of Alberta, 4141 40th St, Red Deer, AB T4N 1A5 403-346-8927

Publications

→ *Perceptions*: p.101

Calgary

☎ **Gay Lines Calgary 403-234-8973**

☎ **Lesbian Information Line/Womyn's Collective of Calgary 403-265-9458**

Accommodation: Hotels, B&B, Resorts, Campgrounds

♀ • Westways Guest House, 216 25th Ave SW; TS2 0L1 403-229-1758

AIDS/HIV Support, Education, Advocacy, Publications

♀ ☆ (&&) AIDS Calgary Awareness Association, #300, 1021 10th Ave SW; T2R 0B7 403-228-0198; 403-228-0161

♂ Feather of Hope Aboriginal AIDS Society, 300 - 1021 10th Ave SW; T2R 0B7 403-288-7719

Bars, Restaurants, Clubs, Discos

♀ • (?&) Detour, 318 17th Ave SW; T2R 0X8 403-228-7999 **BD** Evenings only.

♀ • (?&) Loading Dock, 318 17th Ave SW (rear entrance); T2R 0X8 403-228-7999 3am-2am.

♂ • (&&) RekRoom, 213A 10th Ave SW; T2R IK6 403-265-4749 **BP**f 4pm-3am. Out-of-town guests welcome: ID required.

♂ • Trax, 1130 10th Ave; 403-245-8477

♀ • (?&) Victoria's Restaurant, 306 17th Ave SW; T25 0A8 403-244-9991 **BR**

Bookstores: Gay/Lesbian/Feminist

♀ ○ A Woman's Place, 1412 Centre St S; T2G 2E4 403-263-5256

Erotica (Printed, Visual, Equipment)

♀ • (&) The Erogenous Zone, 3812 Macleod Tr S; T2G 2R2 403-287-3100 Fax 403-287-2619 10am-10pm; Sat & Sun to 6pm.

♀ • (&) Tad's Total Adult Discount Store, 1217-A 9th Ave SE; T2G 0S9 403-237-8237 "Peepshows & preview facilities."

♀ • (&) Tad's Total Adult Discount Store, 1506 14th St SW; T3C 1C9 403-244-8239

Health Clubs, Gyms, Saunas

♂ • Goliath's, 318 17th Ave SW; T2S 0A8 403-229-0911 **P** 24 hrs.

Organizations/Resources: Business & Professional

♀ ★ Calgary Networking Club, PO Box 561 Stn M; T2P 2J2 403-234-8973

Organizations/Resources: Family

♀ ☆ PFLAG Calgary, 96 Gordon Dr SW; T3E 5A8 403-246-3686

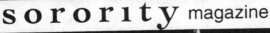

Organizations/Resources: General, Multipurpose, Pride

♀ ★ Lesbian Information Line/Womyn's Collective of Calgary, 223 12th Ave SW #211; T2R 0G9 403-265-9458 "Support/discussion groups, coming out drop-in."

♂ Project Pride Calgary, PO Box 20081; T2P 3H2

Organizations/Resources: Political/Legislative

♂ ★ (?♿) Calgary Lesbian & Gay Political Action Guild (CLAG-PAC), 223 12th Ave SW #209; T2R 0G9 403-266-5318

Organizations/Resources: Sexual Focus (Leather, S/M, etc) & Safe Sex Promotion

♂ ★ (?♿) CLUB Calgary, 223 12th Ave SW #201; T2R 0G9 403-234-8973 "Cowboy, leather, uniform, buddies - club."

Organizations/Resources: Social, Recreational & Support Groups (see also Sport/Dance/Outdoor)

♂ ★ (♿) Southern Alberta Prime Timers Calgary, PO Box 425, Nanton; T0L 1R0 403-646-3162

Organizations/Resources: Sport/Dance/Outdoor

♂ Alpine Frontrunners, Box 22054 Bankers Hall; T2P 4J1 403-234-8973

♂ ★ (♿) Apollo: Friends In Sports Club, PO Box 6481 Stn D; T2P 2E1 403-270-0742 Pub *Apollo Newsletter*.

♂ ★ (♿) Calgary Camp 181 Association, PO Box 702 Stn M; T2P 2J3 403-263-3598

♂ Chinook City Dance Club, G-O 223 12th Ave SW; T2R 0G9 403-266-3710 *d*

Organizations/Resources: Student, Academic, Alumni/ae

♂ ★ ♿♿ Gay, Lesbian & Bisexual Academics, Students & Staff (GLASS), Office #209E, Box 47 MacEwan Hall, 2500 University Dr NW; T2N 1N4 403-246-9214 glass@acs.ucalgary.ca

♀ ★ ♿♿ Gay/Lesbian/Bisexual Collective of Mount Royal College, 4825 Richard Rd SW, Students Association; T3E 6K6 403-686-2352

Organizations/Resources: Transgender & Transgender Publications

T ☆ Illusions Social Club, 6802 Ogden Rd SE Box 2000; T2C 1B4 403-236-7072

Organizations/Resources: Youth (see also Family)

♀ ★ (♿♿) Lesbian & Gay Youth/Calgary, 223 12th Ave SW #200B; T2R 0G9 403-262-1626 Pub *Lesbian & Gay Youth News*.

Performing Arts: Entertainment, Music, Recording, Theater, etc.

♀ ★ Rocky Mountain Singers, PO Box 34034 Westbrook PO; T3C 3W0 403-242-0081

Publications

♂ *Clue! Magazine*, 1039 17th Ave SW #205; 403-245-4512

Real Estate

♀ ● McGowan, Doug, Remax Realty, 159-2515 90th Ave SW; T2V 0L8 403-251-5400 Fax 403-251-6160 24 hrs.

Religious Organizations & Publications

♂ ★ Alleluia Metropolitan Community Church, 201 - 233 12 Ave SW; T2R 0G9 403-264-0320

Switchboards, Helplines, Phone Information

♂ ★ Gay Lines Calgary, 223 12th Ave SW #201; T2R 0G9 403-234-8973 7-10pm; tape 24 hrs.

Travel & Tourist Services (see also Accommodation)

♀ ○ (?♿) Uniglobe Swift Travel, 908 17th Ave SW #112; T2T 0A3 403-244-7887 Fax 403-229-2611

Edmonton

AIDS/HIV Support, Education, Advocacy, Publications

♀ ☆♿♿ AIDS Network of Edmonton Society, 201 - 11456 Jasper Ave; T5K 0M1 403-488-5742; 403-488-5816; Fax 403-488-3735

Bars, Restaurants, Clubs, Discos

♂ ★ ♿♿ Boots 'n Saddle, 10242 106th St; T5J 1H7 403-423-5014 *BLWP* 3pm-2am; Sun 5pm-1am.

♂ Boystown Cafe, 10116 124th St; 403-488-6636 *B*

♂ Rebar, 10551 Whyte Ave; 403-433-3600

♂ ● (?♿) The Roost, 10345 104th St; T5J 1B9 403-426-3150 Fax 403-487-6138 *BDE*

Bookstores: Gay/Lesbian/Feminist

♀ ● Woman to Womon Books, 12404 114th Ave #106; T5M 3M5 403-454-8031

Bookstores: General

♀ ● ♿ Orlando Books, 10640 Whyte Ave; T6E 2A7 403-432-7633

Community Centers (see also Women's Centers)

♂ ★ (♿) Gay & Lesbian Community Centre of Edmonton (GLCCE), PO Box 1852; T5J 2P2 / 11745 Jasper Ave #104 403-488-3234 Mon-Fri 7-10pm; Wed 1-4pm. Pub *GLCCE Newsletter*.

Erotica (Printed, Visual, Equipment)

♂ ● Executive Express, 10120 118th St #201; T5K 1Y4 403-482-7480 Wed-Mon 1-9pm.

Organizations/Resources: Family

♂ ★ (?♿) Gay Fathers & Lesbian Mothers, c/o GLCCE, Box 1852; T5J 2P2 403-482-7421

♀ ★ (?♿) PFLAG, c/o GLCCE PO Box 1852; T5J 2P2 403-462-5958 "Parents, Families & Friends of Lesbians & Gays."

Organizations/Resources: Political/Legislative

♂ ★ Gays & Lesbians Awareness Civil Rights Committee, PO Box 431; T5J 2K1 403-482-7421

Organizations/Resources: Social, Recreational & Support Groups (see also Sport/Dance/Outdoor)

♂ Edmonton Prime Timers, 11444 19th St #1093; T5G 2X6 403-467-8460

♀ ★ Womonspace, 9930 106th St #30; T5K 1C7 403-425-0511 Pub *Womonspace News*.

Organizations/Resources: Student, Academic, Alumni/ae

♂ ★ ♿♿ Gays & Lesbians on Campus (GALOC), Box 75, Student Union Bldg, University of Alberta; T6G 2J7 403-988-4166 Pub *Pink Triangle Supplement*.

Organizations/Resources: Youth (see also Family)

♀ ★ Gay & Lesbian Youth of Edmonton, c/o GLCCE, Box 1852; T5J 2P2 403-488-3234

Religious Organizations & Publications

♂ Dignity Edmonton, PO Box 55; T5J 2G9 403-469-4286 "Gay & Lesbian Catholics & their friends."

AB: Edmonton
105
Mount Lehman : BC

Religious
CANADA
Accommodation

♂ ★ Integrity/Edmonton, PO Box 35010 Oliver Postal Outlet; T5K 2R8 403-452-3482 "Lesbian & Gay Episcopalians & their friends."

♂ ★ & & Metropolitan Community Church of Edmonton, 10342 107th St #151; T5J 1K2 403-429-2321 Fax 403-425-0329 Sun 7.15pm at 10086 McDonald Dr.

Grande Prairie

AIDS/HIV Support, Education, Advocacy, Publications

♀ ☆ South Peace AIDS Council, PO Box 902; T8V 3Y1 403-538-3388 Fax 403-532-1550

Organizations/Resources: General, Multipurpose, Pride

♀ ★ (?&) Peace Gay Association, PO Box 1492; T8V 4Z3 403-539-3325

Jasper

AIDS/HIV Support, Education, Advocacy, Publications

♀ ☆ AIDS: A Positive Co-ordinated Response Society of Jasper, PO Box 1090; T0E 1E0 403-852-5274

Lethbridge

AIDS/HIV Support, Education, Advocacy, Publications

♀ ☆ & Lethbridge AIDS Connection Society, 515 7th St S #421; T1J 2G8 403-328-8186 Fax 403-328-5934

Organizations/Resources: Social, Recreational & Support Groups (see also Sport/Dance/Outdoor)

♂ Lighthouse Social Club, PO Box 24003; T1H 0E0 403-380-4257

Switchboards, Helplines, Phone Information

♀ ☆ & Gay & Lesbian Peer Support Line, c/o Lethbridge AIDS Connection Society, 515 7th St S #421; T1J 2G8 403-329-4666 Staffed Wed 7-10pm; answering machine 24 hrs: all calls returned.

Red Deer

AIDS/HIV Support, Education, Advocacy, Publications

♀ ☆ & & Central Alberta AIDS Network Society, 4935 51st St; T4N 2A8 403-241-2128 Fax 403-436-2352

Bars, Restaurants, Clubs, Discos

♂ ● & & The Other Place, 4752 Ross St #122; T4N 1X2 / Bay 3& 4 5579 47th St; 403-342-6440 *BDf*

Organizations/Resources: General, Multipurpose, Pride

♂ ★ & & Gay & Lesbian Association of Central Alberta (GALACA), PO Box 1078; T4N 6S5 403-340-2198 (recorded message); 403-340-2198 (recorded message)

Organizations/Resources: Youth (see also Family)

♂ Red Deer Youth, 116 - 6834 59th Ave; T4P 1C9 403-341-6823

British Columbia

Province/County Resources

AIDS/HIV Support, Education, Advocacy, Publications

♀ ☆ & Persons With AIDS Society of British Columbia, 1107 Seymour St, Vancouver, BC V6B 5S8 604-893-2250; 604-893-2253 helpline; Fax 604-893-2251 Mon-Fri 10am-5pm; Sat 11am-3pm. Pub *PWA Newsletter*. "Programs for HIV/AIDS Persons in self help/self care settings. Active politically."

Abbotsford: see Fraser Valley

Burnaby: see Vancouver

Duncan: see Vancouver Island Area

Fraser Valley

Organizations/Resources: Social, Recreational & Support Groups (see also Sport/Dance/Outdoor)

♂ ★ Friends in the Valley, PO Box 8000-591, Abbotsford; V2S 6H1 604-859-1567

Grand Forks: see Kootenay Area

Kamloops

AIDS/HIV Support, Education, Advocacy, Publications

♀ ☆ ASK—AIDS Society of Kamloops, 440 Victoria St #3; V2C 2A7 604-372-7585 Fax 604-372-1147

Organizations/Resources: Social, Recreational & Support Groups (see also Sport/Dance/Outdoor)

♂ ★ Gay Community of Kamloops, PO Box 2071; V2B 7K6 604-376-7311

Kelowna

Accommodation: Hotels, B&B, Resorts, Campgrounds

♂ ● The Flags Bed & Breakfast, 2295 McKinley Rd; V1Y 7P9 604-868-2416 (unlisted) "Pool, sauna, Jacuzzi, gardens & barbeque; nudity."

AIDS/HIV Support, Education, Advocacy, Publications

♀ ☆ Kelowna & Area AIDS Resources Education & Support Society (KARES), Box 134, 435 - 2339 Hwy 97 N.; V1X 4H9 604-862-2437 Fax 604-868-8662

Organizations/Resources: Social, Recreational & Support Groups (see also Sport/Dance/Outdoor)

♂ ★ (?&) Okanagan Gay/Lesbian Organization, PO Box 711 Stn A; V1Y 7P4 604-860-8555

Kootenay Area

AIDS/HIV Support, Education, Advocacy, Publications

♀ ☆ & & ANKORS: West Kootenay/Boundary AIDS Network Outreach & Support Society, 903 4th St, Castlegar; V1N 3P3 604-365-2447; 800-421-AIDS; Fax 604-365-5679 Pub *ANKORS Advocate*. (Linda in Grand Forks); 364-0511 (Heather in Trail); 365-4300 (Cindy in Castlegar); 354-6300 (Mary in Nelson)

Organizations/Resources: General, Multipurpose, Pride

♂ ★ & West Kootenay Gays & Lesbians, PO Box 725, Nelson; V1L 5R4 604-354-GAYS Pub *Gayzette*.

Maple Ridge

Organizations/Resources: Social, Recreational & Support Groups (see also Sport/Dance/Outdoor)

♂ ★ (?&) L&G of Meadow Ridge Support & Social Group, PO Box 377; V2X 8K9 604-467-9566

Mount Lehman

Accommodation: Hotels, B&B, Resorts, Campgrounds

♂ ● (?&) Rural Roots B&B, 4939 Ross Rd; V4X 1Z3 604-856-2380

Nelson: see Kootenay Area

BC: Pender Island
Accommodation
106
CANADA
Vancouver Island Area: BC
Organizations: Student

Pender Island

Accommodation: Hotels, B&B, Resorts, Campgrounds

♀ • Eagle Ridge Gulf Island Getaway, c/o Foster & Frost; VON 2M0 604-629-3692

Port Hardy: see Vancouver Island Area

Prince George

Accommodation: Hotels, B&B, Resorts, Campgrounds

♀ • Hawthorne Bed & Breakfast, 829 P.G. Pulp Mill Rd, RR4, S 7, C 10; V2N 2J2 604-563-8299 Fax 604-563-0899

AIDS/HIV Support, Education, Advocacy, Publications

♀ ☆&& Prince George AIDS Society, 1371 4th Ave; V2L 3J6 604-562-1172

Organizations/Resources: Social, Recreational & Support Groups (see also Sport/Dance/Outdoor)

♀ ★ GALA North, 1306 7th Ave #36; V2L 3P1 604-562-6253

Prince Rupert

AIDS/HIV Support, Education, Advocacy, Publications

♀ AIDS Prince Rupert Society, Box 848; V8J 3Y1 604-627-8823 Fax 604-624-4329

Organizations/Resources: General, Multipurpose, Pride

♀ ★ Prince Rupert Gay Group, Box 881; V8J 3Y1 604-627-8900

Revelstoke

Organizations/Resources: Social, Recreational & Support Groups (see also Sport/Dance/Outdoor)

♀ ★ (?&) Lothlorien, Box 8557, Sub #1; V0E 3G0 Social & support group.

Richmond

Organizations/Resources: Sport/Dance/Outdoor

♀ Pacific Rim Yacht Club, 23000 Dyke Rd #2; V6V 2H2 604-682-0118

Salt Spring Island

Accommodation: Hotels, B&B, Resorts, Campgrounds

♀ • The Blue Ewe B&B, 1207 Beddis Road; V8K 2C8 604-537-9344

♀ • Green Rose B&B, 346 Robinson Rd; V8K 1P7 604-537-9927

♀ • Summerhill Guest House, 209 Chu-An Dr; V8K 1H9 604-537-2727 Fax 604-537-4301

Sooke

Accommodation: Hotels, B&B, Resorts, Campgrounds

♀ ○ Ocean Wilderness, 109 West Coast Rd RR#2; V0S 1N0 604-646-2116

Tofino

Accommodation: Hotels, B&B, Resorts, Campgrounds

♀ • West Wind Guest House, 1321 Pacific Rim Hwy, Box 436; V0R 2Z0 604-725-2224

Vancouver Island Area

Accommodation: Hotels, B&B, Resorts, Campgrounds

Victoria

♀ • Back Hills Guest House for Women, 4470 Leefield Road R.R.1, Victoria; V9B 5T7 604-478-9648

♀ ○ (&&) **Lavender Link, 136 Medana St, Victoria; V8V 2H5 604-380-7098**

♀ ○ Oak Bay Guest House, 1052 Newport Ave, Victoria; V8S 5E3 604-598-3812

♀ • Weekender Bed & Breakfast, The, 10 Eberts St, Victoria; V8S 5L6 604-389-1688

AIDS/HIV Support, Education, Advocacy, Publications

♀ ☆&& AIDS Vancouver Island, 733 Johnson St #304, Victoria; V8W 3C7 604-384-2366; 604-384-4554 24 hrs.; Fax 604-380-9411 Pub Update.

♀ ★ Victoria PWA Society, 613 Superior St, Victoria; V8V 1V1 604-383-7494 Fax 604-383-1617

Bars, Restaurants, Clubs, Discos

Victoria

♂ ○ BJ's Lounge, 642 Johnson St, Victoria; V8W 1M6 604-388-0505

♂ • ♿ Rumors Cabaret, 1325 Government St, Victoria; V8W 1Y9 604-385-0566 BDE 9pm-2am; Sun to mdnt.

Bookstores: Gay/Lesbian/Feminist

♀ ☆&& Everywomans Books, 635 Johnson St, Victoria; V8W 1M7 604-388-9411 Mon-Sat 10.30am-5.30pm.

♀ ○ (&) Women's Work, 291 Wallace St, Nanaimo; V9R 5B4 604-754-1878

Counseling/Therapy: Private

♂ • && Teixeira, Bryan, PhD, 5575 W Saanich Rd, Victoria; V8X 4M6 604-727-3451

Health Clubs, Gyms, Saunas

♂ • Steam Works, 582 Johnson St, Victoria; V8W 1M3 604-383-6623 7pm-9am.

Organizations/Resources: General, Multipurpose, Pride

♀ ★ ♿ Central Island Gay & Lesbian Association, PO Box 127, Nanaimo; V9R 5K4 604-751-3060; 604-979-6295 (toll free voice mail); Fax 604-751-3090 Pub Island G.A.L.A. Newsletter. "Sports & other social activities."

Organizations/Resources: Political/Legislative

♀ ☆&& Status of Women Action Group, 506 Fort St #200, Victoria; V8W 1E8 604-383-7322 Fax 604-388-0100

Organizations/Resources: Social, Recreational & Support Groups (see also Sport/Dance/Outdoor)

♂ Hominum Victoria, PO Box 8677, Victoria; V8W 3S2 604-598-4900

♀ ★ (?&) Island Gay & Lesbian Association, Cowichan Valley Branch, mail to IGALA, PO Box 129, Duncan; V9L 3X1 604-748-7689

♀ ★ North Island Gay & Lesbian Support Group/Rural Gay Men's Group, Box 1404, Port Hardy; VON 2P0 604-949-8793

♀ ★ Victoria Prime Timers, PO Box 45030, Victoria; V8Z 7G9 604-727-6669; 604-384-2423 Pub Vintage Views.

Organizations/Resources: Student, Academic, Alumni/ae

♀ ★&& Lesbian Gay Bisexual Alliance, University of Victoria, PO Box 3035, Victoria; V8S 3P3

Publications

♀ • *LesbiaNews: Victoria's Monthly Lesbian Newsletter*, PO Box 5339 Stn B, Victoria; V8R 6S4

Vancouver

☎ Gay & Lesbian Centre Helpline 604-684-6869

Accommodation: Hotels, B&B, Resorts, Campgrounds

♀ • Albion Guest House: a B&B, 592 W 19th Ave; V5Z 1W6 604-873-2287 Fax 604-879-5682

♀ ○ The Buchan Hotel, 1906 Haro St; V6G 1H7 800-668-6654 Fax 604-685-5367
✦ *Buchan Hotel advertisement page 107*

♂ • Colibri Bed & Breakfast, 1101 Thurlow St; V6E 1W9 604-689-5100 Fax 604-682-3925

♀ ○ Columbia Cottage Guest House, 205 W 14th Ave; V5Y 1X2 604-874-5327 Fax 604-879-4547

♀ • (&&) Heritage House Hotel, 455 Abbott St; V6B 2L2 604-685-7777

♀ • Nelson House, 977 Broughton St; V6G 2A4 604-684-9793

♀ • && Royal Hotel, 1025 Granville; V6Z 1L4 604-685-5335 Fax 604-685-5351

♀ • West End Guest House, 1362 Haro St; V6E 1G2 604-681-2889 Fax 604-688-8812
✦ *West End Guest House advertisement page 107*

AIDS/HIV Support, Education, Advocacy, Publications

♀ ☆ & AIDS Vancouver, 1107 Seymour St; V6B 5S8 604-893-2210; 604-687-AIDS; Fax 604-893-2211

West End Guest House

Bed & Breakfast Inn

Catering to discerning travellers of all persuasions. Located in Vanvouver's most enlightened neighbourhood, the West End. Close to clubs, restaurants, shopping, beaches and Stanley Park.

West End Guest House
1362 Haro Street Vancouver B.C.
Canada
Ph 604 681-2889 Fax 604 688-8812
Vancouver's Pink Victorian

In Vancouver's West End

Quality accommodation at modest rates, the Buchan is located only blocks from the heart of downtown Vancouver. As our guest you will be only a short walk from world famous Stanley Park, English Bay and the international culinary delights of Denman street. B.C.'s first completely non-smoking hotel offers clean comfortable rooms where our guests can feel as if they are a part of the community rather than just visitors.

1906 HARO STREET, VANCOUVER, B.C. V6G 1H7
PHONE TOLL FREE 1-800-668-6654 OR FAX (604) 685-5367

BC: Vancouver
AIDS/HIV Support
108
CANADA
Vancouver : BC
Organizations: Social & Support

♀ ☆ ♂ Asian-Support AIDS Project (A-SAP) (A-SAP), c/o AIDS Vancouver, 1107 Seymour St; V6B 5S8 604-893-2210

Bars, Restaurants, Clubs, Discos

♂ Celebrities, 1022 Davie St; 604-689-3180 *D*

♂ • (♂♂) Chuck's Pub, Heritage House Hotel, 455 Abbott St; V6B 2L2 604-685-7777

♂ Denman Station, 860 Denman St; 604-669-3448

♀ Doll & Penny's Cafe, 167 Davie St; V6E 1N2 604-685-3417

♀ ☆♂♂ La Quena Coffeehouse, 1111 Commercial Drive; 604-251-6626 *R* 11am-11pm. "Latin-American flavor restaurant; community organizing centre; educational/political & musical events."

♀ • (♂♂) Lotus Club, Heritage House Hotel, 455 Abbott St; V6B 2L2 604-685-7777 *D* (women only Fri)

♀ • Ms T's, 339 W Pender St; V6E 1T3 604-682-8096 *LW* Mon-Sat 8pm-2am. "All types of Western dancing being taught: line dancing, clogging, 2-stepping.'

♀ o Odyssey, 1251 Howe St; 604-689-5256 *Bd*

♀ • (♂♂) Shaggy Horse, 818 Richards St; V6B 3A9 604-688-2923 *LW* 7pm-2am; Sun to mdnt.

♀ • (♂♂) Streets, Dufferin Hotel, 900 Seymour St; V6B 3L9 604-683-4251 *BDER*

♀ • (♂♂) Uncle Charlie's Lounge, Heritage House Hotel, 455 Abbott St; V6B 2L2 604-685-7777

Bookstores: Gay/Lesbian/Feminist

♀ • Little Sister's Book & Art Emporium, 1221 Thurlow St; V6E 1X4 604-669-1753; 800-567-1662; Fax 604-685-0252 10am-11pm.

♀ ☆ Vancouver Women's Books, 315 Cambie St; V6B 2N4 604-684-0523; 800-610-6222 BC, AB, Yukon & NWT Mon-Sat 10am-6pm. "Everyone welcome."

♀ • ♂ Women In Print, 3566 W 4th Ave; V6R 1N8 604-732-4128

Bookstores: General

♀ o ♂ Black Sheep Books, 2742 W 4th Ave; V6K 1R1 604-732-5087

♀ o Octopus Books, 1146 Commercial Drive; V5L 3X2 604-253-0913

♀ ☆ Spartacus Books, 311 W Hastings St; V6B 1H6 604-688-6138 "Worker-owned non-profit collective."

Broadcast Media

♀ ★ Coming Out Show, CFRO, 337 Carrall St; V6B 2J4 604-684-8494 Thu 7-8pm, 102.7FM.

♀ ★ Lesbian Show, Vancouver Cooperative Radio, 337 Carrall St; V6B 2J4 604-684-8494 Thu 8pm, 102.7FM

♀ ★ WomenVisions, c/o Vancouver Cooperative Radio, 337 Carrall St; V6B 2J4 604-684-8494; 604-684-7561; Fax 604-681-5310 Mon 8pm; Tue 1pm 102.7FM. "Feminist grassroots radio."

Community Centers (see also Women's Centers)

♀ ★ Gay & Lesbian Centre, 1170 Bute St; V6E 1Z6 604-684-5307 11am-6pm; 604-684-6869 7-10pm.; Fax 604-684-5309 10am-10pm. "Services include Library; Health Clinic; Legal Clinic; Counseling & Crisis Information; Coming Out & Youth Groups; AA/SAA; Self Defense."

♀ ★ (?♂) Vancouver Lesbian Connection (VLC), 876 Commercial Drive; V5L 3W6 604-254-8458 Fax 604-254-8115 Tue & Thu noon-7pm, Sat noon-5pm.

Dentists

♀ • ♂ Kardash, David, DMD, 590-1090 W Georgia St; V6E 3V7 604-689-8505

Erotica (Printed, Visual, Equipment)

♀ • (♂) Mack's Leathers, 1043 Granville St; 604-688-6225 11am-7pm; Fri to 9pm; Sat 10am-6pm; Sun noon-6pm.

Health Clubs, Gyms, Saunas

♂ • (♂) Club Vancouver, 339 W. Pender St 416-681-5719 24 hrs.

♂ • Fahrenheit 212 Steam, 971 Richards St; 604-689-9719 *f*

♂ o Richards Street Service Club, 1169 Richards St; V6B 3E7 604-684-6010

Legal Services & Resources

♀ • ♂♂ Benson, Sandra J., 3041 Anson Ave #202, Coquitlam; V3B 2H6 604-878-0408

♀ ★ Lesbian & Gay Immigration Task Force (LEGIT), mail to LEGIT, PO Box 384; V6C 2N2 604-877-7768; 604-856-2453 Pub *LEGIT News.*

♀ • ♂♂ Robb, Kevin James, 207 W Hastings St #610; V6B 1H7 604-681-6322

♀ • ♂♂ Smith & Hughes Law Firm, 1525 Robson St #321; V6G 1C3 604-683-4176

Massage Therapy (Licensed only)

♀ • Sands, Astarte, 1-509 Carrall St; 604-251-5409 "Shiatsu practitioner."

Organizations/Resources: Business & Professional

♀ ★ Gay & Lesbian Business Association of Greater Vancouver, 1810 Alberni #204; V6G 1B3 604-689-5107

♀ ★ (?♂) Lesbian & Gay Benefits Committee, Box 110 1472 Commercial Dr; V5L 3X9 604-876-1465

Organizations/Resources: Ethnic, Multicultural

♀ ★ Atish: Middle East, Africa & South Asian, Box 345, 1027 Davie St; V6E 4L2 604-244-9275 Pub *Awaz-E-Atish.*

♂ ★ Gay Asians of Vancouver Area (GAVA), c/o GLC, 1170 Bute St; V6E 1Z6 604-683-3825

Organizations/Resources: Family

♀ ★♂♂ PFLAG, PO Box 30502 Brentwood Postal Outlet, 201-4567 Lougheed Hwy, Burnaby; V5C 2A0 604-255-4429 "Parents, Families & Friends of Lesbians & Gays."

Organizations/Resources: General, Multipurpose, Pride

♀ ★ Vancouver Pride Society, Box 300, 1195 Davie St; V6E 1N2 604-684-2633 Fax 604-681-4812

Organizations/Resources: Sexual Focus (Leather, S/M, etc) & Safe Sex Promotion

♂ Knights of Malta Dogwood Chapter, PO Box 3116 MPO; V6B 3X6

♂ ★ Vancouver Activists in S/M (VASM), PO Box 4579; V6B 4A1 Pub *Scene.*

♂ ★ Vancouver Jacks, PO Box 2682; V6B 3W8 604-688-9378 x2034 hotline.

Organizations/Resources: Social, Recreational & Support Groups (see also Sport/Dance/Outdoor)

♀ ★ Gay Leisure Link, PO Box 4662; V6B 4A1

♂ ★ Hominum, PO Box 3785; V6B 3Z1 604-684-6869 "Support group for men currently or previously married."

Switchboards, Helplines, Phone Information

♀ ★ Gay/Lesbian Info Line, Box 1661; R3C 2Z6 204-284-5208 Mon-Fri 7.30-10pm.

New Brunswick
Province/County Resources

AIDS/HIV Support, Education, Advocacy, Publications

♀ ☆ ♂♂ AIDS New Brunswick, c/o Victoria Health Centre, 65 Brunswick St, Fredericton, NB E3B 1G5 506-459-7518; 800-561-4009 Mon-Fri 8.30am-4.30pm.

Organizations/Resources: Political/Legislative

♀ ★ New Brunswick Coalition for Human Rights Reform, PO Box 1556 Stn A, Fredericton, NB E3B 5G2 506-457-2156

Aulac

Accommodation: Hotels, B&B, Resorts, Campgrounds

♀ ● Georgian House, RR#3 Sackville; E0A 3C0 506-536-1481 Member of Maritime Rainbow Connections.

Bathurst

Organizations/Resources: General, Multipurpose, Pride

♀ ★ (?♂) Gaies Nor Gays, PO Box 983; EZ3 4H8 506-738-7440 *D*

Campellton

Organizations/Resources: Social, Recreational & Support Groups (see also Sport/Dance/Outdoor)

♀ ★ No Borders/Sans Frontières, PO Box 461 Stn A; E3N 5G2

Fredericton

Bars, Restaurants, Clubs, Discos

♀ ● ♂♂ Kurt's Dance Warehouse, 353 Queen St; 506-453-0740 *D*

Organizations/Resources: Political/Legislative

♀ ★ (?♂) Fredericton Lesbians & Gays (FLAG), PO Box 1556 Stn A; E3B 5G2 506-457-2156 Pub *New Brunswick Gay Guide*.

Organizations/Resources: Social, Recreational & Support Groups (see also Sport/Dance/Outdoor)

♀ ★ (?♂) W.O.M.Y.N.'s Association, PO Box 20082; E3B 6Y8 506-457-2156

Organizations/Resources: Student, Academic, Alumni/ae

♀ Gay & Lesbian Alliance of UNB/UST, c/o Help Centre, UNB SUB, PO Box 4400; E3B 5A3 506-457-2156

Religious Organizations & Publications

♀ New Hope Community Church, c/o Unitarian CHurch, 749 Charlotte St; 506-457-4675

Moncton

Bars, Restaurants, Clubs, Discos

♀ Dans l'fond bar, (basement Nat Bank Bldg) 238 St George St

Organizations/Resources: General, Multipurpose, Pride

♀ ★ Gays & Lesbians of Moncton (GLM), PO Box 7102, Riverview; E1B 1V0 506-855-8064

St John

Accommodation: Hotels, B&B, Resorts, Campgrounds

♀ ● Mahogany Manor, 220 Germain St; E2L 2G4 506-636-8000 Member of Maritime Rainbow Connections.

AIDS/HIV Support, Education, Advocacy, Publications

♀ ☆ ♂♂ AIDS/Saint John, 115 Hazen St; E2L 3L3 506-652-2437 Fax 506-652-2438

Newfoundland
Province/County Resources

Organizations/Resources: General, Multipurpose, Pride

♀ ★ Newfoundland Gays & Lesbians for Equality (NGALE), PO Box 6221, St Johns, NF A1C 6J9 709-753-4297

Corner Brook

Organizations/Resources: Social, Recreational & Support Groups (see also Sport/Dance/Outdoor)

♀ Gay & Lesbian Association for Support (GLAS), PO Box 20002; A2H 6J5 709-634-1066

St Johns

AIDS/HIV Support, Education, Advocacy, Publications

♀ ☆ ♂♂ Newfoundland & Labrador AIDS Committee, Inc, PO Box 626 Stn C; A1C 5K8 / 347 Duvkworth St, 6th Flr 709-579-8656; 800-579-8656

Bars, Restaurants, Clubs, Discos

♀ Back Alley Pub, 164-A Water St; 709-726-6782

♀ Zone 216, 216 Water St; 709-754-2492 *BD*

Bookstores: General

♀ ○ Wordplay Bookstore, 221 Duckworth St; A1C 1G7 709-726-9193; 800-563-9100; http://www.wordplay.com

Organizations/Resources: Social, Recreational & Support Groups (see also Sport/Dance/Outdoor)

♀ Newfoundland Amazon Network (NAN), PO Box 1104; A1C 5M5

Nova Scotia
Province/County Resources

AIDS/HIV Support, Education, Advocacy, Publications

♀ ☆ ♂♂ The AIDS Coalition of Nova Scotia, 5675 Spring Garden Rd #305, Halifax, NS B3J 1H1 902-425-4882; 902-425-AIDS 8am-5pm.

♀ ☆ ♂ Atlantic First Nations AIDS Task Force, PO Box 47049, Halifax, NS B3K 2B0 902-492-4255; 800-565-4255

Organizations/Resources: Ethnic, Multicultural

♀ JUKA, PO Box 36004, Halifax, NS B3J 3S9 902-429-7922 (Nova Scotia Black Gay, Lesbian, & Bisexual Association)

Organizations/Resources: Social, Recreational & Support Groups (see also Sport/Dance/Outdoor)

♂ ★ (?♂) Gay Men's Gathering, PO Box 36054, Halifax, NS B3J 3S9

Publications

♀ ★ *Wayves*, PO Box 34090 Scotia Sq, Halifax, NS B3K 3S1 902-423-6999 wayves@fox.nstn.ca "Covering Atlantic Canada."

Cape Breton

AIDS/HIV Support, Education, Advocacy, Publications

♂ AIDS Coalition of Cape Breton, PO Box 177, Sydney; B1P 6H1 902-567-1766

Organizations/Resources: Social, Recreational & Support Groups (see also Sport/Dance/Outdoor)

♀ ★ (?♂) Island Gay, Lesbian & Bisexual Support, PO Box 469, Florence; B0C 1J0 902-736-0987

Florence: see Cape Breton

Halifax

Accommodation: Hotels, B&B, Resorts, Campgrounds

♀ ○ Bobs' B&B, 2715 Windsor St; B3K 5E1 902-454-4374 Member of Maritime Rainbow Coalition.

♀ ● (?♂) Centretown Bed & Breakfast, 2016 Oxford St; B3L 2T2 (at Quinpool) 902-422-2380 "Non-smoking; air conditioning; Serge parle Français."

♀ ○ Fresh Start Bed & Breakfast, 2720 Gottingen St; B3K 3C7 902-453-6616

Bars, Restaurants, Clubs, Discos

♀ Le Cruz, 5680 Spring Garden Road; 902-422-4530

♀ ● ♂♂ Of Course: A Cafe & Bistro, 5657 Spring Garden Rd; B3J 3R4 902-492-2229 *R*

♀ ● (♂♂) Of Course: A Cafe & Bistro, 1858 Market St; B3J 3L9 902-492-2455 *R*

♀ ● (♂) The Stonewall Tavern, 1560 Hollis St; 902-425-2166; 902-425-2366 *BRE*

♀ ○ The Studio, 1537 Barrington St; 902-423-6866 *BDL*

Bookstores: General

♀ ○ Entitlement: The Book Company, 5675 Spring Garden Road; 902-420-0565 Fax 902-420-3201

♀ ○♂♂ Frog Hollow Books, 5640 Spring Garden Rd; B3J 3M7 902-429-3318

♀ ● ♂ Red Herring Co-op Books, 1578 Argyle St; 902-422-5087

Broadcast Media

♀ ★♂♂ Queer News, c/o CKDU 97.5 FM, 6136 University Ave; B3H 4J2 902-494-6479 (also Fax)

♀ ☆ (♂) The Word Is Out, c/o CKDU 97.5 FM, 6136 University Ave; B3H 4J2 902-494-6479; 902-494-2585 Mon 7-8pm.

Erotica (Printed, Visual, Equipment)

♀ ○ ♂ Atlantic News, 5560 Morris St; 902-429-5468

Meeting/Contact Services, Publications, Talklines

♀ ★ Out To Lunch, 2044 Creighton; B3K 3R2 "Contact service for isolated women."

Organizations/Resources: Sexual Focus (Leather, S/M, etc) & Safe Sex Promotion

♀ Tightrope, PO Box 33067; B3L 4T6

Organizations/Resources: Social, Recreational & Support Groups (see also Sport/Dance/Outdoor)

♂ Wilde In The Streets, PO Box 36054; B3J 3S9 902-425-5486 Fax 902-492-1187

Organizations/Resources: Student, Academic, Alumni/ae

♀ ★♂♂ Bisexual, Gay & Lesbian Association of Dalhousie (BGLAD), SUB #307, 6136 University Ave; B3H 4J2 902-494-1415 Meet Thu 7pm, Room 307.

Publications: Directories, Bibliographies, Guides, Travel

♀ *Greater Halifax Pride Guide*, 3-1563 Walnut St; B3H 3S1

Religious Organizations & Publications

♀ Safe Harbor MCC, PO Box 31108; B3K 5T9 902-461-0035

Kentville

AIDS/HIV Support, Education, Advocacy, Publications

♀ Valley AIDS Concern Group, 28 Webster Ct #201; B4N 1H7 902-679-3515

Lunenburg

Accommodation: Hotels, B&B, Resorts, Campgrounds

♀ ● Brook House, 3 Old Blue Rocks Rd; B0J 2C0 902-634-3826 Member of Maritime Rainbow Connections.

New Glasgow

AIDS/HIV Support, Education, Advocacy, Publications

♀ Pictou County AIDS Coalition, PO Box 964; B2H 5K7 902-752-6218

Shelburne

Accommodation: Hotels, B&B, Resorts, Campgrounds

♀ ● (?♂) Toddle Inn, 163 Water St; 902-875-3229; 800-565-0000 (Check Inns) *R* Member of Maritime Rainbow Connections.

Sydney: see Cape Breton

Wolfville

Organizations/Resources: Social, Recreational & Support Groups (see also Sport/Dance/Outdoor)

♀ ★♂♂ OUTLET, Acadia Women's Centre SUB; B0P 1Z0 902-542-2287 x140

Ontario

Province/County Resources

Organizations/Resources: Political/Legislative

♀ ★ (?♂) Coalition for Lesbian & Gay Rights In Ontario (CLGRO), PO Box 822 Stn A, Toronto, ON M5W 1G3 416-533-6824 Pub *Newsletter*.

Organizations/Resources: Sexual Focus (Leather, S/M, etc) & Safe Sex Promotion

♂ ★ SMAC-SWO (S/M Activists of Southwestern Ontario), 77 Rte 108, RR#1, c/o David F. (Secretary), Lennoxville, QC J1M 2A2 "Gay & bi men; new members & inquiries invited."

Organizations/Resources: Youth (see also Family)

♀ ★ Lesbian Gay Bi Youth Line, PO Box 62 Stn F, Toronto, ON M4Y 2L4 800-268-9688; 416-962-9688 3-11pm.

Edwards

Accommodation: Hotels, B&B, Resorts, Campgrounds

♀● The Stonehouse, 2605 Yorks Corners Rd; K0A 1V0 613-821-3822

Grand Valley

Accommodation: Hotels, B&B, Resorts, Campgrounds

♀● Manfred's Meadow Guest House, RR #1; L0N 1G0 519-925-5306 "100-acre full-service resort 90 minutes NW of Toronto."

Guelph

AIDS/HIV Support, Education, Advocacy, Publications

♀ ☆&& AIDS Committee of Guelph & Wellington County, 265 Woolwich St; N1H 3V8 519-763-2255 Fax 519-763-8125 Pub *Between The Lines.*

Organizations/Resources: Political/Legislative

♀● ★&& Guelph Gay, Lesbian & Bisexual Equality, PO Box 773; N1H 6L8 519-836-4550 Pub *Newsletter.*

Hamilton

AIDS/HIV Support, Education, Advocacy, Publications

♀ ☆& Hamilton AIDS Network (HAN), 143 James St S #900; L8P 3A1 905-528-0854; 800-563-6919; Fax 905-528-6311 Mon-Thu 9am-9pm; Fri to 5pm. Pub *Hamilton AIDS Network News.*

Bars, Restaurants, Clubs, Discos

♂ Cafe 121, 121 Hughson St N; L8R 1G7 905-546-5258 *BR*

♂ Embassy Club, 54 King St E; 905-522-7783 *BD*

Bookstores: Gay/Lesbian/Feminist

♀ ○ Women's Bookstop, 333 Main St West; 905-525-2970

Organizations/Resources: Student, Academic, Alumni/ae

♀● ★& Gay Lesbian Bisexual Association of McMaster, PO Box 313, McMaster University; L8S 1C0 905-525-9140 x27397 Pub *10% Plus.*

Jasper

Accommodation: Hotels, B&B, Resorts, Campgrounds

♀● & Starr Easton Hall, PO Box 215, RR#3; K0G 1G0 613-283-7479 *BR*

Kingston

☎ Kingston Lesbian Gay Bisexual Association 613-545-2960

Bars, Restaurants, Clubs, Discos

♂ Robert's Club Vogue, 477 Princess St; (University Ave) 613-547-2923 *BR*

Organizations/Resources: General, Multipurpose, Pride

♀● ★Lesbian, Gay & Bisexual Pride Committee—Kingston (LCBPC), PO Box 1263; K7L 4Y8 613-545-2960 Fax 613-531-8684 "Organizes June Pride Month, Film Festival."

Organizations/Resources: Youth (see also Family)

♀● & Outright Youth In Kingston, PO Box 2148; K7L 5J9 613-545-2960 (Lesbian & Gay Infoline); 613-545-2960 (Lesbian & Gay Infoline) Meet Wed 7-9pm at 51 Queen's Cres. "Peer support group 26 years & under."

Publications

♂ ★ *Inside Out Newspaper*, PO Box 1263; K7L 4Y8 613-531-8767 Fax 613-531-8684 Monthly community newspaper serving Kingston & South-Eastern Ontario.

Kitchener/Waterloo

AIDS/HIV Support, Education, Advocacy, Publications

♀ ☆&& AIDS Committee of Cambridge, Kitchener, Waterloo & Area (ACCKWA), 123 Duke St E., Kitchener; N2H 1A4 519-570-3687 Fax 519-570-4034

Bars, Restaurants, Clubs, Discos

♂● (&&) Club Renaissance, 24 Charles St W 519-570-2406 *BDf* Wed-Sun 9pm-3am.

Bookstores: General

♀ ○ (?&) Blue Leaf Book Shop, PO Box 1294 Stn C, Kitchener; N2G 4G8 / 93 King St W., 2nd flr 519-570-0950

Organizations/Resources: Student, Academic, Alumni/ae

♂● ★ (?&) Gay & Lesbian Liberation of Waterloo, Federation of Students, University of Waterloo, Waterloo; N2L 3G1 519-884-GLOW

London

☎ London Gayline 519-433-3551

AIDS/HIV Support, Education, Advocacy, Publications

♀ ☆(&&) AIDS Committee of London, 343 Richmond St #200; N6A 3C2 519-434-1601; 519-434-8160 AIDSLine; Fax 519-434-1843 Mon-Thu 9am-9pm; Fri 9am-5pm.

Antiques & Collectables

♂● Antiquities Shoppe, 129 Wellington; N6B 2K7 (at Hill) 519-663-9400

Bars, Restaurants, Clubs, Discos

♂● && 52nd Street Dance Bar/Backstreet Patio, 347 Clarence St; 519-679-4015 *BDELf*

♂● && Embassy Cultural House, 732 Dundas St; 519-438-7127 *R*

♂● ★ (&&) HALO Club, 649 Colborne St; N6A 3Z2 519-433-3762 *D*

♂ Lacey's, 355 Talbot St; 519-645-3197

♀● (&) Strange Angels, 179 Albert St; N6A 1L9 519-432-8484 *BRE*

Bookstores: Gay/Lesbian/Feminist

♀● Womansline Books, 711 Richmond St; N6A 3H1 519-679-3416 Mon-Thu & Sat 10am-5.30pm; Fri to 6pm.

Bookstores: General

♀ ○ & Mystic Bookshop, 616 Dundas St; N5W 2Y8 519-673-5440 "New Age, Occult, Queer Culture, Literature, etc."

Broadcast Media

♂ Rainbow Radio Network, UWO Rm 250 UCC; N6A 3K7 519-661-3601 CHRW 94.7 FM, Tue 10pm-mdnt.

Film & Video

♀● ★&& London Lesbian Film Festival, Box 44030 Market Tower, 151 Dundas St; N6A 5S5 519-858-4466

Funding: Endowment, Fundraising, Scholarship

♀ ★&& Barony of London, 801 Jaina Blvd; N6E 2S1 519-686-4112

ON: London
114
Ottawa/Hull Area: ON
Health Clubs, Gyms, Saunas
CANADA
Organizations: Business

Health Clubs, Gyms, Saunas

⚓ Club London, 722 York St; 519-438-2625

Organizations/Resources: General, Multipurpose, Pride

♀ ★ (&&) Homophile Association of London Ontario (HALO), 649 Colborne St; N6A 3Z2 519-433-3762 Pub *HALO Newsletter*.

Organizations/Resources: Sport/Dance/Outdoor

♀ London Sports Alliance, Box 371 Stn B; N6A 4W1

Organizations/Resources: Student, Academic, Alumni/ae

♀ ★&& uwOUT!, Room 340 UCC, University of Western Toronto; N6A 3K7 519-432-3078

Organizations/Resources: Youth (see also Family)

♀ ★ Positivity About Youthful Sexual Orientation (PAYSO), c/o ACOL, 343 Richmond; N6A 3C2 519-434-1601

Religious Organizations & Publications

♀ ★ Dignity London Dignité, PO Box 1884 CP 1884 Stn Succ. A; N6A 5J4 519-686-7709 (after 5pm) Meet 2nd Mon of month, 7.30-8.30pm, at Halo Club, 649 Colborne St, 2nd flr. "Gay & Lesbian Catholics & their friends."

♀ ★ (&) Holy Fellowship Metropolitan Community Church, PO Box 213 Stn B; N6A 4V8 519-645-0744

Switchboards, Helplines, Phone Information

♀ ★ London Gayline, c/o HALO 649 Colborne St; N6A 3Z2 519-433-3551

Maynooth

Accommodation: Hotels, B&B, Resorts, Campgrounds

♀ ● (&&) Wildewood Guest House, Box 121, Madawaska Rd; K0L 2S0 613-338-3134

Mississauga

Bars, Restaurants, Clubs, Discos

♀ Go West, 105 Lakeshore Road East; 905-891-6911

Niagara Region

AIDS/HIV Support, Education, Advocacy, Publications

♂ ☆&& AIDS Committee of Niagara, 541 Glenridge Ave, St Catharines; L2R 6S5 909-984-8684

North Bay

Organizations/Resources: General, Multipurpose, Pride

♀ ★ (?&) Gay Nipissing, PO Box 1362; P1B 8K5 705-495-4545 Pub *Gay Nipissing Newsletter*. "Dances & social/support meetings; peer counseling phoneline."

Ottawa/Hull Area
Includes Hull, QC

☎ Gayline/Télégai 613-238-1717

Accommodation: Hotels, B&B, Resorts, Campgrounds

Ottawa

♂ ○ Ambiance Bed & Breakfast, 330 Nepean St, Ottawa; K1R 5G6 613-563-0421 "Downtown; walking distance to all activities."

♂ ● Rideau View Inn, 177 Frank St, Ottawa; K2P 0X4 613-236-9309; 800-268-2082; Fax 613-237-6842
◆ *Rideau View Inn advertisement page 115*

AIDS/HIV Support, Education, Advocacy, Publications

♀ ☆&& AIDS Committee of Ottawa/Le Comité du SIDA d'Ottawa, 207 Queen St, 4th flr, Ottawa; K1P 6E5 613-238-5014

♀ ☆&& The Living Room—AIDS Committee of Ottawa, 207 Queen St, 4th flr, Ottawa; K1P 6E5 613-563-0851; 800-461-2182 (WC & ON only) "Drop-in center for persons affected & infected by HIV/AIDS."

Bars, Restaurants, Clubs, Discos

Hull

♂ Le Club & The Club House, 77 rue Wellington, Hull; 819-777-1411 Fri & Sat women; Thu & Sun mixed.

♂ Le Pub de la Promenade, 175 Promenade du Portage, Hull; J8X 2K4 819-771-8810

Ottawa

♂ Briefs, 151 George St, Ottawa; K1N 5W5 613-241-9667

♂ ● (&) Cell Block, 340 Somerset St W., Ottawa; K2P 0J9 613-594-0233 *BEdLL*

♂ ● (&) Centretown Pub, 340 Somerset St W., Ottawa; K2P 0J9 613-594-0233

♂ Club 363, 363 Bank St, Ottawa; 613-237-0708

♂ ★ The Coffeehouse 318 (ALGBO Centre), 318 Lisgar St, Ottawa; K1P 5W9 613-233-1324 Fri: mixed; Sat: women only.

♀ Coral Reef Club, 30 Nicolas, Ottawa; 613-234-5118 Fri women; Sat mixed.

♂ ● Silhouette Piano Bar, 340 Somerset St W., Ottawa; K2P 0J9 613-594-0233 *BE*

Bookstores: Gay/Lesbian/Feminist

♀ ● (?&) After Stonewall, 105 4th Ave, 2nd flr, Ottawa; K1S 2L1 613-567-2221 10am-6pm; Fri to 8pm; Sun noon-5pm.

♀ ● & Mother Tongue Books, 1067 Bank St, Ottawa; K1S 3WP (at Sunnyside) 613-730-2346

♀ ● (&&) Ottawa Women's Bookstore/La Librairie des Femmes, 272 Elgin St, Ottawa; K2P 1M2 613-230-1156 Mon-Wed & Sat 10am-6pm; Thu & Fri to 9pm; Sun 11am-4pm.

Bookstores: General

♀ ○ (&) Octopus Books, 798 Bank St, Ottawa; K1S 3V8 613-236-2589 Mon-Wed & Sat 10am-6pm; Thu & Fri to 9pm.

Erotica (Printed, Visual, Equipment)

♀ ○ Wilde Videos, 631 Somerset St W, Ottawa; K1R 5K3 613-567-4858

Food Specialties, Catering (see also Party/Event Services)

♀ ● The Foodery, Box 5551 Stn F, Ottawa; K2C 3M1 613-728-3918

Health Clubs, Gyms, Saunas

♂ ● Club Ottawa, 1069 Wellington St 613-722-8978 *Bf*

♂ Steam Works, 487 Lewis St, Ottawa; 613-230-8431

Legal Services & Resources

♀ Lesbian & Gay Immigration Task Force Ottawa (LEGIT), mail to LEGIT Ottawa Colin Archibald, 148 Springhurst Ave, Ottawa; K1S 0E5 613-233-5610

♀ ● (&) MacAdam, Philip, BA, LLB, 67 Daly Ave #1000, Ottawa; K1N 6E3 613-234-6759

Organizations/Resources: Business & Professional

♀ ★ Lambda Ottawa, PO Box 1445 Stn B, Ottawa; K1P 6C3 613-233-8212

Organizations/Resources: Family

♂️ ★ Gay Married Men (GMM), PO Box 8933 Stn T, Ottawa; K1G 3J2 "Social/support group."

♂️ Parent Resource Network, c/o Lesbian & Gay Youth/Ottawa-Hull Box 2919 Stn D, Ottawa; K1P 5W9 613-238-1717

Organizations/Resources: General, Multipurpose, Pride

⚥ ★ Association of Lesbians, Gays & Bisexuals of Ottawa (ALGO), PO Box 2919 Stn D, Ottawa; K1P 5W9 / ALGBO Center, 318 Lisgar St 613-233-0152 Pub *GO Info.*

⚥ ★ (♿) Pink Triangle Services, PO Box 3043 Stn D, Ottawa; K1P 6H6 613-563-4818; 613-238-1717 Gayline Speakers Bureau; workshops to assist health care & helping professionals.

Organizations/Resources: Political/Legislative

♂️ ALGB Liberals, PO Box 39 Stn B, Ottawa; K1N 6C3

Organizations/Resources: Sexual Focus (Leather, S/M, etc) & Safe Sex Promotion

♂️ ★ Ottawa Knights, PO Box 9174, Ottawa; K1G 3T9 613-237-9833 (also Fax) Meet 1st Tue of month, 7.30pm, at Ottawa-Carleton Centre, 111 Lisgar St. Bar nights 2nd Sat of month, 9pm-1am, at Cellblock, 340 Somerset St W. "Social/charitable activities."

Organizations/Resources: Social, Recreational & Support Groups (see also Sport/Dance/Outdoor)

⚥ SAGE/Ottawa, c/o Pink Triangle Services PO Box 3043, Stn D, Ottawa; K1P 6H6 613-563-4818

Organizations/Resources: Sport/Dance/Outdoor

⚥ Team/Equipe Ottawa, PO Box 3371 Stn C, Ottawa; K1P 4P2

⚥ ★ Time Out, 151A 2nd Ave, Box 21023, Ottawa; K1S 5N1 (member of International Gay & Lesbian Outdoor Organization; North American Gay Volleyball Association; International Gay Bowling Association)

Organizations/Resources: Youth (see also Family)

♀ ☆ Pink Triangle Youth/Ottawa-Hull, PO Box 3043 Stn D, Ottawa; K1P 6H6 613-563-4818

Performing Arts: Entertainment, Music, Recording, Theater, etc.

♂️ ★ (♿) Ottawa Men's Chorus, PO Box 3010 Stn D, Ottawa; K1P 6H6

Publications

⚥ • (♿) *Capital Xtra!*, 177 Nepean St #303, Ottawa; K2P OB4 613-237-7133

♂️ • (♿) *Malebox*, 177 Nepean St #303, Ottawa; K2P OB4 613-237-7133 Fax 613-237-6651 "Gay erotica & personal ads."

Religious Organizations & Publications

⚥ ★ Dignity Canada Dignité, PO Box 2102 Stn D, Ottawa; K1P 5W8 613-746-7279 Fax 613-746-0353 dignity@web.apc.org Pub *Dignity Journal.* "Support group for Roman Catholic Gays, Lesbians & their friends."

♀ ★ ♂ Metropolitan Community Church/Ottawa, Box 41082, 1910 St Laurent Blvd, Ottawa; K1G 5K9 613-736-1643

Switchboards, Helplines, Phone Information

⚥ ★ Gayline/Télégai, PO Box 3043 Stn D, Ottawa; K1P 6H6 613-238-1717 7-10pm 7 days

Travel & Tourist Services (see also Accommodation)

♀ ○ (♿) Far Horizons, Inc, 190 Maclaren St, Ottawa; K2P 0L6 (at Elgin St) 613-234-6116 Fax 613-563-2593

⚥ • Get AwaY Travel, 380 Elgin St Unit 7, Ottawa; 613-230-2250; 800-699-6193

Port Sydney

Accommodation: Hotels, B&B, Resorts, Campgrounds

⚥ • Divine Lake Resort, RR, Box XD3; P0B 1L0 705-385-1212

Stratford/Woodham

Accommodation: Hotels, B&B, Resorts, Campgrounds

♂️ ○ (♿) Burnside Guest Home, 139 William St, Stratford; N5A 4X9 519-271-7076 "Bed & breakfast."

♂️ ○ The Maples of Stratford, 220 Church St, Stratford; N5A 2R6 519-273-0810

♂️ • Woodham Hall Bed & Breakfast, 26 Baseline Rd E, Woodham; N0K 2A0 519-229-6600

Antiques & Collectables

♂️ • Antiquities Shoppe, 32 Baseline Rd E., Woodham; N0K 2A0 519-225-2800

Sudbury

Organizations/Resources: Social, Recreational & Support Groups (see also Sport/Dance/Outdoor)

⚥ ★ (♿) Sudbury All Gay Alliance (SAGA), PO Box 1092 Stn B; P3E 4S6 / 176 Larch St #304 705-670-2262 Tue 7-10pm. Pub *Northern Pride.* "Social & support groups include Youth group & Gay Parents Committee."

Thunder Bay

AIDS/HIV Support, Education, Advocacy, Publications

♂️ ☆ ♂ AIDS Committee of Thunder Bay (ACT-B), PO Box 24025 Downtown North Postal Outlet; P7A 4T0 807-345-1516

Bookstores: Gay/Lesbian/Feminist

♀ ○ ♂♂ Northern Woman's Bookstore, 65 South Court St; P7B 2X2 807-344-7979 Tue-Sat 11am-6pm.

Women's Centers

♀ ☆ ♂♂ Northern Woman's Centre, 184 Camelot St; P7A 4A9 807-345-7802

ON: Toronto
Accommodation
116
CANADA
Toronto : ON
Gifts, Cards, Novelties

Toronto

☎ Toronto Area Gay & Lesbian Phoneline & Crisis Counseling (TAGL) 416-964-6600

Accommodation: Hotels, B&B, Resorts, Campgrounds

♀ • Acorn House Bed & Breakfast, 255 Donlands Ave; M4J 3R5 416-463-8274

♀ • Catnaps 1892 Downtown Guesthouse, 246 Sherbourne St; M5A 2S1 416-968-2323

♀ • **Mike's Bed & Breakfast, 333 Mutual St; M4Y 1X6 416-944-2611**
✦ *Mike's Bed & Breakfast advertisement page 117*

♂ • (ර්ථ) Muther's Guest House, 508 Eastern Ave; M4M 1C5 416-466-8616

♀ • (ර්ථ) Selby Hotel, 592 Sherbourne St; M4X 1L4 416-921-3142; 800-387-4788

♀ • Toronto Bed & Breakfast, Inc, Box 269, 253 College St; M5T 1R5 416-588-8800; 416-961-3676; Fax 416-964-1756

AIDS/HIV Support, Education, Advocacy, Publications

♀ ☆ රර AIDS Committee of Toronto, 399 Church St; M5B 2J6 416-340-2437

♀ ☆ (ර්) Asian Community AIDS Project, 33 Isabella St #107; M4Y 2P7 416-963-4300 Fax 416-963-4300

♀ ☆ ර Black Coalition For Aids Prevention (Black CAP), 597 Parliament St #103; M4X 1W3 416-926-0122 Fax 416-926-0281

♀ ☆රර Casey House Hospice Inc, 9 Huntley St; M4Y 2K8 416-962-7600

♀ ☆ රර Toronto PWA Foundation, 399 Church St, 2nd flr; M5B 2J6 416-506-1400 Fax 416-506-1404 "AIDS/HIV support, advocacy, financial assistance, drop-in centre, complementary therapies."

Bars, Restaurants, Clubs, Discos

♀ • The 457, 457 Church St; M4Y 2C5 416-923-3469 **BRd** Noon-1am. (mainly men)

♂ Aztec/Tango, 2 Gloucester St; 416-975-8612

♂ Bar 501, 501 Church St

♂ Bijou Bar, 370 Church St; 416-960-1272

♀ Bistro 422, 422 College St

♂ • (රර) Black Eagle, 459 Church St; 416-413-1219 **LW**

♂ • (රර) Boots/Kurbash/The Courtyard, at Hotel Selby, 592 Sherbourne St; M4X 1L4 416-921-3142 Fax 416-923-3177

♂ ○ ර Club Colby's/State II, 5 St Joseph St; M4Y 1J6 416-961-0777

♂ Crews, 508 Church St; M4Y 2C6

♀ El Convento Rico, 750 College St; 416-588-7800

♀ Heavens, 699 Yonge St; 416-968-2832

♀ ○ Hernando's Hideaway, 545 Yonge; 416-929-3629 **R**

♀ ර Joesphine's, 562 Church St; M4Y 2E3 416-962-6255 **R**

♀ Keith's Sport Bar & Grill, 619 Yonge St; 416-922-3068

♀ L.A. Bar & Eatery, 488 Parliament Sr; 416-924-7202

♀ ○ ර Living Well Cafe, 692 Yonge St; 416-922-6770 **BDR**

♀ Mango, 580 Church St; 416-922-6525

♀ P.J.Mellons, 489 Church St; 416-966-3241 **BR**

♂ Pints, 518 Church St; 416-921-8142

♀ Queen's Head Pub, 263 Gerrard St E.; 416-929-9525 **R**

♀ • (රර) Raclette Restaurant & Winebar, 361 Queen St West; M5V 2A4 416-593-0934 **BR**

♂ Remington's, 379 Yonge St; M5B 1S1 416-977-2160

♀ Rose Cafe, 547 Parliament St; 416-928-1495 **BR**

♀ ○ (රර) Second Cup, 546 Church St; M4Y 2E1 416-964-2457 **f**

♂ Sneakers, 502 Yonge St; 416-961-5808

♂ • (රර) Toolbox, 508 Eastern Ave; M4M 1C5 416-466-8616 **RL** 5pm-2am; Sat & Sun noon-2am. "Also leather & toy shop."

♀ • ර Trax V, 529 Yonge St; M4Y 1Y5 416-963-5196 **BR**

♀ • The Warehouse Bar & Grill, 793 Gerrard St E.; M4C 4Z2 (at Logan) 416-465-3687 **D** Wed-Sun 6pm-1am.

♀ ☆ The Woman's Common, 580 Parliament; M4X 1P8 416-975-9079 Free passes for visitors.

♂ ○ Woody's, 467 Church St; M4Y 2C5 416-972-0887 **BR** Noon-1am.

♂ Club Bolero, 2261 Dundas St West; 416-533-2628

Bookstores: Gay/Lesbian/Feminist

♂ • Glad Day Bookshop, 598A Yonge St; M4Y 1Z3 416-961-4161 Fax 416-961-1624

♂ ○ (රර) This Ain't the Rosedale Library, 483 Church St; M4Y 2C6 416-929-9912

♀ ○ (රර) Toronto Women's Bookstore, 73 Harbord St; M5S 1G4 416-922-8744

Bookstores: General

♀ • (රර) The Bob Miller Book Room, 180 Bloor St. West; M5S 2V6 416-922-3557

♀ • ර Chapters Book Shop, 834 Yonge St; 416-975-4370

Broadcast Media

♀ ☆ Frequency Feminist, CKLN Radio, Inc, 380 Victoria St; M5B 1W7 416-595-1477 Sun 11.30am-1pm.

♀ ★ Pink Antenna, CKLN Radio, Inc, 380 Victoria St; M5B 1W7 416-595-1477 Tue 7.30-8pm. "Lesbian & Gay news & current affairs."

Clothes

♀ • Out On The Street, 551 Church St; M4Y 2E2 416-967-2759

Counseling/Therapy: Nonprofit

♀ ☆ University of Toronto Sexual Education & Peer Counseling Centre, 42A St. George St; M5S 2E4 416-591-7949 Mon-Fri 9am-9pm.

Erotica (Printed, Visual, Equipment)

♀ • (?රර) Cinema Bleu, 12 Roy's Sq.; 416-944-9112

♂ ○ (රර) Northbound Leather Ltd, 19 St Nicholas St; M4Y 1W5 416-972-1037 Fax 416-975-1337 Mon, Tue, Wed, Sat 10am-6pm; Thu & Fri to 7.30pm. "Leather, rubber, B&D toys, etc."

♂ • Priape, 465 Church St 2nd flr; M4Y 2C5 416-586-9914 Fax 416-586-0150

Funding: Endowment, Fundraising, Scholarship

♀ ★ (?රර) Lesbian & Gay Community Appeal of Toronto, PO Box 760 Stn F; M4Y 2N6 416-920-LGCA "Umbrella fundraising organization."

Gifts, Cards, Pride & Novelty Items

♀ ○ Amnesia Gifts, 551 Church St; M4Y 2E2 416-925-5009 Fax 416-920-9484

ON: Toronto
Health Care

117
CANADA

Whitby : ON
Bars, Clubs, Restaurants

Health Care (see also AIDS Services)

♂ • ᕼᕼ Fraser, Gregory, 196A Carlton St; M5A 2K8 416-924-0600 Fax 416-924-3304

♂ • ᕼᕼ Genereux, Maurice, M.D., 196A Carlton St; M5A 2K8 416-924-0600 "Comprehensive HIV primary care & home palliation."

♀ ☆ Hassle-Free Clinic, 556 Church St 2nd Floor; M4Y 2E3 416-922-0603 (men); 416-922-0566 (women) "For birth control & sexually transmitted diseases. HIV counseling & testing by appointement; Body Positive support groups for HIV+ men & women."

♂ • ᕼᕼ Kovacs, Colin, M.D., FRCP(c), 196A Carlton St; M5A 2K8 416-924-0600

Health Clubs, Gyms, Saunas

♂ • The Barracks, 56 Widmer St 416-593-0499 24 hrs.

♂ • The Club, 231 Mutual St; 416-977-4629

♂ • The Spa on Maitland, 66 Maitland St 416-925-1571 _Bf_ 24 hrs.

♂ • ᕼᕼ St. Marc Spa, 543 Yonge St, 4th Flr; 416-927-0210

Legal Services & Resources

♀ • ᕼ Coates, Robert G., 120 Carlton St #307; M5A 4K3 416-925-6490

♀ • ᕼᕼ Maloney, Peter, 499 Main St S, Brampton; L6Y 1N7 905-450-0941; 416-410-0360; Fax 905-450-1824 24 hrs. "Criminal defence attorney."

♂ • (ᕼ) Willis, Paul T., 600 Church St; M4Y 2E7 416-926-9806

Organizations/Resources: Business & Professional

♂ ★ ᕼᕼ The Fraternity, 552 Church St, Box 500-29; M4Y 2E3 416-340-1950 "Gay Men's business, social & educational group."

♀ ★ ᕼᕼ Lesbians, Gays, & Bisexuals in Health Care, PO Box 6973 Stn A; M5W 1X7 416-961-8873

Organizations/Resources: Ethnic, Multicultural

♀ ★ Lesbians of Colour, Box 6597 Stn A; M5W 1X4

Organizations/Resources: Family

♀ ★ ᕼᕼ Gay Fathers of Toronto, Box 187 Stn F; M4Y 2L5 416-975-1680

♀ ☆ PFLAG, c/o Mary Jones 35 Willis Dr, Brampton; L6W 1B2 905-457-4570 "Parents, Families & Friends of Lesbians & Gays."

Organizations/Resources: Sexual Focus (Leather, S/M, etc) & Safe Sex Promotion

♂ ★ Spearhead, PO Box 1000, Stn F; M4Y 2N9

Organizations/Resources: Social, Recreational & Support Groups (see also Sport/Dance/Outdoor)

♀ Toronto Rainbow Alliance of the Deaf, PO Box 671 Stn F; M4Y 2N6 Meet 1st Sat of month, 1-4pm, at 519 Church St.

Organizations/Resources: Sport/Dance/Outdoor

♀ ★ (?ᕼ) Out & Out Club, PO Box 331 Stn F; M4Y 2L7 416-925-9872 ext 2800 Pub _Out & Out Newsletter._

♀ ★ (?ᕼ) Triangle Squares, c/o Chris Homer, 28 Sackville Place; M4X 1A4 416-960-5458 _dCW_

Organizations/Resources: Student, Academic, Alumni/ae

♀ ★ ᕼᕼ Bisexual, Lesbian & Gay Alliance at York, Room C449 Student Centre, 4700 Keele St, North York; M3J 1P3 416-736-2100 ext 20494

♀ ★ (?ᕼ) LGB—OUT, 42A St George St; M5S 2E4 416-971-7880 "Lesbians, Gays & Bisexuals of the University of Toronto."

Bed and Breakfast
in the heart of the village

333 Mutual Street
Toronto, Ontario M4Y 1X6

(416) 944-2611

Organizations/Resources: Transgender & Transgender Publications

T _The Transie Times_, 566 Parliament St #3375; M4X 1P8

Organizations/Resources: Youth (see also Family)

♀ ★ ᕼᕼ Lesbian Gay & Bisexual Youth of Toronto, 519 Church St; M4Y 2C9 416-964-1916 Tue 7.30-10pm; Sat 1-4pm. "Social & peer support group for lesbian gay & bisexual youth, totally run by youth."

Publications

♀ _Lickerish_, 363 Sorauren Ave Box 17; M6R 2G5

♂ ★ _Xtra Magazine_, 491 Church St; M4Y 2C6 416-925-6665

Religious Organizations & Publications

♂ ★ Aware, First Christian Reformed Church, 63-67 Taunton Rd; M4S 2P2 416-481-2759 "Support group for lesbians & gays of Christian Reformed background."

♂ ★ ᕼᕼ Christos Metropolitan Community Church, 353 Sherbourne St; M5A 2S3 416-925-7924 Worship Sun 7pm.

♂ ★ ᕼᕼ Congregation Keshet Shalom, PO Box 6103 Stn A; M5W 1P5 416-925-1408 Pub _Koleynu_. "A progressive congregation serving the greater Toronto lesbian & gay community."

♂ ★ ᕼ Dignity Toronto Dignité, Box 6922 Stn A; M5W 1X6 416-763-2300 Fax 416-251-8285 "Support group for Roman Catholic Gays, Lesbians & their friends."

♂ ★ (ᕼᕼ) Integrity/Toronto, PO Box 873 Stn F; M4Y 2N9 416-273-9860 Meets usually 3rd Wed of month, 7.30pm, at Holy Trinity Church, Eaton Centre. "Lesbian & Gay Episcopalians & their friends."

♂ ★ Lutherans Concerned/Toronto, 980 Broadview Ave Apt 2309; M4K 3Y1 416-463-8253

♂ ★ ᕼᕼ Metropolitan Community Church/Toronto, 115 Simpson Ave; M4K 1A1 416-406-6228

Switchboards, Helplines, Phone Information

♀ ★ Toronto Area Gay & Lesbian Phoneline & Crisis Counseling (TAGL), Box 632 Stn F; M4Y 2N6 416-964-6600 Mon-Sat 7-10pm. "Information & peer counseling."

Travel & Tourist Services (see also Accommodation)

♀ • Masters In Travel, Inc, 33 Isabella St #104; M4Y 2P7 416-922-2422 Fax 416-922-3008

♂ • ᕼᕼ Talk Of The Town Travel, 565 Sherbourne St; M4X 1W7 416-960-1393

Waterloo: see Kitchener/Waterloo

Whitby

Bars, Restaurants, Clubs, Discos

♀ The Bar, 110 Dundas St W

Windsor

AIDS/HIV Support, Education, Advocacy, Publications

♀ ☆&& AIDS Committee of Windsor, PO Box 2233; N8Y 4R8 519-973-0222 Fax 519-973-7389 Pub *ACW Newsletter.*

Bars, Restaurants, Clubs, Discos

♂ Happy Tap Tavern, 1056 Wyandotte East; 519-256-8998

♂ • (?&) J.B.'s Bar & Grill, 1880 Wyandotte St E.; N8Y 1E3 519-258-5706 *BRd*

♂ Silhouettes, 1880 Wyandotte St E; N8Y 1E3 519-252-0887 *BR*

Organizations/Resources: Social, Recreational & Support Groups (see also Sport/Dance/Outdoor)

♂ ★ Lesbian/Gay Community Council, PO Box 7002; N9C 3Y6 519-973-4951

Organizations/Resources: Student, Academic, Alumni/ae

♂ ★ Organization of Gay & Lesbian Students, c/o University of Windsor, 401 Sunset; N9B 3P4

Religious Organizations & Publications

♀ MCC of Windsor, PO Box 2052; N8Y 4R5 519-977-6897

Prince Edward Island

Province/County Resources

AIDS/HIV Support, Education, Advocacy, Publications

♀ ☆&& AIDS P.E.I. Community Support Group, PO Box 2762, Charlottetown, PE C1A 8C4 / 199 Grafton St #103; C1A 1L4 902-566-2437 (also fax)

Charlottetown

Performing Arts: Entertainment, Music, Recording, Theater, etc.

♀ Women's Entertainment Productions, PO Box 2031; C1A 7N7 902-566-9733

Switchboards, Helplines, Phone Information

♀ PEI Phoneline, 902-566-9733

Vernon Bridge

Accommodation: Hotels, B&B, Resorts, Campgrounds

♀ • Blair Hall, 902-651-2202; 800-268-7005 Member of Maritime Rainbow Connections.

Quebec

Province/County Resources

Archives/Libraries/History Projects

♂ ★ Archives Gaies du Quebec, CP 395 Succ Place du Parc, Montréal, QC H2W 2N9

Organizations/Resources: Transgender & Transgender Publications

T ☆ FACT (Federation of American & Canadian Transsexuals)/ Quebec Quebec, c/o Patricia Fisher, CP 293, Succ Cote des Neiges, Montréal, QC H3S 2S6

Publications

♀ • *Fugues*, 1212 St Hubert, Montréal, QC H2L 3Y7 514-848-1854 Fax 514-845-7645 Monthly.

♂ • *Guide Gai du Quebec*, CP 915 Succ C, Montréal, QC H2L 4V2 514-523-9463 Fax 514-523-2214

♂ ★&& *Homo Sapiens*, CP 8888 Succ Centre-ville, Montréal, QC H3C 3P8 / Bureau 9210, 1259 Berri 514-987-3039 Fax 514-987-3615

♂ • *RG*, CP 915 Succ C, Montréal, QC H2L 4V2 514-523-9463 Fax 514-523-2214

Chicoutimi

AIDS/HIV Support, Education, Advocacy, Publications

♂ MIENS: Mouvement d'information, d'education et d'entraide dans la lutte contre le sida, CP 723; G7H 5E1 418-693-8983

Bars, Restaurants, Clubs, Discos

♂ Bar L'Excentrique, 332 du Havre; 418-545-9744

♀ Les Divas, 564 blvd Saquenay ouest; 418-693-1179

♂ La Panthere Noire, 294 Ste-Anne

♂ Roscoe Pub, 70 Racine Ouest; 418-698-5811

Drummondville

Bars, Restaurants, Clubs, Discos

♀ Le Chariot, 1110 rue Montplaisir; 819-472-4684

Hull: see Ottawa/Hull Area

Mont-tremblant

Accommodation: Hotels, B&B, Resorts, Campgrounds

♂ • Versant Ouest B&B, 110 Chemin labelle; J0T 1Z0 800-425-6615

✦ *Versant Ouest B&B advertisement page 119*

Montréal

☎ Gai-Ecoute 514-521-1508

☎ Gay Line 514-990-1414

Accommodation: Hotels, B&B, Resorts, Campgrounds

♂ • Auberge du Centre-Ville, Inc, 1070 Mackay St; H3G 2H1 514-938-9393; 800-668-6253; Fax 514-938-9393

♀ o&& Auberge L'Un et L'Autre, 1641 Amherst; H2L 3L4 514-597-0878 *R*

♀ • (?&) Canadian Accommodation Network, PO Box 42-A, Stn M; H1V 3L6 514-254-1250; call first for Fax

♀ • (&) Chablis Guest House, 1641 rue St-Hubert; H2L 3Z1 514-527-8346; 514-523-0053 *BR*

♀ • Chateau Cherrier, 550 Cherrier; H2L 1H3 514-844-0055; 800-816-0055; Fax 514-844-8438 April-December. Bed & breakfast.

♀ • La Conciergerie Guest House, 1019 rue Saint-Hubert; H2L 3Y3 514-289-9297 Fax 514-289-0845

♀ • The Gingerbread House B&B, 1628 St. Christophe St; H2L 4L5 514-597-2804 Fax 514-597-2409 gingerbread.house@gai.com

♀ • Hostellerie Le Chasseur Bed & Breakfast, 1567 rue Saint-André; H2L 3T5 514-521-2238

♀ • (?&) Hotel American, 1042 Rue St-Denis; H2X 3J2 514-849-0616

♀ ○ (♿) Hotel Le Saint-André, 1285 Saint André; H2L 3T1 514-849-7070

♀ ● Hotel Pierre, 169 Sherbrooke est; H2X 1C7 514-289-8519 Fax 514-288-0980

♀ ● Lindsey's Bed & Breakfast for Women, 3974 Laval Ave; H2W 2J2 514-843-4869

♂ ● Le St. Christophe Bed & Breakfast, 1597 St. Christophe; H2L 3W7 514-527-7836

♂ ● Le Stade B&B, PO Box 42-B, Stn M; H1V 3L6 514-254-1250 (Fax available: call first)

♀ ○ Turquoise B&B, 1576 Alexandre-de Seve; 2L2 2V7 514-523-9943

AIDS/HIV Support, Education, Advocacy, Publications

♂ Fondation d'Aide Directe-SIDA, 1422 Panet; H2L 2Z1

Bars, Restaurants, Clubs, Discos

♂ Le 1424 Stanley, Mystique; 514-844-5711

♂ Adonis, Bar, 1681 Ste-Catherine Est; 514-521-1355

♂ Agora, 1160 Mackay; H3H 284 514-934-1428

♂ Black Eagle Bar, 1315 Ste Catherine Est; 514-529-0040

♂ Bar Cajun, 1574 Ste-Catherine est

♂ ○ La California, 514-843-8533

♂ Restaurant Callipyge, 1493 rue Amherst; H2L 3L2 514-522-6144

♂ ○ Campus, 1111 rue Ste-Catherine est; H2L 2G6 514-526-9867

♂ Cabaret Chez Jean-Pierre, 1071 Beaver Hall; 514-878-3570

♂ Citi Bar, 1603 Ontario est

♀ Le Clandestine, 1799 Amherst; 514-528-7918 *BR*

♂ La Club Date, 1218 Ste. Catherine Est; 514-526-5844

♀ Les Entretiens Café, 1577 Laurier Est; 514-521-2934 *R*

♀ L'Exception, 1200 St-Hubert; 514-282-1282 *R*

♀ Exit 2, 4297 St-Denis

♂ K.O.X., Katakombes, K.2, Kaché, 1450 Ste-Catherine est; 514-523-0064

♂ ○ ♿ Max, 1166 rue Ste-Catherine est; H2L 2G7 514-598-5244 *BD* 3pm-3am.

♂ Meteor, 1661 Ste. Catherine Est

♀ Nana Pub, 1365 Ste-Catherine est

♂ Sister's, 1456 Ste-Catherine est

♂ Sky Club, 1474 Ste-Catherine est

♂ Taboo, 1950 est LeMaisonneuve; 514-597-0010

♂ ○ Taverne du Village, 1366 rue Ste-Catherine est; H2L 2H6 514-524-1960

♂ Taverne Normandie, 1295 Amherst; 514-522-2766

♂ Taverne Rocky, 1673 Ste Catherine est

♂ ○ La Track, 1584 rue Ste-Catherine est; H2L 2J2 514-521-1419

Bookstores: Gay/Lesbian/Feminist

♀ ● ♂ L'Androgyne Bookstore, 3636 Boul St Laurent; H2X 2V4 514-842-4765 9am-6pm; Thu & Fri to 9pm. 2 free catalogs: Gay; Lesbian/Feminist.

Versant Ouest

Bed & Breakfast　　　　Mont Tremblant
1-800-425-6615　　　　Québec

Business, Financial & Secretarial

♂ ● Les Fax Express, Box 42-F, Stn M; H1V 3L6 514-254-1250 Fax 514-252-9954

Computer Bulletin Boards

♂ ● S-Tek BBS, PO Box 745 Stn C; H2L 4L5 514-597-2409 modem internet sysop@gai.com 24 hrs.

Erotica (Printed, Visual, Equipment)

♀ ● ♂ Cuir Plus / Leather Plus, 1321 rue Ste-Catherine est; H2L 2H4 514-521-7587

♀ ● ♂ Les Plaisirs d'Amour, 1261 Rue Bleury; H3B 3H9 514-392-1538

♂ ● Priape, 1311 rue Ste-Catherine est; H2L 2H4 514-521-8451 Fax 514-521-1309

♀ ● (♿) Vidéomag Plus, 1243 Rue Bleury; H3B 3H9 514-871-1653

♂ ○ (♿) Wega Complex, 930 rue Ste-Catherine est; H2L 2E7 514-987-5993

Health Care (see also AIDS Services)

♀ ☆ Centre de santé des femmes de Montréal, 16 est boul St-Joseph; H2T 1G8 514-842-8903

Health Clubs, Gyms, Saunas

♂ ● Le 456, 456 LaGauchetiere ouest; H2Z 1E3 514-871-8341

♂ ● Le Sauna L'Oasis, 1390 rue Ste-Catherine est; 514-521-0785

♂ Sauna 226, 226 boul des Laurentides; 514-975-4556

♂ Sauna 5018, 5018 Blvd. St. Laurent; 514-277-3555

♂ Sauna Centre-ville, 1465 Ste-Catherine est; 514-524-3486

♂ ● Sauna St Marc's, 1168 rue Ste-Catherine est; 514-525-8404

Massage Therapy (Licensed only)

♂ ● Tropicales, 514-521-7708 "Licensed California masseurs."

Organizations/Resources: Sport/Dance/Outdoor

♀ ★♿♿ ACC (A Contre-courant), 1860 Boul Rene-Levesque est #304; H2K 4P1 514-522-9323

♂ Equipe-Montréal 94, CP 726 Tour de la Bourse; H4Z 1J9 514-735-8512

Organizations/Resources: Student, Academic, Alumni/ae

♂ L'Alliance gaie Laval-Laurentides, CP 98030, Ste-Thérèse; J7E 5R4 514-334-8218

♂ ★♿♿ Association des Lesbiennes et Gais de l'Université du Québec à Montréal (ALGYQUAM), CP 8888 Succ Centre-ville; H3C 3P8 / Bureau 9210, 1259 Berri 514-987-3039 Fax 514-987-3615

♂ ★ (?♿) Concordia Queer Collective, 1455 De Maisonneuve ouest, c/o CUSA; H3G 1M8 / 2020 Mackay Annex, Rm P-102 514-848-7414 "Collective includes social, activist & queer studies groups."

♂ ★ Lesbians, Bisexuals & Gays of McGill (LBGM), 3480 McTavish #432; H3A 1X9 514-398-6822

Organizations/Resources: Youth (see also Family)

♂ ★ Jeunesse Lambda/Lambda Youth, CP 5514 Succ B; H3B 4P1 514-528-7535

Publications

→ *Fugues*: p.118
→ *RG*: p.118

Religious Organizations & Publications

♂ ★ (⚧) Dignity/Montreal/Dignité, CP 1045 Succ H; H3G 2M9 514-937-6576; 514-597-0554 "Gay & Lesbian Catholics & their friends."

♂ ★ Yakhdav, PO Box 661 Snowdon; H3X 1T7 514-933-7387 Fax 514-487-1725 "Montréal's Gay & Lesbian Jewish Organization."

Switchboards, Helplines, Phone Information

♂ ★ Gai-Ecoute, CP 1006, Succ C; H2L 4V2 514-521-1508 7-11pm.

♂ ★ Gay Line, PO Box 384 Stn H; H3G 2L1 514-990-1414 6.30-10pm. 7-11pm; Fri to 9.30pm.

Travel & Tourist Services (see also Accommodation)

♀ ○ Club Voyages, 981 Rue Duluth Est; H2L 1B9 514-521-3320

♂ ● Voyages Exception-L, 1210 Ste-Catherine Est; H2L 2G9 514-521-2155 Fax 514-521-9991

Women's Centers

♀ ☆⚥⚥ Women's Center of Montreal, 3585 St-Urbain; H2X 2N6 514-842-4780

Québec

Accommodation: Hotels, B&B, Resorts, Campgrounds

♂ ● 727 Guest House, 727 D'Aiguillon; G1R 1M8 418-648-6766 Fax 418-648-1474 Mainly gay men, but lesbians welcome.

♂ ● Le Coureur des Bois, 15 rue Ste-Ursule; G1R 4C7 418-692-1117

AIDS/HIV Support, Education, Advocacy, Publications

♀ ☆ ☆ Mouvement d'information et d'entraide dans la lutte Contre le sida a Québec/AIDS committee of Québec city (MIELS Québec, 175 rue Satin-Jean, Local 200; G1R 1N4 418-649-1720 Fax 418-649-1256

Bars, Restaurants, Clubs, Discos

♂ ● Cafe-Bar L' Amour Sorcier, 789 Cote Ste-Genevieve; G1R 1M8

♂ Le Ballon Rouge, 811 St-Jean; 418-529-6709

♂ Bar de la Couronne, 310 rue de la Couronne; 418-525-6593

♂ Le Drague, 815 St-Augustin; 418-648-0805

♂ Fausse Alarme, 161 rue St-Jean; 418-529-0277

♀ Cafe Restaurant L' Hobbit, 700 rue St-Jean

♂ Bar Male, 770 rue Ste-Genevieve; 418-522-6976

♂ ○ Studio 157/Chez Garbo, 157 Chemin Ste-Foy; G1R 1T1 418-529-9958 *BDR*

Erotica (Printed, Visual, Equipment)

♀ ○ Importations Delta ENR, 875 Rue St-Jean; G1R 1R2 418-647-6808

Health Clubs, Gyms, Saunas

♂ ○ Hippocampe, 31 Rue Mcmahon; G1R 1S3 418-692-1521

♂ Sauna Bloc 225, 225 rue St-Jean; 418-523-2562

♂ ● Sauna St-Jean, 920 rue St-Jean; G1R 1R4 418-694-9724

Organizations/Resources: General, Multipurpose, Pride

♂ ★ La Coalition Gaie et Lesbienne—Québec, CP 155 Succ. Haute-Ville; G1R 4P3 418-523-2259 Pub *Newsletter.*

Organizations/Resources: Student, Academic, Alumni/ae

♂ ★ (⚧) Groupe Gaie de L'Université Laval, CP 2500 Pavillon Lemieux, Cité Universitaire, Ste-Foy; G1K 7P4 514-649-9478 Pub *Calendrier des Activités du Groupe Gai.*

Sherbrooke

AIDS/HIV Support, Education, Advocacy, Publications

♀ ☆ Intervention Regionale et Information Sur Le Sida (IRIS), CP 1766; J1H 5N8 819-823-6704; 800-567-7391

Bars, Restaurants, Clubs, Discos

♂ Les Dames de Coeur, 54 King Est; 819-821-2217

Saskatchewan

Province/County Resources

AIDS/HIV Support, Education, Advocacy, Publications

♀ ☆⚥⚥ PLWA Network of Saskatchewan, PO Box 7123, Saskatoon, SK S7K 4J1 306-373-7766 Mon-Fri 1-5pm Pub *Network Newsletter.* Monthly dances.

Publications

♂ ★ *Perceptions*, PO Box 8581, Saskatoon, SK S7K 6K7 306-244-1930 A Gay/Lesbian Newsmagazine of the Prairies.

Moose Jaw

AIDS/HIV Support, Education, Advocacy, Publications

♀ AIDS Moose Jaw, Inc, c/o 835 6th Ave; S6H 4A3 306-691-0357

Legal Services & Resources

♀ ● ♂ Ocrane, Terrance W., Suite 106, Scott Block, 12 High St E; S6H 0B9 306-694-4922 Fax 306-692-6386

Organizations/Resources: General, Multipurpose, Pride

⚥ Lesbian & Gay Committee of Moose Jaw, PO Box 93; S6H 4N7 306-692-2418

Ravenscrag

Accommodation: Hotels, B&B, Resorts, Campgrounds

♀ ● (⚧) Spring Valley Guest Ranch, Box 10; S0N 0T0 306-295-4124 *R* Bed & breakfast.

Regina

AIDS/HIV Support, Education, Advocacy, Publications

♀ ☆ ♂ AIDS Regina, 1852 Angus St; S4T 1Z4 306-924-8420; 306-525-0905; Fax 306-525-0904

Bars, Restaurants, Clubs, Discos

♂ Mertz Bar & Grill, 1326A Hamilton St; S4R 2B5 306-525-6688

♀ Roca Jack's Coffee House, 1939 Scarth St; S4P 2H1 306-347-2550 Fax 306-791-4825

♂ Scarth Street Station, Gay Community of Regina, Box 3414; S4P 3J8 / 1422 Scarth St 306-522-7343

Organizations/Resources: General, Multipurpose, Pride

♀ ★ (?⚢) Lesbian/Gay Pride Committee of Regina, PO Box 24031; S4P 4J8 306-525-6046

♀ ★ (?⚢) Pink Triangle Community Services, Inc. (PTCS), PO Box 24031; S4P 4J8 306-525-6046

Organizations/Resources: Political/Legislative

♀ ★ EGALE/Regina, PO Box 24031; S4P 4J8

Organizations/Resources: Social, Recreational & Support Groups (see also Sport/Dance/Outdoor)

♀ Lavender Social Club, PO Box 671; S4P 3A3 306-522-7343

♀ Lesbian Association of Southern Saskatchewan (LASS), PO Box 33084; S4T 7X2 306-731-2200

Organizations/Resources: Transgender & Transgender Publications

T Regal Social Association of Regina, Inc, PO Box 3870; S4P 3R8 306-569-9883

Organizations/Resources: Youth (see also Family)

♀ ★ Gay Teen Support Group, PO Box 24031; S4P 4J8 306-522-4293

Performing Arts: Entertainment, Music, Recording, Theater, etc.

♀ Oscar Wilde & Company, c/o 2232 Retallack St; S4T SK6 306-352-2919

Religious Organizations & Publications

♀ ★ Adelfoi Interdenominational Bible Fellowship, PO Box 24031; S4P 4J8 306-949-3383

♀ ★ Dignity Regina Dignité, PO Box 482; S4P 3A2 306-569-3666 "Gay & Lesbian Catholics & their friends."

♀ ★ ⚢ Koinonia, PO Box 3181; S4P 3G7 306-569-3666 Interfaith group.

Saskatoon

☎ **Gay & Lesbian Line 800-358-1833**

Accommodation: Hotels, B&B, Resorts, Campgrounds

♀ ○ ⚥ Brighton House B&B, 1308 5th Ave N.; S7K 2S2 306-664-3278

AIDS/HIV Support, Education, Advocacy, Publications

♀ ☆ ⚢ AIDS Saskatoon, PO Box 4062; S7K 4E3 306-242-5005; 800-667-6876; Fax 306-244-2134

→ PLWA Network of Saskatchewan: p.120

Bars, Restaurants, Clubs, Discos

♀ ● ⚢ Diva's, 110-220 3rd Ave North (alley entrance) 306-665-0100 *BD* 8pm-3am.

Bookstores: General

♀ ● ⚢ Café Browse, 269 3rd Ave S; S7K 1M3 306-664-2665 10am-11pm.

♀ ☆ ⚥ One Sky Books, 259A 3rd Ave S; S7K 1M3 306-652-1571 Fax 306-652-8377 "Specializing in feminist, Aboriginal, & development issues; gay & lesbian titles stocked."

Counseling/Therapy: Private

♀ ● Hellquist, Gens, PO Box 3043; S7K 3S9 306-244-1930

Crafts Galleries, Supplies (see also Art)

♀ ○ Prairie Leathercraft, 224 2nd Ave S; S7K 1K9 306-934-1684 "Leather, beads, craft supplies."

Gifts, Cards, Pride & Novelty Items

♀ ● Out of the Closet, PO Box 8581; S7K 2M8 / 241 2nd Ave S, 3rd flr 306-665-1224

♀ ● ⚥ Trading Post, 226 2nd Ave S.; S7K 1K9 306-653-1769

Health Care (see also AIDS Services)

♀ ★ Gay & Lesbian Health Services, PO Box 8581; S7K 6K7 306-665-1224

Organizations/Resources: Social, Recreational & Support Groups (see also Sport/Dance/Outdoor)

♂ Saskatoon Prime Timers, PO Box 804; S7K 3L7 306-244-2531

Organizations/Resources: Student, Academic, Alumni/ae

♀ ★ ⚢ Gays & Lesbians at University of Saskatchewan, PO Box 369 RPO, University; S7N 4J8 306-244-4782 "Open to students, staff, faculty & alumni/ae."

Religious Organizations & Publications

♀ ★ Dignity Saskatoon, PO Box 7283; S7K 7G5 306-382-3669 "Gay & Lesbian Catholics & their friends."

Switchboards, Helplines, Phone Information

♀ ★ Gay & Lesbian Line, PO Box 8581; S7K 6K7 800-358-1833 Mon-Sat noon-4.30pm; Sat 7.30-10.30pm.

Yukon Territory

Province/County Resources

AIDS/HIV Support, Education, Advocacy, Publications

♀ ☆ (?⚢) AIDS Yukon Alliance, 7221 7th Ave, Whitehorse, YT Y1A 1R8 403-633-2437 Fax 403-668-2447 Pub *SeroNorth*.

Organizations/Resources: General, Multipurpose, Pride

♀ ★ ⚢ Yukon Gay & Lesbian Alliance, PO Box 5604, Whitehorse, YT Y1A 5H4 403-667-7857 (voice mail)

Women Loving Women

For a change in your life, we invite you to try: **THE WISHING WELL**. Features current members' self-descriptions (listed by code), letters, photos, resources, reviews, and more. Introductory copy $5.00 ppd. (discreet first class). A beautiful, tender, loving alternative to "The Well of Loneliness." Confidential, sensitive, supportive, dignified. Very personal. Reliable reputation, established 1974. Free, prompt information. Women are writing and meeting each other EVERYWHERE through:

The Wishing Well
P.O. Box 713090
Santee, CA 92072-3090

(619)443-4818

Travel.
Save Money.
And Make Friends.

HOME SUITE HOM

Hospitality & Home Exchanges for Leisure and Business Travel. Private Bed & Breakfasts. At home and abroad.

For a free brochure: Call 24 hrs,
US & Can.: **1-800-429-4983**
Int'l: **(514) 523-4642**

Or write HOME SUITE HOM
P.O. Box 762, Succ. C, Montreal,
Quebec, Canada H2L 4L6

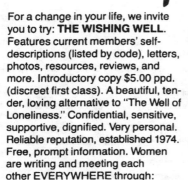

Photo: Mod Bob

Photo: J.J. Green

"Like those frequently trumpeted articles in *Playboy*, good reading can be found twixt the prurient pages."

BOSTON GLOBE, MARCH 15, 1995

SAFE IS FOR SEX.
NOT

1 YEAR (6 issues) $23.95
PLUS FREE EROTIC VIDEO packed with the winners of the Second Annual Gay Men's Safe Sex Video Contest with your paid subscription.

Send check or money order to:
PDA Press, 530 Howard Street, #400, Dept. 50, San Francisco, CA 94105.
Mailed in a plain envelope. Please allow 4-6 weeks for delivery.
Video mailed separately. Canadian, foreign, and RUSH orders,
call 800-478-3268. Sorry, we do not accept credit card orders.

USA National Resources

Accommodation: Reservations & Exchanges (see also Travel)

♀ • (?♿) Camp Sister Spirit, PO Box 12, National Ovett, MS 39464 610-344-1411; 601-344-2005 Pub Resources *Grapevine.* "Feminist education retreat; RV & tent camping, 120 acres; planned group facility for rent late 1994."

♂ • Caritas Bed & Breakfast Network, 75 E Wacker Dr #3600, Chicago, IL 60601 312-857-0801 Fax 312-857-0805

♂ • Casa Panoramica, 800-745-7805 (011-52-322-2-3656 in Mexico) Fax 310-396-7855 "Luxury Bed & Breakfast in Puerto Vallarta, Mexico."
✦ *Casa Panoramica advertisement page 141*

♂ • Home Suite Hom, PO Box 762 Succ. C, Montréal, QC H2L 4L6 514-523-4642; 800-429-4983 US & Canada "Travel & accommodation network for those offering or seeking hospitality & lodging exchange, private B&B, & low cost rentals."
✦ *Home Suite Hom advertisement page 122*

♂ • In Town Reservations, PO Box 1983, Provincetown, MA 02657 / 50 Bradford St 800-67P-TOWN; 508-487-1883; Fax 508-487-6140 "Full service travel agency specializing in arranging accommodations at guest houses, inns, cottages & motels/hotels. No fee for services. Open year round."

♂ • Mi Casa Su Casa, PO Box 10327, Oakland, CA 94610 800-215-CASA Fax 510-268-0299 homeswap@aol.com "International Home Exchange/Hospitality Network; long- & short-term exchanges."

♀ • River Spirit Retreat B & B Reservations, PO Box 23305, St Louis, MO 63156 314-569-5795; 618-462-4051

Accommodation: Residential, Intentional Communities

⚥ ☆ East Wind Community, Rt 3, Box GYP, Tecumseh, MO 65760 417-679-4682 Fax 417-679-4684 "Residential egalitarian intentional community; please contact for details."

♀ ★ (♿) Spinsterhaven, PO Box 718, Fayetteville, AR 72702 Pub *Newsletter.* "A retirement haven for older women & women with disabilities."

Addictive Behavior, Substance Abuse, Recovery

♂ ★ International Advisory Council for Homosexual Men & Women in AA, PO Box 90, Washington, DC 20044-0090

⚥ ☆♿ NALGAP Collection, Rutgers Center of Alcohol Studies Library, Smithers Hall, Busch Campus, Piscataway, NJ 08855-0969 908-445-4442

♂ ★♿ National Association of Lesbian & Gay Alcoholism Professionals (NALGAP), 1147 S Alvarado St, Los Angeles, CA 90006 213-381-8524

♂ • (♂♂) Pride Institute, 800-54-PRIDE "The nation's only accredited chemical dependency treatment center exclusively for Gay, Lesbian & Bisexual People."

♀ ☆ Sex Addicts Anonymous, PO Box 70949, Houston, TX 77270 713-869-4902

♀ ○ Spencer Recovery Center, 343 West Foothill Blvd, Monrovia, CA 91016 818-358-3662; 800-232-5483 "Residential & outpatient care for Gays & Lesbians."

AIDS/HIV Support, Education, Advocacy, Publications

♀ ☆♂♂ ACLU AIDS & Civil Liberties Project, PO Box 1161, Philadelphia, PA 19105 215-592-1513

♀ ☆♂♂ ACT UP/AIDS Coalition to Unleash Power, 135 W 29th St, 10th Flr, New York, NY 10001 212-564-2437 Fax 212-989-1797

♀ ★ Actors Fund of America AIDS Volunteer Program, 1501 Broadway #518, New York, NY 10036 212-221-7300

♀ ☆ AIDS & Cancer Research Foundation, 9601 Wilshire Blvd, 4th Flr, Beverly Hills, CA 90210 800-373-4572

♀ ☆♂♂ AIDS Action Council, 1875 Connecticut Ave NW #700, Washington, DC 20009-5728 202-293-2886 Pub *AIDS Action Update.*

♀ ☆ AIDS and Cancer Research Foundation, 8306 Wilshire #1800, Beverly Hills, CA 90211 800-373-4572 Fax 213-655-1804 "HIV/AIDS education, public awareness & promoting research for AIDS & cancer."

♂ ★ AIDS Info BBS, PO Box 421528, San Francisco, CA 94142-1528 415-626-1246 modem (no voice) Fax 415-626-9415

♂ ★ (♂) AIDS Project: Lambda Legal Defense & Education Fund, 666 Broadway, New York, NY 10012-2317 212-995-8585 Pub *AIDS Update.*

♀ AIDS Research Fund of the Cancer Research Institute, 681 5th Ave, New York, NY 10022 212-688-7515; 800-223-7874

♀ ☆ (?♂) AIDS Theatre Project, 197 E Broadway #U2, New York, NY 10002 212-475-6200 ext 305

♀ • *AIDS Treatment News*, PO Box 411256, San Francisco, CA 94141 415-873-2812 Fax 415-255-4659 "Experimental & alternative treatments for AIDS & HIV-disease. Call for sample issue & invoice with current prices."

♂ ★♂♂ ALLGO/Informe-SIDA, PO Box 6149, Austin, TX 78762-6149 512-472-2001 Fax 512-472-6301 Pub *ALLGO-PASA.* "Bilingual, multicultural HIV/AIDS Education."

♀ ☆♂♂ American College Health Association AIDS Task Force, PO Box 378, University of Virginia, Charlottesville, VA 22908 804-924-2670

♀ ☆ American Foundation for AIDS Research, 733 3rd Ave #12fl, New York, NY 10017-3204; 5900 Wilshire Blvd, Los Angeles, CA 90036-5032; 1828 L St NW #802, Washington, DC 20036-5104 212-682-7440; 213-857-5900 Pub *AIDS/HIV Treatment Directory.* Also publishes "AIDS/HIV Clinical Trial Handbook", addressing most frequently asked questions regarding joining a clinical trial in easy-to-understand language, available English & Spanish.

♀ ☆♂♂ American Red Cross AIDS Education Projects, 1900 25th Ave S, Seattle, WA 98144-4708 206-323-2345

♀ American Run for the End of AIDS, Inc. (AREA), 2350 Broadway, New York, NY 10024 212-592-3683

→ *Art & Understanding.* see PUBLICATIONS page 124

♀ ☆♂♂ Being Alive: People with HIV/AIDS, 3626 W Sunset Blvd, Los Angeles, CA 90026 213-667-3262 Fax 213-667-2735 Pub *Being Alive.*

♀ ☆ Bluelights Campaign, 109 Minna St #125, San Francisco, CA 94105 415-863-3540 "Grassroots AIDS awareness campaign."

♀ ☆ ♂ Body Positive, 19 Fulton St #308B, New York, NY 10038 212-566-7333; 800-566-6599 Hotline; Fax 212-566-4539 Pub *Body Positive Magazine.* "Self-help group for people who are HIV antibody positive."

♀ ☆ ♂ Carl Vogel Foundation, Inc, 1010 Vermont Ave NW #510, Washington, DC 20005-3405 202-638-0750 Fax 202-638-0749 "Non-profit nutritional center & buyers' club for PWAs."

♀ ☆ CDC National AIDS Hotline, 800-342-AIDS 24 hrs; 800-344-SIDA (Spanish Access) 8am-2am; 800-AIDS-TTY (Deaf Access) Mon-Fri 10am-10pm.

♀ ☆ Dental Alliance for AIDS/HIV Care, 101 W Grand Ave #200, Chicago, IL 60610 312-645-4891 Fax 312-222-0329

♂ ★♂♂ Gay Men's Health Crisis, 129 W 20th St, New York, NY 10011 212-807-6665 Hotline; 212-807-6664 office *The Volunteer; Treatment Issues.*

♀ ☆ ♂ Harvey Milk AIDS Education Fund, PO Box 14368, San Francisco, CA 94114 415-773-9544

♂ ☆ (♂♂) HERO, Inc (Health Education Resource Organization), 101 W Read St #825, Baltimore, MD 21201 410-685-1180; 410-945-AIDS 9am-9pm.; Fax 410-752-3353 "Information services."

♀ ☆ Home Nursing Agency AIDS Intervention Project, PO Box 352, Altoona, PA 16603 814-944-2982

♀ International Gay & Lesbian Human Rights Commission, 514 Castro St, San Francisco, CA 94114 415-255-8680

♀ ○ Life Entitlements Corporation, 4 World Trade Center #5270, New York, NY 10048 800-420-1420 "A viatical settlements company."

♀ ☆ *Local AIDS/HIV Services: The National Directory*, US Conference of Mayors, 1620 Eye St NW, Washington, DC 20006 202-293-7330

♀ ☆&⚧ The NAMES Project Foundation, 310 Townsend St #310, San Francisco, CA 94107-1607 415-882-5500

♀ ☆&⚧ National Minority AIDS Council, 300 I St NE #400, Washington, DC 20002-4389 202-544-1076 Fax 202-544-0378

♀ ☆ (?&⚧) National Native American AIDS Prevention Center, 2100 Lakeshore Ave #8, Oakland, CA 94606-1123 510-449-2051; 800-283-2437; Fax 510-444-1593

♂ ★ &⚧ National Task Force on AIDS Prevention, 973 Market St #600, San Francisco, CA 94103 415-356-8100 Fax 415-356-8103 "Primarily HIV prevention/early intervention, education & advocacy for gay men of color; others welcome."

♀ ☆&⚧ Panos Institute, 1717 Massachusetts Ave NW #301, Washington, DC 20036-3001 202-483-0044 Fax 202-483-3059 panos@igc.apc.org Pub *WorldAIDS; SIDAmerica*. "Serving Latina/o populations throughout the Americas; resources for use by policy-makers, nongovernmental organizations, & the media."

♂ ★ &⚧ People of Color Against AIDS Network, 1200 S Jackson St #25, Seattle, WA 98144-2065 206-322-7061

♀ ☆ (?&⚧) Pets Are Wonderful Support (PAWS), 539 Castro St, San Francisco, CA 94114 415-241-1460

♀ ☆ Physicians Association for AIDS Care, 101 W Grand Ave #200, Chicago, IL 60610 312-222-1326 Fax 312-222-0329 Pub *PAACNotes*.

♀ ☆ (?&⚧) Project Inform, 1965 Market St #220, San Francisco, CA 94103-1012 800-822-7422 Hotline Mon-Sat 10am-4pm. "AIDS/HIV treatment information."

♀ ★ ♿ PWA Health Group, 150 W 26th St #201, New York, NY 10001 Pub *Notes From the Underground*.

♀ ★ (?&⚧) The Reimer Foundation, 3023 North Clark 1000, Chicago, IL 60657 312-935-SAFE 24 hrs. Fax 312-288-4844

♀ ★&⚧ San Francisco AIDS Foundation, 25 Van Ness Ave #660, San Francisco, CA 94142-6033 PO Box 426182; 94142-6182 415-863-AIDS (English/Spanish/Filipino hotline); 800-959-1059 (BETA subscriptions); Fax 415-552-9762 beta@sfsuvax1.sfsu.edu Pub *BETA (Bulletin of Experimental AIDS Treatments)*; *Positive News (Filipino, Chinese, English & Spanish)*.

♀ ☆ Seattle AIDS Information BBS, 1202 E Pike #658, Seattle, WA 98122-3934 206-323-4420 (modem only); 206-329-8617 before 11pm (voice only) "National AIDS Bulletin Board Service."

♀ ☆&⚧ Women and AIDS Resource Network, 30 3rd Ave #212, Brooklyn, NY 11217 718-596-6007 Fax 718-596-6041

Archives/Libraries/History Projects

♀ AIDS History Project, PO Box 69679, West Hollywood, CA 90069 310-854-0271 "Archive, museum, library."

♂ ★ Douglas County Gay Archives, PO Box 942, Dillard, OR 97432-0942 503-679-9703

♀ ★ Gay & Lesbian Archives of Washington, DC, PO Box 4218, Falls Church, VA 22044 703-751-7738

♂ ★ ♿ Gay & Lesbian Historical Society of Northern California, PO Box 424280, San Francisco, CA 94142 415-626-0980 Pub *Our Stories*. "Sponsors public programs on lesbian & gay history & maintains extensive archival & periodical collections; oral history project."

♂ ★ ♿ Gerber/Hart Library and Archives, 3352 N Paulina St, Chicago, IL 60657 312-883-3003

♂ ★ Harvey Milk Archives - Scott Smith Collection, 53-B Manchester St, San Francisco, CA 94110-5214 415-824-3449 Fax 415-431-5370 75034,1250@compuserve

♂ ☆ Homosexual Information Center, 115 Monroe St, Bossier City, LA 71111-4539 318-742-4709

♂ ★ International Gay & Lesbian Archives, PO Box 69679, West Hollywood, CA 90069 310-854-0271 Pub *ILGA Bulletin*.

♀ ★ June Mazer Lesbian Collection, 626 N Robertson Blvd, West Hollywood, CA 90069 310-659-2478 "Archive, museum, library."

♀ ♿ Latina Lesbian History Project, PO Box 678, Binghamton, NY 13905-0678

♂ ★ Leather Archives & Museum, 5015 N Clark St, Chicago, IL 60640 312-878-6360 Fax 312-878-5184

♂ ★ (?&⚧) Lesbian & Gay Historical Society of San Diego, PO Box 40389, San Diego, CA 92164 619-260-1522 (previously Lesbian & Gay Archives of San Diego)

♀ ★ ♂♂ Lesbian Herstory Archives/Lesbian Herstory Educational Foundation, Inc, PO Box 1258, New York, NY 10116 718-768-3953 Pub *Lesbian Herstory Archives News.*

♀ ★ Michael Lombardi-NASH (Urania Manuscripts), 6858 Arthour Court, Jacksonville, FL 32211 904-744-7879 "Translations of gay writings, especially of Karl Heinrich Ulrichs."

♀ ★ National Deaf Lesbian & Gay Archives Project, PO Box 14431, San Francisco, CA 94114 415-255-0700 TTY Fax 415-255-9797

♀ ★ ♂♂ Quatrefoil Library, 1619 Dayton Ave #105-107, St Paul, MN 55104 612-641-0969; 612-649-1758 "Over 5000 books; periodicals from 1950s; clippings, newsletters; video & audio tapes, records, games. All welcome to use library; members ($15 yr) can check out many items."

♂ Sexual Minority Archives, PO Box 402 Florence Stn, Northampton, MA 01060 413-584-7616

♀ ★ (♂♂) Stonewall Library & Archives, 330 SW 27th St, Fort Lauderdale, FL 33315 305-522-2317

Art & Photography (see also Graphic Design)

♀ ● ♂♂ Ali Photographics/Gallery, 1642 Euclid Ave, Miami Beach, FL 33139 305-531-8881

♀ ● Stonewall Riots Cartoons, c/o Andrea Natalie, 7100 Blvd East #14N, Guttenberg, NJ 07093

Astrology/Numerology/Tarot/Psychic Readings

♂ ● Lifestyles International Astrological Foundation, 25680 W 12 Mile #203, Southfield, MI 48034 800-358-5757; 800-987-5544 (order line); lifeint92@aol.com

♂ ○ **Personal Psychic, 900-656-4000 ext. 2221**
◆ *Personal Psychic advertisement page 125*

Broadcast Media

♂ ○ (♂♂) ADR Studios, Inc, Skylight Run, Irvington, NY 10533 914-591-5616 "Studio & location audio recording & post production for film, television, albums. Complete sound & acoustic design & installation services."

♂ ★ *The Closet Case Show*, PO Box 790, New York, NY 10108 "Cable TV syndication; Video Festivals; safe-sex erotica with politics."

♀ ★ Dyke TV, PO Box 55 Prince St Stn, New York, NY 10012 212-343-9335 Fax 212-343-9337 *Get Turned On..*

♂ ● ♂♂ Gay Cable Network, 150 W 26th St #703, New York, NY 10001 212-727-8850 Fax 212-229-2347 "Contact for details of programs."

♂ ☆ (♀) HIV Update, a cable series, c/o PAAC 101 West Grand Ave #200, Chicago, IL 60610 312-222-1326 (contact Mabrey Russell Whigham); 312-222-1326 (contact Mabrey Russell Whigham) "Syndicated to 30 major cities."

♀ ★ This Way Out, PO Box 38327, Los Angeles, CA 90038 213-469-5907; 213-874-0874; tworadio@aol.com "Internationally distributed weekly half-hour radio show airing on over 90 stations in 7 countries."

Business, Financial & Secretarial

♂ ● Pink Inc., PO Box 5974, Dept 6281-3, Bethesda, MD 20814-5974 301-493-8646 x4 "Pink Triangle & Rainbow Flag checks with personalized pride messages."

Computer Bulletin Boards

♂ ● **The Backroom BBS, TOSS, Inc. 1412 Ave M #2517, Brooklyn, NY 11230 718-951-8256 (modem); 718-951-8998 (voice)**
◆ *Backroom BBS advertisement page 126*

♂ ★ **Gay/Lesbian Information Bureau (GLIB), PO Box 636, Community Educational Services Foundation, Arlington, VA 22216-0636 703-578-4542 (modem); 703-379-4568 (voice); info@glib.org**

♂ ★ Gay/Lesbian International News Network (GLINN), PO Box 93626, Milwaukee, WI 53203 414-289-8780; 414-289-0789 Voice Mail; Fax 414-289-0789

♂ ● Graffiti Online, 5925 Hwy 78 #D-306, Stone Mountain, GA 30087 404-972-9709 voice; 404-972-4999 modem "Gay & Lesbian Online service."

♂ ● Land of Awes Information Services, PO Box 16782, Wichita, KS 67216-0782 316-269-0913; 316-269-3172 modem; Fax 316-269-4208 "Informing the gay community since 1988."

Computer/Software Sales & Services

♂ ○ (♂♂) Professional Support Software, PO Box 901, West Plains, MO 65775 417-256-4280; 800-880-3454; Fax 417-256-6570 "Fundraising software for/to non-profits."

♂ ● Queen Of Cards, PO Box 33233, Phoenix, AZ 85067 602-246-8277 "Computerized Blackjack."

♂ ● TFI Enterprises, 2025 Hazard #2, Houston, TX 77019-6152 800-925-4834; 713-524-4834; Fax 713-524-1164 st416@jetson.uh.edu

Conferences/Events/Festivals/Workshops (see also Performing Arts)

♀ ● ♂♂ Campfest, RR5, Box 185, Franklinville, NJ 08322 609-694-2037 "The comfortable Womyn's Music Festival: Memorial Day weekend."

♂ ★ National Deaf Lesbian & Gay Awareness Week Project, 150 Eureka St #108, San Francisco, CA 94114 415-255-0700 TTY Fax 415-255-9797 dglc@aol.com

♀ ★ (♂♂) National Women's Music Festival, PO Box 1427, Indianapolis, IN 46206-1427 317-927-9355

♀ ★ North East Women's Musical Retreat, PO Box 550, Branford, CT 06405 203-293-8026

♀ ★♂♂ Ohio Lesbian Festival, c/o Lesbian Business Association, PO Box 02086, Columbus, OH 43202 614-267-3953 "Annual one-day festival featuring nationally known musicians, lesbian craftswomen & merchants, September 9, 1995."

♀ ● (?♂) Womensphere Retreats & Events, RR1 Box 240A, Northwood, NH 03261-9702 603-942-9941

♀ ★♂♂ Womongathering, RR5 Box 185, Franklinville, NJ 08322 609-694-2037 "The festival of Womyn's Spirituality."

Counseling/Therapy: Private

♀ ○ Pride In Recovery: A Treatment Program for Gay Men & Lesbians, Located in the Dallas/Fort Worth Metroplex 800-252-7533

Distributors/Wholesalers

♀ ● ♂♂ Bookpeople, 7900 Edgewater Dr, Oakland, CA 94621 510-632-4700; 800-999-4650 orders only.; Fax 510-632-1281 "Wholesaler of books, audio & video casettes, magazines."

♂ ● Ferne Sales & Mfg Co, Box 113 T.C.B., West Orange, NJ 07052 201-731-0967 "Buttons & bumpers: wholesale only."

♂ ● Good Catch!, PO Box 1756 Old Chelsea Stn, New York, NY 10011 800-77-CATCH Fax 800-98-FAX-US "Manufacturer & distributor of T-shirts, mugs, enamel pins, silver earrings, embroidered hats, etc. The original 'Cum Rag & Cum Towel', postcards & other novelties. Custom orders."

♂ ○ Inland Book Co, Box 120261, East Haven, CT 06512 203-467-4257

♂ ● Prerogative Graphics, 336 Castro St #2, San Francisco, CA 94114 800-707-GEAR Fax 415-255-7194 "Wholesale: Gifts, novelties, jewelry."

♂ ○ Small Changes, PO Box 19046, Seattle, WA 98109 206-382-1980 Fax 206-382-1514

Film & Video

♂ ☆ Cambridge Documentary Films, Inc, PO Box 385, Cambridge, MA 02139 617-354-3677 Fax 617-492-7653 cdf@shore.net

♀ ● Charis Video, PO Box 797, Dept GYP, Brooklyn, NY 11231 "Rent lesbian videos through the mail. USA only."

♂ ● Christian Community Television (CCTV), PO Box 790, New York, NY 10108 "Cable TV & Video Festivals; safe-sex erotica with politics."

♂ ○ First Run Features, 153 Waverly Place, New York, NY 10014 212-243-0600 "Distributors of critically acclaimed gay & lesbian films & home videos. Free catalog."

♀ ★ Foosh Productions, Inc., 2305 Rebel Rd, Austin, TX 78704 512-444-9300

♂ ★ (?♂) Frameline, 346 9th St, San Francisco, CA 94103 415-703-8650

♂ ● Hands On Productions, 633 Post St #500, San Francisco, CA 94109 415-771-2055

♂ ○ Jezebel Productions, PO Box 1348, New York, NY 10011 212-463-0578

♂ ● Man's Hand Films, 633 Post St #500, San Francisco, CA 94109 415-771-2055

♂ ★ New York Lesbian & Gay Film Festival, 462 Broadway #510, New York, NY 10013-2618 212-343-2707 Fax 212-343-0629 Pub *Positive Projections.* "Producers of the Annual New York International Festival of Lesbian & Gay Film; & The National Gay & Lesbian Film Tour."

♂ ● Peper Productions, PO Box 1242, Royal Oak, MI 48068

♂ ● Persona Video, PO Box 14022, San Francisco, CA 94114 415-775-6143 Pub *Out in Video.* "Producer of nonpornographic gay/lesbian videotapes."

♀ ● Pop Video, PO Box 60862, Washington, DC 20039 202-728-0413 "The best non-pornographic lesbian & women's sports videos."

♂ ● Voice and Vision Productions, PO Box 1242, Royal Oak, MI 48068 "Specializing in documenting our 'queer community'."

Food Specialties, Catering (see also Party/Event Services)

♀ ● (?♂) Coyote Cookhouse, 1202 E Pike #544, Seattle, WA 98122-3934 206-324-3731 (also fax) "All natural gourmet salsa & all-purpose salt-free seasoning (more foods to come) sold via retail fairs, wholesale, mail order."

♀ ● Indigo Coffee Roasters, Inc., 660 Riverside Dr, Northampton, MA 01060 413-586-4537; 800-447-5450; Fax 413-586-0019 "Small-batch, wholesale gourmet coffee roaster."

Funding: Endowment, Fundraising, Scholarship

♀ ★ Amazon Autumn, PO Box 2104, Union, NJ 07083 908-354-9052 "Grants to the Lesbian Community. Write for application."

♀ ★♂♂ An Uncommon Legacy Foundation, Inc., 150 W 26th St #503, New York, NY 10001 212-366-6507 Fax 212-366-6509

♀ ★ (♂♂) ASTRAEA National Lesbian Action Foundation, 666 Broadway #520, New York, NY 10012 212-529-8021 "Grants, training, & technical assistance."

♂ ☆ The Funding Exchange, 666 Broadway #500, New York, NY 10012 212-529-5300 "Administers the OUT Fund for Lesbian & Gay Liberation."

♂ Helping Ourselves, PO Box 8980, Boston, MA 02266-8980

♂ ★ Pantheon of Leather Awards, 7985 Santa Monica Blvd #109-368, West Hollywood, CA 90046 213-656-5073

Gardening Services, Landscaping, Supplies & Decoration

♂ ○ Pompeian Studios, 90 Rockledge Rd, Bronxville, NY 10708 914-337-5595; 800-457-5595; Fax 914-337-5661 "Garden statuary (catalog $10) & wrought iron furniture (free brochure)."

Graphic Design/Typesetting (see also Art; Printing)

♂ ● Country Graphics, 13 McDowell St, Hudson Falls, NY 12839 800-600-1660 "Custom T-shirts, etc."

♂ ● (?♂) Helio's Heart, PO Box 3149, Long Beach, CA 90803 310-430-3379; 310-493-1455; Fax 310-594-9739 "Design & screen T-shirts."

Health Care (see also AIDS Services)

♂ ★ Gay & Lesbian Ostomates (GLO), 36 Executive Park #120, Irvine, CA 92714-6744 800-826-0826 Pub *GLO Contact.* Brochure available for Gay/Lesbian Ostomates.

♂ ★ Lesbian & Gay Coalition for Universal Healthcare, 3626 Sunset Blvd, Los Angeles, CA 90026 213-667-3262

♂ ★ Lesbian Health Fund, 273 Church St, San Francisco, CA 94114-1310 415-255-4547 Fax 415-255-4784 "Fund to award grants for Lesbian health research."

♂ ★ (?♂) Lesbian/Gay Health & Health Policy Foundation, mail to LGHHPF, PO Box 168; 308 Westwood Plaza, UCLA, Los Angeles, CA 90095-1647 800-918-6888 izk1sqh@mvs.oac.ucla.edu

♀ ★ ♂ Mautner Project For Lesbians With Cancer, 1707 L St NW 1060, Washington, DC 20036 202-332-5536

♂ ○ **MCA Medical Claims Assistance Co, Inc., 213 20th St, Brooklyn, NY 11232 718-788-0500; 800-232-8090; Fax 718-788-6473**
♦ *MCA Medical Claims Assistance Co, Inc. advertisement page 127*

♀ ★ ♂♂ National Association for Lesbian & Gay Gerontology, 1853 Market St, San Francisco, CA 94103

♀ ★ (♂) National Lesbian & Gay Health Foundation, PO Box 65472, Washington, DC 20035 202-797-3708

Herbalists

♀ • Ron, PO Box 1184, Portsmouth, NH 03802-1184 603-433-5629 "Independent distributor of Neways Products."

Insurance Benefits/Viaticals

♀ • **Ability Life Trust, 668 N Orlando Ave #108, Maitland, FL 32751-4459 800-632-0555 Fax 407-629-0599**
♦ *Ability Life Trust advertisement page 5*

♂ ○ Life Entitlements Corporation, 4 World Trade Center #5270, New York, NY 10048 800-420-1420 "A viatical settlements company."

♂ ○ Lifetime Options, Inc., 2700 S Quincy St #540, Arlington, VA 22206 800-999-5419

♂ ○ **Positive Living Resources, 6016 Westgate Dr #303, Orlando, FL 32835 800-398-5177 Fax 407-298-5350 "A viatical settlement company."**

♀ ○ TLC Funding, 128 W Wallace St, Orlando, FL 32809 407-438-9650; 800-484-5479 (security code 2679)
♦ *TLC Funding advertisement page 124*

Legal Services & Resources

♂ American Civil Liberties Union (ACLU), 132 W 43rd St, New York, NY 10036 212-944-9800

♀ ★ Calm, Inc (Custody Action for Lesbian Mothers), PO Box 281, Narberth, PA 19072 610-667-7508

♀ ★ ♂♂ Equal Marriage Rights Fund, 15 Danton St, Melville, NY 11747-1342 516-271-1092

♀ ★ ♂♂ Gay & Lesbian Advocates & Defenders (GLAD), PO Box 218, Boston, MA 02112 617-426-1350 Pub *GLAD Briefs.* "Serves New England: MA, RI, ME, VT, NH."

♀ ★ ♂ Lambda Legal Defense & Education Fund (LLDEF), Inc, 6030 Wilshire Blvd #200, Los Angeles, CA 90036 213-937-2728 Pub *Lambda Update.*

♀ ♂ Lesbian & Gay Immigration Rights Task Force, Inc. (LGIRTF), c/o LLDEF, 6030 Wilshire Blvd #200, Los Angeles, CA 90036 213-937-2728 x37

♀ Lesbian & Gay Immigration Rights Task Force, Inc. (LGIRTF), c/o National Center for Lesbian Rights, 870 Market St #570, San Francisco, CA 94102 415-392-6257 lgirtf@dorsai.org

♀ Lesbian & Gay Immigration Rights Task Force, Inc. (LGIRTF), PO Box 7741, New York, NY 10116-7741 212-802-7264 lgirtf@dorsai.org

Mailing Lists

♀ ○ Gayellow Pages Mailing Labels, PO Box 533 Village Stn, New York, NY 10014-0533 212-674-0120 "Contents of Gayellow Pages on mailing labels, constantly updated. (NOT a list of individual buyers!)"

♀ ○ National Women's Mailing List, PO Box 68, Jenner, CA 95450 707-632-5763

♀ • Provincetown Purchase Co, 104 Bradford St, Provincetown, MA 02657 508-487-3232; 800-969-2643; Fax 508-487-1605 gabielsma@aol.com "National mailing lists: women & gay-supportive businesses."

♂ ○ Resources Mailing Lists, PO Box 1067 Harvard Sq Stn, Cambridge, MA 02138-1067 617-825-8895

♀ ○ SCS Productions, 244 W 54th St #800, New York, NY 10019 212-362-3515 "Gay & lesbian friendly businesses USA & Canada."

♀ • Strubco, Inc., PO Box 1274 Old Chelsea Stn, New York, NY 10113-0920 212-242-1900 Fax 212-242-1963 "Community Cardpack; gay & AIDS-related mailing lists."

♂ ○ Willowood Press, PO Box 1846, Minot, ND 58702 701-838-0579 Fax 701-838-3933 "Public, college, high school libraries; college English departments."

Massage Therapy (Licensed only)

♂ • ♂ Oak Lawn Myotherapy, 2727 Oak Lawn Ave #107, Dallas, TX 75219 214-528-2390; 800-775-5685 "Catalog of massage products."

Meeting/Contact Services, Publications, Talklines

♂ ○ *Bi-lifestyles*, PO Box 278, Canal St Stn, New York, NY 10013 800-325-4122 "Personal ads & photos."

♀ • **Brunch Buddies, 41 Union Sqare West #511, New York, NY 10003 Fax 212-924-9695 Women: 1-800-2-FIND-US Ext 1 or (212) 242-7800 Ext 1. Men: 1-800-2-FIND-US Ext 2 or (212) 242-7400 Ext 2. HIV+ Men 1-800-2-FIND US Ext 3 or (212) 242-7400 Ext 3. Mon-Fri 7-11pm. "Meeting resource & personal introductions for lesbians, gay men and HIV+ gay men looking for friendship & more serious relationships in the East & Northeast US. See pictures of people before you join."**

♀ ○ ♂ *Continental Spectator*, PO Box 278, Canal St Stn, New York, NY 10013 800-325-4122 "Swingers' magazine; XXX-rated."

♀ • Homo-Writes, Inc., PO Box 632 Gracie Stn, New York, NY 10028 "Introductory correspondence service; computerized matching. SASE for free information."

♂ • ♂ International Wavelength, Inc, 2215-R Market St #829, San Francisco, CA 94114 415-864-6500 Fax 415-864-6615 intwave@netcom.com Pub *Passport.* "Asian/non-Asian cross-cultural exchange; personal ads; news; Asian/Latin erotica."

♀ • *New Beginnings PENPALS*, PO Box 25, Westby, WI 54667-0025

♀ ○ *Shadow Box*, PO Box 411124, St Louis, MO 63141 314-429-7309 "An alternative way to meet new & exciting people: strictly confidential & very discreet. Personal ads."

Meeting/Contact Services & Publications, Talklines: Men Only

♂ ○ *Club Goldenrod*, PO Box 278, Canal St Stn, New York, NY 10013 800-325-4122 "Contact ads & totally uncensored photos."

♂ • *FBB&A*, PO Box 125, Corpus Christi, TX 78403 "Listings for Body-builders & admirers."

♂ ○ *Holiday Bulletin*, PO Box 582209, Minneapolis, MN 55458-2209 "Correspondence club for older men, & younger men (over 21) who appreciate older men. Since 1971."

♂ ★ International Gay Penpals, PO Box 7304 #320, North Hollywood, CA 91603

♂ • (?♂) ISO Club, PO Box 1581, Vienna, VA 22183 800-INSO-JOY *The Fun Times.*

♂ • LL, PO Box 125, Corpus Christi, TX 78403 "Listings for Latin & Hispanics & those interested in meeting them."

♂ ★ Longhaired Bros, PO Box 17931, Rochester, NY 14617 Pub *Bros.*

♂ • Mentors & Protégés, PO Box 11202, Eugene, OR 97440 "Facilitates the estblishment & preservation of relationships between adult men of different ages."

♂ • Northeast Directory, PO Box 2357, Princeton, NJ 08543-2357 "For men over 40. SASE for information."

♂ • Quarterly Interchange, PO Box 42502, San Francisco, CA 94101

♂ ★ Roger's List, PO Box 954, Louisville, KY 40201

♂ • Small, Etc, PO Box 610294, Bayside, NY 11361-0294 Pub *Small Gazette.* "For gay & bisexual men who are small endowed, short in stature, & those who like us. Nationwide membership. SASE for information."

♂ • UM, PO Box 125, Corpus Christi, TX 78403 "Listings for persons interested in foreskins."

♂ ★ United Brothers, PO Box 1733, Louisville, KY 40201 Pub *United Brothers.* "Penpals."

Meeting/Contact Services, Publications, Talklines: Women Only

♀ • (?♭) Golden Threads, PO Box 60475, Northampton, MA 01060-0475 "Contact publication for Lesbian women over 50 (younger welcome); annual celebration for older Lesbians in Provincetown."

♀ • League of Versatile Women, PO Box 1604, Eugene, OR 97440-1604 503-649-6946 24 hrs.

♀ • Matchmakers Introduction Service, PO Box 9974-GY, Colorado Springs, CO 80932 719-574-6554 Pub *Sapphic Sisters.* "Lesbian personal ads. Information $2 (applied to subscription)."

♀ • New Dawn, PO Box 1849, Alexandria, VA 22313 "National/International correspondence club for gay women, established 1980."

♀ • Wishing Well, PO Box 713090, Santee, CA 92072-3090 619-443-4818
✦ Wishing Well advertisement page 122

New Age: Occult, Wicca, Alternative Healing

♀ • (♭♭) Uncommon Hands, c/o Dr SDiane Bogus aka Sister Soul-Joiner 880 E Fremont #736, Sunnyvale, CA 94087 408-738-4623 "Psychic readings by phone. Ask for free brochure."

News Wire Services

♀ ★ GayNet, PO Box 25524, Albuquerque, NM 87125-0524 505-842-5112; 800-524-2963 (new memberships); Fax 505-842-5114 "International Gay & Lesbian news service for the media."

Organizations/Resources: Bisexual Focus

→ *Anything That Moves: Beyond The Myths of Bisexuality*: see **PUBLICATIONS page 129**

♀ ★ (?♭) BiNet USA, PO Box 7327, Langley Park, MD 20787 202-986-7186 rain@glib.org Pub *BiNet USA News.*

♀ ★ ♭♭ Bisexual Resource Center, PO Box 639, Cambridge, MA 02140 617-338-9595 brc@panix.com Pub *Bisexual Resource Guide.*

→ *Switch Hitter.* see **PUBLICATIONS page 129**
♀ ★ Unitarian Universalist Bisexual Network (UUBN), PO Box 10818, Portland, ME 04104

Organizations/Resources: Business & Professional

♀ ★ Alternative Modalities—GLB PT's, PO Box 60313, Florence, MA 01060-0313; *Alternative Modalities.* "Physical Therapists."

♀ ★ American Federation of Teachers National Gay & Lesbian Caucus, PO Box 190983, Miami Beach, FL 33119 305-538-0979 Pub *Open Classroom.*

♀ ★ ♭♭ Association for Gay, Lesbian & Bisexual Issues in Counseling (AGLBIC), PO Box 216, Jenkintown, PA 19046 Pub *AGLBIC News.*

♀ ★ Association of Gay & Lesbian Psychiatrists (AGLP), c/o Roy Harker, Dir. National Office, 209 N 4th St #D-5, Philadelphia, PA 19106 Pub *Newsletter.*

♀ ★ ♭♭ Boeing Employees Association of Gays & Lesbians (BEAGLES), PO Box 1733, Renton, WA 98057 206-781-3587

♀ ☆ COSMEP: The International Association of Independent Publishers, PO Box 420703, San Francisco, CA 94142-0703 415-922-9490; 800-546-3303; Fax 415-922-5566 74217.1707@compuserve.com Pub *COSMEP Newsletter.*

♀ ★ ♭♭ Digital Queers, 584 Castro St #560, San Francisco, CA 94114 info@dq.org

♀ ★ (?♭) G/L PEN, PO Box 580397, Minneapolis, MN 55458-0397 612-866-9609; 612-535-9669 "Postal employees."

♀ ★ Gay & Lesbian Medical Association, 273 Church St, San Francisco, CA 94114-1310 415-255-4547 Fax 415-255-4784

♀ ★ ♭♭ Gay & Lesbian Press Association, PO Box 8185, Universal City, CA 91608-0185 818-902-1476 *The Media Reporter.*

♀ ★ Gay & Lesbian Statisticians' Caucus, c/o Frank Vitrano, US Bureau of the Census, Room 3750-3, Washington, DC 20233 202-347-4207

♀ ★ **Gay Officers Action League (GOAL), PO Box 2038 Canal St Stn, New York, NY 10013 212-996-8808 Pub *GOAL Gazette.* "Social & support services for law enforcement officers."**

♀ ★ Gay, Lesbian & Bisexual Task Force, American Library Association, c/o O.L.O.S., 50 E Huron St, Chicago, IL 60611 "Clearinghouse publications include: Directory of Bookstores specializing in Gay, Lesbian, Feminist books: $2.00; Directory of Publishers of Gay & Lesbian Books: $1.50; Directory of Professional Groups of Gays & Lesbians: $1.50. Request order form for complete list of publications avaiable."

♀ ★ (?♭) Gay/Lesbian Postal Employees Network (GLPEN), PO Box 282982, San Francisco, CA 94128-2982 415-873-4308

♀ ★ Gays & Lesbians In Foreign Affairs (GLIFFA), PO Box 18774, Washington, DC 20036-8774 202-797-5510

♀ ★ (?♭) Gays & Lesbians in Urban Planning & Policy (GALIP), 1705 Lanier Pl NW #402, Washington, DC 20009 202-462-0895 *The GALIP Gazette.*

♀ ★ Gays & Lesbians United for Education, PO Box 19856, Cincinnati, OH 45219 513-242-2491 Pub *Open Classroom: News of Lesbian/Gay Educators.*

♀ ★ GLOBAL: Gay & Lesbian Organizations Bridging Across the Lands, c/o BACW, 55 New Montgomery #606, San Francisco, CA 94105 *The Bridge.*

♀ ★ (?♭) International Gay Travel Association, PO Box 4974, Key West, FL 33041 800-448-8550 Fax 305-296-6633 Pub *IGTA Today.*

♀ ★ (?♭) LEAGUE: Lesbian, Bisexual, & Gay Employees at AT&T, 11900 N Pecos St #30H78, Denver, CO 80234 407-358-5324

♀ ★ Lesbian & Gay Labor Network, PO Box 1159 Peter Stuyvesant Stn, New York, NY 10009 212-923-8690

♀ ★ ♂♂ Lesbian, Gay & Bisexual People in Medicine, 1902 Association Dr, Reston, VA 22091 703-620-6600 "A standing committee of the American Medical Student Association."

♀ ★ LTN (Lesbian Teachers Network), PO Box 301, East Lansing, MI 48826-0301

♀ ★ ♂♂ LVA: Lesbian Visual Artists, 870 Market St #618, San Francisco, CA 94102 415-788-6118 Pub Newsletter. "An international promotional & networking organization, housing a slide registry & producing exhibitions & arts events."

♀ ★ National Education Association Gay & Lesbian Caucus, PO Box 3559, York, PA 17402-0559 717-848-3354

♀ ★ National Gay Pilots' Association, PO Box 27542, Washington, DC 20038-7542 202-660-3852 Pub GPA News.

♀ ★ National Lesbian & Gay Journalists Association, 874 Gravenstein Hwy #4, Sebastopol, CA 95472 707-823-2193 Fax 707-823-4176 execoffice@aol.com Pub Alternatives.

♀ ★ National Lesbian & Gay Law Association, 1555 Connecticut Ave NW #200, Washington, DC 20036-1111 202-389-0161

♀ ★ (?♂) National Organization of Gay & Lesbian Scientists & Technical Professionals (NOGLSTP), PO Box 91803, Pasadena, CA 91109 818-791-7689 Pub NOGLSTP Bulletin.

♀ ☆ ♂♂ Political Staff Workers Union, 5018 Rainier Ave S, Seattle, WA 98118 206-722-2453 Fax 206-723-7691 "Labor union made up of people working for social change organization."

♀ ★ (?♂) Professionals in Film/Video, 336 Canal St, 8th flr, New York, NY 10013 212-387-2022 Pub Newsletter; Networking Directory. Job placement service.

♀ ★ Publishing Triangle, PO Box 114, Prince St Stn, New York, NY 10012 212-572-6142 Pub Newsletter. "An activist-minded networking group of lesbian & gay publishing professionals & writers."

♂ Radical Booksellers' Association, c/o Printers Mark Bookshop, 30A Market Square, Knoxville, TN 37902 615-524-1259

♀ ★ (?♂) Society for the Psychological Study of Lesbian & Gay Issues, 750 1st St NE (American Psychological Association), Washington, DC 20002-4242 202-366-6037 Pub Newsletter..

♀ ☆ Tradeswomen Inc, PO Box 2622, Berkeley, CA 94702 510-649-6160 Pub Tradeswoman Magazine; Trade Trax.

Organizations/Resources: Disability

→ The Disability Rag & Resource: see PUBLICATIONS page 130

→ Dykes, Disability & Stuff: see PUBLICATIONS (Female Readership) page 130

→ Hikané: The Capable Woman: see PUBLICATIONS (Female Readership) page 130

Organizations/Resources: Education, Anti-Defamation, Anti-Violence, Self-Defense

♀ ★ Campaign to End Homophobia, PO Box 438316, Chicago, IL 60643-8316 312-868-8280

♀ ★ Center for Research & Education in Sexuality (CE-RES), San Francisco State University, San Francisco, CA 94132 415-338-1137 Editorial office of Journal of Homosexuality (published by Haworth Press).

♀ ★ (?♂) The Experience, 1223-B S St Francis Dr, Santa Fe, NM 87505-4053 800-966-3896; 505-820-1931; Fax 505-820-7106 "Educational organization supporting personal empowerment & community effectiveness since since 1978. Seminars in various locations."

♀ ★ Gay & Lesbian Advocacy Research Project, PO Box 5085, Columbia, SC 29250

♀ ★ ♂ GLAAD (Gay & Lesbian Alliance Against Defamation), 150 W 26th St #503, New York, NY 10001 212-807-1700 Fax 212-807-1806 Pub GLAAD Bulletin. "GLAAD works for fair, accurate & inclusive images of lesbians, bisexuals, & gay men."

♀ ★ GLAAD (Gay & Lesbian Alliance Against Defamation), 8455 Beverly Blvd #305, Los Angeles, CA 90048 213-658-6775 Fax 213-658-6776

♀ ☆ ♂♂ The Kinsey Institute for Research in Sex, Gender, & Reproduction, Information Services, Morrison Hall #416, Bloomington, IN 47405 812-855-7686 Fax 812-855-8277 libknsy@indiana.edu

♀ ☆ Mariposa Education & Research Foundation, 3123 Schweitzer, Topanga, CA 90290 818-704-4812 Pub Mariposa Newsletter. "Sex research & education."

♀ ☆ ♂♂ Ms. Foundation for Women, 120 Wall St 33rd flr, New York, NY 10005 212-742-2300 Fax 212-742-1653

♀ ★ National Coming Out Day, PO Box 34640, Washington, DC 20043-4640 202-628-4160; 800-866-NCOD

♀ ☆ ♂ National Council for Research on Women, 530 Broadway, 10th flr, New York, NY 10012 212-274-0730 Fax 212-274-0821

♀ ★ New Era Institute, 3282 N 46th St, Milwaukee, WI 53216 414-449-9902 Pub Our Causes Digest. "Research into Gay & Lesbian organizations & their funding; exchanging ideas that work."

♂ • Overlooked Opinions, Inc., 3712 N Broadway #277, Chicago, IL 60613 Pub In Full View. "Opinion Research firm dedicated to assessing the views & opinions of the lesbian, gay & bisexual community."

♀ ★ Pop Against Homophobia (PAH), 545 8th Ave #401, New York, NY 10018 212-560-7130 Fax 212-222-5292

♂ ☆ ♂ Sexuality Information & Education Council of the US (SIECUS), 130 W 42nd St #305, New York, NY 10036-7802 212-819-9770 Pub SIECUS Reports.

Organizations/Resources: Ethnic, Multicultural

♂ African American Gay & Lesbian Studies Center, PO Box 56202, Los Angeles, CA 90056-0202

♀ ★ Asian Lesbians of the East Coast/Asian Pacific Lesbian Network, PO Box 850, New York, NY 10002 212-517-5598

♀ ★ (?♂) Black Gay & Lesbian Leadership Forum, 1219 S LaBrea Ave, Los Angeles, CA 90019 213-964-7820 Fax 213-964-7830

♂ ☆ Black Men's Xchange, PO Box 642365, Chicago, IL 60664-2365 312-824-8222; 800-274-3853 "A group where black men can find love & support from other black men."

→ BLK: see PUBLICATIONS page 130

→ Colorlife! Magazine: see PUBLICATIONS page 130

→ Kuumba: see PUBLICATIONS page 130

→ NABWMT Journal: see PUBLICATIONS page 130

♀ ★ (?♂) National Association of Black & White Men Together, 1747 Connecticut Ave NW, Washington, DC 20009 202-462-3599; 800-NA4-BWMT; Fax 202-462-3690 Black & White Men Together/Men of All Colors Together

♀ ☆ (♂) National Institute for Women of Color (NIWC), PO Box 71567, Washington, DC 20024-1567 202-296-2661

♀ ★ (?♂) National Latino/a Lesbian & Gay Organization (LLEGO), 703 G St SE, Washington, DC 20003-2815 202-544-0092

→ Shamakami: see PUBLICATIONS (Female Readership) page 130

♀ ★ Trikone: Gay & Lesbian South Asians, PO Box 21354, San Jose, CA 95151 408-270-8776 trikone@rahul.net Pub *Trikone Magazine.* "Group for Gay & Lesbian South Asians."

Organizations/Resources: Family

♀ ☆ Catholic Parents Network, 637 Dover St, Baltimore, MD 21230 301-927-8766 Fax 410-864-6948

♀ ☆ Children of Lesbians & Gays Everywhere (COLAGE), 2300 Market St #165, San Francisco, CA 94114 (In Canada PO Box 187 Stn F, Toronto, ON M4Y 2L5) 415-861-KIDS Fax 415-235-83445 Pub *Just For Us; Kids Club Fun Pages.*

→ *The Family Next Door:* see PUBLICATIONS page 131

♀ ★ Gay & Lesbian Parents Coalition International, PO Box 50360, Washington, DC 20091 202-583-8029 Fax 201-783-6204 glpcinat@ix.netcom.com Pub *Network.*

♀ ★ (?♂) Lavender Families Resources Network, PO Box 21567, Seattle, WA 98111 206-325-2643 Voice & TTY. Pub *Mom's Apple Pie.* "Resource network for lesbigay family issues."

♀ ★ (?♂) Momazons, PO Box 82069, Columbus, OH 43202 614-267-0193 Pub *Newsletter.* "For lesbians who have or want children in their lives."

♀ ☆ (?♂) PFLAG: National Office, 1101 14th St NW #1030, Washington, DC 20005 202-638-4200 Pub *PFLAGpole.* "Parents, Families & Friends of Lesbians & Gays; provides support, education & advocacy; various publications, local chapters USA & Canada."

→ *Roots & Wings Adoption Magazine:* see PUBLICATIONS page 131

Organizations/Resources: General, Multipurpose, Pride

♀ ★ (?♂) International Association of Lesbian/Gay Pride Coordinators, 147 Park St #A, San Francisco, CA 94110-5835 415-861-0779

♀ ★ Jewish Lesbian Daughters Of Holocast Survivors, PO Box 75, Hadley, MA 01035-0075

♀ ★ Stonewall 25, Inc., 208 W 13th St, New York, NY 10011-7799 212-439-1031 "Global celebration of Lesbian & Gay Pride & Protest, planned for June 26, 1994."

♀ ☆ ♂ Women's Action Alliance, 370 Lexington Ave #603, New York, NY 10017 212-532-8330

Organizations/Resources: Military/Veterans

♀ ☆ ♂♂ American Friends Service Committee, 915 Salem Ave, Dayton, OH 45406 513-278-4225 Fax 513-278-2778 hawkafsc@aol.com

♀ ★ Committee to Fight Exclusion of Homosexuals from Armed Forces, 115 Monroe St, Bossier City, LA 71111 318-742-4709

♀ ★ Servicemembers Legal Defense Network, PO Box 53013, Washington, DC 20009 202-328-3244 Fax 202-328-0063

♂ ★ (♂♂) Uniformed Services Activity, 2725 13th St NW #101, Washington, DC 20009 0-700-USA-INFO (collect call) Pub *Activity Newsletter.* "Private, professional support group & resource-referral network created to fulfill the morale, welfare, & recreational needs of current/former duty Military & all Law Enforcement or Emergency Services' personnel; plus civilian Defense employees, Civil Air Patrol, & students in ROTC - NROTC Programs. Special services guides, holiday socials; Women's outreach program."

Organizations/Resources: Media (see also Publications)

♀ ★ *Gay Media Task Force,* 71-426 Estellita Dr, Rancho Mirage, CA 92270-4215 619-568-6711

Organizations/Resources: Political/Legislative

♀ ★ Amnesty International Members For Lesbian & Gay Concerns (AIMLGC), 654 C St NE, Washington, DC 20002-6002

♂ Amnesty International USA: Breaking the Silence Campaign, 322 8th Ave, New York, NY 10001 212-807-8400

♀ ★ Gay & Lesbian Americans, PO Box 77533, Washington, DC 20013-7533 202-889-5111 "A diverse, non-partisan coalition of grassroots advocates committed to civil rights for GLBT people, & to a cure for AIDS."

♀ ★ Gay & Lesbian Labor Activist Network (GALLAN), PO Box 1450, Jamaica Plain, MA 02130 Pub *Gallan News.*

♀ ★ ♂ Gay & Lesbian Victory Fund, 1012 14th St NW #707, Washington, DC 20005 202-842-8679 Fax 202-289-3863 "Support of openly gay/lesbian candidates for office."

♀ ★ Human Rights Campaign Fund, 1012 14th St NW #607, Washington, DC 20005 202-628-4160 Fax 202-347-5323 Pub *Momentum; Capitol Hill Update.* "National political organization for Lesbians & Gay Men, devoted to civil rights, AIDS, & other health care issues. Works through lobbying Congress, political action & grassroots organizing."

♀ ★ ♂♂ Log Cabin Republicans, 1101 14th NW #1040, Washington, DC 20005 202-347-5306 Fax 202-347-5224 "National gay Republican lobbying organization affiliated with the Log Cabin Federation."'

♀ ★ ♂♂ National Center for Lesbian Rights, 870 Market St #570, San Francisco, CA 94102 415-392-6257 Fax 415-392-8442 Pub *Quarterly Newsletter.* "Public policy advocacy; community education; legal resources & education."

♀ ★ National Gay & Lesbian Task Force, 2320 17th St NW, Washington, DC 20009 202-332-6483; 202-332-6219 TTY; Fax 202-332-0207 Pub *Task Force Report.*

♀ ☆&& National Organization for Women, Inc, 1000 16th St NW #700, Washington, DC 20036-5705 202-331-0066 Fax 202-785-8576 now@now.org lesb.rts@now.org Pub *National NOW Times*.

♀ ★ (?&) Pro-Life Alliance of Gays & Lesbians, PO Box 33292, Washington, DC 20033-0292 202-223-6697

♀ ☆ Radical Women National Office, 523-A Valencia, San Francisco, CA 94110 415-864-1278

♀ ★ Republicans for Individual Freedoms, PO Box 13162, Atlanta, GA 30324 404-239-1679

Organizations/Resources: Prisoner Resources

♀ ★ Dignity Prison Ministry, 1500 Massachusetts Ave #11 NW, Washington, DC 20005

♀ ★ League for Gay & Lesbian Prisoners, 1202 E Pike St #1044, Seattle, WA 98122-3934 "Support/resource network for gay, lesbian, bisexual, transgender prisoners & their support systems."

♂ ☆ Stop Prisoner Rape, Inc., PO Box 2713 Manhattanville Stn, New York, NY 10027-8817 212-663-5562

Organizations/Resources: Sexual Focus (Leather, S/M, etc) & Safe Sex Promotion

♂ ★ Chest Men Of America (CMA), PO Box 138442, Chicago, IL 60613 312-644-7282

♂ ★ Foot Fraternity, PO Box 24102, Cleveland, OH 44124 216-449-4114

♀ ★ International Mr Leather, 5015 N Clark St, Chicago, IL 60640 312-878-6360 Fax 312-878-5184

♂ ★ Leathermasters International, PO Box 391532, Los Angeles, CA 90027 213-664-6422 "S/M education; social events; professional counseling; introduction service."

♂ ★ Military & Police Uniform Association, PO Box 69A04, Dept GYP, West Hollywood, CA 90069 213-650-5112 Pub *Newsletter*. "Club for men into uniform lifestyle."

♂ ★ (?&) New World Rubber Men, 1602 Lincoln St, Port Townsend, WA 98368-8031 360-385-3811 Pub *Rubber Sheets*.

♂ ★ & North American Man Boy Love Association (NAMBLA), 537 Jones St #8418, San Francisco, CA 94102 212-631-1194; 415-564-2602 Pub *NAMBLA Bulletin*.

♀ ★ Womanlink, 2124 Kittredge #257, Berkeley, CA 94704

Organizations/Resources: Social, Recreational & Support Groups (see also Sport/Dance/Outdoor)

♀ ☆ **Affiliated Bigmen's Club, 584 Castro St #139Y, San Francisco, CA 94114 415-699-7735 The Affiliate. "National umbrella organization for Girth & Mirth clubs."**
✦ Affiliated Bigmen's Club advertisement page 131

♀ ★ Deaf & Hard of Hearing Gay Penpal Network, mail to DHHGPN, PO Box 441, Ashland, MA 01721-0441

♀ ★ Gay & Lesbian History Stamp Club, PO Box 230940, Hartford, CT 06123-0940 203-653-3791 Pub *Lambda Philatelic Journal*.

♂ ★ Gay Naturist International, mail to G.N.I. PO Box 7150, Corte Madera, CA 94976

♀ ★ Gaylaxians International, PO Box 675, Lanham-Seabrook, MD 20703-0675 Pub *Gaylactic Gayzette*. "Promoting Gay/Lesbian/Bisexual Sci-Fi worldwide."

♀ ★ Jewish Lesbian Daughters of Holocaust Survivors, PO Box 8773, Madison, WI 53708-8773 608-256-8883

♀ ★ Lambda Amateur Radio Club, PO Box 91757, Cleveland, OH 44101-3757 216-556-1642 lambdaarc@aol.com

♂ ★ Lambda Car Club International, PO Box 2501, Columbus, OH 43216-2501 Pub *Driveshaft*. "Over 1000 members nationwide interested in old & special interest motor vehicles."

♀ ★ Lesbian, Gay & Bisexual Returned Peace Corps Volunteers, PO Box 14332, San Francisco, CA 94114-4332

♀ ★ Partners Task Force for Gay & Lesbian Couples, PO Box 9685, Seattle, WA 98109-0685 206-935-1206 demian@eskimo.com

♂ ★ Phoebe Snow Society, PO Box 1735, South Hackensack, NJ 07606-1735 "Gay railfans."

♀ ☆ Tahanga Research Association, PO Box 8714, La Jolla, CA 92038-8714 Pub *Nudist East Asia Travel Guide*.

Organizations/Resources: Sport/Dance/Outdoor

♀ The Federation Of Gay Games, 584 Castro St #343, San Francisco, CA 94114

♀ ★ Gay Games, PO Box 5127, New York, NY 10163-5127 212-633-9494 Fax 212-633-9488

♀ ★ International Association of Gay & Lesbian Country Western Dance Clubs, 1608 N Cahuenga Blvd #1282, Hollywood, CA 90028 213-851-3476; 305-977-7589; 617-524-1082; Fax 818-765-3411 *CW*

♀ ★ International Association of Gay Square Dance Clubs, PO Box 15428, Crystal City, VA 22215-0428 800-835-6462 *d*

♀ ★ (?&) International Gay Rodeo Association, 900 E Colfax, Denver, CO 80218 303-832-4472 Fax 303-830-7863

♀ ★ (?&) Lavender Country & Folk Dancers, PO Box 2306, Jamaica Plain, MA 02130-0020 800-LCFD-123 *d* Nongay welcome.

♂ ★ National Gay/Lesbian Outdoor Sports Clubs, PO Box 10644, Greensboro, NC 27404-0644 "Enclose legal sized SASE & donate $1 for worldwide information."
↬ *Pacelines*: see PUBLICATIONS page 132

♀ ○&& RVing Women, 201 E Southern Ave, Apache Junction, AZ 85219-3700 602-983-4678 Pub *Newsletter*. "Also have RV resort in AZ."

♀ ● (?&) Sailing Affairs, 404 E 11th St, New York, NY 10009 212-228-5755 "Sailing lessons, parties, charter vacations, day trips, weekends."

♀ ★ Stonewall Climbers, PO Box 445, Boston, MA 02124 Pub *Newsletter*. "A club for gay, lesbian & bisexual rock & ice climbers & their friends; member sponsored trips worldwide."

♂ ★ Tarheel Outdoor Sports Fellowship, PO Box 10644, Greensboro, NC 27404 910-299-9683 "Friendly athletic high adventure group; send SASE + $1 for information."

♀ ☆ (?&) Women's Motorcyclist Foundation, 7 Lent Ave, Leroy, NY 14482 716-768-6054 Fax 716-768-8014 ginsuewmf@aol.com Pub *Chrome Rose's Review*. "Motorcyclists."

Organizations/Resources: Student, Academic, Alumni/ae

♀ ★ Allegheny College Alumni Caucus for Gay, Lesbian & Bisexual Concerns, c/o Bruce Shewitz, 13051 Cedar Rd, Cleveland, OH 44118 216-371-0709

♀ ★ (&&) Bisexual, Gay & Lesbian Alliance at Pitt, University of Pittsburgh, 502 William Pitt Union, Pittsburgh, PA 15260 412-648-2105

♀ ★ Bucknell GALABI, PO Box 10518, Arlington, VA 22210 703-524-3489

♀ ★ (?&) Center for Lesbian & Gay Studies (CLAGS), CUNY Graduate Ctr, 33 W 42nd St, New York, NY 10036-8099 212-642-2924 Pub *Directory of Lesbian & Gay Scholarship*.

♀ ★ (?♂) Coalition of Lesbian/Gay Student Groups, Inc., PO Box 190712, Dallas, TX 75219 214-761-3802 Fax 214-522-4604 "Student organizing in the Southwest, TX, OK, LA, AR, NM."

♀ ★ Connecticut College B.G.A.L.A. (Alumnae/i), 95 Open Gate Lane, Southport, CT 06490 203-255-5391 Bisexual, Gay & Lesbian Alumni/ae.

♀ ★ Dartmouth Gay & Lesbian Alums, c/o The Center 208 W 13th St, New York, NY 10011-7702 212-330-9189 dartgala@ aol.com

♂ ★ Delta Lambda Phi Fraternity, National Office, 1008 10th St #374, Sacramento, CA 95814 800-587-FRAT

♀ ★ (?♂) Harvard Gay & Lesbian Caucus, PO Box 1809, Cambridge, MA 02238 Pub *Harvard Gay & Lesbian Review.*

♀ ★ Lesbian & Gay Alumnae/i Vassar College (LAGA-VC), Alumnae House, 61 Raymond Ave, Poughkeepsie, NY 12601 914-437-5440 Pub *LAGAVC News.*

♀ ★ ♂♂ National Gay & Lesbian Task Force Campus Project, 6030 Wilshire Blvd #200, Los Angeles, CA 90036 213-934-9030 Fax 213-937-0161

♀ ★ Network of Gay & Lesbian Alumni/Ae Associations/Net-GALA, PO Box 15141, Washington, DC 20003 703-849-0786; 212-807-9584 ext 99 Pub *NetGALA News.*

♀ ★ (?♂) Oberlin Lesbian, Gay & Bisexual Alumni, 105 Bosworth Hall, Oberlin College, Oberlin, OH 44074 Pub *White Squirrel Newsletter.*

♀ ★ Principia Gay & Lesbian Alumni Group, c/o David White, 2900 Connecticut Ave NW, Apt 124, Washington, DC 20008-1404 202-387-7250

♀ ★ Purdue Lesbian, Bi & Gay Alumni Group, PO Box 254, Fredonia, NY 14063-0254 716-881-1878

♀ ★ Queens College (Charlotte, NC) GALA (Alumni/ae), 4219 Ben Gunn Rd, Virginia Beach, VA 23455 804-464-3894

♀ ★ (?♂) Rice University Gay & Lesbian Alumni Association, PO Box 1892, Houston, TX 77251-1892 713-523-0170

♀ ★ Section on Gay & Lesbian Legal Issues, Association of American Law Schools, New York Law School, 57 Worth St, attn Prof. Arthur Leonard, New York, NY 10013 212-431-2156

♀ ★ Society for Lesbian & Gay Philosophy, c/o Prof Chekola, Dept of Philosophy Moorhead State University, Moorhead, MN 56563 218-236-4087

♀ ★ ♂♂ Standing Committee for Lesbian, Gay, & Bisexual Awareness, American College Personnel Association, c/o Jo Campbell, Campus Housing M/C579, 818 S Wolcott Ave, Rm 317 SRH, Chicago, IL 60612-3727 Pub: *Out On Campus, c/o Liz Prince, Director of Susquehanna Hall, UMBC, Baltimore, MD 21228.*

♀ ★ (?♂) University of Southern California Lambda Alumni Association, 830 Childs Way, Box 28, Los Angeles, CA 90089 213-740-5440

♀ ★ William & Mary GALA (Gay & Lesbian Alumni/ae), Inc, PO Box 15141, Washington, DC 20003 202-544-4197 Pub *William & Mary GALA News.*

♀ ★ ♂♂ Yale GALA (Alumnae/i), PO Box 2119, New York, NY 10185 212-382-3311

♀ ★ (♂) Yale GALA/DC, PO Box 15094, Washington, DC 20003-0094

Organizations/Resources: Transgender & Transgender Publications

T ☆ (?♂) **American Educational Gender Information Service, Inc. (AEGIS)**, PO Box 33724, Decatur, GA 30033 404-939-0244 Helpline. aegis@mindspring.com Pub *Chrysalis Quarterly.*

T ★ CDI (Crossdressers International), PO Box 61, Easton, PA 18044 610-570-7389

T ★ *Cross-Talk*, Box 944, Woodland Hills, CA 91365 818-907-3053 Fax 818-347-4190 kymmer@xconn.com

T ○ Crossdresser's InfoGuide, PO Box 566065, Atlanta, GA 30356 404-333-6455 Fax 404-551-0671 "National resource directory & personals, fantasies, catalogs, more. Call anytime."

T ☆ *Grace and Lace Letter*, PO Box 31253, Jackson, MS 39286-1253 601-982-2276

T ○ *He-She Directory*, PO Box 278, Canal St Stn, New York, NY 10013 800-325-4122 "Personal contact ads/photos."

T ☆ ♂ International Foundation for Gender Education, PO Box 367, Wayland, MA 01778 617-899-2212 Pub *TV-TS Tapestry Journal.* "Network of support organizations & services; information; referrals; speakers bureau."

T ● Lee's Mardi Gras Boutique, PO Box 843, New York, NY 10108 / 400 W. 14th St 212-645-1888 "Clothes, underwear, makeup, girdles, corsets; large selection of high heel shoes to size 14."

T ☆ ♂♂ Montgomery Medical & Psychological Institute, PO Box 33311, Decatur, GA 30033 404-603-9426 Pub *Insight.* "Information for transsexuals & other transgenderists; support group meetings, professional referrals, lobbying."

T ★ (?♂) National Harry Benjamin Gender Dysphoric Association, 303-754-7579 "Victims advocacy & specializing in Gender Dysphoria, employment issues, hormonal & sex reassignment."

T ○ Reluctant Press, PO Box 11936, Alexandria, VA 22312 "Books by mail."

T ☆ ♂♂ Renaissance Education Association, Inc., 987 Old Eagle School Rd #719, Wayne, PA 19087 610-975-9119 bensalem@cpcn Pub *Renaissance News & Views.* "Peer support & counseling; all welcome."

T ★ ♂♂ Transsexuals In Prison, mail to TIP, c/o John Prowett, 1517 Court Ave #4, Memphis, TN 38104-2402 Pub *TIP Newsletter.*

T ★ *TransSisters: The Journal of Transsexual Feminism*, 4004 Troost Ave, Kansas City, MO 64110 816-753-7816

T ● ♂♂ Vernon's Specialties/Erotic Variations, PO Box 95189 Dept GYP, Nonantum, MA 02195-0189 / 386 Moody St, Waltham; 02154 617-894-1744 "Everything to create your personal feminine image; large selection of magazines, books, videos. Catalog $20."

Organizations/Resources: Youth (see also Family)

♀ ★ !Out Proud! The National Coalition for Gay, Lesbian & Bisexual Youth, PO Box 24589, San Jose, CA 95154-4589 408-269-6125 Fax 408-269-5328 glbyouth@aol.com

♀ ★ Gay Youth Leadership School, PO Box 121690, Arlington, TX 76012

♀ ★ Lambda Youth Network, PO Box 7911, Culver City, CA 90233 "Referrals; lists of talklines; newsletters, pen pal programs & other services for youth 23 & under. Send $1, large SASE & age for referral list."

♀ ★ National Gay Youth Network, PO Box 846, San Francisco, CA 94101

♀ ★ National Youth Advocacy Alliance, PO Box 121690, Arlington, TX 76012 Pub *Youth Advocacy.* "National youth lobbying organization."

♀ ★ (?♂) Sexual Minority Youth Assistance League (SMYAL), 333 1/2 Pennsylvania Ave SE 3rd flr, Washington, DC 20003-1148 202-546-5940; training & education ext 504; Youth Helpline ext 8 Pub *SMYAL News.* "Serving Lesbian/Gay/Bisexual/Transgender youth, 14-21 years old."

Party/Event Services (see also Food Specialties, Catering)

♀ • Murder By Mail, PO Box 1899, Vineyard Haven, MA 02568 617-489-2171; 508-693-5205 "Mystery parties: customized packages & planning services for home, business, fundraising; 10 to 300 people. Brochure & planning guide $3, or call for information."

Performing Arts: Entertainment, Music, Recording, Theater, etc.

♂ • Aboveground Records, PO Box 2233, Philadelphia, PA 19103 215-732-7494 "Producers of Tom Wilson Weinberg's 'Ten Percent Revue', 'Get Used To It', & other recordings."
✦ Aboveground Records advertisement page 134

♀ • (?♂) Appel Presents..Inc., PO Box 36248, Los Angeles, CA 90036-0248 213-706-6774 Fax 213-930-0194 "Special events, benefits, etc."

♂ • Bent Records, 480 E 17th St, Brooklyn, NY 11226 718-284-4473 "Recordings by Lynn Lavner."

♀ ○ City Sound Productions, 11 Jefferson Ave, Takoma Park, MD 20912 410-265-9000 "Event Management; technical production."

♂ ★ Emma Goldman Gypsy Players (EGGPLANT), PO Box 7382, Sarasota, FL 34278-7382 813-378-4413 (before 10pm EST) "We are an international Radical Faerie travelling theatre troupe."

♀ ★ The Flirtations, PO Box 421 Prince St Stn, New York, NY 10012-0008 212-439-8033 "Openly gay, politically active a cappella men's singing group."

♂ • Fresh Fruit Records, 369 Montezuma #209, Santa Fe, NM 87501 800-IS-FRUIT; 505-989-8647
✦ Fresh Fruit Records advertisement page 135

♂ ★ Gay & Lesbian Association of Choruses, PO Box 65084, Washington, DC 20035 202-467-5830 Fax 202-467-5831
→ Gay Music Guide: see PUBLICATIONS page 134

♂ • Gender Bender Music, PO Box 164, Buffalo, NY 14207 716-836-1801

♀ ★ The Glines, 240 W 44th St, New York, NY 10036 212-354-8899 "Theatre company."

♂ • H. E. Entertainment, PO Box 12151, Fort Wayne, IN 46862 219-432-7027 "Managing Techno & Rock performers & strippers."

♀ • Homos With Attitude, 37 Academy Rd, Somerset, NJ 08873 "Four piece rock band; demo tape available. Write for details & monthly gig updates."

♀ ○ Jade & Queenie, PO Box 536383, Orlando, FL 32853 800-352-1058 "Coomedy, Puppetry & Music."

♀ ○ Lady Adonis, Inc., 7320 Old Clinton Hwy #4, Knoxville, TN 37921 615-938-3345 "Female Revue: full production includes lighting, sound, special effects, choreographed routines. Credits include Warner Bros Motion Picture; MTV; Phil Donahue."

♀ ☆ Ladyslipper Music, PO Box 3124, Durham, NC 27715 919-683-1570; 800-634-4044 orders; Fax 919-682-5601 "Recording & videos by women."

♂ ★ Lesbian & Gay Bands of America, PO Box 57099, Washington, DC 20037-0099 410-675-2308; 410-328-9885

♀ • Olivia Records, 4400 Market St, Oakland, CA 94608 510-655-0364

♂ • OUTmedia, 123 Park Place, Brooklyn, NY 11217 718-789-1776 Fax 718-622-6848 "Personal management agency for lesbian/gay performing arts & entertainment related services."

♂ • ♿ Outright Speakers & Talent Bureau, 15 Danton St, Melville, NY 11747-1342 516-271-1092 "Gay, Lesbian, Bisexual programs for colleges, universities, & events."

♀ • ♿ Piano World/Dallas Pipe Organ, International Music House, 1509 Washington 4th flr, St Louis, MO 63103 314-231-0600; 800-589-5824 "Sales & restoration of vintage antique player pianos, pianos, square grands, pipe organs, reed organs, nickelodeons."

♀ • Pleiades Records, PO Box 7217, Berkeley, CA 94707 510-528-8193 Fax 510-528-9859

♂ • Significant Other Records, PO Box 1341 Old Chelsea Stn, New York, NY 10113-1341 212-366-9078

→ Sing Heavenly Muse!: see PUBLICATIONS (Female Readership) page 134

♀ ☆ (?♂) Sister Singers Network, PO Box 7065, Minneapolis, MN 55407

♀ ★ Taken By The Faeries, 922 El Cajon Way, Palo Alto, CA 94303 415-856-9479 "Queer performance for the new millennium."

Phone Sex

♂ • Gay Live Network, 800-782-7250 "Phone sex; dating line; chat line."

Printing & Promotional Items (see also Art; Graphics/Typesetting)

♂ • B-D Printing & Ad Specialties, 4114 10th Ave, Brooklyn, NY 11219 718-436-0100 Fax 718-436-1425 "Advertising specialties: buttons, pens, etc, imprinted with logos/names."

♂ • B.P. Publishing, PO Box 121690, Arlington, TX 76012 "National newspaper & newsletter publishing."

♀ • Bauer Printing Co., PO Box 512, Paramus, NJ 07653-0512 201-837-8783 "Commercial & social stationery; custom supplies; unusual & custom forms. Free catalog."

♀ • Campus Marketing Specialists, PO Box 30551, Bethesda, MD 20824 301-951-5220; 800-795-4267; Fax 301-654-7939 "Discount prices for custom designed T-shirts/imprinted goods."

♀ • Design Studio 606, 800-582-2862 the.studio@glib.org "Custom promotional & fundraising services & products."

♀ • **Graphic Impressions, PO Box 240, Harrison, NJ 07029 201-484-6116; 800-646-6116; Fax 201-482-6510**

Public Relations/Advertising Agencies

⚥ • (♂♂) LIZA Group, 2765 N Scottsdale Rd #104D, Scottsdale, AZ 85257 602-949-7848 Fax 602-946-1156 "Public speaking/PR re Gay & Lesbian consumer market."

♀ • Rivendell Marketing Company, Box 518, Westfield, NJ 07091-0518 908-232-2021; 212-242-6863; Fax 908-232-0521 "We specialize in securing national advertising for Gay & Lesbian publications."

Publications: Directories, Bibliographies, Guides, Travel

♀ • Alternative Lifestyles Directory, Winter Publishing, PO Box 80667, North Dartmouth, MA 02748 508-999-0078 Fax 508-984-4040 "Directory of hard-to-find publications covering all subjects & fetishes."

⚥ • The Black Book, PO Box 31155, San Francisco, CA 94131 415-431-0171 "Directory of sexuality resources."

⚥ ○ Chapter Z Publishing, Inc., 1888 Emery St NW #220, Atlanta, GA 30318 404-350-6720; 800-849-0406; Fax 404-350-6712 The Gay Community Yellow Pages.

⚥ • Damron Address Book, PO Box 422458, San Francisco, CA 94142-2458 415-255-0404; 800-462-6654 "Annual pocket-sized guide to USA, Canada, Mexico. Mainly men's coverage. Also Damron Road Atlas; Women's Traveller."

⚥ • Directory of Gay & Lesbian Community Publications in the United States & Canada, PO Box 1946, Guerneville, CA 95446

⚥ • The Ferrari Guides, PO Box 37887, Phoenix, AZ 85069 602-863-2408 "Comprehensive resources for Gay & Lesbian travel worldwide: includes Ferrari Travel Planner, Ferrari for Men, Ferrari for Women, Inn Places."

⚥ • Gay Music Guide, Popfront Press, 200 E 10th St #498, New York, NY 10003 212-777-7240 "Lists pop, rock, country, chorale, etc., and refers reader to sources. Book & audio tape."
✦ Gay Music Guide advertisement page 135

⚥ ○ Gayellow Pages, PO Box 533 Village Stn, New York, NY 10014-0533 212-674-0120 "Classified directory of services, businesses, resources, etc in USA & Canada. Various local editions. Also available on mailing labels."

⚥ • The Guide, PO Box 990593, Boston, MA 02199 617-266-8557 "News, travel; directory & maps for bars, etc, US & Canada."

⚥ ★ International Sexual Minorities Information Resource, mail to ISMIR, PO Box 81869, Pittsburgh, PA 15217-0869 412-422-3060; 412-422-1529 (modem dial-in); ismir@ aol.com Pub ISMIR Events Calendar. "ISMIR collects & publishes all regional, national & international events of interest to lesbians, gays, bisexuals, & other sexual minorities."
✦ International Sexual Minorities Information Resource advertisement page 135

⚥ • Not-Straight Guide, PO Box 030487, Fort Lauderdale, FL 33303-0487 800-285-8836 Fax 305-563-2499 "Computerized USA travel, information & service guide."

♂ • Odysseus Travel Planner, PO Box 1548, Port Washington, NY 11050-0306 516-944-5330 Fax 516-944-7540 "USA & international accommodation & travel guide; reservation service for international gay resorts."

⚥ • Our World Travel Magazine, 1104 North Nova Rd #251, Daytona Beach, FL 32117 904-441-5367 Fax 904-441-5604 Monthly.

⚥ • ♿ Out & About Travel Newsletter, 8 W 19th St #401, New York, NY 10011 212-645-6922; 800-929-2268

♀ • Women's Music Plus: Directory of Resources in Women's Music & Culture, 5210 N Wayne, Chicago, IL 60640 312-769-9009 Fax 312-728-7002

Publications: Female & Male Readership

♀ • *The Advocate*, PO Box 4371, Los Angeles, CA 90078-4371 213-871-1225

♀ ★ ♂♀ *Amethyst: A Literary Journal for Lesbians & Gay Men*, 191 Howard St NE, Atlanta, GA 30317 404-473-8750

♀ ★ *Anything That Moves: Beyond The Myths of Bisexuality*, 2404 California St #24, San Francisco, CA 94115 415-703-7977

♀ ☆♂♀ *Art & Understanding*, 25 Monroe St #205, Albany, NY 12210 518-426-9010 Fax 518-436-5354 "The International Magazine of Literature and Art about AIDS."

♀ ○ *Black Sheets*, PO Box 31155, San Francisco, CA 94131-0155 415-824-8377 "Sex-positive 'zine."

♀ • *BLK*, PO Box 83912, Los Angeles, CA 90083-0912 310-410-0808 Fax 310-410-9250 "News & features about, & of interest to, the black lesbian & gay community."

♀ ○ *CDC AIDS Weekly*, PO Box 830409, Birmingham, AL 35283 205-991-6920 "Comprehensive survey of AIDS, therapies; also free computer database as public service."

♀ ★ *Chain of Life*, PO Box 8081, Berkeley, CA 94707 'Newsletter for those who are adopted, considering adoption, have adopted children, or who have relinquished children for adoption; & the movement to open adoption records.'

♀ • *Christopher Street*, PO Box 1475, New York, NY 10008 212-627-2120 "Gay literary magazine."

♀ • *Colorlife! Magazine*, 301 Cathedral Parkway #287, New York, NY 10026 212-222-9794 "Serving the Lesbian/Gay/Two Spirit/Bisexual People Of Color community."

♀ ★ *CTN Magazine*, PO Box 14431, San Francisco, CA 94114 Fax 415-626-9033 ctn@aol.com "National magazine for Deaf, hard-of-hearing, & hearing-signing lesbians, gays, bisexuals."

♀ ☆♂♀ *The Disability Rag & Resource*, PO Box 145, Louisville, KY 40201

♀ • *Echo Magazine*, Ace Publishing, Inc. PO Box 1808, Phoenix, AZ 85001 602-266-0550 Fax 602-266-0773

♀ ○ *Eidos Magazine*, Box 96, Boston, MA 02137-0096 617-262-0096 Fax 617-364-0096 "Sexual freedom tabloid of Erotic entertainment for women, men, couples of all sexual orientations & lifestyles."
+ *Eidos Magazine advertisement page 386*

♀ • *Electronic Gay Community Magazine*, PO Box 16782, Wichita, KS 67216-0782 316-269-0913; 316-269-3172 (modem); Fax 316-269-4208 egcm@f9.n291.z1.fidonet.org "Send us your news releases & we will distribute your story the same day."

♀ ★ *Empathy*, PO Box 5085, Columbia, SC 29250 803-791-1607 "An interdisciplinary journal for persons working to end oppression on the basis of sexual identities."

♀ ★ *Evergreen Chronicles: A Journal of Gay & Lesbian Arts & Cultures*, PO Box 8939, Minneapolis, MN 55408-0939 612-649-4982 bzsura@aol.com

♀ ★ (♂♀) *The Family Next Door*, PO Box 21580, Oakland, CA 94620 510-482-5778 "A newsletter for Lesbian & Gay parents & their friends."
+ *Family Next Door advertisement page 137*

♀ ☆♂♀ *Freedom Socialist Newspaper*, 5018 Rainier Ave S, Seattle, WA 98118 206-722-2453 Fax 206-723-7691 hnoble@eskimo.com "Quarterly socialist, feminist, Trotskyist; covers all social movements."

♀ • *Gay Book Business*, Alamo Square, PO Box 14543, San Francisco, CA 94114 415-863-7410

♀ • *Home Team*, 2215 Market St #R-316, San Francisco, CA 94114-1653

♂ • *Hothead Paisan*, PO Box 214, New Haven, CT 06502 203-865-6113

♀ • *In Newsweekly*, 258 Shawmut Ave, Boston, MA 02118 617-292-0213 Fax 617-426-8246

♀ ○ ♂ *Journal of Gay & Lesbian Social Services*, Haworth Press, 10 Alice St, Binghamton, NY 13904-1580 607-722-5857

♀ ○ *Journal of Gay & Lesbian Psychotherapy*, Haworth Press, 10 Alice St, Binghamton, NY 13904-1580 607-722-5857

♀ ○ ♂ *Journal of Homosexuality*, Haworth Press, 10 Alice St, Binghamton, NY 13904-1580 607-722-5857

♀ • *Kuumba*, PO Box 83912, Los Angeles, CA 90083-0912 310-410-0808 Fax 310-410-9250 "Poetry journal for black lesbians & gay men."

♀ • *L Connection*, 1109 N 21st Ave #104, Hollywood, FL 33020 800-224-9244

♀ • *Lambda Book Report*, 1625 Connecticut Ave NW, Washington, DC 20009 202-462-7924

♀ • *The Leather Journal*, 7985 Santa Monica Blvd #109-368, West Hollywood, CA 90046 213-656-5073 Fax 213-656-3120

♀ ○ *Libido*, PO Box 146721, Chicago, IL 60614 312-275-0842 Fax 312-275-0752

♀ ★ *Living Streams*, PO Box 178, Concord, CA 94522 "Evangelical/Charismatic publication providing a forum for Christian Gays & Lesbians."

♀ • *Monk: The Mobile Magazine*, 175 5th Ave #2322, New York, NY 10010 'Travel/general interest.'

♀ ★ *NABWMT Journal*, c/o David Lott, 222 E Ormsby Ave #1, Louisville, KY 40203 502-637-3781 "A publication of the National Association of Black & White Men Together; includes poetry, essays, art & fiction."

♀ • *New York Native*, PO Box 1475 Church St Stn, New York, NY 10008 212-627-2120 Fax 212-727-9321 "Newspaper."

♀ ★ *Open Hands*, 3801 N Keeler Ave, Chicago, IL 60641 312-736-5526 Fax 312-736-5475 "Resources for Ministries Affirming the Diversity of Human Sexuality."

♀ ○ *Options Magazine*, PO Box 470, Port Chester, NY 10573 "Bisexual magazine for men & women."

♀ ★ ♂♀ *Out On Campus*, c/o Liz Prince, Director of Susquehanna Hall, UMBC, Baltimore, MD 21228 (newsletter of Standing Committee for Lesbian, Gay, & Bisexual Awareness, American College Personnel Association, c/o Jo Campbell, Campus Housing, 818 S. Wolcott Ave, Rm 317 SRH, Chicago, IL 60612-3727)

♀ *Out to Profit*, Washington Business Institute, PO Box 21741, Washington, DC 20078-3866

♀ • *Outlines*, 3059 N Southport, Chicago, IL 60657 312-871-7610 Monthly.

♀ • ♂ *Out*, 110 Greene St #600, New York, NY 10012 212-334-9119; 800-876-1199 subscriptions; Fax 212-334-9227 outmage@aol.com

♀ • *Pacelines*, 43 Upton Street, c/o Bob Bland, Boston, MA 02118 "International Bicycling Newsletter for Gays & Lesbians."

♀ • *POZ*, PO Box 1279, New York, NY 10113-1279 212-242-2163 Fax 212-675-8505 "National lifestyle magazine for people affected by HIV/AIDS."

♀ • ♂ *Project X Magazine*, 37 W 20th St #1007, New York, NY 10011 212-366-6603 Fax 212-645-5489 "Youth culture: fashion, music, etc."

♀ ○ *Roots & Wings Adoption Magazine*, PO Box 638, Chester, NJ 07930 908-637-8828 Fax 908-637-8699

♂ • *Sandmutopian Guardian Magazine*, PO Box 1146, New York, NY 10156 516-842-1711 Fax 516-842-7518 siradam@ ix.netcom.com

♂ ★ *The Second Stone*, PO Box 8340, New Orleans, LA 70182 504-891-7555 "Religious news, information, features."

✦ Second Stone advertisement page 100

♂ ★ *Slippery When Wet*, PO Box 3101, Berkeley, CA 94703

♂ ☆ *Solitary*, PO Box 6091, Madison, WI 53716 608-244-0072 "Quarterly journal for those practicing spiritual traditions alone while seeking dialogue with those who share a similar solitary pagan path."

♂ • *Switch Hitter*, 955 Massachusetts Ave #148, Cambridge, MA 02139

♂ • *Taste Of Latex*, Deena Moore, PO Box 16188, Seattle, WA 98116-0188 Fax 206-937-2066

♂ • (?♂) *VICE*, PO Box 20281, New York, NY 10011-0003 212-727-2787 Fax 212-727-3190

♂ • ♂♂ *Victory!*, 2261 Market St #296, San Francisco, CA 94114-1600 "The national Gay & Lesbian entrepreneur magazine."

♂ *WaveLengths*, Coastline SF Writers Group, PO Box 6554, Portsmouth, NH 03802-6554

♂ *What!!!Quears!!!*, 831 Scott St, San Francisco, CA 94117 415-922-5191 "Newsletter for the deaf."

♂ ★ *Working It Out: The Newsletter for Gay & Lesbian Employment Issues*, PO Box 2079, New York, NY 10108 212-769-2384 Fax 212-721-2680 "Keeps you & your employer informed about law, policy, education & benefits."

♂ • *The X Factor*, Ace Publishing, Inc. PO Box 1808, Phoenix, AZ 85001 602-266-0550 Fax 602-266-0773

Publications: Female Readership

♀ • *Alternate Woman,*, Lonnie Marshall Publications, Box 6002, Thibodaux, LA 70302-6002 504-369-6976

♀ • *At The Crossroads: Feminism, Spirituality and Science Exploring Earthly and Unearthly Reality.*, PO Box 112, St Paul, AR 72760

♀ • *Bad Attitude, Inc.*, PO Box 390110, Cambridge, MA 02139 "Lesbian erotic fiction, nonfiction, poetry, b&w photography."

♀ • *Black Lace*, PO Box 83912, Los Angeles, CA 90083-0912 310-410-0808 Fax 310-410-9250 "Erotic magazine for black lesbians."

♀ • *Bolt*, 1216 Taylor St #21, San Francisco, CA 94108 415-775-9508 "Magazine for alternative young women."

♀ ★ *Brat Attack: Do-It-Yourself S/M*, PO Box 40754, San Francisco, CA 94140-0754 "The Zine for Leatherdykes & Other Bad Girls."

♀ ★ ♂♂ *Common Lives/Lesbian Lives*, PO Box 1553, Iowa City, IA 52244 319-335-1486 "All aspects of Lesbian culture."

♀ ★ *conmocion*, 1521 Alton Rd #336, Miami Beach, FL 33139 305-751-8385

♀ ☆ ♂♂ *Connexions*, PO Box 14431, Berkeley, CA 94701-5431 510-549-3505 "Translations from the international feminist press."

♀ ☆ *The Cutting Edge: A Newsletter for Women Living with Self-Inflicted Violence*, PO Box 20819, Cleveland, OH 44120

♀ • (?♂) *Deneuve*, FRS Enterprises, 2336 Market St #15, San Francisco, CA 94114 415-863-6538 Fax 415-863-1609

♀ • *Dyke Review Magazine*, 584 Castro St #456, San Francisco, CA 94114 415-621-3769 'Literary, controversial, informative, funny.'

♀ ★ *Dykes, Disability & Stuff*, PO Box 8773, Madison, WI 53708-8773 slkaron@facstaff.wisc.edu

♀ • *Fat Girl*, Barbarism 5 Liberty St, San Francisco, CA 94110 415-550-7202

♀ ★ *Feminist Bookstore News*, PO Box 882554, San Francisco, CA 94188 415-626-1556 Fax 415-626-8970

♀ ☆ *Feminist Studies*, Women's Studies Program, University of Maryland, College Park, MD 20742 301-405-7415

♀ • *Girlfriends*, PO Box 713, Half Moon Bay, CA 94019 415-995-2776

♂ • *Girljock*, PO Box 882723, San Francisco, CA 94188 510-452-6252 "Fun women's sports & humor maagazine."

♀ ☆ *Heresies: A Feminist Publication on Art & Politics*, PO Box 1306 Canal St Stn, New York, NY 10013 212-227-2108

♀ ★ *Hikané: The Capable Womon*, PO Box 841, Great Barrington, MA 01230 "Magazine for the networking & empowerment of lesbians with disabilities (and our wimmin allies)."

♀ ☆ *Hurricane Alice: A Feminist Review*, 207 Church St SE, Minneapolis, MN 55455 612-625-1834 "Feminist fiction, poems, book reviews, etc."

♀ ☆ *Iowa Woman Magazine*, PO Box 680, Iowa City, IA 52244 "Literary quarterly: fiction, poetry, interviews, book reviews, etc., by women everywhere. SASE for details."

♀ ★ *Lavender Life*, PO Box 898, Binghamton, NY 13902 607-771-1986

♀ ★ *Lesbian Connection: Ambitious Amazons*, PO Box 811, East Lansing, MI 48826 517-351-5257 "A free, nationwide newsletter for, by & about Lesbians."

♀ ★ *Lesbian Contradiction (LesCon)*, 584 Castro St #356, San Francisco, CA 94114 "A Journal of Irreverent Feminism."

♀ • *The Lesbian Review Of Books*, PO Box 6369, Altadena, CA 91003 818-398-4200 (also fax)

♀ ★ *Lesbian Short Fiction*, 6507 Franrivers Ave; West Hills, CA 91307 818-704-7825 Publication planned to begin Spring 1996

♀ • *Lesbian World Newspaper*, 26151 Lake Shore Blvd #2112, Euclid, OH 44132-1160 216-289-2939 Fax 216-289-5885

♀ ★ *Matrices*, 496 Ford Hall U.MN, Minneapolis, MN 55455 612-625-5074 matrices@gold.tc.umn.edu "A Lesbian Feminist resource/research newsletter."

♀ ★ *Moms*, PO Box 5796, Athens, OH 45701-5796 "A newsletter honoring lesbian motherhood."

♀ • *off our backs*, 2337-B 18th St NW, Washington, DC 20009 202-234-8072 "Feminist newsjournal."

♀ • *On Our Backs*, 530 Howard St #400, San Francisco, CA 94105-3007 415-546-0384 "Lesbian sexuality."

♀ ○ ♿ *Radiance: The Magazine for Large Women*, PO Box 30246, Oakland, CA 94604

♀ • *Rubyfruit Journal*, 2701 E Croyden, Tucson, AZ 85716

♀ ☆ *Sage: A Scholarly Journal on Black Women*, PO Box 42741, Atlanta, GA 30311-0741 404-223-7528

♀ ★ *Shamakami*, PO Box 460456, San Francisco, CA 94146-0456 "Forum for South & Southeast Asian Feminist Lesbians & Bisexual Women."

♀ ☆ *Sing Heavenly Muse!*, PO Box 13320, Minneapolis, MN 55414 "Women's poetry & prose."

♀ ★ (?♿) *Sinister Wisdom, Inc.*, PO Box 3252, Berkeley, CA 94703 "Literature, art & analysis for the lesbian imagination; published since 1976."

♀ ☆ *Sojourner: The Women's Forum*, 42 Seaverns Ave, Jamaica Plain, MA 02130 508-524-0415

♀ ☆ (?♿) *Synapse*, PO Box 95220, Seattle, WA 98145-2220

♀ ☆ *Trivia: A Journal of Ideas*, PO Box 9606, Amherst, MA 01059-9606 "Feminist & lesbian writing: radical, creative, subversive."

♀ • *Virago!*, PO Box 1171, New Market, VA 22844 "The Journal By & For Lesbian Veterans."

♀ • *We Are Visible*, PO Box 1494, Mendocino, CA 95460 707-964-2756 "A magazine for ageful women. News, views, stories, art, etc for women over 55."

♂ ☆ *Woman & Earth*, 70 Terry Rd, Hartford, CT 06105 212-866-8130; 516-368-1652 "Women's issues in America & Russia; ecology & peace."

♀ ○ (♿♿) *Woman of Power Magazine*, PO Box 2785, Orleans, MA 02653 508-240-7877 "Feminism, Spirituality & Politics."

♀ ☆ (♿) *Women's Review Of Books*, Wellesley College Center for Research on Women, Wellesley, MA 02181 617-283-2555

♀ ○ *Women's Work*, 606 Ave A, Snohomish, WA 98290 360-568-5914

Publications: Male Readership

♂ ★ **Able-Together**, PO Box 460053, San Francisco, CA 94146 "Quarterly newsletter for gay & bisexual disabled men and those who care about them."
+ *Able-Together advertisement page 139*

♂ ○ *Adam Gay Video*, 8060 Melrose Ave, Los Angeles, CA 90046 213-653-8080

♂ • *Advocate Men*, PO Box 4371, Los Angeles, CA 90078-4371 213-871-1225

♂ • *All Your Dreams Fulfilled*, PCP, PO Box 3081, Danville, CA 94526 "Gay erotica."

♂ • *American Bear*, PO Box 7083, Louisville, KY 40257 502-894-8573

♂ • *Bandana Magazine*, PO Box 13090, Jersey City, NJ 07303-4090 201-216-0552

♂ • ♿♿ *Bear Magazine*, Brush Creek Media, Inc., 2215R Market St #148, San Francisco, CA 94114 415-552-1506; 800-234-3877 "Magazine for bearded & hairy men & their fans."

♂ ○ *Beau Magazine*, PO Box 470, Port Chester, NY 10573

♂ • **BlackFire**, PO Box 83912, Los Angeles, CA 90083-0912 310-410-0808 Fax 310-410-9250 "Erotic magazine for black gay men."

♂ • *Bulk Male*, PO Box 300352 (Big Bull, Inc.), Denver, CO 80252

♂ • *Celebrate The Self*, PO Box 8888, Mobile, AL 36689 800-304-0077

♂ ☆ (♿) *Changing Men: Issues in Gender, Sex & Politics*, PO Box 908, Madison, WI 53701-0908 816-374-5969 "Journal of the Anti-Sexist Men's Movement."

♂ • *Daddy Bear*, PO Box 2483, Rockville, MD 20847

♂ ○ (♿) *Daddy Magazine*, mail to Ganymede Press, Inc., 1735 Maryland Ave, Baltimore, MD 21201 410-727-5241

♂ • *Dragazine*, PO Box 691664, West Hollywood, CA 90069

♂ • *Drummer*, PO Box 410390, San Francisco, CA 94141-1314 415-252-1195 Fax 415-252-9574

♂ • *DungeonMaster*, PO Box 410390, San Francisco, CA 94141-0390 415-252-1195 Fax 415-252-9574

♂ ★ *Fag Rag*, PO Box 15331, Boston, MA 02215 617-661-7534

♂ ○ *First Hand*, PO Box 1314, Teaneck, NJ 07666 201-836-9177 Fax 201-836-5055

♂ • *Fresh Men*, PO Box 591, Mount Morris, IL 61054-0591

♂ • *Gay Video Guide*, Sabin Publishing 7985 Santa Monica Blvd #109-117, Los Angeles, CA 90046

♂ ★ *Gayme Magazine*, PO Box 15645, Boston, MA 02215 617-695-8015

♂ • *Genre*, 7080 Hollywood Blvd #1104, Los Angeles, CA 90028 213-467-8300 Fax 213-874-1391 "Fashion, travel, lifestyle bimonthly."

♂ ○ *Guys Magazine*, PO Box 1314, Teaneck, NJ 07666 201-836-9177 Fax 201-836-5055

♂ • *Handjobs*, Avenue Services PO Box 390811, Mountain View, CA 94039

♂ ○ ♿ *Honcho*, 462 Broadway, #4000, New York, NY 10013 212-966-8400

♂ • *Hot Shots Magazine*, Sunshine Pub Co, Inc, 7060 Convoy Ct, San Diego, CA 92111 619-278-9080

♂ • *Husky Magazine*, PO Box 471030, San Francisco, CA 94147 415-431-5755

♂ • **In Touch, 13122 Saticoy St, North Hollywood, CA 91605 818-764-2288; 800-637-0101**
+ *In Touch advertisement page 448*

♀ • *In Uniform*, AM Publications, PO Box 3226, Portland, OR 97208-3226 503-228-6935

♂ • *Iniquity*, 28 W 25th St, New York, NY 10010 212-647-0222 Fax 212-647-0236

♂ ★ *James White Review*, PO Box 3356, Minneapolis, MN 55403 612-339-8317 "A gay men's literary quarterly."

♂ • *Jock*, 28 W 25th St, New York, NY 10010 212-647-0222 Fax 212-647-0236

♂ • *Machismo*, 28 W 25th St, New York, NY 10010 212-647-0222 Fax 212-647-0236

♂ • *Mach*, 24 Shotwell, San Francisco, CA 94103 415-252-1195 Fax 415-252-9574 "Heavy Leather/Levi/kink interest."

♂ ○ ♿ *Mandate*, 462 Broadway, #4000, New York, NY 10013 212-966-8400

♂ • *Manhunt Magazine*, Box 8512, FDR Station, New York, NY 10050-8512 212-980-3808 Fax 212-755-6744

♂ ○ *Manscape*, PO Box 1314, Teaneck, NJ 07666 201-836-9177

♂ ○ *Manshots*, PO Box 1314, Teaneck, NJ 07666 201-836-9177

♂ • *Mantalk Magazine*, PO Box 1314, Teaneck, NJ 07666 201-836-9177

♂ • *Mavericks*, PO Box 9543, Santa Fe, NM 87504

♂ ○ *Men's Style*, PO Box 993, Edison, NJ 08818-0993 / 2035 Lincoln Hwy #3001 800-568-2246 Fax 907-287-4210

♂ • *Naked Magazine*, 7985 Santa Monica Blvd #109-232, West Hollywood, CA 90046 800-796-2533

♂ *Numbers*, 28 W 25th St, New York, NY 10010 212-647-0222 Fax 212-647-0236

♂ *Obsession*, 28 W 25th St, New York, NY 10010 212-647-0222 Fax 212-647-0236

♂ ○ ♂ *Playguy*, 462 Broadway, #4000, New York, NY 10013 212-966-8400

♂ • ♂♂ *Powerplay Magazine*, Brush Creek Media, Inc., 2215R Market St #148, San Francisco, CA 94114 415-552-1506; 800-234-3877 'A voyeuristic sex-intimate magazine for gay men.'

♀ • *Pump It Up!*, c/o Mirza Inc, 139 W 4th Ave, Roselle, NJ 07203 908-245-5323 Fax 908-241-6152

♂ • *Raunch*, Tom's Ranch, PO Box 44871, Phoenix, AZ 85064-4871 "Homemade underground 'zine' of male/male & true bi sexual experiences."

♂ ★ *RFD*, PO Box 68, Liberty, TN 37095 615-536-5176
✦ *RFD advertisement page 100*

♂ • *Stars*, 28 W 25th St, New York, NY 10010 212-647-0222 Fax 212-647-0236

♂ • *Steam*, 530 Howard St #400, San Francisco, CA 94105 415-243-3232 Fax 415-243-3233
✦ *Steam advertisement page 122*

♂ ○ *Torso*, 462 Broadway, #4000, New York, NY 10013 212-966-8400

♂ • **Wilde**, 530 Howard St #400, San Francisco, CA 94105-3007 415-243-3232 (also Fax) "Lesbian sexuality."
✦ *Wilde advertisement page 122*

Publishers/Publishing-related Services

♀ • Alyson Publications, 40 Plympton St, Boston, MA 02118 617-542-5679

♀ ☆ (?♂) Astarte Shell Press, PO Box 3648, Portland, ME 04101 207-828-1992 "Books reflecting feminist/womanist perspectives on spirituality, justice, & issues of personal & social life."

♀ ○ Barbo Carlson Enterprises, PO Box 189, Lindsborg, KS 67456-0189 913-227-3276 "Books, pamphlets & pamphlets concerning justice issues, sexuality, discrimination & AIDS."

♀ ○ Big Breakfast Publishing, PO Box 02394, Columbus, OH 43202 "Publisher of *The Complete Garbo Talks*. Free catalog."

♀ • Companion Press, PO Box 2575, Laguna Hills, CA 92654 714-362-9726 "Small gay press specializing in gay- & lesbian-interest film & video books."

♀ ○ Factor Press, PO Box 8888, Mobile, AL 36689 800-304-0077 Publisher of 'Solo Sex: Advanced Techniques.' $16.95 (includes postage & handling). Free brochure available.

♀ ☆ (♂♂) The Feminist Press at The City University of New York, 311 E 94th St, New York, NY 10128 212-360-5790 Pub *Women's Studies Quarterly*.

♂ • (♂) Gay Sunshine Press/Leyland Publications, PO Box 410690, San Francisco, CA 94141 707-996-6082 "Complete catalog of available books: $1 postpaid. Book manuscript submissions: send SASE with 2-page precis."

♀ • Integrity Indexing, 2012 Queens Road West #1, Charlotte, NC 28207 704-335-9936

DISABLED MEN

■ Int'l Qrtly Newsletter serving Gay & Bisexual men

■ **For Able & Disabled Men**
■ **Meet or Correspond**

ABLE-TOGETHER 415-522-9091
Box 460053, San Francisco, CA 94146

♀ • ♂ Kitchen Table: Women of Color Press, PO Box 908, Latham, NY 12110 Fax 518-434-0905

♀ • Lavender Crystal Press, PO Box 8932, Red Bank, NJ 07701 "Lesbian written/focused fiction, non-fiction, photos, art-work."

♀ • M Group Features Syndicate, PO Box 12486, San Antonio, TX 78212-0486 210-737-1404 (also Fax)

♀ • Naiad Press, Inc, PO Box 10543, Tallahassee, FL 32302 904-539-5965

♂ • Pagan Press, 26 St Marks Place, New York, NY 10003 212-674-3321

♂ • Plastic Cow Productions, PO Box 3081, Danville, CA 94526 510-736-2153 "Gay erotica."

♀ • Push Button Publishing, 800-649-7898
✦ *Push Button Publishing advertisement page 143*

♀ • Rising Tide Press, 5 Kivy St, Huntington Station, NY 11746 516-427-1289

♀ • ♂♂ Spinsters Ink, 32 E 1st St #330, Minneapolis, MN 55402 612-727-3119

♀ • Timely Books, 4040 Mountain Creek Rd #1304, Chattanooga, TN 37415 615-875-9447

♂ • Vega Press: African-American Book Publishers, PO Box 784, Sicklerville, NJ 08081 609-728-7809 Fax 609-728-7809

Quilts

♀ ○ **Quilts by Margery**, 25 St Nicholas St, Lynbrook, NY 11563 516-593-4767 "Remember your loved one with a custom designed quilt."
✦ *Quilts by Margery advertisement page 140*

Real Estate

♀ • **Community Real Estate Referrals**, Box 40174, Washington, DC 20016 800-346-5592 "Free referral to gay/gay-supportive realtor in any USA city/state (including Virgin Is. & Puerto Rico). Sorry, no rentals!"

♀ ★ Crossroads Real Estate Referral Network, PO Box 1708, Montclair, NJ 07042 800-442-9735 (4 GAY RELO) "Nationwide real estate referral service."

♀ • Gayrelo, 2008 13th St NW, Washington, DC 20009-4435 800-673-9093 "Nationwide real estate, buying or selling information from gay Realtors."

♀ ○ Network Relocation Services (NRS), 3033 Excelsior Blvd #100, Minneapolis, MN 55416 800-232-4555

Religious Organizations & Publications

♀ ★ *A New Direction (Mormons)*, 1608 N Cahuenga Blvd #B-440, Los Angeles, CA 90028 213-874-8424 waynendir@aol.com "For Gay & Lesbian Mormons, family, friends, etc."

♀ ★ Affirmation/Gay & Lesbian Mormons, PO Box 46022, Los Angeles, CA 90046 213-255-7251 Pub *Affinity*. "Educational, social & support group for lesbian & gay Latter-day Saints, their families & friends."

♀ ★ (?&) Affirmation: United Methodists for Lesbian, Gay & Bisexual Concerns, PO Box 1021, Evanston, IL 60204 708-733-9590

♀ ★ (&&) American Baptists Concerned, 13318 Clairepointe Way, Oakland, CA 94619-3531 510-465-8652 Pub *Voice of the Turtle.*

♀ ☆ American Friends Service Committee Lesbian, Gay, Bisexual Issues Program, 1414 Hill St, Ann Arbor, MI 48104 313-761-8283 Fax 313-761-6022

♀ ★&& Axios: Eastern & Orthodox Christians, PO Box 990 Village Stn, New York, NY 10014-0704 212-989-6211 axiosusa@aol.com Pub *Axios Newsletter.*

♀ ★ Brethren/Mennonite Council For Lesbian & Gay Concerns, PO Box 6300, Minneapolis, MN 55406-0300 612-870-1501 bmcouncil@aol.com Pub *Dialogue.*

♀ ★ (?&) Christian Lesbians OUT Together (CLOUT), PO Box 460808, San Francisco, CA 94146-0808 415-487-5427; 415-550-7796

♀ ★ Conference for Catholic Lesbians, PO Box 436 Planetarium Stn, New York, NY 10024 718-680-6107; 212-663-2963

♀ ★ (?&) Dignity USA, 1500 Massachusetts Ave NW #11, Washington, DC 20005 202-861-0017; 800-877-8797; Fax 202-429-9808 dignity@aol.com Pub *Dignity/USA Journal.* "Gay, Lesbian & Bisexual Catholics & their friends."

♀ ★ (?&) Emergence International: Christian Scientists Supporting Lesbians, Gay Men & Bisexuals, PO Box 6061-423, Sherman Oaks, CA 91413 818-994-6653; 800-280-6653 Pub *Emerge!.* Christian Scientists

♀ ★ Evangelicals Concerned, 311 E 72nd St #1G, c/o Dr Ralph Blair, New York, NY 10021 212-517-3171 Pub *Record; Review.*

♀ ☆ Friends for Lesbian & Gay Concerns, PO Box 222, Sumneytown, PA 18084 215-234-8424 (ask for Bruce); 215-234-8424 (ask for Bruce) Pub *Newsletter.* (Quakers)

♀ ★ GLAD (Gay, Lesbian & Affirming Disciple) Alliance, PO Box 19223, Indianapolis, IN 46219-0223 206-634-9279; 206-324-6231 "Serving the Christian Church (Disciples of Christ) in US & Canada. Regional chapters & educational retreats."

♀ ★ Honesty: Southern Baptists Advocating Equal Rights for Gays & Lesbians, PO Box 7331, Louisville, KY 40257 502-637-7609

♀ ★ Integrity, Inc, PO Box 19561, Washington, DC 20036-0561 201-868-2485 *The Voice of Integrity.* "Lesbian & Gay Justice Ministry of the Episcopal Church."

♀ ★ (?&) Interweave: Unitarian Universalists for Gay, Lesbian, Bisexual & Transgender Concerns, 25 Beacon St, Boston, MA 02108-2800 617-742-2100 x470 Pub *Interweave World.*

→ *Living Streams:* see PUBLICATIONS page 140

♀ ★ Lutherans Concerned/North America, PO Box 10461, Chicago, IL 60610-0461 *The Concord.*

♀ National Congress for Lesbian Christians, PO Box 814, Capitola, CA 95010 800-861-NCLC

♀ ☆ (?&) National Council of Churches, Commission on Family Ministries & Human Sexuality Office, Rev Joe H. Leonard, 243 Lenoir Ave, Wayne, PA 19087-3908

♀ ★ (?&) National Gay Pentecostal Alliance, PO Box 1391, Schenectady, NY 12301-1391 518-372-6001 *The Apostolic Voice.*

♀ ★ National League for Social Understanding, Inc, 4470-107 Sunset Blvd #293, Los Angeles, CA 90027-6305 213-664-6422 (Gay & Lesbian Helpline); 213-664-6422 (Gay & Lesbian Helpline); Fax 213-669-0134 Pub *NLSU News.*

→ *A New Direction (Mormons):* see PUBLICATIONS page 140

♀ ★ New Ways Ministry (Catholic), 4012 29th St, Mount Rainier, MD 20712 301-277-5674 Fax 301-864-6948 Pub *Bondings.*

→ *Open Hands:* see PUBLICATIONS page 140

♀ ★ Phoenix Evangelical Bible Institute, 1035 E Turney, Phoenix, AZ 85014 602-265-2831 "Ministerial training school especially for Gays & Lesbians."

♀ ★ Presbyterians for Lesbian & Gay Concerns, PO Box 38, c/o James Anderson, New Brunswick, NJ 08903-0038 908-249-1016; 908-932-7501 Pub *More Light Update.*

♀ ☆ Reformed Catholic Church (USA), Diocese of the Western Region, c/o Rev. Fr. Rob Havican, OSF, 1800 Lavaca #405, Austin, TX 78701 512-499-0168 revfrrob@io.com frhavian@aol.com

♀ Reformed Church in America Gay Caucus, PO Box 8174, Philadelphia, PA 19101-8174

→ *The Second Stone:* see PUBLICATIONS page 140

♀ ★ & Seventh-day Adventist Kinship International, PO Box 7320, Laguna Niguel, CA 92607 714-248-1299 Pub *SDA Kinship Connection.*

♀ ☆ Silent Harvest Ministries, PO Box 190511, Dallas, TX 75219-0511 214-520-6655 *The Harvester.* "An association of people who serve special ministry needs."

→ *Solitary:* see PUBLICATIONS page 140

♀ ☆ Supportive Congregations Network/Mennonite & Brethren, PO Box 6300, Minneapolis, MN 55406-0300 612-870-1501

♀ ★ (?&) United Lesbian/Gay Christian Scientists, PO Box 2171, Beverly Hills, CA 90212-2171 213-876-1338 Pub *Faith & Understanding.* Christian Scientists

Remember your loved one

Quilts

by Margery

Commemorative Quilt Panels

• *Stock Designs*
• *Custom Designs*
• *Design Service*

FREE COLOR BROCHURE

25 St. Nicholas Street   By Appointment
Lynbrook, NY 11563   (516) 593-4767

♂ ★ ♂ **Universal Fellowship of Metropolitan Community Churches**, 5300 Santa Monica Blvd #304, Los Angeles, CA 90029 213-464-5100 Fax 213-464-2123 Pub *Alert; Keeping In Touch.*

♀ ☆ (♭) Witches/Pagans for Gay Rights, PO Box 408, Shirley, NY 11967-0408

♀ ☆♭♭ Women's Theological Center, PO Box 1200, Boston, MA 02117-1200 617-536-8782

♀ ★ Womland, PO Box 466, Searsport, ME 04974 Pub *Womland Newsletter.* "Spiritual organization for women & children: saving land, women & the planet. Donations appreciated."

♀ ☆ The Womyn's Spirituality Center, 14705 27th Ave NE, Seattle, WA 98155-7414 206-547-3374 Pub *WSC Newsletter.* "Gathering of women & men to explore areas of convergence & diversity between Christianity & Feminism (creating a Feminist-Christian dialog)."

♥ ★ (?♭) World Congress Of Gay & Lesbian Jewish Organizations, PO Box 3345, New York, NY 10008-3345

Security Services

♀ ● Fetsick Distributors, 800-278-8648 "Maxum Defense Spray."

Switchboards, Helplines, Phone Information

♀ ☆ National Runaway Switchboard, 800-621-4000 24 hrs.

Telecommunications: Phones, Paging, Beepers

♀ ○ Planet Communications, 60 Rte 46 E, Fairfield, NJ 07004 800-960-6075 Fax 201-227-5070 "Cellular, paging, long distance, prepaid calling card; 5% supports area nonprofit groups working for social change."

♥ ● **Triangular Communications, 331 Spring Valley Rd, Morganville, NJ 07751 800-972-9122 Fax 908-972-9551**
✦ *Triangular Communications advertisement page 125*

Travel & Tourist Services (see also Accommodation)

♥ ● Club Le Bon, PO Box 444, Woodbridge, NJ 07095 800-836-TOUR "Deluxe lesbian vacations; 'Kool Kids' gay/lesbian family trips."

♥ ● Damron Navigator, 800-643-6558 "Instant access to a world of travel information. $5.95 per month, no per minute fees. Call for details & free 30 day account."

♂ ○ **FPT The Preferred Way in Gay Travel**, NY and NJ offices. 800-624-0207 Fax 201-377-5635, 212-582-6268
✦ *FPT The Preferred Way in Gay Travel advertisement page 141*

♂ ★ Gay Airline & Travel Club, PO Box 69A04, Dept GYP, West Hollywood, CA 90069 213-650-5112 Pub *Newsletter.* "Worldwide organization for those who enjoy traveling, flying, & collecting airline memorabilia or working in the airline/travel industries."

♀ ● (?♭) Her Wild Song, PO Box 515, Brunswick, ME 04011 207-721-9005 "Wilderness journeys for women."

♥ ★ Lesbian & Gay Hospitality Exchange International, PO Box 612 Stn C, Montréal, QC H2L 4K5 Fax 514-523-0806 "International membership network for exchange of hospitality when traveling."

♀ ● (?♭) Mariah Wilderness Expeditions, PO Box 248, Point Richmond, CA 94807 510-233-2303; 800-4-MARIAH

♥ ● (?♭) Mountain Mama Packing & Riding Co, General Delivery, Cañones, NM 87516 505-638-9150

♀ ● (?♭) Olivia Travel, Inc., 4400 Market St, Oakland, CA 94608 510-655-0364; 800-631-6277

♥ ● Peppermint Tours, 1604 SW Fig Tree Ln, Dunnellon, FL 34431-3331 904-589-6885 Fax 904-625-8886 "Motor coach tours; charters; free ground packages."

♥ ● Pride Time Travels, 66 Charles St #283, Boston, MA 02114 617-423-1515; 800-338-6550 "Gay Travel Videos: popular Gay & Lesbian Resorts on VHS."

♥ ★ (?♭) The Travel Club, City Center Box 128, Monroe City, IN 47557 812-743-2919 "Joint discount vacations in a villa/home setting."

♥ ● The Travel Wizard, PO Box 1983, Provincetown, MA 02657 / 50 Bradford St 800-934-TRIP; 508-487-6330; Fax 508-487-6140 "Full service travel agency specializing in air & land arrangements in Provincetown. No fee for our services. Open year round."

♥ ● Undersea Expeditions, PO Box 9455, Pacific Beach, CA 92169 619-270-2900; 800-669-0310 outside San Diego; Fax 619-490-1002

♀ ● Venus Adventures, PO Box 167-Y, Peaks Island, ME 04108-0167 207-766-5655

♀ ☆ Woodswomen Adventure Travel, 25 W Diamond Lake Rd, Minneapolis, MN 55419 612-822-3809 Fax 612-822-3814 Pub *Woodswomen News.*

Weddings/Unions
♀ • Pride, Love, & Union Services, PO Box 283, Woodstock, NY 12491 914-448-3754 Fax 914-448-4076 gaywed@aol.com

MAIL ORDER: Antiques & Collectables
♀ • Friends of the Christmas Fairy, PO Box 883593, San Francisco, CA 94188 415-281-0696 "Christmas ornaments collectors club."

♂ ○ Patsy Comer's Antiques & Jewelry, 7249 Reseda Blvd, Reseda, CA 91335 818-345-1631

♂ • ♿ Replacements Ltd, PO Box 26029, Greensboro, NC 27420 / 1089 Knox Rd 800-562-4462 Fax 910-697-3100 "China, crystal, flatware, collectibles."

MAIL ORDER: Books
♀ • ♿ A Different Light, 151 W 19th St, New York, NY 10011 212-989-4850; 800-343-4002; Fax 212-989-2158
✦ *A Different Light advertisement page 142*

♀ • An Uncommon Vision, 1425 Greywall Lane, Wynnewood, PA 19096 610-658-0953 Fax 610-658-0961 "Mail order only: out of print books; photographs; ephemera about lesbians & women's lives."

♀ • Ariel's Pages, PO Box 2487, New York, NY 10185-2487

♀ • Berdache Books, PO Box 9081, Pittsburgh, PA 15224 412-687-5563

♀ • Blue Delta, 800-649-7898 Pub *True Blue Review.*

♂ ○ ♿ Books etc, 538 Castro St, San Francisco, CA 94114 415-621-8631 Fax 415-387-7162 h18tole@aol.com

♀ • ♿ Dreams & Swords, 6503 Ferguson St, Indianapolis, IN 46220-1148 317-253-9966; 800-937-2706; Fax 317-259-0763 "Send for free catalog."

♂ ○ The Enclave Book Repository, PO Box 507, Dept GYP, Oyster Bay, NY 11771 516-922-1169 "Call or write for free catalog."

⚢ • Everglades Book Company, PO Box 2425, Bonita Springs, FL 33959 941-353-4314 "1st editions, rare, out of print. $3 for book list, applied to first order."
✦ *Everglades Book Company advertisement page 143*

⚢ • (♿) Giovanni's Room, 345 S 12th St, Philadelphia, PA 19107 215-923-2960 Fax 215-923-0813 "Bimonthly lists of new books, one each for gay men & women."

⚢ • Glad Day Bookshop, 673 Boylston St, 2nd floor, Boston, MA 02116 617-267-3010 Fax 617-267-5474 "All available lesbian & gay literature & periodicals."

♀ • Heartland Books, PO Box 1105 H, East Corinth, VT 05040 802-439-5655

♀ • ♿ Herland Book—Cafe, 902 Center St, Santa Cruz, CA 95060 408-42-WOMEN "Mail order books, videos, & gifts."

♀ • Independent Women Books, 36 Laurel Hill Dr, Niantic, CT 06357 "Mail order only: specializing in out-of-print lesbian books."

⚢ ○ Jaguar, 4057 18th St, San Francisco, CA 94114 415-863-4777 Fax 415-863-0235

⚢ • ♿ Lambda Rising, 1625 Connecticut Ave NW, Washington, DC 20009 202-462-6969; 800-621-6969 Pub *Lambda Rising News*. "Books, videos, music, gifts. Catalog free."

♀ • ♿ Lammas Books, 1001 Cathedral St, Baltimore, MD 21201-5403 410-752-1001; 800-955-2662 (mail order only) "Lesbian/gay, women's & children's literature; greeting cards, videos, video rentals, tapes, posters. Resource center for lesbian/gay & progressive communities."

♀ • ♿ Lammas Women's Books & More, 1426 21st St NW, Washington, DC 20036 (at P) 202-775-8218; 800-955-2662

⚢ • (?♿) Newspeak Book & Video, 5 Steeple St, Providence, RI 02903 401-331-3540 "Conspiracy, sex, weirdness; send $1 for catalog."

♀ ★ ⚤ Old Wives' Tales: Women's Visions & Books, 1009 Valencia St, San Francisco, CA 94110 (at 21st St) 800-821-4675 Pub *Women's Voices Events*. "Collectively-run, non-profit bookstore. Commitment to women's & lesbian community in general & women of color in especial. Community referral information."

⚥ • Oscar Wilde Memorial Bookshop, 15 Christopher St, New York, NY 10014 212-255-8097 "World's first Lesbian & Gay Liberation bookshop (founded 1967); free catalog."

⚥ • Our World Too, 11 S Vandeventer, St Louis, MO 63108 314-533-5322; 314-533-6155 Community Access Line (recording) "Over 2000 titles. Mail order catalog."

⚥ • ⚤ Outbooks!, 1239 E Las Olas Blvd, Fort Lauderdale, FL 33301 305-764-4333; 305-764-3255 (roommate referrals) Pub *Outlooks*. "Gay & Lesbian books."

♀ ○ ⚤ Pandora Book Peddlers, 9 Waverly Place, Madison, NJ 07940 201-822-8388

⚥ • Paths Untrodden Book Service, PO Box 3245 Grand Central Stn, New York, NY 10163 212-661-5997 "Catalog $3. Male homosexuality; men's issues; primarily out of print."
◆ *Paths Untrodden Book Service advertisement page 142*

⚥ • ⚤⚤ Perrin & Treggett Booksellers, 3130 Route 10 West, Denville, NJ 07834 201-328-8811; 800-770-8811; Fax 201-328-0999 "Gay & Lesbian books, music, cards, pride items. Recovery, spirituality, self-help. Gift certificates & special orders."

⚥ • Phoenix Rising, 808 Spotswood Ave, Norfolk, VA 23517 804-622-3701
◆ *Phoenix Rising advertisement page 143*

⚥ • Roads Less Traveled, 3017 W State St, Boise, ID 83703 208-384-5075; 800-816-7623 "Books & magazines, videos, & gifts by mail. Free catalog."
◆ *Roads Less Traveled advertisement page 142*

♀ ○ (⚤) Science Fiction, Mysteries & More, 140 Chambers St, New York, NY 10007-1007 212-385-8798 Fax 212-385-8915

⚥ • The Sibylline of Books, 159-A Noe St, San Francisco, CA 94114 415-626-1245 Fax 415-626-9415 ben@magganew.queernet.org

♀ • Sisterhood Bookstore, 1351 Westwood Blvd, Los Angeles, CA 90024 310-477-7300; 800-747-0220

⚥ • St Maur—Bookseller, 820 N Madison, Stockton, CA 95202 209-464-3550 "Gay & Lesbian Fiction; scarce, rare, out-of-print; first editions; single volumes & collections."

♀ • Thunder Road Book Club, PO Box 70, Hackettstown, NJ 07840 908-852-9406 "Mail order lesbian book club; buy 3, get 1 free."

⚥ • Tomes & Treasures, 202 S Howard Ave, Tampa, FL 33606 813-251-9368 "Gay & Lesbian bookstore, with T-shirts, jewelry & Pride items. Write or call for catalog."

⚥ • True Colors, PO Box 780969, San Antonio, TX 78278-0969 / 16106 University Oak #2; 78249 800-745-0555 "Mail order: titles dealing with lesbian & gay issues; call for free newsletter."

⚥ • Womankind Books, 5 Kivy St, Huntington Station, NY 11746 516-427-1289 "Mail order only: free lesbian catalog on request."

♀ ○ Womanvision Books, Inc., PO Box 387, Springfield, PA 19064

♀ • Women's Words Books, 902 B Upper Straw Rd, Hopkinton, NH 03229 603-228-8000 "All areas of women's studies. Mail order only."

♀ • Womontyme Distribution Co., PO Box 50145, Dept GYP, Long Beach, CA 90815-6145 800-247-8903 "Helping Hands Catalog free; self-help books & cassettes books re sexual assault, incest, domestic violence, recovery."

MAIL ORDER: Clothes

⚥ • Don't Panic! Designs, 11264 Playa Court, Culver City, CA 90230 310-915-1682; 800-(800) 45-PANIC mail order; Fax 310-915-0085

⚥ • Good Catch!, PO Box 1756 Old Chelsea Stn, New York, NY 10011 800-77-CATCH Fax 800-98-FAX-US "Manufacturer & distributor of T-shirts, mugs, enamel pins, silver earrings, embroidered hats, etc. The original 'Cum Rag & Cum Towel', postcards & other novelties. Custom orders."

♀ ○ Koala, PO Box 5519, Sherman Oaks, CA 91413 800-238-2941 Fax 818-780-5170 "Exotic swimwear. Free color catalog."

♂ • (⚤) The Leather Man, Inc, 111 Christopher St, New York, NY 10014 212-243-5339 Fax 212-243-5372

♂ • (⚤⚤) Mr S Leather Co, 310 7th St, San Francisco, CA 94103 415-863-7764; 800-746-7677 orders; Fax 415-863-7798

⚥ • Nightsweats & T-cells, 277 Martinel Dr, Kent, OH 44240 216-673-2806; 800-859-8685 "Custom screen-printed T-shirts; HIV owned & operated."

♀ • P.M.S. Hunting Club, PO Box 1267, North Hampton, NH 03862

⚥ ○ Pink Perspective, PO Box 5912, Toledo, OH 43613 419-472-4985 "Clothes; also offer embroidery & screen printing service to organizations."

♀ • ⚥ Pride Of Woodstock, 86 Mill Hill Road; 12498 914-247-0873 "Clothing & jewelry."

♀ • (?⚤) The Rainbow Connection, 501 10th Ave SE, Rochester, MN 55904-4815 / Move planned September 95 to 1235 8th Ave SE (fully wheelchair accessible) 507-282-4768 "Design & manufacture clothing for physically challenged clientele; custom-designed Pride items."

⚥ • We're Everywhere, 3434 N Halsted St, Chicago, IL 60657 800-772-6411 "Free catalog."

MAIL ORDER: Erotica (Printed, Visual, Equipment)

♀ • (⚤) A Taste of Leather, 317-A 10th St, San Francisco, CA 94103 (at Folsom) 415-252-9166; 800-367-0786

⚥ • Adult Erotic Audio Tape Guide, PO Box 423163, San Francisco, CA 94142

⚥ • American Sphincter Society, mail to The DBJ Projects, PO Box 1235, Brattleboro, VT 05302-1235 Pub *Sphincterian Quarterly*. "Homoerotic, anally oriented magazine. For more information send $1 to The DBJ Projects."

⚥ ○ Bijou Video, 1363 N Wells, Chicago, IL 60610 800-932-7111 "Gay/Lesbian adult videos; gay related books, t-shirts, novelties."

♂ ○ The Blue Guide, PO Box 16-Y, Ogdensburg, NJ 07439 201-792-3022 "Guides to adult films & stars: reviews, themes, stars, directors, etc."

⚥ • The Christopher Company, PO Box 5960, Scottsdale, AZ 85261-5960 800-851-0690 Fax 800-851-0069

⚥ • Close-Up Productions, PO Box 691658, West Hollywood, CA 90069 800-697-9009

⚥ • Colt Studios, PO Box 1608GY, Studio City, CA 91614-0608 818-985-5786 Fax 818-985-2145 "Magazines, videos, slides, photosets, calendars, T-shirts, cards."

♀ ○ ⚤ Come Again, 353 E 53rd St, New York, NY 10022 212-308-9394 "Woman-owned erotic emporium; toys, leather, adult books, domestic & foreign fetish magazines, bondage items, oils, erotic lingerie to size 48. Video Shop At Home catalog available; book & magazine catalog $4."

♀ ○ ⚤ Cupid's Treasures, 3519 N Halsted, Chicago, IL 60657 312-348-3884; 800-CUPIDS-0; Fax 312-348-0976

♀ • Eve's Garden, 119 W 57th St #420 (4th flr), New York, NY 10019 212-757-8651 Fax 212-977-4306 "Sexuality boutique created by women for women. Mail order catalog $3.00; free if you mention Gayellow Pages."
✦ *Eve's Garden advertisement page 145*

♀ • Fatale Video, 530 Howard St #400, San Francisco, CA 94105-3007 800-861-4723 "Erotic videos for women by women."

♀ ○ ♂ Forbidden Fruit, 512 Neches, Austin, TX 78701 512-478-8358 "Erotic gifts; leather & safe sex supplies."

♂ • Fox Studio, PO Box 641, Venice, CA 90294 "Gay male videos."

♀ • ♂♂ Good Vibrations, 1210 Valencia #GY, San Francisco, CA 94110 415-974-8980; 800-BUY-VIBE "Books, toys, vibrators."

♀ • ♂ Heaven Sent Me, Inc., 1855 Gaylord St 303-331-6447; 800-472-0022; Fax 303-331-8264

♀ • KW Enterprises, 89 5th Ave #803, New York, NY 10003 212-727-2751 Pub *Bound & Gagged.* "Bondage art, videos, equipment."
✦ *KW Enterprises advertisement page 229*

♀ • (♂) Male Hide Leathers, 2816 N Lincoln Ave, Chicago, IL 60657 312-929-0069 "Leather, videos."

♂ • Malibu Sales, PO Box 93969, Los Angeles, CA 90093-0969 213-468-0390; 800-562-5428 "Books, video, novelties, etc."

♀ ○ Marc Sanders Mail Order, 399 Jayne Ave, Oakland, CA 94610 510-444-3204

♀ • Master's Toy Chest, c/o 139 W 4th Ave, Roselle, NJ 07203 908-245-5323 Fax 908-241-6152

♂ • Mercury Mail Order, 4084 18th St, Dept 9P, San Francisco, CA 94114-2534 415-621-1188 "Latex, lubricants, dildos, leather, etc. Catalog $4."

♂ • MJ Enterprises, PO Box 815, Laramie, WY 82070-0815 "SASE for details of used underwear & cowboy fetish items."

♀ ○ Montana American West Co, PO Box 6395, Dept AD, Bozeman, MT 59715 800-262-9269

♀ • National Marketing Enterprises, Inc., PO Box 030487, Fort Lauderdale, FL 33303-0487 305-566-4200 Fax 305-563-2499 "Catalog X: Tasteful adult catalog for Gays & Lesbians."

♂ • Old Reliable, 1626 N Wilcox Ave #107, Los Angeles, CA 90028 "Videos, photos, audio casettes; wrestling & boxing."

♀ • (♂♂) Passion Flower, 4 Yosemite Ave, Oakland, CA 94611 510-601-7750 Fax 510-658-9645 *The Vine.* "Workshops on many subjects."

♀ • (♂) The Pleasure Place, 1710 Connecticut Ave NW, Washington, DC 20009 202-483-3297; 800-386-2386 "Lingerie, novelties, cards, videos, leather, etc. Catalog $3."

♂ PM Productions, 156 61st St, West New York, NJ 07093 800-336-9696

♂ • Sierra Pacific Productions, PO Box 12109, Marina Del Rey, CA 90295 800-828-4336 "Distributor of adult videos."

♀ ○ ♂ Spartacus Enterprises, 300 SW 12th Ave, Portland, OR 97205 800-666-2604 Fax 503-239-4681 "Custom leather; store & mail order; catalogs $8."
✦ *Spartacus Enterprises advertisement page 384*

♂ • Townsend, Larry, PO Box 302, Beverly Hills, CA 90213 Fax 213-655-7314 "Complete & dependable mail order service for the Leather-SM oriented man."
✦ *Townsend, Larry advertisement page 145*

♀ • Tuff Stuff, 1714 E McDowell Rd, Phoenix, AZ 85006 602-254-9651 "Custom leatherware."

♂ ○ U.S. Male, 14666 Titus St #5t #14, Panorama City, CA 91402-4902 818-902-9697; 800-748-6155 outside CA

♀ ○ Wet Formulas International, PO Box 8069, Van Nuys, CA 91409 818-901-1451; 800-248-4811; Fax 818-901-1463
✦ Wet Formulas International advertisement page 3

♀ ○ ♂ Windfaire Exxxotic Gifts, 3885 Buford Hwy NE, Atlanta, GA 30329 404-634-WIND

MAIL ORDER: Gifts, Cards, Pride & Promotional Items

♀ ● (?♂) 4 R Pride Productions, PO Box 77389, Tucson, AZ 85703-7389 520-579-7000; 800-579-7001; Fax 520-579-1191

♀ ● ♂ Ages of Woman Products, 75 Montgomery St #2E, New York, NY 10002 212-619-3431 "Catalog $2."

♀ ● ♂ Amazon Earthworks, PO Box 248-G, Pacific City, OR 97135-0248 503-392-3900 "Pottery, crystal, healing beads, & sacred art."

♀ ● B.S. Enterprises - Gaytoos, 50 Union St #9, Northampton, MA 01060 413-586-1747 Fax 413-585-0211 "Temporary tattoos; custom design available."

♀ ● Be Proud, PO Box 977, Seaside, OR 97138 800-755-9976; 503-738-4105; Fax 503-738-4105 beproud@aol.com "Manufacturers & wholesale distributors of Gay Pride Products."
✦ Be Proud advertisement page 142

♂ ● The Body Black, PO Box 42628, Los Angeles, CA 90050 213-461-0772

♀ ● BooVà Specialities, PO Box 76014, Pittsburgh, PA 15214-0014 800-38BOOVA Fax 412-322-7398 "Gay/lesbian novelty items; free catalog."

♀ ● (♂) Brushstrokes, 1510-J Piedmont Ave NE, Atlanta, GA 30324 (Ansley Square) 404-876-6567

♀ ● Causemark, 10002 Aurora Ave N #2221, Seattle, WA 98133 "AIDS ribbon bookmarks (laminated) memorializing a donation to the AIDS Research Foundation or a related AIDS group of the buyer's choice."

♀ ● The Christmas Fairy, PO Box 883593, San Francisco, CA 94188 415-281-0696 "Gay themed Christmas ornaments; catalog free."

♀ ● Christopher & Castro Catalog, 349 W 12th St, New York, NY 10014 800-692-8437

♀ ● ♂ Dan Kaufman Graphics, PO Box 4901, Washington, DC 20008 202-466-8878 (IM OUT RU?); 202-466-8878 (IM OUT RU?); Fax 202-466-8879 "Gay/Lesbian/Bi Pride merchandise; write or call for free catalog."

♂ ● Don Ling's Removal Tattoos, PO Box 309, 102 2nd St South, Dept Y, Butterfield, MN 56120 800-247-6817; 507-956-2024; Fax 507-956-2060 "Gay/Lesbian & generic temporary tattoos; wholesale also available."
✦ Don Ling's Removal Tattoos advertisement page 146

♀ ○ Ephemera Buttons & Magnets, PO Box 490, Phoenix, OR 97535 503-535-4195

♀ ● Everyday Feelings, 1814 Bayridge Parkway, Brooklyn, NY 11204 718-331-8573 "The All Occasion Gay & Lesbian Card Line."

♀ ○ ♂ Flag & Banner Company, 543 Dumaine St, New Orleans, LA 70116 504-522-2204; 800-779-FLAG; Fax 504-522-2209

♀ ● Giant Ass Publishing, PO Box 214, New Haven, CT 06502 203-865-6113 "Mail order T-shirts, post cards & comix. Call or fax for free cat-a-log."

♀ ● Greetings From Key West, 1075 Duval St, Duval Square #21, Key West, FL 33040 305-294-1733; 800-KW-GIFTS

♀ • Iris Card Company, PO Box 390543, Dept Y, Cambridge, MA 02139 617-492-3433 "Art Rubberstamps, greeting cards, etc. Catalog $1."

♀ • Ladymead Enterprises, PO Box 1099, Shoreham, NY 11786 "Handmade lesbian gnome figurines. 2 stamps for catalog."

♀ • Lavender Rose ArtWorks, PO Box 6061 Yale Stn, New Haven, CT 06520 203-562-6071

♀ • Looking Out Productions, PO Box 66433, Scotts Valley, CA 95067-6433 800-988-2688 "Women's Romance Greeting Cards/gift items (wholesale). Please send SASE for brochure."

♂ ○ Love Bars, 750 S Spalding Ave #136, Los Angeles, CA 90036 213-933-6986

♀ ○ The Rainbow Connection, PO Box 66307, Houston, TX 77266 713-523-0432

♂ • Respect A Catalog for Gay Men, 1431 2nd Ave #3B, New York, NY 10021 800-881-8496 "Specializing in personalized mugs & t-shirts."

♀ • Seeds Store, Labrys Wilderness Resort, 4115 Scenic Hwy, Honor, MI 49640 616-882-5994 "Free mail order catalog of Landyke Crafts."

♂ ○ Shocking Gray, 1216 E Euclid Ave, San Antonio, TX 78212-4159 800-788-4729

♂ • (?♂) Signs of Pride, PO Box 762, Simpsonville, SC 29681 803-862-6944 Fax 803-862-7833 "SASE for catalog of static cling decals, buttons, etc."

♀ ○ State of Man, PO Box 1933-GY, Studio City, CA 91614-0933 "Calendars, notecards, books."

♀ • Steven Baratz Photography, 2660 3rd St #205, San Francisco, CA 94107 415-647-0247 (also Fax) "Greeting card publisher/distributor."

♂ • Triangle Traders, PO Box 42351, Tucson, AZ 85733-2351 520-795-7345 "'Infinitely Lesbian' & 'Rising Lambda' designs; originators of the Rainbow Ribbon. Notecards, T-shirts, decals, etc."

♂ • United Pride, 1202 E Pike St #725, Seattle, WA 98122 206-467-6267 "Candles (wholesale)."

♂ • Visual Voice, PO Box 8011, Bloomington, IN 47407 800-655-2321 Fax 812-333-7923 "Identities—handcrafted Gay Greeting Cards. Free catalog."

♀ • Woman Made Catalog, PO Box 390923, Mountain View, CA 94039-0923 415-968-1314 kari57755@aol.com

♀ • Yuppifino, 1011 Boren Ave #823, Seattle, WA 98104 206-285-5524 "Gewgaws, gimcracks, knickknacks & bric-a-brac."

MAIL ORDER: Jewelry

♀ • ♂ Bandé Designs, B&E Jewelers, 7102 Castor Ave, Philadelphia, PA 19149 215-742-9823

♀ • Gayla G Jewelry, PO Box 632883, San Diego, CA 92163 619-293-0766

♂ • (?♂) Lielin Jewelers - Moore or Les, PO Box 5607, Virginia Beach, VA 23455 804-464-0105

♂ • Pearl Street, PO Box 22, Provincetown, MA 02657 508-487-2210

♂ • RustiCrafts, 7545 Oak Narrows Rd, Cook, MN 55723-8722 "Dream catchers, dream catcher & beaded-earrings."

♀ • (?♂) Wear With Pride Apparel Company, 488 Whalley Ave, New Haven, CT 06511 203-389-5221

MAIL ORDER: Pet Supplies

♀ • Queer Kitty, 1800 Market St #238, San Francisco, CA 94102 " 'Queer toys for cats!' SASE for brochure; dealer inquiries welcome."

MAIL ORDER: Pharmaceuticals/Health Care Products

♂ ○ ♂♂ APP, Inc., PO Box 9019, Farmingdale, NY 11735 / 197 8th Ave, New York, NY 10011 800-227-1195; 212-691-9050; Fax 516-845-5310 "Prescription/nutrition/infusion."

♀ ○ Community Prescription Service, PO Box 1274 Old Chelsea Stn, New York, NY 10113-0920 800-842-0502; 212-229-9102 "HIV+ owned & operated mail order prescription service."

♀ ○ Family Pharmaceuticals, Box 1288, Mount Pleasant, SC 29464 800-922-3444

♀ ○ MOM: Mail Order Meds, Inc., PO Box 180007, Austin, TX 78718-0007 800-700-6202 Fax 800-700-6106

♦ *MOM: Mail Order Meds, Inc. advertisement inside front cover*

♀ ○ ♂ PX Drugstore, 5160 Vineland Ave #101, North Hollywood, CA 91601-3849 800-752-5721 "Drugs for the immunosuppressed patient: direct billing to insurance company & free overnight UPS delivery."

♀ ○ Stadtlander's Pharmacy, 800-238-7828

♀ ○ US Complete Care, 10 Railroad St, St Marys, PA 15857-1729 800-358-8838 Fax 814-781-3192

MAIL ORDER: Piercing & Body Jewelry

♀ • Gauntlet, Inc., 2377 Market St, San Francisco, CA 94114 415-431-3133

♀ • (?♂) Gauntlet, Inc., 8720 1/2 Santa Monica Blvd, West Hollywood, CA 90069 310-657-6677; 800-RINGS2U Pub *PFIQ (Piercing Fans International Quarterly)*. "Mail order service & publication: erotic piercing & body decoration."

♂ • Silver Anchor Enterprises, Inc., PO Box 760, Dept O, Crystal Springs, FL 33524-0760 813-788-0147; 800-Tit-Ring; Fax 813-782-0180 "Exotic body jewelry catalog $4."

MAIL ORDER: Records

♀ • Art Control, PO Box 415, Lakewood, OH 44107 216-631-6878 "Mail order recordings of electronic, industrial, avant-garde classical & jazz, experimental musics. Write for free catalog."

♂ • OUTcast Productions, 38-11 Ditmars Blvd #234, Astoria, NY 11105 718-728-4794 "Lesbian & gay CDs, records & tapes. Mail order catalog $3."

♦ *OUTcast Productions advertisement page 134*

♀ • (♂♂) Whimsong Records & Publishing, c/o The Whimsy, 1156 Park Lane, West Palm Beach, FL 33417-5957 407-686-1354 "Mainstream & women's music; record production & song publishing; concert & event production & promotion."

MAIL ORDER: Safe Sex Products

♀ ☆ ♂ The Rubber Tree, 4426 Burke Ave N., Dept GP, Seattle, WA 98103 206-633-4750 "Not-for-profit service of Zero Population Growth, specializing in condoms; also lubricants, spermicides, books, latex items, t-shirts, resuable menstrual products, etc. Free catalog."

MAIL ORDER: Video (see also Film & Video)

♂ • ATKOL Video, 912 South Avenue, Plainfield, NJ 07062 908-756-2011 (NJ); 800-88-ATKOL (National)

♂ • Catalina Video Distributing, PO Box 7016, Tarzana, CA 91357-7016 818-708-9200

→ *Gay Video Guide*: see PUBLICATIONS (Male Readership) page 147

Alabama

State/County Resources

AIDS/HIV Support, Education, Advocacy, Publications

♀ ☆ � AIDS Task Force of Alabama, Inc., PO Box 55703, Birmingham, AL 35255 205-592-2437; 205-591-4448 STD/AIDS Information Hotline; Fax 205-592-4998

Organizations/Resources: General, Multipurpose, Pride

♀ ★ (?♂) Gay & Lesbian Alliance of Alabama (GALAA), mail to GALAA, PO Box 36784, Birmingham, AL 35236-6784 205-GALAA-86; 205-424-1005 Pub Community Directory.

Organizations/Resources: Transgender & Transgender Publications

T ☆♀♂ Montgomery Medical & Psychological Institute, Alabama Chapter, PO Box 3361, Montgomery, AL 36109 334-244-9613 "Information for transsexuals & other transgenderists; support group meetings, professional referrals, lobbying."

Publications

♀ ★ ♂ Alabama Forum, 205 32nd St #216, Birmingham, AL 35233-3007 205-328-9228

Real Estate

♂ • Community Real Estate Referrals, 800-346-5592 "Free referral to gay/gay-supportive realtor in any USA city/state (including Virgin Is. & Puerto Rico). Sorry, no rentals!"
✦ Community Real Estate Referrals advertisement back cover

Anniston

AIDS/HIV Support, Education, Advocacy, Publications

♀ ☆ ♂ AIDS Services Center, Inc., PO Box 1392; 36202 205-835-0923 "Services include free HIV clinic for the indigent; professional counseling."

Auburn

AIDS/HIV Support, Education, Advocacy, Publications

♀ ☆ Lee County AIDS Outreach, PO Box 1971; 36831 334-887-5244

Bookstores: General

♀ ○ Behind The Glass, 168 E Magnolia Ave; 36831-1768 334-826-1133 "Bookstore/cafe."

Bookstores: Recovery, Metaphysical, & other Specialty

♀ ○ ♂ Etc., 125 N College St; 36830 334-821-0080 Mon-Fri noon-6pm; Sat 1-6pm. "Books, gifts & jewelry."

Organizations/Resources: Student, Academic, Alumni/ae

♂ ★ (♂) Auburn Gay & Lesbian Association (AGALA), PO Box 821; 36831-0821 334-887-SOFT Meeting Wed 7.30pm, Foy Union.

Birmingham

☎ Gay/Lesbian Information Line, Lambda Inc 205-326-8600

Addictive Behavior, Substance Abuse, Recovery

♂ ★ Live & Let Live AA, PO Box 55372; 35255 205-326-8600 Meets at 205 32nd St S.

AIDS/HIV Support, Education, Advocacy, Publications

♀ ☆ (?♂) Aids In Minorities (AIM), PO Box 1116; 35201 / 1630 4th Ave N 205-323-7949

♀ ☆ (?♂) Birmingham AIDS Outreach, PO Box 550070; 35255 205-322-4197 Pub Outreach Newsletter.

Bars, Restaurants, Clubs, Discos

♀ 22nd St Jazz Cafe, 710 22nd St; 35233 205-252-0407

♂ ○ Bill's Club, 208 N 23rd St; 35203 205-254-8634 P

♂ Buchanan's, 414 21st St S; 35233 205-328-4337 BD

♂ ○ Club 21, 117 N 21st St; 35203 205-322-0469 BDE

♀ Mikatam, 3719 3rd Ave South; 35222 205-592-0790

♂ • Quest Club, 416 24th St S.; 35233 205-251-4313

Bookstores: Gay/Lesbian/Feminist

♂ • Lodestar Books, 2020 11th Ave S; 35205 205-933-1595 Fax 205-939-3356

Erotica (Printed, Visual, Equipment)

♀ ○ (♂) Alabama Adult Books, 901 5th Ave N; 35203 205-322-7323

♀ ○ Birmingham Adult Books, 7610 1st Ave N; 35206 205-836-1580

♀ ○ ♂ Downtown Adult Books, 2731 8th Ave; 35203 205-328-5525 "Bookstore; video sales & rentals; CDs; video arcade, preview booths."

♀ ○ ♂ Jupiter Theatre, 2500 7th Ave S; 35233 205-324-4552 "Adult bookstore/theatre/video arcade; preview booths; adult CD's."

♀ ○ ♂ Pleasure Books East, 7606 1st Ave N; 35206 205-836-7379 "Video arcade, video sales & rentals; preview booths; bookstore, adult CD's."

♀ ○ (♂) Tophat Cinema, 9221 Todd Dr; 35206 205-833-8221 "Adult theatre & bookstore, video sales & rental; screening booths."

Jewelry

♂ • ♂ Crestwood Pawn & Jewelry, 4612 5th Ave S; 35222 205-591-PAWN

Organizations/Resources: Sexual Focus (Leather, S/M, etc) & Safe Sex Promotion

♂ Pendragons Of Birmingham, 210 Lorna Sq #272; 35216

Organizations/Resources: Sport/Dance/Outdoor

♂ ★ Magic City Athletic Association, PO Box 55373; 35255 205-328-5010

♂ New South Softball League, PO Box 55373; 35255 205-328-5010

♂ ★ Southern Shootout, PO Box 55373; 35255 205-595-6315

Organizations/Resources: Student, Academic, Alumni/ae

♂ LGB Awareness League, Birmingham Southern College, PO Box A14; 35254-0001

♂ UAB G/L Student Union, Box 34 Hill University Center, 1400 University Blvd; 35294-1150

Performing Arts: Entertainment, Music, Recording, Theater, etc.

♀ • ♂ Planet Muzica, 725 29th St S; 35233-2809 205-254-9303 (also Fax) "Music, T-shirts, magazines."

Real Estate

♀ ○ First Real Estate Corp: Joe Ross, First Real Estate Corp, 2534 Rocky Ridge Rd; 35243 205-823-7067

♀ ○ Klinner, Jeffrey, Johnson Rast & Hays, 4637-C Highway 280 South; 35242 205-991-8880; 205-979-0262

Religious Organizations & Publications

♀ ★ ♿ Birmingham Community Church, PO Box 130221; 35213 205-849-8505

♀ ★ ♿ Covenant Metropolitan Community Church, PO Box 101473; 35210 / 5117 1st Ave N 205-599-3363

Suntanning

♀ • (?♿) Clara Belle's Tanning Parlor, 211 S 18th St; 35233 205-326-6025

Switchboards, Helplines, Phone Information

♀ ★ ♿ Gay/Lesbian Information Line, Lambda Inc, 205 32nd St S #201; 35233 205-326-8600 7-10pm; TDD available

Dothan

Bars, Restaurants, Clubs, Discos

♀ Chuckie Bee's, 174-A N Foster St; 36303-4540 334-794-0230

Gadsden

Bars, Restaurants, Clubs, Discos

♂ Nitro, 2661 E Meighan Blvd; 35903 205-492-9724

Homewood

Pets & Pet Supplies

♀ ○ Ed's Pet World, 2730 18th St S; 35209 205-879-1331

Huntsville

AIDS/HIV Support, Education, Advocacy, Publications

♀ ☆ (♿) AIDS Action Coalition, PO Box 871; 35804 205-533-2437 The Summit. "Educational, direct services & Support group."

♀ ☆ (♿) Davis Clinic, PO Box 425; 35804 205-533-2437 "For HIV Positive, PWA's & ARC clients lacking resources to obtain medical services elsewhere."

Bars, Restaurants, Clubs, Discos

♀ • Vieux Carre, 1204 Posey St; 35816 205-534-5970 **BDE** 7pm-2am; Sun 4pm-2am.

Bookstores: Gay/Lesbian/Feminist

♀ • ♿ Rainbow's Ltd, 4321 University Dr #400B; 35816 205-722-9220 Mon & Wed-Sat 11am-9pm; Sun 1-6pm.
♦ Rainbow's Ltd advertisement page 149

Counseling/Therapy: Private

♀ • Horn, Martha J, MA, LPC, 500 Wynn Dr #304-A; 35816 205-895-0625 compuserve 75342,305

Organizations/Resources: Business & Professional

♀ ★ (♿) Gay & Lesbian Organization Of Professionals (GALOP), mail to GALOP, PO Box 914; 35804 205-517-6127

Religious Organizations & Publications

♂ ★ ♿♿ Metropolitan Community Church of Huntsville, 3015 Sparkman Dr; 35810 205-851-6914 Pub Joyful Noise.

Mobile

AIDS/HIV Support, Education, Advocacy, Publications

♀ ☆ ♿ Mobile AIDS Support Services, 107 N Ann St; 36604 334-433-6277; 334-432-AIDS

Bars, Restaurants, Clubs, Discos

♀ • ♿ B-Bob's, 6157 Airport Blvd #201 (Plaza De Malaga); 36608 334-341-0102 **BDP**
♦ B-Bob's advertisement page 149

♀ • Gabriel's Downtown, 55 S. Joachim St; 36602 334-432-4900

♂ ○ Golden Rod, 219 Conti; 36602 334-433-9175

♀ ○ Society Lounge, 51 S Conception; 36602 334-433-9141

♂ • Trooper's, 215 Conti St 334-433-7436 **BD**

Erotica (Printed, Visual, Equipment)

♂ ○ Midtown Cinema, 270 Dauphin St, Suite B (entrance in rear); 36602 334-438-9910

Organizations/Resources: Student, Academic, Alumni/ae

♀ ★ ♿♿ Gay, Lesbian, Bisexual Alliance, University of South Alabama, mail to GLB of USA, PO Box 81571; 36608-0002 334-666-9824

Religious Organizations & Publications

♂ ★ (♿) Metropolitan Community Church of Mobile, PO Box 6311; 36660-6311 334-476-4621 Meets Sun 7pm: please call for details.

Montgomery

Accommodation: Hotels, B&B, Resorts, Campgrounds

♀ ○ (♿) Lattice Inn B&B, 1414 S Hull St; 36104 334-832-9931; 800-525-0652

AIDS/HIV Support, Education, Advocacy, Publications

♀ ☆ Montgomery AIDS Outreach, PO Box 5213; 36103 334-269-1002

Bars, Restaurants, Clubs, Discos

♀ Hojons, 215 N Court St; 36104 334-269-9672

Religious Organizations & Publications

♀ ★ ♂ Metropolitan Community Church, PO Box 603; 36101-0603 334-279-7894 Service Sun 5.30pm at Unitarian Fellowship Bldg, 5280 Vaughn Rd.

Pelham

Organizations/Resources: Sexual Focus (Leather, S/M, etc) & Safe Sex Promotion

♂ ★ Steel City Centurions & Bears, PO Box 533; 35124 205-664-0609

Tuscaloosa

AIDS/HIV Support, Education, Advocacy, Publications

♀ ☆ ♂♂ West Alabama Aids Outreach, PO Box 2947; 35403 205-758-2437

Bars, Restaurants, Clubs, Discos

♀ ○ Michael's Lounge, 2201 6th St; 35401 205-758-9223 *BD*

Bookstores: Gay/Lesbian/Feminist

♀ ○ Illusions, 519 College Park; 35401 205-349-5725

Organizations/Resources: General, Multipurpose, Pride

♀ ★ (?♂) Tuscaloosa Lesbian Coalition, PO Box 6085; 35486-6085 205-333-8227 Pub *TLC Newsletter*.

Organizations/Resources: Student, Academic, Alumni/ae

♀ ★ ♂♂ Gay/Lesbian/Bisexual Alliance, University of Alabama (GLBA), mail to GLBA, PO Box 4595; 35486-4595 205-348-7210 glba@ua1vm.us.edu Pub *Lavender Tide*.

Alaska

State/County Resources

☎ Identity, Inc. 907-258-4777

Accommodation: Reservations & Exchanges (see also Travel)

♀ ● (♂♂) Alaska Available B&B Reservations, 7501 Upper O'Malley, Anchorage, AK 99516 800-346-2533

AIDS/HIV Support, Education, Advocacy, Publications

♀ ☆ ♂♂ Alaskan AIDS Assistance Association (AAAA), 1057 W Fireweed Ln #102, Anchorage, AK 99503-1736 907-276-4880; 800-478-AIDS

Organizations/Resources: Business & Professional

♀ ★ Triangle Network, PO Box 82290, Fairbanks, AK 99708 907-389-2528 "Association of travel professionals."

Organizations/Resources: Political/Legislative

♀ Alaskans for Civil Rights, PO Box 201348, Anchorage, AK 99520 907-258-3439

Organizations/Resources: Social, Recreational & Support Groups (see also Sport/Dance/Outdoor)

♀ ★ Identity, Inc., PO Box 200070, Anchorage, AK 99520 907-258-4777 Gay Helpline Monthly potluck socials with programs. Pub *Identity NorthView*.

Organizations/Resources: Sport/Dance/Outdoor

♀ ☆ Alaska Women of the Wilderness, PO Box 773556, Eagle River, AK 99577 907-688-2226 Pub *Alternate Trails*. "Specializing in wilderness programs for women."

Anchorage

Accommodation: Hotels, B&B, Resorts, Campgrounds

♀ ● (♂) Arctic Feather B&B, 211 W Cook Ave; 99501 907-277-3862

♀ ● Aurora Winds Exceptional Bed & Breakfast, 7501 Upper O'Malley; 99516 907-346-2533

♀ ○ ♂ The Lodge At Eagle River, PO Box 90154; 99509 907-278-7575

AIDS/HIV Support, Education, Advocacy, Publications

♀ ☆♂♂ HIV Counselor, Munic. of Anchorage DHHS, PO Box 196650; 99519-6650 / Room 101 907-343-4611 "Free HIV counseling & testing; STD & Hep B testing & treatment."

Bars, Restaurants, Clubs, Discos

♂ ○ Blue Moon, 535 E. 5th Ave; 99501 907-277-0441 *BDE*

♀ ● ♂♂ Raven, 618 Gambell St; 99501 907-276-9672

Bookstores: Gay/Lesbian/Feminist

♀ ● ♂ Bona Dea: The Women's Bookstore, 2440 E Tudor Rd #304; 99507-1129 907-562-4716 Fax 907-562-4325 Mon-Thu 11am-7pm; Fri & Sat 10am-6pm. Community bulletin board & calendar. 'We love to meet visitors!'

Erotica (Printed, Visual, Equipment)

♀ ○ Anchorage Video Mart, 137 W 5th Ave; 99501 907-276-9224

♀ ○ French Quarter, 4028 Mountain View Dr; 99509 907-276-9049 "Video Arcade."

♀ ○♂♂ La Sex Shoppe, 305 W Diamond Blvd; 99508 907-522-1987

♀ ○ Swingers Bookstore, 710 W Northern Lights; 99503 907-561-5039

Health Care (see also AIDS Services)

♀ ☆ ♂♂ STD Clinic, Dept of Health & Human Services, 825 L St, room 101; 99501 907-343-4611

Organizations/Resources: Family

♀ ★ Anchorage Lesbian Families Alliance, 2440 E Tudor, Box 304,, c/o Alaska Woman's Cultural Center; 99507 907-338-5255; 907-278-2198

Organizations/Resources: Social, Recreational & Support Groups (see also Sport/Dance/Outdoor)

♂ The Last Frontier, PO Box 202054; 99520

Performing Arts: Entertainment, Music, Recording, Theater, etc.

♀ ★ (?♂) The Fifteen Percent, PO Box 101201; 99510-1201 907-337-0253

♀ ☆ ♂♂ Out North Theatre, 1325 Primrose St; 99508 907-279-8200

Religious Organizations & Publications

♀ ★ ♂♂ Lamb of God Metropolitan Community Church, 615 Hollywood Dr #5; 99501-1220 (Government Hill) 907-258-5266 Services Sun 11am & 7pm; Wed 7pm; Potluck & movie Tue 7pm.

Travel & Tourist Services (see also Accommodation)

♀ ● Apollo Travel, 1207 W 47th Ave; 99503 907-561-0661; 800-770-0661

Women's Centers

♀ ☆ ♂♂ Alaska Women's Resource Center, 111 W 9th Ave; 99501 907-276-0528 Fax 907-278-8944 Mon-Fri 8.30am-5pm. Pub *AWRC Newsletter*.

Fairbanks

Accommodation: Hotels, B&B, Resorts, Campgrounds

♀ • Alta's Bed & Breakfast, PO Box 82290; 99708 907-457-0246

Bars, Restaurants, Clubs, Discos

♀ ○ Palace Saloon, 3175 College Rd #1; 99709 (near Airport Way & Peeger Rd) 907-456-5960

Juneau

AIDS/HIV Support, Education, Advocacy, Publications

♀ Shanti of Juneau, PO Box 22655; 99802 907-463-5665; 800-478-AIDS

Organizations/Resources: General, Multipurpose, Pride

⚥ ★ (?♿) S.E. Alaska Gay/Lesbian Alliance (SEAGLA), mail to SEAGLA, PO Box 21542; 99802-1542 907-586-4297 Fri 7-9pm. *The Perspective.*

Nikiski

Accommodation: Hotels, B&B, Resorts, Campgrounds

⚥ • (?♿) Moose Haven Lodge, PO Box 8597; 99635 907-776-8535 (also Fax)

Arizona

State/County Resources

Accommodation: Reservations & Exchanges (see also Travel)

♀ • (?♿) Arizona Accommodations, 8900 E Via Linda #101, Scottsdale, AZ 85260 602-860-9338; 800-266-STAY; Fax 602-314-1193 "Arizona accommodations reservations."

Addictive Behavior, Substance Abuse, Recovery

⚥ • (♿) Pride Institute, 800-54-PRIDE "The nation's only accredited chemical dependency treatment center exclusively for Gay, Lesbian & Bisexual People."

AIDS/HIV Support, Education, Advocacy, Publications

⚥ ★ ♿ Arizona AIDS Information Line, 3136 N 3rd Ave, Phoenix, AZ 85013 602-234-2752 10am-10pm.

♀ ★ ♿ Arizona AIDS Project, 4460 N Central Ave, Phoenix, AZ 85012 602-265-3300

♀ ☆ Arizona AIDS Services of the Deaf, 4460 N Central Ave, Phoenix, AZ 85012-1815 602-265-9953 (TTY); 602-265-3300 (voice message); 800-842-4681 Relay (Voice); Fax 602-265-9951

♂ ☆♿ Buyer's Club, 111 E Camelback Rd, Phoenix, AZ 85012-1609 602-265-2437 Fax 602-265-7201 "Health care & nutritional products for men & women at substantial savings."

♂ ☆♿ Community AIDS Council Youth Services, 3136 N 3rd Ave, Phoenix, AZ 85013-4302 602-266-7233 Fax 602-265-0374 "A peer based HIV prevention program which includes discussion groups & workshops for youth under 25 years of age."

♂ ☆♿ Community AIDS Council, 111 E Camelback Rd, Phoenix, AZ 85012-1609 602-265-2437 Fax 602-265-7201 "Early intervention & health promotion."

♂ ☆♿ Gay Men's Sex Project, 3136 N 3rd Ave, Phoenix, AZ 85013-4302 602-265-4677 Fax 602-265-0374 "HIV prevention program."

Insurance (see also Insurance Benefits/Viaticals)

♂ • ♿ Farmers Insurance Group, Murray D Sullivan Agency, Inc., 9700 N 91st St #C-124, Scottsdale, AZ 85258-5036 602-860-0920 Fax 602-860-5723 "Auto, Home, Business & Life Insurance."
✦ *Farmers Insurance Group advertisement page 151*

Organizations/Resources: General, Multipurpose, Pride

♀ ★♿ Lesbian Resource Project, PO Box 26031, Tempe, AZ 85285-6031 602-966-6152 (Voice/TDD) Pub *Women's Center News.*

Organizations/Resources: Social, Recreational & Support Groups (see also Sport/Dance/Outdoor)

⚥ ★ Couples of Arizona, PO Box 7144, Phoenix, AZ 85011 602-831-6432

♂ ★ Southwest Men At Large, PO Box 25951, Tempe, AZ 85285-5951 602-730-8171

⚥ TLGA (Tucson Lesbian Gay Alliance), Box 40301, Tucson, AZ 85717 520-321-0985

Organizations/Resources: Sport/Dance/Outdoor

⚥ ★ (♿) Arizona Gay Rodeo Association, PO Box 16363, Phoenix, AZ 85011 602-265-0618 Pub *Newsletter.*

Publications

⚥ • *Observer,* PO Box 50733, Tucson, AZ 85703-1733 520-622-7176 Fax 520-792-8382

⚥ • *Rubyfruit Journal,* 2701 E Croyden, Tucson, AZ 85716

⚥ • *Western Express,* PO Box 5317, Phoenix, AZ 85010-5317 602-254-1324

Real Estate

♀ • Community Real Estate Referrals, 800-346-5592 "Free referral to gay/gay-supportive realtor in any USA city/state (including Virgin Is. & Puerto Rico). Sorry, no rentals!"
✦ *Community Real Estate Referrals advertisement back cover*

Religious Organizations & Publications

♀ ★ Evangelicals Concerned, PO Box 66906, Phoenix, AZ 85082-6906 602-893-6952

Bisbee

Organizations/Resources: General, Multipurpose, Pride

♀ ★ Lesbian & Gay Alliance of Cochise County, PO Box 818; 85603 520-432-5591 Pub *Out in the Desert.*

Bullhead City

Bars, Restaurants, Clubs, Discos

♀ Lariat Saloon, 1161 Hancock Rd; 86430 602-758-9741 (Gay eves only)

Cottonwood

Accommodation: Hotels, B&B, Resorts, Campgrounds

♀ • Mustang Bed & Breakfast, 4257 Mustang Dr; 86326 520-646-5929 "Children welcome; no pets. Movie theater."

Flagstaff

Bookstores: Gay/Lesbian/Feminist

♀ • Aradia Books, PO Box 266; 86002 / 116 W. Cottage 520-779-3817

Switchboards, Helplines, Phone Information

♀ ★ Gay & Lesbian Switchboard, PO Box 183; 86002 520-522-0442

Glendale: see Phoenix

Phoenix

☎ Lesbian & Gay Community Switchboard 602-234-2752

Accommodation: Hotels, B&B, Resorts, Campgrounds

Phoenix

♀ • (♂♂) Larry's B & B, 502 W Claremont Ave; 85013 602-249-2974

♂ • Royal Villa Apartments, 1102 E Turney Ave; 85014 602-266-6883 "Long & short term."

Addictive Behavior, Substance Abuse, Recovery

♀ ★ ♂ New Creations, 1029 E Turney; 85014 602-265-2831 Meets Mon 7.30pm. "Christian 12-step group."

AIDS/HIV Support, Education, Advocacy, Publications

⚧ Aunt Rita's Foundation, 5501 N 7th Ave #215; 85013-1700 602-265-1659; 602-265-3753

⚧ Volunteers In Direct Aid (VIDA), PO Box 40476; 85067-0476 602-279-VIDA

Art & Photography (see also Graphic Design)

♀ • Edelman, Gregg, freelance photographer: 602-266-7202

Bars, Restaurants, Clubs, Discos

Glendale

♂ JC's Fun One Lounge, 5542 N 43rd Ave, Glendale; 85301 602-939-0528

Phoenix

♂ • ♂ 307 Lounge, 222 E Roosevelt; 85004 602-252-0001 *BE*

♀ Ain't Nobody's Bizness, 3031 E Indian School Road #7; 85016 602-224-9977 *D*

♀ • ♂ Apollo's, 5749 N 7th St; 85014 602-277-9373 8am-1am; Sun 10am-1am.

♂ • Charlie's, 727 W Camelback Rd; 85013 602-265-0224 *BDCW*

♂ • (♂♂) Country Club Bar & Grill, 4428 N 7th Ave; 85013 602-264-4553 *BRD*

♂ • Cruisin' Central, 1011 N Central Ave; 85004 602-253-3376

♀ ♂ The Desert Rose, 4301 N 7th Ave; 85013 602-265-3233 *BDE*

♀ Foster's, 4343 N 7th Ave; 85013 602-263-8313

♂ • Harley's 155, 155 W Camelback Rd; 85013 602-274-8505 *BDE* Noon-1am.

♀ • Incognito, 2424 E Thomas Rd; 85016 602-955-9805 *BDE*

♂ • (♂♂) Johnny MC's, 138 W Camelback Rd; 85013 602-266-0875 *BLW*

♀ Marlys, 15615 N Cave Creek Rd; 85032 602-867-2463

♀ ♂♂ Metro/Bananas, 4102 E Thomas Rd; 85018 602-224-9457

♂ My Favorite Lounge & Grill, 4809 N 27th Ave; 85017 602-242-8102

♀ • Nasty Habits, 3108 E McDowell Rd; 85008 602-267-8707 *BEd*

♂ • ♂ Nu-Towne Saloon, 5002 E Van Buren; 85008 602-267-9959 *BCW*

♂ The Phoenix Eagle, 4531 N 7th St; 85014 602-285-0833

♀ Pookie's Cafe, 4540 N 7th St; 85014 602-277-2121

♂ Pumphouse, 4132 E McDowell Rd; 85008 602-275-3509

♂ Roun' Back, 2107 W Camelback; 85015 602-242-6077

♂ Trax, 1724 E McDowell Rd; 85006 602-254-0231

♀ • Winks, 5707 N 7th St; 85014 602-265-9002 *BRE* 10am-1am.

Scottsdale

♀ • B's West, 7125 5th Ave, Scottsdale; 85251 602-945-9028 *Bd* 1pm-1am.

♀ The Works, 7223 E 2nd St, Scottsdale; 85251 602-946-4141

Bookstores: General

♀ ○ (♂♂) Changing Hands Bookstore, 414 S Mill Ave #109, Tempe; 85281 602-966-0203 changehand@aol.com

Business, Financial & Secretarial

♀ • Word Wizard, PO Box 33233; 85067 602-246-8277 "Word processing & printing."

Community Centers (see also Women's Centers)

♀ ★ ♂♂ Valley of the Sun Gay & Lesbian Community Center, 3136 N 3rd Ave; 85013 602-265-7283 10am-10pm.

Counseling/Therapy: Private

♀ ○ Brinkhoff, Sara, MA, CPC, 5333 N. 7th St #A-202; 85014 602-226-2290

♀ ○ ♂♂ DiBona, Terri L, MC, CPC, 3660 E University Suite 8, Mesa; 85205 602-830-8488

♀ ○ ♂♂ Egge, Conrad, Ph.D., 5727 N 7th St #100; 85014 602-230-2025

♀ • ♂ The Lighthouse Center, 9755 N 90th St #290, Scottsdale; 85258 602-451-0819

♀ • ♂♂ Lovejoy, Gary D., Ph.D., 2701 E Camelback Rd #391; 85016 602-957-2368 & 4450 S. Rural Rd #B-132, Tempe; 85283 756-1669

♀ • ♂♂ Park Central Counseling, 77 E Thomas Rd #215; 85012-3118 602-274-0327

♀ ○♂♂ Peterson, Ronald A., Ph.D., 51 E Lexington Ave; 85012 602-234-3500

Erotica (Printed, Visual, Equipment)

♀ ○ The Adult Shoppe, 111 S 24th St; 85034 602-306-1130

♀ ○ Book Cellar #2, 2103 W Camelback Rd; 85015 602-249-9788

♀ ○ Book Cellar #5, 1421 E McDowell Rd; 85006 602-262-9476

♀ ○ Book Cellar #6, 1838 Grand Ave; 85007 602-262-9251

♀ • Castle Bookstore, 5501 E Washington; 85034 602-231-9837

♂ • ♂ Galerie Leon, 4804 N 7th Ave; 85013 602-263-0463 L

♀ ○ Modern World Adult Bookstore, 1812 East Apache, Tempe; 85281 602-967-9052

♀ ○ Pleasure Palace, 1524 E Van Buren; 85014 602-262-9942

♀ • Tuff Stuff, 1714 E McDowell Rd; 85006 602-254-9651 Tue-Fri 9am-6pm; Sat to 3pm. "Custom leatherware."

Florists (see also Gardening)

♀ • ♂ McDonald Floral & Gifts, Inc., 5223 N Central Ave; 85012 602-277-3335

♀ ○ ♂ Next To Nature, 4700 N Central Ave #122; 85012 602-264-0740; 800-544-6674 Mon-Wed 8am-6pm; Thu & Fri to 7pm; Sat 9am-4pm.

Gifts, Cards, Pride & Novelty Items

♂ • The Freedom Company, 1722 E McDowell Road; 85006 602-252-9493

♂ • Unique On Central, 4700 N Central Ave #105; 85012 602-279-9691 "Cards, gifts, artwork, jewelry, books, cafe." ✦ Unique On Central advertisement page 153

Health Care (see also AIDS Services)

♀ ○ Women's Clinic, 3410 N 4th Ave; 85013 602-241-1966

Health Clubs, Gyms, Saunas

♂ • Flex Complex, 1517 S Black Canyon Hwy; 85009 602-271-9017

Home & Building: Cleaning, Repair, General Contractors

♂ ○ Don Williams Plumbing & Builders Inc, 2719 W Weldon; 85017 602-242-5682

Legal Services & Resources

♀ • ♂ Rea, Roger W., 3601 N 7th Ave #B; 85013 602-248-7921

Organizations/Resources: Bisexual Focus

♀ Arzizona Bisexual Network, 5501 N 7th Ave #1054; 85013 602-352-4023

Organizations/Resources: Business & Professional

♀ ★ ♂♂ Camelback Business & Professional Association, PO Box 2097; 85001-2097 602-225-8444 Fax 520-323-1900

Organizations/Resources: Family

♀ PFLAG, PO Box 37525; 85069-7525 602-843-1404

4700 N. Central, Suite 105 • Phoenix, Arizona 85012 • 279-9691

Organizations/Resources: General, Multipurpose, Pride

♀ ★ Phoenix Lesbian & Gay Pride Committee, PO Box 26139, Tempe; 85285-6139 602-352-7165

Organizations/Resources: Military/Veterans

♂ Southwest Veterans Association, 216 W Cody Dr. #20; 85041-3134 602-755-2928

Organizations/Resources: Political/Legislative

♀ ☆ (?♂) National Organization for Women (NOW), PO Box 16023; 85011 602-948-5014

Organizations/Resources: Sexual Focus (Leather, S/M, etc) & Safe Sex Promotion

♂ Copperstate Leathermen, PO Box 44051; 85064-4501 602-849-8619

♂ NLA: Central Arizona, 4620 N 7th Ave.; 85013

Organizations/Resources: Social, Recreational & Support Groups (see also Sport/Dance/Outdoor)

♂ Arizona Nude Dudes—Phoenix, PO Box 32766; 85064-2766 602-545-8783

♂ ★ East Side Social Club, PO Box 7681, Mesa; 85216-7681 602-380-9610

♂ ★ Stevens-Gregg Foundation, 1238 E Georgia Ave; 85014-2906 602-241-1604 Seniors.

Organizations/Resources: Sport/Dance/Outdoor

♂ ★ Arizona Lambda Yacht Club, 5501 N 7th Ave #1028; 85013 602-266-0550

♂ ★ Desert Adventures, PO Box 2008; 85001 602-266-2267 (CAMP) Pub Trail Marker. "Social & recreation group; 80% of activities involve camping, hiking & other outdoor activities."

♂ ★ ♂ Desert Valley Squares, PO Box 34615; 85067 602-256-2327 d

♂ Sunburst Squares, c/o Charlie's, 727 W Camelback Rd; 85013 602-242-9149 d

Organizations/Resources: Student, Academic, Alumni/ae

♂ ★ Delta Lambda Phi Fraternity, Arizona State University, Box 16 Student Development Office, ASU, Tempe; 85287-3001 800-587-FRAT

Organizations/Resources: Youth (see also Family)

♂ ★ ♂♂ Valley One In Ten (VOIT) Youth Programs, 3136 N 3rd Ave; 85013 602-264-KIDS Wed 7-9pm.

Performing Arts: Entertainment, Music, Recording, Theater, etc.

♂ ★ Grand Canyon Men's Chorale, PO Box 16462; 85011-6462 602-340-7640

Pets & Pet Supplies

♀ ○ Stay 'N Home Pet Sitting, PO Box 10905, Glendale; 85318-0905 602-547-0575 "Overnight pet-sitting in client's home."

TORTUGA ROJA
BED & BREAKFAST
2800 EAST RIVER ROAD
TUCSON, ARIZONA 85718
(520) 577-6822   (800) 467-6822

Publications
→ Western Express: p.151

Religious Organizations & Publications

⚢ ★ (?♂) Affirmation/Gay & Lesbian Mormons: Phoenix, PO Box 26601, Tempe; 85285-6601 602-433-1321 "Mormons."

♂ Boundless Love Community Church, 431 Stapley Dr #23, Mesa; 85204 602-439-0025

⚢ ★♂♂ Casa De Cristo Evangelical Church, 1029 E Turney; 85014 602-265-2831

⚢ Christian Science Group, PO Box 893; 85001 602-371-1102

⚢ ★ (♂) Dignity-Integrity/Phoenix, PO Box 21091; 85036 602-258-2556 "Gay & Lesbian Catholics & Episcopalians & their friends."

⚢ ★ (?♂) Gentle Shepherd Metropolitan Community Church, PO Box 33758; 85067-3758 602-274-6199

♀ ★ ♂ Healing Waters Ministries, 225 W University Dr #105, Tempe; 85281 602-894-8681 "Worshipping with Lesbians & Gays in the East Valley."

⚢ ★ (♂) Lutherans Concerned, PO Box 7519; 85011 602-870-3611

⚢ ★ Mishpachat Am, PO Box 7731; 85011-7731 602-966-5001

⚢ ★ ♂ Oasis Metropolitan Community Church, 2604 N 14th St; 85006-1121

⚢ PLGC/Presbyterians For Lesbian & Gay Concerns, PO Box 61162; 85082 602-275-0506

Switchboards, Helplines, Phone Information

⚢ ★♂♂ Lesbian & Gay Community Switchboard, 3136 N 3rd Ave; 85013 602-234-2752 10am-10pm.

Travel & Tourist Services (see also Accommodation)

♀ • FirsTravel, 5150 N 7th St; 85014 602-265-0666 Fax 602-265-0135

♀ ○ ♂ Valley West Travel, 4907 W Diana Ave, Glendale; 85302 602-934-1238 Fax 602-939-2927

Women's Centers

♀ ☆♂♂ Women's Center, PO Box 26031, Tempe; 85285-6031 602-966-6152 Pub Women's Center News.

Prescott

Bookstores: General

♀ ○ Satisfied Mind, 113 W Goodwin St; 86303-3954 520-776-9766

Organizations/Resources: Social, Recreational & Support Groups (see also Sport/Dance/Outdoor)

⚢ YAG (Support Group), Box 8663, 3200 N Willow Creek Rd; 86301-3720

Scottsdale: see Phoenix

Sedona

Accommodation: Hotels, B&B, Resorts, Campgrounds

♀ ○ (♂) Cozy Cactus, 80 Canyon Circle Dr; 86351 520-284-0082; 800-788-2082

♀ • Paradise Ranch, 135 Kachina Dr; 86336 520-282-9769

♀ • (?♂) Sacred Sedona Lodging, PO Box 3661; 86340 520-204-2422 All welcome.

Travel & Tourist Services (see also Accommodation)

♀ • (?♂) Sacred Sedona Tours, 125 Meander Way; 86336 520-204-2422 All welcome.

Tucson

Accommodation: Hotels, B&B, Resorts, Campgrounds

♀ ○ Casa Alegre Bed & Breakfast Inn, 316 East Speedway; 85705 520-628-1800

♀ ○ Casa Tierra Adobe B & B Inn, 11155 West Calle Pima; 85743 520-578-3058 Fax 520-578-3058

♀ ○ Catalina Park Inn, 309 E 1st St; 85705 520-792-4541

⚢ • (?♂) Montecito House, PO Box 42352; 85733 520-795-7592

⚢ • (?♂) Natural Balance Bed & Breakfast, PO Box 40504; 85717 520-881-4582 "Bed & breakfast; also licensed masseur."

⚢ • **Tortuga Roja B & B, 2800 E River Rd; 85718 520-577-6822; 800-467-6822**
✦ *Tortuga Roja B & B advertisement page 154*

AIDS/HIV Support, Education, Advocacy, Publications

♀ ☆♂♂ El Proyecto Arizona-Sonora, 801 W Congress St; 85745-2817 520-882-3933

♀ ☆♂♂ God's Love In Action (GLIA), 2902 N Geronimo; 85705 520-622-8860

♀ ☆ People with AIDS Coalition of Tucson (PACT), PO Box 2488; 85702-2488 520-770-1710

♀ ☆ Shanti Foundation/Tucson, 300 E 6th St; 85705 520-622-7107

♀ ☆♂♂ Tucson AIDS Project, Inc (TAP), 151 S Tucson Blvd #252; 85716-5523 520-326-AIDS; 800-771-9054; 520-323-9373 (emergency); 502-322-6226 (administration)

Bars, Restaurants, Clubs, Discos

⚢ Ain't Nobody's Bizness, 2900 E Broadway; 85716-5343 520-318-4838

♂ • (♂♂) Club 2520, 2520 North Oracle Rd; 85705 520-882-5799 *BDRCW*

♀ ○ (♂♂) Club Congress, 311 East Congress; 85701 520-622-8848 *BRDEL*

♂ • Graduate, 23 W University Blvd; 85705 520-622-9233

⚢ • ♂ Hours, 3455 E Grant Rd; 85716 520-327-3390 *BDCW*

♂ ○ It's 'Bout Time, 616 N 4th Ave; 85705 520-882-3053

⚢ Paragon, 144 W Lester; 85705-6550 520-622-5560

♂ Stonewall/Eagle, 2921 N 1st Ave; 85719 520-624-8805

♂ • ⚥ Venture-N, 1239 N 6th Ave; 85705 520-882-8224 **BLW** 6am-1am.

Bookstores: Gay/Lesbian/Feminist

♀ • ♂ Antigone Books, 600 N 4th Ave; 85705 520-792-3715

Community Centers (see also Women's Centers)

♀ ★ (⚥) Wingspan: Tucson's Lesbian, Gay & Bisexual Community Center, 422 N 4th Ave; 85705 520-624-1779 *The Center.*

Counseling/Therapy: Private

♀ • ⚥ Hatley, Scott, MS, CSW, 1918 E Edison St; 85719 520-321-1918 "Counseling & psychotherapy; 16 yrs experience with gay men & women."

Erotica (Printed, Visual, Equipment)

♀ ○ Bookstore Southwest, 5754 E Speedway Blvd; 85712-5024 520-790-1550

♀ ○ Caesar's, 2540 N Oracle Rd; 85705 520-622-9479

♀ ○ ♂ Continental, 2655 N Campbell Ave; 85719 520-427-8402

♀ • ♂ Speedway Adult Books & Videos, 3660 E Speedway; 85716 520-795-7467

♀ ○ Tropicana Motor Hotel Adult Bookstore, 617 W Miracle Mile; 85705 520-622-2289

Gifts, Cards, Pride & Novelty Items

♀ • (?⚥) 4 R Pride Productions, PO Box 77389; 85703-7389 520-579-7000; 800-579-7001; Fax 520-579-1191

Organizations/Resources: Family

♀ PFLAG, PO Box 36264; 85740-6264 520-575-8660

Organizations/Resources: Political/Legislative

♀ ★ (?⚥) Lambda Democratic Caucus, PO Box 77389; 85703-7389 520-579-7000

Organizations/Resources: Sexual Focus (Leather, S/M, etc) & Safe Sex Promotion

♂ Desert Leathermen, PO Box 1856; 85702 520-323-9520

Organizations/Resources: Social, Recreational & Support Groups (see also Sport/Dance/Outdoor)

♂ Arizona Nude Dudes—Phoenix, PO Box 64044; 85728-4044

♂ ★⚥ Tucson Prime Timers, c/o George Kaplan, 405 E Wetmore #117-104; 85705-1743 520-887-7493 compuserve 75534,3077 "Social organization for mature gay & bisexual men."

Organizations/Resources: Sport/Dance/Outdoor

♀ Cactus Wrens (Bowling), 1630 S Alvernon; 85711 520-327-6561

♀ ★ (?⚥) G.O./Tucson, 3750 N Country Club Rd #44; 85716-1264 520-325-7607

♀ ★⚥ T-Squares, PO Box 2102; 85702-2102 *d*

Organizations/Resources: Student, Academic, Alumni/ae

♀ ★ ♂ USUA Bisexual Gay & Lesbian Association, University of Arizona, Bldg 19, Rm 215; 85721 520-621-7585 Fax 520-621-6147

Publications

→ *Observer.* p.151

Real Estate

♀ • Eggers, Martin G., PO Box 405; 85702-0405 520-327-1307

♀ • ⚥ Lynn, Gloria & Radecki, Barbara, Sula Rose Shephard Realty, 7920 N Patrick Henry Place; 85741 520-797-1626 Fax 520-544-9649

♀ • Sierra Investments, 3750 N Country Club #44; 85716-1264 520-325-7607

Religious Organizations & Publications

♀ ★⚥ Cornerstone Fellowship, Inc., 2902 N Geronimo; 85705 520-622-4626 Services Sun 9am; 10.30am; Wed 7pm.

♀ ★ Metropolitan Community Church/Tucson, 3269 N Mountain Ave; 85719-2245 520-292-9151

Travel & Tourist Services (see also Accommodation)

♀ ○⚥ Fantasy Travel, 610 E Knox Dr; 85705 520-293-2620

Yuma

Bars, Restaurants, Clubs, Discos

♂ Two Thirty Club, 232 S 4th Ave; 85364-2232 520-782-9225

Erotica (Printed, Visual, Equipment)

♀ • ⚥ Bargain Box, 408 E 16th; 85364 520-782-6742

Arkansas

State/County Resources

☎ Arkansas Gay & Lesbian Task Force Switchboard 501-666-3340

AIDS/HIV Support, Education, Advocacy, Publications

♀ ★ Arkansas AIDS Foundation, 5911 H St, Little Rock, AR 72205-3239 501-663-7833; 800-364-AIDS (AR)

♀ ☆ Helping People With AIDS, PO Box 4397, Little Rock, AR 72204 501-666-6900

Legal Services & Resources

♀ ☆ (♂) American Civil Liberties Union of Arkansas (ACLU), 103 W Capitol #1120, Little Rock, AR 72201 501-374-2660

Organizations/Resources: General, Multipurpose, Pride

♀ ★⚥ Arkansas Gay & Lesbian Task Force, PO Box 45053, Little Rock, AR 72214 501-666-3340 (Little Rock); 800-448-8305 (Statewide) 7.30-10.30pm. Pub *Triangle Rising.*

Organizations/Resources: Political/Legislative

♀ Arkansas Women's Political Caucus, PO Box 2494, Little Rock, AR 72203

Organizations/Resources: Sport/Dance/Outdoor

♀ ★ ♂ Diamond State Rodeo Association, PO Box 806, Little Rock, AR 72203-0806 501-562-4466 Pub *Diamond State Lariat.*

Publications

♀ ★ *Ozark Feminist Review*, PO Box 1662, Fayetteville, AR 72702

Real Estate

♀ • Community Real Estate Referrals, 800-346-5592 "Free referral to gay/gay-supportive realtor in any USA city/state (including Virgin Is. & Puerto Rico). Sorry, no rentals!"
✦ *Community Real Estate Referrals advertisement back cover*

Switchboards, Helplines, Phone Information

♀ ★⚥ Arkansas Gay & Lesbian Task Force Switchboard, 501-666-3340; 800-448-8305 (Statewide) 6.30-10.30pm.

Gardener's Cottage
Eureka Springs, Arkansas
1-800-833-3394
Private • Historic District
Country Decor • Jacuzzi for 2
Full Kitchen • Cable TV
Porch Swing • Hammock

Cedarberry Cottage Bed & Breakfast
3 Kingshighway
Eureka Springs
AR 72632
1-800-590-2424
(501) 253-6115
Eureka's Storybook Inn

El Dorado

AIDS/HIV Support, Education, Advocacy, Publications

♀ South Arkansas Fights Aids, 1616 W Block; 71730

Eureka Springs

Accommodation: Hotels, B&B, Resorts, Campgrounds

♂ • Arbour Glen Victorian B&B Inn, 7 Lema; 72632 800-515-GLEN

♂ ○ **Cedarberry Cottage Bed & Breakfast, 3 Kings Hwy; 72632 501-253-6115**
✦ *Cedarberry Cottage Bed & Breakfast advertisement page 156*

♂ ○ Cliff Cottage and The Place Next Door, A Bed & Breakfast Inn, 13 Armstrong St; 72632 800-799-7409

♀ ○ Golden Gate Cottages, Rte. 5, Box 182; 72632 501-253-5291

♂ • ♿ Greenwood Hollow Ridge Bed & Breakfast, Rt 4, Box 155; 72632 501-253-5283

♂ ○ Maple Leaf Inn Bed & Breakfast, 6 Kingshighway; 72632 501-253-6876; 800-372-6542

♂ • (♿) Pond Mountain Lodge B&B, Rte 1, Box 50; 72632 501-253-5877; 800-583-8043 reservations

♂ • **Rock Cottage Gardens, a bed & breakfast inn, 10 Eugenia St; 72632 (on the Historic Loop) 501-253-8659; 800-624-6646**

♂ ○ **Singleton House Bed & Breakfast, 11 Singleton; 72632 501-253-9111; 800-833-3394 "5 units & private guest cottage available at separate location."**
✦ *Singleton House Bed & Breakfast advertisement page 156*

Accommodation: Reservations & Exchanges (see also Travel)

♀ ○ Bed & Breakfast Reservation Service, 501-253-9111 "Select from 30 inns & cottages. Passion Play & Dinner Train reservations."

Bars, Restaurants, Clubs, Discos

♀ • Center Street Restaurant & Bar, 10 Center St; 72632 501-253-8071 *BRDE* Dinner 5-10pm; bar open 5pm-2am.

♀ Chelsea's Corner Cafe & Bar, 10 Mountain St; 72632 501-253-6723 *BR*

Real Estate

♂ • Century 21 Woodland Real Estate, 58 Kingshighway; 72632 501-253-7321 Ask for Karen Kinsel.

Religious Organizations & Publications

⚥ ★ Metropolitan Community Church of the Living Springs, PO Box 365; 72632 / 17 Elk St 501-253-9337

Fayetteville

AIDS/HIV Support, Education, Advocacy, Publications

♂ ☆ Washington County AIDS Task Force, PO Box 4224; 72702 501-443-AIDS Hotline 7pm-7am.

Archives/Libraries/History Projects

⚥ ★ (♿) Women's Library, 17 1/2 N Block St; 72701-6018 501-521-8496 Open Thu 3.30-6.30pm; Sat noon-2am.

Bars, Restaurants, Clubs, Discos

⚥ • Ron's Place, PO Box 367; 72702-0367 / 523 West Poplar 501-442-3052

Bookstores: General

♂ ○ (♿) Hays & Sanders Bookstore, 25 N Block; 72701 501-442-0832

Bookstores: Recovery, Metaphysical, & other Specialty

♂ ○ ♿♿ Passages, 200 W Dickson; 72701 (moving from 434 N College Ave in March 1995) 501-442-5845

Organizations/Resources: Political/Legislative

⚥ ★ Gay & Lesbian Action Delegation (GLAD), PO Box 2897; 72702 501-521-4509

Organizations/Resources: Student, Academic, Alumni/ae

⚥ ★ ♿♿ Gay, Lesbian & Bisexual Student Association (GLBSA), AU 517; 72701 501-582-3482

Religious Organizations & Publications

⚥ ★ MCC Of The Ozarks, PO Box 92; 72702-0092 501-443-4278

Fort Smith

Bars, Restaurants, Clubs, Discos

⚥ • ♿♿ Court Garden, 305 Garrison Ave; 72901 501-783-9822 *BDEP* 5pm-5am.
✦ *Court Garden advertisement page 157*

⚥ Kinkead's, 1004 1/2 Garrison Ave; 72901-2613 501-783-9347

Hot Springs

Bars, Restaurants, Clubs, Discos

♀ • ♿♿ Our House Lounge & Restaurant, 660 E Grand Ave; 71901-4448 501-624-6868 *BDf* Mon-Fri 7pm-3am; Sat to 2am. "Female impersonator shows monthly; occasionally male strippers."

Little Rock

AIDS/HIV Support, Education, Advocacy, Publications

⚥ ACT-UP/Little Rock, 1419 S Taylor; 72204 501-661-9408

⚥ ☆ ♿ AIDS Support Group Of The Psychotherapy Center, 210 Pulaski; 72201 501-374-3605 Dr Ralph A. Hyman

⚥ RAIN-Arkansas, 2002 S Fillmore St #12; 72204-4909 501-664-4346

Art & Photography (see also Graphic Design)

⚥ • Shields-Marley Studios, 117 S Victory #1315; 72201 501-372-6148 "Commercial photography, specializing in food for advertising & architectural interiors."

Bars, Restaurants, Clubs, Discos

⚥ • ♿ Backstreet Inc., 1021 Jessie Rd, Unit Q; 72202 501-664-2744; 501-666-6900 *DECWP* Opens 9pm.

⚥ • ♿ Discovery III, Inc., 1021 Jessie Rd, Unit Z; 72202 501-664-4784; 501-666-6900 *DEP* Wed-Sun opens 9pm. Memberships available at door.

⚥ ○♿ Michael's (at Little Rock Inn), 601 Center; 72203 501-376-8301

⚥ • Silver Dollar, 2710 Asher Ave; 72204 501-663-9886

Bookstores: Gay/Lesbian/Feminist

⚥ ○♿ Women's Project, 2224 Main St; 72206 501-372-5113

Counseling/Therapy: Private

⚥ • ♿ Gay Counseling Service of the Psychotherapy Center, 210 Pulaski; 72201 501-374-3605 Dr. Ralph A. Hyman Free gay support group Tue 5-6.30pm.

Funding: Endowment, Fundraising, Scholarship

⚥ ★ (?♿) The League, PO Box 56117; 72215

Gifts, Cards, Pride & Novelty Items

⚥ • ♿ Twisted Entertainment, Inc, 7201 Asher Ave; 72204-7657 501-568-4262

⚥ ○ Wild Card, 400 N Bowman; 72212 501-223-9071

Organizations/Resources: Youth (see also Family)

⚥ ★ ♿ PALS (People of Alternative Lifestyles), 210 Pulaski St; 72201 501-374-3605 Meets Wed 6.45-8.15pm. "Teenagers & young adults up to age 22."

Religious Organizations & Publications

⚥ ☆ Holy Cross Ecumenical Catholic Church, 400 S Rosetta St; 72205 501-663-7041

⚥ ★ ♿ Metropolitan Community Church of the Rock, PO Box 1964; 72203-1964 / 2017 Chandler, North Little Rock 501-753-7075

⚥ ★ ♿ Spirit Song Metropolitan Community Church, PO Box 250307; 72225-0307 501-223-2828 Meets Sun 2pm at 1818 Reservoir Rd.

⚥ ☆ ♿ Unitarian Universalist Church, 1818 Reservoir Rock Rd; 72207 501-225-1503

Women's Centers

♀ ☆ ♿ Women's Project, 2224 Main St; 72206 501-372-5113 Fax 501-372-0009 Pub *Transformation*. We also publish the book *Homophobia: A Weapon of Sexism*. (See also Bookstores)

Mountain Home

Organizations/Resources: Social, Recreational & Support Groups (see also Sport/Dance/Outdoor)

⚥ ★ A.B.S., Rte 8, Box 264-A; 72653 (naturist/nudist)

Texarkana

AIDS/HIV Support, Education, Advocacy, Publications

⚥ ☆♿ Texarkana AIDS Project (TAP), PO Box 3243; 75504 501-773-1994

Bars, Restaurants, Clubs, Discos

⚥ • The Gig, 201 East St (Hwy 71 South); 75504 501-773-6900

California

State/County Resources

Accommodation: Reservations & Exchanges (see also Travel)

⚥ • Home Suite Hom, PO Box 762 Succ. C, Montréal, QC H2L 4L6 415-242-9653; 800-429-4983 US & Canada; "Travel & accommodation network for those offering or seeking hospitality & lodging exchange, private B&B, & low cost rentals."

✦ *Home Suite Hom advertisement page 122*

Addictive Behavior, Substance Abuse, Recovery

⚥ • (♿) Pride Institute, 800-54-PRIDE "The nation's only accredited chemical dependency treatment center exclusively for Gay, Lesbian & Bisexual People."

Broadcast Media

⚥ ★ Night Scene, 13 NW 13th Ave, Portland, OR 97209 503-244-NITE Cable access TV show: call for details.

Counseling/Therapy: Nonprofit

♀ ★ ♿ Mark Pope Career Development Center, 760 Market St #962 415-296-8024 Fax 415-296-8021 Pub *Newsletter*. "Nonprofit career counseling for lesbians & gay men. Multicultural staff. Low fee."

Funding: Endowment, Fundraising, Scholarship

⚥ ★ (?♿) Whitman-Brooks Foundation, PO Box 48320, Los Angeles, CA 90048 213-650-5752

Health Care (see also AIDS Services)

⚥ ★ (?♿) Lesbian/Gay Health & Health Policy Foundation, mail to LGHHPF, PO Box 168; 308 Westwood Plaza, UCLA, Los Angeles, CA 90095-1647 800-918-6888 izk1sqh@mvs.oac.ucla.edu

Legal Services & Resources

⚥ ★ ♿ American Civil Liberties Union/Northern California Gay Rights Chapter (ACLU), 1663 Mission St, 4th flr, San Francisco, CA 94103 415-621-2488 Pub *ACLU-NC Gay Rights Chapter Bulletin*.

Legal

♀ ★ ♿ American Civil Liberties Union So. Cal Lesbian & Gay Rights Chapter (ACLU), 1616 Beverly Blvd, Los Angeles, CA 90026 213-977-9500 ext 237

Organizations/Resources: Business & Professional

♀ ★ California Association of Lesbian & Gay Elected Officials (CAL/G EGO), 824 Winslow St #214, Redwood City, CA 94063 415-386-7112

♂ ★ Gay Officers Action League (GOAL), PO Box 69917, Los Angeles, CA 90069 213-612-6577

♀ ★ National Lesbian/Gay Journalists Association/So Cal, PO Box 1552, Los Angeles, CA 90078-1552 213-871-8548 nlgja@aol.com

♀ ★ Southern California Physicians for Human Rights, 31112 Holly Dr, Laguna Beach, CA 92677-2621 714-499-4855

Organizations/Resources: Ethnic, Multicultural

♀ ★ Asian Pacifica Sisters, PO Box 170596, San Francisco, CA 94117 Pub *Phoenix Rising.*

♂ LLEFO California (Latino/a Lesbian & Gay Organization), PO Box 40916, San Francisco, CA 94140

Organizations/Resources: Military/Veterans

♀ ★♿♿ Veterans C.A.R.E., PO Box 26485, Los Angeles, CA 90026-0485 310-529-6969 Fax 213-666-8495 Pub *Veterans C.A.R.E. Aware.* "Working to end military discrimination; upgrade discharges; educate the public; help AIDS patients in VA hospitals."

♀ ★ Veterans C.A.R.E., Inc: Northern California, PO Box 3126, Rohnert Park, CA 94927-3126 707-829-5393

Organizations/Resources: Political/Legislative

♀ ★ Log Cabin California, 932 Rembrandt Drive, Laguna Beach, CA 92651-3443 714-494-6271 Pub *Newsletter.* "Republican political group."

Organizations/Resources: Sport/Dance/Outdoor

♀ ★ Golden State Gay Rodeo Association, 8424A Santa Monica Blvd #250, West Hollywood, CA 90069 619-293-0666

Organizations/Resources: Transgender & Transgender Publications

T ☆ ♿ ETVC (Educational TV Channel), PO Box 426486, San Francisco, CA 94142 510-549-2665

Performing Arts: Entertainment, Music, Recording, Theater, etc.

♀ ★ Taken By The Faeries, 922 El Cajon Way, Palo Alto, CA 94303 415-856-9479 "Queer performance for the new millennium."

Publications

♀ • *Gay & Lesbian Times,* PO Box 34624, San Diego, CA 92163 619-299-6397 Fax 619-299-3430 Southern California: San Diego, Orange & LA Counties.

♀ • *The Lesbian News,* PO Box 5128, Santa Monica, CA 90409-5128 213-656-0258 ext 113

♀ • *OutNOW!,* 45 N 1st St #124, San Jose, CA 95113 408-991-1873 Fax 408-739-3054 jct@netcom.com "News & features for our Northern California community, every other Tuesday."

♀ • *Voice Magazine,* 4086 Alabama St #2, San Diego, CA 92104-2422 619-281-8511 Fax 619-281-9055

Real Estate

♀ • Community Real Estate Referrals, 800-346-5592 "Free referral to gay/gay-supportive realtor in any USA city/state (including Virgin Is. & Puerto Rico). Sorry, no rentals!"
✦ *Community Real Estate Referrals advertisement back cover*

Religious Organizations & Publications

♀ ☆ (?♿) Humanist Community, PO Box 60069, Palo Alto, CA 94306-0069 415-424-8626 Sun 10.45am-noon at Stanford University. Pub *Humanist Community News.*

♀ ☆ UCCL/GC (United Church Coalition for Lesbian/Gay Concerns), 20 Woodside Ave, San Francisco, CA 94127 415-576-1554

Alleghany: see Grass Valley

Anaheim: see Orange County

Arcata

Bookstores: General

♀ ○ Northtown Books, 957 H St.; 95521 707-822-2834

Azusa: see Los Angeles Area

Bakersfield

Addictive Behavior, Substance Abuse, Recovery

♀ ★ Alcoholics Anonymous, Gay/Lesbian, c/o MCC Box 30357; 93385-1357 805-327-3724

Bars, Restaurants, Clubs, Discos

♀ Casablanca, 1030 20th St; 93301 805-324-1384

♂ The Place, 3500 Wilson Rd; 93309 805-834-7431

Religious Organizations & Publications

♀ ★ (♿) Metropolitan Community Church of the Harvest, 2421 Alta Vista; 93305 805-327-3724

Berkeley: see East Bay Area

Beverly Hills: see Los Angeles Area

Big Bear

Real Estate

♀ ○ Olsen, Kirk S., 909-315-8207 70541,2531@compuserve

Brea

Travel & Tourist Services (see also Accommodation)

♀ • All Destinations Travel, Inc., 2810 E Imperial Highway; 92621 714-528-9100

Buena Park: see Orange County

Burbank: see Los Angeles Area

Camarillo: see Santa Barbara/Ventura County Area

Cameron Park: see Sacramento

Campbell: see San Jose Area

Cathedral City: see Palm Springs

Chico

Community Centers (see also Women's Centers)

♀ ★♿♿ Stonewall Alliance of Chico, PO Box 8855; 95927 916-893-3336 Pub *Centerstone.*

Organizations/Resources: Student, Academic, Alumni/ae

♀ ★ Chico State Gay/Lesbian Union, CSUC; 95926

Chinese Camp: see Sonora

Chula Vista: see San Diego Area

Claremont: see San Bernardino/Riverside/Pomona Area

Clearlake
Accommodation: Hotels, B&B, Resorts, Campgrounds
♀ ○ (♿) Blue Fish Cove Resort, PO Box 1252, Clearlake Oaks; 95423-1252 707-998-1769

Colton
Travel & Tourist Services (see also Accommodation)
♂ • (♿) Go Aweigh! Travel, 2584 Carbon Ct, #2; 92324 909-370-4554

Concord: see East Bay Area

Costa Mesa: see Orange County

Cotati
Women's Centers
♀ Sitting Room, 170 E Cotati Ave; 94928 707-664-2140

Culver City: see Los Angeles Area

Cupertino: see San Jose Area

Daly City
Organizations/Resources: Social, Recreational & Support Groups (see also Sport/Dance/Outdoor)
♂ ★ (♿) Golden Gate Connection, PO Box 2328; 94017-0328 415-615-6712 (Hotline) (chapter of Affiliated Big Men's Club)

Davis
Business, Financial & Secretarial
♀ • The Organizer: Lois Richter, PO Box 1011; 95617-1011 916-758-5058 "Editing; office management; computer programming & consulting."

Organizations/Resources: Student, Academic, Alumni/ae
♂ ★ (♿) Bisexuals, Gays, Lesbians at Davis (BGLAD), Box 163 UCD Student Activities Office; 95616 916-757-3848 *The Lavender Cow.*

♂ ★ Delta Lambda Phi Fraternity, University of California, Davis, Student Activities Office, CSU; 95616 800-587-FRAT

Women's Centers
♀ ☆ ♿ Women's Resources & Research Center, 10 Lower Freeborn Hall, UCD Memorial Union; 95616 916-752-3372

Eagle Rock
Grooming Services
♀ • ♿ Robins Beauty Studio, 2042 Colorado Blvd; 90041 213-344-1161 Mon-Sat 9am-5pm; or by appointment.

East Bay Area
☎ Pacific Center for Human Growth 510-548-8283

Accommodation: Hotels, B&B, Resorts, Campgrounds
Berkeley
♀ ○ Elmwood House Bed & Breakfast, 2609 College Ave, Berkeley; 94704 510-540-5123

AIDS/HIV Support, Education, Advocacy, Publications
♀ ACT UP East Bay, PO Box 8074, Oakland; 94608 510-704-0483

♀ ☆ ♿ AIDS Project East Bay, 651 20th St, Oakland; 94612-1312 510-834-8181

♀ ☆ ♿ Diablo Valley AIDS Center, 2253 Concord Blvd, Concord; 94520 510-686-3822

Bars, Restaurants, Clubs, Discos
Berkeley
♀ ☆ ♿ La Peña Cultural Center, 3105 Shattuck, Berkeley; 94703 510-849-2568 Tue-Sat 1pm-mdnt.

Hayward
♂ • Driftwood Lounge, 22170 Mission Blvd, Hayward; 94541 510-581-2050 *CWEd*

♂ • (♿) IJ'S Getaway, 21859 Mission Blvd, Hayward; 94541 510-582-8078 *BDE*

♂ Rumors, 22554 Main St, Hayward; 94540 510-733-2334

♂ • ♿ **Turf Club, 22517 Mission Blvd, Hayward; 94541** 510-881-9877 *BdECWf* 10am-2am.

Oakland
♀ Bella Napoli, 2330 Telegraph Hill, Oakland; 94612 510-893-5552

♂ Bench & Bar, 120 11th St, Oakland; 94607 510-444-2266

♀ ♿ Brick Hut Cafe, 2519 San Pablo Ave 510-486-1124 *R*

♂ Town & Country, 2022 Telegraph Ave, Oakland; 94612 510-444-4978

♀ • ♿ White Horse Inn, 6551 Telegraph Ave, Oakland; 94609 510-652-3820 *BD*

San Leandro
♂ • (♿) Babe's/Bill's The Eagle, 14572 E 14th St, San Leandro; 94578 510-357-7343; 510-351-9974 *BDE* 10am-2am.

Walnut Creek
♂ • ♿ D.J.'s Piano Bar & Grill, 1535 Olympic Blvd, Walnut Creek; 94596 510-930-0300 *BRE* 4pm-2am; Sun 11am-2am. Dinner Wed-Sat 6-10pm; Sun brunch noon-3pm, dinner 4-7pm.

♂ • ♿ JR's Club, 2520 Camino Diablo, Walnut Creek; 94596 510-256-1200 *BD* 5pm-2am; Fri & Sat to 4am. Live entertainment some nights. "Modern, elegant facility with very friendly people."

♂ • ♿ The Twelve-Twenty, 1220 Pine St, Walnut Creek; 94596 510-938-4550 *Bd* 4pm-2am.

Bookstores: Gay/Lesbian/Feminist
♂ • ♿ Boadecia's Books, 398 Colusa Ave, Kensington; 94707 (Kensington/North Berkeley) 510-559-9184 11am-9pm; Sun to 7pm.

♀ • ♿ Mama Bears, 6536 Telegraph Ave, Oakland; 94609 510-428-9684 Bookstore & coffee house.

♀ • (♿) West Berkeley Women's Books, 2514 San Pablo Ave, Berkeley; 94702 510-204-9399

Bookstores: General
♀ ○ ♿ Cody's Books, Inc., 2454 Telegraph Ave, Berkeley; 94704 510-845-7852 10am-9pm; Fri & Sat to 10pm.

♀ ○ (♿) Gaia Bookstore, 1400 Shattuck, Berkeley; 94709 510-548-4172

Business, Financial & Secretarial
♀ • The Facilitator, 2124 Kittredge #257, Berkeley; 94704 510-843-9077 "Professional organizer for home & business."

Community Centers (see also Women's Centers)
♀ ★ Pacific Center for Human Growth, 2712 Telegraph Ave, Berkeley; 94705 510-548-8283; 510-841-6224 Switchboard

Counseling/Therapy: Private

♀ • (♂♂) Boland, Jim, Ph.D., 1466 Hopkins St, Berkeley; 94702 510-524-8540

Erotica (Printed, Visual, Equipment)

♀ ○ Adult Books & Video, 2298 Monument Blvd, Pleasant Hill; 94523 510-676-2982

♀ • ♂♂ Good Vibrations—Berkeley, 2504 San Pablo Ave #FY, Berkeley; 94702 510-841-8987 "Books, toys, vibrators."

♀ • (♂♂) Passion Flower, 4 Yosemite Ave, Oakland; 94611 510-601-7750 Fax 510-658-9645 11am-7pm; Fri & Sat to 8pm; Sun noon-6pm. *The Vine.* "Workshops on many subjects."

Health Care (see also AIDS Services)

♀ ☆♂♂ Berkeley Free Clinic, 2339 Durant Ave, Berkeley; 94704-1670 510-548-2570

♀ ☆♂♂ Berkeley Women's Health Clinic, 2908 Ellsworth, Berkeley; 94705 510-843-6194 "Homeopathy, chiropractic, & Western medical care; sliding scale, insurance, MediCal. Lesbian Clinic (by & for Lesbians) alternate Mon eves: call for appointment."

♀ • MacNair, Barbra, L.Ac., 3021 Telegraph Ave #B, Berkeley; 94705 510-649-8054 "Licensed acupuncturist & herbalist."

Health Clubs, Gyms, Saunas

♂ • Steamworks, 2107 4th St, Berkeley; 94710 510-845-8992 *P*

Jewelry

♀ • ♂ Fisher's Custom Design Jewelry, 1488 Solano Ave, Berkeley; 94706 510-524-0400

Legal Services & Resources

♀ • ♂♂ Tilley, Patricia G., 449 15th St #303, Oakland; 94612 510-541-4753

Organizations/Resources: Ethnic, Multicultural

♀ Black Women's Exchange, 3419 Martin L King Way, Oakland; 94609 510-601-9066

♀ ★ (♂) NIA Collective, PO Box 21462, Oakland; 94620 (collective of Black lesbians)

♂ Umoja, PO Box 4718, Berkeley; 94704-0718 510-286-7992

Organizations/Resources: Family
The Family Next Door, PO Box 21580, Oakland; 94620 510-482-5778 "A newsletter for Lesbian & Gay parents & their friends."

♂ Lesbian & Gay Parenting Group (GLPG), Box 32, 2550 Shattuck Ave, Berkeley; 94704 510-540-5734

Organizations/Resources: General, Multipurpose, Pride

♀ ★♂♂ Queer Resource Center (QRC), 300 Eshleman Hall, UC-Berkeley ((office: Room 407), Berkeley; 94720-4500 510-642-6942; 510-643-8429; qrc@ocf.berkeley.edu Pub *Queer Resource Guide.*

Organizations/Resources: Political/Legislative

♂ ★♂♂ East Bay Lesbian/Gay Democratic Club, PO Box 443, Berkeley; 94701 510-665-7539

Organizations/Resources: Sexual Focus (Leather, S/M, etc) & Safe Sex Promotion

♂ ★ Black Jack, PO Box 10776, Oakland; 94610-0776 800-490-8601

Organizations/Resources: Social, Recreational & Support Groups (see also Sport/Dance/Outdoor)

♂ ★ (?♂) Fremont Men, PO Box 1238, Fremont; 94538 510-713-2455

♂ Hortiphiles, PO Box 19102, Oakland; 94619 415-851-1022

Organizations/Resources: Sport/Dance/Outdoor

♀ ☆ Camping Women/Bay Area, 655 Maud Ave, San Leandro; 94577 510-351-2611

♀ ★ (?♂) Lavender Winds Kite Club, PO Box 5118 #464, Fremont; 94537 510-797-6997 Pub *Newsletter.*

♀ Sierra Club G.L.S./Bay Chapter, 6014 College Ave, Oakland; 94618

♀ ★ Wilderness Women, 5329 Manila Ave, Oakland; 94618 Pub *Newsletter.*

Organizations/Resources: Student, Academic, Alumni/ae

♂ ★♂♂ Boalt Hall/UC Berkeley School of Law Lesbian Gay Bisexual Caucus, 37 Boalt Hall, UC Berkeley, Berkeley; 94720

♂ ★♂♂ Multicultural Bisexual/Gay/Lesbian Alliance (MBLGA), 411 Eshleman Hall, UC Berkeley, Berkeley; 94720 510-642-6942 24 hrs.

Religious Organizations & Publications

♂ ★ (♂) Diablo Valley Metropolitan Community Church, PO Box 139, Concord; 94522-0139 510-945-6859; 510-827-2960

♀ Metropolitan Community Church of Greater Hayward, PO Box 247, San Lorenzo; 94580 510-481-9720

♂ ★ ♂ New Life Metropolitan Community Church, 1823 9th St, Berkeley; 94710-2102 510-843-9355 Sun 12.30pm.

Travel & Tourist Services (see also Accommodation)

♀ ○♂♂ New Venture Travel (John Reynolds), 404 22nd St, Oakland; 94612 510-835-3800 Fax 510-835-7865

Video Sales, Rentals, Services (see also Erotica)

♀ • Very Video, 22523 Mission Blvd, Hayward; 94541 510-881-0185 11am-2am. "Books, mags. gifts, rubber goods, etc."
✦ *Very Video advertisement page 161*

El Cerrito: see East Bay Area

El Monte

Bars, Restaurants, Clubs, Discos

♂ Infinities, 2253 Tyler Ave, South El Monte; 91733 714-575-9164

♂ ○ Sugar Shack, 4101 Arden Drive; 91731 818-448-6579 *Bdf* 3pm-2am.

El Serano: see Los Angeles Area

Escondido: see San Diego Area

Eureka

Bookstores: General

♀ ○ ♂ Booklegger, 402 2nd St; 95501 707-445-1344

Fairfield/Vacaville Area

☎ **Solano County Gay & Lesbian Information Line**
707-448-1010

Bookstores: General

♀ • ♂ Vacaville Book Co, 315 Main St, Vacaville; 95688 707-449-0550 Mon-Sat 10am-8pm.

Organizations/Resources: Social, Recreational & Support Groups (see also Sport/Dance/Outdoor)

♂ ★ ♦ Solano Lambda Men's Association (SLMA), PO Box 9, Vacaville; 95696-0009 707-448-1010

♀ ★ (?♦) Women Preferring Women, PO Box 9, Vacaville; 95696-0009 707-448-1010 message tape.

Switchboards, Helplines, Phone Information

♀ ★ Solano County Gay & Lesbian Information Line, PO Box 9, Vacaville; 95696-0009 707-448-1010 message tape only.

Forestville: see Russian River

Fort Bragg

Bookstores: General

♂ ○ (♦) Windsong Books & Records, 324 N Main St; 95437 707-964-2050

Fresno

☎ Gay United Services Inc. 209-268-3541

AIDS/HIV Support, Education, Advocacy, Publications

♂ ☆♦♦ Central Valley AIDS Team, PO Box 4640; 93744 / 1999 Tuolumne #625 209-264-AIDS Pub *Team Work.* "Support & education; housing for PWA/ARCs."

Bars, Restaurants, Clubs, Discos

♀ The Express, 708 N Blackstone; 93706 209-233-1791

♂ • Palace, 4030 E Belmont Ave; 93702 209-264-8283

♂ • ♦♦ The Red Lantern, 4618 E Belmont; 93702 209-251-5898 *CW*

Bookstores: Gay/Lesbian/Feminist

♀ • (♦♦) Valley Women Books & Gifts, 1118 N Fulton; 93728 209-233-3600 10am-9pm; Sat & Sun to 6pm. *The Inner Word.* "Free lectures, workshops; information referral, etc."

Community Centers (see also Women's Centers)

♂ ★♦♦ Gay United Services Inc., Box 4640; 93744 / 625 N. Palm 209-268-3541

Erotica (Printed, Visual, Equipment)

♂ ○♦♦ Wildcat Books, 1535 Fresno St; 93706 209-237-4525

Organizations/Resources: Political/Legislative

♂ Log Cabin Fresno, 1316 Salam St; 93720 209-261-0835

Travel & Tourist Services (see also Accommodation)

♂ • Travel Address-Galaxsea, 6465 N Blackstone Ave; 93710 209-432-9095

Fullerton: see Orange County

Garden Grove: see Orange County

Glendale: see Los Angeles Area

Grass Valley

Accommodation: Hotels, B&B, Resorts, Campgrounds

♂ • Kenton Mine Lodge, PO Box 942, Alleghany; 95910 916-287-3212 *BR* "Guest house & cabins, 4 hrs from San Francisco."

Grover City

Religious Organizations & Publications

♂ Metropolitan Community Church of the Central Coast, PO Box 1117; 93483-1117 408-481-9376

Gualala

Bookstores: General

♂ • ♦ Gualala Books, PO Box 765; 95445 / 39175 Hwy 1 South 707-884-4255 Mon-Sat 10am-5pm; Sun 11am-4pm.

Guerneville: see Russian River

Hawthorne: see Los Angeles Area

Hayward: see East Bay Area

Healdsburg

Organizations/Resources: Family

♂ ☆♦♦ PFLAG, PO Box 1266; 95448 707-431-8364 "Parents, Families & Friends of Lesbians & Gays."

Hermosa Beach: see Los Angeles

Highland: see San Bernardino/Riverside/Pomona Area

Highland Park: see Los Angeles Area

Hollywood: see Los Angeles Area

Huntington Beach

Counseling/Therapy: Private

♀ • Benjamin, Shela, LCSW, 213-892-8433

Travel & Tourist Services (see also Accommodation)

♂ ○♦♦ Golden Eagle Travel, 17412 Beach Blvd; 92647 213-848-9090 Fax 714-842-6494

♀ • Worldwide Travel & Cruises, 8907 Warner Ave #231; 92647 310-848-5254; 800-690-SHIP; Fax 714-848-9375 worldtrvlz@aol.com "We specialize in all gay travel destinations & cruises."

Idyllwild

Accommodation: Hotels, B&B, Resorts, Campgrounds

♀ • ♿ Fern Village Chalets & Motel, PO Box 886; 92549 909-659-2869

♀ • (♿) The Pine Cove Inn, PO Box 2181; 92549 909-659-5033 Fax 909-659-5033

♂ ○♿♿ Wilkum Inn, PO Box 1115; 92549 909-659-4087

Inglewood: see Los Angeles Area

Irvine: see Orange County

La Jolla: see San Diego Area

La Mirada

Accommodation: Hotels, B&B, Resorts, Campgrounds

♀ • (?♿) Whittier House B&B, PO Box 1799; 90638 213-941-7222

Laguna Beach: see Orange County

Lake Tahoe: see South Lake Tahoe

Lancaster

Bars, Restaurants, Clubs, Discos

♀ • ♿ Back Door, 1255 W Ave I; 93534 805-945-2566 *BD* 6pm-2am.

Religious Organizations & Publications

♀ ★ ♿ Sunrise Metropolitan Community Church of the Hi Desert, PO Box 886; 93584-0886 805-942-7076

Long Beach

☎ ONE in Long Beach 310-434-4455

Addictive Behavior, Substance Abuse, Recovery

♀ ☆ Atlantic Alano Club, 441 E 1st St; 90802-4405 310-432-7476

AIDS/HIV Support, Education, Advocacy, Publications

♀ ☆ (?♿) ACT-UP/Long Beach, 5595 E 7th St #174; 90804

♀ ☆♿♿ Being Alive/Long Beach, 994 Redondo Ave; 90804 310-434-9022 "Resource center for HIV+ people."

Bars, Restaurants, Clubs, Discos

♂ Birds of Paradise Cafe, 1800 E Broadway; 90802 310-590-8773 *BR*

♀ The Brit, 1744 E Broadway; 90802 310-432-9742

♂ The Broadway, 1100 E Broadway; 90804 310-432-3646

♀ • ♿♿ Club 5211/Inspiration, 5211 Atlantic Ave; 90805 310-428-5545 Mon-Thu 10.30am-2am; Fri & Sat 24 hrs.

♂ Club 740, 740 E Broadway; 90802 310-437-7705 *R* 5pm-2am.

♂ Club Broadway, 3348 E Broadway; 90805 310-438-7700

♀ ○ Executive Suite, 3248 E. Pacific Coast Hwy 310-597-3884 *BDE* Thu 8pm-2am; Fri & Sat 7pm-2am; Sun & Mon 6pm-2am.

♂ • ♿♿ Floyd's, 2913-17 E. Anaheim; 90804 310-433-9251 *BCLWd* Tue-Fri 4pm-2am; Sat 6pm-4am; Sun 2am-mdnt. Country/Western.

♀ Inn Kahoots, 1435 E Broadway; 90802 310-432-4146

♂ Mineshaft, 1720 E Broadway; 90802 310-436-2433

♀ • Que Sera, 1923 E 7th St; 90813 310-599-6170 3pm-2am.

♀ • Ripples, 5101 E Ocean Blvd; 90803 310-433-0357 *BDREP*

♂ Silver Fox, 411 Redondo Ave; 90814 310-439-6343

♀ • The Stallion, 5823 Atlantic Ave; 90805 310-422-5997

♀ Sweetwater Saloon, 1201 E Broadway; 90802 310-432-7044

♀ Whistle Stop, 5873 Atlantic Ave; 90805 310-422-7927

♂ • Wolfs, 2020 E Artesia Blvd; 90805 310-422-1928 *L*

♂ • ♿♿ The Zone, 1230 E 223rd St #206, Carson; 90745 310-518-HOMO *P*

Bookstores: Gay/Lesbian/Feminist

♀ • ♿ Pearls Booksellers, 224 Redondo Ave; 90803 310-438-8875 11am-7pm; Sat & Sun noon-5pm.

Bookstores: General

♀ ○ (♿) Bluff Park Rare Books, 2535 East Broadway; 90803 310-438-9830

♂ ○ Chelsea Bookstore, 2501 E Broadway; 90803 310-434-2220

♂ • ♿ Dodds Book Shop, 4818 E 2nd St; 90803 310-438-9948

Broadcast Media

♀ ★ Triangle Express Productions, PO Box 90711; 90809-0711 310-491-1046

Clothes

♀ • ♿♿ The Crypt On Broadway, 1712 E Broadway; 90802 310-983-6560 "Leather clothing."

♀ • ♿ Dick & Jane's Closet, 1734 E Broadway; 90802 310-435-8161 2-8pm; Sat noon-8pm; Sun noon-6pm. "Five percent of profit donated to Long Beach HIV Services."

Community Centers (see also Women's Centers)

♀ ★♿♿ The Center, 2017 E 4th St; 90814 310-434-4455 Mon-Fri 9am-10pm; Sat to 6pm.

Counseling/Therapy: Private

♀ • ♿♿ Thrasher, Bob, MA, 249 E Ocean Blvd #920; 90802-4849 310-435-1749

Erotica (Printed, Visual, Equipment)

♂ • ♿ Condom Wrap, 2038 E 4th St; 90814 310-430-3379 Mon-Sat 11am-8pm. "Condoms, lubricants, lingerie, games, cards, vibrators, dildos, gifts, toiletries."

Florists (see also Gardening)

♂ • Bel Shore Florist, 329 Redondo Ave; 90814 310-433-2485

Gifts, Cards, Pride & Novelty Items

♀ • ♿ Hot Stuff, 2121 E Broadway; 90803 310-433-0692

Legal Services & Resources

♂ • ♿♿ Loftin, A. Stephanie, 3530 Atlantic Ave #100; 90807-4569 310-989-3669

Organizations/Resources: Bisexual Focus

♀ ★♿♿ Bisexual Consultation Service, PO Box 20917; 90801 310-597-2799 gibbin@aol.com

Organizations/Resources: Business & Professional

♀ Community Business Network, 996 Redondo Ave #400; 90804

Organizations/Resources: Family

♀ ☆ ♿ PFLAG Long Beach, PO Box 8221; 90808 310-984-8335 "Parents, Families & Friends of Lesbians & Gays."

Organizations/Resources: General, Multipurpose, Pride

♂ ★ (♿) Long Beach Lesbian & Gay Pride, Inc., PO Box 2050; 90801 310-987-9191

♂ ★♿ ONE in Long Beach, 2017 E 4th St; 90814 310-434-4455 Mon-Fri 9am-10pm; Sat to 6pm. *The Post.*

Organizations/Resources: Political/Legislative

♂ ★ Long Beach Lambda Democratic Club, PO Box 14454; 90803 310-493-9032

Organizations/Resources: Social, Recreational & Support Groups (see also Sport/Dance/Outdoor)

♂ ★♿ Club Sappho, 5520 E 2nd St #1-446; 90803 800-SAP-PHO-1 *P* "Social organization."

Organizations/Resources: Sport/Dance/Outdoor

♂ Great Outdoors/Orange County—Long Beach, PO Box 30171; 90853-0171

Organizations/Resources: Student, Academic, Alumni/ae

♂ ★ Delta Lambda Phi Fraternity, California State University, Long Beach, Student Activities Office, CSU; 90840 800-587-FRAT

♂ ★ Lesbian, Gay & Bisexual Student Union, California State University at Long Beach, 1250 Bellflower Blvd; 90840 310-985-4585

Performing Arts: Entertainment, Music, Recording, Theater, etc.

♂ Gay Men's Chorus of Long Beach, PO Box 92873; 90809-2873 310-437-3031

♂ ★ (?♿) South Coast Chorale, PO Box 92524; 90809 310-349-6919

Pets & Pet Supplies

♀ ○ The Pet Nanny, 6475 E Pacific Coast Hwy #296; 90803 310-431-2233 "Specializing in loving care for 'pampered pets.' Licensed, bonded, insured."

Publications

♂ *The Directory Long Beach*, Turkey Media Services, 4102 E 7th St #621; 90804 310-434-7129

Religious Organizations & Publications

♂ ★ (?♿) Dignity/Long Beach, PO Box 92375; 90809-2375 310-984-8400 "Gay & Lesbian Catholics & their friends."

♂ ★♿ Metropolitan Community Church Long Beach, 5505 E Carson St #343, Lakewood; 90713-3056 310-425-5371 Worship: 2501 Palo Verde Ave, Long Beach.

Thrift/Consignment Stores

♀ ★ ♿ AIDS Assistance Thrift Store, 2238 E 7th St; 90804 310-987-5353

Travel & Tourist Services (see also Accommodation)

♀ ○ Royal Tours & Travel, 1742 East Broadway; 90802 310-983-7370

♀ ○ Touch Of Travel, 3918 Atlantic Ave; 90807 310-427-2144; 800-833-3387

Video Sales, Rentals, Services (see also Erotica)

♀ • ♿ Broadway Video Act II, 3401 E Broadway; 90803 310-433-1920 10am-10pm.

♀ ○ ♿ Broadway Video Rentals & Sales I, 2130 E Broadway; 90803 310-438-8919 10am-10pm.

Los Angeles Area

☎ Los Angeles Gay & Lesbian Community Services Center 213-993-7440

Accommodation: Hotels, B&B, Resorts, Campgrounds

Hollywood

♀ • **Winona Motel, 5131 Hollywood Blvd, Hollywood; 90027 310-213 663-1243 Fax 213-664-7758**
✦ *Winona Motel advertisement page 163*

Los Angeles

♂ • (♿) LA Private Guest House, 2239 Patricia Ave; 90064 310-837-8219 Fax 310-446-0080

Malibu

♀ ○ ♿ Malibu Beach Inn, 22878 Pacific Coast Highway, Malibu; 90265 310-456-6444

West Hollywood

♂ ○ Holloway Motel, 8465 Santa Monica Blvd, West Hollywood; 90069 213-654-2454

♀ ○ ♿ **Le Montrose Suite Hotel, 900 Hammond St, West Hollywood; 90069 310-855-1115; 800-776-0666 reservations**
✦ *Le Montrose Suite Hotel advertisement page 164*

♀ • (?♿) **Le Parc, 733 N West Knoll Dr, West Hollywood; 90069 310-855-8888; 800-5-SUITES; *BR***

♀ ○ ♿ **Ramada West Hollywood, 8585 Santa Monica Blvd, West Hollywood; 90069 310-652-6400; 800-845-8585; Fax 310-652-4207 *BR***
✦ *Ramada West Hollywood advertisement page 165*

♂ • San Vincente Inn, 837 N San Vincente Ave, West Hollywood; 90069 310-854-6915 Fax 310-659-3369

Addictive Behavior, Substance Abuse, Recovery

♀ ☆ Alcoholics Together Center, 1773 Griffith Park Blvd; 90026 213-663-8882

♀ ★♿ **Alcoholism Center for Women, 1147 S Alvarado St; 90006 213-381-8500 Fax 213-381-8525 Pub *ACW Newsletter.*** "Residential & out-participant recovery program, prevention, training & outreach. Ethnic-specific services for African-American & Latina lesbians; lesbian-focused alcohol services since 1974."

AIDS/HIV Support, Education, Advocacy, Publications

♀ ☆ ♿ ACT UP/LA, 3924 W Sunset Blvd #2; 90029 213-669-0702; 213-654-1639 Infoline; Fax 213-669-7302 Pub *Act UP/LA News.*

♀ ☆ ♿ Aid For AIDS, 8235 Santa Monica Blvd #200; 90046 213-656-1107 Pub *Newsletter.*

♀ ☆ ♁♁ AIDS Healthcare Foundation, 6255 W Sunset Blvd 16th flr; 90028 213-462-2273 Fax 213-962-8513 *The Caregiver*. Programs include AHF Clinics, AIDS hospices, & Out of the Closet Thrift Store.

♀ ☆ ♁♁ AIDS Project Los Angeles, 1313 Vine St; 90028 213-962-1600; 800-922-AIDS; Spanish 800-400-SIDA; TDD 800-553-AIDS; Multilanguage 800-922-2438; Mon-Fri 9am-6pm. Pub *Positive Living*. "Services include food program, dental clinic, counseling, education & training, case management, adocacy, community forums, home health, etc."

♀ ★ (♁) Asian Pacific AIDS Intervention Team, 1313 W 8th St #224; 90017 213-353-6055

♀ ☆ ♁♁ Being Alive: People with HIV/AIDS, 3626 W Sunset Blvd; 90026 213-667-3262 Fax 213-667-2735 Pub *Being Alive*.

♀ ☆ Bienestar—Latinos AIDS Proj, 1169 N Vermont Ave; 90029 213-660-9680

♀ ★ Enlightenment, 842 N Curson; 90046 213-651-3005 "Promotion of AIDS awareness; fundraising for AIDS organizations & Gay & Lesbian Pride."

♀ ☆ ♁ LA Shanti Foundation, 1616 N La Brea Ave; 90028-6902 213-962-8197; 213-962-8398 TDD; San Fernando Valley Office (818) 908-8624; Fax 213-962-8299 Office 10am-6pm; support groups days/eves. "One-to-one counseling; HIV education services."

Answering/FAX & Mail Receiving, Shipping & Packaging Services

♂ • ♁♁ West Hollywood Services, 7985 Santa Monica Blvd #109, West Hollywood; 90046 213-656-0257 Fax 213-656-8475 8am-mdnt.

Antiques & Collectables

♀ ○ Patsy Comer's Antiques & Jewelry, 7249 Reseda Blvd, Reseda; 91335 818-345-1631

Archives/Libraries/History Projects

♀ ★ International Gay & Lesbian Archives, PO Box 69679, West Hollywood; 90069 310-854-0271 Pub *ILGA Bulletin*.

♀ ★ June Mazer Lesbian Collection, 626 N Robertson Blvd, West Hollywood; 90069 310-659-2478 "Archive, museum, library."

Bars, Restaurants, Clubs, Discos

Culver City

♀ • (♁) The Connection, 4363 Sepulveda Blvd, Culver City; 90230 310-391-6817 *DE* 2pm-2am; Sat & Sun noon-2am.

♂ JJ's Pub, 2692 S La Cienega Blvd; 90034 310-837-7443

El Serano

♀ Plush Pony, 5261 Alhambra Ave; 90032 213-224-9488

Hawthorne

♀ • (?♁) El Capitan, 13825 S Hawthorne Blvd, Hawthorne; 90250 310-675-3436 *B*

Huntington Park

♀ California De Noche, 7810 Santa Fe, Huntington Park; 90255 213-581-7646

Inglewood

♀ ○ Annex Club, 835 S La Brea Ave, Inglewood; 90301 310-671-7323

♂ Caper Room, 244 S Market St, Inglewood; 90301 310-677-0403

Los Angeles/Hollywood/West Hollywood

♂ The 7702 SM Club, 7702 Santa Monica Blvd; 90046 213-654-3336

♀ && Arena/Circus Disco, 6655 Santa Monica Blvd; 90038 213-462-1291; 213-462-1742; *D* Tue & Fri 9pm-2am.

♀ • && Axis, 652 N Lapeer Dr, West Hollywood; 90069 310-659-0471 *BDP* 9pm-2.30am.

♂ Catch One, 4067 W Pico Blvd; 90019 213-734-8849

♂ • (&) Club Tempo, 5520 Santa Monica Blvd; 90038 213-466-1094 *BDEW*

♂ • & Eagle, 7864 Santa Monica Blvd, West Hollywood; 90046 213-654-3252 *L*

♂ • & Faultline, 4216 Melrose Ave; 90029 213-660-0889 *BLL* 6pm-2am; Sun 2pm-2am.

♀ • && Girlbar: Fridays (at Axis), 652 N Lapeer Dr, West Hollywood; 90069 310-659-0471 *BDE* Fri 9pm-2.30am.

♀ • (?&) Girlbar: Saturdays (at Love Lounge), 657 N Robertson Blvd, West Hollywood; 90069 310-659-0471 *BDE* Sat 9pm-2.30am.

♂ Gold Coast, 8228 Santa Monica Blvd, West Hollywood; 90046 213-656-4879

♂ Hunters, 7511 Santa Monica Blvd; 90046 213-850-9428

♀ Jewel's, 4067 W Pico Blvd; 90019 213-734-8849

♀ o && Joly's Two, 4356 Sunset Blvd; 90029 213-665-6810

♀ • Micky's, 8857 Santa Monica Blvd, West Hollywood; 90069 310-657-1176 *BDR* 11am-2am.

♂ Motherlode, 8944 Santa Monica Blvd, West Hollywood; 90069 310-659-9700

♀ Mugi, 5221 Hollywood Blvd; 90027 213-462-2039

♂ Numbers, 8029 Sunset Blvd, West Hollywood; 90046 213-656-6300 *BR*

♀ o (&) Palms, 8572 Santa Monica Blvd, West Hollywood; 90069 310-652-6188

♂ • Probe, 836 N Highland Ave, Hollywood; 90038 213-461-8301; 310-281-6292 club information hotline; *PD* (after hours Sat only)

♂ Rafters, 7994 Santa Monica Blvd, West Hollywood; 90046 213-654-0396

♀ • Rage, 8911 Santa Monica Blvd, West Hollywood; 90069 310-652-7055 *BDR* Noon-2am.

♀ • Revolver, 8851 Santa Monica Blvd, West Hollywood; 90069 310-659-8851 *BE*

♂ • Score, 107 W. 4th St 213-625-7382 *BDE* 11am-2am.

♂ • Spike, 7746 Santa Monica Blvd; 90046 213-656-9343 *LW*

♂ The Spotlight, 1601 N Cahuenga Blvd; 90028 213-467-2425

♂ • The Study, 1723 N Western Ave; 90027 213-464-9551

♀ • Tempo, 5520 Santa Monica Blvd 213-466-1094 *BDEC* Wed-Sat 8pm-4am; Sun 6pm-4am. Latina Lesbian Night Sun, upstairs only; all other nights gay latin men.

♀ • && Trigo, 8571 Santa Monica Blvd, West Hollywood; 90069 310-652-9263

♂ o Trunks: A Sports Video Bar, 8809 Santa Monica Blvd, West Hollywood; 90069 310-652-1015

♀ o Uncle Bill's Gem, 5556 Santa Monica Blvd; 90038 213-467-0224 6am-2am.

♀ o & Yukon Mining Co, 7328 Santa Monica Blvd, West Hollywood; 90046 213-851-8833 *R* 24 hrs.

♀ • && Little Frida's Coffee Bar, 8730 Santa Monica Blvd, West Hollywood; 90069 310-652-6495

North Hollywood/Studio City

♀ • Apache, 11608 Ventura Blvd, Studio City; 91604 818-506-0404 *BD*

♂ Bullet, 10522 Burbank Blvd, North Hollywood; 91601 818-760-9563 *L*

♀ • & Club 22, 4882 Lankershim Blvd, North Hollywood; 91601 818-760-9792

♀ • && Escapades, 10437 Burbank Blvd, North Hollywood; 91601 818-508-7008 *BDE*

♂ Jox, 10721 Burbank Blvd, North Hollywood; 91601 818-760-9031

♂ • The Lodge, 4923 Lankershim Blvd, North Hollywood; 91601 818-769-7722 *D*

♂ o & Oasis, 11916 Ventura Blvd, Studio City; 91604 818-980-4811 *BDE*

♀ • Oil Can Harry's, 11502 Ventura Blvd, Studio City; 91604 818-760-9749

♂ Queen Mary, 12440 Ventura Blvd, Studio City; 91604 818-506-5619

♂ Rawhide, 10937 Burbank Blvd, North Hollywood; 91601 818-760-9798

♀ • && Rumors, 10622 Magnolia Blvd, North Hollywood; 91601 818-506-9651

♀ • & Venture Inn, 11938 Ventura Blvd, Studio City; 91604 818-769-5400

♀ o Wellington's, 4354 Lankershim Blvd, North Hollywood; 91602 818-980-1430 *BRE*

Sisterhood Bookstore

MAIL ORDER CATALOG FREE
FEMINIST, LESBIAN,
& GAY BOOKS

1351 WESTWOOD BLVD
LOS ANGELES, CA 90024
(310) 477-7300
(800) 747-0220

Redondo Beach

♀ • ♿ The Dolphin, 1995 Artesia Blvd, Redondo Beach; 90278 310-318-3339

♂ J.R. Brian's, 2105 Artesia Blvd, Redondo Beach; 90278 310-371-7859

Reseda

♀ • (♿) Incognito/Valley, 7026 Reseda Blvd, Reseda; 91335 818-996-2976 *BD*

Santa Monica

♂ • The Friendship, 112 W Channel Rd, Santa Monica; 90402 310-454-9080

Silver Lake

♂ Bon Mot, 4022 N Figueroa, Highland Park; 90065 213-222-5963

♂ Bunkhouse, 4519 Santa Monica Blvd; 90029 213-667-9766

♂ Cuffs, 1941 Hyperion Ave; 90027 213-660-2649 *LW*

♂ Detour, 1087 Manzanita St; 90029 213-664-1189

♂ • Gauntlet II, 4219 Santa Monica Blvd; 90029 213-669-9472 *L*

♀ • Houstons, 2538 Hyperion Ave; 90027 213-661-4233 *BRE*

♂ o♿ The Hyperion, 2810 Hyperion Ave; 90027 213-660-1503 *BDE* 11.30am-2am; after hours Sat to 4am.

♂ Le Bar, 2375 Glendale Blvd; 90039 213-660-7595

♂ o Mr. Mike's, 3172 Los Feliz Blvd; 90039 213-669-9640

♂ Silverlake Lounge, 2906 Sunset Blvd; 90026 213-663-9636

Van Nuys/Sherman Oaks

♂ • ♿ Driveshaft, 13641 Victory Blvd, Van Nuys; 91401 818-782-7199

♀ • Gold 9, 13625 Moorpark St, Sherman Oaks; 91423 818-986-0285 11am-2am; Sat & Sun 6am-2am.

♂ • Mag Lounge, 5248 Van Nuys Blvd, Van Nuys; 91401 818-981-6693

♀ Oxwood Inn, 13713 Oxnard St, Van Nuys; 91401 818-997-9666

Venice

♀ o Van Go's Ear, 796 Main St, Venice; 90291 310-314-0022 *R* 24 hrs.

♂ Roosterfish, 1302 Abbot Kinney Blvd, Venice; 90291 310-392-2123

Bookstores: Gay/Lesbian/Feminist

♀ • A Different Light, 8853 Santa Monica Blvd, West Hollywood; 90069 310-854-6601

♀ o Circus of Books, 8230 Santa Monica Blvd; 90046-5916 213-656-6533
♦ *Circus of Books advertisement page 166*

♀ o Circus of Books, 4001 Sunset Blvd; 90029 213-666-1304

♀ • Sisterhood Bookstore, 1351 Westwood Blvd; 90024 310-477-7300; 800-747-0220
♦ *Sisterhood Bookstore advertisement page 166*

♂ • ♿ Unicorn Bookstore, 8940 Santa Monica Blvd, West Hollywood; 90069 310-652-6253 10am-mdnt; Thu to 1am; Fri-Sun to 2am.

Bookstores: General

♀ o♿ Book Soup, 8818 Sunset Blvd; 90046 310-659-3110 Fax 310-659-3410 9am-mdnt.

♀ o ♿ Either/Or Bookstore, 124 Pier Ave, Hermosa Beach; 90254 310-374-2060

♀ o Globe News, 314 W 6th St; 90014 213-622-4390

♀ o ♿ Midnight Special Books, 1318 Third Street Promenade, Santa Monica; 90401 310-393-2923 Fax 310-394-6123 books@msbooks.com 10.30am-11pm.

♀ o Universal News Agency, 1655 N Las Palmas Ave; 90028 213-467-3850

♀ o World Book & News, 1652 Cahuenga Blvd; 90028 213-465-4352

Bookstores: Recovery, Metaphysical, & other Specialty

♀ o Language of the Heart, 502 S 2nd Ave, Covina; 91723 818-858-0997 11am-6pm.

CIRCUS OF BOOKS
Your one-stop source
for gay literature and erotica

Magazines • Fiction • Aromas • Travel Guides
• Videos • Condoms • Leather goods • Novelties

8230 Santa Monica Blvd., West Hollywood, CA 90046
(213) 656-6533

4001 Sunset Blvd., Silverlake, CA 90029
(213) 666-1304

Broadcast Media

⚥ ★ (♑) Overnight Productions, Inc.,, c/o KPFK, 3729 Cahuenga Blvd W., North Hollywood; 91604 818-833-0283 "IMRU" & "Lesbian Sisters" broadcast Sun 10-11pm, 90.7 FM.

Business, Financial & Secretarial

♀ • Ferguson, Dave, Certified Financial Planner,, 8465 Santa Monica Blvd, West Hollywood; 90069 213-848-7161

♀ • Weaver Accountancy Corporation, 7805 W Sunset Blvd #211; 90046 213-850-6599

Clothes

♂ • Don't Panic!, 802 North San Vincente Blvd, West Hollywood; 90069 310-652-3668 Fax 310-652-3966

Community Centers (see also Women's Centers)

⚥ ★ ♿ Los Angeles Gay & Lesbian Community Services Center, 1625 N Schrader Blvd; 90028 213-993-7440; 213-993-7698 TDD; Fax 213-993-7699 Pub *Centernews*.

⚥ ★ (♿) South Bay Lesbian/Gay Community Center, PO Box 2777, Redondo Beach; 90278 / 2009 Artesia Blvd, Suite A 310-379-2850 *The Community News*.

Counseling/Therapy: Nonprofit

♀ ★ (♿) Gay & Lesbian Adolescent Social Services, Inc, 650 N Robertson Blvd #A, West Hollywood; 90069 310-358-8727 "Residential services; foster parenting."

Counseling/Therapy: Private

⚥ • ♿ Reynolds, Jan, MA, MFCC, 6310 San Vicente Blvd #410; 90048 213-937-3787

Dentists

⚥ • ♿ Pickrell, David P., DMD & Schultz, Robert P., DDS, 8619 Santa Monica Blvd, West Hollywood; 90069 310-659-0210 "We specialize in the treatment of HIV & AIDS patients."

♀ • Tamura, Daniel H., DDS, 6200 Wilshire Blvd #1209; 90048 213-937-0197

Erotica (Printed, Visual, Equipment)

♀ ○ ♿ Andy's Adult World, 4624 Whittier Blvd; 90022 213-296-4123 "Adult video & novelties."

⚥ • ♿ Drake's After Midnight Bookstore, 7566 Melrose Ave; 90046 213-651-5600 Fax 213-651-1801 24 hrs.

⚥ • ♿ Drake's West Hollywood, 8932 Santa Monica Blvd, West Hollywood; 90069 310-289-8932 Fax 310-289-1560 10am-1am.

♀ ○ Love Boutique, 2924 Wilshire Blvd, Santa Monica; 90403 310-453-3459

♀ • (♿) Pleasure Chest, 7733 Santa Monica Blvd; 90046 213-650-1022 Fax 213-650-1176 10am-1am.

♂ ○ Twisted Video, 10530 Burbank Blvd, North Hollywood; 91601 818-508-0559 9am-mdnt.

⚥ • ♿ Video and Stuff, 11612 Ventura Blvd, Studio City; 91604 818-761-3162 10am-mdnt.

Exterminators

♀ ○ Adams, Terry, 8060 Melrose Ave; 90046 213-653-8060

Film & Video

⚥ ★ Out on the Screen, 8455 Beverly Blvd #309; 90048 213-951-1247 Fax 213-951-0721

Gifts, Cards, Pride & Novelty Items

♀ ○ ♿ Fantastic Hobbies, 568 E Foothill Blvd #114, Azusa; 91704 818-969-9194 "Hobby shop; also books & gift items."

Graphic Design/Typesetting (see also Art; Printing)

⚥ • In Graphic Detail, 7985 Santa Monica Blvd #181, West Hollywood; 90046 310-874-1726 Fax 213-851-8335

Health Care (see also AIDS Services)

♀ ○ ♿ Citizens Medical Group, 1300 N La Brea; 90028 213-464-1336

⚥ • ♿ Cohan, Gary R., MD, Pacific Oaks Medical Group, 150 N Robertson #300, Beverly Hills; 90211 310-652-2562

⚥ • ♿ Holistic Pain Management Clinic, 10730 Riverside Dr, North Hollywood; 91602 818-769-6041 "Chiropractic, physical therapy, nutritional consultation, etc."

♀ ○ ♿ Keith Medical Group, 6200 Wilshire Blvd #1510; 90048 213-964-1440

♀ • The Lesbian Health Project, 8235 Santa Monica Blvd #308, West Hollywood; 90046 213-650-1508

Health Clubs, Gyms, Saunas

♂ ○ Body Builders Gym, 2516 Hyperion Ave; 90027 213-668-0802

♂ • ♿ Compound, 5636 Vineland Ave, North Hollywood; 91601 818-760-6969

♂ • Flex Bath House, 4424 Melrose Ave; 90046 213-663-5858

♂ • Flex Gym, 4422 Melrose Ave; 90046 213-663-0294

♂ • Hollywood Spa, 1650 Ivar; 90028 213-464-0445 24 hrs.

♂ • Melrose Baths, 7269 Melrose; 90038 213-937-2122

♂ • Midtowne Spa, 615 S Kohler St; 90021 213-680-1838 24 hrs.

♂ • Roman Holiday, 12814 Venice Blvd; 90066 310-391-0200

♂ • Roman Holiday, 14435 Victory Blvd, Van Nuys; 91401 818-780-1320

⚥ • ♿ The Zone, 1037 N Sycamore, West Hollywood; 90048 310-464-8881 *P*

Legal Services & Resources

♀ • ♿ Goodman, Diane M., 15915 Ventura Blvd #201, Encino; 91436 818-386-2889

⚥ ★ ♿ Lambda Legal Defense & Education Fund (LLDEF), Inc, 6030 Wilshire Blvd #200; 90036 213-937-2728 Pub *Lambda Update*.

⚥ ♿ Lesbian & Gay Immigration Rights Task Force, Inc. (LGIRTF), c/o LLDEF, 6030 Wilshire Blvd #200; 90036 213-937-2728 x37

⚥ • (♿) Wissley, Deborah Z., 6454 Van Nuys Blvd #150, Van Nuys; 91401-1445 818-781-9922; 818-980-9373

Ophthalmologists & Optometrists

♀ • ♿ West Hollywood Optometric Center: Dr Mark A. Chung, 8205 Santa Monica Blvd #15, West Hollywood; 90046 213-650-0337

Organizations/Resources: Business & Professional

⚥ ★ Los Angeles Business & Professional Association, PO Box 69982, West Hollywood; 90069 213-896-1444

⚥ ★ (♑) Los Angeles Gay & Lesbian Scientists (LAGLS), PO Box 91803, Pasadena, CA 91109-9813 818-791-7689 Pub *LAGLS Newsletter*.

⚥ ★ (♑) Valley Business Alliance, PO Box 57555, Sherman Oaks; 91413 818-982-2650

Organizations/Resources: Education, Anti-Defamation, Anti-Violence, Self-Defense

♀♂ ★ GLAAD (Gay & Lesbian Alliance Against Defamation), 8455 Beverly Blvd #305; 90048 213-658-6775 Fax 213-658-6776

♀♂ ★ ONE, Inc., PO Box 19028A; 90019-1028 213-735-5252 Pub *Oneletter*. One Institute of Homophile Studies; Graduate school; library.

Organizations/Resources: Ethnic, Multicultural

♀♂ ★ (?♿) Asian/Pacific Lesbians & Gays, 7985 Santa Monica Blvd #109-443; 90046 213-660-2131

♀ Beyond The Bars, 5149 W Jefferson Ave; 90016 213-936-4949

♀♂ ★ Gay & Lesbian Latinos Unidos, PO Box 85459; 90072-0459 213-660-9681 Pub *Unidad*. Radio GLLU, 90.7 FM, Sun 10pm.

♀♂ ★ Gay Asian Pacific Support Network, PO Box 461104; 90046 213-368-6488

♀ ★ Gay Black Female (GBF), 6312 Hollywood Blvd #114; 90028 213-288-6315

♀ ★ ♿♿ Lapis Program, Alcoholism Center for Women, 1147 S Alvarado St; 90006 213-381-8500

♀ ★ Lesbianas Unidas, 805 Westboro, Alhambra; 91803 310-660-9681 Pub *Unidad*.

♀ ★ MACT-Los Angeles, 7985 Santa Monica Blvd #109-136; 90046 213-664-4716 Men of All Colors Together

♀ Makeda, PO Box 78785; 90016 213-935-4105

♀ ★ (?♿) United Lesbians Of African Heritage (ULOAH), 1626 N Wilcox Ave #190; 90028 213-960-5051

Organizations/Resources: Family

♀♂ ★♿♿ Gay Fathers of Los Angeles, 7985 Santa Monica Blvd #109-346, West Hollywood; 90046 213-654-0307

♀ ☆♿♿ PFLAG/Los Angeles, PO Box 24565; 90024 310-472-8952 Meeting 3rd Tue of month. Pub *Newsletter*. "Parents, Families & Friends of Lesbians & Gays."

Organizations/Resources: General, Multipurpose, Pride

♀ ★ Christopher Street West, 7985 Santa Monica Blvd #109-24; 90046 213-656-6553

♀ ★ (♿) South Bay Lesbian & Gay Community Organization, PO Box 2777, Redondo Beach; 90278 / 2009 Artesia Blvd #A 310-379-2850

♀ ★ Uptown Gay/Lesbian Alliance, Box 65111; 90065 213-258-8842

Organizations/Resources: Political/Legislative

♀ ★ Log Cabin Republican Club of Los Angeles, PO Box 480336; 90048 213-486-4232 "Republican organization."

♀ ★ (?♿) Project Rainbow, c/o GLCSC, 1625 Schrader Blvd; 90028 213-621-3180

♀ ★ (?♿) Stonewall Democratic Club, PO Box 26367; 90026-0367 213-969-1735

Organizations/Resources: Sexual Focus (Leather, S/M, etc) & Safe Sex Promotion

♂ ★ (?♿) LA/OC Jacks, PO Box 506, Garden Grove, CA 92626 / PO Box 2626, Los Angeles, CA 90026 714-250-0302

♀ ☆♿♿ NLA: Los Angeles, 7985 Santa Monica Blvd #109-217, West Hollywood; 90046 213-856-5643

♂ Uncut Club, PO Box 2842; 90078

Organizations/Resources: Social, Recreational & Support Groups (see also Sport/Dance/Outdoor)

♀ Butch/Femme Network, PO Box 691593, West Hollywood; 90069 310-379-2850

♀♂ ★ (?♿) Couples Group, PO Box 69954, West Hollywood; 90069 818-797-2568

♂ Girth & Mirth of Los Angeles, PO Box 466, Canoga Park; 91305

♂ ★ Los Angeles Nude Guys (LANG), PO Box 93434; 90093 818-787-LANG Pub *Nude News*. Serving Members in Los Angeles & Orange County.

♂ ★ (?♿) Los Angeles Prime Timers, PO Box 19028A; 90019 213-733-6412

♀♂ ★ Passion Fruits: Gay & Lesbian Vegetarians of L.A., call Rick 818-282-0753 Pub *Fruit Talk*. "Monthly potlucks, hikes, cooking classes & more."

♀♂ ★ Society for Senior Gay & Lesbian Citizens, Inc./Project Rainbow (SSGLC), c/o GLCSC, 1625 N Schrader Blvd; 90028 213-621-3180

♀ ☆♿♿ Sunset Junction Neighborhood Alliance, PO Box 26565; 90026 213-661-7771

Organizations/Resources: Sport/Dance/Outdoor

♂ Arriba Ski Club, PO Box 3213, Hollywood; 90028 818-438-6443

♀♂ ★ Different Spokes of Southern California, PO Box 291875; 90029-1875 213-896-8235 Pub *Hot Links*. "Bicycling club."

♀♂ ★ (?♿) Frontrunners Track Club of LA, PO Box 691772, West Hollywood; 90069 213-460-2554

♀♂ ★ Great Outdoors/Los Angeles, PO Box 1318, Studio City; 91614-0318 818-763-4496

♂ Great Outdoors/Pomona—San Gabriel Valley, PO Box 2516, Covina; 91722-8516

♀♂ ★ ♿ Los Angeles Tennis Assocation, PO Box 481226; 90048

♀♂ ★ Tinseltown Squares, PO Box 691764, West Hollywood; 90069 818-454-1487 *d*

Organizations/Resources: Student, Academic, Alumni/ae

♀♂ ★♿♿ Cal State/Northridge LGBA, 18111 Nordhoff St, Northridge; 91330 818-885-2393 (Campus Activities); 818-885-2393 (Campus Activities)

♀♂ ★ (?♿) GALA: UCLA, 500 Kerkhoff Hall; 90024 / 308 Westwood Plaza 310-825-8053 Multicultural Lesbian Gay & Bisexual Alliance.

♀♂ ★♿♿ Gay & Lesbian Association (GALA of CSULA), 5154 State University Dr #227; 90032 213-224-3595

♀♂ ★ Gay & Lesbian Students Union, Los Angeles Community College, 855 N Vermont Ave.; 90028 213-669-4306

♀♂ ★ ♿ Occidental College Gay & Lesbian Association, 1600 Campus Rd Box 5; 90041 213-259-2560

Organizations/Resources: Transgender & Transgender Publications

▼ ○ Cross Connection, 818-786-8887 (modem) sysop@xconn.com "On-line computer service, sepcializing in information & entertainment for Transgender community & Internet access."

Organizations/Resources: Youth (see also Family)

♀♂ ★ GLASS (Gay & Lesbian Adolescent Social Services), 650 N Roberston Blvd #A, West Hollywood; 90069 310-358-8727

♂ ★ ♂ LA Gay & Lesbian Community Services Center, Youth Services Dept, 1625 N Schrader Blvd; 90028 213-993-7440; 213-993-7698 TDD; Fax 213-993-7699

Performing Arts: Entertainment, Music, Recording, Theater, etc.

♀ ● (?♂) Appel Presents..Inc., PO Box 36248; 90036-0248 213-706-6774 Fax 213-930-0194 "Special events, benefits, etc."

♀ ★ ♂♂ Gay Men's Chorus of Los Angeles, 8470 Santa Monica Blvd, West Hollywood; 90069-4219 213-383-6770 Fax 213-650-0758 Pub Choruspondance.

♂ ★ ♂♂ Great American Yankee Freedom Band of Los Angeles, PO Box 46026; 90046 213-734-3472

♂ ★ VIVA, Lesbian & Gay Latino Artists, 4470 W Sunset Blvd #261; 90027-6018 310-301-8035 Fax 310-301-9326 "Literary, performing & visual arts group oriented to gay/lesbian Latina/Latinos."

Pharmacies/Health Care Supplies

♀ ○ ♂ PX Drugstore, 5160 Vineland Ave #101, North Hollywood; 91601-3849 800-752-5721 "Drugs for the immuno-suppressed patient: direct billing to insurance company & free overnight UPS delivery."

♀ ○ ♂ PX Drugstore, 62546 Wilshire Blvd; 90048 213-936-8221 "Drugs for the immuno-suppressed patient: direct billing to insurance company & free overnight UPS delivery."

♀ ○ ♂♂ Vee's Pharmacy, 8609 Santa Monica Blvd, West Hollywood; 90069 310-657-5180

Publications: Directories, Bibliographies, Guides, Travel

♀ ● Community Yellow Pages, 2305 Canyon Drive; 90068 213-469-4454

Publications

♂ ○ Cuir Magazine, 7985 Santa Monica Blvd #109-368, West Hollywood; 90046 213-656-5073 L

♂ ● Edge Magazine, 6434 Santa Monica Blvd; 90038 213-962-6994 Fax 213-962-2917

♀ ● The Female FYI, 8033 Sunset Blvd #2013; 90046 310-657-5592 Fax 310-657-5594

♂ ● Frontiers News Magazine, 7985 Santa Monica Blvd #109, West Hollywood; 90046 213-848-2222

→ The Lesbian News: p.158

♀ ● Planet Homo, 8080 Santa Monica Blvd #200, West Hollywood; 90069 213-848-2220 Fax 213-656-8784

♂ SBC, Stanley Bennett Clay Productions 1205 4th Ave; 90019 213-732-4242 (for Afrocentric men)

Real Estate

♀ ● Shoush, Julie, 2451 S Azusa Ave, West Covina; 91792 714-964-7990 ex 3212

Religious Organizations & Publications

♂ ★ ♂ Beth Chayim Chadashim, 6000 West Pico Blvd; 90035 213-931-7023 Pub G'Vanim.

♀ ☆ ♂♂ Christ the Shepherd Lutheran Church, 185 W Altadena Dr, Altadena; 91001 818-794-7011

♂ ★ ♂♂ Congregation Kol Ami, 8400 Sunset Blvd #2A, West Hollywood; 90069 213-656-6093 Fax 213-656-6149 Pub Kole-inu.

♀ ☆ (?♂) Crescent Heights United Methodist Church, 7866 W Fountain Ave, West Hollywood; 90046 213-656-5336

♂ ★ (♂♂) Dignity/Los Angeles, PO Box 42040; 90042-0040 213-344-8064 "Gay & Lesbian Catholics & their friends."

♂ Dignity/San Gabriel Valley, 502 Mesa Circle, Monrovia; 91016-1638 "Gay & Lesbian Catholics & their friends."

♂ ★ (♂) Divine Redeemer Metropolitan Community Church, 346 Riverdale Drive, Glendale; 91204 818-500-7124

♂ ★ Evangelicals Together, Inc., 7985 Santa Monica Blvd #109, Box 16; 90046 213-656-8570 Pub ET News. "Groups & events throughout Southern California; workshops, socials, pastoral counseling, AIDS Ministry."

● ★ (♂♂) Free Spirit Metropolitan Community Church at CIW, PO Box 388, Culver City; 90232 213-464-5100 Saturday Worship in Prison 2-4pm.

♂ ★ Gay Buddhist Group (Zen Center), PO Box 29750; 90029 213-461-5042

♂ ★ Holy Trinity Community Church, PO Box 42964; 90042 / 3323 W. Beverly Blvd 213-384-5422

♂ ★ Integrity/Los Angeles, 7985 Santa Monica Blvd #109-113, West Hollywood; 90046 213-662-6301 "Lesbian & Gay Episcopalians & their friends."

♂ ★ Los Angeles Gay & Lesbian Religious Coalition, 7985 Santa Monica Blvd #109, Box 104; 90046 "Coalition of religious organizations & congregations that affirm gay & lesbian persons. Referrals to member groups in LA area."

♂ ★ ♂♂ Lutherans Concerned/Los Angeles, 11225 Magnolia Blvd #290, North Hollywood; 91601 213-665-LCLA 70541.2531@compuserve.com

♂ ★ ♂♂ Metropolitan Community Church For All The Saints, 3621 Brunswick Ave; 90039-1727 213-665-8818

♂ ★ ♂ Metropolitan Community Church In The Valley, 5730 Cahuenga Blvd, North Hollywood; 91601 818-762-1133

♂ ★ ♂♂ New Hope Christian Church, PO Box 316, Van Nuys; 91408 818-765-1590 Pastor Rev. Flo Fleischman.

♀ ★ (♂) PLGC, 3375 Descanso Dr #1; 90026 213-664-4411 "Presbyterians for Lesbian/Gay Concerns."

♂ ★ SDA Kinship, PO Box 745, Glendale; 91209 818-248-1299

♀ ☆ ♂ St John's Episcopal Church, 514 W Adams Blvd; 90007 213-747-6285

♀ ☆ ♂ St Matthew's Evangelical Lutheran Church, 11031 Camarillo St, Studio City; 91602 818-762-2909 Fax 818-762-7439

♂ ★ (?♂) United Lesbian/Gay Christian Scientists, PO Box 2171, Beverly Hills; 90212-2171 213-876-1338 Pub Faith & Understanding. Christian Scientists

♂ ★ ♂ Unity Fellowship Church, 5149 W Jefferson Blvd; 90016 213-936-4948

Travel & Tourist Services (see also Accommodation)

♀ ○ All Travel, 2001 S Barrington Ave #150; 90025 310-312-3368

♂ ○ ♂ Aquarius Travel & Tours, 1149 S Robertson Blvd; 90035-1403 310-475-8851; 310-276-9141

♀ ● Cruise Holidays, 224 S Roberton Blvd, Beverly Hills; 90211 310-652-8521 Fax 310-652-8524

♀ ○ ♂ Cruise Holidays West, 2907 Santa Monica Blvd, Santa Monica; 90404 310-352-8282; 818-889-0204; Fax 310-582-8285

♂ ● ♂♂ Embassy Travel, 906 N Harper Ave #B, West Hollywood; 90046 213-656-5373

♀ ● ♂♂ Firstworld Travel Express, 1990 S Bundy Dr #175, West Los Angeles; 90025 310-820-6868; 800-366-0815; Fax 310-820-2807 "Corporate & leisure gay travel specialists."

♂ • Friends Travel, 322 Huntley Drive #100, West Hollywood; 90048-1919 310-652-9600; 800-GAY-0069

♂ • (♂♂) Gunderson Travel, Inc., 8543 Santa Monica Blvd, West Hollywood; 90069 310-657-3944; 800-899-1944; Fax 310-652-4301

♀ • ♂♂ Mac's Travel, 18738 Amar Rd, Walnut; 91789-4168 818-965-0731; 800-542-4775; Fax 818-913-5379

♀ • ♂♂ Mac's Travel II, 4525 F Towne Center Dr, Baldwin Park; 91706 818-813-0021 Fax 818-813-0591

♂ • (?♂) Mantours-USA, PO Box 36248; 90036-0248 213-706-6774 Fax 213-930-0194

♀ ○ Sta Travel, 7202 Melrose; 90046 213-934-8722

♀ • ♂ Travel Lab, 1943 Hillhurst Ave; 90027-2711 213-660-9811; 800-747-7026

Los Osos: see San Luis Obispo

Mendocino

Accommodation: Hotels, B&B, Resorts, Campgrounds

♀ • Sallie & Eileen's Place, PO Box 409; 95460 707-937-2028 "Vacation cabins for women."

♀ ○ Wittwood, PO Box 229, Comptche; 95427 707-937-5486

Menlo Park: see San Mateo

Mill Valley

Organizations/Resources: Family

♀ ☆ PFLAG/Marin County, PO Box 1626; 94941 415-479-3535 "Parents, Families & Friends of Lesbians & Gays."

Modesto

Bars, Restaurants, Clubs, Discos

♂ Brave Bull, 701 S 9th St; 95354 209-529-6172

♂ Mustang Club, 413 N 7th St; 95354 209-577-9694

Bookstores: General

♀ ○ ♂ The Bookstore Ltd, 2400 Coffee Rd; 95355 209-521-0535

Counseling/Therapy: Private

♀ ○ Sherman, Patricia, MFCC, 502 13th St; 95354 209-529-9080

Erotica (Printed, Visual, Equipment)

♀ ○ ♂ Liberty Books, 1030 Kansas Ave; 95354 209-524-7603

Monrovia: see Los Angeles Area

Monte Rio: see Russian River

Monterey

Accommodation: Hotels, B&B, Resorts, Campgrounds

♀ ○ ♂♂ Monterey Fireside Lodge, 1131 10th St; 93940 408-373-4172

Bars, Restaurants, Clubs, Discos

♂ • After Dark/Backlot, 214 Lighthouse Ave; 93940 408-373-7828

♀ Franco's Norma Jean Bar, 10639 Merritt St, Castroville; 95012 408-633-2090 *BRE* Fri & Sat only.

Morro Bay: see San Luis Obispo

Mountain View: see San Jose Area

Napa

AIDS/HIV Support, Education, Advocacy, Publications

♀ ★♂♂ Napa Valley AIDS Project, 601 Cabot Way; 94559-4731 707-258-AIDS 24 hrs. Fax 707-258-8712 Pub *Gateway*.

Religious Organizations & Publications

♀ ★♂♂ Metropolitan Community Church in the Vineyards, 31 Village Parkway; 94558 707-255-0406

Nice

Organizations/Resources: Military/Veterans

♂ VCARE/Redwood Empire, PO Box 855; 95464-0855 707-274-1303 Gay, Lesbian & Bisexual Veterans Association

North Hollywood: see Los Angeles Area

Northridge: see Los Angeles Area

Oakland: see East Bay Area

Oceanside: see San Diego Area

Ontario: see San Bernardino/Riverside/Pomona Area

Orange County

☎ Gay & Lesbian Community Services Center of Orange County 714-534-0862

Accommodation: Hotels, B&B, Resorts, Campgrounds

Laguna Beach

♂ • (?♂) Coast Inn, 1401 S Coast Highway, Laguna Beach; 92651 714-494-7588

Orange

♂ • ♂♂ Country Comfort Bed & Breakfast, 5104 E Valencia Drive, Orange; 92669 714-532-2802 Fax 714-997-1921

AIDS/HIV Support, Education, Advocacy, Publications

♀ ★♂♂ AIDS Response Program, 12832 Garden Grove Blvd #A, Garden Grove; 92643 714-534-0961 10am-6pm. "Programs especially for gay men."

♀ ○ Center for Special Immunology, 100 Pacifica #100, Irvine; 92718 714-753-0670

Bars, Restaurants, Clubs, Discos

Buena Park

♂ • ♂ Ozz Supper Club, 6231 Manchester Blvd, Buena Park; 90621 714-522-1542 *BRDE* 5pm-2am.

Costa Mesa

♂ Lion's Den, 719 W 19th St, Costa Mesa; 92627 714-645-3830

♂ • Newport Station, 1945 Placentia Ave, Bldg C, Costa Mesa 714-631-0081 *Bd*

♀ Tin Lizzie Saloon, 752 St. Clair St, Costa Mesa; 92626 714-966-2029

Garden Grove

♂ • Frat House, 8112 Garden Grove Blvd, Garden Grove; 92644 714-373-FRAT *BDE*

♂ • (♂♂) Happy Hour, 12081 Garden Grove Blvd, Garden Grove; 92643 714-537-9079 *BD* 2pm-2am; Sat & Sun noon-2am. All welcome.

♂ Nick's, 8284 Garden Grove Blvd, Garden Grove; 92644 714-537-1361

Laguna Beach

♂ • (♂) Boom Boom Room/Hunky's Video Bar, 1401 S Coast Hwy, Laguna Beach; 92651 714-494-7588 Fax 714-494-1735 *BDER* 11am-2am.

⚥ The Cottage, 308 N Coast Hwy, Laguna Beach; 92651 714-494-3023 *B*

⚥ ○ Little Shrimp, 1305 S Coast Hwy, Laguna Beach; 92651 714-494-4111 *BR*

⚥ • (♿) Main Street, 1460 S Coast Hwy, Laguna Beach; 92651 714-494-0056 *BdE* "Piano bar."

Midway City

⚥ Huntress, 8122 Bolsa, Midway City; 92655 714-892-0048

Bookstores: Gay/Lesbian/Feminist

⚥ • ♦ A Different Drummer Bookshop, 1027 N Coast Hwy #A, Laguna Beach; 92651 714-497-6699 10am-7pm; Sat & Sun 11am-5pm.

⚥ • GayMart, 168 Mountain, Laguna Beach; 92651 714-497-9108 "Books, videos, erotica, cards, etc."

Community Centers (see also Women's Centers)

⚥ ★ ♿ Gay & Lesbian Community Services Center of Orange County, 12832 Garden Grove Blvd #A, Garden Grove; 92643 714-534-0862; 714-534-3261 hotline

Erotica (Printed, Visual, Equipment)

⚥ ○ East of Eden, 12065 Garden Grove Blvd, Garden Grove; 92643 714-534-9811

⚥ ○ ♦ Erogenous Zone, 343 N State College Blvd, Fullerton; 92631-4205 714-879-3270

⚥ ○ ♦ Fantasy Video-N-More, 518 S Brookhurst #1-#2, Anaheim; 92804 909-991-4830

⚥ ○ ♦ Garden of Eden, 12061 Garden Grove Blvd, Garden Grove; 92643 714-534-9805

⚥ • (♿) Party House, 8751 Garden Grove Blvd, Garden Grove; 92644 714-534-9996 7am-3am.

⚥ • (♿) Video Horizons, Inc, 31674 Coast Hwy, South Laguna Beach; 92677 714-499-4519

⚥ ○ Video Rental & Preview Center, 8743 Garden Grove Blvd, Garden Grove; 92641 714-534-9922 7am-3am.

Legal Services & Resources

⚥ • Garrett-Norris, Georgia, 414 W 4th St #L, Santa Ana; 92701 714-543-1200; 310-495-2305

Organizations/Resources: Business & Professional

⚥ Orange County Business & Professional Association, PO Box 698, Laguna Beach; 92652 714-494-0215

Organizations/Resources: Family

⚥ ☆ ♦ PFLAG/Orange County, PO Box 28662, Santa Ana; 92799-8662 714-997-8047; 714-997-8047 (calls will be returned); "Parents, Families & Friends of Lesbians & Gays."

Organizations/Resources: General, Multipurpose, Pride

⚥ ★ ♿ Laguna Outreach, Inc., PO Box 1701, Laguna Beach; 92652 714-472-8867 "Educational & special activities; youth, women's, men's, couples rap groups."

Organizations/Resources: Political/Legislative

⚥ ★ Log Cabin Orange County, 4482 Barranca Pkwy 180-115, Irvine; 92714 714-651-9985 "Republican political group."

Organizations/Resources: Sexual Focus (Leather, S/M, etc) & Safe Sex Promotion

♂ • (?♿) LA/OC Jacks, PO Box 506, Garden Grove; 92626 / PO Box 2626, Los Angeles, CA 90026 714-250-0302

Organizations/Resources: Student, Academic, Alumni/ae

⚥ ☆ (?♿) Chapman University Pride Alliance (CUPA), 333 N Glassell, Orange; 92666 714-997-6841

⚥ Cypress College Lambda Student Union, 9200 Valley View, Cypress; 90630 714-826-2220

⚥ ★ ♿ Lesbian, Gay, Bisexual Association, CSU Fullerton, UC 243, Box #67, Fullerton; 92634 714-773-2067

⚥ ★ UC Irvine GLBSU, 102 University Center, Irvine; 92717 714-824-4260 Pub *Q University*.

Publications

⚥ Orange County Blade, PO Box 1538, Laguna Beach; 92654 714-494-4898

Religious Organizations & Publications

⚥ ★ Christ Chapel Metropolitan Community Church, 720 N Spurgeon St, Santa Ana; 92701-3722 714-835-0722

⚥ ★ ♦ Congregation Kol Simcha, PO Box 1444, Laguna Beach; 92652 714-361-8723; 714-551-2072 Pub *Chavurah Quarterly*.

⚥ ★ ♿ Metropolitan Community Church Ocean of Life, 1548D Adams Ave, Costa Mesa; 92626-3894 714-548-2955; 310-690-1830

Travel & Tourist Services (see also Accommodation)

⚥ ○ Ancient Mariner Travel, 14145 Red Hill Ave, Tustin; 92680 714-838-9780

⚥ • (?♿) California Riviera 800, 1400 S Coast Highway, #104, Laguna Beach; 92651 714-376-0305; 800-621-0500; "Hotel reservation service."

⚥ • Travel With Hal, 2227 Atlanta St, Anaheim; 92802 714-537-1553

Pacific Grove

Bookstores: Gay/Lesbian/Feminist

♀ ○ Raven In The Grove, 505 Lighthouse Ave #103; 93950 408-649-6057

Palm Desert: see Palm Springs

Palm Springs

Accommodation: Hotels, B&B, Resorts, Campgrounds

Cathedral City

♂ • Desert Palms Resort, 67-580 E Palm Canyon Dr, Cathedral City; 92234 619-324-5100

♂ • The Villa, 67-670 Carey Rd, Cathedral City; 92234 619-328-7211

Palm Springs

♂ • ♦ Alexander Resort, 598 Grenfall Rd; 92264 619-327-6911; 800-448-6197

♂ • Aruba Hotel, 671 S Riverside Drive; 92264 619-325-8440; 800-84-ARUBA

♂ • Avanti Resort, 715 San Lorenzo Rd; 92264 619-325-7293

♂ • Columns Resort, 537 Grenfall Rd; 92264 619-325-0655; 800-798-0655; Fax 619-322-1436

♂ ○ **Coyote Inn, 234 S Palencio Road; 92262 619-322-9675; 800-269-6830**
   ✦ *Coyote Inn advertisement page 172*

♂ • Desert Knight Hotel, 435 Avenida Olancha; 92264 619-325-5456

♂ ○ **Desert Paradise Hotel, 615 Warm Sands Dr; 92262 619-320-5650; 800-243-7635**
   ✦ *Desert Paradise Hotel advertisement page 172*

COYOTE INN

234 S. Patencio Rd., Palm Springs
619-322-9675   800-269-6830

♀ ○ El Mirasol Villas, 525 Warm Sands Drive; 92264 800-327-2985 Fax 619-325-8931
✦ *El Mirasol Villas advertisement page 173*

♀ • ♿ Enclave Private Resort, 641 San Lorenzo Rd; 92264 619-325-5269; 800-621-6973; Fax 619-320-9535

♀ • (♿) Le Garbo Inn, 287 W Racquet Club Rd; 92262 619-325-6737

♂ • ♿ Hacienda en Sueno Resort, 586 Warm Sands Drive; 92264 800-359-2007

♂ • Harlow Club Hotel, 175 E Alameda; 92262 619-323-3977; 800-223-4073 outside CA

♂ • Inn Exile, 960 Camino Parocela; 92262 619-327-6413; 800-962-0186

♂ • ♿ Inntimate, 556 Warm Sands Dr; 92264 619-778-8334; 800-695-3846

♂ ○ ♿ InnTrigue, 526 Warm Sands Dr; 92264 619-323-7505; 800-798-8781

♂ • Sago Palms Resort Hotel, 595 Thornhill Rd; 92264 800-626-SAGO

♀ • (♿) Smoke Tree Villa Hotel, 1586 E Palm Canyon Dr; 92264 619-323-2231

♂ • Vista Grande Villa Private Resort/Atrium Hotel, 574 Warm Sands Dr; 92264 619-322-2404

♂ • ♿ Warm Sands Villas, 555 Warm Sands Drive; 92264 619-323-3005; 800-357-5695
✦ *Warm Sands Villas advertisement page 173*

AIDS/HIV Support, Education, Advocacy, Publications

♀ ☆ Desert AIDS Project, 750 S Vella Rd; 92264 619-323-2118 Mon-Fri 8am-5pm. Pub *AIDS Matters*.

Bars, Restaurants, Clubs, Discos
Cathedral City
♂ • C.C. Construction Co, 68-449 Perez Rd, Cathedral City; 92234 619-324-4241

♂ • ♿ Choices, 68-325 Perez Road, Cathedral City; 92234 619-321-1145 *BDE* 4pm-2am; Sat & Sun noon-2am.

♀ • (♿) Delilah's, 68657 E Palm Canyon Dr, Cathedral City; 92234 *DE*

♂ The Pub, 68-981 Hwy 111, Cathedral City; 92234 619-324-1032

♂ Spurs Saloon, 36373 Cathedral Canyon Dr, Cathedral City; 92234 619-321-1233

♂ Wolf's Den, 67-625 Highway 111, Cathedral City; 92234 619-321-9688

Palm Desert
♀ Backstreet Deli & Pub, 72-695 Hwy 111, Unit A-7, Palm Desert; 92260 619-341-7966 *R*

Palm Springs
♂ The Club, 1117 N Palm Canyon Drive; 92262-4401 619-778-5310 *BR*

♀ Hamburger Mary's, 226 S Palm Canyon Dr; 92262 619-320-5555 *BR*

♂ Streetbar, 224 E Arenas Road; 92262 619-320-1266

♂ Tool Shed, 600 E Sunny Dunes Rd; 92264 619-320-3299

Rancho Mirage
♀ ○ ♿ Shame On The Moon, 69950 Frank Sinatra Dr, Rancho Mirage; 92270 619-324-5515 *R*

Erotica (Printed, Visual, Equipment)
♂ • Black Moon Leather, 68-449 San Ysidro Ave #7, Cathedral City; 92234 619-328-7773 7pm-2.30am; weekends to 3pm.

♀ ○ Hidden Joy, 68-424 Commercial Rd, Cathedral City; 92234 619-328-1694 10am-3am; Fri & Sat to 4am. "Books, video arcade; video sales & rentals; leather; most gay periodicals."

♀ ○ Perez Video & Books, 68-366 Perez Rd, Cathedral City; 92234 619-321-5597

♂ ○ ♿ Worldwide Adult Bookstore, 68-300 Ramon Rd, Cathedral City; 92234 619-321-1313

Health Clubs, Gyms, Saunas
♂ • CBC Club Palm Springs, 68-449 Perez Rd #1, Cathedral City; 92234 619-324-8588 24 hrs.

DESERT PARADISE HOTEL

CASUAL ELEGANCE

A NEW GENTLEMEN'S RESORT OFFERING
LUSH GARDEN SETTINGS
STYLISHLY DECORATED SUITES
POOLSIDE BREAKFAST
•
615 WARM SANDS DR. • PALM SPRINGS, CALIFORNIA
(619) 320-5650 • (800) 342-7635 (OUTSIDE CA)

Organizations/Resources: Business & Professional

♀ ★ ♑♑ Desert Business Association, PO Box 773; 92263 619-323-5000; 619-325-1978; Pub *DBA Desert Views.*

Organizations/Resources: Political/Legislative

♂ Log Cabin Riverside County, 2284 Temple Hills Dr, Laguna Beach, CA 92651 619-864-9551 "Republican organization."

Organizations/Resources: Social, Recreational & Support Groups (see also Sport/Dance/Outdoor)

♀ ★ (♑) Desert Women's Association/SCWU, PO Box 718, Cathedral City; 92235 619-778-1189 Pub *DWA Newsletter.*

♂ ★ Prime Timers of the Desert, PO Box 3061; 92263-3061 619-328-3326 "Social club for mature men & their admirers."

Publications

♀ • *The Bottom Line,* 1243 Gene Autry Trail #121-122; 92262 619-323-0552

♂ *David,* 68-671 Grove St, Cathedral City; 92234 619-324-4957 Fax 619-324-2857

♀ *Mega Scene,* 611 S Palm Canyon Dr #7B, Cathedral City; 92264 619-327-5178

♂ *MEGA-Scene,* 548 Industrial Place; 92264

♂ *Star Magazine,* 68-671 Grove St, Cathedral City; 92234 619-324-4957

Real Estate

♀ • ♿ TLC Services, PO Box 3337; 92263 619-343-1220 "Relocation & retirement services in Palm Springs."

Religious Organizations & Publications

♂ Chevrat 'Or, c/o Temple Sinai, 43435 Monterey Ave, Palm Desert; 92260 619-568-0558

♂ Christ Chapel of the Desert, 938 Vella Rd; 92264 619-327-2795

♂ Integrity of the Desert, 4741-C E Palm Canyon Dr, Box 149; 92264 619-341-0555 "Lesbian & Gay Episcopalians & their friends."

Travel & Tourist Services (see also Accommodation)

♂ • Rancho Mirage Travel, 71-428 Hwy 111, Rancho Mirage; 92270 619-341-7888; 800-369-1073; Fax 619-568-9202

♀ • San Vicente Travel, 451 E Tahquitz Canyon Way; 92262 619-320-8220 Fax 619-320-7445

Palmdale

Erotica (Printed, Visual, Equipment)

♀ ○ ♿ Sunshine Gifts, 38519 Sierra Hwy; 93550 805-265-0652

Palo Alto

☎ Stanford Lesbian/Gay & Bisexual Community Center, ter 415-725-4222

Bookstores: Gay/Lesbian/Feminist

♀ ○ ♿ Stepping Stones, The Artifactory, 226 Hamilton Ave; 94301 415-583-9685

Community Centers (see also Women's Centers)

♂ ★ (♑♑) Stanford Lesbian/Gay & Bisexual Community Center, PO Box 8265, Stanford; 94309 / on Santa Teresa St, near Tresidder Memorial Union, Stanford Campus 415-725-4222; 415-723-1488; office Mon-Fri noon-4pm; call for evening events.

Organizations/Resources: Family

♀ ☆ ♂ Mid-Peninsula PFLAG, PO Box 8265, Stanford; 94305 415-857-1058 "Parents, Families & Friends of Lesbians & Gays."

Organizations/Resources: Sport/Dance/Outdoor

♂ ★ Gay & Lesbian Sierrans, Loma Prieta Chapter, 3921 E. Bayshore Rd; 94303 408-236-2170

Organizations/Resources: Student, Academic, Alumni/ae

♂ ★ (?♂) Stanford Lesbian/Gay/Bisexual Community Center, PO Box 8265; 94309 415-725-4222 (staff); 415-723-1488 (events line)

Pasadena

AIDS/HIV Support, Education, Advocacy, Publications

♀ ☆ ♂♂ AIDS Service Center, 126 W Del Mar Blvd; 91105-2508 818-796-5633; 800-543-8272; Fax 818-796-8198 Mon-Fri 9am-5pm. Pub Asklepios; Impressions.

Bars, Restaurants, Clubs, Discos

♀ • ♂♂ Club 3772, 3772 E Foothill Blvd; 91107 818-578-9359 *BEW*

♀ • Incognito/Encounters, 203 N Sierra Madre Blvd; 91107 818-792-3735 *BDE* Mainly men; women welcome.

♂ • ♂ Nardi's, 665 E Colorado Blvd; 91101 818-449-3152

♂ • ♂ On The Boulevard, 3199 E Foothill Blvd; 91107 818-356-9304

Bookstores: Gay/Lesbian/Feminist

♀ • ♂ Page One: Books By & For Women, 1196 E Walnut St; 91106 818-798-8418

Counseling/Therapy: Private

♀ • ♂♂ Schoenwether, Paula, PhD, MFCC, 2047 Huntington Dr #C, South Pasadena; 91030-4950 818-441-1789

Herbalists

♂ • ♂ Raub, Karen L., LAc, ND, 2047 Huntington Dr #C, South Pasadena; 91030 818-403-5911

Placerville: see Sacramento

Plymouth

Accommodation: Hotels, B&B, Resorts, Campgrounds

♂ • Rancho Cicada Retreat, PO Box 225; 95669 209-245-4841 "Riverside camping: platform tents & cabins."

Pomona: see San Bernardino/Riverside/Pomona Area

Rancho Mirage: see Palm Springs

Redding

Bars, Restaurants, Clubs, Discos

♂ Club 501, 1244 California St; 96001 916-243-7869

Erotica (Printed, Visual, Equipment)

♂ ○ Adult Books & Video, 2131 Hilltop Dr; 96001 916-223-2675

Redlands: see San Bernardino/Riverside/Pomona Area

Redondo Beach: see Los Angeles

Redway

Travel & Tourist Services (see also Accommodation)

♀ • Kismet Travel, PO Box 974; 95560 707-986-7205; 800-926-7205; Pub Gay Travel Calendar. "Gay destinations our specialty."

Redwood City

AIDS/HIV Support, Education, Advocacy, Publications

♀ ☆ ♂♂ AIDS Community Research Consortium, 1048 El Camino Real #A; 94063 415-364-6563

Bars, Restaurants, Clubs, Discos

♂ • ♂♂ Shouts Bar & Grill, 2034 Broadway; 94063 415-369-9651 *BDR*

Erotica (Printed, Visual, Equipment)

♀ ○ ♂ Golden Gate #3 Books & Video, 739 El Camino Real; 94063 415-364-6913 24 hrs.

Religious Organizations & Publications

♂ ★ ♂♂ MCC of the Peninsula, PO Box 70; 94064-0007 / 2124 Brewster St 415-368-0188

Reseda: see Los Angeles Area

Riverside: see San Bernardino/Riverside/Pomona Area

Russian River

Accommodation: Hotels, B&B, Resorts, Campgrounds

♀ • ♂ Fern Grove Inn, 16650 River Rd, Guerneville; 95446 707-869-9083; 800-347-9083

♂ • (?♂) Fife's Resort, PO Box 45, Guerneville; 95446-0045 707-869-0656; 800-7FIFES1 *BDERCW*

♂ • (♂♂) Heart's Desire Inn At Occidental, PO Box 857, Occidental; 95465-0857 / 3659 Church St 707-874-1047 Fax 707-874-1078 *R*

♂ • Highland Dell Inn, PO Box 370, Monte Rio; 95462-0370 800-767-1759

♂ ○ (♂) Highlands Resort, PO Box 346, Guerneville; 95446 / 14000 Woodland Drive 707-869-0333

♀ ○ House Of A Thousand Flowers, 11 Mosswood Circle, Cazadero; 95421 707-632-5571

♀ • (♂) Huckleberry Springs, PO Box 400, Monte Rio; 95462 800-822-2683 *R*

♀ ○ Mountain Lodge Resort, PO Box 1867, Guerneville; 95446 707-869-3722

♂ • Paradise Cove Resort, 14711 Armstrong Woods Rd, Guerneville; 95446 707-869-2706

♂ • Rio Villa Beach Resort, 20292 Hwy 116, Monte Rio; 95462 707-865-1143

♂ • (♂) The Village Inn, Box 850, Monte Rio; 95462 707-865-2304 *BR*

♂ • The Willows, Box 465, Guerneville; 95446 / 15905 River Rd 800-953-2828; 707-869-2824

♂ • ♂♂ The Woods, Box 1690, Guerneville; 95446-1690 / 16881 Armstrong Woods Rd 707-869-0111

Accommodation: Reservations & Exchanges (see also Travel)

♂ • Redwood Empire Agency, Jim Sorrells, PO Box 1946, Guerneville; 95446 707-869-1146 "Accommodation reservations for the Russian River; also real estate."

Bars, Restaurants, Clubs, Discos

♀ Burdon's, PO Box 259, Guerneville; 95446 / 15405 River Rd 707-869-2615 *R*

♂ ○ Molly's Country Club, Box 349, Guerneville; 95446 / 14120 Old Cazadero Rd 707-869-0511

♂ ○ Rainbow Cattle Co, 16220 Main St 707-869-0206

⚢ O && Ziggurat, 16135 Main St, Guerneville; 95446 707-869-1400 *DE*

Bookstores: General

⚢ ● && The Last Word Newsstand, PO Box 1334, Forestville; 95446 / 14045 Armstrong Woods Rd 707-869-0571 "Also large stock of music on CD & casette."

Organizations/Resources: Business & Professional

⚢ ★ Gay Lesbian Business Association (GLBA), PO Box 2579, Guerneville; 95446 707-869-GLBA

Organizations/Resources: Social, Recreational & Support Groups (see also Sport/Dance/Outdoor)

⚂ Pacific Bears Leather/MC, PO Box 1089, Guerneville; 95446 707-869-3783

Publications

⚂ ● *Manifest Reader*, PO Box 1069, Forestville; 95436 707-823-0322 Fax 707-823-5403

Religious Organizations & Publications

⚢ ★ && Russian River Metropolitan Community Church, PO Box 1055, Guerneville; 95446 / 14520 Armstrong Woods Rd 707-869-0552

Sacramento

Accommodation: Hotels, B&B, Resorts, Campgrounds

⚢ ● Hartley House Inn, 700 22nd St; 95816-4012 916-447-7829

Addictive Behavior, Substance Abuse, Recovery

⚢ Alcoholics Anonymous/Al-Anon, North Hall Group, Box 20125; 95820 / 2751 34th St 916-454-1100

AIDS/HIV Support, Education, Advocacy, Publications

⚢ ☆ && Sacramento AIDS Foundation, 920 20th St, 2nd flr; 95814-3133 916-448-2437

Bars, Restaurants, Clubs, Discos

⚢ O & Buffalo Club, 1831 S St; 95814 916-442-1087

⚂ ● && Faces Bar & Nightclub, 2000 K St; 95814 916-448-7798 *BD* 1pm-2am. All welcome.

⚢ Jammin' Jo's, 2721 Broadway; 95818 916-457-7888

⚂ Mercantile Saloon, 1928 L St; 95814 916-447-0792

⚢ ● && The Mirage, 601 15th St; 95814 916-444-3238 *BD*

⚂ ● & Town House, 1517 21st St; 95814 916-441-5122 *BR* Bar 10am-2am; call for dinner hours.

⚂ Western, 2001 K St; 95814 916-443-9831

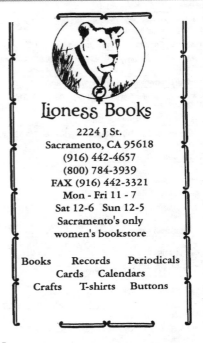

Lioness Books

2224 J St.
Sacramento, CA 95618
(916) 442-4657
(800) 784-3939
FAX (916) 442-3321
Mon - Fri 11 - 7
Sat 12-6 Sun 12-5
Sacramento's only
women's bookstore

Books Records Periodicals
Cards Calendars
Crafts T-shirts Buttons

⚂ O Wreck Room, 2513 Broadway; 95818 916-456-1181

Bookstores: Gay/Lesbian/Feminist

⚢ ● && Lioness Books, 2224 J St; 95816 916-442-4657; 800-784-3939; Fax 916-442-3321 Mon-Fri 11am-7pm; Sat noon-6pm; Sun noon-5pm.

◆ *Lioness Books advertisement page 175*

Bookstores: General

⚢ O Tower Books, 1600 Broadway; 95818 916-444-6688

Bookstores: Recovery, Metaphysical, & other Specialty

♀ O Her Place, 6635 Madison Ave, Carmichael; 95608 916-961-1058

Clothes

♀ • The Empower Wear Company, PO Box 748; 95812 916-925-0312 Fax 916-925-8833

Community Centers (see also Women's Centers)

♂ ★ Lambda Community Center, 1931 L St; 95814 916-442-0185; 916-447-5755

Funding: Endowment, Fundraising, Scholarship

♀ ★ &♂ Sacramento Rainbow Festival, 2000 K St; 95814 916-448-2000; 916-448-7792

Gifts, Cards, Pride & Novelty Items

♀ ○ Postcards Etc., 2101 L St; 95816 916-446-8049 "Cards, gifts, picture framing."

Graphic Design/Typesetting (see also Art; Printing)

♂ • &♂ MGW Typesetting & Graphics, 1725 L St; 95814 916-441-6397

Legal Services & Resources

♀ • &♂ Pearce, M. Jane, 1409 28th St #200; 95816 916-452-3883

Organizations/Resources: Family

♂ ★ Gay Fathers of Sacramento, PO Box 161951; 95816-1951 916-456-DADS

♀ ☆ ♂ PFLAG, PO Box 661855; 95866-1855 916-444-9510 "Parents, Families & Friends of Lesbians & Gays."

Organizations/Resources: Political/Legislative

♀ ★ (?&) Log Cabin Club, 2025 23rd St; 95818-1717 916-737-9383 (Republicans)

♂ ★ &♂ River City Democratic Club, PO Box 161958; 95816-1958 916-448-2383; 916-394-3114

Organizations/Resources: Sexual Focus (Leather, S/M, etc) & Safe Sex Promotion

♀ ☆ Leather & Lace, WMC, Inc, PO Box 163044; 95816 916-489-5656

Organizations/Resources: Sport/Dance/Outdoor

♀ Camping Women/Sacramento, PO Box 13261; 95813

♂ ★ &♂ Capital City Squares, PO Box 19986; 95819 916-929-8697 (George Fox) 4120870@mcimail.com *d*

♂ ★ (?&) Outdoor Adventures (OAS), PO Box 231113; 95823

♂ ★ &♂ Prime 8's, c/o James Ozanich, 1815 Urbana Way; 95833-2646 916-925-4242 0004120870@mcimail *d*

Organizations/Resources: Student, Academic, Alumni/ae

♂ ★ (&♂) Delta Lambda Phi Fraternity/California State University, Sacramento Chapter, Box 59, Student Activities Office; 95819 800-587-FRAT

♂ ★ Gay People's Union, Sacramento City College, Student Activities, 3835 Freeport Blvd; 95822 916-429-7381

Performing Arts: Entertainment, Music, Recording, Theater, etc.

♂ ★ (?&) Sacramento Men's Chorus, PO Box 188726; 95818 916-444-5213

Publications

♂ • &♂ *Dad Guess What Newspaper*, 1725 L St; 95814 916-441-NEWS Twice monthly. "Alternates with Mom Guess What: Pull-out section for social meeting places; personals; 900 numbers, etc."
✦ *Dad Guess What Newspaper advertisement page 175*

♀ • ♂ *The Latest Issue*, 2528 Capitol Ave; 95816 916-448-8504 Fax 916-448-8505

♂ • &♂ *Mom Guess What Newspaper*, 1725 L St; 95814 916-441-NEWS Twice monthly.
✦ *Mom Guess What Newspaper advertisement page 175*

Religious Organizations & Publications

♂ ★ &♂ River City Metropolitan Community Church, PO Box 245125; 95824 916-454-4762

Travel & Tourist Services (see also Accommodation)

♀ ○ Aladdin Travel, 818 K Street Mall; 95814 916-446-0633; 800-433-5386

♀ • Mad About Travel, 930 Bell Ave; 95838 916-567-1958; 800-856-0441

♀ ○ ♂ Red Shoes Travel, 3241 Folsom Blvd; 95816 916-454-4201

♀ • Sports Leisure Travel, 9527A Folsom Blvd; 95827 916-361-2051; 916-485-1931

Women's Centers

♀ ☆ &♂ CSUS Women's Resource Center, 6000 J St, Student Service Center Room 300; 95819 916-278-7388

♀ ☆ ♂ El Dorado Women's Center, 3133 Gilmore St, Placerville; 95667 916-626-1450; 916-626-1131; 800-656-HOPE

St Helena

Accommodation: Hotels, B&B, Resorts, Campgrounds

♀ ★ **The Ink House Bed & Breakfast, 1575 St. Helena Hwy; 94574 510-963-3890; 800-553-4343**

Salinas

Religious Organizations & Publications

♀ ★ (?&) Integrity/El Camino Real, c/o Church of the Good Shepherd, 301 Corral de Tierra; 93908 408-484-2326; 408-294-2026 "Gay & Lesbian Episcopalians & their friends."

San Andreas

Religious Organizations & Publications

♀ ☆ (?&) Integrity of the Sierra, PO Box 110; 95249 209-728-2193 Pub *St. Aelred's Gazette.* "Gay & Lesbian Episcopalians & their friends. Call for details of monthly service, meeting, & potluck."

San Anselmo

Community Centers (see also Women's Centers)

♂ ★ &♂ Spectrum, 1000 Sir Francis Drake Blvd; 94960 415-457-1115

San Bernardino/Riverside/Pomona Area

☎ Gay & Lesbian Center, Inland Empire 909-884-5447

Bars, Restaurants, Clubs, Discos

Pomona

♂ • Alibi East/Back Alley, 225 S San Antonio Ave, Pomona; 91766 909-623-9422

♂ BVD's Dynasty Club, 730-732 W Holt Ave, Pomona; 91768 909-622-7502

♂ • (&) Mary's, 1047 E 2nd St, Pomona; 91766 909-622-1971 *BR*

♂ Robbie's, 390 Pomona Mall, Pomona; 91761 909-620-4371

Riverside

♂ ○ ♂♂ The Menagerie, 3581 University, Riverside; 92501 909-788-8000 *BD* 4pm-2am.

♂ ● ♂♂ Grand Central, 345 W. 7th St; 92401 909-889-5204 *BD* Tue-Sun 7pm-2am.

San Bernardino

♀ Phoenix Alive, 749 W 4th St, San Bernardino; 92410 909-884-0343 *D* (no alcohol)

♂ ● ♂♂ Skylark, 917 Inland Center Drive, San Bernardino; 92408 909-884-2404 *BDLCW*

Bookstores: Gay/Lesbian/Feminist

♀ ○ ♂ Wild Iris Bookstore, 143A Harvard Ave, Claremont; 91711 909-626-8283 Tue-Sat 10am-5.30pm; call for other hours & events. "Women's books, art, music; non-sexist children's books."

Community Centers (see also Women's Centers)

♂ ★ ♂ Gay & Lesbian Center, Inland Empire, PO Box 6333, San Bernardino; 92412 909-884-5447 6.30-10pm; 24 hr information referral

Erotica (Printed, Visual, Equipment)

♀ ○ Bear Facts, 1434 E Baseline, San Bernardino; 92410 909-885-9176 24 hrs. "Books; video arcade; video sales & rentals; most gay periodicals."

♂ ● ♂♂ Mustang Books & Video, 961 N Central, Upland; 91786-3531 909-981-0227

♂ ○ Toy Box, 1999 W Arrow Route, Upland; 91786-7679 909-982-9407

♂ ○ (♂) Video Fantasies, 5327 Mission Blvd, Riverside; 92509 909-782-8056 24 hrs.

Organizations/Resources: Business & Professional

♂ (?♂) GALE/Inland Empire (Gay & Lesbian Educators of So. Cal, Inc.), PO Box 30463, San Bernardino; 92413

Organizations/Resources: General, Multipurpose, Pride

♂ ★ ♂ Pomona/San Gabriel Valley Gay & Lesbian Coalition, 281 S Thomas St #505, Pomona; 91766-1704 909-623-1612

♀ ★ ♂♂ Southern California Women for Understanding/Inland Chapter, PO Box 20246, Riverside; 92516-0246 909-422-3760 (recorded info); 909-422-3760 (recorded info)

Organizations/Resources: Sport/Dance/Outdoor

♂ ★ ♂♂ Great Outdoors/Inland Empire, PO Box 56586, Riverside; 92517-7993 909-888-7993

Organizations/Resources: Student, Academic, Alumni/ae

♂ ★ ♂♂ Gay & Lesbian Student Union, California State University, 5500 University Parkway, San Bernardino; 92407 909-887-7407

♂ ★ ♂♂ Union of Lesbians, Gays & Bisexuals, c/o Commons Main Desk, Uuniversity of California, Riverside; 92521 909-787-3337

Religious Organizations & Publications

♂ ★ Affirmation: United Methodists for Lesbian, Gay & Bisexual Concerns/Inland Empire, 1325 N Claremont, Box 302, Claremont; 91711 909-624-2159

♂ Metropolitan Community Church of the Pomona Valley, PO Box 226, Montclair; 91763 909-392-0422

KEATING HOUSE
2331 2nd Avenue • San Diego, California 92101

Plan a romantic stay in our friendly Victorian Bed & Breakfast in the heart of San Diego! In the morning, we'll serve you a full delicious breakfast.... And for only $50-85 per night!

1-800-995-8644

San Clemente

Organizations/Resources: Sport/Dance/Outdoor

♂ ★ Golden State Squares, c/o Laura Green, 2109 Via Viejo; 92673 714-366-9787 *d*

San Diego Area

☎ Lesbian & Gay Community Center 619-692-GAYS

Accommodation: Hotels, B&B, Resorts, Campgrounds

Palomar Mountain

♀ ○ ♂♂ A Woman's Place, Palomar Mountain 619-742-1593 Fax 619-742-1845 compuserve 72730,436

San Diego

♂ ● Balboa Park Inn, 3402 Park Blvd; 92103 619-298-0823; 800-938-8181; Fax 619-294-8070

♂ ● The Beach Place, 2158 Sunset Cliffs Blvd; 92107 619-225-0746

♂ ○ ♂♂ Clarke's Flamingo Lodge, 1765 Union St; 92101 619-234-6787; 800-822-0133 *BRE*

♂ ● Dmitri's Guesthouse, 931 21st St; 92102 619-238-5547

♂ ○ ♂♂ Downtown Inn Hotel, 660 G Street; 92101 619-238-4100 Fax 619-238-5310

♂ ● ♂ Eagle Crest Hotel, 3942 8th Ave; 92103 619-298-9898

♂ ○ (?♂) Embassy Hotel, 3645 Park Blvd; 92103 619-296-3141

♂ ● ♂♂ Hillcrest Inn, 3754 5th Ave; 92103 619-293-7078; 800-258-2280
♦ Hillcrest Inn advertisement page 177

♀ • (?⚥) **Keating House, 2331 2nd Ave; 92101 619-239-5774; 800-995-8644 "Bed & Breakfast guest house."**
✦ *Keating House advertisement page 177*

♀ • ♿ Park Manor Suites, 525 Spruce Street; 92103 619-291-0999; 800-874-2649; Fax 619-201-8844 **BRE**

♀ ○ ♿♿ Travelodge at the Zoo, 2223 El Cajon Blvd; 92104 619-296-2101

Addictive Behavior, Substance Abuse, Recovery

⚥ ★ (?⚥) Stepping Stone, Hillcrest Community Recovery Service, 3425 5th Ave; 92103 619-295-3995 "A non-residential drug/alcohol program."

⚥ ★ (?⚥) Stepping Stone: Central Residential Recovery Services, 3767 Central Ave; 92105-2506 619-584-4010 "A residential Drug/Alcohol Program."

AIDS/HIV Support, Education, Advocacy, Publications

⚥ ★ ♿♿ AIDS Art Alive, 1043 University Ave #211; 92103 619-338-6395 Pub *AIDS Art Alive Newsletr.* "Community arts program offering juried traveling exhibitions on AIDS-related themes; free art classes for people with AIDS."

♀ ★ Aids Chaplaincy Program, PO Box 34607; 92163 619-294-7753

♀ ★ ♿♿ Aids Foundation San Diego, 140 Arbor Dr; 92103 619-686-5000

♀ ☆ Auntie Helen's Fluff'N Fold, 4028 30th St; 92104 619-584-8438

♀ Being Alive—San Diego, 3960 Park Blvd #H; 92103 619-291-1400

♀ ○ Center for Special Immunology, 2918 5th Ave #300; 92103 619-291-1122

♀ ☆ ♿♿ Owen Clinic, UCSD Medical Center, 200 W Arbor Drt; 92103-8681 619-294-6255

♀ Pets Are Wonderful Support (PAWS), 1278 University Ave Box 178; 92103 619-234-PAWS

♂ ★ ♿ San Diego Community Research Group, 3495 Olive St; 92104-5230 619-291-2437

Archives/Libraries/History Projects

⚥ ★ (?⚥) Lesbian & Gay Historical Society of San Diego, PO Box 40389; 92164 619-260-1522 (previously Lesbian & Gay Archives of San Diego)

Bars, Restaurants, Clubs, Discos

Oceanside

♀ ○ ♿♿ Capri Lounge, 207 N Tremont St, Oceanside; 92054 619-722-7284

Pacific Beach

⚥ ○ ♿ Matador, 4633 Mission Blvd, Pacific Beach; 92109 619-483-6943

San Diego

♂ Bourbon St, 4612 Park Blvd; 92116 619-291-0173

♂ ○ Brass Rail, 3796 5th Ave; 92103 619-298-2233 **BDER**

♂ Caliph Piano Bar, 3102 5th Ave; 92103 619-298-9495

♂ Chee Chee Club, 929 Broadway; 92101 619-234-4404

⚥ • ♿ Cheers, 1839 Adams Ave; 92116 619-298-3269

⚥ • Club Bom Bay, 3175 India St; 92103 619-296-6789 **BDE** 4pm-2am; Fri-Sun 2pm-2am.

♀ ○ ♿♿ Crest Cafe, 425 Robinson Ave; 92103 619-295-2510 **BR**

♂ The Eagle, 3040 North Park Way; 92104-3626 619-295-8072 **L**

⚥ • The Flame, 3780 Park Blvd; 92103 619-295-4163 **D**

♂ • Flicks, 1017 University Ave; 92103 619-297-2056

♂ The Hole, 2820 Lytton St; 92110 619-226-9019

♂ Kickers, 308 University; 92103 619-491-0400 **BD**

♂ • Loft, 3610 5th Ave; 92103 619-296-6407

♂ • ♿♿ North Park Country Club, 4046 30th St; 92104 619-563-9051

♂ Number One Fifth Avenue, 3845 5th Ave; 92103 619-299-1911

♂ Numbers, 3811 Park Blvd; 92103 619-294-9005

♂ Pecs, 2046 University Ave; 92104 619-296-0889

⚥ • Redwing Bar & Grill, 4012 30th St; 92104 619-281-8700 **BR**

♂ Rich's San Diego, 1051 University Ave; 92103 619-497-4588

♂ Shooterz, 3815 30th St; 92104 619-574-0744

♂ SRO, 1807 5th Ave; 92101 619-232-1886

♂ Waterloo Station, 3968 5th Ave; 92103 619-574-9329

♂ • ♿♿ West Coast Production Company, 2028 Hancock St; 92110 619-295-3724 **DE** 9pm-2am.

♂ ○ Wolf's, 3404 30th St; 92104 619-291-3730

Bookstores: Gay/Lesbian/Feminist

⚥ • ♿ Obelisk The Bookstore, 1029 University Ave; 92103 619-297-4171 Fax 619-297-5803 Mon-Thu 11am-10pm; Fri & Sat to 11pm. "Full service community bookstore."

Bookstores: General

♀ ○ Blue Door Bookstore, 3823 5th Ave; 92103 619-298-8610 "Extensive collection of Gay & Lesbian titles."

♀ ○ ♿♿ F Street Escondido, 237 E Grand Ave, Escondido; 92025 619-480-6031 9am-2am.

Broadcast Media

♂ Our World Television, 3976 Park Blvd; 92103 619-297-4975

Business, Financial & Secretarial

♀ • Cundari, Chris, CPA, 1010 University Ave #209; 92103-3361 619-298-9699 Fax 619-298-6168

Clothes

⚥ • ♿ The Crypt on Washington, 1515 Washington; 92103 619-692-9499 "Leather clothing."

♀ • ♿ Moose Leather, 2923 Upas St; 92104 619-297-6935 Tue-Thu noon-9pm; Fri & Sat to 10pm.

Community Centers (see also Women's Centers)

⚥ ★ (♿♿) Lesbian & Gay Men's Community Center, PO Box 3357; 92163 / 3916 Normal St 619-692-2077; 619-692-GAYS; Fax 619-260-3092 Pub *CenterPiece.*

Counseling/Therapy: Private

♀ ○ ♿♿ Fulton, Andrea P., MS, MFCC, 8899 University Center Lane #150; 92122 619-488-5878

⚥ • Karmen, Mel D., Ph.D., 4111 Palmetto Way; 92103 619-296-9442

♀ • Struhl, Laura S., Ph.D., 106 Thorn St; 92103 619-694-0057

Erotica (Printed, Visual, Equipment)

♂ ○ ᗜᗝ Cinema F, 1202 University Ave; 92103 619-298-0854 P 24 hrs. "Private membership theater."

♀ ○ F Street Chula Vista, 1141 3rd St, Chula Vista; 91911 619-447-0381 24 hrs.

♀ ○ F Street Gaslamp, 751 4th Ave; 92101 619-236-0841 24 hrs.

♀ ○ F Street Kearny Mesa, 7865 Balboa; 92111 619-292-8083 24 hrs.

♀ ○ F Street Mira Mesa, 7998 Miramar Rd; 92126 619-549-8014 24 hrs.

♀ ○ ᗜᗝ F Street North Park, 2004 University; 92104 619-298-2644 24 hrs.

♀ ○ ᗝ Gemini, 5265 University Ave; 92105 619-287-1402

♂ ○ ᗜᗝ Hi-Lite Theater & Bookstore, 3203 Hancock St; 92110 619-299-0601 Fax 619-299-2471 9am-2.30am.

♀ ○ ᗜᗝ Midnight Adult Book & Video Center, 316 3rd St, Oceanside; 92054 619-757-7832 24 hrs.

♀ ○ ᗜᗝ Midnight Adult Book & Video, 1407 University Ave; 92103 619-299-7186 24 hrs.

♀ ○ ᗜᗝ Midnight Adult Book & Video, 3604 Midway Dr; 92110 619-222-9973

♀ ○ ᗜᗝ Midnight Adult Book & Video, 4790 El Cajon Blvd; 92115 619-582-1997

♀ ○ ᗝ Midnight Adult Book & Video Center, 1177 Palm Ave, Imperial Beach; 91932 619-575-5081

♀ • ᗝ North Park Adult Video, 4094 30th St; 92104 619-284-4724

♀ ○ ᗝ Pleasureland, 836 5th Ave; 92101 619-237-9056

♀ ○ (?ᗝ) Video Specialties, 2322 S Escondido Blvd, Escondido; 92025 619-745-6697

Funeral Directors/Cemetaries/Mausoleums

♀ ○ ᗜᗝ Park Crest Funeral Home, 2441 University Ave; 92104 619-260-1280 Fax 619-297-5901

Gifts, Cards, Pride & Novelty Items

♀ ○ (ᗝ) Best Wishes, 3830 5th Ave; 92103 619-296-3234 10am-8pm; Sun noon-5pm. "Cards, gifts, jewelry, candy, stationery, giftwrap."

Health Care (see also AIDS Services)

♀ ☆ ᗜᗝ Beach Area Community Health Center, 3705 Mission Blvd; 92109 619-488-0644

♂ • ᗜᗝ Hartmeyer, James A., M.D., 4067 Park Blvd; 92103 619-296-0224

♀ ○ Robert S. Smith Medical Group, 2850 6th Ave 5th flr; 92103 619-296-5590 Fax 619-296-5810

♀ • ᗜᗝ Vrhel, Keith, MD, Park Center for Health, 4067 Park Blvd; 92103 619-296-0224 Fax 619-296-0433

Health Clubs, Gyms, Saunas

♂ Club San Diego, 3955 4th Ave; 92103 619-295-0850

♂ • Dave's Club, 4969 Santa Monica; 92107 619-224-9011

♀ • ᗜᗝ Hillcrest Gym & Fitness Center, 142 University Ave; 92103 619-299-PUMP

♂ • Mustang Spa, 2200 University Ave; 92104 619-297-1661 P

♂ • Vulcan Steam & Sauna, 805 W Cedar St; 92101 619-238-1980 P

Home & Building: Cleaning, Repair, General Contractors

♂ • Barrett Contracting, 7770 Regents Rd #113 / #111; 92122 619-563-6009 Fax 619-450-3680

Interior Design

♀ • (?ᗝ) A Fresh Perspective, PO Box 84555; 92138-4555 619-234-1930 "Residential & commercial interior redesign & organizing services, using existing furnishings. Special understanding & assistance with differently-abled clients."

Legal Services & Resources

♀ ○ (ᗝ) Abeles, Judith, LL.M., PO Box 16612; 92176 619-284-0061 Fax 619-280-5805

♀ ○ Clarno, Mary, Esq, 2150 First Ave; 92101 619-236-8272

♀ ★ ᗜᗝ Lesbian & Gay Men's Center Legal Referral Program, PO Box 3357; 92163 619-692-GAYS

♀ • ᗜᗝ **Moe, Jerome R., 2359 4th Ave #215; 92101 619-234-0045**

Organizations/Resources: Business & Professional

♀ ★ (?ᗝ) Gay & Lesbian Association of County Employees (GALA), PO Box 34393; 92163 619-688-9822 "Public policy & social support group for County government employees in San Diego."

♀ ★ Greater San Diego Business Association, PO Box 33848; 92163-3848 619-296-4543 Fax 619-296-5616

♀ ★ (?ᗝ) San Diego Career Women, PO Box 880384; 92168 619-688-8002

Organizations/Resources: Ethnic, Multicultural

♀ ★ ᗜᗝ Lesbians & Gays of African Descent United (LAGADU), mail to LAGADU, PO Box 620448; 92162 619-496-3372

Organizations/Resources: Family

♀ ☆ ᗜᗝ PFLAG, PO Box 82762; 92138 619-579-7640 "Parents, Families & Friends of Lesbians & Gays."

Organizations/Resources: General, Multipurpose, Pride

♀ ★ (?ᗝ) Gay & Lesbian Association of North San Diego County (GLANC), PO Box 2866, Vista; 92085-2866 619-945-2478 glanc@aol._.com Pub Newsletter. "Social/educational support group."

Organizations/Resources: Political/Legislative

♀ ★ ᗝ Lesbian Rights Task Force, National Organization for Women, PO Box 80292; 92138 619-238-1824

♂ Log Cabin North San Diego County, 1035 E Vista Way #142, Vista; 92084 619-722-0669 (Republicans)

♀ ★ Log Cabin San Diego, PO Box 3242; 92163-3242 619-528-8500 (Republicans)

♀ ★ ᗜᗝ San Diego Democratic Club, PO Box 80193; 92138 619-496-3312

Organizations/Resources: Sexual Focus (Leather, S/M, etc) & Safe Sex Promotion

♀ ☆ (?ᗝ) National Leather Association/San Diego, PO Box 3092; 92163 619-685-5149

Organizations/Resources: Social, Recreational & Support Groups (see also Sport/Dance/Outdoor)

♀ ★ Couples/San Diego, PO Box 33724; 92163 619-286-3141

♂ ★ ᗜᗝ Girth & Mirth of San Diego, PO Box 86822; 92138-8622 619-685-8822 Pub San Diego at Large.

♂ Imperial Court, PO Box 33915; 92163 619-692-1967

⚥ ★ ♿ SAGE of California, Inc. (Seniors Active in a Gay Environment), PO Box 4071; 92164 619-282-1359 24 hrs. Meets 1st Tue of month, 6.30pm, at MCC, 4333 30th St. "Serving Gay & Lesbian seniors & their friends: referrals for legal, health, housing; tourist assistance for travelers; relocation assistance."

Organizations/Resources: Sport/Dance/Outdoor

⚥ ★ (?♂) Finny Dippers SCUBA Club, PO Box 82384; 92138-2384 619-670-8776 finnydip@aol.com

⚥ ★ Front Runners/San Diego, PO Box 3633; 92163-0200 "Running & walking group."

⚥ ★ ♿ Golden State Gay Rodeo Association: San Diego, 3636 4th Ave #310; 92103-4237 619-298-4708

⚥ ★ (?♂) Great Outdoors/San Diego, PO Box 82106; 92138 619-557-0168

⚥ ★ Rainbow Cyclists, PO Box 3344; 92163 619-294-INFO "Bicyclists."

⚥ ★ SAGA Ski Club, PO Box 3203; 92163

Organizations/Resources: Student, Academic, Alumni/ae

♂ ★ Delta Lambda Phi Fraternity, San Diego State University, Box 17 Aztec Center, SDSU; 92182 800-587-FRAT

♂ Delta Lambda Phi Fraternity, San Diego, c/o National Office, 1008 10th St #374, Sacramento, CA 95814 800-587-FRAT

⚥ ★ ♿ Lesbian, Gay & Bisexual Student Union, Box 45, Aztec Center; 92182 619-594-2737

⚥ ★ (?♂) Lesbian/Gay/Bisexual Organization, University of California, San Diego, 0077 - #18, 9500 Gilman Dr, La Jolla; 92093-0077 619-534-4297

Organizations/Resources: Youth (see also Family)

⚥ ★ ♿ Gay Youth Alliance, PO Box 83022; 92138 619-233-9309

Performing Arts: Entertainment, Music, Recording, Theater, etc.

⚥ ★ ♿ Diversionary Theatre, PO Box 370723; 92137 / 4545 Park Blvd 619-574-1060

⚥ ★ ♿ Gay Men's Chorus of San Diego, PO Box 86768; 92138-6768 619-275-ARTS

♂ San Diego Men's Chorus, 3103 Falcon St; 92103 619-296-SONG

Printing & Promotional Items (see also Art; Graphics/Typesetting)

♀ ○ ♿ Imperial Printing & Graphics, 1001 B Ave #201, Coronado; 92118 619-522-6536 Fax 619-435-6013

Publications

⚥ ● Bravo!, PO Box 34646; 92163 619-528-8500 Fax 619-528-8713

→ Gay & Lesbian Times: p.158

♀ ● The North Park Review, PO Box 40174; 92164 619-688-0690

⚥ ★ Update, PO Box 33148; 92163-3148 619-225-0282

→ Voice Magazine: p.158

Real Estate

♀ ○ Keasler, John, 1421 W Lewis St; 92104 619-491-0779

♀ ● Oster, Ron, Realty Executives, 911 Hacienda Dr, Vista; 92083 619-632-4199; 619-758-2300; Fax 619-758-8851 "Commercial/investment/residential."

Religious Organizations & Publications

⚥ ★ (?♂) Affirmation/Gay & Lesbian Mormons: San Diego, PO Box 86469; 92138-6469 619-283-8810 "Mormons."

⚥ ★ (♂) Anchor Ministries, 3441 University Ave; 92104 619-284-8654

⚥ ★ Dignity/San Diego, PO Box 33367; 92163 / Dignity Center, 4561 Park Blvd 619-295-2584 "Gay & Lesbian Catholics & their friends."

⚥ ★ ♿♿ Integrity/San Diego, PO Box 34253; 92163-0801 619-234-1829 "Gay & Lesbian Episcopalians & their friends."

⚥ ★ ♿♿ Metropolitan Community Church in the Country, 3901 Manzanita Dr #C; 92105 619-282-8488 Worship Sun 6pm at 1600 Buena Vista Drive, Vista The Country Prophet.

⚥ ★ ♿ Metropolitan Community Church of San Diego, PO Box 33291; 92163-3291 / 4333 30th St; 92104 619-280-4333 The Prodigal.

⚥ Spirit Eagle Metropolitan Community Church, PO Box 746, Spring Valley; 91976 619-447-4660

⚥ ★ Yachad, PO Box 3457; 92163 619-492-8616

Switchboards, Helplines, Phone Information

⚥ ★ ♿♿ Lesbian & Gay Community Center, PO Box 3357; 92163 619-692-GAYS; 619-692-2077

Travel & Tourist Services (see also Accommodation)

⚥ ● ♿ Firstworld Travel, 7443 Mission Gorge Rd; 92120 619-265-1916 Fax 619-265-1930

♀ ● Happy People Tours, PO Box 620619; 92162 619-236-0984 Fax 619-295-8700 samwarren@aol.com "Gay tours of Baja border cities; Copper Canyon Rail Cruise."

♀ ○ Hillcrest Travel, 431 Robinson Ave; 92103 619-291-0758

♀ ● ♿♿ Jerry & David's Travel, 1025 W Laurel St; 92101 619-233-5199

♀ ○ Midas Travel, 525 University Ave; 92103 619-298-1160

⚥ ● ♿ Mission Center Travel, 3108A 5th Ave 619-299-2720 Member of IGTA.

Women's Centers

♀ ☆ ♿♿ Center for Women's Studies & Services, 2467 E St; 92102 619-233-8984 counseling; 619-233-3088 Crisis Hotline. Pub CWSS Newsletter.

San Francisco/Bay Area

⚥ Gay Area Youth Switchboard 415-386-GAYS

Accommodation: Hotels, B&B, Resorts, Campgrounds

San Francisco

⚥ ● 24 Henry, 24 Henry St; 94114 415-864-5686

⚥ ● Albion House Inn, 135 Gough St; 94102 415-621-0896

♀ ● Amsterdam Hotel, 749 Taylor St; 94108 415-673-3277

♀ ○ Anna's Three Bears, 114 Divisidero St; 94117 415-255-3167; 800-428-8559

♀ ○ (?♂) Atherton Hotel, 685 Ellis St; 94109 415-474-5720; 800-474-5720; BR

♀ ● Bock's Bed & Breakfast, 1448 Willard St; 94117 415-664-6842 Fax 415-664-1109

♀ ○ Carl Street Unicorn House, 156 Carl St; 94117 415-753-5194

♀ ○ Chateau Tivoli: Bed & Breakfast, 1057 Steiner St; 94115 415-776-5462; 800-228-1647

♀ ○ Dakota Hotel, 606 Post St; 94109 415-931-7475 Fax 415-673-4781

♀ ○ Dolores Park Inn, 3641 17th St; 94114 415-621-0482 "Bed & breakfast."

♀ ○ Essex Hotel, 684 Ellis St; 94109 415-474-4664

♀ ○ Gough Hayes Hotel, 417 Gough St; 94102 415-431-9131

♀ ○ Ho Jo Inn, 385 9th St; 94103 415-431-5131

♀ Hotel Triton, 342 Grant Ave; 94108 415-394-0500; 800-433-6611; Fax 415-394-0555

♀ ○&& Hotel Vintage Court, 650 Bush St; 94108 415-392-4666; 800-654-1100; ℟

⚥ • Inn on Castro, 321 Castro St; 94114 415-861-0321
✦ Inn on Castro advertisement page 181

♀ ○ Inn San Francisco, 943 S Van Ness Ave; 94110 415-641-0188; 800-359-0913

♀ ○ King George Hotel, 334 Mason St; 94102 800-288-6005 Fax 415-391-6976 ℟

⚥ • && Leland Hotel, 1315 Polk St; 94109 415-441-5141; 800-258-4458

♀ • nancy's bed, 415-239-5692 "Private lesbian home, close to The Castro & public transit. $20 per woman per night."

♀ ○ Pacific Bay Inn, 520 Jones St; 94102 415-673-0234; 800-343-0880; Fax 415-673-4781

♀ • (&) Pension San Francisco Tourist Hotel, 1668 Market St; 94102 415-864-1271; 800-886-1271; Fax 415-861-8116

♀ ○ & The Phoenix, 601 Eddy St; 94109 415-776-1380

⚥ • San Francisco Cottage, 224 Douglass St; 94114 415-861-3220 Fax 415-626-2633 "Two garden apartments."

⚥ • The Willows Bed & Breakfast Inn, 710 14th St; 94114 415-431-4770 Fax 415-431-5295 (Church/Market Streets)
✦ Willows Bed & Breakfast Inn advertisement page 181

Addictive Behavior, Substance Abuse, Recovery

⚥ ★ 18th Street Services, 217 Church St; 94114 415-861-4898 "Substance abuse counseling for gay/bi men & transgenders."

⚥ ★ Acceptance Place, 673 San Jose Ave; 94110 415-695-1708

♀ ☆&& Iris Center Women's Counseling & Recovery Services, 333 Valencia St #222; 94103 415-864-2364

AIDS/HIV Support, Education, Advocacy, Publications

♀ ACT UP/Golden Gate, 519 Castro St MS-93; 94114 415-252-9200 Fax 415-252-9277

♀ ☆ ACTUP/SF (AIDS Coalition to Unleash Power/San Francisco), PO Box 14844; 94114 415-677-7988

♀ ☆ & AIDS Emergency Fund, 1540 Market St #320; 94102-6035 415-441-6407

⚥ ★ AIDS Info BBS, PO Box 421528; 94142-1528 415-626-1246 modem (no voice) Fax 415-626-9415

♀ ☆ AIDS Legal Referral Panel, 114 Sansome St #1129; 94104 415-291-5454

⚥ ★ DNCB Now!, 2261 Market St #499; 94114 415-954-8896 Fax 415-826-4928

♀ ★ (?&) Pets Are Wonderful Support (PAWS), 539 Castro St; 94114 415-241-1460

♀ ☆ (?&) Project Inform, 1965 Market St #220; 94103-1012 800-822-7422 Hotline Mon-Sat 10am-4pm. "AIDS/HIV treatment information."

INN ON CASTRO

321 castro st · san francisco
ca 94114 · (415) 861·0321

THE WILLOWS BED & BREAKFAST INN

*Your Haven within the Castro,
for Business or Pleasure*

*For brochure or reservations (415) 431-4770
FAX (415) 431-5295
710 Fourteenth St, San Francisco, CA 94114*

⚥ ☆ Project Open Hand, 2720 17th St; 94110 415-558-0600 Mon-Sat 9am-5pm. "Hot meals & groceries for PWA's in San Francisco, Oakland & Berkeley."

⚥ ☆ Proyecto Contra SIDA Por Vida, 2973 16th St; 94103-3633 415-864-7278 Fax 415-255-4954

⚥ ★ ᏸᏸ San Francisco AIDS Foundation, 25 Van Ness Ave #660; 94142-6033 PO Box 426182; 94142-6182 415-863-AIDS (English/Spanish/Filipino hotline); 800-959-1059 (BETA subscriptions); Fax 415-552-9762 beta@sfsuvax1.sfsu.edu ᏸᏸ Pub *BETA (Bulletin of Experimental AIDS Treatments); Positive News (Filipino, Chinese, English & Spanish).*

⚥ ☆ ᏸᏸ Shanti Project, 1546 Market St; 94102 415-864-CARE "Support, advocacy, transportation, recreational activities."

Answering/FAX & Mail Receiving, Shipping & Packaging Services

⚥ ○ ♿ Post Rent-A-Box, 633 Post St; 94109 415-673-6023

Art & Photography (see also Graphic Design)

⚥ • Steven Baratz Photography, 2660 3rd St #205; 94107 415-647-0247 (also Fax)

Bars, Restaurants, Clubs, Discos

San Francisco

♂ • Alta Plaza, 2301 Fillmore St; 94115 415-922-1444 *BRE* All welcome.

♂ Aunt Charlie's Lounge, 133 Turk St; 94102 415-441-2922

♂ Badlands, 4121 18th St; 94114 415-626-9320

♂ Bear, 440 Castro St; 94114 415-861-9427

♀ • ᏸᏸ The Box, 715 Harrison 415-647-8258 *D* Thu 9pm-2am.

♀ • The Cafe, 2367 Market St; 94114 415-861-3846 *R*

⚥ ○ (♿) Cafe Du Nord, 2170 Market St; 94114 415-861-5016 *BRE*

♀ Castro Country Club, 4058 18th St; 94114 415-552-6102 (no alcohol)

♂ • ♿ Castro Station, 456 Castro St; 94114 415-626-7220 Fax 415-626-4069 *BL* 6am-2am.

♀ • ♿ The Cinch, 1723 Polk St; 94109 415-776-4162 6am-2am.

♀ • ᏸᏸ Club Q Women's Dance Party, 177 Townsend St (at 3rd St) 415-647-8258 1st Fri of month, 9pm-3am.

♀ Company, 1319 California St; 94109-4914 415-928-0677

♀ Cove Cafe, 434 Castro St; 94114 415-861-6053 *R*

♂ • Detour, 2348 Market St; 94114 415-861-6053

⚥ • Dottie's True Blue Cafe, 522 Jones St; 94102 415-885-2767 *R*

♂ • The Eagle, 398 12th St; 94103 415-626-0880

♂ • ᏸᏸ The Edge, 4149 18th St; 94114 415-863-4027 Noon-2am.

♀ • ♿ Eichelberger's, 2742 17th St; 94110 415-863-4177 *BRE* 4pm-2am; Sun brunch 11am-3pm.

♀ El Rio, 3158 Mission St; 94110 415-282-3325

♀ Elephant Walk, 500 Castro St; 94114-2512 415-252-8441

♀ • ♿ Esta Noche, 3079 16th St; 94103 415-861-5757

⚥ The French Quarter, 201 9th St; 94103 415-252-7769

♀ • ♿ **The Galleon Bar & Grill, 718 14th St; 94114 415-431-0253** *BRE*

♀ Gangway, 841 Larkin St; 94109 415-885-4441

♂ • (ᏸᏸ) The Gate, 1093 Pine St; 94109 415-885-2852 *BR*

♂ Ginger's Too!, 43 6th St; 94103 415-543-3622

⚥ Ginger's Trois, 246 Kearny St; 94108 415-989-0282

♂ Giraffe, 1131 Polk St; 94109 415-474-1702

⚥ ○ ᏸᏸ Hamburger Mary's, 1582 Folsom St; 94103 415-626-5767 *R*

⚥ Hob Nob, 700 Geary St; 94109-7302 415-771-9866

♂ • Hole In The Wall Saloon, 289 8th St; 94103 415-431-HOWL *L*

⚥ • ᏸᏸ Ivy's Resaurant & Bar, 398 Hayes St; 94102-4421 415-626-3930

♂ Jackhammer, 290 Sanchez; 94114 415-252-0290 *LW*

♀ Josie's Cabaret, 3583 16th St; 94114 415-861-7933 *E* (juice bar)

♀ • ᏸᏸ Kimo's, 1351 Polk St; 94109 415-885-4535 *BDECW* 8am.2am.

⚥ La India Bonita, 3089 16th St; 94103-3417 415-621-9294

♂ • ♿ The Lion's Pub, 2062 Divisadero; 94115 / Sacramento at Divisadero St 415-567-6565 Noon-2am.

♂ ○ Lone Star Saloon, 1354 Harrison; 94103 415-863-9999

♂ Mack, 317 10th St; 94103 415-588-8300

♀ Marlena's, 448 Hayes St; 94102-4309 415-864-6672

♀ • Men's Room, 3988 18th St; 94114 415-861-1310

♂ Metro, 3600 16th St; 94114 415-431-1655 *BR*

♂ Midnight Sun, 4067 18th St; 94114 415-861-4186

♂ • ♿ The Mint, 1942 Market St; 94102 415-626-4726 *BRE* 11am-2am.

♀ Moby Dick, 4049 18th St; 94114 415-861-2482

T ○ Motherlode, 1002 Post St; 94109 415-928-6006

♂ Motorwerks, 4 Valencia St; 94103 415-864-7208

♂ My Place, 1225 Folsom St; 94103 415-863-2329

♂ ○ N' Touch, 1548 Polk St; 94109 415-441-8413 *BDE*

♂ ᏸᏸ Nightshift, 469 Castro St; 94114 415-626-5876 *BL* 6am-2am.

♂ Old Rick's Gold Room, 939 Geary St; 94109 415-441-9211

⚥ P.S. Bar, 1121 Polk St; 94109-5512 415-885-1448

♂ • ♿ Pendulum, 4146 18th St; 94114 415-863-4441

♂ Phoenix, 482 Castro St; 94114 415-552-6827

⚥ Phonebooth, 139 S Van Ness; 94110-4018 415-648-4683

♀ Pilsner Inn, 225 Church St; 94114 415-621-7058

♀ • ᏸᏸ Pleasuredome, 177 Townsend St; 94107 415-985-5256 *BDE*

♂ • ♿ Polk Gulch Saloon, 1100 Polk St; 94109 415-771-2022 *BLW*

♀ • ♿ Polk Rendezvous, 1303 Polk St; 94109 415-673-7934

⚥ • ᏸᏸ QT II, 1312 Polk St; 94109 415-885-1114 *BE* Noon-2am.

♂ Rawhide II, 280 7th St; 94103 415-621-1197

♂ Reflections, 1160 Polk St; 94109 415-771-6262

♂ • Stud, 399 9th St; 94103 415-863-6623

♂ The Swallow, 1750 Polk St; 94109 415-775-4152 10am-2am.

♀ Temple, 520 4th St; 94107 415-978-9488

♂ ○ The Transfer, 198 Church St; 94114 415-861-7499

♂ Trax, 1437 Haight St; 94117 415-864-4213

♂ Twin Peaks, 401 Castro St; 94114 415-864-9470

♀ Uncle Bert's Place, 4086 18th St; 94114 415-431-8616

♀ • ঙঙ Watering Hole Saloon, 1145 Folsom St; 94103 415-864-0309

♀ Without Reservations, 460 Castro St; 94114 415-861-9510 *B*

♀ Wooden Horse, 622 Polk St; 94102 415-441-9278

Bookstores: Gay/Lesbian/Feminist

♀ • ঙঙ A Different Light, 489 Castro St; 94114 415-431-0891; 415-431-6660 computer bb; adl@htg.org

♀ ○ Jaguar, 4057 18th St; 94114 415-863-4777 Fax 415-863-0235 11am-11pm; Fri & Sat to mdnt.
✦ *Jaguar advertisement page 183*

♀ ★ ঙ Old Wives' Tales: Women's Visions & Books, 1009 Valencia; 94110 (at 21st St) 800-821-4675 11am-7pm; Sun to 6pm. Pub *Women's Voices Events.* "Collectively-run, non-profit bookstore. Commitment to women's & lesbian community in general & women of color in especial. Community referral information."

Bookstores: General

♀ • ঙ Books & Company, 1323 Polk St; 94109-4613 415-441-2929

♀ ○ ঙ Books etc, 538 Castro St; 94114 415-621-8631 Fax 415-387-7162 h18tole@aol.com 11am-10am; Fri & Sat to mdnt. "General & rare books; catalogues issued."

♀ ○ City Lights Bookstore, 261 Columbus Ave; 94133 415-362-8193

♀ • ঙ Hog On Ice, 1630 Polk St; 94109 415-771-7909

♀ ○ ঙ The Magazine, 920 Larkin St; 94109-7113 415-441-7737

♀ • ঙঙ Modern Times Bookstore, 888 Valencia; 94110-1739 415-282-9246 11am-8pm; Fri & Sat to 9pm; Sun to 6pm. "General progressive bookstore with gay/lesbian literature."

♀ ○ (ঙ) Stacey's Professional Bookstore, 581 Market St; 94105 415-421-4687 staceysbk@aol.com

Bookstores: Recovery, Metaphysical, & other Specialty

♀ ○ ঙ Lodestar Books, 313 Noe St; 94114 415-864-3746

Broadcast Media

♀ • Electric City, 133 Collingwood; 94114 415-861-7131 "Cable TV program covering all aspects of the gay/lesbian/bi communities. Call for details."

Clothes

♀ • Don't Panic!, 541 Castro St; 94114 415-553-8989

♂ • (ঙঙ) Mr S Leather Co, 310 7th St; 94103 415-863-7764; 800-746-7677 orders; Fax 415-863-7798

Community Centers (see also Women's Centers)

♀ ★ ঙঙ Deaf Lesbian & Gay Center, 150 Eureka St #108; 94114 415-225-0700 TTY Fax 415-255-9797 dlgc@aol.com Pub *Update Newsletter.*

Computer Bulletin Boards

♂ • STUDS Computer Bulletin Board, BBS Services, 1800 Market St #90; 94102 415-495-2929 modem; 415-495-1811 voice.; Fax 415-495-0404

Computer/Software Sales & Services

♀ • Nosh Productions, Inc, 220 Clara St; 94107 415-896-NOSH Fax 415-896-6675 "Full service technology consulting, specializing in software development & systems integration."
✦ *Nosh Productions, Inc advertisement page 183*

Counseling/Therapy: Private

♀ • Psychology & Counseling Associates, 415-863-9559 Fax 415-863-7447

Editing/Writing Services

♀ • Mr. Write - Dennis McMillan, 452 Castro St #5; 94114 415-864-6554

Erotica (Printed, Visual, Equipment)

♂ ○ Arcade Books, 1036 Market St; 94101 415-863-7115

♂ ○ City Entertainment, 960 Folsom St; 94107 415-543-2124

♂ • ঙ Folsom Gulch, 947 Folsom St; 94107 415-495-6402 Sun-Thu 10am-3am; Fri & Sat 24 hrs.

♀ • Frenchy's Sex Shop, 1020 Geary St; 94109 415-776-5940; 415-928-9191

♀ ○ Golden Gate #4 Books & Video, 99 6th St; 94103 415-495-5573

♀ ○ Golden Gate #8 Books & Video, 700 Kearny St; 94108 415-421-5068

♀ ● ♂♂ Good Vibrations, 1210 Valencia #GY; 94110 415-974-8980; 800-BUY-VIBE "Books, toys, vibrators."

♂ ● Grapik Art Productions, PO Box 460142; 94146 Fax 415-928-7193

♀ ○ Kearny #8 Books & Video, 1030 Kearny St; 94133 415-391-9246

♂ ● ♂ Le Salon, Inc., 4126 18th St (off Castro) 552-4213 and 1118 Polk St 415-673-4492 8am-2am.

♀ ○ ♂ Mission Street News & Video, 2086 Mission St; 94110 415-863-7380 24 hrs.

♀ ● ♂♂ Nob Hill Cinema & Video, 729 Bush St; 94108 415-781-9468 "Live shows: male only."

♂ ● ♂ RoB Gallery, 22 Shotwell St; 94103 415-252-1198 Fax 415-252-9574 **L**

♂ ● San Francisco Leather Works, 415-566-7376 "Wholesale & custom leather."

♀ ● (♂) Stormy Leather, 1158 Howard St; 94103 415-626-1672 Noon-6pm; Fri & Sat to 7pm; Sun 2-6pm.

♀ ○ Turk Street News & Video, 66 Turk St; 94102 415-885-2040

♀ ○ Wendell's Leather Shop, 1623 Polk St; 94109 415-474-4104

Gifts, Cards, Pride & Novelty Items

♂ ● ♂ Does Your Mother Know, 4079 18th St; 94114 415-864-3160 10am-10pm.

Graphic Design/Typesetting (see also Art; Printing)

♀ ● Prerogative Graphics, 415-255-7194 "Specialty advertising agency; custom screen printing."

Health Care (see also AIDS Services)

♀ ● Capaldini, Lisa, MD, 533 Castro St; 94114 415-861-3366

♀ ● Owen, William, MD, 45 Castro St #402; 94114-1010 415-861-2400

Health Clubs, Gyms, Saunas

♂ ● City Athletic Club, 2500 Market St; 94114 415-552-6680 Mon-Fri 6am-10pm; Sat & Sun 9am-8pm.

Insurance (see also Insurance Benefits/Viaticals)

♀ ● (♂♂) Schmidt & Schmidt Insurance, 582 Market St, 18th flr; 94104-5319 415-981-3915

Legal Services & Resources

♀ ★ (?♂) Bay Area Lawyers for Individual Freedom, PO Box 421983; 94142-1983 415-956-5764

♀ ● ♂♂ Carl & Wolf, 25 Van Ness Ave #710; 94102 415-621-3988

♂ ● ♂ Cullum & Sena, 45 Polk St, 2nd flr; 94102 415-863-5300 "Specializing in Lesbian/gay adoptions."

♂ ★ Gay/Lesbian Legal Referral Service, Box 421983; 94101-1983 415-621-3900

♀ Lesbian & Gay Immigration Rights Task Force, Inc. (LGIRTF), c/o National Center for Lesbian Rights, 870 Market St #570; 94102 415-392-6257 lgirtf@dorsai.org

♀ ● San Francisco Human Rights Commission, Lesbian Gay Bisexual Transgender Advisory Committee, 25 Van Ness Ave #800; 94102-6033 415-252-2500 Fax 415-431-5764 "City government department handling complaints of discrimination."

♀ ● ♂♂ Wotman, Paul Freud, 414 Gough St #2; 94102 415-864-1900

Meeting/Contact Services, Publications, Talklines

♂ ● David The Matchmater, PO Box 422114; 94142 415-863-9550

Organizations/Resources: Bisexual Focus

♀ ★ Bay Area Bisexual Network, 2404 California St, Box 24; 94115 415-703-7977

Organizations/Resources: Business & Professional

♀ ★♂♂ Bay Area Career Women, 55 New Montgomery St #606; 94105 415-495-5393 Pub *Uncommon Voices.*

♀ ★ Bay Area Lawyers for Individual Freedom (BALIF), PO Box 42-1983; 94142-1983 415-956-5764

♀ ★ (?♂) Bay Area Network of Gay & Lesbian Educators (BANGLE), PO Box 460545; 94146 415-648-8488 Fax 415-824-3944

♀ ★ (?♂) Bay Area Physicians for Human Rights (BAPHR), 4111 18th St #6; 94114 415-558-9353

♀ ★ (?♂) Gay/Lesbian Postal Employees Network (GLPEN), PO Box 282982; 94128-2982 415-873-4308

♀ ★ ♂ Golden Gate Business Association, 1550 California St #5L; 94109-4708 415-441-3651; 800-303-4422; Fax 415-441-1123

♀ Golden State Peace Officers Association, PO Box 14006; 94114-0006 415-281-0601

♀ ★ PG&E Lesbian & Gay Employees Association, PO Box 191311; 94119-1311 415-973-9872

Organizations/Resources: Education, Anti-Defamation, Anti-Violence, Self-Defense

♀ ★♂♂ Community United Against Violence, 973 Market St #500; 94103-1717 415-777-5500; 415-333-HELP 24 hrs.

♀ ★♂♂ Gay & Lesbian Alliance Against Defamation, Inc. (GLAAD/SFBA), 1360 Mission St #200; 94103 415-861-4588 (Defamation Hotline); 415-861-2244; Fax 415-861-4893 glaadsfba@aol.com

♀ ★ (?♂) International Association of Gay & Lesbian Martian Artists, PO Box 590601; 94159-0601

Organizations/Resources: Ethnic, Multicultural

♀ Asians Building Community (ABC), PO Box 590790; 94159

♀ ★ (?♂) Black & White Men Together/San Francisco Bay Area, c/o NTFAP 973 Market St #600; 94103 415-826-BWMT Pub *BWMT-Bridge Newsletter.* Black & White Men Together/Men of All Colors Together

♂ ★ Gay Asian Pacific Alliance/Lavender Godzilla, PO Box 421884; 94142-1884

Organizations/Resources: Family

♀ ☆ (♂) PFLAG, PO Box 640223; 94164-0223 415-921-8850 Helpline "Parents, Families & Friends of Lesbians & Gays."

Organizations/Resources: General, Multipurpose, Pride

♀ ★♂♂ Lesbian/Gay Freedom Day Parade & Celebration Committee, 584 Castro St #513; 94114 415-864-FREE

Organizations/Resources: Political/Legislative

♀ ★ Alice B. Toklas Lesbian & Democratic Club, PO Box 422698; 94142-2698 415-621-3296 Pub *Alice Reports.*

♀ ★♂♂ Harvey Milk Lesbian & Gay Democratic Club, PO Box 14368; 94114-0368 415-773-9545

♀ ☆♂♂ Log Cabin Republican Club of San Francisco, PO Box 14174; 94114 415-664-6714 Pub *Republican Challenge.* "Concerned Republicans for Individual Rights."

♀ ★ Stonewall Gay Democratic Club, 150 Eureka St; 94114

♀ ★ ♏ Wages Due Lesbians, PO Box 14512; 94114 415-626-4114

Organizations/Resources: Sexual Focus (Leather, S/M, etc) & Safe Sex Promotion

♂ ★ The 15 Association, PO Box 421302; 94142 415-673-0452 "Private gay male SM social group."

♂ ★ (♿) Defenders/San Francisco, 415-487-7667 Liturgy Sun 5.30pm. "Gay/Lesbian Catholic outreach to the Leather/Levi community."

♀ ☆ ♏ Outcasts, PO Box 31266; 94131-0266 "Leather & S&M for women only."

♂ Society of Janus, PO Box 6794; 94101 415-985-7117

Organizations/Resources: Social, Recreational & Support Groups (see also Sport/Dance/Outdoor)

♀ ★ Alternative, PO Box 846; 94101-0846 "Social group."

♂ ★ G Forty Plus Club, PO Box 426741; 94142-6741 415-522-1997 "Seniors."

♂ ★ Girth & Mirth of San Francisco International, 176-B Page St; 94102-5811 415-552-1143

♀ ★ Lambda Amateur Radio Club: Golden Gate, PO Box 14073; 94114 Pub Newsletter.

♂ ★ (?♿) San Francisco Bearhug Group, 2261 Market St. #160; 94114-1693 415-647-9127

♂ ★ (?♿) SKiNs (SF Kindred Nudists), PO Box 192492; 94119-2492 "SASE for information."

Organizations/Resources: Sport/Dance/Outdoor

♀ ★ Community Bowling League, 1790 Post St; 94115 415-921-6200

♀ ★ Different Spokes/SF, PO Box 14711; 94114 415-282-1647 "Bicycle club."

♀ ★ ♿♿ Foggy City Dancers, PO Box 14324; 94114 415-905-4546; 415-626-0824 d Pub Foggy City Newsletter. "Square dance club."

♀ ★ (?♿) Gay & Lesbian Sierrans, Sierra Club Bay Chapter, 5237 College Ave, Oakland, CA 94618 510-281-5666

♀ ★ ♏ Gay & Lesbian Tennis Federation/San Francisco, 2215-R Market St #109; 94114 415-282-2453

♀ ★ (?♿) Golden State Gay Rodeo Association: Bay Area Chapter, PO Box 14398; 94114 415-985-5200

♀ Midnight Squares, PO Box 14483; 94114 415-861-1979 d

♀ ★ Northern California Rainbow Divers & SCUBA Club, PO Box 851, San Ramon; 94583 510-522-2348 The Buddy Line.

♀ ★ San Francisco FrontRunners, 1550 California St, #6L200; 94109 415-978-2429 Pub SF Frontrunners Footprint.

♀ ★ San Francisco Hiking Club, PO Box 14065; 94114-0065

♀ ★ Western Star Dancers, 584 Castro St #480; 94114 415-621-6506 dCW

Organizations/Resources: Student, Academic, Alumni/ae

♂ ★ Delta Lambda Phi Fraternity, San Francisco State University, PO Box 94114; 94114 800-587-FRAT

♀ ★ ♿♿ Gay & Lesbian Alliance, San Francisco College, c/o Student Activities San Francisco College; 94112 415-239-3212

♀ ★ Gay Hastings Alliance Gays & Lesbians, Hastings College of the Law, 200 McAllister St; 94102 415-565-4601

♀ ★ ♿♿ Lesbian Gay Bisexual Alliance (LGBA), SFSU Student Union Rm M-100A, 1600 Holloway Ave; 94132 415-338-1952

♀ ★ LIL (Lesbians in Law), c/o Women's Association Law School, Golden Gate College, 536 Mission St; 94105

Organizations/Resources: Transgender & Transgender Publications

♀ ○ Villains, 1672 Haight St; 94117 415-626-5939

Organizations/Resources: Youth (see also Family)

♀ ★ Bay Area Sexual Minority Youth Network (BASMYN), PO Box 460268; 94146-0268 Fax 415-252-5637 Pub Inside Outside.

♀ ★ Gay Youth Community Coalition, PO Box 846; 94101 415-386-4297

Performing Arts: Entertainment, Music, Recording, Theater, etc.

♀ ★ ♿♿ Golden Gate Performing Arts, Inc., PO Box 421491; 94142-1491 415-863-GGPA

♀ ★ (♿♿) Jon Sims Center for the Performing Arts, 1519 Mission St; 94103-2512 415-554-0402 "Performing Arts presenting organization, sponsoring groups; renting office & rehearsal space; Artist in Residence Program."

♀ ☆ The LAB, 1807 Divisadero St; 94115 415-346-4063 Fax 415-346-4567 "Interdisciplinary artists' organization."

⚦ ★&& San Francisco Gay Men's Chorus, PO Box 421491; 94142-1491 415-863-GGPA

⚦ ★&& San Francisco Lesbian/Gay Freedom Band, 150 Eureka St; 94114-2435 415-621-5619

⚦ ★ The Sisters of Perpetual Indulgence, Inc, 584 Castro St #392; 94114-2588 415-864-6722

⚦ ★ (&&) Theatre Rhinoceros, 2926 16th St; 94103 415-552-4100 "Producer & presenter of Gay & Lesbian theater."

Piercing & Body Jewelry

⚦ • **Gauntlet, Inc., 2377 Market St; 94114 415-431-3133**

Publications: Directories, Bibliographies, Guides, Travel

⚦ • The Gaybook, 584 Castro St #632; 94114 415-928-1859 "Referrals to SF Bay Area Gay/Lesbian businesses, organizations & services."

⚦ • Oblivion, 519 Castro St #24; 94114 415-487-5498 Monthly guide to San Francisco's gay nightlife.

Publications

⚦ • 10 Percent, 54 Mint St #200; 94103 415-905-8590

⚦ • 50/50 Magazine, 2336 Market St #20; 94114 415-861-8210; 415-621-1703

⚦ • ♿ Bay Area Reporter, 395 9th St; 94103 415-861-5019

⚦ • Buzz-Tattler, PO Box 421055; 94142 415-864-FAME "Gossip; entertainment."

⚦ Dykespeak, 4104 24th #181; 94114 415-648-6251

⚦ Odyssey Magazine, 584 Castro St #302; 94114-2500 415-621-6514

⚦ • Out & About, 2261 Market St #290; 94114 415-281-3176

⚦ • (&&) San Francisco Bay Times, 288 7th St; 94103-4004 415-626-8121

⚦ • San Francisco Frontiers, 2370 Market St, 2nd Flr; 94114 415-487-6000 Fax 415-487-6060

⚦ • San Francisco Sentinel, 285 Shipley; 94107 415-281-3745 Fax 415-281-3714 Weekly.

⚦ • Savage Male, 564 Mission St Box 345; 94105-2918 800-395-2482

⚦ ★ Shamakami, PO Box 460456; 94146-0456 "Forum for South & Southeast Asian Feminist Lesbians & Bisexual Women."

⚦ • White Crane Newsletter, PO Box 170152; 94117

Religious Organizations & Publications

⚦ ★ Congregation Sha'ar Zahav, 220 Danvers; 94114 415-861-6932 Pub Jewish Gaily Forward. "A progressive Reform synagogue with outreach to Gay & Lesbian Jews, friends, family, & community."

⚦ ★ (&) Dignity/San Francisco, 1329 7th Ave; 94122 415-681-2991 Liturgy Sun 5.30pm. Pub Bridges. "A Faith Community of Gay & Lesbian Catholics & their friends."

♀ ☆ Dolores Street Baptist Church, 938 Valencia St; 94110-2321 415-861-2641 Sun 10am.

⚦ ★ Golden Gate Metropolitan Community Church, 1600 Clay St; 94109 415-567-9080

⚦ ★&& Lutherans Concerned/San Francisco, 566 Vallejo St #25; 94133-4033 415-956-2069 Pub Advent.

⚦ ★ (&) Metropolitan Community Church of San Francisco, 150 Eureka St; 94114-2492 415-863-4434 Sun worship 9 & 11am; 7pm.

⚦ ★ (?&) The Parsonage, 584 Castro St #344; 94114-1465 415-552-2909 "Ministry of the Episcopal Church of California called to advocate justice for Gay & Lesbian people & to witness to the godliness of lesbian/gay love."

♀ ☆ Trinity Episcopal Church, 1668 Bush St; 94109 415-775-1117

⚦ ★&& Unitarian Universalist Gay/Lesbian/Bisexual Caucus, 1187 Franklin; 94109 415-731-3915

Switchboards, Helplines, Phone Information

⚦ ★&& Deaf Lesbian & Gay Event Hotline, 150 Eureka St #108; 94114 415-225-9944 TTY; non-TTY use California Relay 1-800-735-2922 voice dlgc@aol.com

⚦ ★ Gay Area Youth Switchboard, PO Box 846; 94101 415-386-GAYS

♀ ☆ San Francisco Sex Information, PO Box 881254; 94188-1254 415-621-7300 Monn-Fri 3-9pm.

Travel & Tourist Services (see also Accommodation)

♀ ○ Apex World Travel, 256 Sutter St, 7th Fl; 94108 415-421-4460 Fax 415-982-7397

♀ • Carlson Wagonlit Travel, 1245 Market St; 94103 415-558-9796

⚦ • ♿ Cruisin' the Castro, 375 Lexington St; 94110 415-550-8110 "Award winning walking tour of the Castro from an historical perspective; includes history of Gays in SF since 1849 gold rush."

⚦ ○ Navigator Travel, 2047 Market St; 94114 415-864-0401

⚦ ○ Now, Voyager Travel, 4406 18th St; 94114 415-626-1169; 800-255-6951; Fax 415-626-8626

⚦ • Passport To Leisure, 2265 Market St; 94114 415-621-8300

⚦ • Realistic Travel, 301 Arkansas St; 94107-2812 415-824-4501 Fax 415-824-5824 Mon-Fri 10am-6pm.
  ✦ Realistic Travel advertisement page 185

♀ ○ Travel Trends, 431 Castro St; 94114 415-558-6922, 800 558-6920

♀ ○ Winship Travel, 2321 Market St; 94114 415-863-2555

Women's Centers

♀ ☆&& Women's Building, 3543 18th St; 94110 415-431-1180

San Gabriel Valley: see San Bernardino/Riverside/ Pomona

San Jose Area

☎ **Gay & Lesbian Switchboard 408-293-4525**

Accommodation Sharing/Roommates

⚦ • Roomies, PO Box 66856, Scotts Valley; 95067-6856 408-438-1469 Mon-Fri noon-7pm.

AIDS/HIV Support, Education, Advocacy, Publications

♀ ☆ AIDS Legal Services, 111 N St John St #315, San Jose; 95113 408-293-3135 Fax 408-293-0160

♀ ☆ ♿ Necessities & More, Inc., 24 N 5th St, San Jose; 95112 408-293-2437

♀ ☆&& Santa Clara Valley AIDS Health Services, 2400 Moorpark Ave #211, San Jose; 95128 408-885-7000; 408-299-5915 (testing) Mon-Fri 8am-5pm.

Bars, Restaurants, Clubs, Discos

Cupertino

⚦ Silver Fox, 10095 Saich Way, Cupertino; 95014 408-255-3673

Mountain View

⚥ • && Daybreak Bar & Grill, 1711 W. El Camino Real, Mountain View; 94040 415-940-9778 *BRDE* 3pm-2am; Sat & Sun 4pm-2am.

San Jose

♂ ○ 641 Club, 641 Stockton Ave, San Jose; 95126 408-998-1144

⚥ Buck's Southwest Lounge/Corral Room, 301 Stockton Ave, San Jose; 95126 408-286-1176

⚥ • && Club St John, 170 W St John St, San Jose; 95110 408-947-1667 *BDERCW*

♀ • && Greg's Ball Room, 551 W Julian St; 95110-2340 408-286-4388 *BD* 11am-2am.

♂ ○ Mac's Club, 349 S 1st Ave, San Jose; 95113 408-998-9535

♂ • & Renegades, 393 Stockton Ave, San Jose; 95126 408-275-9902

⚥ • & Selections, 1984 Oakland Rd, San Jose; 95131 408-428-0329 Tue-Sun 4pm-2am. Dance Club.

♀ • (&) Wuzzy's, 265 N 1st St, San Jose; 95113 408-995-0222 *R*

Santa Clara

⚥ Savoy, 3546 Flora Vista Ave, Santa Clara; 95051 408-247-7109

♂ • Tinker's Damn, 46 N Saratoga Ave, Santa Clara; 95051 408-243-4595 *BDEf*

Bookstores: Gay/Lesbian/Feminist

⚥ • && Sisterspirit Bookstore/Coffeehouse, 175 Stockton Ave, San Jose; 95126-2760 408-293-9372

Bookstores: General

♀ ○ A Clean Well-Lighted Place for Books, 21269 Stevens Creek Blvd, Cupertino; 95014 408-255-7600

♂ ○ Recycle Bookstore, 138 E Santa Clara St, San Jose; 95113 408-286-6275

Community Centers (see also Women's Centers)

⚥ ★ && Billy DeFrank Lesbian & Gay Community Center, 175 Stockton Ave, San Jose; 95126-2760 408-293-4525 Fax 408-298-8986

Counseling/Therapy: Private

♀ ○ Sherman, Patricia, MFCC, Box 503, Mountain View; 94042 415-968-0897

Erotica (Printed, Visual, Equipment)

♀ • & Leather Masters, 969 Park Ave, San Jose; 95126-3033 408-293-7660

Gifts, Cards, Pride & Novelty Items

⚥ • Woman Made Catalog, PO Box 390923, Mountain View; 94039-0923 415-968-1314 karil57755@aol.com

Health Clubs, Gyms, Saunas

♂ • && Watergarden, 1010 Alameda, San Jose; 95126 408-275-1215 *P*

Legal Services & Resources

⚥ • Fadem, B. J., Esq, 111 N Market St #1010, San Jose; 95113 408-298-4246

♀ ○ Nickerson, Bruce W., 950 S Bascom Ave #1113, San Jose; 95128 408-971-0669

♀ ○ && Yates-Carter, Lynne, 111 W St John St #300, San Jose; 95113 408-294-9544

Organizations/Resources: Business & Professional

⚥ Bay Area Network of Gay/Lesbian Educators, 175 Stockton Ave, San Jose; 95126 408-298-1231

♂ ★ && High Tech Gays, PO Box 6777, San Jose; 95150 408-289-1484 Voicemail; 415-572-9594 BBS

Organizations/Resources: Ethnic, Multicultural

⚥ Lavender Latinas & Friends, 175 Stockton Ave, San Jose; 95126 408-293-4525

Organizations/Resources: Family

♀ ☆ & South Bay PFLAG, PO Box 2718, Sunnyvale; 94087 408-270-8182 "Parents, Families & Friends of Lesbians & Gays."

Organizations/Resources: General, Multipurpose, Pride

⚥ ★ (&&) Gay Pride Celebration Committee of San Jose, 45 N 1st St, Box 86, San Jose; 95113-1034 408-235-1034

Organizations/Resources: Political/Legislative

⚥ ★ Bay Area Municipal Elections Committee (BAYMEC), PO Box 90070, San Jose; 95109 408-297-1024

⚥ Log Cabin Silicon Valley, PO Box 612201, San Jose; 95101-2201 408-294-7469 (Republicans)

Organizations/Resources: Social, Recreational & Support Groups (see also Sport/Dance/Outdoor)

⚥ ★ San Jose Lambda Society of the Deaf, PO Box 90035, San Jose; 95109-3035

Organizations/Resources: Sport/Dance/Outdoor

⚥ ★ El Camino Reelers, PO Box 391373, Mountain View; 94039-1373 415-965-3877 ecr-info@benden.eng.sun.com *d*

Organizations/Resources: Student, Academic, Alumni/ae

⚥ ★ De Anza Gay & Lesbian Alliance, 21250 Stevens Creek Blvd, Cupertino; 95014 408-534-4254

♂ ★ Delta Lambda Phi Fraternity, San Jose State University, PO Box 90001, San Jose; 95109-1110 800-587-FRAT

⚥ San Jose State University Staff for Individual Rights, PO Box 3431, San Jose; 95156-3431

⚥ West Valley College Gay & Lesbian Student Union, 14000 Fruitvale Ave, Saratoga; 95070 408-867-2200 ext 358

Performing Arts: Entertainment, Music, Recording, Theater, etc.

♂ ★ & Silicon Valley Gay Men's Chorus, PO Box 62151, Sunnyvale; 94088 408-275-6344

Printing & Promotional Items (see also Art; Graphics/Typesetting)

♀ • Our Print Shop, 408-B Reynolds Circle, San Jose; 95112 408-452-0570 Fax 408-226-0823

Publications

⚥ ★ (&) Entre Nous Newsletter, PO Box 412, Santa Clara; 95052 408-246-1117

⚥ ★ Our Paper, PO Box 23387, San Jose; 95153-3387 408-452-0570 Fax 408-226-0823 gmrp93a@prodigy.com "The gay family paper of the Santa Clara Valley."

→ OutNOW!: p.158

Publishers/Publishing-related Services

♀ • (?⚢) Woman In the Moon (WIM) Publications, PO Box 2087, Cupertino; 95015-2087 408-738-4623; 408-864-8212 Dr SDiane Bogus; Fax 408-738-4623* (star key) Pub *Newsletter*. "Merit & self-publishing programs. Four poetry & prose contests each year. Free catalog."

Religious Organizations & Publications

♂ ★ (?⚢) Dignity/San Jose, PO Box 2177, Santa Clara; 95055 408-977-4218 *The Catalyst*. "Sponsor of Project Hope AIDS/HIV support ministry; also monthly potluck & other social events."

♂ ★ ⚤ Hosanna Church of Praise, 24 N 5th St, San Jose; 95112 408-293-0708; 408-293-2437

♂ ★ ⚤ Metropolitan Community Church San Jose, PO Box 388, San Jose; 95103-0388 / 65 S. 7th St 408-279-2711 Mon-Thu 10am-5pm; worship Sun 6.30pm, Wed 7.30pm.

♂ Valley West Church of Religious Science, 440 Darryl Dr, Campbell; 95008 408-379-0740

Switchboards, Helplines, Phone Information

♂ ★ ⚤⚤ Gay & Lesbian Switchboard, c/o Billy De Frank Community Center, 175 Stockton Ave, San Jose; 95126 408-293-4525

San Luis Obispo

Accommodation: Hotels, B&B, Resorts, Campgrounds

♀ • Casa De Amigas Bed & Breakfast, 1202 8th St, Los Osos; 93402 805-528-3701

Bars, Restaurants, Clubs, Discos

♂ • ⚤⚤ Breezes Pub & Grill, 11560 Los Osos Valley Rd #160; 93401 805-544-8010 *BDR* Wed-Sat 6pm-2am; Sun 6pm-mdnt.

Bookstores: General

♀ ○ Coalesce Bookstore, 845 Main St, Morro Bay; 93442 805-772-2880

♂ • ⚤⚤ Volumes of Pleasure Bookshop, 1016 Los Osos Valley Rd, Los Osos; 93495 805-528-5565 10am-6pm; Sun 11am-5pm. "General bookstore specializing in Gay/Lesbian books, music, accessories, etc."

Organizations/Resources: Business & Professional

♂ ★ CCBPA, PO Box 14433; 93406 805-546-9394

Organizations/Resources: Political/Legislative

♂ Log Cabin San Luis Obispo, PO Box 608, Avila Beach; 93424 908-549-8644 (Republicans)

Women's Centers

♀ ☆ Women's Resource Center, 1009 Morro St #201; 93401-3227 805-544-9313 Pub *Women's Press*.

San Mateo

AIDS/HIV Support, Education, Advocacy, Publications

♀ ☆ Ellipse Peninsula AIDS Services, 173 South Blvd; 94402 415-572-9702 Mon-Fri 8am-5pm.

♂ ☆⚤⚤ San Mateo County AIDS Program, 3700 Edison St; 94403 415-573-2588 Mon-Fri 8am-5pm.

Bars, Restaurants, Clubs, Discos

♂ • ⚤⚤ B Street/Sassy's, 234-236 S B St; 94401 415-348-4045 *BDE* "3 dance floors."

Bookstores: General

♀ ○⚤⚤ Kepler's Books & Magazines, 1010 El Camino Real, Menlo Park; 94025-4306 415-324-4321

♀ • (⚤⚤) Two Sisters Bookshop, 605 Cambridge Ave, Menlo Park; 94025 415-323-4778

San Pablo

Erotica (Printed, Visual, Equipment)

♀ ○ ⚤ Golden Gate #9 Books & Video, 1966 Rumrill Blvd; 94806 510-620-9639

San Rafael

Religious Organizations & Publications

♂ ⚤ Mother River Spirit (MCC), PO Box 151171; 94915 510-547-8386 Worship Sun 6pm.

Santa Ana: see Orange County

Santa Barbara/Ventura County Area

Accommodation: Hotels, B&B, Resorts, Campgrounds

Santa Barbara

♂ • Glenborough Inn Bed & Breakfast, 1327 Bath St, Santa Barbara; 93101 805-966-0589; 800-962-0589 (reservations only); Fax 805-564-8610

AIDS/HIV Support, Education, Advocacy, Publications

♂ ☆ (⚤⚤) AIDS Project Central Coast, 126 E Haley #A-17, Santa Barbara; 93101 805-963-3636 Fax 805-963-9086 Mon-Fri 10am-5pm. (Agency of Pacific Pride Foundation)

Bars, Restaurants, Clubs, Discos

Santa Barbara

♂ • (?⚢) Club Oasis, 224 Helena Ave, Santa Barbara; 93101 805-966-2464 *BDE* 4pm-2am.

♂ • ⚤ Gold Coast Santa Barbara, 30 W Cota, Santa Barbara; 93101 805-965-6701

Ventura

♀ ○⚤⚤ The Daily Grind Coffeehouse & Newsstand, 607 E Main St #A, Ventura; 93001 805-339-0538 *R* Planning to open Feb 1994.

♂ • Incognito at the Beach, 1644 E Thompson Blvd, Ventura; 93001 805-653-6511 *D*

♂ Paddy Mcdermott's, 577 E Main St, Ventura; 93001 805-652-1071

Bookstores: Gay/Lesbian/Feminist

♂ • (?⚢) Choices Bookstore & Coffeehouse, 901 De La Vina St, Santa Barbara; 93101-3220 805-965-5477 *Ef* Mon 7am-noon; Tue-Fri to 5pm; Sat 9am-5pm.

Bookstores: General

♀ ○ (⚤) Earthling Bookstore, 1137 State St, Santa Barbara; 93101-2712 805-965-0926 10am-11pm.

Business, Financial & Secretarial

♀ • Steketee Office Services, 31 Mission Plaza Dr, Ventura; 93001 805-653-0271 steketee@rain.org "Data entry; mailing list maintenance; hard copy to electronic transfer; income tax preparation."

Community Centers (see also Women's Centers)

♂ ★ ⚤ Gay & Lesbian Community Center, PO Box 2206, Ventura; 93002 / 1995 E Main St, Ventura 805-653-1979; 805-653-2790 AIDS/HIV hotline; Pub *Out 'n About*.

♂ ★ ♿ Gay & Lesbian Resource Center of Ventura County, 363 Mobil Ave, Camarillo; 93010 805-389-1530; 805-646-5884

♂ ★ (♿) Gay & Lesbian Resource Center, 126 E Haley #A-17, Santa Barbara; 93101 805-963-3636 Fax 805-963-9086 Mon-Fri 10am-6pm. Pub *Bulletin.* (Agency of Pacific Pride Foundation)

Legal Services & Resources

♀ • ♿ Lawson, Janet A., 33 S Evergreen Dr, Ventura; 93003 805-861-3840 Fax 805-641-3515

Organizations/Resources: Business & Professional

♂ ★ (?♿) GCBAPA, PO Box 7336, Ventura; 93006 805-388-1545

♂ ★ ♿ Greater Santa Barbara Community Association, PO Box 90907, Santa Barbara; 93190 805-568-3995

Organizations/Resources: Family

♀ ☆ PFLAG/Ventura County, PO Box 5401, Ventura; 93005 805-644-5863 "Parents, Families & Friends of Lesbians & Gays."

Organizations/Resources: General, Multipurpose, Pride

♂ ★ ♿ Gay & Lesbian Alliance of Ventura County, 363 Mobil Ave, Camarillo; 93010 805-389-1530; 805-646-5884 Pub *In The Light.*

♀ ★ ♿ Southern California Women for Understanding/Ventura—Santa Barbara, PO Box 7762, Ventura; 93006 805-644-9564

Organizations/Resources: Political/Legislative

♂ ★ (?♿) Unity Pride Coalition of Ventura County, PO Box 7336, Ventura; 93006 805-650-9546 *The Update.*

Organizations/Resources: Social, Recreational & Support Groups (see also Sport/Dance/Outdoor)

♂ ★ (?♿) Gold Coast Couples, PO Box 3313, Ventura; 93006-0313 805-339-1897

Organizations/Resources: Sport/Dance/Outdoor

♂ ★ Great Outdoors Santa Barbara, PO Box 21051, Santa Barbara; 93121 805-564-3646

Organizations/Resources: Student, Academic, Alumni/ae

♂ ★ Lesbian/Gay/Bisexual Alliance, PO Box 15048 UCSB, Santa Barbara; 93107 805-893-4578

Religious Organizations & Publications

♀ ★ ♿ Grace Chapel Metropolitan Community Church, PO Box 23611, Santa Barbara; 93121-3611

♂ ★ ♿ Metropolitan Community Church Ventura, PO Box 25610, Ventura; 93002 805-643-0502 Sun 6.30pm at 1848 Poli (at Pacific)

Santa Clara: see San Jose Area

Santa Cruz

AIDS/HIV Support, Education, Advocacy, Publications

♀ ☆ ♿ Santa Cruz AIDS Project, PO Box 557; 95061-0557 408-427-3900; 408-427-4999 hotline

Bars, Restaurants, Clubs, Discos

♂ Blue Lagoon, 923 Pacific Ave; 95060 408-423-7117 *BD*

Bookstores: Gay/Lesbian/Feminist

♀ • ♿ Herland Book—Cafe, 902 Center St; 95060 408-42-WOMEN Bookstore 10am-6pm; cafe 8am-6pm. "Mail order books, videos, & gifts."

Bookstores: General

♀ ○ (♿) The Book Loft, 1207 Soquel Ave; 95062 408-429-1812

♀ ○ ♿ Bookshop Santa Cruz, 1520 Pacific Ave; 95060 408-423-0900

♀ ○ Chimney Sweep Books, 419 Cedar St; 95060 408-458-1044 Mon-Sat noon-5pm.

Community Centers (see also Women's Centers)

♂ ★ ♿ Santa Cruz Lesbian, Gay, Bisexual & Transgendered Community Center, PO Box 8280; 95061-8280 / 1328 Commerce Lane; 95060 408-425-LGCC

Organizations/Resources: Bisexual Focus

♀ BiNet, PO Box 934; 95061-0934 408-427-4556

Publications

♂ ★ *Lavender Reader,* PO Box 7293; 95061

Religious Organizations & Publications

♂ ★ (♿) Lavender Road Metropolitan Community Church, PO Box 1764; 95061 408-335-0466 Call for meeting details; call one week ahead for Braille bulletin. Food bank 4th Sun of month, noon-1pm.

Travel & Tourist Services (see also Accommodation)

♀ ○ ♿ Pacific Harbor Travel, 519 Seabright Ave #201; 95062 408-427-5000 Fax 408-425-0709

♀ • (?♿) Travel Experience On Call, PO Box 2588, Aptos; 95001 408-464-8035 Pub *Adventure Travel Newsletter for Women.* "Personal, business/vacation travel for gay men, lesbians & their friends."

Santa Monica: see Los Angeles

Santa Rosa

Bars, Restaurants, Clubs, Discos

♂ Santa Rosa Inn, 4302 Santa Rosa Ave; 95407 707-584-0345

Erotica (Printed, Visual, Equipment)

♀ ○ Santa Rosa Adult Books & Videos, 3301 Santa Rosa Ave; 95407 707-542-8248

Religious Organizations & Publications

♀ ★ ♿ New Hope! Metropolitan Community Church, PO Box 11278; 95406-1278 707-526-HOPE Service Sun 12.15pm at 3632 Airway Dr.

Travel & Tourist Services (see also Accommodation)

♀ ○ ♿ Passport Ticket Travel, 9048 Brooks Rd S, Windsor; 95492 707-838-1557

Saratoga: see San Jose Area

Sebastopol

Travel & Tourist Services (see also Accommodation)

♀ ○ ♿ Stewart-Cole Travel, 6761 Sebastopol Ave; 95472 800-688-3013 Fax 707-823-8423 "We offer sober vacations for recovering AA's; gay only, lesbian only, & mixed."

Sonora

AIDS/HIV Support, Education, Advocacy, Publications

♀ ☆ (?♿) Sierra AIDS Council, PO Box 1062; 95370 209-533-2873 Mon-Fri 10am-3pm.

South Lake Tahoe

Accommodation: Hotels, B&B, Resorts, Campgrounds

♂ • Bavarian House, PO Box 624507, Lake Tahoe; 95754 916-544-4481; 800-431-4411

♀ • (?♿) Holly's Place, PO Box 13197; 96151 916-544-7040

♂ O ♿ Montgomery Inn & Spa, 966 Modesto Ave; 96150 916-544-3871; 800-624-8224

♂ O (♿♿) Scottish Inns, 930 Park Ave; 96150 916-542-3536; 800-628-1829 ext 21; Fax 916-544-1272 *BEd*

♂ • **Secrets of Lake Tahoe**, 924 Park Ave; 96150 916-544-6767; 800-441-6610; Fax 916-541-0735 "Adult accommodations only."
♦ *Secrets of Lake Tahoe advertisement page 190*

♀ • SierraWood Guest House, PO Box 11194, Tahoe Paradise; 96155-0194 916-577-6073

♂ O Silver Shadows Lodge, 1251 Emerald Bay Rd; 96150 916-541-3575

♂ O ♿ Tradewinds Motel & Suites, 944 Friday Ave; 96150 916-544-6459; 800-628-1829; Fax 916-544-1272

Bars, Restaurants, Clubs, Discos

♀ • ♿ Faces, PO Box 487, Zephyr Cove, NV 89448 / 270 Kingsbury Grade 702-588-2333 *D*

Stanford: see Palo Alto

Stockton

AIDS/HIV Support, Education, Advocacy, Publications

♂ ☆ ♿♿ San Joaquin AIDS Foundation, 4410 N Pershing, #C-5; 95207 209-476-8533; 800-FOR-AIDS 24 hrs, N. California

Bars, Restaurants, Clubs, Discos

♀ • ♿ Paradise, 10100 N Lower Sacramento Rd; 95210 209-477-4724 *BD*

Organizations/Resources: General, Multipurpose, Pride

♀ ★ Gay & Lesbian Association, San Joaquin County, 820 N Madison; 95202 209-464-5615 (also Fax)

Religious Organizations & Publications

♂ ★ ♿ Delta Harvest Community Church, 116 W Willow St; 95202-1045 209-469-3853 Sign language interpreted. "All welcome."

Sunnyvale: see San Jose Area

Tarzana

Bars, Restaurants, Clubs, Discos

♀ The Boardman, 5507 Reseda Blvd; 91356 818-881-2777

Erotica (Printed, Visual, Equipment)

♀ O Love Boutique, 18637 Ventura Blvd; 91356 818-342-2400

Travis

Erotica (Printed, Visual, Equipment)

♂ O Parkway Books & Video, 564 Parker Rd; 94535 707-437-9969

Ukiah

Travel & Tourist Services (see also Accommodation)

♀ • Kismet Travel, PO Box 781; 95482 707-462-7521; 800-926-7205; Fax 707-462-9790 Pub *Gay Travel Calendar.* "Gay destinations our specialty."

Upland: see San Bernardino/Riverside/Pomona Area

Vacaville: see Fairfield/Vacaville Area

Vallejo

Bars, Restaurants, Clubs, Discos

♀ • ♿ Q, 412 Georgia St; 94590 707-644-4584 *BD*

Erotica (Printed, Visual, Equipment)

♀ O ♿ Books, Etc: An Adult Variety Store, 540 Georgia St; 94590 707-644-2935

Van Nuys: see Los Angeles Area

Venice: see Los Angeles Area

Ventura: see Santa Barbara/Ventura County Area

Victorville

Bars, Restaurants, Clubs, Discos

♀ • (♿) Westside 15, 16868 Stoddard Wells; 92392 619-243-9600 *CWLd*

Visalia

Religious Organizations & Publications

♀ ★ ♿♿ Metropolitan Community Church of the Sequoias, PO Box 4223; 93278 209-627-2727

Vista: see San Diego Area

Walnut: see Los Angeles Area

Walnut Creek: see East Bay Area

West Covina: see Los Angeles Area

West Hollywood: see Los Angeles Area

Whittier

Religious Organizations & Publications

♀ ★ (♿♿) Good Samaritan Metropolitan Community Church, 11931 Washington Blvd; 90606-2607 310-696-6213

Woodland Hills: see Los Angeles Area

Colorado

State/County Resources

AIDS/HIV Support, Education, Advocacy, Publications

♀ ☆ ♂ Colorado AIDS Project, PO Box 18529, Denver, CO 80218 303-837-0166; 800-333-AIDS

♂ ☆ (?♂) PWA Coalition Colorado, PO Box 300339, Denver, CO 80203 / 1290 Williams St #303 303-329-9397 Fax 303-329-9381 Pub *Resolute: Dedicated to Surviving HIV*.

Community Centers (see also Women's Centers)

♀ ★♂♂ Gay, Lesbian Bisexual Community Center of Colorado, Inc, PO Drawer 18E, Denver, CO 80218-0140 / 1245 E. Colfax #125 303-831-6268 Fax 303-832-1250 glbcscc@tde.com Mon-Fri 10am-10pm; Sat to 7pm; Sun 1-4pm. Pub *Centerlines*.

Organizations/Resources: Business & Professional

♀ ★ Teachers' Group, PO Box 280346, Lakewood, CO 80228-0346 tchrsgrp@aol.com Pub *TG Newsletter*.

Organizations/Resources: Education, Anti-Defamation, Anti-Violence, Self-Defense

♀ ★♂♂ Ground Zero, Inc, PO Box 1982, Colorado Springs, CO 80901-1982 / 125 N Parkside 2nd flr E, Colorado Springs, CO 80909 719-635-6086 Fax 719-635-6106 Pub *Ground Zero Newsletter*.

Organizations/Resources: General, Multipurpose, Pride

♀ Come Out! Colorado, PO Box 13995, Denver, CO 80201 303-399-8300 Fax 303-399-8335 "Dedicated to gay & lesbian visibility."

Organizations/Resources: Political/Legislative

♀ ★♂♂ Equality Colorado, PO Box 300476, Denver, CO 80203 303-839-5540 Fax 303-839-1361 *The Equal Times*.

Organizations/Resources: Social, Recreational & Support Groups (see also Sport/Dance/Outdoor)

♀ ★♂♂ The Lesbian Connection, 2525 Arapahoe Ave #E4-233, Boulder, CO 80302-6710 303-443-1105 Pub *TLC Newsletter*.

Organizations/Resources: Sport/Dance/Outdoor

♀ ★ (?♂) Colorado Gay Rodeo Association (CGRA), PO Box 2558, Denver, CO 80201 303-839-8810

Organizations/Resources: Transgender & Transgender Publications

T ☆ (♂♂) Gender Identity Center of Colorado, Inc, 1455 Ammons St #100, Lakewood, CO 80215-4325 303-202-6466

Publications: Directories, Bibliographies, Guides, Travel

♀ • ♂♂ *Colorado Women's Yellow Pages*, PO Box 22274, Denver, CO 80222-0274 303-296-3447 Fax 303-296-6751 "Women's resource & service guide."

Publications

♀ • *Colorado Community Directory*, PO Box 2270, Boulder, CO 80306-2270 303-443-7768

♀ • ♂ *Colorado Woman News*, PO Box 22274, Denver, CO 80222-0274 303-355-9229

♀ ★ *Lesbians In Colorado*, PO Box 12259, Denver, CO 80212-0259 303-477-6421

♀ ★♂♂ *New Phazes*, PO Box 6485, Colorado Springs, CO 80934-6485 "Lesbian newsletter; women's events, contacts, etc."

Women's - Lesbian-Gay
Books - Music - Gifts
1731 15th St, Boulder
CO 80302

Word Is Out
Women's
Bookstore
303- 449-1415

♀ • *Out Front*, 244 Washington St, Denver, CO 80203-4218 303-778-7900

♀ • ♂♂ *Preferred Stock*, PO Box 18515, Denver, CO 80218 303-839-5410 Fax 303-727-7751

♀ • *Quest*, 430 S Broadway, Denver, CO 80209-1518 303-722-5965 Monthly.

Real Estate

♀ • Community Real Estate Referrals, 800-346-5592 "Free referral to gay/gay-supportive realtor in any USA city/state (including Virgin Is. & Puerto Rico). Sorry, no rentals!"
✦ *Community Real Estate Referrals advertisement back cover*

Aspen

Organizations/Resources: Sport/Dance/Outdoor

♀ ★ Aspen Gay & Lesbian Community, PO Box 3143; 81612-3143 970-925-9249

Aurora: see Denver

Boulder

AIDS/HIV Support, Education, Advocacy, Publications

♂ ☆ (?♂) AIDS Prevention Program, 3450 North Broadway; 80304 303-441-1160

♂ ☆ (?♂) Boulder County AIDS Project, 2118 14th St; 80302-4804 303-444-6121

Bars, Restaurants, Clubs, Discos

♀ • ♂♂ The Yard, 2690-C 28th St (enter on Bluff); 80301 303-443-1987 *BD*

Bookstores: Gay/Lesbian/Feminist

♀ • ♂ Word Is Out Women's Bookstore, 1731 15th St; 80302 303-449-1415
✦ *Word Is Out Women's Bookstore advertisement page 191*

Bookstores: General

♂ ○ Boulder Book Store, 1107 Pearl St; 80302 303-447-2074; 800-244-4651; Fax 303-447-3946 9am-10pm; Sun 10am-8pm.

♂ ○ (♂) Left Hand Books And Records, 1200 Pearl, Lower Level; 80302 303-443-8252

Computer/Software Sales & Services

♀ • Ric Turley Macintosh Consulting, PO Box 2270; 80306-2270 303-830-1275

Erotica (Printed, Visual, Equipment)

♂ ○ Newsstand Adult Bookshop, 1720 15th St; 80302 303-442-9515

CO: Boulder
Erotica

192
USA

Denver : CO
AIDS/HIV Support

Pikes Peak Paradise
Luxury Accommodations

Magnificent Views
Jacuzzi Hot Tubs
Fireplaces
Private Baths
Gay and Lesbian Discount

1-800-354-0989

Gifts, Cards, Pride & Novelty Items
♂ • ♿ Aria, 2047 Broadway; 80302 303-442-5694

Organizations/Resources: Social, Recreational & Support Groups (see also Sport/Dance/Outdoor)
⚥ ★ (♿) Lesbian, Bisexual, & Gay Alliance, UMC At CU Room 28; 80309 303-492-8567

Organizations/Resources: Student, Academic, Alumni/ae
⚥ ★ Campus Lambda Faculty/Staff, Campus Box 55; 80309-0055 303-492-3831

Publications
♀ ○ *Women's Sports & Fitness*, 2025 Pearl St; 80302

Religious Organizations & Publications
⚥ ★ ♿♿ Gay & Concerned Catholics, St Thomas Aquinas University Parish, 904 14th St; 80302 303-443-8383

Colorado Springs
☎ Pikes Peak Gay & Lesbian Community Center Help Line 719-471-4429

Accommodation: Hotels, B&B, Resorts, Campgrounds
♀ • The Hackman House Bed & Breakfast, PO Box 6902, Woodland Park; 80866 719-687-9851

♀ • (♿) Pikes Peak Paradise Bed & Breakfast, PO Box 5760, Woodland Park; 80866 719-687-6656; 800-354-0989
✦ *Pikes Peak Paradise Bed & Breakfast advertisement page 192*

AIDS/HIV Support, Education, Advocacy, Publications
♀ ☆ (?♿) Southern Colorado AIDS Project, PO Box 311; 80901 719-578-9092

Art Galleries/Archives/Restoration, Supplies, Framing
T • (♿) Phoenix Art Restoration, 1715 West Vermijo; 80904 719-473-8842

Bars, Restaurants, Clubs, Discos
⚥ • Hide & Seek Complex, 512 W Colorado; 80905 719-634-9303

♂ ○♿♿ Penthouse Lounge, 1715 N Academy; 80909 719-597-3314 *BD*

♀ True Colors, 1865 N Academy; 80909-2739 719-637-0773

Bookstores: General
♀ ○ Poor Richard's Bookstore, 320 N. Tejon St; 80903

Community Centers (see also Women's Centers)
⚥ ★ (?♿) Pikes Peak Gay & Lesbian Community Center, PO Box 607; 80901-0607 719-471-4429

Counseling/Therapy: Private
♀ ○ Keeffe, Corky, MA, 1425 North Union #201; 80909 719-578-9730

♀ • (♿♿) Lifesigns/Center for Psychotherapy, 10 Boulder Crescent #204; 80903 719-634-2488 Fax 719-633-3513

Erotica (Printed, Visual, Equipment)
♀ • ♿ First Amendment, 220 E Fillmore; 80907 719-630-PORN

♀ ○ Monarch Magazine Exchange, 2214 E Platte Ave; 80909 719-473-2524

Grooming Services
⚥ • Kim Roberts: Dancin' Travelin' Shears, 1513 W Vermijo; 80904 719-386-6301 (500) 346-3387 "Available for haircuts in Chicago, Madison, Denver, Colorado Springs, Guffey."

Organizations/Resources: Student, Academic, Alumni/ae
⚥ ★ ♿ Colorado College Lesbian & Gay Alliance, 902 N Cascade; 80946 719-389-6641

Religious Organizations & Publications
⚥ ★ ♿♿ Pikes Peak Metropolitan Community Church, 730 N Tejon; 80903-1012 719-634-3771

Switchboards, Helplines, Phone Information
⚥ ★ Pikes Peak Gay & Lesbian Community Center Help Line, PO Box 607; 80901-0607 719-471-4429

Travel & Tourist Services (see also Accommodation)
♀ • Uniglobe—Get Out Of Town Travel, Box 6837, Woodland Park; 80866 719-687-1170; 800-343-1549; Fax 719-687-2751

Commerce City
Erotica (Printed, Visual, Equipment)
♂ ○ Pleasures Entertainment Centers, Inc., 6970 Highway 2; 80003 303-289-4606

Denver
☎ Gay & Lesbian Community Center of Colorado, Inc 303-837-1598

Accommodation: Hotels, B&B, Resorts, Campgrounds
♀ ○ Mile High B&B, 303-329-7827; 800-513-7827

⚥ • Victoria Oaks Inn, 1575 Race St; 80218 303-355-1818
✦ *Victoria Oaks Inn advertisement page 193*

AIDS/HIV Support, Education, Advocacy, Publications
♀ Aids HIV Interfaith Network, 1280 Vine St; 80206-2912 303-722-3880

♀ ☆ AIDS/HIV Spiritual Support Group, 980 Clarkson; 80218 303-860-1819

♂ Black Aids Project At Large, 1525 Josephine; 80206 303-388-9780

→ Colorado AIDS Project: p.191

♀ ☆ ♿♿ Denver Aids Prevention, 605 Bannock #217; 80204 303-436-7221

♀ ☆ (?♿) Denver Buyers Club, PO Box 300339; 80203 / 1290 Williams St #303 303-329-9397 Fax 303-329-9381 "Vitamin & herbal supplements, etc."

♀ ☆ & & Denver Aids Prevention, 605 Bannock #217; 80204 303-436-7221

♀ ☆ Jewish Comm Aids Task Force, 300 South Dahlia; 80222 303-321-3399

Answering/FAX & Mail Receiving, Shipping & Packaging Services

♀ • & & Downtown Pack & Ship, 303 16th St #016; 80202-5657 303-572-5050

♀ ○ Terminal Annex Post Office, 1595 Wynkoop St; 80248 303-297-6000

Architectural Services (see also Home/Building)

♀ ○ & & Margaret Smith Architecture, 1228 15th St #215; 80202-1600 303-825-7870

Archives/Libraries/History Projects

♂ ★ & & Terry Mangan Library, PO Drawer 18E; 80218-0140 / 1245 E. Colfax #125 303-831-6268 Fax 303-832-1250

Bars, Restaurants, Clubs, Discos

♂ • & B.J.'s Carousel, 1380 S Broadway; 80210 303-777-9880 **BRE**

♂ Bandits, 255 S Broadway; 80209 303-777-7100

♀ • & & Basil's Cafe, 30 S Broadway; 80209 303-698-1413 **BR**

♀ Blue Note Cafe, 70 S Broadway; 80209-1506 303-744-6774 **R**

♂ The Bobcat, 1700 Logan St; 80213 303-830-0550

♂ Bricks, 1600 E 17th Ave; 80218 303-377-5400

♂ • (&&) Charlie's, 900 E Colfax Ave; 80218 303-839-8890 **BRLW**

♂ Club 22, 22 Broadway; 80203 303-733-2175

♂ Colfax Mining Co, 3014 E Colfax Ave; 80206-1607 303-321-6627

♂ • Colorado Triangle, 2036 Broadway; 80205 303-293-9009 **LW** Mon-Sat 11am-2am; Sun to mdnt.

♂ • (&) Compound & Basix Dance Club, 145 Broadway; 80203 303-722-7977 **BDL** Compound 7am-2am; Basix 9pm-2am.

♂ The Den, 5110 W Colfax; 80204 303-534-9526

♀ • & & The Elle, 716 W Colfax; 80204 303-572-1710 **Df**

♂ • & & Footloose Cafe, 102 S Broadway; 80209 303-722-3430 **BR**

♂ • Garbo's, 116 E 9th Ave; 80203 303-837-8217

♂ Highland Bar, 2532 15th St; 80211 303-455-9978

♂ Matchmaker Pub, 1480 Humboldt St; 80218 303-839-9388

♂ • & & Metro Express Club, 314 E 13th Ave; 80203 303-894-0668 **BDE** Video Bar.

♂ • Mike's, 60 S Broadway; 80209-1506 303-777-0193

♂ Mr Bill's, 1027 Broadway; 80203-2707 303-534-1759

♂ • & & Ms C's, 7900 E Colfax; 80220 303-322-4436 **BDCW**

♂ Outlet Lounge, The, 623 15th St; 80202 303-534-9841

♂ R&R Denver, 4958 E Colfax; 80203 303-320-9337

♂ The Raven, 2217 Welton St; 80205 **D**

♂ Three Sisters, 3358 Mariposa; 80211 303-458-8926

Bookstores: Gay/Lesbian/Feminist

♂ • & Book Garden, 2625 E 12th Ave; 80206 303-399-2004 Mon-Sat 10am-6pm; Sun noon-5pm.

♂ • (?&) Category Six Books, 1029 E 11th Ave; 80218 303-832-6263 Mon-Fri 10am-6pm; Sat & Sun 11am-5pm.

Bookstores: General

♀ ○ & & Tattered Cover, 2955 E 1st Ave; 80206 303-322-7727; 800-833-9327

Broadcast Media

♂ ★ The Lambda Report, PO Box 9742; 80209 303-446-2518 Thu 10.30pm, Channel 12, KBDI-TV

Business, Financial & Secretarial

♂ • Brummett, Martha, 660 Sherman St #302; 80203 303-830-1313 Public Accountant

♀ • (?&) Keene, Carloyn, E.A., 1212 Milwaukee St; 80206 303-394-3273 "Income tax preparation."

Clothes

♂ • (&) Celebrity Vintage Clothing & Costume, 1332 East Colfax Ave; 80218 303-830-0393

Community Centers (see also Women's Centers)

♂ ★ & & Gay, Lesbian Bisexual Community Center of Colorado, Inc, PO Drawer 18E; 80218-0140 / 1245 E. Colfax #125 303-832-1250 Fax 303-839-1361 glbcscc@tde.com Mon-Fri 10am-10pm; Sat to 7pm; Sun 1-4pm. Pub *Centerlines.*

Computer/Software Sales & Services

♀ • (?&) ASK Associates, 875 S Colorado Blvd - #751; 80222 303-757-8949

Counseling/Therapy: Private

♂ • Alkire, Britt, 1461 Milwaukee; 80206 303-339-9144

♀ • & & Bernstein, Gail, PhD, 789 Sherman #430; 80203 303-832-5123

♂ • & Chain, Steven, LCSW, 360 S Monroe St #300; 80209 303-393-7120

♀ ○ & & Cohen, Carol, MA, LPC, 2121 South Oneida #634; 80224 303-759-5126

♀ • (?&) Daugherty & Associates Psychotherapy, 303-754-7579 "Domestic violence victims advocacy & specializing in Gender Dysphoria."

♀ ○ Denver Center For Career & Life Mgt, Ltd, 1441 York St #304; 80206 303-388-6432 "Career/outplacement counseling; career management."

♀ ○ (&) Grundmann, Maryann, PhD, LCSW, 682 Grant St; 80203 303-278-4392

♀ ○ & Hartman, Judith Rachel, PhD, 2160 South Gilpin St; 80210-4615 303-722-2212

CO: Denver
Counseling: Private
194
USA
Denver : CO
Organizations: Social & Support

♀ ○ && Holtby, Michael, LSCW, 309 Cherokee Ave; 80223 303-722-1021

♂ ● && Kelso, Betsy, Psy.D., 1873 S Bellaire #930; 80222 303-757-6969 "Licensed psychologist."

♂ ● && Shell, John, Ph.D., 2250 S Albion St; 80222 303-377-6169

♂ ● Thomson, Deb-Ann, PhD, NCACII, CACII, 2755 S Locust St #207; 80222 303-758-6634

♀ ● && Vitaletti, Robert, PhD, 1616 17th St #567; 80202 303-628-5425

Erotica (Printed, Visual, Equipment)

♂ ● & The Crypt, 131 Broadway; 80203-3916 303-733-3112

♂ ● & The Crypt Cinema, 139 Broadway; 80203-3916 303-778-6584

♀ ○ Emporium of Design, 2028 East Colfax Ave; 80206 303-333-4870

♂ ● Heaven Sent Me, Inc., 1855 Gaylord St 303-331-6447; 800-472-0022; Fax 303-331-8264 Mon-Sat 10am-8pm; Sun noon-6pm.

♀ ● Pleasures Entertainment Centers, Inc., 127 South Broadway; 80209 303-722-5892

Florists (see also Gardening)

♀ ● Bouquets, 2029 E 13th Ave; 80206-2003 303-333-5500 "Also gifts, cards, novelties, etc."

♀ ● Thomas Floral, 1 Broadway #108; 80203 303-744-6400 "Florist; Gay & Lesbian T-shirts; adult gifts; books."

Food Specialties, Catering (see also Party/Event Services)

♀ ○ & Green's Market & Deli, 1312 East 6th Ave; 80218 303-778-8117 8am-7pm; Sun 9am-6pm; 1 hr later in summer. "Organic & gourmet products."

Grooming Services

♀ ● && Bear Valley Merle Norman Cosmetics, 3100 S Sheridan #J-1; 80227 303-936-0278

♀ ● & Headwaves, Inc, 1284 South Pearl; 80210 303-777-7708 10am-7pm.

Health Care (see also AIDS Services)

♀ ● && Broadway Foot & Ankle Clinic, 28 S Broadway At Ellsworth; 80209 303-744-7193

♀ Denver Metro Health Clinic, 605 Bannock St; 80204 303-893-7296

♀ ● (&) Herbal Energy Regeneration, 280 S Pennsylvania St; 80209-1920 303-744-3710 Doctor of Naturopathy.

♀ ● && Kovach, Drew A., MD, ABFP, 8770 Wadsworth Blvd #I, Arvada; 80003 303-431-5409

♀ ☆ && UCHSC Infectious Diseases Clinic, 4200 E 9th Ave #B-163; 80262 303-270-8683

Health Clubs, Gyms, Saunas

♀ ● (?&) Broadway Bodyworks, 160 S Broadway; 80209 303-722-4342

♂ ● (?&) Community Country Club, 2151 Lawrence St; 80205 303-297-2601 P

♂ ● Denver Swim Club, 6923 E Colfax; 80220 303-321-9399

♂ ● Midtowne Spa, 2935 Zuni St; 80211 303-458-8902 P

Home & Building: Cleaning, Repair, General Contractors

♀ ○ Wood Chucks Construction, 238 Columbine #177; 80206 303-388-8119

Insurance (see also Insurance Benefits/Viaticals)

♀ ○ (&&) State Farm Insurance: Tony Richards, 1660 Grant; 80203 303-830-0333

Laundry/Dry Cleaning

♀ ○ && Smiley's, 1060 East Colfax Ave; 80218 303-830-2877

Legal Services & Resources

♀ ● (?&) Buechler, Ruth A., 1764 Gilpin St; 80218 303-321-0946

♀ ○ Celeste, Mary A., 1888 Sherman St #403; 80203 303-863-1711

♂ ● && Henderson, James, 1888 Sherman St #640; 80203 303-830-0038

♂ ● Hundahl, Heidi, 847 Sherman St; 80203 303-839-8600 Fax 303-837-0021

♀ ● && Isaac, Lance Eldon, 1655 Lafayette St #104; 80218-1500 303-866-0909 Fax 303-866-0910

♂ ● Matthews, Liz, 660 Sherman St #302; 80203 303-830-1313

Organizations/Resources: Business & Professional

♂ ★ Colorado Business Council, 432 S Broadway; 80209 303-722-5965

♂ ★ (?&) Colorado Tavern Guild, PO Box 9495; 80209-0495

♂ ★ (?&) LEAGUE: Lesbian, Bisexual, & Gay Employees at AT&T, 11900 N Pecos St #30H78; 80234 407-358-5324

♀ ★ & Rocky Mountain Career Women's Association, PO Box 18156; 80218-0156 303-889-1001

Organizations/Resources: Education, Anti-Defamation, Anti-Violence, Self-Defense

♂ ★ && Anti-Violence Project, c/o GLBCSCC, PO Drawer 18E; 80218-0140 303-831-6268 Fax 303-832-1250 glbcscc@tde.com

♂ ★ && Speaker's Bureau, PO Drawer 18E; 80218-0140 303-831-6268

♀ ★ && Speaker's Project To End Discrimination, 1764 Gilpin St; 80218 303-333-8388; 303-831-8351

Organizations/Resources: Ethnic, Multicultural

♂ B-a-opal, 1525 Josephine St; 80206 303-388-5862

Organizations/Resources: Family

♀ ☆ (?&) PFLAG, PO Box 18901; 80218-0901 303-333-0286 "Parents, Families & Friends of Lesbians & Gays."

Organizations/Resources: Political/Legislative

♂ Log Cabin Club Denver, 1201 Williams St #3-B; 80218-2677 303-355-1663

♀ National Organization for Women (NOW), 1552 Pennsylvania; 80218 303-830-2795

Organizations/Resources: Social, Recreational & Support Groups (see also Sport/Dance/Outdoor)

♂ Capitol Hill United Neighborhoods, 1490 Lafayette St #201; 80218-2392 303-388-2716

♂ ★ (?&) Coming Out/Being Out Group, PO Drawer 18E; 80218 303-831-6268

♀ ★ Every Woman's Coming Out Group, PO Drawer 18E; 80218 303-837-1598

♂ ★ Girth & Mirth of the Rockies, PO Box 2351; 80201 303-784-5814

♂ Men's Coming Out Group, 1630 E 14th Ave; 80218 303-831-6238

♀ ★♂♂ Peer Support Program, PO Drawer 18E; 80218 303-831-6268

♂ Prime Timers, PO Box 9121; 80209-0121 303-922-3639

♂ Rocky Mountain Lambda Lions, PO Box 300416; 80203 303-322-2212

♀ Slightly Older Lesbians, PO Box 100831; 80210 303-331-2547

♀ ★♂♂ Womyncircle, PO Drawer 18E; 80218 303-831-6268

Organizations/Resources: Sport/Dance/Outdoor

♂ ★ 4-players Of Colorado, PO Box 300442; 80203 303-331-2662 "4-wheel Drive Club."

♂ ★ City Bikers Motorcycle Club, PO Box 9816; 80209-0816 303-369-0522 "Motorcylists."

♂ ★ Colorado Outdoor & Ski Association, Box 18598; 80218 303-470-9658

♂ ★ The Group, PO Box 9733; 80209 Pub *Newsletter*. "Social club for gay men."

♀ ★ Rocky Mountain Rainbeaus/Square Dance Club, PO Box 18814; 80218 303-778-1937 ♂ "Square Dance."

♀ ★ Rocky Mountaineers Motorcycle Club, PO Box 2629; 80201 303-733-7047

♀ ★ Women's Outdoor Club, PO Box 300085; 80203 303-699-3312

Organizations/Resources: Youth (see also Family)

♂ ★♂♂ Youth Services/GLBCSCC, PO Drawer 18E; 80218-0140 303-832-1250 Fax 303-839-1361 glbcscc@tde.com

Performing Arts: Entertainment, Music, Recording, Theater, etc.

♀ ★♂♂ Denver Gay Men's Chorus, PO Box 18251; 80218-0251 303-832-DGMC

♀ ★ Denver Women's Chorus, PO Box 2638; 80202 303-274-4177

♀ ★♂♂ Harmony—A Colorado Chorale, PO Box 13256; 80201 303-331-2667

♀ ★ Mile High Freedom Band, Box 9792; 80209-9792 303-744-3808

Pets & Pet Supplies

♀ ● Fish Den, 5055 West 44th Ave; 80212 303-458-0376

Private Investigators

♀ ● (?♂) Q Investigations, 833 Marion St; 80218 303-830-2053 Fax 303-830-2053

Publications

♀ ● ♂♂ *Fag Mag*, 3888 E Mexico Ave #200; 80210 303-753-6969 Fax 303-753-9969

♀ ● *H*, 430 S Broadway; 80209-1518 303-722-5965 Fax 303-698-1183

→ *Out Front*: p.191

→ *Quest*: p.191

♀ ○ *The Rocky Mountain Oyster*, PO Box 27467; 80227 303-985-3034 Fax 303-986-5664 "The sexually correct weekly paper for consenting adults."

Real Estate

♀ ● (♂♂) Club Realty & Investments, 1700 E 17th Ave #103; 80218 303-377-5356

♀ ○ ♂ Mile Hi Estates, Inc., 1133 Race St; 80206 303-839-1738

♀ ● ♂♂ Nelson, Mark, Distinctive Moore Properties, 55 Madison #155; 80206 303-355-7653

♀ ● ♂ Renaissance Realty, Inc, 276 S Pennsylvania St; 80209-1920 303-744-9415 Fax 303-744-9137

♀ ● ♂♂ Rudofsky, Lee, Re/Max, 3700 E Alameda #400; 80209 303-320-1556

Religious Organizations & Publications

♀ ★ (?♂) Axios: Eastern Orthodox Christians, 11635 E Cedar Ave, Aurora; 80012 303-343-9997

♀ ★ Evangelicals Reconciled, PO Box 200111; 80220 303-331-2839

♀ ★ (♂♂) Lutherans Concerned/Denver, PO Box 300343; 80203 303-422-3176

♀ ★ ♂♂ Metropolitan Community Church of the Rockies, 980 Clarkson St; 80218 303-860-1819 Sun worship services 8.55 & 10.55am.

♀ ☆ ♂ St Paul's United Methodist Church, 1615 Ogden St; 80218 303-832-4929

♀ Tikvat Shalom, PO Box 6694; 80206 303-331-2706

Suntanning

♀ ● Tomorrow's Body, 432 S Broadway; 80209 303-777-5660

Travel & Tourist Services (see also Accommodation)

♀ ○ (♂) Imperial Travel, 717 17th St; 80202 303-292-1334

♀ ○ ♂♂ Let's Talk Travel/Carlson Travel Network, 1485 S Colorado Blvd #260; 80222 303-759-1318; 800-934-2506

♀ ○ Metro Travel, 90 Madison St #101; 80206 303-333-6777

Video Sales, Rentals, Services (see also Erotica)

♀ ● ♂ Videotique, 1205 East 9th Ave; 80218 303-861-7465

Durango

Organizations/Resources: Social, Recreational & Support Groups (see also Sport/Dance/Outdoor)

♀ GLAD (Gay & Lesbian Association of Durango), PO Box 1656; 81302 970-247-7778

Englewood

Counseling/Therapy: Private

♀ ○ (♂) Bayes, Marjorie, PhD, 8000 East Prentice #B13; 80111 303-721-8505

Gifts, Cards, Pride & Novelty Items

♀ ○ Magicandles Of Colorado, 2989 South Lincoln; 80110 303-761-0909

Fort Collins

AIDS/HIV Support, Education, Advocacy, Publications

♀ ☆ ♂♂ Northern Colorado AIDS Project/Northern Colorado Health Network, Inc., PO Box 182; 80522 970-223-6227

Bars, Restaurants, Clubs, Discos

♀ ● ♂♂ Nightingales, 1437 E Mulberry St; 80524-3517 970-493-0251 **BD** 4pm-2am.

CO: Fort Collins
Bookstores: Gay/Lesbian/Feminist

196

USA

State/County Resources : CT
Community Centers

Tanrydoon
Bed & Breakfast

"A place for all seasons, in the heart of the Colorado Rockies"

Rich Garlick
(303) 468-1956
463 Vail Circle, Dillon, CO 80435

Bookstores: Gay/Lesbian/Feminist

♀ • ♂ A Quiet Corner Bookstore, 803 E Mulberry St; 80524 970-416-1916

Community Centers (see also Women's Centers)

♀ ★ (♿) Lambda Community Center, 1437 E Mulberry St #1; 80524 970-221-3247

Counseling/Therapy: Nonprofit

♀ ☆ (♿) Crossroads Safehouse, PO Box 993; 80522 970-482-3502

Counseling/Therapy: Private

♀ • Hoole, Ken, MSW, 101 East Pitkin St; 80524 970-221-0272

Organizations/Resources: Student, Academic, Alumni/ae

♀ ★♂♂ Student Organization for Gays, Lesbians & Bisexuals, Box 206 Lory Student Center CSU; 80523 970-491-7232 "Support, education & social programs for the Colorado State University and Fort Collins Communities."

Religious Organizations & Publications

♀ ★ (♂) Metropolitan Community Church Family In Christ, 1205 W Elizabeth St #E-172; 80521 970-221-0811

Travel & Tourist Services (see also Accommodation)

♀ ○ Fort Collins Travel, 333 W Mountain Ave; 80521 970-482-5555

Golden

Counseling/Therapy: Private

♀ ○♂♂ Grundmann, Maryann, PhD, LMSW, 607 Tenth St #201; 80401 303-278-4392

Grand Junction

Bars, Restaurants, Clubs, Discos

♀ • ♂♂ Quincy's Bar, 609 Main St; 81501 970-242-9633 (after 8pm only)

Bookstores: Recovery, Metaphysical, & other Specialty

♀ ○♂♂ Crystal Books & Gifts, 307 Main St; 81501 970-242-5181

Travel & Tourist Services (see also Accommodation)

♀ • Town & Country Travel, 614 Ouray Ave; 81501 970-242-7097

Greeley

Bars, Restaurants, Clubs, Discos

♀ • ♂♂ C Double R Bar, 822 9th St Plaza; 80631 970-353-0900 *BCWdR*

Counseling/Therapy: Private

♀ • ♂♂ Smith, Marilee A., Psy.D., 1750 25th Ave #200; 80631 970-351-6688

Organizations/Resources: Social, Recreational & Support Groups (see also Sport/Dance/Outdoor)

♂ ★ (♿) Greeley Bears, PO Box 907; 80632-0907 970-352-3399 xFUR (Bear Line)

Organizations/Resources: Student, Academic, Alumni/ae

♀ ★ Greeley Gay, Lesbian, & Bisexual Alliance (GOLBA), UNC Student Activities Area; 80651-1484 970-351-2869

Keystone

Accommodation: Hotels, B&B, Resorts, Campgrounds

♀ ○ Tanrydoon Bed & Breakfast, 463 Vail Circle, Dillon; 80435 970-468-1956
✦ *Tanrydoon Bed & Breakfast advertisement page 196*

Moffat

Accommodation: Hotels, B&B, Resorts, Campgrounds

♀ • Harmony Ranch B&B, PO Box 398; 81143 (San Luis Valley) 719-256-4107

Pueblo

Bars, Restaurants, Clubs, Discos

♀ ○ Pirates Cove, 409 N. Union 719-542-9624

Organizations/Resources: General, Multipurpose, Pride

♂ Pueblo After 2, PO Box 1602; 81002 719-564-4004

Religious Organizations & Publications

♀ ★ ♂ Metropolitan Community Church of Pueblo, PO Box 1918; 81002 719-543-6460 *The Beacon.*

Steamboat Springs

Accommodation: Hotels, B&B, Resorts, Campgrounds

♀ ★ Elk River Estates, PO Box 5032; 80477-5032 970-879-7556

Vail

Bookstores: General

♀ ○ Verbatim Bookstore, 450 E Lionshead Cir; 81657-5228 970-476-3032

Organizations/Resources: Social, Recreational & Support Groups (see also Sport/Dance/Outdoor)

♀ ★ SKI GLOV, 970-476-9271

Wheat Ridge: see Denver

Connecticut

State/County Resources

Addictive Behavior, Substance Abuse, Recovery

♂ • (♂♂) Pride Institute, 800-54-PRIDE "The nation's only accredited chemical dependency treatment center exclusively for Gay, Lesbian & Bisexual People."
✦ *Pride Institute advertisement page 122*

Community Centers (see also Women's Centers)

♀ ★♂♂ Triangle Community Center, PO Box 4062, Norwalk, CT 06855 / 25 Van Zant St 203-853-0600 "Membership encompasses Westchester (NY) County; Fairfield County; & as far north as New Haven."

CT: State/County Resources
Counseling: Private

197
USA

State/County Resources : CT
Real Estate

Counseling/Therapy: Private

♀ ○ (?♂) Homosexuality—Gay Issues Counseling & Specialine, 800-286-9900

Home & Building: Cleaning, Repair, General Contractors

♀ • (?♂) Bear Creek Remodelers, PO Box 2476, New Preston, CT 06777 203-672-2345

Organizations/Resources: Business & Professional

♀ ★ Connecticut Association of Physicians for Human Rights, PO Box 652, Sandy Hook, CT 06482

♀ ★ Connecticut Business Guild (CBG), c/o Metroline, 1841 Broad St, Hartford, CT 06114

♀ Educators & Friends of Lesbians & Gays, c/o J Klopfer, 623 Springfield Rd, Somers, CT 06001-1202 203-763-2675

Organizations/Resources: Family

♀ ☆♂♂ PFLAG of Southwestern Connecticut, PO Box 16703, Stamford, CT 06905-8703 203-544-8724; 203-322-5380; Fax 203-968-5380 Meetings 1st & 3rd Weds of month; spouse & exspouse support group 3rd Thu of month. Pub *Voice.* "Parents, Families & Friends of Lesbians & Gays."

Organizations/Resources: General, Multipurpose, Pride

♀ Connecticut PRIDE, PO Box 1173, Hartford, CT 06134 203-278-4163

Organizations/Resources: Political/Legislative

♀ ★ (?♂) Connecticut Coalition for Lesbian & Gay Civil Rights, PO Box 141025, Hartford, CT 06114

Organizations/Resources: Sexual Focus (Leather, S/M, etc) & Safe Sex Promotion

♂ ☆ (?♂) United Leatherfolk of Connecticut, PO Box 281172, East Hartford, CT 06128-1172 ulofct@aol.com

Organizations/Resources: Social, Recreational & Support Groups (see also Sport/Dance/Outdoor)

♀ ★ Lambda Car Club, PO Box 8171, Berlin, CT 06037 "Classic car club (ownership not required). Write for details."

♂ ★ (?♂) Northeast Ursamen, PO Box 2476, New Preston, CT 06777 203-639-4764

Organizations/Resources: Sport/Dance/Outdoor

♀ ★ (?♂) Lavender Contra & Folk Dance Society/CT, 508 Storrs Rd #2, Mansfield Center, CT 06250 203-456-0500 ♂ "Dances held at Wethersfield Grange. No partners or experience necessary."

♀ ★ (♂) Southern New England Friendship Softball League, PO Box 9583, New Haven, CT 06535

♀ ★ (?♂) TEAM Connecticut Pride, PO Box 217, New Haven, CT 06513 203-777-7807 labrys3@aol.com

Organizations/Resources: Youth (see also Family)

♀ ★♂♂ Outspoken, c/o Triangle Community Center, PO Box 4062, Norwalk, CT 06855 / 25 Van Zant St 203-227-1755 Fax 203-226-6087. "Support group for gay, lesbian, bisexual & questioning youth (ages 16-22)

Performing Arts: Entertainment, Music, Recording, Theater, etc.

♀ Another Octave: Connecticut Women's Chorus, PO Box 3208, New Haven, CT 06515 203-466-6263; 203-498-9351

Publications

♀ • (?♂) *Metroline*, 1841 Broad St, Hartford, CT 06114 203-276-6666 Every 2 weeks. "News, features & interviews for the Gay Community; also covers Springfield & Northampton, MA."

♀ • *The Newsletter: A Lesbian Position*, PO Box 9205, New Haven, CT 06533-0205 Monthly.

Real Estate

♀ • Community Real Estate Referrals, 800-346-5592 "Free referral to gay/gay-supportive realtor in any USA city/state (including Virgin Is. & Puerto Rico). Sorry, no rentals!"
◆ *Community Real Estate Referrals advertisement back cover*

♂ • Thompson Realty & Associates, 1845 Summer St, Stamford, CT 06905 203-324-1012 "We cover all of Connecticut."
◆ *Thompson Realty & Associates advertisement page 197*

Religious Organizations & Publications

♀ ★ UCCL/GC (United Church Coalition for Lesbian/Gay Concerns), 147 Virginia Lane, Tolland, CT 06084 203-872-6537

Switchboards, Helplines, Phone Information

♂ ☆ ♿ InfoLine of Connecticut, 1344 Silas Deane Hwy, Rocky Hill, CT 06067-1342 800-203-1234 (TDD accessible) 24 hrs; 203-571-7500 (admin); Fax 203-571-7525 "Information & referral; crisis intervention; advocacy."

Branford

Computer Bulletin Boards

♀ • Lifestyles BBS, 5 Bishop Rd, Dept 143-G; 06405 203-481-4836 (modem); 203-481-4836 (modem); Fax 203-481-6617

Bridgeport

AIDS/HIV Support, Education, Advocacy, Publications

♂ ☆ ♿ Family Services Woodfield, 475 Clinton Ave; 06605 203-368-4291 (Evelyn Figueroa); 203-368-4291 (Evelyn Figueroa); "HIV/AIDS Buddy Program; case management; counseling; Meals On Wheels; education & family support."

♂ ☆ (♿) Scattered Site Housing Program of Catholic Family Services—Bridgeport, 238 Jewett Ave; 06606-2892 203-374-4605 x238 Fax 203-372-5045 "Case management & subsidized housing for individuals & families living with HIV/AIDS."

Bookstores: General

♀ • ♿ Bloodroot, 85 Ferris St; 06605 203-576-9168 "Bookstore & restaurant."

Bristol

Home & Building: Cleaning, Repair, General Contractors

♀ ○ ♂ Rich's Affordable Cleaning & Services, 335 Burlington Ave; 06106 203-589-6606

Colchester

Counseling/Therapy: Private

♀ • ♂ Peck, Janet F., M.S., 244 S Main St; 06415 203-537-3977

Electrical Contractors

♀ • C. A. Conklin Electrical Co., 52 Mill Lane West; 06415 203-537-2709 CT Lic #122210

Collinsville

Bookstores: General

♀ ○ Gertrude & Alice's, 100 Main St; 06022-1100 203-693-3816

Cos Cob: see Greenwich

Coventry

Organizations/Resources: Family

♀ ☆ PFLAG/Coventry, PO Box 752; 06238 203-742-9548

Cromwell: see Hartford

Danbury

AIDS/HIV Support, Education, Advocacy, Publications

♀ ☆ (♿) Interfaith AIDS Ministry of Greater Danbury, 25 West St; 06810 203-748-4077 Pub *Outreach*.

CT: Danbury
Bars, Clubs, Restaurants

199

USA

Hartford : CT
Legal

Bars, Restaurants, Clubs, Discos

♀ • (Ġ) Triangles Cafe, 66 Sugar Hollow Rd; 06810 203-798-6996 **BDEL** 8pm-1am; weekends to 2am.

Bookstores: General

♀ ○ Baileywick Books, 17 Church St, New Milford; 06776 203-354-3865

Counseling/Therapy: Private

♀ • Choices: Margaret Grimes, 203-791-0378

Erotica (Printed, Visual, Equipment)

♀ ○ Fantasy Isle, Mill Ridge Rd; 06811 203-743-1792

Travel & Tourist Services (see also Accommodation)

♀ • Aldis The Travel Planner, 46 Mill Plain Rd; 06811 203-778-9399 Fax 203-744-1139 Mon-Fri 10am-6pm.
♦ Aldis The Travel Planner advertisement page 197

Women's Centers

♀ ☆ Women's Center of Greater Danbury, 2 West St; 06810-7842 203-731-5200

Darien

Organizations/Resources: Youth (see also Family)

♂ ★ Alternative Youth Club/Tri State Area, PO Box 2492; 06820 203-975-9139 "Social & support group for gay or bi males 17-22. Very discreet. Members from Ny, NJ, Ct welcome."

Dayville

Counseling/Therapy: Nonprofit

♀ ☆ ĠĠ United Services, Inc., 1007 N Main St; 06241 203-774-2020

East Hartford: see Hartford
East Norwalk: see Stamford

Enfield

Erotica (Printed, Visual, Equipment)

♀ ○ĠĠ Bookends, 44 Enfield St; 06082 203-745-3988 "Adult books, films, videos, magazines."
♦ Bookends advertisement page 198

Fairfield

AIDS/HIV Support, Education, Advocacy, Publications

♀ ☆ (?Ġ) Circle of Care/Stewart B. McKinney Foundation, Inc., PO Box 338; 06430 203-255-7965

Business, Financial & Secretarial

♀ ○ĠĠ Sweeney, Joseph H, CPA, 140 Sherman St, 5th Flr 203-256-3717 "CPA; attorney; tax planning."

Greenwich

AIDS/HIV Support, Education, Advocacy, Publications

♀ ☆ĠĠ AIDS Alliance of Greenwich, c/o Dept of Health, 101 Field Point Rd; 06836 203-622-6460 Pub Resource Guide.

Counseling/Therapy: Private

♀ • Marino, Joanne M., CCMHC, NCC, 21 Strickland Rd, Cos Cob; 06807 203-869-0216

Guilford

Counseling/Therapy: Private

♂ • Cummings, Brenda H., RDT, 107 State St; 06437 203-453-1204 "Feminist psychotherapy; sliding scale."

Hamden: see New Haven

Hartford

Addictive Behavior, Substance Abuse, Recovery

♀ ☆ĠĠ Community Health Services, 520 Albany Ave; 06120 203-493-6549

♂ ★ĠĠ Project 100/GLB Community Center, 1841 Broad St; 06114-1780 203-724-5542 Fax 203-724-3443 "12-step recovery."

AIDS/HIV Support, Education, Advocacy, Publications

♀ ☆ĠĠ AIDS Program, Hartford Health Dept, 80 Coventry St; 06112 203-543-8822 Services available for Spanish speaking & hearing impaired.

♀ ☆ (?Ġ) AIDS Project/Hartford, Inc, 110 Bartholomew Ave; 06106-2241 203-247-AIDS hotline; 203-951-4833; V/TDD 951-4791; Fax 203-951-4779

Bars, Restaurants, Clubs, Discos

♂ ○ Chez Est, 458 Wethersfield Ave; 06114 203-525-3243

♂ Gotham Lounge, 84 Pope Park Hwy; 06106 203-951-1315

♀ The Loft, 356 Asylum St; 06103 203-278-4747

♂ ○ Nick's Cafe House, 1943 Broad St; 06114 203-522-1573 **BD** 4pm-1am; Fri & Sat to 2am.

♂ Sanctuary, 2880 Main St; 06120 203-724-1277

Bookstores: General

♀ ○ Reader's Feast, 529 Farmington Ave; 06105 203-232-3710 "Feminist bookstore & cafe. Strong gay/lesbian section. All welcome."

Community Centers (see also Women's Centers)

♂ ★ĠĠ Project 100/GLB Community Center, 1841 Broad St; 06114-1780 203-724-5542 Fax 203-724-3443 Pub Newsletter.

Counseling/Therapy: Private

♂ ○ Koplin, James E., M.Ed, MSW, PO Box 1465; 06144 203-724-4204 "Psychotherapist; AIDS/HIV related cases; alcohol & substance abuse with sexual & racial minorities; sliding scale when appropriate."

♂ • Lambda Psychotherapy Associates, 203-635-2393
♀ • Vasso, Loretta M., Ph.D., 674 Prospect Ave; 06105 203-233-6228

♀ • Wallace, Timothy R., Ph.D., 674 Prospect Ave; 06105 203-233-6229

Erotica (Printed, Visual, Equipment)

♀ ○ Aircraft News & Books, 349 Main St, East Hartford; 06118 203-569-2324

♀ ○ĠĠ Danny's Adult World, 35 W Service Rd; 06120 203-549-1896

♀ ○ Red Lantern Books, 1247 Main St, East Hartford; 06118 203-289-5000

Health Care (see also AIDS Services)

♂ ★ĠĠ Hartford Gay & Lesbian Health Collective, Inc, PO Box 2094; 06145-2094 203-278-4163 "Health education; HIV counseling/testing; STD treament, PAP Smears, Health Education, support groups; gay/lesbian youth support group."

Legal Services & Resources

♀ • ĠĠ Cassella, Margaret M., PC, 597 Farmington Ave; 06105-3057 203-236-9999

♀ ○ Feltman, Art, 221 Main St; 06106 203-527-2283

(203) 542-1776 ★ *"A Women's B&B"*
LOON MEADOW FARM
P.O. Box 554, Norfolk, CT 06058

Organizations/Resources: Business & Professional

⚥ Gay Officers Action League (GOAL), PO Box 744; 06142 203-376-3612

Organizations/Resources: Family

⚥ ☆ (?⚤) PFLAG/Hartford, c/o Marie & Bob Calvin, 49 Beechwood Lane, South Glastonbury, CT 06073 203-633-7184 Meets 3rd Wed, 7.30pm, at Immanuel Congregational Church, 10 Woodland St. "Parents, Families & Friends of Lesbians & Gays."

Organizations/Resources: Social, Recreational & Support Groups (see also Sport/Dance/Outdoor)

♂ ★ (?⚤) B&G (Bare & Gay) Club, PO Box 380264, East Hartford; 06138 203-249-0026 dougd628@aol.com "Nudist social group."

⚥ ★ ♂ GEMS, PO Box 22, Manchester, CT 06045-0022 203-724-5542 "Intergenerational group; monthly socials; education & advocacy."

♀ ★ Lesbian Rap Group, c/o Hartford YWCA, 135 Broad St; 06105 203-525-1163

Organizations/Resources: Student, Academic, Alumni/ae

⚥ ★ ♂♂ Eros, Trinity College, Box 702584, 300 Summit St; 06106 203-297-2408

⚥ ★ ♂ Gay & Lesbian Alliance, University of Hartford, c/o Student Association, West Hartford; 06117

⚥ ★ Lesbian/Gay/Bisexual Student Alliance Uconn School of Social Work, 1800 Asylum Ave, West Hartford; 06117 203-523-4841 ext 267

Religious Organizations & Publications

⚥ ★ (?⚤) Am Segulah, PO Box 271522, West Hartford; 06127-1522 800-734-8524 (SEGULAH)

⚥ ★ ♂♂ Dignity/Hartford, PO Box 72; 06141 203-296-9229 *The Good Word.* "Gay & Lesbian Catholics & their friends."

⚥ ★ (♂♀) Metropolitan Community Church of Hartford, 1841 Broad St; 06114 203-724-4605 Sun 10.30am & 7pm.

Travel & Tourist Services (see also Accommodation)

⚥ ○ **All-Ways Travel, 2 Park Place; 06106 203-951-4388, Fax 203 951-4722**

Video Sales, Rentals, Services (see also Erotica)

⚥ • ♂♂ **MetroStore, 493 Farmington Ave; 06105 203-231-8845 Open Mon-Sat. "Video rentals & sales; also gifts, cards, etc."**

Women's Centers

♀ ☆ University of Hartford Women's Center, Gengras SU 200 Bloomfield Ave #213; 06117 203-768-5275

Lakeville

Organizations/Resources: Family

⚥ ☆ (♀) PFLAG/Northwestern CT, PO Box 278, Salisbury, CT 06068-0278 203-435-2738 Meets 3rd Mon, 7pm, at Housatonic Mental Health Center. "Parents, Families & Friends of Lesbians & Gays."

Madison

Organizations/Resources: Family

⚥ ☆ (♀) PFLAG/Shoreline, 66 Bower Rd; 06445 203-453-3895 Meets 4th Mon, 7.30pm, at Unitarian-Universalist Church, 297 Boston Post Rd. "Parents, Families & Friends of Lesbians & Gays."

Manchester

Organizations/Resources: Transgender & Transgender Publications

T ☆ (?⚤) Gender Identity Clinic of New England, 68 Adelaide Rd; 06040 203-646-8651

Women's Centers

♀ ☆ ♂♂ Manchester Community College Women's Center, MS #4, 60 Bidwell St; 06040 203-647-6056

Middletown

Organizations/Resources: Student, Academic, Alumni/ae

⚥ ★ Queer Alliance, Wesleyan University, 190 High St; 06457 203-685-2425

⚥ ★ Wesleyan Gay, Lesbian, Bisexual Alliance (GLBA), 190 High St, Box A; 06457 203-347-9411 ext 2712 or 2540 Meets Wed 10pm while school is in session, 190 High St, 2nd flr.

Women's Centers

♀ ☆ Wesleyan Women's Resource Center, PO Box 6195 Wesleyan Stn; 06457 / 287 High St 203-347-9411 ext 2669

Mystic

Accommodation: Hotels, B&B, Resorts, Campgrounds

⚥ ○ The Adams House, 382 Cow Hill Rd; 06355 203-572-9551; 800-321-0433

⚥ ○ Harbour Inn & Cottage, c/o Charles Lecouras, Jr. Edgemont St; 06355 203-572-9253

Bookstores: Recovery, Metaphysical, & other Specialty

⚥ ○ ♂ Essence, 19 East Main St; 06355 203-536-3918 10am-6pm.

Counseling/Therapy: Private

⚥ • Doran, Linda, MA, RN, CS, 14-14 Mason's Island Rd; 06355 203-536-8804

New Britain

Legal Services & Resources

⚥ • (?⚤) Carifa, Kenneth J., 130 W Main St; 06050 203-225-6464

Organizations/Resources: Student, Academic, Alumni/ae

⚥ Central Connecticut State University Gay & Lesbian Alliance, Box B-17, CCSU Student Center; 06050

Travel & Tourist Services (see also Accommodation)

⚥ • Weber's Travel Service, Inc, 24 Cedar St; 06052 203-229-4846 Mon-Fri 9am-5pm; Sat to noon. Member IGTA.

CT: New Haven
AIDS/HIV Support
201
USA
Stamford : CT
Bars, Clubs, Restaurants

New Haven

AIDS/HIV Support, Education, Advocacy, Publications

♀ ☆&& AIDS Project/New Haven, PO Box 636; 06503 203-624-0947; 203-624-AIDS

Bars, Restaurants, Clubs, Discos

♀ 168 York Street Cafe, 168 York St; 06511 203-789-1915

♀ • & Cafe 11-Fifty, 1150 Chapel St; 06511 203-789-8612 *BDRELW*

♂ Choices, 8 North Turnpike Rd, Wallingford; 06492 203-949-9380

♀ D-V-8, 148 York St; 06511 203-865-6206

♀ Jonathan Michaels Cafe, 1537 Dixwell Ave, Hamden; 06554 203-248-8808

Bookstores: Gay/Lesbian/Feminist

♀ • & Golden Thread Booksellers, 915 State St; 06511 203-777-7807 Tue-Fri 11am-6pm; Sat to 5pm; Sun 1-5pm.

Bookstores: General

♀ ○ & Bookhaven, 290 York St; 06511 203-787-2848

♀ ○ News Haven, 1058 Chapel St; 06510 203-624-1121 Fax 203-230-0402 8am-11pm; Sun to 8pm.

Counseling/Therapy: Private

♀ • **Davidson, Nancy S., PsyD, 436 Orange St; 06511 203-785-8770**

♀ ○&& Krieger, Irwin, MSW, 309 Edwards St; 06511 203-776-1966

♀ • Perlswig, Ellis A., MD, 30 Bryden Terrace, Hamden; 06517 203-777-1876 Psychiatrist.

Erotica (Printed, Visual, Equipment)

♀ ○ Nu Haven Book & Video, 754 Chapel St.; 06511 203-562-5867

Gifts, Cards, Pride & Novelty Items

♀ • (?&) Balloons, 488 Whalley Ave; 06511 203-387-1876 "Balloon deliveries; singing telegrams; event decoration."

Health Care (see also AIDS Services)

♀ ○ Prospect Hill Medical Services, 291 Edwards St; 06511 203-773-9004

♀ ☆&& Women's Health Services, 911 State St; 06511-3926 203-777-4781

Legal Services & Resources

♀ • Luppino, Grace A., PO Box 1167; 06505 203-498-8722

Organizations/Resources: Family

♀ ☆ (&) PFLAG/New Haven Area, c/o P-FLAG/CT 600 Prospect St #H8, New Haven, CT 06511 203-782-9466 Meets 2nd Mon, 7pm, at Congregation Mishkan Israel, 785 Ridge Rd, Hamden. "Parents, Families & Friends of Lesbians & Gays."

Organizations/Resources: General, Multipurpose, Pride

♂ Gay Men's Coalition of Greater New Haven, PO Box 310 Yale Stn; 06520 203-787-4477

Organizations/Resources: Student, Academic, Alumni/ae

♀ • (&) LBG Prism, Southern Connecticut State University, Student Center Box #74, 501 Crescent St; 06515 203-397-9488

♀ ★ (&) Lesbian, Gay & Bisexual Cooperative at Yale, Box 202031 Yale Stn; 06520 203-432-1585

♀ ★ & Yalesbians, PO Box 5051 Yale Stn; 06520 203-438-0388 (Women's Center); 203-438-0388 (Women's Center)

Performing Arts: Entertainment, Music, Recording, Theater, etc.

♂ ★ Connecticut Gay Men's Chorus, 480 Winthrop Ave; 06511 203-787-2835

Publications

→ *The Newsletter: A Lesbian Position*: p.197

Religious Organizations & Publications

♀ ★ Metropolitan Community Church/New Haven, 556 Whalley Ave #1-D; 06511 203-389-6750

Women's Centers

♀ ☆ & Yale Women's Center, PO Box 5051 Yale Stn; 06520 / 198 Elm St 203-432-0388 Pub *From The Center*.

New London

AIDS/HIV Support, Education, Advocacy, Publications

♀ ☆ & Southeastern Connecticut AIDS Project, Inc, 38 Granite St; 06320-5931 203-447-0884

Bars, Restaurants, Clubs, Discos

♂ ○ Frank's Place, 9 Tilley St; 06320 203-443-8883

♀ Heroes Cafe, 33 Golden St; 06320 203-442-HERO

Organizations/Resources: General, Multipurpose, Pride

♀ ★ (&) New London People's Forum, PO Box 386; 06320 203-443-8855 Meet Wed 7.30pm at St James Episcopal Church

New Milford: see Danbury

Norfolk

Accommodation: Hotels, B&B, Resorts, Campgrounds

♀ • (&&) Loon Meadow Farm: A Women's B&B, PO Box 554; 06058 203-542-1776 "Also horse & carriage livery."

✦ *Loon Meadow Farm: A Women's B&B advertisement page 200*

Norwalk: see Stamford

Seymour

Bars, Restaurants, Clubs, Discos

♀ Pier 34, 377 Roosevelt Dr; 06483 203-735-3774

Southington

Erotica (Printed, Visual, Equipment)

♀ ○ & The Source Bookstore, 958 Queen St; 06489 203-621-6255

Stamford

☎ Gay & Lesbian Guideline 203-327-0767

AIDS/HIV Support, Education, Advocacy, Publications

♀ ☆&& Stamford Health Department: AIDS Program, 888 Washington Blvd; 06904 203-967-AIDS

Bars, Restaurants, Clubs, Discos

♂ Art Bar, 84 W Park Place; 06901 203-973-0300 (Sun)

♂ ○ Bar Duval, 85 Woodside St; 06902 203-359-2505

♀ Boppers, 220 Atlantic St; 06901 203-357-0300

Counseling/Therapy: Private

⚥ ● Hyatt, Diane, MSW, CISW, Offices Stamford & Bridgeport. 203-964-1847 "Psychotherapist specializing in but not limited to adult survivors of childhood sexual abuse."

Legal Services & Resources

⚥ ● ♿♿ **Rome, Michael D., Martin & Rome, LLC, 120 East Ave, Norwalk; 06851 203-853-6677 Fax 203-853-6818**

Organizations/Resources: Family

⚥ ☆ (♿) PFLAG/Fairfield County, PO Box 16703; 06905-8703 203-322-5380; 203-544-8724; Meets 1st & 3rd Weds, 7.45pm, at Triangle Community Center, 25 Van Zant St,Room 7C, East Norwalk. "Parents, Families & Friends of Lesbians & Gays."

Switchboards, Helplines, Phone Information

⚥ ★ Gay & Lesbian Guideline, PO Box 8185; 06905 203-327-0767

Storrs

Organizations/Resources: Student, Academic, Alumni/ae

⚥ ★ (?♿) Bisexual, Gay & Lesbian Association, Box U-8, 2110 Hillside Rd, University of Connecticut; 06268 203-486-3679

Women's Centers

♀ ☆♿♿ Women's Center, 417 Whitney Rd, Box U-118; 06269 203-486-4738; 203-486-1546 TDD

Thomaston: see Waterbury

Torrington

AIDS/HIV Support, Education, Advocacy, Publications

⚥ ☆ ♿ Northwestern Connecticut AIDS Project, 100 Migeon Ave; 06790-4815 203-482-1596

Erotica (Printed, Visual, Equipment)

⚥ ○ (?♿) Torrington Video & Book Store, 466 Main St; 06790 203-496-7777 10am-10pm; Fri & Sat to 11pm; Sun noon-10pm.

Trumbull

Addictive Behavior, Substance Abuse, Recovery

⚥ ○♿♿ Regional Recovery Counseling Center, 15 Corporate Dr; 06611 203-261-5040 Fax 203-268-7399

Counseling/Therapy: Private

⚥ ● ♿♿ istvan, john emery, ACSW, CISW, 15 Corporate Dr #3-B; 06611-1378 203-268-8858 Fax 203-268-7399 "Individual & couple psychotherapy; HIV counseling, gender identity issues, end of life issues, consulting. Covered by most insurance, including Medicare."

Funeral Directors/Cemetaries/Mausoleums

⚥ ○ Maple Grove Memorial Park, PO Box 683; 06611 203-336-1718 "Pre-need counseling & affordable purchase programs for the Gay Community."

Vernon

Erotica (Printed, Visual, Equipment)

⚥ ○♿♿ Danny's Adult World, 65 Windsor Ave; 06066 203-872-2125 9.30am-10pm; Fri & Sat to 11pm; Sun moon-9pm.

Waterbury

Art & Photography (see also Graphic Design)

⚥ ○ ♿ C U Photography, 88-90 S Main St; 06702 203-573-1066 "Candid uncensored photo/video for any occasion. Film developing & video transfer/copying services. Portraits; special events; erotic; portfolios."

Bars, Restaurants, Clubs, Discos

⚥ The Brownstone, 29 Leavenworth St; 06702 203-597-1838

⚥ ● Maxie's Cafe, 2627 Waterbury Rd, Thomaston; 06787 203-574-1629 ***BDR*** Wed-Sun 6pm-closing.

Erotica (Printed, Visual, Equipment)

⚥ ○ ♿ Video Book & News, 88 S Main St; 06702 203-573-1116 9.30am-10pm; Fri & Sat to 11pm; Sun noon-10pm.

Religious Organizations & Publications

⚥ ★♿♿ Integrity/Waterbury Area, c/o St John's Church, 16 Church St; 06702 203-482-4239 "Lesbian & Gay Episcopalians & their friends."

Watertown

Organizations/Resources: Sport/Dance/Outdoor

⚥ Mountain Laurel Squares, PO Box 638; 06795 203-274-4380 ***d***

West Hartford: see Hartford

West Haven

Bookstores: Recovery, Metaphysical, & other Specialty

⚥ ○♿♿ **The Sober Camel Book & Gift Shop, 458 Forest Rd; 06516-1342 203-387-5622**

◆ ***Sober Camel Book & Gift Shop advertisement page 202***

CT: Westport
Bars, Clubs, Restaurants

203
USA

Rehoboth Beach : DE
Accommodation

SILVER LAKE

A first class guesthouse

Lake and Ocean Views • Walk to Gay Beach

All Private Baths • CAC • CATV
Continental Breakfast

Two Bedroom Apartments Available
Open All Year

133 Silver Lake Drive
Rehoboth Beach, Delaware
302 226-2115 • 800 842-2115

Westport

Bars, Restaurants, Clubs, Discos
♀ • (&) The Brook Cafe, 919 Post Rd E.; 06880 203-222-2233 *R*

Legal Services & Resources
♀ ○ (&) Altman, Norman D., PO Box 5192; 06881 / 500 Post Road East 203-454-2519

Publications
♂ • *Arena Magazine*, 4 Cedar Road; 06880 203-227-8855

Travel & Tourist Services (see also Accommodation)
♀ ○ & Travelstar Inc, 965 Post Rd E; 06880 203-227-7233 Fax 203-227-3774

Wethersfield

Erotica (Printed, Visual, Equipment)
♀ ○ Wethersfield Video Expo, 1870 Berlin Turnpike; 06109 203-257-8663

Willimantic

Erotica (Printed, Visual, Equipment)
♀ ○ Thread City Book & Novelty, 503 Main St; 06226 203-456-8131 Mon-Sat 11am-9pm; Sun 1-7pm.

Windsor: see Hartford

Delaware

State/County Resources

AIDS/HIV Support, Education, Advocacy, Publications
♀ ★ (?&) Delaware Lesbian & Gay Health Advocates, 601 Delaware Ave #5, Wilmington, DE 19801-1452 302-652-6776; 800-292-0429 Delaware only; Pub *Working for Health in the Human Family*. "Free & confidential counseling & testing service."

Organizations/Resources: Family
♀ ★&& National Association of Women for Understanding, Delaware Chapter, PO Box 404, Montchanin, DE 19710 "Social & educational support group for lesbians."

Organizations/Resources: Social, Recreational & Support Groups (see also Sport/Dance/Outdoor)
♀ ★ (?&) New Moon, 6 Vilone Rd, Wilmington, DE 19805 302-633-6558 "Social group for Lesbians in Delaware."

Real Estate
♀ • Community Real Estate Referrals, 800-346-5592 "Free referral to gay/gay-supportive realtor in any USA city/state (including Virgin Is. & Puerto Rico). Sorry, no rentals!"
✦ *Community Real Estate Referrals advertisement back cover*

Bethany Beach

Accommodation: Hotels, B&B, Resorts, Campgrounds
♀ • (&&) Nomad Village, Inc., Tower Shores Box 1; 19930 302-539-7581 *BD* "Private beach; 3 miles north of Bethany."

Dover

Bars, Restaurants, Clubs, Discos
♀ • && Rumors Restaurant & Nite Club, 2206 N Dupont Hwy; 19901 302-678-8805 *BDERCW* Year-round.

Milton

Accommodation: Hotels, B&B, Resorts, Campgrounds
♀ • (&&) Honeysuckle, Wisteria & Larkspur, 302-684-3284 "Victorian inn & adjoining houses for women only, near the Delaware beaches."

Newark

Organizations/Resources: Sport/Dance/Outdoor
♂ ★ Griffins MC, PO Box 7566; 19714-7566

Organizations/Resources: Student, Academic, Alumni/ae
♀ ★&& Lesbian/Gay/Bisexual Student Union at the University of Delaware, Room 201 Student Center, University of Delaware; 19716 302-831-8066

Rehoboth Beach

Accommodation: Hotels, B&B, Resorts, Campgrounds
♀ ○ The Beach House B&B, 15 Hickman St; 19971 302-227-7074; 800-283-4667
♀ • Cape Suites, 47 Baltimore Ave; 19971 302-226-3342
♀ • The Mallard Guest House, 67 Lake Ave; 19971 302-226-3448
♂ • Rams Head Inn, RD 2, Box 509; 19971-9702 302-226-9171
♀ • Rehoboth Guest House, 40 Maryland Ave; 19971 302-227-4117 May-Oct.

DE: Rehoboth Beach
Accommodation

204

USA

Washington : DC
Accommodation

♂ • ♿ Renegade, Box 11, Rt 1; 19971 302-227-4713

♀ ○ Sand In My Shoes B&B, Canal & 6th St; 19971-2704 800-231-5856

♂ • ♿ The Shore Inn at Rehoboth, 703 Rehoboth Ave; 19971 302-227-8487 (also Fax); 800-597-8899

♂ • ♿ **Silver Lake, 133 Silver Lake Dr; 19971 302-226-2115; 800-842-2115**
♦ *Silver Lake advertisement page 203*

AIDS/HIV Support, Education, Advocacy, Publications

♀ ☆ (♿) Sussex County AIDS Committee, PO Box 712; 19971 302-227-5504

Antiques & Collectables

♀ • **The Glass Flamingo, 46 Baltimore Ave; 19971 302-226-1366**

Art Galleries/Archives/Restoration, Supplies, Framing

♀ • Seashore Galleries, 59 Baltimore Ave; 19971 302-227-7817

Bars, Restaurants, Clubs, Discos

♀ • (♿) Back Porch Cafe, 59 Rehoboth Ave; 19971 302-227-3674 *BR*

♀ Blue Moon Restaurant, 35 Baltimore Ave; 19971 302-227-6515 *R* Mid Feb through late Nov.

♀ ○ ♿ Ground Zero, 50 Wilmington Ave; 19971 302-227-8041 *BRd* 6pm-1am.

♀ • (♿) Mano's Restaurant & Bar, 10 Wilmington Ave; 19971 302-227-6707 *R*

♀ Twig's Restaurant & Bar, 10 N 1st St; 19971 302-227-1547

Bookstores: Gay/Lesbian/Feminist

♀ • (♿) Lambda Rising, 39 Baltimore Ave; 19971 302-227-6969

Bookstores: General

♀ • ♿ Reading Matters, 205 Rehoboth Ave; 19971 302-227-4954

Clothes

♀ • ♿ Splash, 15 N. 1st St; 19971 302-227-9179 "Activewear & casual clothing."

♀ • ♿ Splash, 2 Penny Lane; 19971 302-227-1927 "Active & casual clothing."

Organizations/Resources: General, Multipurpose, Pride

♀ ★ ♿ CAMP Rehoboth, 39B Baltimore Ave; 19971 302-227-5620 Pub *Letters from CAMP Rehoboth.*

Seaford

Bars, Restaurants, Clubs, Discos

♂ ○ ♿ 20 West Dance Club, Rte 20 West (located next to the Canton Inn) 302-628-1155

Wilmington

Bars, Restaurants, Clubs, Discos

♂ The Eight-Fourteen, 814 Shipley St; 19801 302-657-5730

♂ • (♿) Renaissance, 107 W 6th St; 19801 302-652-9435 10am-2am.

♂ • (♿) Roam, 913 Shipley St; 19801 302-658-ROAM

♀ • (♿) Shipley Grill Restaurant, 913 Shipley St; 19801 302-652-7797 *R*

Bookstores: General

♀ ○ ♿♿ The Smoke Shop, Delaware Ave & Dupont St, CMS Bldg; 19806 302-655-2861

Counseling/Therapy: Private

♀ • ♿ McClemens, Mary Anne, MA, LPCMH, Arden Center for Counseling & Self-Esteem Training, 1804 Millers Road; 19810 302-475-3359 maryann98@aol.com

♂ • (♿) Wellington, Susan, MC, 908 N Adams St; 19801 302-658-8808

District of Columbia

Washington Area

☎ Gay & Lesbian Hotline, Whitman-Walker Clinic 202-833-3234

Accommodation: Hotels, B&B, Resorts, Campgrounds

♀ ○ 1836 California, 1836 California St; 20009 202-462-6502 "A Victorian bed & breakfast."
♦ *1836 California advertisement page 204*

♂ • The Brenton, 1708 16th St NW; 20009 202-332-5550

♀ • Calvert House, 1941 Calvert St NW; 20009 202-332-1942

♀ ○ Capitol Hill Guest House, 101 5th St NE; 20002 202-547-1050

♀ ○ **Carlyle Suites Hotel, 1731 New Hampshire Ave NW; 20009 202-234-3200; 800-96-4-LESS**
♦ *Carlyle Suites Hotel advertisement page 207*

DC: Washington
Accommodation

205

USA

Washington : DC
Bars, Clubs, Restaurants

♀ ○ The Embassy Inn, 1627 16th St NW; 20009 202-234-7800; 800-423-9111
♦ *Embassy Inn advertisement page 205*

♀ ○ Kalorama Guest House at Kalorama Park, 1854 Mintwood Pl NW; 20009 202-667-6369 Fax 202-319-1262

♀ ○ Kalorama Guest House at Woodley Park, 2700 Cathedral Ave; 20008 202-328-0860 Fax 202-319-1262

♂ • The Little White House, 2909 Pennsylvania Ave SE; 20020 202-583-4074

♀ ○ ♿ Savoy Suites Hotel, 2505 Wisconsin Ave NW; 20007 202-337-9700; 800-94-4-LESS; *BR*
♦ *Savoy Suites Hotel advertisement page 207*

♀ ○ The William Lewis House, 1309 R St NW; 20009 202-667-4019; 202-462-7574
♦ *William Lewis House advertisement page 206*

♀ ○ The Windsor Inn, 1842 16th St; 20009 202-667-0300; 800-423-9111
♦ *Windsor Inn advertisement page 205*

Addictive Behavior, Substance Abuse, Recovery

♂ • (♿) Pride Institute, 800-54-PRIDE "The nation's only accredited chemical dependency treatment center exclusively for Gay, Lesbian & Bisexual People."

♂ ★ (?♿) Triangle Club, 2030 P St NW; 20036 202-659-8641 11.30am-1.30pm; 5.30pm-12.30am. "12 Step meeting place."

AIDS/HIV Support, Education, Advocacy, Publications

♀ ☆ ACT UP/Washington, 1339 14th St NW #5; 20005 202-328-7965

♀ ★ Aids Resource Center, 1339 14th St NW #5; 20005 202-328-9765 Pub *DCQ*.

♀ ★ (♿) Food & Friends, 1001 First St SE; 20024 202-488-8278 Fax 202-863-1284 "Meal delivery program providing balanced nutrition for individuals homebbound with HIV/AIDS."

♀ ★ Impact-D.C., 300 I St NE #300; 20002 202-546-7228 (5-IMPACT)

♀ ★ Life Link, PO Box 15504; 20003-0504 202-547-7813 Mon-Fri 10am-5pm. "Peer counseling; local organizers of International AIDS Candlelight Memorial; speakers bureau."

♀ ☆ Salud, 1822 Biltmore St NW #24; 20009-1904 202-483-6806; 800-322-SIDA; "Latino community-based organization providing health services including AIDS education & case management for HIV-positive people."

♂ ★ Whitman-Walker Clinic, 1407 S St NW; 20009 202-797-3500

Archives/Libraries/History Projects

♀ ★ Gay & Lesbian Archives of Washington, DC, PO Box 4218, Falls Church, VA 22044 703-751-7738

Automobile Services

♀ ○ Rainbow Auto Body, 1445 Church St NW; 20005 202-332-6222

Bars, Restaurants, Clubs, Discos

♀ ○ Annie's Paramount Steakhouse, 1609 17th St NW; 20009 202-232-0395

♂ • Bachelor's Mill, 1104 8th St SE; 20003 202-544-1931

♂ • Back Door Pub (above Bachelor's Mill), 1104 8th St SE; 20003 202-546-5979

♂ • Badlands, 1415 22nd St NW; 20037 202-296-0505 *BDE*

DC: Washington
Bars, Clubs, Restaurants

206
USA

Washington : DC
Counseling: Private

♂ The Blue Penguin, 801 Pennsylvania Ave SE; 20003 202-547-4568

♀ ○ ♂♂ Brass Rail, 476 K St NW; 20001 202-371-6983

♀ Chief Ike's Mambo Room, 1725 Columbia Rd NW; 20009 202-332-2211 Women's night Sun.

♂ The Circle/Circle Underground, 1629 Connecticut Ave NW; 20036 202-462-5575

♂ • ♂♂ The D.C. Eagle, 639 New York Ave NW; 20001-3626 202-347-6025 *BL*

♂ Delta Elite, 3734 10th St NE; 20017 202-832-9839 *DP*

♀ Escalando/Lone Star West, 2122 P St NW; 20037 202-822-8909 *BD*

♂ • ♂♂ The Fireplace, 2161 P St NW; 20037 202-293-1293 *B* Noon-2am; Fri & Sat to 3am.

♂ • Fraternity House, 2123 Twining Ct NW (rear 2122 P St NW); 20037 202-223-4917 *BDELWC*

♂ The Green Lantern, 1335 Green Court; 20005 202-638-5133

♀ Hung Jury, 1819 H St NW; 20006 202-785-8181

♂ • JR.'S, 1519 17th St NW; 20036 202-328-0090

♂ La Cage Aux Follies, 18 0 St SE; 20003 202-554-3615

♀ • ♂ Mr Henry's, 601 Pennsylvania Ave SE; 20003 202-546-8412 *BR*

♂ • ♂ Mr P's, 2147 P St NW; 20037 202-293-1064 3pm-2am; Fri & Sat to 3am; Sun noon-2am.

♀ • Nob Hill, 1101 Kenyon St NW; 20010 202-797-1101

♀ • Phase One, 525 8th St SE; 20003 202-544-6831

♂ • Remington's, 639 Pennsylvania Ave SE; 20003 202-543-3113

♀ • Straits of Malaya/Larry's Lounge, 1836 18th St NW; 20009 202-483-1483 *BR* Sun-Thu 5.30-10pm; Fri & Sat 5.30pm-11pm; lunch Mon-Fri noon-2pm.

♀ • ♂ Tracks, 1111 1st St SE; 20003 202-488-3320 *D*

♀ Trumpets, 1633 Q St NW; 20009 202-232-4141 *BR*

♀ Utopia Bar & Grill, 1418 U St NW; 20009 202-483-7669 *BR*

♂ Wet, 56 L St SE; 20003 202-488-1202

♂ • Ziegfield's/Secrets, 1345 Half St SE; 20003 202-554-5141 *BDE*

Bookstores: Gay/Lesbian/Feminist

♀ • ♂ Lambda Rising, 1625 Connecticut Ave NW; 20009 202-462-6969; 800-621-6969; 10am-mdnt. Pub *Lambda Rising News.* "Books, videos, music, gifts. Catalog free."

♀ • Lammas Women's Books & More, 1426 21st St NW; 20036 (at P) 202-775-8218; 800-955-2662 10am-10pm; Sun 11am-8pm. All welcome.

Bookstores: General

♀ ○ Atticus Books & Music, 1508 U St NW; 20009 202-667-8148

♀ ○ Bick's Books, 2309 18th St NW; 20009 202-328-2356 10am-11pm; Fri & Sat to mdnt; Sun noon-8pm.

♀ ○ ♂♂ Borders Books & Music, 1801 K St NW; 20006 (entrance L St)

♀ ○ ♂ Kramer Books & Afterwords, 1517 Connecticut Ave NW; 20036 202-387-1400 "Outdoor cafe."

♀ ○ Luna Books, 1633 P St NW (above Cafe Luna); 20036 202-332-2543

♀ ○ ♂ Vertigo Books, 1337 Connecticut Ave NW; 20036 202-429-9272

Counseling/Therapy: Nonprofit

♀ ★ ♂ Whitman-Walker Clinic, 1407 S St NW; 20009 202-797-3500

Counseling/Therapy: Private

♀ • ♂ Dickinson, Pentz & McCall, Associates, 1660 L St NW #303; 20036-5603 202-728-1166 "Work closely with Gay/Lesbian alcohol/drug recovery; specialize in all sexual issues/problems, especially recovery from childhood abuse."

♀ • ♂ Jacobs, Mindy, Ph.D., 201 Massachusetts Ave NE #C2; 20002 202-543-0303

♀ ○ Malkin, Joyce, ACSW, LCSW, 4025 Connecticut Ave NW; 20008 202-363-8119

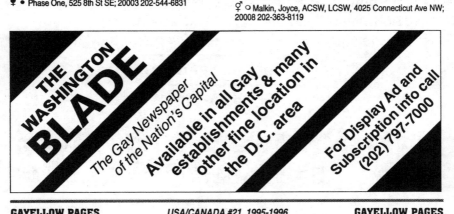

⚲ • (♿) Silverman, Philip J., Ph.D., 3 Washington Circle NW; 20037 202-822-0078

Dentists

⚲ • ♿ Hunter, John S., DDS, 818 18th St NW #240; 20006 202-223-5666

⚲ • ♂ Leight, Arlen Keith, DDS, 1145 19th St NW #714; 20036 202-775-1414

Erotica (Printed, Visual, Equipment)

♂ • Leather Rack, 639 New York Ave NW (3rd flr DC Eagle); 20001-3626 202-347-0666 Noon-1am; Fri & Sat to 2.45am. "Men's retail store: Levis-leather, sportswear, toys, gifts, etc."

⚲ • (♿) The Pleasure Place, 1710 Connecticut Ave NW; 20009 202-483-3297; 800-386-2386; Sun noon-7pm; Mon & Tue 10am-10pm; Wed-Sat to mdnt. "Lingerie, novelties, cards, videos, leather, etc. Catalog $3."

⚲ ○ (♿) The Pleasure Place, 1063 Wisconsin Ave NW; 20007 202-333-8570 Sun noon-7pm; Mon-Tue 10am-10pm; Wed-Sat to mdnt. "Lingerie, novelties, cards, videos, leather, etc."

Gifts, Cards, Pride & Novelty Items

⚲ • Balloon Bouquets of Washington, 202-785-1290; 800-424-2323

⚲ • Nickleby's Cards & Gifts, 1319 Connecticut Ave NW; 20036 202-223-1319

Graphic Design/Typesetting (see also Art; Printing)

⚲ • ♂ Dan Kaufman Graphics, 2025 I St NW #624; 20006 202-466-8878 "Custom design & ad specialties."

Health Care (see also AIDS Services)

⚲ ○ ♂ Brown, Larry, DC, 1330 New Hampshire Ave #114; 20036 202-887-6787

⚲ • Caceres, C.A., MD, 1759 Que St NW; 20009 202-667-5041

⚲ ○ Dotson, Samuel, MD, 650 Pennsylvania Ave SE #250; 20003 202-543-2664

⚲ ○ ♂ Greene, Peter, MD, PC, 1647 Benning Rd NE #303; 20002 202-399-8135

⚲ • ♂ Mackler, Jack, DC, 1712 Eye St NW #1012; 20006 202-857-0003 "Chiropractic health care."

⚲ • Pineda, Desiree, MD, 1759 Que St NW; 20009 202-667-5041

⚲ ★ ♂ Whitman-Walker Clinic, 1407 S St NW; 20009 202-797-3500

Health Clubs, Gyms, Saunas

♂ ○ Club Washington, PO Box 70566; 20024 / 20 O St SE 202-488-7317

Legal Services & Resources

⚲ ★♿ GAYLAW Attorney Referral, 202-842-7732

⚲ • (♿) Grandis, Edward S., Esq, 1735 20th St NW; 20009 202-234-8950

⚲ ○ (♿) McNeil & Ricks, PC, 4614 Wisconsin Ave NW, #2nd flr; 20016-4622 202-686-2600

⚲ ○ ♂ Peters, William, 2141 P St NW #103; 20037 202-463-8492

⚲ • ♿ Steinmetz, Weinberg & Moats, 2141 P. St NW #103; 20037 202-861-0077

DC: Washington
Organizations: Bisexual

208

USA

Washington : DC
Organizations: Transgender

Organizations/Resources: Bisexual Focus

♀ ☆ ♂♂ Bi-Ways, PO Box 959; 20044

Organizations/Resources: Business & Professional

♀ ★ Capital Area Physicians For Human Rights, PO Box 53221; 20009 202-943-5418

♀ ★ ♂♂ Gay & Lesbian Attorneys of Washington (GAYLAW), PO Box 76132; 20013-6132 202-389-1195

♀ ★ Lambda Labor, PO Box 65893; 20035-5893 202-387-7250 "Gay & Lesbian union members & friends in the Washington metropolitan area."

♀ ☆ LETS DC, Local Employment Trading System, PO Box 28477; 20038-8477

♀ Washington Area Gay & Lesbian Educators, 14412 Innsbruck Ct, Silver Spring, MD 20906 301-871-6597

Organizations/Resources: Education, Anti-Defamation, Anti-Violence, Self-Defense

♀ ★ (?♂) Gay Men & Lesbians Opposing Violence (GLOV), PO Box 34622; 20005 202-452-7448 Projects include: Police Dialogue Project; White/Stop! outreach & education project.

♀ ★ (?♂) GLAAD/National Capital Area (Gay & Lesbian Alliance Against Defamation), PO Box 57044; 20036-0614 202-GAY-9500

Organizations/Resources: Ethnic, Multicultural

♀ ★ Asians & Friends, PO Box 18974; 20036 202-387-ASIA

♀ Black Lesbian Gay Pride, Inc (BLGP), mail to BLGP, PO Box 7184; 20024

♂ ★ BWMT (Black & White Men Together), PO Box 73111; 20056-3111 202-452-9173 Black & White Men Together/Men of All Colors Together

♀ DC Coalition Of Black Lesbians & Gay Men, PO Box 77145; 20013-8145 202-488-4771

♀ ★ (?♂) National Association of Black & White Men Together, 1747 Connecticut Ave NW; 20009 202-462-3599; 800-NA4-BWMT; Fax 202-462-3690 Black & White Men Together/Men of All Colors Together

Organizations/Resources: Family

♀ ★ Gay & Lesbian Parents Coalition International, PO Box 50360; 20091 202-583-8029 Fax 201-783-6204 glpcinat@ ix.netcom.com Pub Network.

♂ ★ Gay Fathers Coalition/DC, Box 19891; 20036-0891 301-990-9522

♀ ☆ (?♂) PFLAG of the Washington Metropolitan Area, 1101 14th St NW; 20005 301-439-3524 "Parents, Families & Friends of Lesbians & Gays."

Organizations/Resources: Political/Legislative

♀ ★ Amnesty International Members For Lesbian & Gay Concerns (AIMLGC), 654 C St NE; 20002-6002

♀ ★ (?♂) Capital Area Log Cabin Club, PO Box 57130; 20037 202-488-1561 (Republicans)

♀ ★ DCLARE (DC White Lesbians and Bi Women Against Racism Everywhere), PO Box 28477; 20038-8477

♀ ★ ♂♂ Gay & Lesbian Activists Alliance of Washington, DC, Inc, PO Box 75265; 20013-7526 / 2 Massachusetts Ave 202-667-5139

♀ ★ (?♂) Gays & Lesbians For Individual Liberty (GLIL), PO Box 65743; 20035 202-789-2536

♀ ★ ♂♂ Gertrude Stein Democratic Club, PO Box 21067; 20009

Organizations/Resources: Sexual Focus (Leather, S/M, etc) & Safe Sex Promotion

♀ ☆ The Black Rose, PO Box 11161, Arlington, VA 22210-1161 301-369-7667 The Petal & the Thorn. "S&M support group."

♂ ★ Trident Intl. DC, 5909 Cloverleaf Ave., Clinton, MD 20735 301-297-7539

Organizations/Resources: Social, Recreational & Support Groups (see also Sport/Dance/Outdoor)

♀ ★ Among Friends, 1352 Q St NW; 20009 202-462-4564

♀ ★ (?♂) Bi Centrist Alliance (BCA), Box 2254; 20013-2254 202-828-3065

♀ ★ (?♂) Capital Metro Rainbow Alliance, Inc., PO Box 33257; 20033-0257 301-649-4332 TDD Pub Potomac Prism. "Educational/cultural/Social club for deaf Gays & Lesbians."

♂ ★ Girth & Mirth Club of Washington, DC, PO Box 4814, Falls Church, VA 22044 703-461-9184

♂ ★ Lambda Sci-Fi: DC Area Gaylaxians, PO Box 656; 20044 202-232-3141 Pub Lambda Sc-Fi Newsletter.

♀ Metropolitan Retired Gays/Lesbians, PO Box 70710; 20024 202-543-0325

Organizations/Resources: Sport/Dance/Outdoor

♀ ★ Adventuring, PO Box 18118; 20036-8118

♀ ★ Atlantic States Gay Rodeo Association, PO Box 31208, Bethesda, MD 20824 202-298-0928 MD

♂ ★ (?♂) Centaur Motorcycle Club, PO Box 34193; 20043-4193 L

♂ ★ D.C. Strokes Rowing Club, PO Box 39076; 20016 202-371-8897 (rowing club)

♀ ★ DC Lambda Squares, c/o Nancy Crowell 1209 Linden Pl NE, Washington, DC 20002 202-396-0144 ♂ "Square Dance."

♂ ★ (?♂) Lambda Divers, 202-265-3089 scuba.bear@glib.org

♂ ★ Spartan Motorcycle Club, Box 23623, Alexandria, VA 22304 703-370-5280 "Motorcyclists; members from PA, MD, DC, VA, DE, WV."

♀ Wrestling Club, PO Box 1205; 20013

Organizations/Resources: Student, Academic, Alumni/ae

♂ ★ Delta Lambda Phi Fraternity, Washington DC, PO Box 18662; 20036 800-587-FRAT

♀ ★ Duke GALA, PO Box 19375; 20036-0375 "Support group for Greater Washington DC Metro area Gay & Lesbian graduates of Duke University."

♀ ★ ♂♂ Georgetown Pride, Georgetown University, PO Box 2239 Hoya Stn; 20057 202-687-1592

♀ ★ (♂♂) Organization for Lesbian & Gay Student Rights at The Catholic University of America (OLGSR), UCW 200; 20064 202-635-5291; 202-332-3142

♀ ★ (♂) Yale GALA/DC, PO Box 15094; 20003-0094

Organizations/Resources: Transgender & Transgender Publications

⚥ ☆ TGEA (Transgender Educational Association of Greater Washington), PO Box 16036, Arlington, VA 22215 301-949-3822

Organizations/Resources: Youth (see also Family)

♀ ★ (?⚲) Sexual Minority Youth Assistance League (SMYAL), 333 1/2 Pennsylvania Ave SE 3rd flr; 20003-1148 202-546-5940; training & education ext 504; Youth Helpline ext 8 Mon-Fri 9am-5pm. Pub SMYAL News. Support groups Sat noon-3pm; drop-in Fri 6-8pm. "Serving Lesbian/Gay/Bisexual/Transgender youth, 14-21 years old."

Performing Arts: Entertainment, Music, Recording, Theater, etc.

♀ ★&& D.C.'s Different Drummers, Box 57099; 20037-0099 202-328-9259

♂ ☆&& Gay Men's Chorus of Washington DC, Box 57043; 20037 202-338-SING

♀ ★ Lesbian & Gay Chorus of Washington, DC, PO Box 65285; 20035 202-546-1549

Publications: Directories, Bibliographies, Guides, Travel

♀ ★ Gay & Lesbian Services Guide, 25 16th St SE; 20003 202-546-1549 Fax 202-456-8391 "Annual directory of services, businesses & organizations."

Publications

♀ ★ Lavender Listings, 25 16th St SE; 20003 202-546-1549 "Monthly listing of arts & cultural events."

♀ ● The Washington Blade, 1408 U St NW, 2nd flr; 20009-3916 202-797-7000; 202-234-5400 classifieds; Fax 202-797-4040 Weekly.
✦ Washington Blade advertisement page 206

♀ Woman's Monthly, 2401 H St NW #610; 20037

♀ YOUTH Magazine, Box 34215; 20043 202-234-3562

Real Estate

♀ ● Community Real Estate Referrals, 800-346-5592 "Free referral to gay/gay-supportive realtor in any USA city/state (including Virgin Is. & Puerto Rico). Sorry, no rentals!"
✦ Community Real Estate Referrals advertisement back cover

Record Sales (see also Performing Arts)

♀ ● 12 Inch Dance Records, 2010 P St NW; 20036 202-659-2011

Religious Organizations & Publications

♀ Affirmation (Mormon), PO Box 77504; 20013-7504 202-828-3096

♀ ★ (?⚲) Bet Mishpachah/Gay & Lesbian Synagogue, PO Box 1410; 20013 202-833-1638

♀ ☆ Christ United Methodist Church, 4th & I Sts SW; 20024 202-544-9117

♀ ☆ Church of the Disciples, MCC, 912 3rd St NW; 20001-2511 202-842-4870

♀ ★&& Dignity/Washington, PO Box 53001; 20009 202-387-4516 Mass Sun 4.30 & 7.30pm at St Margaret's Episcopal Church, 1820 Connecticut Ave NW. "Gay & Lesbian Catholics & their families & their friends."

♀ ☆ Dumbarton United Methodist Church, 3133 Dumbarton Ave NW; 20007 202-333-7212

♀ ★&& Faith Temple, 1313 New York Ave NW; 20005 202-544-2766

♀ ★ (&&) Integrity/Washington, DC, PO Box 19561; 20036-0561 301-953-9421 "Gay & Lesbian Episcopalians & their friends."

♀ ★ Lutherans Concerned/Metro Washington, 212 E Capitol St SE; 20001-1036 703-486-3567; 703-971-4342

♀ ★&& Metropolitan Community Church of Washington, 474 Ridge St NW; 20001 202-638-7373 Worship Sun 9 & 11am & 7pm, 5th between M & N Sts NW

♀ ★ (&) Mid-Atlantic Affirmation: United Methodists for Lesbian, Gay & Bisexual Concerns, PO Box 23636; 20026 202-866-6202

♀ ★ (&) PLGC/District of Columbia, c/o Westminster Presbyterian Church, 400 I St SW; 20024 202-667-2679

Switchboards, Helplines, Phone Information

♀ ★ Gay & Lesbian Hotline, Whitman-Walker Clinic, 1407 S St NW; 20009 202-833-3234 7-11pm; 202-332-2192 (Spanish line, Thu only)

Tobacco & Smoke Shops

♀ ● Greybeard's of London, 1365 Connecticut Ave NW; 20026-1801 202-296-0502

Travel & Tourist Services (see also Accommodation)

♀ ○ & Executive Travel Associates/Central Travel, 1101 17th St NW #412; 20006-4707 202-828-3501; 800-562-0189; Member IGTA.

♀ ○ && Mullin Travel, 2424 Pennsylvania Ave NW #118; 20037 202-296-5966

♀ ○ && Passport Executive Travel, 1025 Thos Jefferson St NW; 20007 202-337-7718

Veterinarians

♀ ○ Janes Veterinary Clinic, 520 8th St SE; 20003 202-543-6699

Florida

State/County Resources

Addictive Behavior, Substance Abuse, Recovery

♀ ★ & Florida Roundup, PO Box 7273, Fort Lauderdale, FL 33338-7273 305-463-0040 The Chronicle. "Annual convention for gay men & lesbians who are recovering alcoholics, & their friends."

♀ ● (&&) Pride Institute, 800-54-PRIDE "The nation's only accredited chemical dependency treatment center exclusively for Gay, Lesbian & Bisexual People."

AIDS/HIV Support, Education, Advocacy, Publications

♀ ☆&& Florida AIDS Legal Defense & Education Fund, Inc, 317 1/2 E Park Ave, Tallahassee, FL 32301-1513 904-877-6048

♀ ☆ Florida HIV/AIDS Hotline, PO Box 10950, Tallahassee, FL 32302-0950 800-FLA-AIDS (English); 800-545-SIDA (Spanish); 800-AIDS-101 (Creole)

♀ ☆&& Health Crisis Network, PO Box 370098, Miami, FL 33137-0098 305-751-7751 English Hotline; 305-759-1213 Spanish Hotline 9am-9pm; (305) 758-1971 TDD/TTY

♀ ☆&& Pasco AIDS Support Community Organization (PASCO), PO Box 577, New Port Richey, FL 34665-0577 800-486-8784

♀ ● (?&) Sapphex Learn, 14002 Clubhouse Circle #206, Tampa, FL 33624 813-961-6064 Pub Sexual Health Enlightenment (SHE). "Lesbian's Educational AIDS Resource Network: safer sex workshops, seminars, information kits, etc."

Bookstores: Gay/Lesbian/Feminist

♀ ● Everglades Book Company, PO Box 2425, Bonita Springs, FL 33959 813-353-4314 "1st editions, rare, out of print. $3 for book list, applied to first order."
✦ Everglades Book Company advertisement page 139

Insurance Benefits/Viaticals

♀ • Ability Life Trust, 668 N Orlando Ave #108, Maitland, FL 32751-4459 800-632-0555 Fax 407-629-0599
✦ *Ability Life Trust advertisement page 5*

Organizations/Resources: Business & Professional

♀ ★ Gay & Lesbian Lawyers Association of Florida (GALLA), PO Box 431002, Miami, FL 33143 305-665-3886

Organizations/Resources: Education, Anti-Defamation, Anti-Violence, Self-Defense

♀ (♿) GLAAD/Florida (Gay & Lesbian Alliance Against Defamation, Inc.), PO Box 1985, Winter Park, FL 32790-1985 407-236-9499

Organizations/Resources: Political/Legislative

♀ Florida Liberty Alliance, PO Box 628, Tallahassee, FL 32302 904-877-9303

♀ ☆ Florida National Organization for Women (NOW), 3700 Belle Vista Dr, St Petersburg Beach, FL 33706 813-360-1225

♀ ★ (♿) Human Rights Task Force, 1222 S Dale Mabry #652, Tampa, FL 33629 813-273-8769

Organizations/Resources: Social, Recreational & Support Groups (see also Sport/Dance/Outdoor)

♂ ★ (♿) Girth & Mirth of Florida, PO Box 21022, Fort Lauderdale, FL 33335 305-791-9794 "For chubby men & their admirers (over age 21)."

Organizations/Resources: Sport/Dance/Outdoor

♀ ★ Florida Sunshine Athletic Association, PO Box 14481, Fort Lauderdale, FL 33302 305-754-1923 Pub *Sunsations*. Non-gay welcome.

♀ ★ SAA Scuba, PO Box 14481, Fort Lauderdale, FL 33302 305-754-1923 Non-gay welcome.

Organizations/Resources: Transgender & Transgender Publications

T ★ ♿ Montgomery Medical & Psychological Institute, Florida Chapter, PO Box 141133, Gainesville, FL 32614 904-462-4826 "Information for transsexuals & other transgenderists; support group meetings, professional referrals, lobbying."

Performing Arts: Entertainment, Music, Recording, Theater, etc.

♂ ★ ♿ Gay Men's Chorus of South Florida, PO Box 9772, Fort Lauderdale, FL 33310-9772 305-777-3199; 305-757-7464; Meets Wed 7-10pm at 2800 W Oakland Park Blvd #105, Oakland Park; 33311.

Publications: Directories, Bibliographies, Guides, Travel

♀ • OUT Pages, 1323 SE 17th St #528, Fort Lauderdale, FL 33316 305-524-0547 "Community oriented: South Florida gay & gay friendly listings."

Publications

♀ • ♿ David Magazine, 801 SW 27th Ave, Fort Lauderdale, FL 33312-2907 305-583-4744 Weekly. "Entertainment guide for the Gay/Lesbian community of S. Florida."

♀ • Florida Travel Connection Magazine, 118 S Westshore Blvd #168, Tampa, FL 33609 813-288-0121

♀ • The Gazette, PO Box 2650, Brandon, FL 33509-2650 813-689-7566 "Florida's monthly Gay & Lesbian News Magazine."

♀ • (♿) Hotspots Magazine, 5100 NE 12th Ave, Fort Lauderdale, FL 33334 305-928-1862 Fax 305-772-0142 Weekly.

♀ • ♿ Mama Raga, PO Box 1002, Gainesville, FL 32602 "North Central Florida Lesbian networking: events, articles, directory of Lesbian Craftswimmin, etc."

♀ ○ Portfolio Magazine, 23 Palafox Place, Pensacola, FL 32501 904-435-7646 Fax 904-434-6706 "Arts & Entertainment."

♀ • TWN (The Weekly News), 901 NE 79th St, Miami, FL 33138 305-757-6333
✦ *TWN (The Weekly News) advertisement page 210*

Real Estate

♀ • Community Real Estate Referrals, 800-346-5592 "Free referral to gay/gay-supportive realtor in any USA city/state (including Virgin Is. & Puerto Rico). Sorry, no rentals!"
✦ *Community Real Estate Referrals advertisement back cover*

Boca Raton

Accommodation: Hotels, B&B, Resorts, Campgrounds

♀ • Floresta Historic Bed & Breakfast, 755 Alamanda St; 33486 407-391-1451

Bars, Restaurants, Clubs, Discos

♀ • ♿ Choices, 21073 Powerline Rd; 33433 407-482-2195 *BDE*

Organizations/Resources: Social, Recreational & Support Groups (see also Sport/Dance/Outdoor)

♀ ★ ♿ Boca Lesbian Rap Group, PO Box 485, Deerfield Beach, FL 33443 407-368-6051 Meeting Tue 7.30pm, Unitarian Church, 2601 St Andrews Blvd, Boca Raton.

Organizations/Resources: Student, Academic, Alumni/ae

♀ Lambda United/LGBA, c/o Student Activities Fla Atlantic Univ Ctr Room 203, 777 Glades Rd; 33431 407-347-5467

FL: Boca Raton
Organizations: Social & Support

211
USA

Boca Raton : FL
Organizations: Social & Support

THE COPA

U.S. 1 & S.E. 28TH ST. • FT. LAUDERDALE. FLORIDA • 305-463-1507
623 DUVAL STREET • KEY WEST. FLORIDA • 305-296-8521

Religious Organizations & Publications

♀ ★ ♂♂ Metropolitan Community Church: Church of Our Savior, 4770-C NW 2nd Ave; 33431 407-998-0454 *The Other Six Days.*

Travel & Tourist Services (see also Accommodation)

♀ ○ Elkin Travel, 885 E Palmetto Park Rd; 33432 407-368-8788; 800-226-TRIP

Bradenton

Accommodation: Hotels, B&B, Resorts, Campgrounds

♂ ○ ♿ Bungalow Beach Resort, 2000 Gulf Dr N, Bradenton Beach; 34217 813-778-3600

Brandon: see Tampa Bay Area

Clearwater: see Tampa Bay Area

Cocoa/Cocoa Beach Area

Accommodation: Hotels, B&B, Resorts, Campgrounds

Cocoa Beach

♀ • Triangle Palms Guest House, 131 Sunny Lane, Cocoa Beach; 32931 407-799-2221 Fax 407-799-2131

AIDS/HIV Support, Education, Advocacy, Publications

♂ ★ (?♿) AEGIS, PO Box 542404, Merritt Island; 32954-2404 407-453-4764 Hotline 24 hrs. "Housing for HIV positive males."

Bars, Restaurants, Clubs, Discos

Cocoa Beach

♀ Blondie's on the Beach, 5450 N Atlantic Ave, Cocoa Beach; 32931 407-783-5339

Organizations/Resources: Social, Recreational & Support Groups (see also Sport/Dance/Outdoor)

♂ ★ Men of Brevard, PO Box 1333, Cocoa; 32923 407-777-9443

Religious Organizations & Publications

♀ Breaking the Silence Metropolitan Community Church, PO Box 1585, Cocoa; 32923 407-631-4524

Coral Gables: see Miami Area

Daytona Beach

Accommodation: Hotels, B&B, Resorts, Campgrounds

♀ • (?♿) The Villa, 801 N Peninsula Dr; 32118 904-248-2020

AIDS/HIV Support, Education, Advocacy, Publications

♀ ★ (?♿) Outreach, Inc of Daytona Beach, 119 S Palmetto Ave; 32114-4319 904-672-6069 "We house a Special Immunology Center, Outreach offices, North Florida Aids Network, HIV+ support groups."

Bars, Restaurants, Clubs, Discos

♀ • (?♿) 769 Club, 769 Alabama St; 32014 904-253-4361 11am-3am; Sat & Sun 5pm-3am.

♀ • ♂♂ The Barracks, 952 Orange Ave; 32114 904-254-3464 *BDLW*

♂ ○ (♿) Beachside Club, 415 Main St; 32118 904-252-5465 10am-3am.

♀ ○ ♂ Hollywood Lounge/Barn Door/Wild Olive Restaurant, 615 Main St; 32118 904-252-3776 *BRDE* 11am-3am.

Health Care (see also AIDS Services)

♀ VD Clinic, 501 Clyde Morris; 32114 904-258-7000

Organizations/Resources: Business & Professional

♀ ★ (?♿) Daytona Beach Business Guild, PO Box 263148; 32118 904-322-8003

Religious Organizations & Publications

♀ ★ ♂♂ Hope Metropolitan Community Church, PO Box 15151; 32115 904-254-0993

Fort Lauderdale

Accommodation: Hotels, B&B, Resorts, Campgrounds

Fort Lauderdale

♀ • (?♿) Admiral's Court Resort & Motel, 21 Hendrick's Isle; 33301 305-462-5072; 800-248-6669; Fax 305-763-8863

♀ • ♿ Bahama Hotel, 401 N Atlantic Blvd; 33304 305-467-7315; 800-622-9995; Fax 305-467-7319 *BR*

♀ • (♿) Big Ruby's Tropical Guesthouse, 908 NE 15th Ave; 33304 305-523-7829 Fax 305-563-9953 *BR*
◆ Big Ruby's Tropical Guesthouse advertisement page 213

♂ • ♂♂ Blue Dolphin, 725 N Birch Rd; 33304 305-565-8437; 800-893-BLUE

♀ • King Henry Arms, 543 Breakers Ave; 33304 305-561-0039; 800-205-KING; "Private baths, pool, cable TV, AC, direct-dial phones, continental breakfast; one block from ocean."

♀ • (?♿) La Casa Del Mar B&B, 3003 Granada; 33304 800-739-0009 Fax 305-467-7439

♀ • (♿) Rainbow's Inn, Ft Lauderdale Beach 800-881-4814 Fax 305-881-4814 "Women only. Courtesy pickup/delivery from airport. Private pool. Near parks, mall, bars, restaurants."

♂ • ♿ The Royal Palms, 2901 Terramar; 33304 305-564-6444; 800-237-PALM; "Luxury accommodation, steps from beach."

Addictive Behavior, Substance Abuse, Recovery

♀ ★ Lambda South, Inc., PO Box 030339; 33303-0339 / 1231A E. Las Olas Blvd 305-761-9072

AIDS/HIV Support, Education, Advocacy, Publications

♀ ACT-UP/Fort Lauderdale, PO Box 7437; 33338-7437

♀ ○ ♂♂ Center For Special Immunology, 1625 SE 3rd Ave #600; 33316 305-767-9444 "Comprehensive treatment & research center for HIV disease."

♀ ☆ ♂♂ Center One, 3015 N Ocean Blvd #111; 33308-7300 305-537-4111

♀ ★ Pets Are Wonderful Support (PAWS), Inc. of South Florida, PO Box 451358, Sunrise; 33345-1358 305-537-9423 Fax 305-741-9889 "Helping people living with AIDS to care for their pets."

♀ ☆ ♂♂ Poverello/PWA Food Bank & Thrift Shop, 2297 Wilton Dr; 33305-2131 305-943-3993 Mon-Sat 10am-4.30pm.

♀ ☆ PWA Coalition of Broward County, 2302 NE 7th Ave; 33305 305-565-9119 Pub *PWA Coalition Newsline.*

Archives/Libraries/History Projects

♀ ★ (♂♂) Stonewall Library & Archives, 330 SW 27th St; 33315 305-522-2317

Bars, Restaurants, Clubs, Discos

Fort Lauderdale

♂ • Boots Bar, 2708 SW 9th St 305-792-9177

♂ Bus Stop, 2203 S Federal Hwy; 33316 305-761-1782

♂ • ♿ The Bushes, 3038 N Federal Hwy; 33306 305-561-1724 9am-2am.

FL: Fort Lauderdale
Bars, Clubs, Restaurants
213
USA
Fort Lauderdale : FL
Gifts, Cards, Novelties

♀ • ♿ Chardees Dinnerclub, 2209 Wilton Dr; 33305-2131 305-563-1800 **BREd** 4.30pm-2am. "Restaurant, dinnerclub with 2 bars; live entertainment nitely; big-name celebrities 6 times a year."

♂ Club Caribbean Resort, 2851 N Federal Highway; 33306 305-565-0402

♀ ♿♿ Club Cathode Ray, PO Box 030520; 33303-0520 305-462-8611

♀ • **The Copa Nightclub, 2800 S Federal Highway; 33316** 305-463-1507 **BDER**
✦ Copa Nightclub advertisement page 211

♀ ○ The District, 120 SW 3rd Ave; 33312 305-764-1111

♂ • (♿) The Eagle, 1951 Power Line Rd; 33311 305-462-6380 **BLLLW**

♂ • End Up Lounge, 3521 W Broward Blvd; 33312 305-584-9301 **BDLL**

♀ • ♿ Everglades Bar, 1931 S Federal Hwy; 33316 305-462-9165 **BD**

♂ • Hideaway, 2022 NE 18th St; 33305 305-566-8622 **Bd** 7am-2am; Sat to 3am; Sun noon-2am.

♂ Johnny's Village Inn, 1116 W Broward Blvd; 33312 305-522-5931

♂ The Jungle, 545 S Federal Hwy; 33301 305-832-9550

♀ Le Bar, 1914 E Oakland Park Blvd; 33306 305-563-0721

♂ Lefty's, 710 N Federal Hwy; 33304 305-763-6467

♀ • ♿♿ The Otherside of Ft Lauderdale, 2283 Wilton Dr; 33305 (NE 4th Ave) 305-565-5538 **BDE** 5pm-2am. Men welcome.

♂ • Side Street, 1753 N Andrews Ave Ext.; 33311 305-525-2007 **Bd** 4pm-2am.

♂ ○ Stanley's, 626 S Federal Hwy; 33301 305-523-9769

♂ • ♿♿ The Stud, 1000 W State Rd 84; 33315 305-525-STUD **BDELL** 4pm-2am; Sat to 3am; Sun noon-2am.

♀ • ♿♿ Studio West, 3543 North Pine Island Rd; 33351 305-742-8863 **BDEf**

Pompano Beach

♀ • Adventures, 303 SW 6th St, Pompano Beach; 33060 305-782-9577 **D**

Wilton Manors

♂ ○ (♿) Club Classics, 2004 Wilton Dr (NE 4th Ave), Wilton Manors; 33305 305-564-0209 **BD**

Bookstores: Gay/Lesbian/Feminist

♀ • ♿ Outbooks!, 1239 E Las Olas Blvd; 33301 305-764-4333; 305-764-3255 (roommate referrals); Pub Outlooks. "Gay & Lesbian books."

Bookstores: General

♀ ○ (?♿) Clark's Out of Town News, 303 S Andrews Ave; 33301 305-467-1543 8am-8pm; Sat & Sun to 7pm.

♀ • (♿) News - Books - Cards, 7126 N University Dr, Tamarac; 33321 305-726-5544 Mon-Sat 9am-6.30pm.

Bookstores: Recovery, Metaphysical, & other Specialty

♀ • (♿♿) Ricke's, 916 N Federal Hwy; 33304 305-525-3455 Fax 305-525-2963 "New Age: astrological, Tarot reading."

Broadcast Media

♂ Queer Talk, WFTL RADIO PO Box 100819; 33310 305-733-1400; 800-874-3454

Clothes

♀ ○ Audace, 813 E Las Olas Blvd; 33301 305-522-7503

♀ • J. Miles Clothing, 1023 E Las Olas Blvd; 33301 305-462-2710

♀ • ♿ Trader Tom's of North America, Inc., 930 N Federal Hwy; 33304-2707 305-763-4630 "Swimwear, activewear, & gay memorabilia."

Community Centers (see also Women's Centers)

♀ ★ Gay & Lesbian Community Center, 1164 E Oakland Park Blvd; 33334 305-463-9515 Fax 305-779-2691 The Center Voice.

Counseling/Therapy: Private

♀ • ♿♿ Center For Identity Development South, Ltd., 4400 W Sample Rd #244, Pompano Beach; 33073 305-345-5525

Erotica (Printed, Visual, Equipment)

♀ ○ (♿♿) Broward Adult Books, 3419 W Broward Blvd; 33312 305-792-4991

♀ ○ Omni Adult Bookstore, 3224 West Broward Blvd; 33312 305-584-6825

♀ ○ Pink Pussycat Boutique, 921 Sunrise Lane; 33304 305-563-4445

♀ • ♿ Trader Tom's Fantasy Depot, 914 N Federal Hwy; 33304 305-524-4759 "Leather clothing & accessories; adult toys & novelties; body piercing jewelry; magazines, S&M, fetish."

Gifts, Cards, Pride & Novelty Items

♀ • Alternatives Pride & Video Store, 710 W Broward Blvd; 33312 305-463-6006

FL: Fort Lauderdale

Gifts, Cards, Novelties

214

USA

Fort Myers : FL

Bars, Clubs, Restaurants

⚢ • (?⚦) Fallen Angel, 3045 N Federal Hwy (Store #98 Coral Center); 33301 305-563-5230 11am-8pm; Fri & Sat to 10pm; Sun 1-5pm. "Books, cards, specialized leather items; piercing jewelry."

⚢ • Grand Central Stationery, 1227 East Las Olas Blvd; 33301 305-467-2998

Health Care (see also AIDS Services)

⚢ ○ Gutierrez, Frank, M.D., 3075 NE Commercial Blvd #101; 33308 305-771-2120

⚢ ○⚦⚦ Richmond, Gary J., M.D., 315 SE 14th St; 33316 305-524-2250 Fax 305-524-5833

⚢ ☆⚦⚦ STD Clinic, 3698 NW 15th St; 33311 305-797-6900

Health Clubs, Gyms, Saunas

⚣ Club Fort Lauderdale, 400 W Broward Blvd; 33312 305-525-3344

⚣ ○⚦⚦ Clubhouse II, 2650 E Oakland Park Blvd; 33306 305-566-6750

Legal Services & Resources

⚢ ⚦⚦ American Civil Liberties Union Broward Chapter (ACLU), PO Box 350533; 33335 305-920-7715

Organizations/Resources: Business & Professional

⚢ ★⚦⚦ Broward Women In Network, PO Box 9744; 33310-9744 305-537-0866 The Winner.

Organizations/Resources: Ethnic, Multicultural

⚣ Asians & Friends of Florida, PO Box 1207; 33301

Organizations/Resources: Family

⚢ ☆ PFLAG, PO Box 290871, Davie; 33329 305-434-2993

⚢ PFLAG, 10405 Sunrise Lakes Blvd, Sunrise; 33322 305-741-3648

Organizations/Resources: General, Multipurpose, Pride

⚣ ★ Pride South Florida, PO Box 2048; 33303 305-771-1653 "Local planning group for the June 26, 1994, Celebration of Lesbian & Gay Pride & Protest to be held in New York City."

Organizations/Resources: Military/Veterans

⚢ ★ Florida Gold Coast Chapter GLB Vets, 3210 Seaward Dr, Pompano Beach; 33062 305-782-1095 Pub Forward March. "Servicing social & benevolent needs of military active service personnel & veterans."

Organizations/Resources: Political/Legislative

⚢ ★⚦⚦ Dolphin Democratic Club, 1402 E Las Olas Blvd #163; 33301-2336 305-763-1530

⚣ GUARD (Gays United To Attack Repression & Discrimination), PO Box 11357; 33339 305-570-5791

⚢ ★ Log Cabin Club/Broward County, PO Box 1281; 33302 305-563-3626 Pub Logger. "Republicans & Libertarians."

⚢ ☆ (?⚦) NOW Broward County, PO Box 23640; 33307 305-485-7005

Organizations/Resources: Sexual Focus (Leather, S/M, etc) & Safe Sex Promotion

⚣ ★ Saber M.C., PO Box 14441; 33302 305-779-2825 "A brotherhood of levi/leathermen."

Organizations/Resources: Social, Recreational & Support Groups (see also Sport/Dance/Outdoor)

⚢ ★ Broward United Against Discrimination, c/o Steve Irving 4750 SW 36th St, Unit Q, Davie; 33314 305-327-9839

⚢ ★ SAGE of Broward County, Inc., PO Box 11704; 33339-1704 305-786-5893 "A social & support organization for gays, lesbians & bisexuals of all ages dedicated to serving the senior community."

♀ ★ Women In Network, PO Box 9744; 33310-9744 305-537-0866

Organizations/Resources: Sport/Dance/Outdoor

⚣ Fort Lauderdale Frontrunners, PO Box 7064; 33338 305-566-8413

⚣ ★ (?⚦) Southern Country South Florida, PO Box 23512; 33307 305-977-7589 dCW "Country Western dance."

Organizations/Resources: Youth (see also Family)

⚣ Broward Gay & Lesbian Youth Group, 4611 S University Dr; 33328 305-764-5436

Performing Arts: Entertainment, Music, Recording, Theater, etc.

⚣ ⚦ Flamingo Freedom Band, 2249 SW 33rd Terrace; 33312 305-792-1320

Publications

♀ The Fountain, 10097 Cleary Blvd #520, Plantation; 33324 305-791-6929

→ Hotspots Magazine: p.210

→ OUT Pages: p.210

⚣ Scoop, 1126 S Federal Hwy #381; 33326 305-764-2323

Religious Organizations & Publications

⚢ ★ (?⚦) Dignity, PO Box 22884; 33335 305-463-4528 "Gay & Lesbian Catholics & their friends."

⚣ Interweave, Unitarian Universalist Church, 3970 NW 21st Ave; 33309 305-484-6734

⚣ Rodfei Shalom Fellowship, 8469 W Oakland Park Blvd, Sunrise; 33351 305-572-0902

⚢ ★⚦⚦ Sunshine Cathedral Metropolitan Community Church, 330 SW 27th St; 33315 305-462-2004; 305-467-3385

Travel & Tourist Services (see also Accommodation)

⚢ ○ Dolphin Travel, 2509 N Andrews Ave; 33311 305-566-6539

⚢ • Life Style Tours, PO Box 23964; 33307

⚢ ○ ⚦ Universal/Carlson Travel, 215 S Andrews Ave; 33301 305-525-5000 Fax 305-524-6642

⚢ ○ Up Up & Away - Tom, 701 E Broward Blvd; 33301 305-523-4944; 800-234-0841

Fort Myers

☎ SW FL Support, Inc 941-332-2272

Accommodation: Hotels, B&B, Resorts, Campgrounds

⚢ ⚦⚦ Golf View Motel, 3523 Cleveland Ave; 33901 941-936-1858

AIDS/HIV Support, Education, Advocacy, Publications

⚢ ☆⚦⚦ Comprehensive AIDS Clinic, 2231B McGregor Blvd; 33901 941-334-1448

⚢ ☆⚦⚦ Lee County Health Unit, 3920 Michigan Ave; 33916 941-332-9501

Bars, Restaurants, Clubs, Discos

♀ The Alternative, 4650 Cleveland Ave; 33907 941-277-7002

⚣ • ⚦⚦ Bottom Line, 3090 Evans Ave; 33901 941-337-7292 BDEL

FL: Fort Myers
Bars, Clubs, Restaurants

215
USA

Gainesville : FL
Bars, Clubs, Restaurants

⚲ • ♿ Office Pub, 3704 Cleveland Ave; 33901 941-936-3212 *BCLd*

⚲ Velvet Turtle Restaurant & Lounge, 1404 Cape Coral Pky, Cape Coral; 33904 941-549-9000 *BR*

Computer Bulletin Boards

⚲ • The Beach Board BBS, PO Box 181; 33902 941-278-2893 (voice); 813-337-5480 2400 baud; 337-4950 14.4K; Fax 813-337-7470

Computer/Software Sales & Services

⚲ • Ward's Computer Consulting Service, PO Box 181; 33902 941-278-2893 Fax 813-337-7470; data 337-5480

Erotica (Printed, Visual, Equipment)

⚲ ○♿ Tender Moments Lingerie, 4635-3 Coronado Parkway, Cape Coral; 33904 941-945-1448 Mon-Fri 10am-6pm; Sat to 4pm. "Lingerie & adult toys."

Laundry/Dry Cleaning

⚲ ○♿ U-Turn Coin Laundry, 2412 Cortez Blvd; 33901 941-334-7111

Organizations/Resources: Social, Recreational & Support Groups (see also Sport/Dance/Outdoor)

⚲ ★ (♿) SW FL Support, Inc, PO Box 546; 33902 941-332-2272 Pub *Support-line*.

Performing Arts: Entertainment, Music, Recording, Theater, etc.

⚲ ★ Southwest Florida Gay & Lesbian Chorus, PO Box 60623; 33906 941-432-9225

⚲ ★♿ Southwest Florida Gay & Lesbian Chorus, PO Box 60623; 33906 941-458-1382

Religious Organizations & Publications

⚲ ★ ♿ St John the Apostle Metropolitan Community Church, PO Box 6779; 33911-6779 941-278-5181; 813-433-1007

Travel & Tourist Services (see also Accommodation)

⚲ ○♿ Geraci Travel, 2132 First St; 33901 941-334-1161; 800-741-1161

Fort Pierce

Publications

♂ *Cruisin!*, PO Box 12597; 33479-2597

Fort Walton Beach

Bars, Restaurants, Clubs, Discos

⚲ • (♿) Frankly Scarlett/Choo Choo's Pub, 223 Hwy 98E 904-664-2966 *BDE* 4pm-3am.
  ✦ *Frankly Scarlett/Choo Choo's Pub advertisement page 215*

Gainesville

☎ Gay Switchboard 904-332-0700

Bars, Restaurants, Clubs, Discos

⚲ • Ambush/Melody Club, 4130 NW 6th St; 32601 904-376-3772

⚲ • ♿ The Quake, 7118 W University Ave; 32607 904-332-2553 *BREd* 4pm-2am.

⚲ University Club, 18 E University Ave; 32601 904-378-6814

Bookstores: Gay/Lesbian/Feminist

♀ • ♂ Iris Books, 802 W University Ave; 32601 904-375-7477

Bookstores: General

♀⚥ ○ ♂ Goerings' Book Center, 1310 West University Ave; 32603 800-726-1487 10am-9pm; Sun to 5pm.

Organizations/Resources: Bisexual Focus

♀⚥ Gainesville Bisexual Alliance, PO Box 14151; 32604-2151 904-355-6359

Organizations/Resources: Family

♀⚥ ☆ PFLAG of Gainesville/Ocala, PO Box 140176; 32614 904-377-8131 "Parents, Families & Friends of Lesbians & Gays."

Organizations/Resources: General, Multipurpose, Pride

♀ ★ ♂♂ Gainesville Community Alliance, PO Box 159; 32602 904-373-3557 Pub *Community Ties.*

Organizations/Resources: Political/Legislative

♀⚥ Human Rights Council of North Central Florida, PO Box 2112; 32602 904-372-5192

Organizations/Resources: Sport/Dance/Outdoor

♀ ★ Lavender Menace Women's Sports, c/o Barron, 3003 SE 35th St; 32641 904-375-4596

Organizations/Resources: Student, Academic, Alumni/ae

♀ ★ ♂♂ Lesbian, Gay & Bisexual Student Union of the University of Florida, PO Box 118505; 32611-8505 904-392-1665 x310

Organizations/Resources: Youth (see also Family)

♀⚥ Queer Youth, PO Box 12971; 32604-0971 904-338-3593

Performing Arts: Entertainment, Music, Recording, Theater, etc.

♀⚥ ★ (?♂) Gainesville Pride Chorus, PO Box 13087; 32604 904-371-7096

Publications

♀ ★ *Gay, Lesbian, & Bi Resource Guide to Gainesville*, PO Box 12971; 32604-0971 904-332-0700 tgs4edit@aol.com

→ *Mama Raga*: p.210

Religious Organizations & Publications

♀ ★ ♂♂ Trinity Metropolitan Community Church, PO Box 140535; 32614 904-495-3378

♀⚥ ☆ ♂♂ United Church of Gainesville, 1624 NW 5th Ave; 32603 904-378-3500

Switchboards, Helplines, Phone Information

♀⚥ ★ Gay Switchboard, PO Box 12002; 32604-0002 904-332-0700 Staffed 6-11pm; computerized answering system other times.

Holiday

Religious Organizations & Publications

♀⚥ ★ ♂♂ Metropolitan Community Church—Spirit of Life, 4810 Mile Stretch Dr; 34690 813-942-8616

Hollywood

Accommodation: Hotels, B&B, Resorts, Campgrounds

♀⚥ ○ Maison Harrison Bed & Breakfast, 1504 Harrison St; 33020 305-922-7319

Bars, Restaurants, Clubs, Discos

♀⚥ ○ ♂♂ Club 21, 2920 SW 30th Ave, Hallandale; 33009 305-458-0021

♀ Partners, 625 E Dania Blvd, Dania; 33004 305-921-9893

♀ Zachary's Pub, 2217 N Federal Hwy; 33019 305-920-5479

Organizations/Resources: Political/Legislative

♀⚥ ★ The Monitor, Gay Watch, PO Box 221207; 33022-1207 305-920-4233 *The Monitor.* "Keeping the First Amendment alive in the Homosexual Community."

Organizations/Resources: Sport/Dance/Outdoor

♀⚥ South Florida Mustangs, PO Box 462; 33022 305-899-1710 *d*

Jacksonville

AIDS/HIV Support, Education, Advocacy, Publications

♀⚥ ☆ ♂♂ Main Street Clinic, 962 N Main St; 32202 904-798-4810

♀⚥ ☆ STD Clinic, Duval County Public Health Unit, 515 W 6th St #14; 32206 904-633-3620

Bars, Restaurants, Clubs, Discos

♀⚥ • Bo's Coral Reef, 201 5th Ave N., Jacksonville Beach; 32250 904-246-9874

♂ ○ Bootrack, 4751 Lenox Ave; 32205 904-384-7090

♀ • ♂♂ Ezell's, 910 King St; 32204 904-388-0394 *R*

♀ HMS Bar, 1702 E 8th St; 32206

♀⚥ • In Touch Tavern, 10957 Atlantic Blvd; 32225 904-642-7506 *BR* Noon-2am. Beer & wine only.

♂ • (♂♂) The Junction, 1261 King St; 32204 904-388-3434 2pm-2am.

♀⚥ • Metro, 2929 Plum St; 32205 800-380-8719 *BDE*
✦ *Metro advertisement page 216*

♀ My Little Dude (Jo's), 2952 Roosevelt Blvd; 32205 904-388-9503

♀⚥ Park Place, 2712 Park; 32205

♀⚥ • ♂♂ The Third Dimension, 711 Edison Ave; 32204 904-353-6316 *BDE*

Counseling/Therapy: Private

♀⚥ ○ Allison, Judith S., M.Ed, MSH, 5645 Nettie Rd; 32207 904-733-3310

Health Clubs, Gyms, Saunas

♂ • Club Jacksonville, 1939 Hendricks Ave; 32207 904-398-7451

FL: Jacksonville
Massage Therapy
217
USA
Key West : FL
Accommodation

Massage Therapy (Licensed only)

♀ • (?&) Health Techs, 434 3rd St N., Jacksonville Beach; 32250 904-247-0527

Organizations/Resources: Youth (see also Family)

♀ ★ (?&) Jacksonville Area Sexual Minority Youth Network (JASMYN), PO Box 23778; 32241-3778 904-565-1668 (Gay Youth Information line)

Publications

♀ C.O.E. (Calendar of Events), PO Box 43335; 32203

Religious Organizations & Publications

♀ ★&& St Luke's Metropolitan Community Church, 126 E 7th St; 32206-4510 904-358-6747

Key West

Accommodation: Hotels, B&B, Resorts, Campgrounds

♂ • (&) Alexander's Guest House, 1118 Fleming St; 33040 305-294-9919

♀ ○ Atlantic Shores Motel, 510 South St; 33040 305-296-2491

♀ • Big Ruby's Guesthouse, 409 Appelrouth Lane; 33040-6534 305-296-2323; 800-477-RUBY; Fax 305-296-0281

♀ • Blue Parrot Inn, 916 Elizabeth St; 33040 305-296-0033

♀ • **Brass Key Guesthouse, 412 Frances St; 33040-6950 800-932-9119**

♀ • The Captain Saunders House, 322 Elizabeth St; 33040 305-296-8800

♀ ○ Chelsea House, 707 Truman Ave; 33040 305-296-2211; 800-845-8859; Fax 305-296-4822

♀ • Coconut Grove Guest House, 817 Fleming St; 33040 305-296-5107

♀ • Colours Key West: The Guest Mansion, 410 Fleming St; 33040 800-93GLOBAL Fax 305-534-0362

♂ • Curry House, 806 Fleming; 33040 305-294-6777

♂ • Cypress House, 601 Caroline St; 33040 800-525-2488
✦ Cypress House advertisement page 217

♀ • (&) Duval House, 815 Duval St; 33040 305-294-1666; 800-22-DUVAL

♀ • Heron House, 512 Simonton St; 33040 305-294-9227

♂ • Island House for Men, 1129 Fleming St; 33040 305-294-6284 Fax 305-292-0051 *LW*

♀ ○ Key Lodge Motel, 1004 Duval St; 33040 305-296-9915

♀ • The Knowles House, 1004 Eaton St; 33040 305-296-8132; 800-352-4414; Fax 305-294-3273

♀ ○&& La Casa De Luces, 422 Amelia St; 33040 305-296-3993; 800-432-4849

♂ • Lighthouse Court, 902 Whitehead St; 33040 305-294-9588

♂ • && Lime House Inn, 219 Elizabeth St; 33040 305-296-2978; 800-374-4242; Fax 305-294-5858
✦ Lime House Inn advertisement page 217

♀ ○ (?&) Merlinn Guest House, 811 Simonton St; 33040 305-296-3336

♀ ○ The Mermaid & The Alligator, 729 Truman Ave; 33040 305-294-1894; 800-773-1894; "A mixed guest house welcoming gay business."
✦ Mermaid & The Alligator advertisement page 217

♂ • Newton Street Station, 1414 Newton St; 33040 305-294-4288; 800-248-2457; Fax 305-292-5062

♂ • Oasis Guest House & Coral Tree Inn, 823 Fleming St; 33040 305-296-2131; 800-362-7477

♀ ○&& Pilot House Guest House, 414 Simonton St; 33040 305-294-8719; 800-648-3780

Key West Express

Enjoy the convenience of our non-stop flights between Key West and Southwest Florida. Fly to **Naples** from the **Key West International Airport** in only 40 minutes. For travelers originating in Southwest Florida, parking at Naples Airport is free. For reservations and information call your local travel agent or Cape Air toll free at **1-800-352-0714.**

Cape Air
FLYING FOR FLORIDA & THE KEYS

12.303

♀ • Pines Key West, 521 United St; 33040 305-296-7467; 800-282-PINE
✦ Pines Key West advertisement page 217

♀ • The Rainbow House, 525 United St; 33040 305-292-1450; 800-749-6696

♂ • (&) Sea Isle Guest House, 915 Windsor St; 33040 305-294-5188; 800-995-4786; Fax 305-296-7143

♀ • Seascape, 420 Olivia St; 33040 305-296-7776 Fax 305-296-7776

♀ • Simonton Court Historic Inn & Cottages, 320 Simonton St; 33040 305-294-6386; 800-944-2687; Fax 305-293-8446

♀ ○ (?&) The Treetop Bar, 1125 Duval St; 33040 305-294-4737

♀ • Tropical Inn, 812 Duval St; 33040 305-294-9977

Answering/FAX & Mail Receiving, Shipping & Packaging Services

♀ • The Mail Spot, 1075 Duval St; 33040 305-292-9559 Fax 305-292-3082 "Mailing & shipping service; Western Union money orders, etc."

Art & Photography (see also Graphic Design)

♀ • Ed Cox Photography, PO Box 6564; 33041 305-294-9000

Bars, Restaurants, Clubs, Discos

♂ 801 Bar, 801 Duval St; 33040 305-294-4737

♀ ○ & Antonia's Restaurant & Catering, 615 Duval St; 33040 305-294-6565; 305-294-6464 catering; *R*

♀ • && Appelrouth Grill, 416 Appelrouth Lane; 33040 305-296-9483 *R*

♀ Club International, 900 Simonton St; 33040 305-296-9230

♀ • (?&) Copa Key West, 623 Duval St; 33040 305-296-8521 *BDER*
✦ Copa Key West advertisement page 211

♀ Donnie's/Cocktails, 618 Duval St; 33040 305-294-5620

♀ ○&& Mangos, 700 Duval St; 33040 305-292-4606 *R* 8am breakfast to mdnt.

♂ • Numbers, 1029 Truman Ave; 33040 305-296-0333 *BDELWC*

♂ ○ & One Saloon, 524 Duval St; 33040 305-296-8118 *BDE*

♀ ○ Savannah, 915 Duval St; 33040 305-296-6700 *BR*

♀ Square One, 1075 Duval St; 33040 305-296-4300 *R*

♀ Tea By The Sea, 510 South; 33040 305-296-2491

♀ ○ & Yo Sake, 722 Duval St; 33040 305-294-2288 "Japanese restaurant & sushi bar."

Bookstores: Gay/Lesbian/Feminist

♀ • SandCastles, 1219 Duval St; 33040 305-292-3048

Bookstores: General

♀ ○&& Bargain Books & News Stand, 1028 Truman Ave; 33040 305-294-7446 7am-6pm. "Full line of Gay/Lesbian magazines & newspapers."

♀ ○ & Blue Heron Books, 538 Truman Ave; 33040 305-294-3508 10am-10pm; Sun to 9pm.

♀ • (&) Caroline Street Books, 800 Caroline St #7; 33040 305-294-3931 Fax 305-294-8658

♀ ○ Key West Island Bookstore, 513 Fleming St; 33040 305-294-2904

Erotica (Printed, Visual, Equipment)

♀ ○ Alligator News & Books, 716 Duval St; 33040-7453 305-294-4004

FL: Key West
Erotica

219

USA

Miami Area: FL
Accommodation

♀ ○ ♂ Key West Video, 528 Duval St; 33040 305-292-4113 24 hrs.

♀ • Leather Master, 418A Appelrouth Lane; 33040 305-292-5051

Gifts, Cards, Pride & Novelty Items

♀ • Greetings From Key West, 1075 Duval St, Duval Square #21; 33040 305-294-1733; 800-KW-GIFTS

Health Care (see also AIDS Services)

♀ • ♂ Old Town Medical Center/Immune Care of Key West, 520 Southard St; 33040 305-296-4868 Fax 305-296-4868

Organizations/Resources: Business & Professional

♀ ★ ♂♂ Key West Business Guild, PO Box 1208; 33041 305-294-4603; 800-535-7797; Fax 305-296-8132

Organizations/Resources: General, Multipurpose, Pride

♀ ★ (?♂) KW Lesbian & Gay Pride Alliance, PO Box 310; 33041 305-293-0494 Fax 305-294-9044

Publications

♀ • Southern Exposure Guide, 819 Peacock Plaza #575; 33041 305-294-6303 Monthly.

Religious Organizations & Publications

♀ ★ Metropolitan Community Church, 1215 Petronia St; 33040 305-294-8912 Services Sun 9.30 & 11am; Wed Communion 7pm.

Travel & Tourist Services (see also Accommodation)

♂ • Hanns Ebensten Travel, Inc, 513 Fleming St; 33040 305-294-8174 "Tour operator."

♀ • (?♂) Key West Reservation Service, Box 1689; 33041-1689 / 628 Fleming St 305-294-7713; 800-327-4831 US & Canada;; Fax 305-296-6291 "Reservation service for accommodation: hotels, motels, condos, vacation homes, free to tourists."

Lake Worth: see Palm Beach Area

Lakeland
Area code changes to 941 during 1995

Accommodation: Hotels, B&B, Resorts, Campgrounds

♀ • (♂) Sunset Motel, 2301 New Tampa Hwy, US 92 W; 33801 941-683-6464

Bars, Restaurants, Clubs, Discos

♀ Roy's Green Parrot, 1030 E Main St; 33801 941-683-6021

Organizations/Resources: General, Multipurpose, Pride

♀ ★ (?♂) Polk Gay/Lesbian Alliance, PO Box 8221; 33802-8221 941-644-0085 Pub PGLA News.

Lantana: see West Palm Beach

Largo

Organizations/Resources: Social, Recreational & Support Groups (see also Sport/Dance/Outdoor)

♀ TBBC Wrap-Up, PO Box 1986; 34649 813-996-4738

Madeira Beach: see Tampa Bay Area

Melbourne

Bars, Restaurants, Clubs, Discos

♂ • (♂) Saturday's, 4060 W New Haven Ave; 32901 407-724-1510 D

Miami Area

☎ Gay, Lesbian & Bisexual Community Hotline of Greater Miami 305-759-3661

☎ Switchboard of Miami, Inc 305-358-HELP

Accommodation: Hotels, B&B, Resorts, Campgrounds
Miami Beach

♀ • ♂ The Bayliss, 504 14th St, Miami Beach; 33139 305-534-0010

♀ ○ Brigham Gardens, 1411 Collins Ave, Miami Beach; 33139 305-531-1331 Fax 305-538-9898

♀ • (?♂) European Guest House Miami Beach, 721 Michigan Ave, Miami Beach; 33139 305-673-6665 Fax 305-672-7442 "Luxury rooms; full buffet breakfast; Jacuzzi; remote cable; walk to beaches, bars, & Art Deco."

♂ • Island House, Three Beach/South Beach locations. 305-864-2422; 800-382-2422

♀ • (♂) The Jefferson House, 1018 Jefferson Ave, Miami Beach; 33139 305-534-5247

♂ • Normandy South, Miami Beach 305-674-1197

♀ ○ (?♂) Waldorf Towers Hotel, 860 Ocean Drive, Miami Beach; 33139 305-531-7684; 800-933-BEACH; Fax 305-672-6836 BR

♀ ○ Winterhaven Hotel, 1400 Ocean Dr, Miami Beach; 33139 305-531-5571; 800-395-2322; Fax 305-536-3337 BD

FL: Miami Area
Accommodation
220
USA
Miami Area: FL
Erotica

Accommodation: Reservations & Exchanges (see also Travel)

♀ • **South Beach Destinations, 4110 El Prado Blvd, Coconut Grove; 33133 305-666-0163; 800-443-8224; Fax 305-666-3210**

◆ *South Beach Destinations advertisement page 219*

♀ • South Florida Hotel Network, 1688 Meridian Ave #1016, Miami Beach; 33139 800-538-3616; 305-538-3616 local; Fax 305-538-5858

AIDS/HIV Support, Education, Advocacy, Publications

♂ ☆ (♿) Body Positive Resource Center, 175 NE 36th St, Miami; 33137 305-576-1111 Fax 305-576-0604

♀ ○ Center for Special Immunology, 400 Arthur Godfrey Rd, Miami Beach; 33140 305-672-5009

♀ ☆ (♿) Community Research Initiative of South Florida, 1320 S Dixie Hwy #485, Miami; 33146-2926 305-667-9296 Fax 305-667-8686 "Conduct HIV related clinical research trials."

♀ ☆♿ Health Crisis Network, PO Box 370098, Miami; 33137-0098 305-751-7775; 305-751-7751; Fax 305-756-7880

♀ ★ (♿) Miami Beach HIV/AIDS Project, c/o LGBCC, PO Box 1679, Miami Beach; 33119-1679 / 1335 Alton Rd 305-672-2347

♀ ☆ ♿ PWA Coalition of Dade County, 3890 Biscayne Blvd, Miami; 33137-3731 305-573-6010 Pub *PWAC Monthly Newsletter.*

Art & Photography (see also Graphic Design)

♀ • ♿ Ali Photographics/Gallery, 1642 Euclid Ave, Miami Beach; 33139 305-531-8881 By appointment only. Mail order catalog available.

Bars, Restaurants, Clubs, Discos

Miami Beach

♀ 821 Club, 821 Lincoln Rd, Miami Beach; 33139 305-673-8551

♀ Amnesia International, 136 Collins Ave, Miami Beach; 33139 305-531-5535

♀ BASH, 655 Washington Ave, Miami Beach; 33139 305-538-BASH

♂ • ♿ Gertrude's, 826 Lincoln Rd, Miami Beach; 33139 305-538-6929 *BR* 10am-11pm. Coffee house, wine bar.

♂ • ♿ Hombre, 925 Washington Ave, Miami Beach; 33139 305-538-STUD *B* 5pm-5am.

♀ The Kremlin, 727 Lincoln Rd, Miami Beach; 33139 305-673-3150

♀ Les Bains, 753 Washington Ave, Miami Beach; 33139 305-532-8768

♀ Lucky's, 1969 71st St, Miami Beach; 33139 305-868-0901

♀ The Palace Bar & Grill, 1200 Ocean Dr, Miami Beach; 33139 305-531-9077 *BR*

♂ Paragon, 245 22nd St, Miami Beach; 33139 305-534-1235 *D* Tue & Sat 9.30pm-sunrise.

♀ Starfish Restaurant, 1427 West Ave, Miami Beach; 33139 305-673-1717

♀ Ted's Hideaway South, 124 2nd St, Miami Beach; 33139

♀ Twist, 1057 Washington Ave, Miami Beach; 33139 305-53-TWIST

♂ Warsaw, 1450 Collins Ave, Miami Beach; 33139 305-531-4555 *D*

♂ Westend, 942 Lincoln Rd, Miami Beach; 33139 305-538-WEST

Miami

♀ • Cheers, 2490 SW 17th Ave, Miami; 33145 305-857-0041 *BDR*

♂ ○ The Eagle, 1252 Coral Way, Miami; 33134 305-860-0056

♂ • ♿ O'Zone, 6620 Red Road, Miami; 33143 (SW 57th Ave) 305-667-2888 *BDE* 9pm-5am.

♂ On The Waterfront, 3615 NW South River Dr, Miami; 33142 305-635-5500

♂ Southpaw Saloon, 7005 Biscayne Blvd, Miami; 33138 305-758-9362

♂ Sugar's, 17060 W Dixie Hwy, Miami; 33181

North Miami Beach

♂ • ♿ Boardwalk, 17008 Collins Ave N., North Miami Beach; 33160 305-354-8617 *BDE* 7am-5am (before & after hours)

Bookstores: Gay/Lesbian/Feminist

♀ • ♂ GW Miami Beach, 720 Lincoln Rd Mall, Miami Beach; 33139 305-534-4763 Fax 305-534-9177

♀ • ♂ Lambda Passages, 7545 Biscayne Blvd, Miami; 33138 305-754-6900 11am-9pm; Sun noon-6pm.

Bookstores: General

♀ ○ Book Depot, 1638 Euclid Ave, Miami Beach; 33139 305-538-0747; 800-438-2750; Fax 305-538-9666 andyes@aol.com 11am-7pm. "New & used books."

♀ ○ Westchester News, 8659 Coral Way, Miami; 33155 305-264-6210

Bookstores: Recovery, Metaphysical, & other Specialty

♀ • ♿ The 9th Chakra, 817 Lincoln Rd, Miami Beach; 33139 305-538-0671 "New Age books, tapes, etc; free healing meditations & discussion groups."

Clothes

♂ • ♂ Cabana Joe Unique Beachwear, 1200 Ocean Dr, Miami Beach; 33139 (10th St at Ocean Dr) 305-532-4510 10am-8pm.

♀ • Don't Panic!, 1249 Washington Ave, Miami Beach; 33139 305-531-7223

♀ ○ Zoo 14, 933 Washington Ave, Miami Beach; 33139 305-538-HARD

Community Centers (see also Women's Centers)

♀ ★ (♿) Lesbian Gay & Bisexual Community Center, PO Box 1679, Miami Beach; 33119-1679 / 1335 Alton Rd 305-531-3666

Computer/Software Sales & Services

♀ • South Beach Computers, 2421 Lake Pancoast Dr, Miami Beach; 33140 305-531-9702

Counseling/Therapy: Private

♀ • ♿ Arocha, Jorge, LCSW, 2000 S Dixie Hwy #103, Miami; 33133 305-285-8900

Erotica (Printed, Visual, Equipment)

♀ ○ 72nd St Book & Video, 10494 SW 72nd St, Miami; 33173 305-271-5919

♀ ○ Bird Road Book & Video, 6833 Bird Rd, Miami; 33155 305-661-9103

♀ ○ Biscayne Books & Video, 11711 Biscayne Blvd, Miami; 33181 305-895-9009

♀ Condomania, 758 Washington Ave, Miami Beach; 33139 305-531-7872

♀ ○ Dixie Erotic Book & Video, 9818 S Dixie Hwy, Miami; 33156 305-661-5888

FL: Miami Area
Erotica

221

USA

Miami Area: FL
Organizations: Student

♀ ○ Happy Books, 9514 S Dixie Hwy, Miami; 33156 305-670-9203

♀ ○ J&R Book & Video, 7455 Bird Rd, Miami; 33155 305-262-6570

♀ ○ Le Jeune Books, 928 SW 42nd Ave, Miami; 33134 305-443-1913

♀ ○ Lisa Book & Video, 14817 W Dixie Hwy, Miami; 33181 305-940-9759

♂ ○&& Perrine Book & Video, 18093 S Dixie Hwy, Miami; 33157 305-233-3913

♀ ○ Pink Pussycat Boutique, 3419 Main Hwy, Coconut Grove; 33133 305-448-7656

♂ ● Pleasure Chest at Club Body Center, 2991 Coral Way, Miami; 33133 305-448-2214

♀ ● && Stadium Book & Video, Inc., 17381 NW 27th Ave, Opa Locka; 33055 305-623-8933 Sun-Thu 9am-mdnt; Fri & Sat to 1am. "Peeps, viewing rooms; video sales & rentals, etc."

♀ ○ Ted's News, 8744 Mills Dr, Miami; 33183 305-274-6397

♀ ○ Trail Books, 7350 SW 8th St, Miami; 33144 305-262-4776

Florists (see also Gardening)

♀ ● ♂ Flowers & Flowers, 925 Lincoln Rd, Miami Beach; 33139 305-534-1633; 800-274-1633; Fax 305-534-0122

♀ ● Stephen Nevitt Florist, 600 NE 72 Terrace, Miami; 33138 305-757-8383; 800-757-8383; Fax 305-754-2876 "Florist; erotic chocolates; gifts."

Grooming Services

♀ ● (&&) Salon 1000, 1000 West Ave, Miami Beach; 33139 305-531-4614

Health Care (see also AIDS Services)

♀ ☆ && Prevention, Education & Treatment (PET) Center, 615 Collins Ave, Miami Beach; 33139 305-538-0525 Mon-Fri 8am-5pm. "STD; early intervention treatment of HIV spectrum disease."

♀ ☆ && Public Health Clinic, 1350 NW 14th St, Miami; 33125 305-324-2434

Health Clubs, Gyms, Saunas

♂ ○ Club Miami, 2991 Coral Way, Miami; 33133 305-448-2214

Laundry/Dry Cleaning

♀ ○ Clean Machine Laundry, 226 12th St, Miami Beach; 33139 305-534-9429

Legal Services & Resources

♀ && American Civil Liberties Union of Florida (ACLU), 225 NE 34th St #102, Miami; 33137 305-576-2336

♀ ● ♂ Finesilver, Michael I., 420 Lincoln Rd #372, Miami Beach; 33139 305-672-7000 Criminal defense.

Massage Therapy (Licensed only)

♂ ● Tyrell, Jim, LMT, 305-250-0061 (beeper); 305-867-1424

Meeting/Contact Services, Publications, Talklines

♀ ● Les Connection, PO Box 16-4836, Miami; 33116 305-829-6941

♂ ★ Miami Beach Hardbodies, 305-865-9499

Organizations/Resources: Business & Professional

♀ Gay & Lesbian Psychotherapist Group, c/o Larry Harmon, PhD, 2000 S Dixie Hwy #103, Miami; 33133 305-285-8900

♀ ★ Lesbian, Gay & Bisexual Addiction Professionals Group, c/o Larry Harmon, PhD, 2000 S Dixie Hwy #103, Miami; 33133 305-285-8900

♀ ★ South Beach Business Guild, PO Box 394, Miami Beach; 33119 305-234-SBBG

♀ ★ United Teachers of Dade Gay & Lesbian Caucus, 2929 SW 3rd Ave (UTD office), Miami; 33129 305-854-0220 x251

Organizations/Resources: Ethnic, Multicultural

♀ ★ (?&) Black & White Men Together/South Florida, PO Box 15581, Miami; 33101-5581 305-364-4528

♀ ★ Gay & Lesbian Association of Cuban Exiles (GLACE), 4700 NW 7th St #463, Miami; 33126 305-541-6097

♀ Las Salamandras de Ambiente, 3277 SW 22nd Ter, Miami; 33145-3109 305-380-8585

Organizations/Resources: Family

♀ LesBiGay Parents of Our Kids, 830 NE 71st St, Miami; 33138 305-758-0392

♂ PFLAG, 6930 SW 64th Ave, Miami; 33143-3239 305-666-0770

♂ PFLAG North Miami Beach, PO Box 292091, Davie, FL 33329 305-389-0378

Organizations/Resources: Political/Legislative

♂ Dade Action PAC, PO Box 431151, Miami; 33143 305-460-3140

♂ Dan Bradley Democratic Club, PO Box 127, Coconut Grove; 33133 305-444-4647

♀ ☆&& National Organization For Women (NOW), PO Box 611146, North Miami Beach; 33161-1146 800-417-9777

♂ NOW FIU Chapter, FIU, University Park Campus DM212, Miami; 33199 305-348-2408

♂ NOW North Miami, PO Box 611796, North Miami; 33161 305-936-5926

♂ Safeguarding American Values for Everybody, PO Box 454406, Miami; 33145 305-460-5772

Organizations/Resources: Social, Recreational & Support Groups (see also Sport/Dance/Outdoor)

♀ ★ ♂ Friday Night Womyn's Group, PO Box 570-132, Miami; 33157 305-253-3740 (Geraldine) Meets 3rd Fri of month, 8pm, at Lesbian & Gay Community CEnter, 1335 Alton Rd, South Miami Beach. *The InformHer.*

♂ SAGE Chapter Miami, c/o LG&B Community Center 1335 Alton Road, Miami Beach; 33109 305-531-3666

♀ ☆ (?&) WOMB (Women of Miami Beach), PO Box 190776, Miami Beach; 33119 305-538-2617

Organizations/Resources: Sport/Dance/Outdoor

♀ ● Rainbow Adventures, Sailing Charters, 800-881-4814 Fax 305-881-4814 "Sunset, full & half day, private charters on Biscayne Bay. Transportatipn available from hotel."

♀ ★ (?&) Southeastern Great Outdoors, PO Box 142123, Coral Gables; 33114-2123 305-667-2222

♀ Sunshine Athletic Association Dade Chapter, PO Box 430007, South Miami; 33143 305-662-3998

Organizations/Resources: Student, Academic, Alumni/ae

♀ ★ && GLBC/University of Miami, c/o Volunteer Services, PO Box 249116, Coral Gables; 33124 305-284-4483

⚨ Stonewall Student Union, Student Activities Florida Intl Univ, GC340, University Park, Miami; 33199 305-348-2137; 305-822-2825

Public Relations/Advertising Agencies

♀ • The Berkeley Studio, 5925 North Bay Rd, Miami Beach; 33140 305-867-9585

Publications

♀ LIPS, 16345 W Dixie Hwy #389, North Miami Beach; 33160 305-534-4830 Fax 305-538-0263

⚨ • Newzette, The Associates, PO Box 472382, Miami; 33147-2382

♂ Outpost, 1000 Lincoln Ave, Miami Beach; 33139 305-588-9700

⚨ Planet Homo, 1521 Alton Road #349, Miami Beach; 33139 305-672-homo

→ TWN (The Weekly News): p.210

◆ TWN (The Weekly News) advertisement page 210

♂ ○ Wire, 1638 Euclid Ave, Miami Beach; 33139 305-538-3111 Weekly newspaper.

Religious Organizations & Publications

⚨ ★ && Christ Metropolitan Community Church, 7701 SW 76th Ave, Miami; 33143 305-284-1040

♂ ☆ && Church of Religious Science, 8905 SW 87th Ave, 2nd flr, Miami; 33176 305-274-0571

⚨ ★ (&) Congregation Etz Chaim, 19094 West Dixie Hwy, North Miami Beach; 33180 305-931-9318 Shabbat services Fri 8.30pm.

♂ Eastside Unitarian Universalist Church, c/o Rev Al Boyce, 4218 NE 2nd Ave, Miami; 33137-3520 305-576-1412

⚨ ★ (&&) Grace Church of Miami Shores, 10390 NE 2nd Ave, Miami; 33138 305-758-6822

Switchboards, Helplines, Phone Information

⚨ ★ Gay, Lesbian & Bisexual Community Hotline of Greater Miami, c/o Lambda Passages, 7545 Biscayne Blvd, Miami; 33138 305-759-3661

♂ ☆ && Switchboard of Miami, Inc, 75 SW 8th St, Miami; 33130 305-358-HELP

Thrift/Consignment Stores

♂ ☆ PWAC Thrift Shop, 286 NE 39th St, Miami; 33137 305-571-2000

Travel & Tourist Services (see also Accommodation)

♂ • Interworld African Safaris, 673 NE 73rd St, Miami; 33138 305-751-7960; 800-237-4225; Fax 305-751-6362

♂ ○ Palm Travel: Don or Vicki, 1911 NE 172nd St, North Miami Beach; 33162 305-944-4000; 800-749-1900; Fax 305-948-6000

⚨ • && Professional Travel Management, Inc, 195 SW 15th Rd #403, Miami; 33129 305-858-5522; 800-568-4064

♂ ○ && Vision Travel, 2222 Ponce De Leon, Coral Gables; 33134 305-444-8484; 800-654-4544

Miami Springs

Organizations/Resources: Political/Legislative

⚨ NOW South Miami, 425 LaVilla Dr; 33166 305-888-2548

Organizations/Resources: Social, Recreational & Support Groups (see also Sport/Dance/Outdoor)

♀ Feminist Alternative, 425 LaVilla Dr; 33166 305-888-2548

Miramar

AIDS/HIV Support, Education, Advocacy, Publications

♂ ACT-UP/Miami, 2411 Largo Dr; 33023 305-787-1311

Naples

AIDS/HIV Support, Education, Advocacy, Publications

♀ ☆ && Collier AIDS Resource & Education Service, Inc. (CARES), 1090 6th Ave N; 33940-5604 941-263-2303 Fax 941-263-8460 Pub Newsletter.

Bars, Restaurants, Clubs, Discos

♀ • & Cafe Flamingo, 947 3rd Ave N; 33940 941-262-8181 *B*

⚨ • (&) The Galley, 509 3rd St S; 33940 941-262-2808 *BR* Disco weekends.

♂ The Galley Restaurant & Lounge, 509 3rd St S; 33940 941-262-3968 *BR*

Bookstores: Gay/Lesbian/Feminist

⚨ • Lavenders—the Alternative Source, Pine Ridge Plaza, 5600 Trail Blvd #4; 33963-2894 941-594-9499

Bookstores: General

♂ ○ Book Nook, 824 5th Ave S; 33940 941-262-4740 8.30am-6pm; Sun 8am-2.30pm.

Transportation: Limousine, Taxi, Etc.

♂ ○ (?&) **Cape Air, Barnstable Municipal Airport, East Ramp, Hyannis, MA 02601 800-352-0714; 508-771-6944; (Member IGTA) "Non-stop, scheduled flights between Naples & Key West. Also serving Cape Cod, Nantucket & Martha's Vineyard, MA in the Northeastern US."**

◆ Cape Air advertisement page 218

Ocala

Bars, Restaurants, Clubs, Discos

⚨ • The Connection, 3331 Pine Ave; 34471 (off Hwy 441) 904-620-2511

Orlando

☎ Gay/Lesbian Community Services of Central Florida 407-843-4297

Accommodation: Hotels, B&B, Resorts, Campgrounds

Orlando

⚨ • & Garden Cottage Bed & Breakfast, PO Box 533953; 32853 407-894-5395 Fax 407-894-3809

♀ • Leora's B's Bed & Breakfast, PO Box 6094; 32853 407-649-0009

⚨ • Parliament House Motor Inn, 410 North Orange Blossom Trail; 32805 407-425-7571 *BDE* 11am-2am; restaurant 24 hrs. "Female impersonation shows."

♂ Power House/Stable/Cantina de La Luna, at Parliament House 410 N Orange Blossom Trail; 32805 407-425-7571 *BDE*

Art Galleries/Archives/Restoration, Supplies, Framing

♂ • (&&) Scott Laurent Galleries, 348 Park Ave N., Winter Park; 32789 407-629-1488 Fax 407-644-2717 Mon-Wed 11am-6pm; Thu-Sat to 9pm; Sun noon-5pm. "Art gallery; picture framing."

Bars, Restaurants, Clubs, Discos

Longwood

♂ The Ruby Slipper, 664 S Hwy 17-92, Longwood; 32750 407-339-1611

FL: Orlando
Bars, Clubs, Restaurants

223
USA

Orlando : FL
Organizations: Family

Out & About Books & Gifts

930 N. Mills Ave
Orlando, FL 32803
(407) 896-0204
Mon-Sat
11am-8pm

Orlando

♀ • Cactus Club, 1300 N Mills Ave; 32803 407-894-3041

♀ • City Lights Disco Cabaret, 3400 S Orange Blossom Trail; 32809 407-422-6826 *DE* Noon-2am.

♀ • ♿ The Club, 578 N Orange Ave; 32801 407-426-0005 *BD*

♀ Connections, 1517 N Orange Blossom Trail; 32804 407-841-4030

♀ Dekko's, 46 N Orange Ave; 32804

♀ The Edge, 100 W Livingston; 32801

♀ • ♿ Faces, 4910 Edgewater Dr; 32810 407-291-7571 *BD* 4pm-2am. Beer & wine. 'Gay gentlemen welcome.'

♂ • ♿ Full Moon Saloon, 500 N. Orange Blossom Trail; 32805 407-648-8725 *LCWd*

♂ ○ ♿ Hank's, 5026 Edgewater Dr; 32810 407-291-2399 *L*

♂ • ♿ The Orlando Eagle, 3400 S. Orange Blossom Trail; 32809 407-843-6334; 407-420-9015, 839-0204; *BDLW* 2pm-2am.

♂ Secrets Night Club & Lounge, 745 Bennett Rd; 32803 407-649-8442

♀ • (♿) Southern Nights, 375 S Bumby Ave; 32803 407-898-0424 *BDE* 4pm-2am.

♂ Uncle Walt's, 5454 International Drive; 32819 407-351-4866

Winter Park

♀ • ♿ Phoenix, 7124 Aloma Ave, Winter Park; 32792 407-678-9220 3pm-2am.

Bookstores: Gay/Lesbian/Feminist

♀ • (♿) Out & About Books, 930 N Mills Ave; 32803 407-896-0204 11am-8pm; Sun 1-6pm. "Gay & Lesbian books, cards, caldendars, jewelry; Art Gallery, & much more."
♦ *Out & About Books advertisement page 223*

Bookstores: General

♀ • ♿ Alobar Books & Music, 709 W Smith St; 32804 407-841-3050 10am-9pm; Sun noon-5pm. "We accept trade-ins on books, CDs, records."

♀ ○ ♿ Bookstop, 303 East Altamonte Drive, Altamonte Springs; 32701 407-339-6555

Broadcast Media

♂ Family Values, PO Box 561504; 32856-1504 407-646-2398

Community Centers (see also Women's Centers)

♀ ★ ♿ Gay/Lesbian Community Services of Central Florida, PO Box 533446; 32853-3446 / 714 E. Colonial Drive 407-843-4297 (THE-GAYS) computer hotline 24 hrs; 407-425-4527 office; Fax 407-423-9904 Mon-Fri 11am-9pm; Sat noon-5pm. *The Triangle.*

Erotica (Printed, Visual, Equipment)

♀ • Absolute Leather, 3400 S Orange Blossom Trail; 32809 407-843-8168; 800-447-4820

♀ • ♿ Liberty Video, 4408 N Orange Blossom Trail; 32804 407-294-1919 9am-2am.

♀ ○ (♿) The Original Book Store, 2203 Orange Blossom Trail; 32805 407-648-4546 Sun-Wed 8.30am-2.30am; Thu-Sat 24 hrs.

Health Care (see also AIDS Services)

♀ ☆ (♿) Women's Health Center, Inc, 1030 Herman Ave; 32803 407-896-2022; 407-422-0606; FL only (800) 432-8517

Health Clubs, Gyms, Saunas

♂ New Image Fitness Center, 3400 S Orange Blossom Trail; 32805 407-420-9890

Insurance Benefits/Viaticals

♀ ○ **Positive Living Resources, 6016 Westgate Dr #303; 32835 800-398-5177 Fax 407-298-5350 "A viatical settlement company."**

♀ ○ TLC Funding, 128 W Wallace St; 32809 407-438-9650; 800-290-8171; Viatical settlement company
♦ *TLC Funding advertisement page 121*

Jewelry

♂ • Jewelry Etc, 5685 Red Bug Lake Road, Winter Springs; 32708 407-699-0680

Legal Services & Resources

♀ ○ ♿ Fagin, Suellen D., 300 Garfield Ave #100, Winter Park; 32789 407-645-1779

♂ ○ Slaughter, David B., PO Box 922; 32802 407-843-8390

Organizations/Resources: Business & Professional

♀ ★ ♿ Metropolitan Business Association, PO Box 150364, Altamonte Springs; 32715-0364 407-420-2182

Organizations/Resources: Family

♀ ★ (♿) Gay & Lesbian Parents Coalition International/Central Florida Chapter, PO Box 561504; 32856-1504 407-420-2191

♀ ☆ ♿ PFLAG, PO Box 141312; 32814-1312 407-896-0689; 407-236-9177; "Parents, Families & Friends of Lesbians & Gays."

Organizations/Resources: Political/Legislative

♀ ★ ♿ Rainbow Democratic Club, PO Box 532041; 32853-2041 407-236-9476 Fax 407-299-8376 Pub *Newsletter*.

Organizations/Resources: Social, Recreational & Support Groups (see also Sport/Dance/Outdoor)

♀ ★ LCN (Loving, Committed Network), PO Box 149512; 32814-9512 407-648-4154 Pub *LCN Express*.

Organizations/Resources: Sport/Dance/Outdoor

♀ ★ (?♿) Challengers International M.C., PO Box 883; 32802-0883 407-382-3332 "Motorcylists."

♂ ★ (?♿) Conquistadors M.C., PO Box 555591; 32855-5591 407-648-2156

♀ ★ Gay & Lesbian Orlando Water Skiers (GLOWS), PO Box 970, Goldenrod; 32733-0970 407-679-0507

♀ ● Horn, Jeff D., 407-895-3722 "Tennis lessons, groups & privates, by USPTA certified professional."

Publications

♀ ● *Watermark*, PO Box 533655; 32853 407-481-2243 Fax 407-481-2246

Religious Organizations & Publications

♀ ★ (?♿) Integrity/Central Florida, PO Box 530031; 32853-0031 407-332-2743 "Lesbian & Gay Episcopalians & their friends."

♀ ★ ♿ Joy Metropolitan Community Church, PO Box 3004; 32802-3004 / 2351 S. Ferncreek 407-894-1081

Palm Beach Area

☎ Compass, Inc. 407-966-3050

Accommodation: Hotels, B&B, Resorts, Campgrounds

West Palm Beach

♀ ● (♿) Hibiscus House Bed & Breakfast, 501 30th St, West Palm Beach; 33407 407-863-5633

♀ ● West Palm Beach Bed & Breakfast, 419 32nd St, West Palm Beach; 33407-4809 (Old Northwood) 407-848-4064 Fax 407-848-2422

AIDS/HIV Support, Education, Advocacy, Publications

♀ ☆ (♿) AIDS Walk For Life, c/o The Whimsy, 1156 Park Lane, West Palm Beach; 33417-5957 407-686-1354 "Annual AIDS benefit & entertainment."

♀ ☆ ♿ Comprehensive AIDS Program, PO Box 18887, West Palm Beach; 33416-8887 / 3706 Broadway 407-881-9040

♀ ☆ ♿ Hope House, PO Box 6905, West Palm Beach; 33405-0905 407-697-2600

♀ ☆ Palm Beach County AIDS/HIV Center, 3518 Broadway, West Palm Beach; 33407 407-845-4444

♀ ☆ ♿ People With AIDS Coalition of Palm Beach, PO Box 2107, West Palm Beach; 33402-2107 407-655-3322; 800-499-8033; Pub *On A Positive Note*.

Art Galleries/Archives/Restoration, Supplies, Framing

♀ ● Christopher Street Gallery, Inc, 5603 S Dixie Hwy, West Palm Beach; 33405 407-547-4578

Bars, Restaurants, Clubs, Discos

Lake Worth

♀ ● ♿ InnExile, 6 South J St, Lake Worth; 33460 305-582-4144 *BDE* 3pm-2am; Sun to mdnt. Beer & wine only. Video nightclub.

♀ K&E, 29 S Dixie Hwy, Lake Worth; 33460 305-533-6020 *BR*

Lantana

♂ Zippers, 308 N Dixie Hwy, Lantana; 33462 305-588-9028

West Palm Beach

♂ The 5101, 5101 S Dixie Hwy, West Palm Beach; 33405 407-858-2379

♀ ○ ♿ Chatters Cocktail Lounge, 2677 Forest Hill Blvd #112, West Palm Beach; 33406 407-966-1590

♀ Enigma, 109 N Olive, West Palm Beach; 33401 407-832-5040

♀ ● (?♿) The Flip Side, 5004 S Dixie Hwy, West Palm Beach; 33405 407-533-9922 *BR*

♂ ● ♿ H.G. Roosters, 823 Belvedere Rd, West Palm Beach; 33401 407-832-9119 Open 1pm.

♀ ○ ♿ Heartbreaker Dance Club, 2677 Forest Hill Blvd #110, West Palm Beach; 33406 407-966-1590 *Df*

♀ Illusion Bar, 4340 Forest Hills Blvd, West Palm Beach; 33408 407-966-0075

♀ ○ Kozlow's, 6205 Georgia Ave, West Palm Beach; 33401 407-533-5355 *CW* 10am-3am.

Bookstores: General

♀ ○ ♿ Changing Times Bookstore, 911 Village Blvd #806, West Palm Beach; 33409 407-640-0496

Community Centers (see also Women's Centers)

♀ ★ ♿ Compass, Inc., 2677 Forest Hill Blvd #106, West Palm Beach; 33405-5941 407-966-3050; 407-966-3777 24 hrs.; Fax 407-966-0039 Pub *Compass Points*. "Support groups, cultural events, teen support groups, library, bookstore."

Counseling/Therapy: Private

♀ ● ♿ Platt, Keith Allen, LCSW, Comprehensive Wellness Institute, 2601 N. Flagler Dr #212 407-835-3934

Health Care (see also AIDS Services)

♀ ☆ ♿ Palm Beach County Health Department STD Program, PO Box 29, West Palm Beach; 33402-0029 / 705 N Olive 407-653-2066

Organizations/Resources: Family

♀ PFLAG South Florida, 7652 Mansfield Hollow, Delray Beach; 33446 407-495-9950

♀ ★ ♿ PFLAG West Palm Beach, 683 Pelican Way, Delray Beach; 33483 407-272-1634

Organizations/Resources: General, Multipurpose, Pride

♀ ☆ (♿) The Whimsy (A Safe Haven), 1156 Park Lane, West Palm Beach; 33417-5957 407-686-1354 "A multi-service provider: music & literature archive; private organization base & meeting place; statewide referral & resource provider; private camping for tents, vans, RVs; Rustron Music Productions."

Organizations/Resources: Political/Legislative

♀ ★ (♿) Atlantic Coast Democratic Club, c/o The Whimsy, 1156 Park Lane, West Palm Beach; 33417-5957 407-686-1354

♀ ★ (♿) Lesbian Caucus of the National Women's Political Caucus, c/o The Whimsy, 1156 Park Lane, West Palm Beach; 33417-5957 407-686-1354 "5 county network: SE coastal Florida."

♀ ★ (♿) Lesbian Task Force of NOW, Palm Beach County, c/o The Whimsy, 1156 Park Lane, West Palm Beach; 33417-5957 407-686-1354

Organizations/Resources: Social, Recreational & Support Groups (see also Sport/Dance/Outdoor)

♂ SAGE of the Palm Beaches, 3590 South Ocean #107, Palm Beach; 33480 305-585-3467

♂ ☆ ᕹᕹ Seniors & Sunshine, 3273 Grove Rd, Boynton Beach; 33435 407-588-0774 5

Organizations/Resources: Sport/Dance/Outdoor

♂ Gay Bowling League, c/o Verdes Tropicana Bowling 1801 Belvedere Rd, West Palm Beach; 33406 407-433-8674

♂ Gay Soccer, 5328 Crystal Anne Dr, West Palm Beach; 33417 407-683-6073

♂ ★ (?ᕹ) Gay Volleyball, PO Box 1208, West Palm Beach; 33402 407-683-3505 Also Gay Aerobics.

Organizations/Resources: Youth (see also Family)

♂ ★ ᕹᕹ COMPASS Teen Program, 2677 Forest Hill Blvd #106, West Palm Beach; 33406 407-966-0318; 407-966-3050

Publications

♀ • The Community Voice, PO Box 17975, West Palm Beach; 33416 407-471-1528

Religious Organizations & Publications

♂ Congregation Yeladim Shel Yisrael, c/o COMPASS, 2677 Forest Hill Blvd #108, West Palm Beach; 33406 407-967-4267

♀ ★ ᕹ Dignity/Palm Beach, PO Box 3014, Tequesta; 33469 305-744-1591; 407-751-3468 (pager); Meets in Palm Beach Gardens. "Gay & Lesbian Catholics & their friends. Transgender welcome."

♂ Integrity, c/o St Georges Center 21 W. 22nd St, Riviera Beach; 33404 407-627-1409

♀ ★ ᕹᕹ Metropolitan Community Church of the Palm Beaches, PO Box 18527, West Palm Beach; 33416 407-687-3943 Pub Emerald Wave.

Switchboards, Helplines, Phone Information

♀ ☆ Centerline, PO Box 3588, Lantana; 33465 407-930-1234 (toll free in Palm Beach County); 407-547-1000; "Crisis/suicide hotline, telephone counseling. Phone information & referral."

Thrift/Consignment Stores

♀ ☆ ᕹ The Red Ribbon Guild, PO Box 18887, West Palm Beach; 33416-8887 / 4900 S. Dixie Hwy; 33405 407-588-6808 Tue-Sat 10am-4pm. "Assists PWAs through Comprehensive AIDS Program."

Panama City

AIDS/HIV Support, Education, Advocacy, Publications

♀ ☆ Bay AIDS Services & Information Coalition (BASIC), PO Box 805; 32402 904-785-1088

Bars, Restaurants, Clubs, Discos

♀ • Fiesta Room, 110 Harrison Ave; 32401 904-763-9476 BDE 7pm-4am. "Drag shows."

♀ • ᕹᕹ La Royale Lounge, 100 Harrison Ave; 32401 904-763-9110 BDE 3pm-4am.

Religious Organizations & Publications

♀ ★ Family of God Metropolitan Community Church, 1139 Everitt Ave; 32401 904-784-4851

Pensacola

AIDS/HIV Support, Education, Advocacy, Publications

♀ ☆ ᕹᕹ Escambia AIDS Services & Education (EASE), PO Box 13584; 32591-3584 904-435-7841 Mon-Fri 8.30am-4.30pm.

♀ ☆ ᕹᕹ HRS AIDS Program, PO Box 12604; 32574-2604 / 2251 N. Palafox St 904-444-8654 Mon-Fri 8am-5pm.

Art Galleries/Archives/Restoration, Supplies, Framing

♀ ○ Soho Gallery, 23 Palafox Place; 32501 904-435-7646 Mon-Sat 10am-6pm.

Bars, Restaurants, Clubs, Discos

♀ • ᕹᕹ Bayside Coffeehouse, 424 E Government St; 32501 904-432-4848 7am-11pm.

♀ ○ Dainty Del Steak & Seafood Restaurant, 286 N Palafox St; 32501 904-438-1241 B 10am-11pm.

♂ ○ (ᕹ) Numbers Pub, 200 S Alcaniz; 32501 904-438-9004 BDLW 3pm-3am.

♀ • The Park Pub, 312 E Government St; 32501 904-434-3441 BE 11am-3am.

♀ • (ᕹᕹ) Red Carpet, 937 New Warrington Rd; 32506 904-453-9918 BDE 2pm-3am.

♂ • ᕹᕹ Roundup, 706 E Gregory St; 32501 904-433-8482

♀ ○ Sluggo's, 15 E. Intendencia St 904-433-9292 BE Tue-Sat 8pm-2.30am; Sun 9pm-2.30am. "Live progressive music."

Bookstores: Recovery, Metaphysical, & other Specialty

♀ ○ ᕹᕹ Silver Chord Bookstore, 10901 Lillian Hwy; 32506 904-453-6652 1-7pm; Sat 11am-7pm. "Metaphysical & Alternate Lifestyles."

Florists (see also Gardening)

♀ ○ ᕹᕹ Botany Hut, 1500 W Garden; 32501 904-435-1500

♀ ○ Passionflower, 202 Palafox Pl; 32501 904-435-1090 Mon-Fri 10am-5pm; Sat to 2pm.

Gifts, Cards, Pride & Novelty Items

♀ • ᕹ Just For Us, 12 S Palafox St; 32501 904-432-5777 Mon-Thu 10am-7pm; Fri & Sat to 9pm; Sun noon-6pm. "Pensacola's unofficial tourist information center."

Grooming Services

♀ • ᕹ Guys 'n' Dolls Hair Stylists & Tanning Salon, 939 New Warrington Rd; 32506 904-457-6092

Organizations/Resources: General, Multipurpose, Pride

♀ ★ Christopher Street South, Inc, PO Box 2752; 32513-2752 904-433-0353 Fax 904-4434-3384 Pub CSS Quarterly.

♀ ★ West Florida Pride Committee, 415 N Alcaniz St; 32501 904-433-0931 Pub Gulf Coast Community News.

Organizations/Resources: Political/Legislative

♀ ☆ Escambia County Greens Lesbian, Bisexual, Gay/Questioning Queer Caucus, PO Box 10294; 32524-0294 904-474-1495

Organizations/Resources: Social, Recreational & Support Groups (see also Sport/Dance/Outdoor)

♀ ☆ Women's Social Organization, PO Box 34461; 32507 904-492-5719

Real Estate

♀ ○ Greenwell, Susan, 1708 E Cervantes; 32503 904-434-8511

♀ • Neal & Associates, Inc., 2258 LaVista Str; 32504 904-433-0353 Fax 904-434-3384

Religious Organizations & Publications

♂ ★ Holy Cross Metropolitan Community Church, 415 N Alcaniz St; 32501 904-433-8528 Sun 11am; Wed 7pm.

Pinellas Park: see Tampa Bay Area

Port Richey

Bars, Restaurants, Clubs, Discos

♂ BT'S, 7737 Grand Blvd; 34667 813-841-7900

Ruskin

Accommodation: Hotels, B&B, Resorts, Campgrounds

♀ ○ (&&) Ruskin House Bed & Breakfast, 813-645-3842

St Augustine

Accommodation: Hotels, B&B, Resorts, Campgrounds

♀ • & The Pagoda, 2854 Coastal Hwy; 32084 904-824-2970 "Women's cultural center with rooms for female visitors."

Bookstores: Recovery, Metaphysical, & other Specialty

♀ • Dream Street Bookstore, 64 Hypolita St; 32084 904-824-8536 dream_st_2@aol.com "New Age books & gifts."

Sarasota

Accommodation: Hotels, B&B, Resorts, Campgrounds

♂ • M-T-In Bed & Breakfast, 3684 Country Place Blvd; 34233-2116 813-927-1619 "Nudity & smoking permitted."

♀ ○ Normandy Inn, 400 N Tamiami Trail; 34236-4822 813-366-8979; 800-282-8050

Addictive Behavior, Substance Abuse, Recovery

♀ ☆&& First Step, Inc, 2800 Bahia Vista St #200; 34239 813-366-5333 "Includes confidential HIV pre- & post-test counseling; significant other programs."

Bars, Restaurants, Clubs, Discos

♀ Club Chada, 2941 Tamiami Trail; 34234 813-355-1404

♂ • && H. G. Rooster's, 1256 Old Stickney Pt Rd; 34242 813-346-3000 *BD* 3pm-2am.

♂ • && Ricky J's, 1330 Martin Luther King Way 813-953-5945 *BDELWC* 4pm-2am.

♂ ○ The X at Bumpers, 1927 Ringing Blvd; 34236 813-951-0335 *BE*

Bookstores: General

♀ ○ Read All Over, 2245 Bee Ridge Road; 34239 813-923-1340

Counseling/Therapy: Private

♀ ○&& Twitchell, Carol, Psy.D., 2055 Wood St #200; 34237 813-365-9424

Organizations/Resources: General, Multipurpose, Pride

♂ ★ Gay & Lesbian Alliance (GALA), PO Box 15851; 34277

Organizations/Resources: Sport/Dance/Outdoor

♂ ★ Lambda Camping & R.V. Club, PO Box 315; 34230-0315

Religious Organizations & Publications

♀ ☆ (&&) Church of the Trinity Metropolitan Community Church, 7225 N Lockwood Ridge Rd; 34243-4526 813-355-0847 Mon-Fri 10am-4pm; Services Sun 10am.

♂ Integrity/Southwest Florida, c/o St Boniface Church, 5615 Midnight Pass Rd; 34242-1721 813-349-5616 "Lesbian & Gay Episcopalians & their friends."

St Petersburg: see Tampa Bay Area

Tallahassee

Bars, Restaurants, Clubs, Discos

♂ Brothers, 926-7 Tharpe St; 32303 904-386-2399

♂ ○ (&) Club Park Ave, 115 E Park Ave; 32301 904-933-5459

Bookstores: Gay/Lesbian/Feminist

♀ • & Rubyfruit Books, 666-4 W Tennessee St; 32304 904-222-2627

Health Care (see also AIDS Services)

♀ ☆&& VD Clinic, Leon County Health Dept, PO Box 2745; 32316 904-487-3155

Organizations/Resources: Student, Academic, Alumni/ae

♂ ★&& Lesbian/Gay/Bisexual Student Union, Florida State University, 201 Oglesby Union; 32306-4027 904-644-8804 "Rap groups, library, referrals, speakers, socials."

Publications

♂ • *Community News*, PO Box 14682; 32317 904-671-7982 "North Florida's newspaper serving the Lesbian, Gay, Bi & Transgender community."

Tampa: see Tampa Bay Area

Tampa Bay Area

☎ Gay Hotline, Inc 813-229-8839

☎ The Line 813-586-4297

Accommodation: Hotels, B&B, Resorts, Campgrounds

Pass-A-Grill Beach

♀ ○ Barge House, Box 46526, Pass-A-Grill Beach; 33741 813-360-0729 *BR*

St Petersburg Beach

♂ • Cape House, 2800 Pass-A-Grille, St Petersburg Beach; 33706 813-367-6971 "Bed & breakfast inn."

St Petersburg

♂ • Garden Guesthouses, 920 4th St S., St Petersburg; 33701 813-821-3665

Tampa

♂ • Gram's Place Bed/Breakfast Guesthouse, 3109 N Ola Ave, Tampa; 33603 813-221-0596 (also fax); 813-221-0596 (also fax)

Treasure Island

♀ • The SeaOats & Dunes, 12625 Sunshine Lane, Treasure Island; 33706 813-367-7568

Accommodation Sharing/Roommates

♀ • ර&ර Roommate Referral Network, USF Gay/Lesbian/Bisexual Coalition, CTR 2466, 4202 E. Fowler Ave; 33620 813-974-GAYS

Addictive Behavior, Substance Abuse, Recovery

♀ ★ර&ර G.A.Y.S. (Go After Your Sobriety), meets at King of Peace MCC, 3150 5th Ave N, Wed 8pm, OD, OB; Fri 8pm OD. 813-347-1965

♀ ★ Getting It Together (AA), meets at Good Samaritan (rear Cottage), 6085 Park Blvd, Pinellas Park

AIDS/HIV Support, Education, Advocacy, Publications

♀ ★ ACT-UP/Tampa Bay, 1222 S Dale Mabry Dept. 953, Tampa; 33629-5009 813-882-5359

♀ ★ (?රර) Habitat Society Foundation Inc., PO Box 20305, Tampa; 33622 813-839-5493 Fax 813-839-3216

♀ ★රරර Metropolitan Charities Inc. AIDS Services, 3150 5th Ave N, St Petersburg; 33703 813-321-3854

♀ ☆ PWA Coalition of Tampa Bay, PO Box 9731, Tampa; 33674-9731 813-238-2887

♀ ☆ ර Tampa AIDS Network, 11215 N Nebraska Ave, Tampa; 33612 813-978-8683 "Services include case management; food bank; financial/legal assistance."

Art Galleries/Archives/Restoration, Supplies, Framing

♀ ★ (රර) **Beaux Arts, 2635 Central Ave, St Petersburg; 33713-3722 813-328-0702** "Art gallery; live performances & open stage Sat 8pm & Sun 2.30pm; quality gay films plus dancers (call for times); Apollo Cinema Club (private)."

Automobile Services

♀ • ර Window Tinting by Carol Walther, 1489 S Missouri Ave, Clearwater; 34616 813-443-4372 "We tint windows/glass on Autos, homes, businesses."

Bars, Restaurants, Clubs, Discos

Clearwater

♀ ර Lost & Found, 5858 Roosevelt Blvd, Clearwater; 34620 813-539-8903 *BD* 4pm-2am. "Multi-bar complex; separate game room."

♀ • Pro Shop Pub, 840 Cleveland St, Clearwater; 34615 813-447-4259

♀ ○රර Rocky's Pub, 18425 U.S. 19 North, Clearwater; 34624 813-531-4431 *BEdf* 11am-2am; Sun 1pm-2am.

♀ Rumors, 16100 Fairchild Dr, Clearwater; 34627 813-531-8817

Dunedin

♂ 1470 West, 325 Main St, Dunedin; 34698 813-736-5483

Gulfport

♀ ○ Sharp A's, 4918 22nd Ave S./Gulfport Blvd South, Gulfport; 33707 813-327-4897

Madeira Beach

♂ • රර **Back Room, Surf & Sand, 14601 Gulf Blvd, Madeira Beach; 33708 813-392-2814**
✦ *Back Room, Surf & Sand advertisement page 226*

Pinellas Park

♀ Rainbow Club & Restaurant, 7790 US 19 North, Pinellas Park; 34665 813-546-2384

St Petersburg

♀ The Connection, 3100 3rd Ave N, St Petersburg; 33713 813-321-2112

♂ • DT's (Dallas Time Inc), 2612 Central Ave, St Petersburg; 33712 813-327-8204 *Bd*

♂ • **Golden Arrow, 10604 Gandy Blvd, St Petersburg; 33702 813-577-7774**
✦ *Golden Arrow advertisement page 227*

♂ • ර Hank's Hideaway, 8302 W 4th St, St Petersburg; 33702 *BD*

♂ The Saint, 10568 Gandy Blvd, St Petersburg; 33702 813-579-1570

Tampa

♂ 2606, 2606 N Armenia, Tampa; 33607 813-875-6693

♂ Angel's, 4502 S Dale Mabry, Tampa; 33611 813-831-9980

♀ The Annex, 2408 W Kennedy Blvd, Tampa; 33609 813-254-4188

♀ • රර Baxter's/Moody's Cafe, 4010 S Dale Mabry Hwy, Tampa; 33611 813-831-6537 *BRDE* Noon-3am. Wed, Sat, Sun afternoons Country-Western; live shows Sun after 10pm.

♀ Bridge Club, 5519 1/2 W Hillsborough Ave, Tampa; 33614

♀ Cherokee Club, 1320 E 9th Ave (above Cafe Creole), Tampa; 33605 813-247-9966

♀ City Side, 3810 Neptune St, Tampa; 33629 813-254-4666

♀ The Cove, 3703 Henderson Blvd, Tampa; 33609 813-875-3290

♂ Hammer Jax, 901 N Franklin St, Tampa; 33602 813-221-5299

♂ Howard Avenue Station, 3003 N Howard Ave, Tampa; 33607 813-254-7194

♂ • ♂♂ Keith's, PO Box 280513, Tampa; 33682-0513 / 14905 N. Nebraska Ave; 33613 813-971-3576 _Bd_ 1pm-3am.

♀ KiKiKi III, 1908 W Kennedy Blvd, Tampa; 33606 813-227-8000

♀ Northside Lounge, 9002 N Florida Ave, Tampa; 33604 813-931-3396

Ybor City

♀ ○ Tracks, 1430 E 7th Ave, Ybor City; 33605 813-247-2711

Bookstores: Gay/Lesbian/Feminist

♂ • ♂♂ Affinity Books, 2435 9th St North, St Petersburg; 33704 813-823-3662; 800-355-3662

♀ • (♂) Brigit Books, 3434 4th St N #5, St Petersburg; 33704 813-522-5775 10am-8pm; Fri & Sat to 6pm; Sun 1-5pm. "New & used books, music, giftts, T-shirts. Bulletin board; resource center."

♂ • ♂♂ Lifestyle Books, King of Peace MCC, 3150 5th Ave N, St Petersburg; 33713-7610 813-323-5857 Fax 813-327-7670 Thu 7-9pm; Sun 9-10am & 11.30am-noon; or by arrangement. "Gay, Lesbian & Bisexual books; non-fiction, self-help, recovery, sex education, 12-step books & meditations; novelties; greeting cards; Bibles."

♂ • Tomes & Treasures, 202 S Howard Ave, Tampa; 33606 813-251-9368 Mon-Sat 11am-8pm; Sun noon-6pm. "Gay & Lesbian bookstore, with T-shirts, jewelry & Pride items. Write or call for catalog."

Bookstores: General

♀ • On The Move: A Mobile Bookstore, PO Box 2985, St Petersburg; 33731 813-223-9171 "Feminist & peace activist."

♀ ○ Three Birds Bookstore & Coffee Room, 1518 7th Ave, Tampa; 33605 813-247-7041

Business, Financial & Secretarial

♂ • Fischer, Lawrence A., CPA, 8487 9th St N, St Petersburg; 33702 813-577-6072

♀ • McGarry, Patrick, Personal Financial Planner, American Express Financial Advisor, 18167 US 19 N, Harbourside Building #100, Clearwater; 34624 813-535-6481

Counseling/Therapy: Private

♀ ○ (♂) Brewer, Sue A., MSW, LCSW, 1700 Park St N #109, St Petersburg; 33710 813-347-3680

♀ ○ ♂ Cotter, Nell, 1700 Park St N #109, St Petersburg; 33710 813-345-8847 "Gay & lesbian couples therapy; weekly lesbian issues therapy group."

♀ ○ Counseling Services of Brandon, 207 E Robertson #G, Brandon; 33511 813-654-0166

♀ • ♂ McEwen, Chase, ACSW, LCSW, 104 E Fowler Ave #A, Tampa; 33612 813-932-9300

♀ ○ (♂♂) Phoenix Counseling Center, Inc., 1404 W Busch Blvd, Tampa; 33612 813-933-6904 " Out-patient psychological counseling."

Erotica (Printed, Visual, Equipment)

♂ ○ Buddies Video, 4322 W Crest Ave, Tampa; 33614 813-876-8083 24 hrs.
♦ _Buddies Video advertisement page 229_

♀ ○ ♂ Fourth Street Bookmart, 1427 4th St S, St Petersburg; 33704 813-821-8824

♀ ○ Pussycat II, 39468 US Hwy 19 North, Tarpon Springs; 34689 813-942-4587

Film & Video

♂ • ★ ♂♂ Pride Film Festival, 1222 S Dale Mabry #602, Tampa; 33629-5009 813-837-4485 "Ten-day film & video festival held in the historic Tampa Theatre, late Sept/early Oct."

Florists (see also Gardening)

♀ • (?♂) Artistic Florist of Tampa, Inc., 2509 W Busch Blvd, Tampa; 33618 813-932-6116

Gardening Services, Landscaping, Supplies & Decoration

♀ • Affordable Lawn Care, 813-238-5017

Gifts, Cards, Pride & Novelty Items

♀ • Paradise Trading Co, 110 1/2 129th Ave, Madeira Beach; 33708 813-392-5902

Health Clubs, Gyms, Saunas

♂ • Club Tampa, 215 N 11th St, Tampa; 33602 813-223-5181

Home & Building: Cleaning, Repair, General Contractors

♀ ○ Custom Clean, Inc., 813-931-7636 "Housecleaning catering to Gay & Lesbian needs."

Legal Services & Resources

♀ ☆ ♂♂ American Civil Liberties Union Tampa Chapter (ACLU), PO Box 1481, Tampa; 33601-1481 813-221-1423

♂ • ♂ Chatham, L. Charlyne, 1489 S Missouri Ave, Clearwater; 34616 813-443-6928

♀ • ♂♂ Clark, James, PA, 201 N MacDill Ave, Tampa; 33609-1523 813-874-7020 Fax 813-872-9219

♂ • DuFour, George Allen, 4610 Central Ave, Tampa; 33603 813-239-1001

♂ ○ (♂) Pope & Henninger, 2037 1st Ave N, St Petersburg; 33713 813-896-6633

Organizations/Resources: Business & Professional

♂ ★ ♂♂ Tampa Bay Business Guild, 1222 South Dale Mabry #656, Tampa; 33629 813-237-3751

Organizations/Resources: Ethnic, Multicultural

♂ ★ (?♂) Bay Area Men of All Colors Together, 1222 S Dale Mabry #918, Tampa; 33629-5009 813-831-7454

Organizations/Resources: Political/Legislative

♂ ★ Log Cabin Club of Tampa Bay, PO Box 869, Oldsmar; 34677 813-855-0852; 813-933-8638; "Republican organization."

Organizations/Resources: Sexual Focus (Leather, S/M, etc) & Safe Sex Promotion

♂ ★ Suncoast Leather Club, PO Box 2772, St Petersburg; 33731

Organizations/Resources: Social, Recreational & Support Groups (see also Sport/Dance/Outdoor)

♀ ★ ♂♂ Womyn's Energy Bank, PO Box 15548, St Petersburg; 33733-5548 813-823-5353 Pub _Womyn's Words._

♂ • ★ ♂♂ Bay Bash: Uniting The Bay, 18425 U.S. 19 North, Clearwater; 34624 813-429-6678 "Traveling monthly party raising $50,000 for AIDS. Co-sponsored by the local bars."

Organizations/Resources: Sport/Dance/Outdoor

♂ Front Runners, 3225 S MacDill Ave, Box 191, Tampa; 33629 813-891-7098

♂ • ★ Tampa Bay Wrestling Club, PO Box 21552, St Petersburg; 33742-1552

Organizations/Resources: Student, Academic, Alumni/ae

♀ ★ ♿ University of South Florida Gay/Lesbian/Bisexual Coalition, CTR 2466, 4202 E Fowler Ave, Tampa; 33620 813-974-GAYS *The Pink Triangle*.

Performing Arts: Entertainment, Music, Recording, Theater, etc.

♂ ★ ♿ Tampa Bay Gay Men's Chorus, 1222 S Dale Mabry Hwy #602, Tampa; 33629-5009 813-837-4485

Printing & Promotional Items (see also Art; Graphics/Typesetting)

♂ • WORDSPlus, PO Box 2650, Brandon; 33509-2650 813-689-7566 "Printing, copywriting, typesetting; graphic design."

Publications

♀ *Encounter*, 1222 South Dale Mabry Hwy #913, Tampa; 33629 813-877-7913

→ *The Gazette*: p.210

♀ *Stonewall*, 3225 S MacDill Ave S-220, Tampa; 33629 813-891-7098

Religious Organizations & Publications

♀ ★ (♿) Beth Rachameem Synagogue, 1222 S Dale Mabry, Box 609, Tampa; 33629 813-726-3482 Shabbat services Fri 8pm at MCC Church. Pub *Nu? News*.

♀ ★ ♿ Dignity/Tampa Bay, PO Box 24806, Tampa; 33629 813-238-2868 Pub *Reflections*. "Gay & Lesbian Catholics & their friends."

♀ ★ ♿ King of Peace Metropolitan Community Church, 3150 5th Ave N., St Petersburg; 33713 813-323-5857 Fax 813-327-7670 Services Sun 10am; Prayer & Communion service Thu 6.30pm; prayer time Wed noon; weekly dinner Thu 7.30pm; CODA Mon 8pm; AA Wed & Fri 8pm; OA Fri 7.30pm. Pub *Vision Magazine*. Also Lifestyle Bookstore.

♀ ★ (♿) Metropolitan Community Church of Tampa, 408 E Cayuga St, Tampa; 33603-3702 813-239-1951 Fax 813-239-2018

Switchboards, Helplines, Phone Information

♀ ★ ♿ Gay Hotline, Inc, 1222 South Dale Mabry #608, Tampa; 33629 813-229-8839

♀ ★ The Line, PO Box 14323, St Petersburg; 33733 813-586-4297 Gay Information services of Pinellas, with Community Events Calendar and Volunteers 7-11pm; computer information system 24 hrs.

Travel & Tourist Services (see also Accommodation)

♂ • Fantasy Adventures Travel, 138 Beach Dr NE, St Petersburg; 33701 813-821-0880

♂ ○ International House Of Travel, 40966 Us Highway 19 N, Tarpon Springs; 34689 813-938-1511; 813-842-6458

♂ ○ ♿ The Travel Source, 3000 Gulf To Bay Blvd #501, Clearwater; 34619 813-725-9557; 800-943-5592; Fax 813-724-8039

West Palm Beach: see Palm Beach Area

Winter Park: see Orlando

Georgia

State/County Resources

Addictive Behavior, Substance Abuse, Recovery

♀ • (♿) Pride Institute, 800-54-PRIDE "The nation's only accredited chemical dependency treatment center exclusively for Gay, Lesbian & Bisexual People."

Legal Services & Resources

♀ ★ ♿ Lesbian/Gay Rights Chapter, American Civil Liberties Union (ACLU) of Georgia, 142 Mitchell St SW #301, Atlanta, GA 30303 404-523-6201

Organizations/Resources: Business & Professional

♀ ★ Georgia Association of Physicians for Human Rights, PO Box 13132, Atlanta, GA 30324 404-231-2251 Pub *GAPHR Newsletter*.

Organizations/Resources: Political/Legislative

♂ Log Cabin Georgia, PO Box 56149, Atlanta, GA 30343-0149 404-557-3300

♀ ★ Republicans for Individual Freedoms, PO Box 13162, Atlanta, GA 30324 404-239-1679

Publications

♀ • ♂ *Etcetera Magazine*, PO Box 8916, Atlanta, GA 30306 404-525-3821 Fax 404-525-1908 Weekly. "Distributed in FL, AL, NC, SC, TN & GA."

♀ • *Southern Voice*, 1095 Zonolite Rd, Atlanta, GA 30306 404-876-1819

♀ *Venus*, PO Box 89238, Atlanta, GA 30312 404-622-8069 Fax 404-622-8089 A Magazine for Lesbians & Gays of Color.

Real Estate

♀ • Community Real Estate Referrals, 800-346-5592 "Free referral to gay/gay-supportive realtor in any USA city/state (including Virgin Is. & Puerto Rico). Sorry, no rentals!"
♦ *Community Real Estate Referrals advertisement back cover*

Albany

Bars, Restaurants, Clubs, Discos

♀ Michaels, 116 S Harding; 31701 912-435-8703

Athens

Bars, Restaurants, Clubs, Discos

♀ ○ ♿ 40 Watt Club, 285 W Washington St; 30601 706-549-7871 *BD* Mon-Sat 6pm-2am. "Alternative rock club."

♀ Boneshakers, 433 E Hancock Ave; 30601 706-543-1555

♀ ○ (♿) Downstairs Cafe, 140 E Clayton St; 30601 706-549-4416 *RE*

♀ ○ ♿ The Globe, 199 N Lumpkin St; 30601 706-353-4721 *BLLf*

Bookstores: General

♀ ○ Barnett's Bookstore, 147 College Ave; 30601 706-353-0530

Organizations/Resources: Social, Recreational & Support Groups (see also Sport/Dance/Outdoor)

♀ ★ (♿) Lesbian Support Group (LSG), PO Box 7864; 30604 706-546-4611

Atlanta

☎ Atlanta Gay Center Helpline 404-892-0661

Accommodation: Hotels, B&B, Resorts, Campgrounds

♂ • (♿) Hidden Creek Bed & Breakfast, 201 N Mill Road; 30328 404-705-9545

♀ ○ (♿) Midtown Manor - Victorian Guest House, 811 Piedmont Ave NE; 30308 404-872-5846; 800-724-4381

♀ • (♿) Our Home, 1451 Sanden Ferry Dr, Decatur; 30033 404-491-0248

Addictive Behavior, Substance Abuse, Recovery

♀ ☆ (♿) Sexual Compulsives Anonymous, PO Box 76961; 30358 404-239-8048

AIDS/HIV Support, Education, Advocacy, Publications

♀ ☆ (♿) ACT UP/Atlanta, 828 W Peachtree St NW #206A; 30308-1146 404-874-6782

♀ ☆ (♿) AID Atlanta, 1438 West Peachtree St NW; 30309 404-872-0600 Fax 404-875-6799 Pub *Infolines*. "AIDS multi-service agency."

♀ ★ AIDS Education/Services for Minorities (AESM), PO Box 87227; 30337 404-753-2900 Fax 404-752-5610

♂ Brothers Back 2 Back, Inc., PO Box 11366; 30310 404-593-580-

♂ The Names Project/Atlanta, PO Box 1018; 30301 404-605-7386

Art & Photography (see also Graphic Design)

♀ • Haver, Charles, 449 Moreland #216; 30307 404-524-8221

Bars, Restaurants, Clubs, Discos

♀ ○ Armory, 836 Juniper NE; 30309 404-881-9280

♀ ○ Backstreet Atlanta, 845 Peachtree St (rear); 30308 404-873-1986 *BD* 24 hrs.

♀ Bellissima, 688 Spring St NW; 30308

♂ Blakes, 227 10th St NE; 30309 404-892-7535

♂ ♿ Buddies, 2345 Cheshire Bridge Rd #1; 30324 404-634-5895

♀ • (♿) Buddies Midtown, 239 Ponce de Leon NE; 30308 404-872-2655

♂ ○ Bulldog & Co, 893 Peachtree St (rear); 30309 404-872-3025

♂ ○ ♿ Burkhardt's Pub, 1499 Piedmont Ave; 30309 404-872-4403

♀ • ♿ The Chamber, 2115 Faulkner Rd NE; 30324 404-248-1612 *BDEL*

♀ Chaps, 917 Peachtree St; 30309 404-815-0606

♀ Coronet Club, 5275 Roswell Rd; 30305 404-250-1534

♀ ○ ♂ Dusty's Barbecue, 1815 Briarcliff Rd; 30329 404-320-6264 11am-9.30pm; Fri & Sat to 10.30pm.

♀ • (♿) Eagle Saloon & Cafe, 306 Ponce de Leon Ave NE; 30308 404-873-2453 *BRdLL* "All welcome, especially leather, fetish, S/M."

♂ The Heretic, 2069 Cheshire Bridge; 30324 404-325-3061 *LW*

♀ ○ ♿ Hoedown, 1890 Cheshire Bridge Rd; 30324 404-874-0980

♀ Loretta's, 708 Spring St NW; 30308 404-874-8125

♀ Masquerade, 695 North Ave NE; 30308 404-577-8178

GA: Atlanta

231

Atlanta : GA

Bars, Clubs, Restaurants

USA

Organizations: Social & Support

♂ • The Metro, 48 6th St NE; 30308 404-874-9869

♂ • ♿ Model T, 699 Ponce De Leon NE #11; 30308 404-872-2209 *CW* Noon-4am.

♂ Moreland Ave Restaurant & Tavern, 1196 Moreland Ave SE; 30315 404-622-4650 *BR*

♂ • ♿ New Order, 1544 Piedmont Ave NE (Ansley Mall); 30324 404-874-8247

♂ Opus I, 1086 Alco St; 30324 404-634-6478

♂ • ♿ The Otherside of Atlanta, 1924 Piedmont Rd; 30324 404-875-5238 *BDP* Opens 5pm; Sun 1pm.

♂ The Pearl Garden, 111 Luckie St; 30303 404-659-4055

♂ Peppers by Frank Powell, 980 Piedmont Ave NE; 30309 404-872-4000

♂ • (♿) The Phoenix, 567 Ponce de Leon; 30308 404-892-7871 *BCW* 9am-4am.

♀ Players, 800 Sandtown Road, Marietta; 30060 404-429-9115

♂ Revolution, 293 Pharr Road; 30301 404-816-5455

♂ • Scandals, 1510-G Piedmont Rd NE; 30324 404-875-5957 *B* 11am-4am.

♀ Shahan's Saloon, 735 Ralph McGill Blvd NE; 30312 404-523-1535

♂ ○ (♿) Spectrum, 1492B Piedmont; 30309 (Ansley Sq) 404-875-8980 *BRDE*

♂ ○ Velvet, 89 Park Place NE; 30303 404-681-9936 Mon only; call for details.

♂ Visions, 2043 Cheshire Bridge Rd NE; 30327 404-248-9712

Bookstores: Gay/Lesbian/Feminist

♀ • ♿ Charis Books & More, 1189 Euclid Ave NE; 30307 404-524-0304

♂ • ♿ Outwrite Bookstore & Coffeehouse, 931 Monroe Dr #108; 30308 (Midtown Promenade Shopping Center) 404-607-0082

Bookstores: General

♀ ○ Oxford Books, 2345 Peachtree Rd NE; 30305 404-262-3332

Broadcast Media

♂ ★ Southern Gay Dreams, PO Box 5332 c/o WRFG; 30307 404-523-3471

Clothes

♀ • The Boy Next Door Menswear, 1447 Piedmont Ave NE; 30309 404-873-2664

Community Centers (see also Women's Centers)

♀ ★ **Atlanta Gay Center, 71 12th St; 30309 404-876-5372; 404-892-0661 (TDD capable) 6-11pm.**

Counseling/Therapy: Nonprofit

♀ ☆♿ Atlanta Women's Counseling Collective, 280 Elizabeth St #A-113; 30307 404-524-1427

Counseling/Therapy: Private

♀ ○♿ Ansley Therapy Associates, 1904 Monroe Dr NE #120; 30324 404-874-8294

♀ • ♿ Hawkins, Brenda, EdD, 3684 Stewart Rd #A-2; 30340-2760 404-986-4247

Erotica (Printed, Visual, Equipment)

♀ ○ (♿) CondomArt, 632 N Highland; 30306 404-875-5665 11am-11pm; Fri & Sat to mdnt; Sun noon-7pm.

♀ ○ CondomArt, 632 N Highland Ave NE; 30306 404-875-5665

♂ • (♿) Mohawk Leather At Eagle Saloon, 306 Ponce De Leon Ave NE; 30308 404-873-2453 *L* 8pm-2am; Fri-Sun 7pm-3am.

♀ ○ ♿ Windfaire Exxxotic Gifts, 3885 Buford Hwy NE; 30329 404-634-WIND Mon-Sat 10am-9pm; Sun 1-6pm.

Gifts, Cards, Pride & Novelty Items

♀ • (♿) Brushstrokes, 1510-J Piedmont Ave NE; 30324 (Ansley Square) 404-876-6567 10am-10pm; Fri & Sat to 11pm. "Magazines, T-shirts, condoms, lubricants, jewelry."

♀ • Poster Hut, 2175 Cheshire Bridge Rd NE; 30324 404-633-7491

Health Care (see also AIDS Services)

♀ ☆♿ Feminist Women's Health Center, 580 14th St NW; 30318 800-877-6013 (US toll free) Mon-Fri 9am-5pm; Sat 10am-2pm. "Donor insemination services regardless of sexual orientation; anonymous AIDS testing."

♂ • ♿ Ostrow, Stosh, MD, 13 Corporate Sq NE #107; 30329-1905 404-325-2273

Legal Services & Resources

♀ • ♿ Mackinson & Katz, 2 Decatur Towncenter, 125 Clairemont Ave #430, Decatur; 30030 404-371-1255 (voice/TDD) Fax 404-373-6781

Organizations/Resources: Ethnic, Multicultural

♂ ★ Black & White Men Together, PO Box 1334; 30301-1334 404-892-2968 Black & White Men Together/Men of All Colors Together

♂ Latinos En Accion, PO Box 15388; 30333 404-621-5743

♀ Positive Black Lesbians United (PBLU), PO Box 655 Avondale Estates; 30302 404-250-7950

Organizations/Resources: Family

♀ ☆♿ PFLAG/Atlanta, PO Box 8482; 31106-8482 404-662-6475 "Parents, Families & Friends of Lesbians & Gays."

Organizations/Resources: Sexual Focus (Leather, S/M, etc) & Safe Sex Promotion

♀ ★ NLA/Atlanta, PO Box 78131; 30357-8131

Organizations/Resources: Social, Recreational & Support Groups (see also Sport/Dance/Outdoor)

♀ ★ Atlanta Couples Together, PO Box 54311; 30308-0311

♂ ★♿ Atlanta Prime Timers, PO Box 29487; 30359-0487 404-734-2490 Pub *Apt-ltudes.*

♀ ★♿ Fourth Tuesday, PO Box 7817; 30309 404-662-4353 "Networking for lesbian professionals & entrepreneurs."

♂ ★ GANG (Greater Atlanta Naturist Group), PO Box 7546; 30357 "Nudist/Naturist group."

♀ ★ Hospitality Atlanta, PO Box 55410; 30308

♂ ★ Hotlanta River Expo, Inc, PO Box 8375; 30306 404-377-9669; 404-874-EXPO

♂ ★ Lambda Car Club/Dogwood Region, PO Box 11705; 30355 404-901-9447 "Enjoyment of old & special interest motor vehicles."

♂ ★ Men Meeting Men Seminars, PO Box 95312; 30347 404-874-8294

♂ The Outsouth Foundation, PO Box 8569; 30306 404-874-8761

♂ ★ Southern Bears, Inc., PO Box 13964; 30324 404-908-3381

Organizations/Resources: Sport/Dance/Outdoor

♀ ★ Atlanta Venture Sports, PO Box 7718; 30309 404-242-4899

♀ ★ Southeast Gay Rodeo Association, PO Box 7881; 30357-0881 404-760-8126

Organizations/Resources: Student, Academic, Alumni/ae

♀ ★ && Agnes Scott Lesbian & Bisexual Alliance, PO Box 76, Decatur; 30030

♀ ★ && Alliance of Lesbian, Gay, & Bisexual Students, Georgia State University, Box 1817 University Center; 30303 404-605-7681

♂ ★ Delta Lambda Phi Fraternity, Atlanta, c/o National Office 1008 10th St #374, Sacramento, CA 95814 800-587-FRAT

♀ ★ && Emory Lesbian/Gay Organization (ELGO), PO Box 23515; 30322 404-727-6692

♀ ★ && Georgia Tech's Gay & Lesbian Alliance, 50291 Georgia Tech Stn; 30332-0458 404-497-0684

Performing Arts: Entertainment, Music, Recording, Theater, etc.

♀ ★ && Atlanta Gay Men's Chorus, PO Box 77114; 30357 404-977-6310

♀ ★ Southeastern Arts, Media, & Education Project, Inc (SAME), 191 Howard St NE; 30317 404-609-9590

Pharmacies/Health Care Supplies

♀ ○ && Lambda Apothecary, 595 Piedmont Ave; 30308 404-875-9717 Fax 404-875-1754

Printing & Promotional Items (see also Art; Graphics/Typesetting)

♀ • Copies Etcetera, 427 Moreland Ave #700; 30307 404-525-3821 Fax 404-525-1908

♀ • (?&) Gilchrist Printing Co, 541 Ashworth Dr, Riverdale; 30274 404-603-7177 Fax 404-428-3273

Publications

→ Etcetera Magazine: p.230

♀ HotSpots Magazine, PO Box 421622; 30342-8622

♀ • Southern Voice, PO Box 18215; 30316 404-876-1819

Religious Organizations & Publications

♀ ★ ♂ All Saints Metropolitan Community Church of Atlanta, PO Box 13968; 30324 404-622-1154

♀ ★ && Congregation Bet Haverim, PO Box 54677; 30308-0677 404-642-3467

♀ ★ (?&) Dignity/Atlanta, PO Box 14342; 30324 404-409-0203 "Gay & Lesbian Catholics & their friends."

♀ ★ Emergence/Atlanta, 3282 Chestnut Oaks Dr NE, Marietta; 30062-2126 404-565-2126 "Lesbian & Gay Christian Scientists."

♀ ★ First Existentialist Congregation, 470 Candler Park Dr NE; 30307 404-378-5570 "Call for details of services & various other programs & activities."

♀ ★ && First Metropolitan Community Church of Atlanta, 1379 Tullie Rd NE; 30329 404-325-4143 Fax 404-325-1372

♀ ★ && Integrity/Atlanta, PO Box 13603; 30324-0603 404-642-3183 Meeting 2nd & 4th Fri, 7.30pm, at All Saints Episcopal Church, 634 W. Peachtree St. Pub Ex Umbris. "A Gay & Lesbian Justice Ministry of the Episcopal Church."

♀ ★ (?&) Lutherans Concerned Atlanta, PO Box 13673; 30324 404-636-7109

♀ ★ (?&) PLGC, PO Box 8362; 30306 404-373-5830 "Presbyterians for Lesbian/Gay Concerns."

♀ Unitarian-Universalist Lesbian & Gay Community (UULGC), 1911 Cliff Valley Way; 30329 404-634-5134

Switchboards, Helplines, Phone Information

♀ ★ (?&) **Atlanta Gay Center Helpline, 63 12th St; 30309 404-892-0661 (TDD capable) 6-11pm.**

Travel & Tourist Services (see also Accommodation)

♀ • Conventional Travel, 1658 Lavista Road; 30329-3602 404-315-0107; 800-747-7107; Fax 404-315-0206

♀ • ♂ Different Directions Travel, 314 Pharr Rd; 30305 404-262-1011

♀ • George Hearn Holidays, 404-636-4312 Fax 404-982-9161

♀ • && Travel Affair, 1205 Johnson Ferry Rd, #116, Marietta; 30068 404-977-6824; 800-332-3417

♂ ○ Trips Unlimited, 1004 Virginia Ave NE; 30306 404-872-8747

Augusta

Bars, Restaurants, Clubs, Discos

♀ • && The Walton Way Station/Reflections, 1632 Walton Way; 30904 706-733-2603 **BDE** Mon-Fri 8.30pm-3am; Sat to 2am.

Religious Organizations & Publications

♀ ★ ♂ Metropolitan Community Church Augusta, 609 Shartom Dr; 30907-4715 706-860-7131 Worship Sun 7.15pm, 3042 Eagle Dr.

Bowdon

Bars, Restaurants, Clubs, Discos

♀ • Rainbow Pub, 1174 W Hwy 166; 30108 404-258-7766 (Call ahead for details)

Carrollton

AIDS/HIV Support, Education, Advocacy, Publications

♂ ☆ (&&) Positive Response, Inc, 109 John Wesley Plaza; 30117 404-214-AIDS Pub P.R. Newsletter.

Columbus

Bars, Restaurants, Clubs, Discos

♀ • Fountain City Yacht Club, 1214 1st Ave 706-322-8682

Religious Organizations & Publications

♀ Family of God Metropolitan Community Church, PO Box 2201; 31902 706-327-7414

Covington

Accommodation: Hotels, B&B, Resorts, Campgrounds

♂ ○ (?&) 2119—The Inn, 2119 Emory St; 30233 404-787-0037

Dahlonega

Accommodation: Hotels, B&B, Resorts, Campgrounds

♀ • Triangle Pointe, Rte 4, Box 242; 30533 706-867-6029 Fax 706-867-6030 "A mountain B&B in new home."

Demorest

Organizations/Resources: Social, Recreational & Support Groups (see also Sport/Dance/Outdoor)

♀ Mountain Catalyst, PO Box 199; 30535 706-778-3996

Gainesville

Accommodation: Hotels, B&B, Resorts, Campgrounds

♀ • (♨) Bon Secour, 1719 Cove Pt; 30501 404-535-6530

Macon

AIDS/HIV Support, Education, Advocacy, Publications

♀ ★♨ Central City AIDS Network, Inc., 530 First St; 31201-2819 912-750-8080; 800-374-2437

♂ ★♨ The Rainbow Center, 530 First St; 31201 912-750-8080; 800-374-2437

Bars, Restaurants, Clubs, Discos

♀ • (♨) Topaz, 695 Riverside Dr; 31201 912-750-7669 *BDELWf*

Savannah

Architectural Services (see also Home/Building)

♀ • Snyder, Daniel E., 216 E Gaston St; 31401 912-238-0410

Bars, Restaurants, Clubs, Discos

♀ The Bar Bar, 312 W St Julian; 31401 912-231-1910

♀ • Butcher Shop, 301 W Bay St; 31402 912-232-9431 *BR*

♂ • Club I Jefferson, 1 Jefferson St; 31401 912-232-0200 *BDER* 5pm-3am.

♂ • Faces II Tavern & Deli, 17 Lincoln St; 31401 912-233-3520 *BRLCW* noon-3am; Sun to 2am.

Bookstores: General

♂ ○ (♨) Stardust Book Emporium, 11 W York St; 31401 912-236-1441 Mon-Sat 10am-6pm. "Specializing in metaphysical."

Counseling/Therapy: Private

♀ • ♂ Womack, Martha B, PhD, 125 1/2 E Jones St; 31401 912-231-0420

Erotica (Printed, Visual, Equipment)

♀ • (♨) Captain Video, 7 W York St; 31401 912-232-2951

♀ ○ Home Run Video & News, 4 E Liberty; 31401 912-236-5192

Organizations/Resources: Family

♀ PFLAG, PO Box 2442; 31402 912-352-4758

Organizations/Resources: General, Multipurpose, Pride

♂ ★ First City Network, Inc, PO Box 2442; 31402-2442 912-236-2489 Pub *Network News*.

Religious Organizations & Publications

♂ Metropolitan Community Church Savannah, PO Box 14624; 31416 912-925-3731

Stone Mountain

Religious Organizations & Publications

♂ Christ Covenant Metropolitan Community Church, 798 Ray's Rd #100; 30083 404-297-0350

Valdosta

Bars, Restaurants, Clubs, Discos

♂ • ♨ Club Paradise, I-75 & Hwy 84 Interchange 912-242-9609 *BDE* Tue-Sat 8pm-3am.

Counseling/Therapy: Private

♀ ○ Curtis, John H., Ph.D., 1100 Williams St; 31601 912-244-5721

Hawaii

Statewide/County Resources

☎ Gay Community Directory 808-532-9000

Accommodation: Reservations & Exchanges (see also Travel)

♂ ○ (?♨) Bed & Breakfast Honolulu (Statewide), 3242 Kaohinani Dr, Honolulu, HI 96817 808-595-7533; 800-288-4666 (US & Canada); Fax 808-595-2030

AIDS/HIV Support, Education, Advocacy, Publications

♂ ★ ♂ AIDS Project Hawaii, PO Box 8425, Honolulu, HI 96815 808-926-2122 Fax 808-531-4635

♀ ☆ PWA Coalition: Hawaii, Box 11752, Honolulu, HI 96828 808-948-4PWA Pub *Living Now News*.

Funding: Endowment, Fundraising, Scholarship

♀ • (?♨) Imperial Court of All Hawaii, PO Box 91030, Honolulu, HI 96835 808-942-7513

Organizations/Resources: Education, Anti-Defamation, Anti-Violence, Self-Defense

♂ ★ Gay & Lesbian Education & Advocacy Foundation (GLEA), PO Box 37083, Honolulu, HI 96837-0083 808-532-9000 ext 201, voice & fax

Organizations/Resources: Political/Legislative

♂ ★ (?♨) Hawaii Equal Rights Marriage Project, 1820 University Ave, Room 8, Honolulu, HI 96822 808-942-3737 Fax 808-926-1000

Organizations/Resources: Social, Recreational & Support Groups (see also Sport/Dance/Outdoor)

♂ Org. of Hawaii Arts 'n Athletics-OHANA, PO Box 90543, Honolulu, HI 96835 808-926-6157; 808-373-9000

Organizations/Resources: Sport/Dance/Outdoor

♂ Hawaii Softball Federation, 666 Prospect St #202, Honolulu, HI 96813 808-845-7921; 808-536-4912

♂ Island Triathlon & Bike, 569 Kapahulu Ave, Honolulu, HI 96816 808-732-7227

♂ ★ (?♨) Organization of Hawaii Arts 'n' Athletics (OHANA), PO Box 90543, Honolulu, HI 96835 808-926-6157; 808-373-9000; Pub *OHANA News*.

Publications: Directories, Bibliographies, Guides, Travel

♂ • The Pages, 2851A Kihei Pl, Honolulu, HI 96816 808-737-6400 Fax 808-735-8825 Annual; $4.

Publications

♂ • Island Lesbian Connection, Ste 171 Box 356, Paia, HI 96779 808-575-2681 Fax 808-579-8556 "All-island newsletter, bi-monthly. Sample $2; sliding scale subscription $10-20."

♂ • Island Lifestyle Magazine, 2851A Kihei Place, Honolulu, HI 96816 808-737-6400 Fax 808-735-8825 Monthly. "Monthly magazine for local & visiting Gays & Lesbians."

♂ The Jungle Vine, PO Box 4056, Hilo, HI 96720

Real Estate

♂ • Community Real Estate Referrals, 800-346-5592 "Free referral to gay/gay-supportive realtor in any USA city/state (including Virgin Is. & Puerto Rico). Sorry, no rentals!"
♦ Community Real Estate Referrals advertisement back cover

Religious Organizations & Publications

♀♂ ★ Affirmation/Gay & Lesbian Mormons, PO Box 75131, Honolulu, HI 96836-0131 808-239-4995 "Mormons."

Switchboards, Helplines, Phone Information

♀♂ ☆ ♦ Gay Community Directory, PO Box 37083, Honolulu, HI 96837-0083 808-532-9000 "24 hr taped listing of Gay & Gay Supportive community services, AIDS information; referrals to Gay supportive businesses. Free calssifieds on line."

Travel & Tourist Services (see also Accommodation)

♀♂ • (?♿) Pacific Ocean Holidays, PO Box 88245, Honolulu, HI 96830 808-923-2400 Fax 808-923-2499 "Gay Hawaii Vacation Packages."

Aiea

Convenience Stores

♀♂ • C 'n' N Mini Mart & Liquors, Aiea Shopping Center; 96701 808-487-2944

Erotica (Printed, Visual, Equipment)

♀♂ • ♿ Suzie's, Aiea Shopping Center #242, 2nd flr; 96701 808-486-3103

Hawaii (Big Island)

Accommodation: Hotels, B&B, Resorts, Campgrounds

♀ • Butterfly Inn, Box J, Kurtistown; 96760 808-966-7936; 800-54-MAGIC; Bed & Breakfast for women.

♀♂ • Huliaulea Bed & Breakfast, PO Box 1030, Pahoa; 96778 808-965-9175

♀♂ • ♿ Kalani Honua Retreat By the Sea, RR2 Box 4500, Pahoa-Kehena; 96778 808-965-7828; 800-800-6886 reservations only; *Rd* "Conference & retreat center."

♀♂ • RBR Farms, PO Box 930, Captain Cook; 96704 808-328-9212

♀ ○ ♿ Samurai House, 89-5929 Mamalahoa Hwy, Captain Cook; 96704 808-328-9210

♀♂ • Wood Valley B & B Inn, PO Box 37, Pahala; 96777 808-928-8212

Organizations/Resources: Social, Recreational & Support Groups (see also Sport/Dance/Outdoor)

♀♂ ★ (?♿) Gays & Lesbians of Hawaii Island (GALOHI), PO Box 639, Kailua Kona; 96745 808-329-0049 Pub *B.I.G. Newsletter.*

♀ Jungle Vine, PO Box 29, Kurtistown; 96760 808-968-6614; 808-935-6984

Kauai

Accommodation: Hotels, B&B, Resorts, Campgrounds

♀♂ • (♿) Anohola Beach Club, PO Box 562, Anahola; 96703 808-822-6966

♀ ○ Hale Kahawai Bed & Breakfast, 185 Kahawai Place 808-822-1031 Fax 808-823-8220

♀ ○ Mahina Kai, PO Box 699, Anahola; 96703 808-822-9451

♀♂ • Pali Kai, PO Box 450, Kilauea; 96754 808-828-6691 "Bed & Breakfast."

♀♂ • ♿ Royal Drive Cottages, 147 Royal Drive, Kapaa; 96746 808-822-2321

Bars, Restaurants, Clubs, Discos

♀♂ Sideout, 4-1330 Kuhio Hwy, Kapaa; 96746 808-822-0082

Maui

Accommodation: Hotels, B&B, Resorts, Campgrounds

♀♂ • (♿) Camp Kula-Maui B&B, PO Box 111, Kula; 96790 808-878-2528

♀♂ • Golden Bamboo Ranch, 1205A Kaupakalua Road, Haiku; 96708 808-572-7824

♀♂ • Hale Makaleka, 539 Kupulau, Kihei; 96753 808-879-2971

♂ • Hana Plantation Houses, Box 248, Hana; 96713 800-248-4262

♀♂ • ♿ Huelo Point Flower Farm B & B, PO Box 1195, Paia; 96779-1195 808-572-1850

♀♂ • (♿) Kailua Maui Gardens, S.R. Box 9, Haiku; 96708 800-258-8588

♀♂ • (♿) The Triple Lei, Box 959, Kihei; 96753 808-874-8645; 800-871-8645; Fax 808-875-7324 Bed & breakfast.
♦ *Triple Lei advertisement page 235*

Accommodation: Reservations & Exchanges (see also Travel)

♂ • Royal Hawaiian Accommodations & Activities, PO Box 424, Puunene; 96784 800-659-1866 Fax 808-875-0623

Organizations/Resources: Social, Recreational & Support Groups (see also Sport/Dance/Outdoor)

♀♂ • (?♿) Both Sides Now, PO Box 5042, Kahului; 96732 808-872-6061 oim@tdp.org Pub *Out in Maui.*

Organizations/Resources: Sport/Dance/Outdoor

♂ • Maui Surfing School, PO Box 424, Puunene; 96784 808-875-0625; 800-851-0543; Fax 808-875-0623

Organizations/Resources: Youth (see also Family)

♀♂ ★ ♿ Maui Lesbian/Gay Youth Project, Ste 171 Box 356, Paia, HI 96779 808-573-1093 (Joe); 808-575-2681 (Karen); Fax 808-579-8556 "All-island newsletter, bi-monthly. Sample $2; sliding scale subscription $10-20."

Religious Organizations & Publications

♀♂ New Liberation Metropolitan Community Church, PO Box 347, Puunene; 96784 808-879-6193

Travel & Tourist Services (see also Accommodation)

♂ • (?♿) Personal Maui, PO Box 1328, Haiku; 96708 808-572-1589 "Guide & driver: I show you my favorite Maui 'secret' places in your rented car."

Weddings/Unions

♂ • Royal Hawaiian Weddings, PO Box 424, Puunene; 96784 800-659-1866 Fax 808-875-0623

Oahu

Accommodation: Hotels, B&B, Resorts, Campgrounds

♂ • Ali'i Bluffs Windward B & B, 46-251 Ikiiki St, Kaneohe; 96744 808-235-1124

♂ ○ Bed & Breakfast in Manoa Valley, 2651 Terrace Drive, Honolulu; 96822 808-988-6333

♂ ○ Coconut Plaza Hotel, 450 Lewers St, Honolulu; 96815 808-923-8828; 800-882-9696
♦ *Coconut Plaza Hotel advertisement page 235*

♀♂ • Hotel Honolulu, 376 Kaiolu St, Honolulu; 96815 (Waikiki) 808-926-2766; 800-426-2766

♀♂ • The Mango House, 2087 Iholena St, Honolulu; 96817-2105 808-595-6682 (also Fax); 800-77-MANGO; "The only Lesbian bed & breakfast on Oahu."

♀ ○ Waikiki AA Studios, 3242 Kaohinani Dr, Honolulu; 96817 808-595-7533; 800-288-4666 (US & Canada); Fax 808-595-2030

♀ • (?⚲) Waikiki Vacation Condos, 1860 Ala Moana Blvd #108, Honolulu; 96815 808-946-9371; 800-543-5663

AIDS/HIV Support, Education, Advocacy, Publications

↦ PWA Coalition: Hawaii: p.233

Bars, Restaurants, Clubs, Discos

♀ ○ ⚲⚲ Bananas Cafe, 2139 Kuhio Ave, Honolulu; 96815 *BR*

♀ ○ ⚲ Caffè Guccinni, 2139 Kuhio Ave, Honolulu; 96815 808-922-5287 *BR*

♂ Fusion Waikiki, 2260 Kuhio St, 3rd flr, Honolulu; 96815 808-924-2422 (after-hours)

♀ • ⚲⚲ Hamburger Mary's/Dirty Mary's, 2109 Kuhio Ave, Honolulu; 96815 808-922-6722 *BR*

♂ • ⚲⚲ Hula's Bar & Lei Stand, 2103 Kuhio Ave, Honolulu; 96815 808-923-0669 *BD* 10am-2am.

♀ ○ (?⚲) Jungle/Xtension, 311 Lewers St, Honolulu; 96815 808-922-7808 *BDRE* Lunch 11am-3pm; dinner 6-10pm; nightclub 10pm-4am.

♀ ○ Malia's Waikiki Grill, 311 Lewers St, Honolulu; 96815 808-922-7808 *BRD* 11am-4am. Live music SUN & Mon.

♀ Metropolis, 611 Cooke St, Honolulu; 96813 808-593-2717

♀ Windows on Eaton Square, 444 Hobron Ln, Honolulu; 96815 808-946-4442

Bookstores: General

♀ ○ Pacific Book House, 435 Atkinson Dr, Honolulu; 96814-4729 808-942-2242

♀ ○ Walden Books, 212 Waikiki Shopping Plaza, 2250 Kalakaua Ave, Honolulu; 96815 808-922-4154

Broadcast Media

♀ ★ Out & About, PO Box 61790, Honolulu; 96839 808-737-9034 Fax 808-737-6982

Community Centers (see also Women's Centers)

♀ ★ (⚲) Gay & Lesbian Community Center, 1820 University Ave, 2nd flr, Honolulu; 96822 808-951-7000 Fax 808-926-1000 Pub *Honolulu Outlook.*

Counseling/Therapy: Private

♀ • Bridge, Michael, PhD, 1188 Bishop St #2605, Honolulu; 96813 808-526-2605

Erotica (Printed, Visual, Equipment)

♀ ○ Submission, 1831 Ala Moana Blvd #110, Honolulu; 96815 808-942-0670

Gifts, Cards, Pride & Novelty Items

♀ • 80% Straight Inc, 2139 Kuhio Ave, 2nd flr, Honolulu; 96815 808-923-9996 10am-mdnt.

Health Clubs, Gyms, Saunas

♂ • Koko Pacific, Ltd, 2139 Kuhio Ave, 2nd flr, Honolulu; 96815 (Waikiki) 808-923-1852 24 hrs.

Organizations/Resources: Education, Anti-Defamation, Anti-Violence, Self-Defense

♀ ★ (⚲) Anti-Violence Project of Oahu, 1820 University Ave, 2nd flr, Honolulu; 96822 808-951-7000 Fax 808-926-1000 "Hate crime recording; homophobia workshops."

Organizations/Resources: General, Multipurpose, Pride

♀ ★ Pride Parade & Rally Council, Inc (PPRC), PO Box 37083, Honolulu; 96837 808-532-9000 ext 203

Organizations/Resources: Political/Legislative

♀ ★ ⚲ Gay Rights Task Force, PO Box 37083, Honolulu; 96837-0083 808-532-9000

Organizations/Resources: Social, Recreational & Support Groups (see also Sport/Dance/Outdoor)

♂ Gay Men's Nudist Club, PO Box 15385, Honolulu; 96830 808-735-4114 "Nudist/Naturist group."

♀ ★ Lesbian Support Group, c/o GLCC, 1820 University Ave, 2nd flr, Honolulu; 96815 808-951-7000 "Confidential women's support group for Lesbians, Bi-Sexual Women & those questioning their sexuality."

Organizations/Resources: Youth (see also Family)

♀ ★ ⚲ Gay & Lesbian Teen Task Force, c/o GLCC 1820 University Ave, Room 8, Honolulu; 96822 808-951-7000

Pets & Pet Supplies

♀ ○ Pet's Central, 2333 Alahao Place, Honolulu; 96819 808-848-1688

Publications

→ *Island Lifestyle Magazine*: p.233

Religious Organizations & Publications

♀ ★ (?⚲) Dignity/Honolulu, PO Box 3956, Honolulu; 96812-3956 808-536-5536 "Gay & Lesbian Catholics & their friends."

♂ ★⚲⚲ Ke Anuenue O Ke Aloha Metropolitan Community Church, PO Box 23334, Honolulu; 96823-3334 808-942-1027 Sun 11am, Dole Cannery Square, 7pm, 1212 University Ave.

♀ ☆⚲⚲ Religious Science Church/Honolulu, 1120 Maunahea St #275, Honolulu; 96817 808-521-0855

♂ UULGC, 2500 Pali Hwy, Honolulu; 96817 808-623-4726

Transportation: Limousine, Taxi, Etc.

♂ ● Dave's Hololulu Island Pride Taxi & Tours, Airport greeting & hotel transfer, by appointment 800-330-5598; 808-732-6518; "Unique personalized 'limo-van' at taxi rates."

Travel & Tourist Services (see also Accommodation)

♀ ● ⚲⚲ Second Floor Tickets & Tours, 2250 Kalakaua #K-5, Honolulu; 96815 808-924-3006 Fax 808-941-2407 "Discount prices for all Oahu activities; outer island specials."

♀ ● (?⚲) Tickets To Go, 1910 Ala Moana Blvd #B, Honolulu; 96815 808-942-7785 Fax 808-949-3935

♀ ○ Travel Travel, 320 Ward Ave #204, Honolulu; 96814 808-596-0336 Fax 808-591-6639

♀ ● Vacations-Hawaii Inc, 1314 S King St #1062, Honolulu; 96814 808-593-9911

Idaho

State/County Resources

AIDS/HIV Support, Education, Advocacy, Publications

♀ ☆ Idaho AIDS Foundation, PO Box 421, Boise, ID 83701 208-345-2277; 800-677-AIDS

Organizations/Resources: Political/Legislative

♀ ★⚲⚲ Idaho for Human Dignity, Inc., PO Box 768, Boise, ID 83701-0768 Fax 208-344-4458

♂ ★ (?⚲) Log Cabin Club of Idaho, 1117 Kimberley Lane, Boise, ID 83712 208-368-9789

Organizations/Resources: Social, Recreational & Support Groups (see also Sport/Dance/Outdoor)

♀ Idaho Women's Network, PO Box 1385, Boise, ID 83701 208-344-5738

Performing Arts: Entertainment, Music, Recording, Theater, etc.

♂ ★ Idaho Freedom Chorus, PO Box 7593, Boise, ID 83707-7593 208-323-0974

Publications

♂ ★ *Diversity*, PO Box 323, Boise, ID 83701 208-336-3870; 208-323-0805

♂ ★ *PLUS*, PO Box 4534, Coeur d'Alene, ID 83814

Real Estate

♂ ● Community Real Estate Referrals, 800-346-5592 "Free referral to gay/gay-supportive realtor in any USA city/state (including Virgin Is. & Puerto Rico). Sorry, no rentals!"
✦ *Community Real Estate Referrals advertisement back cover*

Religious Organizations & Publications

♂ Affirmation, PO Box 72, Eagle, ID 83616

Boise

Bars, Restaurants, Clubs, Discos

♀ Earth Food Cafe, 2907 W State St; 83702-2240 208-342-7169

♀ Emerald City/Oz, 415 S 9th St; 83702 208-342-5446

♂ The Oly, 1108 Front St; 83702 208-342-1371

♀ ● ⚲⚲ Partners, 2210 Main St; 83702 208-331-3551 *BD* 4pm-2am.

♀ ○ Rick's Cafe Americain at The Flicks, 646 Fulton St; 83702 208-342-4288 *R*

Bookstores: Recovery, Metaphysical, & other Specialty

♀ ○ ⚲ Blue Unicorn, 1809 W State St; 83702 208-345-9390 "New Age; Gay/Lesbian section."

Community Centers (see also Women's Centers)

♂ ★ The Community Center (TCC), PO Box 323; 83701 208-336-3870

Counseling/Therapy: Private

♂ ● ⚲⚲ Boise Counseling Center, Steven I Lanzet, M.ED., LPC, 815 Park Blvd #310; 83712 208-345-4660

♀ ○ ⚲ Garrison, Ruth, M.Ed, LPC,, 1818 E State; 83702 208-342-1651

Organizations/Resources: General, Multipurpose, Pride

♂ ★ (?⚲) Your Family, Friends & Neighbors, Inc., PO Box 768; 83701-0768 208-344-4295 "Promoter of gay & lesbian visibility."

Organizations/Resources: Student, Academic, Alumni/ae

♂ ★ Delta Lambda Phi Fraternity, Boise State University, Box 145 Student Activities, BSU, 1910 University Dr; 83725 800-587-FRAT

Real Estate

♀ ○ Stamos & Associates, 3133 Hillway Dr; 83702-0961 208-338-9668 Fax 208-385-0178

Religious Organizations & Publications

♀ ★ Metropolitan Community Church at Boise, PO Box 1959; 83701 208-342-6764 mccboise@aol.com

Caldwell

Erotica (Printed, Visual, Equipment)

♀ ○ Adult Shop, 716 Arthur Ave; 83605 208-454-2422

Coeur d'Alene

AIDS/HIV Support, Education, Advocacy, Publications

♂ ★⚲⚲ North Idaho AIDS Coalition, c/o Hospice, W 280 Prairie Ave; 83814 208-769-6254

Organizations/Resources: Student, Academic, Alumni/ae

♀ ★ (?⚲) North Idaho College Lesbian, Gay & Bisexual Alliance, PO Box 2622; 83816-2622 208-769-3328

Grangeville

Organizations/Resources: Political/Legislative

⚥ Central Idaho for Human Rights, PO Box 328; 30 208-983-8706

Idaho Falls

Organizations/Resources: Family

⚥ PFLAG, PO Box 50191; 83403-0191

Lava Hot Springs

Accommodation: Hotels, B&B, Resorts, Campgrounds

⚥ ○ Bar H Ranch, PO Box 297, Driggs; 83422 208-354-2906 "Working cattle ranch near Jackson Hole, WY; trail rides, pack trips, etc. Mostly women; men welcome."

Moscow

Organizations/Resources: General, Multipurpose, Pride

⚥ ★ Idaho Rural Outreach Network for Gays & Lesbians (IRON-GAL), PO Box 3182; 83843 208-882-1973

Organizations/Resources: Political/Legislative

♀ ★ Palouse Lesbian Avengers (IRONGAL), PO Box 3182; 83843 208-882-1973 "Direct action group committed to lesbian visibility & survival."

Organizations/Resources: Social, Recreational & Support Groups (see also Sport/Dance/Outdoor)

⚥ ★ Inland Northwest Gay People's Association (INWGPA), PO Box 8135; 83843 208-882-8034 *The Alliance.*

Women's Centers

♀ ☆ (?♿) Women's Center, University of Idaho; 83844-1064 208-885-6616

Nampa

Counseling/Therapy: Private

♀ • ♿ Mannion, Kris, MS, 516 3rd St S.; 83651 208-465-5311

Pocatello

Bars, Restaurants, Clubs, Discos

♀ The Mainlander, 304 N Main St; 83204 208-232-9603

Erotica (Printed, Visual, Equipment)

♂ ○ Pegasus Unusual Books, 246 W Center St; 83204 208-232-6493

♂ ○ Silver Foxx, 143 S 2nd Ave; 83201-6446 208-234-2477

Illinois

State/County Resources

Addictive Behavior, Substance Abuse, Recovery

⚥ • (♿) Pride Institute, 800-54-PRIDE "The nation's only accredited chemical dependency treatment center exclusively for Gay, Lesbian & Bisexual People."

Organizations/Resources: Political/Legislative

⚥ ★ Illinois Gay & Lesbian Task Force, PO Box A3728, Chicago, IL 60690-3728 312-975-0707

⚥ ★ IMPACT: Illinois' Gay & Lesbian Political Action Committee, 909 W Belmont #201, Chicago, IL 60657 312-528-5868 Fax 312-528-5776

Organizations/Resources: Sport/Dance/Outdoor

⚥ Illinois Gay Rodeo Association, PO Box 14878, Chicago, IL 60614-0878 312-642-1675

Publications

⚥ • *Windy City Times,* Sentury Publications, 970 W Montana #2FL, Chicago, IL 60614 312-935-1790 Fax 312-935-1853

Real Estate

⚥ • Community Real Estate Referrals, 800-346-5592 "Free referral to gay/gay-supportive realtor in any USA city/state (including Virgin Is. & Puerto Rico). Sorry, no rentals!"
✦ *Community Real Estate Referrals advertisement back cover*

Alton: see St Louis Area

Bloomington/Normal

Bookstores: Gay/Lesbian/Feminist

⚥ • Once Upon A Time, 311 N Main St, Bloomington; 61761 309-828-3998

Organizations/Resources: Student, Academic, Alumni/ae

⚥ ★ ♿♿ Gay & Lesbian Alliance, Illinois State University, Illinois State University, Normal; 61761-6901 217-438-2GAY Mon-Fri 11am-5pm.

Blue Island: see Chicago

Calumet City: see Chicago

Carbondale

Organizations/Resources: Student, Academic, Alumni/ae

⚥ ★ ♿♿ Gays, Lesbians, Bisexuals & Friends, OSD, 3rd Floor Student Center, Southern Illinois University; 62901 618-453-5151 Prideline Mon-Fri 5-9pm.

Champaign/Urbana Area

☎ Lesbian, Gay & Bisexual Switchboard 217-384-8040

AIDS/HIV Support, Education, Advocacy, Publications

♂ ☆ Gay Community AIDS Project, PO Box 713, Champaign; 61824-0713 217-351-AIDS

Bars, Restaurants, Clubs, Discos

Champaign

♀ • Chester St, 65 Chester St, Champaign; 61820 217-356-5607 5pm-1am.

♀ • ♿ Fiesta Cafe, 216 S First St, Champaign; 61820 217-352-5902 *B* 11am-1am.

Bookstores: General

♀ ○ Horizon Bookstore, 1115 1/2 W Oregon St, Urbana; 61801-3715 217-328-2988

♀ ○ (?♂) Jane Addams Book Shop, 208 N Neil St, Champaign; 61820 217-356-2555 10am-5pm; Sun 1-5pm. Pub *Women's Newsletter*.

Business, Financial & Secretarial

♀ • ♿ Ryan, Edward J., Accounting & Consulting, 41 E University Ave #2B2, Champaign; 61824-0441 217-356-0076 Fax 217-356-2961

Organizations/Resources: Political/Legislative

♂ ★ (?♂) Champaign County Lesbian, Gay & Bisexual Task Force, 217-344-0910

Organizations/Resources: Social, Recreational & Support Groups (see also Sport/Dance/Outdoor)

♂ ★ Alternate Current, PO Box 2641 Stn A, Champaign; 61825-2641 "Write for list of events."

♂ ★ (?♂) The Symposium, 1011 S Wright St, Champaign; 61820 217-384-8040; 217-333-1187; Fri 8-10pm.

Chicago's Bookstore for Gay Literature

unabridged BOOKSTORE

3251 North Broadway   Chicago   (312) 883-9119

Organizations/Resources: Student, Academic, Alumni/ae

♂ ★ (?♂) People for Lesbian, Gay Bisexual Concerns, University of Illinois, Urbana-Champaign, PO Box 2027 Stn A, Champaign; 61825-2027 217-384-8040 Mon-Fri 8-10pm. Gay, Lesbian & Bisexual Faculty Staff Association at University of Illinois at Urbana-Champaign.

Religious Organizations & Publications

♂ † Integrity/East Central Illinois, 1011 S Wright St, Champaign; 61820 217-344-1924 "Lesbian & Gay Episcopalians & their friends."

♀ ☆ ♂ New Jewish Agenda, c/o Hillel Foundation, 503 E John St, Champaign; 61820 217-344-1328

Switchboards, Helplines, Phone Information

♂ ★ ♂ Lesbian, Gay & Bisexual Switchboard, PLGBC, 284 Illini Union, 1401 W Green St, Urbana; 61801 217-384-8040

Chicago

☎ In Touch Hotline 312-996-5535

☎ Lesbian/Gay Helpline, Horizons Community Services 312-929-HELP

Accommodation: Hotels, B&B, Resorts, Campgrounds

Chicago

♀ ○ City Suites Hotel Chicago, 933 W Belmont Ave; 60657 312-404-3400

♂ • Lions Inn, 1473 W Catalpa; 60640 312-769-3119

♂ • Magnolia Place Bed & Breakfast, 5353 N Magnolia; 60640 312-334-6860

♂ • Old Town Bed & Breakfast, 1451 N North Park Ave; 60610-1226 312-440-9268

♀ ○ Park Brompton Hotel, 528 W Brompton Pl; 60657 312-404-3499

♀ ○ Surf Hotel, 555 W Surf Stn Pl; 60657 312-528-8400

♀ • Villa Toscana Guest House, 3447 N Halsted; 60657 312-404-2643; 800-404-2643

Addictive Behavior, Substance Abuse, Recovery

♂ ★ Alcoholics Anonymous, Gay Groups, 621 W Belmont Ave; 60657 312-346-1475

♂ ○ Lifestyles, Charter Barclay, 4700 N Clarendon Ave; 60640 800-877-6848

♂ ★ (?♂) Newtown Alano Club, 4403-07 N Clark St; 60640 312-271-NTAC 11am-11pm; Sat 8am-11pm; Sun 10am-11pm. "12 Step Recovery Club."

AIDS/HIV Support, Education, Advocacy, Publications

♀ ☆ AIDS Education Project/AIDS Volunteer Companion Network, 2045 W Washington; 60614 312-477-4709

♀ ☆ (?♂) AIDS Foundation of Chicago, 411 S Wells St #300; 60607-3924 312-642-5454

♀ ☆ (?♂) AIDS Legal Council of Chicago, 220 S State St #1330; 60604 312-427-8990

♀ ★ (?♂) AIDS Ministries, Holy Covenant MCC, 17 W Maple, Hinsdale; 60521-3495 708-325-8488

♀ ☆ ♿ AIDS Pastoral Care Network, 4753 N Broadway #800; 60640 312-334-5333 *The Spirit*.

♀ ○ Center for Special Immunology, 2835 N Sheffield Ave #104; 60657 312-296-2400

♀ ☆ ♿ Chicago House & Social Service Agency, Inc, 913 W Belmont; 60657 312-248-5200 Fax 312-248-5019 "AIDS housing."

IL: Chicago
AIDS/HIV Support

239

USA

Chicago : IL
Bars, Clubs, Restaurants

♂ ☆ HealthWorks Theatre, 3171 N Halsted St, 2nd flr; 60657-4435 312-929-4260

♀ ★ (♿) Howard Brown Health Center, 945 W George St; 60657 312-871-5777 "Sexually transmitted disease testing & treatment; HIV testing & counseling."

♂ ☆ (?♿) Kupona Network, 4611 S Ellis; 60653-3624 312-536-3000 Fax 312-536-8355

♀ ☆♿♿ Open Hand Chicago, 909 W Belmont Ave #100; 60657 312-665-1000 "Home delivered meals & nutritional services for Persons with AIDS/HIV."

♂ ☆ Stop AIDS Chicago, 909 N Belmont; 60657 312-871-3300 Mon-Thu 10am-10pm; Fri 10am-6pm.

Answering/FAX & Mail Receiving, Shipping & Packaging Services

♂ ○ ♿ Mail Center of Chicago, Inc, 601 S LaSalle St; 60605 312-922-1788 "Private lockbox/remailing service."

Architectural Services (see also Home/Building)

♀ ● Tatum, Raymond Terry, 718 W Melrose; 60657 312-327-9886 "Historic preservation consultant; also architectural research & writing."

Archives/Libraries/History Projects

♀ ★ ♿ Gerber/Hart Library and Archives, 3352 N Paulina St; 60657 312-883-3003

Art & Photography (see also Graphic Design)

♀ ● Photography By Jade, Carol Stream, IL. 708-231-5641

Bars, Restaurants, Clubs, Discos

Calumet City

♂ Bank Lounge, 200 State St, Calumet City; 60409 708-891-9651

♂ Dick's R U Crazee, 48 154th Place, Calumet City; 60409 708-891-2996

♀ Inntrigue, 582 Stateline Road, Calumet City; 60479 708-868-5240

♂ ● ♿ Mr B's Club, 606 State Line, Calumet City; 60409 708-862-1221 **BdLW** 1pm-2am; weekends to 3am. DJ Fri & Sat. Video bar; free pool table.

♀ ● Patch, 201 155th St, Calumet City; 60409 708-891-9854

♀ ● (?♿) Pour House, 103 155th Place, Calumet City; 60409-4617 708-891-3980

Chicago

♀ Annex III, 3160 N Clark St; 60657 312-327-5969

♂ Anvil, 1137 W Granville Ave; 60626 312-973-0006

♀ ● Baton Show Lounge, 436 N Clark St; 60610 312-644-5269

♂ ● ♿♿ Berlin, 954 W Belmont; 60657 312-348-4975 **BDE** 5pm-4am.

♂ ● Buck's Saloon, 3439 N Halsted; 60657 312-525-1125

♀ ● ♿ Buddies, 3301 N Clark St; 60657 312-477-4066 **BRCWLW**

♂ Cell Block, 3702 N Halsted; 60613 312-665-8064 **L**

♀ ● Charmers, 1502 W Jarvis; 60626 312-465-2811

♀ ● ♿♿ Chicago Eagle, 5015 N Clark St; 60640 312-728-0050 Fax 312-878-5184 **BL** 8pm-4am; Sat to 5am.

♂ Clark's on Clark, 5001 N Clark; 60640 312-728-2373

♀ ● Closet, 3325 N Broadway; 60657 312-477-8533

♀ Dandy's, 3729 N Halsted; 60613 312-525-1200

♂ Different Strokes, 4923 N Clark; 60640 312-989-1958

♀ ♿ Escapades, 6301 S Harlem Ave; 60638 312-229-0886

♀ ● Gentry, 712 N Rush; 60611 312-664-1033 **BE**

♀ ○ Gentry on Halsted, 3320 N Halsted St; 60657 312-348-1053

♂ ● InnExile, 5758 W 65th St; 60638 (Midway Airport area) 312-582-3510

♀ ○ Jeffery Pub, 7041 S Jeffery; 60649 312-363-8555

♂ Legacy '21, 3042 W Irving Park Rd; 60618 312-588-9405

♂ ○ ♿ Little Jim's, 3501 N Halsted; 60657 312-871-6116

♀ Lost & Found, 3058 W Irving Park Rd; 60618 312-463-9617

♂ ● ♿♿ Lucky Horseshoe Lounge, 3169 N Halsted; 60657 312-404-3169; 800-443-3169; 2pm-2am; Sat & Sun 3pm-closing; Fri 5pm-closing. Male dancers nightly.

♂ Manhandler, 1948 N Halsted; 60614 312-871-3339

♂ ○ Manhole, 3458 N Halsted St; 60657 312-975-9244 **BdLLLW**

♂ Martin's Den, 5550 S State St; 60621 312-363-9470

♀ Neo, 2350 N Clark; 60657 312-528-2622 **BD**

♂ ● ♿♿ The North End, 3733 N Halsted; 60613 312-477-7999 **BEL**f 4pm-2am; Sat 2pm-3am; Sun 2pm-2am.

♂ Numbers, 6406 N Clark; 60626 312-743-5772

♀ Off The Line, 1829 W Montrose; 60670 312-528-3253

♀ ● (♿♿) Paris Dance/Luna Park Cafe, 1122 W Montrose Ave; 60613 312-769-0602 **BDef** 5pm-2am; Sat 2pm-3am; Sun noon-2am. Men welcome.

♀ • (&) Roscoe's Tavern & Cafe, 3354-6 N Halsted; 60657 312-281-3355 *BDR*

♂ • (?&) Second Story Bar, 157 E. Ohio St 312-923-9536 *B* Noon-2am; Sat 3pm-3am; Sun 3pm-2am.

♂ • Sidetrack, The Video Bar, 3349 N Halsted; 60657 312-477-9189

♀ ○ Smart Bar, 3730 N Clark St; 60613 312-549-4140

♀ The Other Side, 3655 N Western; 60618 312-404-8156

♂ Touché, 6412 N Clark; 60626 312-465-7400

♂ Traveler's Rest, 1138 W Granville Ave; 60626 312-262-4225

♂ Visions, 3432 W Irving Park Rd; 60618 312-539-5229

♀ ○&& Vortex, 3631 N Halsted; 60613 312-975-6622; 312-975-0600; *BDE* 9pm-4am; Sat to 5am.

♀ Winner's, 4530 N Lincoln; 60625

Elk Grove Village

♂ Hunters, 1932 E Higgins Rd, Elk Grove Village; 60007 708-439-8840

Forest Park

♂ • Hideaway II, 7301 W Roosevelt Rd, Forest Park; 60130 708-771-4459 *BD*

♂ Nutbush City Limits, 301 N Harlem Ave, Forest Park; 60130 708-366-5117

Franklin Park

♀ Temptations, 10235 W Grand Ave, Franklin Park; 60131 312-455-0008

Bookstores: Gay/Lesbian/Feminist

♀ • A Book For All Seasons, 114 S Bloomingdale Rd 2nd Flr, Bloomingdale; 60108 708-893-9866

♀ • **People Like Us Books, 3321 N Clark; 60657 312-248-6363 Fax 312-248-1550 plubooks@aol.com 10am-9pm. "Chicago's only exclusively Gay & Lesbian bookstore."**
♦ *People Like Us Books advertisement page 239*

♀ • ♂ Prairie Moon, Ltd, 8 N Dunton, Arlington Heights; 60005 708-342-9608

♀ • ♂ The Pride Agenda Bookstore, 1109 Westgate, Oak Park; 60301 708-524-8429

♀ • ♂ Women & Children First, 5233 N Clark; 60640 312-769-9299

Bookstores: General

♀ ○&& Barbara's Bookshop, 3130 N Broadway; 60657 312-477-0411

♀ ○&& Healing Earth Resources, 2570 N Lincoln Ave; 60614 312-EARTH59

♀ • ♂ Left Bank Bookstall, 104 S Oak Park Ave, Oak Park; 60302 708-383-4700

♀ • Moon Mystique, 614 W Belmont; 60657 312-665-9016 Fax 312-665-9116 in@ripco.com 10am-10pm; Sun to 8pm.

♂ ○ ♂ Quimby's, 1328 N Damon; 60622 312-342-0910 11am-10pm; Sun noon-8pm.

♀ • **Unabridged Books, 3251 N Broadway; 60657 312-883-9119 10am-10pm; Sun to 8pm. "Extensive Gay & Lesbian literature."**
♦ *Unabridged Books advertisement page 238*

Business, Financial & Secretarial

♀ • (&) Murphy, Deborah, CPA, 3442 N Southport; 60657 312-404-8401

Community Centers (see also Women's Centers)

♀ ★&& Horizons Community Services, Inc, 961 W Montana; 60614 312-472-6469; 312-929-HELP 6-10pm; Anti-Violence Hotline 313-871-CARE; Mon-Thu 9am-10pm; Fri to 5pm; Sat 10am-3pm. "Programs for adults & youth, HIV/AIDS affected, victims of violence. Counseling, psychotherapy, legal info & referral, advocacy."

♂ ★ (?&) Midwest Men's Center of Chicago (MMC/C), PO Box 2547; 60690 312-348-3254 Pub *Men Nurturing News.*

Counseling/Therapy: Nonprofit

♀ ☆ (?&) Community Counseling Centers of Chicago, 4740 N Clark; 60640 312-769-0205 "Se habla Espanol. Insurance/Medicare/Medicaid accepetd."

Counseling/Therapy: Private

♀ • && Frisch, Hannah, Ph.D., 4933 S Dorchester; 60615 312-924-5057 (Also 203 N. Wabash; 4145 N. Greenview)

♀ • Power, John C., RN, MSW, ACSW, 718 W Melrose; 60657-3418 312-327-9886 "Hypnotherapy."

Erotica (Printed, Visual, Equipment)

♂ ○ Bijou Theatre, 1349 N Wells; 60610 312-943-5397 24 hrs.

♀ ○ ♂ Cupid's Treasures, 3519 N Halsted; 60657 312-348-3884; 800-CUPIDS-0; Fax 312-348-0976 11am-mdnt; Fri & Sat to 1am.

♀ • (&) Male Hide Leathers, 2816 N Lincoln Ave; 60657 312-929-0069 "Leather, videos."

♂ ○ Over 21, 1347 N Wells; 60610 312-337-8730

♂ • ♂ Pleasure Chest, 3143 N Broadway; 60657 312-525-7151

♂ ○ Ram Bookstore, 3511 1/2 N Halsted St; 60657 312-525-9528

♂ ○ Zebulon Books, 24 W 777 Lake St, Roselle; 60172 708-980-6088

Film & Video

♀ ★ (&&) Chicago Lesbian & Gay International Film Festival, c/o Chicago Filmmakers, 1543 W. Division St; 60622-3337 312-384-5533 Fax 312-384-5532 chifilm@tezcat.com

Gifts, Cards, Pride & Novelty Items

♀ • Gay Mart, 3457 N Halsted; 60657 312-929-4272 11am-11pm. "A gay department store."

♂ ○ The Paper Trail, 5307 N Clark St; 60640 312-275-2191

Health Care (see also AIDS Services)

♀ ☆ Chicago Women's Health Center, 3435 N Sheffield Ave; 60657 312-935-6126

♂ ○&& Coynik, David J., MD, PC, 30 N Michigan Ave #517; 60602 312-984-3540

♂ ○ Mavrinac, Maureen, MD, 711 W North Ave #209; 60610 312-280-0996

Health Clubs, Gyms, Saunas

♂ • Man's World, 4740 N Western Ave; 60625 312-728-0400

♂ • (&&) Mans Country, 5015 N Clark St; 60640 312-878-2069 Fax 312-878-5184 *P* 24 hrs. "Bath & entertainment complex, 3 floors."

♂ • (?&) Unicorn Club/Chicago Body Shop, 3246 N Halsted St; 60657 312-929-6080; 312-248-7717; *P*

Legal Services & Resources

♀ ○ ♂ Brunswick, Keefe & Deer, 2428 Vermont #417, Blue Island; 60406-0417 708-385-5500 Mon-Fri 9am-5pm; Sat by Appt.

IL: Chicago
Legal

241

USA

Chicago : IL
Organizations: Transgender

♂ ★ ♂♂ Lambda Legal Defense & Education Fund (LLDEF), Inc, 17 E Monroe #212; 60603 312-759-8110 Fax 312-641-1921

♀ ● ♂♂ Weaver, Alexander, 36 W Randolph St #800; 60601 312-578-0222

Organizations/Resources: Business & Professional

♀ ☆ Chicago Women In Trades, 37 S Ashland; 60607 312-942-1444

♂ ★ (?♂) Gay & Lesbian Physicians of Chicago, PO Box 14864; 60614 312-670-9630

♂ ★ Gay Association of Technicians, Engineers & Scientists, Box 14700; 60614-0700

♂ ★ Lesbian & Gay Bar Association of Chicago (LAGBAC), PO Box 06498; 60606-0498 312-404-9574

♂ ★ (♂♂) Professionals Over 30, PO Box 146681; 60614 312-409-1590 Pub *Newsletter*.

Organizations/Resources: Disability

♂ ★ (♂) Rainbow Bridge Organization, PO Box 42, Itasca, IL 60143-0042 312-488-0159 "Social & educational organization to unite persons with and without disabilities within the gay, lesbian & bisexual community."

Organizations/Resources: Education, Anti-Defamation, Anti-Violence, Self-Defense

♀ ★ Institute of Lesbian Studies, PO Box 25568; 60625

Organizations/Resources: Ethnic, Multicultural

♂ Active Proud Black Lesbians & Gays, PO Box 198573; 60619 312-493-3848

♀ African American Womyn's Alliance, PO Box 198573; 60619 312-324-5120

♂ ★ Asians & Friends of Chicago, PO Box A3916; 60690-3916 312-248-2444

♂ ★ ♂♂ Black & White Men Together, 2863 N Clark St (Community Center); 60657 312-334-2012; 800-NA4-BWMT; Fax 312-907-0083 Pub *Newsletter*. "Gay multiracial organization for all people."

♂ ☆ Black Men's Xchange, PO Box 642365; 60664-2365 312-824-8222; 800-274-3853; "A group where black men can find love & support from other black men."

♂ Brotherrs, 6540 S Woodlawn; 60637 312-667-8313 Pub *Voices*.

♂ Chicago Black Lesbians & Gays, 5828 N Winthrop; 60660-3512 312-257-8669; 312-871-2117

♂ ★ Gay & Lesbian South Asians / SANGAT Chicago, PO Box 268463; 60626 312-506-8810

♀ ★ (?♂) Yahimba, 1012 1/2 Dodge, Evanston; 60202 708-328-7715

Organizations/Resources: Family

♀ ☆ (♂) PFLAG, PO Box 11023; 60611 312-472-3079 "Parents, Families & Friends of Lesbians & Gays."

♀ ☆ ♂♂ PFLAG, 17 W Maple c/o Holy Covenant MCC, Hinsdale; 60521-3495 708-325-8488 "Parents, Families & Friends of Lesbians & Gays."

Organizations/Resources: General, Multipurpose, Pride

♂ ★ (♂) Fox Valley Gay Association, PO Box 393, Elgin; 60120 708-392-6882 Mon-Fri 7-10pm. Pub *Fox Tales*.

♂ ★ (♂) North Suburban Gay Association, PO Box 465, Wilmette; 60091 708-251-8853

♂ ★ **Pride Chicago, PO Box 14131; 60614 312-348-8243 "Organizers of the Annual Gay & Lesbian Pride Parade."**

♂ ★ West Suburban Gay Association, PO Box 161, Glen Ellyn; 60138 708-790-9742 Information Hotline

Organizations/Resources: Political/Legislative

♂ ★ Democratic Socialists of America, Lesbian/Gay/Bisexual Commission, c/o Chicago DSA, 1608 N Milwaukee #403; 60647 312-384-0327 Pub *Socialism & Sexuality*.

♂ Log Cabin CARGO, 128 Timbertrail, Streamwood; 60107 312-372-6615 "Republican organization."

Organizations/Resources: Sexual Focus (Leather, S/M, etc) & Safe Sex Promotion

♂ ★ Chest Men Of America (CMA), PO Box 138442; 60613 312-644-7282

♂ Windy City Hellfire Club, PO Box 5426; 60680

Organizations/Resources: Social, Recreational & Support Groups (see also Sport/Dance/Outdoor)

♂ Chi Town Society, PO Box 416825; 60641

♂ ★ (?♂) Girth & Mirth Chicago, Inc., PO Box 14384; 60614 312-327-1585

♂ ★ (?♂) Great Lakes Bears, PO Box 578840; 60657-8849 312-509-5135 Pub *Scratching Post*.

♂ ★ Lambda Car Club: Lake Michigan Region, PO Box 268534; 60626

♂ ★ Lincoln Park Lagooners, 3712 N Broadway, Box 278; 60613 312-883-0253

♀ ★ ♂♂ Mountain Moving Coffeehouse, 1545 W Morse; 60626 312-581-6455 Sat 7pm-mdnt (closed 1st Sat of month). "Live entertainment."

♂ ★ Reading Group, c/o A. Smalling, 1260 W Loyola Ave; 60626 312-262-3513

Organizations/Resources: Sport/Dance/Outdoor

♂ ★ Chi-Town Squares, PO Box 14897; 60614 312-357-3100 *dCW* "Square Dance."

♂ ★ ♂ Frontrunners/Frontwalkers Chicago, PO Box 148313; 60614-8313 312-409-2790

♂ ★ Metropolitan Sports Association, PO Box 578039; 60657 312-665-8008

♂ ★ Open Road Riders of Chicagoland, PO Box 14033; 60614 708-795-1803 "Motorcylists."

♂ ★ Windy City Athletic Association, PO Box 14142; 60614 312-327-5969

♀ ★ Women Together In Sports, PO Box 366, Hinsdale; 60521 708-323-8583

Organizations/Resources: Student, Academic, Alumni/ae

♂ ★ ♂♂ Northwestern University Bisexual, Gay & Lesbian Alliance, 1999 Sheridan Rd, Evanston; 60201 708-491-2375

♂ ★ (?♂) PRIDE at UIC/Spectrum, PO Box 4348 M/C 118; 60680 312-996-4424 Mon-Fri 9am-5pm.

♂ ★ ♂ University of Chicago Gay & Lesbian Alliance, 1212 E 59th St, Room 207; 60637 312-702-9734

♂ ★ ♂ Uppity Les/Bi/Gays, 1212 E 59th St, Room 207 c/o GALA; 60637 "Coalition devoted to progressive political action."

Organizations/Resources: Transgender & Transgender Publications

T ☆ (?♂) Chicago Gender Society, PO Box 578005; 60657 708-863-7714

IL: Chicago
Organizations: Youth

242
USA

De Kalb : IL
Organizations: Student

Organizations/Resources: Youth (see also Family)

♀ ☆ Chicago Runaway Switchboard, 3080 N Lincoln; 60657 800-621-3230 "Youth services."

Party/Event Services (see also Food Specialties, Catering)

♀ • Events a la Carte, 5716 N Hermitage Ave; 60660-3907 312-275-4018 "Also Gay & Lesbian Unions (weddings)."

Performing Arts: Entertainment, Music, Recording, Theater, etc.

♀ • Backdoor Promotions, 803 W Cornelia #200; 60657-2723 312-871-3070

♀ ★ (丙) Chicago Gay Men's Chorus, 6246 N Glenwood Ave #2; 60660-1830 312-275-7294

♀ • Music Magic Mobile Entertainment, PO Box 1571, Des Plaines; 60017 708-530-2206 "Mobile Disc Jockey for all occasions."

♂ ★ (丙) Windy City Gay Chorus/Windy City Performing Arts, 3023 N Clark St #329; 60657 312-404-WCGC Fax 312-404-6815

Pharmacies/Health Care Supplies

♀ ○ 丙 Save-Rite Pharmacy, 3479 N Broadway; 60657 312-525-0766 8am-10pm; Sun to 8pm.

Publications

♀ Bridges, PO Box 49119; 60649 312-493-7662

♂ • (丙) Gay Chicago Magazine, 3121 N Broadway; 60657-4522 312-327-7271 Fax 312-327-0112 Weekly.

♀ Girl Talk, PO Box 268446; 60626-8446 312-743-4724 Fax 312-973-6070

♀ Mala Leche, 3712 N Broadway #334; 60613 312-784-0609

♂ • Outlines, 3059 N Southport; 60657 312-871-7610 Monthly.

→ Windy City Times: p.237

♀ ○ (丙) Women in Business Yellow Pages, 7358 Lincoln Ave #150; 60646 708-679-7800

Real Estate

♂ • 丙 Smith, Richard, RE/MAX Realty Group, 4305 N Lincoln Ave; 60618 312-334-3347; 800-342-2344; Fax 312-907-1827 "10% at closing (max $250) donated to the AIDS charity of your choice when you mention this ad."

Religious Organizations & Publications

♂ ★ Chicago Interfaith Congress, PO Box 60039; 60660 312-784-2635 "Union of 15 Gay/Lesbian religious organizations."

♂ ★ Church of the Resurrection Metropolitan Community Church, 5540 S Woodlawn; 60637-1623 312-288-1535

♂ ★ 丙 Congregation Or Chadash, c/o 2U, 656 W Barry Ave; 60657 312-248-9456

♂ ★ Emergence/Midwest: Gay Christian Scientists, PO Box 2547; 60690 Christian Scientists

♂ Gentle Spirit Metropolitan Community Church, PO Box 597350; 60659-7350 312-972-2278

♂ ★ Good Shepherd Parish Metropolitan Community Church, 615 W Wellington Ave; 60657-5305 312-427-8708 24 hr Info Line for Metro Chicago MCCs. Worship service Sun 7pm.

♂ ★ 丙丙 Holy Covenant Metropolitan Community Church, 17 W Maple, Hinsdale; 60521-3495 708-325-8488 Worship service Sun 6pm. The Covenant.

♂ ★ 丙 Integrity/Chicago, Inc, PO Box 2516; 60690-2516 312-348-6362 "Gay & Lesbian Episcopalians & their friends."

♂ ★ 丙 Joy of Life Metropolitan Community Church, PO Box 1161, North Chicago; 60064 312-263-5197 The Forward Look.

♂ ☆ Lincoln Park Presbyterian Church, 600 W Fullerton Parkway; 60614-2690 312-248-8288 "A 'More Light' congregation, inclusive of all persons, regardless of sexual orientation."

♂ ★ (丙) Lutherans Concerned/Chicago, PO Box 10197; 60610 312-342-1647

♂ ★ PLGC/Chicago, c/o Lincoln Park Presb. Church, 600 W Fullerton Parkway; 60614-2690 312-784-2635 "Presbyterians for Lesbian/Gay Concerns."

♀ ☆ 丙丙 Unitarian Universalist Lesbian & Gay Concerns, c/o Second Unitarian Church, 656 W Barry Ave; 60657 312-549-0260

♂ ★ (丙) United Church of Christ Coalition for Lesbian/Gay Concerns, c/o Mark A. Palermo, 6171 N Sheridan Rd #2701; 60660-2858 312-338-0452

Switchboards, Helplines, Phone Information

♀ ☆ In Touch Hotline, c/o Couseling Center, (MLC 333) U of IL at Chicago, 601 S Morgan; 60607 312-996-5535

♂ ★ 丙丙 Lesbian/Gay Helpline, Horizons Community Services, 961 W Montana; 60614 312-929-HELP

Travel & Tourist Services (see also Accommodation)

♂ • All Points Travel Service, 3405 N Broadway; 60657 312-525-4700; 800-PRIDE 29

♂ ○ 丙丙 Associated United Travel Services, 4746 W Peterson Ave; 60646-5706 312-736-9292 Fax 312-737-9964 "Wholesale cruises: Europe & Caribbean."

♂ • Concierge Exclusif, 75 E Wacker Dr #3600; 60601 312-849-3604 Fax 312-857-0805 "Personalized assistance for Chicago's Gay & Lesbian visitors: hotels, tours, theatre, sporting events, etc."

♂ • Envoy Travel, 740 N Rush St; 60611 312-787-2400

♂ • 丙 Foremost Travel, 150 S Wacker Dr; 60606 312-346-6643 Fax 312-346-3899

♂ • 丙 Horizon: Experts In Travel, 7012 W North Ave; 60635 312-237-1178 Fax 312-237-3127 "Specialists in Gay/Lesbian cruises & destinations."

♀ ○ 丙 Presidential Travel, 605 E Roosevelt Rd, #105, Wheaton; 60187 708-690-0570

♂ ○ Sunset Travel, 732 W Fullerton; 60614 312-929-8155; 800-621-1274; Fax 312-929-2821

♂ • (?丙) Toto Tours, 1326 W Albion #3-W; 60626 312-274-8686 Fax 312-274-8695 "Specializing in worldwide travel for 'Friends of Dorothy' since 1990."

♀ • (丙) Yellow Brick Road Travel, 1500 West Balmoral Ave; 60640 312-561-1800; 800-642-2488; Fax 312-561-4497 Mon-Fri 9.20am-6pm; Sat 10am-3pm.

Video Sales, Rentals, Services (see also Erotica)

♀ • R.J.'s Video, 3452 N Halsted; 60657 312-871-1810

Women's Centers

♀ ★ (?丙) Kinheart Women's Center, 2214 Ridge Ave, Evanston; 60201 708-491-1103

Cicero: see Chicago

De Kalb

Organizations/Resources: Student, Academic, Alumni/ae

♂ ★ (?丙) Lesbian/Gay/Bisexual Coalition Northern Illinois University, Holmes Student Center, Room 256A; 60115 815-753-0584 Pub Prideletter.

IL: Decatur
Erotica

243
USA

Springfield : IL
Bookstores: General

Decatur

Erotica (Printed, Visual, Equipment)

♀♂ ○ Adult Books & Cinema X, 145 N Main St; 62521 217-423-9540

Travel & Tourist Services (see also Accommodation)

♀♂ ○ Village Travel, 3008 N Water; 62526 217-875-5640

Des Plaines: see Chicago

East St Louis: see Saint Louis, MO

Edwardsville

Organizations/Resources: Student, Academic, Alumni/ae

♀ ★ ♂♂ Gay & Lesbian Association of Students at SIU-E, PO Box 1168; 62026 618-692-2686

Elgin: see Chicago

Elk Grove Village: see Chicago

Evanston: see Chicago

Forest Park: see Chicago

Franklin Park: see Chicago

Galesburg

Erotica (Printed, Visual, Equipment)

♀♂ ○ Galesburg Adult Book & Video, 595 N Henderson St; 61401 309-342-7019

Organizations/Resources: Social, Recreational & Support Groups (see also Sport/Dance/Outdoor)

♀ ★ Peer Support Group (GLBCA), Knox College Box K-1590; 61401 "For Knox College students & youth in the area wishing a deal confidentially with gay & lesbian issues."

Organizations/Resources: Student, Academic, Alumni/ae

♀ ★ Gay, Lesbian & Bisexual Community Alliance (GLBCA), Knox College Box K-1648; 61401

♀ ★ Queer Theory Discussion Group (GLBCA), Knox College Box K-1648; 61401

Glen Ellyn: see Chicago

Granite City: see Saint Louis, MO

Hinsdale: see Chicago

Lincolnwood

Travel & Tourist Services (see also Accommodation)

♀♂ • Edward's Travel Advisors, 7301 N Lincoln Ave; 60646 708-677-4434 Fax 708-677-4421

Lombard: see Chicago

Metropolis: see Paducah

Mundelein: see Chicago

Nauvoo

Accommodation: Hotels, B&B, Resorts, Campgrounds

♀♂ ○ Ed-Harri-Mere, Box 367, 290 N Page St; 62354 217-453-2796

Normal: see Bloomington/Normal

Oak Park: see Chicago

Park Forest

Religious Organizations & Publications

♀ Metropolitan Community Church South Suburban Fellowship, PO Box 0488; 60426-0488 219-322-0049

Peoria

Bars, Restaurants, Clubs, Discos

♀ ○ Quench Room, 631 W Main; 61606 309-676-1079

♀ • Red Fox Den, 800 N Knoxville; 61602 309-674-8013 4pm-4am.

Health Care (see also AIDS Services)

♀♂ ☆ ♂♂ Peoria City County Health Dept., 2116 N Sheridan Rd; 61604 309-679-6028 "STD Clinic; anonymous HIV testing site."

Religious Organizations & Publications

♀ ★ ♂♂ Spirit of Life Metropolitan Community Church, PO Box 1614; 61656-1614 309-676-3330

Quincy

Bars, Restaurants, Clubs, Discos

♀ • (?♂) Irene's Cabaret, 124 N. 5th St 217-222-6292 *BDECW*

Religious Organizations & Publications

♀ ★ (♂♂) Metropolitan Community Church/Illiamo, PO Box 5141; 62305-5141 217-224-2800 Pub *Lamplighter*.

Rock Island

Bars, Restaurants, Clubs, Discos

♀ • Augie's, 313 20th St; 61201 309-788-7389

♀ JR's, 325 20th St; 61201 309-786-9411

♀ ○ Madison Square, 319 20th St; 61201 309-786-9400

Rockford

Accommodation: Hotels, B&B, Resorts, Campgrounds

♀ • Travlur Lounge & Motel, 7125 W State St; 61102-1003 815-964-7005 Bar 7pm-2am; Sun 4-11pm.

AIDS/HIV Support, Education, Advocacy, Publications

♀♂ ☆ ♂ AIDS Care Network, 221 N Longwood St #105; 61107-4171 815-968-AIDS Pub *Bridges*.

Bars, Restaurants, Clubs, Discos

♀ • The Office, 513 E State St; 61104 815-965-0344 5pm-2am.

Roselle: see Chicago

Schaumburg

Bars, Restaurants, Clubs, Discos

♀ Fourteen Fifty East/Flash, 1450 E Algonquin Rd; 60173 708-397-4564; 708-397-4521

Springfield

Bars, Restaurants, Clubs, Discos

♀ New Dimensions, 3036 Peoria Rd; 62702 217-753-9268

♀ • Smokey's Den, 411 E Washington; 62701 217-522-0301

Bookstores: General

♀ • Sundance, 1428 E Sangamon Ave; 62702 217-788-5243 (also Fax)

aQuaRius BOOKS
for a feminist future

306 SOUTH WASHINGTON St.
BLOOMINGTON, IN.
47401   812-336-0988

Organizations/Resources: General, Multipurpose, Pride

♀ ★ (?⚢) Springfield Area Lesbian Outreach (SALO), PO Box 5487; 62705 217-528-SALO

Religious Organizations & Publications

♀ ★ (⚤) Faith Eternal Metropolitan Community Church, PO Box 4824; 62708-4824 217-525-9597

Urbana: see Champaign/Urbana Area

Villa Park

Organizations/Resources: Social, Recreational & Support Groups (see also Sport/Dance/Outdoor)

♀ ★ ⚤♂ Review, PO Box 7406; 60181 708-620-6946 "Bi & Gay Married Men's Group."

Wilmette: see Chicago

Indiana

State/County Resources

AIDS/HIV Support, Education, Advocacy, Publications

♀ ☆ Indiana CARES, Inc, 3951 N Meridian St #101, Indianapolis, IN 46208 317-920-1200; 800-276-6443

Organizations/Resources: Political/Legislative

♂ ★⚤♂ Justice, PO Box 2387, Indianapolis, IN 46206 317-634-9212; 800-634-9212; "Statewide coordinating group."

Organizations/Resources: Social, Recreational & Support Groups (see also Sport/Dance/Outdoor)

♂ ★ Hoosier Bears of Indiana, Inc., PO Box 531311, Indianapolis, IN 46253-1311 317-299-3535 Pub *Bear-Trax.*

♂ ★ (?⚢) Out & About Indiana, 133 W Market St #105, Indianapolis, IN 46204 317-547-0615 Fax 317-574-0228
◆ *Out & About Indiana advertisement page 245*

Organizations/Resources: Sport/Dance/Outdoor

➔ Tri-State Gay Rodeo Association: p.369

Organizations/Resources: Transgender & Transgender Publications

T ☆⚤♂ IXE (Indiana Crossdressers Society), PO Box 20710, Indianapolis, IN 46220 317-876-5635 "Serving TS, TV & TG persons & their SO's."

Publications

♂ ● *The Indiana Word,* 225 E North St, Tower 1 #2800, Indianapolis, IN 46204 317-579-3075

♂ ★ (?⚢) *OUTlines: Out & About Indiana,* 133 W Market St #105, Indianapolis, IN 46204 317-537-0615 Fax 317-574-0228
◆ *OUTlines: Out & About Indiana advertisement page 245*

Real Estate

♂ ● Community Real Estate Referrals, 800-346-5592 "Free referral to gay/gay-supportive realtor in any USA city/state (including Virgin Is. & Puerto Rico). Sorry, no rentals!"
◆ *Community Real Estate Referrals advertisement back cover*

Bloomington

☎ Gay & Lesbian Switchboard 812-855-5OUT

Bars, Restaurants, Clubs, Discos

♂ ○ Bullwinkle's, 201 S College; 47401 812-334-3232

♂ ● The Other Bar, 414 S Walnut; 47403 812-332-0033 *BdE* Mon-Thu 4pm-1am; Fri to 2pm; Sat noon-2am. Beer & wine only.

Bookstores: Gay/Lesbian/Feminist

♀ ● ♂ Aquarius Books For A Feminist Future, 306 S Washington St; 47401-3529 812-336-0988 11am-6pm; Sat 10am-5pm; Sun 1-5pm.
◆ *Aquarius Books For A Feminist Future advertisement page 244*

Bookstores: General

♂ ○ Morgenstern Booksellers, 2650 E 3rd; 47401 812-331-2066

Broadcast Media

♀ ☆ WFHB, PO Box 1973; 47402 812-323-1200

Gifts, Cards, Pride & Novelty Items

♂ ● Visual Voice, PO Box 8011; 47407 800-655-2321 Fax 812-333-7923 "Identities—handcrafted Gay Greeting Cards. Free catalog."

Organizations/Resources: Student, Academic, Alumni/ae

♀ ★ (?⚢) GLB Student Support Services, Indiana University 705 E 7th St; 47405 812-855-4252 Fax 812-855-4465 qlb.serve@indiana.edu "Resource center for IU students."

♂ ★⚤♂ OUT Indhania University Bloomington's Gay, Lesbian & Bisexual People's Union, IMU Rooms 48-L & M; 47405 812-855-5688

Religious Organizations & Publications

♂ Integrity/Bloomington, PO Box 3232; 47402-3232 812-339-0426 "Lesbian & Gay Episcopalians & their friends."

♂ Spinoza, PO Box 6112; 47407 812-333-7973

Switchboards, Helplines, Phone Information

♂ ★⚤♂ Gay & Lesbian Switchboard, 812-855-5OUT

Crown Point

Travel & Tourist Services (see also Accommodation)

♂ ○ Fantasy Travel, 608 W 93rd Ct; 46307 219-663-8144

Evansville

AIDS/HIV Support, Education, Advocacy, Publications

♀ ☆⚤♂ AIDS Resource Group of Evansville, Inc., Old Courthouse #301, 201 NW 4th St; 47708-1357 812-421-0059 Pub *ARG Newslettter.*

Bookstores: General

♂ ○ ♂ A.A. Michael Books, 1541 S Green River Road; 47700 812-479-8979

Organizations/Resources: Family

♂ ★ Evansville Gay/Lesbian Parents Coalition, PO Box 2794; 47728-0794

Organizations/Resources: General, Multipurpose, Pride

♀ ★ (?♿) Tri-State Alliance, PO Box 2901; 47728-0901 812-474-4853 Pub *Tri-State Newsletter*.

Religious Organizations & Publications

♀ ★ Tri-State Metropolitan Community Church, PO Box 3382; 47732 812-429-3512

Fort Wayne

☎ Gay/Lesbian Helpline 219-744-1199

AIDS/HIV Support, Education, Advocacy, Publications

♀ ☆♿ AIDS Task Force, Inc, 2124 Fairfield Ave; 46802-5158 219-744-1144

Bars, Restaurants, Clubs, Discos

♀ • (♿) After Dark, 231 Pearl St; 46802 219-424-6130 *BDEf* Mon-Sat 3pm-3am.

Community Centers (see also Women's Centers)

♀ ★ Fort Wayne Gay/Lesbian Resource Center & Archives, 3426 Broadway; 46807 219-744-1199 7.30-10pm at Up The Stairs Community Center.

♀ ★ (♿) Up The Stairs Community Center, 3426 Broadway; 46807 219-744-1199 Mon-Thu 7-10pm; Fri & Sat to mdnt; Sun 7-9pm.

Health Care (see also AIDS Services)

♀ ☆♿ STD Clinic, Room 505, City-County Bldg, 1 E Main St; 46802-1810 219-449-7504 STD clinic & HIV testing, by appointment.

Religious Organizations & Publications

♀ ★ Dignity, PO Box 11988; 46862 219-484-6492 "Promoting spiritual development, personal growth & friendship."

♀ ★ New World Church & Outreach Center, Box 11553; 46859 / 222 E. Leith St 219-456-6570

♀ ★ Open Door Chapel, 3426 Broadway; 46807 219-744-1199 Worship Sun 7pm.

♀ ☆♿ Task Force on Homosexuality, First Presbyterian Church, 300 W Wayne St; 46802 219-744-1199

Switchboards, Helplines, Phone Information

♀ ★ Gay/Lesbian Helpline, 219-744-1199 Mon-Thu 7-10pm; Fri & Sat to mdnt; Sun to 9pm.

Goshen

AIDS/HIV Support, Education, Advocacy, Publications

♀ ☆♿ Oaklawn, PO Box 809; 46527 219-533-1234

Indianapolis

☎ Gay/Lesbian Switchboard/Community Referral Service 317-639-5937

Accommodation: Hotels, B&B, Resorts, Campgrounds

♀ ○ North Meridian Inn, 1530 N Meridian St; 46202 317-634-6100; 800-233-4639 reservations; Fax 317-634-4814 *BR*

♀ ○ The Nuthatch B&B, 7161 Edgewater Place; 46240 317-257-2660

♀ ○ Saint Cecelia Guest House, 317-630-4315

AIDS/HIV Support, Education, Advocacy, Publications

♀ ☆♿ Damien Center, 1350 N Pennylvania; 46202 317-632-0123; 317-632-4259 TDD; Fax 317-632-4362 "Educational & support facility for persons infected with HIV/AIDS and their families of choice."

♀ ☆ Indiana AIDS Hotline, PO Box 2152; 46206 317-257-HOPE 7-11pm.

♀ ☆ (♿) Infectious Diseases Clinic Free Anonymous AIDS Test Site, 1101 W 10th St; 46202 317-635-TEST

Bars, Restaurants, Clubs, Discos

♀ • ♿ The 151 Club, 151 W 14th St; 46202 317-767-1707 *BD* Mon-Sat 5pm-3am. Female Exotic Dancers.

♀ 501 Tavern, 501 N College; 46202 317-632-2100

♀ ● (ᕃᕃ) Brothers Bar & Grill, 822 N Illinois St; 46204 317-636-1020 *BR*

♀ ♿ Coffee Zon, 137 E Ohio; 46204 317-684-0432 *RE*

♀ ● (?ᕃ) Jimmy's, 924 N Pennsylvania; 46204 317-638-9039 *BRE*

♂ ○ (ᕃᕃ) Metro, 707 Massachusetts Ave; 46204 317-639-6022 *BD*

♂ ● ♿ Our Place, 231 E 16th St; 46202 317-638-8138 *BDLW*

♂ ● ᕃᕃ The Ten, 1218 N Pennsylvania Ave; 46202 317-638-5802 *DE* Drag shows.

♂ Tomorrow's, 2301 N Meridian; 46208 317-925-1710

♂ ★ (ᕃ) Unicorn Club, 122 W 13th St; 46202 317-262-9195 *PB* 6pm-3am. Male dancers.

♂ ○ Varsity Lounge, 1517 N Pennsylvania; 46202 317-635-9998

Bookstores: Gay/Lesbian/Feminist

♀ ● ♿ Dreams & Swords, 6503 Ferguson St; 46220-1148 317-253-9966; 800-937-2706; Fax 317-259-0763 Mon-Fri 10am-6pm; Sat 10.30am-5pm; Sun noon-5pm. "Send for free catalog."
♦ *Dreams & Swords advertisement page 245*

Bookstores: General

♀ ○ ᕃᕃ Borders Book Shop, 5612 Castleton Corner Ln; 46250 317-849-8660 9am-10pm; Sun 11am-6pm.

Counseling/Therapy: Nonprofit

♂ ★ Lee, C. David, MA, 1253 N Morgantown Rd, Greenwood; 46142 317-887-8476

Counseling/Therapy: Private

♀ ○ Applegate, Eric, MS, 2625 North Meridian #18; 46208 317-925-1881

♀ ○ Passages Psychological Services, 6311 Westfield Blvd #303; 46220 317-251-1110

♀ ● (?ᕃ) Wishmire, Christopher J., ACSW, 927 E Westfield Blvd #A; 46220 317-255-8973

Erotica (Printed, Visual, Equipment)

♀ ● ♿ Bookland, 137 W Market St; 46204 317-639-9864

Gifts, Cards, Pride & Novelty Items

♀ ○ Just Cards, 145 E Ohio St; 46204 317-638-1170 Mon-Fri 9am-5.30pm; Sat 10am-5pm.

Health Clubs, Gyms, Saunas

♂ ● ᕃᕃ Club Indianapolis, 620 N Capitol; 46204 317-635-5796

♂ ● The Works, 4120 N Keystone Ave; 46205-2843 317-547-9210

Legal Services & Resources

♀ ○ King, J. Bradley, Esq, 847 Woodruff Place E Dr; 46201-1923 317-634-8868

Organizations/Resources: Business & Professional

♂ ★ (?ᕃ) Indianapolis Business Outreach Association (IBOA), PO Box 501915; 46250 317-726-9746; 317-925-9126

Organizations/Resources: Family

♂ ★ Gay & Lesbian Parents Coalition of Indianapolis, PO Box 831; 46206 317-925-8092; 317-253-2280

Organizations/Resources: Sexual Focus (Leather, S/M, etc) & Safe Sex Promotion

♂ NLA Indianapolis/Circle City Leather, Box 1632; 46206-1632

Organizations/Resources: Student, Academic, Alumni/ae

♂ ★ ᕃᕃ The IUPUI Advocate, Box 37, University Library 006A, 815 W Michigan St; 46202 317-274-8206

Organizations/Resources: Transgender & Transgender Publications

T Tran Sexuals & Genders of America, mail to TSGA, 133 W Market St #179; 46204 317-259-1427

Organizations/Resources: Youth (see also Family)

♂ ★ Indianapolis Youth Group, PO Box 20716; 46220-0716 317-541-8726; 800-347-TEEN; Pub *IYG Reachout*.

Publications

→ *The Indiana Word*: p.244
♂ ● *SARJ Guide*, 771 Massachusetts Ave; 46204 317-637-2368; 800-959-0453; "Indianapolis' weekly bar rag."

Religious Organizations & Publications

♂ ★ Affirmation: United Methodists for Lesbian, Gay & Bisexual Concerns, 33 E 32nd St; 46205 317-925-0043

♂ ★ ᕃᕃ Dignity/Central Indiana, PO Box 431; 46206 "Gay & Lesbian Catholics & their friends."

♀ ☆ ♿ Disciples Peace Fellowship, PO Box 1986; 46206 317-353-1491; 317-352-8294

♂ ★ Jewish Support Group, Judy Wolf 5413 Graceland Ave; 46208 317-251-5413

♂ ★ ᕃᕃ Metropolitan Community Church, PO Box 19392; 46219-0392 317-895-4934

Switchboards, Helplines, Phone Information

♂ ★ Gay/Lesbian Switchboard/Community Referral Service, Box 2152; 46206 317-639-5937 7-11pm

Travel & Tourist Services (see also Accommodation)

♀ ● (?ᕃ) Bon Voyage Adventures, Inc., 2908 Sunmeadow Way; 46208 317-293-3719; 317-899-9900 (voice mail); "Specializing in cruises & travel packages for gay men."

♀ ● UniWorld Travel, Inc., 1010 E 86th St #65-E; 46240 317-573-4919

Lafayette

AIDS/HIV Support, Education, Advocacy, Publications

♀ ★ ♿ Project AIDS Lafayette (PAL), PO Box 5375; 47903 / 810 North St (rear entrance) 317-742-2305; 800-524-3229 in state.; "AIDS/HIV services, case management, community outreach, counseling, advocacy."

Bars, Restaurants, Clubs, Discos

♀ ○ Sportsman, 644 Main St; 47901 317-742-6321

Erotica (Printed, Visual, Equipment)

♀ ○ ᕃᕃ Fantasy Gift Shop, 119 N River Rd; 47906 317-743-5042

♀ ○ ᕃᕃ Fantasy Gift Shop, 2311 Concord Rd; 47905 317-474-2417

Organizations/Resources: Social, Recreational & Support Groups (see also Sport/Dance/Outdoor)

♂ ★ Dignity/Lafayette, PO Box 4665; 47903 Pub *Newsletter*.. "Non-denominational discussion/support/social group (not associated with Catholic Dignity)."

Organizations/Resources: Student, Academic, Alumni/ae

♂ ★ ᕃᕃ The Purdue Lesbigay Network, Box 512, Purdue Memorial Union, West Lafayette; 47906 "Student-faculty-staff-and-community organization."

Lake Station

Bars, Restaurants, Clubs, Discos

♀ The Station House, 2417 Rush St; 46405 219-962-1017

Michigan City

Travel & Tourist Services (see also Accommodation)

♀ ○ Athena Travel Services, 1099 N Karwick Rd; 46360 219-879-4461; 219-873-2360

Muncie

Bars, Restaurants, Clubs, Discos

♀ Carriage House, 247 Kilgore Ave; 47305 317-282-7411

♀ Mark III, 107 E Main St; 47305 317-282-8273

Organizations/Resources: Student, Academic, Alumni/ae

♀ ★ ♂♂ Ball State Lesbian, Bisexual, Gay Student Association, Student Center Box 16; 47306 317-28-LBGSA (office); Safeline (Hotline) 317-285-SAFE Mon-Thu 5-10pm; 317-285-6615 (student center); d000lgbsa@bsu.edu Pub *Family Values*.

Notre Dame

Organizations/Resources: Student, Academic, Alumni/ae

♀ ★ ♂♂ Gays & Lesbians at Notre Dame/St Mary's College, Box 194; 46556

Richmond

Bars, Restaurants, Clubs, Discos

♀ ○ ♂ Coachman Lounge, 911 Main St; 47374 317-966-2835 *BD* 3pm-3am.

Organizations/Resources: Student, Academic, Alumni/ae

♀ ★ Earlham Lesbian, Bisexual & Gay People's Union, Drawer 279 Earlham College; 47374 317-983-1436

South Bend

Addictive Behavior, Substance Abuse, Recovery

♀ ☆ ♂ AA (Gay Group), c/o First Unitarian Church, 101 E Northshore Drive; 46617

Bars, Restaurants, Clubs, Discos

♀ • ♂ Seahorse II Cabaret, 1902 Western Ave; 46619 219-237-9139

♀ Starz Bar & Restaurant, 1505 S Kendall St; 46613 219-288-7827

♀ Truman's, 100 Center, Mishawaka; 46544 219-259-2282

Erotica (Printed, Visual, Equipment)

♀ • Little Denmark Books & Videos, 3002 Western Ave; 46619 219-233-9538

Health Care (see also AIDS Services)

♀ ☆ ♂ St Joseph County Health Dept, County-City Bldg, 227 W Jefferson Blvd, 9th Flr; 46601 219-284-9725 8-11.30am; 1-4pm. "HIV counseling & testing; STD clinic."

Organizations/Resources: Social, Recreational & Support Groups (see also Sport/Dance/Outdoor)

♀ ★ Support Group/Open Arms, PO Box 845, Mishawaka; 46544 Monthly.

Organizations/Resources: Student, Academic, Alumni/ae

♀ ★ ♂♂ OUT at Indiana State University South Bend, Rm U100F, 1700 Mishawaka Ave; 46615 219-237-4125

Women's Centers

♀ ☆ ♂ IUSB Women's Center, Northside 0005, 1825 Northside Blvd; 46615 219-237-4494

Terre Haute

Organizations/Resources: Family

♀ PFLAG—Wabash Valley Chapter, 135 Aikman Place; 47803 812-232-5188

Organizations/Resources: Student, Academic, Alumni/ae

♀ ★ Alliance for Bisexual Lesbian & Gay Students & Allies (ABL-GSA), Box 18 HMSU; 47809 812-231-3724

Organizations/Resources: Youth (see also Family)

♀ IGY-TH, PO Box 2065; 47802-0065 812-231-6829

Iowa

State/County Resources

Addictive Behavior, Substance Abuse, Recovery

♂ • (♂♂) Pride Institute, 800-54-PRIDE "The nation's only accredited chemical dependency treatment center exclusively for Gay, Lesbian & Bisexual People."

AIDS/HIV Support, Education, Advocacy, Publications

♀ ☆ All Iowa AIDS Benefit, c/o Cornhaulers PO Box 305, Des Moines, IA 50302 515-282-7787

Organizations/Resources: Social, Recreational & Support Groups (see also Sport/Dance/Outdoor)

♂ ★ Bear Paws of Iowa, PO Box 2774, Iowa City, IA 52244-2774

♂ ★ (?♂) Iowa Bareskins, PO Box 266, Des Moines, IA 50301-0266 "Nonsexual gay male nudist group."

Publications: Directories, Bibliographies, Guides, Travel

♀ ★ *GLBA Resource Directory*, PO Box 1761, Ames, IA 50010

Publications

♀ *PEN Magazine*, PO Box 1693, Des Moines, IA 50306 515-265-3214

Real Estate

♀ • Community Real Estate Referrals, 800-346-5592 "Free referral to gay/gay-supportive realtor in any USA city/state (including Virgin Is. & Puerto Rico). Sorry, no rentals!"
♦ *Community Real Estate Referrals advertisement back cover*

Religious Organizations & Publications

♀ ★ ♂♂ UCCL/GC (United Church Coalition for Lesbian/Gay Concerns), PO Box 67 c/o Conklin, Nashua, IA 50658-0067 515-435-5068

Ames

☎ Gay & Lesbian Info Line 515-294-2104

☎ Open Line 515-233-5000

AIDS/HIV Support, Education, Advocacy, Publications

♀ ☆ AIDS Coalition Story County, 113 Colorado Ave; 50014-3403 515-292-5487

Erotica (Printed, Visual, Equipment)

♂ ○ Pleasure Palace II, 117 Kellogg St; 50010 515-232-7717

Organizations/Resources: General, Multipurpose, Pride

♀ ★ ♿ GLB Ames (Gays, Lesbians, Bisexuals of Ames, PO Box 1761; 50010-1761 515-233-5000; 515-292-7000 Open Line; 294-2104 Gay & Lesbian Information Line; Pub *GLB Ames Newsletter*.

Organizations/Resources: Student, Academic, Alumni/ae

♀ ★ ♿ Lesbian/Gay/Bisexual Alliance, 39 Memorial Union; 50011 515-294-2104 *The Rainbow Connection*.

Switchboards, Helplines, Phone Information

♀ ★ ♿ Gay & Lesbian Info Line, 39 Memorial Union, c/o Gay/Lesbian/Bisexual Alliance; 50010 515-294-2104 Mon 6-9pm

♀ ☆ Open Line, c/o American Red Cross, 426 5th St; 50010 515-233-5000

Women's Centers

♀ ☆ ♿ Margaret Sloss Women's Center, Sloss House, Iowa State University; 50011 515-294-4154 Mon-Fri 8am-5pm.

Bettendorf

Religious Organizations & Publications

♀ ★ Lutherans Concerned, Box 773; 52722-0773

Cedar Falls: see Waterloo

Cedar Rapids

AIDS/HIV Support, Education, Advocacy, Publications

♀ ☆ ♿ Rapids Aids Project, American Red Cross, Grant Wood Red Chapter 3601 42nd St NE; 52402-7111 319-393-9579

Bars, Restaurants, Clubs, Discos

♀ ○ Side Saddle Saloon, 525 H St SW; 52404 319-362-2226 *BDEf*

Community Centers (see also Women's Centers)

♀ ★ ♿ GLRC (Gay & Lesbian Resource Center), PO Box 1643; 52406 319-366-2055 Pub *GLRC News*.

Religious Organizations & Publications

♀ ☆ ♿ All Faiths Metropolitan Community Church, PO Box 412; 52406 319-396-9207

Council Bluffs

Erotica (Printed, Visual, Equipment)

♀ ○ Off Broadway Emporium, 3216 1st Ave; 51501 712-328-2673

Organizations/Resources: Transgender & Transgender Publications

T ☆ River City Gender Alliance, PO Box 680; 51502

Davenport

AIDS/HIV Support, Education, Advocacy, Publications

♀ ☆ ♿ AIDS Project Quad Cities, Inc., 605 N Main St #6A; 52803-5245 319-324-8638

Bookstores: Recovery, Metaphysical, & other Specialty

♀ ● Crystal Rainbow, 1025 W 4th St; 52802-3510 319-323-1050 Mon-Sat 10am-6pm.

Publications

♀ *River Bend Vision*, PO Box 4078; 52808-4078

Religious Organizations & Publications

♀ ★ (♿) Metropolitan Community Church Quad Cities, 3019 Harrison St; 52803-1033 319-324-3281 Services Sun 11am & Wed 7pm.

Decorah

Organizations/Resources: Social, Recreational & Support Groups (see also Sport/Dance/Outdoor)

♀ ★ (♿) Aware/FLAG, Dr. Bruce Wrightsman FPO 57 Luther College; 52101-1045 319-387-1277

Des Moines

☎ Gay & Lesbian Resource Center 515-279-2110

AIDS/HIV Support, Education, Advocacy, Publications

♀ Aids Project Of Central City, 414 12th St; 50309 515-284-0245

♀ ★ Buddy Program, Iowa Chapter Red Cross, 2116 Grand Ave; 50312-5382 515-244-6700

♀ ☆ H.E.R.O.E.S., 1329 22nd St #1; 50311 515-280-6422 "We provide education, information & referral to women, children, & families infected or affected by HIV/AIDS."

Bars, Restaurants, Clubs, Discos

♀ ● ♿ Blazing Saddle, 416 E 5th St; 50309 515-246-1299

♀ ● The Garden, 112 SE 4th St; 50315 515-243-3965 *BD*

♀ ● Playpen, 424 E Locust St; 50309 515-243-9626 *BDE*

♀ ○ (♿) Side Saddle Cafe, 418 E 5th St; 50309 515-280-7723

Bookstores: General

♀ ○ Borders Book Shop, 1821 22nd St, West Des Moines; 50265 515-223-1620

♀ ☆ ♿ Peace Resource Center, 4211 Grand Ave; 50312 Mon-Fri 9.30am-4pm.

Business, Financial & Secretarial

♀ ● Schmacker, John, CPA, 857 17th St; 50314-1127 515-282-7925

Community Centers (see also Women's Centers)

♀ ★ ♿ Gay & Lesbian Resource Center, PO Box 7008; 50309-7008 / 4211 Grand Ave; 50312 515-279-2110; 515-277-1454 Gay & Lesbian Information Line; Pub *OUTword*.

Counseling/Therapy: Private

♀ ● Central Iowa Gender Institute, PO Box 12164; 50312-9403 515-277-7754

Erotica (Printed, Visual, Equipment)

♀ ○ Bachelor's Library, 2020 E Euclid; 50317 515-266-7992

♀ ○ Gallery Bookstore, 1114 Walnut St; 50309-3426 515-245-9164

Funding: Endowment, Fundraising, Scholarship

♀ ★ Only With Love, PO Box 21036; 50321-9401 515-282-7158 "We raise funds for medical emergencies of all kinds in the Gay/Lesbian community."

Gifts, Cards, Pride & Novelty Items

♀ ● ♿ The Other Side, 414 E 5th St; 50309 515-280-6076

Organizations/Resources: Family

♀ ♿ PFLAG, c/o GLRC, PO Box 7008; 50309-7008 515-274-4851 Mon-Fri 9.30am-4pm. "Parents, Families & Friends of Lesbians & Gays."

Organizations/Resources: Sexual Focus (Leather, S/M, etc) & Safe Sex Promotion

♂ ★ Cornhaulers L & L Club, PO Box 632; 50303-0632

Organizations/Resources: Social, Recreational & Support Groups (see also Sport/Dance/Outdoor)

♀ Women's Cultural Collective, PO Box 22063; 50325-9402 515-277-1454

Organizations/Resources: Student, Academic, Alumni/ae

⚥ ♂ Drake University Alternative Lifestyles, c/o GLRC, Box 7008; 50309-7008 515-226-1428 Mon-Fri 9.30am-4pm.

Performing Arts: Entertainment, Music, Recording, Theater, etc.

♂ Des Moines Men's Chorus, 1900 44th St; 50310-3007 515-255-1654

Religious Organizations & Publications

⚥ ★ ♂ Church of the Holy Spirit Metropolitan Community Church, PO Box 8426; 50301-8426 515-284-7940 Worship 6pm.

Women's Centers

♀ ☆ (⚧) Young Women's Resource Center, 554 28th St; 50312-5222 515-244-4901 "Particular outreach to 12-21 yr old lesbians."

Dubuque

AIDS/HIV Support, Education, Advocacy, Publications

♀ ☆ Dubuque Regional AIDS Coalition, 1306 Main St; 52001 319-589-4181; 800-637-2919

Evansdale

Organizations/Resources: Social, Recreational & Support Groups (see also Sport/Dance/Outdoor)

♂ Gay Men's Support Group, PO Box 3133; 50707-0133 319-233-4766

Fort Dodge

Erotica (Printed, Visual, Equipment)

♀ ○ Mini Cinema, 15 N 5th St; 50501 515-955-9756

Grinnell

Organizations/Resources: General, Multipurpose, Pride

⚥ ★ ♿ Stonewall Coalition, PO Box U-5; 50112 stoneco@ac.grin.edu Mon-Thu 4-11pm; Fri to 6pm; Sat 1-4pm.

Organizations/Resources: Student, Academic, Alumni/ae

⚥ ★ ♿ Stonewall Resource Center, PO Box U-5, Grinnell College; 50112 515-269-3327 srcenter@ac.grin.edu Mon-Thu 4-11pm; Fri to 6pm; Sat 1-4pm.

Iowa City

☎ Les Bi Gayline 319-335-3251

AIDS/HIV Support, Education, Advocacy, Publications

♀ ☆ ♿ AIDS Project, 1105 Gilbert Ct; 52240 319-356-6040

♂ ★ ♿ IA Ctr AIDS Resources & Education (ICARE), PO Box 2989; 52244-2989 319-338-2135

Bars, Restaurants, Clubs, Discos

⚥ • ♿ 6:20 Club, 620 S. Madison; 52240 319-354-2494 *Bd* Thu-Sat 9pm-2am.

Bookstores: General

♀ • Moon Mystique, 114 1/2 East College St #16; 52240 319-338-5752 10am-9pm; Sun noon-6pm.

♀ ○ ♿ Prairie Lights Bookstore, 15 S Dubuque St; 52240 319-337-2681 Mon-Fri 9am-9pm; Sat & Sun to 5pm. Readings Fri & Sun eves: call for info.

♂ ○ ♿♿ University Bookstore, University of Iowa; 52242 319-335-3179

Erotica (Printed, Visual, Equipment)

♀ ○ Pleasure Palace I, 315 Kirkwood; 52244 319-351-9444

Organizations/Resources: Business & Professional

⚥ ★ University of Iowa Lesbian, Gay & Bisexual Staff & Faculty Association, 130 N Madison St; 52242 319-335-1125

Organizations/Resources: General, Multipurpose, Pride

⚥ ★ ♿♿ Lesbian Alliance, Women's Resource Center, 130 N Madison; 52240 319-335-1486

Organizations/Resources: Student, Academic, Alumni/ae

♀ ★ ♿♿ Spectrum, U of Iowa Memorial Union, SAC; 52242 319-354-1703

Switchboards, Helplines, Phone Information

⚥ ★ ♿♿ Les Bi Gayline, Gay, Lesbian, & Bisexual People's Union, Univ of Iowa Memorial Union, SAC; 52242 319-335-3251

Women's Centers

♀ ☆ ♿♿ Women's Resource & Action Center, 130 N Madison; 52245 319-335-1486 Pub *WRAC Newsletter*.

Mason City

AIDS/HIV Support, Education, Advocacy, Publications

♀ ☆ ♿♿ North Iowa AIDS Project, Gloria Billings, 232 2nd St SE; 50401-3906 515-423-0025

Organizations/Resources: Social, Recreational & Support Groups (see also Sport/Dance/Outdoor)

⚥ ★ GLNCI/North Central Iowa, PO Box 43; 50402 Pub *Newsletter*.

Mount Vernon

Organizations/Resources: Student, Academic, Alumni/ae

⚥ Cornell Gay/Lesbian Alliance, Old Sem Cornell College; 52314-1098 319-895-4224

Sioux City

Bars, Restaurants, Clubs, Discos

⚥ • Kings & Queens, 417 Nebraska; 51101 712-252-4167 *BD*

⚥ Three Cheers, 414 20th St; 51104 712-255-8005

Waterloo

AIDS/HIV Support, Education, Advocacy, Publications

♂ AIDS Coalition Of N.E. Iowa, Hawkeye CH. Red Cross PO Box 1680; 50704-1680 319-234-6831

Bars, Restaurants, Clubs, Discos

♀ The Bar Ltd, 555 Eastgate Dr; 50703-5417 319-232-0543

⚥ • Stilettos, 1125 W Donald St; 50703 319-234-6752 *BRDE* 5pm-2am.

Erotica (Printed, Visual, Equipment)

♀ ○ ♂ Danish Book World II, 1507 Laporte Rd; 50702-271 319-234-9340 24 hrs.

Organizations/Resources: Family

♀ ☆ PFLAG/Waterloo, 317 Hartman Ave; 50701-2332 319-234-6531 "Parents, Families & Friends of Lesbians & Gays."

Organizations/Resources: General, Multipurpose, Pride

♀ ★ (♂) Access In Northeast Iowa, PO Box 1682; 50704 319-232-6805 Pub *Access Line*.

Organizations/Resources: Social, Recreational & Support Groups (see also Sport/Dance/Outdoor)

♂ Gentle Healer Ministries, PO Box 1893; 50704-1893 319-233-4766

♂ ★ (?♂) Menz Nite OUT, PO Box 1682; 50704 319-266-3891

♀ ★ (?♂) Women's Collective, PO Box 1682; 50704 319-233-7529

Organizations/Resources: Student, Academic, Alumni/ae

♀ ★ ♂♂ University of Northern Iowa Gay/Lesbian Outreach (UNIGLOW), c/o Counseling Center, SSC 213, Cedar Falls; 50613 319-273-2676

Religious Organizations & Publications

♀ ★ ♂♂ Church of New Hope Metropolitan Community Church, 1218 Stratford Ave; 50701-1957 / Unitarian Society Bldg 3912 Cedar Heights Dr, Cedar Falls 319-234-1981

Wellsburg

AIDS/HIV Support, Education, Advocacy, Publications

♀ Names Project Cedar Valley, Mary Zimmerman Box Q; 50680-0564 515-869-3638

Kansas

State/County Resources

Meeting/Contact Services, Publications, Talklines

♀ ● *Personally Speaking*, PO Box 16782, Wichita, KS 67216-0782 316-269-0913 Fax 316-269-4208

Organizations/Resources: Political/Legislative

♀ ★ Equality Kansas, PO Box 116, Topeka, KS 66601 Pub *Common Ground*. "Loosely organized network of political activists."

Organizations/Resources: Sport/Dance/Outdoor

♂ Kansas Gay Rodeo Association, PO Box 16703, Wichita, KS 67216-0703

Publications

♀ ● *The Parachute*, PO Box 11347, Wichita, KS 67202 316-651-0500; 800-536-6519

Real Estate

♀ ● Community Real Estate Referrals, 800-346-5592 "Free referral to gay/gay-supportive realtor in any USA city/state (including Virgin Is. & Puerto Rico). Sorry, no rentals!"
◆ *Community Real Estate Referrals advertisement back cover*

Religious Organizations & Publications

♀ ★ UCCL/GC (United Church Coalition for Lesbian/Gay Concerns), 5933 Holmes, Kansas City, MO 64110 816-363-6744

Emporia

Travel & Tourist Services (see also Accommodation)

♀ ● Travel Source, 310 E 14th Ave; 66801 316-342-2854; 800-532-9248

Hays

Organizations/Resources: Social, Recreational & Support Groups (see also Sport/Dance/Outdoor)

♂ Western Kansas Gay & Lesbian Services, 600 Park St, Weist Hall; 67601 913-628-5514

Kansas City: see Kansas City, MO

Lawrence

Bars, Restaurants, Clubs, Discos

♂ The Barefoot Iguana, 925 Iowa, Hillcrest Shopping Center; 66044-1836 913-794-1666

♂ ○ Hide Away, 106 N Park St W; 66044-3060 913-841-4966

♂ ○ ♂♂ Teller's Restaurant & Bar, 746 Massachusetts; 66044 913-843-4111 *BR*

Bookstores: General

♂ ○ Terra Nova Books, 920 Massachusetts St; 66044 913-832-8300

Organizations/Resources: Family

♂ ☆ (?♂) PFLAG Lawrence, PO Box 1284; 66044 913-842-0225

Organizations/Resources: Student, Academic, Alumni/ae

♀ ★ ♂♂ LesBiGay Services of Kansas, 410 Kansas Union, Box 13, University of Kansas; 66045 913-864-3091 lbgsok@ukanaix.cc.ukans.edu Weekly meetings; non-students welcome. *The Vanguard.* Non-students welcome.

Manhattan

Switchboards, Helplines, Phone Information

♂ ★ Flint Hills Alliance: Gay, Lesbian, Bisexual Info Line, PO Box 2018; 66502-0023 913-587-0016

Shawnee Mission: see Kansas City Area

Topeka

☎ Gay Rap Telephone Line of Topeka 913-233-6558

AIDS/HIV Support, Education, Advocacy, Publications

♂ ☆ ♂♂ Topeka AIDS Project, 1915 SW 6th St; 66606 913-232-3100

Bars, Restaurants, Clubs, Discos

♂ ○ Classics, 124 SW 8th St; 66603 913-357-1960

♂ ● (♂♂) Expressions, 110 SE 8th St; 66603 913-233-3622 *BDCWP*

Organizations/Resources: Social, Recreational & Support Groups (see also Sport/Dance/Outdoor)

♀ ★ ♂♂ LIFT (Lesbians in Friendship Together), c/o Metropolitan Community Church, PO Box 4776; 66604-0776 / SE Indiana Ave at 25th St 913-232-6196 Meets 3rd Thu, 6pm.

Religious Organizations & Publications

♂ ☆ ♂♂ Metropolitan Community Church/Topeka & Manhattan Outreach, PO Box 4776; 66604-0776 913-271-8431

Switchboards, Helplines, Phone Information

♀ ★ Gay Rap Telephone Line of Topeka, PO Box 223; 66601 913-233-6558

Wichita

☎ **Wichita Gay Info Line 316-269-0913**

AIDS/HIV Support, Education, Advocacy, Publications

♀ ☆ AIDS Referral Services (ARS), 1809 N Broadway St #E; 67214-1146 316-264-AIDS

Bars, Restaurants, Clubs, Discos

♂ • Harbor Restaurant, 3201 S Hillside; 67216 316-681-2746 *B*

♂ • Our Fantasy/South Forty, 3201 S Hillside; 67216 316-682-5494 *DCW*

♂ R & R's Brass Rail, 2828 E 31st St S.; 67216 316-684-9009

♂ • ♿ T Room, 1507 E Pawnee; 67211 316-262-9327 *BdP* Noon-2am.

Bookstores: Gay/Lesbian/Feminist

♀ • ♿ Visions & Dreams, 2819 E Central Ave; 67214 316-686-6700 11am-7pm; Sun noon-6pm. Lesbian networking.

Erotica (Printed, Visual, Equipment)

♀ ○ Adult Entree, 220 E 21st St; 67214 316-832-1816

♀ ○ Plato's Bookstore, 1306 E Harry St; 67211 316-269-9036

♀ ○ T.B's Camelot, 1515 S Oliver; 67218 316-688-5343

Organizations/Resources: Education, Anti-Defamation, Anti-Violence, Self-Defense

♀ ★ (?♿) Wichitans for Advancement through Education (W.A.E.), PO Box 16782; 67216-0782 316-269-0913 noon-10pm.

Organizations/Resources: General, Multipurpose, Pride

♀ ★ Wichita Gay/Lesbian Alliance, PO Box 2845; 67201 316-267-1852

Publications: Directories, Bibliographies, Guides, Travel

♀ Community Directory/KFHD, PO Box 2845; 67201

Religious Organizations & Publications

♀ ★ First Metropolitan Community Church of Kansas, 156 S Kansas Ave; 67211 316-267-1852 Pub *Victory!*.

♀ ☆ Wichita Praise & Worship Center, PO Box 11347; 67202 / 754 S Pattie St 316-627-6270

Switchboards, Helplines, Phone Information

♀ Wichita Gay Info Line, PO Box 16782; 67216-0782 316-269-0913 noon-10pm. Fax 316-269-4208

Kentucky

State/County Resources

AIDS/HIV Support, Education, Advocacy, Publications

♀ ★ ♿ HIV-AIDS Legal Project, 810 Barret Ave #652, Louisville, KY 40204 800-574-8199 Fax 502-574-5497

♀ ★ ♿ KIPWAC (Kentuckiana People With Aids Coalition), 810 Barret Ave, Louisville, KY 40204 502-574-5493 Pub *KIPWAC Update.*

♀ ☆ Northern Kentucky AIDS Consortium, 610 Medical Village Dr, Covington, KY 41017 606-291-0770

Archives/Libraries/History Projects

♀ ★ Kentucky Gay & Lesbian Archives & Library, PO Box 4264, Louisville, KY 40204 502-636-0935

Legal Services & Resources

♀ ☆ ♿ American Civil Liberties Union of Kentucky (ACLU), 425 W Muhammad Ali Blvd, Louisville, KY 40202 502-581-1181

Organizations/Resources: Political/Legislative

♀ ★ (?♿) Kentucky Fairness Alliance, PO Box 1523, Frankfort, KY 40602 606-431-0513

♂ Log Cabin Kentucky, 1556 Alexandria Dr #4B, Lexington, KY 40504

Organizations/Resources: Social, Recreational & Support Groups (see also Sport/Dance/Outdoor)

♂ Bluegrass Bears, PO Box 37001, Louisville, KY 40233-7001

Organizations/Resources: Sport/Dance/Outdoor

♀ ★ ♿ Tri-State Gay Rodeo Association, PO Box 5401, Cincinnati, OH 45205-0401 513-581-2512

Publications

♂ • *The Kentucky Word*, 225 E North St, Tower 1 #2800, Indianapolis, IN 46204 317-579-3075

♂ ★ *The Letter*, PO Box 3882, Louisville, KY 40201 502-772-7570 (Advertising & administration); 502-636-0935 (news)

Real Estate

♂ • **Community Real Estate Referrals**, 800-346-5592 "Free referral to gay/gay-supportive realtor in any USA city/state (including Virgin Is. & Puerto Rico). Sorry, no rentals!"
✦ *Community Real Estate Referrals advertisement back cover*

Religious Organizations & Publications

♀ ★ (?♿) PLGC, 1435 S 3rd St, Louisville, KY 40208 502-637-4734 "Presbyterians for Lesbian/Gay Concerns."

Bowling Green

Organizations/Resources: Student, Academic, Alumni/ae

♂ ★ Western Kentucky University Lambda, PO Box 8335; 42101

Lexington

☎ **Gay/Lesbian Services Organization (GLSO) 606-231-0335**

AIDS/HIV Support, Education, Advocacy, Publications

♀ ☆ (?♿) AIDS Volunteers, PO Box 431; 40585 606-254-2865 Pub *AVOL News.*

Bars, Restaurants, Clubs, Discos

♂ • (♿) The Bar Complex, 224 E Main St; 40507 606-255-1551 *BRDE* Mon-Fri 4pm-1am; Sat after hours to 3.30am. Featuring: Living Room Lounge; Guilded Cage Cabaret; Johnny Angel Discotheque.

♂ • ♿ Crossings, 117 N. Limestone; 40507 606-233-7266 *LWf* 4pm-1.30am.
✦ *Crossings advertisement page 252*

♀ Joe's Fleur de Lys Cafe & Bar, 120 South Upper St; 40507 606-252-7946 *BR*

Bookstores: General

♂ ○ The Hypnotic Eye, 387 Rose St; 40508-3053 606-255-8987

KY: Lexington
Bookstores: General
252
USA
Louisville : KY
Organizations: Political

♂ ○&& Joseph-Beth Booksellers, 3199 Nicholasville Rd; 40503 606-273-2911 Fax 606-272-6948 9am-9pm; Fri & Sat to 10pm; Sun noon-6pm.

Erotica (Printed, Visual, Equipment)

♀ ○ Kentucky After Dark, 933 Winchester Rd; 40505 606-252-0357

♂ • The Rack, 117 N. Limestone (Crossings basement); 40507 606-233-7266 Mon-Sat 4.30pm-1am.

Gifts, Cards, Pride & Novelty Items

♀ ○ & Jesters, 351 W Short St; 40507 606-252-6510

Organizations/Resources: General, Multipurpose, Pride

♀ ★ (?&) Gay/Lesbian Services Organization (GLSO), PO Box 11471; 40575 606-231-0335 Pub *GLSO News*. "Social & support group."

Organizations/Resources: Sexual Focus (Leather, S/M, etc) & Safe Sex Promotion

♂ ★ Bluegrass C.O.L.T.S (Circle Of Leathermen Together), PO Box 12403; 40583 606-233-7266

Organizations/Resources: Student, Academic, Alumni/ae

♀ ★&& UK Lambda, PO Box 647, UK Main Station; 40506 lambda@ukcc.uky.edu

Religious Organizations & Publications

♂ Lexington's Metropolitan Community Church, 1013 Reilus Court; 40517 606-271-1407

Travel & Tourist Services (see also Accommodation)

♀ ○&& Pegasus Travel, Inc, 2040 Idle Hour Center, Richmond Rd; 40502 606-268-4337; 800-228-4337

Louisville

AIDS/HIV Support, Education, Advocacy, Publications

♀ ★&& Community Health Trust, Inc, PO Box 4277; 40204 502-574-5496 Fax 502-574-5497 Pub *Heart Beat*.

Bars, Restaurants, Clubs, Discos

♂ • (&&) The Club, 227-229 E Market St; 40202 502-585-2086 *BDE*

♂ The Connection, 120 S Floyd; 40202 502-585-5752

♀ Magnolia Bar & Grille, 1398 S 2nd St; 40208 502-637-9052 *BR*

♂ Murphy's Place, 306 E Main St; 40202-1216 502-587-8717

♂ • && Sparks, 104 W Main St; 40202 502-587-8566 8pm-4am; disco weekends.

♂ Tad's, 501 E Jefferson St; 40202 502-589-3649

♂ Teddy Bear's, 1148 Garvin Place; 40203 502-589-2619

♂ Tryangles, 209 S Preston St; 40202 502-583-6395 *CW*

♂ ○ (&&) Tynkers Bar & Cafe, 657 West Shipp St; 40208 502-636-9271 *BR*

Bookstores: General

♀ ○ (&) Carmichael's Bookstore, 1295 Bardstown Rd; 40204 502-456-6950

♀ ○ & Hawley-Cooke, Gardiner Lane Center; 40205 502-456-6660

♀ ○ & Hawley-Cooke Booksellers, 27 Shelbyville Rd Plaza; 40207 502-893-0133

Erotica (Printed, Visual, Equipment)

♂ ○&& Blue Movies, Inc., 244 W Jefferson St; 40202 502-585-4627

Legal Services & Resources

♀ ○ Plotnik, Kenneth C., 607 W Ormsby Ave; 40203 502-636-0361

♀ ○ (?&) Stewart, Karen L., 1167 E Broadway #300; 40204 502-589-2986

Massage Therapy (Licensed only)

♂ ○ Koch, George, 502-485-1385 "Licensed massage therapist for men; ask about rooms to rent for travelers."

Organizations/Resources: Disability *Disability Rag*, PO Box 145; 40201

Organizations/Resources: Ethnic, Multicultural

♂ ★ Men of All Colors Together, PO Box 1838; 40201 502-366-2949

Organizations/Resources: Family

♀ ☆ (&) PFLAG, PO Box 5002; 40255-0002 502-329-0229 Meets at First Lutheran Church, 417 E Broadway. "Parents, Families & Friends of Lesbians & Gays."

Organizations/Resources: General, Multipurpose, Pride

♂ ★&& Gays & Lesbians United for Equality (GLUE), PO Box 992; 40201-0992

♂ ★ Pride Committee, PO Box 1504; 40201-1504 "Plans annual march held during Pride Week; other activities supporting the local gay/lesbian/bisexual rights movement."

Organizations/Resources: Political/Legislative

♀ ★&& Fairness Campaign, PO Box 3431; 40201-3431 502-893-0788 Pub *Newsletter*.

Organizations/Resources: Sexual Focus (Leather, S/M, etc) & Safe Sex Promotion

♀ ★ (?⚤) Louisville Nightwings, PO Box 32051; 40232-2051 *PLL*

Organizations/Resources: Social, Recreational & Support Groups (see also Sport/Dance/Outdoor)

♂ ★ Kentuckiana Gay Nudists (KGN), PO Box 3721; 40201-3721 "Nudist/Naturist group."

Organizations/Resources: Student, Academic, Alumni/ae

♀ ☆ ⚤⚤ Feminists at Louisville Presbyterian Theological Seminary, 1044 Alta Vista Rd, LPTS; 40205-1798

♀ ★⚤⚤ GLOBAL (Gay Lesbian or Bisexual Alliance), SAC W301, University of Louisville; 40292 502-852-4556; 502-852-3918

Organizations/Resources: Youth (see also Family)

♀ ★⚤⚤ Louisville Youth Group, PO Box 4664; 40204 502-589-3316

Performing Arts: Entertainment, Music, Recording, Theater, etc.

♂ ★⚤⚤ Voices of Kentuckiana, Inc., PO Box 72; 40201 502-327-4099

Pets & Pet Supplies

♀ ● Pets Palace, 7 Bon Air Manor; 40220 502-452-6912

Publications

♥ ● *The Furies*, 2054 Frankfort Ave; 40206-2029 502-899-3551; 800-899-3582

→ *The Letter*: p.251

Religious Organizations & Publications

♀ ★ ALLEGRO: Alliance of Lesbian & Gay Religious Organizations, PO Box 4034; 40204 502-473-1458

♀ Alliance For Lesbian & Gay Religious Organization (Allegro), PO Box 4034; 40204 502-581-1829

♀ ★ B'Nai Shalom, PO Box 6861; 40206-0861 502-896-0475

♀ ☆⚤⚤ Central Presbyterian, 318 W Kentucky Ave; 40203 502-587-6935 Worship Sun 11am.

♥ ★ Conference for Catholic Lesbians, PO Box 4778; 40204-0778 502-895-0930

♀ ★ ♿ Dignity/Louisville, PO Box 4778; 40204 502-473-1458 "Gay & Lesbian Catholics & their friends."

♀ Integrity/Kentuckiana, c/o St George's Episcopal Church, 1202 S 26th St; 40202 502-584-6658 "Lesbian & Gay Episcopalians & their friends."

♀ ★ (?⚤) Lutherans Concerned, PO Box 7692; 40257-0692 502-897-5719

♀ ★⚤⚤ Metropolitan Community Church/Louisville, PO Box 32474; 40232-0474 / 4222 Bank St 502-775-6636

♀ ☆(⚤⚤) **Third Lutheran Church, 1864 Frankfort Ave; 40206 502-896-6383 Sun 10.45am.**

♀ ☆ ♿ Trinity Lutheran Church, 1432 Highland Ave; 40204 502-587-8395

Newport

AIDS/HIV Support, Education, Advocacy, Publications

♀ Northern Kentucky AIDS Task Force, N. KY Dist. Health Dept, 401 Park Ave; 41071 502-491-6611

Paducah

Bars, Restaurants, Clubs, Discos

♀ ● ♿ Club DV8, PO Box 1657; 42001 / 1200 N. 8th St 502-443-2545 *BDE* 9pm-3am.

♀ ● ⚤⚤ Moby Dick, 500 Broadway; 42001 (5th St) 502-442-9076 *Bdf* 5pm-3am.

Organizations/Resources: Family

♀ ☆ PFLAG, 2942 Clay St; 42001 502-442-7972; 502-575-3325

Religious Organizations & Publications

♀ ★ (♿) Metropolitan Community Church, PO Box 188; 42002 502-441-2307

Louisiana
State/County Resources

Addictive Behavior, Substance Abuse, Recovery

♀ ● (⚤⚤) Pride Institute, 800-54-PRIDE "The nation's only accredited chemical dependency treatment center exclusively for Gay, Lesbian & Bisexual People."

AIDS/HIV Support, Education, Advocacy, Publications

♀ ☆ ♿ NO/AIDS Task Force, 1407 Decatur St, New Orleans, LA 70116 504-945-4000; 504-944-AIDS AIDS Hotline; (800) 99-AIDS-9; Noon-8pm. Pub *Newsline*.

Archives/Libraries/History Projects

♀ ☆ Homosexual Information Center, 115 Monroe St, Bossier City, LA 71111-4539 318-742-4709

Legal Services & Resources

♀ ☆ (?⚤) American Civil Liberties Union: Louisiana Affiliate (ACLU), PO Box 70496, New Orleans, LA 70172 504-522-0617 Fax 504-522-0618

Organizations/Resources: Business & Professional

♀ ★ Gay & Lesbian Business & Professional Association, 940 Royal St, Box 350, New Orleans, LA 70116 504-271-0631

Organizations/Resources: Political/Legislative

♀ ★ Louisiana Electorate of Gays & Lesbians (LEGAL), PO Box 70344, New Orleans, LA 70172 504-525-7117

Publications

♀ ● *AMbush Magazine*, PO Box 71291, New Orleans, LA 70172-1291 504-522-8049 "Gay/Lesbian entertainment & news."

⚥ • *Impact*, PO Box 52079, New Orleans, LA 70152 504-944-6722 Every 2 weeks.

Real Estate

⚥ • Community Real Estate Referrals, 800-346-5592 "Free referral to gay/gay-supportive realtor in any USA city/state (including Virgin Is. & Puerto Rico). Sorry, no rentals!"
✦ *Community Real Estate Referrals advertisement back cover*

Religious Organizations & Publications

♀ ☆ Presbyterians for Lesbian & Gay Concerns/Louisiana, c/o 2285 Cedardale, Baton Rouge, LA 70808 "Presbyterians for Lesbian/Gay Concerns."

Alexandria

AIDS/HIV Support, Education, Advocacy, Publications

♀ ☆ (♿) Central Louisiana AIDS Support Services (CLASS), 824 16th St; 71301 318-442-1010; 800-444-7993; Mon-Fri 8.30am-3pm. "Free anonymous HIV testing."

Bars, Restaurants, Clubs, Discos

♂ E.T.'s Bar & Lounge, 1615 Elliott St; 71301 318-484-9362

⚥ Rumours, 1205 England Dr; 71303 318-448-9371

♂ • Unique Bar & Lounge, 3117 Masonic Dr; 71301 318-445-9622 *BD* Mon-Sat 5pm-2am.

Organizations/Resources: General, Multipurpose, Pride

⚥ ★ Le Beau Monde, PO Box 3036, Pineville; 71361 318-442-3747

Baton Rouge

Accommodation: Hotels, B&B, Resorts, Campgrounds

⚥ • Brentwood House, PO Box 40872; 70835-0872 504-924-4989 Fax 504-924-1738

AIDS/HIV Support, Education, Advocacy, Publications

♀ ☆ (?♿) Friends For Life—Capital Area HIV/AIDS Services, Inc, 4521 Jamestown Ave #13; 70808-3234 504-923-2277; 800-923-2279 (LA only); Fax 504-928-9393

Bars, Restaurants, Clubs, Discos

⚥ Argon, 2160 Highland Rd; 70802 504-336-4900

♀ Buddies, 450 Oklahoma St; 70802 504-364-1191

♀ ○ ♂ Club Scandalous, 5828 Airline Hwy; 70805 504-356-9331 *D* Tue-Sat 6pm-2am.

♂ • George's Place, 860 St Louis St; 70802 504-387-9798 "Some Country Western; occasional entertainment. Private club, but visitors welcome."

⚥ • Hide-A-Way Club, 7367 Exchange Place; 70806 504-923-3632 *BdE* Tue-Sat 7pm-2am.

♂ Mirror Lounge, 111 Riverside Mall; 70802 504-387-9797

Bookstores: General

♀ ○ Hibiscus Bookstore, 635 Main St; 70802 504-387-4264 Call for hours.

Counseling/Therapy: Private

⚥ • ♿ Leinweber & Associates, 5800 One Perkins Place, Bldg #9; 70808 504-768-1694

Legal Services & Resources

⚥ • Bryan, Gail A., 5150 Bull Run Dr; 70817 504-756-3281

♀ • Ham, Chad B., Esq, 1346 Main St; 70802 504-381-7289 Fax 504-387-2267

Organizations/Resources: Social, Recreational & Support Groups (see also Sport/Dance/Outdoor)

♂ ★ KREWE of Apollo/Baton Rouge, PO Box 3591; 70821 504-924-1386

Religious Organizations & Publications

♀ ☆ (?♿) Church Of Mercavah, PO Box 666703; 70896 504-665-7815

⚥ ☆♿ Interweave, c/o Unitarian Church 8470 Goodwood Blvd; 70806 504-926-2291

⚥ ★ (♿) Joie de Vivre Metropolitan Community Church, PO Box 64996; 70896-4996 504-383-0450 Meets Sun 11am at 333 E. Chimes

Travel & Tourist Services (see also Accommodation)

♀ • Good Time Tours, 655 Main St; 70802 504-336-4681 Fax 504-336-4729

⚥ • Good Time Tours, 635 Main St; 70802 504-336-4681 Fax 504-336-4729

♀ • Trips Unlimited, Inc., 9930 Florida Blvd #G; 70815 504-927-7191 Fax 504-927-7194

Harvey: see New Orleans

Houma

Bars, Restaurants, Clubs, Discos

♂ Kixx, 112 N Hollywood; 70364 504-876-9587

Kenner: see New Orleans

Lafayette

AIDS/HIV Support, Education, Advocacy, Publications

♀ ☆ (?♿) Arcadia CARES, PO Box 91446; 70509 800-354-AIDS Fax 318-235-4178 Pub *Arcadia CARES Newsletter*. "Relief, education & support for all HIV-reactive."

Bars, Restaurants, Clubs, Discos

⚥ C'est Le Guerre, 607 N. University Ave 318-235-9233

⚥ Club Majestic, 408 Maurice St; 70550 318-234-7054

♀ Frank's, 1803 Jefferson; 70501 318-235-9217

⚥ Old Blue Note, 115 Spring St; 70501 318-234-9232

Gifts, Cards, Pride & Novelty Items

♀ • ♂ LoveWorks, 3607C Ambassador Caffery Parkway; 70503 318-988-5000 "Lingerie, swimwear, adult toys, gifts, cards, novelties."

Organizations/Resources: Family

♂ PFLAG/Lafayette, PO Box 31078; 70503 318-984-2216 "Parents, Families & Friends of Lesbians & Gays."

Organizations/Resources: Social, Recreational & Support Groups (see also Sport/Dance/Outdoor)

⚥ ★ ♿ Krewe of Apollo de Lafayette, PO Box 53251; 70505-3251

Religious Organizations & Publications

⚥ ★ ♿ Metropolitan Community Church of Lafayette, PO Box 92682; 70509 / 211 Garfield St 318-232-0546

LA: Lake Charles
AIDS/HIV Support

255
USA

New Orleans : LA
Accommodation

Lake Charles

AIDS/HIV Support, Education, Advocacy, Publications

♀ ☆ (♿) Southwest Louisiana AIDS Council, 435 10th St; 70601-6092 318-439-5145; 800-256-5145 outside Lake Charles area

Bars, Restaurants, Clubs, Discos

♂ • ♿ Crystal's, 112 W. Broad St; 70601 318-433-5457 *D* Wed & Sat 9pm-2am; Fri 9pm-4am.

Bookstores: General

♀ ○ Pappy's, 2627 Ryan St; 70601 318-436-2819

Organizations/Resources: Social, Recreational & Support Groups (see also Sport/Dance/Outdoor)

♀ ★ (?♿) Krewe of Illusions, PO Box 1228; 70602

Religious Organizations & Publications

♂ ★ ♿ Metropolitan Community Church, PO Box 384; 70602 318-439-9869

Metairie: see New Orleans

Monroe

Addictive Behavior, Substance Abuse, Recovery

♂ Lambda Recovery, 2121 Justice St; 71201 318-361-3849

AIDS/HIV Support, Education, Advocacy, Publications

♀ ☆ GO CARE, 2121 Justice St; 71201 318-325-1092

Bars, Restaurants, Clubs, Discos

♂ • (♿) Hott Shotz, 110 Catalpa St; 71201 318-388-3262 *BD*

New Orleans

Accommodation: Hotels, B&B, Resorts, Campgrounds

New Orleans

♀ • A Private Garden B&B, 1718 Philip St.; 70113 504-523-1776

♂ • Another Country Guest House, 2026 Burgandy St; 70116 504-949-5384

♂ • Avalon Guest House, 1212 Magazine St; 70130 504-561-8400; 800-783-9977

♂ • Bon Maison Guest Apartments, 835 Bourbon St; 70116 504-561-8498

♀ ○ Bourgoyne House, 839 Bourbon St; 70116 504-524-3621; 504-525-3983
✦ Bourgoyne House advertisement page 255

♂ • Chartres Street House, 2517 Chartres St; 70117 504-945-2339

♂ • (♿) Fourteen Twelve Thalia: A Bed & Breakfast, 1412 Thalia; 70130 504-522-0453
✦ Fourteen Twelve Thalia: A Bed & Breakfast advertisement page 255

♀ • French Quarter Reservation Service, 940 Royal St #263; 70116 504-523-1426

♀ ○♿ The Frenchmen, 417 Frenchman St; 70116 504-948-2166; 800-831-1781

♂ • Guest House Deja Vu, 1835-37 N Rampart St; 70116 800-867-7316; 504-945-5912
✦ Guest House Deja Vu advertisement page 256

♀ • Lafitte Guest House, 1003 Bourbon St; 70116 504-581-2678; 800-331-7971

♀ • **Macarty Park Guest House, 3820 Burgundy St; 70117 504-943-4994; 800-521-2790; "Cottages & rooms rented by the night; continental breakfast; parking & swimming pool."**
✦ Macarty Park Guest House advertisement page 256

♀ • Mazant Guest House, 906 Mazant; 70117 504-944-2662

♀ ○ Mentone Bed & Breakfast, 1437 Pauger St; 70116 504-943-3019

♀ ○ (?♿) New Orleans Guest House, 1118 Ursulines; 70116 504-566-1177; 800-562-1177

♀ • Rainbow House B&B, 2311-2315 N Rampart St; 70117 504-943-5805; 800-783-7004; Fax 504-943-6376

♀ • (?♿) Rober House, 822 Ursulines St; 70116-2422 504-529-4663

♀ • **Rue Royal Inn, 1006 Royal St; 70116 504-524-3900; 800-776-3901; Fax 504-558-0566**
✦ Rue Royal Inn advertisement page 255

♀ • (♿) Ursuline Guest House, 708 Ursulines; 70116 504-525-8509; 800-654-2351; Fax 504-525-8408

♀ ○ Vieux Carre Rentals, 841 Bourbon St; 70116 504-525-3983

Addictive Behavior, Substance Abuse, Recovery

♀ Lambda Center/New Orleans, 2106 Decatur; 70116 504-947-0548

AIDS/HIV Support, Education, Advocacy, Publications

♂ ☆ New Orleans PWA Coalition, PO Box 2616; 70176-2616 504-944-3663

♀ ★ ♿ Project Lazarus, Box 3906; 70177-3906 504-949-3609

Air Conditioning & Heating Services

♀ • Affiliated Air Conditioning & Heating Service, 1837 N Rampart St; 70116 504-945-5912

Bars, Restaurants, Clubs, Discos

Harvey

♂ The Full Moon, 424 Destrehan Ave, Harvey; 70058 504-341-4396

Marrero

♂ • X-is, 1302 Allo St, Marrero; 70072 504-340-0049

Metairie

♂ Angles, 2301 N Causeway Blvd, Metairie; 70001 504-834-7979

♂ • (♿) The Four Seasons / The Out Back, 3229 N Causeway, Metairie; 70002 504-832-0659 *BDCW* 3pm-4am.

New Orleans

♂ Another Corner/Boots, 2601 Royal St; 70117 504-945-7006

♂ • (?♿) Big Daddy's, 2513 Royal; 70116 504-948-6288 *Bd*

♂ • Bourbon Pub & Parade Disco, 801 Bourbon St; 70116 504-529-2107 *BD*

♂ Buffa's, 1001 Esplanade Ave; 70116 504-945-9373 *B*

♀ Bus Stop Bar, 542 N Rampart; 70112 504-522-3372

♂ • Cafe Lafitte In Exile, 901 Bourbon St; 70116 504-522-8397

♂ • (♿) Charlene's/Over C's, 940 Elysian Fields; 70117 504-945-9328 *BD* Tue-Sat open 5pm; Sun open 2pm.

♀ • Clover Grill, 900 Bourbon St; 70116 504-523-0904 *R*

♂ Corner Pocket, 940 St Louis; 70112 504-568-9829

♂ • (?♿) The Country Club, 634 Louisa St; 70117 504-945-0742 *BP* Pool & sundeck 10am-6pm Apr15-Oct15.

♂ • FootLoose, 700 N Rampart St; 70116 504-524-7654 *BEd*

♂ Friendly Bar, 2301 Chartres St; 70117 504-943-8929

♂ ○ Golden Lantern, 1239 Royal St; 70116 504-529-2860

♀ • Good Friends, 740 Dauphine; 70116 504-566-7191

♂ ♿ Heartbreak Bar, 625 St. Philip St; 70116 504-568-1631

♀ La Peniche, 1940 Dauphine St; 70116 504-943-1460 *R*

Beautiful rooms and cottages just 5 minutes from the French Quarter. Private baths, TV, phone, some with kitchens. From $45-89.

♀ ○ ♂ Mama Rosa's Pizza, 616 N Rampart; 70112 504-523-5546 _R_

♂ ○ The Mint, 504 Esplanade Ave; 70116-2017 504-525-2000

♀ Mona Lisa Cafe, 1212 Royal St; 70116 504-522-6746 _R_

♂ • ♂ MRB, 515 St. Philip St; 70116 504-586-0644

♂ Oz, 800 Bourbon St; 70116 504-593-9491

♀ • Petunias Restaurant, 817 St Louis St; 70112 504-522-6440 _R_

♂ Phoenix/Men's Room, 941 Elysian Fields; 70117 504-945-9264

♀ • (♿) **Quarter Scene Restaurant, 900 Dumaine St; 70116 504-522-6533 _R_ Wed-Mon 6am-mdnt; fri & Sat 24 hrs. Closed Tue.**

♂ • Rawhide, 740 Burgundy St; 70116 504-525-8106 _LW_

♂ Roundup, 819 St Louis St; 70112 504-561-8340

♂ • ♂♂ **Rubyfruit Jungle, 640 Frenchmen St; 70116 504-947-4000 _BDEW_**

♀ ○ St Ann's Cafe & Deli, 800 Dauphine; 70116 504-529-4421 _R_ 24 hrs.

♂ ○ TT's, 820 N Rampart St; 70116 504-523-8521

♀ The Wild Side, 439 Dauphine; 70112 504-529-5728

♂ ○ Wolfendale's, 834 N Rampart St; 70116 504-524-5749

♂ Ziggie's, 718 N Rampart St; 70116 504-566-7559

Bookstores: Gay/Lesbian/Feminist

♀ • **Faubourg-Marigny Bookstore, 600 Frenchmen St; 70116 504-943-9875**
✦ _Faubourg-Marigny Bookstore advertisement page 257_

Bookstores: General

♀ ○ Bookstar, 414 North Peters; 70130 504-523-6411

♀ ○ Sidney's Newsstand, 917 Decatur St; 70116 504-524-6872

Bookstores: Recovery, Metaphysical, & other Specialty

♀ • Moore Magic, 1212 1/2 Royal; 70116

Community Centers (see also Women's Centers)

♂ ★ (♿) Lesbian & Gay Community Center of New Orleans, 816 N Rampart St; 70116 504-522-1103 Fax 504-527-5334

Counseling/Therapy: Private

♂ • (♿) **Mayers, Terry F., M.Ed, BCSW, ACSW, 1412 Thalia; 70130 504-524-5973**

♀ • (?♿) Simon, Liz, BCSW, 3500 St Charles Ave #209; 70115 504-899-6024

Erotica (Printed, Visual, Equipment)

♀ ○ Airline Books, 1404 26th St, Kenner; 70062 504-468-2931

♀ ○ Gargoyles Leather, 1205 Decatur; 70116 504-529-4387

♀ ○ (♿) Lenny's News, 5420 Magazine St; 70115 504-897-0005 7am-10pm.

♀ ○ (♿) Lenny's News, 622 S Carrollton Ave; 70118 504-866-5127 8am-11pm.

♀ • ♂ Panda Bear, 415 Bourbon St; 70130 504-529-3593

♂ • (♿) Second Skin Leather, 521 rue St Philip; 70116 (Above & below body piercing salon) 504-561-8167 Fax 504-561-5662 Noon-10pm; Sun to 6pm. "Leather, latex, toys, body piercing."

♀ ○ Tom's Toybox, 907 Bourbon St; 70116 504-523-7827

Food Specialties, Catering (see also Party/Event Services)

♀ ○ ♂♂ Bagel Works, 132 Carondelet St; 70130 504-523-7701 _R_ Mon-Fri 7am-5pm; Sat 8am-3pm.

Gifts, Cards, Pride & Novelty Items

♀ ○ ♂ Flag & Banner Company, 543 Dumaine St; 70116 504-522-2204; 800-779-FLAG; Fax 504-522-2209

♂ ○ New Orleans Gay Mart, 808 N Rampart St; 70116 504-523-5876

Grooming Services

♀ • (?♿) The Bourbon Cuts, Ltd, 909 Bourbon St; 70116 504-523-6848 9am-9pm; Sat to 6pm; Sun noon-5pm. "All hair services including body shaving & waxing."

Health Care (see also AIDS Services)

♀ • ♂ Downtown Chiropractic, 828 Perdido St; 70112 504-525-4502

♀ ○ Wellness Medical Office, 2001 Burgundy St; 70116 504-948-3631

Health Clubs, Gyms, Saunas

♂ Club New Orleans, 515 Toulouse St; 70130 504-581-2402

♂ Midtown Spa, 700 Baronne St; 70113 504-566-1442

Legal Services & Resources

♀ • ♂ Reeder, Jeffrey T., 938 Lafayette #419; 70113 504-558-0433

♀ • (♿) Winder, Jeffrey S., 3456 Cleary Ave #210, Metairie; 70002 504-887-1874 Fax 504-887-1862 "A limited portion of this law practice is devoted to the representation of disable/disadvantaged clients on a sliding scale."

FM BOOKS

The finest in Gay, Lesbian, and Feminist Literature

Faubourg Marigny Bookstore

600 Frenchmen Street
New Orleans, Louisiana 70116

(504) 943-9875

Organizations/Resources: Family

♀ ☆ (♿) PFLAG/New Orleans, PO Box 15515; 70175 504-895-3936; 504-581-2749; *The Banner.* "Parents, Families & Friends of Lesbians & Gays."

Organizations/Resources: General, Multipurpose, Pride

♀ ★ Celebration (Louisiana Conference), PO Box 51877; 70151 504-586-1006 A production of LaGala, Inc.

♀ ★ New Orleans Alliance of Pride, PO Box 52343; 70152-2343 504-943-7455

Organizations/Resources: Political/Legislative

♂ Forum For Equality, PO Box 850096; 70185-0096

♀ ★ (♿) New Orleans Lesbian Avengers, PO Box 791375; 70179-1375 504-365-3069 Pub *Lesbian Avenger Communiqué.*

♀ ☆♿ New Orleans National Organization For Women (NOW), PO Box 72125; 70172-2125

Organizations/Resources: Social, Recreational & Support Groups (see also Sport/Dance/Outdoor)

♀ Acadiana Rainbow Society of the Deaf, PO Box 57166; 70157 504-889-0138 (TDD)

♂ Greater New Orleans Prime Timers, PO Box 71611; 70172-1611 504-525-3299

Organizations/Resources: Student, Academic, Alumni/ae

♀ ★ Gay & Lesbian Alliance at the University of New Orleans, Lakefront, Office of Campus Activities; 70148 504-286-6349

Performing Arts: Entertainment, Music, Recording, Theater, etc.

♂ ★ (♿) New Orleans Gay Men's Chorus, PO Box 19365; 70179 504-245-8884

Piercing & Body Jewelry

♀ • (♿) Rings Of Desire—Body Piercing, 1128 Decatur St; 70116 504-524-6147 Elayne "Angel" Binnie, Master Piercer.

Publications

→ *AMbush Magazine*: p.254
→ *Impact*: p.254

Real Estate

♀ • Renaissance Realty, 1835 N Rampart St; 70116 800-867-7316; 504-945-5912

Religious Organizations & Publications

♀ ★ Grace Fellowship, PO Box 70555; 70172 / 3151 Dauphine St 504-944-9836

♀ ☆ (♿) Task Force for Gay & Lesbian Concerns of the 1st Unitarian Church, 1800 Jefferson Ave; 70115 504-865-7005 (men); 504-822-3278 (women)

♀ ★ UCCL/GC (United Church Coalition for Lesbian/Gay Concerns), 944 Joyce St, Marrero; 70072-2306 504-341-4608

♀ ★ (♿) Vieux Carre Metropolitan Community Church, 1128 Saint Roch Ave; 70117-7716 504-945-5390 Sun 11am.

Travel & Tourist Services (see also Accommodation)

♀ • (♿) Alternative Tours & Travel, 1001 Marigny St; 70117-8414 504-949-5815; 800-576-0238

♀ • Avalon Travel Advisors, 1206 Magazine St 504-561-8400; 800-783-9977; Fax 504-581-1306 sfcf11a@prodigy

Shreveport

AIDS/HIV Support, Education, Advocacy, Publications

♂ ACT-UP/Shreveport, PO Box 44525; 71134-4525

♀ ☆♿ Philadelphia Center, PO Box 44454; 71134-4454 318-222-6633 9am-4pm. "An AIDS/HIV resource center."

♀ ☆♿ YWCA AIDS Minority Community Outreach, 700 Pierre Ave; 71103 318-226-8717

Bars, Restaurants, Clubs, Discos

♂ Cell Block, 1605 Marshall; 71101 318-226-9084 *D*

♂ ○♿ Central Station, 1025 Marshall St; 71101-3746 318-222-2216 *D*

♀ Korner Lounge, 800 Louisiana Ave; 71101 318-222-9796

Gifts, Cards, Pride & Promotional Items

♀ ○ Fun Shop, PO Box 16; 71161 / 1601 Marshall St 318-226-1308 "Gifts, cards, novelties, videos, magazines, costumes, Mardi Gras supplies. Local information."

Gifts, Cards, Pride & Novelty Items

♀ ○ Fun Shop Too, 9434 Mansfield Rd; 71118 318-688-2482

Health Care (see also AIDS Services)

♀ ○♿ Spurlock, William Marcus, MD, PO Box 44454; 71134 / 1534 Elizabeth #440 318-222-8300 "Medical care including HIV/AIDS."

Organizations/Resources: Social, Recreational & Support Groups (see also Sport/Dance/Outdoor)

♂ ★ Krewe of Apollo/Shreveport, PO Box 4918; 71134

♂ ★ (♿) Shreveport Prime Timers, PO Box 44543; 71134-4543 318-868-9574

Religious Organizations & Publications

♀ ★ Victory Fellowship Metropolitan Community Church, PO Box 4200; 71134 318-861-3482

Vinton: see Lake Charles

Maine

State/County Resources

☎ Gay/Lesbian Phoneline 207-498-2088

AIDS/HIV Support, Education, Advocacy, Publications

♀ ☆ ♿ The AIDS Project (TAP), 22 Monument Sq, 5th Flr, Portland, ME 04101 800-851-AIDS; 207-774-6877

♀ ☆♿ Aids Response Seacoast, 1 Junkins Ave, Portsmouth, NH 03801-4511 603-433-5377; 800-375-1144 (NH & ME); Fax 603-431-8520

♀ ☆♿ PWA Coalition of Maine, 696 Congress St, Portland, ME 04102-3371 207-773-8500

♀ ☆ ♿ Waldo-Knox AIDS Coalition, PO Box 956, Belfast, ME 04915 207-338-1427

Conferences/Events/Festivals/Workshops (see also Performing Arts)

♀ ★ Maine Lesbian & Gaymen's Symposium, c/o PO Box 990, Caribou, ME 04736 207-498-2088 TDD/Voice Annual statewide conference since 1973; usually Memorial Day weekend.

Organizations/Resources: Bisexual Focus

♀ ★ Unitarian Universalist Bisexual Network (UUBN), PO Box 10818, Portland, ME 04104

ME: State/County Resources
259
Bucksport : ME

Organizations: Business
USA
Counseling: Private

Organizations/Resources: Business & Professional

♀ Maine Lesbian & Gay Law Association (LeGal), PO Box 443, Portland, ME 04112 207-829-3379

Organizations/Resources: General, Multipurpose, Pride

♀ ★ Apollo Society, PO Box 5301, Portland, ME 04101 207-773-5726 "New England's lesbian & gay atheists, free-thinkers, ethical humanists & Hellenes."

Organizations/Resources: Political/Legislative

♀ ★♂♂ Maine Lesbian/Gay Political Alliance, PO Box 232, Hallowell, ME 04347 800-55-MLGPA (Maine only); 207-761-3732

Publications

♀ ★ *Apex: A Point of Departure*, PO Box 4743, Portland, ME 04112 207-282-8091

Real Estate

♀ • Community Real Estate Referrals, 800-346-5592 "Free referral to gay/gay-supportive realtor in any USA city/state (including Virgin Is. & Puerto Rico). Sorry, no rentals!"
♦ *Community Real Estate Referrals advertisement back cover*

Religious Organizations & Publications

♀ ★ (?♂) Am Chofshi, 207-833-6004 "Maine's Lesbian, Gay & Bisexual Jewish Organization."

Switchboards, Helplines, Phone Information

♀ ★ Gay/Lesbian Phoneline, Box 990, Caribou, ME 04736 207-498-2088 Wed 7-9pm (Maine); 8-10pm (NB)
♀ ★ Mid-Coast Maine Gay Men's HelpLine, 207-863-2728; 207-863-2974; Mon-Fri 6-9pm. "Also youth group information."

Auburn

Counseling/Therapy: Private

♀ • ♂♂ Eule, Norma Kraus, LCSW, 10 Minot Ave; 04210 207-784-8747

Organizations/Resources: Youth (see also Family)

♀ Outright Central Maine, PO Box 802; 04212 800-339-4042

Augusta

Bars, Restaurants, Clubs, Discos

♀ • (?♂) Papa Joe's, 80 Water St; 04330 207-623-4041 *BD* Tue-Sat 7pm-1am. Country Western Wed; restaurant Fri & Sat.

Grooming Services

♀ • Carl's Place Hair Styling, 69 Arsenal St; 04330 207-623-5131

Organizations/Resources: Transgender & Transgender Publications

T ☆ The Outreach Institute of Gender Studies & Fantasia Fair, 126 Western Ave #246; 04330 207-621-0858 Pub *Journal of Gender Studies*.

Religious Organizations & Publications

♀ ★ Northern Lights Metropolitan Community Church, PO Box 2845; 04338-2845 207-453-9750

Bangor

AIDS/HIV Support, Education, Advocacy, Publications

♀ ACT-UP/Bangor, RR 1 Box 1280, Dixmont; 04932-9727 207-947-3947

♀ ☆ ♂ Eastern Maine AIDS Network (EMAN), PO Box 2038; 04402-2038 / Fleet Center, 80 Exchange St 207-990-3626 Mon-Fri 8.30am-4.30pm. Pub *Network News*. "HIV Antibody testing; case management."

Bars, Restaurants, Clubs, Discos

♀ ♂ Riverfront Lounge, 193 Broad St; 04401 207-947-1213

Organizations/Resources: General, Multipurpose, Pride

♀ Downeast Lesbian/Gay Organization (DELGO), Unitarian Church, 126 Union St; 04401 207-942-6503

Organizations/Resources: Social, Recreational & Support Groups (see also Sport/Dance/Outdoor)

♀ ★ Gay/Lesbian Community Network, PO Box 212; 04402 207-862-5907

Organizations/Resources: Youth (see also Family)

♀ ★ Outright, Too, PO Box 212; 04402 207-285-7180

Bar Harbor

Accommodation: Hotels, B&B, Resorts, Campgrounds

♀ ○ (♂) Eastern Bay Cottages, RR1 Box 1545; 04609 207-288-9223
♀ • Manor House Inn, 106 West St; 04609 207-288-3759 Mid-April to mid-November.

Organizations/Resources: Social, Recreational & Support Groups (see also Sport/Dance/Outdoor)

♀ ★ (?♂) Out On MDI, PO Box 367, Southwest Harbor; 04609-0367 207-288-2502 "Social/support groups serving the Aradia National Park/Downeast Maine area."

Belfast

Publications

♀ *Fruits of Our Labors*, PO Box 125; 04915

Boothbay Harbor

New Age: Occult, Wicca, Alternative Healing

♀ • Enchantments, 16 McKown St; 04538 207-633-4992 10am-5pm.

Bridgton

Organizations/Resources: Social, Recreational & Support Groups (see also Sport/Dance/Outdoor)

♂ ★ Mountain Valley Men, Box 36, Center Conway, NH 03813-0036 207-925-1034

Brunswick

AIDS/HIV Support, Education, Advocacy, Publications

♀ ☆ Merrymeeting AIDS Support Services, PO Box 57; 04011-0057 207-725-4955

Counseling/Therapy: Private

♀ • (?♂) Bellville Counseling Associates, PO Box 186; 04011-0186 207-729-8727

Bucksport

Counseling/Therapy: Private

♀ • Poulin, Roberta, MS, LCPC, PO Box 1433; 04416 207-496-6405

Legal Services & Resources
♀ ○ Buchanan, Brenda M., PO Box 1426; 04416 / 128 Main St 207-469-1033

Camden
Real Estate
♀ ○ && Nadeau, Susan, Camden Hills Realty, PO Box 561; 04843 207-338-3266 (also Fax); 800-763-3266

Cape Neddick: see Ogunquit

Caribou
Accommodation: Hotels, B&B, Resorts, Campgrounds
♀ • (&&) The Westman House: A Bed & Breakfast, Box 1231; 04736 207-896-5726

Community Centers (see also Women's Centers)
♀ ★&& NLN Community Services Center of Northern Maine, PO Box 990; 04736-0990 / 398 S Main St; 04736 207-498-2088

Organizations/Resources: General, Multipurpose, Pride
♀ ★ Northern Lambda Nord, PO Box 990; 04736-0990 207-498-2088 (TTY & voice) Pub *CommuniQué*. "Bilingual (French & English); news & information for Northern Maine, Western Brunswick, & Temiscouata, Quebec."

Damariscotta
Bookstores: General
♂ • Laughing Moon Bookstore, PO Box 1084; 04543 /Main St 207-563-5537 Tue-Sat 10am-5pm.

Dexter
Accommodation: Hotels, B&B, Resorts, Campgrounds
♂ • (&&) Brewster Inn, 37 Zions Hill; 04930 207-924-3130 "Bed & breakfast; closed January."

Ellsworth
Accommodation: Hotels, B&B, Resorts, Campgrounds
♂• • Carriage House Inn, 64 Birch Ave; 04605 207-667-3078; 800-669-5795; Fax 207-667-3079

AIDS/HIV Support, Education, Advocacy, Publications
♀ ☆ (&) Down East AIDS Network (DEAN), 114 State St; 04605 207-667-3506

Legal Services & Resources
♀ ○ Kuriloff, Roberta S., 20 Oak St; 04605 207-667-3107

Gardiner
Counseling/Therapy: Private
♀ ○ Molvig, Karen, Psy.D., 103 Brunswick Ave; 04345 207-582-1559 Licensed Psychologist.

Hallowell
Organizations/Resources: Family
♀ ☆ PFLAG, 23 Winthrop St; 04347 207-623-2349; 207-729-0519; "Parents, Families & Friends of Lesbians & Gays."

Harrison
Accommodation: Hotels, B&B, Resorts, Campgrounds
♀ ○ (?&) Maine-ly For You, RR2 Box 745; 04040 207-583-6980 Two Women events held each summer.

Kennebunk
Accommodation: Hotels, B&B, Resorts, Campgrounds
♀ ○ (&) Arundel Meadows Inn, PO Box 1129; 04043 207-985-3770

Legal Services & Resources
♀ ○ & Coles, Ronald R., 62 Portland Rd, PO Box 1028; 04043 207-985-6561

Lewiston
AIDS/HIV Support, Education, Advocacy, Publications
♀ (?&) AIDS Coalition of Lewiston—Auburn (ACLA), PO Box 7977; 04243-7977 207-786-4697

Bars, Restaurants, Clubs, Discos
♂ • Sportsman Athletic Club, 2 Bates St; 04240 207-784-2251

Erotica (Printed, Visual, Equipment)
♂ ○ Adult Bookstore, 314 Lisbon St; 04240 207-784-5961

♂ • Paris Adult Bookstore, 297 Lisbon St; 04240 207-784-6551; 207-783-6677

Lincolnville
Accommodation: Hotels, B&B, Resorts, Campgrounds
♂ ○ Old Massachusetts Homestead Campground, PO Box 5, Lincolnville Beach; 04849 207-789-5135 "Campground; cabins."

♀ • Sign Of The Owl, 243 Atlantic Hwy, Northport; 04849 207-338-4669 "Bed & breakfast; also antique & gift shop specializing in Orientalia & Victoriana."

Lovell
Accommodation: Hotels, B&B, Resorts, Campgrounds
♀• • Stone Wall Bed & Breakfast, RR 1, Box 26; 04051 207-925-1080; 800-413-1080; Open all year.

Ogunquit
Accommodation: Hotels, B&B, Resorts, Campgrounds
♂ ○ (&) Admiral's Inn, PO Box 2241; 03907 / 70 S. Main St; 03907 207-646-7093

♀ • Grenadier Motor Inn, PO Box 903; 03907 / 64 S. Main St 207-646-3432

♀ • The Heritage Of Ogunquit, PO Box 1295; 03907 207-647-7787 "Primarily women; men welcome."

♂• • The Inn at Tall Chimneys, PO Box 2286; 03907 / 94 Main St 207-646-8974

♂• • The Inn at Two Village Square, PO Box 864, 135 US Rte 1; 03907 207-646-5779 April-Oct.

♀ ○ Leisure Inn, PO Box 2113; 03907 / 6 School St 207-646-2737

♀ • Moon Over Maine, PO Box 1478; 03907 / 6 Berwick Rd 207-646-MOON; 800-851-6837; moonmaine@aol.com

♀ ○ Ogunquit House, PO Box 1883; 03907 / 7 Kings Highway 207-646-2967

♀ • Yellow Monkey Guest House, PO Box 478; 03907-0478 / 168 Main St 207-646-9056
♦ *Yellow Monkey Guest House advertisement page 261*

Bars, Restaurants, Clubs, Discos
♀ • (&) Cafe Amore, PO Box 725; 03907 / 37 Shore Rd 207-646-6661 *R*

ME: Ogunquit
Bars, Clubs, Restaurants

261
USA

Portland : ME
Organizations: Transgender

YELLOW MONKEY

GUEST HOUSES and MOTEL UNITS
EFFICIENCIES, T.V.s, AIR CONDITIONING
WALKING DISTANCE TO OCEAN BEACH AND TOWN

Continental Breakfast

VICTOR CAFFESE   **168 Main Street**
PETER WINN   **Ogunquit**
Maine 03907

(207) 646-9056

A Friendly Place to Meet People
Fitness Room & Large Jacuzzi

♂ • The Club, PO Box 856; 03907-0856 / 13 Main St 207-646-6655 *BD* May-Oct Mon-Fri 9pm-1am; Sat & Sun 4pm-1am.

♀ ○ (?⚤) Front Porch Cafe & Garden Club Lounge, Box 2279; 03907 / Ogunquit Square 207-646-3976 *BR*

♀ Maxwell's Pub, 27 Main St; 03907 207-6460-2345

♀ ○ The Old Village Inn, 30 Main St; 03907 207-646-7088

♀ Shore Cafe, 22 Shore Road; 03907 207-646-6365

Clothes

♀ • (⚤) Drop Anchor, PO Box 1991; 03907-1991 / 24 Main St; 03907 207-646-1615 "Clothes, sunglasses, sports watches, etc."

Food Specialties, Catering (see also Party/Event Services)

♀ • Bread & Roses Bakery, Inc., PO Box 1972; 03907 / 28A Main St 207-646-4227

Organizations/Resources: Social, Recreational & Support Groups (see also Sport/Dance/Outdoor)

♀ ★ (?⚤) Out & About, PO Box 695, Cape Neddick; 03902-0695

Old Orchard Beach

Tattoos

♀ ○ ⚤ Mad Hatter's Tattoo Studio, Box 716; 04064 / 50 Old Orchard St 207-934-4090

Pembroke

Accommodation: Hotels, B&B, Resorts, Campgrounds

♀ • Yellow Birch Farm, Box 248A Youngs Cove Road; 04666 207-726-5807

Portland

Addictive Behavior, Substance Abuse, Recovery

♀ Gay/Lesbian Alcoholics Anonymous, c/o Williston West Church, 32 Thomas St; 04102

♀ • ⚤⚤ Intown Counseling Center, 477 Congress St; 04101 207-761-9096 "Alcohol/substance abuse; other addictive behavior; Adult Children of Alcoholics issues & co-dependency."

AIDS/HIV Support, Education, Advocacy, Publications

♀ ★ (?⚤) ACT-UP/Portland, PO Box 1931; 04104-1931 207-828-0566

Bars, Restaurants, Clubs, Discos

♀ • (⚤) Blackstones, 6 Pine St; 04102 207-775-2885

♀ • ⚤⚤ The Chart Room Saloon, PO Box 7435; 04101 / 117 Spring St 207-774-9262 *BCWL*

♀ ○ Limelight, 3 Spring St; 04101 207-773-3315

♂ Moon Dance Club, 425 Fore St; 04101 207-772-1983

♀ • ⚤ Woodfords Cafe, 129 Spring St; 04101 207-772-1374 *R*

Bookstores: General

♀ ○ ⚤ Bookland Of Mill Creek, Mill Creek Shopping Center, South Portland; 04106 207-799-2659

♀ ○ Books Etc., 38 Exchange St; 04101 207-774-0626 9.30am-6pm; summers & Dec to 9pm; Sun noon-5pm.

♀ • Drop Me A Line, 615-A Congress St; 04101 207-773-5547 Mon-Sat 10am-6pm; Sun to 5pm.

Convenience Stores

♀ • ⚤ Gervais & Sun, 133 Spring St; 04101 207-874-6426

Counseling/Therapy: Private

♀ ○ (⚤) Watson, Jacob, M.A., 491 Stevens Ave; 04103 207-870-8656 "Licensed Clinical Professional Counselor, specializing in loss & transition. (Senior staff member: Elisabeth Kubler-Ross Center.)"

♀ • Womanspace Counseling Center, 236 Park Ave; 04102 207-871-0377

♀ ○ Zavasnik, Victoria, PH.D, Back Cove Counseling Center 527 Ocean Ave; 04103 207-775-6598

Erotica (Printed, Visual, Equipment)

♀ ○ (⚤) Congress Book Shop, 668 Congress St; 04101 207-774-1377

♀ ○ ⚤ Treasure Chest, 2A Pine St; 04101 207-772-2225

Florists (see also Gardening)

♀ • (⚤) I Love Flowers, 320 Fore St; 04101 207-774-5882

Legal Services & Resources

♀ • Lavin, Paul, Esq, PO Box 443; 04112 / 22 Monument Sq #206 207-772-4114

Organizations/Resources: Education, Anti-Defamation, Anti-Violence, Self-Defense

♀ ★⚤⚤ The Matlovich Society, PO Box 942; 04104 "Cultural organization: discussions; presentations."

Organizations/Resources: Family

♀ ☆ ⚤ PFLAG Portland Chapter, PO Box 8742; 04104 207-774-3441 "Parents, Families & Friends of Lesbians & Gays."

Organizations/Resources: General, Multipurpose, Pride

♀ ★ Portland Roundup, PO Box 5245 Stn A; 04101-5245

Organizations/Resources: Military/Veterans

♀ Matlovich Society, PO Box 942; 04101 207-773-4444

Organizations/Resources: Sexual Focus (Leather, S/M, etc) & Safe Sex Promotion

♀ Harbor Masters, Inc., PO Box 4044; 04101

Organizations/Resources: Sport/Dance/Outdoor

♀ ★ (?⚤) Time Out, PO Box 11502; 04104 207-871-9940

Organizations/Resources: Student, Academic, Alumni/ae

♀ ★ (⚤⚤) Alliance for Sexual Diversity, USM, 96 Falmouth St; 04103-4899 207-874-6956

Organizations/Resources: Transgender & Transgender Publications

T ☆ (?⚤) Transsupport, Box 17622; 04101

Organizations/Resources: Youth (see also Family)

♂ Outright: Portland Alliance of Gay & Lesbian Youth, PO Box 5077; 04101-0777 207-774-TALK

Publications

♂ *Community Pride Reporter*, 142 High St #634; 04101 207-879-1342

Religious Organizations & Publications

♂ ★ (?♿) Dignity, PO Box 8113; 04104 "Gay & Lesbian Catholics & their friends."

♀ ☆ Feminist Spiritual Community, PO Box 3771; 04104 207-797-9217

♂ ★ Metropolitan Community Church/Portland, PO Box 1671; 04104

Travel & Tourist Services (see also Accommodation)

♀ ● Adventure Travel, Inc, PO Box 6610, Scarborough; 04070-6610 207-885-5060; 800-234-6252

Women's Centers

♀ ☆ (?♿) U.S.M. Women's Forum, 86 Winslow St; 04103 207-874-6593 Pub *Herizons*.

South Harpswell

Potteries

♀ ● (♿) Ash Cove Pottery, Ash Cove Rd; 04079 207-833-6004

Stonington

Accommodation: Hotels, B&B, Resorts, Campgrounds

♀ ● Sea Gnomes' Home, PO Box 33; 04681 / Church St 207-367-5076 June thru Sept.

Tenants Harbor

Accommodation: Hotels, B&B, Resorts, Campgrounds

♀ ○ (?♿) **East Wind Inn**, Box 149; **04860-0149 207-372-6366; 800-241-VIEW**

Waterville

Erotica (Printed, Visual, Equipment)

♀ ○ Priscilla's, 18 Water St; 04901 207-873-2774

♀ ○ Treasure Chest II, 5 Sanger Ave; 04901-4851 207-873-7411

Organizations/Resources: Student, Academic, Alumni/ae

♂ ★♂♿ The Bridge: Colby's Gay/Lesbian/Bisexual/Straight Coalition, c/o Stu-A, Colby College; 04901 207-872-3000

Maryland

State/County Resources

Addictive Behavior, Substance Abuse, Recovery

♂ ● (♿♿) **Pride Institute, 800-54-PRIDE** "The nation's only accredited chemical dependency treatment center exclusively for Gay, Lesbian & Bisexual People."

Legal Services & Resources

♂ ★♂♿ GAYLAW Attorney Referral, 202-842-7732

Organizations/Resources: Business & Professional

→ Lambda Labor: p.208

Organizations/Resources: Military/Veterans

♂ ★ (♿) Gay & Lesbian Veterans of Maryland, 211 E Lombard St #169, Baltimore, MD 21218 410-889-4158 Gay, Lesbian & Bisexual Veterans Association

Organizations/Resources: Political/Legislative

♂ ★ (?♿) Free State Justice Campaign, PO Box 13221, Baltimore, MD 21203 410-837-7282 "Advocates for civil rights for lesbians, gays & bisexuals within Maryland."

Organizations/Resources: Sport/Dance/Outdoor

♂ ★ (?♿) Atlantic States Gay Rodeo Association, PO Box 31208, Bethesda, MD 20824 202-298-0928

Real Estate

♂ ● **Community Real Estate Referrals, 800-346-5592 "Free referral to gay/gay-supportive realtor in any USA city/state (including Virgin Is. & Puerto Rico). Sorry, no rentals!"**
✦ *Community Real Estate Referrals advertisement back cover*

Religious Organizations & Publications

♂ ★ SDA Kinship International, Region 2, 12221 Berry St, Wheaton, MD 20902 301-248-1299 hjohnson@usuhsb.usuhs.mil

Annapolis

Accommodation: Hotels, B&B, Resorts, Campgrounds

♀ ○ One-Four-Four Bed & Breakfast, 144 Prince George St; 21401 410-268-8053

♀ ○ William Page Inn, 8 Martin St; 21401 410-626-1506 Bed & breakfast.

AIDS/HIV Support, Education, Advocacy, Publications

♂ Positive Seekers, PO Box 426, Crownsville; 21032 410-849-2530

Erotica (Printed, Visual, Equipment)

♂ ○ 2020, 2020-C West St; 21401 410-266-0514

Organizations/Resources: Family

♂ PFLAG/Annapolis, PO Box 722, Crownsville; 21032 410-849-FLAG "Parents, Families & Friends of Lesbians & Gays."

Baltimore Area

☎ Gay & Lesbian Switchboard 410-837-8888

Accommodation: Hotels, B&B, Resorts, Campgrounds

Baltimore

♀ ○ Abacrombie Badger B&B, 58 W Biddle St, Baltimore; 21201 410-637-1660 Fax 410-244-8415 *B*

♀ ○ Chez Claire, 17 W Chase St, Baltimore; 21201 410-837-0996; 410-685-4666; "Bed & breakfast."

♀ ○ **Mr. Mole Bed & Breakfast, 1601 Bolton St, Baltimore; 21217 410-728-1179**

Addictive Behavior, Substance Abuse, Recovery

♂ ★ Chase & Brexton Gay Group AA, 241 W Chase St, Baltimore; 21201 410-837-5445; 410-837-8888; Mon 8.30pm: Beginners.

♂ ★ ♂ Live & Let Live Group/Alcoholics Anonymous, St Vincent De Paul Church, 120 N. Front St (enter on Fallsway) Sat 8.30pm.

♂ ★ Narcotics Anonymous, Meet Tue 8pm at Mt Vernon Methodist Church, Charles & Monument Sts.

♂ ★ Narcotics Anonymous, 410-837-5445; 410-837-8888; Meet Sun 11.30am at GLCCB, 241 W Chase St, 2nd flr.

AIDS/HIV Support, Education, Advocacy, Publications

♀ ★ AIDS Action Baltimore, Inc, 2105 N Charles St, Baltimore; 21218 410-837-AIDS

♂ ☆ AIDS Interfaith Residential Services, 5000 York Rd, Baltimore; 21212-4437 410-433-1109 "Housing."

♀ ☆♿ AIDS Legislative Committee, PO Box 1322, Baltimore; 21203-1322 410-889-2885

♀ ★ ♿ The Chase-Brexton Clinic, 101 W Read St #211, Baltimore; 21201 410-837-2050 Mon-Thu 9am-9pm; Fri to 4pm. "HIV counseling, testing, primary health care, home visits, research, etc; STD clinic; women's gyn self-help clinic; psychotherapy services & support groups."

♀ ☆ Moveable Feast, PO Box 38445, Baltimore; 21231 410-243-4604 (meals delivery service)

♀ ☆ (♿) People With AIDS Coalition, 101 Read St #808, Baltimore; 21201 410-625-1677 Pub *News & Views*.

Art & Photography (see also Graphic Design)

♀ ● Moonlight Studios, 1728 Langford Rd, Baltimore; 21207 410-944-0006 Fax 410-944-1602 "Photography; black & white film processing & custom printing; illustration; desktop typesetting & graphic design."

Bars, Restaurants, Clubs, Discos

Baltimore

♀ ● Allegro, 1101 Cathedral St, Baltimore; 21201 410-837-3906 "Men's Night Tue; Women's Night Thu."

♂ ● Baltimore Eagle, 2022 N Charles St, Baltimore; 21218 (enter on 21st St) 410-82-EAGLE *L*

♀ ● Carole's Crow's Nest, 834 S Luzerne, Baltimore; 21224 410-732-4373

♀ Central Station, 1001 N Charles St, Baltimore; 21201 410-752-7133

♂ ● Club Atlantis, 615 Fallsway, Baltimore; 21202 (nr Centre St) 410-727-9099 *BE* Tue-Sun 4pm-2am (call ahead for Mon openings).

♀ ● (♿) Club Mardi Gras, 228 Park Ave, Baltimore; 21201 410-625-9818

♂ ● Drinkery, 205 W Read St, Baltimore; 21201 410-669-9820

♀ ○ The Hippo, 1 W Eager St, Baltimore; 21201 410-547-0069 *D*

♂ ● Lynn's of Baltimore, 774 Washington Blvd, Baltimore; 21230 410-727-8924 Mon-Fri 4pm-1am; Sat 11am-1am.

♂ ● P.T. Max, 1735 Maryland Ave, Baltimore; 21201 410-539-6965 *BDRL*

♂ ○ Park Sportsman's Bar, 412 Park Ave, Baltimore; 21201 410-727-8935

♀ ● Port In A Storm, 4330 E Lombard St, Baltimore; 21224 410-732-5608

♂ ○ Senator, 614 N Howard St, Baltimore; 21201 410-727-9620

♀ ● ♿ Stagecoach Saloon & Restaurant, 1003 N Charles St, Baltimore; 21201 410-547-0107; 800-394-1779; Fax 410-547-0461 *BRECW* 4pm-2am; Sun 11.30am-2am.
✦ *Stagecoach Saloon & Restaurant advertisement page 263*

♂ ○ Unicorn, 2218 Boston St, Baltimore; 21224

♀ Zig Zags, 3717 Eastern Ave, Baltimore; 21200 410-522-3168

♀ ● Zippers, 511 Gorsuch Ave, Baltimore; 21218 410-366-9006 11am-2am; Sat & Sun noon-2am. "Neighborhood gay bar."

Bookstores: Gay/Lesbian/Feminist

♀ ● ♿ Lambda Rising, 241 W Chase St, Baltimore; 21201 410-234-0069 10am-1o0m. "Gay & Lesbian literature, music, videotapes, cards, jewelry, etc; Women's Studies; etc. Work by local artists; readings & signings by local & national authors."

♀ ● ♿♿ Lammas Books, (old 31st St Bookstore) 1001 Cathedral St, Baltimore; 21201-5403 410-752-1001; 800-95-LAMMA (mail order only); 11am-8pm; Thu-Sat to 10pm; Sun to 7pm. "Lesbian/gay, women's & children's literature; greeting cards, videos, video rentals, tapes, posters. Resource center for lesbian/gay & progressive communities."

Bookstores: General

♀ ○ Atomic Books, 229 W Read St, Baltimore; 21201 410-728-5490 Fax 410-669-4179 atomicbk@clark.net

♂ ○ ♿ Mystery Loves Company, 1730 Fleet St, Baltimore; 21231 410-276-6708 Tue-Sat 11am-6pm; Sun noon-5pm.

♂ ○ ♿ Normal's Books & Music, 429 E 31st St, Baltimore; 21228 410-243-6888

Community Centers (see also Women's Centers)

♀ ★ (♿) Gay & Lesbian Community Center, 241 W Chase St, Baltimore; 21201 410-837-5445; 410-837-8888 for events & activities); TDD 837-8529; Fax 410-837-8512

Counseling/Therapy: Nonprofit

♀ ★ ♿ The Chase-Brexton Clinic, 101 W Read St #211, Baltimore; 21201 410-837-2050 Mon-Thu 9am-9pm; Fri to 4pm. "HIV counseling, testing, primary health care, home visits, research, etc; STD clinic; women's gyn self-help clinic; psychotherapy services & support groups."

Counseling/Therapy: Private

♂ • (♿) Chesapeake Psychological Services, 28 W Allegheny Ave #1304, Towson; 21204-3919 410-321-1091

♀ • ♿ Lehne, Gregory K., Ph.D., 4419 Falls Rd, Baltimore; 21211 410-366-0642

Dentists

♀ • Burt, Robert J., DDS, 6201 Eastern Ave, Baltimore; 21224 410-633-5776

Erotica (Printed, Visual, Equipment)

♀ ○ Book Nook, 1825 N Charles St, Baltimore; 21201 410-752-5778

♀ ○ Broadway News Center, 301 S Broadway, Baltimore; 21231 410-342-9590

♀ ○ Le Salon, 18 Custom House Ave, Baltimore; 21202 410-347-7555 Noon-3am; Mon to mdnt.

♥ • Leather Underground, 136 W Read St, Baltimore; 21201 410-528-0991 Mon-Thu 11am-7pm; Fro to 8pm; Sat 10am-6pm.

Health Care (see also AIDS Services)

♥ ★ ♿ Chase-Brexton Health Services, 1001 Cathedral St #3-FL, Baltimore; 21201-5403 410-837-2050 Mon-Thu 9am-8pm; Fri to 5pm. Pub *Celebrate Life*. "HIV counseling, testing, primary health care, home visits, research, etc; STD clinic; women's gyn self-help clinic; psychotherapy services & support groups."

♀ ○ ♿ Effron, Philip, MD, GBMC Physicians Pavilion #615, 6565 N Charles St, Baltimore; 21204 410-339-4650

♀ ○ ♿ Horn, Janet, MD, 10755 Falls Rd #310, Lutherville; 21093 301-582-2644

♀ ○ ♿ Page, Carlos J., MD, 101 W Read St #305, Baltimore; 21201 410-244-8484

♀ • (♿) Westrick, Samuel J., MD, 3100 St Paul St #5, Baltimore; 21218 410-243-5544

Legal Services & Resources

♀ ○ ♿ Dee, Lynda, Esq, 111 N Charles St #500, Baltimore; 21201-3808 410-332-1170 Fax 410-837-0288

♀ • (♿) Fields, Jane, 1210 S Charles St, Baltimore; 21230 410-625-0191

♥ ○ McKenzie, Ann, 772 Washington Blvd, Baltimore; 21230 410-752-2696; 410-728-2600

♀ • Singleton, Ann E., 45 Walden Mill Way, Baltimore; 21228 410-744-2500

Organizations/Resources: Business & Professional

→ Lambda Labor: p.208

♥ ★ (♿) PLUS (Professionals Like Us), c/o GLCCB, 241 W Chase St, Baltimore; 21201 410-837-5445 Fax 410-837-8512

Organizations/Resources: Ethnic, Multicultural

♂ ★ ♂ Black & White Men Together, PO Box 33186, Baltimore; 21218 410-542-6218; 301-336-3767

♥ ★ Womyn of Color of GLCCB, 241 W Chase St, Baltimore; 21201 410-837-8888 Feminist Study, Discussion & Rap Group Fri, 8-10pm, 4th flr.

Organizations/Resources: Family

♥ Gay Fathers Coalition of Baltimore, PO Box 553, Forest Hill; 21030 410-909-0920

♀ ☆ ♿ PFLAG/Baltimore, PO Box 5637, Baltimore; 21210 410-433-FLAG "Parents, Families & Friends of Lesbians & Gays."

Organizations/Resources: General, Multipurpose, Pride

♥ ★ ♂ Baltimore Gay Alliance, 1504 E Baltimore St, Baltimore; 21231-1424 410-276-8468

Organizations/Resources: Political/Legislative

♥ ★ (♿) Baltimore Justice Campaign, PO Box 13221, Baltimore; 21203 410-889-1223

Organizations/Resources: Social, Recreational & Support Groups (see also Sport/Dance/Outdoor)

♥ BLADeaf, Inc., PO Box 22444, Baltimore; 21203-4444 410-523-8396 TTY/TDD

♥ ★ MAGE (Mid Atlantic Gaylactic Entities), PO Box 1008, Sykesville; 21784 Pub *Mage's Crystal*. "Social club with interests in science fiction, fantasy & horror, serving Baltimore's Metro Area."

Organizations/Resources: Sport/Dance/Outdoor

♥ ★ Chesapeake Squares, PO Box 1633, Baltimore; 21203 410-833-3617 *d*

♥ ★ Frontrunners/Baltimore, PO Box 22181, Baltimore; 21203-4181 Write for information.

Organizations/Resources: Student, Academic, Alumni/ae

♥ ★ ♿ Bisexual, Gay & Lesbian Alliance at JHU, SAC, Johns Hopkins U, 3400 N Charles St, Baltimore; 21218 410-516-4088

♀ ★ ♿ The Freedom Alliance of UMBC, University Center Box 26, 5401 Wilkens Ave, Baltimore; 21228-5394 410-455-1901; 410-242-8720; njudki1@umbc8.umbc.edu Pub *Closet Space*.

♥ ★ Towson State University Gay & Lesbian Outreach, 7800 York Rd #404, Towson; 21204 410-830-4007

Organizations/Resources: Youth (see also Family)

♥ ★ (♿) Sufficient As I Am (SAIM), 241 W Chase St, Baltimore; 21201 410-837-5445 "A program for persons ages 14-24, sponsored by the Gay & Lesbian Community Center of Baltimore."

Performing Arts: Entertainment, Music, Recording, Theater, etc.

♥ ★ Baltimore Men's Chorus, PO Box 2401, Baltimore; 21203-2041 410-467-6233

♀ New Wave Singers, PO Box 2012, Baltimore; 21203 410-665-7973

Pharmacies/Health Care Supplies

♀ • Medical Arts Pharmacy, 816 Cathedral St, Baltimore; 21201 410-837-2696

Publications

♥ • *Baltimore Alternative*, PO Box 2351, Baltimore; 21203 410-235-3401

♥ ★ (♿) *BGP (Baltimore Gay Paper)*, Box 22575, Baltimore; 21203 410-837-7748 Fax 410-837-8512

Real Estate

♀ ○ (♿) Lowe, Vincent P., Prudential Preferred Properties, 4635 Falls Rd, Baltimore; 21209 410-771-0099; 800-771-LOWE; Fax 410-433-9095 9am-6pm; weekends by appt.

Religious Organizations & Publications

♥ ★ Adath Rayoot, Jewish Gays of Central Maryland, c/o GLCC Box 22575, Baltimore; 21203 / 241 W. Chase St 410-685-0736

♂ Archdiocesan Gay/Lesbian Outreach (AGLO), 2034 Park Ave, Baltimore; 21217 410-728-2638

♥ • (♿) Dignity/Baltimore, PO Box 1243, Baltimore; 21203-1243 410-325-1519 "Gay & Lesbian Catholics & their friends."

⚥ ★ (?⚫) First New Covenant Fellowship Church, 5 W Fort Ave, Baltimore; 21230-4407 410-523-7789 Worship Sun 2.15pm at Dorguth United Methodist Church, 527 Scott St

⚥ ★ (?⚫) Integrity/Baltimore, c/o Emmanuel Church, 800 Cathedral St, Baltimore; 21201 410-732-0718 Service every 3rd Fri, 7.30pm, followed by pot-luck dinner. Pub *Walking With Integrity.* "Lesbian & Gay Episcopalians & their friends."

⚥ ★ Lutherans Concerned/Baltimore-Washington, Box 23271, Baltimore; 21203-5271 410-225-0563

⚥ ★ ⚫⚫ Metropolitan Community Church of Baltimore, 3401 Old York Rd, Baltimore; 21218 410-889-6363 Services signed for the hearing-impaired.

Switchboards, Helplines, Phone Information

⚥ ★ Gay & Lesbian Switchboard, 241 W Chase St, Baltimore; 21201 410-837-8888; 410-837-8529 TDD; Fax 410-837-8512

Travel & Tourist Services (see also Accommodation)

⚥ • Adventures In Travel, 3900 N Charles St, Baltimore; 21218 410-467-1161

⚥ ○ (?⚫) Mt. Royal Travel, Inc., 1303 North Charles St., Baltimore; 21201 410-685-6633

Women's Centers

⚥ ★ (?⚫) Womonspace, 241 W Chase St, Baltimore; 21203 410-837-5445; 410-837-8888

Beltsville

Travel & Tourist Services (see also Accommodation)

⚥ ★ (⚫) Your Travel Agent Of Beltsville, Inc., 10440 Baltimore Blvd; 20705 301-937-0966; 800-TRAVLER; Fax 301-937-4211 Member IGTA.
♦ *Your Travel Agent Of Beltsville, Inc. advertisement page 265*

Bethesda/Rockville Area

Art Galleries/Archives/Restoration, Supplies, Framing

⚥ Red Capricorn Art Gallery & Coffeehouse, 12222 Rockville Pike, Rockville; 20852 301-230-1429

Bookstores: General

⚥ ○ ⚫⚫ Borders Books & Music, 11301 Rockville Pike, White Flint Mall, Kensington; 20895-1021 301-816-1067 Fax 301-816-8940 9am-11pm; Sun 11am-8pm.

Bookstores: Recovery, Metaphysical, & other Specialty

⚥ ○ ⚫ Miracles Recovery Books & Gifts, 825-B Rockville Pike, Rockville; 20852-1214 301-340-8785

Business, Financial & Secretarial

⚥ • (?⚫) Moss, Natalie B., CPA, PO Box 4294, Rockville; 20850 301-495-9223

Erotica (Printed, Visual, Equipment)

⚥ ○ ⚫ Night Dreams of Maryland, Inc., 825-I Rockville Pike, Rockville, MD 20850 800-AROUSE-U; 301-340-2211; "Large selection of adult toys, creams, lotions, lingerie, menswear, books, gag gifts, etc."
♦ *Night Dreams of Maryland, Inc. advertisement page 431*

Health Care (see also AIDS Services)

⚥ • Timm, Patricia, 301-946-0156 "Physical therapy."

Legal Services & Resources

⚥ • ⚫⚫ Maddox & Shelton, 1335 Rockville Pike #255, Rockville; 20852 301-738-9494

Organizations/Resources: Social, Recreational & Support Groups (see also Sport/Dance/Outdoor)

⚀ Rainbow Relief, PO Box 30191, Bethesda; 20824 301-951-9040

Real Estate

⚥ • ⚫⚫ Barrister Title Services, Inc., 1335 Rockville Pike #255, Rockville; 20852 301-738-9494

Boonesboro: see Hagerstown

Boyds

Religious Organizations & Publications

⚥ ★ ⚫⚫ Open Door Metropolitan Community Church, PO Box 127; 20841-0127 / 15817 Barnesville Rd 301-601-9112 Fax 301-916-0618 Worship Sun 9am, 10.30am & 7pm. "Also alcohol- & smoke-free community center."

College Park

Organizations/Resources: Student, Academic, Alumni/ae

⚥ ★ ⚫⚫ Lesbian, Gay & Bisexual Alliance, University of Maryland, 3107 Adele Stamp Union; 20742 301-314-8467 Pub *LGBA Newsletter.*

Columbia

AIDS/HIV Support, Education, Advocacy, Publications

⚥ ☆ AIDS Alliance of Howard County, c/o Hospice Services, 5537 Twin Knolls Rd #433; 21045 410-313-2333

Health Care (see also AIDS Services)

⚥ • (?⚫) Spivey, Clayton Elizabeth, L.Ac., 8342 Old Montgomery Rd; 21045-2640 410-799-5883 "Traditional Acupuncture."

Organizations/Resources: Social, Recreational & Support Groups (see also Sport/Dance/Outdoor)

⚥ ★ Gay & Lesbian Community of Howard County, PO Box 2115; 21045

Cumberland

Accommodation: Hotels, B&B, Resorts, Campgrounds

⚥ ○ Red Lamp Post, 849 Braddock Rd; 21502 301-777-3262

Fort Meade

Erotica (Printed, Visual, Equipment)

⚥ ○ Annapolis Road Books, 1656 Old Annapolis Rd; 21113 410-674-9414

MD: Frederick
Bars, Clubs, Restaurants
266
USA
Wheaton : MD
Organizations: General

Frederick

Bars, Restaurants, Clubs, Discos

♀ ○ (♂♀) Talons, 5854 Urbana Pike; 21701 301-698-1990 *BDE*

Bookstores: General

♀ ○ Bradley Books, 318 N Market St; 21701 301-662-9886

Organizations/Resources: General, Multipurpose, Pride

♂ ★ Triangles, PO Box 748; 21705-0748 301-694-8933

Gaithersburg

Organizations/Resources: Family

♀ ★ (?♂) GLPC—MW (Gay & Lesbian Parents Coalition), c/o Jim Fagelson 14908 Piney Grove Court; 20878 301-762-4828

Travel & Tourist Services (see also Accommodation)

♀ ● Monarch Travel Center, 9047 Gaither Road; 20877 301-258-0989; 800-800-4669

Hagerstown

Bars, Restaurants, Clubs, Discos

♀ ● Deer Park Lodge, 21614 National Pike, Boonsboro; 21713 301-790-2760 *BR*

Hollywood

Organizations/Resources: Social, Recreational & Support Groups (see also Sport/Dance/Outdoor)

♂ Southern Maryland Social Group, PO Box 616; 20636

Hyattsville

Erotica (Printed, Visual, Equipment)

♀ ○ Silver News, 2488 Chillum Rd; 20782 301-779-1024

Laurel

Bookstores: General

♀ ○ Route 1 News Agency, 106 Washington Blvd; 20707 301-725-9671

Health Care (see also AIDS Services)

♀ ● Brandt, Edna M., Lic.Ac., 657A Main St; 20707-4067 301-953-3413 "Board certified registered acupuncturist."

Organizations/Resources: General, Multipurpose, Pride

♀ ★ (?♂) Gay People of Laurel, PO Box 25; 20725 301-776-6891 "Social & support."

Religious Organizations & Publications

♀ ★ (?♂) Capital Area Interweave (Unitarian Universalists), PO Box 25; 20725 301-776-6891 "Social & support."

Port Deposit

Accommodation: Hotels, B&B, Resorts, Campgrounds

♂ ○ Haviland Hill Bed & Breakfast, 2464 Frenchtown Rd; 21904 410-378-8385

Randallstown

Legal Services & Resources

♀ ● (♂♀) Brager, Elliott A., 8627 Liberty Rd; 21133 410-655-4757 Fax 410-655-4776

Rockville: see Bethesda/Rockville Area

Salisbury

Erotica (Printed, Visual, Equipment)

♀ ○ Salisbury News Agency, 616 S Salisbury Rd; 21801 410-543-4469

Silver Spring

Bookstores: General

♀ ○ ♂ Max Wonder, 9421 Georgia Ave; 20910-1435 301-585-3333

Counseling/Therapy: Private

♀ ○ Briscoe, C. Elaine, LCSW, 8630 Fenton St #224; 20910 301-942-3237

♀ ● Zeiger, Robyn S., Ph.D., CPC, 9920 Cottrell Terrace; 20903 301-445-7333

Funeral Directors/Cemetaries/Mausoleums

♀ ● Rapp Funeral Services, 933 Gist Ave; 20910 301-565-4100

Organizations/Resources: Business & Professional

♀ ★ National Lesbian & Gay Journalists Association, 8258 Bradford Rd; 20901 301-585-5545 Fax 301-585-4234

Travel & Tourist Services (see also Accommodation)

♀ ○ Travel Central, 8209 Fenton St; 20910 301-587-4000

Takoma Park

Bookstores: General

♀ ○ ♂♀ Chuck & Dave's Books, 7001 Carroll Ave; 20912 301-891-2665

Organizations/Resources: General, Multipurpose, Pride

♀ ★ (?♂) Takoma Park Lesbians & Gays (TPLAG), PO Box 5243; 20913 301-891-DYKE "Social group holds monthly potluck brunches; call for details."

Wheaton

Counseling/Therapy: Private

♀ ● ♂♀ Ruth, Richard, Ph.D., 11303 Amherst Ave #1; 20902 301-933-3072

Organizations/Resources: General, Multipurpose, Pride

♀ ★ Gay & Lesbian Interest Consortium of Montgomery County (GLIC), PO Box 2737; 20915-2737 301-231-3550 glicofmc@aol.com

MA: State/County Resources
Addictive Behavior
267
USA
Amherst/Berkshire/Northampton Area: MA
Accommodation

Massachusetts

State/County Resources

Addictive Behavior, Substance Abuse, Recovery

♀ • (⅃⅃) Pride Institute, 800-54-PRIDE "The nation's only accredited chemical dependency treatment center exclusively for Gay, Lesbian & Bisexual People."

AIDS/HIV Support, Education, Advocacy, Publications

♀ ☆ ⅃⅃ AIDS Action Committee, 131 Clarendon St, Boston, MA 02116 617-437-6200; 800-235-2331 in MA; Youth Only AIDS Line in MA (800) 788-1234

♂ ★ HIV Essex County Referral Line, 508-462-6839 "Referrals to HIV & AIDS services, information, & support north of Boston."

♀ ☆ ⅃⅃ Multicultural AIDS Coalition, Inc, 801-B Tremont St, Boston, MA 02118 617-442-1MAC Fax 617-442-6622

Archives/Libraries/History Projects

♀ Sexual Minority Archives, PO Box 402 Florence Stn, Northampton, MA 01060 413-584-7616

Legal Services & Resources

♀ ☆ ⅃⅃ Civil Liberties Union of Western Massachusetts, 39 Main St, Northampton, MA 01060 413-586-9115

♀ ★ (?⅃) Massachusetts Lesbian/Gay Bar Association (MLGBA), PO Box 9072, Boston, MA 02114

Meeting/Contact Services, Publications, Talklines

♀ ★ LINC (Lesbians Inviting New Connections), PO Box 11, Ashby, MA 01431

Organizations/Resources: Political/Legislative

♀ ★ Coalition for Lesbian & Gay Civil Rights, PO Box 205, Boston, MA 02133-0205 617-776-6956

♀ ★ Log Cabin/Massachusetts, PO Box 1465 Back Bay Annex, Boston, MA 02117-1465 617-576-9746 "Republican organization."

♀ ☆ (?⅃) Massachusetts National Organization for Women, 971 Commonwealth Ave, Boston, MA 02215 617-782-9183 Pub *MA NOW Newsletter.*

Organizations/Resources: Social, Recreational & Support Groups (see also Sport/Dance/Outdoor)

♂ ★ Girth & Mirth of New England, PO Box 6041, Boston, MA 02209 617-387-0762 Pub *Newsletter.* "A club for big men & their admirers."

Visit LESBIANVILLE!

Tin Roof Bed & Breakfast

5 minutes from downtown Northampton

413 • 586 • 8665

cats in residence   *non-smoking*

♂ New England Bears, c/o Bill Sanderson 281 Liberty St, Lowell, MA 01851

Organizations/Resources: Sport/Dance/Outdoor

♀ ★ (?⅃) Lavender Country & Folk Dancers, PO Box 2306, Jamaica Plain, MA 02130-0020 800-LCFD-123 ♂ Nongay welcome.

Publications: Directories, Bibliographies, Guides, Travel

♂ • *New England Community Guide/Pink Pages,* KP Media Group, 66 Charles St #283, Boston, MA 02114 617-423-1515 Fax 617-423-7147 kpmedia@aol.com

Publications

♀ • (⅃) *Bay Windows,* 1523 Washington St, Boston, MA 02118 617-266-6670 "Weekly; New England Gay & Lesbian newspaper."

♂ ★ *Gay Community News,* 25 West St, Boston, MA 02111-1213 617-426-4469 (Planning to resume publication Fall 1993)

♀ • *The Lesbian Calendar,* mail to TLC, 351 Pleasant St, Box #132, Northampton, MA 01061 413-586-5514 "Monthly listing of events by, for, about Lesbians in Western New England. Sample with ad rates $3."

♂ • *The Valley Gay Men's Calendar,* mail to TLC, 351 Pleasant St, Box #132, Northampton, MA 01061 413-586-5514 "Monthly listing of events by, for, about Gay Men in Western New England. Sample with ad rates $3."

Real Estate

♀ • Community Real Estate Referrals, 800-346-5592 "Free referral to gay/gay-supportive realtor in any USA city/state (including Virgin Is. & Puerto Rico). Sorry, no rentals!"
✦ *Community Real Estate Referrals advertisement back cover*

Religious Organizations & Publications

♀ ★ Lutherans Concerned/New England, c/o Randall Rice, 108 1/2 Chestnut St, Waltham, MA 02154-0404 617-893-2783

♂ UCCL/GC (United Church Coalition for Lesbian/Gay Concerns), PO Box 403, Holden, MA 01520 508-856-9316

Travel & Tourist Services (see also Accommodation)

♂ • The Travel Wizard, PO Box 614, Provincetown, MA 02657 / 50 Bradford St 800-934-TRIP; 508-487-6330; Fax 508-487-6140 "Full service travel agency specializing in arranging accommodations throughout at guest houses, inns, cottages & motels/ hotels. No fee for services. Open year round."

Acushnet: see New Bedford

Amherst/Berkshire/Northampton Area

☎ Gay & Lesbian Info Services 413-731-5403

Accommodation: Hotels, B&B, Resorts, Campgrounds

Amherst

♀ • The Ivy House Bed & Breakfast, 1 Sunset Court, Amherst; 01002 413-549-7554

Goshen

♀ • Innamorata, PO Box 113, Goshen; 01032 413-268-0300

Hadley

♀ • Tin Roof Bed & Breakfast, PO Box 296, Hadley; 01035 413-586-8665
✦ *Tin Roof Bed & Breakfast advertisement page 267*

Ware

♀ ○ Wildwood Inn, 121 Church St, Ware; 01082 413-967-7798 "Bed & breakfast; 40 minutes from Northampton."

Williamstown

♂ • River Bend Farm, 643 Simonds Rd (Rte 7), Williamstown; 01267 413-458-3121

Addictive Behavior, Substance Abuse, Recovery

♂ ★ (?♂) Gay & Lesbian AA, 175 Wendell Ave, Pittsfield; 01201 413-443-7903 Meets Fri 7.30pm at U.U. Church.

AIDS/HIV Support, Education, Advocacy, Publications

♀ ★ (?♂) Affected By AIDS Support Group, 175 Wendell Ave, Pittsfield; 01201 413-443-7905; 413-442-1838

♀ ☆♂♂ AIDS Allies, 93 Mill Park, Springfield; 01108 413-747-5144

♀ ☆ AIDS Information Collective, Hampshire College, Amherst; 01002 413-549-4600

♀ ★♂♂ American Red Cross/Berkshire AIDS Coalition, 480 West St, Pittsfield; 01201 413-442-1506; 800-332-2030

Bars, Restaurants, Clubs, Discos

Chicopee

♂ Eclipse, 13 View St, Chicopee; 01020 413-534-3065

♀ Our Hideaway, 16 Bolduc Lane, Chicopee; 01013 413-534-6436

Northampton

♀ • ♂ North Star Seafood Bar & Restaurant, 25 West St, Northampton; 01060 413-586-9409 *BR*

Springfield

♂ David's, 397 Dwight St, Springfield; 01103 413-734-0566

♂ Just Friends, 23 Hamden St, Springfield; 01103 413-781-5878

♂ ○ The Pub, 382 Dwight St, Springfield; 01103 413-734-8123

♂ Speakeasy's, 300 Washington St, Springfield; 01103 413-746-0203

Bookstores: Gay/Lesbian/Feminist

♀ ★ ♂ Food For Thought Books, 106 N Pleasant St, Amherst; 01002-1703 413-253-5432

♀ • ♂♂ Lunaria Feminist Bookstore, 90 King St, Northampton; 01060 413-586-7851 (voice & TTY/TDD) Tue, Wed, Fri 10am-6pm; Thu to 8pm; Sat 10am-5pm; Sun noon-5pm; closed Mon.

Bookstores: General

♀ ○♂♂ Beyond Words Bookshop, 189 Main St, Northampton; 01060 413-586-6304 9.30am-9pm; Fri & Sat to 10.30pm; Sun noon-5pm.

Bookstores: Recovery, Metaphysical, & other Specialty

♀ • ♂♂ Oasis, 63 Main St, Amherst; 01002 413-256-4995 "Tools for Transformation."

Broadcast Media

♀ ☆♂♂ Women's Media Project, WMUA, 102 Campus Center, Univ. Mass, Amherst; 01003 413-545-2876

Counseling/Therapy: Nonprofit

♂ ★ (?♂) Lesbian, Bisexual, & Gay Men's Counseling Collective, 433 Student Union, Box 41, UMass Amherst, Amherst; 01003 / Room 406-G 413-545-2645 "Free lending library."

Counseling/Therapy: Private

♀ • ♂♂ Lambda Resources for Women & Men, 16 Center St #503, 516, Northampton; 01060 413-586-2590; 413-586-7377

♀ ○ LifeCourse Counseling Center, Amherst & Springfield 413-252-2822

Erotica (Printed, Visual, Equipment)

♀ ○ Springfield Book & Video, 292 Worthington St, Springfield; 01103 413-781-6833

Food Specialties, Catering (see also Party/Event Services)

♀ • **Indigo Coffee Roasters, Inc., 660 Riverside Dr, Northampton; 01060 413-586-4537; 800-447-5450; Fax 413-586-0019 "Small-batch, wholesale gourmet coffee roaster."**

Gifts, Cards, Pride & Novelty Items

♂ • ♂ Pride & Joy, 20 Crafts Ave, Northampton; 01060 413-585-0683

♀ • Wild Iris, 7 Old South St, Northampton; 01060 413-586-7313

Insurance (see also Insurance Benefits/Viaticals)

♀ • Landis, Maureen, Woodward & Grinnell Insurance, PO Box 538, Northampton; 01061-0538 413-369-4761

Massage Therapy (Licensed only)

♂ • ♂ Connective Tissue Therapy, 25 Main St #211, Northampton; 01060 413-586-2981

Moving/Transportation/Storage

♀ • Stuff-It Storage, 222 Russel St (Rte 9) "Self-storage."

Organizations/Resources: Business & Professional

♂ G.A.L.E. Network, PO Box 930, Amherst; 01004-0930 413-253-3054

♂ ★ Northampton Area Lesbian & Gay Business Guild, PO Box 593, Northampton; 01061 413-585-0683

Organizations/Resources: Education, Anti-Defamation, Anti-Violence, Self-Defense

♂ ★♂♂ Face to Face: A Gay, Lesbian & Bisexual Speakers Bureau, PO Box 118, Amherst; 01004-0118 413-253-3054

Organizations/Resources: Family

♀ ☆♂♂ PFLAG Williamstown/Berkshire, 29 Stringer Ave, Lee; 01238 413-243-2382 Pub *Newsletter.* "Parents, Families & Friends of Lesbians & Gays."

♀ ☆ ♂ PFLAG/Pioneer Valley, PO Box 55, South Hadley; 01075-0055 413-532-4883 "Parents, families, spouses & friends of lesbians, gays, bisexuals."

♂ ★ (?♂) *Valuable Families*, PO Box 111, Williamsburg; 01096

Organizations/Resources: General, Multipurpose, Pride

♂ ★ (♂♂) Valley Gay Alliance, PO Box 80051, Springfield; 01138-0051 413-736-2324 Meets 7.30pm, 1st Tue, at U.U. Church, 245 Porter Lake Dr, Springfield. Pub *VGA Gayzette.*

Organizations/Resources: Political/Legislative

♂ ★ (?♂) Lesbian/Gay/Bisexual Political Alliance of Western Massachusetts, mail to LGBPAWM, PO Box 4436, Springfield; 01101 Fax 413-585-0683

Organizations/Resources: Sexual Focus (Leather, S/M, etc) & Safe Sex Promotion

♀ ★ ♂ Shelix, PO Box 416 Florence Stn, Northampton; 01060-0416 Pub *Newsletter.* "We support safe, centered, consensual & loving woman-focused S/M for Lesbians, bisexual women, & transvestites & transexuals."

Organizations/Resources: Social, Recreational & Support Groups (see also Sport/Dance/Outdoor)

♂ Greater Springfield Gay Nudists, mail to WILL, 1981 Memorial Dr #146, Chicopee; 01020

♂ Kaleidoscope, PO Box 1004, Williamsburg; 01096

MA: Amherst/Berkshire/Northampton Area
Organizations: Social & Support

269
USA

Boston Area: MA
Accommodation

♀ ★ (?占) Myriad Network, PO Box 288, Williamstown; 01267-0288 Pub *Myriad Network News.* "Networking for social, support, political & economic purposes; all welcome, including transgender."

Organizations/Resources: Sport/Dance/Outdoor

♀ ★ Venture Out, PO Box 60271, Northampton; 01060 413-584-4781 Pub *Venture Out Newsletter.* "Non-competitive outdoor social events."

Organizations/Resources: Student, Academic, Alumni/ae

♀ ★ Bi-the-Way, SU Box 3223, Williams College, Williamstown; 01267

♀ ★ (?占) Gay, Lesbian, & Allied Student Society, North Adams State College, North Adams; 01247 413-664-4511

♀ ★ Hampshire College Queer Community Alliance, Hampshire College Box 5001, Amherst; 01002-5001 413-549-4600 "Call for details of weekly meetings, etc."

♀ ★ (?占) Lesbian, Bisexual, Gay Alliance (LBGA), Student Union Box 66, University of Massachusetts, Amherst; 01003 413-545-0154

♀ ★ Program for Gay/Lesbian & Bisexual Concerns, UMASS, Crampton House/SW, Amherst; 01003-1799 413-545-4824 (413) 54-LAMDA pglbc@stuaf.umass.edu

♀ ★ (?占) Smith College Lesbian Bisexual Alliance, Stoddard Annex Smith College, Northampton; 01063 413-585-4907

♀ Springfield Technical College GLBA, PO Box 9000, Springfield; 01101-9000 413-781-7822 x3828

♀ ★ Williams Bisexual, Gay & Lesbian Union, SU Box 3209, Williams College, Williamstown; 01267 413-597-2413

Publications

♀ ★ *Berkshire Alternatives,* PO Box 508, North Adams; 01247-0508

♀ ○ 占占 *Valley Women's Voice,* 321 Student Union Building, U. Mass, Amherst; 01003 413-545-2436

Real Estate

♀ ● Hutchins Realty, 43 Gothic St, Northampton; 01060 413-586-4663 Fax 413-586-5550

♂ ○ 占占 Town & Country Realtors, 90 Conz St, Northampton; 01060 413-585-0400 Fax 413-585-8774

Religious Organizations & Publications

♀ ★ 占 Integrity/Western Massachusetts, PO Box 5051, Springfield, MA 01101-5051 413-737-4786 Meets last Sun of month, 7pm, Grace Church, Amherst. "Lesbian & Gay Episcopalians & their friends."

Switchboards, Helplines, Phone Information

♀ ★ Community Prideline, 413-584-4848

♀ ★ Gay & Lesbian Info Services, PO Box 80891, Springfield; 01138-0891 413-731-5403

Travel & Tourist Services (see also Accommodation)

♂ ● Adventura Travel, 122 Main St, Northampton; 01060 413-584-9441

♂ ● Adventura Travel, 233 N Pleasant St, Amherst; 01002 413-549-1256

Women's Centers

♀ ☆ (?占) Everywoman's Center, Wilder Hall, U Mass, Amherst; 01003 413-545-0883

♀ ☆ (?占) Women's Services Center, 146 1st St, Pittsfield; 01201 413-499-2425; 413-443-0089 hotline 24 hrs.; Pub *Newsletter.*

Arlington: see Boston Area

Ashfield
Antiques & Collectables

♂ ● Blue Jet Antique Toys, Ranney Corner Rd; 01330 413-628-3213

Ashland
Organizations/Resources: Sport/Dance/Outdoor

♂ ★ Triangle Scuba Dive Club, PO Box 191; 01721-0191 508-881-5019 tridive@world.std.com

Attleboro
Organizations/Resources: Social, Recreational & Support Groups (see also Sport/Dance/Outdoor)

♀ ★ (?占) Triborough Triangles, PO Box 776, Norton; 02766-0776

Barre
Accommodation: Hotels, B&B, Resorts, Campgrounds

♂ ● The Jenkins House Bed & Breakfast Inn, PO Box 779; 01005 / 7 West St, Barre Common/Rt 122 508-355-6444 *R*

Berkshire: see Amherst/Berkshire/Northampton Area

Boston Area
☎ Boston Gay & Lesbian Helpline 617-267-9001

Accommodation: Hotels, B&B, Resorts, Campgrounds
Boston

♂ ● Amsterdammertje B&B, Box 865, Boston; 02203 / 126 Darrow St, Quincy 617-471-8454 (also Fax) "At the ocean; 15 mins to downtown. No smoking."

♂ ○ 占占 The Buckminster, 645 Beacon St, Boston; 02215 617-236-7050; 800-727-2825; *R*

♂ ● (?占) Chandler Inn, 26 Chandler St (at Berkeley), Boston; 02116 617-482-3450; 800-842-3450; *B*
♦ *Chandler Inn advertisement page 271*

♂ ○ The Farrington Inn, PO Box 364 Allston Stn, Boston; 02134 / 23 Farrington Ave 800-767-5337 Fax 617-783-3869

♂ ○ Four Sixty Three Beacon Street Guest House, 463 Beacon St, Boston; 02115 617-536-1302 Fax 617-247-8876
♦ *Four Sixty Three Beacon Street Guest House advertisement page 269*

⚧ • Oasis Guest House, 22 Edgerly Rd, Boston; 02115 617-267-2262 Fax 617-267-1920
◆ *Oasis Guest House advertisement page 270*

Cambridge

♀ • Bed & Breakfast, 617-876-1501

Dedham

♀ • Iris Bed And Breakfast, PO Box 4188, Dedham; 02027 617-329-3514

Accommodation Sharing/Roommates

⚧ • (♿) The Roommate Connection, 50 Union St, Newton Centre; 02159-2223 and 316 Newbury St, Boston; 02115 800-APT-SHAR; 617-527-4190; 24 hrs.

Addictive Behavior, Substance Abuse, Recovery

⚢ Lesbian Al-Anon, Women's Center, 46 Pleasant St, Cambridge; 02139

♀ ☆ Women's Program of CASPAR, Inc, 6 Camelia Ave, Cambridge; 02139 617-661-1316; 617-661-5855 TTY; 9am-5pm; group sessions eves.

AIDS/HIV Support, Education, Advocacy, Publications

⚨ ACT-UP/Boston, Box 483 Kendall Sq Stn, Boston; 02142 617-492-2887

Architectural Services (see also Home/Building)

⚢ • Mulliken, Jeffrey, Architect, 18 Brattle St, Cambridge; 02138-3728 617-864-8744 Fax 617-661-0613

Bars, Restaurants, Clubs, Discos

Boston

⚨ • 119 Merrimack, 119 Merrimac St, Boston; 02114 617-367-0713

⚨ ○ (♿) Avalon/Axis, 13-15 Lansdowne St, Boston; 02215 617-262-2424 *BD* 9am-2am.

⚨ Bobby's, 59 Canal St, Boston; 02114 617-248-9520

⚨ Boston Eagle, 520 Tremont, Boston; 02116 617-542-4494

⚨ Chaps, 27-31 Huntington Ave, Boston; 02116 617-266-7778

⚧ • ♿ Club Cafe, 209 Columbus Ave, Boston; 02115 617-536-0966 *BRE*

♀ Coco's Lazy Lounge & Dance Club, 965 Massachusetts Ave, Boston; 02218 617-427-7807 Thu-Sat.

♀ ○ Esme, 116 Boylston St, Boston; 02116 (enter 3 Boylston Place) 617-482-7799 (Sundays for Women)

⚧ ○ **Fritz at Chandler Inn, 26 Chandler St (at Berkeley), Boston; 02116 617-482-4428**

⚨ Jacques, 79 Broadway, Boston; 02116 617-426-8902

⚨ ○ Jox/Luxor/Mario's, 69 Church St, Boston; 02116 617-423-6969

⚨ Napoleon Club, 52 Piedmont, Boston; 02116 617-338-7547

⚨ Playland Cafe, 21 Essex St, Boston; 02111 617-338-7254 *R*

⚨ ○ Quest, 1270 Boylston St, Boston; 02115 617-424-7747

⚨ • ♿ Ramrod, 1254 Boylston St, Boston; 02215 617-266-2986 *BLW*

⚨ Sporter's, 228 Cambridge St, Boston; 02114 617-742-4084 *LL* 3pm-2am.

⚨ Venus De Milo, 11 Lansdowne St, Boston; 02115 617-421-9595

Cambridge

⚧ • ♿ Campus/ManRay, 21 Brookline St, Cambridge; 02139 617-864-0400 *BD* Wed=-Sat 9pm-1am. Thu gay men; Sat lesbian; other nights at least 50% gay."

⚨ ○ Paradise, 180 Massachusetts Ave, Cambridge; 02139 617-864-4130

Chelsea

♀ Club #9-11, 9-11 Williams St, Chelsea; 02150 617-884-9533

Bookstores: Gay/Lesbian/Feminist

⚢ • ♿ Crones' Harvest, 761 Centre St, Jamaica Plain; 02130 617-983-9530 10am-7pm; Sun noon-6pm.

⚨ • Glad Day Bookshop, 673 Boylston St, 2nd floor, Boston; 02116 617-267-3010 Fax 617-267-5474 "All available lesbian & gay literature & periodicals."
◆ *Glad Day Bookshop advertisement page 273*

♀ • ♿ New Words, 186 Hampshire St, Cambridge; 02139 617-876-5310; 617-876-3340 TDD; Mon-Fri 10am-8pm; Sat to 6pm; Sun noon-6pm. "Feminist books; includes lesbian titles. Also jewelry, music, cards, & more."
◆ *New Words advertisement page 272*

⚨ • We Think the World Of You, 540 Tremont St, Boston; 02216 (between Berkeley & Clarendon) 617-423-1965 Fax 617-350-0083

Bookstores: General

⚧ ○ ♿ Brookline Booksmith, 279 Harvard St, Brookline; 02146 617-566-6660

⚧ ○ (♿) Globe Corner Bookstore, 1 School St, Boston; 02108 617-523-6658; 800-358-6013; "Books & Maps for the Traveller."

MA: Boston Area
Bookstores: General

271
USA

Boston Area: MA
Gifts, Cards, Novelties

⚥ ○ Globe Corner Bookstore, 49 Palmer St, Cambridge; 02138 617-497-6277; 800-358-6013; "Books & Maps for the Traveller."

⚥ ○ ⅃⅃ Harvard Book Store, 1256 Massachusetts Ave, Cambridge; 02138 617-661-1515 9.30am-11pm; Sun noon-8pm.

⚥ Lucy Parsons Center Books, 3 Central Sq, Cambridge; 02139-3310 617-497-9934 Tue-Fri noon-7pm; Sat & Sun noon-5pm. Free community space eves. "Independent radical bookstore."

⚥ • (?⅃) Unicorn Books, 1210 Massachusetts Ave, Arlington; 02174 617-646-3680

⚥ ○ Wordsworth, 30 Brattle St, Cambridge; 02138 617-354-5201

Community Centers (see also Women's Centers)

⚲ ★ ⅃⅃ Bisexual Community Resource Center, PO Box 609, Cambridge; 02140 617-338-9595

⚲ ★ ⅃⅃ Boston Lesbian & Gay Community Center, PO Box 69, West Medford; 02156-0069 617-247-2927 10am-10pm.

Computer/Software Sales & Services

⚥ ○ Hosken & Associates, 617-445-8130

Counseling/Therapy: Nonprofit

⚥ ☆ Focus, Inc, 186 1/2 Hampshire St, Cambridge; 02139 617-876-4488

Counseling/Therapy: Private

⚥ • Chin, Frederick, M.Ed., 617-469-3702 "Holistic Lifestyle Consultation & support services."

⚲ • Hencken, Joel D., Ph.D., 1105 Mass Ave #2D, Cambridge; 02138 617-864-7711

⚥ • (?⅃) Kleinberg/Livingston, 1131 Beacon St #1, Brookline; 02146 617-731-8539; 617-734-5779

⚲ • Mass Bay Counseling Associates, 321 Columbus Ave, 6th flr, Boston; 02116 617-739-7832

⚲ • ⅃⅃ Rosenberg, Miriam, MD, Ph.D, 508-358-7512

⚥ ○ ⅃⅃ Spadola, Madeline, Psy.D., CADAC, Behavior Management Services, 75 Kneeland St 11th flr, Boston; 02111 617-636-5725

Crafts Galleries, Supplies (see also Art)

⚥ • (?⅃) Cory Glass Works, 38 Cornish St, Lawrence; 01841-1226 508-688-5520 By appointment.

Dentists

⚥ • ⅃ Bankhead, Richard R., DDS, 1259 Hyde Park Ave, Hyde Park; 02136 / 1682 Centre St, West Roxbury; 02132 (617) 325-0101 617-364-5500

Erotica (Printed, Visual, Equipment)

♀ • Grand Opening!, 318 Harvard St #32 (2nd Flr), Brookline; 02146 617-731-2626 Mon-Sat 10am-7pm; Sun noon-5pm.

⚥ ○ Lifestyles for the 90's, 269 Moody St, Waltham; 02154 and 7 Spring St, W. Roxbury 617-891-6060

⚥ ○ Love Toy Books, 646 Washington St, Boston; 02111 617-451-2168

Gardening Services, Landscaping, Supplies & Decoration

⚥ ○ Suburban Service Co, 617-444-6723 "Landscape service."

Gifts, Cards, Pride & Novelty Items

⚥ • Copley Flair, 583 Boylston St, Boston; 02116 617-247-3730

CHANDLER INN
Inn Town Bed & Breakfast

A Bed & Breakfast hotel in the heart of the city... perfect for a traveler seeking a small, friendly spot at an affordable price. Our 56 contemporary rooms are equipped with private bath, color TV and telephone.

$69-$74 • Dbl. $79-$84
Includes continental breakfast

26 Chandler at Berkeley, Boston, MA 02116

(617) 482-3450   (800) 842-3450

B · O · S · T · O · N

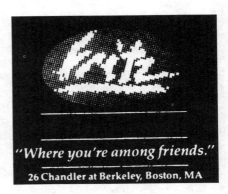

"Where you're among friends."

26 Chandler at Berkeley, Boston, MA

HOURS:
Mon-Fri 10-8
Sat 10-6
Sun Noon-6

New Words
A Women's Bookstore

186 Hampshire St., Cambridge MA 02139
(617) 876-5310
Full Mail-Order Services Available

Health Care (see also AIDS Services)

♀ ★ **Fenway Community Health Center, 7 Haviland St, Boston; 02115 617-267-0900 "Services include General Medicine, Counseling, Substance Abuse Treatment, HIV Education & testing."**

♀ • (?♂) Moulton, David, DC, 45 Newbury St #333, Boston; 02116 617-266-8584

♀ • ♂♂ Russell & Harris Medical Group, PC, 142 Berkeley St, Boston; 02116 617-247-7555

♀ • Stoler, David, DC, 124 Harvard St #7, Brookline; 02146 617-731-3306

♀ ○ Taylor, Robert, MD, 1755 Beacon St, Brookline; 02146 617-232-1459

Health Clubs, Gyms, Saunas

♂ • ♂♂ Safari Club, 90 Wareham St, Boston; 02118 617-292-0011

Home & Building: Cleaning, Repair, General Contractors

♀ • Little Bear & Company, Jill Stewart, Contractor, 617-776-0038 "Painting, surface restoration."

Legal Services & Resources

♀ ○ Donahue & Grolman, 321 Columbus Ave, Boston; 02116 617-859-8966

♂ • **Israel, Laurie, Esq, 1318 Beacon St #14, Brookline; 02146 617-277-3774**

♀ ★ (?♂) Lambda Research Project, Harvard Law School, 23 Everett St #20, Cambridge; 02138 617-495-4087 Fax 617-495-1110

♀ • (♂♂) Triantafillou & Guerin, P.C., 101 Rogers St #405, Cambridge; 02142 617-577-1505 Fax 617-577-1012

♀ • Wilson, Susan, BSN, MPH, JD, 1318 Beacon St #14, Brookline; 02146 617-277-2101

Organizations/Resources: Bisexual Focus

♀ ★ ♂♂ Biversity Boston, 95 Berkeley St #613, Boston; 02116 617-338-9595 Pub *Biversity Calendar*.

♀ ★ ♂♂ Boston Bisexual Women's Network, PO Box 639, Cambridge; 02140 617-338-9595 Pub *Bi Women*.

Organizations/Resources: Business & Professional

♀ ★ ♂♂ BGLAD: Boston Gay & Lesbian Architects & Designers, c/o Boston Society of Architects, 52 Broad St, Boston; 02109 617-951-1433 "Open to all design disciplines; professionals & students; membership in BSA not required."

♀ ★ ♂♂ Boston Professional Alliance, Inc., 398 Columbus Ave #262, Boston; 02116 Pub *Diogenes*.

♂ ★ Gay & Lesbian Caucus/National Writers Union: Boston Local, PO Box 1073, Harvard Sq Stn, Cambridge; 02238

♀ ★ ♂♂ Greater Boston Business Council, PO Box 1059, Boston; 02117-1059 617-236-GBBC Pub *Newsletter*.

♀ ★ LEAGUE: Lesbian, Bisexual & Gay United Employees at AT&T, 99 Bedford St Floor 4, Boston; 02111 908-582-3545

♀ ★ (?♂) Lesbian Lawyers & Legal Workers, Box 85, West Medford; 02156 508-483-3685

Organizations/Resources: Education, Anti-Defamation, Anti-Violence, Self-Defense

♀ ★ Gay, Lesbian & Bisexual Speakers Bureau, PO Box 2232, Boston; 02107 617-354-0133

Organizations/Resources: Ethnic, Multicultural

♀ Alliance of Massachusetts Asian Lesbians & Gay Men, PO Box 543 Prudential Stn, Boston; 02199

♀ ★ Baltic Women, PO Box 99, North Quincy; 02171

Organizations/Resources: Family

♀ ☆ PFLAG/Boston, PO Box 44-4, Boston; 02144 617-547-2440 "Parents, Families & Friends of Lesbians & Gays."

Organizations/Resources: General, Multipurpose, Pride

♀ ★ ♂♂ Dorchester Gay & Lesbian Alliance (GALA), PO Box 329, Dorchester; 02122 617-825-3737 "Social, support & neighborhood association; may cease functioning owing to lack of support."

Organizations/Resources: Political/Legislative

♀ ☆ (?♂) Boston National Organization for Women, 971 Commonwealth Ave, Boston; 02215 617-782-1056

♀ ★ ♂♂ Greater Boston Lesbian & Gay Political Alliance, PO Box 65 Back Bay Annex, Boston; 02117 617-338-4297 Pub *Alliance News*.

Organizations/Resources: Social, Recreational & Support Groups (see also Sport/Dance/Outdoor)

♂ ★ B.A.N.G., PO Box 180036, Boston; 02118-0036 617-695-8113; 800-257-0358; "Gay Male Nudist Group. SASE for information."

♀ ★ Gaylactic Network, PO Box 127, Brookline; 02146 "Science Fiction & Fantasy fans."

♀ ★ (?♂) Older Lesbian Energy, Box 1214, Arlington; 02174

♀ ★ People United for More Practical Solutions (PUMPS, Inc), 6 Clinton St #B, Cambridge; 02139 617-765-2598

♀ ★ ♂♂ Prime Timers, PO Box 180010, Boston; 02118-0001 617-338-5305 Pub *Prologue*. "Social group for older gay & bisexual men; monthly events."

♀ ★ (?♂) Watertown (GLOW), Gays & Lesbians of, PO Box 384, Watertown; 02272-0384

Organizations/Resources: Sport/Dance/Outdoor

♀ Beantown Softball League, PO Box 428, Boston; 02215

♀ ★ (?♂) Chiltern Mountain Club, PO Box 407-Y, Boston; 02117-0407 617-859-2843 (Tripline) "Hikers, skiers, bicyclists, & others interested in outdoor activities welcome."

♂ ★ Frontrunners/Boston, PO Box 423 Back Bay Annex, Boston; 02117 617-266-6294 Keith

♀ Moving Violations Women's Motorcycle Club (MVMC), PO Box 2356, Cambridge; 02238 617-695-8093 "Motorcyclists."

MA: Boston Area
273
Framingham: MA
Organizations: Student
USA
Organizations: Student

Organizations/Resources: Student, Academic, Alumni/ae

⚲ Babson Gay & Lesbian Alliance, PO Box 631 Babson Park, Wellesley; 02157

⚲ ★ ♿ Boston University Gay Lesbian Bisexual Caucus, Boston University School of Law, 765 Commonwealth Ave, Boston; 02115 617-353-8974

⚲ ★ ♿ Brandeis Triskelion, Box 32-L Brandeis U, Waltham; 02254-9110 617-736-4761

⚲ ★ ♿ Gay & Lesbian Alliance at Suffolk University (GALAS), Suffolk University, Beacon Hill, Boston; 02114 617-573-8226

⚲ ★ Gays & Lesbians at Andover Newton Theological School (GLANTS), 210 Herrick Rd, Newton Centre, Boston; 02159

⚲ ★ (♿) Gays, Lesbians, Bisexuals & Friends at MIT (GAMIT), MIT 50-306, 142 Memorial Dr, Cambridge; 02139 617-253-5440

⚲ ★ (♿) Harvard Law School Lambda, 23 Everett St #20, Cambridge; 02138 617-495-4087

⚲ ★ ♿ Lesbian, Gay & Bisexual Center, University of MA/Boston, 100 Morrissey Blvd, Dorchester; 02125-3393 617-287-7983

⚲ ★ Lesbian, Gay & Bisexual Community at Boston College, 617-552-2979

⚲ ★ ♿ Northeastern School of Law Lesbian, Gay & Bisexual Caucus, 400 Huntington Ave, Boston; 02115

Organizations/Resources: Youth (see also Family)

⚲ ★ Peer Listening Line, Fenway Community Health Center, 7 Haviland St, Boston; 02115 617-267-2535; 800-399-PEER (within MA; voice & TTY); Mon-Fri 4-10pm. "Youth-staffed hotline for gay, lesbian, bisexual, transgender or questioning youth."

Private Investigators

♀ ○ Suburban Service Co, 617-444-6723 "Investigations; bodyguards; security officers."

Publications

♂ ★ Gayme, PO Box 5645, Boston; 02215 617-695-8015

⚲ Harvard Gay & Lesbian Review, PO Box 180722, Boston; 02218 617-499-9570

⚲ ● New England Community Guide/Boston Pink Pages, 66 Charles St #283, Boston; 02114 617-423-1515 "Local gay/lesbian resource directory."

♀ ○ Paramour Magazine, PO Box 949, Cambridge; 02140-0008 617-499-0069

Religious Organizations & Publications

⚲ ★ ♿ Am Tikva, Box 11, Cambridge; 02238 617-493-3105 (also Fax) Pub Kol Am Tikva. "Boston's community of Lesbian, Gay & Bisexual Jews."

⚲ ★ (♿) Dignity/Boston, 95 Berkeley St #616, Boston; 02116-6203 617-423-9558 Sun Mass Sun 5.30pm, at St John the Evangelist, 35 Bowdoin St, Beacon Hill "Gay, Lesbian & Bisexual Catholics & their friends."

⚲ Gay & Lesbian Support Group, Church of the Covenant, 67 Newbury St, Boston; 02116 617-266-7480

⚲ ★ Integrity/Boston-Metro, 12 Quincy Ave, Quincy; 02169 617-479-5719; 617-773-0310; "Lesbian & Gay Episcopalians & their friends."

⚲ ★ Metropolitan Community Church of Boston, PO Box 15590 Kenmore Stn, Boston; 02215 617-288-8029 Meets Sun 7pm at 131 Cambridge St, Beacon Hill.

Switchboards, Helplines, Phone Information

⚲ ★ Boston Gay & Lesbian Helpline, Fenway Community Health Center, 7 Haviland St, Boston; 02115 617-267-9001 (voice & TTY) 4-11pm; Sat & Sun 6-11pm.

GLAD·DAY
BOOKSHOP
673 BOYLSTON ST.
BOSTON, MA 02116
(617)   267-3010
OPEN 7 DAYS
Lesbian & Gay Literature

Travel & Tourist Services (see also Accommodation)

♀ ● ♿ Creative Travel, PO Box 57, Jamaica Plain; 02130 / 765 Centre St 508-524-7700 Fax 617-524-4935

♀ ○ Five Star Travel Services, 164 Newbury St, Boston; 02116 617-536-1999; 800-359-1999

⚲ ● ♿ Forex Travel, 76 Arlington St, Boston; 02116 617-482-2900

♀ ● ♿ Fresh Pond Travel of Sudbury, 5 Concord Rd, Sudbury; 01776 508-443-5141; 800-338-1763

Video Sales, Rentals, Services (see also Erotica)

♀ ○ The Video Lab, Margie Chebotariov, videographer 617-493-3105 (also Fax)

Women's Centers

♀ ☆ ♿ Women's Center, 46 Pleasant St, Cambridge; 02139 617-354-8807 Voice & TTY. Mon-Thu 10am-10pm; Fri to 8pm; Sat 11am-4pm. Pub On Our Way.

Brookline: see Boston Area

Cambridge: see Boston Area

Chelmsford

Art & Photography (see also Graphic Design)

♀ ● ♿ Elizabeth's Country, 171 Westford St; 01824 508-256-8556 By appointment. "Customized country art in various media."

Pets & Pet Supplies

♀ ● ♿ Best Friends Grooming, 171 Westford St; 01824 508-256-6860 Mon-Sat 7am-7pm. "Complete pet grooming."

Chelsea: see Boston Area

Chestnut Hill: see Boston Area

Chicopee: see Amherst/Berkshire/Northampton Area

Dorchester: see Boston Area

Edgartown: see Martha's Vineyard Area

Florence: see Amherst/Berkshire/Northampton Area

Framingham

Bookstores: General

♀ ○ ♿ Borders Book Shop, 85 Worcester Road, Framingham; 01701 508-875-2321 9am-10pm; Sun noon-6pm.

Organizations/Resources: Student, Academic, Alumni/ae

⚲ ★ Framingham State College GLAF (Gays, Lesbians & Friends), College Center 508, 100 State St, Framingham; 01701

MA: Framingham
Organizations: Youth
274
USA
North Truro : MA
Accommodation

Organizations/Resources: Youth (see also Family)

♀ ★ (?♂) Framingham Regional Alliance of Gay & Lesbian Youth (FRAGLY), PO Box 426, Framingham; 01701 508-655-7183

Gloucester

Bookstores: General

♀ ○ The Bookstore, 61 Main St; 01930 508-281-1548

Great Barrington

Organizations/Resources: Disability Hikan: The Capable Womon, PO Box 841; 01230 "Magazine for lesbians & our wimmin friends; to promote & facilitate networking & empowerment for disabled wimmin."

Greenfield

Bookstores: General

♀ ○ ♿ World Eye Bookshop, 60 Federal St; 01301 413-772-2186 9am-7pm; Fri to 9pm; Sat to 6pm; Sun noon-5pm.

Hadley: see Amherst/Berkshire/Northampton Area

Haverhill

Bookstores: Gay/Lesbian/Feminist

♀ • Radzukina's Gifts, Books & Music for Womyn, 714 N. Broadway; 01832 508-521-1333 "Fine arts & crafts made by womyn; books, music & other items of interest to womyn. Primarily Lesbian, but all welcome."

Holbrook: see Boston Area

Hyannis

Bars, Restaurants, Clubs, Discos

♂ • ♿ Mallory Dock/Duval Street, 477 Yarmouth Rd; 02601 508-775-9835 maldoc@ccsnet.com *BDEf*

Transportation: Limousine, Taxi, Etc.

♂ ○ Nantucket Airlines, Nantucket Memorial Airport 508-790-0300; 800-635-8787; "26 daily flights between Nantucket Island & Hyannis, Cape Cod."

Jamaica Plain: see Boston Area

Lawrence: see Boston Area

Lenox: see Amherst/Berkshire/Northampton Area

Lowell & Merrimack Valley

Counseling/Therapy: Private

♂ ○ ♿ Merrimack Valley Counseling, 184 Pleasant Valley St, Methuen; 01844-5855 508-687-4383

Erotica (Printed, Visual, Equipment)

♀ ○ Tower Newsstand, 101 Gorham St, Lowell; 01852 508-452-8693 6am-1am; Fri & Sat to 3am.

Organizations/Resources: Student, Academic, Alumni/ae

♀ ★ Gay Outreach Association for Lowell Students (GOALS), South Box 59, I University Ave, Lowell; 01854 508-452-3679

Lynn

Bars, Restaurants, Clubs, Discos

♀ Fran's Place, 776 Washington St; 01901 508-595-8961

♂ Joseph's, 191 Oxford St; 01901 508-599-9483 *BR*

Manomet

Grooming Services

♂ ○ ♿ Backstage Hair Designers, Inc., 767 State Rd; 02345 508-224-7344

Marblehead

Organizations/Resources: General, Multipurpose, Pride

♀ ★ North Shore Gay & Lesbian Alliance, Box 806; 01945 617-745-3848

Marlborough

Organizations/Resources: Social, Recreational & Support Groups (see also Sport/Dance/Outdoor)

♀ ★ (?♂) Wobbles (West of Boston Lesbians), PO Box 292; 01752 508-386-7737 (Janis).; 508-386-7737 (Janis).; Pub *Wobbles Newsletter*. Monthly activities for women.

Martha's Vineyard Area

Accommodation: Hotels, B&B, Resorts, Campgrounds

♀ ○ Captain Dexter House of Edgartown, Box 2798, 35 Pease's Point Way, Edgartown; 02539 508-627-7289

Home & Building: Cleaning, Repair, General Contractors

♀ ○ Ward, Robin, PO Box 16, Vineyard Haven; 02568 800-693-2027; 508-693-2027

Organizations/Resources: Social, Recreational & Support Groups (see also Sport/Dance/Outdoor)

♀ ★ Island Lesbian & Gay Association, PO Box 1809, Vineyard Haven; 02568 508-693-3563 Pub *Stone Walls*.

Public Relations/Advertising Agencies

♀ ○ Ward, Robin, PO Box 16, Vineyard Haven; 02568 800-693-2027; 508-693-2027; "Copywriter & consultant."

Medford: see Boston Area

Methuen: see Lowell & Merrimack Valley

Monterey

Organizations/Resources: Youth (see also Family)

♀ ★ ♿ Gay Youth Action/GLUB Club, PO Box 481; 01245

New Bedford

Bars, Restaurants, Clubs, Discos

♀ Leplace, 20 Kenyon St 508-992-8156

♀ Puzzles, 428 N Front St; 02746 508-991-2306

North Adams: see Amherst/Berkshire/Northampton Area

North Dartmouth

Bars, Restaurants, Clubs, Discos

♂ • ♿ Fiddlesticks, 460 Old Fall River Rd; 02747 508-998-9139 *BDLf*

North Truro

Accommodation: Hotels, B&B, Resorts, Campgrounds

♀ ○ Cape View Motel, PO Box 114; 02652 508-487-0363; 800-224-3232; Mid April to mid October.

Northampton: see Amherst/Berkshire/Northampton Area

MA: Provincetown
Accommodation

275
USA

Provincetown : MA
Accommodation

Provincetown

Accommodation: Hotels, B&B, Resorts, Campgrounds

⚥ • Admiral's Landing, 158 Bradford St; 02657 508-487-9665 Fax 508-487-4437 Open all year. "Centrally located; parking; breakfast & afternoon snacks. Pet-friendly cottages available."
✦ *Admiral's Landing advertisement page 277*

♂ ○ Ampersand Guesthouse, PO Box 832; 02657 508-487-0959

♀ • Anchor Inn Beach House, 175 Commercial St; 02657 508-487-0432

⚥ ○ Angels' Landing, 353 Commercial St.; 02657 508-487-1600

⚥ • Beaconlite Guesthouse, 12 Winthrop St; 02657 508-487-9603; 800-696-9603
✦ *Beaconlite Guesthouse advertisement page 278*

♀ • Boatslip, 161 Commercial St; 02657 508-487-1669

♀ • Bradford Gardens Inn, 178 Bradford St; 02657 508-487-1616; 800-432-2334

⚥ • ♿ The Brass Key/Provincetown, 9 Court St; 02657 508-487-9005; 800-842-9858

⚥ ○ The Buoy, 97 Bradford St; 02657 508-487-3082

♀ ○ Burch House, 116 Bradford St; 02657 508-487-9170 "Home away from home."

♀ ○ (♿) Captain Lysander Inn, 96 Commercial St; 02657 508-487-2253 Open all year.

♂ • Captain's House, 350A Commercial St; 02657 508-487-9353; 800-457-8885 reservations; "Private & shared baths."
✦ *Captain's House advertisement page 276*

♂ • Carl's Guest House, 68 Bradford St; 02657-1363 508-487-1650 reservations; 800-348-CARL free brochure & rates recording
✦ *Carl's Guest House advertisement page 276*

♀ • (♿) Check'er Inn Resort, 25 Winthrop St; 02657 508-487-9029; 800-894-9029; "Women's guesthouse & apartments offering fine acommodations in a friendly & private environment."

♂ • Chicago House, PO Box 953; 02657 / 6 Winslow St 508-487-0537; 800-733-7869

♂ • Christopher Inn, 8 Dyer St; 02657 508-487-1920; 800-828-7896; "Mainly men but women welcome."

♂ • Coat of Arms, 7 Johnson St; 02657 508-487-0816

♂ ○ Crown & Anchor Inn, PO Box 111; 02657 / 247 Commercial St 508-487-1430 *BDER*

MA: Provincetown
Accommodation

276
USA

Provincetown : MA
Accommodation

⚲ • Dexter's Inn, 6 Conwell St; 02657 508-487-1911

⚲ • Dunes Motel & Apartments, PO Box 361; 02657 / Bradford St Extn 508-487-1956

⚲ ○ Dusty Miller Inn, 82 Bradford St; 02657 508-487-2213

⚲ • **Elephant Walk Inn, 156 Bradford St; 02657 508-487-2543; 800-889-WALK**
✦ *Elephant Walk Inn advertisement page 275*

♂ • Elm House, 9 Johnson St; 02657 508-487-0793

⚲ • Fairbanks Inn, 90 Bradford St; 02657 508-487-0386

⚲ • **Flamingo Bay, 27 Conwell St; 02657 508-487-0068; 800-FLAMBAY**
✦ *Flamingo Bay advertisement page 275*

CARL'S GUEST HOUSE
provincetown

"...where strangers become friends."
Comfortable, Clean, Friendly.
Free Brochure & Rates Message
Write/Call: 1-800-348-CARL
For reservations and/or questions
Call: **(508) 487-1650**
68 Bradford St., Provincetown, MA 02657

The
Captain's House
in
Provincetown   **GUESTS**

~~~~~~⚬~~~~~~

350A Commercial Street • MA 02657
508-487-9353

1-800-457-8885

- *Private and Shared Baths*
- *Cable Color TV*
- *Private Patio*
- *Center of Town*
- *Immaculate Accommodations*

♀ • Four Bays, 166 Commercial St; 02657 508-487-0859 Fax 508-487-6571

⚲ • Four Bays Guest House, 166 Commercial St; 02657 508-487-0859 Fax 508-487-6571 Non-smokers guest house.

⚲ • Gabriel's, 104 Bradford St; 02657 800-9-MY-ANGEL Fax 508-487-1605 gabrielsma@aol.com

⚲ • Gifford House Inn, 9-11 Carver St; 02657 508-487-0688 *BDE*

♀ • The Gull Walk Inn, 300A Commercial St; 02657 508-487-9027

⚲ • Harbor Hill at Provincetown, 4 Harbor Hill Rd; 02657 508-487-0541 Fax 508-487-9804 Open all year.

⚲ • Hargood House at Bay Shore, 493 Commercial St; 02657 508-487-9133

⚲ • Haven House, 12 Carver St; 02657 508-487-3031

⚲ ○ Heritage House, 7 Center St; 02657 508-487-3692

⚲ ○ (?♿) Holiday Inn, Rte 6A Box 392; 02657 508-487-1711; 800-422-4224

⚲ • (?♿) **Lady Jane's Inn, 7 Central; 02657 508-487-3387**

♂ • **The Lamplighter Inn, 26 Bradford St; 02657 800-263-6574; 508-487-2529; Fax 508-487-0079**

⚲ ○ Land's End Inn, 22 Commercial St; 02657 508-487-0706

⚲ ○ Lotus Guest House, 296 Commercial St; 02657 508-487-4644

♂ • Moffett House, 296A Commercial St; 02657 508-487-6615

♀ • Monument House, 129 Bradford St; 02657 508-487-9664

⚲ ○ Normandy House, 184 Bradford St; 02657 508-487-1197

♀ • Pilgrim House, 336 Commercial St; 02657 508-487-0889

♀ • Plums Bed & Breakfast Inn, 160 Bradford St; 02657 508-487-2283

⚲ ○ Provincetown Inn & Conference Center, PO Box 619; 02657 / 1 Commercial St 508-487-9500; 800-WHALEVU

♂ • The Ranch, Box 26; 02657 / 198 Commercial St 800-942-1542 *LW*

⚲ • (?♿) Renaissance Apartments, 46 Commercial St; 02657 508-487-4600 "Furnished apartments; weekly rental."

⚲ • **Revere Guest House, 14 Court St; 02657-2114 508-487-2292**
✦ *Revere Guest House advertisement page 275*

⚲ • (?♿) Richmond Inn, 4 Conant St; 02657 508-487-9193

⚲ • Roomers, 8 Carver St; 02657 508-487-3532

The COMMONS
Guest House ❧ Bistro ❧ Bar
386 Commercial Street
Provincetown, MA 02657
508-487-7800   800-487-0784

MA: Provincetown
Accommodation

277
USA

Provincetown : MA
Accommodation

♂ • Rose and Crown Guesthouse, 158 Commercial St; 02657 508-487-3332

♂ ○ Sandpiper Beach House, 165 Commercial St. Po Box 646; 02657 508-487-1928

♂ • Sea Drift Inn, 80 Bradford St; 02657 508-487-3686 _LW_

♀ ○ Sea Side Apartments, 357 Commercial St; 02657 508-487-0227

♀ • Seventy Bradford Street Guest House, 70 Bradford St; 02657 508-487-4966

♀ • ShireMax Inn, 5 Tremont St; 02657 508-487-1233

♀ • Six Webster Place, 6 Webster Place; 02657 508-487-2266; 800-6WEBSTER

♀ • **Somerset House, 378 Commercial St; 02657 800-575-1850 Fax 508-487-4746**

♀ • **Swanberry Inn, 8 Johnson St; 02657 508-487-4242; 800-VIP-SWAN**

♀ • ♿ **The Commons Guest House & Bistro, 386 Commercial St 800-487-0784; 508-487-7800; _BRE_**
✦ _The Commons Guest House & Bistro advertisement page 276_

♀ • **Three Peaks: A Victorian B&B, 210 Bradford St; 02657 508-487-1717; 800-286-1715**

♀ • **Trade Winds Inn, 12 Johnson St; 02657 508-487-0138 "Guest house."**

♀ • **Watership Inn, 7 Winthrop St; 02657 508-487-0094; 800-330-9413; Open year round.**
✦ _Watership Inn advertisement page 277_

♂ • West End Inn, 44 Commercial St; 02657 508-487-9555; 800-559-1220; Open all year.

♀ • White Wind Inn, 174 Commercial St; 02657 508-487-1526

♀ • The Willows, PO Box 937; 02657 / 25 Tremont St 508-487-0520

♀ ○ Windamar House, 568 Commercial St; 02657 508-487-0599

Accommodation: Reservations & Exchanges (see also Travel)

♀ • (♿) Citywide Reservation Services, Inc., 25 Huntington Ave #500, Boston, MA 02116 800-468-3593; 617-267-1440 in MA; "Gay/Lesbian Guesthouse & Inn listings for Boston, Provincetown, Ogunquit, NYC, Fire Island, Ogunquit; immediate reservations, no charge."

♂ • In Town Reservations, PO Box 1983; 02657 / 50 Bradford St 800-67P-TOWN; 508-487-1883; Fax 508-487-6140 "Full service travel agency specializing in arranging accommodations at guest houses, inns, cottages & motels/ hotels. No fee for services. Open year round."
✦ *In Town Reservations advertisement page 278*

♀ • Provincetown Reservation System, 293 Commercial St; 02657 800-648-0364 Fax 508-487-4887
✦ *Provincetown Reservation System advertisement page 279*

AIDS/HIV Support, Education, Advocacy, Publications

♀ ★ ♿ Provincetown Harbor Swim 4 Life, PO Box 819; 02657 508-487-3684

♀ ☆ ♿ Provincetown Positive PWA Coalition, Box 1465; 02657 508-487-3998

Antiques & Collectables

♀ • Remembrances of Things Past, 376 Commercial St; 02657 508-487-9443

Bars, Restaurants, Clubs, Discos

♂ • Atlantic House, 4-6 Masonic Place; 02657 508-487-3821

♂ ○ (♿) Back Street, Gifford House Hotel, 9-11 Carver St; 02657 508-487-0688

♀ • ♿ Cafe Blase, PO Box 293; 02657 / 328 Commercial St 508-487-9465 *B* 9am-1am.

♀ ○ Cafe Edwige, 333 Commercial St; 02657 508-487-2008 *B*

⚥ • ♿ Crown & Anchor (Crown Club, Red Rooster), Box 111; 02657 / 247 Commercial St 508-487-1430

♀ ○ Front Street Restaurant, 230 Commercial St; 02657 508-487-9715 *B*

♀ • Landmark Inn Restaurant, 404 Commercial St; 02657 508-487-9319 *B*

⚥ • Love Shack, 67 Shank Painter Road; 02657 508-487-4444

♀ ○ ♿ Napi's Restaurant, 7 Freeman St; 02657 508-487-1145 *B*

♀ ○ Ocean's Inn, PO Box 442; 02657-0442 / 386 Commercial St; 02657 508-487-0358

⚥ ○ ♿ Pied Piper, PO Box 984; 02657 / 193A Commercial St; 02657 508-487-1527

♀ ○ Post Office Restaurant/Cabaret, 303 Commercial St; 02657 508-487-3892; 508-487-6400;

♀ ○ ♿ Sebastian's Restaurant, 177 Commercial St; 02657 508-487-3286 *B*

♀ ○ Town House, 291 Commercial St; 02657 508-487-0295

Bookstores: Gay/Lesbian/Feminist

⚥ • Now Voyager, PO Box 551; 02657 357 Commercial St; 02657 508-487-0848 11am-11pm in season.

⚥ • **Womencrafts, 376 Commercial St; 02657 508-487-2501**
✦ *Womencrafts advertisement page 279*

Bookstores: General

♀ ○ ♿ The Little Store, 205 Commercial St; 02657 508-487-0208

♀ • Provincetown Bookshop, 246 Commercial St; 02657 508-487-0964

⚥ • ♿ Recovering Hearts, 4 Standish St; 02657 508-487-4875 "Bookstore & gift gallery."

Business, Financial & Secretarial

♀ • Public Business Supply, Women Printers, 70 Shank Painter Rd.; 02657 508-487-6750

MA: Provincetown
Business Services

279
USA

Provincetown : MA
Transportation: Limousine, Taxi

Clothes

♀ • Don't Panic!, 192 Commercial St; 02657 508-487-1280 Fax 508-487-6034

Conferences/Events/Festivals/Workshops (see also Performing Arts)

♀ ★ Sirens Workshop Center, 104 Bradford St; 02657 800-9-MY-ANGEL; 508-487-3232; Fax 508-487-1605 gabrielsma@aol.com "Holistic learning center for women."

Erotica (Printed, Visual, Equipment)

♀ • (&) 1st Old Store, 227 Commercial St; 02657 508-487-1010

Gifts, Cards, Pride & Novelty Items

♀ ○ Cape Card, 230 Commercial St; 02657 508-487-2029

♀ • Pride's Presents, 182 Commercial St; 02657 508-487-1127

♀ Sand Castles By The Sea, 234 Commercial St; 02657 508-487-4346

♀ • (&) Ten Thousand Things, 2 Standish St; 02657 508-487-4875 10am-11pm.

Jewelry

♀ • ♂ T-Bear Bros., Silversmiths, 134 Commercial St; 02657-2014 508-487-6129

Legal Services & Resources

♂ ○ Garfield, Roslyn, Atty, 115 Bradford St, Box 618; 02657 508-481-3787

Massage Therapy (Licensed only)

♀ • J. Critchley Massage Studio, 7 Carnes Lane; 02657 508-487-3684 "Licensed Massage Therapist."

♀ • ♂♂ Jay Critchley/Massage Studio, PO Box 819; 02657 508-487-3684

Organizations/Resources: Business & Professional

♀ ★ Provincetown Business Guild, PO Box 421; 02657 508-487-2313 Pub *Provincetown Business Guild Directory*.

Publications

♀ ○ *Provincetown Advocate*, PO Box 93; 02657 508-487-1170

Real Estate

♀ ○ All Provincetown Sales & Rentals, 309 Commercial St; 02657-2202 508-487-9000

♀ • Atlantic Bay Real Estate, 166 Commercial St; 02657 508-487-2430

♀ • (&) Beachfront Realty, PO Box 665; 02657 / 145 Commercial St 508-487-1397

♂ • Provincetown Properties, PO Box 1983; 02657 / 50 Bradford St 508-487-3276 "Sales & rentals of residential & commercial properties; vacation rentals a specialty."

♂ • Roslyn Garfield Associates, 115 Bradford St, Box 618; 02657 508-487-1308

Transportation: Limousine, Taxi, Etc.

♂ ○ (&) Cape Air, Barnstable Municipal Airport, East Ramp, Hyannis, MA 02601 800-352-0714; 508-771-6944.; (Member IGTA) "Daily scheduled service from Boston to Provincetown, Nantucket, Martha's Vineyard & Hyannis, & from New Bedford to Nantucket & Martha's Vineyard. Also providing non-stop flights between Key West & Naples, FLA."

✦ *Cape Air advertisement page 277*

MA: Provincetown

Travel

280

USA

Worthington : MA

Accommodation

Planning to go through the book and copy all those names and addresses for a mailing? You need

GAYELLOW PAGES ON MAILING LABELS
Updated daily. Old addresses eliminated. New addresses added.

Cost averages 10 cents per label and we will BUY BACK any that bounce within sixty days of your purchase for the price of a first class stamp!

Send fax number or a self-addressed stamped envelope for details:
PO Box 533 Village Station, New York, NY 10014-0533
(212) 674-0120 Fax (212) 420-1126

Travel & Tourist Services (see also Accommodation)

♀ ○ (?♿) Portuguese Princess Whale Watch, PO Box 1469; 02657 508-487-2651; 800-442-3188 New England; Fax 508-487-6458 April-Oct: daily cruises; also Gay Men's Harbor Cruises & Women's Harbor Cruises July & Aug eves.

♀ ○ Timbuktu Travel Agency, PO Box 369, Orleans, MA 02653-0369 508-487-3413

♂ • The Travel Wizard, PO Box 1983; 02657 / 50 Bradford St 800-934-TRIP; 508-487-6330; Fax 508-487-6140 "Full service travel agency specializing in air & land arrangements in Provincetown. No fee for our services. Open year round."

♀ • Your Way Travel, 145 Commercial St; 02657 508-487-2992 Fax 508-487-2994

Quincy: see Boston Area

Randolph

Bars, Restaurants, Clubs, Discos

♂ • Randolph Country Club, 44 Mazzeo Dr; 02368 617-961-2414

Salem

Accommodation: Hotels, B&B, Resorts, Campgrounds

♀ • Goddess of the Sea B&B, 508-745-6157 "Near all historic sites."

Bars, Restaurants, Clubs, Discos

♀ Carmelina's Restaurant & Bar, 98 Wharf St, Pickering Wharf; 01970 508-744-0472

Women's Centers

♀ ☆ (?♿) Florence Luscomb Women's Center, Salem State College, 352 Lafayette St; 01970 508-741-6600 ext 6555

Somerville: see Boston Area

South Hadley: see Amherst/Berkshire/Northampton Area

Springfield: see Amherst/Berkshire/Northampton Area

Swansea

Bookstores: General

♀ ○ ♿ Newsbreak, Rt. 6, Stuarts Plaza; 02777 508-675-9380 Fax 508-679-3336 8am-9pm; Sun 7.30am-6pm.

Taunton

Bars, Restaurants, Clubs, Discos

♀ • Farrell's, 60 Weir St; 02780 508-822-0404 *Bd* 3pm-1am; Fri & Sat to 1.30pm.

Tyngsboro

Bars, Restaurants, Clubs, Discos

♂ • ♿ DiRocco's Tall Pines Inn, 147 Frost Rd; 01879 508-649-9134 *BD* Fri-Sun 8pm-2am.

Vineyard Haven: see Martha's Vineyard Area

Wakefield

Travel & Tourist Services (see also Accommodation)

♀ ○ Alternative Travel, 413 Lowell St; 01880 617-246-7480

Waltham: see Boston Area

Ware: see Amherst/Berkshire/Northampton Area

Watertown: see Boston Area

Wayland: see Boston Area

Wellesley: see Boston Area

Williamsburg: see Amherst/Berkshire/Northampton Area

Williamstown: see Amherst/Berkshire/Northampton Area

Worcester

AIDS/HIV Support, Education, Advocacy, Publications

♀ ☆ Health Awareness Services, 405 Grove St; 01605-1270 508-756-7123 "Education to schools & community groups about AIDS; special outreach to Gay/Lesbian Youth."

Bars, Restaurants, Clubs, Discos

♂ • Club 241, 241 Southbridge St; 01608 508-755-9311

♂ • ♿ The MB Lounge, 282 Main St 508-799-4521

Erotica (Printed, Visual, Equipment)

♀ ○ (♿) Myrtle Bookstore, 42 Myrtle St; 01608 508-755-7541

♀ ○ United Book, 290 Main St; 01608 508-752-9293

Organizations/Resources: General, Multipurpose, Pride

♂ ★ Worcester County Lesbian & Gay Alliance, PO Box 427; 01614-0427 508-829-9898

Organizations/Resources: Student, Academic, Alumni/ae

♂ ★ (?♿) Clark University Bisexual, Lesbian & Gay Alliance (Bi-LAGA) (BiLGALA), 950 Main St, Box B-5; 01610-1477 508-793-7287

Organizations/Resources: Youth (see also Family)

♂ ★♿ Supporters of Worcester Area Gay & Lesbian Youth, PO Box 592 West Side Stn; 01602 508-755-0005

Religious Organizations & Publications

♂ ★♿ Morning Star Metropolitan Community Church, 231 Main St, Cherry Valley; 01611 508-892-4320 *The Eagle Connection.*

♂ ★ Unitarian Universalists for Bisexual, Gay & Lesbian Concerns, PO Box 592 West Side Stn; 01602 508-755-0005

Worthington

Accommodation: Hotels, B&B, Resorts, Campgrounds

♀ • Little River Farm, 967 Huntington Rd; 01098 413-238-4261

Michigan

State/County Resources

Addictive Behavior, Substance Abuse, Recovery

♀ • (ᕲᕲ) **Pride Institute, 800-54-PRIDE** "The nation's only accredited chemical dependency treatment center exclusively for Gay, Lesbian & Bisexual People."

AIDS/HIV Support, Education, Advocacy, Publications

♀ ☆ᕲᕲ HIV/AIDS Advocacy Program, 106 W Allegan #210, Lansing, MI 48933-1706 800-288-5923

Organizations/Resources: Political/Legislative

♀ Log Cabin Club of Southeastern Michigan, 18530 Mack Ave #113, Grosse Pointe Farms, MI 48236 810-478-6054

♂ Log Cabin Michigan, PO Box 10037, Lansing, MI 48901 517-694-1167

♂ Michigan Coalition for Human Rights (MCHR), 4800 Woodward Ave, Detroit, MI 48201

♂ ★ Michigan Lesbian/Gay Democratic Caucus, PO Box 1708, Royal Oak, MI 48068-1708

Organizations/Resources: Social, Recreational & Support Groups (see also Sport/Dance/Outdoor)

♂ ★ (?ᕲ) Great Lakes Gaylaxians, c/o 1106 E 5th St, Royal Oak, MI 48067-2902 810-541-8198 *The Newsletter That Dare Not Speak Its Name.* "Science fiction fans."

Publications

♂ ★ *Between The Lines*, PO Box 7594, Ann Arbor, MI 48107 313-741-5159 Fax 313-741-5162 "Michigan's Gay & Lesbian newspaper."

Real Estate

♂ • **Community Real Estate Referrals, 800-346-5592** "Free referral to gay/gay-supportive realtor in any USA city/state (including Virgin Is. & Puerto Rico). Sorry, no rentals!"
✦ *Community Real Estate Referrals advertisement back cover*

Ann Arbor

Bars, Restaurants, Clubs, Discos

♀ ○ (ᕲᕲ) The Nectarine, 516 E Liberty; 48104 313-994-5436 *BD* 9pm-2am.

Bookstores: Gay/Lesbian/Feminist

♂ • ᕲ Common Language, 215 S Fourth Ave; 48104 313-663-0036 Noon-8pm; Sun to 4pm.

Bookstores: General

♀ ○ Borders Books & Music, 612 E Liberty St; 48104 313-668-7652; 313-668-7100 (music); Fax 313-668-2455 9am-10pm; Fri to 11pm; Sun 10am-8pm.

♀ ○ᕲᕲ Webster's Books, 2607 Plymouth Road; 48105 313-662-5086

Bookstores: Recovery, Metaphysical, & other Specialty

♀ ○ (?ᕲ) Crazy Wisdom Bookstore, 206 N 4th Ave; 48104 313-665-2757 "Specializes in women's spirituality, uddhism, transpersonal psychology, wholistic health & bodywork."

Counseling/Therapy: Private

♀ • Baker, Karen, ACSW, 410 E William; 48104 313-668-3085

♀ • ᕲᕲ **Dargel, Robert H., ACSW, LMFT, 3055 Plymouth Rd #201; 48105 313-996-0918**

♂ ○ Tenbusch, Lynne G., Ph.D., 2301 S Huron Pkwy; 48104-5133 313-973-3232

♂ • (ᕲ) Wilton, Jim, MSW, CSW, 513 Oswego; 48104-2624 313-663-5021

Massage Therapy (Licensed only)

♀ • (?ᕲ) Rosenberg, David, 209 W Kingsley 313-662-6282 Certified Massage Therapist

Organizations/Resources: Family

♀ ☆ᕲᕲ PFLAG/Ann Arbor, PO Box 7471; 48107-7471 313-769-1684 "Parents, Families & Friends of Lesbians & Gays."

Organizations/Resources: Student, Academic, Alumni/ae

♂ ★ᕲᕲ **Lesbian & Gay Bisexual Programs Office, 3116 Michigan Union, UM 530 S State St; 48109-1349 313-763-4186 Fax 313-747-4133 lgbpo.staff@umich.edu**

Publications

→ *Between The Lines:* p.281

Religious Organizations & Publications

♀ ☆ American Friends Service Committee Lesbian, Gay, Bisexual Issues Program, 1414 Hill St; 48104 313-761-8283 Fax 313-761-6022

♀ ☆ᕲᕲ Guild House Campus Ministry, 802 Monroe St; 48104 313-662-5189 "Campus ministry working for peace, justice, & environmental integrity."

Battle Creek

Bars, Restaurants, Clubs, Discos

♂ ○ The Rascals, 910 North Ave; 49017 616-962-7276

Bay City

Erotica (Printed, Visual, Equipment)

♂ • A.C.E. Book Store, 210 3rd St; 48708 517-893-3981

Belleville

Bars, Restaurants, Clubs, Discos

♂ ○ᕲᕲ Granny's Place, 9800 Haggerty; 48111 313-699-8862 *BR*

Birmingham: see Detroit

Chelsea

Organizations/Resources: Political/Legislative

♂ LGLC (Libertarians For Gay & Lesbian Concerns), Box 447; 48118

Dearborn: see Detroit

Detroit

☎ Affirmations 800-398-4297

AIDS/HIV Support, Education, Advocacy, Publications

♀ ☆ Midwest AIDS Prevention Project (MAPP), 702 Livernois St, Ferndale; 48220 810-545-1435

Bars, Restaurants, Clubs, Discos

♂ ○ Back Pocket, 8832 Greenfield; 48228 313-272-8374 *BR*

♂ • ᕲᕲ Backstreet, 15606 Joy Rd; 48228 313-272-8959 *D*

♂ Body Shop, 22061 Woodward, Ferndale; 48220 810-398-1940 *BR*

♂ • ᕲ Chains Bar, 6228 Michigan 313-897-3650 *BLd*

MI: Detroit
Bars, Clubs, Restaurants

282

USA

Detroit: MI
Organizations: General

♂ Cruisin' Again, 1641 Middlebelt Road, Inkster; 48141 313-729-8980

♂ Deck, 14901 E Jefferson; 48215 313-822-1991

♂ • ♿ Detroit Eagle, 1501 Holden; 48208 313-873-6969 *BDLWf*

♀ • (♿) Gigi's, 16920 W Warren; 48227 313-584-6525 *BDE* Noon-2am. (Lower Deck shows; Upper Deck dancing)

♂ Gold Coast, 2971 E 7 Mile Rd; 48234 313-366-6135

♂ Hayloft Saloon, 8070 Greenfield; 48228 313-581-8913

♀ Ken's, 18931 W Warren Ave; 48208 313-336-2080

♀ The Male Box, 3537 E Seven Mile Road; 48234 313-892-5420

♀ Maxie's, 14060 Telegraph Rd; 48239 313-538-1645

♀ • ♿ Menjo's, 928 W McNichols; 48203 313-863-3934 *D*

♀ • ♿ Numbers, 17518 Woodward Ave NE; 48203 313-868-9145 *P* Thu-Sun 1-5am (afterhours club)

♂ Off Broadway East/Men's Room, 12215 Harper St; 48213 313-521-0920

♂ Other Side, 16801 Plymouth Rd; 48227 313-836-2324

♀ • ♿♿ Pronto! A Deli & Catering Company, 608 S Washington, Royal Oak; 48067 810-544-7900 Fax 810-544-0123 *R*

♀ Punchinello's, 184 Pierce, Birmingham; 48009 810-644-5277 *R*

♀ • Railroad Crossing, 6640 E 8 Mile Rd; 48234 313-891-1020 *Bd* Wed-Sat 7pm-2am; Sun 5pm-2am.

♀ • (♿♿) The Rhinoceros, 265 Riopelle; 48207 313-259-2208 *BDRE*

♀ Splash, 14526 W Warren, Dearborn; 48126 313-582-0639 *D*

♀ • ♿ Stingers Lounge & Grill, 19404 Sherwood; 48234 313-892-1765 *BR* 11am-2am; Sun 2pm-2am.

♀ Sugarbakers, 3800 E Eight Mile Rd.; 482 313-892-5203

♂ Tiffany's on the Park, 17436 Woodward Ave; 48203 313-883-7162

♀ • ♿ Times Square Station, 1431 Times Square; 48226 313-963-0874 *BDf*

♂ Woodward, 6426 Woodward; 48203 313-872-0166 *D*

♀ Zippers, 6221 East Davison; 48212 313-892-8120

Bookstores: Gay/Lesbian/Feminist

♀ • ♿ Chosen Books of Michigan, 120 W 4th St, Royal Oak; 48067 810-543-5758 Noon-10pm. "Lesbian/Gay & Feminist literary bookstore."
✦ *Chosen Books of Michigan advertisement page 283*

Clothes

♀ ○ ♿♿ Faith Glamour/Gallery, 315 S Center, Royal Oak; 48067 810-548-4945 Mon-Sat 11am-7pm. "Fetish Glam apparel, shoes, accessories. Monthly showings by local & national exotic artists."

Community Centers (see also Women's Centers)

♀ ★ Affirmations, 195 W 9 Mile Rd, Ferndale; 48220 800-398-4297 Switchboard Sun-Fri 4.30-11pm; 810-398-7105

Counseling/Therapy: Nonprofit

♀ • ♿ East Side Ministry of Social Services, 9162 Crane; 48213 / office 1510 Hurlbut 313-331-0033

Counseling/Therapy: Private

♂ • Kinsel, Kevin, MSW, CSW, PC, 108 E 5th St, Royal Oak; 48067 810-541-6830

Erotica (Printed, Visual, Equipment)

♀ ○ 24 Hour Video, 17520 Woodward Ave; 48203 313-869-9524 "Gay adult video rental."

♂ • ♿ Complex Video, Ltd, (at TNT Health Club) 13333 W 8 Mile Rd; 48235 313-341-5322 *P*

♀ ○ (♿) Escape Bookstore, 18728 W Warren; 48228 313-336-6558

♀ ○ Irving Art Theater & Video, 21220 Fenkell; 48223 313-531-2368

♀ ○ ♿ Noir Leather, 415 S Main St, Royal Oak; 48067 810-541-3979 11am-8pm; Sat to 7pm; Sun 1-5pm. "Fetish clothing; S&M & B&D accoutrements; piercing jewelry."

♀ ○ (♿) Uptown Video Club, 16541 Woodward, Highland Park; 48203 313-869-9477 "Bookstore & video club."

♀ ○ ♿ Uptown Video Club, 16401 W 8 Mile Rd; 48235 313-836-0647 "Bookstore & video club."

♀ ○ ♿ Vintage Noir, 124 W 4th St, Royal Oak; 48067 810-543-8733 (USED) 1-8pm; Sat noon-9pm; Sun 1-5pm "Vintage alternative clothing, jewelry, & specialty items."

♂ ○ (♿) Wood-Six Theater, 16549 Woodward Ave; 48203-2819 313-883-5233

♀ ○ Worldwide Magazines, 16140 Woodward Ave, Highland Park; 48203 313-866-6020

Film & Video

♀ • ♿♿ The Ladies Film Society, PO Box 1242, Royal Oak; 48068 810-546-9677 "Monthly lesbian-focused film series."

Florists (see also Gardening)

♀ • ♿♿ Blossoms Fresh Flower Market, 175 W Maple, Birmingham; 48009 810-548-7900

Health Clubs, Gyms, Saunas

♂ • ♿ TNT Health Club, 13333 W 8 Mile Rd; 48235 313-341-5322 *P*

Legal Services & Resources

♀ ○ Greenspon, Scheff & Washington, PC, One Kennedy Square #2137; 48226 313-963-1921

Organizations/Resources: Business & Professional

♀ GLEAM, PO Box 271, Royal Oak; 48068

Organizations/Resources: Education, Anti-Defamation, Anti-Violence, Self-Defense

♀ ★ (♿) The Triangle Foundation, 19641 W Seven Mile Rd; 48219 313-537-3323

Organizations/Resources: Ethnic, Multicultural

♂ • ♿ BWMT (Black & White Men Together) Detroit, PO Box 441562; 48244-1562 810-569-8595 Black & White Men Together/Men of All Colors Together

♂ ★ Men Of Color Motivational Group, PO Box 11499; 48211 810-691-1486

Organizations/Resources: Family

♀ ☆ ♿ PFLAG/Detroit, PO Box 145, Farmington Hills; 48332 810-656-2875 "Parents, Families & Friends of Lesbians & Gays."

Organizations/Resources: General, Multipurpose, Pride

♀ ★ (♿) Detroit Area Gay/Lesbian Council (DAG/LC), 29209 Northwestern Hwy #507, Southfield; 48034-1024 818-988-0242

♀ ★ (♿♿) South East Michigan Pride, Inc (S.E.M.P.), PO Box 1915, Royal Oak; 48068-1915 810-825-6651

MI: Detroit
Organizations: Social & Support

283
USA

Grand Rapids : MI
Community Centers

Organizations/Resources: Social, Recreational & Support Groups (see also Sport/Dance/Outdoor)

♂ ★ Girth & Mirth of Detroit, PO Box 39523, Redford; 48239 313-531-3907

♂ ★ (?&) Motor City Bears, PO Box 1894, Royal Oak; 48068-1894 810-988-0227

Organizations/Resources: Sport/Dance/Outdoor

♀ ★ Cadillac Squares, 9521 Chinavere Rd, Newport; 48166 313-586-8638 khermona@macomb.lib.mi.us d

Performing Arts: Entertainment, Music, Recording, Theater, etc.

♂ ★ Detroit Together Men's Chorus, 2441 Pinecrest Drive, Ferndale; 48220 810-544-3872

♀ ★ Great Lakes Men's Chorus, PO Box 336, Royal Oak; 48068 810-399-SING

Publications

♀ • ♂ Cruise Magazine, 660 Livernois Ave, Ferndale; 48220 810-545-9040

♀ • Metra, PO Box 71844, Madison Heights; 48071-0844 810-543-3500

Religious Organizations & Publications

♀ ★ ♂ Dignity/Detroit, PO Box 32874; 48232 313-563-0892 "Gay & Lesbian Catholics & their friends."

♀ Divine Peace Metropolitan Community Church, PO Box 71938, Madison Heights; 48071 810-544-8335

♀ ★ Integrity/Detroit, c/o Emmanuel Episcopal Church 18320 John R St; 48203 313-459-7319 Meets 2nd & 4th Sun, 5.15pm, Emmanuel Episcopal Church. "Gay & Lesbian Episcopalians & their friends."

♀ Metropolitan Community Church Detroit, Box 836, Royal Oak; 48068 810-399-7741

♀ ★ ♂♂ Simcha, PO Box 652, Southfield; 48037 810-353-8025 Jewish group.

Travel & Tourist Services (see also Accommodation)

♀ • Ken's Travel Bureau, 24738 Donald Ave, Redford; 48239 313-531-3907

Douglas: see Saugatuck

East Lansing: see Lansing

Escanaba

Bars, Restaurants, Clubs, Discos

♀ o Club Xpress, 904 Ludington St; 49829 BD

Fennville: see Saugatuck

Ferndale: see Detroit

Flint

Bars, Restaurants, Clubs, Discos

♂ Club Merry Inn, 2402 N Franklin; 48506 810-234-9481

♀ o Club Triangle, 2101 S Dort Hwy; 48507 810-767-7550

♀ The Copa, 565 S Saginaw; 48502 810-235-2500

♂ Fox's Den, G-5412 S Dort Hwy; 48507 810-787-8821

♀ State Bar, 2512 S Dort Hwy; 48507 810-767-7050

Legal Services & Resources

♀ o (&) Fallis, Carol A., PC, 107 S Walnut St; 48530 810-750-8862

Organizations/Resources: Family

♀ PFLAG/Flint, PO Box 90722, Burton; 48509-0722 810-631-4910 "Parents, Families & Friends of Lesbians & Gays."

Religious Organizations & Publications

♀ ★ ♂♂ Redeemer Metropolitan Community Church of Flint, 1665 N Chevrolet Ave; 48504 810-238-6700 Sun 6pm; Thu 7pm. "All functions are chemical- & alcohol-free."

Gladwin

Counseling/Therapy: Private

♀ • (&) Gould, William D., MA, PO Box 151; 48624 / 400 N Antler St 517-426-2351

Grand Rapids

☎ Lesbian & Gay Community Network of Western Michigan 616-458-3511

AIDS/HIV Support, Education, Advocacy, Publications

♀ ☆ ♂♂ Grand Rapids AIDS Resource Center, PO Box 6603; 49516 616-459-9177 Fax 616-459-3432 Pub Communique. "Information, referral, food bank, buddy program, emergency financial help, transportation."

Bars, Restaurants, Clubs, Discos

♂ Apartment, 33 Sheldon NE 616-451-0815

♂ The Cell, 76 S Division; 49503 616-454-4499

♀ o ♂♂ Club 67, 67 S Division Ave; 49503 616-454-8003 BDE 3pm-2am.

♀ • (?&) Diversions Video Bar & Grill, 10 Fountain NW; 49503 616-451-3800 BDRE Restaurant Mon-Fri 11am-10pm; Video & Dance Bar 7 nights to 2am.
♦ Diversions Video Bar & Grill advertisement page 283

Bookstores: Gay/Lesbian/Feminist

♀ • ♂ Sons & Daughters, 962 Cherry St SE; 49506 616-459-8877 Noon-mdnt; Sat & Sun 10am-mdnt.

Bookstores: Recovery, Metaphysical, & other Specialty

♀ o ♂ Earth & Sky, 6 Jefferson SE; 49503 616-458-3520

Community Centers (see also Women's Centers)

♀ ★ ♂ Lesbian & Gay Community Network of Western Michigan, 909 Cherry St SE; 49506-1403 616-458-3511 Mon-Fri 6-10pm. Pub Network News. "Community advocacy; library; referral line; speakers bureau."

MI: Grand Rapids
Health Clubs, Gyms, Saunas

284

USA

Lansing: MI
Organizations: Social & Support

Health Clubs, Gyms, Saunas

♂ • (Ġ) Diplomat Health Club, 2324 S Division Ave; 49507 616-452-3754

Organizations/Resources: Political/Legislative

♀ ★ Lesbian/Gay Political Action Network, PO Box 3775; 49501-3775 Pub *Panorama*.

♀ Log Cabin West Michigan, 539 Fairview NE; 49503 616-456-6602

Religious Organizations & Publications

♀ ☆ (?Ġ) Bethel Christian Assembly, PO Box 6935; 49516 616-459-8262 "Pro-gay & lesbian evangelical church."

♀ ★ĠĠ Dignity, PO Box 1373; 49501 616-454-9779 "Gay & Lesbian Catholics & their friends."

♀ ★ (Ġ) Reconciliation Metropolitan Community Church, 300 Graceland NE; 49505 616-364-7633

Travel & Tourist Services (see also Accommodation)

♀ • Ġ Kresnak, Karen, Travel Agent, Vacation Depot, 973 Cherry SE; 49506 616-454-4339 Fax 616-454-4972 Member of IGTA.

Hamtramck

Bars, Restaurants, Clubs, Discos

♀ Falcon Club, 3515 Caniff; 48212 313-368-6010

Highland Park: see Detroit

Honor

Accommodation: Hotels, B&B, Resorts, Campgrounds

♀ • Labrys Wilderness Resort, 4115 Scenic Hwy; 49640 616-882-5994

Gifts, Cards, Pride & Novelty Items

♀ • Seeds Store, Labrys Wilderness Resort, 4115 Scenic Hwy; 49640 616-882-5994 "Free mail order catalog of Landyke Crafts."

Jackson

Bars, Restaurants, Clubs, Discos

♀ Club 405, 405 Biddle St; 49203 517-788-9853

Kalamazoo

☎ Kalamazoo Gay/Lesbian Resource Center 616-345-7878

AIDS/HIV Support, Education, Advocacy, Publications

♀ ☆ĠĠ CARES, 628 S Park St; 49007 616-381-2437; 800-344-1695 (SE Michigan only)

♀ KABS (Kalamazoo AIDS Benefit Services), PO Box 20023; 49003 616-344-1695

Bars, Restaurants, Clubs, Discos

♀ • ĠĠ Brothers Beta Club, 209 E Stockbridge Ave; 49001-2841 616-345-1960 *BDEP* 4pm-2am. "Membership club; visitors welcome. Resident gay theater company."

♀ • ĠĠ The Zoo, 906 Portage St; 49001 616-342-8888 *BD* 4pm-2am.

Bookstores: Gay/Lesbian/Feminist

♀ • Ġ Pandora Books for Open Minds, 226 W Lovell; 49007 616-388-5656

Erotica (Printed, Visual, Equipment)

♀ • (Ġ) Triangle World & The Leather Palace, 551 Portage Rd; 49007-5323 616-373-4005 Tue-Sun noon-10pm.

Organizations/Resources: Family

♀ ★ Our Kids, c/o Pandora's Books & Music 226 W Lovell; 49007 616-388-5656 "Gay parents."

♀ ☆ Ġ PFLAG, PO Box 1201, Portage; 49081-1201 "Parents, Families & Friends of Lesbians & Gays."

Organizations/Resources: General, Multipurpose, Pride

♀ ★ Kalamazoo Gay/Lesbian Resource Center, PO Box 51532; 49005 616-345-7878 Pub *Newsletter*.

Organizations/Resources: Social, Recreational & Support Groups (see also Sport/Dance/Outdoor)

♀ Gay, Lesbian & Bisexual Support Group, Kalamazoo College 1200 Academy St; 49006-3291

Organizations/Resources: Student, Academic, Alumni/ae

♀ ★ (?Ġ) Alliance for Bisexual, Lesbian & Gay Strength, Western Michigan University, PO Box 226, Faunce Student Services B106; 49008 616-387-2134

Organizations/Resources: Youth (see also Family)

♀ ★ (?Ġ) Kalamazoo Lesbian/Gay/Bi Youth Group, PO Box 51532; 49005 616-345-7878

Publications

♀ • *Lavender Morning*, PO Box 729; 49005 616-685-5377 Monthly.

Religious Organizations & Publications

♀ ★ĠĠ Phoenix Community Church, PO Box 2222; 49003-2222 616-381-3222 Sun 6pm. (United Church of Christ)

Lansing

Bars, Restaurants, Clubs, Discos

♂ Club 505, 505 E Shiawasee; 48912-1213 517-374-6312

♂ Club Paradise, 224 S Washington Sq; 48933 517-484-2399

Bookstores: General

♀ ○ Community Newscenter #1, 418 Frandor Shopping Center; 48912 517-351-7562

♀ • ĠĠ The Real World Emporium, 1214-16 Turner St; 48906 517-485-BOOK; 517-485-2665; *ER* "Community store & cafe for Lesbian & Gay people & friends."

Counseling/Therapy: Private

♀ ○ Railey, Julie C., ACSW, 1218 Red Oak Lane #3, East Lansing; 48823 517-332-1449

Organizations/Resources: Family

♀ ☆ĠĠ PFLAG/Lansing, PO Box 35, Okemos; 48805 517-349-3612 (Mary) "Parents, Families & Friends of Lesbians & Gays."

Organizations/Resources: General, Multipurpose, Pride

♀ ★ Ġ Lesbian Alliance, PO Box 6423, East Lansing; 48826 517-394-1454 TDD available.

Organizations/Resources: Political/Legislative

♀ Log Cabin Central Michigan, PO Box 10037; 48901 517-374-4733

Organizations/Resources: Social, Recreational & Support Groups (see also Sport/Dance/Outdoor)

♂ ★ Capitol Men's Club, PO Box 4361, East Lansing; 48826-4361 517-484-6342 Pub *Newsletter*. "Social & support group."

MI: Lansing
Organizations: Student

285

USA

Traverse City : MI
Organizations: Social & Support

Organizations/Resources: Student, Academic, Alumni/ae

♀ ★ ♿ Alliance of Lesbian-Bi-Gay Students (ALBGS), 442 Student Union, Michigan State University, East Lansing; 48824 517-353-9795; 517-353-5255

Publications

♀ ★ *Lesbian Connection: Ambitious Amazons*, PO Box 811, East Lansing; 48826 517-371-5257 "A free, nationwide newsletter for, by & about Lesbians."

Religious Organizations & Publications

♀ Dignity, PO Box 1265, East Lansing; 48826 "Gay & Lesbian Catholics & their friends."

♀ ★ Ecclesia, PO Box 6311, East Lansing; 48826

Switchboards, Helplines, Phone Information

♀ Lesbian & Gay Hotline, 517-332-3200

Travel & Tourist Services (see also Accommodation)

♀ • ♿ Anderson International Travel Service, 1308 Michigan Ave, East Lansing; 48823 517-337-1301; 800-723-1233

Marquette

AIDS/HIV Support, Education, Advocacy, Publications

♀ ☆ ♿ Continuum of Care Program, AIDS Services, Marquette County Health Dept, 184 US Hwy 41 East, Negaunee; 49866 906-475-7651 : AIDS Hotline Financial assistance for outpatient medical services & agency referrals for HIV positive individuals in the Upper Peninsula.>

Bookstores: General

♀ • (♿) Sweet Violets, 413 North 3rd St; 49855 906-228-3307 Mon-Sat 10am-6pm. "Books, greeting cards, jewelry, music, smudges."

Organizations/Resources: Student, Academic, Alumni/ae

♀ ★ Gay/Lesbian/Bisexual Student Union, Northern Michigan University SAO Box 4; 49855 906-227-2407 blbsu@nmu.edu

Midland

Accommodation: Hotels, B&B, Resorts, Campgrounds

♀ ○ Jay's B & B, 4429 Bay City Rd; 48640 517-496-2498

Mount Clemens

Bars, Restaurants, Clubs, Discos

♀ Mirage, 27 N Walnut St.; 48043 810-954-1919

Bookstores: General

♀ ○ O'Shea's Bookstore, 43 Gratiot Ave; 48043 810-469-9254

Mount Pleasant

Organizations/Resources: Student, Academic, Alumni/ae

♀ ★ Central Michigan Gay Liberation, Inc, Box 34, Warriner Hall, Central Michigan Univ; 48859 517-774-3822

Muskegon Heights

Bars, Restaurants, Clubs, Discos

♀ • ♿ R's 3236 Club & Discoteque, 3236 Hoyt St; 49444-3156 *DE* Tue-Sun 9pm-2am.

Muskegon

Bookstores: Gay/Lesbian/Feminist

♀ • ♿ It's Your Pleasure, 3228 Glade St; 49444 616-639-7348 "Fireplace with tables; Cappuccino, Espresso, desserts served."

Counseling/Therapy: Nonprofit

♀ ★ Wolf Clan Counseling, 345 W Grand Ave; 49441 616-726-6224

Owendale

Accommodation: Hotels, B&B, Resorts, Campgrounds

♀ • Windover Resort, 3596 Blakely; 48754 517-375-2586

Plymouth: see Detroit

Pontiac

Bars, Restaurants, Clubs, Discos

♀ • ♿ Club Flamingo, 352 Oakland Ave; 48342 810-253-0430 *D* 2pm-2am.

Port Huron

Bars, Restaurants, Clubs, Discos

♀ Seekers, 3301 24th St; 48060 810-985-9349

Richmond

Real Estate

♀ ○ Threet, Mary Ann, ReMax Country 810-727-4456

Royal Oak: see Detroit

Saginaw

Bars, Restaurants, Clubs, Discos

♀ Bambi's, 1742 E Genessee Ave; 48601-2403 517-752-9179

Saugatuck

Accommodation: Hotels, B&B, Resorts, Campgrounds

♀ • Campit, 6635 118th Ave, Fennville; 49408 616-543-4335

♀ • ♿ Douglas Dunes Resort, PO Box 369, Douglas; 49506 616-857-1401 *BDRE*

♀ • Kirby House, PO Box 1174; 49453 / 294 W. Center St 616-857-2904

♀ • Newnham Suncatcher Inn, PO Box 1106; 49457 / 131 Griffith 616-857-4249

♀ • ♿ Volare Inn, 3291 Blue Star Hwy 616-857-4269 Fax 616-857-7308 Open all year.

Traverse City

Bars, Restaurants, Clubs, Discos

♀ • Side Traxx Nite Club, 520 Franklin St; 49684 616-935-1666 *BE* Mon-Sat open 6pm; Sun open 2pm; teadance.

Bookstores: General

♀ • ♿ Bookie Joint, 120 S Union St; 49684 616-946-8862 Mon-Sat 10am-6m. "Primarily used paperbacks; specializing in gay & women's music & gay/lesbian literature; large selection gay/lesbian periodicals; jewelry, T-shirts, buttons, etc."

Organizations/Resources: Social, Recreational & Support Groups (see also Sport/Dance/Outdoor)

♀ ★ ♿ Friends North, PO Box 562; 49685-0562 616-946-1804 Pub *Networking 45 North*.

Wyandotte

Religious Organizations & Publications

♀ ☆ Mariavite Old Catholic Church - Province of North America, 2803 10th St; 48192-4994 313-281-3082 "A traditional Independent Catholic Church serving all people. Youth counseling, friendship club; other services available."

Ypsilanti

Bars, Restaurants, Clubs, Discos

♂ Flick's, 1435 E Michigan Ave; 48198 313-483-2840

Erotica (Printed, Visual, Equipment)

♂ • ♂♂ Magazine Rack, 515 W Cross; 48197 313-482-6944

Home & Building: Cleaning, Repair, General Contractors

♀ • D. L. Church Construction, 105 Babbitt St; 48198 313-483-1237 Fax 313-483-7059

Organizations/Resources: Student, Academic, Alumni/ae

♀ ★ (?♂) Lesbian/Gay/Bisexual Student Association (LGBSA), c/o Office of Campus Life, 221 Goodison Hall; 48197

Religious Organizations & Publications

♀ ★♂♂ Tree of Life Metropolitan Community Church, 218 N Adams St; 48197-2507 Pub *Branches*.

Minnesota

State/County Resources

AIDS/HIV Support, Education, Advocacy, Publications

♀ ★♂♂ ACT-UP/Gay Liberation Front/Minnesota, PO Box 50201 Loring Stn, Minneapolis, MN 55405 612-870-8026

♀ ★♂♂ Minnesota AIDS Project, 205 W 2nd St #306, Duluth, MN 55802 218-727-AIDS

♀ ☆♂♂ Minnesota AIDS Project, 1400 Park Ave S, Minneapolis, MN 55404 612-341-2060; 800-248-AIDS; Metro 873-AIDS; Fax 612-341-4057

♀ ☆♂♂ Minnesota AIDS Project, 1500 NE 1st Ave #200-B, Rochester, MN 55906 507-282-8771

New Age: Occult, Wicca, Alternative Healing

♀ ○ Evenstar School of Sacred Paths, 2401 University Ave W., St Paul, MN 55114-1507 612-644-3727

Organizations/Resources: Family

♀ ☆♂♂ Minnesota PFLAG, PO Box 8588, Minneapolis, MN 55408-0588 612-458-3240 Pub *Newsletter*. "Parents, Families & Friends of Lesbians & Gays."

♀ ☆♂♂ Southern Minnesota PFLAG, 2205 Elton Hills Dr NW, Rochester, MN 55901-1564 507-282-0484 "Parents, Families & Friends of Lesbians & Gays."

Organizations/Resources: Social, Recreational & Support Groups (see also Sport/Dance/Outdoor)

♂ ★ (?♂) Minnesota Polar Bares, PO Box 581953, Minneapolis, MN 55458-1953 mpbconnect@aol.com "Social nudist group."

Publications

♀ • ♂♂ Gaze Magazine, 2344 Nicollet Ave #30, Minneapolis, MN 55404 612-871-7479 Fax 612-871-0525

♀ ★ (?♂) WomenWorks, PO Box 300106, Minneapolis, MN 55403 612-377-9114 Pub *WomenWorks Newsletter*. "Social & networking."

Real Estate

♂ • Community Real Estate Referrals, 800-346-5592 "Free referral to gay/gay-supportive realtor in any USA city/state (including Virgin Is. & Puerto Rico). Sorry, no rentals!"
✦ *Community Real Estate Referrals advertisement back cover*

Religious Organizations & Publications

♀ ☆ (?♂) Catholic Pastoral Committee on Sexual Minorities (CPCSM), 1118 Farrington St, St Paul, MN 55117-4802 612-340-0618

♂ ★ UCCL/GC (United Church Coalition for Lesbian/Gay Concerns), 134 W 43rd St, Minneapolis, MN 55409

Albert Lea

Organizations/Resources: General, Multipurpose, Pride

♂ ★ (?♂) Albert Lea Gay & Lesbian Outreach, PO Box 341; 56007

Bloomington: see Minneapolis/St Paul Area

Collegeville: see Minneapolis/St Paul Area

Crystal: see Minneapolis/St Paul Area

Duluth

Accommodation: Hotels, B&B, Resorts, Campgrounds

♀ • Stanford Inn, 1415 E Superior St; 55805 218-724-3044

Bookstores: Recovery, Metaphysical, & other Specialty

♀ ○ Journeys Marketplace, 30 E Superior; 55802 218-722-5798

Community Centers (see also Women's Centers)

♀ • Aurora: A Northland Lesbian Center, 32 E 1st St 218-722-4903

♂ ★ (?♂) Northland Gay Men's Center, 8 N 2nd Ave East #309; 55802 218-722-8585

Health Care (see also AIDS Services)

♀ ☆♂♂ Duluth Community Health Center, 2 E 5th St; 55805 218-722-1497

Organizations/Resources: Student, Academic, Alumni/ae

♀ ★ University Lesbian, Gay, Bisexual Alliance, Kirby Student Center, UMD, 10 University Dr; 55812

Hill City

Accommodation: Hotels, B&B, Resorts, Campgrounds

♀ • Northwoods Retreat, 5749 Mt Ash Drive; 55748 218-697-8119; 800-767-3020

Kenyon

Accommodation: Hotels, B&B, Resorts, Campgrounds

♀ • (♂♂) Dancing Winds Farm, 6863 CO #12 Blvd; 55946-4125 507-789-6606

Mankato

Organizations/Resources: Education, Anti-Defamation, Anti-Violence, Self-Defense

♀ ★♂♂ Alliance for Justice, PO Box 124; 56002 507-625-7532; 800-269-9940

Organizations/Resources: General, Multipurpose, Pride

♀ ★♂♂ Lesbian, Gay, Bisexual Center, MSU, Box 4; 56002-8400 507-389-5131 8am-5pm. "Support, outreach, education, resources, etc, for LGBT people & their allies in the area."

MN: Mankato
Organizations: General

287
USA

Minneapolis/St Paul Area: MN
Community Centers

Marshall

Religious Organizations & Publications

♀ ★&& Lutherans Concerned/Integrity: SW Minnesota, PO Box 3013; 56258 800-235-3708

Minneapolis/St Paul Area

☎ Gay & Lesbian Hotline 612-822-8661

Accommodation: Hotels, B&B, Resorts, Campgrounds

Minneapolis

♀ • Hotel Amsterdam, 828 Hennepin Ave, Minneapolis; 55429 612-288-0459; 800-649-9500

Somerset

♀ • (&) The Country Guest House, 1673 38th St, Somerset, WI 54025 (30 mins from Mpls./St Paul) 715-247-3520

St Paul

♀ • BeYourself Inn - Twin Cities, 1093 Snelling Ave South, St Paul; 55116 612-698-3571 Fax 612-699-3840 "Bed & Breakfast primarily serving gay men."

•♂ • Como Villa Bed & Breakfast, 1371 W Nebraska Ave, St Paul; 55108 612-647-0471

Addictive Behavior, Substance Abuse, Recovery

♀ Blaisdell Women's AA Group, 1900 Nicollet Ave, Minneapolis; 55403 612-871-7400

♀ ★ Brothers & Sisters Al-Anon, Plymouth Congregational Church, 1900 Nicollet Ave, Minneapolis; 55403 Meets Fri 7-8.45pm.

♀ Lesbian Al-Anon Group, 1900 Nicollet Ave, Minneapolis; 55403 612-871-7400

♀ Lesbian/Gay AA On Campus, Boynton Health Services Ctr, Room 402, University of Minnesota, Mpls, Minneapolis; 55455

♀ ★&& Live & Let Live AA Group, 265 Oneida St, St Paul; 55102 612-292-8049

AIDS/HIV Support, Education, Advocacy, Publications

♂ ☆ Aids Emergency Fund: "Every Penny Counts", PO Box 582943, Minneapolis; 55458-2943 612-331-7733

♂ Direct Aid, PO Box 10635, St Paul; 55110 612-429-9792

♂ ☆&& Minnesota American Indian AIDS Task Force, 1433 E Franklin Ave #1, Minneapolis; 55404 612-870-1723

♂ ☆ Open Arms of Minnesota, Inc, 5005 Bryant Ave S., Box 179, Minneapolis; 55419 612-827-2624 "Food delivery program for people with HIV/AIDS."

♂ ★&& PWAlive Publications, Inc, PO Box 80216, Minneapolis; 55408-8216 612-640-PWAS "Treatment updates, personal stories, arts, memorials, etc."

Archives/Libraries/History Projects

♀ ★&& Quatrefoil Library, 1619 Dayton Ave #105-107, St Paul; 55104 612-641-0969; 612-649-1758; "Over 5000 books; periodicals from 1950s; clippings, newsletters; video & audio tapes, records, games. All welcome to use library; members ($15 yr) can check out many items."

Bars, Restaurants, Clubs, Discos

Minneapolis

♂ • & 19 Bar, 19 W. 15th St 612-871-5553

♂ • Brass Rail Lounge, 422 Hennepin Ave, Minneapolis; 55401 612-333-3016

♂ o && Gay Nineties, 408 Hennepin Ave, Minneapolis; 55401 612-333-7755 "Seven bars under one roof, including Happy Hour, Club Casablanca; Country Western Bar, Casablanca Show Lounge, Leather Bar."

♂ Ruby's Cafe, 1614 Harmon Place, Minneapolis; 55403 612-338-2089 R

♂ • && The Saloon, 830 Hennepin Ave, Minneapolis; 55403 612-332-0835 BDR 9am-1am; Fri & Sat to 3am; Sun noon-2am.

St Paul

♂ • (&&) Club Metro, 733 Pierce Butler Route, St Paul; 55104 612-489-0002 BDRE

♂ • && Innuendo, 510 N Robert St, St Paul; 55101 612-224-8996 Mon-Sat 4pm-1am.

♂ o Over The Rainbow, 249 W 7th St, St Paul (Planning to open August 1995)

♂ • && Rumours, 490 N Robert St, St Paul; 55101 612-224-0703 BDR 4pm-1am; Sat & Sun noon-1am.

♂ • Town House Country, 1415 University Ave, St Paul; 55104 612-646-7087 BdCW 2pm-1am; Sat & Sun noon-1am. The Queer Steer Review. "Free dance lessons Sun & Tue-Fri."

Bookstores: Gay/Lesbian/Feminist

♂ • A Brother's Touch, 2327 Hennepin Ave, Minneapolis; 55405 612-377-6279 Mon-Tue 11am-7pm; Wed-Fri to 9pm; Sat to 6pm; Sun noon-5pm.
+ A Brother's Touch advertisement page 289

♀ • & Amazon Bookstore Inc, 1612 Harmon Place, Minneapolis; 55403 612-338-6560

Bookstores: General

♂ • Denmark Books, 459 W 7th St, St Paul; 55102 612-222-2928

♂ o (&&) Hungry Mind Bookstore, 1648 Grand Ave, St Paul; 55105 612-699-0587

♂ o (&&) Odegard Books Saint Paul, 857 Grand Ave, St Paul; 55105 612-222-2711; 800-247-0635

♂ o Shinder's Readmore Bookstore, 733 Hennepin Ave, Minneapolis; 55403 612-333-3628

Bookstores: Recovery, Metaphysical, & other Specialty

♀ o Evenstar Bookstore, 2401 University Ave W., St Paul; 55114-1507 612-644-3727

Broadcast Media

♂ ★&& Fresh Fruit, KFAI, 1808 Riverside Ave, Minneapolis; 55454-1035 612-341-3144 Fax 612-341-4281 Thu 7.30-8.30pm. Mpls 90.3FM; St Paul 106.7FM.

♂ ★ Green & Yellow TV, PO Box 40, Eagle Lake, MN 56024 800-821-5456 Weekly one-hour cable tv magazine program.

Business, Financial & Secretarial

♂ • (?&) ROR Financial Services, Inc., 1515 W Lake St, Minneapolis; 55408 612-822-7192 "Income tax preparation."

Community Centers (see also Women's Centers)

♀ ★&& Brian Coyle Community Center, 420 15th Ave S, Minneapolis; 55454 612-338-5283 Fax 612-338-8421 Mon-Fri 9am-8pm; Sat 10am-5pm.

Counseling/Therapy: Nonprofit

♀ ★ ♿ Lesbian & Gay Counseling Program of Family & Children's Service, 414 S 8th St, Minneapolis; 55404 612-339-9101 Fax 612-339-9150 By appt. "Since 1974: affirmative, professional counseling, community education, training & consultation to professionals. Sliding fee or insurance. Internship opportunities for graduate students."

Counseling/Therapy: Private

♀ • (?♿) Benowitz, Mindy, PhD, LP, 1730 Clifton Place #205, Minneapolis; 55403 612-870-0398

♂ ○ (♿) Frederickson & Associates, 821 Raymond Ave, St Paul; 55114 612-646-8373

♀ • Holman, Patricia L., M.A., Nokomis Psychotherapy Associates 5161 Bloomington Ave South, Minneapolis; 55417 612-721-3767

♂ • ♿ Northland Therapy Center, 2324 University Ave W #100, St Paul; 55114 612-641-1009

♂ • Valgemae, Allan, MD, Adult Psychiatry Clinic, 914 S 8th St #0157, Minneapolis; 55404 612-347-2218 Fax 612-373-1859

Dentists

♀ ○ Lowry Hill Dental Clinic, 1516 West Lake St #302, Minneapolis; 55408 612-822-1484

Erotica (Printed, Visual, Equipment)

♂ ○♿ Broadway Book & Video, 901 Hennepin Ave, Minneapolis; 55403 612-338-7303

♂ ○ Buns 'N Roses, 300 3rd St South, Minneapolis; 55415 612-338-3724

♂ ○♿ Sex World Book & Video, 241 2nd Ave North, Minneapolis; 55401 612-672-0556

Funding: Endowment, Fundraising, Scholarship

♀ ★ (?♿) Gamma, Inc., 310 E 38th St #133C, Minneapolis; 55409-1300 612-825-9870 "Social organization for all gay men, sponsoring monthly member-organized events."

♂ ★ Philanthrofund Foundation, 1619 Dayton Ave #327, St Paul; 55104-6206 612-645-2287

Gifts, Cards, Pride & Novelty Items

♀ • (♿) Basket Barn, 3748 Cedar Ave S, Minneapolis; 55407 612-729-6156

Graphic Design/Typesetting (see also Art; Printing)

♂ • Designed To Sell, PO Box 47538, Minneapolis; 55447-0538 612-557-9399 Fax 612-557-8951 "Advertising from design to placement."

Health Care (see also AIDS Services)

♀ ☆ ♿ Red Door Clinic, 525 Portland Ave, Minneapolis; 55415 612-348-6363; 612-347-AIDS

Jewelry

♂ • Bolos By Barb, 1515 W Lake St, Minneapolis; 55408 612-822-7192

Legal Services & Resources

♀ • ♿ Burris, Jonathan, Esq, 701 4th Ave S #500, Minneapolis; 55415 612-337-9576

♂ ★ Minnesota Gay & Lesbian Legal Assistance, PO Box 75224, St Paul; 55175 612-879-1925

♂ • ♿ Piepkorn, Timothy L., 247 3rd Ave S, Minneapolis; 55415 612-340-9323

♂ • ♿ Viitala, Ann C., Esq, 701 4th Ave S, Minneapolis; 55415 612-337-9518

Massage Therapy (Licensed only)

♂ ○ Pearson, Bret, 612-673-9482 Member AMTA.

Organizations/Resources: Bisexual Focus

♂ ★ (?♿) Bisexual Connection, PO Box 13158, Minneapolis; 55414

Organizations/Resources: Business & Professional

♂ ★ (?♿) G/L PEN, PO Box 580397, Minneapolis; 55458-0397 612-866-9609; 612-535-9669; "Postal employees."

♂ ★ GALLOP (Gay & Lesbian Leads Organization Of Professionals), 1515 W Lake St, Minneapolis; 55408 612-822-7192

Organizations/Resources: Education, Anti-Defamation, Anti-Violence, Self-Defense

♀ ○ Brandl/Bendickson Self-Defense, PO Box 40340, St Paul; 55104-8340 612-729-4621

Organizations/Resources: Ethnic, Multicultural

♂ Voces de Ambiente, PO Box 50285, Minneapolis; 55405

Organizations/Resources: Family

♂ Minnesota Families, Box 11386, St Paul; 55111 612-377-8141

♂ PFLAG/St Cloud, PO Box 7641, St Cloud; 56302 218-259-4238; 612-252-5789; "Parents, Families & Friends of Lesbians & Gays."

Organizations/Resources: General, Multipurpose, Pride

♂ ★ Gays South of Lake Street, PO Box 8663, Minneapolis; 55408

♂ ★ ♿ Twin Cities Lesbian-Gay-Bisexual-Transgender Pride Committee, PO Box 2104, Minneapolis; 55402-0104 612-339-5329

Organizations/Resources: Political/Legislative

♂ Minnesota Independent-Republican Log Cabin Club, 2732 Grand Ave S #201, Minneapolis; 55408-1415 612-871-2509 "Republican organization."

Organizations/Resources: Sexual Focus (Leather, S/M, etc) & Safe Sex Promotion

♂ ★ ATONS of Minneapolis, PO Box 2311, Minneapolis; 55402 612-738-7343; 612-8825-3478; L

♂ ★ Black Guard of Minneapolis, PO Box 8989, Minneapolis; 55408

♂ ★ (♿) Knights of Leather, PO Box 582601, Minneapolis; 55458-2601 612-870-7473 L

Organizations/Resources: Social, Recreational & Support Groups (see also Sport/Dance/Outdoor)

♂ ★ Gay & Lesbian Community Action Council, 310 E 38th St #204, Minneapolis; 55409 612-822-0127; 800-800-0350; Fax 612-822-8786

♂ ★ (?♿) Girth & Mirth/Twin Cities, PO Box 4288, Hopkins, MN 55343 612-934-4332

♂ ★ ♿ GLEAM (Gay & Lesbian Elders Active In Minnesota), PO Box 6515, Minneapolis; 55406-6515 612-721-8913

♂ ☆ ♿ The Men's Center, 3249 Hennepin Ave #55, Minneapolis; 55408 612-822-5892 Pub Men Talk.

♀ ★ Minnesota Leather Den, PO Box 29348, Brooklyn Center; 55430 612-561-6526 L "Women's leather club not orientated to S/M lifestyles."

♂ ★ MnBear, 2344 Nicollet Ave #30 Box B, Minneapolis; 55404 612-871-1924 Pub Growler Newsletter. "Social group for large men, hairy men, & their admirers."

MN: Minneapolis/St Paul Area
289
Minneapolis/St Paul Area: MN

Organizations: Social & Support
USA
Real Estate

♂ ★ (?♿) North Country Gaylaxians, 1248 St. Clair #8, St Paul; 55105 Pub *North Country News*. "Science Fiction & Fantasy fans."

♂ ★ North Woods Radical Faerie Circle, 1807 Elliot Ave S #3, Minneapolis; 55404 612-334-1948 "Group of Faerie identified gay & bisexual men; urban events & rural gatherings."

♀ ★ (?♿) Out To Brunch, PO Box 2495 Loop Stn, Minneapolis; 55402 612-822-4432 "Social group."

Organizations/Resources: Sport/Dance/Outdoor

♀ ★ Front Runners Minneapolis/St Paul, Box 3850, Minneapolis; 55403 612-724-2211

♀ Goodtime Bowling Association, Box 425, Minneapolis; 55458 612-529-0480

♀ Minnesota Wild Roses, PO Box 3664, Minneapolis; 55403-0664 612-339-4161 *d*

♀ North Star Gay Rodeo Association, 1515 W Lake St, Minneapolis; 55408 612-827-6336

♀ ★ Northern Lights Women's Softball League, PO Box 11573, St Paul; 55111 612-488-9214

♀ ★ (?♿) Outwoods, PO Box 8855, Minneapolis; 55408

Organizations/Resources: Student, Academic, Alumni/ae

♂ ★♿ The 10% Group, Box 5855, St John's University, Collegeville; 56321 218-363-3791

♂ ★ (?♿) Delta Lambda Phi Fraternity/University of Minnesota, PO Box 13122, Minneapolis; 55414-5122 800-587-FRAT; 612-879-4340; dlp@gold.tc.umn.edu

♀ ★♿ Gay, Lesbian, Bisexual, Transgender Programs Office, University of Minnesota, 425 Walter Library, 117 Pleasant St SE, Minneapolis; 55455 612-625-6042 (voice/TTY)

♀ ★ (?♿) Lesbian, Gay, Bisexual & Transgender Resource Center, St Cloud State University, Colbert House North, St Cloud; 56301-4498 218-654-5166 Fax 612-654-5505 Thu 7-9pm. "Social/support groups, referrals, & programming of events for campus & community."

♀ ★ (♿) Lesbian/Gay/Bisexual/Transgender Resource Center (LGBTRC), St Cloud State University, 412 1st Ave S, Colbert House, St Cloud; 56301-4498 218-654-5166 Fax 218-654-5505

♀ ★♿ Macalester Gays, Lesbians, Bisexuals United, Macalester College Union 205, 1600 Grand Ave, St Paul; 55105 612-696-6248

♀ ★♿ Normandale Community College Lesbian/Gay Network, 9700 France Ave S., Bloomington; 55431 612-832-6544

♀ ★♿ United Theological Seminary Lesbian & Gay Caucus, 3000 5th St NW, New Brighton; 55112 612-633-8703

♀ ★♿ University Bi & Transgender Community, 235 Coffman Union, 300 Washington Ave SE, Minneapolis; 55455 612-626-2344; 612-625-6908; ubtc@gold.tc.umn.edu

♀ ★♿ University Lesbians, c/o U-YW, 244 Coffman Union, 300 Washington Av SE, Minneapolis; 55455 612-625-1611

♀ University of Minnesota Lesbian/Gay Law Students Association, University of Minnesota Law Center, 229 19th Ave S., Minneapolis; 55454 612-625-1000

♀ William Mitchell College of Law Gay/Lesbian Association, 875 Summit Ave, St Paul; 55105 612-646-3966

Organizations/Resources: Transgender & Transgender Publications

T City of Lakes Crossdressers Club, Box 16265, Minneapolis; 55416

Organizations/Resources: Youth (see also Family)

♀ ★♿ District 202, 2524 Nicollet Ave, Minneapolis; 55404 612-871-5559 Fax 612-871-1445 dist202@aol.com

Performing Arts: Entertainment, Music, Recording, Theater, etc.

♀ ☆ Calliope Women's Chorus, PO Box 80077, Minneapolis; 55408-8077 612-871-1952; 612-874-9804

♀ ★ Minnesota Freedom Band, PO Box 300140, Minneapolis; 55403-5140

♀ ★ One Voice Mixed Chorus, PO Box 2290, Minneapolis; 55402 612-344-9663

♂ ★♿ Twin Cities Gay Men's Chorus, 528 Hennepin Ave #504, Minneapolis; 55403-1810 612-891-9130

Publications

♀ • *FocusPoint*, PO Box 80637, Minneapolis; 55408-8637 612-874-9000 Fax 612-374-2170

→ *Gaze Magazine*: p.286

♀ *Inforum*, PO Box 47538, Minneapolis; 55447-0538 612-557-9399 Fax 612-557-8951 (May be suspended for reorganization.)

♀ ○♿ *Minnesota Women's Press*, 771 Raymond Ave, St Paul; 55114 612-646-3968

♀ • *Q Monthly*, 10 S 5th St, Minneapolis; 55402 612-321-7300 Fax 612-321-7333

Real Estate

♂ • ♿ Burnet Realty, Michael McGee, 3033 Excelsior Blvd, Minneapolis; 55416 612-920-4706 Fax 612-924-4706

Religious Organizations & Publications

♀ ★ Affirmation/Great Lakes (Mormon), PO Box 3878, Minneapolis; 55403 612-641-8666 "Mormons."

♀ ★ ♂ Affirmation: United Methodists for Lesbian, Gay & Bisexual Concerns, 101 E Grant St, Minneapolis; 55403 612-874-6613

♀ ★ ♂ All God's Children Metropolitan Community Church, 3100 Park Ave, Minneapolis; 55407 612-824-2673

♀ ★ (♈) Dignity/Twin Cities, PO Box 3565, Minneapolis; 55403 612-827-3103 "Gay & Lesbian Catholics & their friends."

♀ Integrity/Twin Cities, c/o University Episcopal Center, 317 17th Ave SE, Minneapolis; 55414 612-825-2301 "Lesbian & Gay Episcopalians & their friends."

♀ ★ ♂♂ Lutherans Concerned/Twin Cities, 100 N Oxford St, St Paul; 55104-6540 612-866-8941 Worship/social 3rd Fri of month, 7.30pm.

♀ ★ ♂♂ Spirit of the Lakes Ecumenical Community Church (UCC), 2930 13th Ave S., Minneapolis; 55407 / 2930 13th Ave S. 612-724-2313 Worship Sun 10am; Wed 7pm.

♀ ★ ♂♂ Wingspan Ministry, St Paul-Reformation Lutheran Church, 100 N Oxford St, St Paul; 55104 612-224-3371 Fax 612-224-6228

Switchboards, Helplines, Phone Information

♀ CERNET, PO Box 80637, Minneapolis; 55408 612-377-8141

♀ ★ Gay & Lesbian Hotline, 612-822-8661 noon-mdnt.; 800-800-0907

Travel & Tourist Services (see also Accommodation)

♀ • ♂♂ Kenwood Travel, 2101 Hennepin Ave South #113, Minneapolis; 55405-2769 612-871-6399 Fax 612-871-8502 Member of IGTA.

♀ • (♈) Spirit International Travel Club, 1515 W Lake St, Minneapolis; 55408 800-873-4784

♀ • (♈) Time Out Travel, 1515 W Lake St, Minneapolis; 55408 800-373-7244 Fax 612-823-7446

♀ ○ Travel About, 400 S Cedar Lake Road, Minneapolis; 55405 612-377-8955

♀ • ♂♂ The Travel Company of Minnesota, Inc, 2800 University Ave SE, Minneapolis; 55414-3293 612-379-9000; 800-328-9131

Women's Centers

♀ ☆ (♈) Chrysalis: A Center for Women, 2650 Nicollet Ave, Minneapolis; 55408-1662 612-871-0118; 612-871-2603

Moorhead

Organizations/Resources: Student, Academic, Alumni/ae

♀ ★ ♂♂ 10% Society, MSU Box 266; 56563 218-236-2227

Morris

Organizations/Resources: Student, Academic, Alumni/ae

♀ ★ (♈) Blue Light Special, c/o E-Quality UMM Mail #45 SC; 56267 612-589-6080 "Support/community group."

♀ ★ (♈) E-Quality, UMM Mail #45 SC; 56267 612-589-6080

♀ ★ (♈) Safe Haven Program, c/o UMM Counseling Office, University of Minnesota, Morris; 56267 612-589-6080 "Group of staff, faculty, administration, residence hall advisors & other student groups (trained in sensitivity issues & supplies with informational & support-service oriented pamphlets) which agree to designate their office as a Safe Haven."

New Brighton: see Minneapolis/St Paul Area

Northfield

Organizations/Resources: Student, Academic, Alumni/ae

♀ ★ ♂♂ Lesbian/Gay/Bisexual Community Carleton College, Carleton College; 55057 507-663-4265; 507-663-4154

Rochester

Organizations/Resources: General, Multipurpose, Pride

♀ ★ ♂ Gay & Lesbian Community Services, PO Box 454; 55903 / 1500 1st Ave NE 507-281-3265 Pub *Rochester Gayzette.*

St Cloud: see Minneapolis/St Paul Area

St Paul: see Minneapolis/St Paul Area

Mississippi

State/County Resources

☎ Community Services Network, Inc 601-924-3333

Accommodation: Hotels, B&B, Resorts, Campgrounds

♀ • (♈) Camp Sister Spirit, PO Box 12, Ovett, MS 39464 610-344-1411; 601-344-2005; Pub *Grapevine.* "Feminist education retreat; RV & tent camping, 120 acres; planned group facility for rent late 1994."

AIDS/HIV Support, Education, Advocacy, Publications

♀ ★ Adopt-A-Friend Project, Mississippi Phoenix Coalition, Inc., PO Box 2055, Jackson, MS 39225 601-924-3333

♀ ☆ ♂♂ MS Persons With AIDS Project, Inc., Drawer 8457, Jackson, MS 39284-8457 601-371-3019 24 hrs.

Legal Services & Resources

♀ ☆ (♂♂) American Civil Liberties Union Of Mississippi (ACLU), PO Box 2242, Jackson, MS 39225-2242 601-355-6464

Organizations/Resources: Family

♀ ☆ PFLAG, Jackson, MS, PO Box 7854, Jackson, MS 39284-7854 601-924-3333

Organizations/Resources: General, Multipurpose, Pride

♀ ★ Mississippi Phoenix Coalition, Inc., PO Box 2055, Jackson, MS 39225 601-924-3333 8.30am-10pm. Fax 601-354-2251

Organizations/Resources: Political/Legislative

♀ ★ Mississippi Gay & Lesbian Task Force, Inc, PO Box 7737, Jackson, MS 39284-7737 601-924-3333

Organizations/Resources: Social, Recreational & Support Groups (see also Sport/Dance/Outdoor)

♂ ★ Prime Timers, PO Box 59071, Jackson, MS 39284-9071 601-924-3333 Pub *Newsletter.* "Social & support group for gay men 35 & over."

Organizations/Resources: Transgender & Transgender Publications

T ☆ *Grace and Lace Letter*, PO Box 31253, Jackson, MS 39286-1253 601-982-2276

Real Estate

♀ • **Community Real Estate Referrals, 800-346-5592** "Free referral to gay/gay-supportive realtor in any USA city/state (including Virgin Is. & Puerto Rico). Sorry, no rentals!"
✦ *Community Real Estate Referrals advertisement back cover*

Switchboards, Helplines, Phone Information

♀ ★ Community Services Network, Inc, PO Box 7737, Jackson, MS 39284-7737 601-924-3333 Action Line 24 hrs.

Biloxi

AIDS/HIV Support, Education, Advocacy, Publications

♀ South Missippi Aids Task Force, 466 Caillavet St; 39530 601-435-1234

Bars, Restaurants, Clubs, Discos

♀ Joey's, 1708 Beach Blvd (Hwy 90); 39530 601-435-5639

Community Centers (see also Women's Centers)

♀ ★ G L Friendly, 311 Caillavet St; 39530-2044 601-435-2398

Erotica (Printed, Visual, Equipment)

♀ ○ The Adult Bookstore, 1620 Pass Road; 39531 601-435-2802

Organizations/Resources: General, Multipurpose, Pride

♀ Mississippi Gay & Lesbian Task Force/Gulf Coast Chapter, 311 Caillavet St; 39530 601-435-2398

Religious Organizations & Publications

♀ Metropolitan Community Church of the Gulf Coast, PO Box 5304; 39533 601-897-1950

Greenville

Bookstores: General

♀ ○ ♂ The Book Store, 323 Washington Ave; 38701 601-332-2665 Fax 601-335-6767

Hattiesburg

Organizations/Resources: Student, Academic, Alumni/ae

♀ Gay Lesbian Bi Student Organization (GLBSO), USM PO Box 8471; 39406

Jackson

Addictive Behavior, Substance Abuse, Recovery

♀ ★ (♂♀) Lambda AA, PO Box 8342; 39284-8342 601-924-3333

Bars, Restaurants, Clubs, Discos

♀ ○ (♂♀) Club Colours, 200 N. Mill St; 39201 (corner of Mill & Amitt) 601-353-2041

♂ • (♂) Jack's Construction Site, 425 N. Mart Plaza 601-362-3108 *BLCWdf* Opens 5pm.

♀ • Jaded Entertainment Emporium, 2460 Terry Rd; 39204 601-371-0478

♀ • (♂♀) Sugarbaker's, 208 W Capitol; 39201 601-352-0022 *BECWd* Wed, Fri, Sat & Sun from 9pm.

Erotica (Printed, Visual, Equipment)

♀ ○ Heritage Video, 1515 Terry Rd; 39204 601-354-5555

Organizations/Resources: Social, Recreational & Support Groups (see also Sport/Dance/Outdoor)

♀ Magnolia Lambda Car Club, PO Box 1812; 39215-1812 601-924-3333

→ Prime Timers: p.290

Organizations/Resources: Student, Academic, Alumni/ae

♀ MS State GLBF, PO Box 6220; 39262 601-325-0700

Publications

♀ ★ *The Mississippi Voice*, PO Box 7737; 39284-7737 601-924-3333

Religious Organizations & Publications

♀ ★ ♂♂ Metropolitan Community Church of the Rainbow, 5565 Robinson Rd Ext Ste L; 39204-4163 601-366-1815

♂ ★ ♂ St Stephen's Community Church, PO Box 97793; 39288-7793 601-939-7181 Meets Sun 5pm, at Unitarian Church, 4872 N. State St, Jackson

Meridian

Bars, Restaurants, Clubs, Discos

♀ • ♂ Crossroads & Ollie Mae's, Exit 42 Savoy Rd 601-655-8415 *BDRECW*

Missouri

State/County Resources

Addictive Behavior, Substance Abuse, Recovery

♀ • (♂♀) Pride Institute, 800-54-PRIDE "The nation's only accredited chemical dependency treatment center exclusively for Gay, Lesbian & Bisexual People."

AIDS/HIV Support, Education, Advocacy, Publications

♀ ☆ ♂♂ AIDS Project of the Ozarks, 1901 E Bennett St #D, Springfield, MO 65804-1419 417-881-1900 Mon-Fri 9am-5pm; Helpline to 9pm. Serving 29 counties in SW Missouri.

♂ ☆ (?♂) Mid-MO AIDS Project, 3900 Clark Ln Lot 167, Columbia, MO 65202-2494 314-875-AIDS Fax 314-442-0058

Legal Services & Resources

♀ ☆ ♂♂ American Civil Liberties Union of Kansas & Western Missouri (ACLU), 706 W 42nd St, Kansas City, MO 64111 816-756-3113

Organizations/Resources: General, Multipurpose, Pride

♂ ★ (?♂) Missouri Task Force for Gay & Lesbian Concerns (MOTF), PO Box 563, Columbia, MO 65205-0563 800-576-5128

Organizations/Resources: Political/Legislative

♀ Log Cabin Club, 1425 Summergate Pkwy, St Charles, MO 63303 314-447-9709 (Republicans)

♀ ☆ (?♂) Ozarks Human Rights Coalition, PO Box 901, West Plains, MO 65775 417-257-1747

♂ ★ ♂♂ Triangle Coalition Political Action Committee, c/o GALA-MU, A022 Brady Commons, Univ of Missouri, Columbia, MO 65211 314-882-4427

Organizations/Resources: Sport/Dance/Outdoor

♀ ★ Missouri Gay Rodeo Association, mail to MGRA Inc, PO Box 3234, Joplin, MO 64803-3234

Publications

♂ • *Current News*, 809 W 34th St #1, Kansas City, MO 64111-7010 816-561-2679

♂ • *News-Telegraph*, PO Box 14229A, St Louis, MO 63178-1229 314-664-6411; 816-561-6266; Fax 314-664-6303; KC fax (816) 561-2623 newstele@aol.com Kansas City office: PO Box 10085, Kansas City, MO 64171 Distribution covers Missouri, Arkansas, Kansas, southern Illinois, western Tennessee.

MO: State/County Resources
292
Kansas City Area: MO
Publications
USA
Bars, Clubs, Restaurants

A Message Board For Personal Ads

Eclectics

Columbia's Safer Sex Shop
1122-A Wilkes Blvd.
Columbia
MO 65201

Free Condoms
& Educational
Materials

Arcade
Magazines
Gifts & Cards
Antique Memorabilia
Leather

(314) 443-0873
We Buy Used Magazines and Tapes

♂ ★ SoMo News Connection, c/o Mike Bromberg, Rt 3, Box 6B2, Tecumseh, MO 65760 417-679-4682 (afternoons) Fax 417-679-4684 "Please send stamp for sample issue."

Real Estate

♂ ● Community Real Estate Referrals, 800-346-5592 "Free referral to gay/gay-supportive realtor in any USA city/state (including Virgin Is. & Puerto Rico). Sorry, no rentals!"
◆ Community Real Estate Referrals advertisement back cover

Cape Girardeau

AIDS/HIV Support, Education, Advocacy, Publications

♀ ☆&& AIDS Project of Southeast Missouri (APSEMO), PO Box 1132; 63702-1132 314-339-9588; 800-704-AIDS

Bars, Restaurants, Clubs, Discos

♂ ● Independence Place, 5 S Henderson; 63701 314-334-2939 BD

Bookstores: General

♀ ○ Metro News, 415 Broadway; 63701 314-335-8633

Columbia

☎ Lesbian & Gay Helpline 314-449-4477

Bars, Restaurants, Clubs, Discos

♂ ● && Contacts—The Bar, 514 E Broadway; 65201 314-443-0281 D Mon-Fri 5pm-1.30am; Sat 8pm-1.30am.

♂ Styx Inc., 3111 Bus 63 South; 65201 314-499-1828

Bookstores: General

♀ ○ & Wellspring, 1027 E Walnut St; 65201 314-443-4340 "Metaphysical books."

Broadcast Media

♂ ○ (&) KOPN Radio 89.5 FM, 915 E Broadway; 65201 314-874-5676 Sun 5.30-6.30pm: The Gaydar Show; Wed 10pm-mdnt: Womenergy (Lesbian music & issues); Sun 2.30-5pm: Moon of Artemis (Feminist issues & music by women); Sun 5-5.30pm: The Feminist News.

Erotica (Printed, Visual, Equipment)

♀ ○ & Eclectics, 1122-A Wilkes Blvd; 65201 314-443-0873 11am-mdnt.
◆ Eclectics advertisement page 292

Organizations/Resources: Political/Legislative

♂ ★ Columbia Stonewall Coalition, c/o Womenergy/Gaydar, KOPN, 915 E Broadway; 65201 314-449-4477

Organizations/Resources: Social, Recreational & Support Groups (see also Sport/Dance/Outdoor)

♀ ★ (?&) Coming Out Collective, PO Box 48; 65205-0048 314-442-4174; 314-445-5981

♂ Dignity, 701 Maryland Ave c/o Newman Center; 65201 314-449-5424 "Social group."

Organizations/Resources: Student, Academic, Alumni/ae

♀ ★ && Triangle Coalition, A022 Brady Commons, University of Missouri; 65211 314-882-4427 "Lesbians, Gays, Bisexuals, Transsexuals, Transgenderists."

Religious Organizations & Publications

♂ ★ Christ The King Agape Church, 515 Hickman Ave; 65201 314-443-5316

♂ ★ && United Covenant Mission Church, PO Box 7152; 65205 314-449-7194

Switchboards, Helplines, Phone Information

♀ ★ Lesbian & Gay Helpline, 314-449-4477

Women's Centers

♀ ☆&& MU Women's Center, 229 Brady Commons; 65211 314-882-6621

Joplin

Bars, Restaurants, Clubs, Discos

♂ Partners Dance Bar, 722 S Main St; 64801 417-781-9313

♂ Partners Western Lounge, 720 S Main St; 64801 417-781-6453

Kansas City Area

Includes Kansas City, KS

☎ Gay Talk 816-931-4470

Accommodation: Hotels, B&B, Resorts, Campgrounds

Kansas City, Missouri

♀ ○ Doanleigh Wallagh Inn, 217 E 37th St; 64111 816-753-2667 "Bed & breakfast inn."

Overland Park, Kansas

♂ ★ (&&) B & B In KC, 9215 Slater, Overland Park, KS 66212-3826 913-648-5457

Addictive Behavior, Substance Abuse, Recovery

♂ ★&& Live & Let Live AA, PO Box 411111; 64141-1111 816-531-9668; 816-471-7229: Central AA Information Service

AIDS/HIV Support, Education, Advocacy, Publications

♂ ★ Condom Crusaders, 706 W 42nd #107; 64111 816-561-9717

♀ ☆&& Good Samaritan Project, 3030 Walnut St; 64106 816-561-8784

♀ ☆&& Heartland AIDS Resource Council, 2615 Holmes St; 64108-2744

Antiques & Collectables

♀ ● Adrienne's Midtown Flea Market, 3308 Troost Ave; 64109 816-561-4777

Bars, Restaurants, Clubs, Discos

Kansas City, Kansas

♂ ● View on the Hill, 204 Orchard, Kansas City; 66101 913-371-9370

MO: Kansas City Area
Bars, Clubs, Restaurants

293

USA

Kansas City Area: MO
Printing

Kansas City, Missouri

Arabian Knights, 3314 Gillham Plaza; 64109 816-531-9312

Buddies, 3715 Main St; 64111 816-561-2600

Cabaret, 5024 Main St; 64112 816-753-6504 *DER*

Dixie Belle Complexx, 1922 Main St; 64108 816-471-2424 *BRDL*

• && The Edge, 323 W 8th St (entrance in rear); 64105 816-221-8900 *BDE* Mon-Sat 8pm-3am. "Mostly gay men's club with lesbians & straight mix."

• && Jamie's Sports Bar, 528 Walnut St; 64106 816-471-2080 *BRDECW* 8am-1.30am.

• K.C. Eagle—Billy's Place, 1818 Main St; 64108 816-472-6366 *BRDELL* 11am-3am.

Mari's, 1809 Grand Ave; 64108 816-283-0511 *R*

○ (&) Metropolis American Grill, 303 Westport Rd; 64111 816-753-1550 *R*

Missie B's, 805 W 39th St; 64111 816-561-0625

The Other Side, 3611 Broadway; 64111 816-931-0501

• Side Kicks, 3707 Main St; 64111 816-931-1430 *CW*

Tools, 518 E 31st St; 64108 816-753-0263 *BR*

Tootsie's, 3601 Broadway; 64111 816-756-3538

Whistle Stop, 1321 Grand Blvd; 64106 816-221-8008 *D*

Overland Park, Kansas

• The Fox, 7520 Shawnee Mission Pkwy, Overland Park; 66202 913-384-0369 *Bd* Noon-2am.

Bookstores: General

○ && Borders Book Shop, 9108 Metcalf, Overland Park; 66212 913-642-3642 8am-10pm; Fri & Sat to 11pm; Sun 11am-7pm.

Community Centers (see also Women's Centers)

Lesbian Gay Community Center, PO Box 412681; 64141 816-374-5945

Computer Bulletin Boards

• Lobo After Dark, 6300 Main St #405; 64113 816-737-5500; 816-737-9600 Modem: 32 lines; 24 hrs.; Fax 816-737-1100

Counseling/Therapy: Private

• & Lambda Counseling Services, 5128 Brookside Blvd; 64112-2736 816-531-7133

○ && McCarthy, Mark, MS, LPC, 4520 Madison #200; 64111 816-931-0011

Erotica (Printed, Visual, Equipment)

• Adrienne's Bookstore & Arcade, 3314 Troost Ave; 64109 816-561-8996

○ (&&) Hollywood at Home, 9063 Metcalf, Overland Park; 66212 913-649-9666

○ (&&) Ray's Playpen, 3235 Main St; 64111 816-753-7692

Gifts, Cards, Pride & Novelty Items

• **Larry's Gifts & Cards, 205 Westport Rd; 64111 816-753-4757** 10am-7pm; Sat to 6.30pm; Sun to 5pm.
+ *Larry's Gifts & Cards advertisement page 293*

Health Care (see also AIDS Services)

☆ && KC Free Health Clinic, 2 E 39th St; 64111 816-753-5144 Pub *KC Free Health Clinic Newsletter.*

☆ STD Clinic, 2301 Locust; 64108 816-474-4901

Health Clubs, Gyms, Saunas

♂ • (&) 1823 Club, 1823 Wyandotte St; 64108 *Pf*

Legal Services & Resources

○ && Bogler, Steven Kent, 818 Grand Ave #200; 64106 816-842-9850

Organizations/Resources: Education, Anti-Defamation, Anti-Violence, Self-Defense

GLAAD-KC, PO Box 7214; 64113-0214 816-374-5927

Organizations/Resources: Ethnic, Multicultural

★ (?&) Asians & Friends, PO Box 7521; 64113 816-822-7127

♂ ★ Men of All Colors Together/Kansas City, PO Box 412432; 64141 816-931-4470 Pub *MACt-KC Newsletter.*

Organizations/Resources: Family

★ (&) Gay & Lesbian Parents Coalition/GALA, 6241 Blue Ridge Blvd; 64133-4107 816-356-9589

Organizations/Resources: General, Multipurpose, Pride

★ Gay & Lesbian Services Network, 706 W 42nd St #107; 64111-3199 816-561-9717 (Gay Talk) 5pm-1am. "Programs include Gay Talk Hotline; Condom Crusaders (safer sex/AIDS education outreach); Speakers program; Project Pride."

★ && Project Pride, 706 W 42nd St #107; 64111-3199 816-561-9717

Organizations/Resources: Political/Legislative

★ && Human Rights Project, PO Box 32812; 64111-2812 816-753-1672 Fax 816-753-3880 Pub *HRP Newsletter.* "Political action group."

Organizations/Resources: Social, Recreational & Support Groups (see also Sport/Dance/Outdoor)

KC Couples, PO Box 13576, Shawnee Mission; 66212 913-753-3551

☆ (?&) L'Cha Dodi of the JCRB/AJC, 5801 West 115th St, Overland Park; 66211-1824 816-756-3333

♀ ★ Womontown, PO Box 090811; 64109 913-791-8058

Organizations/Resources: Sport/Dance/Outdoor

★ Greater Kansas City Gay & Lesbian Outdoor Club, PO Box 412232; 64141-2232

Printing & Promotional Items (see also Art; Graphics/Typesetting)

○ Markline Promotional Wear, 8261 State Ave, Kansas City; 66112 913-299-4621 Fax 913-299-4622

♂ • Seneca Printing, 6241 Blue Ridge Blvd; 64133 816-356-9589

Publications

♀ • ♂ *News-Telegraph, KC Office*, PO Box 10085; 64171-0085 816-561-6266 Fax 816-561-2623

Religious Organizations & Publications

♀ ★ (♿) Affirmation: United Methodists for Lesbian, Gay & Bisexual Concerns, 5709 Virginia Ave; 64110-2855 816-363-6892

♂ ★ (♿♿) GLAD-KC (Disciples of Christ), PO Box 414711; 64141

♀ ★ (♿) Metropolitan Community Church of Johnson County, 12510 W 62nd Terrace #106, Shawnee Mission; 66216 913-631-1184 Services Sun 10.30am; Wed 7.30pm; Christian Education Sun 9am.

♂ ★ ♿ Metropolitan Community Church, PO Box 10087; 64171-0087 / 3801 Wyandotte 816-931-0750

♀ ★ New Jerusalem Fellowship Ministries, PO Box 10476; 64171 816-756-3667

Switchboards, Helplines, Phone Information

♀ ★ Gay Talk, 706 W 42nd St #107; 64111-3199 816-931-4470 5pm-1am.

Veterinarians

♀ • ♂ Rainbow Pet Hospital, 4468 Rainbow Blvd, Kansas City, KS 66103 913-831-2034

Video Sales, Rentals, Services (see also Erotica)

♀ • ♂ Video Westport, 208 Westport Rd; 64111 816-561-6397

St Charles

Bookstores: General

♀ ○ Bargain Books, 3010 N Hwy 94; 63301 314-723-9598; 800-834-4127

Women's Centers

♀ ☆ (?♿) The Women's Center, PO Box 51; 63302 314-946-6854 "Thirty day residential program for victims of domestic violence."

St Joseph

Bars, Restaurants, Clubs, Discos

♂ ○ Avis' Lounge, 705 Edmond St; 64501 816-364-9748

Organizations/Resources: General, Multipurpose, Pride

♀ ★ Midland Empire Task Force, PO Box 8233; 64508-8233 816-364-8376

St Louis Area
Includes East St Louis

☎ Gay & Lesbian Hotline, Challenge Metro 314-367-0084

Accommodation: Hotels, B&B, Resorts, Campgrounds

St Louis

♀ • (♿) **Brewers House Bed & Breakfast, 1829 Lami St;** 63104 314-771-1542

♀ • St. Louis Guesthouse, 1032-38 Allen Ave; 63104 314-773-1016

AIDS/HIV Support, Education, Advocacy, Publications

♂ ★ ACT-UP/Saint Louis, PO Box 16899; 63105 314-727-6792

♀ ☆ Blacks Assisting Blacks Against AIDS (BABAA), 1307 Washington Ave #400; 63103-1926

♀ ☆ (?♿) Doorways, PO Box 4652; 63108 314-454-9599 "AIDS/HIV housing."

♀ ☆♿♿ Food Outreach, Inc., 4579 Laclede Ave #309; 63108 314-367-4461

♂ ★ Pets Are Wonderful Support (PAWS), 4579 Laclede Ave #306; 63108 314-351-8047

♀ ★♿♿ St Louis Effort for AIDS (EFA), 5622 Delmar #104E; 63112-2646 314-367-2382 Pub *Frontline*. "Support for People With AIDS, HIV; families, lovers, spouses."

Antiques & Collectables

♀ • Windsor Antiques, 2222 Cherokee; 63118 314-773-3135; 800-752-8118; 9.30-6pm; 11.30-6pm.

Bars, Restaurants, Clubs, Discos
Alton

♀ • (♿♿) Alton Metro, 602 Belle St; 62002 618-465-8687 *DE* 4pm-1.30am.

Belleville

♂ Char-pei Lounge, 400 Mascoutah Ave, Belleville; 62220 618-236-0810 (evenings; call ahead)

♀ Lil's Second Time Around, 317 Mascoutah Ave, Belleville; 62220 618-233-9452

East St Louis

♂ • Faces/Upstage, 130 4th St, East St Louis, IL 62201 618-271-7410 *BDEL*

Granite City

♂ • ♂ Club Zips, 3145 W Chain Of Rocks Road, Granite City; 62040 618-797-0700 Fax 618-797-2200 *BD*

St Louis

♀ Attitudes, 4100 Manchester Ave; 63110 314-534-3858

♂ Bacchus, 6 Sarah St; 63108 314-531-1109

♀ • Charles Street Station, 412 N Tucker Blvd; 63108 314-241-2444 *BRE*

♀ • (♿) Clementine's, 2001 Menard St; 63104 314-664-7869 *BRLW*

♂ Club 747, 1624 Delmar; 63103 314-621-9030

♂ • ♿♿ The Complex, 3511 Chouteau; 63103 314-722-2645 *BDR* 11am-3am.

♂ The Drake, 3502 Papin St; 63101 314-685-1400

♂ Eagle/Outpost, 17 S Vandeventer; 63108 314-535-4100

♀ • Ernie's Class Act Restaurant & Lounge, Inc., 3756 S Broadway; 63118 314-664-6221 *BDR* 11am-1.30am.

♂ Fallout, 1324 Washington; 63103 314-421-0003 *D*

♂ Front Page, 2330 Menard Ave; 63104 314-664-2939

♀ Gabriel's, 6901 S Broadway; 63111 314-832-0656

♀ The Grey Fox Pub, 3503 S Spring; 63116 314-772-2150

♂ • (♿) Loading Zones, 16 S Euclid; 63108 314-361-4119

♀ • ♿♿ Magnolia's Restaurant & Bar, 5 S Vandeventer; 63108 314-652-6500 *BDR* 4pm-3am. 2nd floor Western Bar & Cafe.

♀ Merlie's, 2917 S Jefferson; 63104 314-771-4974

Bookstores: Gay/Lesbian/Feminist

♀ • **Our World Too, 11 S Vandeventer; 63108 314-533-5322;** 314-533-6155 **Community Access Line (recording); "Over 2000 titles. Mail order catalog."**
✦ *Our World Too advertisement page 295*

Bookstores: General

♀ ○ (&) Books-N-Things, 1 S Old Orchard; 63119 314-961-3755

♂ ○ (&) Daily Planet News, 243 N Euclid; 63108 314-367-1333

♀ ● (&) Left Bank Books and Coffee, 399 N Euclid; 63108 314-367-6731

♂ ○ (&) Pages Video & More, 10 N Euclid; 63108 314-361-3420

Community Centers (see also Women's Centers)

♥ ★ && The Center, PO Box 4589; 63108 / 438 N Skinker Blvd 314-997-9897; 314-725-3122

Computer Bulletin Boards

♥ ★ GA-PRO, 314-231-0062 2400 Baud; free access.

Counseling/Therapy: Private

♥ ● Murrell, Pat, MSW, LCSW, PO Box 23305; 63156 618-462-4051; 314-569-5795

♀ ● (&&) Rogers, Linda L., PhD, 231 S Bemiston Ave #925, Clayton; 63105 314-727-1907

♀ ○ ♂ Snyder, Robert, Ph.D., 225 S Meramac #321T; 63105 314-727-9088

♥ ● Tetlow, Ellen, LCSW, 214 S Meramac, Clayton; 63105 314-863-6303

♀ ● (?&) Wagner, Dick, MSW, ACSW, 10349 Watson Rd; 63127 314-965-1942

Florists (see also Gardening)

♀ ● (&) Cumberworth's Fine Flowers, 1909 Park Ave; 63104 314-231-7407

♂ ● Windsor Florist, 2220 Cherokee; 63118 314-773-8080; 800-752-8118; 9.30-6pm; 11.30-6pm.

Gifts, Cards, Pride & Novelty Items

♀ ● (?&) Friends & Luvers Boutique, 3550 Gravois Avenue; 63118 314-771-9405 Fax 314-771-9431 10am-10pm; Sun noon-7pm. "Separate showroom for adult toys. Video sales & rentals."

♀ ● Heffalumps, 387 N Euclid St; 63108 314-361-0544

Health Care (see also AIDS Services)

♀ ● (?&) Matakoa-Williams, Richard, N.T., 314-664-8251 "Naturopathic Therapist; alternative healing; herbalist."

♥ ● && Williamson, Catherine, RNC, 2340 Hampton Ave; 63139 314-647-2200 "Women's Health Care Nurse Practitioner."

Health Clubs, Gyms, Saunas

♂ ● Club St Louis, 2625 Samuel Shepherd Dr; 63103 314-533-3666

Legal Services & Resources

♀ ● && Delta Legal Services, PC, 7352 Forsyth, Clayton; 63105 314-863-4297 Fax 314-863-5150

♂ ● (&&) Fisk, Jay D., 100 N Euclid #608; 63108 314-361-3039

♀ ● Keesee, David R., 4144 Lindell #506; 63108 314-535-6770

♀ ○ Lohr, Robert J., 8011 Clayton Rd; 63117 314-727-7100 "Criminal defense & personal injury."

♀ ● (?&) Marshall, Steve, 4658 Nebraska; 63111 314-353-1311

♀ ○ && Toko, Gale L., 7352 Forsyth Blvd; 63105-2154 314-863-8555 "Emphasis on domestic relations, estate planning; bankruptcy."

♀ ● (?&) Wysack, Kathryn J., 3203A South Grand #D; 63118 314-771-4494

Meeting/Contact Services, Publications, Talklines

♀ ○ *Shadow Box*, PO Box 411124; 63141 314-429-7309 "An alternative way to meet new & exciting people: strictly confidential & very discreet. Personal ads."

Organizations/Resources: Business & Professional

♥ ★ Gateway Business & Professional Alliance, PO Box 23037; 63156-3037 314-993-7533

Organizations/Resources: Ethnic, Multicultural

♥ ★ (?&) People of All Colors Together, PO Box 775402; 63177-5402 314-995-4683

Organizations/Resources: Family

♀ ☆ && PFLAG, 7443 Cromwell Dr; 63105 314-821-3524 "Parents, Families & Friends of Lesbians & Gays."

Organizations/Resources: General, Multipurpose, Pride

♥ ★ Pride St. Louis, 3810 S Broadway; 63118-4608

Organizations/Resources: Political/Legislative

♥ Lesbian & Gay Alliance for Justice, PO Box 1926; 63118 314-664-4896

♀ ★ (?&) Privacy Rights Education Project (PREP), PO Box 24106; 63130 314-862-4900 Fax 314-862-8155

Organizations/Resources: Social, Recreational & Support Groups (see also Sport/Dance/Outdoor)

♥ ★ ♂ GAMMA Support Group, 314-567-2076 "Confidential (non-sexual) support group for gay men who are married, separated or divorced."

♂ ★ Gay Men's Support Group, c/o Metropolitan Community Church, 1120 Dolman Ave; 63104 314-231-9100 Meets Tue 7.30pm.

♀ ★ Kindred Spirits, PO Box 160225; 63116-8225 Pub *Lavender Dragon.* "Science fiction/fantasy fan club by & for gays, lesbians, & bisexuals; meets 1st Sun of month, 2pm, at Blue Moon Coffee House, 3710 Gravois."

Organizations/Resources: Sport/Dance/Outdoor

♀ ★ (♿) TEAM St Louis, PO Box 1926; 63118 314-997-9877

Organizations/Resources: Student, Academic, Alumni/ae

♀ ★ (♿) Gay & Lesbian & Bisexual Community Alliance, Washington University, 1 Brookings Dr., Campus Box 1128; 63130 314-935-5349

♂ ★♿♿ Gay & Lesbian Olin Business School Alliance (GLOBAL), 1 Brookings Dr., Campus Box 1133, c/o Washington University; 63130 314-935-6315

♀ ★ Lesbian/Gay Campus Organization, 267 University Center, 8001 Natural Bridge Rd; 63121-4499 314-553-5380

♂ ★ Principia Gay & Lesbian Alumni Group, c/o David White, 2900 Connecticut Ave NW, Apt 124, Washington, DC 20008-1404 202-387-7250

Organizations/Resources: Youth (see also Family)

⚥ Growing American Youth, Box 7226 c/o MCC; 63177 314-533-5322

Performing Arts: Entertainment, Music, Recording, Theater, etc.

♂ ★ (♿) Gateway Men's Chorus, 2102 Russell Blvd; 63104-2607 314-771-GWMC

♀ • ♿ Piano World/Dallas Pipe Organ, International Music House, 1509 Washington 4th flr; 63103 314-231-0600; 800-589-5824; "Sales & restoration of vintage antique player pianos, pianos, square grands, pipe organs, reed organs, nickelodeons."

Publications

♀ • *Lestalk*, Rose Publications, PO Box 63188; 63163 314-773-3220 (also Fax; please call first) ltalk@aol.com

♂ • *News-Telegraph*, **PO Box 14229A; 63178-1229 314-664-6411; 816-561-6266; Fax 314-664-6303; KC fax (816) 561-2623 newstele@aol.com Kansas City office: PO Box 10085, Kansas City, MO 64171 Distribution covers Missouri, Arkansas, Kansas, southern Illinois, western Tennessee.**

♀ *TWISL (This Week In St. Louis),* PO Box 8086, Alton; 62002 618-465-9370

Religious Organizations & Publications

♀ ★♿♿ Agape Church of St Louis, 2026 Lafayette Ave; 63104 314-664-3588 *The St Louis Agapian.*

♂ ★ (♿♿) Dignity/St Louis, PO Box 23093; 63156 314-997-9897 x63

♂ ★ (♿) Metropolitan Community Church of Greater St Louis, PO Box 7226; 63177-7226 314-231-9100

♀ ★♿♿ Metropolitan Community Church of Living Faith, 6501 Wydown Blvd, Clayton; 63105 314-726-2855

♂ ★ (♿) UCCL/GC (United Church Coalition for Lesbian/Gay Concerns), PO Box 21812; 63109 314-776-4483

Switchboards, Helplines, Phone Information

♀ ★ Gay & Lesbian Hotline, Challenge Metro, PO Box 23227; 63156 314-367-0084 6-10pm. "We also have a Speaker's Bureau."

Travel & Tourist Services (see also Accommodation)

♀ • ♿ Dynamic Travel, Inc., 7750 Clayton Rd #105; 63117 314-781-8400; 800-237-4083

♂ • Lafayette Square Travel, 1801 Lafayette Ave; 63104 314-776-8747 1-800-727-1480

♀ • Rainbow Vacationers, 7359 Carleton; 63130 314-726-5832 "Information & referral on lesbian travel (not travel agents)."

♂ ○ ♀ Trips Unlimited, 4501 Maryland Ave; 63108 314-361-1176

Veterinarians

♀ • ♿ Kingsbury Animal Hospital, 420 N Skinker Blvd; 63130 314-721-6251

Women's Centers

♀ ☆♿♿ UMSL Women's Center, 211-212 Clark Hall, 8001 Natural Bridge Rd; 63121 314-553-5380

♀ ☆ (♿♿) Women's Resource Center, PO Box 1128 Washington University; 63130 314-935-7583 "Library; meeting space."

♀ ☆♿♿ Women's Self Help Center, 2838 Olive St; 63103 314-531-9100; 314-531-2003 hotline

Springfield

Bars, Restaurants, Clubs, Discos

♂ • ♿♿ Club 1105, 1109 E Commercial; 65803-3254 417-831-9043 *DCW* Mon-Sat 4pm-4.30am.

♂ The Colosseum, 2100 E Pythian; 65802 417-869-5451

♀ Joint at Black Forest Inn, 2185 S Campbell Ave; 65807 417-882-6755 *BR*

♀ • (♿) Martha's Vineyard, 219 W Olive; 65806 417-864-4572 *B*

♀ The Peanut Gallery & Lounge, 424 N Booneville; 65806 417-865-1266

♂ The Stables, 620 W College St; 65806 417-862-6363

Bookstores: General

♀ ○ Renaissance Books, 1337 East Montclair; 65804 417-883-5161

♀ ○ Sunshine News, 3537 W Sunshine; 65807 417-831-2298

Organizations/Resources: Political/Legislative

♀ ★ (♿) COHAB, PO Box 225; 65801

Religious Organizations & Publications

⚥ Metropolitan Community Church In The Ozarks, PO Box 2782; 65801 417-865-6539

Montana
State/County Resources

AIDS/HIV Support, Education, Advocacy, Publications

♂ CritiCare, PO Box 1253, Billings, MT 59103 406-255-7467

Organizations/Resources: General, Multipurpose, Pride

♀ ★ Pride!, PO Box 775, Helena, MT 59624-0775 406-442-9322 Fax 406-442-5589

Organizations/Resources: Political/Legislative

♀ ☆ Montana Human Rights Network, PO Box 1222, Helena, MT 59624 406-442-5506

♀ ☆ Montana Women's Lobby, PO Box 1099, Helena, MT 59624 406-449-7917; 406-549-4466 Missoula

Real Estate

♂ • Community Real Estate Referrals, 800-346-5592 "Free referral to gay/gay-supportive realtor in any USA city/state (including Virgin Is. & Puerto Rico). Sorry, no rentals!"
✦ *Community Real Estate Referrals advertisement back cover*

Billings

AIDS/HIV Support, Education, Advocacy, Publications

♀ ☆ Yellowstone AIDS Project, PO Box 1748; 59103 406-252-1212

Bookstores: General

♂ • ♿ Barjon's Books, 2718 3rd Ave N.; 59101 406-252-4398 Mon-Sat 9.30am-5.30pm. "A Deli for the Mind."

Erotica (Printed, Visual, Equipment)

♀ ○ Adult Bookstore, 2702 Minnesota Ave; 59101 406-245-4293

♀ ○ Studio One Theatre & Bookstore, 2709 Montana; 59101 406-259-0051

Religious Organizations & Publications

♂ ★ ♿ Family of God Metropolitan Community Church, PO Box 23003; 59104 406-245-7066 Worship Sun 11am & Wed 7pm at 645 Howard. Pub *Family Ties.*

Bozeman

Erotica (Printed, Visual, Equipment)

♀ • Ms Kitty's Adult Shop, 12 N Willson St; 59715 406-586-6989

Organizations/Resources: Student, Academic, Alumni/ae

♂ ★ ♿♿ Lambda Alliance of Gay Men & Lesbians, c/o Women's Center, Hamilton Hall #15; 59717 406-994-3836 (messages); 406-994-3836 (messages); Mon-Fri 9am-4pm.

Women's Centers

♀ ☆ ♿♿ Women's Center, Hamilton Hall #15, Montana State University; 59717 406-994-3836 Mon-Fri 9am-4pm. Pub *Womanifesto.*

Butte

AIDS/HIV Support, Education, Advocacy, Publications

♀ ☆ ♿♿ Butte AIDS Support Services, PO Box 382; 59703 406-494-6125 24 hrs.

Great Falls

Religious Organizations & Publications

♂ ★ Metropolitan Community Church—Shepherd of the Plains, PO Box 2162; 59403 / 1505 17th Ave SW; 59404 406-771-1070

Kalispell

Organizations/Resources: General, Multipurpose, Pride

♂ ★ ♿♿ Flathead Valley Alliance, PO Box 2730; 59903 406-758-6707 donnfar@aol.com

Missoula

Bars, Restaurants, Clubs, Discos

♀ Am-Vets Club, 225 Ryman; 59802 406-728-3137 (more gay eves)

♂ • ♿♿ The Catalyst Espresso Shop, 111 N Higgins Ave; 59801 406-542-1337

Bookstores: General

♀ ○ (♿) Freddy's Feed & Read, 1221 Helen Ave; 59801 406-549-2127 Take-out deli.

♀ ☆ ♿ University Center Bookstore, UOM, Campus Drive; 59806 406-243-4921

Erotica (Printed, Visual, Equipment)

♀ ○ ♿♿ Fantasy for Adults Only, 210 E. Main St; 59801 406-543-7760 8am-1.30am; Fri & Sat to 3am; Sun 10am-mdnt.

♀ ○ Fantasy For Adults Only, 2611 Brooks St; 59801 406-543-7510 8am-1.30am; Fri & Sat 24 hrs.

Organizations/Resources: Political/Legislative

♀ ☆ (?♿) Missoula Advocates For Social Justice, PO Box 9294; 59807 406-721-3206 (also fax)

Organizations/Resources: Student, Academic, Alumni/ae

♂ ★ ♿♿ Lambda Alliance, PO Box 7611; 59807 406-523-5567 "Western Montana's Gay/lesbian/bisexual support group."

Women's Centers

♀ ☆ ♿♿ University of Montana Women's Center, UC 211, University of Montana; 59812 406-243-4153 Pub *Montana Women's Resource Newsletter.*

Ronan

Accommodation: Hotels, B&B, Resorts, Campgrounds

♂ • ♿ North Crow Vacation Ranch, 2360 N Crow Rd; 59864 406-676-5169 "Cabin sleeps 8 people; also tipis & campsites. Ranch house rental $300 week."

Nebraska

State/County Resources

Addictive Behavior, Substance Abuse, Recovery

♂ • (♿♿) Pride Institute, 800-54-PRIDE "The nation's only accredited chemical dependency treatment center exclusively for Gay, Lesbian & Bisexual People."

AIDS/HIV Support, Education, Advocacy, Publications

♀ ☆ ♂ Nebraska AIDS Project, 3610 Dodge St #110W, Omaha, NE 68131-3218 402-342-4233; 800-782-AIDS Mon-Fri 9-5pm; daily 6-11pm.

Funding: Endowment, Fundraising, Scholarship

♀ ★ Imperial Court of Nebraska, PO Box 3772, Omaha, NE 68103

Organizations/Resources: Family

♀ (♂♂) Central Nebraska PFLAG, 1320 8th Ave, Holdrege, NE 68949 308-995-5490 "Parents, Families & Friends of Lesbians & Gays."

Organizations/Resources: Political/Legislative

♀ ★♂♂ Coalition for Gay/Lesbian Civil Rights, PO Box 94882, Lincoln, NE 68509-0548

Organizations/Resources: Sport/Dance/Outdoor

♂ ICE BOWL, PO Box 3622, Omaha, NE 68103-0622

Publications

♀ ★ *The New Voice*, PO Box 3512, Omaha, NE 68103

♀ • *Times of the Heartland*, 2442 Whitmore St, Omaha, NE 68112-3134 402-341-6900

Real Estate

♀ • Community Real Estate Referrals, 800-346-5592 "Free referral to gay/gay-supportive realtor in any USA city/state (including Virgin Is. & Puerto Rico). Sorry, no rentals!"
◆ *Community Real Estate Referrals advertisement back cover*

Imperial

Bookstores: General

♀ ○ ♂ Phil's Fun Stuff/Bookbarn, PO Box 789; 69033-0789 / 616 Broadway 402-575-1261 10am-6pm; often to mdnt, but call ahead. "Books, magazines, newspapers, music, office supplies, gifts, candy, fishing & sporting goods, & more."

Kearney

AIDS/HIV Support, Education, Advocacy, Publications

♀ Nebraska AIDS Project, 3423 2nd Ave; 68847

Organizations/Resources: General, Multipurpose, Pride

♀ ★ GLAGN, PO Box 2401; 68848-2401 308-384-7235 Pub *GLAGN Newsletter*.

Lincoln

Bars, Restaurants, Clubs, Discos

♂ Panic, 200 S 18th St; 68528 402-435-8764

♀ • ♂♂ Q, 226 S 9th St; 68508 402-475-2269 *BDER*

Erotica (Printed, Visual, Equipment)

♀ ○ Adult Books & Cinema X, 921 O St; 68505 402-435-9323

Organizations/Resources: Family

♀ ☆♂♂ PFLAG Cornhusker, PO Box 30128; 68503-0128 402-467-4599 24 hrs. "Parents, Families & Friends of Lesbians & Gays."

Organizations/Resources: Social, Recreational & Support Groups (see also Sport/Dance/Outdoor)

♂ Information for Older Gay People, PO Box 22043; 68542-2043 402-488-4178

♀ ★♂♂ Lesbian Discussion Group, Women's Center, 340 Nebraska Union; 68588 402-472-2597 "Men welcome, but services primarily for women of all sexual orientations."

Organizations/Resources: Student, Academic, Alumni/ae

♂ ★ (?♂) Gay Men's Support Group, University Health Center Room 213; 68588-0618 402-472-7450 "Confidential support group run by trained counselors."

♀ ★♂♂ Gay/Lesbian Resource Center/GLSA, Nebraska Union Room 234; 68588-5644 402-472-5644

Omaha

☎ A.N.G.L.E., Inc 402-558-5303

Bars, Restaurants, Clubs, Discos

♀ ♂♂ The Chesterfield, 1901 Leavenworth St; 68102-3126 402-345-6889

♂ DC's Bar, 610 S 14th St; 68102-3207 402-344-3103

♀ ○ ♂ Diamond Bar, 712 S 16th St; 68102 402-342-9595 *Bd* 9am-1am; Sun noon-1am.

♂ Gilligan's Pub, 1823 Leavenworth; 68102 402-449-9147

♂ • The Max/Stosh's Saloon, 1417 Jackson St; 68102 402-346-4110

♂ The Run, 1715 Leavenworth St; 68102 402-449-8703

Bookstores: Recovery, Metaphysical, & other Specialty

♀ ○♂♂ New Realities, 1026 Howard St; 68102 402-342-1863 Mon 11am-5pm; Tue-Thu to 9pm; Fri & Sat to 10pm; Sun noon-5pm. "Gay & Lesbian; Recovery, Self-help, New Age; Native American books; gifts, etc."

Organizations/Resources: Business & Professional

♂ EAGLE-Omaha, P. Phalen, 1299 Farnham, 12th flr; 68102

Organizations/Resources: Ethnic, Multicultural

♂ ★ Onyx Images, PO Box 31026; 68132-9998

Organizations/Resources: Family

♀ (?♂) PFLAG Omaha, 2912 Lynnwood Dr; 68123 402-291-6781 omahapflag@aol.com "Parents, Families & Friends of Lesbians & Gays. Current services include straight spouse support group & a family HIV/AIDS support group."

Organizations/Resources: General, Multipurpose, Pride

♀ ★ ♂ A.N.G.L.E., Inc, PO Box 31375; 68131-0375 402-558-5303

Organizations/Resources: Political/Legislative

♀ ★ Citizens for Equal Protection, PO Box 65548; 68155 402-398-3027

♀ ★ Queer Nation, PO Box 34463; 68134-0463 402-451-7987

Organizations/Resources: Sexual Focus (Leather, S/M, etc) & Safe Sex Promotion

♀ (?♂) Omaha Players Club, PO Box 34463; 68134 402-451-7987 Pub *Chain Mail*.

Organizations/Resources: Sport/Dance/Outdoor

♂ ★ Omaha Frontrunners/Walkers, PO Box 4583; 68104-0583 402-496-3658

Organizations/Resources: Youth (see also Family)

♀ ★♂♂ Parents FLAG Omaha Youth Support Group, 2912 Lynnwood Dr; 68123 402-291-6781 omahapflag@aol.com

NE: Omaha
Performing Arts
299
USA
Las Vegas : NV
Legal

Performing Arts: Entertainment, Music, Recording, Theater, etc.

♀ ☆ ♂ River City Mixed Chorus, PO Box 3267; 68103-0267 402-341-SING

Publications

♥ *Womenspace*, PO Box 24712; 68124-0712

Religious Organizations & Publications

♥ ★ Metropolitan Community Church, PO Box 3173; 68103-0173 / 819 S. 22nd St 402-345-2563

♥ ★ (?♂) Presbyterians for Lesbian & Gay Concerns, c/o Evans 3810 S 13th St #22; 68107 402-733-1360 "Presbyterians for Lesbian/Gay Concerns."

Scottsbluff

Organizations/Resources: Social, Recreational & Support Groups (see also Sport/Dance/Outdoor)

♥ Panhandle Gay & Lesbian Support Group, PO Box 1046; 69361

Nevada

State/County Resources

AIDS/HIV Support, Education, Advocacy, Publications

♀ ☆♂ Aid for AIDS/Nevada (AFAN), 1111 Desert Ln, Las Vegas, NV 89102-2305 702-382-2326; 702-474-2437 hotline; Pub *AFANews*.

♂ Names Project of S. Nevada, 1111 Desert Ln, Las Vegas, NV 89102-2305 702-736-6762

Organizations/Resources: Political/Legislative

♀ ★ (?♂) Nevadans for Constitutional Equality, 3765 E Desert Inn Rd, Las Vegas, NV 89121 702-435-9301 "We also produce Gay & Lesbian music, comedy, plays & cultural events."

Organizations/Resources: Sport/Dance/Outdoor

♀ ★ (?♂) Nevada Gay Rodeo Association, 2350 S Jones Blvd #101 Ste 924, Las Vegas, NV 89102 702-593-3193

Publications

♥ ● ♂ *Bugle*, PO Box 14580, Las Vegas, NV 89114-4580 702-369-6260 Fax 702-369-9325

Real Estate

♀ ● ♂ American Dream Realty & Investment, 3765 E Desert Inn Rd, Las Vegas, NV 89121 702-435-9301; 800-435-9305; Fax 702-435-6210 "We also produce Gay & Lesbian music, comedy, plays & cultural events."

♥ ● Community Real Estate Referrals, 800-346-5592 "Free referral to gay/gay-supportive realtor in any USA city/state (including Virgin Is. & Puerto Rico). Sorry, no rentals!"
✦ *Community Real Estate Referrals advertisement back cover*

Crystal Bay

Accommodation: Hotels, B&B, Resorts, Campgrounds

♥ ● Lakeside B 'n' B Tahoe, PO Box 1756; 89402 702-831-8281

Henderson: see Las Vegas

Las Vegas

Accommodation: Hotels, B&B, Resorts, Campgrounds

♂ ● ♂ Desert Oasis, 3567 E Hacienda; 89120-1215 702-436-0113 "Quiet, Spanish-style bed & breakfast; clothing-optional heated pool/spa; close to bars & casinos."

♂ ○ Las Vegas Private Bed & Breakfast, G.A.L.A. Tours at A to Z Bargain Travel 3133 S Industrial at Stardust; 89109 702-369-8671; 702-384-1129; (800) 346-5999

AIDS/HIV Support, Education, Advocacy, Publications

→ Aid for AIDS/Nevada (AFAN): p.299

♀ ● ♂♂ Lambda Health Care, 2300 W Charleston #259; 89102 702-877-8600

Bars, Restaurants, Clubs, Discos

♥ ● Angles-N-Curves, 4633 Paradise Rd 702-741-1947; 702-791-0100; 24 hrs. "Videos, slots, pool table. Mostly men but women always welcome."

♥ ♂ Backdoor Lounge, 1415 E Charleston Blvd; 89104 702-385-2018

♥ Backstreet, 5012 Arville Rd; 89118 702-876-1844

♂ ● (♂) Badlands Saloon, 953 E Sahara #22-B; 89104 702-792-9262 *BW*

♂ Buffalo, 4640 Paradise Rd #12; 89109 702-733-8355

♥ The Cave, 5740 W Charleston Blvd; 89103 702-878-0001

♥ Curves, 4633 Paradise Rd (behind Angles); 89109 702-791-1947

♂ ○ Eagle, 3430 E Tropicana; 89121 702-458-8662

♥ Faces, 701 E Stewart; 89101 702-386-7971

♥ ● The Gipsy Show & Dance Bar, 4605 Paradise Rd; 89109 702-733-9677; 702-731-1919; *DE* Tue-Sun 10pm-5am.

♂ Goodtimes, 1775 E Tropicana Ave; 89119 702-736-9494

♂ ● Snick's, 1402 S 4th St; 89104 702-385-9298

♀ Texas Rodeo Saloon, 3430 E Tropicana Ave; 89121 702-456-5525

♀ Vicious Rumors, 6370 Windy St; 89119 702-896-1993

Bookstores: Gay/Lesbian/Feminist

♥ ● ♂ Get Booked, 4643 Paradise Rd; 89109 702-737-7780 10am-2pm. "Books, cards, magazines, condoms, t-shirts, etc."

Community Centers (see also Women's Centers)

♥ The Center, PO Box 60301; 89160 702-733-9800

Erotica (Printed, Visual, Equipment)

♀ ○ ♂ Desert Adult Books, 4350 Las Vegas Blvd N.; 89115 702-643-7982

Funding: Endowment, Fundraising, Scholarship

♥ ★ Golden Rainbow, PO Box 94138; 89193 702-384-2899 Fax 702-384-3914

♥ ★ Green Walrus Screenworks, 2160 W Charleston #L-333; 89102 702-242-0220 "Custom garment screenprinting."

Health Care (see also AIDS Services)

♀ ● ♂♂ Crooks, Kathryn, MD, 2810 W Charleston #F-54; 89102 702-870-0808

Legal Services & Resources

♀ ○ Aimar, Don, Esq, 2217 Paradise Rd; 89104 702-734-2984 Fax 702-734-1825

NV: Las Vegas
Organizations: Business
300
USA
State/County Resources : NH
Conferences/Events/Festivals

If you can't find the
NAME   PLACE   SUBJECT
you're looking for,
PLEASE TRY THE INDEX

Organizations/Resources: Business & Professional

♀ ★ Lambda Business Association, 1801 E Tropicana #9; 89119 702-593-2875 Fax 702-362-6006 lambdabus@aol.com Pub *Lambda Business Directory*.

♂ ★ Las Vegas Men's Club, PO Box 60631; 89160-0631 702-593-1173

Organizations/Resources: Ethnic, Multicultural

♂ ★ (?&) Latino Pyramid, PO Box 545; 89125-0545 702-369-8127 x765

Organizations/Resources: Family

♀ ☆ PFLAG, PO Box 20145; 89112 702-438-7838 "Parents, Families & Friends of Lesbians & Gays."

Organizations/Resources: General, Multipurpose, Pride

♀ LV Lesbian & Gay Pride Association, 5015 W Sahara #125; 89102 702-593-1523

Organizations/Resources: Political/Legislative

♀ Log Cabin/Las Vegas, PO Box 13439; 89112-3439 702-798-6804 "Republican organization."

Organizations/Resources: Social, Recreational & Support Groups (see also Sport/Dance/Outdoor)

♂ Las Vegas Bears, PO Box 34263; 89133-4263 702-658-7548

Organizations/Resources: Sport/Dance/Outdoor

♂ Desert Brotherhood MC, PO Box 71145; 89170

♀ Neon Squares, PO Box 46161; 89114-6161 702-253-9435; 702-732-7559; *d* "Square Dance."

♂ Satyricons Motorcycle Club, PO Box 19357; 89132-0357 702-733-8355

Organizations/Resources: Student, Academic, Alumni/ae

♂ ★ && Delta Lambda Phi Fraternity, University of Nevada at Las Vegas, 912 E Sahara, Box 60301; 89160 800-587-FRAT; 702-733-9800; "Inquiries SASE only."

Real Estate

♀ • American Dream Realty & Investment, 3187 S Eastern Ave #5; 89122 702-735-9300 "Full service real estate."

Religious Organizations & Publications

♀ && Metropolitan Community Church, PO Box 3488, North Las Vegas; 89036-3488 702-384-2325

Travel & Tourist Services (see also Accommodation)

♀ • & A To Z Bargain Travel, 3133 S Industrial Rd; 89109 702-369-8671

Reno

Bars, Restaurants, Clubs, Discos

♂ 1099 Club, 1099 S Virginia; 89502 702-329-1099

♀ • The Alley Club, 100 N Sierra; 89501 (1st St between Sierra & Virginia) 702-333-2808 24 hrs. Mostly men.

♂ • (&&) Bad Dolly's, 535 East 4th St; 89512 702-348-1983 *DWE* Mon-Thu 3pm-3am; weekends 24 hrs. Disco Fri; CW Tue, Thu, Sat. Quality live entertainment twice a month.

♂ Bar West, 210 W Commercial Row; 89501 702-786-0878

♂ Five Star Saloon, 132 West St; 89501 702-329-2878

♀ ○ Shouts Bar, 145 Hillcrest Dr; 89509 702-829-7667

♀ Visions, 340 Kietzke Lane; 89509 702-786-5455

Bookstores: Gay/Lesbian/Feminist

♀ • (&&) Grapevine Books, 1450 S Wells Ave; 89502-2971 702-786-4869

Bookstores: General

♀ ○ & Bold Print, 3432 Lakeside Dr; 89509 702-829-BOLD 10am-8pm; Sat & Sun to 6pm.

Funding: Endowment, Fundraising, Scholarship

♀ ★ The Trellis Foundation, PO Box 33004; 89533-3004 702-747-2849 *The Blossom Report*. "Support growth in the Lesbian Community in the areas of education, business, research, public affairs, the arts."

Health Clubs, Gyms, Saunas

♂ Steve's Gym, 1030 W 2nd St; 89503 702-323-8770

Organizations/Resources: Social, Recreational & Support Groups (see also Sport/Dance/Outdoor)

♂ ★ Knights of Malta Western Chapter, PO Box 7726; 89510

Publications

♀ • *Lesbian Voices*, PO Box 33004; 89533-3004

♀ • *Reno Informer*, 5150 Mae Anne Ave #213-185; 89523 702-826-2257

Religious Organizations & Publications

♀ ★ (?&) Metropolitan Community Church of the Sierra, PO Box 21192; 89515-1192 702-826-3177

New Hampshire

State/County Resources

☎ Gay Info Line of New Hampshire 603-224-1686

Addictive Behavior, Substance Abuse, Recovery

♀ • (&&) Pride Institute, 800-54-PRIDE "The nation's only accredited chemical dependency treatment center exclusively for Gay, Lesbian & Bisexual People."

AIDS/HIV Support, Education, Advocacy, Publications

♀ ☆ (?&) AIDS Community Resource Network (ACORN), PO Box 2057, Lebanon, NH 03766 603-448-2220 "Serves the Upper Valley region of New Hampshire & Vermont."

♂ ☆&& Aids Response Seacoast, 1 Junkins Ave, Portsmouth, NH 03801-4511 603-433-5377; 800-375-1144 (NH & ME); Fax 603-431-8520

♀ ☆ New Hampshire AIDS Foundation, PO Box 59, Manchester, NH 03105 / 10 Middle St 603-623-0710 Pub *Rally*.

Conferences/Events/Festivals/Workshops (see also Performing Arts)

♀ • (?&) Womensphere Retreats & Events, RR1 Box 240A, Northwood, NH 03261-9702 603-942-9941

Counseling/Therapy: Private

♀ ○ ♂ People Living With Illness, PO Box 227, Newfields, NH 03856 603-778-3011 "We specialize in chronic illness groups, AIDS groups, behavioral medicine groups."

Legal Services & Resources

♂ ★ Coalition to End Discrimination, PO Box 74, Concord, NH 03302 603-536-4011

Organizations/Resources: Family

♀ ☆ (?♿) PFLAG:NH, PO Box 386, Manchester, NH 03105 603-623-6023 Pub *PFLAG NH Newsletter*. "Parents, Families & Friends of Lesbians & Gays. Support groups in Concord, Stratham, Nashua, Seacoast, Peterborough, Plymouth, Hanover."

Organizations/Resources: Political/Legislative

♂ ★ Citizens Alliance for Gay & Lesbian Rights (CALGR), PO Box 730, Concord, NH 03302-0730 603-224-1686 Pub *Breathing Space*.

Organizations/Resources: Sexual Focus (Leather, S/M, etc) & Safe Sex Promotion

♂ ★ The Norsemen, PO Box 556, Manchester, NH 03105-0556 603-641-3450

Organizations/Resources: Social, Recreational & Support Groups (see also Sport/Dance/Outdoor)

♀ ★ (♿♿) Nashua Women In Touch, PO Box 3541, Nashua, NH 03061 603-883-9228

→ Social Alternative for Gay Men (SAM): p.424

Real Estate

♂ • Community Real Estate Referrals, 800-346-5592 "Free referral to gay/gay-supportive realtor in any USA city/state (including Virgin Is. & Puerto Rico). Sorry, no rentals!"
◆ *Community Real Estate Referrals advertisement back cover*

Switchboards, Helplines, Phone Information

♂ ★ (?♿) Gay Info Line of New Hampshire, 26 S Main St Box 181, Concord, NH 03301 603-224-1686 "Complete social, legal, educational, therapeutic & other referrals. Calendar of events available on request."

Ashland

Accommodation: Hotels, B&B, Resorts, Campgrounds

♀ • Country Options, 27-29 N Main St; 03217 603-968-7958

Bartlett

Accommodation: Hotels, B&B, Resorts, Campgrounds

♀ • (?♿) The Notchland Inn, Harts Location; 03812 603-374-6131; 800-866-6131; Fax 603-374-6168 *B*

Bath

Accommodation: Hotels, B&B, Resorts, Campgrounds

♂ • Evergreen Bed & Breakfast, Route 302; 03740 603-747-3947 "Four guest rooms; 2 with working fireplaces; hot tub; gay only! 2 1/2 hours from Montréal."
◆ *Evergreen Bed & Breakfast advertisement page 301*

Bethlehem

Accommodation: Hotels, B&B, Resorts, Campgrounds

♂ • (♿♿) The Highlands Inn, Box 118GP; 03574 603-869-3978
◆ *Highlands Inn advertisement page 301*

Bridgewater

Accommodation: Hotels, B&B, Resorts, Campgrounds

♀ • The Inn on Newfound Lake, 1030 Mayhew Tpk (Rte 3A); 03222 603-744-9111; 800-745-7990; Fax 603-744-3894

Center Harbor

Accommodation: Hotels, B&B, Resorts, Campgrounds

♀ • (♿♿) Red Hill Inn, RFD #1 Box 99M; 03226 603-279-7001 Fax 603-279-7003 *BR* 8am-11pm.

NH: Colebrook
Accommodation
302
USA
Manchester : NH
Counseling: Private

Over 10,000 square feet

Everybody welcome

FRONT RUNNER

22 Fir St
Manchester
NH 03101
(603) 623-6477

Colebrook

Accommodation: Hotels, B&B, Resorts, Campgrounds

♂ • Columbia Hills B&B, Box 258; 03576-0258 603-237-5550 richl10730@aol.com

Concord

Counseling/Therapy: Nonprofit

♀ ☆ (?♿) Womankind Counseling Center, 21 Green St; 03301 603-225-2985

Counseling/Therapy: Private

♀ • Foley, Lyn, MSW, ACSW, 30 S Main St; 03301 603-224-5600

Health Care (see also AIDS Services)

♀ ☆ (♿) Concord Feminist Health Center, 38 S Main St; 03301 603-225-2739 Pub *WomenWise.* "Gyn services; HIV/AIDS testing & counseling & STD clinics for women and men; Lesbian support group; abortion services."

Legal Services & Resources

♀ • ♿ Fraas, Linda E., 15 N Main St #206; 03301 603-225-0477

Conway

Organizations/Resources: Social, Recreational & Support Groups (see also Sport/Dance/Outdoor)

♂ ★ Mountain Valley Men, Box 36, Center Conway; 03813-0036 207-925-1034

Durham

Organizations/Resources: Student, Academic, Alumni/ae

♂ ★♿ The Alliance, Rm 7, Memorial Union Bldg, University of New Hampshire; 03824 603-842-4522 "A student support group for gay, lesbian, bisexual & transgendered people."

Franconia

Accommodation: Hotels, B&B, Resorts, Campgrounds

♀ ○ Bungay Jar Bed & Breakfast, Box 15 Easton Rd; 03580 603-823-7775 Fax 603-444-0100 Brochure available.

♀ • Raynor's Motor Lodge, Box 10; 03580 / Main St 603-823-5651; 800-634-8187 reservations only

Hanover

Organizations/Resources: Student, Academic, Alumni/ae

♀ ★♿ Dartmouth Gay/Lesbian/Bisexual Organization (DaGLO), 5057 Collis Center, Dartmouth College; 03755 603-646-3636

Religious Organizations & Publications

♀ ★♿ MCC in the Mountains, PO Box 264, White River Junction, VT 05001 603-448-3754 Fax 603-448-4076

Keene

Addictive Behavior, Substance Abuse, Recovery

♀ ★♿ Pink Triangle Group: Gay & Lesbian AA, Cheshire Medical Center 603-357-4300 Meets Sat 7-8.30pm, Auditorium A

Bookstores: Recovery, Metaphysical, & other Specialty

♀ • ♿ Oasis, 45 Central Square; 03431 603-352-5355 "Tools for Transformation."

Counseling/Therapy: Nonprofit

♀ ★♿ Gay Community Counseling, PO Box 1124; 03431 603-357-5544

Organizations/Resources: Social, Recreational & Support Groups (see also Sport/Dance/Outdoor)

♀ Monadnock Area Womyn (MAW), PO Box 6345; 03431 603-357-5757

♂ ★ (?♿) Monadnock Gay Men (MGM), PO Box 1124; 03431 603-357-5544 Pub *MGM Newsletter.*

Organizations/Resources: Student, Academic, Alumni/ae

♂ Lesbian-Bisexual-Gay Alliance, Keene State College; 03431

Organizations/Resources: Transgender & Transgender Publications

T ☆ Cheshire Counseling Associates, PO Box 1124; 03431 603-357-5544 "Transvestite/Transsexual & Gender Identity counseling; support group."

Lebanon

Organizations/Resources: Social, Recreational & Support Groups (see also Sport/Dance/Outdoor)

♀ ☆ Amelia Earhart, PO Box 746; 03766 Pub *Newsletter.*

Switchboards, Helplines, Phone Information

♀ Women's Information Service (WISE), 79 Hanover St; 03766 603-448-5525

Manchester

Accommodation: Hotels, B&B, Resorts, Campgrounds

♀ • Manchester House, B & B, 305 Taylor St; 03103 603-644-2303

Bars, Restaurants, Clubs, Discos

♀ Club Merrimac, 201 Merrimac; 03103 603-623-9362

♀ • ♿ **Front Runner, 22 Fir St; 03101 603-623-6477** *BDEPL*
  ✦ *Front Runner advertisement page 302*

♀ • (♿) Sporters, 361 Pine St; 03101 603-668-9014 *B*

Counseling/Therapy: Private

♀ • (?♿) Barr, Patricia K., Ph.D., 69 Bay St; 03104-3005 603-647-2366 "Certified psychologist. Insurance accepted."

NH: Manchester
Counseling: Private

303
USA

State/County Resources : NJ
Funeral Directors

♂ • ᕕᕗ Lamothe, Denise C., Psy.D., 311 Highlander Way; 03103 603-627-3739

♂ • ᕕᕗ Whiting, Joyce, ACSW, 795 Elm St #518; 03101 603-666-4299

Plymouth

Organizations/Resources: Student, Academic, Alumni/ae

♂ ★ (ᕕ) ALSO (Alternative Lifestyles Support Org), Plymouth State College, PO Box 492; 03264-0492 603-535-2796 "Open to all Gays, Lesbians, & bisexuals."

Portsmouth

Bars, Restaurants, Clubs, Discos

♀ ○ ᕕ Blue Strawbery, 29 Ceres St; 03801 603-431-6420

♂ • ᕕᕗ Desert Hearts, Rte. 1 Bypass North; 0380 1 603-431-5400 *PDE*

♂ ★ Members, 53 Green St 603-436-9451 *BDP*

Bookstores: Gay/Lesbian/Feminist

♀ ○ Lady Iris, 10 Ladd St; 03801-4010

Counseling/Therapy: Nonprofit

♀ ☆ᕕᕗ Sexual Assault Support Services, 7 Junkins Ave; 03801 603-436-4107 hotline 24 hrs. "Crisis line; education; prevention."

Counseling/Therapy: Private

♀ ○ᕕᕗ Seacoast Resource Associates, Orchard Park, 875 Greenland Rd #3-B; 03801-4162 603-431-1900; 603-431-8186 (Tax: seasonal)

Erotica (Printed, Visual, Equipment)

♀ ○ The Fifth Wheel, Rt 1 Bypass North; 03801 603-436-1504

♀ ○ ᕕ Peter's Palace, Rt 1 Bypass North; 03801 603-436-9622 9am-11pm; Sun noon-8pm.
♦ *Peter's Palace advertisement page 303*

Gifts, Cards, Pride & Novelty Items

♀ • For A Song, PO Box 353, Rye Beach, NH 03871-9998 603-436-0583 "Songs written for all occasions. Mention this listing for 20% discount."

Organizations/Resources: Social, Recreational & Support Groups (see also Sport/Dance/Outdoor)

♂ ★ Seacoast Gay Men, PO Box 1394; 03802-1394 Meets Mon 7pm (except holidays) at U-U Church, 292 State St.

New Jersey

State/County Resources

☎ Gay Helpline of New Jersey (Gay Activist Alliance in Morris County) 201-285-1595

☎ Gay Helpline of New Jersey 201-692-1794

Addictive Behavior, Substance Abuse, Recovery

→ Carrier Foundation: p.303

♂ • (ᕕᕗ) Pride Institute, 800-54-PRIDE "The nation's only accredited chemical dependency treatment center exclusively for Gay, Lesbian & Bisexual People. Out patient program in NYC."

♀ ☆ Together Inc: NJ Drug Hotline, 7 State St, Glassboro, NJ 08028 800-225-0196 24 hrs.

AIDS/HIV Support, Education, Advocacy, Publications

♀ ☆ AIDS Benefit Committee of NJ, PO Box 1443, Plainfield, NJ 07061 908-561-4359

♀ ☆ AIDS Coalition of Southern New Jersey, 607 White Horse Pike, Audubon, NJ 08106 609-573-7900 Fax 609-573-7904

♀ ★ AIDS Network of Hunterdon County, 101 Voorhees Rd, Glen Gardner, NJ 08826 908-638-4785

♀ ☆ᕕᕗ HIV Confidential Testing Service, Annex, Community Service Building, Route 31, Flemington, NJ 08822 908-806-4893

♀ ☆ (?ᕕ) Hyacinth AIDS Foundation, 103 Bayard St, 3rd Fl, New Brunswick, NJ 08901-2121 800-433-0254 in NJ; 908-755-0021; Mon-Fri 9m-5pm; Hotline Mon-Fri 10am-10pm; Sat 11am-5pm. "New Jersey's leading AIDS Service Agency."

♀ ☆ Names Project/New Jersey, 330 Broadway, Union Beach, NJ 07735 908-739-4863 "Official chapter of the International AIDS Memorial Quilt."

Counseling/Therapy: Nonprofit

♂ ☆ Carrier Foundation, PO Box 147, Belle Mead, NJ 08502 908-281-1626; 800-933-3579; "Private, non-profit hospital offering full range of services for psychiatric & addictive illnesses."

Film & Video

♂ ★ Gay & Lesbian Arts Society (GALAS), PO Box 1291, Montclair, NJ 07042 "Organizers of the NJ Lesbian/Gay Film Festival."

Funeral Directors/Cemetaries/Mausoleums

♀ • ᕕ S. J. Priola Parsippany Funeral Service, 49 Whippany Rd 201-335-4700

Insurance Benefits/Viaticals

♀ ○ **Alpha Premium Viatical Services, PO Box 1534, Morristown, NJ 07962 800-6060-911**

Legal Services & Resources

♂ ☆ American Civil Liberties Union/New Jersey (ACLU), 2 Washington Place, Newark, NJ 07102 201-642-2084

Organizations/Resources: Business & Professional

♀ ★ LEAGUE: Lesbian, Bisexual & Gay United Employees at AT&T, 107 Harter Rd, Morristown, NJ 07960 908-582-3545

♀ ★ (?♿) Lesbian & Gay Educators of New Jersey, PO Box 8932, Red Bank, NJ 07701-8932 Pub *Newsletter*.

♀ Lesbian & Gay Lawyers Association, PO Box 580, Seaside Park, NJ 08752-0580

♀ ★ (?♿) Lesbians & Gays in Telecommunications, PO Box 8143, Red Bank, NJ 07701

♀ ★ NASW/NJ Committee on Lesbian & Gay Issues, 110 W State St, Trenton, NJ 08608-1183

♀ ★ **Gay Officers Action League—New Jersey Division (GOAL), PO Box 254, Fairview, NJ 07022 908-775-2793; 201-941-9144; Fax 908-545-5677 "Fraternal, Social & Support Group for employees of the Criminal Justice System."**

Organizations/Resources: Family

♀ ☆ ♿ PFLAG North Jersey, PO Box 244, Belleville, NJ 07109 201-267-8414 "Parents, Families & Friends of Lesbians & Gays."

Organizations/Resources: General, Multipurpose, Pride

♀ ★ (♿) Gay Activist Alliance in Morris County, PO Box 137, Convent Station, NJ 07961-0137 201-285-5504 Fax 201-538-8882 Meets Mon 8.45-10pm at Morristown Unitarian Fellowship, Normandy Hts Rd, Morristown. Pub *Challenge*; *NJ Pride*.

♀ ★ ♿ Gay Activists Alliance of New Jersey, PO Box 1734, South Hackensack, NJ 07606 201-692-1794 Meets Wed 8.30pm in Teaneck: call for details.

♀ ★ Jersey Pride, PO Box 11335, New Brunswick, NJ 08906-1335 908-651-7743 (NJ1-PRIDE) The parade committee of the Lesbian & Gay Coalition.

♀ ★ Lesbian Union of Central Jersey, Box 87, Plainsboro, NJ 08536 609-799-8928

♀ ★ ♿ New Jersey Lesbian & Gay Coalition, PO Box 11335, New Brunswick, NJ 08906-1335 908-828-6772 Pub *News Jersey*.

♀ ★ Organization for Gay Awareness, PO Box 1291, Montclair, NJ 07042 201-746-6196 "Information & referral."

Organizations/Resources: Political/Legislative

♀ ★ Gay & Lesbian Political Action & Support, PO Box 11406, New Brunswick, NJ 08916-2536 908-985-9371 Fax 908-985-2437

♀ ★ (?♿) Lesbian Rights Task Force of Essex County NOW, PO Box 201, Maplewood, NJ 07040 201-761-4479 "Focusing on Lesbian/Gay rights; also other feminist issues."

♀ ★ Log Cabin Club/New Jersey, mail to LCC/NJ, PO Box 4102, Wayne, NJ 07474 201-742-0242

♂ ☆ Voters for Civil Liberties, PO Box 1431, New Brunswick, NJ 08903-1431

Organizations/Resources: Social, Recreational & Support Groups (see also Sport/Dance/Outdoor)

♀ ★ Delaware Valley Couples, PO Box 553, Collingswood, NJ 08108 908-364-8431 (Lakewood); 215-639-1024 (Philadelphia); Pub *Newsletter*.

♂ ★♿ Gay, Lesbian or Bisexual Alliance of Cumberland County, Inc. (GLOBAL), mail to GLOBAL of Cumberland County Inc., PO Box 541, Millville, NJ 08332-0541 609-563-1872 Pub *GLOBAL News*.

♂ ★ Gays & Lesbians of Atlantic County (GALA), PO Box 459, Northfield, NJ 08225-0459

♂ ★ (♿) Girth & Mirth of Delaware Valley, PO Box 1381, Marlton, NJ 08053 609-786-4166

♂ ★♿ Lesbians & Gays of Burlington County, PO Box 1492, Medford, NJ 08055-1429

♂ ★♿ LesBiGays of Cape May County, PO Box 641, Cape May Court House, NJ 08210-0641

♂ ★ The NEW Group, PO Box 1542, Asbury Park, NJ 07712 908-870-9424; 908-892-1061; Pub *G.O.A.L.S.*. "Social & community oriented group in the Monmouth County area."

♂ ★♿ Ocean (County) Lesbian-Gay Alliance, Inc., PO Box 285, Toms River, NJ 08754-0285 908-240-5554

♂ ★ Poconos Action Lambda Society, mail to PALS, Box 1375, Milford, PA 18337 PA

♂ ★ ♂ Prime Timers, Box 291 Midtown Stn, New York, NY 10018-0291 212-787-0329

Organizations/Resources: Transgender & Transgender Publications

⚧ ☆ (?♿) Connecticut Outreach Society, PO Box 163, Farmington, CT 06034 203-657-4344

Organizations/Resources: Youth (see also Family)

♀ ★ (?♿) Gay & Lesbian Youth in New Jersey (GALY-NJ), PO Box 137, Convent Station, NJ 07961-0137 201-285-1595 (GAAMC Helpline) 7.30-10.30pm. Meets Sat 1.30-4.30pm in several locations: call for details. For ages 16-21.

Performing Arts: Entertainment, Music, Recording, Theater, etc.

♂ ★ (?♿) Delaware Valley Men's Chorus, PO Box 21, Princeton, NJ 08542-0021

♀ ★♿ Labrys Productions, PO Box 494, Somerville, NJ 08876 908-725-5562 "Bringing cultural events to the NJ Lesbian Community."

Publications

♀ ● *Lavender Express*, PO Box 514, Harrison, NJ 07029 201-439-1593 Fax 201-385-1916 Monthly. "New Jersey's Lesbian Journal since 1978."

♀ ● *Network Magazine: for the 10% Plus*, 2 Julie Dr, Edison, NJ 08820 908-754-2288 Fax 908-754-1924 "Monthly magazines about everyday issues for everyday lesbians & gay men."
♦ *Network Magazine: for the 10% Plus advertisement page 305*

♀ ● *Womyn's Monthly*, PO Box 1584, Wall, NJ 07719 908-974-1526

Real Estate

♀ ● **Community Real Estate Referrals, 800-346-5592 "Free referral to gay/gay-supportive realtor in any USA city/state (including Virgin Is. & Puerto Rico). Sorry, no rentals!"**
♦ *Community Real Estate Referrals advertisement back cover*

Religious Organizations & Publications

♀ ★ New Jersey Lesbian & Gay Havurah, PO Box 2576, Edison, NJ 08818 908-549-6032

♀ ★ (?⚲) **The Oasis, Cathedral House, 24 Rector St, Newark, NJ 07102 201-621-8151 Fax 201-622-3503** *The Wellspring.* "An outreach of the Episcopal Diocese of Newark to & with Lesbians & Gay Men, their families & friends."

♀ ★ Presbyterians for Lesbian & Gay Concerns, PO Box 38, c/o James Anderson, New Brunswick, NJ 08903-0038 908-249-1016; 908-932-7501; Pub *More Light Update.*

Switchboards, Helplines, Phone Information

♀ ★ Gay Helpline of New Jersey (Gay Activist Alliance in Morris County), 201-285-1595 7.30-10.30pm.

♂ ★ Gay Helpline of New Jersey, PO Box 1734, South Hackensack, NJ 07606 201-692-1794 7.30-10.30pm.

Telecommunications: Phones, Paging, Beepers

♀ ○ Planet Communications, 60 Rte 46 E, Fairfield, NJ 07004 800-960-6075 Fax 201-227-5070 "Cellular, paging, long distance, prepaid calling card; 5% supports area nonprofit groups working for social change."

♀ • **Triangular Communications, 331 Spring Valley Rd, Morganville, NJ 07751 800-972-9122 Fax 908-972-9551**
✦ *Triangular Communications advertisement page 122*

Annandale

AIDS/HIV Support, Education, Advocacy, Publications

♀ ☆⚲⚲ The AIDS Network, Box 594; 08801 908-638-4785; 800-262-0733

Asbury Park

Antiques & Collectables

♀ • Of Rare Vintage, 718 Cookman Ave; 07712 908-988-9459 10am-5pm; closed Tue & Sun.

Bars, Restaurants, Clubs, Discos

♀ ○ Bond Street Bar, 208 Bond St; 07712 908-776-9766 **BR**

♀ • Down The Street, 230 Cookman Ave; 07712 908-988-2163 **BRDE** Noon-2am.

♀ ○ The Hitching Rail Bar & Restaurant, 106 2nd Ave; 07712 908-774-5200

♀ ○ Key West, 611 Hech St; 07712 908-775-9694

♂ Teddy's Pub, 402-404 Emery St; 07712 908-775-3250

Community Centers (see also Women's Centers)

♀ ★ (⚲) Gay & Lesbian Community Center of New Jersey, PO Box 1316; 07712 / 515 Cookman Ave 908-774-1809; 908-775-4GAY; Fax 908-774-5513

Exterminators

♀ • Bug Busters, Asbury Park; Monmouth County 908-775-0840

Gifts, Cards, Pride & Novelty Items

♀ ○ ⚲ Shellcraft Shop, 70 Main Ave, Ocean Grove; 07756 908-775-1930

♀ ○ Small Wonders, 76 Main Ave, Ocean Grove; 07756 908-774-6330

Interior Design

♀ ○ Blotner Window Fashions, PO Box 973; 07712 / 611 Bangs Ave 908-775-1200

Legal Services & Resources

♀ ○ Leslie, Grace, 704 Main St; 07712 908-775-0014 Fax 908-775-3169

♀ • Mrozik, Albert J., Jr, 18 Locust Dr; 07712-4911 908-774-7987

Organizations/Resources: Family

♀ ☆ Monmouth/Ocean Counties Parents FLAG, PO Box 1542; 07712 908-905-6823 Meet 2nd Wed of month, 7.30pm, at St Anselm Church, Wayside, NJ.

Organizations/Resources: Social, Recreational & Support Groups (see also Sport/Dance/Outdoor)

♀ ★ The Asbury Park Garden Club, 502 4th Ave; 07712 908-774-6162 "We are dedicated to beautification projects throughout our neglected city."

Real Estate

♀ • ⚲ Burns Bradshaw Realty Co, 1508 Main St; 07712 908-776-6844; 908-775-7996

♀ ○ Cassel, Ron, 401 2nd Ave; 07712 908-774-1860

♀ • The More The Merrier, 1207 Bond St; 07712 908-775-0840; 908-774-7987; Fax 908-775-2793

Atlantic City

Accommodation: Hotels, B&B, Resorts, Campgrounds

♂ • Ocean House, 127 S Ocean Ave; 08401 609-345-8203

♀ • Surfside Guest House House & Sundeck Bar, 18 S Mt Vernon Ave; 08401 609-347-0808

AIDS/HIV Support, Education, Advocacy, Publications

♀ ★⚲⚲ South Jersey AIDS Alliance, 1301 Atlantic Ave; 08401-7247 609-347-8799; 800-281-AIDS in NJ

Bars, Restaurants, Clubs, Discos

♀ • Brass Rail Tavern, 12 S Mt Vernon Ave; 08401 609-348-0192 *BR* 24 hrs.

♀ Entertainer's Club, 169 Westminster; 08401 609-344-9223

♂ • (?♂) Reflections, 181-185 S. Carolina Ave; 08404-7244 609-348-1115 *BD* Bar 24 hrs; disco 11pm-5am.

♂ • Rendezvous Lounge, 137 S New York Ave; 08401 609-347-8539; 609-347-8539; *BLW* 3pm-3am.

♀ • Studio Six Dance Club, 14 S Mt Vernon Ave; 08401 609-348-0192 *BDE* 10pm-6am "Dance/video club; new cabaret bar & show room."

Erotica (Printed, Visual, Equipment)

♀ ○ Atlantic City News Agency, 101 S Illinois Ave; 08401 609-344-9444

Bayonne: see Jersey City

Belle Mead

Legal Services & Resources

♀ • (♂♂) Singer, William S., Esq, 2230 Rte 206, PO Box 134; 08502 908-359-7873

Veterinarians

♀ • ♂♂ Newman, Christine, DVM, Harlingen Veterinary Clinic, 2162 Rte 206 S; 08502 908-359-2000

Belleville: see Newark

Bellmawr

Community Centers (see also Women's Centers)

♀ ★ (?♂) Rainbow Place, PO Box 682; 08099-0682 / 1103 N Broad St; 08906 609-848-2455 allen219@aol.com

Organizations/Resources: Social, Recreational & Support Groups (see also Sport/Dance/Outdoor)

♀ ★ GLOW, PO Box 1372; 08099-5372 609-933-2947 "Social organization for over-40 Lesbians."

Berlin

Erotica (Printed, Visual, Equipment)

♀ ○ Red Barn Adult Bookstore, Rt 73; 08009 609-767-1525

Blackwood

Addictive Behavior, Substance Abuse, Recovery

♀ • ♂ Focused Counseling Services, Inc., 8 N Black Horse Pike; 08012 609-228-8910

Bloomfield

Clothes

♀ • (?♂) Creations by Nightwing, 39 Oakland Ave; 07003-3462 201-680-8757 "Handcrafted clothing."

Bloomingdale

Meeting/Contact Services, Publications, Talklines

♀ • (?♂) Gal-a-vanting, PO Box 268; 07403 201-838-5318

Brick Town

Counseling/Therapy: Private

♀ • Garcia, Diane, PhD, 478 Manchester Ave; 08723-5225 908-920-8110

Erotica (Printed, Visual, Equipment)

♀ ○ Unisex Adult Bookstore, 2148 Rte 88E; 08723 908-295-0166

Brick

Travel & Tourist Services (see also Accommodation)

♀ ○ **Monarch Travel, 291 Herbertsville Road; 08724 908-840-2233 Fax 908-840-5511 Mon-Fri 9.30am-5.30pm; Sat 10am-1pm (closed Jul & Aug).**

Camden

Religious Organizations & Publications

♀ ★ ♂ Caritas, 609-228-7438 "Support group."

Cherry Hill

Bars, Restaurants, Clubs, Discos

♀ ○ ♂ Gatsby's Niteclub & Driveshaft Lounge, 760 Cuthbert Blvd; 08002 609-663-8744 *DE* 8.30pm-3am.

Counseling/Therapy: Nonprofit

♀ ★ (♂♂) Hicks, Walter Dean, PhD, CAS, 1101 N Kings Hwy #301; 08034 609-482-5695

Counseling/Therapy: Private

♀ ○ (♂) Ross, Joellyn, Ph.D., 1930 E Marlton Pike, J-49 Executive Mews; 08003 609-424-1065

Legal Services & Resources

♀ ○ Shreter, Stephanie, Esq, 1930 E Marlton Pike #L-61, The Executive Mews; 08003 609-424-2244

Clementon

Bookstores: Recovery, Metaphysical, & other Specialty

♀ ○ ♂♂ Enchanted Cottage, Rte 30 Mall/Market, 260 White Horse Pike; 08021 609-346-1199; 609-783-0685

Collingswood

Counseling/Therapy: Private

♀ ○ Gershman, Leonard F., Ph.D., FAACS, 1001 Park Ave; 08108-3236 609-858-6247

Cranford

Health Care (see also AIDS Services)

♀ • ♂ Banda, Geraldine M., DC, 347 Lincoln Ave E.; 07016 908-276-3440

Denville

Bookstores: Recovery, Metaphysical, & other Specialty

♀ • ♂♂ **Perrin & Treggett Booksellers, 3130 Route 10 West; 07834 201-328-8811; 800-770-8811; Fax 201-328-0999 "Gay & Lesbian books, music, cards, pride items. Recovery, spirituality, self-help. Gift certificates & special orders."**
✦ *Perrin & Treggett Booksellers advertisement page 307*

Computer/Software Sales & Services

♀ • **Mighty Mouse Electronics, 39 Cedar Lake East; 07834 201-625-3307 (also fax) "Repair CD players, VCRs, fax machines, copiers, computers, printers."**

Counseling/Therapy: Private

♀ • (?♂) Lafferty, Norma, MSW, ACSW, LCSW, 201-586-3694

Erotica (Printed, Visual, Equipment)

♀ • Video Emporium, 3049 Rte 10; 07834 201-361-9440

Dover

AIDS/HIV Support, Education, Advocacy, Publications

♀ ☆ ᕀᕀ AIDS Center at Hope House, 19-21 Belmont Ave; 07801-0851 201-361-7555; 201-361-7443; *The Olive Branch.* "Comprehensive AIDS Psychosocial services."

Dumont: see Teaneck

East Brunswick: see New Brunswick

East Orange: see Orange

Edgewater

Bars, Restaurants, Clubs, Discos

♂ ★ (ᕀᕀ) Morgan's, 8921 River Rd; 07020 201-941-4164 **BDE** Tue-Sun 9pm-3am.

Edison

Erotica (Printed, Visual, Equipment)

♂ ○ Adult Bookstore, 1851 State Hwy 27; 08817 908-985-9619

Real Estate

♀ ○ Clausen, Claudia, CRS, GRI, 358 Rt 18, East Brunswick 908-494-6800; 908-293-6482 pager; "Serving Middlesex & Somerset & Union Counties."

Egg Harbor City

Erotica (Printed, Visual, Equipment)

♂ ○ Adult World, 25 White Horse Pike; 08215 609-965-1110

Elizabeth

Bars, Restaurants, Clubs, Discos

♀ The Rose L Pub, 639 W 1st St, Roselle; 07203 908-245-3350

Legal Services & Resources

♀ ○ ᕀᕀ Bergen, Bruce H, Esq, c/o Krevsky, Silber & Brown, Box 1111; 07207-1111 / 288 North Broad St 908-352-2430 Fax 908-352-2413

Real Estate

♀ ○ Brewster Realty: Don Maroun, 635 Westfield Ave; 07208 908-820-8888; 908-353-4647

Travel & Tourist Services (see also Accommodation)

♀ ○ Approved Travel, 177 Elmora Ave; 07202 908-352-4244 Fax 908-352-7137

Elmwood Park

Health Care (see also AIDS Services)

♀ ○ Greenspan, Bernard, DO, PA, 1 Broadway; 07407 201-796-9336

Fairview

Bars, Restaurants, Clubs, Discos

♀ The Warehouse, 201 Broad Ave; 07022 201-945-7034

Fanwood

Organizations/Resources: Political/Legislative

♀ ★ Log Cabin Club of Central New Jersey, PO Box 484; 07023 908-988-6673

Far Hills

Counseling/Therapy: Private

♀ • Bedminster Counseling Center, PO Box 511; 07931 / Far Hills Professional Bldg, 43 Rt 202 908-781-0847

Florham Park

Travel & Tourist Services (see also Accommodation)

♀ ○ FPT The Preferred Way in Gay Travel, NY and NJ offices. 800-624-0207 Fax 201-377-5635, 212-582-6268
✦ *FPT The Preferred Way in Gay Travel advertisement page 146*

Fort Lee

Health Care (see also AIDS Services)

♀ ○ ᕀ Brauner, Gary J., MD, 1625 Anderson Ave; 07024 201-461-5522

Glen Ridge

Organizations/Resources: Social, Recreational & Support Groups (see also Sport/Dance/Outdoor)

♀ Upscale Sistas, PO Box 8072; 07028 201-523-1477

Glen Rock

Legal Services & Resources

♀ ○ Guston, Debra E., 55 Harristown Rd; 07452 201-447-6660

Guttenberg

Art & Photography (see also Graphic Design)

♀ • Natalie, Andrea, 201-662-7124 "Freelance cartoonist."

Hackettstown

Organizations/Resources: General, Multipurpose, Pride

♀ ★ Warren County Pride, PO Box 7188; 07840 201-442-0600; 201-442-1919; warren.county.pride@glitch.com

Hamburg

Legal Services & Resources

♀ • ᕀ Agnelli, Kathleen M., 118 Rt 23 North; 07419 201-827-7973

Hasbrouck Heights

Legal Services & Resources

♀ • ᕀᕀ Auriemma, Marianne F., Esq, 240 Boulevard; 07604 201-288-9084

Hawthorne

Piercing & Body Jewelry

♀ • (?ᕀ) Pleasurable Piercings, Inc., 417 Lafayette Ave; 07507 201-238-0305 Fax 201-238-9564

Pamela Sheldrick
Vivian Scheinmann

The multicultural feminist bookstore

9 Waverly Place, Madison NJ 07940

Pandora
Book Peddlers

(201) 822-8388

9 Waverly Place, Madison, NJ 07940 (201) 822-8388

Highland Park: see New Brunswick

Highlands

Accommodation: Hotels, B&B, Resorts, Campgrounds

⚥ ● Sea Bird Inn, Box 395, 60 Bay Ave; 07732 908-872-0123

Hoboken

Bars, Restaurants, Clubs, Discos

⚥ ○ (♿) Cafe Louis, 505 Washington St; 07030 201-659-9542 ***BR***

⚥ Excalibur, 1000 Jefferson St; 07030 201-795-1023; 201-795-1161; (late night only)

⚥ ○ Maxwell's, 1039 Washington St; 07030 201-656-9632

Counseling/Therapy: Private

⚥ ● ♿ Bergman, Tod, MSW, 324 Garden St; 07030 201-795-4050

Howell

Erotica (Printed, Visual, Equipment)

⚥ ○ Howell Adult Book Store, 6825 Hwy 9 North; 07731-3327 908-363-9680

Irvington

Erotica (Printed, Visual, Equipment)

⚥ ○ Best Adult Bookstore, 166 Prospect Ave; 07111 201-372-0130

Jersey City

Accommodation: Hotels, B&B, Resorts, Campgrounds

⚥ ● **P&P Bed & Breakfast, 290 Barrow St; 07302 201-435-0181**

Bars, Restaurants, Clubs, Discos

⚥ Uncle Joe's, 154 1st St; 07302 201-653-9173

⚥ ○ Wiggles, 175 21st St, Bayonne; 07002 201-436-2121 (Thu-Sun)

Counseling/Therapy: Private

⚥ ● **Institute for Personal Growth, 8 S 3rd Ave, Highland Park, NJ 08904-2510 908-246-8439 Fax 908-246-8081**

⚥ ● Nichols, Margaret, Ph.D., 281 Pavonia Ave; 07302 201-798-5926

Organizations/Resources: Social, Recreational & Support Groups (see also Sport/Dance/Outdoor)

⚥ Gay Friends & Neighbors/Jersey City, PO Box 3146; 07303 201-333-2000

Kinnelon

Insurance (see also Insurance Benefits/Viaticals)

⚥ ● Digiacomo, Maryellen, 31 Kiel Ave; 07405 201-838-2982 "Specializing in financial planning & insurance for the professional."

Lakewood

Erotica (Printed, Visual, Equipment)

⚥ ● Adult Books, 1359 River Rd; 08701 908-367-5622

Lambertville

Accommodation: Hotels, B&B, Resorts, Campgrounds

⚥ ● (?♿) Chimney Hill Farm Bed & Breakfast, 207 Goat Hill Road; 08530 609-397-1516

⚥ ○ ♿♿ The Inn At Lambertville Station, 11 Bridge St; 08530 609-397-4400; 800-524-1091

Erotica (Printed, Visual, Equipment)

⚥ ● Joy's Books, Rt 165, #103; 08530 609-397-2907

Little Falls

Art & Photography (see also Graphic Design)

⚥ ● **Giulianna Marie Studios, Studios in West Paterson & New York City 201-785-0555; 212-642-8071; "Portraits, headshots, portfolios, fashion, commercial."**

Little Ferry

Legal Services & Resources

⚥ ● (?♿) Wooldridge, Ann A., Esq, 11 Grove St; 07643 201-641-6864

Livingston

Counseling/Therapy: Private

♀ ○ **Women's Counseling/Psychotherapy Services, 60 Compton Ave, Verona, NJ 07044 201-992-9190; 201-857-2808 Verona; 201-631-8188 Morristown**

Lodi

Jewelry

⚥ • (?⚤) Golden Gayte Designs, Fine Diamonds & Jewelry, 201-340-7642 "Custom work on request."

Madison

Bookstores: Gay/Lesbian/Feminist

♀ ○ ♂ Pandora Book Peddlers, 9 Waverly Place; 07940 201-822-8388
♦ *Pandora Book Peddlers advertisement page 308*

Mahwah

Organizations/Resources: Student, Academic, Alumni/ae

⚥ ★♂♂ Gay, Lesbian, Bisexual Coalition of Ramapo College, 501 Ramapo Valley Rd; 07430 201-529-7468

Maplewood

Legal Services & Resources

♀ • Gale, Lynn P., Esq, 484 Irvington Ave; 07040 201-763-4297

Religious Organizations & Publications

⚥ ★ Dignity/Metro NJ, St George's Church, 550 Ridgewood Rd; 07040 201-761-7321 "Gay & Lesbian Catholics & their friends."

Maywood

Counseling/Therapy: Private

♀ • Williams, Kevin James, MSW, 453 Golf Ave; 07607 201-843-2954

Health Care (see also AIDS Services)

♀ • ♂ Eustace, Timothy J., DC, 140 W Pleasant Ave; 07607 201-843-3111

Millburn

Counseling/Therapy: Private

♀ • ♂♂ Alternative Approach Counseling & Psychotherapy Center, 55 Main St; 07041 201-736-8785
♀ ○ Levin, E. Betty, MA, 117 Sagamore Rd; 07041 201-763-1035

Mine Hill: see Dover

Montclair

Addictive Behavior, Substance Abuse, Recovery

♀ • Butler, Angela, Psy.D., 17 Carteret St, Upper Montclair; 07043 201-783-9779

AIDS/HIV Support, Education, Advocacy, Publications

♀ NJ Aids Connection, PO Box 162; 07042 201-481-1412

Bookstores: General

♀ ○ Montclair Book Center, 221 Glenridge Ave; 07042 201-783-3630 10am-8pm; Sun noon-6pm.

Counseling/Therapy: Nonprofit

♀ ☆ ♂ Drop-In Center, Montclair State College, Upper Montclair; 07043 201-893-5271 24 hrs walk-in & phone: peer counseling & referrals.

Counseling/Therapy: Private

♀ • ♂♂ Alternative Approach Counseling & Psychotherapy Center, 50 Church St; 07042 201-736-8785

⚥ • ♂ Center for Identity Development, 31 Trinity Place; 07042 201-744-6386
⚥ • Giachetti, Diane, CSW, ACSW, 201-783-4116
⚥ • Institute for Personal Growth, 8 S 3rd Ave, Highland Park, NJ 08904-2510 908-246-8439 Fax 908-246-8081
⚥ ○ Kopacsi, Rosemarie, PhD, ACSW, 460 Bloomfield Ave #209 201-338-4834 "Individual & couples therapy."
⚥ • Lewinter, Beth C., MSW, CSW, 37 N Fullerton Ave #303; 07042 201-783-6351
♀ ○ Madura, Karen, MSW, 209 Cooper Ave, Upper Montclair; 07043 201-744-4444
♀ ○ Wolverton, Gwen, PsyD, 1 Upper Mountain Ave; 07042 201-746-1414

Erotica (Printed, Visual, Equipment)

♀ ○ Dressing For Pleasure Boutique, 590 Valley Rd 201-746-5466 Tue-Sat. "Fetish clothing & bondage equipment."

Legal Services & Resources

♀ • (♂) Molina, Wanda, Esq, 460 Bloomfield Ave; 07042 201-792-1466

Organizations/Resources: Social, Recreational & Support Groups (see also Sport/Dance/Outdoor)

♀ ★ (♂) Always On Sunday, PO Box 1708; 07042 201-783-7699 "Social & networking."

Real Estate

♀ • (♂♂) Henry & Co., Realtors, Jaan, PO Box 708; 07042 201-746-9200; 201-783-7699

Morristown

Counseling/Therapy: Private

♀ ○♂♂ Allen Wells Center for Pychotherapy & Healing, 102 Ogden Place; 07960 201-539-0301

Organizations/Resources: General, Multipurpose, Pride

⚥ ★ (?⚤) Gay Activist Alliance in Morris County, PO Box 137, Convent Station, NJ 07961-0137 201-285-1595 Helpline 7.30-10.30pm. Meets Mon 8.45-10pm at Morristown Unitarian Fellowship, Normandy Hts Rd, Morristown.

♂ ★ (?⚤) Men's Rap Group, Gay Activist Alliance in Morris County, PO Box 137, Convent Station; 07961-0137 201-285-1595 Helpline 7.30-10.30pm. Rap groups 7.15 & 7.30 precede main meeting 8.45pm at Morristown Unitarian Fellowship, 21 Normandy Hts Rd, Morristown.

♀ ★ (?⚤) Womyn's Network, Gay Activist Alliance in Morris County, PO Box 137, Convent Station; 07961-0137 201-285-1595 Helpline 7.30-10.30pm. Meets Mon 7.30-8.30pm at Morristown Unitarian Fellowship, 21 Normandy Hts Rd, Morristown.

Organizations/Resources: Sport/Dance/Outdoor

♀ ★ Alliance Ski Club, PO Box 123; 07960

Neptune

AIDS/HIV Support, Education, Advocacy, Publications

♀ ☆♂♂ AIDS Support Team, 71 Davis Ave; 07753 908-776-4700 Mon-Fri 9am-5pm.

New Brunswick

Accommodation: Reservations & Exchanges (see also Travel)

♀ • Rentorations Limited, 908-247-4966 "Private & shared apartments & houses to rent in historic buildings."

NJ: New Brunswick
Bars, Clubs, Restaurants
310
USA
Orange: NJ
Bars, Clubs, Restaurants

Bars, Restaurants, Clubs, Discos

♂ ○ &♿ The Den, 700 Hamilton St, Somerset; 08873 908-545-7329 *BD* 8pm-2am.

♀ ○ &♿ The Frog And The Peach, 29 Dennis St; 08901 908-846-3216 *BR*

♀ ● &♿ J. August's Cafe, 100 Jersey Ave; 08901 908-545-4646 Fax 908-545-0113 *R* Mon-Fri 7am-5pm.

♀ ○ &♿ Stage Left: An American Café, 5 Livingston Ave; 08901 908-828-4444 *BR*

♂ ● &♿ Tod's Dance Club & Cafe, 2 George's Rd 908-545-8990 *BDE* Thu 8pm-2am; Fri & Sat 8pm-3am.

Bookstores: General

♀ ○ All About Books, 409 Raritan Ave, Highland Park; 08904 908-247-8744

♂ ○ (&♿) Chapter One Books, 128 Raritan Ave, Highland Park; 08904 908-828-7648 10.20am-11pm.

Broadcast Media

♂ ★ &♿ Gay Spirit/Generation Queer, 86 Albany St; 08903 908-932-8800 Fax 908-932-1768; 828-4222 Tue 9-11pm, 88.7 WRSU-FM.

Community Centers (see also Women's Centers)

♀ Pride Center of New Jersey, PO Box 1431; 08903 908-846-CCDC

Counseling/Therapy: Private

♂ ● Institute for Personal Growth, 8 S 3rd Ave, Highland Park; 08904-2510 908-246-8439 Fax 908-246-8081

♀ ○ Swack, Mary Travers, LCSW, ACSW, Offices in Florham Park, Paramus & Tewkesbury 201-377-4911; 908-236-2468

Health Care (see also AIDS Services)

♀ ● &♿ Stypka, Trish, DC, 1075 Hamilton St, Somerset; 08873 908-828-7070

Home & Building: Cleaning, Repair, General Contractors

♀ ● Kafka, Moe, 908-247-4966 "Specializing in restoration & detail work on historic homes & antique furniture."

Interior Design

♀ ● Lemontree Productions, 177 Hamilton St; 08901 908-246-1292

Organizations/Resources: General, Multipurpose, Pride

♂ ★ &♿ Lesbians & Gay Men of New Brunswick, PO Box 1949; 08903-1949 908-247-0515 Meets 2nd & 4th Tue 8pm at Friends Meeting House, 109 Nichol Ave.

♀ ★ (?&) More Than You Can Count, PO Box 4178, Highland Park; 08904 908-819-0601

Organizations/Resources: Student, Academic, Alumni/ae

♂ ★ &♿ Rutgers University Lesbian, Gay & Bisexual Alliance, SAC Box 91; 08903 908-932-1306 Pub *Queer Chatter*.

Publications

→ *Network Magazine: for the 10% Plus*: p.304

Record Sales (see also Performing Arts)

♀ ● &♿ Quantum X Music, Kilmer Square, 86 Albany St; 08901 908-828-2121 10am-9pm; Sun noon-6pm. "CDs, cassettes, vinyl, accessories, jewelry, body piercing."

Religious Organizations & Publications

♂ ★ &♿ Dignity/New Brunswick, PO Box 10781; 08906-0781 908-254-7942 "Gay & Lesbian Catholics & their friends."

♂ ★ (&♿) Metropolitan Community Church of Christ the Liberator, PO Box 10494; 08906 908-846-8227

Women's Centers

♀ ☆ Women's Support & Survival Center, 56 College Ave; 08903 908-828-7273

Newark

AIDS/HIV Support, Education, Advocacy, Publications

♀ ☆ &♿ AIDS Helpline, St Michael's Medical Center, 268 M. L. King Blvd; 07102 201-596-0767; 201-877-5525; Mon-Fri 8.30am-4.30pm.

♀ ☆ Newark Community Health Centers, Inc, PO Box 1960; 07101 201-565-0355

Bars, Restaurants, Clubs, Discos

♂ ● First Choice, 533 Ferry St; 07105 201-465-1944 *BDEf* "Dancers; female impersonator shows."

♂ ○ Murphy's, 59 Edison Place; 07102 201-622-9176

Organizations/Resources: Ethnic, Multicultural

♂ ★ SHADES, Edward Robinson, 4 Little St, 2nd Floor; 07107 201-485-5689 Monthly meetings for Gay Men of African Descent.

Printing & Promotional Items (see also Art; Graphics/Typesetting)

♀ ● Graphic Impressions, PO Box 240, Harrison; 07029 201-484-6116; 800-646-6116; Fax 201-482-6510

♂ ● Peacock Printing, 207 Railroad Ave, Harrison; 07029 201-481-9497 "Silkscreening on all suitable surfaces. Customizing our specialty."

Newfoundland

Gifts, Cards, Pride & Novelty Items

♀ ● Scents of Pride, 8 Oak Ridge Road; 07435 201-697-3013 "Gift baskets; aromatherapy."

North Bergen

Massage Therapy (Licensed only)

♂ ● &♿ Lader, Amy, 8200 Blvd East #31K; 07047 201-662-9054 "Licensed therapeutic massages; certified Reflexology."

Oak Ridge

Bars, Restaurants, Clubs, Discos

♂ ● Yacht Club, 366 Berkshire Valley Rd; 07438 201-697-9780

Oakland

Organizations/Resources: Social, Recreational & Support Groups (see also Sport/Dance/Outdoor)

♀ ★ &♿ Feminine Connection, Oakland 201-337-7506 "Social group for Lesbians."

Orange

Bars, Restaurants, Clubs, Discos

♀ ● Rah-Rah's Pub/Mama T's Pizza, 51 S. Day St; 07050 (call for directions) 201-676-1399 *Bdf* 4pm-2am; Fri & Sat to 3am; sandwiches & pizza till mdnt; finger foods, cheese, wings, etc." "All lifestyle undisco friendly bar. Mostly men weekdays; mixed Fri-Sun. Compact disc jukebox: 2400 songs. Video, pool, bowls, darts. No cover. Parking lot monitored by camera."

NJ: Orange
Health Care

311
USA

Princeton : NJ
Organizations: Social & Support

Health Care (see also AIDS Services)

♀ • ♂♂ Belt, Steven, MD, 100 Northfield Ave, West Orange; 07052 201-731-1535

Palisades Park

Florists (see also Gardening)

♂ • The Gay Rose, Box 12; 07650 201-592-1268; 800-843-4297; Fax 201-592-0114

Passaic

Home & Building: Cleaning, Repair, General Contractors

♀ • Courageous Cleaners Of Montclair, 228 Gregory Ave; 07055 201-778-9035

Paterson

Bars, Restaurants, Clubs, Discos

♂ ○♂♂ Colt Lounge, 5 Colt St; 07505 201-523-9701 *BDER* 11am-3am.

Pennington

Travel & Tourist Services (see also Accommodation)

♀ • (♂) Hobbit Travel Services, 1 Michael Way; 08534 609-737-2257; 800-815-4555; Fax 609-737-2344

Perth Amboy

Bars, Restaurants, Clubs, Discos

♂ • The Colosseum, 7090 State Hwy 35 N; 08879 (at Rte 9N, Sayreville) 908-316-0670

♂ • The Other Half, 547 Kennedy St; 08861 908-826-8877

Organizations/Resources: Sport/Dance/Outdoor

♀ • Doc's Yacht Kare Enterprise, 908-324-2177

Plainfield

Accommodation: Hotels, B&B, Resorts, Campgrounds

♀ ○ The Pillars B&B, 922 Central Ave; 07060 908-753-0922; 800-37-2REST; "Secluded Victorian mansion; easy access to NYC & Sandy Hook. Private baths; full breakfast."
✦ *Pillars B&B advertisement page 311*

Bars, Restaurants, Clubs, Discos

♀ • ♂ The Gin Mill, 308 Wachtung Ave; 07050 908-755-4000 *BDE* 10am-1am; Fri & Sat to 2am; Sun 1pm-1am.

Counseling/Therapy: Private

♀ • Walker, Sylvia, MSW, LCSW, 908-561-6073 "Special training & experience working with PWA's, Sero-positive individuals, & Significant Others."

Health Care (see also AIDS Services)

♀ ○ Powderly, Mary K., MD, FACOG, 190 Greenbrook Rd, North Plainfield; 07060 908-756-6812

Legal Services & Resources

♀ ○ (♂) **Gargano, Francine A., Esq, 113 Watchung Ave, North Plainfield; 07060 908-753-2079**

Real Estate

♂ ○ Realty World—PAR Agency, Inc., Violette Brown, Broker, 356 Park Ave, Scotch Plains; 07076 908-322-4700 Fax 908-322-4742

Video Sales, Rentals, Services (see also Erotica)

♂ • ATKOL Video, 912 South Avenue; 07062 908-756-2011 (NJ); 800-88-ATKOL (National)
✦ *ATKOL Video advertisement page 311*

Princeton

Counseling/Therapy: Private

♂ • (♿) Bunker Hill Consultation Center, 7 Three Acre Lane; 08540 609-497-0899 Mon-Fri 9am-9pm.

Organizations/Resources: Social, Recreational & Support Groups (see also Sport/Dance/Outdoor)

♂ ★ ♂ Gay People Princeton, PO Box 2303; 08543 Meets Thu 8-10.30pm at Princeton Unitarian Church, 50 Cherry Hill Rd.

Organizations/Resources: Student, Academic, Alumni/ae

⚥ ★ (?♿) Lesbian, Gay & Bisexual Alliance, Princeton University, 306 Aaron Burr Hall; 08544 609-258-4522

Red Bank

Bookstores: General

⚥ ○ Earth Spirit, 16 W Front St; 07701 908-842-3855

Counseling/Therapy: Private

⚥ • (♿) **Banks, Daphnee, CSW, MSW, ACSW, 248 Broad St; 07701 908-530-8483**

⚥ • **Institute for Personal Growth, 8 S 3rd Ave, Highland Park, NJ 08904-2510 908-246-8439 Fax 908-246-8081**

⚥ ○♿♿ **Swomley, David Neal, PhD, 10 W Bergen Pl #108; 07701 908-219-6655**

◆ *Swomley, David Neal, PhD advertisement page 312*

Ringwood

Accommodation: Hotels, B&B, Resorts, Campgrounds

♀ • Ensanmar, 2 Ellen St; 07456 201-831-0898; 201-835-0546

River Edge

Bars, Restaurants, Clubs, Discos

♂ ○ Feathers, 77 Kinderkamack Rd; 07661 201-342-6410

Massage Therapy (Licensed only)

♀ • Evergreen Body Therapy, 201-779-1434 "Licensed Massage Therapist (serving women & gay men); also Reflexology, Shiatsu, Reiki. Home visits."

Organizations/Resources: General, Multipurpose, Pride

♀ ★ (♿) Lesbian Awareness, mail to A.B.L. PO Box 4414; 07661-4414 201-779-1434

Rockaway

Organizations/Resources: Social, Recreational & Support Groups (see also Sport/Dance/Outdoor)

⚥ ★ (?♿) New Jersey Rainbow Alliance of the Deaf, Inc., PO Box 596; 07866 800-852-7897 for relay service; 201-857-2555 TDD only.; "Hearies are welcomed."

Rocky Hill

Travel & Tourist Services (see also Accommodation)

⚥ • ♿ Travel Registry, Inc., 127 Washington St; 08553 609-921-6900; 800-346-6901

Roselle: see Elizabeth

Seabrook

Addictive Behavior, Substance Abuse, Recovery

⚥ ☆ (♿♿) Seabrook House, PO Box 5055 Polk Ln; 08302-5055 800-582-5968 "Detox & rehabilitation program, in- & out-patient."

Sewell

Organizations/Resources: Student, Academic, Alumni/ae

⚥ ★ (?♿) IMRU of Gloucester County College, PO Box 227; 08080 609-468-5000 ext 750

Short Hills

Massage Therapy (Licensed only)

♂ ○ ♿ Caraglia, Ralph, MA, CMT, JFK Parkway 201-482-5941 "Certified massage therapist: Swedish, Shiatsu, sports & stress management."

Shrewsbury

Counseling/Therapy: Private

⚥ ○ **Reskof, Jane A, MSW, ACSW, CSW, 21 White St; 07702 908-758-6366**

Somerville

Counseling/Therapy: Private

♀ ○ **Stein, Virginia Kramer, MA, 357 William St; 08876 908-722-6343**

South Amboy

Bars, Restaurants, Clubs, Discos

⚥ Sauvage, 1 Victory Plaza; 08879 908-727-6619

Stratford

Erotica (Printed, Visual, Equipment)

⚥ ○ White Horse Bookstore, 906 White Horse Pike; 08084 609-435-9662

Summit

Addictive Behavior, Substance Abuse, Recovery

⚥ • **Smith, Deborah S., 47 Maple St L-27; 07901 / 22 Maple Ave, Morristown; 07960 908-277-9599; 908-580-0797; "Certified Drug & Alcohol Counselor; also specialize in counseling on gay/lesbian/bisexual issues."**

NJ: Teaneck
Counseling: Private
313
USA
State/County Resources : NM
AIDS/HIV Support

Teaneck

Counseling/Therapy: Private

♀ ○ Kupferman, Roz Yager, BS, MA, PSY.A., 304 Winthrop Rd; 07666 201-837-6381

Toms River

Counseling/Therapy: Private

♀ ○ (?⚲) Hepburn, Fran, MSW, CADC, 1518 Hwy 37E #5; 08753 908-270-2952

Trenton

Bars, Restaurants, Clubs, Discos

♂ • Buddies Pub, 677 South Broad; 08611 609-989-8566 *BEf*

♀ • ♿ Casa Lido, 120 S Warren St; 08608 609-394-8158 *BDR* 7am-2am; restaurant 7am-3pm.

♂ Club 21, 499 Center St; 08611 609-392-9188

Counseling/Therapy: Private

♀ • ♿ Achievement Center of Hamilton, 2622 Nottingham Way, Hamilton; 08619 609-587-8774

Gardening Services, Landscaping, Supplies & Decoration

♀ • City Yard & Garden, 1003 Indiana Ave; 08638 800-882-6342 "Small scale gardenscapes & yard maintenance."

Organizations/Resources: Social, Recreational & Support Groups (see also Sport/Dance/Outdoor)

♀ ☆ (?⚲) Supported and Independent Leisure Services, 1003 Indiana Ave; 08638 800-882-6342 "Leisure assistance for developmentally disabled, their families & riends. Call or write for details."

Union City

Bars, Restaurants, Clubs, Discos

♂ • XTC, 509 22nd St; 07087 201-863-9515 *BD* 8pm-3am.

Union

Bars, Restaurants, Clubs, Discos

♀ • ♿ Cactus Club, 1731 Route 22 West; 07083 908-688-0101 *D*

Computer/Software Sales & Services

♀ • Scantastics, 340 Nottingham Way; 07083 201-216-0552 "Electrofiling services for the office environment."

Voorhees

Travel & Tourist Services (see also Accommodation)

♀ ○ (♿) Emerald Travel Network, 36 Evesham Road, Avian Plaza; 08043 609-424-0975 Fax 609-424-0991

Washington Township

Counseling/Therapy: Private

♀ ○ Gordon, Donna L., MA, NCPsyA, 63 Horizon Court; 07675 201-652-2957

Wayne

Counseling/Therapy: Private

♀ • ♿ H.E.L.P. Inc, 1065 Alps Rd; 07470-3707 and 184 Rivervale Rd #14, River Vale 201-305-7638 (also Fax) "PWAs & their family members welcome. Services to gay teenagers; member of PFLAG. Special rated fee to gays & family of $25 per counseling hour."

There is NO CHARGE to be listed in Gayellow Pages. Please send a business-size stamped self-addressed envelope to the address below for an application.

Gayellow Pages
PO Box 533 Village Station, New York, NY 10014-0533

Insurance (see also Insurance Benefits/Viaticals)

♂ • Martorano, Mary Grace & Prince, Ginny, Prudential Insurance & Financial Services, 33 Littlewood Court; 07470 201-942-8744 Fax 201-904-0360

Organizations/Resources: Student, Academic, Alumni/ae

♂ ★ (♿) William Paterson College Coalition of Lesbians, Gays & Friends, Student Center, William Paterson College; 07470 201-595-3427

West Orange: see Orange

Westfield

Public Relations/Advertising Agencies

♀ • Rivendell Marketing Company, Box 518; 07091-0518 908-232-2021; 212-242-6863; Fax 908-232-0521 "We specialize in securing national advertising for Gay & Lesbian publications."

Real Estate

♀ ○ Duncan Smythe, Caldwell Banker/Schlott Realtors, 209 Central Ave; 07090 908-233-5555; 908-233-7405 (eves); Fax 908-233-8780

Westmont

Counseling/Therapy: Nonprofit

♂ ★ (♿♿) Hicks, Walter Dean, PhD, CAS, 216 Haddon Ave #608; 08108-2814 609-854-3155

Woodbridge

Organizations/Resources: Sexual Focus (Leather, S/M, etc) & Safe Sex Promotion

♂ ★ Pocono Warriors, PO Box 1483; 07095-0970 908-750-2638 *L*

Travel & Tourist Services (see also Accommodation)

♀ ○ Gulliver's Travel, 76 Main St; 07095 908-636-1120; 800-836-TOUR

Woodcliff Lake

Counseling/Therapy: Private

♀ ○ Panozzo, David, CSW, 201-476-1816 "Specializing in Gay/Bisexual & HIV issues."

New Mexico

State/County Resources

Addictive Behavior, Substance Abuse, Recovery

♂ • (♿♿) Pride Institute, 800-54-PRIDE "The nation's only accredited chemical dependency treatment center exclusively for Gay, Lesbian & Bisexual People."

AIDS/HIV Support, Education, Advocacy, Publications

♀ ☆ ♿ New Mexico AIDS Services, 4200 Silver Ave SE #D, Albuquerque, NM 87108 505-266-0911 Pub *Volunteer*.

♀ ☆ ♂♂ **New Mexico Association of People Living with AIDS (NMPALA), 111 Montclaire SE, Albuquerque, NM 87108-2623 505-266-0342; 800-658-6717; 9am-5pm.** Pub *NMPLA News*.

Organizations/Resources: Political/Legislative

♂ Log Cabin New Mexico, PO Box 4769, Albuquerque, NM 87196 505-244-1824

Organizations/Resources: Sport/Dance/Outdoor

♂ ★ ♂♂ New Mexico Gay Rodeo Association, PO Box 35381, Albuquerque, NM 87176 505-255-5045

♂ New Mexico Outdoors, 9604 Lona Lane NE, Albuquerque, NM 87111 505-822-1093

Publications

♂ ★ ♂ *Out! Magazine*, PO Box 27237, Albuquerque, NM 87125-7237 505-243-2540 Fax 505-842-5114 outmag@ swcp.com Monthly.

Real Estate

♂ • Community Real Estate Referrals, 800-346-5592 "Free referral to gay/gay-supportive realtor in any USA city/state (including Virgin Is. & Puerto Rico). Sorry, no rentals!"
✦ *Community Real Estate Referrals advertisement back cover*

Religious Organizations & Publications

♂ ★ ♂ Dignity/New Mexico, PO Box 27294, Albuquerque, NM 87125 505-898-3343; 800-877-8797; "Gay & Lesbian Catholics & their friends."

Travel & Tourist Services (see also Accommodation)

♀ • (?♂) Mountain Mama Packing & Riding Co, General Delivery, Cañónes, NM 87516 505-638-9150

Albuquerque

☎ **Common Bond Gay & Lesbian Information Line 505-266-8041**

Accommodation: Hotels, B&B, Resorts, Campgrounds

♂ • ♂♂ Dave's Bed & Breakfast on the Rio Grande, PO Box 27214; 87125-7214 505-247-8312 *L* "Mainly men; casual & private home for gays & leatherfolk."

♂ ○ Rio Grande House, 3100 Rio Grande Blvd NW; 87107 505-345-0120

♀ • The W.E. Mauger Estate B&B, 701 Roma Ave NW; 87102 505-242-8755

If you can't find the
NAME   PLACE   SUBJECT
you're looking for,
PLEASE TRY THE INDEX

♀ • ♂ Whiptail Inn, PO Box 4723; 87196 505-247-9461

AIDS/HIV Support, Education, Advocacy, Publications

→ New Mexico AIDS Services: p.313

♂ ☆ ♂♂ New Mexico Association of People Living with AIDS/Albuquerque (NMAPLA), 111 Montclaire SE; 87108-2623 505-266-0342; 800-658-6717; 9am-5pm.

Bars, Restaurants, Clubs, Discos

♀ Albuquerque Mining Co, 7209 Central Ave NE; 87108-2013 505-266-8465

♂ • (♂♂) Albuquerque Social Club, PO Box 80554; 87108 / 4021 Central Ave NE 505-255-0887 *LWP* Noon-2am. Country/ Western dancing.

♀ • ♂♂ Chef Du Jour, 119 San Pasquale SW; 87104-1147 505-247-8998 *R*

♀ Club On Central, 10030 Central SE; 87123 505-291-1550

♂ • Corky's, 2428 San Mateo Place NE; 87110 505-884-6800 *PCWD*

♂ ○ Cuffs, at The Ranch, 8900 Central St SE; 87123 505-275-1616

♀ • Foxes Lounge, 8521 Central Ave NE; 87108 505-255-3060

♂ ○ The Ranch, 8900 Central St SE; 87123 505-275-1616 11am-2am.

Bookstores: Gay/Lesbian/Feminist

♀ • ♂♂ Full Circle Books, 2205 Silver SE; 87106 505-266-0022; 800-951-0053; Mon-Fri 10am-6pm; Sat & Sun to 5pm.

♀ • ♂♂ **Sisters' & Brothers' Bookstore, 4011 Silver Ave SE; 87108-2643 505-266-7317; 800-687-3480**
✦ *Sisters' & Brothers' Bookstore advertisement page 314*

Bookstores: General

♀ ○ ♂ Living Batch Bookstore, 106 Cornell Dr SE; 87106 505-262-1619

♀ ○ ♂ Newsland Bookstore, 2112 Central Ave SE; 87106 505-242-0694

Business, Financial & Secretarial

♀ • ♂ Bedford, Dave, PO Box 27214; 87125 505-247-8312 "Tax preparation & accounting."

♂ • (?♂) To The Penny Bookkeeping Services, 820 Mildred St NE; 87123 505-298-7075

Community Centers (see also Women's Centers)

♀ ★ ♂ **Common Bond Gay & Lesbian Community Center, PO Box 26836; 87125 / 4013 Silver Rd SE 505-266-8041 7-10pm; Sat & Sun Noon-2pm (lesbian only)**

Erotica (Printed, Visual, Equipment)

♀ ○ ♂ Harris Newsstand, 5319 Menaul NE; 87110 505-880-8696 Fax 505-254-3835 9am-11pm; Fri & Sat to mdnt.

♂ • Nebula Boooks, 9132 Central SE; 87123 505-275-7727 10am-mdnt

Florists (see also Gardening)

♀ • **Flowers By Martha Lee, 5019 Lomas NE; 87110 505-256-3518; 800-634-2149; Mon-Fri 8am-5.30pm Mon-Fri; Sat 9-5pm.** "European Vase, Exotics & High-Style Arrangements."

Food Specialties, Catering (see also Party/Event Services)

♀ • Red Silk Caterers, 618 High St SE; 87102 505-764-8300

Legal Services & Resources

♀ • Atkins, Loretta Libby, 507 Roma NW; 87102 505-243-6808 Fax 505-247-4976

♀ • (?⚥) Cohen, Ruth B., 123 Richmond Drive SE; 87106 505-256-7742

♂ • ⚥⚥ Roybal, Randall, 1720 Louisiana Blvd NE #305; 87110 505-255-7711

♀ • ⚥⚥ Work, Claudia D., 1720 Louisiana Blvd NE #305; 87110 505-255-7711 Fax 505-255-8811

News Wire Services

♀ ★ GayNet, PO Box 25524; 87125-0524 505-842-5112; 800-524-2963 (new memberships); Fax 505-842-5114 "International Gay & Lesbian news service for the media."

Organizations/Resources: Business & Professional

♀ ★⚥⚥ Duke City Business & Professional Association, PO Box 27207; 87125 505-897-1443

Organizations/Resources: Political/Legislative

♀ New Mexico Progressive Political Action Committee (NM Pro-PAC), PO Box 36874; 87176 505-345-9132

Organizations/Resources: Social, Recreational & Support Groups (see also Sport/Dance/Outdoor)

♂ ★ ♂ Gay Men's Rap Group, c/o Common Bond 4013 Silver Ave SE; 87106 505-266-8041 Wed 7-9pm.

♂ ★ Hijos Del Sol, PO Box 112, Sandia Park; 87047 505-299-9282

♀ ★⚥⚥ Lesbian Support/Rap Group, c/o Full Circle Books, 2205 Silver Ave SE; 87106 505-266-0022

Organizations/Resources: Sport/Dance/Outdoor

♀ ★ ♂ Wilde Bunch, PO Box 40393; 87196-0393 505-266-8746; 505-877-6519; ♂ Mon & Wed 7-9.30pm at Albuquerque Social Club. Pub *Wilde Times.* "Square dance group; all welcome."

Organizations/Resources: Student, Academic, Alumni/ae

♀ ★⚥⚥ Lesbian, Bisexual & Gay Alliance, PO Box 100 Student Union Bldg, UNM; Room 24A; 87131 505-277-6739

Publications

♀ ○ *Hembra*, PO Box 40572; 87196

→ *Out! Magazine*: p.314

♀ • *The Weekly Rainbow*, PO Box 4769; 87196 505-244-1824 Fax 505-244-1679 summers@rt66.com

Religious Organizations & Publications

♀ Emmanuel Metropolitan Community Church, PO Box 80192; 87108 505-268-0599

♂ ★⚥⚥ Metropolitan Community Church of Albuquerque, 2404 San Mateo Place NE; 87110 505-881-9088 Fax 505-881-8089 Pub *MCC Alive.*

Switchboards, Helplines, Phone Information

♀ ★ Common Bond Gay & Lesbian Information Line, PO Box 26836; 87125 505-266-8041 7-10pm

Travel & Tourist Services (see also Accommodation)

♂ ○ American Express Travel, 6600 Indian School Rd NE, Bldg C #1; 87110 505-883-3677 Fax 505-884-0008

Video Sales, Rentals, Services (see also Erotica)

♂ • (⚥⚥) Blue Angel Videos, 4013 Silver SE; 87108

Women's Centers

♀ ⚥⚥ University of New Mexico Women's Center, 1160 Mesa Vista Hall; 87131 505-277-3716

Belen

Bars, Restaurants, Clubs, Discos

♂ Fiorello's, 921 River Rd; 87002 505-864-7636 *BR*

Clovis

Organizations/Resources: Social, Recreational & Support Groups (see also Sport/Dance/Outdoor)

♀ ★ (?⚥) Clovis/Portales Common Bond, PO Box 663; 88101 505-356-2656

Corrales

Accommodation: Hotels, B&B, Resorts, Campgrounds

♂ ○ ♂ Corrales Inn Bed & Breakfast, PO Box 1361; 87048 505-897-4422

Galisteo

Accommodation: Hotels, B&B, Resorts, Campgrounds

♂ ○ ♂ Galisteo Inn, HC 75, Box 4; 87540 505-466-4000

Las Cruces & Mesilla

AIDS/HIV Support, Education, Advocacy, Publications

♂ ☆⚥⚥ New Mexico Association of People Living with AIDS/Las Cruces (NMAPLA), 101 N Alameda #14, Las Cruces; 88001 505-524-0013; 800-658-6717; 10am-5pm.

Counseling/Therapy: Private

♂ ○ (⚥) Lehman, James, ACSW, LISW, Jardin Escondido Counseling Center, 570 W Griggs Ave, Las Cruces; 88005 505-524-3614

Organizations/Resources: Bisexual Focus

♀ ★ Gay & Lesbian Student Association, New Mexico State University, PO Box 4639, Las Cruces; 88003

Organizations/Resources: Social, Recreational & Support Groups (see also Sport/Dance/Outdoor)

♀ ★ (⚥) Sabra Lesbian Coalition, c/o Box 992, Mesilla; 88046 Meetings twice a month in Las Cruces.

Religious Organizations & Publications

♂ ★ (?⚥) Koinonia, PO Box 168, Mesilla; 88046 505-521-1490 "Ecumenical spirituality group."

Mesilla: see Las Cruces

Pecos

Accommodation: Hotels, B&B, Resorts, Campgrounds

♀ • (♿) Wilderness Inn, PO Box 1177; 87552 505-757-6694

Santa Fe

Accommodation: Hotels, B&B, Resorts, Campgrounds

♀ • (?♿) Heartseed B&B Retreat Center & Spa, PO Box 6019; 87502-6019 505-471-7026

♀ ○ Open Sky B&B, 134 Turquoise Trail; 87505 800-244-3475

♀ • ♿ Rocking S Ranch, Rte 2, Box 278; 87505 505-438-7333

♀ ○ (♿) Temple Of Light, 2407 Camino Capitan; 87505 505-471-4053 "Bed & breakfast."

♂ • The Triangle Inn, PO Box 3235; 87501 505-455-3375

Accommodation: Reservations & Exchanges (see also Travel)

♀ ○ Jamelos Properties, 1116 South Luna Circle; 87501 505-988-3399 8am-9pm.

Addictive Behavior, Substance Abuse, Recovery

♂ Live & Let Live AA, PO Box 674; 87504 505-982-0685; 505-986-0223

AIDS/HIV Support, Education, Advocacy, Publications

♀ ☆♿ AIDS Wellness Program & Clinic, VNS, 811 St Michael's Dr; 87501 505-983-1822 "Full service HIV medical clinic, providing confidential primary medical care (sliding fee scale) & free anonymous HIV testing."

♀ ★♿ Hand In Hand, 1229-C St Francis Dr; 87505 505-820-AIDS Fax 505-820-2100 "Home care & practical suppport for HIV+ people."

♀ ☆♿ New Mexico Association of People Living with AIDS/ Santa Fe (NMAPLA), 1223-B St Francis Dr; 87505 505-820-3437; 800-658-6717; 10am-5pm.

♀ ☆ Santa Fe Cares/AIDS WALK Santa Fe, 1223 B St Francis Dr; 87505 505-986-3820; 505-989-9255; Fax 505-986-6120

Bars, Restaurants, Clubs, Discos

♀ • ♿ Edge, 135 W Palace, 3rd Floor; 87501 505-986-1700 (also Fax) *BRECW* Opens noon.

Bookstores: General

♂ • ♿ Galisteo News, 201 Galisteo St; 87501 505-984-1316

Broadcast Media

♂ ★ Out, Loud, & Proud Gay Talk Radio, c/o Pride Committee 369 Montezuma 399; 87501 505-989-6672 Fax 505-982-1341 aol.shepodd Sun 10-11am, KVSF-AM 1260.

Counseling/Therapy: Private

♂ • ♿ Bromberg, Paula N., Ph.D., South West Medical Life Center, 23 Frasco Rd; 87505-8842 505-466-1872; 508-487-4048 (Jul-Sept); "Sacred psychology & transformational therapy. Individuals, couples: relationships."

Dentists

♀ • Parker, Richard, DDS, 1210 Luisa St #7; 87505-4175 505-982-9222 Fax 505-982-7114 parkerdds@aol.com

Legal Services & Resources

♀ ○♿ Polich, Judith, J.D., PO Box 6019; 87502-6019 505-471-8059

Organizations/Resources: General, Multipurpose, Pride

♂ ★ Santa Fe Lesbian, Gay & Bi Pride Committee, 369 Montezuma 399; 87501 505-989-6672 Fax 505-982-1341 aol.shepodd

Organizations/Resources: Sport/Dance/Outdoor

♂ ○ Hawk, I'm Your Sister, PO Box 9109; 87504 505-984-2268 "Women's Wilderness Canoeing."

♂ ★♿ High Desert Stars, PO Box 707, Tesuque; 87574 505-989-8627 *d* "Square dance club."

Travel & Tourist Services (see also Accommodation)

♀ • Spirit Journeys, PO Box 5307; 87502-5307 505-351-4004 Fax 505-351-4999

Taos

Accommodation: Hotels, B&B, Resorts, Campgrounds

♀ • (?♿) The Ruby Slipper, PO Box 2069; 87571 / 416 La Lomita 505-758-0613 "Guest house."

♀ • Taos Stone House, PO Box DD, Valdez; 87580 505-776-2146; 800-771-2189

Bookstores: General

♀ • ♿ Taos Book Shop, 122D Kit Carson Rd; 87571 505-758-3733 9am-6pm.

Thoreau

Accommodation: Hotels, B&B, Resorts, Campgrounds

♀ ★♿ Zuni Mountain Lodge, HC-62, Box 5114; 87323-9515 505-862-7769 Bed & breakfast.
♦ *Zuni Mountain Lodge advertisement page 315*

Travel & Tourist Services (see also Accommodation)

♂ • ♿ Zuni Mountain Tours, HC-62, Box 5114; 87323-9408 505-862-7769 "Day & extended tour service; private small group escort (for tours)."

University Park

Organizations/Resources: Social, Recreational & Support Groups (see also Sport/Dance/Outdoor)

♂ Gay Men's Support Group, PO Box 4639; 88003

Vallecitos

Accommodation: Hotels, B&B, Resorts, Campgrounds

♀ ★♿ Vallecitos Retreat, PO Box 226; 87581 505-582-4226

NY: State/County Resources
Addictive Behavior

317

USA

Albany: NY
Accommodation

New York
State/County Resources

Addictive Behavior, Substance Abuse, Recovery

⚥ • (⚭) **Pride Institute, 800-54-PRIDE "The nation's only accredited chemical dependency treatment center exclusively for Gay, Lesbian & Bisexual People. Outpatient program in NYC."**

AIDS/HIV Support, Education, Advocacy, Publications

♀ ☆ ⚡ ADAP Plus, PO Box 2052 Empire Stn, Albany, NY 12220 800-542-2437 "Federally funded primary medical care program administered by the NYS Dept of Health. Very simple & confidential application process. Over 250 hospitals, clinics & physicians participating."

♀ ☆⚭⚭ AIDS Community Resources, 627 W Genessee St, Syracuse, NY 13204 315-475-2430; 800-343-AIDS; Pub *Newsletter.*

♀ ☆⚭⚭ AIDS Community Services of Western New York, 121 W Tupper St, Buffalo, NY 14201-2142 716-847-2441 9am-9pm. *The AIDS Newsletter.*

♀ ☆ ⚡ AIDS Drug Assistance Program (ADAP), PO Box 2052 Empire Stn, Albany, NY 12220 800-542-2437 "Federally funded drug assistance program administered by the NYS Dept of Health. Very simple & confidential application process. Now cover 180 medications to treat HIV illness."

♀ ★ ⚡ AIDS Treatment Data Network, 611 Broadway #613, New York, NY 10012 800-734-7104; 212-260-8868 Español; Fax 212-260-8869 aidstreatd@aol.com Pub *Experimental Treatment Guide.* "Treatment & experimental study information; counseling & professional training; library & directories."

♀ ☆ (?⚭) AIDS-Related Community Services (ARCS), 473 Broadway, Newburgh, NY 12550 914-562-5005 (office); 800-992-1442 AIDSLINE; "Serving Orange & Ulster Counties."

♀ ☆ (?⚭) AIDS-Related Community Services, c/o Public Health Nursing, Box 590 Infirmary Rd, Liberty, NY 12754 914-292-0100 x2713 (office); 800-992-1442 AIDSLINE; "Serving Sullivan County."

♀ ☆⚭⚭ AIDS-Related Community Services (ARCS), 89 Market St, Poughkeepsie, NY 12601 914-471-0707; 800-992-1442 AIDSLINE; "Serving Dutchess County."

♀ ☆⚭⚭ AIDS-Related Community Services (ARCS), c/o PCMH, 47 Brewster, Carmel, NY 10512 914-225-2700 x127; 800-992-1442 AIDSLINE; "Serving Putnam County."

♀ ☆ (⚭⚭) AIDS-Related Community Services (ARCS), 2269 Saw Mill River Rd, Bldg 1S, Elmsford, NY 10523-3814 914-345-8888; 800-992-1442; Fax 914-785-8227 Pub *ARCS News.*

♀ ☆ ⚡ AIDS-Related Community Services (ARCS), 228 North Main St, Spring Valley, NY 10977 914-356-0570; 800-992-1442 AIDSLINE; "Serving Rockland County."

♀ ☆ ⚡ HIV Home Care Uninsured Fund, PO Box 2052 Empire Stn, Albany, NY 12220 800-542-2437 "Federally funded HIV home care program administered by the NYS Dept of Health. Very simple & confidential application process. Over 400 home care agencies participating."

♀ ○ (⚭) Northern Lights Alternatives-NY, 601 W 50th St #5FL, New York, NY 10019-7003 212-765-3202 *The Northern Light.* "AIDS Mastery Workshop; Children's Care Program; AIDS Training Program."

♀ ☆⚭⚭ Southern Tier AIDS Program, Inc, 122 Baldwin St, Johnson City, NY 13790-2148 607-798-1706; 800-333-0892

Organizations/Resources: Business & Professional

⚥ ☆ Gay & Lesbian Issues Committee, NYS Chapter, National Association of Social Workers, 225 Lark St, Albany, NY 12210 518-463-4741 Pub *Resource Directory.*

Organizations/Resources: General, Multipurpose, Pride

⚥ ★ Governor's Office of Lesbian & Gay Concerns, Executive Chamber, State Capitol, Albany, NY 12224 518-870-8604

Organizations/Resources: Political/Legislative

⚥ ★ ⚡ Empire State Pride Agenda, 611 Broadway #907A, New York, NY 10012-2608 212-673-5417 Fax 212-673-6128 & 79 Central Ave, Albany, NY 12204 (518) 433-0134 'New York State's Gay & Lesbian lobby & political action committee.'

⚥ ★⚭⚭ Governor's Office of Lesbian & Gay Concerns, Executive Chamber, State Capitol, Albany, NY 12224 518-486-3168

Organizations/Resources: Social, Recreational & Support Groups (see also Sport/Dance/Outdoor)

⚥ ★ Poconos Action Lambda Society, mail to PALS, Box 1375, Milford, PA 18337 PA

♂ ★ ⚡ Prime Timers, Box 291 Midtown Stn, New York, NY 10018-0291 212-787-0329

Publications

♀ ○ *Common Ground*, PO Box 287, Buffalo, NY 14224-0287 716-675-1433 "Western New York Women's Newsjournal."

⚥ • **In The LIFE, PO Box 921, Wappingers Falls, NY 12590-0921 914-227-7456 "Mid-Hudson Valley's Lesbian & Gay newspaper."**
✦ *In The LIFE advertisement page 352*
→ *Network Magazine: for the 10% Plus:* p.305
✦ *Network Magazine: for the 10% Plus advertisement page 304*

⚥ • *On The Wilde Side*, 106 Cain Dr, Brentwood, NY 11717 516-435-0005 Fax 516-435-0808 "Resource guide NY, NJ, CT."

♀ • **Sappho's Isle, 960 Willis Ave, Albertson, NY 11507 516-747-5417 "Solely Lesbian publication, featuring current events & entertainment."**
✦ *Sappho's Isle advertisement page 344*

Real Estate

⚥ • **Community Real Estate Referrals, 800-346-5592 "Free referral to gay/gay-supportive realtor in any USA city/state (including Virgin Is. & Puerto Rico). Sorry, no rentals!"**
✦ *Community Real Estate Referrals advertisement back cover*

Religious Organizations & Publications

⚥ ★ Dignity: Region Two, 6 Campo Ave, Selden, NY 11784-1704 516-781-5942 "Gay & Lesbian Catholics & their friends."

⚥ ★ United Church of Christ Coalition for Lesbian/Gay Concerns, 333 Argonne Dr, Buffalo, NY 14217-2417 716-877-0459

Travel & Tourist Services (see also Accommodation)

⚥ • American Outdoor Adventures, PO Box 299, Laurens, NY 13796 607-431-9509 "Mountain & Road bike: singles, couples, tours. Rental equipment available. Ask for Nick."

Albany & Capital Area
Accommodation: Hotels, B&B, Resorts, Campgrounds

Albany

♀ • Yellow House Inn, PO Box 6477; 12206 518-434-8581

Bolton Landing

♀ • Scenic View Campgrounds, Route 9N, Bolton Landing; 12814 800-734-0161

Addictive Behavior, Substance Abuse, Recovery

♂ ○ && Al-Care, 445 New Karner Rd; 12205 518-456-8043

♂ ★ Gay Alcoholics Anonymous, PO Box 131; 12201 518-462-6138 7-11pm. Meets Sun 7.30pm at Gay Community Center, 332 Hudson Ave; Men's open discussion Mon 7.30pm.

AIDS/HIV Support, Education, Advocacy, Publications

♂ ☆ && AIDS Council of Northeastern NY, 88 4th Ave; 12202-1422 518-434-4686; 800-660-6886

♂ ○ Child's HomeHealth AIDS Home Care Program, 25 Hackett Blvd; 12208-3499 518-487-7342

♂ ★ Our Brothers Keepers Foundation, PO Box 1872; 12201-1872 "Monthly socials, brunches, or events to raise money for direct patient services to persons with HIV/AIDS."

Automobile Services

♀ ○ (&) **Albany Fleet Service, 120 Catherine St; 12202 518-426-0952**

Bars, Restaurants, Clubs, Discos

Albany

♀ Club Oz, 326 Central Ave 518-434-4288 *D*

♀ ● Donnie's Cafe 75, 75 Central Ave; 12206 518-436-0378 7am-3pm; Sat & Sun 3am-3pm.

♀ ○ ♂ El Loco Mexican Cafe, 465 Madison Ave; 12210 518-436-1855

♀ Longhorns, 90 Central Ave; 12206 518-462-4862 *LCW*

♀ ● Oh Bar, 304 Lark St; 12210 518-463-9004

♀ Power Company, 238 Washington Ave; 12210 518-465-2556 *D*

♀ ● Water Works Pub, 76 Central Ave; 12206 518-465-9079 *BD* 4pm-4am; Fri-Sun 3pm-4am.

Schenectady

♀ Blythewood, 50 N Jay St, Schenectady; 12305 518-382-9755 *BR*

♀ ○ ♂ Clinton Street Pub, 159 Clinton St, Schenectady; 12305 518-382-9173 *BWd*

Business, Financial & Secretarial

♀ ● (?&) Gordon, Anthony M., CPA, 2 Oakwood Place, Delmar; 12054 518-439-0994

Community Centers (see also Women's Centers)

♀ ★ Capital District Lesbian & Gay Community Center, PO Box 131; 12201-0131 / 332 Hudson Ave 518-462-6138 Mon-Thu 7-10pm; Fri & Sat to 11pm; Sun 2-10pm. Pub *Community Newsletter*.

Counseling/Therapy: Private

♀ ○ Capital District Center for Dissociative Disorders, PO Box 9136; 12209 518-462-0213

♀ ● && Choices Counseling Associates, 266 Delaware Ave, Delmar; 12054 (near Albany) 518-439-9270 Transgender welcome.

♀ ● Crouch, Katherine Eustis, CSW, 127 N Allen St; 12203 518-456-5845

♀ ○ Crowe, John F., CRC, CAC, 305 Hamilton St; 12210 518-436-1578

♀ ● && Journeys, 321 Washington Ave; 12206 518-446-1127

♀ ○ O'Brien, Maureen, CSW, ACSW, PO Box 9136; 12209 518-462-0213; 518-447-5715

♀ ○ (?&) Shapiro, Jonathan, PsyD, 305 Hamilton St; 12210 518-462-6139

Erotica (Printed, Visual, Equipment)

♀ ○ (&) Adult Education Books, 1115 State St, Schenectady; 12308

♀ ○ (&) Another World, 145 Erie Boulevard, Schenectady; 12308

♀ ○ Continental Books, 1455 State St, Schenectady; 12308

♀ ○ && King Video, 14 King St; Troy; 12180 518-272-4714 24 hrs.

♀ ● Savage Gifts & Leather, 88 Central Ave; 12208 518-434-2324

♀ ○ Troy Video Expo, 516 River St, Troy; 12180 518-272-7577

Gifts, Cards, Pride & Novelty Items

♀ ● Romeo's Gifts, 299 Lark St; 12210 518-434-4014 11am-9pm; Sun noon-5pm.

Grooming Services

♀ ○ **Hair Replacement Systems, 1710 Central Ave; 12205-4701 518-371-4957; 800-872-0790**

Legal Services & Resources

♀ ○ Coughtry, Jo Ann E., 1221 Central Ave; 12205 518-482-4740 Fax 518-355-6268

♀ ● (?&) Kelly, Eileen M., 98 South Pine Ave; 12208-2215 518-438-5237

♀ ● && Latimer, Suzanne L., Esq, 31 Henkes Lane, Latham; 12110 518-785-8150 Fax 518-475-0766

Organizations/Resources: Sexual Focus (Leather, S/M, etc) & Safe Sex Promotion

♀ ★ Stars M.C., PO Box 2484; 12220 518-436-4917 *L*

Organizations/Resources: Social, Recreational & Support Groups (see also Sport/Dance/Outdoor)

♀ ★ (?&) Alternate Universe Gaylaxians, PO Box 66054; 12206-0607 518-272-3748 *The Alternate Universe.* "Gay & Lesbian Science Fiction & Fantasy fandom."

Organizations/Resources: Sport/Dance/Outdoor

♀ ★ Two Rivers Outdoor Club, Inc, PO Box 6217; 12206 518-449-0758

Organizations/Resources: Student, Academic, Alumni/ae

♀ ★ (?&) Lesbian/Gay/Bisexual Caucus, SASU, 300 Lark St; 12210 518-465-2406

♀ ★ && Lesbian/Gay/Bisexual Alliance SUNY Albany (LGBA), CC116 1400 SUNY Albany; 12222 518-442-5672 Meeting Tue 8.30pm on CC375.

♀ ★ && Rensselaer Gay, Lesbian & Bisexual Alliance, PO Box 146, Troy; 12181-0146 518-271-2655 Fax 518-276-6920 Radio show 'Sounds Gay' on WRPI 91.5 FM.

Organizations/Resources: Transgender & Transgender Publications

T ☆ Transgenderists Independence (TGIC), PO Box 13604; 12212-3604 518-436-4513

Organizations/Resources: Youth (see also Family)

♀ ★ Lesbian & Gay Youth Group, PO Box 131; 12201 518-462-6138

Printing & Promotional Items (see also Art; Graphics/Typesetting)

♀ ● ♂ Communication Services, 8 Thurlow Terrace; 12203 518-463-3522 Fax 518-426-3961 comservlp@aol.com Mon-Fri 9am-6pm. "Direct Mail Fundraising services."

NY: Albany & Capital Area
Real Estate

319

Buffalo : NY
Bars, Clubs, Restaurants

USA

Real Estate

♀ • Zimmerman, Kate, PO Box 8645; 12208 518-459-6401

Religious Organizations & Publications

♂ ☆&& Congregation Berith Sholom, 167 3rd St, Troy; 12180 518-272-8872

♂ ★ (&) Dignity/Capital District, PO Box 11204, Loudonville; 12211-0204 518-436-8546 "Gay & Lesbian Catholics & their friends."

♂ ★ Integrity/Albany, 518-446-1548 "Lesbian & Gay Episcopalians & their friends."

♂ ★ (?&) Lighthouse Apostolic Church, PO Box 1391, Schenectady; 12301-1391 518-372-6001

♂ & Metropolitan Community Church of the Hudson Valley, 40 Duncan Dr, Latham; 12110 518-785-7941

Travel & Tourist Services (see also Accommodation)

♂ • && Atlas Travel Center, Inc., 1545 Central Ave; 12205 518-464-0271

♂ • & Capital Travel, Inc., 271 Lark St; 12210 518-434-9900; 800-800-9009

♀ • (&&) The Travel Company, 41 State St #110; 12207 518-433-9000 Fax 518-433-9038

Video Sales, Rentals, Services (see also Erotica)

♂ • & Video Central, 37 Central Ave; 12210 518-463-4153 10am-10pm; Thu-Sun to 11pm. "Also Gay & Lesbian magazines & guides."

Women's Centers

♀ ☆&& The Women's Building, 79 Central Ave; 12206 518-465-1597 Mon-Fri 10am-5pm; some eves & wkends. Pub *Women's Building News.*

Amherst: see Buffalo

Angelica

Accommodation: Hotels, B&B, Resorts, Campgrounds

♂• • Jones Pond Campground, RD #1 Box 214 / 9835 Old State Rd; 14709-9729 716-567-8100 *LWd*

Annandale on Hudson

Organizations/Resources: Student, Academic, Alumni/ae

♀ ★ Bard Bisexual, Lesbian & Gay Alliance, Bard College; 12504 518-758-6822

Ballston Spa: see Saratoga/Lake George Area

Bellmore: see New York City Area

Binghamton

Accommodation: Hotels, B&B, Resorts, Campgrounds

♂ • Flamingo Arms, 201 State St; 13901 607-723-1507 "Guest house."

♂ • (?&) Hillside Campgrounds, PO Box 726; 13902 717-756-2007 *DP* "Located between Binghamton & Scranton, PA."

Bars, Restaurants, Clubs, Discos

♂ • Risky Business Video Bar, 203 State St; 13901 607-723-1507 *BDE* 5pm-1am.

♀ Squiggy's, 34 Chenango St; 13901 (back of Weeks & Dickinson) 607-722-2299

Counseling/Therapy: Private

♀ ○ Cohen, Lillian, CSW, 265 Main St; 13905-3930 607-729-5616

Erotica (Printed, Visual, Equipment)

♀ ○ & Allies Blvd Bookstore East, 483 Court St; 13904 607-724-9749

♀ ○ Allies Blvd Bookstore Downtown, PO Box 452; 13902 / 140 Washington St 607-724-8659

♂ ○ North Street Bookshop, 17 Washington Ave, Endicott; 13760 607-785-9606

Gifts, Cards, Pride & Novelty Items

♀ ○ & E&R Gifts & Graphics, PO Box 541; 13902 / 215 Main St; 13905 607-729-5305 "Gifts, cards, New Age, Occult."

Organizations/Resources: Social, Recreational & Support Groups (see also Sport/Dance/Outdoor)

♂ ★ Gay & Lesbian Support Group, PO Box 597; 13905 607-723-6680

♂ ★ SYOL (Save Your Own Lives), PO Box 728 Westview Stn; 13905 607-729-1921 Pub *Amethyst.*

Organizations/Resources: Student, Academic, Alumni/ae

♂ ★&& Lesbian/Gay/Bisexual Union (LGBU) SUNY-Binghamton, c/o SA Box 2000; 13901 607-777-2202 Pub *LGBU Newsletter.*

Women's Centers

♀ ☆&& Women's Center, PO Box 354; 13902 607-724-3462 Women's Eventline

Brockport

Organizations/Resources: Student, Academic, Alumni/ae

♂ && Alternative Lifestyles, SUC Brockport, c/o Student Government; 14420 716-395-5546

Bronx: see New York City Area

Brooklyn: see New York City Area

Buffalo

Addictive Behavior, Substance Abuse, Recovery

♂ ★ Open Mind Group (AA), PO Box 395 Ellicott Stn; 14205 Meets Wed 8.30pm at Ascension Church, 16 Linwood Ave.

AIDS/HIV Support, Education, Advocacy, Publications

♀ ☆&& AIDS Alliance of Western New York, 777 Main St; 14203 716-852-6778

→ AIDS Community Services of Western New York: p.317

Astrology/Numerology/Tarot/Psychic Readings

♀ ○ Rich, Lynne, PFMA, 1155 Orchard Park Rd, West Seneca; 14224 Pub *Constant Change.* "Write for details & complimentary copy of newsletter."

Bars, Restaurants, Clubs, Discos

♂ • && Buddies, 31 Johnson Park; 14201 716-855-1313 *BDE* 1pm-4am.

♂ ○ && Cathode Ray, 26 Allen St; 14202 716-884-3615 1pm-4am. "Video bar."

♂ • (&&) Club Heat, 153 Delaware Ave; 14202 716-842-6825 *BDE* Wed-Sun 10pm-4am.

♂ Compton's After Dark, 1239 Niagara St; 14213 716-885-DARK

♀ Lavender Door, 32 Tonawanda St; 14213 716-874-1220

♂• • Stage Door, 20 Allen St; 14202 716-886-9323 *BEd* Open 5pm.

♀ ○ (&) Zippers/Back Pocket, 884 Main St; 14202 716-886-8135 *BR* Women first floor, men 2nd floor. 'Volleyball court; patio.'

Bookstores: General

♀ ○ (ᕉ) Talking Leaves, 3158 Main St; 14214 716-837-8554 Mon-Sat 10am-6pm.

♀ ○ (ᕉᕉ) Village Green Bookstore, 765A Elmwood Ave; 14222-1600 716-884-1200 Fax 716-884-3007

♀ ○ Village Green Bookstore, 3670 McKinley Parkway, Blasdell; 14219-2658 716-827-5895

Counseling/Therapy: Private

♀ • Dincher, Kevin P., MA, MFCC, 56 York St; 14213-2537 716-881-2278

Erotica (Printed, Visual, Equipment)

♀ ○ Video Variety, 83 W Chippewa; 14202 716-856-8936

♀ ○ ᕉ Village Book & News, 3102 Delaware Ave, Kenmore; 14217 716-887-5027

Gifts, Cards, Pride & Novelty Items

♀ • ᕉ Apparel Plus, Ltd., 483 Elmwood Ave; 14222 716-883-0498

♂ • Ditson's Pink Triangle News, PO Box 722 Ellicott Stn; 14205-0722 716-845-6971 Call for details.

Health Clubs, Gyms, Saunas

♂ • New Morgan Sauna, Inc, 655 Main St; 14203 716-852-2153

Organizations/Resources: Ethnic, Multicultural

♂ ★ Shades, PO Box 1591; 14205 716-896-1770

Organizations/Resources: Family

♀ ☆ (ᕉ) P-FLAG/Western New York, PO Box 861; 14225 716-883-0384 "Parents, Families & Friends of Lesbians & Gays."

Organizations/Resources: General, Multipurpose, Pride

♂ ★ Buffalo Gay & Lesbian Community Network, 2316 Delaware #267; 14216 716-883-4750 Pub Network News.

♂ ★ Gay Positive Men's Group of Buffalo, 2316 Delaware Ave #267; 14216 716-884-8670

♂ ★ Pride/Western New York, PO Box 621; 14207 716-883-4750

Organizations/Resources: Student, Academic, Alumni/ae

♂ ★ ᕉᕉ Graduate Gay & Lesbian Alliance, 362 Student Union, SUNY Buffalo, Amherst; 14260 716-645-3063

♂ ★ Lesbian Gay Bisexual Alliance Buffalo State College, 1300 Elmwood Ave, Cassety 204; 14222-1095

♂ ★ ᕉᕉ Lesbian, Gay, Bisexual Alliance, 362 Student Union, SUNY-Buffalo, Amherst; 14260 716-645-2950 Fax 716-645-2112 "Coming out support group; coffee house; peer support."

Organizations/Resources: Youth (see also Family)

♂ ★ ᕉᕉ Gay & Lesbian Youth Services of Western New York, 190 Franklin St; 14202 716-855-0221 Hotline 24 hrs. Mon, Wed, Fri 6-9pm; Sat 1-5pm.

Publications

♂ QWER Quarterly, PO Box 664; 14226-0664

♂ • Volumé, PO Box 106 West Side Stn; 14213-0106 716-885-4580

Religious Organizations & Publications

♂ ★ Dignity/Buffalo, Inc, PO Box 75 Ellicott Stn; 14205 716-833-8995 "Gay & Lesbian Catholics & their friends."

♂ ★ Integrity/Western New York, c/o Church of the Ascension, 16 Linwood Ave; 14209 716-884-6362 "Lesbian & Gay Episcopalians & their friends."

♂ ★ (?ᕉ) Pink Triangle Christian Fellowship, PO Box 722 Ellicott Stn; 14205-0722 716-845-6971 Wed 7.30pm & Wed 7-9pm. Pub Spiritworks. "An informal Christian fellowship with SPIRIT!"

Transportation: Limousine, Taxi, Etc.

♂ • Absolute Elegance Limo, 24 Allen St; 14202 716-883-5303

Travel & Tourist Services (see also Accommodation)

♂ • ᕉᕉ Destinations Unlimited, 130 Theater Place; 14202 716-855-1955; 800-528-8877; Fax 716-855-0016

♂ ○ ᕉ Earth Travelers, Inc, 683 Dick Road, Cheektowaga; 14225 716-685-2900; 800-321-2901

♂ • Heidie's Travel & Tour, 2308 Seneca st; 14210 716-821-1991 Fax 716-826-5658

Cairo

AIDS/HIV Support, Education, Advocacy, Publications

♂ ☆ ᕉᕉ AIDS Task Force Greene County, PO Box 505; 12413 518-622-2964

Carmel

Legal Services & Resources

♂ • Schoenfeld, Laura G., 914-225-0985

Catskill Mountains Area

Accommodation: Hotels, B&B, Resorts, Campgrounds

Palenville

♂ • Palenville House Bed & Breakfast, PO Box 465, Palenville; 12463-0465 / Jct Rts 23A & 32A 518-678-5649

Rock Hill

♂ • **Stonewall Acres, Box 556, Rock Hill; 12775-0556 914-791-9474; 800-336-4208 (Metro NYC area); "Guest house in the Catskills, 90 minutes from NYC; on 13 acres, with pool & cottages. Hot tub. Comfortable rooms for couples/singles or full house rental for small groups & families."**

White Lake

♂ • (?ᕉ) Bradstan Country Hotel, PO Box 312, White Lake; 12786 914-583-4114 BE

Chatham

Legal Services & Resources

♂ • (ᕉ) Katz, Pamela S., RD1, Box 11B, White Mills Rd; 12037 518-392-9497

Cherry Grove: see New York City Area

Clinton: see Utica

Cooperstown

Accommodation: Hotels, B&B, Resorts, Campgrounds

♂ • Country Memories, Rte 80 Lake Road, Box 430, Springfield Center; 13468 315-858-2691

♂ • (?ᕉ) The Owls' Nest Inn Bed & Breakfast, Box 185, Edmeston; 13335 / 4 West St. 607-965-8720

♂ • Toad Hall Bed & Breakfast, RD 1 Box 120, Fly Creek; 13337 607-547-5774

Art Galleries/Archives/Restoration, Supplies, Framing

♂ • Toad Hall Shop & Gallery, 63 Pioneer St; 13326 607-547-4044

NY: Cortland
Bookstores: General

321

USA

Ithaca : NY
Organizations: Ethnic, Multicultural

Cortland

Bookstores: General

♀ ○ Basil's Bookstore, 12 1/2 Main St; 13045 607-756-9409

Cuba

Accommodation: Hotels, B&B, Resorts, Campgrounds

♀ • Rocking Duck Inn, 28 Genesee Parkway; 14727 716-968-3335

Bars, Restaurants, Clubs, Discos

♀ • ♿ Valley Point Restaurant, 46 Genesee St; 14727 716-968-3911

Delmar: see Albany

East Hampton: see New York City Area

East Windham

Accommodation: Hotels, B&B, Resorts, Campgrounds

♀ ○ ♿ Point Lookout Mountain Inn, Rt 23 Box 33; 12439 518-734-3381 Fax 518-734-6526 *R* Restaurant open to public 11am-10pm.

East Worcester

Bars, Restaurants, Clubs, Discos

⚥ ○ (♿) Boots Place, 60 Main St; 12064-0773 607-397-8326 Fax 607-397-8331 *BC* (Sat from 10pm only; call for details).

Elmira

Accommodation: Hotels, B&B, Resorts, Campgrounds

♀ • Rufus Tanner House, 60 Sagetown Road, Pine City, NY 14871-9137 607-732-0213

Bars, Restaurants, Clubs, Discos

⚥ • The David, 511 Railroad Ave; 14901 607-733-2592 *BD* Noon-1am. "Mostly gay men; all welcome."

Erotica (Printed, Visual, Equipment)

♀ ○ Deluxe Book Bargains, 123 Lake St; 14901 607-734-9656

Endicott: see Binghamton

Fairport

Bookstores: General

♀ ○ Village Green Bookstore, 587 Moseley Rd; 14450-3347 716-425-7950 Fax 716-425-4968

Fayetteville

Counseling/Therapy: Private

.T ○ ♿ Deming, Alison, 208 Redfield Ave; 13066 315-637-8990 "Relationship therapy; gender, orientation & lifestyles."

Fire Island Pines: see New York City Area

Fleischmanns

Accommodation: Hotels, B&B, Resorts, Campgrounds

♀ • (♿) River Run Bed & Breakfast Inn, Main St; 12430 914-254-4884 "50 percent gay-owned & 100 percent friendly!"

Fly Creek: see Cooperstown

Fredonia

Organizations/Resources: Student, Academic, Alumni/ae

⚥ ★ B-GLAD (Bisexual, Gay, Lesbian Alliance for Diversity), SUC Fredonia, Campus Center; 14063 Non-gay participants welcome.

⚥ ★ Purdue Lesbian, Bi & Gay Alumni Group, PO Box 254; 14063-0254 716-881-1878

Switchboards, Helplines, Phone Information

⚥ ★ Chautauqua Gay Lesbian & Bi Infoline, Box 254; 14063 716-679-3560

Geneva

Organizations/Resources: Social, Recreational & Support Groups (see also Sport/Dance/Outdoor)

⚥ ★ ♿ The Finger Lakes Social Group, Box 941; 14456 315-536-7753

Religious Organizations & Publications

♀ ★ (♿) PLCG/Geneva, PO Box 278, Dresden; 14441-0278 315-536-7753 "Presbyterians for Lesbian/Gay Concerns."

Glen Wild: see Catskill Mountains Area

Glens Falls: see Saratoga/Lake George Area

Greenwood Lake

Bars, Restaurants, Clubs, Discos

⚥ • The Livingroom of Greenwood Lake, PO Box 1806; 10925 / Jersey Ave, half mile south light in village 914-477-8184

Hempstead: see New York City Area

Herkimer

Clothes

♀ ○ Atomic Boutique, 105 S Main St; 13350

Highland: see Poughkeepsie/Kingston Area

Hudson Falls: see Saratoga/Lake George Area

Ithaca

Accommodation: Hotels, B&B, Resorts, Campgrounds

♀ • Pleasant Grove Bed & Breakfast, 1779 Trumansburg Rd, Jacksonville; 14854 607-387-5420; 800-398-3963
♦ *Pleasant Grove Bed & Breakfast advertisement page 322*

Bars, Restaurants, Clubs, Discos

♀ ○ (♿) Apple Blossom Cafe, 308 Stewart Ave; 14850 607-277-4770 *R*

⚥ • ♿ Common Ground, 1230 Danby Rd, Rt 96B; 14850 607-273-1505 *BDR*

Bookstores: General

♀ ○ (♿) The Bookery, Dewitt Bldg, 215 N Cayunga St; 14850 607-273-5055 "Travel books downstairs; used & rare upstairs."

♀ • ♿ Borealis Bookstore, 113 N Aurora St; 14850-4301 607-272-7752

Erotica (Printed, Visual, Equipment)

♀ ○ Book Sale Gallery, 103 W State St; 14850 607-272-9882

Organizations/Resources: Ethnic, Multicultural

⚥ Gay, Bisexual, Lesbians of Color, Cornell University, 535 Willard Straight Hall; 14853

Ithaca & the Finger Lakes Wine Country

PLEASANT GROVE
BED & BREAKFAST
800-398-3963
Jacksonville, NY 14854-0009

Organizations/Resources: General, Multipurpose, Pride

♀ ★ ♿ Ithaca Lesbian, Gay & Bisexual Task Force, PO Box 283; 14851-0283 607-277-4614 Pub *Outlines*.

Organizations/Resources: Social, Recreational & Support Groups (see also Sport/Dance/Outdoor)

♀ Ithaca Gay Lesbian Activities Board (IGLAB), PO Box 6634; 14850-6634

Organizations/Resources: Student, Academic, Alumni/ae

♀ ★ Cornell Lesbian, Gay & Bisexual Alliance, Box 45, 207 Willard Straight Hall; 14853 607-255-6482

Women's Centers

♀ ☆ (?♿) Cornell Women's Center, PO Box 71, Willard Straight Hall; 14853 607-255-9611

♀ Women's Community Center, 100 W Seneca St; 14850 607-272-1247

Jamestown

Bars, Restaurants, Clubs, Discos

♀ Nite Spot, 201 Windsor St; 14701

♀ • ♿♿ Sneakers, 100 Harrison St; 14701 716-484-8816 *BD* 3.30pm-2am.

Organizations/Resources: Social, Recreational & Support Groups (see also Sport/Dance/Outdoor)

♀ ★ ♿ 10% Network, 716-484-7285 (John)

Kenmore: see Buffalo

Kingston: see Poughkeepsie/Kingston Area

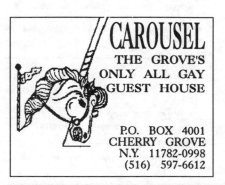

CAROUSEL
THE GROVE'S ONLY ALL GAY GUEST HOUSE
P.O. BOX 4001
CHERRY GROVE
N.Y. 11782-0998
(516) 597-6612

Lake George: see Saratoga/Lake George Area

Naples

Accommodation: Hotels, B&B, Resorts, Campgrounds

♀ • ♿♿ Landmark Retreat Bed & Breakfast, 6004 Route 21; 14512 716-396-2383 "We welcome groups for workshops. Our view offers serenity & healing."

New Paltz

Accommodation: Hotels, B&B, Resorts, Campgrounds

♀ ○ Churchill Farm, 39 Canaan Road; 12561 914-255-7291

Bookstores: General

♀ ○ ♿ Ariel Booksellers, 3 Plattekill Ave; 12561 914-255-8041 9am-6pm; Sun noon-5pm.

♀ • ♿ The Painted Word, 36 Main St; 12561 914-256-0825 11am-8pm; Sun noon-8pm. "Books, T-shirts, cards, magazines, gifts."

Organizations/Resources: Student, Academic, Alumni/ae

♀ ★ ♿♿ BiGAYLA (Bisexual, Gay, & Lesbian Alliance) at New Paltz, Student Union Bldg room 332; 12561 914-257-3097; 914-257-5081

Women's Centers

♀ Sojourner's Wimmins Gathering Place, PO Box 398; 12561

New York City Area

☎ Gay & Lesbian Help-Line 914-948-4922

☎ Gay & Lesbian Switchboard 212-777-1800

☎ Gay & Lesbian Switchboard of Long Island (GLSB of LI) 516-737-1615

☎ Lesbian Switchboard 212-741-2610

☎ Middle Earth Crisis Center 516-679-9000

☎ New York City Gay & Lesbian Anti-Violence Project 212-807-0197

☎ Response of Suffolk County 516-751-7500

☎ Youth Environmental Services 516-799-3203

Accommodation: Hotels, B&B, Resorts, Campgrounds

Fire Island

♂ • Belvedere Guest House, Box 26, Cherry Grove, Fire Island; 11782 / Bay View Walk 516-597-6448 Gay men only.
✦ *Belvedere Guest House advertisement page 323*

♂ • Botel, Fire Island Pines, Fire Island; 11782 516-597-6500

♂ • Carousel Guest House, PO Box 4001, Cherry Grove; 11782-0998 / 185 Holly Walk 516-597-6612
✦ *Carousel Guest House advertisement page 322*

♀ ○ ♿♿ Cherry Grove Beach Hotel, PO Box 537, Sayville; 11782-0537 516-597-6600 *BDE* Handicap rooms available.

♀ • ♿♿ Dune Point, Box 78, Cherry Grove, Fire Island; 11782 516-597-6261 "Deluxe apartments, rooms, studio rentals."

♀ Fire Island Pines, 9B Ocean Walk, Fire Island; 11782 516-597-6767

♂ ○ Holly House, Box 96, Cherry Grove, Fire Island; 11782 516-597-6911

♀ ○ Seacrest, Box 53, Cherry Grove, Fire Island; 11782 516-597-6849

NY: New York City Area
Accommodation

323
USA

New York City Area : NY
Accommodation

Long Island

♂ • **Cozy Cabins Motel, PO Box 848, Wainscott; 11975 / East Hampton 516-537-1160**

⚢ • && **One-Three-Two North Main, 132 North Main St, East Hampton; 11937 516-324-2246**

⚢ • && Sag Harbor Bed & Breakfast, 516-725-5945; 212-505-7869; Labor Day to Memorial Day; shares Memorial Day to Labor Day.

Manhattan

♂ • **333 W. 88th Associates, 333 W 88th St; 10024 212-724-9818** "Bed & breakfast apartments."

♂ • **Abingdon B&B, 13 8th Ave; 10014 212-243-5384 Fax 212-807-7473** "Non-smoking rooms; no pets."
✦ *Abingdon B&B advertisement page 324*

NY: New York City Area
Accommodation

324
USA

New York City Area: NY
Addictive Behavior

♀ • Bed & Breakfast—Manhattan, 212-866-6422 (call before 9pm) "Exclusively for women."

♂ • The Blue Rabbit, 730 St Nicholas Ave; 10031 212-491-3892 "International travelers'hostel in Harlem's Sugar Hill section. Communal. Lesbian/Gay travelers welcome!"

♂ • Chelsea Mews Guest House, 344 W 15th St; 10011 212-255-9174
♦ *Chelsea Mews Guest House advertisement page 323*

♂ • Chelsea Pines Inn, 317 W 14th St; 10014 212-929-1023 Fax 212-645-9497 "Charming bed & breakfast inn, Greenwich Village/Chelsea area. Advance reservation advised. All major credit cards."
♦ *Chelsea Pines Inn advertisement page 324*

♀ • Colonial House Inn, 318 W 22nd St; 10011 212-243-9669; 800-689-3779; Fax 212-633-1612 ckuest house. Rates include continental breakfast. All rooms with color TV, phones, A/C; some with fireplaces & refrigerators. Roof sundeh. 24-hr concierge."
♦ *Colonial House Inn advertisement page 323*

♀ ○ Holiday Inn Downtown-Soho, 138 Lafayette St; 10013 (Corner of Howard St) 212-966-8898 Fax 212-966-3933
♦ *Holiday Inn Downtown-Soho advertisement page 323*

♂ • Incentra Village House, 32 8th Ave; 10014 (Abingdon Sq) 212-206-0007 "Landmark house in heart of Village. All rooms private baths & kitchenette. Mainly gay men but others welcome."

♀ ○ Riverside Tower Hotel, 80 Riverside Drive; 10024 (80th St) 800-724-3136

♀ • Sugar Hill International House, 722 St Nicholas Ave; 10031 212-926-7030 infohostel@aol.com "Youth hostel for international travelers located in a brownstone in Harlem's Sugar Hill section. Gay/Lesbian travelers welcome."

♀ • A Village Bed & Breakfast, 131 E 15th St #2N; 10003 212-387-9117 "Various bed & breakfast apts in the Village."

Staten Island

♀ • White Pickets, PO Box 161, Staten Island; 10304 718-727-9398 "Bed & breakfast. All welcome, especially naturists/nudists."

Rockland, Westchester, Dutchess, Orange Counties

♀ ○ The Villa Bed & Breakfast, 90 Rockledge Rd, Bronxville; 10708 914-337-7050; 800-457-5595; Fax 914-337-5661

Accommodation: Reservations & Exchanges (see also Travel)

Manhattan

♀ • Home Suite Hom, PO Box 762 Succ. C, Montréal, QC H2L 4L6 212-995-3138; 800-429-4983 US & Canada; "Travel & accommodation network for those offering or seeking hospitality & lodging exchange, private B&B, & low cost rentals."
♦ *Home Suite Hom advertisement page 122*

♀ • ♂ (?♂) The Manhattan Bed & Breakfast Reservation Center, PO Box 2646, Southampton; 11969-2646 212-977-3512
♦ *Manhattan Bed & Breakfast Reservation Center advertisement page 324*

Accommodation Sharing/Roommates

♀ • ♿ Gay Roommate Service, 133 W 72nd St #504; 10023 212-580-7696 Mon-Fri noon-7.30pm (call for appointment). "Serving the gay & lesbian community since 1976. Many shares always available. Fee $100; no fee if you have apartment & need roommate."

Addictive Behavior, Substance Abuse, Recovery

Long Island

♀ • Moskowitz, Eileen, CAC, NCAC II, 516-496-0802

♀ ☆ & SNG Counseling Center, 3375 Park Ave #2005, Wantagh; 11793 516-781-1911 "Outpatient drug abuse center. Professional mental health staff. Sliding fee scale. Individual, group, couple, family counseling; intensive dat treatment."

Manhattan

● ★ Al-Anon, Lesbian/Gay Community Center, 208 W 13th St; 10011 212-620-7310

♂ ★ (?&) Alcoholics Anonymous, Lesbian/Gay Community Center, 208 W 13th St; 10011 212-620-7310 "Many meetings each week; consult bulletin board or call for details."

♂ ★ Alcoholics Anonymous New Group, 657 Washington St; 10014 212-924-5628 Fri 7pm beginners, 8.30pm closed; Sun 3pm & 6pm closed, beginners 5pm.

♂ ★ Lambda West AA Group, Rutgers Presbyterian Presbyterian Church, 236 W 73rd St; 10023 212-877-8190

♀ ○ Marschall, Rick, CSW, CAC, 161 W 16th St; 10011 212-620-7155

♀ ○ **Mediplex Holliswood Hospital, 8737 Palermo St, Jamaica; 11423 718-776-3005; 800-486-3005**

♂ ★ Nar-Anon, Lesbian/Gay Community Center, 208 W 13th St; 10011 212-620-7310 Mon 8pm.

♂ ★ Narcotics Anonymous, Lesbian/Gay Community Center, 208 W 13th St; 10011 212-620-7310 Tue 7.30pm, Thu 5.45pm, Fri 6pm, Sun 2.15pm.

♂ ★ Overeaters Anonymous, Lesbian/Gay Community Center, 208 W 13th St; 10011 212-620-7310 Wed 6.15pm, Fri 8pm, Sat 5pm; gay men Thu 8pm & Sun 7pm; lesbians Sun 12.30pm.

♂ ★ Overeaters Anonymous: East Side Gay Group, Gracie Square Hospital, 420 E 76th St; 10021 Mon: Beginners 7pm, Discussion 7.30pm.

♂ ★ (&) Project Connect, c/o The Center, 208 W 13th St; 10011 212-620-7310 Mon-Fri 10am-11pm. "Alcoholism/Drug Prevention & Intervention Services. Transgender welcome."

♂ ★ Pyramid Place, 814-816 Amsterdam Ave; 10036 212-662-6700 "Live-in therapeutic community; facility of Project Return."

♀ ● **Realization Center, 19 Union Sq W, 7th flr; 10003 212-627-9600**

♀ Women in Need, Inc., 406 W 40th St; 10018

Queens

♂ ★ Flushing Gays & Lesbians in Recovery, c/o Unitarian Universalist Church, 147-54 Ash Ave, Flushing; 11355 212-683-3900 Wed 7.30-8.45pm.

Rockland, Westchester, Dutchess, Orange Counties

♂ ★ & West Nyack Gay & Lesbian AA Group, West Nyack Church of Religious Science, 96 Straw Town Rd, West Nyack; 10994 914-358-4961

AIDS/HIV Support, Education, Advocacy, Publications

Bronx

♀ ☆ && Bronx AIDS Services, 1 Fordham Plaza #903, Bronx; 10458 718-295-5605 Fax 718-733-3429

● ★ && Bronx Lesbian AIDS Task Force, PO Box 1738, Bronx; 10451

Brooklyn

♀ ☆ && Brooklyn AIDS Task Force, CSP, 465 Dean St, Brooklyn; 11217 718-783-0883 Fax 718-638-0191 9.30am-5.30pm.

♀ ☆ The Oustationed Program, Bedford-Stuyvesant Community Mental Health Center, 1360 Fulton St #B02, Brooklyn; 11216 718-398-7790 Fax 718-636-1601 "Support groups for Men/ Women & Couples who are HIV Positive."

♀ ★ (&) TOUCH AIDS Community Dinners, PO Box 401032, Brooklyn; 11240 718-518-2806

Long Island

♀ ☆ The AIDS Collective, Inc., PO Box 7, Greenport; 11944-0007 516-477-2447

♀ ☆ && East End HIV/AIDS Center, 2 Goodfriend Dr Bldg #1, East Hampton; 11937 516-329-6800

♀ ☆ && Long Island Association for AIDS Care, Inc. (LIACC), PO Box 2859, Huntington Station; 11746 516-385-AIDS; 516-385-2451 business; Pub LIAAC Newsletter. "Support groups, case management, free legal clinic, prevention education, advocacy, meal delivery, transportation, etc; weekly confidential information meeting for HIV+ people & partners."

♀ ☆ The NAMES Project Long Island, PO Box 7, Greenport; 11944-0007 516-477-2447

♀ ☆ People With AIDS Coalition of Long Island, Inc, 1170 Rte 109, Lindenhurst; 11757-1002 516-225-5797; 516-225-5700 Life-Line; Fax 516-225-5796 Mon-Fri 10am-6pm; Sat 11am-3pm.

♀ ☆ (&&) Thursday's Child, 80 Terry St, Patchogue; 11772 516-447-5044 Fax 516-288-4735 Independent housing.

♀ ★ && Uveges, Bruce A., Esq, 300 Rabro Dr #142, Hauppauge; 11788 516-234-3232

Manhattan & New York City Area

♀ ☆ && ACT UP/AIDS Coalition to Unleash Power, 135 W 29th St, 10th Flr; 10001 212-564-2437 Fax 212-989-1797

♀ ★ Actors Fund of America AIDS Volunteer Program, 1501 Broadway #518; 10036 212-221-7300

♀ AIDS Education & Program Services, NYC Dept Of Health, 311 Broadway 4th flr; 10007 212-285-4625

♀ ☆ AIDS Memorial in the Village, PO Box 843; 10014-0843 718-565-6789

♀ AIDS Research Fund of the Cancer Research Institute, 681 5th Ave; 10022 212-688-7515; 800-223-7874

♀ ☆ (&) AIDS Resource Center (ARC), 275 7th Ave, 12th flr; 10001 212-633-2500 Fax 212-633-2932 9.30am-5.30pm.

♀ AIDS Service Center of Lower Manhattan, 80 5th Ave #405; 10011 212-645-0875

♀ ☆ (?&) AIDS Theatre Project, 197 E Broadway #U2; 10002 212-475-6200 ext 305

♀ ● **Always Your Choice, 80 E 11th St #437; 10003 212-677-1777 Testing & counseling.**

♀ ☆ American Foundation for AIDS Research, 733 3rd Ave #12fl, New York, NY 10017-3204; 5900 Wilshire Blvd, Los Angeles, CA 90036-5032; 1828 L St NW #802, Washington, DC 20036-5104 212-682-7440; 213-857-5900; Pub AIDS/HIV Treatment Directory. Also publishes "AIDS/HIV Clinical Trial Handbook", addressing most frequently asked questions regarding joining a clinical trial in easy-to-understand language, available English & Spanish.

♀ ☆ && **American Indian Community House HIV/AIDS Project, 404 Lafayette St, 2nd Flr; 10003 212-598-0100**

♀ ☆ && APICHA (Asian & Pacific Islander Coalition on HIV/ AIDS), 275 7th Ave, 12th flr; 10001 212-620-7287 Fax 212-620-7323

♀ ☆ Bailey House/AIDS Resource Center, 180 Christopher St; 10014 212-337-3000

♀ Broadway Cares/ Equity Fights Aids, 165 W 46th St #1600; 10036 212-840-0770

♂ ★ (&) Center Bridge AIDS Bereavement Program, The Center, 208 W 13th St; 10011 212-620-7310 Mon-Fri 10am-6pm.

♀ ☆&& Division Of AIDS Services, Human Resources Administration, 241 Church St, 1st flr; 10013 212-645-7070

♣ ★&& **Gay Men's Health Crisis, 129 W 20th St; 10011 212-807-6665 Hotline; 212-807-6664 office;** *The Volunteer;* **Treatment Issues.**

♀ ☆&& God's Love We Deliver, Inc, 895 Amsterdam Ave; 10025 212-865-6500 "Hot meals for homebound people with HIV/AIDS; comprehensive nutrition education & counseling for asymptomatic & symptomatic people with HIV/AIDS."

♀ ☆&& Harlem United Community AIDS Center, Inc, 207 W 133rd St; 10030 212-491-9000 Fax 212-491-9069

♀ ☆&& Housing Works, 594 Broadway #700; 10012 212-966-0466 Fax 212-966-0869 "Permanent housing, support services & advocacy for homeless people living with AIDS & HIV."

♀ ○ Life Entitlements Corporation, 4 World Trade Center #5270; 10048 800-420-1420 "A viatical settlements company."

♂ ★ (?&) Men of Color AIDS Prevention Program (MOCA), 125 Worth St Box 67; 10013 / New York City Department of Health, Office of Gay & Lesbian Health Concerns 212-788-4403

♀ ☆ (&) Minority Task Force on AIDS, 505 8th Ave, 16th flr; 10018 212-563-8340; 212-727-5161; 864-4046; "Housing; legal services; case management; meal programs."

♀ ☆ & Miracle House, PO Box 30931; 10011-0109 212-799-0563 ext 229 Fax 212-645-0461 "Provides housing & support to out-of-town family & friends of NYS people with AIDS."

♀ ☆&& Office of AIDS Discrimination Issues, NYS/DHR, 55 W 125th St, 12th Flr; 10027 212-961-8624; 212-961-8999 (TDD); 800-532-AIDS; Fax 212-523-AIDS

♀ ★ Positive Action of New York, 351 W 18th St #133; 10011-4402 212-268-4196

♀ ☆ POWARS: Pet Owners With AIDS/ARC Resource Service Inc, Box 1116 Madison Square Stn; 10159 212-744-0842

♀ ☆ & PWA Coalition of New York, Inc, 50 W 17th St, 8th flr; 10011 212-647-1415; 212-647-1420; 800-828-3280; Fax 212-647-1419 Mon-Fri 10am-6pm. Pub *PWACNY Newsline; SIDAahora.* "AIDS educational, medical referral service; support groups; AIDS treatment information."

♀ ★ & PWA Health Group, 150 W 26th St #201; 10001 Pub *Notes From the Underground.*

♣ ★ (?&) South Asian AIDS Action, PO Box 1326; 10009 212-349-3293

♀ Stand-Up Harlem, Inc, 145 W 130th St; 10027 212-926-4072

♀ ☆&& Upper Manhattan Task Force on AIDS, Inc, 55 W 125th St #1103; 10027 212-369-5800 Fax 212-369-5874 "Also volunteer progarm & scattered site housing."

♣ ☆&& Women At Risk, c/o Community Counseling & Mediation Center, 252 7th Ave, 11th flr; 10001 212-255-5477

♀ Women In Crisis, 360 W 125th St #11; 10027 212-316-5200

Queens

♀ ☆ & AIDS Center of Queens County (ACQC), 97-45 Queens Blvd #1220, Rego Park; 11374 / 175-61 Hillside Ave, 4th flr, Jamaica; 11432 / 21-17 Mott Ave, 5th flr, Far Rockaway; 11691 718-896-2500; 718-739-2525 Jamaica; TDD 718-896-2985; Far Rockaway 718-868-8645; Fax 718-275-2094 Mon-Fri 9am-9pm; Sat 10am-4pm; Jamaica Mon, Thu, Fri 9am-6pm, Tue & Wed 9am-8pm.

♣ ☆ (?&) HOPE (HIV-AIDS Outreach Prevention & Education), Center For Children & Families Inc. 8912 162nd St, Jamaica; 11432-5072 718-262-9180

♀ ☆ Hope Program, Center for Children & Families, Inc, 89-12 162nd St, Jamaica; 11432 718-262-9180 Fax 718-297-8059

Staten Island

♀ ☆ (&) Staten Island AIDS Task Force, 29 Hyatt St, Staten Island; 10301 718-981-3366

Rockland, Westchester, Dutchess, Orange Counties

♀ ACT UP/Westchester, PO Box 1964, SUNY Purchase, Purchase; 10577 914-241-1544

♀ ☆ Project Hope, 1059 Main St, Peekskill; 10566 914-737-1498 Fax 914-737-1752 Mon-Fri 9am-5pm. "Adult drop-in center for those infected, affected & at risk for HIV. Various support groups."

Answering/FAX & Mail Receiving, Shipping & Packaging Services

♀ ○ Aerobeep & Voicemail Services, 267 5th Ave #801; 10016 212-679-0000

♀ • & Broadway Mail & Phone Service, 1328 Broadway #1054; 10001 212-268-7145 Fax 212-268-7144 "We also do mailings for businesses & organizations."

♀ • Mail Call Rent-A-Box, 227 E 56th St #400; 10022 212-753-2357 Fax 212-888-6828

♀ • Message Bureau, Inc., 37 Union Square West 212-255-3155 "Voice mail; remote access via beeper."

♀ • Your Neighborhood Office, 332 Bleecker St; 10014 212-989-8303

Antiques & Collectables

♀ • & Uplift Antiques, 506 Hudson St; 10014 212-929-3632

Architectural Services (see also Home/Building)

♣ ★ (&) OLGAD: The Organization of Lesbian & Gay Architects & Designers, PO Box 927 Old Chelsea Stn; 10113 212-475-7652 "All design fields, preservationists, builders, & students welcome."

Art & Photography (see also Graphic Design)

♀ • Cruse, Howard, 718-639-4951 "Freelance cartoonist."

♣ • (&) Discreet Photographers, 718-381-8304 Willam Joseph. "For dancers, bodybuilders, actors, & others; private scenes & portraits."

♀ • Fotografia, 21 Howard St; 10013 212-966-0498 Fax 212-226-1085 By appointment. "Professional photo studio; high quality lab work; photoreproduction; publicity; freelance assignments."

♀ • & Koala Studios, 2026 Route 112, Medford; 11763 516-654-1831 Tue-Fri 10am-5.30pm; Sat 11am-4pm. "Photography: portraits, special events, commercial."

♀ • (&) Lee Snider/Photo Images, 221 W 82nd St #9D; 10024 212-873-6141 Fax 212-787-5337

♀ • Maynard, John, 524 E 13th St; 10009-3526 212-475-0195 (call Mon-Fri 7-5.30pm) "Sign-painter; not for businesses serving liquor or drugs."

Art Galleries/Archives/Restoration, Supplies, Framing

♀ • A Clean, Well Lighted Place, 363 Bleecker St; 10014 212-255-3656

♣ ★ (&) Leslie-Lohman Gay Art Foundation, 127 Prince St, Basement; 10012 212-673-7007 Tue-Sat noon-6pm. "Archive facility & gay art exhibits."

♀ ○ McFrame Co, 410 W 47th St; 10036 212-582-2756 "Picture framing, by appointment."

♀ • Toad Hall at ABC Carpet & Home, 888 Broadway 4th flr; 10003 212-473-3000 x281

Astrology/Numerology/Tarot/Psychic Readings

♀ • Robert, 212-864-3753 "Tarot Encouragement."

♀ • (?⚲) Yaa Asantewaa, Eva, PO Box 1133; 10009-9998 212-505-0426 "Tarot; creative visualization; meditation; chakras; stress management."

Bars, Restaurants, Clubs, Discos

Bronx

⚥ G.T.'s, 2768 Webster Ave (198th St), Bronx; 10458

Brooklyn

⚥ • 1 Hot Spot, 1 Front St, Brooklyn; 11201 718-852-0139 **B**

⚥ ○ Celebrity's, 8705 3rd Ave, Brooklyn; 11209 718-745-9652

⚥ • **Spectrum, 802 64th St, Brooklyn; 11220 718-238-8213 _BD_ Wed-Sun 9pm-4am.**

Fire Island

⚥ • ⚲⚲ Cherry's/Cherry's Pit, 158 Bayview Walk, Cherry Grove; 11782 516-597-6820 **BRDE**

⚥ ○⚲⚲ Ice Palace, Cherry Grove, Fire Island; 11782 516-597-6600 **BDE**

⚥ • Monstro/The Queen & I, Box 81, Cherry Grove, Fire Island; 11782 / Ocean Walk 516-597-6888 **BDR** Noon-4am.

⚥ ○ ⚲ Pines Pavillion, Harbor Walk, Fire Island Pines, Fire Island; 11782 **D**

♀ • (?⚲) **Top of the Bay, PO Box 134, Cherry Grove, Fire Island; 11782 / Dock Walk 516-597-6699 _BR_ Noon-4am.**

♀ Yacht Club at Botel, Fire Island Pines, Fire Island; 11782

Long Island: Nassau

⚥ • ⚲⚲ Bedrock, 121 Woodfield Rd, West Hempstead; 11552 516-486-9516 **BDE** "Mainly women but all welcome."

⚥ • ⚲ Blanche, 47-2 Boundary Ave, S. Farmingdale; 11735 516-694-6906 **BE** 8pm-4am; Sun from 4pm. "Cocktail lounge, piano bar & gin mill."

♀ Club Chameleon, 4020 Long Beach Rd, Island Park; 11558 516-669-4083

⚥ ○ Libations, 3547 Merrick Road, Seaford; 11783 516-679-8820

⚥ • Pal Joey's, 2457 Jerusalem Ave, North Bellmore; 11710 516-785-9301

⚥ • Silver Lining, 175 Cherry Lane, Floral Park; 11001 516-354-9641 **BD**

Long Island: Suffolk

♀ Bayman's Katch Restaurant, 220 Montauk Hwy, Sayville; 11782 516-599-0744 **R**

⚥ • (⚲⚲) Bunkhouse, 192 N Main St, Sayville; 11782 516-567-9834

⚥ • (⚲) Club 608, 608 Sunrise Hwy, West Babylon; 11704 516-661-9580 8pm-4am.

⚥ • (⚲) Club Swamp & Annex Restaurant, PO Box 369, Wainscott; 11975 / Montauk Hwy 516-537-3332 **BDR**

⚥ • Forever Green, 841 N. Broome Ave, Lindenhurst; 11757 516-226-9357 **BD** Opens 8pm.

⚥ ○ ⚲ Kiss, Rose Drive, Lake Ronkonkoma 516-467-4264 **BDR** 8pm-4am; Sun 5pm-4am.

⚥ • Long Island Eagle, 94 N Clinton Ave, Bay Shore; 11706 516-698-2750 **L** "Levi-leather bar; home of the Long Island Ravens MC."

⚥ ○ (⚲) Mallory Sq. Restaurant, Box 626, Sayville; 11782 / Cherry Grove Ferry Dock 516-589-0810 **BRd** May-Oct, from 7am.

⚥ • ⚲ Thunders, 1017 E Jericho Turnpike, Huntington Station; 11746 516-423-5241 **BDELW**

Manhattan

⚥ • ⚲ 9 Jones Street Restaurant, 9 Jones St; 10014 212-989-1220 **BR**

♀ Ballroom, 353 W 28th St; 10001 (7th/8th Aves) 212-244-3005 Cabaret; $15 minimum (2 drinks).

⚥ The Bar, 68 2nd Ave; 10003 (4th St) 212-674-9714

♀ • BarDo, 34 Downing St; 10014 (Bedford St) 212-627-1580

⚥ • ⚲ **Black Sheep Cafe, 344 W 11th St; 10014 (Washington St) 212-242-1010 _B_ 6-11.30pm; Brunch Sat & Sun noon-4pm.**

♀ Blue Angel, 323 W 44th St; 10036 212-262-3333 Cabaret.

⚥ Boiler Room, The, 86 E 4th St; 10003 212-254-7536

⚥ • (⚲) Boots & Saddle, 76 Christopher St; 10014 (7th Ave S) 212-929-9684 **BLW** 8am-4am; Sun noon-4am.

♀ • Brandy's Piano Bar, 235 E 84th St; 10021 (2nd/3rd Ave) 212-650-1944

⚥ • ⚲ The Break, 232 8th Ave; 10011 (22nd St) 212-627-0072 **B** 2pm-4am.

♀ • ⚲ C.J. Blanda, 209 7th Ave; 10011 (22nd St) 212-206-7880

♀ ○ Cafe Elsie, 358 W 47th St; 10036 212-765-7653 **R**

♀ ○ **Caffe Torino, 139 W 10th St; 10014 212-675-5554 _BR_**

♀ Cajun, 129 8th Ave; 10011 212-255-6529

⚥ • Candle Bar, 309 Amsterdam Ave: 10023 (74th/75th St) 212-874-9155 2pm-4am.

⚥ Cats Too, 232 W 48th St; 10036 (Broadway/8th Ave) 212-245-5245

⚥ • (?⚲) Cell Block 28, 28 10th Ave; 10014 (13th St) 212-255-6758 **LWP** Juice bar club. Contact for details.

⚥ Champs, 17 W 19th St; 10011 (5th/6th Aves) 212-633-1717 **BD** Wed-Sat 10pm-4am; Sun 6pm-4am.

♀ ○ Chelsea's Choice Coffee & Teas, 210 7th Ave; 10011 212-206-8033 & 58 3rd Ave (212) 777-2463 8am-11pm. "Espresso bar."

♀ • **Chez Michallet, 90 Bedford St; 10014 (Grove) 212-242-8309 _B_ Tue-Sat 5.30-11pm.**

♀ ○ **Chez Suzette, 363 W 46th St; 10036 212-581-9717; 212-974-9002; _R_ "Country French cuisine."**
♦ **Chez Suzette advertisement page 328**

⚥ ○ Claire Restaurant, 156 7th Ave; 10011 (19th/20th Sts) 212-255-1955 **BR** Noon-2am.

♀ • ⚲ Cleo's, 656 9th Ave; 10036 (45th/46th Sts) 212-307-1503 8am-4am; Sun noon-4am.

⚥ • Club 58, 40 E 58th St; 10022 212-308-1546; 212-644-7437; **BDE** 4pm-4am.

♀ • Club Edelweiss, 580 11th Ave; 10036 (43rd St) 212-629-1021 **BDE**

⚥ • **Crazy Nanny, 21 7th Ave South; 10014 212-929-8356**
♦ **Crazy Nanny advertisement page 328**

⚥ • ⚲ Crowbar, 339 E 10th St; 10009 212-420-0670 **BDE** Drag shows.

♀ ○ Cubby Hole, 281 W 12th St; 10014 (4th St) 212-243-9041

♀ Danny's Skylight Room/Grand Sea Palace, 346 W 46th St; 10036 212-265-8133 **R**

NY: New York City Area
Bars, Clubs, Restaurants
328
USA
New York City Area : NY
Bars, Clubs, Restaurants

♀ • ♂♂ David's Potbelly Stove Cafe, 94 Christopher St; 10014 212-727-9068 *R* 24 hrs. "Courtyard dining."

♂ Dick's Bar, 192 2nd Ave; 10003 212-475-2071

♀ ○ (♿) Don't Tell Mama, 343 W 46th St; 10036 (8th/9th Ave) 212-757-0788 *BE* 4pm-4am. "Piano bar & cabaret."

♂ ○ Dugout Bar, 185 Christopher St; 10014 212-242-9113

♀ ○ Duplex, 61 Christopher St; 10014 212-255-5438 *BE* 4pm-4am. "Piano bar, cabaret."

♂ • (♿) Eagle's Nest, 142 11th Ave; 10011 (21st St) 212-691-8451 *BLW* 10pm-4am.

♀ Eight of Clubs, The, 230 W 75th St; 10023 212-580-7398

♀ • Eighty Eight's, 228 W 10th St; 10014 212-924-0088 *BE* 4pm-4am; Sun brunch noon-4.30pm. "Piano bar; cabaret."

CHEZ SUZETTE

since 1967

country french cuisine
open seven days
lunch & dinner
prix fixe luncheon special
pre-theater/after theater

212 581-9717
800 371-9475

363 west 46th street, new york, ny 10036

Crazy Nanny's

A Place for Gay Women Biological or Otherwise

21 7TH AVENUE SOUTH
(corner of Leroy St)
New York, NY 10014

Events: (212) 366-6312
Bar: (212) 929-8356
Fax: (212) 807-9195

♂ • (♿) The Falcon Club, 42 W 33rd St; 10001 212-279-0179 *BP*

♀ ○ Fedora's, 239 W 4th St; 10014 212-242-9691 *R*

♀ ○ Five Oaks, 49 Grove St; 10014 212-243-8885 *R*

♀ • ♿ Food Bar, 149 8th Ave; 10011 (17th St) 212-243-2020 *R*

♂ • G.H. Club, 353 E 53rd St; 10022 212-223-9752 *BE* 4pm-1am; Fri & Sat to 2am.

♂ • The Hangar, 115 Christopher St; 10014 212-627-2044

♂ • Hangout, 675 Hudson St; 10014 (9th Ave) 212-242-9292

♀ Henrietta Hudson, 438 Hudson St; 10014 212-243-9079

♀ Joe L's Uptown Bar, 4488 Broadway (192nd St); 10034 212-567-8555

♀ • Judy's Restaurant & Cabaret, 49 W 44th St; 10036 212-764-8930 *BRE* Mon-Fri noon-2am; Sat 5pm-2am.

♀ • Julie's, 204 E. 58th St; 10022 2nd/3rd Aves 212-688-1294

♀ • Julius, 159 W 10th St; 10014 (Waverly) 212-243-1928

♂ ○ Keller's, 384 West St; 10014 (Barrow) 212-243-1907

♂ • King, 579 6th Ave (17th St); 10011 212-366-5464 Fax 212-206-8398

♀ • ♿ Kiss Bar & Grill, 142 W 10th St; 10014 212-242-6444 *BR*

♀ • Lucky Cheng's, 24 1st Ave; 10009 212-473-0516 *BRE* "Asian-California cuisine, served by drag queen waitresses."

♂ The Lure, 409 W 13th St; 10014 212-741-3919 8pm-4am. (Weekend dress code: leather, levi, uniform, etc)

♀ • M Bar & Lounge, 256 E 49th St; 10017 (2nd/3rd Aves) 212-935-2150 Fax 212-935-8377

♀ ○ Manatus Restaurant, 340 Bleecker St; 10014 Christopher/ W. 10th) 212-989-7042 *R*

♀ ○ ♿ Marie's Crisis, 59 Grove St; 10014 (Bleecker) 212-243-9323 *BE* 2pm-4am.

♀ ○ Mayfair, 964 1st Ave; 10022 (53rd St) 212-421-6216 *BR*

♀ • ♂♂ Mike's Club Cafe, 400 W 14th St; 10014 212-691-6606 *BRE*

♀ • The Monster, 80 Grove St; 10014 (Sheridan Sq) 212-924-3558 *BD*

♂ Nuts & Bolts, 101 7 Ave S; 10014 (corner Grove St) 212-620-4000

♀ ○ One If By Land, 17 Barrow St; 10014 212-228-0822 *R*

♀ • One Potato, 518 Hudson St; 10014 212-691-6260 *R* noon-4am.

♀ • (♿) Paris Commune, 411 Bleecker St; 10014 (Between Bank & W 11th St) 212-929-0509 *R* "Casual French bistro, serving lunch, brunch & dinner daily. MC & Visa."

♀ Pegasus, 119 E 60th St; 10022 212-888-4702

♀ ○ Pennyfeather's, 95 7th Ave S.; 10014 (Sheridan Sq) 212-242-9567 *R* 24 hrs.

♂ • ♿ Pieces, 8 Christopher St; 10014 212-929-9291 *BE*

♀ ○ Pyramid Cocktail Lounge, 101 Ave A; 10009 (6th/7th Sts) 212-420-1590 4pm-4am.

♂ • Rawhide, 212 8th Ave; 10011 (21st St) 212-242-9332 *LW*

♀ Raymond's Cafe, 88 7th Ave; 10011 (15th/16th Sts) 212-929-1778 *R*

♀ ○ Restaurant Florent, 69 Gansevoort St; 10014 212-989-5779 24 hrs. "French food plus. Greatly varied clientele, from truck drivers at breakfast to upper East Siders."

NY: New York City Area
Bars, Clubs, Restaurants

329
USA

New York City Area : NY
Bars, Clubs, Restaurants

⚥ Rose's Turn, 55 Grove St; 10014 212-366-5438

⚥ ● Rubyfruit Bar & Grill, 531 Hudson St; 10014 (Charles & 10th St) 212-929-3343; 212-929-1155

T Sally's II, At The Carter Hotel, 252 W 43rd St; 10036 212-944-6000 Ext 212

♂ Savoy, 355 W 41st St; 10036 212-560-9635

⚥ ○ (♿) Sazerac House, 533 Hudson St; 10014 (Charles St) 212-989-0313 *B*

⚥ ● (♿) Sneakers, 392 West St; 10014 (Christopher/10th St) 212-242-9830 Noon-4am.

♂ ○ South Dakota, 405 3rd Ave; 10016 (28th/29th Sts) 212-684-8376 3pm-4am; weekends 2pm-4am.

♂ ● **Spike, 120 11th Ave; 10011 (20th St) 212-243-9688** *L* 3pm-4am; Sun brunch 1-5pm.
✦ *Spike advertisement page 329*

♂ ● ♿ Splash Bar, 50 W 17th St; 10011 off 6th Ave 212-691-0073 *BE* 3pm-4am; Sat & Sun 2pm-4am.

♂ ○ Star Sapphire, 400 E 59th St; 10022 (1st Ave) 212-688-4710

⚥ Stella's, 268 W 47th St (Between 8th & Broadway); 10036 (8th Ave/Broadway) 212-997-4041

♂ Stonewall, 53 Christopher St; 10014 212-463-0950

⚥ ● **Thomas Scott on Bedford, 72 Bedford St; 10014 212-627-4011** *B*
✦ *Thomas Scott on Bedford advertisement page 329*

♂ Tool Box, 1748 2nd Ave; 10028 (91st St) 212-427-3106

11th Avenue at 20th St.
243-9688

Thomas Scott's
on Bedford

⭐⭐⭐
Next Magazine

72 Bedford Street · New York, N.Y. 10014 · 212 · 627 · 4011

Rated **VERY GOOD** to **EXCELLENT** for Food, Service and Decor."
Zagat's Restaurant Guide - 1995

"Dare I say the **BEST** gay restaurant in New York City".
Private Lives, Jason Reeves

"Reminiscent of the little restaurants that flourish in London and Paris"
Sheldon Landwehr, N.Y. Post

" the Best Rack of Lamb in America"   "Romantic, intimate ambiance for Lovers of all ages."
The Native, Keith Willete   The Villager, Feb. 1994

" I half expected to see one of those signs ' Established 1868',
and to find Thomas the Great-Grandson of the Original Chef."
Greenwich Village Press, Chef Rossi

FULL SERVICE OFF-PREMISE CATERING

NY: New York City Area
Bars, Clubs, Restaurants
330
USA
New York City Area: NY
Bookstores: Gay/Lesbian/Feminist

Corporation

Spaces for
Imagination

Lesbian and Gay Literature

Creative Visions

Books, Periodicals
Newspapers

548 Hudson Street,

Coffee Bar

New York City

Performance Space
Promotional and
Informational Material

(212) 645-7573

♂ • The Townhouse, 236 E 58th; 10022 212-754-4649 Piano bar.

♀ • The Townhouse Restaurant, 206 E 58th; 10022 212-826-6241 *R* 4pm-2am; Sat to 4am.

♂ Tunnel Bar, 116 1st Ave; 10003 (7th St) 212-777-9232

♀ Two Potato, 143 Christopher St; 10014 212-242-9304

♂ • Ty's, 114 Christopher St; 10014 (Bleecker/Hudson Sts) 212-741-9641 1pm-4am.

♂ • Uncle Charlie's, 56 Greenwich Ave; 10011 (6th/7th Aves) 212-255-8787 *BE* 3pm-4am. "Video bar."

♀ Universal Grill, 44 Bedford St; 10014 (7th Ave) 212-989-5621 *R*

♀ • Wonder Bar, 505 E 6th St; 10003 (Ave A/Ave B) 212-777-9105 *BE* 8.30pm-4am.

♀ • ⚫ The Works, 428 Columbus Ave; 10024 (81st St) 212-799-7365 *B* 2pm-4am.

Queens

♂ Bachelor's Tavern, 81-12 Roosevelt Ave, Jackson Heights; 11372 718-458-3131

♂ ○ Breadstix, 113-24 Queens Blvd, Forest Hills; 11375 (76th Rd) 718-263-0300 *BR*

♀ Bum-Bum Bar, 63-14 Roosevelt Ave, Woodside; 11377

♀ • ⚫ Club Reflexions, 69-45 51st Ave, Woodside; 11373 718-429-8834 *DEf* 8pm-4am.

♀ ○ Duque's, 72-19 Roosevelt Ave, Jackson Heights; 11372 718-639-7418

♀ • Field Of Dreams, 108-15 Liberty Ave, Richmond Hill; 11419 718-845-9703 7pm-4am.

♀ • Friends Tavern, 78-11 Roosevelt Ave, Jackson Heights; 11372 (78th St) 718-397-7256 *BE* 4pm-4am.

♀ • (⚫) Hatfield's, 126-10 Queens Blvd, Kew Gardens; 11415 (83rd Ave) 718-261-8484 *BDE* 9pm-4am.

♀ ○ Love Boat, 77-02 Broadway, Elmhurst; 11372 718-429-8670

♀ Lucho's Club, 38-19 69th St, Woodside; 11377 (off Roosevelt Ave) 718-899-9048; 718-899-9320

♂ ○ ⚫⚫ Magic Touch, 73-13 37th Rd, Jackson Heights; 11372 718-429-8605 *BDE* 4pm-4am.

♀ • Montana Saloon, 40-08 74th St, Jackson Heights; 11372 (Broadway) 718-429-9356 10am-4am.

Staten Island

♀ ○ (⚫⚫) Sandcastle, 86 Mills Ave, Staten Island; 10305 (South Beach) 718-447-9365

Rockland, Westchester, Dutchess, Orange Counties

♀ • (⚫) Barz Club Cafe, 327 Route 9W, Upper Nyack; 10960 914-353-4444 *BDRE* 5pm-4am; Sat & Sun with Piano Brunch at noon. "Sophisticated dance club for gay men & women."

♀ • The Coven Cafe, 162 Main St, Nyack; 10960 914-358-9829 *BDR* (private club Wed)

♀ • (⚫) Folderol II, PO Box 239, Westtown; 10998 / Rte 284, Westtown; 10998 914-726-3822 *BR* Sun noon-7pm; Mon, Wed-Sat from 5pm.

♀ • ⚫ Harlee's, 590 Nepperhan Ave, Yonkers; 10703 914-965-6900 Opens 10pm.

♀ • The Old Homestead, 325 N Main St, Portchester; 10573 914-939-0758 *BR* 8am-4pm.

♀ ○ Stutz, 202 Westchester Ave, White Plains; 10601 914-761-3100

Farmingdale

♀ The Runway, 400 Route 109, Farmingdale; 11736 516-293-5879

Bookstores: Gay/Lesbian/Feminist

Brooklyn

♀ • A Room Of Our Own, 444 9th St, Brooklyn; 11215 718-499-2223
✦ *A Room Of Our Own advertisement page 330*

Long Island

♀ • Womankind Books, 5 Kivy St, Huntington Station; 11746 516-427-1289 "Mail order only: free lesbian catalog on request."

NY: New York City Area
Bookstores: Gay/Lesbian/Feminist

331
USA

New York City Area : NY
Business Services

Bookstores: Gay/Lesbian/Feminist

Manhattan

♀ • ⚲ **A Different Light, 151 W 19th St; 10011 212-989-4850; 800-343-4002; Fax 212-989-2158**
♦ *A Different Light advertisement page 331*

♂ • **Creative Visions, 548 Hudson St; 10014 212-645-7573 11am-11pm. "Also performance space & art gallery."**
♦ *Creative Visions advertisement page 330*

♂ • Oscar Wilde Memorial Bookshop, 15 Christopher St; 10014 212-255-8097 "World's first Lesbian & Gay Liberation bookshop (founded 1967); free catalog."

Bookstores: General

Brooklyn

♀ ○ Book Link, 99 7th Ave, Brooklyn; 11215 718-783-6067

♀ ○ Book Link Too, 320 7th Ave, Brooklyn; 11215 718-965-9122

♀ ○ Community Bookshop, 143 7th Ave, Brooklyn; 11215 718-783-3075

Long Island

♂ • ⚲ Book Hampton, 14 Main St, East Hampton; 11937 516-324-4939

♂ • ⚲ Book Hampton, 93 Main St, Southampton; 11968 516-283-0270

♂ ○ ⚲⚲ Borders Book Shop, 3350 Hempstead Turnpike, Levittown; 11756

♂ ○ ⚲⚲ Borders Books & Music, 5151 Sunrise Highway, Bohemia; 11716

Manhattan

♂ ○ Casa Magazines, Global News, Inc. 22 8th Ave; 10014 (12th St) 212-645-1197

♂ • Mags 'R' Us, 116 Christopher St; 10014 212-929-1250 12.30pm-mdnt.

♂ ○ ⚲ Saint Marks Bookshop, 31 3rd Ave; 10003 212-260-7853

♂ ○ (⚲) Science Fiction, Mysteries & More, 140 Chambers St; 10007 212-385-8798 Fax 212-385-8915

♂ ○ Shakespeare & Co, 716 Broadway; 10003 212-529-1330

♂ ○ Spring Street Books, 169 Spring St; 10012 212-219-3033

♂ • **Three Lives & Co, Ltd, 154 W 10th St; 10014 212-741-2069**

♂ ○ Verso Books, 128 8th Ave; 10011 212-620-3141 10am-10.30pm; Sat to 11pm; Sun 11am-9pm. "Snacks; coffee & water bar."

Rockland, Westchester, Dutchess, Orange Counties

♂ ○ (⚲) Books & Things, 3 North Broadway, Tarrytown; 10591 914-631-2966 Mon-Sat 9.30am-5.30pm.

♂ • (⚲) Reading, Writing & Wrapping, 30 E Parkway, Scarsdale; 10583-4192 914-723-1278 Fax 914-723-1542 Mon-Sat 9am-6.30pm; Thu to 8pm.

Bookstores: Recovery, Metaphysical, & other Specialty

Manhattan

♂ ○ (⚲) Choices - The Recovery Bookshop, 220 East 78th St; 10021 212-794-3858

♂ • Esoterica New Age Bookstore, 61 4th Ave; 10003 212-529-9808

Rockland, Westchester, Dutchess, Orange Counties

♂ ○ **New Spirit Books, 128 Main St, Nyack; 10960 914-353-2126**

Broadcast Media

♀ ★ Gay & Lesbian Independent Broadcasters (GLIB), 505 8th Ave, c/o WBAI Box 18; 10018 212-473-1689

♂ ★ (⚲) Gay Broadcasting System, 178 7th Ave #A3; 10011 212-243-1570 "*Out In The Nineties* Manhattan Cable Channel 16."

♀ ★ (⚲⚲) Lavender Wimmin Radio Show, WUSB 90.1FM Suny At Stonybrook, Stony Brook; 11794 516-632-6901 Thu 6-7pm, 90.1FM.

♀ ★ LESBIAN CENTRAL, c/o GLAAD, 150 W 26th St #503; 10001 212-807-1700 Fax 212-807-1806 Cable Ch. 34 (MNN). Contact for current schedule. "Lesbian TV talk show, sponsored by GLAAD."

♂ ★ Long Island Rainbow Connection TV Show, PO Box 301, Upton; 11973 516-399-3891 (also Fax) "Long Island's Lesbian & Gay Political Action Committee."

Business, Financial & Secretarial

♂ • AAA Expert Typing, 212-866-6422

♂ • ⚲ **Beauchamp Business Services, 5619 14th Ave #1C, Brooklyn; 11219-4611 718-851-1612 "Special attention given to low income workers, new persons entering the work force, & immigrants. Se habla español."**

♂ • BGS Services, 718-459-3690; 212-631-1192; "Accounting, tax & computer consulting."

♂ • ⚲ Christopher Street Financial, Inc, 80 Wall St #1214; 10005 212-269-0110

♂ • **Crowe, J.J, 229 E. 24th St #3; 10010-3840 212-779-4004 "Public accountant."**

♀ ○ Graham, Sally, Ph.D., 24 E 12th St #601; 10003 212-807-0543; 212-803-5412; "Typing: dissertations, theses, term papers."

♂ • ♂♂ Human Resource Solutions, Inc, 521 5th Ave #1700; 10175-0003 212-316-2800 Fax 212-316-6994 "Management consulting; career counseling."

♀ • ♂ **Krause, Alice M., E.A., 682 Broadway; 10012 212-473-5269 "Tax preparation & financial counseling for individuals & self-employed. Delinquent tax matters & estate taxes."**

♀ ○ Lee, Susan, 212-633-1516 "Tax: individuals & freelancers."

♂ • Mathematronics, 205 W 95th St #3E; 10025-6322 212-222-2777 "Computer services for small businesses, including mailing labels."

♀ ○ **Monjure, Ted, MBA, CPA, 200 W 15th St; 10011 212-989-4743**

♂ • Rowan, Arnold, CPA, PO Box 304 Village Stn; 10014 212-675-7352

♀ • (?♂) Saladino, F. Scott, CPA, 48 Mystic Circle, Bay Shore; 11706 516-665-8161

♀ • Seabury, Robert, 38 Garfield Place, Brooklyn; 11215-1904 718-499-7955; 212-242-3900; "Bookkeeping service for small businesses & individuals."

♀ • Small, Stan, E.A., 89 5th Ave #309; 10003 212-627-4585 "Tax Preparation & Accounting Services."

♂ • ♂ Telltype Tape Transcription, 75 Montgomery St #2E; 10002 212-619-3431; 212-619-0925 modem

♀ • ♂ Woloshen & Herman, 853 Broadway #1101; 10003 212-843-3486 "Accounting & tax service."

Child Care

♀ • City Sitters, Inc., 212-475-8747 (Ms. Ronnie J. Schultz) "Professional babysitting service (since 1984); member of Center Kids; brochure on request."

Clothes

Fire Island

♂ • Rodayo Drive Clothing, Lewis & Ocean Walk, Cherry Grove; 11782 516-597-7044

Manhattan

♀ ○ Chelsea Army & Navy Store, 110 8th Ave; 10011 15th/16th Sts 212-645-7420

♂ • Don't Panic!, 98 Christopher St; 10014 212-989-7888 Fax 212-989-8395

♀ ○ Fifty-Ninth Street Army & Navy Store, 221 E 59th St; 10022 212-755-1855

♂ • **Good Catch!, PO Box 1756 Old Chelsea Stn; 10011 800-77-CATCH Fax 800-98-FAX-US "Manufacturer & distributor of T-shirts, mugs, enamel pins, silver earrings, embroidered hats, etc. The original 'Cum Rag & Cum Towel', postcards & other novelties. Custom orders."**

♀ • (♂) The Leather Man, Inc, 111 Christopher St; 10014 212-243-5339 Fax 212-243-5372

♀ • (♂) The Loft, 89 Christopher St; 10014 212-691-2334

♀ • ♂ New York Bodyworks, 45 Christopher St; 10014 645-0301

♀ ○ P. Chanin, 152 8th Ave; 10011 800-PChanin☞

♀ ○ Saint Michael's Emporium, 156 E. 2nd St #1; 10009 212-995-8359 "Leather."

♀ ○ Second Avenue Army & Navy Store, 1598 2nd Ave; 10028 83rd St 212-737-4661

♂ • Shades of The Village, 33-D Greenwich Ave; 10014 212-255-7767 "Sunglasses & hats."

♀ ○ Steve Cobb's Haberdashery, 110 E 7th St 212-473-6844 Fax 212-941-7464

♀ ○ Village Army & Navy Store, 328 Bleecker St; 10014 212-242-6655

♂ ○ World, 75 Christopher St; 10014 212-627-6754

Community Centers (see also Women's Centers)

Brooklyn

♀ ★♂♂ Shades of Lavender, 470 Bergen St, Brooklyn; 11217 (Park Slope) 718-499-0352 Fax 718-638-0191 Pub *Lavender Notes*.

Long Island

♀ ★ The Long Island Center, 1170 Rt 109, PWAC Building, Lindenhurst; 11757 516-226-3445 Pub *Center Lines*.

Manhattan

♀ ★ **Lesbian & Gay Community Services Center, 208 W 13th St; 10011 212-620-7310 9am-11pm. Pub *Center Voice*.**
✦ *Lesbian & Gay Community Services Center advertisement page 333*

Rockland, Westchester, Dutchess, Orange Counties

♀ ★ The Loft: Lesbian & Gay Community Services Center, Inc., PO Box 1513, White Plains; 10602 / 255 Grove St, White Plains; 10601 914-948-4922 *The Loft Community News*. "Weekly rap groups for Gay/Bi Men & Lesbian/Bi Women."

Computer Bulletin Boards

♀ • **The Backroom BBS, TOSS, Inc. 1412 Ave M #2517, Brooklyn; 11230 718-951-8256 (modem); 718-951-8998 (voice)**
✦ *Backroom BBS advertisement page 125*

♀ ○ Erotic Visions BBS, Box 203; 10013 718-296-8151 "Adult computer communication."

Computer/Software Sales & Services

♀ • (♂) Integral Consulting, 256 W 10th St #2D; 10014-2525 212-807-9584 (also fax) "Training, developing & networking for Macintosh/PC."

♀ • **Nerd Word Productions, Park Slope 718-789-6520 "Advice on computer needs for home & business; on & off-site training for children & adults; installation, maintenance & repairs (including DEC printers; Banyan Vines); manuscripts, flyers, color scanning."**

♀ • Schultz, Ms. Ronnie, 212-544-1113 "Macintosh computer training, trouble shooting, upgrades."

Conferences/Events/Festivals/Workshops (see also Music)

♀ ★ Christopher Street Festival Committee, 92-16 Whitney Ave #210, Elmhurst; 11373-2281 718-565-6789

Counseling/Therapy: Nonprofit

Brooklyn

♀ ★ Roche, James J., MA, NBCC, Offices Chelsea/West Village & Brooklyn. 718-230-0697 "Licensed Marriage & Family Therapist; Licensed Rehabilitation Coiunselor."

♀ ☆ (?♂) The Answer Is Loving Counseling Center, 1964 E 35th St, Brooklyn; 11234 718-998-2305

Long Island

♀ ★ Allmen, Robert J., MS, M.Div., PO Box 436, Central Islip; 11722 516-723-0348 "Certified/licensed counselor available for private psychotherapy or couple counseling, for personal or relation issues. Will travel."

NY: New York City Area
Counseling: Nonprofit

333
USA

New York City Area: NY
Counseling: Private

Manhattan & New York City Area

♀ ★ (?♿) Center for Nontraditional Families, 111 W 90th St; 10024 212-721-1012 "Counseling & mediation services for Lesbian & Gay couples; single parent families; blended & adoptive families. Offices throughout the Metropolitan Area."

♀ ★ ♿♿ The Columbia Center for Lesbian, Gay & Bisexual Mental Health, 16 E 60th St #400; 10022 212-326-8441 Fax 212-326-8590 Mon-Fri 8am-8pm. "A program of Columbia University's Department of Psychiatry: individual & group psychotherapy, medications & consultations offered."

♀ ★ ♿♿ Identity House, PO Box 572 Old Chelsea Stn; 10011-0572 / 39 W. 14th St #205 212-243-8181 Sun, Mon, Tue 6-10pm. "Peer counseling; open rap groups; therapy referrals; short-term counseling; workshops."

♀ ★ Institute for Human Identity, Inc, 118 W 72nd St, First Floor; 10023 212-799-9432 "Complete psychotherapeutic services; individual, couple & group therapy. Licensed & certified professionals on staff. Sliding scale fees based on ability to pay. Insurance accepted."

♀ ★ Ninth Street Center, 151 1st Ave Box 25; 10003 212-228-5153 Pub Ninth Street Center Journal. "Peer counseling; Psychology Discussion Group; books by Paul Rosenfels."

→ SAGE (Senior Action in a Gay Environment): p.349

♀ ☆ (?♿) Women's Psychotherapy Referral Service, 25 Perry St. 212-595-6655; 212-242-8597; "Referrals to qualified, nonsexist psychotherapists. Sliding scale fees. Insurance accepted."

♀ ☆ (?♿) Women's Psychotherapy Referral Service, 25 Perry St; 10025 212-595-6655; 212-242-8597

Counseling/Therapy: Private

Bronx

♀ ● Creutzberg, Gilbert, MA, CRC, 5800 Arlington Ave, Riverdale; 10471 718-884-3744 "Certified Rehabilitation Counselor, specializing in vocational counseling, resume writing."

Brooklyn

♥ ● Gorra, Georgine, DSW, 646 Baltic St, Brooklyn; 11217 718-783-8247 "Doctor of Social Welfare licensed by NYS, providing consultation & therapy for individuals, couples, & children. Specializing in anxiety & depression. Insurance accepted."

♀ ○ ♂ Herzog, Mary, MPS, CAC, ATR, 166 Prospect Park W #4L, Brooklyn; 11215 & 373 Bleecker St, NYC 718-788-0908 "Treatment of bereavement issues, addictive behavior & creative work blocks."

♀ ○ Juran, Shelley, Ph.D., Brooklyn Heights 718-625-6526 "NYS licensed psychologist. Specialist in gender identity, sex roles, sexuality."

♀ ○ ♂ Miller, Theresa V., CSW, BCD, 7111 5th Ave, Brooklyn; 11209 718-745-6550 "Individual & couple psychotherapy."

♀ ● Milo, Gennaro, Ph.D., 718-232-3448 "Cognitive-behavioral therapy, stress management, phobias; short-term psychotherapy; religious issues."

♥ ● Weiss, Shelly, CSW, Park Slope & Village locations 718-789-1776 Fax 718-622-6848

♀ ○ Zelterman, Irene, CSW, Park Slope 718-832-3739 "Individuals & couples. Adults & children. Experienced working with depression, anxiety, eating disorders, as well as victims of childhood & recent trauma. Insurance reimbursable. Sliding scale."

Long Island

♀ ● ♿♿ Affirmations Psychotherapy & Counseling, 278 E Main St, Smithtown; 11787 516-265-2900 Mon-Fri 9am-9pm. "Individual & group counseling for People With AIDS & their partners; Gay & Lesbian substance abusers & partners; parenting, coming out, etc."

♀ ● (♿) Aspinall, John, CSW, 18 Karen Court, Oyster Bay; 11771 516-922-6155 "Insurance reimbursement; sliding scale."

♥ ● Begelman, Hedda, MSW, RCSW, North Massapequa office: 516-795-1320 "Individual, group, couples therapy for the Gay/Lesbian Community. NYS licensed. Insurance eligible."

♀ ● Blume, E. Sue, CSW, Freeport office 516-379-4731 "Individual & relationship therapy for women; bereavement; children of alcoholics; therapy & education for incest survivors & their lovers; author of Secret Survivors: Uncovering Incest & Its Aftereffects in Women."

♀ ○ ♿♿ Capone, C. Thomas, PhD, 6 Meadow Ridge, Woodbury; 11797 516-367-1016

♀ ○ ♿♿ Capone, Julie, CSW, 6 Meadow Ridge, Woodbury; 11797 516-367-1016

♥ ● D'Amico, Jane, MSW, CSW, CAC, 333 Main St #C, Roslyn; 11576 516-621-3033

♀ ● (?♿) Flaherty, Patricia A., MSW, CSW, 97 Norman Ave, Amityville; 11701 516-264-0087 Evenings & Sat. "Individual & couple counseling; call for information about groups.

♥ ● Gay Counseling Center of Long Island, PO Box 1133, Massapequa; 11758 516-795-0151 "Individual, group, couples therapy. NYS licensed. Insurance eligible."

♀ ● Landry, Patricia K., CSW, BCD, 271 Merrick Ave, East Meadow; 11554-1549 516-794-2626 "Psychotherapy; couple counseling."

♀ ● (?♿) Lanzone, Joseph, CSW, CSAC, 41A North Broadway, Nyack; 10960 914-627-6309

♀ ● ♿♿ Miller, Marianne S., PhD, & Associates, Huntington, LI 516-424-5705 "NYS licensed psychologusts serving adults, adolescents & children-.

♀ • ♂♂ Passages Counseling Center, 3680 Rte 112, Coram; 11727-4133 Ronkonkoma & Moriches locations. 516-698-9222 "NYS Licensed Agency; relationships; alcohol & drug abuse; gay/lesbian support groups. Medicaid, most insurance, sliding scale fees."

♀ • Rubinstein, Joan, M.D., 640 Belle Terre Rd, Bldg E, Port Jefferson; 11777 516-331-0715 Fax 516-331-1775

♀ • Saegert, Linda, Psychotherapist, 516-825-2289

♀ • Schlesinger, Jay, PhD, 13 North Dorado Circle, Hauppauge; 11788 / 1919 Middle Country Rd, Centerreach 516-582-2188 Licensed psychologist.

♀ ○ Weene, Kenneth A., Ph.D., 85 Cold Spring Rd, Syosset; 11791 516-496-8023 "Group, individual, relationship therapy."

Manhattan

♀ ○ Asnien, Carolyn, MA, Upper West Side 212-749-4171 "Psychotherapy: individuals & couples."

♀ • ♂ Beckham, Dixie, CSW, ACSW, Chelsea Psychotherapy Associates, 80 8th Ave #1305; 10011 212-206-0045

♀ • (♂) Bisexual Counseling Service, 599 West End Ave #1-A; 10024 212-595-8002 Bi/Gay Infoline.

♀ • Blair, Ralph, 311 E 72nd St #1G; 10021 212-517-3171

♀ • Bloom, Daniel, JD, CSW, 31 W 10th St; 10011 212-674-0404

♀ • (?♂) Borras, Mildred, PhD, 18 E 93rd St; 10128 212-289-0123 Bilingual: Spanish/English

♀ ○ Byrum, Mildred L., Ph.D., 26 W 9th St; 10011 212-674-1091

♀ • Canarelli, Joseph, CSW, 222 E. 5th St #313; 10003 212-529-8940

♀ • Capson, Stephen, Psy.D., 412 6th Ave; 10011 (9th St) 212-769-8299 "Individuals, couples, HIV issues."

♀ • (♂♂) Chelsea Psychotherapy Associates, 80 8th Ave #1305; 10011 212-206-0045 "Individual, couple & group therapy."

♀ • Clarke, Judith N., MSW, ACSW, BCD, 27 W 8th St; 10011 212-254-7256 "NYS certified; sliding scale fees. Specializing in individual & couples work."

♀ • ♂ Coss, Clare, CSW, 212-662-4609 "Individual & couple counseling. Insurance reimbursable."

♀ • Davidson, Nancy S., PsyD, 168 5th Ave, 2nd flr; 10011 212-502-0170

♀ • (♂♂) Davies, Ann C., CSW, 315 Central Park W #2N (at 91st St) 212-873-3422 "12 step, recovery work; menopausal women's midlife issues."

♀ • Driscoll, Robert, CSW, 8 Stuyvesant Oval; 10009 212-228-2745

♀ • Eden, Carl, CSW, CAC, 80 Charles St #5W; 10014 212-929-7178 "Experienced with Dependency, Trans-gender; HIV, Creative Blocks. Individual & couple work. Free consult."

♀ • Feller, Deborah, ACSW, CSW, NCAC II, 26 W 9th St #2D; 10011 212-979-2979

♀ ○ Felshin, Elaine, Ph.D., W. 56th St 212-533-4092 "Certified & licensed psychologist; Supervisor: Institute for Human Identity."

♀ ○ Fontanella, Robert, CSW, 43 W 12th St; 10011 212-741-2739

♀ • Frankel, Susan I., CSW, BCD, 710 West End Ave #PHA; 10025-6808 212-866-5756

♀ ○ Gair, Susan, MSW, CSW, 315 Central Park West; 10024 212-799-5436

♀ • ♂♂ Gay Center for Counseling & Psychotherapy, 31 Washington Sq W, Penthouse E; 10011 212-780-9400

♂ • Gay Men's Psychotherapy Referral Service, Locations in NYC Metropolitan area. 212-388-2738 "Individual, couple & group therapy."

♀ • Gay Psychological Services, 412 Ave Americas; 10011 212-265-1974

♀ • Gibbons, William G., ME.D., CAC, PO Box 8584, JAF Station; 10016 212-332-9897

♀ • ♂ Giorgianni, Paul, CSW, 165 E 32nd St; 10016 212-532-2599

♀ ○ (♂) Goldberg, Jonathan, Ph.D., 342 W 85th St #1A; 10024 212-496-0535 "Long-term analytic cases only."

♀ • ♂ Gotham Psychotherapy Associates, East & West Side locations 212-903-4033 "Specializing in lesbian/gay lifestyles."

♀ ○ Gottlieb, Andrew R., RMT, CSW, 80 E 11th St; 10003 718-624-0263

♀ ○♂♂ Graham, Lorna, 212-749-6043 "Counseling, Rieki; crystal healing; meditation taught."

♀ ○ Graham, Sally, Ph.D., 24 E 12th St #601; 10003 212-807-0543; 212-803-5412; "Medicaid, Medicare, & insurance accepted. HIV welcome."

♀ • Griffin, David Lindsey, CSW, CAC, 333 W 57th St #102; 10019 212-582-1881

♀ • ♂♂ Horowitz, Richard, CSW, CAC, 45 Christopher St #17-F; 10014 212-780-9400

♀ • (♂♂) Isaacs, Robert, CSW, 115 Washington Place #4; 10014 212-229-0090 "Individual, couple, group therapy; sliding fee; insurance accepted."

♀ • Jarratt, Kent D., ACSW, 26 W. 9th St #1D; 10011 212-674-7370 "Specialist in addictions; sexual compulsivity; certified hypnotherapist."

♀ • ♂ Jones, Linda, CSW, ACSW, 80 E 11th St #1003; 10003 212-982-9232; 201-858-4743; "Couples, individuals, & family therapy. Sliding scale. NYS Certified."

♀ ○ ♂ Kassan, Lee D., MA, 56 7th Ave #12H; 10011 212-989-3613

♂ • Kerner, Bruce, Psy.D., 230 Park Ave #315; 10169 212-682-1288 "Licensed psychologist; individual & group therapy. Free consultation."

♀ • Koppel, Mark A., Ph.D., 172 W 79th St; 10024 212-362-7027; Purdys Rd, Purdys, NY 10578 (Westchester) (914) 277-7809

♀ ○ (?♂) Lathrop, Brian A., NCPsy. A., 63 Downing St #4A; 10014 212-727-9797 By appointment.

♀ • Lesko, Kathryn, PhD, 24 E 12th St #704B; 10003-4474 212-243-7825 "Licensed psychologist. Individuals, couples, groups, HIV issues; insurance reimbursable."

♀ • ♂ Liechenstein, Rev Joyce, PhD, 444 E 20th St #7H; 10009 212-673-4427

♀ • Manhattan Psychotherapy, 20 W. 72nd St #1103; 10023 212-724-8767

♀ • ♂ Marks, Linda Nathan, 212-529-7579

♀ ○ Marschall, Rick, CSW, CAC, 161 W 16th St; 10011 212-620-7155

♀ ○ McCoul, Maryann D., MA, CAS, 200 W 18th St #3F; 10011 212-645-2113 "Psychotherapist; sliding scale fees."

♀ • McGovern, Maureen, MSW, 247 W 15th St; 10011 212-929-1498 "Psychotherapist/Psychodramatist. Sliding scale; most insurance accepted."

NY: New York City Area
Counseling: Private

335
USA

New York City Area: NY
Erotica

♂ • Melillo, Peter A., CSW, ACSW, 80 8th Ave #1305 718-446-6644 "Sliding fee scale; most insurance."

♀ • Meyers, Joyce Z., CSW, Village/Soho area. 212-229-0335 "Traditional & spiritual approach to healing; individuals, couples, groups; incest recovery groups."

♀ • **Mind-BodyWork, 917-876-4969 (voice beeper) "Deep tissue & full-body stress reduction."**

♀ • **Nussdorf, Gerrie, Ph.D., Greenwich Village 212-691-1818 "Licensed psychologist; individual & couple; substance abuse; insurance reimbursable."**

♀ • ♂♂ Page, Ken, CSW, 853 Broadway #1717; 10003 212-420-0394 "Psychotherapy, including 12-Step Recovery Work, Spirituality, & Body/Mind Therapy."

♀ • **Pantaleo, Michael, CSW, CAC, 222 W 14th St #3C; 10011 212-691-2312**

T • **Patti, Vincent-John, ACSW, 226 E 13th St #3; 10003 212-475-3623 "Psychotherapist who also specializes in working supportively with the S/M-Leather Community."**

♀ • ♂ **Pearl, Alan, MD, 135 W 70th St; 10023 212-724-5188**

♀ • ♂♂ Pincus, Florence Volkman, 311 1/2 W 20th St; 10011 212-924-7104

♀ ○ Quadland, Michael C., Ph.D., 10 Downing St #1P; 10014-4737 212-691-1617; 203-355-3538 (Sherman, CT); "Certified sex therapist & licensed psychotherapist."

♂ ○ Rahmani, Kamran, MD, 61 W. 9th St #1A; 10011 212-666-1864 "Psychotherapy with Gay/Lesbian people."

♀ • Raphael, Jerry, Ph.D., Greenwich Village: 212-529-4563 "Individual & couple psychotherapy for Gay Men & Lesbian Women."

♀ • ♂ Roberts, Lynne, CSW, ACSW, 212-749-1596

♀ • (?♂) Romano, G. Nino, CSW, MSW, 153 Waverly Place #1110; 10014 914-242-2896 "New growth through self-discovery. Sliding scale. Also Mid-Hudson location."

♀ • (♂) Ruderman, Jerome M., JD, MS, 142 West End Ave #22M; 10023 212-769-2097; 212-877-7344

♀ ○ **Scherma, Robert F., Psy.D., 412 Ave of Americas #500; 10011 (W. 9th St) 212-969-0988 "Psychotherapy for gay, lesbian, bisexual community. Insurance reimbursable."**

♀ ○ ♂ Schmidt, Beverly A., RCSW, 145 4th Ave, Apt 3M; 10003; and East Hampton (Springs), L.I. 212-677-0551; 516-329-0474; Flexible schedule: weekend hours available in East Hampton.

♀ • ♂ Semler, Conrad S., ACSW, CSW, 301 E 22nd St; 10010 212-260-2590 "Individual psychotherapy; couple counseling."

♀ • (♂♂) Shaw, Nanette, Ph.D., 212-505-7869; 516-725-5945; "Individuals, couples, groups."

♀ • ♂♂ Shaw, Nanette, PhD, 310 E 12th St; 10003 212-505-7869; 516-725-5945

♀ • ♂♂ **Shernoff, Michael, CSW, ACSW, 80 8th Ave #1305; 10011 212-675-9563 "Individual, couple, group & family therapy; supervision of therapists."**

♀ • Silverstein, Charles, Ph.D., 233 W 83rd St; 10024 212-799-8574

♀ • (♂) Steinhorn, Audrey, 125 Riverside Dr; 10024 212-877-5486

♀ ○ (♂) **Stevens, Lynne, CSW, BCD, 159 W 95th St; 10025 212-222-9563**

♀ • ♂ Vinson, Joyce, CSW, 31 W. 11th St, NYC (212) 675-7429; and 124 Main St, Village Green Prof Bldg, Huntington; 11746 516-689-9456

♀ • ♂♂ Williams, Mark, Ph.D., 200 Park Ave S #916; 10003 212-254-0529; 212-691-6161 eves

♀ • **Wind, Mark N., MA, CAC, CSAC, NCAC II, 10 W 15th St #609; 10011-6821 212-929-4390**

♀ • **Witchel, Joy E., CSW, CAC, Greenwich Village Office 212-477-8258**

♀ • ♂♂ Women's Therapy Resources, 300 Mercer St #3M; 10003 212-533-0081 "Individual, couple, group therapy."

Queens

♀ ○ Eisenberg, Edith, ACSW, 110-21 73rd Rd, Forest Hills; 11375 718-263-0779

♀ • Grabowski, Robert, RCSW, ACSW, 109-23 71st Rd 718-261-1346 Evening appointments available. "Psychotherapist; interpersonal approach. Board Certified Diplomate."

♀ • **Keegan, Betty, 114-06 Queens Blvd, Forest Hills 718-335-2622**

♀ ○ Lippman, Susan, CSW, Jackson Heights 718-639-5969 "Quality supervision for psychotherapists; reasonable fees."

♀ ○ ♂ Metamorphosis, PO Box 6260, Long Island City; 11106-0260 718-728-4615 "Psychotherapy, counseling, evaluations, referrals. Individual, family & group support. By appointment only."

Staten Island

♀ • Noone, Kenneth, CSW, CAC, 718-720-3970

♀ • Verhey, Gregory, MSW, CSW, 1346 Victory Blvd, Staten Island; 10301 718-447-3473

Rockland, Westchester, Dutchess, Orange Counties

♀ • Rosa, Lydia E., CSW, 922 Harmon Dr, Larchmont; 10538-1800 914-834-2128

Dentists

Manhattan

♀ • ♂♂ DeBonis, William B, DDS, 200 W 57th St #1402; 10019 212-333-2650

♀ • Drs Sengos, Rosenberg & Associates, 45 W 10th St; 10011 212-982-5883

♀ • ♂ Iott, Michael C., DDS, PC, 487 3rd Ave; 10016 212-686-2907

♀ • **Mandarine, Vincent, DDS, 315 8th Ave; 10001 (25th St) 212-243-3989**

♀ • **Wolf, John W., DDS, PC, 55 W 21st St #4th Fl; 10010-6809 212-366-5900 Mon-Sat 8am-8pm.**

Editing/Writing Services

♀ • (?♂) Yaa Asantewaa, Eva, PO Box 1133; 10009-9998 212-505-0426 "Writer; editor; writing workshops."

Employment Services

♀ • ♂♂ **Allante Personnel Agency, 70-A Greenwich Ave, Ste #120; 10011 212-229-0600**

Entertainment-Related Services (see also Music, Organizations/Resources: Performing

♀ ○ The Kenny Dash Revue, Box 163, Bethpage; 11714 718-490-3578; 718-343-3420; 516-931-8502

♀ • **OUTmedia, 123 Park Place, Brooklyn; 11217 718-789-1776 Fax 718-622-6848 "Personal management agency for lesbian/gay performing arts & entertainment related services."**

Erotica (Printed, Visual, Equipment)

Long Island

♂ ○ Adult Shop, 6083 Sunrise Hwy, Holbrook; 11741 516-472-9519

♀ ○ (?⚲) Adult Videos & More, 146A West Sunrise Hwy, Lindenhurst; 11757 516-226-7253 Mon-Thu 9am-11pm; Fri & Sat to mdnt; Sun 2-10pm.

♂ • ♂ Cupid's Video Boutique, 786 Grand Blvd, Deer Park; 11729 516-586-0066

♂ • ♂♂ Heaven Sent Me, 108 Cain Dr, Brentwood; 11717 516-434-4777 24 hrs.
* *Heaven Sent Me advertisement page 337*

♀ ○ Video Novelty, 3316 Rte 112, Medford; 11763 516-736-3643

Manhattan

♀ ○ ♂ Adult Entertainment Center, 488 8th Ave; 10001 212-947-1590

♂ • Ann Street Adult Entertainment Center, 21 Ann St; 10038 212-267-9760
* *Ann Street Adult Entertainment Center advertisement page 336*

♀ ○ Badlands Video, 388 West St; 10014 212-255-1110

♂ • Banana Video, 55 W 38th St; 10018 212-768-7965 "All the latest male releases; sales, screening rooms."
* *Banana Video advertisement page 338*

♂ • Christopher Street Bookshop, 500 Hudson St; 10014 212-463-0657 24 hrs. (See display ad inside back cover.)
* *Christopher Street Bookshop advertisement inside back cover*

♀ ○ ♂ Come Again, 353 E 53rd St; 10022 212-308-9394 Mon-Fri 11am-8.30pm; Sat to 7pm. "Woman-owned erotic emporium; toys, leather, adult books, domestic & foreign fetish magazines, bondage items, oils, erotic lingerie to size 48. Video Shop At Home catalog available; book & magazine catalog $4."
* *Come Again advertisement page 336*

♀ ○ ♂ Come Again 2, 50 W 33rd St; 10001 212-268-0387 "We carry short dresses, long slinky dresses, lingerie, thongs, stockings, bondage equipment."

♀ ○ (?⚲) Condomania, 351 Bleecker St; 10014 212-691-9442 11am-11pm; Thu-Sat to mdnt.

♀ ○ Courageous Books, 250 W 42nd St; 10036 212-944-1050

♂ ○ Eros I Cinema, 732 8th Ave; 10036 212-581-4594

♀ ○ Etcetera News, 337 Bleecker St; 10014 212-6757952 "Magazines & videos."

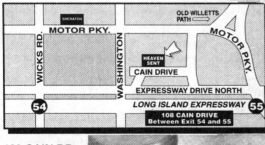

NY: New York City Area

338

New York City Area: NY

Erotica

USA

Food Specialties & Catering

♀ • Eve's Garden, 119 W 57th St #420 (4th flr); 10019 212-757-8651 Mon-Sat noon-7pm. "Sexuality boutique created by women for women. Mail order catalog $3.00."
✦ *Eve's Garden advertisement page 141*

♂ ○ Gaiety Burlesk, 201 W 46th St; 10036 212-221-8868

♀ • Gay Pleasures, 546 Hudson St; 10014 212-255-5756
✦ *Gay Pleasures advertisement page 339*

♀ ○ Harmony Video, 139 Christopher St; 10014 212-366-9059

♂ ○ International Film & Video, 453 W 47th St; 10036 212-245-8039

♂ • Les Hommes Bookshop, 217 W 80th St, 2nd Flr; 10024
✦ *Les Hommes Bookshop advertisement inside back cover*

♂ ○ New Kings Cinema, 356 W 44th St; 10036 212-582-8714

♀ ○ (?⚢) The Noose, 261 W 19th St; 10011 212-807-1789 *LW*

♀ ○ Peep World Underground, 155 W 33rd St; 10001 212-643-8907

♀ ○ ♿ Pink Pussycat Boutique, 167 W 4th St; 10014 212-243-0077

♀ ○ ♿ Pleasure Chest, 156 7th Ave South; 10014 212-242-2158 1pm-1am. "Erotic specialist store."

♀ ○ Pleasure Palace, 733A 8th Ave; 10036 (46th St) 212-265-5213 24 hrs.

♀ ○ Purple Passion, 242 W 16th St; 10011 212-807-0486 "Fetish clothing & accessories."

♀ ○ Serendib Video, Inc, 755 6th Ave; 10010 212-229-1316

♂ ○ ♿ Seventh Ave Gifts & Video, 113 7th Ave S.; 10014 212-741-1161 Noon-mdnt.

♂ ○ Seventh Avenue Tobacco, 130 7th Ave South; 10014 212-242-5067 Noon-mdnt.

♂ • Show Palace, 672 8th Ave; 10036 212-944-7867
✦ *Show Palace advertisement page 339*

♀ ○ Two-Fifty Book Center, 250 W 42nd St; 10036 212-354-1513

♂ ○ Unicorn, 277-C W 22nd St; 10011 212-924-2921
✦ *Unicorn advertisement page 339*

♀ ○ (♿) Visual Video, 725 6th Ave; 10010 (23rd/24th St) 212-620-7862

♂ • Vital Video, 119 Christopher St; 10014 212-627-5700 9am-4am; Fri & Sat 24 hrs.

♀ ○ World of Video, 178-80 7th Ave S; 10014 212-691-1281 "Video only; no books."

♀ ○ Xtasy Down Under Male Emporium, 691 8th Ave; 10036 212-262-0178 24 hrs.

Queens

♀ ○ Dee Two Video, Inc., 86-10 Roosevelt Ave, Jackson Heights; 11372 718-507-7207

Florists (see also Gardening)

Manhattan

♀ • ♿ The Gay Rose, 96 Greenwich Ave; 10011 212-691-8113

♀ • Grey-Knowles Flowers Ltd., 218 E 27th St; 10016 212-LE2-7661

♀ • Hatleberg/DeCastro Orchids, 43 8th Ave; 10014 (2 blocks south of 14th St) 212-463-9577 By appointment.

♀ • McManus Florist, 69 8th Ave; 10014 212-243-2958; 800-477-3939; "Distinctive floral designs; silk & fresh."

Food Specialties, Catering (see also Party/Event Services)

♀ • Crystal Caterers, PO Box 536, Bronx; 10475 800-231-1093

Funding: Endowment, Fundraising, Scholarship

⚥ ☆ The Heyday Company, 149 5th Ave, 12th flr; 10010 212-353-2553 Fax 212-353-2288 Consultatio.

⚥ ★ Stonewall Community Foundation, c/o Jim Pepper, 250 W 89th St #5F; 10024 212-353-2552

⚥ Stonewall Community Foundation, 825 3rd Ave #3315; 10022 212-685-1586

Funeral Directors/Cemetaries/Mausoleums

⚥ ○ (♿) Crestwood Memorial Chapel, Inc, 33 Spring St; 10012 212-431-6712

♀ ○ **David Funeral Home, Inc, 718-729-3400 "Serving all five boroughs. Pre-need consultation available."**

Gardening Services, Landscaping, Supplies & Decoration

♂ ○ Pompeian Studios, 90 Rockledge Rd, Bronxville; 10708 914-337-5595; 800-457-5595; Fax 914-337-5661 "Garden statuary (catalog $10) & wrought iron furniture (free brochure)."

Gifts, Cards, Pride & Promotional Items

Brooklyn

♀ ○ ♿ Scribbles, 115 7th Ave, Brooklyn; 11215 718-783-1706

Fire Island

♀ ○ Melbamar, Harbor Walk, Fire Island Pines 516-597-6441

Manhattan

♀ ○ Alternate Card Shop, 85 Christopher St; 10014 212-645-8966

♂ ○ Candle Shop, 118 Christopher St; 10014 212-989-0148 "Beeswax, oil lamps, scented candles, etc."

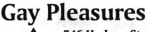

Gifts, Cards, Pride & Novelty Items
Manhattan

♀ • Cardeology, 452 Amsterdam Ave; 10024 (81/82 Sts) 212-873-2491 "Cards, gifts, balloons."

♀ • Crystal Gardens, 21 Greenwich Ave; 10014 212-366-1965 "Crystals, gifts, tapes, books, etc."

♀ • (&) Exotiqa, 284 Columbus Ave; 10023 212-721-4394 10am-10pm. "International arts & crafts."

♀ • & Greetings, 45 Christopher St; 10014 212-242-0424 11am-11pm. "Outrageous, artistic, & erotic gay cards, gifts, novelties."

♀ ○ Lucy Anna, 502 Hudson St; 10014 212-645-9463 "Folk art gifts & New Age products."

♀ • Rainbows & Triangles, 192 8th Ave; 10011 212-627-2166

♀ • Singing Telegram - Anytime, 244 W 22nd St; 10011 212-929-8609

Graphic Design/Typesetting (see also Art; Printing)

♀ • (&) ALP Horizons—Graphic Design Services, PO Box 740673, Rego Park; 11374 718-275-8868 Fax 718-275-5717

♀ • (&) Bence, Sandra, 677 West End Ave; 10025 212-866-2593 "Full service desktop publishing."

♀ • Charisma Graphics, 276 5th Ave #805; 10001-4509 212-696-1750 Fax 212-696-1751

♀ • Fotografia Graphics, 21 Howard St; 10013 212-966-0498

♀ • (?&) Graphic Arts Studio, 718-624-4680 "Affordable professional graphic design."

♀ • **Type-Right, Inc., 370 Lexington Ave #1511; 10017 212-490-9523 "Word processing, desktop publishing, resumes; IBM & Mac."**

Grooming Services

♀ • Zipper at 227, 227 E 56th St, 3rd flr; 10022-3754 212-754-2270 "Hair, facial, maicure, pedicure, waxing."

Brooklyn

♀ ○ Mannarino, Billie, Manhattan & Brooklyn. 212-388-2687; 718-998-9608; "Electrolysis: disposable probes only. Facials; waxing; massages. Reasonably priced."

Manhattan

♂ • Hay, Kenneth, 420 W 24th St Apt 1E; 10011-1333 212-727-1850 "Affordable electrolysis: Village location."

♀ ○ Yorkville Electrolysis, 212-427-2420 Free consultation; by appointment only.

Health Care (see also AIDS Services)
Brooklyn

♀ Black Women's Health Project, PO Box 401037, Brooklyn; 11240 212-439-8749

♀ • & Fries, Isabelle S., DC, 209 12th St, Brooklyn; 11215 718-788-3513

♀ • (?&) Hennessey, N. Patrick, MD, 142 Joralemon St, Brooklyn Hts 718-797-3333 "Dermatology; dermatologic surgery; sexually transmitted diseases."

♀ ○ **Salvati, Steven W., MD, 914 Bay Ridge Pkway, Brooklyn; 11228 718-748-7150 "Internal medicine/HIV specialist; testing, counseling, & treatment."**

Long Island

♀ ○ & Banks, Scott J., DC, 233 E Main St, Huntington; 11743 516-271-0770

♀ ○ Boffert, Joyce, DC, 516-496-0802

♀ ☆ Health House: A Women's Resource Center, Inc., 190 Blydenburg Rd, Islandia; 11722 516-342-9401

Manhattan

♀ • & Alpert, Michelle, DO, 89 5th Ave #604; 10003 212-675-9343 "Osteopathic physician; general & family medicine, holistic & traditional."

♀ ○ && Bihari, Bernard, MD, 29 W 15th St, Ste L; 10011 212-929-4196

♀ ○ & **Brauner, Gary J., MD, 125 E 63rd St; 10021 212-421-5080**
✦ **Brauner, Gary J., MD advertisement page 341**

♀ ○ & Brook, Daniel D., MD, 185 West End Ave #1N; 10023 212-580-8680

♂ ★ Columbia University Gay Health Advocacy Project, 400 John Jay Hall; 10027 212-854-2878 "Columbia University affiliated only."

♂ ★ Community Health Project, 208 W 13th St; 10011 212-675-3559

♀ ○ Deutchman, Gary, DC, 52 W 86th St; 10024 212-874-9033

♀ ○ Empire Chiropractic, 350 5th Ave; 10118 212-563-2966

♀ ○ && Fontana, Larry, MD, 36 E 23rd St 10th Flr; 10010 212-420-1303

♀ ○ Fonville, T. W., MD, 29 5th #1A; 10003 212-674-1020

♀ • Franchino, Charles A., DC, 30 5th Ave; 10011 212-673-4331

♂ • & **Friedman, Loretta T., RN, DC, 28 E 10th St #1J; 10003 212-475-7902 Fax 212-475-7905**

♀ • & Gertel, Rose, DC, 2 5th Ave #5; 10011 212-353-1100

♀ • && Goldberg, Edward S., MD, 121 E 60th St; 10022 (Park Ave) 212-980-8800 "Internal medicine, gastroenterology, nutrition."

♀ • & Greenberg, Elizabeth, DC, 89 5th Ave #604; 10003 212-627-2660

♀ ☆ **Guttman Breast Diagnostic Institute, 55 5th Ave; 10003 212-463-8733**

♀ • Heldeman, Marvin D., MD, 42 W 72nd St; 10023 212-873-0909 "Dermatology & venereal disease; see ad."

♀ • **Hellman, Ronald E., MD, 129 Barrow St Apt GA; 10014 212-255-5209**

♀ • (?&) **Hennessey, N. Patrick, MD, 650 1st Ave; 10016 212-683-6470 "Dermatology; dermatologic surgery; sexually transmitted diseases."**

♀ ○ && Horowitz, Mark E., M.D., 67 Broad St; 10004 212-482-2400

♀ • James, Frederick, DC, 853 Broadway #1717; 10003 212-473-2273 "Chiropractic care & massage therapy."

♂ • **Kessler, Debra, DC, 10 Downing St #IU; 10014 212-645-8151 "Holistic Chiropractic; traditional & low force techniques; nutritional counseling."**

♂ • Keyes, Craig W., MD / Chieffe, Russell A., RPAC, 200 E 74th St; 10021 212-737-3620 "General internal medical, HIV care."

♀ ○ && Konig, Michael, Ph.D., DC, 59 W 19th St #4D; 10011-4202 212-645-1961

♀ ★ (?&) Lesbian Health Project, 125 Worth St Box 67; 10013 / New York City Department of Health, Office of Gay & Lesbian Health Concerns 212-788-4310 "Education & referrals for lesbian & bisexual women."

♂ • (&&) Leveillee, Thomas H., DC, 210 5th Ave #7fl; 10011 212-685-5857

NY: New York City Area
Health Care

341
USA

New York City Area: NY
Health Care

♀ ○ Lopez, Wanda E., DC, 120 E 56th St #930; 10022-3607 212-319-3433

♀ ○ **Manhattan Podiatry Associates, PC, 133 E 54th St; 10022 212-759-9090 and 67 Broad St; 10004 785-1717**

♀ ○ Margolin, Steven, DC, 14 E 34th St, 2nd Flr; 10016 212-725-8626

♀ ○ ♂♂ Marks-Nelson, Harriet, BSN, RN, 914-997-8957 "Gerontologist; PRI exams; Memory Consultant."

♂ ● Martin, Craig A., DC, 250 W 57th St #1132; 10107 212-307-7669 "Chiropractor."

♀ ○ MCA Medical Claims Assistance Co, Inc., 213 20th St, Brooklyn; 11232 718-788-0500; 800-232-8090; Fax 718-788-6473 Mon-Thu 10am-5pm.
◆ *MCA Medical Claims Assistance Co, Inc. advertisement page 127*

♀ ● ♂♂ **Medical & Dental Associates, 141 5th Ave #2FL; 10010-7105 212-533-2400 Fax 212-533-6607**

♂ ★♂♂ New York City Department of Health, Office of Gay & Lesbian Health Concerns, 125 Worth St Box 67; 10013 212-788-4310 Fax 212-788-5243 "Improving the public health of lesbian, gay & bisexual New Yorkers through efforts in policy, planning, & education."

♂ ★ (?♂) Provider Education Project, 125 Worth St Box 67; 10013 / New York City Department of Health, Office of Gay & Lesbian Health Concerns 212-788-4399 "Training & consultation for health care providers on lesbian, gay & bisexual issues."

T ● Schooler, C.P, MD, 425 W 23rd St; 10011 212-243-1224 "Services include pre-operative treatment for transsexuals."

♀ ★ ♂ St Marks Women's Health Collective, PO Box A711; 10163-0711 Clinic at 9 2nd Ave. 212-228-7482

♂ ● ♂ Stefanick, Gary F., DC, 49 W 12th St #1E; 10011 212-243-3080

♂ ● Unger, Kenneth W., MD, 12A Sheridan Square; 10014 212-929-2370 Fax 212-675-1191

♀ ● ♂♂ Waitkevicz, Joan, MD, 13 E 15th St; 10003 212-645-4790 "Internist; special interests in lesbian/gay health issues & geriatrics. Spanish spoken. Medicare participating."

♂ ● Wiebersch, D. Sean, MA, CHy, 250 W 57th St #1132; 10107 212-307-7669 "Sex counseling & hypnosis."

♀ ☆ (?♂) Women's Health Action Mobilization (WHAM!), PO Box 733; 10009 212-560-7177 *The Urban Herbalist.*

♂ ☆ Youth Health Services, 1918 1st Ave, Draper Hall, 14th flr; 10029 212-230-7408

Queens

♀ ● ♂♂ Bay Meadows Chiropractic, Joyce Boffert, DC, 58-47 Francis Lewis Blvd, Bayside; 11364 718-428-3388

Staten Island

♀ ● ♂ May, Debra L., DC, 1055 Hylan Blvd, Staten Island; 10305 718-44-SPINE "Traditional & non-force techniques; acute & chronic pain; specializing in headaches."

Rockland, Westchester, Dutchess, Orange Counties

♀ ○ (♂♂) Elliott, Holly E, DC, Chiropractor, Suite 1A, 12 Old Mamaroneck Rd, White Plains; 10605; also Somers Chiropractic Center, Rte 202, Somers; 10589 914-948-6677

♀ ○ Posillico, Albert J., DC, 280 Dobbs Ferry Road, White Plains; 10607 914-949-3734

♀ ○ ♂♂ Somers Chiropractic Center, Route 202, Somers; 10589 914-276-BACK; 914-276-2179

♂ • ♿ Sutter, Madge, MS, CACHt, White Plains 914-949-5253; 800-484-7243-8470 out of area; "Clinical Hypnotherapy; International Medical & Death Hypnotherapy Assoc.; Alternatives for Creative Transitions."

Health Clubs, Gyms, Saunas

Manhattan

♀ • ♿ American Fitness Center, 128 8th Ave; 10011 (16th St) 212-627-0065 Fax 212-627-1847 6am-mdnt.

♂ • Chelsea Gym, 267 W 17th St; 10011 212-255-1150

♀ • Dolce, Tony, 201-963-8196 "Body building programs. Sliding scale for HIV/AIDS clients."

♀ • East Side Club, 227 E 56th St; 10022 212-753-2222 24 hrs.

♀ • (?♿) Fire Sign Fitness, Personal training 212-645-5234

♀ • ○ Studio Fitness, 51 W 14th St #2F; 10011 212-691-6144

♂ • Wall Street Sauna, 1 Maiden Lane; 10038 212-233-8900 Mon-Fri 11am-8am; San noon-6pm.

♂ West Side Club, 27 W 20th St, 2nd floor; 10010 212-691-2700

Queens

♂ ○ ♿ **Northern Sauna & Health Club, 33-61 Farrington St, Flushing; 11354 718-445-9775 Noon-mdnt.**

Home & Building: Cleaning, Repair, General Contractors

♀ ○ **Apple Restoration & Waterproofing, 132 Bedford Ave, Brooklyn; 11211 718-599-5055 Fax 718-599-3588**

♀ • Climbing The Walls, 914-337-3279 "Professional paperhanging."

♀ ○ Corporate Building Services, 3 Avon Ave, Farmingville; 11738 516-928-0749

♀ • Gay Lady Contractor, 212-475-4363 "Electrical, carpentry, painting, plumbing."

♀ ○ JNL Commercial Cleaning, 84 Daly Rd, East Northport; 11731 516-462-2643

♀ ○ Kwality Master Cleaners, 8 Main St, Hastings on Hudson; 10706 914-478-7200 Tue-Sat 10am-5pm. "Restoration services (fire, smoke, odor, water); floor refinishing; dry cleaning, oriental rugs & W.W. carpet cleaning; general maintainance & cleaning services."

♀ • Painters Alliance, 34-57 82nd St #4E, Jackson Heights; 11372 718-457-5740 "Interior painting."

♀ • **Well Hung Paperhanging, Manhattan only. 212-744-6606**

Hypnotherapy

♀ • Jarratt, Kent D., ACSW, 26 W. 9th St #1D; 10011 212-674-7370 "Specialist in addictions; sexual compulsivity; certified hypnotherapist."

♂ ○ ♿ Sutter, Madge, MS, CACHt, 914-949-5253; 800-484-7243-8470 out of area; "Clinical Hypnotherapy; International Medical & Death Hypnotherapy Assoc.; Alternatives for Creative Transitions."

Insurance (see also Insurance Benefits/Viaticals)

♀ ○ Bielat & Bielat, Inc., 19 W 44th St; 10036 212-575-1277 Fax 212-575-1279

♀ ○ Casswood Insurance Agency, Ltd, 227 E 56th St #201; 10022 212-593-4200

♀ ○ (♿) Cohrt, Connie, CLU, ChFC, Prof. Comp. Planners, 261 Madison Ave #400; 10016 212-697-1355

♀ • **Granville, Bernard, 124 W 79th St; 10024 212-580-9724 Fax 212-580-8895 "A full-service broker: Life/Property, Personal/Business, Health/Disability; Individual/Groups."**
◆ *Granville, Bernard advertisement page 342*

♂ • MM Associates, 718-846-5168

Insurance Benefits/Viaticals

♀ ○ Life Entitlements Corporation, 4 World Trade Center #5270; 10048 800-420-1420 "A viatical settlements company."

Interior Design

♀ • Center Courte Designs, 1517 E 59th St, Brooklyn; 11234 718-763-8896; 212-529-2733; "Complete decorating service."

♂ ○ Edward Cohen, Inc., 350 E 54th St #4D; 10022 212-371-1554 "Small spaces a speciality."

Jewelry

♂ • Gallery Eclectic, 43 Greenwich Ave; 10014 212-924-4314

♂ • Halloran, Ellen M., PO Box 825 Village Stn; 10014 212-982-0098 By appointment only. "Specializing in rings for partners."

♀ • ♿ Out of Our Drawers, 184 7th Ave S; 10014 212-929-4473 "Ear piercing: your choice with or without pain!"

♀ • **Stick, Stone & Bone, 111 Christopher St; 10014 212-807-7024**

♀ • Vita Mfg, 274 Astor Dr, Sayville; 11782 516-563-2553 "Costume jewelry: manufacturing & wholesale."

Legal Services & Resources

Brooklyn

♀ • (♿) Herman, Lori Sue, 718-338-6018

♀ ○ **Law Offices of Ruth Gursky & Barbara Odwak, 32 Court St, Brooklyn; 11201 718-875-1611**

♀ • Salen, Elizabeth, Esq, 294 Windsor Place, Brooklyn; 11218 718-499-5477

Long Island

♀ • ♿ Frankel, Bryan, Esq, 1 Grant Ave, Islip; 11751 516-581-1111

♀ • ♿♿ **Konits & Uveges, PC, 300 Rabro Dr #142, Hauppauge; 11788 516-234-3232 Fax 516-234-3757**
♀ ○ Schwartz, Alan J., 100 Garden City Plaza, Garden City; 11530-3208 516-248-6311 Fax 516-742-4106

♀ ○ **Simenowitz, Steven H, 1 Suffolk Sq, Islandia; 11722-1534 516-232-3117**

♀ • (?♿) **Stone, Judith Ellen, Esq, 2819 Harbor Rd, Merrick; 11566 516-623-0897 Fax 516-867-7936**

Manhattan & New York City Area

♀ ○ Altman, Norman, 122 E 42nd St #1700; 10017 212-551-1032

♂ American Civil Liberties Union (ACLU), 132 W 43rd St; 10036 212-944-9800

♀ • ♿ Bing, Steven E., 1 Madison Ave; 10010 212-447-0200

NY: New York City Area
343
New York City Area : NY
Legal
USA
Meeting/Contact Services

♀ • ♂♂ Bohn, Ted, PO Box 317 Planetarium Stn; 10024 212-787-0319 "Attorney at Law, licensed to practice in NY, NJ, PA, VT, WV."

♀ Center for Consitutional Rights, 666 Broadway; 10012 212-614-6464

♂ ★ (?♂) The Center Mediation Service, 208 W 13th St; 10011 212-713-5089

♀ ○ Darvin, Iris M., Esq, 40 E 42nd St; 10165 212-922-1410

♂ • (?♂) Dworkin, Eric J., 60 E 8th St #33J; 10003 212-388-0605 "Immigration."

♂ • (♂) Greenbaum, Richard, 15 W 84th St; 10024 212-799-2983

♀ • ♂ Jeselsohn, Paul, Esq, 799 Broadway #542; 10003 212-477-2400

♂ ★ ♂ Lambda Legal Defense & Education Fund (LLDEF), Inc, 666 Broadway #1200; 10012-2317 212-995-8585 Fax 212-995-2306 "Legal assistance in matters of interest to lesbian/gay people as a group: test case situations only. Intake service for referrals & information available. Volunteers welcome: please contact Volunteer Coordinator for further information."

♀ • (?♂) Lavery, Michael J., 106 Perry St; 10014 212-691-2356 "General criminal & civil practise (excluding matrimonial & personal injury)."

♀ Lesbian & Gay Immigration Rights Task Force, Inc. (LGIRTF), PO Box 7741; 10116-7741 212-802-7264 lgirtf @ dorsai.org

♂ ★ Lesbian & Gay Law Association of Greater New York (LeGal-GNY), 799 Broadway #340; 10003-6811 212-353-9118; 212-459-4873 (lawyer referral service); Pub Law Notes. "Professional association for Gay & Lesbian Lawyers, Law Students & Legal Workers."

♀ ○ Levine, Rebecca S., 200 E 27th St; 10016 212-683-3645

♀ ○ McCann, Timothy M., 300 Rector Place #8-O; 10280 212-945-4811

✦ McCann, Timothy M. advertisement page 343

♂ • Morrison & Henderson, 15 Park Row #2035; 10038 212-385-0301 "Landlord/tenant; Social Security; criminal defense; family."

♀ • Rabney, Randy E., 90 John St, 7th flr; 10038 212-619-1770

♀ ○ Roven, Janice G., 101 W 23rd St; 10011 212-255-1346

♀ • Silverstein Langer Lipner & Newburgh, 500 5th Ave, Suite 1205; 10110 212-302-5100

♀ • ♂ Sommer, Kenneth A., Esq, 350 5th Ave #7720; 10118 212-967-5383

♀ ○ Stewart, Geoffrey S., 162 Charles St; 10014 212-255-3137

♀ ○ Stewart, Lynne F., 162 Charles St; 10014 212-243-3196

♀ • Teitelbaum, Shelley, 13 1st Ave; 10003 212-473-7080

♀ • Terzian, George Anthony, 500 5th Ave #1205; 10110 212-302-5111

♂ • ♂♂ Tesler, Richard E., Esq., 2109 Broadway #202A; 10023 212-362-6961 "Wills & Real Estate. Your at-home or off hour appointment is easily made."

♀ • ♂ Turkel Forman & Zimmerman, PC, 30 E 40th St; 10016 212-447-7800

♀ • ♂ Weiss, Buell & Bell, 350 5th Ave #1210; 10118 212-967-5710

♀ • ♂♂ Yassky & Lederle, PC, 5 Beekman St #920; 10038-2206 212-732-5153

Queens

♀ ★ Marsh, Tom, 142-22 59th Ave, Flushing; 11355 718-539-1108 "Juris Doctor, Social Security appeals, Notary Public; referrals for wills, immigration & domestic issues. (Consultant; fundraising for private non-profit organizations; political campaigs for women.)'

Lighting

♀ ○ (♂) Say It In Neon, 288 3rd Ave, Brooklyn; 11215-1815 718-625-1481

Mailing Lists

♀ ○ SCS Productions, 244 W 54th St #800; 10019 212-362-3515 "Gay & lesbian friendly businesses USA & Canada."

Massage Therapy (Licensed only)

♂ • (♂♂) Barbara Mitchell, Huntington, LI 516-549-0283 "Medical/Sports/Rehab: Shiatsu; Swedish Massage; Reflexology; Aromatherapy. Women & gay men welcome."

♀ • Chirichella, MaryAnn, 516-876-8468 "Licensed massage therapist. Stress management, meditation & relaxation classes. Westbury."

Meeting/Contact Services, Publications, Talklines

♂ • Brunch Buddies, 41 Union Sqare West #511, New York, NY 10003 Fax 212-924-9695 Women: 1-800-2-FIND-US Ext 1 or (212) 242-7800 Ext 1. Men: 1-800-2-FIND US Ext 2 or (212) 242-7400 Ext 2. HIV+ Men 1-800-2-FIND US Ext 3 or (212) 242-7400 Ext 3. Mon-Fri 7-11pm. "Meeting resource & personal introductions for lesbians, gay men and HIV+ gay men looking for friendship & more serious relationships in the East & Northeast US. See pictures of people before you join."

✦ Brunch Buddies advertisement page 344

NY: New York City Area
Meeting/Contact Services

344
USA

New York City Area : NY
Moving/Transportation/Storage

⚢ ● ManMate, PO Box 901 Ansonia Stn; 10023 800-622-MATE; 212-580-9595 Mon-Fri 7-11pm.; "Personalized introduction service for men interested in friendships or more serious relationships with other men, in NY, NJ, CT, PA & DE since 1985."

✦ *ManMate advertisement page 344*

♀ ★ (?⚧) Mid-Town Lunch Club, PO Box 387; 10028 212-289-1741

♀ ★ (?⚧) Wall Street Lunch Club, PO Box 387; 10028 212-289-1741

♀ ● Womanpagers Networking Club, PO Box 690290, Bronx; 10469-0760 718-515-6936 "Dating, friendship & travel club for Lesbian & Bisexual Women in NY, NY, PA."

Messenger Services

♀ ○ A To Z Couriers Inc, 317 W 13th St; 10014 212-691-4012

♀ ○ **USA Four Star Courier, 94 E 7th St; 10009 212-460-8121 Fax 212-460-8054**

Moving/Transportation/Storage

♀ ○ Ace Van/Zebra Van, 212-254-9289 "Last minute Man & Van. Low rates."

⚢ ○ Adonis Moving & Storage, 425 Central Park West #4A; 10025 212-387-2083

♀ ● All Star Moving & Storage Inc, 318 E 11th St; 10003 212-254-2638

⚢ ● ⚧ Amazon Movers, 240 Lafayette St; 10012 212-343-9415

⚢ ● Joanna Hopkinson Movers, 236 Harrison Ave, Jersey City, NJ 07304 201-434-5309

♀ ○ ⚧ Manhattan Fine Art Storage, 55 Vandam St; 10013 212-757-4700

♀ ○ (?⚧) Manhattan Mini Storage, 212-766-7243 (S-T-O-R-A-G-E) "Ten locations in Manhattan only."

♀ ● **Moving Man Inc, 429 W 127 St; 10027 212-254-8188**
✦ *Moving Man Inc advertisement page 345*

♀ ○ Muller Moving & Storage, Inc., 109 E 2nd St; 10009 800-BIG-VANS (NY State only); 212-674-6631, 677-6685; Fax 212-260-0880 "Local & long distance."

♀ ○ Niva Moving, 800-246-NIVA

♀ ○ **Optimal Moving, Inc., 201 Lincoln Rd, Brooklyn; 11225 718-693-3838; 212-208-0195; 800-649-3088**

♀ ○ Spectrum Mini-Storage, 800-LOCK-SAF E "Self-storage; open 7 days. Free pick-up & delivery. One month free."

NY: New York City Area
Moving/Transportation/Storage

345
USA

New York City Area : NY
Moving/Transportation/Storage

Let This Man Manage Your Next Move

Whether your move is cross-town, cross-country or across the globe, we provide quality moving and storage services for household and corporate moves

(212) 662-4000
Moving Man, Inc, of New York

Agents for Paul Arpin Van Lines

New Age: Occult, Wicca, Alternative Healing

♀ • (?♂) Spirit Crossroads, PO Box 1133; 10009-9998 212-505-0426 "Workshops on spirituality, holistic health, creativity, human potential, abuse recovery. SASE for brochure. Tarot services. Speakers bureau."

Office Supplies (see also Computer)

♀ • Axys Imaging, 160 W 71st St #10-B; 10023 212-595-6917 "Toner cartridges for laser printers & copiers at 40% off list."

Ophthalmologists & Optometrists

♀ • Cotlowitz, Daniel I., 122 Washington Place; 10014 212-242-6592 "Eye examinations; eyeglass prescriptions; contact lens specialist."

✦ *Cotlowitz, Daniel I. advertisement page 341*

Organizations/Resources: Bisexual Focus

Manhattan & New York City Area

♂ ★ BiRequest, PO Box 577 Cooper Stn; 10276-0577 212-714-7714

♂ ★ New York Area Bisexual Network, PO Box 497 Times Square Stn; 10108 212-459-4784 "The cutting edge of the Sexual Evolution."

Organizations/Resources: Business & Professional

Manhattan & New York City Area

♂ AGGL (Art Group For Gay & Lesbian Artists), 324 E 13th St #14; 10003 212-644-4984; 212-243-0510

♂ ★ Association of Lesbian & Gay Faculty, Administrators & Staff at NYU, c/o Henry Wiemhoff, 10 W 76th St #1C; 10023

♂ ★ (?♂) Coalition of Lesbian & Gay City Employees, PO Box 1256; 10008 212-802-4731

♂ Committee on Lesbian & Gay Concerns/NYC NASW, 545 8th Ave 6th flr; 10018

♂ District Council 37 Lesbian & Gay Issues Committee, 125 Barclay St #784; 10007 212-815-7575

♂ ★ ♂♂ FIRE-FLAG/GEMS, (Fire-Fighters Lesbian & Gay), Inc., c/o The Center, 208 W 13th St; 10011 914-762-6261 Fax 914-762-8391

✦ *FIRE-FLAG/GEMS, (Fire-Fighters Lesbian & Gay), Inc. advertisement page 347*

♂ ★ (?♂) Gay & Lesbian Analysts (GALA), PO Box 20293 London Terrace Stn; 10011-9998 212-645-2232

♂ ★ (?♂) Gay & Lesbian Psychiatrists of New York (GLPNY), PO Box 20293 London Terrace Stn; 10011-9998 212-265-5539

♂ ★ Gay Officers Action League (GOAL), PO Box 2038 Canal St Stn; 10013 212-996-8808 Pub *GOAL Gazette*. "Social & support services for law enforcement officers."

♂ ★ H.P. GALA (Housing Police Gay & Lesbian Association), PO Box 312; 10002-9998 212-533-2779

♂ ★ Lesbian & Gay Law Association of Greater New York, PO Box 1899 Grand Central Stn; 10163 212-459-4873 (referral service to Gay/Lesbian lawyers in NY Metro Area.' "Professional association for Gay & Lesbian Lawyers, Law Students & Gay Legal Workers."

♂ ★ ♂ Lesbian & Gay Teachers' Association, NYC, PO Box 021052, Brooklyn; 11202-0023 914-428-9602 (Elissa); 718-596-1864 (Ron; please call before 9.30pm); Meets 1st Wed of month, 6pm, at Lesbian & Gay Community Services Center, 203 W. 13th St. Pub *LGTA Newsletter*.

♂ ★ National Lesbian & Gay Nurses Association, 208 W 13th St; 10011-7799 718-933-1158 (Fax *51) Pub *Lavender Lamps*. "Global celebration of Lesbian & Gay Pride & Protest, planned for June 26, 1994."

♂ ★ New York Advertising & Communications Network, 332 Bleecker St #149; 10014 212-517-0380 Pub *Newsletter*.

♂ ★ (?♂) New York Bankers Group, Inc, PO Box 867; 10274-0867 212-807-9584 x24 Pub *Newsletter/Networking Bulletin*.

♂ ★ (&) OLGAD: The Organization of Lesbian & Gay Architects & Designers, PO Box 927 Old Chelsea Stn; 10113 212-475-7652 "All design fields, preservationists, builders, & students welcome."

♀ Second Thursday Networking Women, 245 8th Ave #1200; 10011 212-517-0180

♂ ★ ♂♂ Stonewall Business Association, PO Box 387; 10028-0007 212-629-1764 "Business & professional group for all individuals & businesses, targeted to strengthen productivity & economic development of its members."

Rockland, Westchester, Dutchess, Orange Counties

♂ ★ Gay & Lesbian Business & Professionals Guild, PO Box 8392, White Plains; 10602-8392 914-633-3472

Organizations/Resources: Disability

Manhattan & New York City Area

♀ ☆ ♂♂ Disabled In Action of Metropolitan New York, PO Box 30954 Port Authority Stn; 10011-0109 718-261-3737 Pub *DIA Activist*.

♂ ★ ♂♂ Education in a Disabled Gay Environment, Inc (E.D.G.E.), PO Box 305 Village Stn; 10014 212-929-7178

Rockland, Westchester, Dutchess, Orange Counties

♂ ★ Westchester Disabled On The Move, 984 N Broadway, Suite L-1, Yonkers; 10701 914-968-4717 "Call for details of monthly meetings."

Organizations/Resources: Education, Anti-Defamation, Anti-Violence, Self-Defense

Manhattan & New York City Area

♀ ☆ Brooklyn Women's Martial Arts/The Center for Anti-Violence Education, 421 5th Ave, Brooklyn; 11215 718-788-1775

♂ CLGRI (Community Lesbian & Gay Rights Institute), 28 E 4th #7W; 10003-7004 212-289-1741

♂ ★ ♂ GLAAD (Gay & Lesbian Alliance Against Defamation), 150 W 26th St #503; 10001 212-807-1700 Fax 212-807-1806 Pub *GLAAD Bulletin*. "GLAAD works for fair, accurate & inclusive images of lesbians, bisexuals, & gay men."

♂ ★ ♂♂ Hetrick-Martin Institute, 2 Astor Place 3rd flr; 10003 212-674-2400 Fax 212-674-8650 "Training & education on HIV/AIDS & issues of sexual orientation; peer education; educational materials."

♀ ☆ (?♂) Karate School for Women, 149 Bleecker St; 10012 212-982-4739

♂ ★ Lesbian Avengers, c/o The Center, 208 W 13th St; 10011 212-967-7711 ext #3204

♂ ★ ♂♂ New York City Gay & Lesbian Anti-Violence Project, 647 Hudson St; 10014 212-807-0197 City-wide Crime Victim Assistance Hotline 24 hrs.

♂ ★ Out Of The Closet Foundation, Inc, PO Box 20084 Cherokee Stn; 10028 212-472-3573

♂ ★ Queer Nation, The Center, 208 W 13th St; 10011 212-260-6156

NY: New York City Area
Organizations: Education

347
USA

New York City Area : NY
Organizations: General

♀ ☆ **Sanctuary for Families**, PO Box 3344; 10008 212-349-6009 Fax 212-349-6810 "Social & legal services for battered women & their children; crisis support group specifically for battered lesbians."

Organizations/Resources: Ethnic, Multicultural
Manhattan & New York City Area

⚥ **African-Ancestral Lesbians United for Societal Change, Inc.**, c/o The Center 208 W. 13th St; 10009 212-359-5459

♀ ★ **Armenian Sisters**, c/o Zaum, 147 W 14th St #13; 10011

♂ ★ **Asians & Friends/New York**, PO Box 3361; 10163 718-488-0630

♀ **Bisexual Women of Color Group**, PO Box 497; 10108 212-459-4784

♀ ★ **BLAGH: Bisexual, Lesbian & Gay Haitians**, mail to BLAGH, PO Box 1302; 10159-1302 718-965-3354

♀ ★&& **Caribbean-identified Lesbian/Gay Alliance**, 100 S Oxford, Brooklyn; 11217 718-797-1218 Pub *CiLGA Newsletter.*

♀ ★ **Clann An Uabhair G.L.S.A.**, PO Box 30024; 10011-0101 718-622-1535 Gay & Lesbian Scottish Association

♂ ★&& **Gay Asian/Pacific Islander Men of NY (GAPIMNY)**, PO Box 1608; 10113 212-727-0965

♂ ★ ♂ **Gay Men of African Descent, Inc.**, 666 Broadway #520; 10012-2317 212-420-0773 Fax 212-982-3321 Pub *GMAD Calendar.* "Social; recreational; consciousness raising."

♂ **Hombres/Latino Gay Men of New York**, PO Box 1103; 10025-1103 212-663-9148

♀ ★ **Irish Lesbian & Gay Organization (ILGO)**, c/o The Center, 208 W 13th St; 10011 212-967-7711 x3078 (ILGO Hotline) Meets 1st Mon of month, 8pm. "Support for Irish & Irish-American Lesbians & Gays in New York."

⚥ ★ **Las Buenas Amigas**, c/o The Center, 208 W 13th St; 10011-7702 201-868-7816; 212-287-8367; 718-622-5889; Pub *Las Buenas Amigas Boletin.* "Latina Lesbian group."

♀ ★ **Latinos & Latinas de Ambiente/NY (LLANY)**, c/o The Center, 208 W 13th St; 10011 718-588-0201 Pub *Arco Iris.*

⚥ **Lesbian & Gay People of Color Steering Committee**, c/o The Center 208 W. 13th St; 10009 212-222-9794; 212-620-7310

♂ ★ (?&) **Men Of All Colors Together/New York (MACT/NY)**, PO Box 1518 Ansonia Stn; 10023 212-330-7678 Pub *MACT/NY Information Bulletin.*

♀ **National Coalition of Black Lesbians & Gays/New York Chapter**, c/o 505 8th Ave, 16th flr; 10018 212-563-8340

♀ ★ **Petalouthas**, PO Box 532 Peter Stuyvesant Stn; 10009 718-891-3842 "Society for Women & Men of Hellenic Ancestry."

♂ ★ (?&) **South Asian Lesbian & Gay Association**, 170 E 3rd St #2G; 10009 212-475-6486

Organizations/Resources: Family
Long Island

♂ ★ **Gay Fathers of Long Island**, PO Box 2483, Patchogue; 11772-0879 516-447-1833 (Brian)

♀ ☆&& **P-FLAG/LI, Inc.**, c/o 109 Browns Rd, Huntington; 11743 516-938-8913 "Parents, Families & Friends of Lesbians & Gays."

Manhattan & New York City Area

♂ ★ **Gay Fathers I**, c/o R. Boxer 194 Riverside Dr #7C; 10025 212-874-7727

♂ ★&& **Gay Fathers' Forum of Greater NY**, PO Box 1321 Midtown Stn; 10018-0725 212-721-4216

♀ ☆ **P-FLAG/New York City**, PO Box 553 Lenox Hill Stn; 10021-0034 212-463-0629; 516-889-6619; Pub *Newsletter.* "Parents, Families & Friends of Lesbians & Gays."

♀ ★ **Second Generation**, 57 2nd Ave #51; 10003 212-673-2926 dcherubin@nyp.org "Gay kids of gay parents."

Queens

♀ ☆&& **P-FLAG/Queens Chapter**, PO Box 580460, Flushing; 11358 718-271-6663 Meet 1pm, 3rd Sun of month, at Church on the Hill, 35th Ave & 167th St, Flushing.

Rockland, Westchester, Dutchess, Orange Counties

♂ ★ **Gay Fathers of Westchester (GFW)**, PO Box 686, Croton Falls; 10519 914-948-4922

♀ ☆ **P-FLAG/Westchester**, c/o Rose Dinolfo, 3 Leatherstocking Lane, Mamaroneck; 10543 914-698-3619 "Parents, Families & Friends of Lesbians & Gays."

Organizations/Resources: General, Multipurpose, Pride
Bronx

♀ ★&& **Bronx Lesbians United in Sisterhood**, PO Box 1738, Bronx; 10451 212-330-9196

Long Island

♀ ★ **Long Island Pride**, PO Box 531, Upton; 11973 516-579-6382 "Organizer of the annual Long Island Pride Parade & Show, 2nd Sun in June."

♂ **Pride Coalition Of Long Island**, 14 Cary Place, Freeport; 11520 516-378-8280

Manhattan & New York City Area

♀ ☆ ♂ **Crystal Quilt, Inc.**, 532 LaGuardia Pl #321; 10012 212-941-4994 "Support groups, workshops, cultural events for women; contact for details."

NY: New York City Area
Organizations: General

348
USA

New York City Area : NY
Organizations: Social & Support

♂ ★ (?&) Heritage of Pride Inc, 154 Christopher St #1D; 10014 212-807-7433 "Volunteer organization producing NYC's annual Lesbian & Gay Prode Eevnts: the March, Rally, Pridefest & Dance."

Queens

♂ ★ (?&) Queens Gays & Lesbians United (Q-GLU), PO Box 4669, Sunnyside; 11104 718-205-6605

♂ ★ Queens Lesbian & Gay Pride Committee (QLGPC), PO Box 580445, Flushing; 11358-0445 718-460-4064 Meet 7.30pm, 1st Thu of month, at Queens Borough Hall, 120-55 Queens Blvd Rm 213 Pub *Newsletter*.

Organizations/Resources: Military/Veterans

Manhattan & New York City Area

♂ ★ ♂ Gay, Lesbian, Bisexual Veterans of Greater New York, 346 Broadway #811; 10013 212-349-3455

Organizations/Resources: Political/Legislative

Brooklyn

♂ ★ (?&) Lambda Independent Democrats of Brooklyn, 309 5th Ave #434, Brooklyn; 11215-4811 718-361-3322

Long Island

♂ ★ CERF-PAC (Citizens for Equal Rights Fund Political Action Committee), PO Box 301, Upton; 11973 516-399-3891 Pub *CERF-PAC*. "Long Island's Lesbian & Gay Political Action Committee."

♂ ★ ♂ East End Gay Organization for Human Rights (EEGO), PO Box 708, Bridgehampton; 11932-0077 516-324-3699 Pub *In Brief*. "Year round social & political activities."

♀ Log Cabin Long Island, 76 Cambridge Ave, Garden City; 11530 516-528-3014

♂ ★ Long Island Lavender Action Collective, PO Box 708, Mineola; 11501-0708 516-751-0941 Pub *Pulse*.

Manhattan & New York City Area

♂ ★ && Coalition for Lesbian & Gay Rights, 208 W 13th St; 10011 212-627-1398

♀ ★ Feminists for Animal Rights, Box 694 Cathedral Stn; 10025 212-866-6422 Pub *Newsletter*. "Women's group which applies nonexploitative feminist principles to all living creatures."

♂ ★ Gay & Lesbian Independent Democrats, c/o The Center, 208 W 13th St; 10011-7702 212-633-0985 Meet 2nd Wed of month, 8pm, at 208 W. 13th st. Pub *GLID News*.

♂ ★ Log Cabin Club/New York City, PO Box 1690; 10159-1690 212-886-1893 "Serving Gay & Lesbian Republicans."

♀ ★ National Center For Lesbian Rights, New York office, 462 Broadway #500A (Public Policy Office); 10013 212-343-9589 Fax 212-343-9687

♀ ☆ NOW-NYC Lesbian Rights Committee, 22 W 21st St, 7th flr; 10010-6904 212-807-0721

♀ ☆ Radical Women, 32 Union Sq East #907; 10003 212-677-7002 Fax 212-491-4634

♂ ★ Republicans for Individual Freedoms, PO Box 290, Mamaroneck; 10543 404-239-1679 (national)

♂ ★ (&) Stonewall Democratic Club, PO Box 1750 Old Chelsea Stn; 10011 212-969-8854

♀ ☆ (?&) Women's Democratic Club of New York City, PO Box 656; 10011

Queens

♂ ★ (?&) Gay Human Rights League of Queens County, PO Box 521224, Flushing; 11352-1224 718-463-2938 (Bill Page)

Rockland, Westchester, Dutchess, Orange Counties

♂ ★ && Log Cabin Club—Hudson Valley, c/o 5-9 Steven Dr, Ossining; 10562 914-762-6261 Fax 914-762-8391 "Gay Republicans of Westchester, Rockland, Orange, Putnam, Ulster & Dutchess."

Organizations/Resources: Sexual Focus (Leather, S/M, etc) & Safe Sex Promotion

Manhattan & New York City Area

⚥ ★ Defenders/Dignity, PO Box 1146; 10011 908-324-6475

♀ ☆ ♂ The Eulenspiegel Society, Box 2783 Grand Central Stn; 10163 212-388-7022 Pub *TES Newsletter*.

♂ ★ Gay Male S/M Activists, 332 Bleecker St #D23; 10014 212-727-9878 Pub *Newslink*.

♀ ★ Hot Ash, PO Box 20147, London Terrace; 10011 718-789-6147 "Cigar fetish club."

♂ ★ Iron Guard B.C., PO Box 291 Village Stn; 10014 "Leather/Levi Brotherhood."

♂ ★ (&) Jacks Of Color, 212-222-9794; 718-625-6093; "A safe sex club for Men Of Color. Parties 1st Sat of month."

♀ ★ Lavender & Lace, 332 Bleecker St, Box F4; 10014 / 28 9th Ave (downstairs) 212-255-6758 *LWP* Social & play group. Contact for details.

♀ ★ && Lesbian Sex Mafia, PO Box 993, Murray Hill Station; 10056

♀ ☆ National Leather Association (NLA): Metro New York, PO Box 1084; 10156 212-597-0019 *The Inquisitor*.

♂ ★ North American Man Boy Love Association (NAMBLA), PO Box 174 Midtown Stn; 10018 212-807-8578

♂ ☆ Renegades, PO Box 1457; 10013

Organizations/Resources: Social, Recreational & Support Groups (see also Sport/Dance/Outdoor)

Bronx

♂ ★ && Gay Men of the Bronx (GMOB), PO Box 511, Bronx; 10451 718-792-8078; 718-378-3497 (Spanish); Pub *GMOB Update*. "Multi-ethnic, multi-cultural organization comm,itted to creating a supportive community in the Bronx."

Long Island

♂ ★ (?&) Gaymen & Lesbians in Brookhaven (GLIB), PO Box 203, Brookhaven; 11719-0203 516-286-6867 (touchtone only) Men's group 1st & 3rd Sun, 4pm; Women's group 1st & 3rd Thu, 8pm. Pub *GLIB News*. "Serving all of Long Island. Social, cultural, & educational activities."

♂ ★ Long Island Gay Men's Group, PO Box 433, Levittown; 11756 516-694-2407

Manhattan & New York City Area

♂ ★ (?&) Broadway Night Out, PO Box 387; 10028 212-289-1741 "Theater party club."

♂ ★ Le Cercle français lesgay, PO Box 4154, College Point; 11356 718-353-3941 (leave message) Meets alternate Weds at Lesbian & Gay Community Services Center, 203 W. 13th St

♂ ★ Club Frottage (Social Networking), PO Box 2119 Cathedral Stn; 10025 *P*

♂ ★ (?&) Couples Together, 212-662-3080 Outdoor activities & meetings run by Gay Circles. "Social & support organization for couples in committed Gay or Lesbian relationships."

♂ ★ Gay Circles, PO Box 2004; 10009 212-242-9165 "8-week series of discussion groups in a safe space."

♀ ★ Gay Women's Alternative, Meets at Universalist Church, 4 W. 76th St Oct-June 1st Thu of month, 8pm. 212-595-8410

♂ ★♿♿ Girth & Mirth of New York, Inc., PO Box 10, Dept Y, Pelham; 10803 914-699-7735 Pub *Fat Apple Review*. "For gay chubby men & their admirers."

T ★♿♿ Imperial Queens of NY, LI & NJ, 70-A Greenwich Ave Suite 120; 10011 212-627-6100/229-0487; 516-889-1999; Pub *Imperially Yours*. "Since 1969, a social club/support group for T/V's, D/Q's, T/S's, D.K's, & admirers."

⚥ ★ ♿ Lavender Heights, c/o Cornerstone Center 178 Bennett Ave; 10040 212-927-5174 Pub *Lavender Heights News*. "Lesbian/Gay Neighbors of Washington Heights & Inwood."

⚥ ★ Lesbian & Gay Foreign Language Club, PO Box 4154, College Point; 11356 718-353-3941 (leave message) Meets 2nd Tue of month at Lesbian & Gay Community Services Center, 203 W. 13th St

♂ ★ Males Au Naturel, 332 Bleecker St Box 133; 10014 212-535-3914 P Pub *MAN to MAN*. "Gay male, non-sexual nudist club."

♂ ★ (?♿) New York Bears, 332 Bleecker St #F4; 10014 718-367-7484 "Bears, Cubs, & their admirers."

⚢ ★ New York Femmes, PO Box 580281 Stn A, Flushing; 11358 212-388-2736

♂ ★ ♿ Prime Timers, Box 291 Midtown Stn; 10018-0291 212-929-1035 *The Prime Timer*.

⚥ ★ SAGE (Senior Action in a Gay Environment), 305 Fashion Ave FL 16; 10002-6008 212-741-2247 "Social services for Gay & Lesbian Seniors. Counseling, rap groups & workshops. Drop-In Senior Center daily. Friendly Visitor Services to homebound elderly. AIDS & the Elderly Program. Monthly brunches & socials."

⚢ ★ (?♿) SAL (Social Activities for Lesbians), PO Box 150118, Brooklyn; 11215 718-630-9505

⚢ ★ (?♿) Theater/Dinner/Etc!, 718-998-2536 (before 10pm) "Theater, dinner, etc. for women 35+ (flexible) in a smoke-free environment."

⚥ ★ Twentysomething, PO Box 396 Old Chelsea Stn; 10011 212-439-8051 (Hotline)

⚢ ★ (?♿) Women About, PO Box 280 J.A.F.; 10116 212-642-5257 24 hrs. Pub *Meanderings*. "Adventure social club for lesbians. Detailed calendar of indoor/outdoor social activities & quarterly newsletter."

♀ Womyn Who Dare Network, PO Box 3763 Grand Central Stn; 10063

Queens

♀ ★ All The Queens Women, Inc, PO Box 4278 Parkside Stn, Flushing; 11375 718-380-2210 "Rap group."

♀ Woman United, Caller Box 6703, Flushing; 11367 718-263-5668

Staten Island

⚥ ★♿♿ Lambda Associates of Staten Island, GPO Box 665, Staten Island; 10314 718-979-8890

Rockland, Westchester, Dutchess, Orange Counties

⚥ ★♿♿ Gay & Lesbian Alliance in Orange County, PO Box 1557, Greenwood Lake, NY 10925 914-782-1525 Meeting Tue 8pm at St. Paul's Episcopal Church, Main St & Maple Ave, Chester, NY

⚥ OCGLA (Orange County Gay/Lesbian Alliance), PO Box 623, Chester; 10918-0623 914-782-1525

⚥ ★ (?♿) RLGA (Rockland Lesbian Gay Alliance), PO Box 549, Nyack; 10960 914-358-0161

Organizations/Resources: Sport/Dance/Outdoor

Long Island

♂ ★ Long Island Ravens M.C., c/o L.I. Eagle, 94 N Clinton Ave, Bay Shore; 11706 516-666-6901 L Meets at L.I. Eagle, 94 Clinton Ave, Bay Shore.

Manhattan & New York City Area

⚥ ★ Big Apple Softball League, PO Box 475 FDR Stn; 10150-0475 718-625-8095

♂ ★ Excelsior M.C., PO Box 1386; 10274-1130 LL "Motorcylists."

⚥ ★ Front Runners New York, PO Box 87 Ansonia Stn; 10023-0087 212-724-9700 "Distance; Track & Field; Race Walking."

⚥ ★ (?♿) Gay & Lesbian Sierrans of New York City, mail to GLS-NY, c/o Ketay Agency, 1501 Broadway #1910; 10036 212-691-1083

⚥ ★ Gotham Sports Association, PO Box 172, Elmsford; 10523 516-488-2425

⚥ ★ Knights Wrestling Club, PO Box 720161, Jackson Heights; 11372 718-639-5141

⚥ ★ Metro Gay Wrestling Alliance, Inc (MGWA), 500 W 43rd St #14F; 10036 212-563-7066 Pub *Wrestlespeak*.

♂ ★ Ramblers Soccer Club, c/o 175 W 76th St, Apt 15D; 10023 212-724-7992

♀ ★ Sirens Motorcycle Club, c/o The Center, 208 W 13th St; 10011 212-673-8975 "Women Motorcylists."

⚥ ★ Sundance Outdoor Adventure Society, PO Box 2737; 10163-2737 212-598-4726 Pub *Crosswinds*.

⚥ ★ (?♿) Times Squares, PO Box 1229 Ansonia Stn; 10023 212-675-5475 dCW "Gay & Lesbian Square Dance club. Instruction; weekly club night."

Organizations/Resources: Student, Academic, Alumni/ae

Bronx

⚥ Einstein Association of Gays, Lesbians & Bisexuals (EAGLB), c/o Dr Frank Lilli, Dept of Molecular Genetics, Albert Einstein College of Medicine, Bronx; 10461

⚥ ★ Lesbian & Gay Support Group, Fordham University, Station 37, Box 480, Bronx; 10458

Brooklyn

⚥ ★ ♿ Brooklyn College Gay & Lesbian Alliance, Brooklyn College Student Activities, James Hall, Brooklyn; 11210-2889 718-951-4234

⚥ ★♿♿ Gay, Lesbian & Bisexual Alliance of Kingsborough, 2001 Oriental Blvd, Brooklyn; 11235 718-368-5400

⚥ Gays, Lesbian & Bisexuals at Pratt, Pratt Institute, OSA, Chapel Hall, Brooklyn; 11205 718-636-3422

Long Island

⚥ ★♿♿ Hofstra Lesbian, Gay, & Bisexual Alliance, c/o Dean of Students Office, 200 Hofstra University, Hempstead; 11550 516-463-6301

⚥ ★♿♿ Lesbian, Gay & Bisexual Alliance, Student Union 045A, SUNY at Stony Brook, Stony Brook; 11794 516-632-6469

Manhattan & New York City Area

⚥ ★ ♿ Barnard College/Columbia Lesbian Bisexual Gay Coalition, 303 Earl Hall, Columbia University; 10027 212-854-1488 "Dances in Earl Hall on 1st Fri of month. Listing of all non-straight campus events on phoneline."

⚥ ★ Bisexual, Gay & Lesbian Law Students at NYU, 240 Mercer St; 10012 212-998-6574

♂ ★&& Bisexual, Lesbian, & Gay Alliance at City College NY, Finley Student Center, Convent Ave & W 135th St; 10031 212-650-8234

♂ ★ Cardozo Gay & Lesbian Law Student Alliance, 55 5th Ave; 10003

♂ ★ (?&) Center for Lesbian & Gay Studies (CLAGS), CUNY Graduate Ctr, 33 W 42nd St; 10036-8099 212-642-2924 Pub *Directory of Lesbian & Gay Scholarship.*

♂ ★ Columbia Bisexual, Gay & Lesbian Alumni/ae (BiGALA), c/o LBGC, 394 Earl Hall, Columbia University; 10027

♂ ★ & Gay & Lesbian Union at NYU, Loeb Student Center, 566 LaGuardia Pl #810; 10012 212-998-4938

♂ ★ Gay Academic Union: New York Chapter, PO Box 480 Lenox Hill Stn; 10021-0033 212-864-0361 Pub *Gai Saber Monographs.* "Scholarly correspondence invited, all languages."

♂ ★ Gay Students Alliance at Baruch College, 137 E 22nd St, Box 321; 10010

♂ ★&& Lambda Lesbian & Gay Student Association, John Jay College, 445 W 59th St; 10019 212-237-8738; 212-237-8732

♂ ★&& Lesbian & Gay Students Association, New York Law School, 57 Worth St; 10013 212-431-2100

♂ The New School Gay, Lesbian, Bisexual Collective, 66 W 12th St; 10011

♂ Pride at MMC, Marymount Manhattan College, Student Government 221 E 71st St; 10021 212-517-0496

Queens

♂ ★&& Gay & Lesbian Union at Queens College, 65-30 Kissena Blvd, SUB Room 215, Flushing; 11367-0904 718-520-1866

♂ Lesbians At Queens College, 65-30 Kissena Blvd, Flushing; 11367 718-263-5668

♀ ☆ (&&) Queens College Womyn's Center, SU 215, 65-30 Kissena Blvd c/o Student Union Queens College, Flushing; 11367 / 65-30 Kissena Blvd, Student Union 210A 718-263-5668

♂ ★ Queensboro Community College Lesbian & Gay Male Alliance, Queensboro Community College of CUNY, Bayside; 11364 718-631-6212

Staten Island

♂ ★ College of Staten Island Lesbian, Gay & Bisexual Alliance, Campus Center Room 217, 2800 Victory Blvd, Staten Island; 10314 718-982-3107

Rockland, Westchester, Dutchess, Orange Counties

♂ ★&& Gay/Lesbian/Bisexual Union SUNY Purchase, c/o Campus Life, 735 Anderson Hill Rd, Purchase; 10577-1400 914-251-6976

Organizations/Resources: Transgender & Transgender Publications

Manhattan & New York City Area

T ☆ Gender Identity Project, c/o The Center, 208 W 13 St; 10011 212-620-7310 "Transgender peer counseling services."

T Girls Night Out, PO Box 369, Brooklyn; 11235

T ☆ Greater New York Gender Alliance, co Lynda Frank, 330 W 45th St #3H; 10036 212-765-3561 6-10pm.

T ● Lee's Mardi Gras Boutique, 565 10th Ave; 10036 212-947-7773 "Books only."

T ● Lee's Mardi Gras Boutique, PO Box 843; 10108 / 400 W. 14th St 212-645-1888 "Clothes, underwear, makeup, girdles, corsets; large selection of high heel shoes to size 14."

T ○ & Metamorphosis, PO Box 6260, Long Island City; 11106-0260 718-728-4615 "Psychotherapy, counseling, evaluations, referrals. Individual, family & group support. By appointment only."

T ☆ & NYCGA (New York City Gender Alliance), c/o Fem Fashions, 9 W 31st St #7R; 10001 212-629-5750 (by appt only)

T ○&& Yelsky, Miriam, Ph.D., 350 W 24th St; 10011 212-243-0261

Organizations/Resources: Youth (see also Family)

Long Island

♂ ★&& Bridges, PO Box 1084, Shoreham; 11786 516-924-3640 "Lesbian Gay Bisexual youth group."

♂ ★ (?&) Long Island Gay & Lesbian Youth, Inc, PO Box 977, c/o David Kilmnick, CSW, Levittown; 11756 516-627-3340 (Nassau); 516-579-6382 (Suffolk); "Sponsors twelve or more support youth support groups across Long Island; counseling, community education, advocacy & outreach."

♂ ★ Pride For Youth, c/o Middle Earth Crisis Center, 2740 Martin Ave, Bellmore; 11710 516-679-9000 24 hour hotline "Support group for Gay & Lesbian Youth; community outreach; 24 hr hot line."

♂ ★&& Unity, PO Box 1084, Shoreham; 11786 516-924-3640 "20 something Lesbian Gay Bisexual Union."

Manhattan & New York City Area

♂ ★ Community Health Project Health Outreach To Teens, 208 W 13th St; 10011 212-255-1673 Mon-Fri 10am-7pm.

♂ ★ (?&) Hetrick-Martin Institute, 2 Astor Place 3rd Flr; 10003 212-674-2400; 212-674-8695 TTY; Fax 212-674-8650 Mon-Fri 9am-7pm. Pub *HMI Report Card.* "Social Service agency for lesbian, gay & bisexual youth."

♂ ★ (&) Neutral Zone Youth Center, 162 Christopher St 212-924-3294; 212-627-2585 (also Fax: call first); Tue-Thu 3-10.30pm; Fri-Sat 4pm-1am. *The Youth Voice.* "LesbiGay youth under 22. Drop-in; referral; counseling; family support; social & discussion groups."

♂ ★ (&) Neutral Zone Youth Center, c/o Greenwich Village Youth Council, St #208; 10014 212-924-3294; 212-627-2585 (also Fax, call first); Call for address & hours. *The Youth Voice.* "Drop-in; referral; counseling; family support; social & discussion groups for lesbian gay bisexual transgender youth under 22."

♂ ★ (?&) Youth Enrichment Services of the Lesbian & Gay Community Services Center (YES), 208 W 13th St; 10011 212-620-7310 Fax 212-924-2657 Sat 3.30-6pm. Pub *OutYouth.*

Rockland, Westchester, Dutchess, Orange Counties

♂ Gay & Lesbian Youth of Hudson Valley, PO Box 216, Congers; 10920 914-948-4922

Performing Arts: Entertainment, Music, Recording, Theater, etc.

♂ ★ AFREE Artists Collective, c/o J. Brown PO Box 2119; 10025

♀ ○ (?&) Barentyne, Ross, 160 W 73rd St; 10023 212-580-5890 "Vocal coach; accompanist."

♀ ● Dawn, Rick, 260 W 15th St; 10011 212-243-4524 "Pianist, musical director; vocal coach."

♀ ● (?&) Epstein, Audrey Lynn, 212-439-9763 "Piano instruction/music theory; vocal coach; entertainment on piano; accompanist for individuals & ensembles. Own portable piano-keyboard, etc."

♀ ★ Gay Performances Company, PO Box 1647 Old Chelsea Stn; 10011 212-595-1445

♀ ○ Horowitz, Leonard, 212-799-3747 "Piano/music instruction."

NY: New York City Area
Performing Arts

351
USA

New York City Area : NY
Pharmacies/Health Supplies

♂ ★ (♀♂) Lesbian & Gay Big Apple Corps Marching & Symphonic Band, c/o TriMusicAngle, 332 Bleecker St #K48; 10014 718-768-8256 "Marching, concert & swing band ensembles available for parties, events, etc. Non-musicians welcome."

♀ ○ Logen, Carol, 119 W 80th St #4R; 10024 212-877-1211 "Acting & singing coaching."

♀ ● M.K. Music & Orchestra, 235 E 95th St #33D; 10128 212-362-2828

♀ ● Orlick, Phil, 41 5th Ave; 10003 212-777-8929 "Singing coach for R&B, top 40, jazz."

♂ ● Supersound DJ Service, Inc., PO Box 780022, Maspeth; 11378 718-326-7213 Fax 718-326-4153

♀ ● (♀♂) WOW (Women's One World) Cafe, 59-61 E 4th St; 10003 212-460-8067 "Performance space: all welcome."

Performing Arts: Entertainment, Music, Theater, etc. ▾

Long Island

♂ ★ (♀♂) Long Island Pride Chorus, 158 Rule St, Franklin Sq; 11010 516-366-1855 (Randall); 516-538-4546 (Louisa); "Warm & friendly group of people expressing love of themselves & their community through music."

Manhattan & New York City Area

♂ Gay Gotham Chorus, 275 W 96th St #32A; 10025 212-663-7748

♀ ★ The Glines, 240 W 44th St; 10036 212-354-8899 "Theatre company."

♂ ★♂♂ Lavender Light Gospel Choir, 70-A Greenwich Ave #315; 10011 212-714-7072

♂ ★ New York City Gay Men's Chorus, 55 Christopher St, 2nd flr; 10014-3530 212-924-7770 Fax 212-924-6660 Pub *Chorus Lines*. "Concerts signed for the hearing-impaired."

♂ ★ (♂) Stonewall Chorale, PO Box 920 Old Chelsea Stn; 10011 212-262-9544

Pets & Pet Supplies

Manhattan

♀ ● (♂) Animal World—We Deliver, 219 E 26th St; 10010 212-685-0027 Mon-Sat 10am-7pm.

♀ ● Dog-O-Rama, 123 4th Ave; 10003 212-353-9186 Mon-Fri 8.30am-6pm; Sat 10am-6pm. "Dog grooming; pet supplies; puppies."

♀ ● Towne-House Grooming & Pet Supplies, 249 W 18th St; 10011 212-929-2910

Queens

♀ ● A Dog's Best Friend, 62-78 Woodhaven Blvd, Rego Park; 11374 718-335-0110

Rockland, Westchester, Dutchess, Orange Counties

♀ ● (♂) Dog's Place / Dog Grooming, 981 Main St, New Rochelle; 10801 914-636-2020

Pharmacies/Health Care Supplies

♀ ○ APP-NY, 197 8th Ave; 10011 212-691-9050 Fax 212-691-9052

♀ ○ McKay Drugs, 55 5th Ave; 10003 212-627-2300
♦ *McKay Drugs advertisement page 351*

♀ ○ New London Pharmacy, 246 8th Ave; 10011 212-243-4987

♀ ○ Price Mark Drugs, 336 E 86th St; 10028 212-249-2504 "Free citywide delivery."

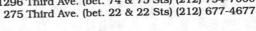

NY: New York City Area
Pharmacies/Health Supplies

352
USA

New York City Area : NY
Publications: Directories & Travel

Sappho's Isle

News • Opinion • Lifestyle

Health • Leisure • Travel

Gay News from
A Woman's
Perspective

Women's News
From A Gay
Perspective

960 Willis Avenue
Albertson, NY 11507
516-747-5417

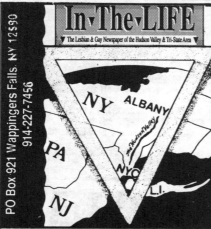

PO Box 921 Wappingers Falls, NY 12590
914-227-7456

In▼The▼LIFE

The Lesbian & Gay Newspaper of the Hudson Valley & Tri-State Area

NY   ALBANY

PA

NJ   NYC   L.I.

The ***HOTTEST*** lesbian and gay newspaper for
the Hudson Valley and surrounding area.
• Received recognition and honors
Only $18 / 12 issues will keep you in touch
with what's going on.
Call for a FREE copy
• News, Feature Stories & Monthly Columns
• Places to Go & Stay • Listing of Events & Happenings

♀ ○ ♿ Stadtlanders Pharmacy Wellness Center, 126 8th Ave;
10011 212-807-8798 Fax 212-645-1429

♀ ○ Village Apothecary, 346 Bleecker St; 10014 212-807-7566

Piercing & Body Jewelry

Manhattan

♂ • (♿) Venus Modern Body Arts, Inc., 199 E 4th St; 10009 212-473-1954 Noon-9pm. "Body piercing/tattooing; all body modifications & accessories, hardware."

Printing & Promotional Items (see also Art; Graphics/Typesetting)

♀ • B-D Printing & Ad Specialties, 4114 10th Ave, Brooklyn; 11219 718-436-0100 Fax 718-436-1425 "Advertising specialties: buttons, pens, etc, imprinted with logos/names."
✦ *B-D Printing & Ad Specialties advertisement page 352*

♀ • Grayscale Graphics & Design, 201-864-3539 "Advertisements & other design work; large library of male physique images available if needed. Special hand-holding care for beginners!'

♂ • Magic Circle Printing Company, 13 E 17th St 4th floor; 10003 212-675-3043

♂ ○ Milo Printing Co, 193 Ave A; 10009 212-254-5811 Fax 212-254-5906

♂ • Newsletter Press, 135 W 20th St, 3rd flr; 10011 212-463-7800 Fax 212-463-7803

♂ • ♿ SuperScript Desktop Publishing Plus, 245 W 104th St #16C; 10025-4280 212-866-0789

♂ • ♿ Tower Press Communications, 80 8th Ave #902; 10011 212-807-9800 Fax 212-807-9843 Pub *Pride Guide: Annual Calendar & Resource.* "Graphic design, typesetting, computer graphics; printing (1-6 colors) & mailing services."

♂ ○ Westprint, 873 Washington St; 10014 212-989-2948

Public Relations/Advertising Agencies

♀ • Athey, Levine & Ost Creative Consultants, 214 W 29th St; 10001 212-967-7070

⚥ • ♿ Karlsberg, Michele, 47 Dongan Hills Ave, 1st flr, Staten Island; 10306 718-351-9599 "Specializing in publicity for large & small presses, & independent authors."

Publications: Directories, Bibliographies, Guides, Travel

♀ ○ *Gayellow Pages,* PO Box 533 Village Stn; 10014-0533 212-674-0120 "Classified directory of services, businesses, resources, etc in USA & Canada. Various local editions. Also available on mailing labels."

Publications

♀ • *Clique Magazine*, Meadowlark Productions 81 Pondville Road #342, Bronxville; 10708 Fax 718-652-1928

♂ • *Dirty*, J & H Publications, 140 Bergen St, Brooklyn; 11217 718-858-4303 "Adult-related fiction & photography; personals; catalogs of adult services."

♀ • *The Greenwich Village Press*, 319 8th St, Brooklyn; 11215 718-768-2048 Fax 718-499-5972 "Issues & concerns of the Lesbian & Gay Community of NYC; Downtown Arts & Lifestyles."

♀ • *Homo Xtra*, 19 W 21st St #504; 10010 212-627-0747

♂ ○ *LISP*, 245 8th Ave, Box 392; 10011

♀ • **Long Island Pride Press, PO Box 2303, North Babylon; 11703-0303 516-225-7900 Fax 516-225-7918 "11 monthly issues plus Pride Guide Annual Edition in May."**
✦ *Long Island Pride Press advertisement page 353*

♀ • *Metrosource*, 622 Greenwich St #5F; 10014 212-691-5127

♀ • ♿ *Michael's Thing Magazine*, 240 West End Ave #4D; 10023 212-724-3691

♀ • *My Comrade*, 326 E 13th St #15; 10003

♀ • *New York Native*, PO Box 1475 Church St Stn; 10008 212-627-2120 Fax 212-727-9321 Weekly. "Newspaper."

♀ *New York Triangle*, Box 478, 147 Second Ave; 10003

♀ • *Next Magazine*, 101 Lafayette St, 5th flr; 10013 212-226-6556 Fax 212-226-2777

♀ • *Parlee Plus*, PO Box 430, Babylon; 11702 516-587-8669 Monthly. "General & Gay entertainment; gay news."

♀ ★ *Radical Chick*, The Center 208 W 13th St; 10011 "Feminist newspaper."

♀ *Stonewall News*, PO Box 816, Madison Square Station; 10159 212-627-2120

♀ • (?♿) *VICE*, PO Box 20281; 10011-0003 212-727-2787 Fax 212-727-3190

Publishers/Publishing-related Services

♂ • ♿ Willow Communications, 75 Montgomery St #2E; 10002 212-619-3431; 212-619-0925 modem; "Publishing & Personal Communications support services."

Quilts

♀ ○ **Quilts by Margery, 25 St Nicholas St, Lynbrook; 11563 516-593-4767 By appointment only. "Remember your loved one with a custom designed quilt."**
✦ *Quilts by Margery advertisement page 138*

Real Estate

♀ • A Summer Place Realty, PO Box 4062, Cherry Grove; 11782 / Lewis & Ocean Walk 516-597-6140; 212-752-8074; 10am-8pm. "Serving Cherry Grove & Fire Island Pines."

♂ • (?♿) **Coleman Neary Realty Ltd., 57 W 16th St; 10011 212-633-2727 Fax 212-989-1207 "Rentals & sales of residential properties in Chelsea, Greenwich Village, & surrounding areas."**

♀ ○ Fire Island Land Co, Cherry Grove; 11782 516-597-6040
✦ *Fire Island Land Co advertisement page 353*

♀ • **Howard, Bob, Real Estate, PO Box 5297, Fire Island Pines, NY 11782 / 37 Fire Island Blvd 516-597-9400; 212-819-9400 (winter)**
✦ *Howard, Bob, Real Estate advertisement page 355*

♀ • ♿ **Island Properties Real Estate & Management, PO Box 5272, Fire Island Pines; 11782-5272 / 37 Fire Island Blvd 516-597-6900**
✦ *Island Properties Real Estate & Management advertisement page 354*

♂ • Justis Properties, 224 W 4th St; 10014 212-807-7700 "Rentals; sales; property management."

♂ ○ **Munnell, Shirley, Licensed Real Estate Broker 516-597-6467; 516-589-1978 winter**

♂ • Oele, Paul, c/o DeMax Metro, 3317 Merrick Rd, Wantagh; 11793 516-826-9300 Fax 516-826-3836

♂ ○ Pines Harbor Realty, PO Box 219, Fire Island Pines, Sayville; 11782 516-597-7575 Fax 516-597-7504 "Sales; seasonal & short term rentals in Fire Island Pines, Water Island, Cherry Grove. Licensed NY State mortage broker."

BOB HOWARD
R E A L   E S T A T E ,   I N C.
LICENSED REAL ESTATE BROKER

FIRE ISLAND PINES

APPOINTMENTS • INFORMATION
212-819-9400
•
516-597-9400

FOR THE SEASON • FOR THE MONTH • FOR THE WEEK • FOR SALE

FOR YOU!

FROM SOMEONE YOU KNOW

Record Sales (see also Performing Arts)

♀ ○ ♂ Decadance Records, 119 W 23rd St; 10011 212-691-1013 Fax 212-692-7207

Religious Organizations & Publications

Bronx

♂ St Ann's Church of Morrisania - Gay & Lesbian Ministry, 295 St Ann's Ave, Bronx; 10454 718-585-6325

Brooklyn

♂ ★ Dignity/Brooklyn, PO Box 021313, Brooklyn; 11202-1313 718-769-3447 Eucharist & potluck supper 3rd Sat of month at parish house of St Ann & the Holy Trinity, 122 Pierrepont St. "Gay & Lesbian Catholics & their friends."

♂ ★ First Unitarian Church of Brooklyn, Lesbian, Gay, Bisexual Concerns Committee, 50 Monroe Place, Brooklyn; 11201 718-624-5466

Long Island

♂ ★ Allmen, Rev. Robert J., MS, M.Div., PO Box 436, Central Islip; 11722 516-723-2012 "Pastor of Good Shepherd American Catholic Church, available for baptisms, masses, spiritual counseling, & rites of union."

♂ ★ (?♂) Circle of "More Light", OSHPC, Box 203, Brookhaven; 11719-0203 516-286-0542 Worship & study group, 1st Mon, 8pm.

♂ ★ Dignity/Nassau, PO Box 48, East Meadow; 11554 516-781-6225 Pub Dignity/Nassau News. "Gay, Lesbian & Bisexual Catholics & their friends."

♂ Gay & Lesbian Unitarian Universalists, c/o UUF of Stony Brook, PO Box 602, Stony Brook; 11790 516-399-4967

Manhattan & New York City Area

♂ ★♂♂ Axios: Eastern & Orthodox Christians, PO Box 990 Village Stn; 10014-0704 212-989-6211 axiosusa@aol.com Pub Axios Newsletter.

♀ ☆ (♂) Beth Am, The People's Temple, 178 Bennett Ave; 10040 (One block west of Broadway at 189th St) 212-927-2230 "A dynamic Reform synagogue."

♂ ★ Christian Science Group, c/o 444 3rd Ave #4; 10016 212-532-8379

♂ ★♂♂ Congregation Beth Simchat Torah, 57 Bethune St; 10014-1791 212-929-9498 Pub Gay & Lesbian Synagogue News.

♂ ★ Dignity/Big Apple, Inc., PO Box 1028 Old Chelsea Stn; 10011 212-818-1309 Meets Sat 8pm, Lesbian & Gay Community Services Center, 208 W. 13th St. Pub Outlook. "Gay & Lesbian Catholics & their friends."

♂ ★♂♂ Dignity/New York, PO Box 1554 FDR Stn; 10150 212-627-6488 Liturgy Sun 7.30pm, St John's Church, 218 W. 11th St (corner Waverly Place), followed by social. Pub Calendar, This Week. "Gay & Lesbian Catholics & their friends."

♂ ★ Evangelicals Concerned, 311 E 72nd St #1G, c/o Dr Ralph Blair; 10021 212-517-3171 Pub Record; Review.

♂ ★ (♂) Gay & Lesbian Quakers, 15 Rutherford Place; 10003-3791 212-475-0195; 212-979-0170; "Religious Society of Friends (Quakers)."

♀ ★ (?♂) GLAD Alliance (Gay, Lesbian & Affirming Disciples), 1453-A Lexington Ave; 10128-2506 212-289-3016 "Supportive community for lesbians, gay men & bisexuals & their families & friends in the Christian Church (Disciples of Christ)."

♂ ★ Gold, Rev. August Olivia, Interfaith Minister/Wedding & Commitment Ceremonies, Park Ave, NYC 212-387-8221 Mon-Fri 10am-7pm.

♂ ★ The Good Shepherd Christian Fellowship, PO Box 4154, College Point; 11356 718-353-3941 eves & weekends. Meeting 1st & 3rd Mon, 6-9pm, at the Center, 208 W 13th St. The Good Shepherd.

♂ Iglesia de la Comunidad Metropolitana Cristo Rey, 4455 Broadway #3G; 10040 212-942-6428

♂ ★ ♂ Integrity/New York, PO Box 5202; 10185-0043 718-720-3054 Pub Outlook. Eucharist & social gathering Thu 7.30pm, St Luke's in the Fields, Hudson St. 'Gay & Lesbian Episcopalians & their friends.'

♀ ☆ ♂ Kathexis Coven, PO Box 408, Shirley; 11967-0408 mthorn@aol.com "Traditional Witchcraft coven; referrals made to other groups in the area; SASE for info."

♂ ★ ♂ Maranatha: Riversiders for Lesbian/Gay Concerns, c/o Riverside Church, 490 Riverside Drive; 10027 212-222-5900 ext 290

♂ ★ (♂) Metropolitan Community Church of New York, 446 W 36th St; 10018 212-629-7440 Fax 212-629-7441 Worship Sun 10pm & Pm.

♂ ★ PLGC/NYC, 740 West End Ave c/o Bisson; 10025 212-866-3580 "Presbyterians for Lesbian/Gay Concerns."

♀ ★ (♂) Potluck!, c/o Allen V. Harris 1010 Park Ave; 10028-0991 212-288-3246 4th Fri of month, 7pm: call for details. "An ecumenical gathering for food & friendship."

♀ ☆♂♂ Rutgers Presbyterian Church, 236 W 73rd St; 10023 212-877-8227 Worship Sun 11am. "A More Light Church."

♀ ☆ Saints Community Church, 13 Chester Ave, Brooklyn; 11218 718-633-7781 "Inclusive weekly worship in Manhattan. Contact for details."

♂ ★ ♂ Seventh-Day Adventist Kinship International, NY Chapter, PO Box 20595; 10025 212-662-8656

♀ ☆ ♂ Stephen Wise Free Synagogue - Lesbian & Gay Concerns Group, 30 W 68th St; 10023 212-877-4050

♀ ☆ Temple of Miraculous Perception, 237 W 100 St #3R; 10025 212-222-2874

♂ ★ (?♂) United Church of Christ Coalition for Lesbian/Gay Concerns, c/o Craig Hoffman, 1453A Lexington Ave; 10128 212-289-3016

♀ ☆ (?♂) Washington Square United Methodist Church, 135 W 4th St; 10012 212-777-2528 "AIDS ministry; diverse community service program."

♀ ☆ (♂♂) West-Park Presbyterian Church, 165 W 86th St; 10024 212-362-4890 "A More Light Church, welcoming Gays & Lesbians to all aspects of the church's life & leadership."

♀ ☆ (♂) Witches/Pagans for Gay Rights, PO Box 408, Shirley; 11967-0408

Queens

♂ ★ Unitarian Universalist Church of Flushing—Gay, Lesbian & Bisexual Concerns Committee, 147-54 Ash Ave, Flushing; 11355 718-353-3860

Rockland, Westchester, Dutchess, Orange Counties

♂ ★ Chek, Rev. V., MSC, PO Box 324, Piermont; 10968 914-358-2687 Fax 914-358-7002 "Interfaith minister; 'Life Partner Packages' commitment ceremonies; counseling."

♂ ★ ♂ Integrity of Westchester, PO Box 2038, White Plains; 10602-2038 914-949-4367 The Grapevine. Eucharist & program 2nd Wed of month, 7.30pm, at Grace Episcopal Church, 33 Church St. "Gay & Lesbian Episcopalians & their friends."

Suntanning

♀ ● ♂ Scarsdale Tan Spa, Ltd., 390 Central Park Ave, Scarsdale; 10583 914-472-2273

NY: New York City Area
Switchboards & Helplines

357
USA

New York City Area : NY
Video Sales, Rentals, Services

Switchboards, Helplines, Phone Information

♂ ★ (?♿) Gay & Lesbian Help-Line, PO Box 1905, White Plains; 10602 914-948-4922 7-10pm.

♂ ★ **Gay & Lesbian Switchboard, 212-777-1800**

♂ ★ Gay & Lesbian Switchboard of Long Island (GLSB of LI), PO Box 1312, Ronkonkoma; 11779 516-737-1615 7-11pm.

♀ ★ Lesbian Switchboard, 212-741-2610 Mon-Fri 6-10pm.

♂ ★ ♿♿ Middle Earth Crisis Center, 2740 Martin Ave, Bellmore; 11710 516-679-9000 24 hrs

♂ ★ New York City Gay & Lesbian Anti-Violence Project, 647 Hudson St; 10014 212-807-0197 Crime Victim Assistance City-wide Hotline 24 hrs

♀ ☆ Response of Suffolk County, PO Box 300, Stony Brook; 11790 516-751-7500 24 hrs.

♀ ☆ Youth Environmental Services, 30 Broadway, Massapequa; 11758 516-799-3203

Thrift/Consignment Stores

Manhattan

♂ ★ Out Of The Closet Thrift Shop, 220 E 81st St; 10028 212-472-3573

Transportation: Limousine, Taxi, Etc.

♀ ○ (?♿) Churchill Luxury Stretch Limousines, 176 S 12th St, Lindenhurst; 11757 516-226-5328

♀ ● (?♿) Hot Cherry's & Creamy Peaches, 88-52 Myrtle Ave #2, Glendale; 11385 718-847-8109; 917-988-1268 beeper; "Limousine service."

Travel & Tourist Services (see also Accommodation)

♀ ● All Continent Tours, 227 E 56th St 4th flr; 10022-3754 212-861-5325; 516-292-7914; 9am-6.30pm. "Daily hand delivery in NYC & LI: no charge."

♀ ● Ami-Co Travel, 234 E Montauk Hwy, Lindenhurst; 11757 516-957-6666 Member IGTA.

♀ ● **Choice Travel, 979 Central Park Ave, Scarsdale; 10583 914-472-5100; 800-49-CHOICE outside NY; Fax 914-725-6534**

♂ ● **D.C. Worldwide Travel, 251 W 19th St; 10011 212-243-PLAY**

♀ ○ Deville Travel Service, 7818 3rd Ave, Brooklyn; 11209-3606 718-680-2700 Fax 718-680-2743

♀ ○ Dix Hills Travel, 868 East Jericho Turnpike, Huntington Station; 11746 516-673-6333 Fax 516-673-4114

♀ ● ♿♿ Frankel Travel, 350 5th Ave #1004; 10118 212-714-1700 Fax 212-714-1377

♂ ● Islanders/Kennedy Travel, 183 W 10th St; 10014 212-247-3222; 800-988-1181; "Gay travel agency & party events."

♀ ○ J. Bette Travel, 4809 Ave N #279, Brooklyn; 11234 718-241-3872 Fax 718-241-3481

♀ ● **Kennedy Travel, 267-10 Hillside Ave, Floral Park; 11004 718-347-7433 (NYC); 800-237-7433**

♂ ● (?♿) Our Family Abroad, 40 W 57th St #430; 10019 212-459-1800; 800-999-5500

♂ ● Out Everywhere!, PO Box 4571, Great Neck; 11023 516-482-1405 Fax 516-466-2847

♂ ● Pied Piper Travel, 330 W 42nd St #1601; 10036 212-239-2412; 800-TRIP-312; "Gay group cruises on the QE2 our specialty."

♂ ○ (?♿) Pink Pyramid Tours, PWT & Cruises, 2 W 45th St #1101; 10036 212-869-3890; 800-874-1811; Fax 212-869-5932

GAY+LESBIAN SWITCHBOARD OF NY

(212) 777-1800

Volunteers alway welcome

♂ ● Pride Tours, 267-10 Hillside Ave, Floral Park; 11004 718-368-8412

♂ ● ♿ Qui/Palmer Travel, 540 Palmer Rd, Yonkers; 10701-5207 914-965-5051 "Ask for Jacqui."

♀ ○ ♿ Solid Gold Travel, Inc, 718-597-7867 Fax 718-767-7204

♀ ○ (♿♿) Specialty Travel, 185 Medford Ave, Patchogue; 11772 516-289-5070; 516-758-0060

♀ ○ ♿ Stevens Travel Management, 432 Park Ave S., 9th Flr; 10016 212-696-4300; 800-275-7400 (Fred Shames ext 211); Fax 212-696-0591

♀ ○ T.R.I.P. Tours Ltd, 11 Grace Ave, Great Neck; 11021 516-487-9400; 800-553-7494

♀ ● ♿ Tan Spa Travel, 390 Central Park Ave, Scarsdale; 10583 914-472-2273 Fax 914-227-4059

♂ ● Tour Du Jour, 28 W 44th St #900; 10036 212-789-9129; 800-654-3117 outside NY State; "Specializing in national & international gay events."

♂ ● **Travel Masters of NY, 20 Lakeview Ave, Rockville Centre; 11570 516-766-0707; 800-MORE-TVL; Fax 516-766-5126**

♀ ○ The Travel People, Inc, 35 Greenwich Ave; 10014 212-675-6566 Fax 212-627-0452 10am-6.30pm.

♀ ○ ♿ Travel Tammaro, 139-15 83rd Ave #125, Briarwood; 11435 718-805-0907 "All destinations. Ticket & travel documents delivered to any location."

♀ ● Triangle Travel, 5 Beekman St #920; 10038 212-608-1000; 800-572-5266; Fax 212-608-2980

♀ ○ TTD The Travel Department, 15 Penn Plaza; 10001 212-279-3939; 800-660-3939; Fax 212-279-6469

♀ ○ Yampolsky, Michael, Battery Travel Associates, Inc., 132 Nassau St #822; 10038 212-587-0088 Fax 212-349-4102

Veterinarians

Brooklyn

♀ ● ♿ Animal Clinic of New York, 1623 1st Ave; 10028 212-628-5580

♀ ○ ♿ Animal Clinic of Sunset Park, 5908 5th Ave, Brooklyn; 11220 718-492-9090

Manhattan

♀ ○ Novick, Richard M., DVM, PC, 267 W 25th St; 10001 212-691-9270

Video Sales, Rentals, Services (see also Erotica)

♂ ● ♿ Spur Productions, 150 W 26th St #703; 10001 212-727-8850 Fax 212-229-2347 "Complete video production, location & studio, 3 cameras & in-house editing. Duplication: special quantity rates to Gay Community."

NY: New York City Area
Video Sales, Rentals, Services

358

USA

Poughkeepsie/Kingston Area: NY
Counseling: Private

♂ • Third Avenue Video Haven, 220 E 14th St; 10003 212-475-4223 "Sales & rentals."

Women's Centers

Long Island

♀ ★ (?⚥) Women's Alternatives Community Center, PO Box 232, Westbury; 11590-0232 516-483-2050 Call for information.

Niagara Falls

Accommodation: Hotels, B&B, Resorts, Campgrounds

♀ ○ Olde Niagara House, 610 4th St; 14301 716-285-9408 "Niagara's oldest Bed & Breakfast."

Erotica (Printed, Visual, Equipment)

♀ ○ Unique News, 1907 Main St; 14305 716-282-9282

Organizations/Resources: Social, Recreational & Support Groups (see also Sport/Dance/Outdoor)

⚥ ★ (?⚥) G.A.L.S. (Gay & Lesbian Support), PO Box 1464, M.P.O.; 14302

Oneonta

Clothes

♀ ○ Atomic Boutique, 100 Main St; 13820

Organizations/Resources: General, Multipurpose, Pride

♀ ★ LGCN (Lesbian & Gay Concerns Network), c/o Unitarian Universalist Church, 12 Ford Ave; 13820 607-432-1289

Organizations/Resources: Student, Academic, Alumni/ae

⚥ ★ GOAL: Gay Organization for Alternative Lifestyles, c/o Student Assoc, Hunt Union Bldg, SUNY; 13820

Ontario

Travel & Tourist Services (see also Accommodation)

♀ ○ Catherine's Travel Service, 528 Haley Road; 14519 315-524-8733

Oswego

Organizations/Resources: Student, Academic, Alumni/ae

⚥ ★ ⚥ Gay & Lesbian Alliance SUC-Oswego, c/o Student Association, Hewitt Union Rm 225; 13126 315-341-2955

Women's Centers

♀ ☆ Oswego Women's Center, 243 Hewitt Union, SUNY-Oswego; 13126 315-341-2967

Owego

Travel & Tourist Services (see also Accommodation)

♀ • ⚥ Tioga Travel, 189 Main St; 13827 607-687-4144

Pawling

Counseling/Therapy: Private

♀ ○ ⚥ Walsh, Eileen M., MS, Old Route 22, Box 50; 12564 914-855-5306

Plattsburgh

Bars, Restaurants, Clubs, Discos

⚥ ○ Blair's Cocktail Lounge, 30 Marion St; 12901 518-561-9071 *BD*

Erotica (Printed, Visual, Equipment)

♀ ○ ⚥ Triple A Video, 622 N Margaret St; 12901

Organizations/Resources: Student, Academic, Alumni/ae

⚥ ★ ⚥ Lesbian, Gay & Bisexual Alliance at Plattsburgh, SUNY Plattsburgh, Angell College Center; 12901 518-564-3200

Port Ewen: see Poughkeepsie/Kingston Area

Potsdam

☎ Reachout of St Lawrence County, Inc 315-265-2422

Organizations/Resources: Student, Academic, Alumni/ae

⚥ ★ ⚥ Lesbian/Gay/Bisexual Association at SUNY Potsdam, Barrington Student Union; 13676 315-267-2184

Switchboards, Helplines, Phone Information

♀ ☆ Reachout of St Lawrence County, Inc, PO Box 5051; 13676 315-265-2422

Poughkeepsie/Kingston Area

Accommodation: Hotels, B&B, Resorts, Campgrounds

Newburgh

♀ ○ (⚥) Stockbridge Ramsdell Bed & Breakfast, 158 Montgomery St, Newburgh; 12550 914-561-3462

Stone Ridge

♀ ○ (?⚥) Hasbrouck House Bed & Breakfast, PO Box 76, Stone Ridge; 12484 914-687-0736

Antiques & Collectables

♀ ○ (⚥⚥) Skillypot Antique Center, 41 Broadway, Kingston; 12401 914-338-6779 11am-5pm; closed Wed.

♀ ○ (⚥) Tiques & Stuff, 41 Broadway, Kingston; 12401 914-338-6779

Art Galleries/Archives/Restoration, Supplies, Framing

♀ • Ascent Fine Art II, 38 S Perry St #2, Poughkeepsie; 12601-3011 914-473-7864 By appointment.

Bars, Restaurants, Clubs, Discos

Highland

⚥ • (⚥) Prime Time, Rt 9W, Highland: 12528 914-691-8550 *BDE*

Kingston

⚥ • Campus, 731 Broadway; 12401 914-339-0730

Port Ewen

⚥ • ⚥⚥ The Club, 100 Broadway (at Rt 9W) 914-334-9657 *BDE*

Poughkeepsie

♂ ○ ⚥ Congress Tavern, 411 Main Mall E, Poughkeepsie; 12601 914-486-9068; 914-486-9531; *Bfd*

Wappingers Falls

♀ The Clever Hen, 114 Old Post Road, Wappingers Falls; 12590 914-298-9380

⚥ ○ Club FX, Duchess Shopping Plaza, Rte 9, behind Dunkin Donuts 914-297-1585 *DE* Thu-Sat 9pm-4am; Sun 6pm-2am. (Name may change)

Bookstores: General

♀ ○ Author Author, 37 Broadway, Kingston; 12401-6059 914-339-1883; 914-339-1889

Counseling/Therapy: Private

⚥ • Barker, Stephanie L., MSW, CSW, 123 Main St, Kingston; 12401 914-336-0756

♀ • ⚥⚥ Steinhorn, Audrey, 24 Davis Ave, Poughkeepsie; 12603 914-452-0374

Erotica (Printed, Visual, Equipment)

⚥ ○ Hamilton Book, 216 N Hamilton St, Poughkeepsie; 12601 914-473-1776

Legal Services & Resources

⚥ ○ Levine & Htoo, Esq., 290 Hooker Ave, Poughkeepsie; 12603 914-452-2366

Organizations/Resources: Business & Professional

⚦ Mid Hudson G&L Professional Alliance, PO Box 3727, Poughkeepsie; 12603

Organizations/Resources: Family

⚥ ☆ Mid-Hudson PFLAG, PO Box 880, Pleasant Valley; 12569 914-221-9559 "Parents, Families & Friends of Lesbians & Gays."

Organizations/Resources: Political/Legislative

♀ ☆&& Ulster County NOW, PO Box 4182, Kingston; 12401 914-688-2169

Organizations/Resources: Social, Recreational & Support Groups (see also Sport/Dance/Outdoor)

⚦ ★ Newburgh Neighbors Network, 914-561-0283; 914-561-5047

⚦ Visibility Project, PO Box 44, Rosendale; 12472 914-338-5087

Organizations/Resources: Sport/Dance/Outdoor

♀ ★ (?&) WOMBATS, Jenny Krouse, PO Box 291, Rosendale; 12472 914-658-9720 "Women's Mountain Bike and Tea Society."

Organizations/Resources: Student, Academic, Alumni/ae

⚦ ★ & BIGALA: Bisexual, Gay & Lesbian Alliance, Vassar College Maildrop 271, 124 Raymond Ave, Poughkeepsie; 12601

⚦ ★&& Poughkeepsie GALA (Gay & Lesbian Association), PO Box 289, Hughsonville; 12537 518-431-6756 Pub *GALA Connection.*

Religious Organizations & Publications

⚦ ★&& Dignity-Integrity/Mid-Hudson, PO Box 356, Lagrangeville; 12540-0356 914-724-3209 Pub *Koinonia.* "Gay & Lesbian Catholics, Episcopalians, & their friends."

Veterinarians

♀ ○ Yasson, Michele, DVM, CVA, PO Box 291, Rosendale; 12472 914-658-3923 "Acupuncture & homeopathy only."

Video Sales, Rentals, Services (see also Erotica)

⚥ • The Alternative Video Shop, 26 Main St, Rosendale 914-658-3875 Fax 914-658-3875 10am-10pm; Fri & Sat to 11pm; Sun noon-10pm.

Purchase: see New York City Area

Rochester Area

☎ Gay Alliance of Genesee Valley (GAGV) 716-244-8640

AIDS/HIV Support, Education, Advocacy, Publications

⚥ ☆&& AIDS Rochester, Inc, 1350 University Ave #C, Rochester; 14607-1622 716-442-2220 (V/TDD)

⚥ ☆ HPA (Helping People With AIDS), Inc., PO Box 1543, Rochester; 14603-1543 716-987-1853

Bars, Restaurants, Clubs, Discos

⚦ • & Anthony's 522, 522 E Main St, Rochester; 14604 716-325-2060 *BD* Noon-2am.

♂ • Avenue Pub, 522 Monroe Ave, Rochester; 14607 716-244-4960

♂ • Bachelor Forum, 670 University Ave, Rochester; 14607-1232 716-271-6930 *BDLW*

⚦ Bobby's, 379 Lake Ave, Rochester; 14608 716-458-8160

⚦ • (&&) Club Mahara, 10-12 S Washington, Rochester; 14614 716-423-9748 *BD*

⚦ Club Marcella, 123 Liberty Pole Way, Rochester; 14604 716-454-5963

⚦ • && Common Grounds, 139 State St, Rochester; 14614 716-232-9303 *BLd*

♂ Gallery, 113 State St, Rochester; 14614 716-232-1734

♀ ○ & Heaven Nightclub, 50 Liberty Pole Way, Rochester; 14604 716-262-4340 *D* 9pm-2am.

⚦ • (&) Mother's 40 Union, 40 South Union St, Rochester; 14607 716-325-6216 Fax 716-288-2802 *BRD* 2pm-2am; restaurant 5pm-2am.

♂ Pandora's, 90 Liberty Pole Way, Rochester; 14604 716-232-5440

♂ The Stages, 88 Liberty Pole Way, Rochester; 14604 716-232-5070 *BDE*

⚦ ○ Tara Cocktail Lounge, 153 Liberty Pole Way, Rochester; 14604 716-232-4719 Noon-2am.

Bookstores: General

⚥ ○ Park Avenue Bookstore, 370 Park Ave, Rochester; 14607 716-271-6120

⚥ • & Silkwood Books, Inc, 633 Monroe Ave, Rochester; 14607 716-473-8110 Tue& Wed 11am-6pm; Thu-Sat to 9pm; Sun noon-5pm.

⚥ ○ (&) Village Green Bookstore, 766 Monroe Ave, Rochester; 14607-3296 716-442-1151

⚥ ○ (&&) Village Green Bookstore, 1954 West Ridge Rd, Rochester; 14626 716-723-1600 Fax 716-723-1669

⚥ ○ Worldwide News, 100 St Paul, Rochester; 14604 716-546-7140

Counseling/Therapy: Private

⚦ • Debes, Barbara, MS, 545 Park Ave, Rochester; 14607 716-271-4610

Erotica (Printed, Visual, Equipment)

⚥ ○ Dundalk News, 561 State St, Rochester; 14608 716-325-2248 24 hrs. "Private video viewing booths. We carry Gay & Lesbian fiction & nonfiction; Rainbow Coalition & CHEF children's books. AIDS library. Alternative lifestyle resource center."

⚥ ○&& Hudson Video & News, 1462 Hudson Ave, Rochester; 14621 716-342-8310 24 hrs. "Private video viewing booths. We carry Gay & Lesbian fiction & nonfiction; Rainbow Coalition & CHEF children's books. AIDS library. Alternative lifestyle resource center."

⚥ • & Monroe Show World, 587 Monroe Ave, Rochester; 14607 716-473-0160

⚥ ○ New Clinton Book Mart, 115 Clinton Ave N., Rochester; 14604-1411 716-325-9322

⚥ ○ & North End News, 490 Monroe Ave, Rochester; 14607 716-271-1426

♂ • Rochester Custom Leathers, 274 N Goodman St, Rochester; 14607 (Village Gate Sq) 716-442-2323

⚥ ○ (&) State Street Bookstore, 109 State St, Rochester; 14614 716-263-9919

NY: Rochester Area

360

Rochester Area: NY

Erotica

USA

Video Sales, Rentals, Services

♀ ○ Times Square Books, 57 Mortimer St, Rochester; 14604-1317 716-325-9570

Gifts, Cards, Pride & Novelty Items

♀ ○ Chatterly's, 667 Monroe Ave, Rochester; 14607 716-473-6918 11am-9pm; Sat to 7pm; Sun noon-6pm.

Gifts, Cards, Pride & Promotional Items

♀ ○ ♿ Parkleigh, 215 Park Ave, Rochester; 14607 716-244-4842

Gifts, Cards, Pride & Novelty Items

♀ • Pride Connection, 728 South Ave, Rochester; 14620 716-242-7840 10am-9pm; Sun noon-6pm. "Gifts, cards, books, videos."

Grooming Services

♀ • (♿) Hair Force, 1100 Atlantic Ave, Rochester; 14600 716-224-9090

Health Clubs, Gyms, Saunas

♂ • Rochester Spa & Body Club, 109 Liberty Pole Way, Rochester; 14604 716-454-1074 24 hrs.

Home & Building: Cleaning, Repair, General Contractors

♀ • Saltzman, Kenneth R., 716-654-6174 "Painter."

Legal Services & Resources

♀ ○ Dunn, Andrew S., 36 W Main St, 495 Executive Office Bldg, Rochester; 14614 716-262-2190 Fax 716-325-4156

♀ ○ ♿ Krieger, Lawrence, Attorney at Law, 1 E Main St #400, Rochester; 14614 716-325-2640

Organizations/Resources: Business & Professional

♀ ★ (?♿) Bar Association for Human Rights of Western New York (BAHR-WNY), 96 Mount Vernon Ave, Rochester; 14620-2150 716-244-3038

♀ ★ Gays & Lesbians at Xerox (GALAXE), PO Box 25382, Rochester; 14625 716-473-5982

Organizations/Resources: Family

♂ ★ Gay Married Men's Support Group, PO Box 10041, Rochester; 14610

♀ ☆ (?♿) P-FLAG/Rochester, 179 Atlantic Ave, c/o GAGV, Rochester; 14607-1255 716-436-7051 Pub Newsletter. "Parents, Families & Friends of Lesbians & Gays."

Organizations/Resources: General, Multipurpose, Pride

♀ ★ Gay Alliance of Genesee Valley (GAGV), 179 Atlantic Ave, Rochester; 14607-1255 716-244-8640

Organizations/Resources: Political/Legislative

♀ ★ ♿ Rochester Lesbian & Gay Political Caucus, 179 Atlantic Ave, Rochester; 14607-1255 716-234-5050 Meets 2nd Mon, 7pm. "Non-partisan lobbying & educational group."

Organizations/Resources: Sexual Focus (Leather, S/M, etc) & Safe Sex Promotion

♂ ★ Rochester Rams, PO Box 1727, Rochester; 14603 716-244-9812 (Leather/Levi club; home bar Bachelor Forum)

♂ ★ T.O.M., PO Box 10514, Rochester; 14610-0514 "JO group."

Organizations/Resources: Social, Recreational & Support Groups (see also Sport/Dance/Outdoor)

♀ ★ ♂ G.L.S.G., PO Box 211, Penn Yan; 14527

♀ Lambda Kodak, PO Box 14067, Rochester; 14614 716-234-4388

♀ ★ (♿) OMEGA (Older Mature & Gay Action/Advocacy), PO Box 10292, Rochester; 14610-0292 716-223-2748

♀ ★ T.L.C. The Lesbian Connection, mail to T.L.C., Michele & Sandy Rea, Box 397, Manchester; 14504 716-289-3197

Organizations/Resources: Sport/Dance/Outdoor

♀ ○ (♿) Freewheelers Bicycle Shop & Personal Fitness Center, 1149 Culver Rd, Rochester; 14609 716-473-3724

♀ Out & About, c/o GAGV, 179 Atlantic Ave, Rochester; 14607-1255

Organizations/Resources: Student, Academic, Alumni/ae

♀ ★ ♿ Bisexual-Gay & Lesbian Association of RIT, c/o Student Directorate/Ritreat, 1 Lomb Memorial Drive, Rochester; 14623 716-475-3296

♀ ★ (?♿) Gay, Lesbian, Bisexual & Friends Association (GLBFA) University of Rochester, Wilson Commons #101J, Rochester; 14627 716-275-9379

Organizations/Resources: Transgender & Transgender Publications

♂ ☆ (♿) Rochester CD Network, PO Box 92055, Rochester; 14692 716-251-2132 24 hrs. Pub CD-News. "Non-sexual support group for crossdressers & their wives or girlfriends. Educational library. Monthly meetings."

Organizations/Resources: Youth (see also Family)

♀ ★ Lesbian & Gay Youth of Rochester, 179 Atlantic Ave c/o GAGV, Rochester; 14607-1255 716-251-9604

Performing Arts: Entertainment, Music, Theater, etc.

♂ ★ ♿ Rochester Gay Men's Chorus, 121 N Fitzhugh St #433, Rochester; 14614-1214 716-423-0650

Publications

♀ ★ (?♿) The Empty Closet, 179 Atlantic Ave, Rochester; 14607-1255 716-244-9030

Religious Organizations & Publications

♀ ★ (?♿) Dignity/Integrity Rochester, 17 S Fitzhugh St, Rochester; 14614 716-262-2170 "Gay & Lesbian Catholics & Episcopalians & their friends."

♀ ★ Nayim, PO Box 18053, Rochester; 14618 716-461-3386

♀ ★ ♂ Open Arms Metropolitan Community Church, 875 E Main St, Rochester; 14605 716-271-8478

♀ ★ ♿ Presbyterians for Lesbian & Gay Concerns, c/o Carter, 111 Milburn St, Rochester; 14607-2918 716-271-7649 ralph_carter.parti@pcusa.org Meets 1st Thu, 7.30pm, 3rd Presbyterian, 4 Meigs St.

Travel & Tourist Services (see also Accommodation)

♀ ○ Breslin, Ray, De Prez Travel, 325 Westminster Rd, Rochester; 14607 716-234-3615 Fax 716-442-8309

♀ ○ ♿ De Prez Travel Bureau, 145 Rue De Ville, Rochester; 14618-5684 716-442-8900

♀ • (?♿) Great Expectations Travel Services, 1649 Monroe Ave, Rochester; 14618 716-244-8430

♀ ○ Park Ave Travel Inc, 25 Buckingham St, Rochester; 14607 716-256-3080 Fax 716-473-7436

Video Sales, Rentals, Services (see also Erotica)

♂ • Video Channel, 667 Monroe Ave, Rochester; 14607 716-442-1140 11am-9pm; Sat to 7pm; Sun noon-6pm.

Rosendale: see Poughkeepsie/Kingston Area

NY: Saranac Lake
Accommodation

361

USA

Syracuse : NY
Organizations: Student

Saranac Lake

Accommodation: Reservations & Exchanges (see also Travel)

♀ ○ (♿) **Adirondack Bed & Breakfast Reservations Service**, 10 Park Place; 12983 518-891-1632; 800-891-1632

Saratoga Springs: see Saratoga/Lake George Area

Saratoga/Lake George Area

Accommodation: Hotels, B&B, Resorts, Campgrounds

Lake George

♀ • ♿ King Hendrick Motel, RR3 Box 3340, Lake George; 12845 / Rte 9 518-792-0418 April to November.

Bars, Restaurants, Clubs, Discos

Ballston Spa

♀ ○ Serendipty's, 2839 Rte 9, Ballston Spa; 12020 518-584-6077

Glens Falls

♀ Alternatives, 22 South St, Glens Falls; 12801 518-792-9441 *BD*

♀ • Martini's, 70 South St, Glens Falls; 12801 518-798-9808

Bookstores: General

♀ Bookworks, 456 Broadway, Saratoga Springs; 12866 518-587-3228

♀ ○ ♿ Nahani, 482 Broadway, Saratoga Springs; 12866 518-587-4322

Gardening Services, Landscaping, Supplies & Decoration

♀ • Legend Landscaping: Connie Schmitz, 2743 Rt 29, Middle Grove; 12850-1302 518-882-9885

Graphic Design/Typesetting (see also Art; Printing)

♀ • **Country Graphics, 13 McDowell St, Hudson Falls; 12839 800-600-1660 "Custom T-shirts, etc."**

Health Care (see also AIDS Services)

♀ ○ ♿ Allison, Lynn, DC, 20 Front St, Ballston Spa; 12020 518-884-9395

Organizations/Resources: General, Multipurpose, Pride

♀ ★ Network North, PO Box 118, Saratoga Springs; 12866 518-583-3834 networknor@aol.com Pub *Network North News*.

♀ ★ (♿) Saratoga Gay Coalition, PO Box 333, Clifton Park; 12065-0333 518-798-3304

Schenectady: see Albany & Capital Area

Sharon Springs

Accommodation: Hotels, B&B, Resorts, Campgrounds

♀ • The Turnaround Spa House, 201 Washington St; 13459 518-284-2271; 212-628-9008; *R*

Somers: see New York City Area

Spring Valley

Bars, Restaurants, Clubs, Discos

♀ • (♿) Hideaway, 105 S Pascack Rd; 10977 914-425-0025 *BDEf* 9pm-4am; Sun 4pm-4am.

Travel & Tourist Services (see also Accommodation)

♀ • (♿) Trade Wind, 6 Jay Street; 10977 914-352-4134 Fax 914-352-4134

Staten Island: see New York City Area

Stony Brook: see New York City Area

Stormville: see Poughkeepsie/Kingston Area

Syracuse

☎ Gayline 315-422-5732

☎ Gayphone 315-443-3599

AIDS/HIV Support, Education, Advocacy, Publications

→ AIDS Community Resources: p.317

♀ ☆ H.O.P.E., Inc., PO Box 6728; 13217-6728 / 205 Hickory St 315-474-3616 (Fax ext. 333)

Bars, Restaurants, Clubs, Discos

♂ Armory Pub, 400 S Clinton; 13202 315-471-9059

♀ • Claudia's UBU, 1203 Milton Ave; 13204 315-468-9830 *BDR* 4pm-2am; Sun 1pm-2am.

♂ • (♿) Mr. T's, 218 N Franklin St; 13202 (entrance on Herald Place) 315-471-0376 *BD*

♀ • My Bar, 205 N West St; 13204 315-471-9279 *BRE* 11am-2am; Sat 10am-2am. "Neighborhood type bar, family owned & run."

♀ • ♿ Ryan's Someplace Else, 408-410 Pearl St; 13202 315-471-9499 *BD*

♀ • ♿ Trexx, 319 N Clinton St; 13202 (Harold Pl) 315-474-6408 *BD* Tue-Thu & Sun 6pm-2am; Fri & Sat to 4pm.

♀ • ♿♿ Tu Tu Venue, 731 James St; 13202 315-475-8888 *BR*

Bookstores: Gay/Lesbian/Feminist

♀ • My Sisters' Words, 304 N McBride St; 13203 315-428-0227 "Lesbian/feminist publications."

Bookstores: General

♀ ☆ Front Room Bookstore, Syracuse Peace Council, 924 Burnet Ave; 13203 315-472-5478 Mon-Fri noon-6pm; Sat 10am-3pm.

Counseling/Therapy: Private

♀ ○ (♿) Graham, Sharon, 213 Cambridge St; 13210 315-445-9633

Erotica (Printed, Visual, Equipment)

♀ ○ Burnet Bookstore, 303 Burnet Ave; 13203 315-471-9230

♀ ○ ♿ Salt City Book & Video, 2807 Brewerton Rd; 13212-4100 315-454-0629

Organizations/Resources: Business & Professional

♀ ★ ♿♿ Gay & Lesbian University Employees (GLUE), PO Box 922 University Stn; 13210

Organizations/Resources: Social, Recreational & Support Groups (see also Sport/Dance/Outdoor)

♀ GLAS (Gay & Lesbian Alliance Of Syracuse), PO Box 1675; 13201 315-422-5732

♂ The Stonewall Committee, 246 E Water St; 13202

Organizations/Resources: Student, Academic, Alumni/ae

♀ ★ ♿♿ Gay & Lesbian & All Student Association, Onondaga Community College, Rt 173; 13215

♀ ★ Syracuse University Gay, Lesbian, Bisexual Student Association, 750 Ostrom Ave; 13244-4350 315-443-3599 Gayphone 7-11pm.

NY: Syracuse
Organizations: Transgender

362

USA

Woodstock : NY
Weddings/Unions

Organizations/Resources: Transgender & Transgender Publications

T Eon (Expressing Our Nature), 523 Onondaga St; 13204 315-475-5611

Performing Arts: Entertainment, Music, Recording, Theater, etc.

♂ ★ ♂♂ Syracuse Gay & Lesbian Chorus, Inc, PO Box 6796; 13217 315-476-4329

Publications

♀ • *The Pink Paper*, PO Box 6462; 13217-6462 315-479-9644

Real Estate

♀ • Severance, Scott, 919 Salt Springs Rd; 13224 315-446-2867 "Residential real estate sales."

Religious Organizations & Publications

♀ ★ ♂♂ May Memorial Unitarian Universalists for Lesbian & Gay Concerns, May Memorial Unitarian Society, 3800 E Genessee St; 13214 315-446-2867

♀ ★ ♂♂ Ray of Hope Metropolitan Community Church, PO Box 6955; 13217-6955 315-762-8397 Worship Sun 6pm at 819 Madison St.

Switchboards, Helplines, Phone Information

♀ ★ Gayline, PO Box 738; 13201-0738 315-422-5732 Mon-Fri 7.30-9.30pm.

♀ ★ Gayphone, c/o Gay, Lesbian, Bisexual Student Association, 750 Ostrom Ave; 13244-4350 315-443-3599 7-11pm.

Women's Centers

♀ ☆ ♂♂ Syracuse University Women's Center, Schine Center 126, 303 University Place; 13244 315-423-4268

♀ ☆ ♂ Women's Information Center, 601 Allen St; 13210 315-478-4636 Pub *Info News*.

Troy: see Albany & Capital Area

Tupper Lake

Organizations/Resources: Social, Recreational & Support Groups (see also Sport/Dance/Outdoor)

♀ ★ Adirondack GABLE, 620 Panther Mtd Rd; 12986 518-359-7358

Utica

Addictive Behavior, Substance Abuse, Recovery

♀ ★ Lambda Acceptance Group, Alcoholics Anonymous, Meets Thu 7.30pm at First Presbyterian Church, 1605 Genesee St

AIDS/HIV Support, Education, Advocacy, Publications

♀ ☆ Mid-New York AIDS Coalition, 1644 Genessee St; 13502-5428 315-724-3921 Mon, Wed, Fri 11am-2am.

Bars, Restaurants, Clubs, Discos

♀ Carmen D's, 812 Charlotte St; 13501 315-735-3964

♀ ○ Lipstix, 1724 Oriskany Blvd West; 13502 315-724-9231

♂ • That Place, 216 Bleecker St; 13503 315-724-1446 *BDLW*

Clothes

♀ ○ Atomic Boutique, 112 Varick St; 13502

Erotica (Printed, Visual, Equipment)

♀ • ♂ Adult World, 319 Oriskany Blvd, Yorkville; 13495

Gifts, Cards, Pride & Novelty Items

♀ ○ Balls Card Shop, 2 Lafayette St; 13502 315-733-7005 Mon-Fri 4am-4.30pm; Sat, Sun, holidays 4am-noon.

Organizations/Resources: General, Multipurpose, Pride

♀ ★ ♂ Greater Utica Lambda Fellowship, PO Box 122; 13503 Pub *Gulf Gayzette*.

Organizations/Resources: Sexual Focus (Leather, S/M, etc) & Safe Sex Promotion

♂ ★ ♂ Utica Tri's, MC, PO Box 425; 13503

Publications

♀ ★ (?♂) LIP (Lesbian Interest Pages) Newsletter, PO Box 761; 13503-0761 315-942-4035; 315-336-3197 Warmline

Religious Organizations & Publications

♀ Community, PO Box 352; 13503-0352 315-738-0599 (Catholic)

♀ ★ Dignity/Mid New York, PO Box 352; 13503 315-738-0599 dignitymny@aol.com "Gay & Lesbian Catholics & Friends."

Wappingers Falls: see Poughkeepsie/Kingston Area

West Haverstraw

Travel & Tourist Services (see also Accommodation)

♀ ○ Noah's Ark Travel, 33A Roosevelt Dr; 10993 914-429-7556; 800-633-NOAH; Fax 914-942-2417

White Plains: see New York City Area

Woodstock

Accommodation: Hotels, B&B, Resorts, Campgrounds

♀ ○ (?♂) The Woodstock Inn, 38 Tannery Brook Rd; 12498 914-679-8211

Bookstores: General

♀ ○ ♂ Golden Notebook, 29 Tinker St; 12498 914-679-8000 11am-7pm; summer to 9pm.

Real Estate

♀ • Village Green Realty, 5 Rock City Road; 12498 914-679-2255 Fax 914-679-2715
✦ *Village Green Realty advertisement page 362*

Weddings/Unions

♀ • Pride, Love, & Union Services, PO Box 283; 12491 914-448-3754 Fax 914-448-4076 gaywed@aol.com

Yonkers: see New York City Area

Yorkville: see Utica

North Carolina

State/County Resources

Funding: Endowment, Fundraising, Scholarship

⚥ ★ && Gaslight Productions, Bourbon Street, Inc., PO Box 26222, Winston-Salem, NC 27114 910-724-4644 Fax 910-722-3099 *The Gaslight*. "Produces & promotes fund raisers for various gay/AIDS related charities on a state level."

Legal Services & Resources

♀ ☆ ♂ American Civil Liberties Union of North Carolina (ACLU), PO Box 28004, Raleigh, NC 27611 919-834-3390; 919-834-3466; Fax 919-828-3265 aclunc@nando.net

Organizations/Resources: Business & Professional

⚥ ★ North Carolina Gay & Lesbian Attorneys (NC-GALA), PO Box 2164, Durham, NC 27702

Organizations/Resources: Political/Legislative

⚥ ★ ♂ Lesbian & Gay Democrats of North Carolina, PO Box 307, Chapel Hill, NC 27514 919-929-4053

⚥ ★ (?&) NC Pride PAC, PO Box 28768, Raleigh, NC 27611-3763 919-829-0343 NC Pride Political Action Committee for Lesbian & Gay Equality

⚥ ★ && North Carolina Coalition for Gay & Lesbian Equality, PO Box 61392, Durham, NC 27715 919-286-1378

Organizations/Resources: Sexual Focus (Leather, S/M, etc) & Safe Sex Promotion

♂ ★ (?&) Carolina Punishment, mail to CP, c/o G/M-NC PO Box 38032, Greensboro, NC 27438 Pub *CP News*. "Social group for spanking enthusiasts."

Organizations/Resources: Social, Recreational & Support Groups (see also Sport/Dance/Outdoor)

♂ ★ (?&) Girth & Mirth of North Carolina, PO Box 38032, Greensboro, NC 27438 704-274-2100 Pub *Carolina Chubby Review*. "Chubby chaser group."

Organizations/Resources: Sport/Dance/Outdoor

♂ ★ Tarheel Outdoor Sports Fellowship, PO Box 10644, Greensboro, NC 27404 910-299-9683 "Friendly athletic high adventure group; send SASE + $1 for information."

Publications

♂ • && *Blue Nights*, PO Box 221841, Charlotte, NC 28222 704-531-9988 Fax 704-531-1361

⚥ ★ *Community Connections*, PO Box 18088, Asheville, NC 28814 704-285-8861

⚥ • && *Front Page*, PO Box 27928, Raleigh, NC 27611 919-829-0181
✦ *Front Page* advertisement page 363

⚥ • && *Q-Notes*, PO Box 221841, Charlotte, NC 28222 704-531-9988 Fax 704-531-1361

Real Estate

⚥ • Community Real Estate Referrals, 800-346-5592 "Free referral to gay/gay-supportive realtor in any USA city/state (including Virgin Is. & Puerto Rico). Sorry, no rentals!"
✦ *Community Real Estate Referrals* advertisement back cover

Asheville

☎ Asheville Gay & Lesbian Information Line 704-253-2971

Accommodation: Hotels, B&B, Resorts, Campgrounds

⚥ • The Bird's Nest, 41 Oak Park Rd; 28801 704-252-2381

♀ ○ The Inn On Montford, 296 Montford Ave; 28801 704-254-9569

⚥ • The Old Mill, PO Box 252, Bat Cave; 28710 / Hwy 74/64/9 704-625-4256

AIDS/HIV Support, Education, Advocacy, Publications

♀ ☆ (?&) Mountain AIDS Coalition, PO Box 1862; 28802 704-253-4647

♀ ★ && PWA Support Groups, Box 5978, c/o All Souls Episcopal Church; 28813 704-277-7815; 704-669-2635

♀ ☆ && Western North Carolina AIDS Project, PO Box 2411; 28802 704-252-7489

Art Galleries/Archives/Restoration, Supplies, Framing

♀ • && Blue Spiral 1, 38 Biltmore Ave; 28801 704-251-0202 Mon-Sat 10am-5pm.

♀ • New Morning Gallery, 7 Boston Way; 28803 704-274-2831 10am-6pm; Sun noon-5pm. Annual Village Art & Craft Fair every August.

Bars, Restaurants, Clubs, Discos

♀ • ♂ Cahoots, 12 Grove St; 28801 704-252-2838 **BDREP**

♀ • Hairspray Cafe & Club Metropolis, 38 N French Broad Ave; 28801 704-258-2027 **BDE** 7pm-3am.

⚥ • && O'Henry's of Asheville, 59 Haywood St; 28801 704-254-1891 **BDEPLW** 11am-2am; Sun 1am-2am.

⚥ Scandals, 12 Grove St; 28801 704-252-2838

NC: Asheville
Bookstores: General

364

USA

Charlotte : NC
Organizations: Business

Bookstores: General

♀ • ♿ Downtown Books & News, 67 N Lexington; 28801 704-253-8654 8am-6pm; Sun 6am-6pm. "Magazines; used books; out-of-town papers, natal charts."

♂ • ♿ Malaprop's Bookstore/Cafe, 61 Haywood; 28801 704-254-6734; 800-441-9829; 9am-8pm; Fri & Sat to 10pm; Sun noon-6pm. "Cafe offers light menu, beer & wine; store also sells cassettes & CDs of regional & women's music; community bulletin board; free movies & entertainment on weekends."

Bookstores: Recovery, Metaphysical, & other Specialty

♀ • ♿ Crystal Visions, PO Box 8, Naples; 28760 / Highway 25 704-687-1193

Counseling/Therapy: Private

♂ ○ Harrison, James, Ph.D., 492 Sunset Dr; 28804 Clinical psychologist.

Organizations/Resources: Ethnic, Multicultural

● ★ ♿ La Lucha, PO Box 1246; 28802 704-251-0475 "Lesbians who self-identify as being of color working to raise social/political consciousness. Monthly potlucks."

Organizations/Resources: Family

♀ ★ ♿♿ Western NC P-FLAG, PO Box 5978; 28813 704-277-7815; 704-669-2635; "Parents, Families & Friends of Lesbians & Gays."

Organizations/Resources: General, Multipurpose, Pride

♀ ★ ♿♿ Southern Appalachian Lesbian & Gay Alliance (SALGA), PO Box 197; 28802 704-645-5908

Organizations/Resources: Social, Recreational & Support Groups (see also Sport/Dance/Outdoor)

♀ ★ (♿) CLOSER (Community Liaison Organization for Support, Education, & Reform), PO Box 2911; 28802 704-277-7815

Organizations/Resources: Transgender & Transgender Publications

T Phoenix, PO Box 18332; 28814

Organizations/Resources: Youth (see also Family)

♀ ★ (♿♿) OutFit (Youth Support Group), c/o All Souls Parish, PO Box 5978; 28813 704-277-7815; 704-669-2635

Religious Organizations & Publications

♀ ★ ♿ Metropolitan Community Church/Asheville, PO Box 25278; 28813 704-687-9568

Switchboards, Helplines, Phone Information

♀ ★ Asheville Gay & Lesbian Information Line, c/o SALGA, PO Box 197; 28802 704-253-2971

Blowing Rock

Accommodation: Hotels, B&B, Resorts, Campgrounds

♂ • ♿♿ Stone Pillar B & B, PO Box 1881; 28605 / 144 Pine St 704-295-4141

Boone

AIDS/HIV Support, Education, Advocacy, Publications

♀ Hope HIV Support Group, Rt. 5, Box 549A; 28607 704-264-4109

Organizations/Resources: Family

♀ ☆ P-FLAG/Boone, Rt. 5, Box 549A; 28607 704-264-4109 "Parents, Families & Friends of Lesbians & Gays."

Organizations/Resources: Student, Academic, Alumni/ae

♀ B-GLAD, ASU Box 8979; 28608 704-265-2452

Religious Organizations & Publications

♀ ★ ♿♿ MCC of the High Country, PO Box 504; 28607 704-963-8582

Canton

Accommodation: Hotels, B&B, Resorts, Campgrounds

♂ ○ (♿) The Mountain Bungalow, Rte #2, Box 442; 28716 704-648-7702

Chapel Hill: see Triangle Area

Charlotte

☎ Gay & Lesbian Switchboard of Charlotte 704-535-6277

AIDS/HIV Support, Education, Advocacy, Publications

♀ ☆ ♿♿ Metrolina AIDS Project, PO Box 32662; 28232 800-289-AIDS; 704-333-AIDS Hotline Mon-Fri 9.30am-8.30pm; office 333-1435 Mon-Fri 9am-5pm.

♀ ☆ ♿♿ Project Outreach UFS, United Way Building, 301 S Brevard St; 28202 704-332-9034

♀ The Refuge, PO Box 31564; 28231 704-372-5499

Bars, Restaurants, Clubs, Discos

♂ • ♿♿ Chasers, 3217 The Plaza; 28205 704-339-0500 *P*

♀ • ♿♿ Liaisons, 316 Rensselaer; 28203 704-376-1617 *PBf* 4pm-1am.

♂ ○ Oleen's, PO Box 35676; 28235 / 1831 South Blvd 704-373-9604

♀ Scorpio, 2301 Freedom Drive; 28266 704-373-9124

♀ • ♿♿ Ye Olde Wishing Gate, 1501 Elizabeth Ave; 28204 704-339-0350 *B*

Bookstores: Gay/Lesbian/Feminist

♀ • ♿♿ Rising Moon Books & Beyond, 316 East Blvd; 28203 704-332-RISE Mon-Thu 10am-7pm; Fri & Sat to 6pm; Sun 1-6pm.

♀ • White Rabbit Books/Charlotte, call ahead for new address. 704-377-4067

Bookstores: General

♀ ○ Paper Skyscraper, 300 East Boulevard; 28203 704-333-7130

Erotica (Printed, Visual, Equipment)

♀ ○ Independence News, 3205 The Plaza; 28205 704-332-8430

Legal Services & Resources

♀ • ♿♿ Koenig, Jeffrey Grant, 1130 E 3rd St #400; 28204-2624 704-335-5471 Fax 704-335-5472

♀ • ♿♿ Southern Center for Law and Justice, PO Box 18804; 28218 / 4037 E Independence Blvd #565 704-567-5530 "Gay & Lesbian Law Project; Women's Law Project; general civil practice."

Organizations/Resources: Business & Professional

♀ ★ ♿♿ Charlotte Business Guild, PO Box 35445; 28235-5445 704-565-5075

Organizations/Resources: Education, Anti-Defamation, Anti-Violence, Self-Defense

♂ ★ Speakers Bureau, 2634-E Park Rd; 28209 704-332-3834

Organizations/Resources: Ethnic, Multicultural

♂ ★ BWMT-Charlotte, PO Box 29061; 28229-9061 704-563-0067 Black & White Men Together/Men of All Colors Together

Organizations/Resources: Family

♀ ☆&& P-FLAG, 5815 Charing Place; 28211 704-364-1474 "Parents, Families & Friends of Lesbians & Gays."

Organizations/Resources: General, Multipurpose, Pride

♂ ★&& Metrolina Community Service Project, PO Box 11144; 28220 704-535-6277

Organizations/Resources: Political/Legislative

♀ ☆ (?&) National Organization For Women (NOW), PO Box 37204; 28237

Organizations/Resources: Social, Recreational & Support Groups (see also Sport/Dance/Outdoor)

♂ **★&& Collections, 226 Baldwin Ave; 28204 704-333-SEEK Mon-Fri 6-10pm; Sat special events & workshops 1-4pm; Sun 4-8pm. "Meeting rooms; lending library; art gallery; information network."**

♂ ★&& Married Men's Group, PO Box 19524; 28219

♀ Older Wiser Lesbians (OWLS), PO Box 12072; 28220 704-376-4745

♂ ★&& Prime Timers Charlotte, PO Box 11202; 28220-1202 704-561-2257 "Mature gay & bisexual men 40 & over."

♀ ★ WOW!, PO Box 12072; 28220 704-563-7716

Organizations/Resources: Youth (see also Family)

♂ ★ Time Out Youth, 4037 E Independence Blvd #633; 28205-7375 704-537-5050 Fax 704-358-0164

Performing Arts: Entertainment, Music, Recording, Theater, etc.

♂ ★&& Charlotte Gay Men's Chorus, PO Box 11301; 28220 704-536-3967

♀ ★ One Voice, PO Box 9241; 28299 704-548-0771

Religious Organizations & Publications

♂ (?&) Integrity/Charlotte, PO Box 12204; 28220-2204 704-548-0987 "Lesbian & Gay Episcopalians & their friends."

♂ ★ (&) Lutherans Concerned of Charlotte, PO Box 9562; 28299 704-527-5753 *The Clarion.*

♂ ★ & Metropolitan Community Church/Charlotte, 4037 E Independence Blvd #300; 28205-7375 704-563-5810 Sun worship at 10.45am & 7.30pm.

♂ ★&& New Life Metropolitan Community Church, PO Box 221404; 28222 704-343-9070

Switchboards, Helplines, Phone Information

♂ ★ Gay & Lesbian Switchboard of Charlotte, PO Box 11144; 28220 704-535-6277 6.30-10.30pm.

Travel & Tourist Services (see also Accommodation)

♀ ○ **Atlantis Travel, 4801 E Independence Blvd #711; 28212 704-566-9779; 704-535-7649; Fax 704-535-7649**

Dallas

Organizations/Resources: Family

♀ P-FLAG Southeast Region, Box 722; 28034 704-922-9273 "Parents, Families & Friends of Lesbians & Gays."

Fairview

Accommodation: Hotels, B&B, Resorts, Campgrounds

♀ ● (&) Mountain Laurel B 'n B, 139 Lee Dotson Rd; 28730 704-628-9903

Fayetteville

Bars, Restaurants, Clubs, Discos

♂ ● & Oz, 2540 Gillespie St; 28306 910-485-2037 *BD* 9pm-3am.

Erotica (Printed, Visual, Equipment)

♂ ○&& Christie's, 3800 Sycamore Road; 28303 910-860-1776

♀ ○ (&) Fort Video & News, 4431 Bragg Blvd; 28303 910-868-9905 24 hrs.

♀ ○ President News, 3712 Bragg Blvd; 28303

Organizations/Resources: Social, Recreational & Support Groups (see also Sport/Dance/Outdoor)

♂ ★ **Lambda Association of Fayetteville, PO Box 53281; 28305 910-497-4577**

Flat Rock

Organizations/Resources: Family

♀ ☆ P-FLAG, Rt.2, Box 105 L; 28731 704-696-8250 "Parents, Families & Friends of Lesbians & Gays."

Gastonia

Erotica (Printed, Visual, Equipment)

♀ ● & 321 News & Video, 1410 N Chester St; 28052 704-866-0075

♀ ○ Gastonia Video News, 414 W Main St; 28052 704-867-9262

Travel & Tourist Services (see also Accommodation)

♀ ● && All Travel, Inc., 1708 E Garrison Blvd #A; 28054 704-853-1111

Greensboro

☎ Alternative Resources of the Triad 910-274-2100

AIDS/HIV Support, Education, Advocacy, Publications

♀ ☆&& Alamance CARES, PO Box 909, Burlington; 27216 910-570-5325

♀ ☆ & Triad Health Project, PO Box 5716; 27435 910-275-1654

Antiques & Collectables

♀ ● && Replacements Ltd, PO Box 26029; 27420 / 1089 Knox Rd 800-562-4462 Fax 910-697-3100 "China, crystal, flatware, collectibles."

Bars, Restaurants, Clubs, Discos

♂ ● (&) The Palms, 413 N. Eugene; 27401 910-272-6307 *PDE* Sun-Thu 9pm-2.30am; Fri & Sat to 3am.

♀ ○&& Sunset Cafe, 4608 W Market St; 27407 910-855-0349 *BR* Mon-Fri lunch 11.30am-2am; dinner Tue-Sat 5.30-9.30pm; Sun dinner only 5-9pm. Catering available.

NC: Greensboro
Bars, Clubs, Restaurants

366

USA

Sanford : NC
Erotica

THE DUCKETT HOUSE
INN & FARM

P.O. Box 441
Hot Springs
NC 28743
(704) 622-7621

♂ • (৬) Warehouse 29, 1011 Arnold St; 27405 910-333-9333 *BDELWCP*

Bookstores: General

♀ ○ (৬) White Rabbit Books, 1833 Spring Garden St; 27403 910-272-7604 Fax 910-272-9015 10am-6pm; Sat to 7pm; Sun 1-6pm.

Community Centers (see also Women's Centers)

♀ ★ The HELP Center, 382 W Harden St #2, Burlington; 27215 910-226-0094 chingle@aol.com *The HELP Letter.*

Erotica (Printed, Visual, Equipment)

♀ ○ ♂ Gents, 3722 High Point Rd; 27407 910-855-9855

♀ ○ (৬) New Vision Video, 507 Mobile St; 27406 910-274-6443

♀ ○ Outlet Video And News, 2223 Maple Ave, Burlington; 27215 910-229-0757

♀ • The Toy Store, 2416-B High Point Rd; 27403 910-547-8697 (TOYS) Mon-Thu 10am-5pm; Fri & Sat to 8pm. "Lingerie, adult novelties, leather goods, preference jewelry, adult tapes."

♀ ○৬৬ Treasure Box Video & News, 1203 E Bessemer Ave; 27405 910-373-9849 24 hrs.

Organizations/Resources: Business & Professional

♀ ★ Triad Business & Professional Guild, PO Box 4755; 27404-4753 910-274-2100

Organizations/Resources: Ethnic, Multicultural

♂ ★ (?৬) MACT/Greensboro—Triad, PO Box 14327; 27415 910-274-9259 Black & White Men Together/Men of All Colors Together

Organizations/Resources: Family

♀ ☆৬৬ P-FLAG, PO Box 49126; 27419 910-274-2100 "Parents, Families & Friends of Lesbians & Gays."

Organizations/Resources: Political/Legislative

♀ ★৬৬ Alamance Gay & Lesbian Alliance (AGALA), PO Box 743, Haw River; 27258-0094 704-578-5441

Organizations/Resources: Sexual Focus (Leather, S/M, etc) & Safe Sex Promotion

♀ ★ (?৬) Tarheel Leather Club, PO Box 16457; 27416-0457 910-272-6307 Pub *Tar & Feathers.*

Organizations/Resources: Student, Academic, Alumni/ae

♀ ★ (?৬) Gay & Lesbian Student Association, Box 27 Elliott University Center, UNCG; 27412 910-334-5110

Organizations/Resources: Youth (see also Family)

♀ ★ GLASS, PO Box 4442; 27404 910-274-2100 "Youth group for Gay & Lesbian teenagers."

Pets & Pet Supplies

♀ • Critter Care, 910-275-7128

Religious Organizations & Publications

♀ ★৬৬ St. Mary's Metropolitan Community Church, PO Box 5808; 27435-0808 910-272-1606

Switchboards, Helplines, Phone Information

♀ ★৬৬ Alternative Resources of the Triad, PO Box 4442; 27404 910-274-2100 "Support groups, events, etc."

Travel & Tourist Services (see also Accommodation)

♀ • Carolina Travel, Carolina Circle Mall; 27405 800-289-9009 (ask for David)

Greenville

Bars, Restaurants, Clubs, Discos

♀ • Paddock Club, 1008-B Dickenson Ave 919-758-0990

Hickory

AIDS/HIV Support, Education, Advocacy, Publications

♀ ☆ (৬) ALFA: Aids Leadership Foothills Area, PO Box 2987; 28603 704-322-1447

Bars, Restaurants, Clubs, Discos

♀ ○ Club Cabaret, 101 North Center St; 28601 704-322-8103

Religious Organizations & Publications

♀ ★ ♂ Metropolitan Community Church, c/o Unitarian Church Of Hickory, 109 11th Ave NW; 28601 704-324-1960

Hot Springs

Accommodation: Hotels, B&B, Resorts, Campgrounds

♀ ○ (৬) Duckett House Inn & Farm, PO Box 441; 28743 704-622-7621

✦ *Duckett House Inn & Farm advertisement page 366*

Jacksonville

Bars, Restaurants, Clubs, Discos

♀ • ♂ Friends Lounge, 1551 Lejeune Blvd; 28540 910-353-9710 *PDE*

♀ The Mirage, 2125 Richlands Highway; 28540 910-346-8724

Kure Beach

Accommodation: Hotels, B&B, Resorts, Campgrounds

♀ • ৬৬ The Ocean Princess Inn, 824 Fort Fisher Blvd S; 28449 910-458-6712; 800-762-4863

Ocracoke

Accommodation: Hotels, B&B, Resorts, Campgrounds

♀ ○ The Lightkeepers Guest House, PO Box 597; 27960 919-928-1821 "Open May-Dec. Reasonable rates, light kitchen use. 15 miles of undeveloped beach."

Raleigh: see Triangle Area

Sandy Ridge

Counseling/Therapy: Private

♀ • Smith, Kathryn R., M.Ed, 910-871-2966

Sanford

AIDS/HIV Support, Education, Advocacy, Publications

♀ ☆৬৬ Lee County AIDS Task Force (LCATF), PO Box 4262; 27331-4262

Erotica (Printed, Visual, Equipment)

♀ ○ Sanford Video & News, 667 Horner Blvd; 27330 919-774-9124

Triangle Area

☎ Gay & Lesbian Helpline of Wake County 919-821-0055

☎ Lesbian & Gay Health Project 919-286-4107

Accommodation: Hotels, B&B, Resorts, Campgrounds

Chapel Hill

♀ • Joan's Place, 1443 Poinsett Dr, Chapel Hill; 27514 919-942-5621 "Bed & breakfast for women."

AIDS/HIV Support, Education, Advocacy, Publications

♀ ☆&& AIDS Community Residence Association, PO Box 61584, Durham; 27715-1584 919-479-4834

♀ ☆&& AIDS Service Agency, PO Box 16574, Chapel Hill; 27516 919-967-0009 "Support, education, advocacy, housing."

♀ ☆ (&&) AIDS Service Agency of Wake County, PO Box 12583, Raleigh; 27605 919-834-2437 Mon-Fri 9am-5pm; HIV testing Thu 6-9pm.

♀ ☆&& Duke AIDS Research & Treatment Center, Box 3284, Duke University Medical Center, Durham; 27710 919-684-5260

♀ ☆&& People With HIV/AIDS Support Group, PO Box 3203, c/o LGHP, Durham; 27715-3203 919-286-4107; 919-286-7475

♀ ☆ Wake County Dept of Health, 10 Sunnybrook Rd, Raleigh; 27620-4049 919-250-3950 (testing & conseling); 919-250-3999 HIV early intervention; 250-4510 AIDS case management; Fax 919-250-0443

Art & Photography (see also Graphic Design)

♀ • (?&) Kirby, Kenda R., Medical Illustrator, 1106 Buchanan, Durham; 27701 919-286-1570 "Freelance medical, scientific & technical illustrator."

♀ • (&&) Smith, Patti, Chapel Hill 919-967-0436 "Photography: weddings, Holy Unions, advertising, etc."

Bars, Restaurants, Clubs, Discos

Chapel Hill

♀ • && Crook's Corner, 610 W Franklin St, Chapel Hill; 27516 919-929-7643 *R* Dinner 6-10.30pm; Sun brunch 10.30am-2pm. Outdoor dining available.

Durham

♂ Boxer's, 5504 Chapel Hill Blvd, Durham; 27707-3319 919-489-7678

♂ • & Competition, 711 Rigsbee Ave, Durham; 27701 919-688-3002 *PD*

♀ Flipper's Bar & Grill, 1117 Broad St, Durham; 27705 919-286-0669 *BR*

♂ Gentlemen's Corner, 704 Rigsbee, Durham; 27701 (opening planned at press time)

♂ o (&&) Power Company, 315 W Main St, Durham; 27701 919-683-1151 *BDEP*

Raleigh

♂ • && Capital Corral (CC), 313 W Hargett St, Raleigh; 27601 919-755-9599

♂ • & Club 1622, 1622 Glenwood Ave, Raleigh; 27608 919-832-9082 *D*

♀ Irregardless Cafe, 901 W Morgan St, Raleigh; 27603 919-833-8898 *BR*

♂ • && Legends, 330 W. Hargett St, Raleigh; 27601 919-831-8888 *BDEP*

Bookstores: General

♀ ☆ & Internationalist Books, PO Box 951, Chapel Hill; 27514 / 408 W. Rosemary St; 27516 919-942-1740 Noon-6pm; Sat 10am-6pm. "Community resource & bulletin board."

♀ o&& Regulator Bookshop, 720 9th St, Durham; 27705 919-286-2700 "Large selection of gay-interest books & magazines; special orders welcome."

♀ o The Newsstand, 1821 Martin Luther King Parkway, Durham; 27705

♀ o The Newsstand, 225 S Elliott Rd, Village Plaza, Chapel Hill; 27514 919-929-4642

♀ o The Newsstand, 300 E Main St, Carboro; 27510 919-942-4920

♀ o The Newsstand, Northgate Mall, Guess Rd, Durham 919-286-4522

♀ o The Newsstand, Park West Crossing, Hwy 55, Durham 919-544-5278

♀ o The Newsstand, Triangle Factory Shops, Morrisville 919-460-9188

♀ o **White Rabbit Books & Things, 309 W Martin St, Raleigh; 27601 919-856-1429**

Clothes

♀ • Innovations, 517 Hillsborough St, Raleigh; 27603 919-833-4833 "Leather clothes & accessories."

♀ o Time After Time, 414 W Franklin St, Chapel Hill; 27514 919-942-2304 "Vintage thrift shop."

Counseling/Therapy: Private

♂ • && Androgyny Center, 2301 Stonehenge Dr #109, Raleigh; 27615 919-848-0500

♂ • Hedberg, Catherine, MA, 300-200 Parham St #E, Raleigh; 27601 919-755-9796 "Specializing in sexual abuse/incest recovery; depression; coming out."

Erotica (Printed, Visual, Equipment)

♀ o Castle Video & News, 1210 Downtown Blvd, Raleigh; 27603 919-836-9189

♂ o (&) Christie's, 2802 Guess Road, Durham; 27705 919-620-6881

♀ o Pegasus, 6804 Davis Circle, Raleigh; 27612 919-782-2481

Gifts, Cards, Pride & Novelty Items

♀ • (&) Cameron's, University Mall, Chapel Hill; 27514 919-942-5554 Mon-Sat 10am-9pm. "Gifts; cards; contemporary American crafts."

Health Care (see also AIDS Services)

♂ ★ Lesbian & Gay Health Project, PO Box 3203, Durham; 27715-3203 919-286-4107 Pub *Newsletter*.

Legal Services & Resources

♀ o&& Edelstein & Payne, Attorneys, PO Box 28186, Raleigh; 27611-8186 919-828-1456

Organizations/Resources: Business & Professional

♂ ★ Triangle Area Gay Scientists, PO Box 1137, Chapel Hill; 27514 919-929-4997

Organizations/Resources: Ethnic, Multicultural

♂ ★ (?♿) Triangle/Men of All Colors Together, PO Box 3411, Durham; 27702-3411 919-929-8843 "Gay-affirmative men's social organization promoting interracial friendship & education about racism."

Organizations/Resources: Family

♀ ☆♿♿ P-FLAG, PO Box 10844, Raleigh; 27605-0844 919-380-9325 "Parents, Families & Friends of Lesbians & Gays."

Organizations/Resources: General, Multipurpose, Pride

♀ ☆ Coalition 807, PO Box 5961, Raleigh; 27650-5961

Organizations/Resources: Social, Recreational & Support Groups (see also Sport/Dance/Outdoor)

♀ ★ Triangle Area Lesbian Feminists, PO Box 2272, Durham; 27702 919-688-4398

♀ Triangle Lesbian & Gay Alliance, Box 3295, Durham; 27705-1295 919-929-4053

Organizations/Resources: Student, Academic, Alumni/ae

♀ ★♿♿ B-GLAD: Bisexuals, GayMen, Lesbians & Allies for Diversity, Box 39 Carolina Union CB#5210, Chapel Hill; 27599 919-962-4401 Pub *Lambda*.

♀ ★♿♿ NC State Lesbian/Gay Student Union, PO Box 7314-NCSU, Raleigh; 27695 919-829-9553

Organizations/Resources: Youth (see also Family)

♀ ★♿♿ A Safer Place Youth Network (aspyn), PO Box 28913, Raleigh; 27611-8913 919-851-9544

♀ ★ (♿) Outright: Triangle Area Gay, Lesbian & Bisexual Youth, PO Box 3203, Durham; 27715-2396 919-286-2396; 800-879-2300 Statewide; outright@aol.com "Support, social & educational program for gay, lesbian & bisexual youth, 13-22."

Real Estate

♀ ○♿♿ **Menges, Tom, GRI, CRS, Howard Perry & Walston Realtors, 5509 Creedmoor Rd, Raleigh; 27612 919-781-5556; 800-880-5899; ncrealtor1@aol.com**

Religious Organizations & Publications

♀ ★ (?♿) Affirmation: United Methodists for Lesbian, Gay & Bisexual Concerns, PO Box 5961, Raleigh; 27650 919-850-9380

♀ ★ (?♿) Dignity/Triangle, PO Box 51129, Durham; 27717-1129 919-836-8793 "Gay, Lesbian, & Bisexual Catholics & their friends."

♀ Integrity/Raleigh, c/o Church of the Good Shepherd, PO Box 28024, Raleigh; 27611 919-828-8831 "Lesbian & Gay Episcopalians & their friends."

♀ ★ (?♿) Lesbian & Gay Jews/Shabbat, 919-286-7801; 919-490-5125

♀ ★ ♿ Lutherans Concerned/Triangle, PO Box 665, Apex; 27502 919-387-0824 Meeting in Raleigh.

♀ ★ ♿ St John's Metropolitan Community Church, PO Box 5626, Raleigh; 27650 919-834-2611 Sun worship 11am & 7.15pm at 805 Glenwood Ave.

♀ ★ Triangle Lesbian & Gay Concern, c/o Unitarian Fellowship, 3313 Wade Ave, Raleigh; 27607 919-781-7635

Switchboards, Helplines, Phone Information

♀ ★ Gay & Lesbian Helpline of Wake County, PO Box 36207, Raleigh; 27606-6207 919-821-0055 7-10pm.

Travel & Tourist Services (see also Accommodation)

♀ ● Rainbow Travel, PO Box 31288, Raleigh; 27622-1288 919-571-9054; 800-633-9350

♀ ○ Sunset Travel, PO Box 31288, Raleigh; 27622-1288 919-787-2511; 800-633-9350; Fax 919-782-1936

Video Sales, Rentals, Services (see also Erotica)

♀ ○ Visart Video, 1821 Martin Luther King Parkway, Durham; 27705

♀ ○ Visart Video, 225 S Elliott Rd, Village Plaza, Chapel Hill; 27514 919-929-4584

♀ ○ Visart Video, 300 E Main St, Carboro; 27510 919-932-1945

♀ ○ Visart Video, 3405-A Hillsborough Rd, Durham; 27705 919-382-0650

♀ ○ Visart Video, Weaver Dairy Road, Timberline Village, Chapel Hill; 27514 919-929-7634

Women's Centers

♀ ★ ♿ Our Own Place, Inc., PO Box 27702-5443, Durham; 27702-5443 919-286-9966 "Lesbian resource, educational & social center. All women welcome."

♀ ☆ (♿♿) The Women's Center, PO Box 1057, Chapel Hill; 27514 / 210 Henderson St 919-968-4610 *The Women's Center Newsletter*.

Wilmington

☎ Gay & Lesbian Switchboard 910-675-9222

Accommodation: Hotels, B&B, Resorts, Campgrounds

♀ ● ♿ **The Inn On Orange, 410 Orange St; 28401 910-815-0035; 800-381-4666**

♀ ● (?♿) Southern Heritage, 614 S 2nd St; 28401 910-251-9501

AIDS/HIV Support, Education, Advocacy, Publications

♀ ★♿♿ GROW, A Community Service, 341-11 S College Rd #182; 28403 910-675-9222

♀ ☆♿♿ UNC-W Committee on AIDS, 601 S College Rd; 28403 910-395-3119

Bars, Restaurants, Clubs, Discos

♀ The Manor, 208 Market St; 28401 910-251-9220 *BDE*

♀ ○ Mickey Ratz, 115 S Front St; 28401 910-251-1289

Organizations/Resources: Sexual Focus (Leather, S/M, etc) & Safe Sex Promotion

♀ ★ (?♿) Menamore Levi/Leather Club, PO Box 7364; 28406 910-675-9222 x534

Organizations/Resources: Social, Recreational & Support Groups (see also Sport/Dance/Outdoor)

♀ ★ (♿♿) Between Ourselves, 2148 Harrison St; 28401-6922

Religious Organizations & Publications

♀ ★ St Jude's Metropolitan Community Church, 4326 Market St #170; 28403 910-657-9222 x622; 910-762-5833; Worship Sun & Wed 7pm.

Switchboards, Helplines, Phone Information

♀ ★♿♿ Gay & Lesbian Switchboard, c/o GROW, 341-11 S College Rd #182; 28403 910-675-9222

Winston-Salem

AIDS/HIV Support, Education, Advocacy, Publications

♀ ☆ (?♿) AIDS Task Force of Winston-Salem, 713 S Marshall St #8; 27101-5808 910-723-5031

Bars, Restaurants, Clubs, Discos

♀ ○ && Bourbon Street, 916 Burke St; 27101 910-724-4644 Fax 910-722-3099 *BDEP* 9pm-4am.

Organizations/Resources: Family

♀ ☆ P-FLAG/Winston Salem, PO Box 15477; 27113 910-723-6345 "Parents, Families & Friends of Lesbians & Gays."

Organizations/Resources: Social, Recreational & Support Groups (see also Sport/Dance/Outdoor)

♀ ★ (?&) LUNA (Lesbians Up for New Adventures), PO Box 15321; 27113

Real Estate

♀ ○ Crouse, Bonnie, 2001 Boone Ave; 27103 910-722-0421

Religious Organizations & Publications

♀ ☆&& U-U Lesbian & Gay Concerns Task Force, Unitarian Universalist Fellowship, 2873 Robinhood Rd; 27106 910-723-7633

Switchboards, Helplines, Phone Information

♀ ★&& Alternative Resources of the Triad, 910-748-0031 7-10pm.

North Dakota

State/County Resources

AIDS/HIV Support, Education, Advocacy, Publications

♀ ★ (&) Dakota Life Foundation, PO Box 2, Fargo, ND 58107-0002 701-287-AIDS Helpline. Pub *Turning Points*. "AIDS education; PLWA housing."

Fargo

AIDS/HIV Support, Education, Advocacy, Publications

♀ Dakota AIDS Project, PO Box 2; 58107 701-287-AIDS

Erotica (Printed, Visual, Equipment)

♀ ○&& Adult Books & Cinema, 417 Northern Pacific Ave; 58102 701-232-9768

Organizations/Resources: General, Multipurpose, Pride

♀ ★ Prairie Lesbian & Gay Community, PO Box 83, Moorhead, MN 56560 701-235-7335

Grand Forks

Erotica (Printed, Visual, Equipment)

♀ ○ Plain Brown Wrapper II, 102 S 3rd St; 58201 701-772-9021

Organizations/Resources: Student, Academic, Alumni/ae

♀ UND G&L Coalition, PO Box 8055; 58202

Mandan

Bookstores: Gay/Lesbian/Feminist

♀ ○ Bookstore of Mandan, 116 E Main St; 58554 701-663-9013

Minot

Bookstores: Gay/Lesbian/Feminist

♀ ○&& Risque's I, 1514 S Broadway; 58701 701-839-9033

Ohio

State/County Resources

Addictive Behavior, Substance Abuse, Recovery

♀ • (&&) Pride Institute, 800-54-PRIDE "The nation's only accredited chemical dependency treatment center exclusively for Gay, Lesbian & Bisexual People."

AIDS/HIV Support, Education, Advocacy, Publications

→ AIDS Foundation Miami Valley: p.369

♀ (&&) AIDS Foundation Miami Valley, PO Box 3539, Dayton, OH 45401 513-277-2437 Fax 513-277-7619 Pub *Quest*.

♀ ☆ Ohio Aids Coalition (OAC), PO Box 10034, Columbus, OH 43201 614-445-8277 Fax 614-445-8283 Pub *Wellness Times*.

♀ ☆ & Ohio AIDS Hotline, c/o Columbus AIDS Task Force, 1500 W 3rd Ave #329, Columbus, OH 43212 800-332-AIDS; 800-332-3889 TTY; 9am-9pm; Sat & Sun 10am-6pm.

Archives/Libraries/History Projects

♀ ★ (?&) Ohio Lesbian Archives, c/o Crazy Ladies, 4039 Hamilton Ave, Cincinnati, OH 45223 513-541-1917 By appointment.

Conferences/Events/Festivals/Workshops (see also Music)

♀ ★&& Ohio Lesbian Festival, c/o Lesbian Business Association, PO Box 02086, Columbus, OH 43202 614-267-3953 "Annual one-day festival featuring nationally known musicians, lesbian craftswomen & merchants, September 9, 1995."

Legal Services & Resources

♀ ☆ American Civil Liberties Union of Ohio (ACLU), 1223 W 6th St, Cleveland, OH 44113 216-781-6276

Organizations/Resources: Business & Professional

♀ ★ Ohio Human Rights Bar Association, PO Box 10655, Columbus, OH 43201

Organizations/Resources: Family

♀ ☆ (&) P-FLAG/Miami Valley NW, 416 Medallion Drive, Greenville, OH 45331 513-548-6730

Organizations/Resources: Military/Veterans

♀ ☆&& American Friends Service Committee, 915 Salem Ave, Dayton, OH 45406 513-278-4225 Fax 513-278-2778 hawkafsc@aol.com "Gay & Lesbian staff members offer counseling on military issues: Gay/Lesbian persecution. All services free & confidential."

Organizations/Resources: Political/Legislative

♀ Log Cabin Ohio, 1025 Highland St, Columbus, OH 43201 614-224-7648

Organizations/Resources: Sport/Dance/Outdoor

♀ ★&& Tri-State Gay Rodeo Association, PO Box 5401, Cincinnati, OH 45205-0401 513-581-2512 Pub *Newsletter*. (Ohio, Kentucky, Indiana)

Publications

♀ • Dinah, PO Box 1485, Cincinnati, OH 45201 "News & articles relevant to lesbians; also poetry."

♀ • Gay People's Chronicle, PO Box 5426, Cleveland, OH 44101 216-631-8646 Fax 216-631-1082 chronohio@aol.com "Biweekly newspaper covering news, arts, & opinions in Cleveland & Columbus."

♀ • & Gaybeat, 772 N High St #103, Columbus, OH 43215-1457 800-701-9901 Fax 614-463-4238 Biweekly.

OH: State/County Resources
Publications
370
USA
Cincinnati : OH
Accommodation

♀ • *The Ohio Word*, 225 E North St, Tower 1 #2800, Indianapolis, IN 46204 317-579-3075

Real Estate

♀ • Community Real Estate Referrals, 800-346-5592 "Free referral to gay/gay-supportive realtor in any USA city/state (including Virgin Is. & Puerto Rico). Sorry, no rentals!"
♦ *Community Real Estate Referrals advertisement back cover*

Religious Organizations & Publications

♀ ★ (և.&) PLGC/N. Ohio Chapter, 1689 Glenmont, Cleveland, OH 44118 216-932-1458 "Presbyterians for Lesbian/Gay Concerns."

♀ ★&& United Church Coalition for Lesbian/Gay Concerns: Ohio, 18 N College St, Athens, OH 45701 614-593-7301

Akron

AIDS/HIV Support, Education, Advocacy, Publications

♀ ☆ (?&) Northeast Ohio Task Force on AIDS, 667 N Main St; 44310 216-375-2000; 216-375-AIDS hotline 24 hrs

♀ ☆ (?&) Positive Connection Support Center, 667 N Main St; 44310 216-375-2000 Mon-Fri 2-8pm. Pub *Postive Connection Newsletter*.

♀ ☆ (?&) Summit AIDS Housing Corp, 667 N Main St; 44310 216-375-2134 Mon-Fri 8am-8pm.

Bars, Restaurants, Clubs, Discos

Akron

♂ • 358 Club, 358 S Main St; 44311 216-434-7788

♂ • Adams Street Bar, 77 N Adams St; 44304 216-434-9794 *DLW*

♀ • Annex, 803 N Main St; 44310 216-762-2747 *BE*

♀ Dr Dan's, 1225 Sweitzer; 44301 216-773-0008

♀ Interbelt, 70 N Howard St; 44308 216-253-5700

♀ • & Roseto Social-Fraternal Club, 627 S Arlington St; 44306 216-724-4228 *PEDC*

♀ • & Tear-Ez Lounge, 360 S Main St; 44311 216-376-0011

Health Clubs, Gyms, Saunas

♂ Akron Steam & Sauna, 41 S Case; 44305 216-794-5424

♂ • Club Akron, Inc, 1339 E Market St; 44305 216-784-0309 24 hrs.

Organizations/Resources: Family

♀ ★&& P-FLAG/Akron, 702 N Revere Rd; 44333-2915 216-923-1883 "Parents, Families & Friends of Lesbians & Gays."

Religious Organizations & Publications

♀ ★ (&) Cascade Community Church, 1190/1196 Inman St; 44306 216-773-5298 Sunday School 11.30am; worship Sun 2pm; discussion Wed 7.30pm. All welcome. Pub *Cascade Newsletter*.

♀ ★&& Emmanuel Fellowship Church, 60 N. Arlington St 216-376-8725

♀ ★ & Lutherans Concerned/Northeast Ohio Chapter, PO Box 67114, Cuyahoga Falls; 44222 216-928-6041

♀ ★ (&) New Hope Temple, 1215 Kenmore Blvd; 44314 216-745-5757 Pub *Beacon of Light*.

Ashtabula

Bars, Restaurants, Clubs, Discos

♀ • && The Leeward, 1022 Bridge St (Ohio 531); 44004 216-964-9935 *Bdf*

Counseling/Therapy: Private

♀ ○&& Great Lakes Counseling, PO Box 132; 44005-0132 216-992-5995 Fax 216-992-5949

Athens

AIDS/HIV Support, Education, Advocacy, Publications

♀ ☆ (?&) Athens AIDS Task Force, 18 N College St; 45701 614-592-4397 Mon-Fri 9am-4pm.

Organizations/Resources: Social, Recreational & Support Groups (see also Sport/Dance/Outdoor)

♀ • ★ Open Doors: Ohio University's Gay, Lesbian, & Bisexual Student Union, 18 N College St; 45701 614-594-2385 opendoor@lihus.cs.ohio.edu

Organizations/Resources: Student, Academic, Alumni/ae

♀ • ★ LGBC (Lesbian, Gay, & Bisexual Commission) of Student Senate, 308 Baker Center, 20 E Union St; 45701 614-593-4049 lgbc@lihus.cs.ohiou.edu

Bowling Green

Organizations/Resources: Student, Academic, Alumni/ae

♀ • ★ (&&) Lesbian & Gay Alliance, Bowling Green State University, University Hall Box 22; 43403-0001 419-372-0555 Mon, Wed, Fri 7-10pm. "All activities open to the community."

♀ ☆ (?&) Women for Women, 315D Student Services, Bowling Green State University; 43403 419-372-2281

Canton

Bars, Restaurants, Clubs, Discos

♂ 540 Club, 540 Walnut St; 44702 216-456-8622

♀ Boardwalk, 1227 W Tuscawaras; 44702 216-453-8000

♀ Dar's Bar, 1120 W Tuscawaras; 44702 216-454-9128

♀ La Casa Lounge, 508 Cleveland Ave NW; 44702 216-453-7432

♀ Miss Tina's Golden Gate, 236 Market Ave N; 44702 216-454-0440

♀ Sidestreet Cafe, 2360 Mahoning Rd NE; 44705-1963 216-453-8055

♀ Sonny's Alibi, 425 Court Ave NW; 44702 216-453-4646

Chillicothe

Bars, Restaurants, Clubs, Discos

♀ • && Beemer's, 64 Enterprise Pl; 45601 614-775-9660 *D* 4pm-2.30am.

Cincinnati

☎ Gay & Lesbian Community Switchboard 513-651-0070

Accommodation: Hotels, B&B, Resorts, Campgrounds

Cincinnati

♀ • Prospect Hill Bed & Breakfast, 408 Boal St; 45210 513-421-4408

OH: Cincinnati
AIDS/HIV Support

371

USA

Cincinnati : OH
Religious

AIDS/HIV Support, Education, Advocacy, Publications

♀ ☆ (?♿) AIDS Coalition To Unleash Power (ACT UP)/Cincinnati, 408 Ludlow Ave #56; 45220 513-861-6171

♀ ☆ ♿ AIDS Volunteers of Cincinnati, 2183 Central Parkway; 45214 513-421-2437 Pub *AVOC Newsletter.*

♀ ☆ ♿ Caracole, 1821 Summit Rd #201; 45237-2820 513-761-1480 "Housing for Persons With AIDS."

♀ ☆ Greater Cincinnati AIDS Consortium, PO Box 19353; 45219 513-558-4259

Bars, Restaurants, Clubs, Discos

Cincinnati

♀ ○ (♿) Carol's Corner Cafe, 825 Main St; 45202 513-651-BOOP *BR* 11am-2.30am; Sat 4pm-2.30am; food served until 1am; Sun brunch 11am-pm.

♂● ● The Dock, 603 Pete Rose Way; 45202 513-241-5623 *BDEL*

♂● ○ Golden Lions, 340 Ludlow Ave; 45220 513-281-4179

♀ ● (♿) Pipeline, 241 W Court St; 45202 513-241-5678 4pm-2.30am.

♂ ● (♿) Shooters, 927 Race St; 45202 513-381-9900 *DCW* 4pm-2.30am.

♂● ○ ♿ Simon Says, 428 Walnut St; 45202 513-381-8196

♂● ● ♿ Spurs, 326 E 8th St; 45202 513-621-BOOT *LW* 4pm-2.30am.

♂ The Subway, 609 Walnut St; 45205 513-421-1294

Bookstores: Gay/Lesbian/Feminist

♀ ● ♿ Crazy Ladies Bookstore, 4039 Hamilton Ave; 45223 513-541-4198 "Books by, for, & about women; lesbian & gay literature; children's non-sexist books."

♂ ● Pink Pyramid, 36A West Court St; 45202 513-621-PINK **Mon-Thu 11am-9pm; Fri & Sat 11am-11pm.**
✦ Pink Pyramid advertisement page 375

Bookstores: General

♀ ○ Fountain Square News, 101 E 5th St; 45202 (4th & Walnut) 513-421-4049 "Magazines & newspapers."

Broadcast Media

♂ ★ (♿) Alternating Currents, PO Box 6126, WAIF-FM; 45206 513-961-8900 office; 513-749-1444 studio line during show; Sat 3-5pm, 88.3FM.

Community Centers (see also Women's Centers)

♂ ★ ♿ Greater Cincinnati Gay/Lesbian Center, PO Box 141061; 45250-1061 513-651-0040

Counseling/Therapy: Nonprofit

♀ ☆ (?♿) Women Helping Women, Inc., 216 E 9th St; 45202 513-381-5610 24 hr crisis line; 513-381-6003; "Crisis center for victims of rape, incest & domestic violence."

Counseling/Therapy: Private

♀ ○ Ashland Psychological Services, 2334 Ashland Ave; 45206 513-861-8365

Erotica (Printed, Visual, Equipment)

♂ ● ♿ Acme Leather & Toy Company, 326 E 8th St; 45202 513-621-7390 Tue, Thu & Sun 7pm-1am; Fri & Sat 10pm-2.30am.

♀ ● ♿ Kinks, 1118 Race St; 45210-1919 513-651-2668

Gifts, Cards, Pride & Novelty Items

♀ ● LeftHanded Moon, 48 E Court St; 45202 513-784-1166

Health Care (see also AIDS Services)

♀ ☆ ♿ STD Clinic, 3101 Burnet Ave; 45229 513-352-3138

Legal Services & Resources

♀ ★ (?♿) American Civil Liberties Union of Ohio, Cincinnati Chapter (ACLU), 103 Wm. Howard Taft Rd; 45219 513-961-5566

Organizations/Resources: Business & Professional

♂ ★ ♿ Queen City Careers Association, PO Box 3663; 45201-3663 513-579-9877 "Gay/Lesbian Chamber of Commerce."

Organizations/Resources: Family

♀ ☆ ♿ P-FLAG/Greater Cincinnati, PO Box 19634; 45219-0634 513-721-7900 Meeting 2nd Tue of month, 7.30pm, at Mt Auburn Presbyterian Church, 103 W.H. Taft Rd. "Parents, Families & Friends of Lesbians & Gays."

Organizations/Resources: General, Multipurpose, Pride

♂ ★ (?♿) Greater Cincinnati Gay/Lesbian Coalition, PO Box 19158; 45219 513-557-2904

♀ ★ (?♿) Stonewall Cincinnati, PO Box 954; 45201 513-541-8778 Pub *Newsletter.* "Service, educational organization & political action committee."

Organizations/Resources: Political/Legislative

♂ Log Cabin Cincinnati, PO Box 19472; 45219 513-723-9722

Organizations/Resources: Social, Recreational & Support Groups (see also Sport/Dance/Outdoor)

♂ River Bears, PO Box 431; 45201

♀ ★ Slightly Older Lesbians, c/o Crazy Ladies, 4039 Hamilton Ave; 45223 513-541-4198

Organizations/Resources: Sport/Dance/Outdoor

♂ Greater Cincinnati Sports Association, Box 6296; 45206 513-751-2513

Organizations/Resources: Student, Academic, Alumni/ae

♂ ★ ♿ U.C. Alliance of Lesbian, Gay & Bisexual People, 211 Tangeman Center/Mail Location #136; 45221-0136 513-556-1449

Organizations/Resources: Transgender & Transgender Publications

♂ ☆ Cross-Port, PO Box 54657; 45254-0657 513-474-9557 Pub *Cross-Port InnerView Newsletter.*

Performing Arts: Entertainment, Music, Recording, Theater, etc.

♀ ★ Cincinnati Men's Chorus, PO Box 3061; 45201 513-579-9877

Publications

♂ ● *Nouveau Midwest*, PO Box 3176; 45201 513-621-9500

Real Estate

♀ ● Bastian, Bob, CRS, GRI, West Shell Realtors, 9150 Winton Rd; 45231 513-931-5900; 513-221-2112

Religious Organizations & Publications

♂ ★ Dignity/Cincinnati, PO Box 983; 45202 513-557-2111 Worship 1st & 3rd Sat, 7.30pm, at The Community Friends (Quaker) Meeting House, 3960 Winding Way (near Xavier University). "Gay & Lesbian Catholics & their friends."

♂ ★ ♿ Integrity/Greater Cincinnati, 4905 Chalet Dr #11; 45217-1445 513-242-7297 Pub *Newsletter.* "Lesbian & Gay Episcopalians & their friends."

⚥ ★ (?&) New Spirit Metropolitan Community Church, 65 E Hollister St; 45219-1703 513-241-8216

Switchboards, Helplines, Phone Information

⚥ ★ Gay & Lesbian Community Switchboard, PO Box 141061; 45250-1061 513-651-0070 6-11pm.

Travel & Tourist Services (see also Accommodation)

⚥ • Victoria Travel, 3330 Erie Ave; 45208 513-871-1100; 800-626-4932

Women's Centers

♀ ☆&& University of Cincinnati Office of Women's Programs & Services, 340 Tangeman Center; 45221-0179 513-556-4401

Cleveland

🕾 Cleveland Lesbian/Gay Hotline 216-781-6736

AIDS/HIV Support, Education, Advocacy, Publications

♀ ☆& AIDS Taskforce of Greater Cleveland, 2250 Euclid Ave; 44115 216-621-0766 Mon-Fri 9am-5pm.

♀ ☆&& The Living Room, Box 6177; 44101 / 1410 W. 29th St 216-522-1998 Fax 216-522-0025

Archives/Libraries/History Projects

♀ ☆&& What She Wants Feminist Library, PO Box 18465; 44118 / 3130 Mayfield Rd 216-321-3054

Bars, Restaurants, Clubs, Discos

⚥ • (?&) 5-Cent Decision, 4365 State Rd; 44109 216-661-1314 *Bd* 4pm-2.30am; 7pm-2.30am.

251-3330 Since 1984
A Store of Erotic Hardware & Romantic Software

Body Language

Books, Magazines, Videos, Leather & Accessories

3291 W. 115th St.   Hours:
Cleveland, Ohio 44111   Mon.-Sat. Noon-9PM
(1/2 block North of Lorain)   Sunday Noon-5PM

THE GRID (216)623-0113
1281 W.9th ST.
CLEVELAND, OH 44113
10 min. from downtown in the Warehouse District
VISA/MC/ATM Parking & Security

Open Daily at 4:00pm.
Multi-level, Multi-Sensory Entertainment!

Experience the HOTTEST Downtown Dance Floor!
GRID Dick Dancers take it off every week!
Friendliest Staff in town!
Where EVERYONE is Welcome!

⚥ • The Grid, 1281 W 9th St; 44113 216-623-0113 *BD* Opens 4pm. Women's Day Sun 4-9pm.
✦ *Grid advertisement page 372*

♀ • (&&) Hi & Dry In, 2207 W 11th St; 44113-3605 216-621-6166 *BR*

♂ JJ's Club Phoenix, 2032 W 25th St; 44113 216-621-1752

♂ • Leather Stallion Saloon, 2205 St Clair Ave; 44114 216-589-8588 *BLW* 3pm-2.30am.

♂ • & Legends, 11719 Detroit Ave, Lakewood; 44107 216-226-1199 *BD*

♂ Memoirs, 11213 Detroit; 44102 216-221-8576

⚥ Muggs, 11633 Lorain Ave; 44111 216-252-6172

⚥ • (&&) Numbers, 620 Frankfort Ave; 44113 216-621-6900 *DLL* Wed-Sun 10pm-3am.

⚥ • && Ohio City Oasis, 2909 Detroit Ave; 44113 216-574-2203 Fax 216-771-7814 *BDE* 5.30am-2.30am.

♂ Over The Rainbow, 9506 Detroit; 44102 216-651-9399

♀ Paradise Inn, 4488 State Road; 44109 216-741-9899

♀ • (&) Rec Room, 15320 Brookpark Rd; 44135 216-433-1669 *Bdf*

♂ Rockies, 9208 Detroit Ave; 44102 216-961-3115

♀ Scarlet Rose's Lounge, 2071 Broadview Road; 44109 216-741-9819

♂ ○ Tomahawk, 11217 Detroit Ave; 44102 216-521-5443 *BLW*

⚥ Too's Attraxions, 6757 W 130th St; 44130 216-842-0020

⚥ • ○ & U4IA Nite Club, 10630 Berea Rd; 44102 216-631-7111 *D* Wed, Fri-Sun from 9.30pm.

♂ Visions, 1229 W 6th St; 44113 216-566-0060

Bookstores: General

♀ ○ Bookstore on West 25th, 1921 W 25th St; 44113 216-566-8897

♀ • (&) Gifts of Athena, 2199 Lee Rd; 44118 216-371-1937 Mon & Wed-Fri 10am-8pm; Sat 10am-6pm; Sun noon-5pm.

♀ ○ The Pavilion Mall Booksellers, 24031 Chagrin Blvd; 44122 216-831-5035

Community Centers (see also Women's Centers)

⚥ ★&& Lesbian & Gay Community Center of Greater Cleveland, PO Box 6177; 44101 / 1418 W. 29th; 44113 216-522-1999; 216-861-5454 hotline

Erotica (Printed, Visual, Equipment)

♀ ○ 95th Street News, 9500 Lorain Ave; 44102 216-631-4010 7.30am-11pm; Sun noon to 9pm.

♀ ○ Bank News, 4025 Clark; 44109 216-281-8777

⚥ • & Body Language, 3291 W 115th St; 44111 216-251-3330 Fax 216-476-3825
✦ *Body Language advertisement page 372*

♀ ○ & Detroit Avenue News, 6515 Detroit Ave; 44102 216-961-3880 8am-11pm; Sun noon to 9pm.

Health Clubs, Gyms, Saunas

♂ Club Body Center, 1448 W 32nd St; 44113 216-961-2727

⚥ • (?&) Flex, 1293 W 9th St; 44113 216-696-0595 *P*
✦ *Flex advertisement page 373*

Home & Building: Cleaning, Repair, General Contractors

♀ • Walls By Cento, 216-721-4649; 800-435-5178; "Painting & restoration."

Legal Services & Resources

♀ ● ♿ Savren, Joy B., 1836 Euclid Ave #308; 44115 216-771-6597

Organizations/Resources: Bisexual Focus

♂ ★ ♿ Bisexual & Married Gay Men, PO Box 770932, Lakewood; 44107-0041 216-529-9139 (Doug)

♀ ★ (♿) Women's Support Group, PO Box 594, Northfield; 44067 216-467-6442 (9am-9pm please); 216-467-6442 (9am-9pm) "Meets on Cleveland's West side; welcomes all women, including heterosexual with questions about bisexuality & lesbianism."

Organizations/Resources: Ethnic, Multicultural

♂ ★ (?♿) African-American Lesbian/Gay/Bisexual Caucus, CLGCC, PO Box 6177; 44101 216-522-1999 Pub *Response.*

♂ ★ Black & White Men Together, PO Box 5144; 44101-0144 216-397-2968 Black & White Men Together/Men of All Colors Together

♀ Sistahparty, PO Box 6177; 44101 216-348-3215

Organizations/Resources: Family

♂ ★ (?♿) Gay Fathers, PO Box 91853; 44101 216-621-0228

♀ ☆ P-FLAG, 14260 Larchmere Blvd; 44120 216-321-7413; 216-460-9078; "Parents, Families & Friends of Lesbians & Gays."

Organizations/Resources: General, Multipurpose, Pride

♂ ★ Cleveland Lesbian/Gay Pride Committee, PO Box 91031; 44101 216-226-4973

♂ ★ (♿) Northern Ohio Coalition, Inc, PO Box 15065; 44115-0065 216-771-0369

Organizations/Resources: Political/Legislative

♀ Greater Cleveland National Organization for Women (NOW), 4207 Lorain Ave #4; 44113 216-281-4225

♂ Log Cabin Club Northeast Ohio, PO Box 94100; 44101-6100 216-281-7925 (Republicans)

♂ Stonewall Cleveland, PO Box 5936; 44101 216-741-9105

Organizations/Resources: Social, Recreational & Support Groups (see also Sport/Dance/Outdoor)

♂ ★ (?♿) Cleveland Couples Together, PO Box 771102, Lakewood; 44107-0047 216-734-7980

♂ ★ NEON (North East Ohio Naturists), PO Box 770911, Lakewood; 44107 "Social, educational, recreational men's nudist club."

♂ ★ ♿ Sign of Rainbow, PO Box 6253; 44101-1253 "Social organization for deaf/hard of hearing and hearing gay, lesbian, bisexual, straight."

Organizations/Resources: Sport/Dance/Outdoor

♀ ★ (♿) Cleveland City Country Dancers, PO Box 5592; 44101 216-691-4664 *dCW* Wed 7.30-10.30pm at Lesbian/Gay Community Center, 2905 W. 29th St. "Western & Folk Dancing."

Organizations/Resources: Student, Academic, Alumni/ae

♂ CSU Lambda Delta Lambda, CSU, UC 301, Box 79; 44115 216-261-8645

♂ ★ ♿ CWRU Gay Lesbian Bisexual Alliance, c/o Student Activities Office, Thwing SAO, 11111 Euclid Ave; 44106-7103 216-368-2679; 216-368-8840; xx425@po.cwru.edu

Performing Arts: Entertainment, Music, Theater, etc.

♂ ★ ♿ North Coast Men's Chorus, PO Box 15181; 44115 216-473-8919 Signing for hearing impaired.

Performing Arts: Entertainment, Music, Recording, Theater, etc.

♀ ☆ Oven Productions, Box 18175; 44118 216-321-7799

Printing & Promotional Items (see also Art; Graphics/Typesetting)

♀ ● (♿) Alice Paul Printers & Mail Service, PO Box 5426; 44101 216-631-8646 Fax 216-631-1082

Publications

♂ ● *Cleveland For You & Akron Too!,* For You Productions, PO Box 760 Edgewater Branch, Lakewood; 44107 216-221-1940; 800-560-8712

♂ ● *Gay People's Chronicle,* PO Box 5426; 44101 216-631-8646 Fax 216-631-1082 chronohio@aol.com "Biweekly newspaper covering news, arts, & opinions in Cleveland & Columbus."

♂ ★ ♿ *Now Cleveland Magazine,* Box 406 Edgewater Branch, Lakewood; 44107-0406 216-771-0369

Real Estate

♂ ● Realty One: John Lauro, 20515 Shaker Blvd; 44122 216-975-2056; 216-991-8400

Religious Organizations & Publications

♂ ★ ♿ Chevrei Tikva, PO Box 18120; 44118-0120 216-932-5551 Meets 1st & 3rd Fri, 8.30pm, Unitarian Society, Lancashire Rd, Cleveland Hts.

OH: Cleveland
Religious

374
USA

Columbus : OH
Counseling: Private

Religious

⚣ ★ (?&) Common Bond, PO Box 91853; 44101 "Ex-Jehovah's Witnesses."

⚣ ★ Dignity/Cleveland, PO Box 91697; 44101 216-531-4469 "Gay & Lesbian Catholics & their friends."

⚣ ★ Emmanual Christian Fellowship Church, 10034 Lorain Ave; 44111-5429 216-651-0129 Tue-Thu noon-7pm; worship Sun 10.45am; Bible study Wed 7pm. Call for details of 12-step Support Groups, etc.

Switchboards, Helplines, Phone Information

⚣ ★&& Cleveland Lesbian/Gay Hotline, PO Box 6177; 44101 216-781-6736 7-11pm; Sat 5-8pm; Sun 7-10pm.

Thrift/Consignment Stores

⚢ ○ Affordable Treasure, 16806 Madison Ave, Lakewood; 44107 216-521-7253 Mon-Sat 11am-6pm.

Travel & Tourist Services (see also Accommodation)

⚢ ○ Ade Travel International, Inc., 510 Euclid Ave., Suite 1 Euclid Arcade; 44115 216-484-7872 x1644 Fax 216-771-5552

⚢ ○ && Sundance Travel, Inc., 6650 Pearl Rd #300; 44130-3836 216-842-1994

⚣ ○ & The Travel Place, 22965 Lorain Rd; 44126 216-734-1886; 800-484-7858 x1886

Columbus
☎ Stonewall Union 614-299-7764

Accommodation: Hotels, B&B, Resorts, Campgrounds
Columbus

⚣ • The Gardener's House, 556 Frebis Ave; 43206 614-444-5445 "Bed & breakfast; five minutes from downtown."

Glenford

⚥ • Springhill Farm, 5704 Highpoint Rd, Glenford; 43739 614-659-2364

Logan

⚣ • && Summit Lodge Resort & Guest House, PO Box 951-GY, Logan; 43138 / 26500 Wildcat Rd, Rockbridge; 43149 614-385-6822 "Clothing optional."

Addictive Behavior, Substance Abuse, Recovery

⚢ • (?&) Laufersweiler, Donald, MS, CCDC, LPCC, 918 S Front St; 43206 614-445-8277

♀ ☆ (&) Sober Strong Free, c/o Women's Outreach for Women 1950-H N 4th St; 43201 Alcoholics Anonymous meets Fri 8pm.

⚢ ☆&& Southeast Counseling Services, 1455 S 4th St; 43207 614-444-0800 Fax 614-444-1036 By appointment. "Chemical dependency services."

♀ ☆ (&&) Women's Outreach for Women, 1950-H N 4th St; 43201 614-291-3639 "Prevention & education services for women; we house a variety of 12-step meetings, a few of which are Lesbian specific."

AIDS/HIV Support, Education, Advocacy, Publications

⚢ ★&& Columbus AIDS Task Force, 1500 W 3rd Ave #329; 43212 614-488-2437; 800-332-AIDS; 800-DEAF-TTY

⚢ ★ (&) Community Free Job List/Crisis Center, 2456 W Broad St; 43204 614-870-6460

⚢ ☆&& HIV Counseling Program: Southeast Counseling Services, 1455 S 4th St; 43207 614-445-3330 By appointment.

⚢ ☆&& OSU Hospitals AIDS Clinical Trials Unit, 456 W 10th Ave #4725; 43210 614-293-8112

⚢ ★ (&&) Pater Noster Houses, 2456 W Broad St; 43204 614-870-6460 "Housing for ARC/AIDS-positive adults & children, operated by Community Free Job List/Crisis Center."

Automobile Services

⚢ • && Alternative Auto Care, 585 W 2nd Ave; 43215-1140 614-294-0580

Bars, Restaurants, Clubs, Discos
Columbus

⚣ Club 20, 20 E Duncan; 43202 614-261-9111

⚣ • & Columbus Eagle Bar, 232 N 3rd St; 43215 614-228-2804 **BD** 5pm-2.30am. Leather/Western in Eagle's Nest.

⚣ • & Eagle In Exile, 893 N. 4th St 614-294-0069 **BLW** Wed-Sat 9pm-2.30am. Leather/Levi dress code enforced Fri & Sat.

⚣ ○ Herby's Tavern, 349 Marconi; 43215 614-464-2270

⚢ Imaginations Too, 283 E Spring St; 43215-2627 614-242-2407

⚣ The Red Dog, 196 1/2 E Gay St (rear); 43215 614-224-7779

⚢ Slammers, 202 E Long; 43215-1830 614-221-8880

⚥ Summit Station, 2210 Summit St; 43201 614-261-9634

⚣ • (&) Tradewinds II, 117 E Chestnut; 43215 614-461-4110 **BD** Tue-Sun 4pm-2.30am.

⚣ ○ (?&) Tremont Lounge, 708 S High St; 43206 614-445-9365 **Bd** 7am-2.30am; Sun 1-9pm.

⚣ • & Trends/Garage Disco, 40 E Long St; 43215 614-461-0076 **D**

⚢ • && Wall Street, 144 N Wall St; 43215 614-464-2800 **DE**

Bookstores: Gay/Lesbian/Feminist

⚢ • An Open Book, 749 N High St; 43215 614-291-0080

♀ • & Fan The Flames Feminist Bookstore, 3387 N High St; 43202 614-447-0565 Tue-Fri 11am-7pm; Sat & Sun noon-6pm. "Lesbians & gay men welcome."

⚢ • & Pink Pyramid, 772 N High St #103; 43215-1457 (side entrance) 614-297-1500 Mon-Fri 11am-7pm.
♦ *Pink Pyramid advertisement page 375*

Bookstores: General

⚢ ○ Disco Book Store, 973 Harrisburg Pike; 43223 614-274-9716

⚢ ○ & Nickleby's Bookstore Cafe, 1425 Grandview Ave; 43212 614-488-2665

Broadcast Media

⚢ ★ (?&) Stonewall Union Lesbian/Gay Pride Report, Box 10814; 43201-7814 614-299-7764 Fax 614-299-4408 Mon & Sat 11.30pm, on cable access, Channel 21.

Business, Financial & Secretarial

⚢ • Delphia Carr Accounting Systems, 1435 Grandview Ave; 43212 614-487-1112 Fax 614-431-0059

Community Centers (see also Women's Centers)

⚢ ★&& Stonewall Community Center, PO Box 10814; 43201 / 47 W. 5th Ave 614-299-7764 Fax 614-299-4408 (also TTY) Mon-Fri 9am-5pm; Sat to 1pm.

Counseling/Therapy: Private

⚢ • Affirmations: A Center for Psychotherapy & Growth, 918 S Front St; 43206 614-445-8277; 800-285-9397

⚢ • Clintonville Counseling Services, 3840 N High St; 43214 614-261-1126

OH: Columbus
Counseling: Private

375

USA

Columbus : OH
Publications

♀ • (♂♂) Columbus Psychological Services, 24 E Weber Rd; 43202 614-262-2444

♀ ○ Crane, Meral, PO Box 02008; 43202 614-451-0111

♂ • ♂ Fuller, Kayla, LISW, & Daniels, Patricia, MA, LPC, 3620 N High St #303; 43214 614-261-0060

♀ ○ Schwartz, Judith, Ph.D., 11 E Kossuth St, Village Counseling, Inc; 43206 614-444-7714

♀ • (♂) Shannon, Joseph W., Ph.D., 1155 W 3rd Ave; 43212 614-297-0422 8am-8pm; Sat 8am-2pm.

Gifts, Cards, Pride & Novelty Items

♀ ○ Hausfrau Haven, 769 S 3rd St; 43206 614-443-3680 "Gifts, cards, books, wine."

♀ ○ (♂) Kukala's, 636 North High St; 43215 614-228-TEES 11.30am-6.30pm; Thu to 7pm. "Cards, gifts, custom tees; body piercing & jewelry; some leather."

Health Clubs, Gyms, Saunas

♂ • Club Columbus, 1575 E Livingston Ave; 43205 614-252-2474

♀ ○♂♂ World Gym East, 5508 E. Livingston Ave; 43232 614-863-9090 6am-11pm; Sun 10am-6pm.

Legal Services & Resources

♀ • ♂♂ Eby, James, 50 W Broad St; 43215 614-228-2605

♀ ○ Fishman & Fey Co,, LPA, 395 E Broad St #31U; 43215-3877 614-228-1164 "Domestic; custody; real estate."

Organizations/Resources: Bisexual Focus

♂ ★ (?♂) Bi-Lines, PO Box 14773; 43214 614-341-7105 (John); 614-341-7105 (John)

Organizations/Resources: Business & Professional

♀ ★♂♂ Lesbian Business Association, PO Box 02086; 43202 614-267-3953

Organizations/Resources: Education, Anti-Defamation, Anti-Violence, Self-Defense

♀ ★♂♂ Stonewall Union Anti-Violence Project, PO Box 10814; 43201 614-299-7764 "Self-defense classes; statistics gathering; documentation; victim advocacy & support."

Organizations/Resources: Ethnic, Multicultural

♂ ★ Black & White Men Together/Columbus, PO Box 151276; 43215 614-221-2734 Black & White Men Together/Men of All Colors Together

Organizations/Resources: General, Multipurpose, Pride

♀ ★♂♂ **Stonewall Union, PO Box 10814; 43201-7814 614-299-7764 Fax 614-299-4408 Pub Stonewall Union Journal.** "Unity group for political, educational & social events."

Organizations/Resources: Political/Legislative

♀ ★ (?♂) Log Cabin Club Of Columbus, PO Box 12126; 43212 (Republicans)

♂ ★♂♂ Society for Individual Rights of Ohio, Inc., Box 951, Logan; 43138 614-385-6822

Organizations/Resources: Sexual Focus (Leather, S/M, etc) & Safe Sex Promotion

♀ ☆ (?♂) Briar Rose, PO Box 163143; 43216

♂ Centurions, PO Box 15456; 43215-0456

♂ ☆ National Leather Association/Columbus, c/o Eagle In Exile, 893 N 4th St; 43201

Organizations/Resources: Social, Recreational & Support Groups (see also Sport/Dance/Outdoor)

♂ ★ (?♂) Columbus Couples Together, PO Box 2723; 43216-2723 614-341-7498

♂ G/L/B Support Group, PO Box 1136, Delaware; 43015 614-363-0431

♂ ★ (?♂) GAP, PO Box 16369; 43216 614-447-6531

Organizations/Resources: Sport/Dance/Outdoor

♂ ★ (?♂) Capital City Cycling Club, PO Box 02028; 43202 "Bicyclists."

♂ Columbus Stompers, 1601 W 5th Ave., Box 235; 43212 614-487-8976 ♂ "Square Dance."

Organizations/Resources: Student, Academic, Alumni/ae

♂ ★♂♂ Bisexual, Gay & Lesbian Alliance (B-GALA), 340 Ohio Union, 1739 High St; 43210 614-292-9212

Organizations/Resources: Transgender & Transgender Publications

T ☆ (♂♂) Central Ohio Gender Dysphoria Program, PO Box 02008; 43202 614-451-0111

♀ ☆ Crystal Club, PO Box 287, Reynoldsburg; 43068

Organizations/Resources: Youth (see also Family)

♂ ★♂♂ Kaleidoscope Youth Coalition (KYC), PO Box 8104; 43201 614-447-7199; 800-291-9190

♂ ☆ (♂♂) Phoenix Pride Youth Group, Southeast Recovery & Mental Health Services 1455 S 4th St; 43207 614-444-0800 Fax 614-444-1036 Pub Phoenix Pride. "Support group for Lesbian/Gay/Bisexual youth, ages 15-21."

Performing Arts: Entertainment, Music, Recording, Theater, etc.

♂ ★ (?♂) Columbus Gay Men's Chorus, PO Box 18131; 43218 614-228-2462

Publications: Directories, Bibliographies, Guides, Travel

♂ ★♂♂ Lavender Listings, PO Box 10814; 43201 614-299-7764 Fax 614-299-4408 "Annual directory of Gay/Lesbian & friendly businesses, organizations & services."

Publications

♀ ○ The Free Press, 203 E Broad St; 43215-3701 614-221-2792

⚦ • *Gay People's Chronicle*, PO Box 12235; 43212 614-253-4038 Fax 614-253-1367 chronohio@aol.com "Biweekly newspaper covering news, arts, & opinions in Columbus & Cleveland."

→ *Gaybeat*: p.369

♀ ☆ *Lesbian Health News*, mail to LHN, PO Box 12121; 43212

⚦ • *The Word Is Out!*, PO Box 02106; 43202 Lesbian Voices of Columbus

Real Estate

♀ • ♿ Luebbe, Darla, & Ferret, Lorraine, Realtors, c/o King Thompson/Holzer-Wollam, 550 Cleveland Ave, Westerville; 43081 614-523-0808 Fax 614-882-6824

Religious Organizations & Publications

⚦ ★ Christ United Evangelical Church, PO Box 141264; 43214 614-297-6317

♂ ☆ Evangelicals Concerned, PO Box 360491; 43236 614-235-GAYS

♀ ☆♿ First Unitarian Universalist Church, 93 W Weisheimer; 43214 614-267-4946 Sun 9 & 11.15am at 93 W. Weisheimer Rd.

⚦ ★ (?♿) Friends for Lesbian & Gay Concerns, 614-488-2096 "For lesbians, gay men, bisexuals, & their friends who seek spiritual community in the Religious Society of Friends (Quakers)."

⚦ ★ G & L Jewish Group, PO Box 06119; 43206-0119

♂ ★♿ Gay Men's Support Group, c/o Newman Center, 64 W Lane Ave; 43201 614-291-4674

⚦ ★♿ Integrity/Central Ohio, PO Box 292625; 43229 614-237-2844 Pub *Newsletter*. "Lesbian & Gay Episcopalians & their friends."

⚦ ★ New Creation Metropolitan Community Church, PO Box 141212; 43214-6212 614-294-3026

⚦ ★ (?♿) Spirit of the Rivers Ecumenical Community Church, PO Box 10333; 43201 614-470-0816 "Includes Christians from many denominations: founded on liberation theology."

♂ ★ (?♿) United Church Coalition for Lesbian/Gay Concerns, 614-291-6581; 614-488-2096; "Recognized special interest group within the United Church of Christ committed to ministry with & justice for Lesbians, gay men, bisexuals, their families & friends."

Travel & Tourist Services (see also Accommodation)

♀ •♿ TravelPlex East, 555 Officenter Place #100; 43230 614-337-3155

Video Sales, Rentals, Services (see also Erotica)

♀ • Metro Video, 848 N High St; 43215 614-291-7962 11am-mdnt; Sun noon-mdnt. "Mainstream, adult & gay/lesbian interest sections."

Dayton

AIDS/HIV Support, Education, Advocacy, Publications

♀ ☆♿ Community Unity Health & Wholeness Project, PO Box 4021; 45401 513-228-4031 "AIDS & breast cancer outreach of Metropolitan Community Church Dayton Parish."

Bars, Restaurants, Clubs, Discos

Dayton

⚦ Dugout, 619 Salem Ave; 45406 513-274-2394

⚦ The Edge, Inc., 909 Patterson Rd; 45419 513-294-0713 *BDLCW* 5pm-2.30am. "Leather Shoppe included."

♂ •♿ The Foundry, 34 N. Jefferson St; 45402 513-461-5200 *DL*

⚦ Jessie's After Dark, 121 N Ludlow St; 45402 513-223-2582

⚦ Stage Door, 44 N Jefferson; 45402 513-223-7418

Kettering

⚦ • 1470 West, 1470 W Dorothy Lane, Kettering; 45409 513-293-0066

⚦ Rustic Cabin Inn, 2320 Wilmington Pike, Kettering; 45420-1434 513-253-7691

Bookstores: General

♂ o♿ Books & Co, 350 East Stroop Rd; 45429 513-298-6540

Bookstores: Recovery, Metaphysical, & other Specialty

♂ • ♀ Earth Song Herbal Sundries Co., 6500 N Dixie Dr; 45414-3310 513-264-1774

Erotica (Printed, Visual, Equipment)

♂ o Exotic Bookstore, 444 E 5th St; 45402 513-228-3584

Gifts, Cards, Pride & Novelty Items

⚦ •♿ Q! Gift Shop, Inside Jessie's, 121 N. Ludlow St 513-223-4438 Wed-Sat 10pm-2am; Sun to mdnt.

Health Care (see also AIDS Services)

♂ ☆♿ Communicable Disease Clinic, Combined Health District, 451 W 3rd St; 45422-1280 513-225-4249

Organizations/Resources: Family

♂ ☆ Miami Valley NW Chapter of P-FLAG, 1219 Northmoor Dr, Greenville; 45331 513-547-1433 "Parents, Families & Friends of Lesbians & Gays."

Organizations/Resources: Political/Legislative

⚦ ★ Serenity, Inc., PO Box 3032; 45401-3032 513-274-1616 Pub *Rightfully Proud.*

⚦ ★♿ Sexual Orientation Civil Rights PAC, PO Box 3511; 45401 513-278-GAYS

Performing Arts: Entertainment, Music, Recording, Theater, etc.

♂ Dayton Men's Chorus, c/o 665 Salem Ave; 45406 513-253-3031

Real Estate

⚦ •♿ Short, Doug, Re/Max Pro-formance Realty, Inc., 1810 Sugar Run Trail, Bellbrook; 45305-1150 513-848-4663 Fax 513-848-8086

Religious Organizations & Publications

⚦ ★ ♿ Community Gospel Church, PO Box 1634; 45401 513-252-8855 Meets 10am at 546 Xenia Ave. "A gay-positive, open church."

⚦ ★♿ Dignity/Dayton, PO Box 55; 45401 513-277-7706 "Gay & Lesbian Catholics & their friends."

⚦ ★ ♿ Metropolitan Community Church/Dayton Parish, PO Box 4021; 45401-4021 / 1630 E. 5th St 513-228-4031

Elyria

Organizations/Resources: Transgender & Transgender Publications

T Alpha Omega Chapter-Tri Ess, PO Box 954; 44036

Glenford: see Columbus

Kent

Bookstores: General

♂ o The News & Photo Shop, 407 E Main St; 44240 216-678-5499

OH: Kent
Clothes

377
USA

Toledo : OH
Fund... ...ndowment; Fundraising

Clothes

♀ • Nightsweats & T-cells, 277 Martinel Dr; 44240 216-673-2806; 800-859-8685; "Custom screen-printed T-shirts; HIV owned & operated."

Organizations/Resources: Student, Academic, Alumni/ae

♀ ★ ♂♂ Kent Lesbian, Gay, Bisexual Union (LBGU-KENT), Box 17, Student Activities, Kent State University; 44242 216-672-2068

Kettering: see Dayton

Lakewood: see Cleveland

Lima

Bars, Restaurants, Clubs, Discos

♀ • Somewhere In Time, 804 W North; 45801 419-227-7288

Lorain

Bars, Restaurants, Clubs, Discos

♂ • Nite Club, 2223 Broadway; 44052 216-245-6319 *BLLf*

Community Centers (see also Women's Centers)

♀ ★ Lorain Lesbian/Gay Center, PO Box 167; 44052 216-988-5326 Pub *Hotlines*.

Organizations/Resources: Family

♀ ☆ P-FLAG, PO Box 167; 44052 216-988-8215 "Parents, Families & Friends of Lesbians & Gays."

Mansfield

AIDS/HIV Support, Education, Advocacy, Publications

♀ North Central Ohio AIDS Foundation, 611 Cliffside Drive; 44904-1501 419-522-9357

Bars, Restaurants, Clubs, Discos

♀ Alternatives, 138 W 3rd St; 44902 419-522-0044 *R*

Mentor

Community Centers (see also Women's Centers)

♀ ★ Mentor Center (HUGS East), PO Box 253; 44061-0253 216-974-8909

Newark

Bars, Restaurants, Clubs, Discos

♀ • The Lavender Rose, 380 Sereco Ave; 43055 614-349-7023 *BR*

Oberlin

Organizations/Resources: Student, Academic, Alumni/ae

♀ ★ (?♂) Oberlin College Lesbian Gay Bisexual Union, Wilder Hall, Box 88; 44074 216-775-8179 Pub *SNAP: It's A Queer Thing.*

Oxford

Organizations/Resources: Student, Academic, Alumni/ae

♀ ★ Miami University Gay/Lesbian/Bisexual Alliance, 381 Shriver Center; 45056 513-529-3823

Parma

Organizations/Resources: Transgender & Transgender Publications

T ☆ Paradise Club, PO Box 29564; 44129 216-586-9292

Sandusky

Bars, Restaurants, Clubs, Discos

♀ X-centricities, 306 W Water St; 44880 419-624-8118

Springfield

AIDS/HIV Support, Education, Advocacy, Publications

♀ ★ (?♂) A Touch of Love, Inc, 2226 Columbus Ave; 45503 513-322-2631

♀ ☆ Clark County American Red Cross, 1830 N Limestone St; 45503 513-399-3872 Fax 513-399-6111 "Imteragency forum on AIDS/HIV; support group."

♀ ☆ (♂♂) Clark County Health Dept. & Education, 529 E Home Rd; 45503 513-328-5624 "AIDS education; testing, & counseling Thu pm only."

Bars, Restaurants, Clubs, Discos

♀ • Chances, 1912-1914 Edwards Ave; 45503 513-324-0383 *BE*

♂ • (♂) Why Not III, 5 N Murray St; 45503 513-322-4208; 513-324-9758; *BDEW* 8.30pm-1am; Fri & Sat to 2.30am.

Religious Organizations & Publications

♀ ★ (?♂) Community Church of Truth, PO Box 3005; 45501-3005 513-325-7691

Steubenville

Bookstores: General

♀ ○ Steubenville News, 426 Market St; 43952-2853 614-282-5842

Toledo

AIDS/HIV Support, Education, Advocacy, Publications

♀ ☆ ♂♂ David's House Compassion, Inc., PO Box 391; 43697-0391 419-244-6682; 419-244-6682; Fax 419-249-2741

♀ ☆ ♂♂ David's House/NOVA Program, PO Box 391; 43697-0391 419-244-6682; 419-244-NOVA; Mon-Fri 9-5pm.

Bars, Restaurants, Clubs, Discos

♀ • Blu Jeans, 3606 W Sylvania; 43623 419-474-0690 *BR* 2pm-2.30am.

♀ • ♂♂ Bretz Bar, 2012 Adams; 43624 419-243-1900 *BDEf* 2pm-4.30am.

♀ Caesar's Showbar, 133 N Erie St; 43624 419-241-5140

♂ Hooterville Station, 119 N Erie; 43624 419-241-6981

♂ • Rustler Saloon, 4023 Monroe (rear); 43606 419-472-8278 2pm-2.30am.
♦ *Rustler Saloon advertisement page 377*

♀ Scenic, 702 Monroe; 43624 419-241-5997

Funding: Endowment, Fundraising, Scholarship

♀ ★ John Domrose Foundation for Personal Rights, PO Box 4642; 43610-0642

Gifts, Cards, Pride & Novelty Items

♀ ○ Tallulah's, 6940 W Central Ave; 43617 419-843-7707

Health Clubs, Gyms, Saunas

♂ ● Diplomat Health Club, 1313 N Summit; 43604 419-255-3700

Organizations/Resources: General, Multipurpose, Pride

♀ ★ (♿) Lavender Triangle, PO Box 178079; 43615 419-531-0644 Pub *Women's Vineline.*

♂ ★ Toledo Area Gay & Lesbian Affiliation (TAGALA), PO Box 4642 Old West End Stn; 43610-0642 419-243-9351 Pub *TAGALA Newsletter.*

Organizations/Resources: Political/Legislative

♀ Gays & Lesbians United (G.L.U.), PO Box 6552; 43612-0552

Organizations/Resources: Student, Academic, Alumni/ae

♀ ★♿ Gay & Lesbian Student Union, University of Toledo, 3503-D Student Union Bldg., Univ Of Toledo; 43606-3390 419-537-7975

Religious Organizations & Publications

♀ ★ Dignity/Toledo, PO Box 1388; 43603 419-242-9057 "Gay & Lesbian Catholics & their friends."

♀ ★ ♿ Integrity/Toledo, c/o St Marks Church, 2272 Collingwood Blvd; 43620 419-476-5877; 419-243-5641; Meeting 2nd Sun of month, 4pm; call for details of social events. "Gay & Lesbian Episcopalians & their friends."

♀ ★ Lutherans Concerned/Toledo, PO Box 12225; 43612-0225 419-476-3148

♀ ★ (♿) Metropolitan Community Church, Good Samaritan Parish, 720 W Delaware Ave; 43610 419-244-2124 Service Sun 11am & 6pm; Bible Study Wed 7.30pm.

♀ ★ ♿ Silver Owls, c/o Dignity/Toledo, PO Box 1388; 43603 419-242-9057

Travel & Tourist Services (see also Accommodation)

♀ ● Great Ways Travel, Inc., 4625 W Bancroft; 43615 419-536-8000; 800-729-9297

Warren: see Youngstown

Yellow Springs

Bars, Restaurants, Clubs, Discos

♀ ○♿♿ Winds Cafe, 215 Xenia Ave; 45387 513-767-1144 *BR* Mon-Sat lunch 11.30am-2pm, dinner 6-10pm; Sun 10am-2pm.

Organizations/Resources: Student, Academic, Alumni/ae

♀ ★ ♿ Lesbian & Gay Rights Caucus, Antioch School of Law, 795 Livermore St; 45387 513-265-9500

Youngstown

Bars, Restaurants, Clubs, Discos

Warren

♀ ● Alley Bar, 441 E Market St (rear entrance), Warren; 44481 216-394-9483 *Bd* 2pm-2.30am.

♂ The Crazy Duck, 121 Pine Ave, Warren; 44481 216-394-3825

♂ ● ♿ Purple Onion, 136 Pine Ave, Warren; 44481 216-399-2097 *BDf*

Youngstown

♀ ● ♿♿ Sophie's II, 2 E LaClede; 44507 216-782-8080 *BDEf* 4pm-2.30am.

♂ ● (♿) Troubador Lounge, 2618 Market St 216-788-4379

Erotica (Printed, Visual, Equipment)

♂ ○ Uptown Bookstore, 2597 Market St; 44507 216-783-2553

Organizations/Resources: Ethnic, Multicultural

♂ ★ BWMT, PO Box 1131; 44501-1131 216-782-3483 Black & White Men Together/Men of All Colors Together

Oklahoma
State/County Resources

Legal Services & Resources

♂ ☆ (♿) American Civil Liberties Union of Oklahoma (ACLU), 600 NW 23rd St #104, Oklahoma City, OK 73103-1416 405-524-8511

Organizations/Resources: Bisexual Focus

♂ Oklahoma Bisexual Network, PO Box 2714, Norman, OK 73070 405-945-2903

Organizations/Resources: Political/Legislative

♀ ★ ♂ Oklahoma Gay & Lesbian Political Caucus, PO Box 61186, Oklahoma City, OK 73146 405-791-0202 Pub *OGLPC Reporter.*

Organizations/Resources: Sport/Dance/Outdoor

♀ ★ Oklahoma Gay Rodeo Association, PO Box 12485, Oklahoma City, OK 73157 405-943-0843

Publications

♀ ● Gayly Oklahoman, PO Box 60930, Oklahoma City, OK 73146 405-528-0800 Bi-monthly.

Enid

Bars, Restaurants, Clubs, Discos

♂ The Par-T, 3203 S Van Buren St (US 81); 73703

Lawton

Bars, Restaurants, Clubs, Discos

♂ The Downtowner, 116 SW 1st Ave; 73501 405-357-1430

♂ Ingrid's, 1104 NW Cache Rd; 73507 405-353-1488

Erotica (Printed, Visual, Equipment)

♂ ○ Ingrid's Bookstore, 1124 NW Cache Rd; 73507 405-353-1488

Religious Organizations & Publications

♂ Great Plains Metropolitan Community Church, PO Box 63; 73502 405-357-7899

Norman: see Oklahoma City

Oklahoma City

☎ Oasis Gay, Lesbian & Bisexual Community Resource Center 405-525-2437

Accommodation: Hotels, B&B, Resorts, Campgrounds

♀ ● ♿ Habana Inn, 2200 NW 39th Expressway St; 73112 405-528-2221 *BDRLCW*

AIDS/HIV Support, Education, Advocacy, Publications

♂ ★ (♿) AIDS Support Program, PO Box 12185; 73157-2185 405-525-6277

OK: Oklahoma City
AIDS/HIV Support
379
USA
Oklahoma City : OK
Travel

AIDS/HIV Support

♂ ☆ 👬 HIV Prevention & Education Services, Red Rock Mental Health Center, 4400 N Lincoln Blvd; 73105-5105 405-425-0399; 405-425-0321

♂ ★ 👬 Monday Night Clinic, 4400 N. Lincoln Blvd 405-843-8378; 405-427-5812 during clinic only.; Mon 7-8.30pm. "Free anonymous HIV testing, no appointment necessary; other testing available at cost."

♂ ★ (👬) Oklahoma City Foundation for AIDS Research, 2136 NW 39th St; 73112-8830 405-843-8378 HIV treatment clinic. Please call first for instructions.

♂ ★ 👬 Testing The Limits, 2136 NW 39th St; 73112 405-843-8378 (THE-TEST) Noon-mdnt. "Free anonymous AIDS testing."

Bars, Restaurants, Clubs, Discos

♂ ○ Angles, 2117 NW 39th St; 73112 405-524-3431 __BDE__ Hi-NRG dance, video Wed-Sun; show Sun.

♂ ● 👬 Bunkhouse Club & Restaurant, 2800 NW 39th Expressway; 73112 405-943-0843 __BRCW__

♀ ○ Coyote Club, 2120 NW 39th St; 73112 405-521-9533 __BD__ "Sand volleyball court with outdoor music. Country/Western Thu."

♂ ● Finish Line/Gushers, 2200 NW 39 Expressway; 73112 405-525-0730 __BDERW__

♂ ● Hi Lo Club & Piano Bar, 1221 NW 50th St; 73118 405-843-1722 __Bd__ 4pm-2am.

♂ KA's, 2024 NW 11th; 73106 405-525-3991

♂ Levi's, 2807 NW 36th St; 73112 405-947-LEVI

♂ The Neon Moon, 2805 NW 36th St; 73112 405-947-3422

♂ ○ Park, 2117 NW 39th St; 73112 405-528-4690 Hi-NRG, disco, video.

♀ ● (👬) The Porthole Lounge, 3630 NW 39th; 73112 405-949-9837 __Bd__ Tue-Sat 7pm-2am; Sun 4pm-2am.

♂ Tramps, 2201 NW 39th St; 73112 405-528-9080

♂ ○ Wreck Room, 2127 NW 39th; 73112 405-525-7610 __D__ After hours dancing.

Bookstores: Gay/Lesbian/Feminist

♀ ○ 👬 Herland Sister Resources, Inc, 2312 NW 39th St; 73112 405-521-9696 10am-6pm; Sun 1-6pm. Pub *Herland Voice.* "Feminist bookstore & women's center; producer of various events, concerts, retreats, etc."

Community Centers (see also Women's Centers)

♂ ★ (👬) Oasis Gay, Lesbian & Bisexual Community Resource Center, 2135 NW 39th St; 73112 405-525-2437 Nopon-5pm & 7-10pm.

Counseling/Therapy: Nonprofit

♀ ☆ 👬 Red Rock Mental Health Center, 4400 N Lincoln Blvd; 73105-5105 405-425-0399

Counseling/Therapy: Private

♀ ○ 👬 Art Therapy, 123 E Tonhawa St #104, Norman; 73069 405-364-2008

♂ ● 👬 Hunter, Shirley, M.Ed., Lakeshore Medical & Office Bldg, 4301 NW 63rd Ave #202; 73116 405-848-5429 "Licensed professional counselor."

♀ ● 👬 Prater, Larry M., MD, 1110 N Classen Blvd #318; 73106-6808 405-232-5453 "In-patient & out-patient counseling."

Dentists

♀ ● Browning, Debra K., DDS, 13321 N Meridian Ave #302; 73120-8356 405-755-4099

Erotica (Printed, Visual, Equipment)

♀ ○ 👬 Naughty 'n Nice, 3121 SW 29th St; 73119 405-686-1110

Gifts, Cards, Pride & Novelty Items

♀ ● Geoffrey's Cards & Gifts, 7650 N Western; 73116 405-843-0833

♂ ● 👬 Isn't That Special, call for events & locations. 405-690-5294; 405-690-6204; Noon-mdnt; weekends 3pm-2am. "Tanning & massage therapy available below store."

♀ ● Jungle Red (in Habana Inn), 2200 NW 39th Expressway St; 73112 405-524-5733 Fax 405-524-4951 2pm-2am.

Legal Services & Resources

♀ ● 👬 Hanks, Donald G., 1400 N Shartel; 73103 405-525-3001

Organizations/Resources: Family

♀ P-FLAG, PO Box 75914; 73147 405-948-6084

Organizations/Resources: General, Multipurpose, Pride

♀ ★ 👬 Gay & Lesbian Outreach, Red Rock Mental Health Center, 4400 N Lincoln Blvd; 73105-5105 405-425-0399

♀ Pride Network, PO Box 12415; 73157-2415 405-794-3035; 405-942-6250

♀ ★ (?👬) Simply Equal, PO Box 5684, Norman; 73070 405-945-2908

♀ Simply Equal/OKC, PO Box 61306; 73146-1306 405-521-9696

Organizations/Resources: Student, Academic, Alumni/ae

♀ ★ (?👬) OU Gay, Lesbian & Bisexual Alliance, 306 Ellison Hall, 633 Elm Ave, Norman; 73019-0350 405-325-4GLA

Organizations/Resources: Youth (see also Family)

♀ ★ (👬) Young Gay & Lesbian Alliance of Oklahoma City, Oasis Resource Center, 2135 NW 39th St; 73112 405-525-2437 Sun 7.30pm; serving gay, lesbian & bisexual young adults up to 24 years.

♀ ★ 👬 Young Gay & Lesbian Alliance, Red Rock Mental Health Center, 4400 N Lincoln Blvd; 73105-5105 405-425-0399

Publications

→ *Gayly Oklahoman*: p.378

Religious Organizations & Publications

♀ ★ (?👬) Church of Christ for Gays, PO Box 75481; 73147 405-528-8417

♀ ★ Dignity-Integrity Oklahoma City, PO Box 25473; 73125 405-636-4388; 405-789-5212; "Gay & Lesbian Catholics, Episcopalians, & their friends."

♀ ★ 👬 Lighthouse Metropolitan Community Church, PO Box 26221; 73126-0221 / 3629 NW 19th St 405-942-2822 Sun services 10.30am.

♀ ★ New Horizons Metropolitan Community Church, PO Box 12457; 73157-2457 (Planning to move.) 405-942-6313 "Pastoral & trained Lay Christian Counselor available by appointment."

♀ ☆ 👬 Oklahoma City Friends Meeting, 312 SE 25th St; 73129 405-632-7574; 405-631-4174; "Religious Society of Friends (Quakers)."

Travel & Tourist Services (see also Accommodation)

♀ ○ Prestige Travel, 7652 N Western; 73118-1611 405-842-8880; 800-299-1733

OK: Oklahoma City
Women's Centers

380
USA

State/County Resources : OR
Organizations: General

Women's Centers

♀ ☆&& Women's Resource Center, Inc, PO Box 5089, Norman; 73070 / 226 E.Gray 405-364-9424; 405-360-0590

Stillwater

AIDS/HIV Support, Education, Advocacy, Publications

♀ ☆ & Community AIDS Action Network, c/o Action, Inc, PO Box 282; 74076 405-624-2544; 405-624-2533; Fax 405-624-5004

Organizations/Resources: Student, Academic, Alumni/ae

♂ Gay, Lesbian & Bisexual Community Association of OSU, Student Union 040 Box 601; 74078 405-744-5252

Tulsa

☎ TOHR Gay/Lesbian Helpline 918-743-GAYS

AIDS/HIV Support, Education, Advocacy, Publications

♀ ★ HIV Resource Consortium, 4154 S Harvard #H-1; 74135 918-749-4194 Fax 918-749-4213 Mon-Fri 9-5pm. "AIDS/HIV intake & referral, assistance, care teams, mental health, free & anonymous HIV testing & counseling."

Bars, Restaurants, Clubs, Discos

♂ Bad Boyz, 1229 S Memorial Dr; 741 918-835-5083

♀ Lola's, 2630 E 15th St; 74104 918-749-1563

♀ Metropole, 1902 E 11; 741 918-587-8811

♂ • & New Age Renegade, 1649 S Main; 74119 918-585-3405 *BED*

♂ Rex, 6101 E Admiral Pl; 74115 918-835-1055

♂ • (&&) Silver Star Saloon, 1565 S Sheridan; 74112 918-834-4234 *BCWd*

♂ • Time and Time Again, 1515 S Memorial Dr; 74112 918-660-8299

♂ ○ TNT's, 2114 S Memorial; 74129 918-660-0856

♂ Toolbox Too, 1338 E 3rd; 74120 918-584-1308

♀ U.B.U./The Alley, 3340 S Peoria; 741 918-744-0896 *D*

Business, Financial & Secretarial

♀ • Kirby, Kelly, CPA, PC, PO Box 14011; 74159-1011 918-747-5466

Erotica (Printed, Visual, Equipment)

♀ ○ Elite Adult Books, 814 S Sheridan; 74112 918-838-8503

♀ ○ & Whittier Bookstore, 1 N Lewis Ave; 74110 918-592-0767

Gifts, Cards, Pride & Novelty Items

♂ • Tomfoolery!, 1565 S Sheridan; 74112 918-832-0233 Thu & Sun 9.30pm-mdnt; Fri & Sat 9.30pm-2am. "Gay/Lesbian news magazines, giftys, jewelry, etc."

Organizations/Resources: Family

♀ ☆&& Tulsa P-FLAG, PO Box 52800; 74152 918-749-4901 (hotline 24 hrs); 918-749-4901 (hotline 24 hrs); Pub *FLAG of Green Country*. "Parents, Families & Friends of Lesbians & Gays."

Organizations/Resources: General, Multipurpose, Pride

♂ ★&& TOHR Resource Center, PO Box 52729; 74152 918-743-4297; 918-749-4194 Free/Anonymous HIV testing Clinic

Organizations/Resources: Political/Legislative

♂ Log Cabin Tulsa, PO Box 4140; 74159 918-832-0233

♂ ★&& Tulsa Oklahomans for Human Rights, PO Box 52729; 74152 918-743-GAYS 8-10pm. Pub *TOHR Reporter*.

Organizations/Resources: Social, Recreational & Support Groups (see also Sport/Dance/Outdoor)

♂ Tulsa Prime Timers, PO Box 52118; 74152-0118 918-437-2878

Organizations/Resources: Sport/Dance/Outdoor

♂ ★ OK Spoke Club, PO Box 9165; 74157 "Bicyclists."

Publications

♂ • *Tulsa Family News*, PO Box 4140; 74159 918-832-0233

Religious Organizations & Publications

♂ ★&& Dignity-Integrity/Tulsa, PO Box 701044; 74170-1044 918-298-4648 Pub *D/I Newsletter*. "Gay, Lesbian, & Bisexual Catholics, Episcopalians, & their friends."

♀ ★ (&&) Family of Faith Metropolitan Community Church, 5451-E S Mingo; 74146 918-622-1441

♂ ★ Metropolitan Community Church, PO Box 4187; 74159 / 1623 N. Maplewood 918-838-1715

Switchboards, Helplines, Phone Information

♂ ★ TOHR Gay/Lesbian Helpline, PO Box 52729; 74152-2729 918-743-GAYS 8-10pm.

Oregon

State/County Resources

Addictive Behavior, Substance Abuse, Recovery

♂ • (&&) Pride Institute, 800-54-PRIDE "The nation's only accredited chemical dependency treatment center exclusively for Gay, Lesbian & Bisexual People."

Broadcast Media

♂ ★ Night Scene, 13 NW 13th Ave, Portland, OR 97209 503-244-2489 Cable access TV show: call for details.

Organizations/Resources: Bisexual Focus

♀ ☆ (?&) Bisexual Network of Oregon (BiNet-Oregon), PO Box 2593, Portland, OR 97208-2593 503-236-4941 (also fax); 503-236-4941 (also fax); Pub *Northwest BiWays*. "Educational, political, support & social group for bisexual women & men."

Organizations/Resources: Business & Professional

♂ Cascade Union of Educators (CUE), PO Box 2122, Beaverton, OR 97075

♂ ★ (?&) Oregon Gay & Lesbian Law Association, PO Box 876, Portland, OR 97207 503-229-3988

Organizations/Resources: Education, Anti-Defamation, Anti-Violence, Self-Defense

♂ ★ Anti-Violence Project Line, PO Box 5931, Portland, OR 97218 503-796-1703; 800-796-1703 outside Portland; 24 hrs. "Provides advocacy & referrals to victims & survivors of homophobic-biased violence."

♀ ★&& Northwest Speak Out Project, 921 SW Morrison St #506, Portland, OR 97205-2734 503-223-4992 Fax 503-223-5098 osop@aol.com

Organizations/Resources: General, Multipurpose, Pride

♂ ★ Lambda Eastern Oregon Association, PO Box 382, Baker City, OR 97814 Pub *LEOA Newsletter*. "Networking service association."

OR: State/County Resources
Organizations: Political

381

USA

Corvallis : OR
Bookstores: General

Organizations/Resources: Political/Legislative

⚥ Log Cabin Oregon, PO Box 7537, Aloha, OR 97007 503-642-7292

♀ ☆ (♂♀) National Organization for Women (NOW), 651 SE Reed Market Rd, Bend, OR 97702-2230 Pub *NOW News.*

♂ ☆ Support Our Communities PAC, PO Box 40625, Portland, OR 97240-0625 503-222-6151 Fax 503-222-6418

Organizations/Resources: Social, Recreational & Support Groups (see also Sport/Dance/Outdoor)

⚥ Gentle Giants of Oregon, PO Box 83332, Portland, OR 97283-0332 503-981-4281

Organizations/Resources: Sport/Dance/Outdoor

⚥ ★ (♂♀) Outdoor Activities Group, PO Box 5505, Eugene, OR 97405-0505 503-484-2147 Pub *Outdoor Newsletter.*

Organizations/Resources: Youth (see also Family)

♂ Oregon Sexual Minority Youth Network (OSMYN), PO Box 162, Portland, OR 97207-0162 503-228-5976; 800-676-9638

Publications

⚥ ★ *Just Out*, PO Box 14400, Portland, OR 97214-0400 503-236-1252 Fax 503-236-1257 Twice monthly. "News & entertainment; also annual Just Out Pocketbook: A Directory of Gay & Lesbian Resources."

⚥ ★ *Northwest Community News*, PO Box 663, Salem, OR 97308 503-363-0006

Real Estate

⚥ • Community Real Estate Referrals, 800-346-5592 "Free referral to gay/gay-supportive realtor in any USA city/state (including Virgin Is. & Puerto Rico). Sorry, no rentals!"
✦ *Community Real Estate Referrals advertisement back cover*

Aloha

Travel & Tourist Services (see also Accommodation)

♂ ○ ♿ Travel Corner, 17175 SW T.V. Highway; 97006 503-649-9867; 800-327-0840

Ashland/Medford Area

Accommodation: Hotels, B&B, Resorts, Campgrounds

Ashland

♂ • Country Willow B&B Inn, 1313 Clay St, Ashland; 97520 503-488-1590; 800-WILLOWS; Fax 503-488-1611

⚥ • (♂♀) Willow-Witt Ranch Country Guest House, 658 Shale City Rd, Ashland; 97520 503-776-1728; 503-734-9522

Bars, Restaurants, Clubs, Discos

Ashland

♂ • Cook's Playbill Club, 66 E Main St, Ashland; 97520 503-488-4626

Bookstores: General

♂ ○ Bloomsbury Books, 290 E Main St, Ashland; 97520-1831 503-488-0029

Organizations/Resources: Family

♀ ☆ Rogue Valley Parents, Families & Friends of Gays, PO Box 13, Ashland; 97520 503-488-3436; 503-482-4017; Fax 503-482-4017 Pub *Jefferson Banner.* "Parents, Families & Friends of Lesbians & Gays."

Organizations/Resources: Student, Academic, Alumni/ae

⚥ Gay/Lesbian Alliance at Southern Oregon State College, c/o Stevenson Union, Siskyou Blvd, Ashland; 97550 503-552-7702

Performing Arts: Entertainment, Music, Recording, Theater, etc.

♀ ☆ (♂♀) Womansource, PO Box 335, Ashland; 97520 503-482-2026 Coffeehouse 1st Fri of month. "Sponsorship of women artists, performers."

Astoria

AIDS/HIV Support, Education, Advocacy, Publications

♂ ☆ Clatsop County AIDS Coalition, PO Box 455; 97103 503-338-7501

Bend

☎ The GALON 503-388-2395

AIDS/HIV Support, Education, Advocacy, Publications

♂ ★ Central Oregon AIDS Support Team, PO Box 9184; 97708 503-389-4330

Art Galleries/Archives/Restoration, Supplies, Framing

♂ • (♿) Buffet Flat, 64990 Deschutes Market Rd; 97701 503-389-6391

♂ • ♿ The Funny Farm, 64992 Deschutes Market Rd; 97701-9797 503-389-6391

Organizations/Resources: General, Multipurpose, Pride

⚥ ★ The GALON, PO Box 5672; 97708-5672 503-388-2395 24 hrs. "Meeting place; library; social contact."

Organizations/Resources: Social, Recreational & Support Groups (see also Sport/Dance/Outdoor)

⚥ ★ (♂♀) Another Side, PO Box 5672; 97701 503-388-2395 Pub *Another Side.*

Canyonville

Accommodation: Hotels, B&B, Resorts, Campgrounds

♀ ★ Oregon Women's Land Trust (OWL) Farm, PO Box 133, Days Creek; 97429 "All women welcome. Please write for details."

Central Point

Religious Organizations & Publications

⚥ Metropolitan Community Church of the Siskiyous, 8165 Gold Ray Rd; 97502 503-770-7966

Corvallis

AIDS/HIV Support, Education, Advocacy, Publications

♂ ☆ (♂♀) Valley AIDS Information Network, PO Box 971; 97339 503-752-6322

Bookstores: General

♂ ○ ♿ Grass Roots, 227 SW 2nd St; 97333 503-754-7668

♀ ○ Monroe Avenue Book Bin, 2305 NW Monroe; 97330 503-753-8398

Organizations/Resources: Political/Legislative

♂ ★ ♂ After 8, PO Box 1828; 97339-1828 503-752-8157 "Lesbian, gay, & bisexual advocacy, education, information & referral. All welcome."

Organizations/Resources: Student, Academic, Alumni/ae

♀ ★ ♂ Lesbian, Gay & Bisexual Alliance, Oregon State University, Student Activities Center; 97331 503-737-6363

Publications

♀ ★ *Ladies Home Companion*, PO Box 1828; 97339 "Local newsletter."

Women's Centers

♀ ☆ ♂ OSU Women's Center, Benton Annex, OSU; 97331-2503 503-737-3186

Dillard: see Roseburg

Eugene

Accommodation: Hotels, B&B, Resorts, Campgrounds

♂ ● Westwind Retreat Bed & Breakfast, 30 miles south of Eugene 503-942-4414; 800-GAY0069
◆ *Westwind Retreat Bed & Breakfast advertisement page 381*

AIDS/HIV Support, Education, Advocacy, Publications

♀ ☆ (♂♂) Acorn House, PO Box 5360; 97405 503-342-2830 Pub *Friends of Acorn*. "Foster home for persons with AIDS."

♀ ○ (?♂) HIV Alliance, Inc., PO Box 5513; 97405-0513 503-342-5088 Fax 503-342-1150 Pub *HIV Alliance Update*.

Bars, Restaurants, Clubs, Discos

♂ ● (♂) Club Arena/Perry's, 959 Pearl St; 97401 503-683-2360 *BDR* 7pm-2.30am. Video bar.

Bookstores: Gay/Lesbian/Feminist

♂ ★ ♂♂ Mother Kali's Books, 720 E 13th Ave; 97401 503-343-4864

Bookstores: General

♀ ● ♂♂ Baba Yaga's Dream, 1235 Willamette St; 97401 503-683-3842 Bookstore & coffeehouse.

♀ ○ ♂ Hungry Head Books, 1212 Willamette St; 97401 503-485-0888 Mon-Sat 11am-6pm.

Bookstores: Recovery, Metaphysical, & other Specialty

♀ ● ♂ Peralandra Books & Music, 199 E 5th St; 97401 (Station Square) 503-485-4848 Mon-Sat 10am-6pm. "Specializing in books on personal & planetary healing. Lesbian, Gay & Feminist sections; distribution point for local Lesbian/Gay newspaper."

Erotica (Printed, Visual, Equipment)

♀ ○ ♂ Sweet Sensations, 2727 Willamette Ave 503-345-5065 10am-10pm; Fri & Sat to mdnt; Sun noon-8pm.

Funding: Endowment, Fundraising, Scholarship

♂ ★ ♂♂ Imperial Sovereign Court of the Emerald Empire, PO Box 3243; 97403

Organizations/Resources: Family

♀ ☆ ♂♂ P-FLAG, PO Box 11137; 97440 503-689-1630 "Parents, Families & Friends of Lesbians & Gays."

Organizations/Resources: General, Multipurpose, Pride

♂ ★ ♂♂ Lesbian, Gay, Bisexual Alliance, #319 EMU, Univ. of Oregon; 97403 503-686-3360

Publications

♀ ○ (?♂) *Womyn's Press*, PO Box 562; 97440 503-689-3974 "Eclectic feminist newspaper."

Religious Organizations & Publications

⚥ Baleboosteh, PO Box 11134; 97440

♀ ☆ ♂♂ Clergy & Laity Concerned, PO Box 10837; 97440-0837 503-485-1755

♂ ★ ♂♂ Metropolitan Community Church/Eugene, PO Box 10091; 97440-2091 / 1414 Kincaid St 503-345-5963 Worship Sun 4pm at First Congregational Church, Condon Chapel, 23rd & Harris St. Pub *Common Ground*.

Travel & Tourist Services (see also Accommodation)

♀ ○ Global Affair, 285 E 5th Ave; 97401 503-343-8595; 800-755-2753

Women's Centers

♀ ☆ ♂♂ Women's Resource & Referral, Women's Center, Suite 3, EMU, University of Oregon; 97403 503-346-4095

Grants Pass

Accommodation: Hotels, B&B, Resorts, Campgrounds

♀ ★ (?♂) Womanshare, PO Box 681; 97526 503-862-2807 "Feminist country retreat."

Organizations/Resources: Political/Legislative

♀ ☆ Josephine County Human Rights Alliance, PO Box 182; 97526 503-479-0633 Pub *JCHRA Newsletter*.

Klamath Falls

AIDS/HIV Support, Education, Advocacy, Publications

♀ ☆ (?♂) Klamath County AIDS/HIV Support & Education Council, 1035 Main St; 97601 503-883-AIDS

Organizations/Resources: Social, Recreational & Support Groups (see also Sport/Dance/Outdoor)

♂ ★ (?♂) Klamath Area Lambda Association, mail to KALA PO Box 43; 97601 / 1035 Main St, alley entrance. 503-883-2437 Pub *KALA Newsletter*.

La Grande

Organizations/Resources: Student, Academic, Alumni/ae

⚥ Gay & Lesbian Alliance of Eastern Oregon State College, Hoke College Center, SAO, 8th St at K Ave; 97850

Lincoln City

Accommodation: Hotels, B&B, Resorts, Campgrounds

♀ ○ Lincoln Lodge, 2735 NW Inlet; 97567 503-994-5007; 800-866-9925; Ocean front.

Medford: see Ashland/Medford Area

Newport

Accommodation: Hotels, B&B, Resorts, Campgrounds

♀ ● Green Gables Bed & Breakfast, 156 SW Coast St; 97365 503-265-9141

Bookstores: General

♀ ● Green Gables Bookstore, 156 SW Coast St; 97365 503-265-9141 Thu-Mon 10am-5pm.

OR: Pacific City
Organizations: Social & Support

383
USA

Portland : OR
Broadcast Media

Pacific City

Organizations/Resources: Social, Recreational & Support Groups (see also Sport/Dance/Outdoor)

⚥ Tillamook County Gala, PO Box 592; 97135

Portland

Accommodation: Hotels, B&B, Resorts, Campgrounds

♀ ○ The Mark Spencer Hotel, 409 SW 11th Ave; 97205 503-224-3293; 800-548-3934; Fax 503-223-7848

⚥ • Sullivan's Gulch B&B, 1744 NE Clackamas St; 97232 503-331-1104
✦ *Sullivan's Gulch B&B advertisement page 383*

Addictive Behavior, Substance Abuse, Recovery

♀ ○ ♿ ASAP Treatment Services, Inc, 2130 SW 5th Ave #100; 97201-4943 503-224-0075

⚥ ★ Live & Let Live Club, 2802 SE Ankeny; 97214 503-231-3760; 503-231-4829

AIDS/HIV Support, Education, Advocacy, Publications

♀ ☆ ♿ Cascade AIDS Project, 620 SW 5th Ave #300; 97204-1418 503-223-5907; 800-777-AIDS; Mon-Fri 10am-9pm; Sat & Sun noon-6pm.

♀ Esther's Pantry, PO Box 42005; 97242-0005 503-236-4475

♀ ☆ (?♿) Tod's Corner, PO Box 69553; 97201 503-245-7428

Art Galleries/Archives/Restoration, Supplies, Framing

♀ ○ Photographic Image Gallery, 208 SW 1st Ave; 97204 503-224-3543 "Art gallery; picture framing; books & posters."

Automobile Services

♀ ○ Ferguson Autobody & Paint, Inc., 2454 E Burnside; 97214 503-232-3600

Bars, Restaurants, Clubs, Discos

♂ • CC Slaughter's, 1014 SW Stark St; 97205 503-248-9135 *LL* 5pm-2.30am; Sun 3pm-2.30am.

♀ ○ ♿ Choices Pub, 2845 SE Stark; 97214 503-236-4321 4pm-1am; Fri & Sat to 2am; Sun 4pm-mdnt. Beer & wine only.

⚥ • (♿) City Nightclub, 13 NW 13th Ave; 97209 503-224-CITY *DE* Wed, Thu, Sun 10pm-2am; Fri & Sat to 4am "Alcohol-free all-age dance club with show, after hours."

⚥ • ♿ Crow Nightclub, 4801 SE Hawthorne Blvd; 97215 503-232-2037 *DRLE*

♀ Cup & Saucer Cafe, 3568 SE Hawthorne Blvd; 97214 503-236-6001 *R*

♀ • ♿♿ Darcelle's XV, 208 NW 3rd Ave; 97209 503-222-5338

♂ Dirty Duck Tavern, 439 NW 3rd Ave; 97209 503-224-8446

♂ The Eagle, 1300 W Burnside; 97209 503-241-0105

⚥ • ♿♿ Fish Grotto/Boxxes/Brig/Panorama, 1035 SW Stark; 97205 503-226-4171 *BDR*

♀ • ♿ Hamburger Mary's, 840 SW Park Ave; 97205 503-223-0900

♀ ○ Hobo's, 120 NW 3rd St; 97209 503-224-3285 *R*

⚥ • ♿ Joq's Tavern, 2512 NE Broadway; 97232 503-287-4210
✦ *Joq's Tavern advertisement page 383*

♀ • ♿♿ Old Wives' Tales, 1300 E Burnside; 97214 503-238-0470

♂ • (♿) Ray's Ordinary Bar & Grille, 317 NW Broadway; 97209 503-222-RAYS *BR*

♂ Scandals Tavern, 1038 SW Stark; 97205 503-227-5887

♂ • ♿ Silverado, 1217 SW Stark; 97205 503-224-4493 *BREL-CEd*

⚥ • (♿♿) Starky's, 2913 SE Stark; 97214 503-230-7980 *BR* 11am-2.30am.

Bookstores: Gay/Lesbian/Feminist

⚲ • ♿♿ Widdershins Books, 1996 SE Ladd Ave; 97214 503-232-2129

Bookstores: General

♀ ○ In Other Words/Women's Books & Resources, 3734 SE Hawthorne Blvd; 97214 503-232-6003

♂ ○ ♿♿ Laughing Horse Books, 3652 SE Division; 97202-1546 503-236-2893

♀ ○ Looking Glass Books, 318 SW Taylor St; 97204 503-227-4760 Mon-Fri 9am-6pm; Sat 10am-6pm.

♀ ○ ♿♿ Powell's Travel Store, 701 SW 6th, Pioneer Courthouse Square; 97204 503-228-1108

♀ ○ Twenty-Third Avenue Books, 1015 NW 23rd Ave; 97210 503-224-5097

Broadcast Media

⚲ ☆ ♿♿ Bread & Roses Show, KBOO Radio, 20 SE 8th; 97214 503-231-8032 Tue 9-10pm. *Bread & Roses Show..* "Feminist public affairs program."

→ Night Scene: p.380

♀ ☆ ♿♿ Womansoul, KBOO Radio, 90.7FM, 20 SE 8th; 97214 503-231-8032

OR: Portland
Business Services

384

USA

Portland : OR
Organizations: Political

SPARTACUS LEATHERS

THE COMPLETE LEATHER AND ADULT TOY STORE

HOURS: Mon. - Sat. 10 a.m. - 11 p.m.
Sun. 12 p.m. - 8 p.m.

Voice (503)224-2604 : Fax (503)239-4681

300 S.W. 12th Avenue
Portland, Oregon 97205

Business, Financial & Secretarial

♀ ○ Brown, Eric D., Waddell & Reed Financial Services, 500 NE Multnomah #278 503-282-6701

Community Centers (see also Women's Centers)

♀ ★ ♂♂ Phoenix Rising Foundation, Inc., 620 SW 5th Ave #710; 97204-1422 503-223-8299 "Counseling, psychiatric medication evaluation; advocacy; HIV services; information & referrals."

Computer Bulletin Boards

♀ • Hot Pockets BBS, PO Box 3921; 97208 503-232-9027

Counseling/Therapy: Nonprofit

♀ ★ ♂♂ Phoenix Rising Foundation, Inc., 620 SW 5th Ave #710; 97204-1422 503-223-8299 Fax 503-223-1861 "Mental health agency, serving all sexual minorities."

Dentists

♀ • ♂♂ Lopez, John, DMD, 511 SW 10th Ave #708; 97205 503-228-4122

Erotica (Printed, Visual, Equipment)

♂ ○ ♂♂ Blue Spot Video, 3232 NE 82nd Ave; 97220 503-251-8944

♂ • (♂) The Crimson Phoenix, 1876 SW 5th Ave; 97201 503-228-0129 "Sexuality bookstore/condom store."

♂ • ♂♂ Fantasy For Adults Only, 3137 NE Sandy Blvd; 97232 503-239-6969 24 hrs. "Video arcade; magazines; video rentals & sales."

♂ • (♂♂) Harts Movie Arcade, 330 SW 3rd; 97204 503-224-2338

♂ ○ (♂) The Leatherworks, 2908 SE Belmont; 97214-4025 503-234-2697

♂ ○ Sin City Adult Books, 838 SW 3rd Ave; 97204 503-223-6514

♂ ○ ♂ **Spartacus Enterprises, 300 SW 12th Ave, Portland, OR 97205 800-666-2604 Fax 503-239-4681 Mon-Sat 10am-9pm. "Custom leather; store & mail order; catalogs $8."**
♦ *Spartacus Enterprises advertisement page 384*

If you can't find the
NAME   PLACE   SUBJECT
you're looking for,
PLEASE TRY THE INDEX

Gifts, Cards, Pride & Novelty Items

♀ • ♂♂ It's My Pleasure, 4526 SE Hawthorne; 97215 503-236-0505 "Women's resources, gifts, books, arts & crafts, safer sex resources, etc."

♀ ○ The Jellybean, 721 SW 10th Ave; 97205 503-222-5888

Grooming Services

♀ ○ ♂♂ Techniques Hair Salon, 34 NW 1st #106; 97209

Health Clubs, Gyms, Saunas

♂ Club Portland, 303 SW 12th Ave; 97205 503-227-9992

♂ ○ Olympic Steam Bath Downtown, 509 SW 4th Ave; 97204 503-227-5718

Legal Services & Resources

♀ ☆ ♂ American Civil Liberties Union (ACLU), PO Box 40585; 97240-0585 503-227-3186

♀ • (♂♂) Cumfer, Cynthia, 316 NE 28th; 97232 503-234-4282

♀ ○ ♂♂ Kramer & Toth-Fejel, 520 SW 6th #1010; 97204 503-243-2733

♀ • ♂♂ Merrill, Ben, 1020 SW Taylor St #330; 97205-2588 503-222-9830 Fax 503-274-8575

♀ • Simon, Emily, 620 SW 5th Ave #1204; 97204 503-241-1553 Fax 503-241-2587

♂ • ♂♂ Woodworth, Bradley J., 1500 SW 1st Ave #920; 97201-5823 503-273-9146

Organizations/Resources: Education, Anti-Defamation, Anti-Violence, Self-Defense

♀ ★ ♂♂ Equity Foundation, PO Box 5696; 97228 503-220-0628 Fax 503-222-5062 equityfund@aol.com

Organizations/Resources: Ethnic, Multicultural

♀ Asian/Pacific Islander Lesbians & Gays, PO Box 824; 97207 503-232-6408

Organizations/Resources: Family

♀ ☆ ♂♂ Parents FLAG/Portland, PO Box 8944; 97207-8944 503-232-7676

Organizations/Resources: General, Multipurpose, Pride

♀ ★ Lesbian & Gay Pride, Inc, PO Box 6611; 97228 503-232-8233

♀ ★ (♂♂) Lesbian Community Project, PO Box 5931; 97228 503-223-0071 Tue-Thu 10am-4pm, & by appointment. Pub *On Track.* "Multi-cultural, multi-issue organization that advocates for the Lesbian community."

Organizations/Resources: Military/Veterans

♀ Veterans for Human Rights, 208 SW Stark St #306; 97204 503-223-1373 Fax 503-241-0059 veteran@agora.rdrop.com

Organizations/Resources: Political/Legislative

♂ Coalition for Human Dignity (CHD), PO Box 40344; 97240 503-281-5823

♀ National Organization For Women/Portland, 921 SW Morrison St #443; 97205-2734

♀ ☆ Radical Women, 1819 NW Everett #201; 97209 503-228-3090 Pub *Radical Women Manifesto, etc..* "We promote the leadership of women, lesbians & women of color. Men welcome to work with us."

♀ ★ Right To Privacy Political Action Committee, 921 SW Morrison #518; 97205 503-228-5825

Organizations/Resources: Social, Recreational & Support Groups (see also Sport/Dance/Outdoor)

♂ ★ Cascade Bears, 625 SW 10th Ave #125; 97205 503-323-6071

♂ ★ ♂ Gay Men's Community Project, PO Box 40741; 97240-0741 503-331-2282 "Project-oriented group: social & visible PR activities."

♂ Portland Metro Club, 9961 SW Walnut Apt 17; 97223-5152 503-598-3442

⚥ Portland Power & Trust, Box 3781; 97208

Organizations/Resources: Sport/Dance/Outdoor

♂ ★ ♂ Portland Community Bowling Association, PO Box 851; 97207

♂ ★ (♂♀) Rosetown Ramblers, Box 5352; 97228 503-231-6062 *d* "Square Dance."

⚥ Wrestling Club Of Portland, PO Box 40066; 97240-0066

Organizations/Resources: Transgender & Transgender Publications

T ☆ (♂♀) Northwest Gender Alliance, PO Box 4928; 97208 503-774-8463

Performing Arts: Entertainment, Music, Recording, Theater, etc.

♂ ★ ♂ Portland Gay Men's Chorus, PO Box 3223; 97208-3223 503-284-5386

Performing Arts: Entertainment, Music, Theater, etc.

♀ ★ (♂♀) Portland Lesbian Choir, PO Box 8212; 97207 503-241-8994

Publications

⚥ *Alternative Connection*, PO Box 1145; 97207-1145 503-236-3055

→ *Just Out:* p.381

Real Estate

♀ ○ ♂♀ Bridgetown Realty, 1000 NE Multnomah; 97232 503-287-9370 Fax 503-281-2037

Religious Organizations & Publications

⚥ ★ Affirmation: United Methodists for Lesbian, Gay & Bisexual Concerns, PO Box 12673; 97212 503-234-8854

⚥ ★ ♂ American Friends Service Committee/Gay & Lesbian Program, 2249 E Burnside; 97214 503-230-9430 "Religious Society of Friends (Quakers)."

⚥ ★ Dignity/Portland, PO Box 6708; 97228-6708 503-295-4868 "Gay & Lesbian Catholics & their friends."

⚥ ★ ♂ Evangelicals Concerned of Portland, PO Box 40741; 97240-0741 503-232-7451

♀ ★ (♂♀) Integrity/Columbia-Willamette, PO Box 12543; 97212-0543 503-288-5949 (also fax) bruceintc@aol.com "Lesbian & Gay Episcopalians & their friends."

♀ ☆ Metanoia Peace Community United Methodist Church, 2116 NE 18th Ave; 97212-4609 503-281-3697

⚥ ★ ♂ Metropolitan Community Church of Portland, 2400 NE Broadway St; 97232 503-281-8868

⚥ ★ (♂) Reach Out! - Gay ex-Jehovah's Witnesses, PO Box 1173, Clackamas; 97015

♀ ☆ ♂♀ SisterSpirit, PO Box 9246; 97207 503-294-0645 Pub *Spirited Women.* "Women from various backgrounds & traditions sharing spirituality."

Yachats, OR (503)547-3227
The
See Vue Ocean Lodging

Travel & Tourist Services (see also Accommodation)

♀ • Advantage Travel Service, 812 SW Washington St #200; 97205 503-225-0186; 800-688-6690

⚥ • ♂♀ In Touch Travel, 121 SW Morrison #270; 97224 503-223-1062

♀ ○ ♂ Kaz Travel Services, Inc., 1975 SW 1st Ave #K; 97201 503-223-4585; 800-637-3874

♀ • ♂♀ Mikuni Travel Services, 1 SW Columbia St #1010; 97258 503-227-3639; 800-248-0624; Fax 503-227-0602

♀ • ♂♀ Travel Agents International, 917 SW Washington St; 97205 503-223-1100; 800-357-3194

Video Sales, Rentals, Services (see also Erotica)

♀ ○ ♂ Hard Times West, 311 NW Broadway; 97209 503-223-2398 24 hrs.

Rogue River

Accommodation: Hotels, B&B, Resorts, Campgrounds

⚥ • Whispering Pines Bed & Breakfast/Retreat, 9188 W Evans Creek Rd; 97537 503-582-1757; 800-788-1757

Roseburg

AIDS/HIV Support, Education, Advocacy, Publications

♀ ☆ ♂♀ Douglas County AIDS Council, 3035 Laurel Springs Dr; 97470-1311 503-440-2761 Pub *Bow To One Another.* "Housing for People with HIV/AIDS."

Archives/Libraries/History Projects

⚥ ★ Douglas County Gay Archives, PO Box 942, Dillard; 97432-0942 503-679-9703

Herbalists

⚥ • Annie Ocean Witchcrafted Botanicals, 925 Raven Lane; 97470 503-672-0525

Religious Organizations & Publications

♀ ☆ (?♂) Metropolitan Community Church, Box 2125; 97470-0449 503-440-1496

Salem

Bars, Restaurants, Clubs, Discos

⚥ • ♂♂ Sneakers Bar/Seasons Restaurant, 300 Liberty SE; 97301 503-363-0549 ***BDR*** 4pm-2.30am.

Bookstores: General

♀ ○ ♂ Rosebud & Fish Community Bookstore, 524 State St; 97301 503-399-9960 10am-7pm; Sun noon-5pm.

Erotica (Printed, Visual, Equipment)
♀ ○ Bob's Adult Bookstore, 3655 Portland Rd NE; 97303 503-363-3846

Organizations/Resources: Social, Recreational & Support Groups (see also Sport/Dance/Outdoor)
♀ ★ (&) Prime Of Life Club, PO Box 663; 97308 503-363-0006

Publications
→ *Northwest Community News*: p.381

Religious Organizations & Publications
♀ ★ Dignity/Willamette Valley, PO Box 532; 97308 503-363-0006 "Gay & Lesbian Catholics & their friends."

♀ ★ & Sweet Spirit Metropolitan Community Church, PO Box 13969; 97309 / 1410 12th St SE 503-363-6618

Springfield
Erotica (Printed, Visual, Equipment)
♀ ○ & Exclusively Adult, 1166 S A St; 97477 503-726-6969 24 hrs.

♀ ○ & Exclusively Adult, 1166 S A St; 97477-5209 503-726-6969

Tiller
Accommodation: Hotels, B&B, Resorts, Campgrounds
♀ • (&) Kalles Family RV Ranch, 233 Jackson Creek Rd; 97484 503-825-3271 "Campground: all amenities."

Waldport
Accommodation: Hotels, B&B, Resorts, Campgrounds
♀ • (&) Cliff House Bed & Breakfast, PO Box 436; 97394 503-563-2506

Yachats
Accommodation: Hotels, B&B, Resorts, Campgrounds
♀ ○ (?&) Oregon House, 94288 Hwy 101; 97498 503-547-3329

♀ • (&) The See Vue, 95590 Hwy 101; 97498 503-547-3227
✦ *See Vue advertisement page 385*

♀ ○ Yachats Inn, PO Box 307; 97498 503-547-3456

PA: State/County Resources
Addictive Behavior

387

USA

Dubois : PA
Organizations: Family

Pennsylvania

State/County Resources

Addictive Behavior, Substance Abuse, Recovery

♀ ☆ (?♂) Lambda Recovery Program, Livengrin Foundation, 4833 Hulmeville Rd, Bensaiem, PA 19020 215-638-5200; 800-245-4746

♂ • (♂♂) Pride Institute, 800-54-PRIDE "The nation's only accredited chemical dependency treatment center exclusively for Gay, Lesbian & Bisexual People."

AIDS/HIV Support, Education, Advocacy, Publications

♀ ☆♂♂ AIDS Law Project of Pennsylvania, 1211 Chestnut St #1200, Philadelphia, PA 19107 215-587-9377

♀ ☆ (♂) Venango-Forest AIDS Support, PO Box 834, Oil City, PA 16301 800-359-2437

Organizations/Resources: Business & Professional

♂ ★ National Education Association Gay & Lesbian Caucus, PO Box 3559, York, PA 17402-0559 717-848-3354

Organizations/Resources: Political/Legislative

♂ ★ ♂ League of Gay & Lesbian Voters (State HQ), 5100 Penn Ave #3rd FL, Pittsburgh, PA 15224-1616 412-661-6670

♀ ☆ ♂ Pennsylvania Council for Sexual Minorities, 238 Main Capitol Bldg, Governor's Office, Harrisburg, PA 17120 412-624-5046

Organizations/Resources: Social, Recreational & Support Groups (see also Sport/Dance/Outdoor)

♂ ★ Lesburbia, PO Box 293, Montgomeryville, PA 18936 Pub *Lesburbia.* "Various social events in various locations in Bucks & surrounding counties; write for details."

♂ ★ Poconos Action Lambda Society, mail to PALS, Box 1375, Milford, PA 18337 Pub *Spread the Word.* "Networking gay men & lesbians in NE PA, SE NY, NW NJ."

Publications

♂ • *Au Courant Newsmagazine,* PO Box 42741, Philadelphia, PA 19101-2741 215-790-1179 Weekly.

Real Estate

♂ • Community Real Estate Referrals, 800-346-5592 "Free referral to gay/gay-supportive realtor in any USA city/state (including Virgin Is. & Puerto Rico). Sorry, no rentals!"
◆ *Community Real Estate Referrals advertisement back cover*

Religious Organizations & Publications

♂ ★ (♂) Dignity/NE Penna, PO Box 379, Hamlin, PA 18427 717-829-1341 "Gay & Lesbian Catholics & their friends."

♂ ★ Gay, Lesbian & Bisexual Spiritual Fellowship, 1805 8th Ave, Altoona, PA 16602 814-949-5852 Pub *Reconciliation.*

♂ ★ (?♂) UCCL/GC (United Church Coalition for Lesbian/Gay Concerns), PO Box 6315, Philadelphia, PA 19139 215-724-1247

Travel & Tourist Services (see also Accommodation)

♀ ○ Pocono Whitewater Rafting, Ltd, Rt 903, Jim Thorpe, PA 18229 717-325-3656

Allentown: see Lehigh Valley Area

Altoona

☎ Gay, Lesbian & Bisexual Helpline 814-942-8101

Counseling/Therapy: Nonprofit

♀ ☆♂♂ Family & Children's Service, 2022 Broad Ave; 16601 814-944-3583 Fax 814-944-8701

Organizations/Resources: General, Multipurpose, Pride

♀ ★♂♂ Gay, Lesbian & Bisexual Task Force, c/o Family & Childrens Service 2022 Broad Ave; 16601 814-944-3583

Organizations/Resources: Political/Legislative

♂ ★ League of Gay & Lesbian Voters/Altoona-Johnstown Regional Chapter, PO Box 209, Stoystown, PA 15563 814-949-5852

Switchboards, Helplines, Phone Information

♂ ★♂♂ Gay, Lesbian & Bisexual Helpline, c/o Family & Childrens Service 2022 Broad Ave; 16601 814-942-8101 Thu-Sun 7-10pm.

Bethlehem: see Lehigh Valley Area

Boyers

Accommodation: Hotels, B&B, Resorts, Campgrounds

♂ • (♂♂) Camp Davis, 311 Red Brush Road; 16020 412-637-2402 "Membership only."

Bradford

Organizations/Resources: Student, Academic, Alumni/ae

♂ University of Pitt-Bradford BiGALA, 300 Campus Dr #235 Commons; 16701 814-362-7654

Bridgeport

Bars, Restaurants, Clubs, Discos

♂ ○ Lark Hotel & Bar, 302 DeKalb; 19405 610-275-8136 *BD*

Bryn Mawr

Organizations/Resources: Student, Academic, Alumni/ae

♂ ★ Bryn Mawr/Haverford Bisexual, Gay, & Lesbian Alliance (BGALA), Box 1725, Bryn Mawr College; 19010

Buckingham

AIDS/HIV Support, Education, Advocacy, Publications

♀ ☆ F.A.C.T. Bucks County, PO Box 616; 18112 215-598-0750

Carlisle

Organizations/Resources: Student, Academic, Alumni/ae

♀ ☆♂♂ Dickinson College Allies, c/o Health Education PO Box 4888; 17013 717-240-1835 "Student/staff/faculty organization. Everyone welcome!"

Downingtown

Accommodation: Hotels, B&B, Resorts, Campgrounds

♀ • (?♂) Baker & Babbage, Glen Isle Farm 800-269-1730 Fax 610-269-9191

Dubois

Organizations/Resources: Family

♀ ☆ (♂) P-FLAG Dubois, 1191 Treasure Lake; 15801 814-371-8962

Duryea: see Pottstown

East Stroudsburg: see Stroudsburg/Poconos Area

Easton: see Lehigh Valley Area

Edinboro

Organizations/Resources: Student, Academic, Alumni/ae

♀ ★ ♂♂ Identity/EGO, Edinboro University, Heather Hall; 16444 814-732-2555

Emlenton

Accommodation: Hotels, B&B, Resorts, Campgrounds

♀ ○ Apple Alley Bed & Breakfast, PO Box 130; 16373 / 214 River Ave 412-547-8499; 412-867-9636

Ephrata

Travel & Tourist Services (see also Accommodation)

♀ ● ♂♂ Zeller Travel, 4213 Oregon Pike; 17522 717-859-4710; 800-331-4359

Erie

AIDS/HIV Support, Education, Advocacy, Publications

♀ Friends From The Heart, Well Being 710 Beaumont Ave; 16505 814-838-0123

Bars, Restaurants, Clubs, Discos

♀ Cup-A-Ccinos, 18 North Park Row; 16501 814-456-1151 *BR*

♀ The Embers, 1711 State St; 16501 814-459-1711

♀ ● ♂♂ La Bella Bistro, 556 W 4th St; 16507 814-454-3616; 814-454-2400; *R* Lunch 11am-2am; dinner 5-10pm. BYOB.

♀ Lizzy Borden's II, 3412 W 12th St; 16505 814-833-4059

♀ Pie-In-The-Sky Cafe, 463 W 8th St; 16502 814-459-8638 *R*

Erotica (Printed, Visual, Equipment)

♀ ○ Eastern Adult Books, 1313 State St; 16501 814-459-7014

♀ ○ Filmore News, 2757 W 12th St; 16505 814-833-2667

Organizations/Resources: General, Multipurpose, Pride

♀ ★ Erie Gay Coalition, PO Box 3063; 16508-0063 814-456-8933 Mike; 814-453-2785 Deb; Fax 814-452-1392 mikemahler@aol.com 70331,1622 Pub *Erie Gay Community Newsletter.*

Organizations/Resources: Political/Legislative

♀ ★ League of Gay & Lesbian Voters/Erie Regional Chapter, PO Box 8083; 16505-0083 814-833-3258 (also Fax, please call first) kidithart@aol.com

Organizations/Resources: Social, Recreational & Support Groups (see also Sport/Dance/Outdoor)

♀ ★ ♂ Closet Culture, PO Box 10274; 16514-0274 814-825-0530 "Social & Support for the LesBiGay Community."

Organizations/Resources: Student, Academic, Alumni/ae

♀ ★ ♂ Trigon: Lesbian, Gay & Bisexual Coalition, c/o College Mailroom, Box 1054, Behrend College, Station Rd; 16563 814-898-7050

Organizations/Resources: Transgender & Transgender Publications

T Erie Sisters, 2115 W 8th St #261; 16505

Religious Organizations & Publications

♀ ★ ♂♂ Integrity/Northwest Pennsylvania, PO Box 1782; 16507-0782 814-774-0903 "Lesbian & Gay Episcopalians & their friends."

Travel & Tourist Services (see also Accommodation)

♀ ○ Camelot Travel & Tours, PO Box 3874; 16508 814-835-3434 (also Fax)

Gettysburg

Erotica (Printed, Visual, Equipment)

♀ ○ Bequest Books, 2108 Chambersburg Road (Rt 30 West); 17325 717-337-2062

Organizations/Resources: Student, Academic, Alumni/ae

♀ ★ ♂♂ Gettysburg College Lambda Alliance, Box 2282, Gettysburg College; 17325

Video Sales, Rentals, Services (see also Erotica)

♀ ○ Video Plus, 3930 Chambersburg Rd, Biglerville; 17307 717-334-7038

Greensburg: see Pittsburgh Area

Harrisburg

☎ Gay & Lesbian Switchboard of Harrisburg 717-234-0328

Addictive Behavior, Substance Abuse, Recovery

♀ ★ ♂♂ Lambda Group/AA, PO Box 15602; 17105-5602 717-234-5390 Closed (non-smoking) meetings Mon 8pm & Fri 8.30pm, at Friends Meeting House, 6th & Herr Sts.

Bars, Restaurants, Clubs, Discos

♀ ● ♂♂ B-TLS, 891 Eisenhower Blvd 717-939-1123 *BDE* Wed 6-11pm; Thu & Fri to 2am; Sat 3pm-2am.

♀ The Courtyard, 706 N 3rd St (rear); 17102 717-236-7555

♀ ● Neptune/Paper Moon Restaurant, 268 North St; 17101 717-233-3078 *R*

♀ ○ Stallions, 706 N 3rd St (rear); 17102 717-232-3060 *BDR* 4pm-2am; Sat 7pm-2am; disco Tue-Sun 10pm-2am.

♂ ● ♂ Strawberry Cafe, 704 N 3rd St; 17101 717-234-4228 *R*

Business, Financial & Secretarial

♀ ● Miller, Daniel C., MBA, CPA, 200 North St; 17101-1121 717-234-2250

Counseling/Therapy: Private

♀ ● (♿) Drummond Counseling Center, 44 Oak Park Rd #101; 17109 717-545-1616

♀ ○ ♂♂ T. B. Associates, 1600 Hummel Ave, Camp Hill; 17011-3707 717-761-6649 "Gay/Lesbian stress management & career/vocational issues. Individual, relationship & family therapy. Notary Public."

♀ ○ Weinberger, Bette R., ACSW, 240 Division St; 17110 717-233-7153

Gifts, Cards, Pride & Novelty Items

♀ ○ Bare Wall Gallery, 712 Green St; 17102-3097 717-236-8504 10am-6pm; Sat to 5pm; Sun 10am-1pm. "Gifts, cards, video rental: foreign & classic features; mainstream Gay/Lesbian films (no porn)."

Organizations/Resources: Family

♀ ☆ ♂ Central Pennsylvania P-FLAG, c/o Tressler Lutheran Social Services, Box 2001, Mechanicsburg; 17055 717-795-0330 "Parents, Families & Friends of Lesbians & Gays."

Organizations/Resources: General, Multipurpose, Pride

♂ ★ Pennsmen, PO Box 401; 17108

PA: Harrisburg
Organizations: General
389
USA
Lehigh Valley Area: PA
Erotica

♀ ★ Pride Coalition of Central Pennsylvania, PO Box 60668; 17106-0668 717-545-8411

Organizations/Resources: Transgender & Transgender Publications

T ☆ ♐♐ Renaissance Lower Susquehanna Valley Chapter, PO Box 2122; 17105 717-780-1578 bensalem@cpcn "Peer support & counseling; all welcome."

Performing Arts: Entertainment, Music, Recording, Theater, etc.

♂ Harrisburg Men's Chorus, PO Box 3302; 17105 717-232-9299

Publications

♀ ★ *Lavender Letter*, PO Box 60184; 17106-0184 717-732-8010

Religious Organizations & Publications

♀ ★ ♂ Dignity/Central Pennsylvania, PO Box 297 Federal Square Stn; 17108 "Gay & Lesbian Catholics & their friends."

♀ ★ (♐♐) Metropolitan Community Church of the Spirit, PO Box 11543; 17108 717-236-7387 Pub *Spirit Wings*.

Switchboards, Helplines, Phone Information

♀ (♐♐) Gay & Lesbian Switchboard of Harrisburg, PO Box 872; 17108-0872 717-234-0328 Mon-Fri 6-10pm. Pub *Outlook*.

Havertown

Counseling/Therapy: Private

♀ • Cardell, Mona, Ph.D., 1618 Rose Glen Rd; 19083 610-446-9625 Licensed Psychologist.

Hellam: see York

Johnstown

Bars, Restaurants, Clubs, Discos

♀ Lucille's, 520 Washington St; 15901 814-539-4448

King Of Prussia: see Philadelphia Area

Kingston: see Wilkes Barre

Kutztown

Accommodation: Hotels, B&B, Resorts, Campgrounds

♀ • Grim's Manor Bed & Breakfast, 10 Kern Rd; 19530 610-683-7089

Lancaster

Accommodation: Hotels, B&B, Resorts, Campgrounds

♀ • Cedar Spring Farm Bed & Breakfast, 1125 Osceola Rd, Drumore; 17518 717-548-2006

♀ • (♂) DalEva Farms, Box 6, Drumore; 17518 717-548-3163 "Women's B&B in PA Dutch country; children & pets welcome."

Bars, Restaurants, Clubs, Discos

♀ • Sundown Lounge, 429 N Mulberry St; 17603 717-392-2737 *BD* Mon-Sat 8pm-2am.

♀ • Tally-Ho Tavern/Loft Restaurant, 201 W Orange St; 17604 717-299-0661 *BR*

Erotica (Printed, Visual, Equipment)

♀ ○ (♂) Den of Pleasures, 53 N Prince St; 17603 717-299-1779

♀ ○ Erotic Forum, 227 N Prince St; 17603 717-393-9772

Organizations/Resources: General, Multipurpose, Pride

♀ ★ The Pink Triangle Coalition, PO Box 176; 17608-0176

Organizations/Resources: Sport/Dance/Outdoor

♀ ★ Susquehanna Club, PO Box 10122; 17605-0122 "Hiking & Camping club."

Lebanon

Graphic Design/Typesetting (see also Art; Printing)

♀ • (?♂) Aries Creative Design Concepts, Harry Long, 1130 Church St; 17046-4662 717-273-3404 "Illustration: fine art; male nudes."

Lehigh Valley Area

Accommodation: Hotels, B&B, Resorts, Campgrounds

Allentown

♀ ○ Hamilton House B&B, 22 S 18th St, Allentown; 18104 610-433-3919

AIDS/HIV Support, Education, Advocacy, Publications

♀ ★ ♐♐ AIDS Services Center, 60 W Broad St #205, Bethlehem; 18018-5721 610-974-8701 Fax 610-974-8703 Pub *Positive Plus*.

♀ ☆ (?♂) Fighting AIDS Continuously Together (FACT), PO Box 1028, Allentown; 18105 610-820-5519

♀ ★ (?♂) Footprints In Time, Box 1565, Allentown; 18105 610-376-1510 Pub *Footnotes*. "HIV/AIDS housing & services, advocacy, education."

Bars, Restaurants, Clubs, Discos

Allentown

♀ • Candida, 247 N 12th St, Allentown; 18102 610-434-3071

♀ • Stonewall Bar/Moose Lounge, 28-30 N 10th St, Allentown; 18101 610-432-0215; 610-432-0706; *BDER* 2pm-2am.

Bethlehem

♀ • ♂ Diamonz, 1913 W Broad St, Bethlehem; 18018 610-865-1028 *BDER*

Reading

♀ Nostalgia, 1101 N 9th St, Reading; 19604 610-372-5557

♂ • Red Star, 11 S 10th St, Reading; 19602 610-375-4116

♂ • Scarab Bar, 724 Franklin St, Reading; 19602 610-375-7878

Bookstores: General

♀ • (♂) Lavender Hearts, 13 N 9th St, Reading; 19601 610-372-1828

Business, Financial & Secretarial

♀ ○ Foley, Brian E., Public Accountant, 1240 Turner St, Allentown; 18102 610-434-9852

Counseling/Therapy: Nonprofit

♀ ☆ (?♂) Women's Counseling Services of Berk County, Inc., 739 Washington St, Reading; 19601-3535 610-372-7234

Counseling/Therapy: Private

♀ ○ ♐♐ Kiernan, Mary, M.Ed, 3005 Brodhead Rd #23, Bethlehem; 18017 610-974-8787

♀ • (♂) Marish, Jacqueline, M.A., 1322 Center St, Bethlehem; 18018 610-865-1006

Erotica (Printed, Visual, Equipment)

♀ • Green Door, 1164 Pembroke Rd, Bethlehem; 18017 610-865-5855

Gifts, Cards, Pride & Novelty Items

♥ • Drop Me A Line, 919 Hamilton Mall, Allentown; 18101 610-435-7481

Grooming Services

♀ • ⚤ Shear Dimensions Hair Studio, 1601 Liberty St, Allentown; 18102 610-435-2224

Legal Services & Resources

♥ • Black, Steve, 1322 Center St, Bethlehem; 18018 610-865-7890

Organizations/Resources: Business & Professional

♥ ★ GLEE (Gay & Lesbian Empowered Employees), mail to GLEE, 338 N 8th St, Allentown; 18102

Organizations/Resources: Family

♥ ★ (?⚤) Gay & Lesbian Parents, 610-439-8755

♀ ☆⚤ P-FLAG, 610-439-8755 Meets 2nd Sun, 3.30pm, Unitarian Church, 701 Lechauweki Ave, Fountain Hill "Parents, Families & Friends of Lesbians & Gays."

Organizations/Resources: General, Multipurpose, Pride

♥ ★ (⚤) Lambda Alive, PO Box 4313, Reading; 19606 610-589-4854

♥ ★ Lehigh Valley Gay & Lesbian Task Force, PO Box 20253, Lehigh Valley; 18002-0253 610-515-1551

♥ ★ Pride of the Lehigh Valley, PO Box 20804, Lehigh Valley; 18002 610-264-9369 "Sponsors of the annual Lehigh Valley Pride Celebration."

Organizations/Resources: Political/Legislative

♥ ★ League of Gay & Lesbian Voters, Lehigh Valley Chapter, PO Box 20781, Lehigh Valley; 18002-0781 610-437-2294

Organizations/Resources: Social, Recreational & Support Groups (see also Sport/Dance/Outdoor)

♂ ★ ⚤ Gay Men of the Lehigh Valley, 610-439-8755 Meets 2nd & 4th Sats, 7pm, Unitarian Church, 701 Lechauweki Ave, Fountain Hill

♥ ★ (?⚤) GLORA: Gay & Lesbian Organization of Reading & Allentown, PO Box 1952, Allentown; 18105-1952 The Tassel.

♥ ★ ⚤ Lehigh Valley Lesbians, 610-439-8755 Meets 3rd Tues, 7pm, Unitarian Church, 701 Lechauweki Ave, Fountain Hill

Organizations/Resources: Sport/Dance/Outdoor

♥ ★ The Velvet Spikers, PO Box 21862, Lehigh Valley; 18002 610-434-2966

Organizations/Resources: Student, Academic, Alumni/ae

♥ ★ ⚤ Lehigh University LesBiGay Alliance, c/o Chaplain's Office, 110 Johnson Hall, 36 University Dr, Bethlehem; 18015 610-758-3877

♥ ★ ⚤ Northampton Co. Community College Gay, Lesbian & Bi Student Union, Green Pond Rd 3835, Bethlehem; 18017

Organizations/Resources: Youth (see also Family)

♥ ★ (?⚤) Your Turf, 610-439-8755 Gay & Lesbian Youth Group, 16-22, Fri 7pm. Call for meeting location.

Performing Arts: Entertainment, Music, Theater, etc.

♂ ★ Lehigh Valley Gay Men's Chorus, PO Box 20712, Lehigh Valley; 18002-0712 610-821-0578 lvgmc@aol.com

Real Estate

♀ • Hoover, Gail, 610-433-7919

Religious Organizations & Publications

♥ ★ Grace Covenant Fellowship, 247 N 10th St, Allentown; 18102 610-740-0247 Worship Sun 10.45am.

♥ ★ Integrity/Bethlehem, PO Box 5181, Bethlehem; 18015-5181 610-758-8642 "Lesbian & Gay Episcopalians & their friends."

♀ ★ ♂ Metropolitan Community Church of the Lehigh Valley, 1345 Linden #3, Allentown; 18102 610-439-8755 Worship Sun 7pm at Unitarian church, 701 Lechauweki Ave, Bethlehem Pub Valley Star.

Lemoyne: see Harrisburg

Levittown

Counseling/Therapy: Private

♀ • ⚤ Fillman, James M., MA, 1400 New Rodgers Rd #108; 19058 / 855 W Main St, Lansdale, PA 215-428-0670

Marshalls Creek: see Stroudsburg/Poconos Area

Meadville

Organizations/Resources: Student, Academic, Alumni/ae

♥ ★ The Committee In Support Of Gay, Lesbian, Bisexual People, Box 186, Allegheny College; 16335 814-332-4358; 814-332-4375

Milanville

Accommodation: Hotels, B&B, Resorts, Campgrounds

♀ ○ Milanville House, PO Box 19; 18443 717-729-8236; 212-532-1028

Milford

Accommodation: Hotels, B&B, Resorts, Campgrounds

♥ • K'saan, 212-663-2963; 718-680-6107

Bars, Restaurants, Clubs, Discos

♀ • Dimmick Inn, 101 E Hartford St; 18337 717-296-4021 *R*

Mountville

Religious Organizations & Publications

♥ Vision of Hope Metropolitan Community Church Lancaster, 130 E Main St; 17554 717-285-9070

New Hope

Accommodation: Hotels, B&B, Resorts, Campgrounds

♥ • (?⚤) Back Street Inn, 144 Old York Rd; 18938 215-862-9571 Bed & breakfast.

♂ • The Fox & The Hound Bed & Breakfast of New Hope, 246 West Bridge St; 18938 215-862-5082; 800-862-5082
✦ Fox & The Hound Bed & Breakfast of New Hope advertisement page 391

♀ • Lexington House, 6171 Upper York Rd; 18938 215-794-0811 Bed & breakfast.

♀ • (⚤) Raven Hall, 385 W Bridge St; 18938 215-862-2081

♥ • Riverside, 58 N Main St; 18938 215-862-0216 "Luxury accommodations on the river, near the center of town."

Bars, Restaurants, Clubs, Discos

♥ ○ ⚤ The Cartwheel Restaurant & Nightclub, 437 Old York Rd; 18938 215-862-0880 *BDR* 4pm-2am; Sun 11.30am-2am.

♥ ○ The Prelude, 408-A York Rd; 18938 215-862-3600 *BDR*

♀ • (占占) Raven, 385 W Bridge St; 18938 / Rte 179 215-862-2081

♀ • (占占) Wildflowers Restaurant & Garden Cafe, 8 W Mechanic St; 18938 215-862-2241 *R*

Bookstores: Gay/Lesbian/Feminist

♀ • **Book Gallery, 19 W Mechanic St; 18938 215-862-5110**

Bookstores: General

♀ ○ Farley's Bookstore, 44 S Main St; 18938 215-862-2452

♀ • Mystickal Tymes, 127 S Main St; 18938 215-862-5629 "New Age; metaphysical & herbal books & supplies; movie memorabilia."

♀ ○ Village Green Bookstore, 16 S Main St, Doylestown; 18901 215-230-7610 Fax 215-230-7615

Erotica (Printed, Visual, Equipment)

♀* • Grownups, 2 E Mechanic St; 18938 215-862-9304

Gifts, Cards, Pride & Novelty Items

♀ • Ember'Glo Gifts, 27 W Mechanic St; 18938 215-862-2929 "Eclectic emporium of gifts, cards & novelties."

♀ • (占) Galerie Metamorphosis, 352 W Bridge St (York Place); 18938 215-862-5005 "The gay general store: cards, books, gifts."

♀ ○ Now And Then Shop, 15 E Bridge St; 18938 215-862-5777

Legal Services & Resources

♀* • Kisner, Gary, Esq, 142 E Court St, Doylestown; 18901 215-230-8830 "General legal services for primarily gay/lesbian clients."

New Kensington: see Pittsburgh Area

New Milford

Accommodation: Hotels, B&B, Resorts, Campgrounds

♀* • (占) Oneida Camp & Lodge, PO Box 537; 18834 717-465-7011 *PDEL* "Campground for tents, trailers, RVs, etc; guesthouses & cabins for rent. Also information center, library, meeting center for AA groups & meditation groups. Counseling available."

Norristown

Bars, Restaurants, Clubs, Discos

♂* • Double Header Bar & Dance Club, 354 West Elm St; 19401 610-277-1070 *BDELL*

Legal Services & Resources

♀ • Connor, Carla E., Esq., 43 E Marshall St; 19401 610-272-4222 "General practice; emphasis on personal injury, worker's compensation, family law, DUI cases."

Philadelphia Area

☎ Philadelphia Gay Switchboard 215-546-7100

☎ Tell-A-Woman 215-564-5810

Accommodation: Hotels, B&B, Resorts, Campgrounds

♀ ○ Antique Row Bed & Breakfast, Center City Philadelphia 215-592-7802 Fax 215-592-9692

♀ • Gaskill House, 312 Gaskill St, Philadelphia; 19147 215-413-2887

♀ ○ 占占 Travelodge Hotel - Stadium, 2015 Penrose Ave, Philadelphia; 19145 215-755-6500 Fax 215-465-7517

♀ ○ Uncle's, 1220 Locust St, Philadelphia; 19107 215-546-6660
♦ *Uncle's advertisement page 391*

A Bed & Breakfast
246 West Bridge Street, New Hope, PA 18938
(215) 862-5082

The Fox & Hound of New Hope

| Sun-Thurs | Fri-Sat |
| $60-$80 | $110-120 |

Addictive Behavior, Substance Abuse, Recovery

♀ ★ Gay Alcoholics Anonymous, c/o Recovery Clubhouse, 202 S 12th St, Philadelphia; 19107 215-545-7006 or AA Intergroup 574-6900

♀ ★ Narcotics Anonymous, 2125 Chestnut St, Philadelphia; 19103 215-735-7063

♀ ★ Recovery Clubhouse, 202 S 12th St, Philadelphia; 19107 215-545-7006 or AA Intergroup 574-6900 All welcome.

AIDS/HIV Support, Education, Advocacy, Publications

♀ ☆ (?占) ACT UP/Philadelphia, PO Box 15919, Philadelphia; 19103-0919 215-731-1844 Fax 215-731-1845 jdavids@cpp.pha.pa.us

♀ ☆ 占占 ActionAIDS, Inc, 1216 Arch St, Philadelphia; 19107 215-981-3300

PA: Philadelphia Area
AIDS/HIV Support

392

USA

Philadelphia Area: PA
Erotica

♀ ☆ ♂ AIDS Information Network, 1211 Chestnut St, 7th flr, Philadelphia; 19106 215-922-5120 AIDS Library of Philadelphia; Critical Path Project; Safeguards Project; Youth Health Empowerment Project.

♀ ☆ The Names Project Philadelphia, 328 S 15th St, Philadelphia; 19102 215-735-NAMES Meet Thu 6.30pm at We The People, 425 S. Broad St. "AIDS Memorial Quilt: education, outreach, Quilt display."

♀ ☆ Philadelphia AIDS Task Force/Philadelphia Community Health Alternatives, 1642 Pine St, Philadelphia; 19103-6711 215-545-8686; 215-732-AIDS

♂ ★ ♂♂ The Safe Guards, AIDS Information Network, 32 N 3rd St, Philadelphia; 19106 215-922-5597; 215-922-7999 TDD; Fax 215-922-6762 "Safe sex workshops, forums, prevention education."

Archives/Libraries/History Projects

♂ ★ Lesbian & Gay Library/Archives of Philadelphia, 201 S Camac St, Philadelphia; 19107 215-732-2220 lglap@aol.com

Bars, Restaurants, Clubs, Discos

♂ ○ 247 Bar, 247 S 17th St, Philadelphia; 19103 215-545-9779 *BE*

♂ ● 24th Ward Young Men's Association, 1221 St James, Philadelphia; 19107 215-735-5772 Fax 215-732-1530 *P* "Private club to provide a safe social setting for the gay community."

♀ The Astral Plane, 1706-8 Lombard St, Philadelphia; 19146 215-546-6230

♀ ● Backstage, 614 S 4th St, Philadelphia; 19147 215-627-9887

♂ ● (♿) Bike Stop, 204-206 S Quince St, Philadelphia; 19107 215-627-1662 *BDL* 11am-2am; Sat & Sun noon-2am.

♂ ○ BJP's, 53rd & Market, Philadelphia; 19131 215-747-4953 *BR*

♀ Black Banana, 247 Race St, Philadelphia; 19106 215-925-4433

♀ ● (♿) Cafe on Quince, 202 S Quince St, Philadelphia; 19107 215-592-1750 Fax 215-627-9639 *R* Tue-Sun 11am-11pm.

♂ ● (♿) Cheap Art Cafe, 260 S 12th St, Philadelphia; 19107 215-735-6650 *R*

♂ ● Club Tyz, 1418 Rodman St; 19146 215-546-4195 *PDLW* Open to 3am.

♂ ● CR Bar, 6405 Market St, Upper Darby; 19082 610-352-9762

♀ ● (♿) Hepburn's, 254 S 12th St, Philadelphia; 19107 215-545-8484 *BRED* 4pm-2am; Sun noon-2am.

♂ Key West, 207 S Juniper, Philadelphia; 19107 215-545-1578

♂ Les Femmes, 209 S Juniper St, Philadelphia; 19107 215-545-5476

♂ ● MSA Club, 6405 Market St, Upper Darby; 19082

♂ Post, 1705 Chancellor St, Philadelphia; 19103 215-985-9720

♂ ● Raffles, 243 S Camac St, Philadelphia; 19107 215-545-6969 *BCD*

♀ Revival, 22 S 3rd St, Philadelphia; 19106 215-627-4825

♂ ● Rodz Bar, 1418 Rodman St, Philadelphia; 19146 215-546-1900 *BRE* 5pm-2am; Sun noon-2am.

♀ ○ **Uncle's, 1220 Locust St, Philadelphia; 19107 215-546-6660**
♦ *Uncle's advertisement page 391*

♂ Venture Inn, 255 S Camac St, Philadelphia; 19107 215-545-8731

♀ ● Waldorf Cafe, 506 S 20th St, Philadelphia; 19146 (Lombard St) 215-985-1836 *BR* 5pm-2am.

♂ Westbury, 261 S 13th St, Philadelphia; 19107 215-546-5170

♂ ● ♂♂ **Woody's, 202 S 13th St, Philadelphia; 19107 215-545-1893 *BDRC* 11am-2am.**

Bookstores: Gay/Lesbian/Feminist

♂ ● (♿) **Giovanni's Room, 345 S 12th St, Philadelphia; 19107 215-923-2960 Fax 215-923-0813 Mon, Tue, Thu 11.30am-9pm; Wed to 7pm; Fri to 10pm; Sat 10am-10pm; Sun 1-7pm. Mail order Mon-Sat 10am-7pm; Sun 1-7pm. "Bi-monthly lists of new books, one each for gay men & women."**
♦ *Giovanni's Room advertisement page 393*

Bookstores: General

♀ ● Afterwords, 218 S 12th St, Philadelphia; 19107 215-735-2393

♀ ○ ♂♂ Borders Book Shop, 1727 Walnut St, Philadelphia; 19103 215-568-7400 7am-10pm; Sat 9am-9pm; Sun 11am-7pm.

♀ ○ Robin's Books, 1837 Chestnut St, Philadelphia; 19103 215-567-2615

♀ ● Wooden Shoe Books & Records, 112 S 20th St, Philadelphia; 19103 215-569-2477 "A collectively organized, all volunteer anarchist bookstore."

Broadcast Media

♂ ★ Amazon Country, WXPN-FM (88.5), 3905 Spruce St, Philadelphia; 19104 215-898-6677 Sun 8-9pm.

♂ ★ Gaydreams Radio, WXPN-FM, 3905 Spruce St, Philadelphia; 19104 215-898-6677 88.5FM, Sun 9-10pm.

Clothes

♀ ○ Leather Rose, 201 S 13th St, Philadelphia; 19107 215-985-2344; 215-985-BEGG; "Leather, lace & latex."

Community Centers (see also Women's Centers)

♂ ★ Penguin Place: Gay/Lesbian Community Center of Philadelphia, 201 S Camac St, Philadelphia; 19107 215-732-2220

Counseling/Therapy: Nonprofit

♀ ☆ ♂ Women's Therapy Center, 1930 Chestnut St #1703, Philadelphia; 19103 215-567-1111

Counseling/Therapy: Private

♂ ○ (?♂) Carter, B. F., Ph.D./Lambda Resources, 7 Bala Ave #209, Bala Cynwyd; 19004 610-667-9060

♂ ● ♂ Eiberson, Jeffrey, PhD, 1326 Spruce St, Philadelphia; 19107 215-546-1767

♀ ○ Slutsky, Sidney S., Ed.D., Cottman Professional Bldg, 1936 Cottman Ave, Philadelphia; 19111 215-722-1404

♀ ○ Victor, Hope R., Ph.D., 512 S 4th St, Philadelphia; 19147 215-925-0330

Erotica (Printed, Visual, Equipment)

♂ ● **Adonis Cinema Complex, 2026 Sansom St, Philadelphia; 19103 215-557-9319 24 hrs. "Multi-level theater."**
♦ *Adonis Cinema Complex advertisement page 393*

♀ ○ Adult World, 1236 Arch St, Philadelphia; 19107 215-972-9031

♂ ● Book Bin East, 942 Market St, Philadelphia; 19103 215-922-8208

♀ ○ (♂♂) Cupid's Treasures, 2025 Sansom St, Philadelphia; 19103 215-563-4430 Fax 215-587-9336 Noon-mdnt.

♀ ● Danny's Adam & Eve, 133 S 13th St, Philadelphia; 19107 215-925-5041

PA: Philadelphia Area
393
Philadelphia Area: PA
Erotica
USA
Health Care

♀ • Edward's Books, 1319 Arch St, Philadelphia; 19107 215-563-6171

♀ ○ Pleasure Chest, 2039 Walnut St, Philadelphia; 19103 215-561-7480

♂ ○ Sansom Cinema, 120 S 13th St (upstairs), Philadelphia; 19107 215-545-9254

♂ ○ The Tomcat Store, 120 S 13th St, Philadelphia; 19107 215-985-9725

♀ ○ Venus Video, 6307 Passyunk Ave, Philadelphia; 19153 215-937-1545

Florists (see also Gardening)

♀ • Bloomies, 1200 Spruce St, Philadelphia; 19107 215-732-3262 9am-8pm.

Health Care (see also AIDS Services)

♀ ○ (♿) A Chiropractic Orthopedic Practice, 512 S 4th St, Philadelphia; 19147 215-923-5577

♀ ☆ ♿ Elizabeth Blackwell Health Center for Women, 1124 Walnut St, Philadelphia; 19107 215-923-7577 "Services include anonymous HIV counseling & testing; domor insemination for for single & lesbian women."

♀ • ♿ Muurahainen, Norma E., MD, PhD, 1740 South St #305, Graduate Hospital, Philadelphia; 19146 215-790-6030 Fax 215-790-6010 "HIV, Nutrition & Internal Medicine."

♀ • ♿ Ondercin, Joseph, PA-C, 1740 South St #305, the Graduate Hospital, Philadelphia; 19146 215-790-6030 Fax 215-790-6010

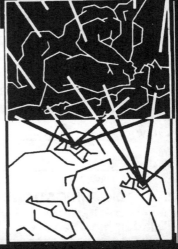

PA: Philadelphia Area
Health Care

394
USA

Philadelphia Area: PA
Organizations: Family

♀ • ♂♂ **Turner, John L., MD, 1740 South St #305, The Graduate Hospital, Philadelphia; 19146 215-790-6030 Fax 215-790-6010**
✦ *Turner, John L., MD advertisement page 395*

♀ • ♂♂ Walton, Lori, PA-C, 1740 South St #305, Graduate Hospital, Philadelphia; 19146 215-790-6030 Fax 215-790-6010

♀ • (?♂) Watkins, Mark T., DO, 1202 Locust St #201, Philadelphia; 19107 215-545-0170

Health Clubs, Gyms, Saunas

♂ ○ Chancellor Athletic Club, 1220 Chancellor St, Philadelphia; 19107 215-545-4098

♂ • **Club Body Center/Gym Philly, 120 S 13th St, Philadelphia; 19107 215-735-9568**

Home & Building: Cleaning, Repair, General Contractors

♀ • Action Builders & Remodelers, 1418 S 7th St, Philadelphia; 19147 215-389-3100

♀ • Cook's Cleaning Service, 215-752-0121; 215-752-5453 emergency; "Commercial/residential; insured & bonded. 10% discount."

♀ • Handyman Company of Delaware Valley, Inc, 1420 S 7th St, Philadelphia; 19147 215-462-2828 "General contracting."

Jewelry

♀ • ♂ Bandé Designs, B&E Jewelers, 7102 Castor Ave, Philadelphia; 19149 215-742-9823

Legal Services & Resources

♀ ☆ ♂♂ American Civil Liberties Union (ACLU), PO Box 1161, Philadelphia; 19105-1161 215-592-1513

♀ • **Black, Steve, 333 S Camac St, Philadelphia; 19107 215-735-0852**

♀ • Greenberg, Michael C., Esq., 834 Chestnut St #320, Philadelphia; 19107 215-238-9518

Organizations/Resources: Bisexual Focus

♀ ☆ (?♂) BiUnity, PO Box 41905, Philadelphia; 19101-1905 215-724-3663 (7BI-FONE)

Organizations/Resources: Business & Professional

♀ ★ (?♂) Building Perspectives: Gay & Lesbian Architects, Designers & Building Professionals, PO Box 2102, Philadelphia; 19103 215-790-0192

♀ ★ GALA Visual Arts, PO Box 54217, Philadelphia; 19105 215-413-1445

♀ Greater Philadelphia Professional Network (GPPN), PO Box 42366, Philadelphia; 19101 215-336-9676

♀ ★ Greater Roundtable of Women Professionals, mail to GROWP, PO Box 35010, Philadelphia; 19128-0510 610-789-4938 "Social organization for Lesbian professionals."

♀ Wisdom (Women In Science, Dentistry, Or Medicine), PO Box 29629, Philadelphia; 19144-0929

Organizations/Resources: Ethnic, Multicultural

♀ ★ Gelede Sisters, 4913 Woodcrest Ave, Philadelphia; 19131 215-878-6875 "Black Lesbian support group."

♂ ★ (?♂) MACT/Philadelphia (Men of All Colors Together), PO Box 42257, Philadelphia; 19101 610-277-6595

Organizations/Resources: Family

♀ ☆ P-FLAG, PO Box 15711, Philadelphia; 19103 215-572-1833 "Parents, Families & Friends of Lesbians & Gays."

PA: Philadelphia Area
Organizations: General

395
USA

Philadelphia Area: PA
Publications

Organizations/Resources: General, Multipurpose, Pride

♀ ★ (♂♀) Diversity of Pride, PO Box 395, Philadelphia; 19105 215-351-5315 "Organize the June Pride Festival & parade."

♀ ★♂♂ Philadelphia Lesbian & Gay Task Force, 1616 Walnut St #1005, Philadelphia; 19102 215-772-2005 (Discrimination & Violence Hotline)

♀ ★ POPEC (Pride of Philadelphia Election Committee), 505 S 4th St, Philadelphia; 19147-1506 215-625-9477

♀ ★ Triangle Interests, PO Box 35145, Philadelphia; 19128 215-487-3716 Fax 215-844-6309

Organizations/Resources: Political/Legislative

♀ ★ League of Gay & Lesbian Voters: Greater Philadelphia Chapter, 12 West Willow Grove Ave #117, Philadelphia; 19118-3952 215-242-5746; 610-941-0837

♀ ★ Log Cabin Club of Philadelphia, PO Box 34704, Philadelphia; 19101 215-339-6771 Fax 215-339-0672 (Republicans)

♀ Philadelphia Equal Rights Coalition, 4519 Osage, Philadelphia; 19143

Organizations/Resources: Sexual Focus (Leather, S/M, etc) & Safe Sex Promotion

♀ Female Trouble, PO Box 30145, Philadelphia; 19103 215-844-5733

Organizations/Resources: Social, Recreational & Support Groups (see also Sport/Dance/Outdoor)

♀ ★ Delaware Valley Couples, PO Box 553, Collingswood, NJ 08108 908-364-8431 (Lakewood); (215) 639-0144 (Philadelphia); 908-364-8431 (Lakewood); (215) 639-0144 (Philadelphia)

♂ ★ Humboldt Society: Lesbian & Gay Naturalists, 2030 Fitzwater St, Philadelphia; 19146-1333 215-985-1456 Pub *Newsletter*.

♀ LCDC (Lesbian Community Of Delaware County), PO Box 193, Media; 19063

♀ ★ Les Femmes Unies, PO Box 42833, Philadelphia; 19101 215-657-5138

♀ ★ Olde Chester County Brunch Bunch, c/o Bob Santangelo, 171 Summit Rd, Malvern; 19355 Write for details.

♀ ★ (♂) Sisterspace of the Delaware Valley, 542A S 48th St, Philadelphia; 19143-2029 215-476-8856 Fax 215-747-7565 "Contact for details of Sisterspace Pocono Weekend."

Organizations/Resources: Sport/Dance/Outdoor

♂ ★ City of Brotherly Love Softball League, PO Box 53836, Philadelphia; 19105 215-238-0224

♂ ★ Frontrunners/Philadelphia, PO Box 30115, Philadelphia; 19103 215-545-6990

♂ ★ GO! Philadelphia, PO Box 15784, Philadelphia; 19103 215-969-8948

♂ Independence Squares, PO Box 41867, Philadelphia; 19101-1867 215-862-5989 *d*

♂ North American Gay Amateur Athletic Alliance (NAAGA), c/o Jim Doetzel 1035 Spruce St #112, Philadelphia; 19107 215-925-4586

♂ ★ (♂♂) Spartans Wrestling Club, Drake Box #43, 1512 Spruce St, Philadelphia; 19102 215-546-0735 Wed 7-10pm.

♂ ★ Team Philadelphia, 201 S Camac St, Philadelphia; 19107 215-732-2220 "Philadelphia's delegation to the Gay Games."

♂ ★ Vanguards M.C., PO Box 2308, Philadelphia; 19103

♀ ★ Wild Heart Adventures/Wilderness Womyn, 6914 Ridge Ave, Philadelphia; 19128 215-483-7937

Organizations/Resources: Student, Academic, Alumni/ae

♀ ★ ♂ Lesbian, Gay & Bisexual Alliance at Penn, 243 Houston Hall, 3417 Spruce St, Philadelphia; 19104-6306 215-898-5270

♀ ★ Penn GALA, 3537 Locust Walk, 3rd flr, Philadelphia; 19104-6225

♀ ★♂♂ Temple Lambda Alliance, Box 116 Student Activities Center, Room 205, 13th St & Montgomery Ave, Philadelphia; 19122 215-232-4522

♀ Temple Law Students For Lesbian/Gay Rights, Klein Law Center, Room 118D, Temple University, Philadelphia; 19122

Organizations/Resources: Transgender & Transgender Publications

T *International Transcript/CDS*, Box 61263, King Of Prussia; 19406-1263

Performing Arts: Entertainment, Music, Recording, Theater, etc.

♀ ★ OutMusic/Philadelphia, c/o Penguin Place, PO Box 12814, Philadelphia; 19108 215-732-2220 "Monthly performance & open mike for singers/songwriters/musicians."

♂ ★ Philadelphia Gay Men's Chorus, PO Box 58842, Philadelphia; 19102-8842

Publications: Directories, Bibliographies, Guides, Travel

♀ • *Greater Philadelphia Lavender Pages*, 205 W Mt Pleasant Ave #1, Philadelphia; 19119 215-247-1018 "Resource guide meeting the needs of the Delaware Valley Lesbian, Bisexual, Gay, & Transgendered Community."

Publications

→ *Au Courant Newsmagazine*: p.387

♀ ☆ ♂ *Labyrinth*, 4722 Baltimore Ave, Philadelphia; 19143 215-724-6181 Monthly. "The Philadelphia Women's Paper," also quarterly women's information & resources guide."

♂ • *Philadelphia Gay News*, 505 S 4th St, Philadelphia; 19147-1506 215-625-8501
✦ *Philadelphia Gay News advertisement page 394*

Religious Organizations & Publications

♂ ★ ♂ Congregation Beth Ahavah, PO Box 7566, Philadelphia; 19101 / 8 Letitia St 215-923-2003 *The Shofar.*

♂ ★ ♂♂ Dignity/Philadelphia, PO Box 53348, Philadelphia; 19105 215-546-2093 *The Independence.* "Gay & Lesbian Catholics & their friends."

♂ ★ Integrity/Philadelphia, c/o Holy Trinity Church, 1904 Walnut St, Philadelphia; 19103 215-382-0794 1st Wed of month, 7pm: Holy Eucharist 7pm; 3rd Wed of month, 7pm: discussion group & Evening Prayer. "Gay & Lesbian Episcopalians & their friends."

♂ ★ ♂♂ Metropolitan Community Church of Philadelphia, PO Box 8174, Philadelphia; 19101-8174 / 2125 Chestnut St 215-563-6601 Services Sun 7pm.

♀ ☆ Unitarian Universalist Church in Mt Airy, Stenton Ave & Gorgas Lane, Philadelphia; 19150 215-247-2561

Switchboards, Helplines, Phone Information

♂ ★ Philadelphia Gay Switchboard, PO Box 2091, Philadelphia; 19103 215-546-7100

♀ ☆ (♂♂) Tell-A-Woman, 1530 Locust St, Box 322, Philadelphia; 19102 215-564-5810 "24-hr tape of local forthcoming events, including lesbian activities & services."

Travel & Tourist Services (see also Accommodation)

♂ • Good Companions Travel & Tour, 1105 Cooper Ct, #200-A, Voorhees, NJ 08043 609-772-9269

♀ ○♂♂ Jewel Travel, 225 S 15th St #829, Philadelphia; 19102 215-546-8747; 800-755-3935

♀ ○ Lambda Travel, 21 S 5th St #545, Philadelphia; 19106 215-925-3011

♀ • Wilson, Pat, IGTA, Will Travel, 118 S Bellevue Ave, Langhorne; 19047 215-741-4492; 800-443-7460; Fax 215-741-5156

Video Sales, Rentals, Services (see also Erotica)

♀ ○ Spruce Street Video, 1201 Spruce St, Philadelphia; 19107 215-985-2955 Fax 215-545-6484

Women's Centers

♀ ★ ♂♂ P.E.A.R.L. (Penn's Eagerly Awaited Radical Ladies), Penn Women's Center, 119 Houston Hall, 3417 Spruce St, Philadelphia; 19104-6306 215-898-8611 "A support group for lesbians, bisexual women, & their friends."

♀ ☆ ♂♂ Penn Women's Center, 119 Houston Hall, 3417 Spruce St, Philadelphia; 19104-6306 215-898-8611

Pitman

Religious Organizations & Publications

♂ ★ ♂♂ Christiansbrunn Kloster, RD1, Box 149; 17964 Pub *Newsletter.* "Self-sustaining religious farming community of gay Harmonists, the Guardian Angels of the Garden. Free work retreats."

Pittsburgh Area

☎ Gay & Lesbian Community Center of Pittsburgh 412-422-0114

Accommodation: Hotels, B&B, Resorts, Campgrounds
Pittsburgh

⚥ • The Guest House, 1907 Lowrie St, Pittsburgh; 15212 412-321-4427

♂ • (?♂) The Inn on the Mexican War Streets, 1606 Buena Vista St, Pittsburgh; 15212-3926 412-231-6544

Addictive Behavior, Substance Abuse, Recovery

⚥ Sex & Love Addicts Anonymous, Box 99485, Pittsburgh; 15233 412-441-0956

AIDS/HIV Support, Education, Advocacy, Publications

♀ ★ ♂♂ Persad Center, Inc, 5150 Penn Ave, Pittsburgh; 15224-1627 412-441-9786 "Complete AIDS services program."

♀ ☆ (♂♂) Pitt AIDS Center for Treatment (PACT), University of Pittsburgh Medical Center, 200 Lothrop St, Pittsburgh; 15213 412-647-7220 Fax 412-647-7951 "Primary medical care for persons with HIV/AIDS."

♂ ★ Pitt Men's Study, University of Pittsburgh, PO Box 7319, Pittsburgh; 15213 412-624-2008

♀ ☆ (♂♂) Pitt Treatment Evaluation Unit (PTEV), University of Pittsburgh Medical Center, 200 Lothrop St, Pittsburgh; 15213 412-647-8125 Fax 412-687-4625 "Participation in studies of promising new treatments for HIV/AIDS."

♀ ☆ ♂♂ Pittsburgh AIDS Task Force, Inc, 905 West St, 4th flr, Pittsburgh; 15221 412-242-2500 Pub *Update.*

♀ ☆ ♂♂ Shepherd Wellness Community, Church of the Good Shepherd, PO Box 5619, Pittsburgh; 15207 412-421-8747; 412-421-8743

Bars, Restaurants, Clubs, Discos
Greensburg

♂ • Safari Lounge, 108 W Pittsburgh St, Greensburg; 15601 412-837-9948

Homestead

♂ Bubba's, 128 8th Ave, Homestead; 15120 412-461-9700

Mount Pleasant

♀ ○ Yuppie's, 241 E Main St, Mount Pleasant; 15666 412-547-0430

Pittsburgh

♂ ○ Brewer's Hotel, 3315 Liberty, Pittsburgh; 15201 412-681-7991

♂ • ♂ C.J. Deighan's, 2506 West Liberty Ave, Pittsburgh; 15226-1725 412-561-4044 *BDf*

♂ Donnie's Place, 1226 Herron Ave, Pittsburgh; 15219 412-682-9869 *BD*

♂ The Eagle, 1740 Eckert St, Pittsburgh; 15212 412-766-7222

♂ • ♂♂ Holiday Bar, 4620 Forbes Ave, Pittsburgh; 15213 412-682-8598

♂ House of Tilden, 941 Liberty Ave, Pittsburgh; 15222 412-391-0804 *DP*

♂ • ♂ Images, 965 Liberty Ave, Pittsburgh; 15222 412-391-9990 *BR* 7pm-2am.

♂ Jazi's, 1241 Western Ave, Pittsburgh; 15233 412-323-2721 *BRL*

♂ • ♂ New York, New York, 5801 Ellsworth Ave, Pittsburgh; 15232 412-661-5600 *BR*

⚥ • Pegasus, 818 Liberty Ave, Pittsburgh; 15222 412-281-2131 *BDE* Mon-Fri 4pm-2am; Sat 8pm-2am.

⚥ • க Real Luck Cafe, 1519 Penn Ave, Pittsburgh; 15222 412-566-8988 *BDR*

♀ Sunset Strip Cafe, 2117 Penn Ave, Pittsburgh; 15222-4419 412-261-2333

Bookstores: Gay/Lesbian/Feminist

♀ • க Gertrude Stein Memorial Bookshop, 1003 E Carson St, Pittsburgh; 15203 412-481-9666 Thu & Fri 5.30-8pm; Sat noon-6pm; Sun noon-3pm.

Bookstores: General

♀ ○ Bookstall, 3604 5th Ave, Pittsburgh; 15213 412-683-3030

♀ ○ Borders Book Shop, 1775 N Highland Rd, Pittsburgh; 15241 412-835-5583

♀ • Saint Elmo's Outwords, 2214 E Carson St, Pittsburgh; 15203 (Planning to move to 2208 Carson in April 95: check ahead.) 412-431-9100 9.30am-9.30pm. "Also video rental."

Broadcast Media

♂ Gay Cable Network, PO Box 6399, Pittsburgh; 15212 412-734-8961

Business, Financial & Secretarial

♀ ○ Lange, James, CPA, 2008 Murray Ave, Pittsburgh; 15217 412-521-2732

Community Centers (see also Women's Centers)

⚥ ★ Gay & Lesbian Community Center of Pittsburgh, PO Box 5441, Pittsburgh; 15206 / 5860 Forward Ave 412-422-0114 Pub *GLCC Community Newsletter.*

Counseling/Therapy: Nonprofit

⚥ ★ க Persad Center, Inc, 5150 Penn Ave, Pittsburgh; 15224-1627 412-441-9786 "Professional individual, relationship, & family therapy for all sexual minorities. Education, Community organizations & research services. Complete AIDS services program."

Counseling/Therapy: Private

♀ ○ Carlett, David G., LSW, Park Plaza Suite #217, 128 N Craig St, Pittsburgh; 15213 412-681-3733

⚥ • க Skinner & Claudette Kulkarni, James, PhD, MSW, 5830 Ellsworth Ave #302, Pittsburgh; 15232 412-734-5550

Erotica (Printed, Visual, Equipment)

♀ ○ Boulevard Books, 346 Blvd of Allies, 2nd flr, Pittsburgh; 15222 412-261-9119

♀ ○ க Golden Triangle News, 816 Liberty Ave, Pittsburgh; 15222 412-765-3790

Film & Video

⚥ ★ (?க) Pittsburgh International Lesbian & Gay Film Festival, PO Box 9007, Pittsburgh; 15224 412-687-0609

Funding: Endowment, Fundraising, Scholarship

⚥ ★ க Lambda Foundation, PO Box 5169, Pittsburgh; 15206 412-521-5444 "Foundation for granting funds to Gay & Lesbian organizations & projects, & AIDS-related services organizations & projects."

Gifts, Cards, Pride & Novelty Items

♀ ○ The Essex, 122 Meyran Ave, Pittsburgh; 15213 412-687-2299

Graphic Design/Typesetting (see also Art; Printing)

♀ • Graphics A La Carte, 747 South Ave, Pittsburgh; 15221-2939 412-243-3341

Grooming Services

♀ ○ Intrigues Salon of Pittsburgh, 330 3rd Ave, Pittsburgh; 15222 412-471-3150

Health Care (see also AIDS Services)

⚥ • க க MacKenzie, Laurel J., DC, 1139 S Braddock Ave, Pittsburgh; 15218 412-371-9311

Health Clubs, Gyms, Saunas

♂ • Arena Health Club, 2025 Forbes Ave, Pittsburgh; 15219 412-471-8548

Legal Services & Resources

♀ ☆ American Civil Liberties Union (ACLU), 237 Oakland Ave, Pittsburgh; 15213 412-681-7736

♀ ○ (?க) Hens-Greco & Associates, 2021-B Murray Ave, Pittsburgh; 15217 412-422-7400

♀ ○ க க Robison, Jonathan B., 429 Forbes Ave, 712 Allegheny Bldg, Pittsburgh; 15219 412-338-9900

⚥ • Sanchas, Vera S., Esq, 1227 S Braddock Ave, Pittsburgh; 15218 412-371-8811

Meeting/Contact Services, Publications, Talklines

⚥ • Computer Info, PO Box 15755, Pittsburgh; 15244 "Women meet Women confidentially. Discreet mail-out service."

Organizations/Resources: Business & Professional

♂ Thurday Night Live, PO Box 23700, Pittsburgh; 15222-6700 412-363-5865

Organizations/Resources: Ethnic, Multicultural

♂ ★ Asians & Friends/Pittsburgh, PO Box 16455, Pittsburgh; 15242-0755 412-681-1556 Pub *Ring of Fire.*

♂ BWMT-Pittsburgh, PO Box 8772, Pittsburgh; 15221 412-242-7361 Black & White Men Together/Men of All Colors Together

Organizations/Resources: Family

♀ ☆ (க க) PFLAG/Pittsburgh, PO Box 54, Verona; 15147 412-795-2186 "Parents, Families & Friends of Lesbians & Gays."

Organizations/Resources: General, Multipurpose, Pride

♂ Three Rivers Pride Committee/Pittsburgh Pride, PO Box 81207, Pittsburgh; 15217 412-422-3060

Organizations/Resources: Political/Legislative

⚥ ★ க க Gertrude Stein Political Club of Greater Pittsburgh, 429 Forbes Ave, 712 Allegheny Bldg, Pittsburgh; 15219 412-784-9157

⚥ ★ க League of Gay & Lesbian Voters/Pittsburgh, 5100 Penn Ave #3rd FL, Pittsburgh; 15224-1616 412-362-8406

♀ TRI-PAC, 414 S Craig St #282, Pittsburgh; 15213 412-661-3244

Organizations/Resources: Sexual Focus (Leather, S/M, etc) & Safe Sex Promotion

♂ ★ (?⚲) Pitt B.C., PO Box 19091, Pittsburgh; 15213 412-734-5663

♂ ★ Three Rivers Leather Club, PO Box 5485, Pittsburgh; 15206 Pub *Gauntlet.*

Organizations/Resources: Social, Recreational & Support Groups (see also Sport/Dance/Outdoor)

♂ Burgh Bears, Box 1451, Pittsburgh; 15230-1451 412-521-BEAR

♀ ★ (?⚲) Couples of the Pittsburgh Area (COPA), 1622 Braddock Ave, Pittsburgh; 15218-1638 412-247-1545 (women); 371-6269 (men Fax 412-731-2894 xhbc2ao@prodigy.com

♀ ★ Horse of a Different Color, PO Box 99321, Pittsburgh; 15233 *CW*

♂ Pittsburgh Men's Collective, 2226 Delaware Ave, Pittsburgh; 15218 412-243-7658; 412-421-6405

♀ ★ (?⚲) Rainbow Social Club, PO Box 8368, Pittsburgh; 15218 412-661-4041; 412-731-4781

Organizations/Resources: Sport/Dance/Outdoor

♂ Pittburgh Motorcycle Club, PO Box 17198, Pittsburgh; 15235

♂ Pittsbugh Outdoors Club, PO Box 39, Wexford; 15090 412-935-6588

♀ Pittsburgh Gay Games Delegation, PO Box 99987, Pittsburgh; 15233

♀ ★ ♂ Steel City Softball League, 606 N Negley Ave, Pittsburgh; 15206

♀ ★ TREAT (Three Rivers Eastern Area Tournament), PO Box 99604, Pittsburgh; 15233

Organizations/Resources: Student, Academic, Alumni/ae

♀ ★ CMU-OUT, c/o Skibo Information Desk, Carnegie Mellon University, Pittsburgh; 15213 412-268-8794 Meets Fri 7.30pm, Baker Hall 254C

♀ Gay & Lesbian Law Caucus at University of Pittsburgh School of Law, 3900 Forbes Ave, Pittsburgh; 15213 412-648-1388

♀ Visions—AC, c/o Community College of Allegheny County, OSA, 808 Ridge Ave, Pittsburgh; 15212 412-237-2675

Organizations/Resources: Transgender & Transgender Publications

T ☆ (?⚲) Transpitt, PO Box 3214, Pittsburgh; 15230 412-224-6015 Pub *Rhapsody Newsletter.*

Organizations/Resources: Youth (see also Family)

♀ ★ (?⚲) Pittsburgh Youth Services, Inc., PO Box 2047, Pittsburgh; 15230-2047 412-471-9392 Pub *Youthquake.*

Performing Arts: Entertainment, Music, Theater, etc.

♀ ★ (?⚲) Pittsburgh Queer Theatre, PO Box 9103, Pittsburgh; 15224 412-734-8437

♂ ★ ♂ Renaissance City Choir, PO Box 10282, Pittsburgh; 15232-0282 412-471-8208

Publications

♀ • (⚲) *Out*, 747 South Ave, Pittsburgh; 15221-2939 412-243-3350 Fax 412-243-4067
✦ *Out advertisement page 397*

Religious Organizations & Publications

♀ ★ Affirmation: United Methodists for Lesbian, Gay & Bisexual Concerns, Box 10104, Pittsburgh; 15232-0104 412-683-5526

♂ ★ (?⚲) Bet Tikvah, c/o Persad Center, Inc, 5150 Penn Ave, Pittsburgh; 15224-1627 412-441-9786 "Synagogue & Community for Lesbian, Gay & Bisexual Jews & their friends."

♀ ★ Dignity/Pittsburgh, PO Box 362, Pittsburgh; 15230 412-362-4334 "Gay & Lesbian Catholics & their friends."

♀ ★ Integrity, PO Box 5619, Pittsburgh; 15207-0619 412-421-8747; 412-731-2192; "Gay & Lesbian Episcopalians & their friends."

♀ ★ Lutherans Concerned/Pittsburgh, PO Box 81866, Pittsburgh; 15217-0866 412-521-7746 (Timothy or Jim); 412-521-7746 (Timothy or Jim)

♀ ★ ⚲⚲ Metropolitan Community Church, 4836 Ellsworth Ave, Pittsburgh; 15213 412-683-2994

♀ Pittsburgh Friends (Quaker), 4836 Ellsworth Ave, Pittsburgh; 15213 412-683-2669

♀ ★ ⚲⚲ PLGC/Presbyterians for Lesbian/Gay Concerns, PO Box 9022, Pittsburgh; 15224-0022

♀ Three Rivers UULGBC, c/o 1st UU Church, Ellsworth & Morewood Aves, Pittsburgh; 15213 412-343-2523

Travel & Tourist Services (see also Accommodation)

♀ ○ ⚲⚲ Alternative Travels, 900 Penn Ave, Pittsburgh; 15222 412-263-2930 Fax 412-471-1594

Port Matilda: see State College

Reading: see Lehigh Valley Area

Sciota: see Stroudsburg/Poconos Area

Scotrun: see Stroudsburg/Poconos Area

Scranton

Bars, Restaurants, Clubs, Discos

♀ ○ The Silhouette, 523 Linden St; 18503

Slippery Rock

Organizations/Resources: General, Multipurpose, Pride

♀ Alternative Lifestyles Union, PO Box 444; 16057 412-738-2930

Spring Grove: see York

State College

☎ Gay & Lesbian Switchboard 814-237-1950

AIDS/HIV Support, Education, Advocacy, Publications

♀ ☆ ⚲⚲ The AIDS Project, 301 S Allen St #102; 16801 814-234-7087; 800-233-AIDS

Bars, Restaurants, Clubs, Discos

♀ Players, 112 W College St; 16801 814-237-4350 (Sun only)

Bookstores: General

♀ ○ ⚲⚲ Svoboda's Books, 227 W Beaver Ave; 16801 814-237-6171 Fax 814-237-3934 svobooks@aol.com 9am-7pm; Thu & Fri to 9pm; Sat 10am-6pm; Sun 11am-5pm.

Bookstores: Recovery, Metaphysical, & other Specialty

♀ ○ Tower Of Glass, 137 W Beaver Ave; 16801 814-234-4338

PA: State College
Organizations: Political

399
USA

Tionesta : PA
Organizations: Social & Support

Organizations/Resources: Political/Legislative

♀ ★ (?♂) League of Gay & Lesbian Voters/State College Regional Chapter, PO Box 10986; 16805 814-237-1950 (switchboard)

♀ ☆ Penn State ABOUT FACE, HUB Communication File, University Park; 16802 717-865-3327

Organizations/Resources: Sport/Dance/Outdoor

♀ ★ (?♂) State College Frontrunners, Jeff Gould, PO Box 10532; 16805-0532 814-234-8523 jmg159@psuvm.psu.edu

Organizations/Resources: Student, Academic, Alumni/ae

♀ ★ (♂♂) Lesbian, Gay & Bisexual Student Alliance, Penn State University, 310 Hetzel Union Building, University Park; 16802 717-237-1950; 814-865-3327

Switchboards, Helplines, Phone Information

♀ ★ Gay & Lesbian Switchboard, PO Box 805; 16804 814-237-1950 6-9pm.

Women's Centers

♀ ☆♂♂ Centre Co. Women's Resource Center, 140 W Nittany Ave; 16801 814-234-5222; 814-234-5050 hotline 24 hrs

Stroudsburg/Poconos Area

Accommodation: Hotels, B&B, Resorts, Campgrounds

East Stroudsburg

♂ • (♂) Rainbow Mountain Resort, RD 8, Box 8174, East Stroudsburg; 18301 717-223-8484 Fax 717-421-3453 BDER
✦ Rainbow Mountain Resort advertisement page 399

Marshalls Creek

♂ • Curt & Wally's Guest House, PO Box 219, Marshalls Creek; 18335 717-223-1395

Scotrun

♀ ○ Blueberry Ridge, McCarrick / Moran RR 1, Box 67, Scotrun; 18355 717-629-5036

♂ • Stoney Ridge, 717-629-5036

Counseling/Therapy: Private

♂ ○ (?♂) Wielgus, Joan S., MS, HCR #1 Box 344 Skyview Circle, Sciota; 18354-9737 610-992-5135 Pocono & W. NJ area; 717-477-2573 Wilkes Barre Area.; "Licensed & certified for all addictions & relationship problems. 12 step oriented."

Meeting/Contact Services, Publications, Talklines

♀ • Sapphic Alliances, 615 Main St #B-10, Stroudsburg; 18360-2025

Organizations/Resources: Student, Academic, Alumni/ae

♀ ★ ♂ East Stroudsburg University GLBSO, Box 68 University Center ESU, East Stroudsburg; 18301 717-424-3748

Tionesta

Organizations/Resources: Social, Recreational & Support Groups (see also Sport/Dance/Outdoor)

♂ NW PA G & L Task Force, PO Box 213; 16353-0213

University Park: see State College

Upper Darby: see Philadelphia Area

West Chester

Addictive Behavior, Substance Abuse, Recovery

♂ ☆ Here's A Place For Us Group, West Chester 307 Club, 1311 West Chester Pike; 19380 610-696-9557 AA meeting Sat 10-11am.

Organizations/Resources: Student, Academic, Alumni/ae

♀ ★♂♂ Lesbian Gay & Bisexual Association, West Chester University, Box 2331 West Chester University; 19383 610-436-6949

West Grove

Bars, Restaurants, Clubs, Discos

♀ • ♂♂ Trib's Waystation, 627 W Baltimore Pike; 19390 610-869-9067 Fax 610-869-0395 _CW_ 11am-12.30am; Fri-Sun to 2am.

White Haven

Bars, Restaurants, Clubs, Discos

♀ • ♂♂ Combinations, PO Box 293; 18661 / Towanda St 717-443-8616 _BDR_ Wed-Sat 8pm-2am.

Wilkes Barre

Accommodation: Hotels, B&B, Resorts, Campgrounds

♂ • Grey Oaks Bed & Breakfast, 298 E South St; 18702 717-829-7097 (eves); 717-829-7097 (eves)

Bars, Restaurants, Clubs, Discos

♀ ○ Rumors Lounge, 1170 Hwy 315, Fox Ridge Plaza; 18702 717-825-7300 4pm-2am; Sun to 4pm-2am.

♂ • ♂♂ Selections, 45 Public Square Wilkes-Barre Center,; 18701 717-829-4444 _DERCW_ Mon-Sat from 7pm.

♀ • Vaudevilla, 465 Main St, Edwardsville; 18704 717-287-9250 _BDEL_ Mon-Sat 7pm-2am.

Williamsport

☎ Gay & Lesbian Switchboard of North Central Pennsylvania 717-327-1411

AIDS/HIV Support, Education, Advocacy, Publications

♀ ☆ AIDS Resource Alliance, Inc., 507 W 4th St; 17701-6003 717-322-8448

Bars, Restaurants, Clubs, Discos

♀ ○ Peachie's Court, 320 Court St; 17701 717-326-3611

♀ Rainbow Room, 761 W 4th St; 17701

Organizations/Resources: Family

♀ ☆ Central Susquehanna P-FLAG, 717-742-9350 "Parents & Friends of Lesbians & Gays (P-FLAG)."

Organizations/Resources: General, Multipurpose, Pride

♀ ★ Susquehanna Lambda, PO Box 2510; 17703 717-327-1411 Pub _Colours._

Switchboards, Helplines, Phone Information

♀ ★ Gay & Lesbian Switchboard of North Central Pennsylvania, PO Box 2510; 17703 717-327-1411 Mon-Fri 6-9pm.

York

AIDS/HIV Support, Education, Advocacy, Publications

♀ ☆ YHESSI, 101 E Market St; 17401 717-846-6776 Fax 717-854-0377 Mon-Fri 8am-5pm (Spanish/English)

♂ ☆ York Area Aids Coalition, PO Box 5001; 17405 717-846-6776

Bars, Restaurants, Clubs, Discos

♀ • (♨) 14 Karat, 659 W Market St; 17404 717-843-9159 _Bdf_ Mon-Sat 7pm-2am.

♂ • ♂ Altland's Ranch, PO Box 4131, Spring Grove; 17362 717-225-4479

♂ • Mackley's Mill, 305 S Broad St, Hellam; 17406 717-757-6778 _BR_

Bookstores: Gay/Lesbian/Feminist

♀ • ♂ Her Story: A Women's Bookstore, 2 W Market St, Hellam; 17406 (Hallam, York County) 717-757-4270 11am-7pm; Sat 9am-5pm; Sun noon-5pm.

Counseling/Therapy: Private

♂ • (♨) Drummond Counseling Center, 2001 E Market St; 17402 717-757-6511

Erotica (Printed, Visual, Equipment)

♂ • Cupid's Connextion, 244 N George St; 17401 717-846-5029 9am-2am; Fri & Sat to 5pm.

Organizations/Resources: General, Multipurpose, Pride

♂ ★ (?♨) York Area Lambda, PO Box 2425; 17405-2425 717-292-1665; 717-846-9636

Puerto Rico

State/County Resources

AIDS/HIV Support, Education, Advocacy, Publications

♂ ★ (♨) Community Network for Clinical Research on AIDS (PR CONCRA), One Stop Station Box 30, 103 University Ave, San Juan, PR 00925 809-753-9443 Fax 809-753-2894

Real Estate

♂ • **Community Real Estate Referrals, 800-346-5592 "Free referral to gay/gay-supportive realtor in any USA city/state (including Virgin Is. & Puerto Rico). Sorry, no rentals!"**
♦ _Community Real Estate Referrals advertisement back cover_

San Juan

Accommodation: Hotels, B&B, Resorts, Campgrounds

♂ • ♂♂ Atlantic Beach Hotel, 1 Calle Vendig; 00907 (Condado) 809-721-6900 Fax 809-721-6917 _BR_

♂ Beach Buoy Inn Guest House, 1853 McLeary, Ocean Park; 00911 809-728-8119

♂ • ♂ Casablanca Guest House, 57 Caribe, Condado; 00907 809-722-7319

♂ • Condado Inn & Terrace Restaurant, 6 Condado Ave; 00907 (Condado) 809-724-7145

♂ • ♂ Embassy Guest House Condado, Calle Seaview #1126; 00907 809-725-2400; 809-725-8284

♂ ○ L'Habitation Beach Guest House, 1957 Italia, Ocean Park; 00911 809-727-2499 Fax 809-727-2599 _B_

♂ ○♂♂ Numero Uno on the Beach, 1 Calle Santa Ana, Ocean Park; 00911 809-726-5010; 809-727-9687; _BR_

♂ • ♂ **Ocean Park Beach Inn/3 Elena Guest House, 3 Calle Elena; 00911 809-728-7418; 800-292-9208; Fax 809-728-7418** _BR_

PR: San Juan
Accommodation
401
USA
Newport : RI
Bars, Clubs, Restaurants

♀ ○ Ocean Walk Guest House, 1 Atlantic Place; 00911 809-728-0855; 800-468-0615
♦ *Ocean Walk Guest House advertisement page 401*

AIDS/HIV Support, Education, Advocacy, Publications

♀ Instituto del SIDA de San Juan, 1386 Avenida Fernandez Juncos; 00909 809-723-2424

Bars, Restaurants, Clubs, Discos

♂ ○ (&) Barefoot Bar, 2 Calle Vendig; 00907 (Condado) 809-724-7230

♀ Cups at the Barn, Calle San Mateo 1708, Santurce; 00911 809-268-3570

♀ Junior's Club, Calle Condado #602, Parada 17 1/2, Santurce; 00907 809-722-5663

♀ • Panache Restaurant, 1127 Seaview; 00907 809-725-8284 *B*

♂ • Terrace Restaurant, 6 Condado Ave; 00907 (Condado) 809-724-7145 *B*

♂ • Vibrations, PO Box 41273 Minillas Station; 00940 / 51 Ave Barranquitas

Santurce

♀ Krash!, 1257 Ponce De Leon, Santurce 809-722-1131

Health Clubs, Gyms, Saunas

♂ • Steamworks, 205 Calle Luna, 2nd Flr; 00903 809-725-4993

Organizations/Resources: Family

♀ ☆ P-FLAG, Box 116, 1505 Loiza St, Santurce; 00911 809-724-0390 "Parents, Families & Friends of Lesbians & Gays."

Organizations/Resources: General, Multipurpose, Pride

♀ Amigas Y Amigos De Los Derechos Humanos, 106 Ave De Diego, Box 242, Santurce; 00907 809-790-0672

♀ ★ Colectivo de Lesbianas Feministas, Apartado 1003 Estacion Viejo San Juan; 00902

Real Estate

♀ ○ San Miguel Properties, 1959 Calle Loiza #821, Santurce; 00911 809-727-6350 (also Fax)

Vieques

Accommodation: Hotels, B&B, Resorts, Campgrounds

♀ • && New Dawn's Caribbean Retreat & Guest House, PO Box 1512; 00765 809-741-0495 *BR*

Rhode Island

State/County Resources

☎ Gay/Lesbian Helpline of Rhode Island 401-751-3322

AIDS/HIV Support, Education, Advocacy, Publications

♀ ☆ (&&) Rhode Island Project/AIDS, 95 Chestnut St, 3rd flr, Providence, RI 02903-4161 401-831-5522; 800-726-3010

Broadcast Media

♀ ○ & WALE 990 AM, 1185 N. Main St, Providence, RI 02904-1824 401-521-0990 "Exclusive gay, lesbian & bisexual live, local call-in issues talk show."

Ocean Walk ♁♁♁♁
Guest House

Atlantic Place No. 1
San Juan
Puerto Rico 00911

Directly on the best beach.
Pool, large sundeck
bar and grill.

(800) 468-0615 (809) 726-0445
FAX (809) 728-6434

Meeting/Contact Services, Publications, Talklines

♀ ○ Local Swingers, PO Box 1398, Providence, RI 02901 401-521-5333

Organizations/Resources: General, Multipurpose, Pride

♂ ★ (&) Network of Rhode Island, PO Box 40212, Providence, RI 02940-0212

Organizations/Resources: Political/Legislative

♀ ★ && Rhode Island Alliance for Lesbian & Gay Civil Rights, PO Box 5758 Weybosset Hill Stn, Providence, RI 02903-0758 401-521-GAYS rialliance@aol.com

Real Estate

♀ • Community Real Estate Referrals, 800-346-5592 "Free referral to gay/gay-supportive realtor in any USA city/state (including Virgin Is. & Puerto Rico). Sorry, no rentals!"
♦ *Community Real Estate Referrals advertisement back cover*

Religious Organizations & Publications

♀ ★ (?&) United Church of Christ Coalition for Gay & Lesbian Concerns, RI Conference, 15 Oak Ave, Riverside Congregational Church, Providence, RI 02915 401-433-2039

Switchboards, Helplines, Phone Information

♀ ★ Gay/Lesbian Helpline of Rhode Island, PO Box 5671, Providence, RI 02903 401-751-3322

Coventry: see Providence

Kingston

Organizations/Resources: Student, Academic, Alumni/ae

♀ ★ & URI Gay/Lesbian/ Bisexual Association, 346 Memorial Union, c/o Student Senate; 02881 401-792-2097 Pub *3 Dollar Bill.*

Newport

Accommodation: Hotels, B&B, Resorts, Campgrounds

♀ ○ The Brinley Victorian Inn, 23 Brinley St; 02840 401-849-7645 Open all year.

♂ • Hydrangea House Inn & Art Gallery, 16 Bellevue Ave; 02840 401-846-4435; 800-945-4667; Fax 401-846-6602 bandbinn@aol.com

♀ • (?&) The Melville House, 39 Clarke St; 02840 401-847-0640 Fax 401-847-0956 innkeepri@aol._.com

Bars, Restaurants, Clubs, Discos

♀ • David's, 28 Prospect Hill St; 02840 401-847-9698 *BD*

♂ • & Raffles, 3 Farewell St; 02840 401-847-9663

RI: Pawtucket
Counseling: Nonprofit

402
USA

Woonsocket : RI
Bars, Clubs, Restaurants

Pawtucket

Counseling/Therapy: Nonprofit

♀ ★ (?⅖) Women's Growth Center, 97 Knowles St; 02860 401-728-6023

Providence

Addictive Behavior, Substance Abuse, Recovery

♂ ★ Gay Group of AA, 114 George St, St Stephen's Church; 02906 401-438-8860

AIDS/HIV Support, Education, Advocacy, Publications

♀ ☆ ♿ ACT-UP/Rhode Island, PO Box 3156; 02906 401-461-4191

Bars, Restaurants, Clubs, Discos

♂ Birds Of A Feather, 681 Valley St; 02908 401-331-8355

♀ • ♿ Blinky's Video Dance Bar, 125 Washington St; 02903 401-272-6950 **BD**

♀ ○ (♿) Deville's Cafe, 10 Davol Square; 02903 401-251-7166 **BDf**

♂ • ♿ Galaxy, 123 Empire St; 02903 401-831-9206 Opens noon.

♂ ○ Generation X, 235 Promenade St; 02908 401-521-7110

♂ ○♿ Gerardo's/One Franklin Square, 1 Franklin Square; 02903 401-274-5560 4pm-2am.

♂ • In Town, 95 Eddy St; 02903 401-621-8739

♂ Mirabar, 35 Richmond St; 02903 401-331-6761

♂ Skippers, 70 Washington St; 02903 401-751-4241

♀ Stars, 220 Weybossett; 02903 401-861-2600

♂ Tramps, 70 Snow St; 02903 401-421-8688

♂ • Union Station, 69 Union St; 02903 401-331-2291

♂ • Yukon Trading Co, 124 Snow St; 02903 401-274-6620 **BLDF** 4pm-1am; Fri & Sat to 2pm.

Bookstores: General

♀ • (?⅖) Newspeak Book & Video, 5 Steeple St; 02903 401-331-3540 Mon-Sat 11am-9pm. "Conspiracy, sex, weirdness; send $1 for catalog."

Erotica (Printed, Visual, Equipment)

♂ ○ Back Street Video, 112 Mathewson St; 02903 401-521-7905

♂ ○ Upstairs Bookshop, 206 Washington St; 02903 401-272-3139

Health Clubs, Gyms, Saunas

♂ • Club Providence, 257 Weybosset St; 02903 401-274-0298

Organizations/Resources: Sexual Focus (Leather, S/M, etc) & Safe Sex Promotion

♂ ★ Enforcers, RI, PO Box 5770; 02903-0770 "Safe, sane & consensual discussion & pursuit of Leather/SM & Fetish activities; fundraising programs for philanthropic ventures."

Organizations/Resources: Student, Academic, Alumni/ae

♀ ★ (?⅖) Brown University G/L/B Graduate Student Group, Box 1829, c/o Sarah Doyle Center; 02912 401-863-2189

♂ ★ ♿ Lesbian/Gay/Bisexual Alliance, Brown University, PO Box 1930 SAO, Brown University; 02912 401-863-3062

♂ ★ Rhode Island College Gay, Lesbian, or Bisexual Equity Alliance (GLOBE), 600 Mt Pleasant Ave, Student Union; 02908

Religious Organizations & Publications

♂ ★♿ Dignity/Providence, PO Box 2231, Pawtucket, RI 02861 401-727-2657 Pub *Gaudeamus*. "Gay & Lesbian Catholics & their friends."

Travel & Tourist Services (see also Accommodation)

♂ ○ Travel Concepts, 1 Regency Plaza #906; 02903-3158 401-453-6000; 800-983-6900; Fax 401-453-0222

Women's Centers

♀ ☆ (?⅖) Sarah Doyle Women's Center, Box 1829 Brown University; 02912 / 185 Meeting St 401-863-2189

Smithfield

Bars, Restaurants, Clubs, Discos

♂ • Bullwinkle/Loft Country Club, 325 Farnum Pike; 02917 401-231-3320 **BR**

Warwick

Erotica (Printed, Visual, Equipment)

♂ ○ Warwick Video Expo, 2318 Post Rd; 02888 401-739-3080

Westerly

Accommodation: Hotels, B&B, Resorts, Campgrounds

♀ ○ (?⅖) The Villa, 190 Shore Rd; 02891 401-596-1054

Woonsocket

Bars, Restaurants, Clubs, Discos

♀ ○ Club 91, 91 Main St; 02895 401-766-2414

♂ • Kings & Queens, 285 Front St; 02895 401-762-9538

It's impossible to publish a completely current directory:
Things change constantly,
especially while the book is on press.
You can help by telling us as soon as possible
about any corrections or changes you notice.

Gayellow Pages,
PO Box 533 Village Station, New York, NY 10014-0533
Fax (212) 420-1126 (if possible before noon or after 6pm)

SC: State/County Resources
AIDS/HIV Support
403
USA
Columbia : SC
Organizations: Family

South Carolina

State/County Resources

AIDS/HIV Support, Education, Advocacy, Publications

♀ ☆ (?♂) Palmetto AIDS Life Support Services of South Carolina, Inc. (PALSS), PO Box 12124, Columbia, SC 29211 803-779-7257; 800-723-7257

♂ ☆ South Carolina AIDS Education Network, Inc, 2768 Decker Blvd #98, Columbia, SC 29206 803-736-1171

Organizations/Resources: Business & Professional

♀ ★ South Carolina Gay & Lesbian Business Guild, mail to SCGLBG, PO Box 7913, Columbia, SC 29202-7913 803-929-0114

Organizations/Resources: General, Multipurpose, Pride

♀ ★ South Carolina Gay & Lesbian Pride Movement, Inc, PO Box 12648, Columbia, SC 29211 803-771-7713 Pub *GLPM Community News.*

♀ South Carolina Women's Consortium (SCWC), PO Box 11738, Columbia, SC 29211-2284

Publications

♂ • ♂♂ *Blue Nights,* PO Box 221841, Charlotte, NC 28222 704-531-9988 Fax 704-531-1361 NC

♀ • ♂♂ *Front Page,* PO Box 27928, Raleigh, NC 27611 919-829-0181 NC

♀ • ♂♂ *Q-Notes,* PO Box 221841, Charlotte, NC 28222 704-531-9988 Fax 704-531-1361

♀ • *Virago,* PO Box 11193, Columbia, SC 29211 803-256-9090 "Lesbian Newsletter."

Real Estate

♀ • Community Real Estate Referrals, 800-346-5592 "Free referral to gay/gay-supportive realtor in any USA city/state (including Virgin Is. & Puerto Rico). Sorry, no rentals!"
♦ *Community Real Estate Referrals advertisement back cover*

Charleston

Accommodation: Hotels, B&B, Resorts, Campgrounds

♀ • 1854 B&B, Terry Fox 34 Montagu St; 29401 803-723-4789

♀ • Charleston Beach Bed & Breakfast, PO Box 41, Folly Beach; 29439 803-588-9443
♦ *Charleston Beach Bed & Breakfast advertisement page 403*

♂ • Charleston Columns Guesthouse, 8 Vanderhorst St; 29403 803-722-7341

AIDS/HIV Support, Education, Advocacy, Publications

♂ ☆ ♂ Low Country Palmetto AIDS Support Services (LOWCOUNTRY PALSS), PO Box 207; 29402 803-577-2437

Bars, Restaurants, Clubs, Discos

♂ • (♂) Arcade Club, 5 Liberty St; 29401 803-577-9160 *BRDE*

♂ • Dudley's, 346 King St; 29401 803-723-2784

Organizations/Resources: Sexual Focus (Leather, S/M, etc) & Safe Sex Promotion

♂ ★ Trident Knights, PO Box 31622; 29417 803-769-2094

Organizations/Resources: Social, Recreational & Support Groups (see also Sport/Dance/Outdoor)

♀ ★ Lowcountry Gay/Lesbian Info Alliance, PO Box 98; 29401 803-720-8088

Religious Organizations & Publications

♀ ★ ♂♂ Metropolitan Community Church of Charleston, 2010 Hawthorne Dr #10; 29406 803-747-6736

Columbia

Bars, Restaurants, Clubs, Discos

♂ • ♂ Affairs, 712 Huger St; 29201 803-779-4321

♀ Alcatraz, 1801 Main St; 29200 803-749-7100

♀ • ♂♂ Capital Club, 1002 Gervais St; 29201 803-256-6464 *P*

♀ ○ Lil Rascals, 1109 Assembly; 29201 803-771-0121 *PL* 5pm-6am. Strippers.

♂ Metropolis, 188 Blanding; 29201-3518 803-799-8727

♂ Shandon Club, 2406 Devine St; 29200 803-771-0339

♀ • ♂ Traxx, 416 Lincoln St; 29201 803-256-1084 *BDP*

Bookstores: General

♀ • (?♂) Bluestocking Books, 829 Gervais St; 29201 803-929-0114 Mon-Sat 10am-6pm; Sun 1-6pm. "Specializing in women authors."

Community Centers (see also Women's Centers)

♀ ★ The South Carolina Gay & Lesbian Community Center, PO Box 12648; 29211 / 1108 Woodrow St 803-771-7713 Fri 7-11pm; Sat & Sun 1-8pm; Wed 1-6pm.

Counseling/Therapy: Private

♂ ○ Bradford, Patricia Allen, ACSW, LISW, 2927 Devine St #230; 29205 803-771-9515

Erotica (Printed, Visual, Equipment)

♀ Big E X-citing Emporium, 4333 Fort Jackson Blvd; 29205 803-738-3703

♂ ○ Video X-Press, 2729 Two Notch Road; 29202 803-771-0504

Legal Services & Resources

♀ • ♂♂ Strickland Law Firm, PA, PO Box 2086; 29202 803-256-1318 Fax 803-256-6808 "Specializing in collections, commercial & retail."

Organizations/Resources: Family

♂ ☆ P-FLAG Columbia, 493 Hickory Hill Dr; 29210 803-772-7396 "Parents, Families & Friends of Lesbians & Gays."

Publications

♀ • *In Unison*, PO Box 8024; 29202 803-771-0804

Real Estate

♀ • (?♿) **Hubbard Group Residential Real Estate & Insurance, PO Box 9361; 29290 803-783-8888 Fax 803-783-5244**

Religious Organizations & Publications

♀ ★ ♿ Community Fellowship MCC, PO Box 8753; 29202 803-256-2154 Meets at 1111 Belleview #2.

♀ ★ ♿♿ Lutherans Concerned South Carolina, PO Box 8828; 29202-8828 803-796-8271

Florence

Bars, Restaurants, Clubs, Discos

♀ • ♿ Zippers, 3027 E Palmetto St 803-679-3289

Greenville

AIDS/HIV Support, Education, Advocacy, Publications

♀ ☆ ♿♿ AID Upstate, PO Box 105; 29602 803-455-2040; 800-755-2040 toll free upstate SC; Fax 803-455-2042 "Case management; direct services."

Bars, Restaurants, Clubs, Discos

♀ • ♿♿ The Castle, 8 Le Grand Blvd 803-235-9949 8pm-4am. All welcome.

♀ New Attitude, 706 Washinton St; 29601 803-233-1387

♀ • ♿♿ R&R Corral, 404 Airport Rd; 29607 803-298-0039 *PLWCd*

Bookstores: General

♀ ○ Wittershins Bookstore & Cafe, 233 North Main St., #10 Hammond Square; 29601 803-242-6677

Counseling/Therapy: Private

♀ • (?♿) Holder & Associates, 152 Broughton Dr; 29609-3839 803-242-1360

♀ ○ (?♿) Whitehead, Judy C., ACSW, 250 S Pleasantburg Dr; 29607 803-242-3924

Organizations/Resources: General, Multipurpose, Pride

♀ ★ (?♿) Upstate Women's Community, PO Box 6652; 29606 803-271-4207

Religious Organizations & Publications

♀ ★ (♿♿) Metropolitan Community Church/Greenville, PO Box 6322; 29606-6322 803-233-0919

Hilton Head Island

Bars, Restaurants, Clubs, Discos

♀ ★♿♿ MJ's/Moonjammer's, #1 Heritage Plaza 803-842-9195 *P* Opens 8pm.

Myrtle Beach

Bars, Restaurants, Clubs, Discos

♀ • ♿ Illusions, 1012 S Kings Hwy; 29577 803-448-0421 *BDE*

♀ • ♿♿ Time Out!, 520 8th Ave N; 29577 803-448-1180 *BEPd* Opens 6pm.

Erotica (Printed, Visual, Equipment)

♀ • Big Six Video & Books & XXX Superstore, 1450 W. Hwy 501 803-444-8000 24 hrs.

♀ ○ Maxwell's News & Video, 2027 Hwy 501; 29577 803-626-3140

♀ ○ Video Max, 942 Lake Arrowhead Road; 29572 803-449-3265 24 hrs.

Gifts, Cards, Pride & Novelty Items

♀ ○ ♿ Lotions & Lace XXX Superstore, 1450 Hwy 501 West (Big Six Video Complex) 803-946-9466 Fax 803-946-9777 24 hrs.

Religious Organizations & Publications

♀ Metropolitan Community Church Myrtle Beach, PO Box 3032; 29578 803-347-0177

Pawleys Island

Organizations/Resources: Family

♀ P-FLAG, PO Box 1761; 29585 803-237-2878 "Parents, Families & Friends of Lesbians & Gays."

Rock Hill

Bars, Restaurants, Clubs, Discos

♀ The Hide-A-Way, 405 Baskins Rd; 29730 803-328-6630

Organizations/Resources: Student, Academic, Alumni/ae

♀ GLOBAL, c/o Student Development Office, Winthrop Univ; 29733 803-323-4503

Spartanburg

Bars, Restaurants, Clubs, Discos

♀ Cheyenne's Cattlemen's Club, 995 Asheville Hwy; 29303 803-573-7304

South Dakota

State/County Resources

Organizations/Resources: General, Multipurpose, Pride

♀ SDGLBF (South Dakota Gay Lesbian Bi Federation), 13121 S Creekview Rd, Rapid City, SD 57702 605-343-5577; 800-354-3417 In State Only

Publications

♀ • *Left of Center*, Box 88812, Sioux Falls, SD 57105 605-361-7043

Real Estate

♀ • **Community Real Estate Referrals, 800-346-5592** "Free referral to gay/gay-supportive realtor in any USA city/state (including Virgin Is. & Puerto Rico). Sorry, no rentals!"
   ✦ *Community Real Estate Referrals advertisement back cover*

Religious Organizations & Publications

♀ ★ UCCL/GC (United Church Coalition for Lesbian/Gay Concerns), Rt 1 Box 76, Lake Preston, SD 57249 605-847-4623

Hill City

Bookstores: General

♀ • Oriana's Bookcafé, PO Box 479; 57745 / Main Street 605-574-4878; 800-524-4954; Pub *Bookcafé News*. "Bookstore & full service restaurant; conference & meeting spacew available."

Rapid City

Erotica (Printed, Visual, Equipment)

♀ ○ Monument Books, 912 Main St; 57701 605-397-9877

SD: Sioux Falls
Bars, Clubs, Restaurants

405
USA

Chattanooga : TN
Religious

Sioux Falls

Bars, Restaurants, Clubs, Discos

♂ • (?&) Touche'z, 323 S. Phillips Ave; 57102 605-335-9874 *DELC*

Erotica (Printed, Visual, Equipment)

♀ ○ Studio One, 311 N Dakota Ave; 57102 605-332-9316

Religious Organizations & Publications

♀ ★ St Francis & St Clare Metropolitan Community Church, PO Box 266; 57101-0266 605-332-3966

Tennessee

State/County Resources

Addictive Behavior, Substance Abuse, Recovery

♂ • (&&) Pride Institute, 800-54-PRIDE "The nation's only accredited chemical dependency treatment center exclusively for Gay, Lesbian & Bisexual People."

Legal Services & Resources

♀ ☆ American Civil Liberties Union of Tennessee (ACLU), PO Box 120160, Nashville, TN 37212 615-320-7142

Meeting/Contact Services, Publications, Talklines

♂ ○ *Alternative Lifestyles*, 6324 Papermill Dr #4H, Knoxville, TN 37919 615-588-2995

Organizations/Resources: Social, Recreational & Support Groups (see also Sport/Dance/Outdoor)

♂ ★ Girth & Mirth of Tennessee, PO Box 121886, Nashville, TN 37212-1886 615-297-6386

Publications

♂ • *Query*, PO Box 24241, Nashville, TN 37202-4241 615-259-4135 "Tennessee's Lesbian & Gay Newsweekly."
◆ *Query advertisement page 405*

♂ • *XENOGENY*, PO Box 60716, Nashville, TN 37206 615-228-6572

Real Estate

♂ • Community Real Estate Referrals, 800-346-5592 "Free referral to gay/gay-supportive realtor in any USA city/state (including Virgin Is. & Puerto Rico). Sorry, no rentals!"
◆ *Community Real Estate Referrals advertisement back cover*

Chattanooga

Bars, Restaurants, Clubs, Discos

♂ ○ ♿ Alan Gold's, 1100 McCallie Ave 615-629-8080

♂ Chuck's II, 27 1/2 W Main St; 37402 615-265-5405

Organizations/Resources: Family

♀ ☆ (&) P-FLAG of Greater Chattanooga, PO Box 17252; 37415 615-875-5750; 615-622-3813; Meets 3rd Sun of month, 2.30pm, at TN Bible Inst, Corner of McCallie & Central. "We help families heal."

Religious Organizations & Publications

♂ ★ Integrity/Chattanooga, PO Box 4956; 37405 615-756-7352 "Lesbian & Gay Episcopalians & their friends."

♂ ★ ♿♿ Metropolitan Community Church of Chattanooga, 1601 Foust St; 37404 615-629-2737 Worship Sun 11am & 7pm.

TN: Clarksville
Bars, Clubs, Restaurants

406

USA

Memphis : TN
Erotica

Clarksville

Bars, Restaurants, Clubs, Discos

⚥ • P's, 539 Franklin St; 37040 615-503-9840 Disco weekends.

Erotica (Printed, Visual, Equipment)

♀ ○ ♿ Southern Secrets, 19 Crossland Ave; 37040 615-648-0365

Cookeville

Organizations/Resources: General, Multipurpose, Pride

⚥ ★ Middle Tennessee Gay & Lesbian Alliance, PO Box 101; 38503-0101

Greeneville

Accommodation: Hotels, B&B, Resorts, Campgrounds

♂ • Timberfell Lodge, 2240 Van Hill Rd; 37745 615-234-0833; 800-437-0118; Open all year.
♦ Timberfell Lodge advertisement page 405

Johnson City
Area code changes to 423 September

AIDS/HIV Support, Education, Advocacy, Publications

♀ ★ (♿) HIV Network, Inc., PO Box 1512; 1995 37605-1512 615-928-8888 "HIV/AIDS information; support groups for NE TN & SW VA."

Bars, Restaurants, Clubs, Discos

⚥ ★ ♿ New Beginnings Restaurant & Nightclub, 2910 N. Bristol Hwy 615-282-4446 *BRDE* Tue-Thu 9pm-3am; Fri & Sat 8pm-3am.

Religious Organizations & Publications

♀ ★ ♂ Metropolitan Community Church of the Tri-Cities, PO Box 1612; 37605-1612 615-926-4393; 615-349-7707

Knoxville
☎ Gay & Lesbian Helpline 615-521-6546

AIDS/HIV Support, Education, Advocacy, Publications

♀ ☆ (♿) AIDS Response Knoxville (ARK), 109 Northshire Dr SW #411; 37919-4925 615-523-2437 Fax 615-546-2437 "Support, education & service."

Bars, Restaurants, Clubs, Discos

⚥ • ♂ Carousel II, 1501 White Ave; 37916 615-522-6966

⚥ Old Plantations, 837 N 5th Ave; 37917 615-637-7132

⚥ • Trumps, 4541 Kingston Pike; 37919 615-584-4884 *BDE* Tue-Sun 9.30pm-3am. "Female impersonation shows Wed, Fri-Sun nights."

Bookstores: General

♀ ○ Chelsea Station News, 103 W Jackson Ave; 37902 615-522-6390

♀ ○ Davis-Kidd Booksellers, 113 N Peters Rd; 37923 615-690-0136

♀ ○ Printer's Mark Bookshop, 30-A Market Sq; 37902 615-524-1259 Mon-Thu 11am-6.30pm; Fri & Sat to 10pm.

Religious Organizations & Publications

⚥ ★ ♂ Metropolitan Community Church, PO Box 2343; 37901-2343 615-521-6546

Switchboards, Helplines, Phone Information

⚥ ★ Gay & Lesbian Helpline, PO Box 2343; 37901-2343 615-521-6546 7-11pm (staff permitting)

Travel & Tourist Services (see also Accommodation)

♀ ○ ♿ Bryan-Lawson Travel, PO Box 10612; 37939-0612 615-588-8166

Memphis
☎ Gay & Lesbian Switchboard 901-728-GAYS

AIDS/HIV Support, Education, Advocacy, Publications

♀ ☆ (♿) Friends For Life—HIV Resources, PO Box 40389; 38174-0389 901-458-AIDS

Bars, Restaurants, Clubs, Discos

⚥ Amnesia, 2866 Poplar; 38111 901-454-1366

⚥ Apartment Club, 343 Madison; 38103 901-525-9491

♀ • ♂ Club 501/505, 111 N Claybrook; 38104 901-274-8655 *BDELCW* Sun-Thu noon-3.30am; Fri & Sat to 6am. Beer only.

⚥ ○ Cross Roads, 102 N Cleveland; 38104 901-725-8156 *BE*

⚥ The Edge, 532 S Cooper; 38104 901-272-3036

♂ • ♿ J-Wag's Lounge, 1268 Madison Ave; 38104 901-725-1909 24 hrs.

⚥ Mad Dog Mary's Saloon & Grill, 92 N Avalon St; 38104 901-276-0009 *BDE* Tue-Sun 8p 38104 Beer & wine

♀ Nikita's Bar & Grill, 2117 Peabody Ave; 38104 901-272-1700

♀ P & H Cafe, 1532 Madison Ave; 38104 901-274-9794

⚥ • ♂ Pipeline, 1382 Poplar; 38104 901-726-5263 *BLLd* 2pm-3am. "Large variety of import beers."

♀ Sunshine Lounge, 1379 Lamar; 38104 901-272-9843

♀ Western Steak House & Lounge, 1298 Madison Ave; 38104 901-725-9896

⚥ WKRB In Memphis, 1528 Madison; 38104 901-278-9321

⚥ X-scape, 227 Monroe; 38103 901-528-8344

Bookstores: Gay/Lesbian/Feminist

♀ • ♿ Meristem, 930 S Cooper; 38104 901-276-0282 Wed-Sat 10am-6pm; Sun 1-5pm. "Feminist books & gifts; clearinghouse for women's & lesbian/gay events."

Broadcast Media

⚥ ★ ♿ Gay Alternative, PO Box 41773; 38104-1773 Mon 6-7pm, WEVL-FM 90.

Community Centers (see also Women's Centers)

⚥ ★ ♿ Memphis Gay & Lesbian Community Center, PO Box 41074; 38174 / 1486 Madison Ave; 38104 901-726-5790; 901-728-4297 Switchboard 7.30-11pm; "Video nights; dances; counseling; meditation classes."

Counseling/Therapy: Private

♀ ○ Collins, Etheldreda, LCSW, BCD, 2670 Union Ave, Extd, #601; 38112 901-323-6500

Erotica (Printed, Visual, Equipment)

♀ ○ Airport Bookmart, 2214 Brooks Rd E; 38132 901-345-0657
♦ Airport Bookmart advertisement page 407

♀ ○ Cherokee Video Mart, 2947 Lamar; 38114 901-744-7494 24 hrs.

♂ ○ ♂ Paris Adult Theater, 2432 Summer Ave; 38112 901-323-2665 24 hrs. "Adult books, novelties; video arcade; adult walk-in theatre."

Legal Services & Resources

♀ ● ♂ MacKenzie, Susan, 100 N Main #2518; 38103 901-526-0809

♀ ○ ♂♂ Ross, Robert, 100 N Main St #3310; 38103 901-525-0417 Fax 901-523-9444

♀ ○ ♂ Stark, Kelly, 44 N 2nd St #600; 38103 901-521-9996

Organizations/Resources: Bisexual Focus

♀ ★ ♂♂ Memphis Bisexual Alliance, 1517 Court St #4; 38104-2402

Organizations/Resources: Ethnic, Multicultural

♂ ★ ♂ Black & White Men Together/Memphis, Inc., PO Box 42157; 38174-2157 901-452-5894 Black & White Men Together/Men of All Colors Together

Organizations/Resources: Family

♀ ☆ (?♂) P-FLAG/Memphis, PO Box 172031; 38187-2031 901-761-1444 "Parents, Families & Friends of Lesbians & Gays."

Organizations/Resources: General, Multipurpose, Pride

♀ ★ ♂♂ Memphis Pride, Inc, PO Box 3956; 38173 901-726-4887; 901-725-9179

Organizations/Resources: Political/Legislative

♀ ☆ ♂ National Organization For Women (NOW), PO Box 40982; 38174-0982 901-276-0282

Organizations/Resources: Sexual Focus (Leather, S/M, etc) & Safe Sex Promotion

♀ ★ Alliance, 4372 Kerwin Dr; 38128 *L*

♂ ★ Tsarus, PO Box 41082; 38174-1082 Pub *Times of the Pyramid*. "Private membership leather/levi club; fundraising for local charities."

Organizations/Resources: Social, Recreational & Support Groups (see also Sport/Dance/Outdoor)

♀ ★ ♂ Mystic Krewe of Aphrodite, PO Box 41822; 38174-1822

♂ Wings, PO Box 41784; 38174-1784

Organizations/Resources: Sport/Dance/Outdoor

♀ Cotton Pickin Squares, c/o Prescott Memorial Baptist Church, 3952 Blue Spruce, Lakeland; 38002 901-387-1567 *d*

Organizations/Resources: Student, Academic, Alumni/ae

♀ ★ ♂♂ Students for Bisexual, Gay, & Lesbian Awareness (BGALA), Box 100, Office of Greek Affairs, MSU; 38152 Meets Thu 7pm at UC Center

Organizations/Resources: Transgender & Transgender Publications

T ★ ♂♂ Memphis TransGender Alliance, PO Box 11232; 38111-0232 901-352-2612 4th Sat of month, 1-4pm, at the Community Center. Pub *Powder & Pearls*. "Total support services for transgendered persons."

Performing Arts: Entertainment, Music, Recording, Theater, etc.

♂ Lambda Men's Chorus, 1698 Belvedere Ct; 38104 901-278-1190

Publications

♀ ● ♂ *Triangle Journal News*, PO Box 11485; 38111-0485 901-454-1411

Religious Organizations & Publications

♀ ★ ♂♂ Integrity/Memphis, c/o Calvary Church 102 N 2nd St; 38103 901-525-6602 Pub *Newsletter*. "Lesbian & Gay Episcopalians & their friends."

Switchboards, Helplines, Phone Information

♀ ★ Gay & Lesbian Switchboard, PO Box 41074; 38174-1074 901-728-GAYS

Veterinarians

♀ ● ♂♂ Mobile Veterinary Care, 480 Pruitt Rd, Oakland; 38060 502-465-2699 "Housecall veterinarian, greater Memphis area; weekend & evenings hours available."

Video Sales, Rentals, Services (see also Erotica)

♀ ● Starsearch Video, 1411 Poplar Ave; 38104 901-272-STAR

Murfreesboro

Organizations/Resources: Student, Academic, Alumni/ae

♀ ★ ♂♂ MTSU Lambda Association, MTSU Box 624; 37132 615-780-2293 Pub *Lambda Outlook*.

Nashville

Accommodation: Hotels, B&B, Resorts, Campgrounds

♀ ● The Savage House Inn, 167 8th Ave N.; 37203 615-244-2229

Bars, Restaurants, Clubs, Discos

♀ ♂ Chez Colette, 300 Hermitage Ave; 37210 615-256-9134

TN: Nashville
Bars, Clubs, Restaurants

408
USA

Sewanee : TN
Accommodation

Check out our honeymooners package and Fall and Winter rates

Lee Valley Farm

142 Drinnon Lane
Rogersville,
TN 37857

(615) 272-4068
E-mail: Lees farm @aol.com

The No-Attitude, Stress-Free Mountain Retreat
Ride
Hike - Fish
Party - Chill Out - Sleep
Soak - Make Love
Pig Out on to-die-for
country cookin'
Since 1980

♂ • Chute Complex, 2535 Franklin Rd; 37204 615-297-4571

♀ The Connection, 901 Cowan St; 37207-5625 615-742-1166

♂ Crazy Cowboy II, 2311 Franklin Rd; 37204 615-269-5318

♂ • Gaslite Lounge, 167 1/2 8th Ave N.; 37203 615-254-1278

♂ • (♿) Jungle Lounge, 306 4th Ave S.; 37201 615-256-9411

♀ Pyramids, 701 4th Ave S; 37210 615-259-9514

♀ Ralph's Rutledge Hill Tavern, 515 2nd Ave S.; 37210 615-256-9682

♀ Roxy's, 4726-A Nolensville Rd; 37211 615-333-9010

♀ • Townehouse Restaurant, 165 8th Ave N.; 37203 615-254-1277 *B*

♂ • ♿ Victor/Victoria's, 111 8th Ave N.; 37203 615-244-7256 *BDRLW* 3pm-3am.

♀ • ♿ World's End, 1713 Church St; 37203 615-329-3480 *BRd* 4pm-2am.

♂ Ynonah's, 1700 4th Ave S; 37210 615-251-0980

Bookstores: General

♀ ○ ♿ Davis-Kidd Booksellers, 4007 Hillsboro Rd; 37215 615-385-2645

♀ ○ ♿ Dragonfly Books, 1701 Portland Ave; 37212 615-292-5699 Mon-Sat 11am-7pm; Sun 1-5pm.

Broadcast Media

♀ ★ ♿ Gay Cable Nash, 703 Berry Rd; 37204-2803 615-297-0008 Tue & Sat 9-10pm; Sat 8-9pm Viacom Cable, Channel 19. "National & local news & events concerning the National & Nashville Gay & Lesbian Community."

Community Centers (see also Women's Centers)

♀ ★ ♿ The Center for Lesbian & Gay Community Services, 703 Berry Rd; 37204-2803 615-297-0008 24 hrs.

Computer/Software Sales & Services

♀ • Triangle Computer Consultants, 1813 Fatherland St; 37206 615-228-9579 Fax 615-251-1108

Erotica (Printed, Visual, Equipment)

♀ ○ Carousel Books, 5606 Charlotte Ave; 37209 615-352-0855

♀ ○ Odyssey Book Store, 700 Division St; 37203 615-726-0243

Gifts, Cards, Pride & Novelty Items

♀ ○ Mosko's & The Muncheonette, 2204 Elliston Pl; 37203 615-327-2658 8am-mdnt. "Newsstand & food to go."

Health Care (see also AIDS Services)

♂ ○ (♿) Johnson, James E., MD, PO Box 110519; 37222-0519 615-781-2170

♀ • ♿ Sanders, Roy Q., MD, Mental Health Cooperative, 275 Cumberland Bend; 37228 615-726-3340

Organizations/Resources: General, Multipurpose, Pride

♀ ★ ♿ Nashville Women's Alliance, PO Box 120834; 37212 615-297-0008

Organizations/Resources: Political/Legislative

♀ ☆ National Organization For Women (NOW), PO Box 120523; 37212

Organizations/Resources: Social, Recreational & Support Groups (see also Sport/Dance/Outdoor)

♂ Conductors, PO Box 40261; 37204

Organizations/Resources: Transgender & Transgender Publications

T ☆ ♿ Tennessee Vals, PO Box 92335; 37209-2335 615-664-6883 Open transgender support group every 2nd Sat.

Organizations/Resources: Youth (see also Family)

♀ ★ ♿ One-In-Teen Youth Services, 703 Berry Rd; 37204 615-297-0008

Publications

→ *Query*: p.405

Religious Organizations & Publications

♀ ★ ♿ Integrity/Middle Tennessee, PO Box 121172; 37212 615-383-6608 "Lesbian & Gay Episcopalians & their friends."

♀ ★ ♿ Metropolitan Community Church/Nashville, PO Box 60406; 37206-0406 1021 Russell St; 37206 615-262-0922 Services Sun 11am & 7pm.

Travel & Tourist Services (see also Accommodation)

♀ ○ Embassy Travel Services, 50 Music Sq W #505; 37203-3227 615-320-5202; 800-548-1031 in TN

♀ • Sterling Travel, 325 Plus Park Blvd #200-C; 37217 615-399-3626; 800-449-2479; Fax 615-399-3431

♀ ○ TravelPlex, 1602 21st Ave South; 37212-3125 615-321-3321; 800-325-8123; Fax 615-329-8145

New Market

Organizations/Resources: Social, Recreational & Support Groups (see also Sport/Dance/Outdoor)

♀ ★ (♿) Smoky Mountain Gay & Lesbian Support, mail to SMGLS, 2001 Highlander Way; 37820 615-932-4138

Rogersville

Accommodation: Hotels, B&B, Resorts, Campgrounds

♀ • Lee Valley Farm, 142 Drinnon Lane; 37857 615-272-4068 "No-attitude, stress-free mountain retreat; camping, cabins, pool, horses, hottub. All meals included."
♦ *Lee Valley Farm advertisement page 408*

Sewanee

Accommodation: Hotels, B&B, Resorts, Campgrounds

♂ • Boxwood Cottage, 293 Anderson Cemetery Rd; 37375 615-598-5012 "Bed & breakfast for Gay Men only. Western/Leather especially welcome."

Texas

State/County Resources

Addictive Behavior, Substance Abuse, Recovery

♀ • (♂♂) Pride Institute, 800-54-PRIDE "The nation's only accredited chemical dependency treatment center exclusively for Gay, Lesbian & Bisexual People."

AIDS/HIV Support, Education, Advocacy, Publications

♂ Texas AIDS Network, PO Box 2395, Austin, TX 78768 512-447-8887

Legal Services & Resources

♀ ☆ American Civil Liberties Union of Texas (ACLU), PO Box 132047, Houston, TX 77219-2047 713-942-8146 Fax 713-942-0131

Meeting/Contact Services, Publications, Talklines

♂ • FBB&A, PO Box 125, Corpus Christi, TX 78403 "Listings for Body-builders & admirers."

♂ • LL, PO Box 125, Corpus Christi, TX 78403 "Listings for Latin & Hispanics & those interested in meeting them."

♂ • UM, PO Box 125, Corpus Christi, TX 78403 "Listings for persons interested in foreskins."

Organizations/Resources: Ethnic, Multicultural

♂ People of Color Caucus, 227 Congress #250, Austin, TX 78701 512-473-8335

Organizations/Resources: General, Multipurpose, Pride

♂ Texas Conference of Clubs, PO Box 667071, Houston, TX 77266-7071 713-522-5508

Organizations/Resources: Political/Legislative

♀ ★ (♂) Lesbian/Gay Rights Lobby of Texas, PO Box 2579, Austin, TX 78768-2579 512-474-5475 The Lobby Report.

♀ ★ Log Cabin PAC of North Texas, PO Box 191033, Dallas, TX 75219-8033 214-520-6655 "Republican organization."

♀ ★ ♂ Texas Human Rights Foundation, PO Box 49740, Austin, TX 78765 512-479-8473; 800-828-6417 AIDS Legal Assistance; Mon-Fri 10am-6pm. Pub THRF News. "Dedicated to fighting discrimination against lesbian, gay & HIV-infected persons."

Organizations/Resources: Social, Recreational & Support Groups (see also Sport/Dance/Outdoor)

♀ ★ Gay Service Network, PO Box 2585, Austin, TX 78768 512-445-7270 "Information, support & roommate referral services."

Organizations/Resources: Sport/Dance/Outdoor

♀ ★ Texas Gay Rodeo Association, 3527 Oak Lawn #259, Dallas, TX 75219

Publications

♀ • Dimensions, PO Box 856, Lubbock, TX 79408 806-797-9647

♀ • ♂♂ Houston Voice, 811 Westheimer #105, Houston, TX 77006 713-529-8490 Fax 713-529-9531

♀ • (♂) The Texas Triangle, 1615 W 6th St, Austin, TX 78703 512-476-0576 Fax 512-472-8154
✦ Texas Triangle advertisement page 409

♀ • ♂♂ This Week in Texas (TWT), 811 Westheimer #111, Houston, TX 77006-3942 713-527-9111 News & entertainment.

Real Estate

♀ • Community Real Estate Referrals, 800-346-5592 "Free referral to gay/gay-supportive realtor in any USA city/state (including Virgin Is. & Puerto Rico). Sorry, no rentals!"
✦ Community Real Estate Referrals advertisement back cover

Religious Organizations & Publications

♀ ☆ Reformed Catholic Church (USA), Diocese of the Western Region, c/o Rev. Fr. Rob Havican, OSF, 1800 Lavaca #405, Austin, TX 78701 512-499-0168 revfrrob@io.com frhavian@aol.com

Abilene

AIDS/HIV Support, Education, Advocacy, Publications

♂ T.C.H.P. STD/AIDS Clinic, 317 Pecan St; 79602 915-676-7824

Bars, Restaurants, Clubs, Discos

♀ ○ Just Friends, 201 S. 14th St; 79602 915-672-0882 **BDE**

Religious Organizations & Publications

♀ ★ (♂) Exodus Metropolitan Community Church, PO Box 3274; 79604-3274 / 904 Walnut St 915-672-7922

Alvin

AIDS/HIV Support, Education, Advocacy, Publications

♂ AIDS Coalition of Alvin, 1404 W Snyder; 77511 713-331-1689

The Winners:
- Newsweek - The NY Times
- Nightline - CNN
- The Texas Triangle -

Every week, more than 30,000 Texans read *The Texas Triangle*– the only Texas newspaper to be recognized as a major award winner at the National Gay and Lesbian Journalists Association's annual convention.
Call today for a complimentary copy and advertising information.

1615 West 6th Street
Austin, Texas 78703
512.476.0576
fax 512.476.0576

TX: Amarillo
Bars, Clubs, Restaurants

410

USA

Austin : TX
Organizations: Political

Amarillo

Bars, Restaurants, Clubs, Discos

♂ ○ Alexanders, 1219 W 10th St; 79101 806-372-7414

♂ Classifieds, 519 E 10th Ave; 79101-3609 806-374-2435

♂ Maggie's Disco, 1515 S Harrison St; 79101-4221 806-371-9312

♂ Old Plantation (OP's), 500 W 16th St; 79101 806-379-9613

♂ Ritz, 323 W 10th St; 79101 806-372-9382

♀ Sassy's, 309 W 6th; 79101 806-374-3029

Bookstores: Gay/Lesbian/Feminist

♀ • Washington Square Cafe & Bookstore, 1607 S. Washington; 79102 806-373-5885 _REf_

Erotica (Printed, Visual, Equipment)

♀ ○ (♂♂) Adult Etc II, Rte 2, Box 970 (Exit 80 I-40 East); 79101 806-335-3155

♀ ○ Studio One, 9000 Triangle Dr; 79107-7812 806-372-0648

Organizations/Resources: General, Multipurpose, Pride

♂ Amarillo Lesbian/Gay Alliance, PO Box 9361; 79105 806-373-5725

Religious Organizations & Publications

♂ ★ Metropolitan Community Church, PO Box 1276; 79105-1276 / 2123 S. Polk St 806-372-4557

Arlington: see Dallas/Fort Worth Area

Austin

Addictive Behavior, Substance Abuse, Recovery

♂ ★ ♂ Live & Let Live AA, 2700 W Anderson Ln #412; 78757-1132 512-453-1441

AIDS/HIV Support, Education, Advocacy, Publications

♀ ☆ ♂♂ AIDS Services of Austin, PO Box 4874; 78765 512-451-2273; 512-452-AIDS info & referral.; Mon-Fri 9am-6pm.

♀ ☆ ♂ CARE Program, 1633 E 2nd St; 78702 512-473-CARE Fax 512-476-0217

♂ E.C. Wood Foundation, PO Box 608; 78767-0608 512-451-9807

♀ ☆ ♂ HIV Wellness Center, 502 Oakland Ave #B; 78703-5114 512-472-2753

♀ ★ ♂♂ Project Transitions, Inc., PO Box 4826; 78765-4826 512-454-8646 Pub _Project Transitions Update_. "Residential AIDS hospice serving Austin/Travis County."

Bars, Restaurants, Clubs, Discos

♂ Auntie Mame's, 912 Red River; 78701 512-478-4511

♂ ○ Bout Time, 9601 N. IH 35; 78753 512-832-5339 _Bd_ 11am-2am; Sun noon-2am.

♂ • ♂♂ Chain Drive, 504 Willow St; 78701-4220 512-480-9017

♂ Charlie's, PO Box 13004; 78711 / 1301 Lavaca Ave 512-474-6481

♂ • ♂♂ **Club 404, 404 Colorado St; 78701 512-476-8297** _BDE_ **(after hours gay & straight)**
♦ **_Club 404 advertisement page 411_**

♀ ○ Common Market Cafe, 1600 S Congress Ave; 78701 512-416-1940

♂ Cowboys, 705 Red River St; 78701 512-478-7091

♂ DJ's, 611 Red River; 78701 512-476-3611

♂ Fifth Street Station, 505 E 5th St; 78701 512-478-6065

♀ ♂♂ Hollywood, 113 San Jacinto Blvd; 78701 512-480-9627 _CWd_

♀ • **Nexus, 305 W 5th St; 78701 512-472-5288**

♂ Oil Can Harry's, 211 W 4th; 78701 512-320-8823

♂ Proteus, 501 E 6th St; 78701 512-472-8922

Bookstores: Gay/Lesbian/Feminist

♀ • ♂ Book Woman, 918 W 12th St; 78703 512-472-2785 Mon-Wed 10am-6pm; Thu-Sat to 9pm.

♀ • ♂ Celebration!, 108 W 43rd St; 78751 512-453-6207 "Feminist, spiritual gifts & books."

♂ • ♂♂ **Liberty Books, 1014B N. Lamar Blvd; 78703 512-495-9737**

♂ • Lobo Book Store, 3204A Guadalupe; 78705 512-454-5406 10am-10pm.

Bookstores: General

♀ ○ Congress Avenue Booksellers, 716 Congress Ave; 78701 512-478-1157

Counseling/Therapy: Nonprofit

♂ ★ (?♂) Waterloo Counseling Center, 2525 Wallingwood Dr #1500; 78746-6923 512-329-9922

Erotica (Printed, Visual, Equipment)

♀ ○ ♂ Forbidden Fruit, 512 Neches; 78701 512-478-8358 11am-11pm; Sun 1-7pm. "Erotic gifts; leather & safe sex supplies."

♀ • ♂ Oasis Bookstore, 9601 N Interregional Hwy 35; 78753 512-835-7208

♀ • ♂ Pleasureland, 613 W 29th St; 78705 512-478-2339

♀ ○ Uptown Forbidden Fruit, 2514 Guadalupe St; 78705 512-478-8542 "Leather; lotions; lingeries & fetish wear."

Health Care (see also AIDS Services)

♀ ☆ ♂♂ Austin Health & Human Services STD Clinic, 15 Waller; 78702 512-469-2070

♀ ☆ ♂ David Powell HIV Assessment & Treatment Clinic, 1000 Toyath St; 78703 512-479-6121

Legal Services & Resources

♀ • ♂ Fitzwater, Martha, Esq, 1201 W 24th St; 78705 512-473-3733 (Austin); 210-299-4448 (San Antonio); Fax 512-473-2730

Organizations/Resources: Business & Professional

♂ ★ Austin Stonewall Chamber of Commerce, PO Box 49976; 78765 512-707-3794

Organizations/Resources: Ethnic, Multicultural

♂ ★ (♂♂) Austin Latino/a Lesbian & Gay Organization, Inc (ALLGO), PO Box 6149; 78762-6149 512-447-1809 Pub _ALLGO Pasa_.

♂ ★ ♂♂ Ebony Connection, PO Box 1428; 78767 512-926-3786 "Educational, cultural, social & support for Black Lesbians & Gays."

Organizations/Resources: General, Multipurpose, Pride

♂ Austin Lesbian Gay Pride Commission, PO Box 402064; 78704 512-479-9431

Organizations/Resources: Political/Legislative

♂ ★ (?♂) Austin Lesbian/Gay Political Caucus, PO Box 822; 78767 512-474-0750; 512-462-9888; Fax 512-474-4511 Pub _ALCPC Newsletter_.

TX: Austin
Organizations: Sexual

411
USA

Corpus Christi : TX
Bars, Clubs, Restaurants

Organizations/Resources: Sexual Focus (Leather, S/M, etc) & Safe Sex Promotion

⚥ ☆ (♂♂) NLA: Austin, PO Box 684013; 78768-4013 512-370-4713 Pub *Newsletter*.

Organizations/Resources: Social, Recreational & Support Groups (see also Sport/Dance/Outdoor)

♂ ★ (?♂) Austin Gay Nudists, mail to A.G.N. PO Box 684101; 78768-4101 "Nudist/Naturist group."

♂ Classic Chassis Car Club, PO Box 12553; 78711

♂ ★♂♂ Prime Timers International, PO Box 14892; 78761-4892 512-927-1133

Organizations/Resources: Sport/Dance/Outdoor

⚥ ★ Adventuring Outdoor Club, PO Box 9700 #128; 78766 512-445-7216

⚥ ★ Team Austin/Gay Games, PO Box 161701; 78716 512-447-6408; 512-450-0230

⚥ ★ Texas Gay Rodeo Association, PO Box 1511; 78767 512-835-5314

Organizations/Resources: Youth (see also Family)

⚥ ★ Out Youth Austin, 425 Woodward; 78704 512-472-9264; 800-96-YOUTH; Pub *Inside Out Youth*.

Performing Arts: Entertainment, Music, Recording, Theater, etc.

⚥ ★ (?♂) Capital City Men's Chorus, PO Box 50082; 78763 512-477-7464

Pharmacies/Health Care Supplies

⚥ ○ MOM: Mail Order Meds, Inc., PO Box 180007; 78718-0007 800-700-6202 Fax 800-700-6106
◆ *MOM: Mail Order Meds, Inc. advertisement inside front cover*

Publications

⚥ • *Fag Rag*, c/o Snaxus Productions PO Box 1034; 78767 512-416-0100 Fax 512-416-6981

→ *The Texas Triangle*: p.409
◆ *Texas Triangle advertisement page 409*

Religious Organizations & Publications

⚥ ★ (♂♂) Affirmation: United Methodists for Lesbian, Gay & Bisexual Concerns, 7403 Shoal Creek Blvd; 78757 512-451-2329

⚥ ★ Dignity/Austin, PO Box 2666; 78768 512-467-7908 "Gay & Lesbian Catholics & their friends."

⚥ ★ (?♂) Integrity/Austin, PO Box 4327; 78765-4327 512-445-6164; 512-447-4779 TTY; Pub *Integrity/Austin News*. "Episcopalians for Gay & Lesbian Concerns."

⚥ Metropolitan Community Church Austin, 425 Woodward St; 78704 512-416-1170

♂ Mishpachat Am Echad, PO Box 9591; 78766 512-451-7018

Travel & Tourist Services (see also Accommodation)

⚥ • ♂♂ Creative Travel Center, 8650 Spicewood Springs Rd #210; 78759-4318 512-331-9560 Fax 512-331-6230

Video Sales, Rentals, Services (see also Erotica)

⚥ • ♂♂ Tapelenders Video, 3926 Cedar Springs #120, Dobie Mall lower level; 78705 512-472-4206 10am-11pm; Sun noon-11pm.

Austin's Most Popular Dance Club for Everyone 18+!

404 Colorado
Austin, TX 78701
10pm-? W/T/F/S/S
☎ 512-476-8297

SIX BARS, CATWALK CRUISING, LATEST VIDEOS, HOT DANCERS OUTDOOR PATIO, DRINK SPECIALS & SEXY BASEMENT LOUNGE

Bandera

Accommodation: Hotels, B&B, Resorts, Campgrounds

⚥ • Desert Hearts Cowgirl Club, HC3, Box 650; 78003 210-796-7446 "Adult women's guest ranch; 50 miles NW of San Antonio."

Beaumont

Bars, Restaurants, Clubs, Discos

⚥ • (♂) Copa Disco, 304 Orleans 409-832-4206 *D* 9pm-2am.

♂ Sundowner, 497 Crockett St; 77701 409-833-3989

Carrollton

Religious Organizations & Publications

♂ SDA Kinship, PO Box 110116; 75011-0116 214-416-1358

College Station

AIDS/HIV Support, Education, Advocacy, Publications

⚥ ☆ Brazos Valley AIDS Foundation, PO Box 9209; 77842-0209 409-260-2437

Bars, Restaurants, Clubs, Discos

♂ Club 202, 202 S Bryan Av, Bryan; 77803 409-823-6767

Organizations/Resources: Student, Academic, Alumni/ae

⚥ ★♂♂ Gay, Lesbian & Bisexual Aggies, MSC Student Finance Center #789, Texas A&M University; 77843-1237 409-847-0321

Corpus Christi

Accommodation: Hotels, B&B, Resorts, Campgrounds

⚥ • (?♂) Anthony's Bed & Breakfast, 732 S Pearl St, Rockport; 78382 512-729-6100; 800-460-2557

AIDS/HIV Support, Education, Advocacy, Publications

⚥ ☆♂♂ Coastal Bend AIDS Foundation, Box 331416; 78463 512-814-7001; 512-814-2001 Hotline 24 hrs.

Bars, Restaurants, Clubs, Discos

⚥ • Club Unity, 4125 Gollihar Rd; 78415 512-851-1178

♂ • ♂ Hidden Door, 802 S Staples; 78404 512-882-0183 11am-2am; Sun noon-2am.

⚥ Members Only, 1314 Ayers; 78404 512-882-3647

♂ Numbers, 1214 Leopard St; 78401 512-887-8445 (Latina)

⚥ Rumors, 601 N Chaparral St; 78401 512-887-4994

⚥ UBU, 4701 Ayers St; 78415 512-853-9693

Organizations/Resources: Sexual Focus (Leather, S/M, etc) & Safe Sex Promotion

♂ Silver Dolphins LLC, PO Box 6129; 78466-6129

Religious Organizations & Publications

⚥ ★ ♿♿ Metropolitan Community Church of Corpus Christi, 1315 Craig St; 78404 512-882-8255 Worship Sun 11am.

Dallas/Fort Worth Area

☎ **Gay & Lesbian Information Line 214-368-6283**

☎ **Lesbian Information Line 214-528-2426**

Accommodation: Hotels, B&B, Resorts, Campgrounds

Dallas

⚥ ● **The Inn On Fairmount, 3701 Fairmount, Dallas; 75219 214-522-2800 Fax 214-522-2898**
◆ ***Inn On Fairmount advertisement page 413***

Hamilton

♀ ○ (?♿) **Hamilton Guest Hotel, 109 N Rice, Hamilton; 76531 817-386-8977**

Addictive Behavior, Substance Abuse, Recovery

⚥ Lambda Group of AA, 2727 Oak Lawn #101, Dallas; 75219 214-522-6259

AIDS/HIV Support, Education, Advocacy, Publications

♀ ☆ ♿ AIDS Arms, 4300 MacArthur #160, Dallas; 75209 214-521-5191 Fax 214-528-5879 8.30am-5pm. "AIDS Service Organization, Case Management, referral services for Dallas County residents with AIDS or HIV symptomatic. Client brochure in Spanish & English."

♀ ☆ ♿♿ AIDS Funding Association, 4300 MacArthur #130, Dallas; 75209 214-954-0508 Fax 214-526-2137

♀ ☆ AIDS Interfaith Network, 4300 MacArthur Ave #LB14, Dallas; 75209-6544 214-559-4899

♀ ★ (?♿) AIDS Mastery - Dallas, PO Box 36125, Dallas; 75235 214-526-LIFE

♀ ★ ♿♿ AIDS Outreach Center, 1125 W Peter Smith, Fort Worth; 76104 817-335-1994 Fax 817-335-3617

♀ ☆ ♿♿ AIDS Resource Center, 2701 Reagan, Dallas; 75219 214-521-5124 Pub *AIDS Update*.

♀ ☆ (?♿) AIDS Services of Dallas, PO Box 4338, Dallas; 75208 214-941-0523 Fax 214-941-8144 "Services include medically supportive housing for PWAs; licensed by State of Texas as a Special Care Facility."

♀ ○ Center for Special Immunology, 4140 Lemmon Ave #267, Dallas; 75219 214-528-2727

♀ ○ Center for Special Immunology, 6500 Greenville Ave #430, Dallas; 75206 214-696-0414

Archives/Libraries/History Projects

⚥ ★ (♿) Dallas Gay/Lesbian Historic Archives, PO Box 190869, Dallas; 75219 214-821-1653; 214-528-9254

Bars, Restaurants, Clubs, Discos

Arlington

♂ Arlington 651, 1851 W. Division 817-275-9651 **D**

⚥ Tomboys, 2315 S Cooper St, Arlington; 76015 817-461-4475

Dallas

♂ Backstreet, 4020 Maple Ave, Dallas; 75219 214-522-4814 **D**

♂ Bamboleo's, 5027 Lemmon Ave, Dallas; 75204 214-520-1124

♂ ○ Big Daddy's/Anchor Inn, 4024 Cedar Springs, Dallas; 75219 214-528-4098

♂ Brick Bar, 4117 Maple, Dallas; 75219 214-521-2024

⚥ Buddies, 3415 Mahanna, Dallas; 75209 214-526-8720 **D**

⚥ Club Boxx Office, 2515 N Fitzhugh Ave, Dallas; 75204 214-828-2665

⚥ Club Regency, 2525 Wycliff #130, Dallas; 75219 214-520-8822 **Bd**

♂ ● Crews Inn, 3215 N Fitzhugh, Dallas; 75204 214-526-9510

⚥ ● ♿♿ Dallas Eagle, 2515 Inwood #107, Dallas; 75235 214-357-4375 **BLL** 4pm-2am; Fri & Sat to 4am.

♀ Desert Moon, 5039 Willis Ave, Dallas; 75206 214-828-4471

♂ Hidden Door, 5025 Bowser, Dallas; 75209 214-526-0620

♂ ● Hideaway Club, Inc., 4144 Buena Vista, Dallas; 75204 214-559-2966

♂ John L's, 2525 Wycliffe Ave, Dallas; 75219 214-520-2525

⚥ ● ♿♿ JR's Bar & Grill, 3923 Cedar Springs Rd, Dallas; 75219 214-380-3808 **BR**

⚥ ○ ♿ Jugs, 3810 Congress, Dallas; 75219 214-521-3474 **DECW**

⚥ Las Mariposas, 2513 N Fitzhugh Ave, Dallas; 75204 214-826-2806

⚥ The Metro, 2204 Elm St, Dallas; 75201 214-742-2101

♂ (?♿) Moby Dick, 4011 Cedar Springs 214-520-MOBY

♂ ○ Numbers, 4024 Cedar Springs, Dallas; 75201 214-521-7861

♂ Pub Pegasus, 3326 N Fitzhugh, Dallas; 75204 214-559-4663

⚥ The Rock, 2815 Main St, Dallas; 75226 214-698-9401

♂ Round-Up Saloon, 3912 Cedar Springs, Dallas; 75219 214-522-9611 **D**

⚥ Side 2 Bar, 4006 Cedar Springs Rd, Dallas; 75235 214-528-2026

⚥ Spankee's Club, 7650 Shady Brook Lane, Dallas; 75213 214-739-4760

♂ The Splash!, 4025 Maple Ave, Dallas; 75219 214-522-9283

⚥ ● ♿♿ Sue Ellen's, 3903-5 Cedar Springs Rd; 75219 214-380-3386 **BD**

♂ ● ♿ Throckmorton Mining Company, 3014 Throckmorton, Dallas; 75219 214-521-4205

♂ ● ♿ The Trestle, 412 S. Haskell Ave; 75226 214-826-9988 **BLLW** 8pm-2am; after hours Fri & Sat to 4am.

⚥ ● ♿♿ Village Station, 3911 Cedar Springs; 75219 214-526-0690 **BD**

♂ Zippers, 3333 N Fitzhugh, Dallas; 75204 214-526-9519

Fort Worth

♂ ● 651 Club, 651 S Jennings Ave, Fort Worth; 76104 817-332-0745

♀ Across The Street, 700 S Jennings, Fort Worth; 76104 817-332-0192

♂ Ashburn's, 3012 E Rosedale St, Fort Worth; 76105 817-534-6630

⚥ Copa Cabana, 1002 S Main St, Fort Worth; 76104

⚥ Corral, 621 Hemphill St, Fort Worth; 76104 817-335-0196

⚥ DJ's, 1308 Saint Louis Ave, Fort Worth; 76104 817-927-7321 **BR**

⚥ Magnolia Station, 600 W Magnolia Ave, Fort Worth; 76104 817-332-0415

Wylie

⚥ • ♿ Wilderzone, 3535 Stonewall Road, Wylie; 75098-6263 214-475-2434 *DLCWf* Fri-Sun only, open 7pm. Nude male shows Fri & Sat 9pm-2am.

Bookstores: Gay/Lesbian/Feminist

⚥ • **Crossroads Market & Bookstore, 3930 Cedar Springs, Dallas; 75219 214-521-8919**

⚥ • (♿) Lobo After Dark, 4008C Cedar Springs, Dallas; 75219 214-522-1132

⚥ ★ Sources of Hope Gifts & Books, PO Box 35466, Dallas; 75235 / c/o Cathedral of Hope, 5910 Cedar Springs Road, Dallas; 75235 800-501-4673 Fax 214-352-6099

Broadcast Media

⚥ ★ Cathedral of Hope TV, Cathedral of Hope MCC, PO Box 35466, Dallas; 75235 214-351-1901 x114 Fax 214-351-6099

⚥ ★ Just For The Record, PO Box 35373, Dallas; 75235-0373 214-351-1901 (Public Access) *Newsletter.*.

⚥ ★ Lambda Weekly Radio, PO Box 35031, Dallas; 75235 520-1375 Sun 2-4pm, KNON, 89.3.

Clothes

♀ • **Leather By Boots, 3014 Throckmorton, Dallas; 75219 214-522-2737 Fax 713-523-0432 Noon-8pm.**
✦ *Leather By Boots advertisement page 413*

♀ • **Leather By Boots, 4038 Cedar Springs, Dallas; 75219 214-528-3865 Fax 214-523-0432 Mon-Sat noon-8pm.**
✦ *Leather By Boots advertisement page 413*

♀ • ♿ Shades of Grey Leather, 3928 Cedar Springs Rd 214-521-GREY

♀ • ♿♿ Union Jack, 3920 Cedar Springs Rd, Dallas; 75219 214-528-9600 Mon-Tue 10am-7pm; Wed-Sat to 10pm; Sun 11am-7pm.

Community Centers (see also Women's Centers)

⚥ ★ ♿♿ Gay/Lesbian Community Center, PO Box 190869, Dallas; 75219 / 2701 Reagan; 75219 214-528-9254

⚥ Lesbian Resource Center, PO Box 180446, Dallas; 75218 214-821-3999

Counseling/Therapy: Nonprofit

⚥ ★ ♿♿ Oak Lawn Community Services, PO Box 191069, Dallas; 75219 214-520-8108 Mon-Fri 9am-9pm. "Mental health services/substance abuse/AIDS support services."

Erotica (Printed, Visual, Equipment)

♀ ○ Eros, 2555 Walnut Hill Lane, Dallas; 75229 214-351-3654

♂ ○ **Now Alternatives of New Fine Arts (La Cage), 1720 W Mockingbird Ln (rear entrance), Dallas; 75235 214-630-7071**

♀ ○ Video Stop, 2006 Market Center, Dallas; 75207 214-747-4722

♀ ○ Videoland, 10857 Harry Hines Bl, Dallas; 75220 214-358-6559

Gifts, Cards, Pride & Novelty Items

♀ • ♿ Babylon, 4008D Cedar Springs, Dallas; 75219 214-522-5887 Mon-Sat noon-8pm; Sun to 5pm. "Jewelry, cards, gifts; Holy Union specialist."

♀ ○ ♿ Off The Street, 3921 Cedar Springs, Dallas; 75219 214-521-9051

Health Care (see also AIDS Services)

♀ ● ♂♂ Oaklawn Physicians Group, 3514 Cedar Springs Road, Dallas; 75219 214-520-1810

Health Clubs, Gyms, Saunas

♂ ● Club Dallas, 2616 Swiss Ave, Dallas; 75204 214-821-1990

♂ ● ♂♂ Crossroads Gym, 4001 Cedar Springs Rd #D, Dallas; 75219 214-522-9376

♂ ○ Midtowne Spa Dallas, 2509 Pacific, Dallas; 75226 214-821-8989

Legal Services & Resources

♀ ● ♂♂ Stewart, Charles L., 3500 Oak Lawn #400, Dallas; 75219 214-521-3804

Massage Therapy (Licensed only)

♂ ● ♂ Oak Lawn Myotherapy, 2727 Oak Lawn Ave #107, Dallas; 75219 214-528-2390; 800-775-5685; "Massage clinic & retail store of wellness & massage products."

Organizations/Resources: Bisexual Focus

♂ BiNet, PO Box 190869, Dallas; 75219 214-504-6612

Organizations/Resources: Business & Professional

♂ Dallas Tavern Guild, 3900 Lemmon Ave #220, Dallas; 75219 214-824-2787

Organizations/Resources: Education, Anti-Defamation, Anti-Violence, Self-Defense

♂ ★ (?♿) GLAAD/Dallas (Gay & Lesbian Alliance Against Defamation, Inc.), PO Box 190869, Dallas; 75219 214-521-5342 x816

♂ ★ Welcome Wagon, Deb Elder, PO Box 190132, Dallas; 75219 214-979-0017 "Service whereby visitors or relocators may be mailed newspapers & general information on the Dallas Gay & Lesbian community."

Organizations/Resources: Ethnic, Multicultural

♂ ★ (?♿) Asians & Friends, PO Box 9142, Dallas; 75209 214-480-5906 Pub Bamboo Quill.

♂ ★ Men Of All Colors Together, PO Box 190611, Dallas; 75219-0611 214-521-4765

Organizations/Resources: Family

♂ ★ (?♿) Gay/Lesbian Parents of Dallas, PO Box 154031, Irving; 75015-4031 214-259-9862

♂ ★ (?♿) Tarrant County Parents Group, PO Box 48382, Watauga; 76148-0382 817-656-8056

Organizations/Resources: General, Multipurpose, Pride

♂ ★ ♂♂ Dallas Gay & Lesbian Alliance, PO Box 190712, Dallas; 75219 / 2701 Reagan 214-528-4233 Fax 214-522-4604

♂ ★ ♂♂ Tarrant County Lesbian/Gay Alliance, Inc, 3327 Winthrop #243, Fort Worth; 76116 817-763-5544; 817-763-8382: Teen Project Hotline; Pub Alliance News.

Organizations/Resources: Political/Legislative

♂ ♂♂ Lesbian Visionaries, PO Box 191443, Dallas; 75219-8443 214-521-5342

♀ ☆♂♂ Lesbian/Gay Political Coalition of Dallas, PO Box 224424, Dallas; 75222 214-526-6724

♀ ★ Metroplex Republicans/Log Cabin, PO Box 191033, Dallas; 75219-8033 214-520-6655 "Republican organization."

Organizations/Resources: Sexual Focus (Leather, S/M, etc) & Safe Sex Promotion

♀ ☆ ♂♂ National Leather Association: Dallas Chapter, PO Box 7597, Dallas; 75209 214-521-5342 ext 820 The Newsleather.

Organizations/Resources: Social, Recreational & Support Groups (see also Sport/Dance/Outdoor)

♂ Couples/Metro Dallas, PO Box 803156, Dallas; 75280 214-504-6775

♂ Dallas Silver Sabres, PO Box 190179, Dallas; 75219 214-642-7881

♂ ★ Dallas/Forth Worth Prime Timers, PO Box 191101, Dallas; 75219-8101 214-350-6150

♂ Gay & Lesbian Gardeners, PO Box 190552, Dallas; 75219 214-339-0787

♂ ISR Court de Dallas, PO Box 190464, Dallas; 75219 214-521-8446

Organizations/Resources: Sport/Dance/Outdoor

♂ Battalion Motorcycle Corps, PO Box 191227, Dallas; 75219

♂ Dallas Motorcycle Club, 2139 W Lovers Ln, Dallas; 75253 214-630-2550

♀ ★ (?♿) Oak Lawn Ski Club, PO Box 7438, Dallas; 75209 214-380-7987

♂ Rainbow Skydive Club, PO Box 543062, Dallas; 75254 214-357-9880

♂ ★ (?♿) Team Dallas Aquatics, PO Box 190869, Dallas; 75219-0712 214-821-1653 "Umbrella group for gay sports groups."

♂ ★ Trinity Dallas Aquatics, PO Box 190768, Dallas; 75219

Organizations/Resources: Student, Academic, Alumni/ae

♂ ★♂♂ Gay/Lesbian Association of UTA, PO Box 19348-77, Arlington; 76019 817-794-5140

Organizations/Resources: Transgender & Transgender Publications

T ☆ Delta Omega/Metroplex Cross Dressers Support Group, PO Box 1021, Arlington; 76004 817-261-3253; 214-264-7103; "Crossdressers & wives."

Organizations/Resources: Youth (see also Family)

♂ ★ Gay Lesbian Bisexual Young Adults, PO Box 190712, Dallas; 75219 / 2701 Reagan St 214-521-5342 x260 Pub Youth Street News.

♂ ★ Hope House, PO Box 35466, Dallas; 75235 214-351-5657 Fax 214-351-1007 "Transitional living services for youth (up to 21): includes residential services."

Performing Arts: Entertainment, Music, Recording, Theater, etc.

♂ ★ ♂ Oak Lawn Band, Greater Dallas Music Foundation, PO Box 190973, Dallas; 75219 214-993-8997

Publications

♂ ● *Dallas Voice*, 3000 Carlisle St #200, Dallas; 75204 214-754-8710 Fax 214-969-7271 Weekly.

Real Estate

♀ ● Elder, Deb, Uptown Realtors, 2612 Boll St, Dallas; 75204 214-979-0017 Fax 214-660-0936 "Relocation specialist."

♂ ● Hewitt, Kathy, Vice President, Realtor, Uptown Realtors, 2612 Boll St, Dallas; 75204 214-979-0057 Fax 214-660-0941 "Residential sales & leasing."

Religious Organizations & Publications

♀ ★ ♂♂ Agapé Metropolitan Community Church of Fort Worth, PO Box 15247, Fort Worth; 76119-0247 / 4615 SE Loop 820 817-535-5002 Mon-Thu 11am-6pm. Pub *Agape News*. Worship Sun 9 & 11am; AIDS & other support groups.

♀ ★ ♂♂ **Cathedral of Hope Metropolitan Community Church, 5910 Cedar Springs Rd, Dallas; 75235 214-351-1901 Fax 214-351-6099 Sat 6.30pm; Sun 9 & 11am, 6.30pm; Wed 6.30pm.**
♦ *Cathedral of Hope Metropolitan Community Church advertisement page 415*

♀ Christian Gays in Fellowship EC, PO Box 120611, Arlington; 76012 817-446-1555

♀ ★ ♂♂ Congregation Beth El Binah, PO Box 191188, Dallas; 75219-8188 214-497-1591 Pub *Kibbitz*.

♂ ★ ♂♂ Dallas Affirmation: United Methodists for Lesbian, Gay & Bisexual Concerns, PO Box 190987, Dallas; 75219-0987 214-528-4913

♀ ★ Dignity/Dallas, PO Box 190133, Dallas; 75219-0133 214-521-5342 x832 "Gay & Lesbian Catholics & their friends."

♀ ★ ♂ Dignity/Fort Worth, 4503 Bridge Rd, Fort Worth; 76103 817-283-8588 "Gay & Lesbian Catholics & their friends."

♀ ★ Holy Trinity Community Church, 4402 Roseland Ave, Dallas; 75204 214-827-5088

♀ Integrity/Dallas, PO Box 190351, Dallas; 75219-0351 214-520-0912 "Lesbian & Gay Episcopalians & their friends."

♀ ★ ♂♂ Trinity Metropolitan Community Church, 331 Aaron Ave #125, Arlington; 76012 817-265-5454

Switchboards, Helplines, Phone Information

♀ ★ Gay & Lesbian Information Line, PO Box 191069, Dallas; 75219 214-368-6283 7.30pm-mdnt; 214-520-8108 to volunteer

♀ ★ ♂♂ Lesbian Information Line, PO Box 191443, Dallas; 75219 214-528-2426 (recorded events, updates, referrals for Lesbian & Gay Men)

Travel & Tourist Services (see also Accommodation)

♀ ○ Travel Friends, 8080 N Central #320, Dallas; 75206 214-891-8833

Video Sales, Rentals, Services (see also Erotica)

♀ ● ♂♂ Tapelenders Video, 3926 Cedar Springs, Dallas; 75219 214-528-6344 9am-mdnt; Sun noon-11pm.

Del Valle

Erotica (Printed, Visual, Equipment)

♂ ○ Highway 71 News, 5246 E Hwy 71; 78617 915-247-4070

Denison

Bars, Restaurants, Clubs, Discos

♀ Good Time Lounge, 2520 N Hwy 75A; 75020 903-463-9944

♂ Quad Angles, 5006 S Farm Road; 75020 903-786-9996

Denton

AIDS/HIV Support, Education, Advocacy, Publications

♀ ★ ♂ Harvest Ecumenical AIDS Resource Team, 5900 South Stemmons; 76205 817-321-2332

TX: Denton
Bars, Clubs, Restaurants
416
USA
Houston Area: TX
AIDS/HIV Support

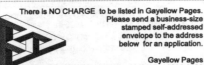

There is **NO CHARGE** to be listed in Gayellow Pages. Please send a business-size stamped self-addressed envelope to the address below for an application.

Gayellow Pages
PO Box 533 Village Station, New York, NY 10014-0533

Bars, Restaurants, Clubs, Discos

♀ Bedo's, 1215 E University Dr; 76201-2152 817-566-9910 *P*

Organizations/Resources: Student, Academic, Alumni/ae

♀ ★ (?♂) Courage: The Lesbian/Gay/Bisexual Student Organization of UNT, c/o Student Activities Center, UNT Box 5067; 76203 817-565-6110

Religious Organizations & Publications

♀ ★ ♂ Harvest Metropolitan Community Church, 5900 South Stemmons; 76205 (I-35 at Exit 460) 817-321-2332 Sun 10.30am.

El Paso
☎ **LAMBDA Services 915-562-4297**

AIDS/HIV Support, Education, Advocacy, Publications

♀ ☆♂♂ Southwest Aids Committee, 1505 Mescalero Dr; 79925-2019 915-772-3494

Bars, Restaurants, Clubs, Discos

♀ ○ Briarpatch, 204 E Rio Grande; 79902 915-546-9100 *BR*

♀ Candie's, 4512 Alemeda Ave; 79905 915-546-9475

♀ Old Plantation, 219 S Ochoa; 79901 915-533-6055

♀ San Antonio Mining Co, 800 E San Antonio Ave; 79901 915-533-9516

♀ U Got It, 216 S Ochoa; 79901 915-533-9310

♂ Whatever Lounge, 701 Paisano Dr; 79901 915-533-0215; 915-546-9010

Erotica (Printed, Visual, Equipment)

♀ ○ ♂ Green Door, 211 Stockyard Rd; 79927 915-858-3174 9am-1am.

♀ ○ ♂ Trixx Adult Cinema & Bookstore, 2230 Texas; 79901 915-532-6171

Meeting/Contact Services, Publications, Talklines

♀ ☆ Gentle Quest Swing Club, PO Box 4594; 79914 915-821-1997

♀ ● (?♂) New Age Dating Service, PO Box 3977; 79923 915-592-3716

Organizations/Resources: Education, Anti-Defamation, Anti-Violence, Self-Defense

♀ ★ LAMBDA Services Anti-Violence Project, PO Box 31321; 79931-0321 915-562-4297 24 hrs.

Organizations/Resources: Family

♀ P-FLAG, PO Box 1761; 79949 915-592-2218 "Parents, Families & Friends of Lesbians & Gays."

Organizations/Resources: General, Multipurpose, Pride

♀ ★ Gay & Lesbian Community Council, PO Box 12248; 79912 915-757-6201

Organizations/Resources: Social, Recreational & Support Groups (see also Sport/Dance/Outdoor)

♀ ★ (?♂) LAMBDA Services Lesbian & Bisexual Womyn Support Group, PO Box 31321; 79931-0321 915-562-4297 24 hrs.

Organizations/Resources: Youth (see also Family)

♀ ★♂♂ LAMBDA Services Youth OUTreach, PO Box 31321; 79931-0321 915-562-4297 24 hrs.

Religious Organizations & Publications

♂ Metropolitan Community Church El Paso, PO Box 3121; 79903 915-524-1227

Switchboards, Helplines, Phone Information

♀ ★ LAMBDA Services, PO Box 31321; 79931-0321 915-562-4297 24 hrs. Fax 915-533-1357

Fort Worth: see Dallas/Fort Worth Area

Galveston

AIDS/HIV Support, Education, Advocacy, Publications

♂ AIDS Coalition of Coastal Texas, 1419 Tremont St; 77550-4519 409-763-AIDS

♀ Community Care for AIDS-UTMB, 12th & Mechanic, Rt J-28; 77550 409-938-2202; 409-761-3038

Bars, Restaurants, Clubs, Discos

♀ Evolution, 2214 Mechanic St; 77550 409-763-4212 *BD*

♂ ● Kon-Tiki, 315 Tremont (23rd St); 77550 409-763-6264 *BD* 4pm-2am. "Mostly men."

♀ ● ♂ Robert's Lafitte, 2501 Ave Q; 77550 409-765-9092 *BdE* 10am-2am.

Gun Barrel City

Bars, Restaurants, Clubs, Discos

♀ 231 Club, 231 W Main; 75147 903-887-2061

Harlingen

Bars, Restaurants, Clubs, Discos

♀ ● (♂♂) Zippers, 319 W Harrison St; 78550 210-412-9708 *Bd*

Houston Area
☎ **Gay & Lesbian Switchboard of Houston 713-529-3211**

Accommodation: Hotels, B&B, Resorts, Campgrounds

Houston

♀ ● The Lovett Inn, 501 Lovett Blvd, Houston; 77006 713-522-5224; 800-779-5224

♂ ● Montrose Inn, 408 Avondale, Houston; 77006 713-520-0206; 800-357-1228
✦ Montrose Inn advertisement page 417

AIDS/HIV Support, Education, Advocacy, Publications

♀ ☆♂♂ AIDS Alliance of the Bay Area, 17511 El Camino Real #159, Houston; 77058-3049 713-488-4492

♀ ★ AIDS Equity League, PO Box 980307, Houston; 77098-0307 713-529-9966 Fax 713-871-0093

♀ ☆ ♂ AIDS Foundation Houston, Inc., 3202 Weslayan St, Houston; 77027-5113 713-623-6796; 713-524-AIDS; 9am-9pm. Pub *Lifeline*.

♀ ★ (?♂) AIDS Talk Houston TV, 3333 W Alabama St #116, Houston; 77098-1706 713-902-2231 Fax 713-942-7621

TX: Houston Area
AIDS/HIV Support
417
USA
Houston Area: TX
Broadcast Media

♂ ☆ Amigos Volunteers & Education & Services (AVES), 4126 Southwest Fwy #1717, Houston; 77027-7316 713-626-2837 Fax 713-626-2848

♂ Bering Support Network, PO Box 540517, Houston; 77254-0517 713-526-1017

♀ ☆ ♿ Bureau of HIV/STD Prevention, Dept of Health & Human Services, 8000 N Stadium Dr, 5th flr, Houston; 77054 713-794-9020 Hotline Pub *Houston AIDS Surveillance Update.*

♂ ★ Colt 45's AIDS Trouble Fund, PO Box 66804, Houston; 77266-6804 713-526-6077

♂ ☆ Design Industries Foundation For AIDS/Houston (DIFFA), PO Box 131605, Houston; 77219-1605 713-522-9445

♂ ☆ ♿ Houston Regional HIV/AIDS Resource Group, 811 Westheimer St #201, Houston; 77006-3942 713-526-1016

♂ ☆ ♿ NAMES Project Houston, PO Box 66595, Houston; 77266-6595 713-526-2637 (52-NAMES) Fax 713-526-1859

♂ ☆ (♿) People With AIDS Coalition Houston, Inc., 3400 Montrose Blvd #106, Houston; 77006 713-522-2674 Fax 713-522-2679 Pub *Among Friends.*

Archives/Libraries/History Projects

♂ ★ ♿ MCC Library, Metropolitan Community Church of the Resurrection, 1919 Decatur, Houston; 77007 713-861-9149

Bars, Restaurants, Clubs, Discos

Houston

♂ 611 Hyde Park Pub, 611 Hyde Park, Houston; 77006 713-526-7070

♂ Bacchus, 2715 Waughcrest St, Houston; 77006 713-523-3396

♂ Berryhill II, 15346 Kuykendahl, Houston; 77090 713-587-8810

♂ • (♿) Brazos River Bottom, 2400 Brazos, Houston; 77006 713-528-9192

♂ • Briarpatch, 2294 W Holcombe Blvd, Houston; 77005 713-665-9678

♂ Chances, 1100 Westheimer, Houston; 77006 713-523-7217

♀ Charlie's Coffee Shop, 1100 Westheimer, Houston; 77006 713-522-3332 *R*

♂ ○ Club 403, 403 Westheimer, Houston; 77006 713-523-0030

♂ • ♿ Cousins, 817 Fairview, Houston; 77006 713-528-9204 *BECWf*

♂ E/J's, 2517 Ralph St, Houston; 77006 713-527-9071

♂ Ean's, 112 E Travis St, Houston; 77002-1715 713-227-0505

♂ • Gentry, 2303 Richmond Ave, Houston; 77098 713-520-1861 2pm-2am; Sat & Sun noon-2am.

♂ • ♿ Heaven, 810 Pacific St, Houston; 77006 713-521-9123 *D*

♀ Inergy, 6121 Hillcroft St, Houston; 77081 713-771-9611 *D*

♂ • ♿ J.R.'s Bar & Grill, 804-808 Pacific St, Houston; 77006 713-521-2519 *B*

♀ ○ Java Java Cafe, 911 W 11th St, Houston; 77008 713-880-5282

♂ Lazy J, 312 Tuam St, Houston; 77006 713-528-9343

♂ Mailbox Bar/El Buzon, 4215 Washington Ave, Houston; 77007 713-864-2977

♂ ○ Mary's, 1022 Westheimer, Houston; 77006 713-527-9669

♂ ○ ♿ Missouri Street Station, 1117 Missouri; 77006 713-524-1333 4pm-2am; Sun 2pm-2am.

Montrose Inn

FOR GAY MEN

COMFORTABLE ■ BASIC

Walk to 13 Gay Bars

408 AVONDALE
HOUSTON, TX 77006
(713) 520-0206
(800) 357-1228
MOST ROOMS $49

♂ • ♿ Montrose Mining Company, 805 Pacific St, Houston; 77006 713-529-7488 *BL*

♀ • (♿) Ms B's, 9208 Buffalo Speedway; 77025 713-666-3356 *Bd* 4pm-2am.

♂ • ♿ Outpost, 2818 Richmond, Houston; 77098 713-520-8446

♂ • (♿) Pacific Street, 710 Pacific, Houston; 77006 713-523-0213 *BDL* 9pm-2am; Fri & Sun 7pm-2am.

♀ Past Time, 617 Fairview St, Houston; 77006-2903 713-529-9669

♀ Penthouse Club, 3400 Montrose, 10th flr, Houston; 77006 713-522-0745 *BR*

♂ QT's, 534 Westheimer, Houston; 77006 713-529-8813

♀ • ♿ The Ranch, 9218 Buffalo Speedway, Houston; 77025 713-666-3464 *CW*

♂ • ♿ Rich's, 2401 San Jacinto, Houston; 77002 713-759-9606 *D*

♂ • ♿ Ripcord, 715 Fairview, Houston; 77006 713-521-2792

♀ • (♿) The Toy Box, 1419 Richmond Ave, Houston; 77006 713-529-3367

♀ • ♿ Venture-N, 2923 S Main St, Houston; 77002 713-522-0000 *BLLEd* Noon-2am.

♀ • ♿ XTC, 9200 Buffalo Speedway, Houston; 77025 713-666-3464 *BD*

Bookstores: Gay/Lesbian/Feminist

♀ • Crossroads Market & Bookstore, 610 W Alabama, Houston; 77006 713-942-0147

♀ • Inklings: an alternative bookshop, 1846 Richmond Ave, Houston; 77098 713-521-3369 Tue-Sat 10.30am-6.30pm; Sun noon-5pm. "Books & music for the feminist, gay & lesbian communities."

♀ • Lobo Book Store, 1424C Westheimer St, Houston; 77006 713-522-5156 10am-10pm.

Broadcast Media

♀ ★ After Hours, KPFT 90.1 FM, 419 Lovett, Houston; 77006-4018 713-526-5738 Sat 12 mdnt.

♂ Alternative Broadcasting Service, PO Box 980845, Houston; 77098-0845 713-526-3425 Fax 713-522-5115

♀ ★ Fem TV (Feminist Television), PO Box 66604, Houston; 77266-6604 713-755-7766

♂ ☆ ♿ KTRU 91.7FM, PO Box 1892, Houston; 77251-1892 713-527-4098 Fax 713-527-4093

TX: Houston Area
Broadcast Media

418

USA

Houston Area: TX
Organizations: General

Metropolitan Community Church of the Resurrection

**Metropolitan Community Church
of the Resurrection**
1919 Decatur St
Houston, TX 77007-7698
(713) 861-9149
"Experience God's Unconditional Love"

⚧ ★ Lesbian & Gay Voices, KPFT 90.1 FM, 419 Lovett, Houston; 77006-4018 713-526-4000 Fax 713-529-1223 lgvoices@ aol.com Fri 6-8pm.

Clothes

⚧ ● Basic Brothers, 1232 Westheimer, Houston; 77006 713-522-6626

⚧ ● **Leather By Boots, 2424 Montrose, Houston; 77006 713-526-2668 Fax 713-523-0432 Noon-8pm.**
◆ *Leather By Boots advertisement page 413*

⚧ ● **Leather By Boots, 715 Fairview, Houston; 77006 713-526-0444 Fax 713-523-0432 8pm-2am.**
◆ *Leather By Boots advertisement page 413*

⚧ ● **Leather Forever, 711 Fairview, Houston; 77006 713-526-6940 Noon-8pm.**
◆ *Leather Forever advertisement page 413*

Computer Bulletin Boards

⚧ ● The Fluorescent Igloo, 2025 Hazard #2, Houston; 77019-6152 713-524-7342 st416@jetson.uh.edu

Computer/Software Sales & Services

⚧ ● TFI Enterprises, 2025 Hazard #2, Houston; 77019-6152 800-925-4834; 713-524-4834; Fax 713-524-1164 st416@jet-son.uh.edu

Counseling/Therapy: Nonprofit

⚧ ★&& Montrose Counseling Center, 701 Richmond Ave, Houston; 77006-5511 713-529-0037; 713-529-6634 TDD; 8am-9pm.

Counseling/Therapy: Private

⚧ ● && DAPA: Family of Choice, PO Box 131019, Houston; 77219-1019 800-822-2272

Erotica (Printed, Visual, Equipment)

⚧ ○ Fountainview News, 5887 Westheimer Rd, Houston; 77057 713-781-7793

⚧ ○&& Southeast Cinema, Inc., 1636 Federal Rd, Houston; 77015 713-451-5470 10am-mdnt.

Furniture

⚧ ● Abba Interiors, 7138 Myrtle, Houston; 77087 713-921-7401 "Upholstery/refinishing/furniture restoration."

Gifts, Cards, Pride & Novelty Items

⚧ ○ Hollywood Food Store, 1660 Westheimer, Houston; 77006 713-528-3234 "Food, beer, wine, gifts, cards, magazines, books, etc."

⚧ ○ Hollywood Food Store, 2501 Montrose, Houston; 77006 713-524-7052 "Food, beer, wine, gifts, cards, magazines, books, etc."

⚧ ● && Loveworks, 25170 I-45 North #3A, Spring; 77386 713-292-0070

⚧ ● Unique Boutique Gifts & Gallery, 4317 Montrose, Houston; 77006 713-526-5266 Noon-8pm.

Health Care (see also AIDS Services)

⚧ ● && Duren, Crad, MD, 1213 Hermann Dr #430, Houston; 77004 713-520-0653 Fax 713-520-0654

Health Clubs, Gyms, Saunas

⚥ ● Club Houston, 2205 Fannin, Houston; 77002 713-659-4998

⚥ ○ (?&) Midtowne Spa Houston, 3100 Fannin, Houston; 77004 713-522-2379

Jewelry

⚧ ○ (&) Crystal Castle, 228 Westheimer; 77006 713-526-6165 Tue-Sat 10am-6pm; Thu to 8pm.

Legal Services & Resources

⚧ ○&& Craft, E. Ross, 811 Westheimer #200, Houston; 77006 713-526-0141

⚧ ● Moore & Hunt, PO Box 300788, Houston; 77230 / 3608 Audubon Place 713-522-4282

⚧ Southeast Texas Legal Clinic, PO Box 667007, Houston; 77266-7007 713-523-7852

Organizations/Resources: Business & Professional

⚧ ★ Bar Association for Human Rights, PO Box 270664, Houston; 77077-0664 713-524-5549

⚧ Houston Organization of Bar Owners, 710 Pacific, Houston; 77006 713-523-0213

⚀ ★ (?&) Lesbians in Business (LiB), mail to LiB, PO Box 66748, Houston; 77266-6748 713-529-0077

Organizations/Resources: Education, Anti-Defamation, Anti-Violence, Self-Defense

⚧ ★ (?&) Diana Foundation, PO Box 66523, Houston; 77266-6523 713-639-2000

⚧ ★ Q-Patrol, Inc., PO Box 58131, Houston; 77258-0131 713-871-8519

Organizations/Resources: Ethnic, Multicultural

⚀ Amiga de Houston, PO Box 980134, Houston; 77098 713-527-0941

⚧ ★ (?&) Asians & Friends of Houston, Inc, PO Box 740346, Houston; 77274-0346 713-772-3757

⚧ ★ Paz Y Liberacion, PO Box 66450, Houston; 77266-6450

Organizations/Resources: Family

⚧ ★ (&) Gay Fathers/Fathers First of Houston, PO Box 981053, Houston; 77098-1053

⚧ Houston Gay & Lesbian Parents, PO Box 35709-262, Houston; 77235-5709 713-980-7995

⚧ ☆&& P-FLAG, PO Box 692444, Houston; 77269-2444 713-862-9020 "Parents, Families & Friends of Lesbians & Gays."

Organizations/Resources: General, Multipurpose, Pride

⚧ ★ Pride Committee of Houston, PO Box 66071, Houston; 77266-6071 713-529-6979 Fax 713-529-1223 Pub *Pride News-letter.*

Organizations/Resources: Military/Veterans

♂ Texas Gay Veterans of Houston, PO Box 66135, Houston; 77266-6135 713-522-3477

Organizations/Resources: Political/Legislative

♀ ★ Houston Gay & Lesbian Political Caucus, PO Box 66664, Houston; 77266-6664 713-521-1000

♂ Log Cabin/Houston, PO Box 131104, Houston; 77219-1104 713-529-9100 (Republicans)

Organizations/Resources: Sexual Focus (Leather, S/M, etc) & Safe Sex Promotion

♀ ☆ (?⚢) National Leather Association: Houston, PO Box 66553, Houston; 77266-6553 713-527-9666 Fax 713-528-2850

Organizations/Resources: Social, Recreational & Support Groups (see also Sport/Dance/Outdoor)

♂ Agora, 5338 Creekbend Dr, Houston; 77096-5314 713-729-4527

♂ ★ Astro Rainbow Alliance of the Deaf, Inc., PO Box 66136, Houston; 77266-6136 713-869-4369; 713-869-2287 via (800) 735-2988

♂ Bay Area Gays & Lesbians (BAGAL), 13703 Segrest, Houston; 77047-4726 713-734-1170

♀ ★ (?⚢) Classic Chassis Car Club/Houston, PO Box 981102, Houston; 77098-1102 713-683-1867

♂ Just For Us, PO Box 35709-262, Houston; 77235-5709 713-666-8260

♀ ★ ♂♂ LOAF (Lesbians Over Age 50), PO Box 980601, Houston; 77098-0601 713-661-1482 "Social & Support group."

♂ ★ (♂) Lone Star Nudist Group, PO Box 66621, Houston; 77266-6621 713-866-8847 "Nudist/Naturist group."

♂ ★ ♂ Men's Network, 713-529-0037

♀ ★ Old Lesbians Organizing for Change (OLOC), PO Box 980422, Houston; 77089 Pub *OLOC Reporter*.

♂ ★ (?⚢) Prime Timers/Houston, PO Box 980612, Houston; 77098-0612 713-867-3903

♂ ★ The Royal, Sovereign, & Imperial Court of the Single Star of Houston, Inc., PO Box 980444, Houston; 77098-0444

Organizations/Resources: Sport/Dance/Outdoor

♀ ★ Chain Gang Bicycle Club, PO Box 130064, Houston; 77219-0064 713-863-1860 "Bicyclists."

♂ ★ FrontRunners Houston, 713-522-8021

♂ ★ Houston Outdoor Group, PO Box 980893, Houston; 77098-0893 713-526-7688 (KAMPOUT)

♀ ★ **Houston Women's Softball League, 12233 Palmfree, Houston; 77034 "Please write for details."**

♂ ★ ♂♂ Houston Wrestling Club, PO Box 131134, Houston; 77219-1134 713-453-7406

♀ ★ Lambda Rollerskating Club, 7414 Puerta Vallarta, Houston; 77083 713-933-5818 "Indoor & outdoor skating."

♀ ★ (?⚢) Montrose Country Cloggers, PO Box 875, Humble; 77347 713-987-8277 **d**

♀ ★ Montrose Softball League, PO Box 541954, Houston; 77254-1954 713-867-3913

♂ ★ ♂♂ TEAM Houston, PO Box 66405, Houston; 77266-6405

Organizations/Resources: Student, Academic, Alumni/ae

♂ ★ ♂♂ Delta Lambda Phi—University of Houston, 4800 Calhoun CA Box #219, Houston; 77204-0001 713-524-7966

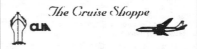
♂ ★ ♂♂ Gays & Lesbians of Rice (GALOR), PO Box 1892, Houston; 77251-1892 713-527-4097

♂ ★ ♂♂ GLOBAL: the Gay, Lesbian & Bisexual Alliance at UH, mail to GLOBAL, 4800 Calhoun, Box 314, Houston; 77204-3650 713-743-7539

♀ ★ (?⚢) Rice University Gay & Lesbian Alumni Association, PO Box 1892, Houston; 77251-1892 713-523-0170

Organizations/Resources: Youth (see also Family)

♀ ★ ♂ Houston Area Teen Coalition of Homosexuals (HATCH), PO Box 667053, Houston; 77266-7053 713-942-7002

♀ ☆ (♂) Houston Institute for the Protection of Youth (HIPY), PO Box 130843, Houston; 77219-0843 / 604 Westheimer 713-942-YUTH; 713-524-5224

Performing Arts: Entertainment, Music, Theater, etc.

♂ Gay Men's Chorus of Houston, PO Box 541004, Houston; 77254-1004 713-531-7464

Public Relations/Advertising Agencies

♀ ● (?⚢) Locklin Agency Advertising & Promotion, 3333 W Alabama #116, Houston; 77098 713-942-7600 Fax 713-942-7621

Publications

♂ *Maleman*, Blueboy Inc., 3400 Montrose #207, Houston; 77006 713-528-MALE

♀ ● *OutSmart*, 3406 Audubon Place, Houston; 77006-4412 713-520-7237

Religious Organizations & Publications

♀ ★ Dawn of Faith Christian Church, 8405-K Alameda-Genoa Rd, Houston; 77075 713-991-6766

♀ ★ ♂♂ Dignity/Houston, PO Box 66821, Houston; 77266-6821 / 1307 Yale #H 713-880-2872 Liturgy Sat 7.30pm; Sun 5.30pm. "Gay & Lesbian Catholics & their friends."

♀ ☆ ♂♂ First Unitarian Universalist Church, 5200 Fannin St, Houston; 77004-5899 713-526-5200

♀ ★ ♂ Houston Mission Church, PO Box 131371, Houston; 77219-1371 / 1505 Nevada at Commonwealth 713-529-8225

♀ ★ (?⚢) **Integrity/Houston, PO Box 66008, Houston; 77266-6008 713-432-0414 Pub *Marginal Notes*. "Gay & Lesbian Episcopalians & their friends."**

♀ ★ (♂) Kingdom Community Church, 4404 Blossom, Houston; 77007 713-862-7533 Fax 713-868-2089

♀ ★ ♂♂ Kolbe House, PO Box 66669, Houston; 77266-6669 713-522-8182

♀ ★ ♂ Lutherans Concerned—Houston, 2515 Waugh Dr, Houston; 77006 713-528-3269

TX: Houston Area
Religious

420
USA

Merkel : TX
Erotica

⚢ ☆&& Maranatha Fellowship MCC, PO Box 667032, Houston; 77266-7032 713-528-6756

⚢ ★ (&&) **Metropolitan Community Church of the Resurrection, 1919 Decatur, Houston; 77007-7698 713-861-9149** Services Sun 8.30am & 10.45am; Wed 7pm.
◆ *Metropolitan Community Church of the Resurrection advertisement page 418*

⚢ ★ (?&) Mishpachat Alizim, PO Box 980136, Houston; 77098-0136 713-748-7079

♀ ☆&& Unitarian Universalists for Lesbian/Gay Concerns, First UCC of Houston, 5200 Fannin St, Houston; 77004-5899 713-526-5200

Switchboards, Helplines, Phone Information

♀ ☆ Crisis Hotline, PO Box 130866, Houston; 77219-0866 713-228-1505

⚢ ★ Gay & Lesbian Switchboard of Houston, PO Box 66469, Houston; 77266-6469 713-529-3211 4.30pm-mdnt.

Travel & Tourist Services (see also Accommodation)

⚢ ○ Advance Damron Vacations, 10700 Northwest Freeway #160, Houston; 77092 713-682-2650; 800-695-0880

♂ ● I.D. Travel, 1717 St James Place #150, Houston; 77056 713-850-9332; 800-856-9332; Fax 713-850-8426

⚢ ● Sandra Wilkins Travel, 713-526-4471 (also Fax) "Expert planning for the demanding gay & lesbian traveler."

⚢ ● && **Sojourns/A World Travel Service, 3400 Montrose #909, Houston; 77006 713-528-2299; 800-530-2299; Fax 713-528-6767**

♀ ○&& **World Travel—The Cruise Shoppe, 2323 S Shepherd Dr #111, Houston; 77019 713-942-7447; 800-747-5174; Fax 713-523-4297**
◆ *World Travel—The Cruise Shoppe advertisement page 419*

Women's Centers

♀ ☆&& Houston Area Women's Center, 3101 Richmond #150, Houston; 77098-3013 713-528-2121; 713-528-7273; Fax 713-535-6363 Pub *Catalyst*.

Kempner

Organizations/Resources: Social, Recreational & Support Groups (see also Sport/Dance/Outdoor)

⚢ ★ (&&) Fort Hood Area Chapter GLACT, PO Box 279; 76539 512-932-2718; 800-833-2718

Laredo

Bars, Restaurants, Clubs, Discos

♀ The Discovery, 2019 Farragut St; 78078 210-722-9032

Organizations/Resources: General, Multipurpose, Pride

⚢ Forward Foundation, PO Box 420142; 78042-0142 210-791-0606

Longview

Bars, Restaurants, Clubs, Discos

⚢ ● && Choices, 446 Eastman Rd 903-753-9221 ***PBDE*** 3pm-2am.

Erotica (Printed, Visual, Equipment)

♀ ○ Newsland, 301 E Marshall; 75601 903-753-4167

Religious Organizations & Publications

⚢ ★ (&) Church With A Vision Metropolitan Community Church, PO Box 1287; 75606-1287 / 420 E. Cotton St; 75601 903-753-1501 Service Sun 10am.

Lubbock

AIDS/HIV Support, Education, Advocacy, Publications

♀ ☆ South Plains AIDS Resource Center, PO Box 6949; 79493 806-796-7068; 806-792-7783 info line

Bars, Restaurants, Clubs, Discos

♀ ○ Oz, 1806 Clovis Rd; 79415 806-741-1047

⚢ The Place, Main St & Avenue X; 79401 806-744-4222

Community Centers (see also Women's Centers)

⚢ ★ && Community Outreach Center, PO Box 64746; 79464-4746 / 102 Avenue S 806-762-1019

Counseling/Therapy: Private

♀ ○ Pair, Beverly, LPC, NCC, 5215 79th St; 79424 806-794-4520 Fax 806-763-6098

Erotica (Printed, Visual, Equipment)

♀ ○ Crystal Cinema, 1408 N Ave Y; 79415 806-765-7107

♀ ○ (&&) Fantasy Adult Theatre & Bookstore, 6125 Slaton Hwy 806-745-3044 "Peep shows & preview booths."

Grooming Services

♀ ● && Shear Envy, 4407 71st; 79424 806-799-7771 (ask for Natalie)

Legal Services & Resources

♀ ● & Gore, Richard R., 1005 Broadway; 79401-3368 806-762-1690 Fax 806-762-0654

Organizations/Resources: Family

♀ ☆&& P-FLAG, PO Box 94493; 79493-4493 806-799-5466

Organizations/Resources: General, Multipurpose, Pride

⚢ ★&& **Lubbock Lesbian/Gay Alliance, PO Box 64746; 79464-4746 806-791-4499 Pub *Lambda Times*.**

Organizations/Resources: Student, Academic, Alumni/ae

⚢ ★ Gay/Lesbian Student Association, Texas Tech University, mail to GLBS, 1919 17th, Apt D; 79401 806-742-2527 "Social/support group, primarily for students but others welcome."

Publications

→ *Dimensions*: p.409

Religious Organizations & Publications

⚢ ★ && Metropolitan Community Church, 5501 34th St; 79407-3309 806-792-5562 Worship Sun 11am & 6pm; Bible Study 9am; Children's Church 11am; Prayer Group Sun 5pm; Worship also Wed 7.30pm.

McAllen

Bars, Restaurants, Clubs, Discos

♀ ○ Just Terry's, 1500 N. 23rd 210-682-CHER

⚢ ○ PBD Disco, 2908 Ware Rd at Daffodil 210-682-8019 *D*

⚢ Tenth Avenue, 1820 N 10th St; 78501 210-682-7131

Merkel

Erotica (Printed, Visual, Equipment)

♀ ○ Adult Etc I, 9210 I-20 (exit 270); 79536 915-928-3894

Odessa

Bars, Restaurants, Clubs, Discos

⚢ • ⚤ **Mining Company, 409 N Hancock Ave; 79761 915-580-6161** *BDECW* **Wed-Sun 9pm-2am. Tejano music.**

⚢ Miss Lillie's Nite Spot, 8401 Andrews Hwy; 79765 915-366-6799

Port Aransas

Accommodation: Hotels, B&B, Resorts, Campgrounds

⚢ • Sea Horse Inn, PO Box 426; 78373-0426 512-749-5221

Rockport: see Corpus Christi

San Angelo

AIDS/HIV Support, Education, Advocacy, Publications

⚥ ☆ (⚤) San Angelo AIDS Foundation, Inc., 1121 S Bryant Blvd; 76903-7241 915-658-3634

Bars, Restaurants, Clubs, Discos

⚢ ○ **Silent Partners, 3320 Sherwood Way; 76901 915-949-9041**

San Antonio

☎ **LISA (Lesbian Information San Antonio) 210-828-LISA**

☎ **San Antonio Gay & Lesbian Switchboard 210-733-7300**

Accommodation: Hotels, B&B, Resorts, Campgrounds

⚥ ○ The Garden Cottage Guesthouse, 800-235-7215

⚢ • The Painted Lady Guesthouse, 620 Broadway; 78215 210-220-1092

⚥ • Park Motel, 3617 Broadway; 78209 210-826-3245

Addictive Behavior, Substance Abuse, Recovery

⚢ • Lambda Club AA, 8546 Broadway St #255; 78217-6340 210-824-2027

AIDS/HIV Support, Education, Advocacy, Publications

⚢ ★ The Blue Light Candle, PO Box 12444; 78212-0444 210-655-8431

⚥ ☆ Names Project, PO Box 120123; 78212 210-737-0408; 210-824-4768

⚥ PWA Coalition, 12125 Jones-Maltsberger #210; 78247 210-545-HELP

⚥ ☆ (⚤) San Antonio AIDS Foundation, 818 E Grayson St; 78208-1013 210-225-4715 Fax 210-224-7730 "Medical/hospice care."

Archives/Libraries/History Projects

⚢ ★ The Happy Foundation, 411 Bonham; 78205 210-227-6451

Bars, Restaurants, Clubs, Discos

⚢ • 2015 Place, 2015 San Pedro Ave; 78212 210-733-3365 *BdE* 2pm-2am.

⚢ • B.B.'s Pub, 5307 McCullough Ave; 78212 210-828-4222 *BD*

⚢ Bamboleo's Latin Fever, 1812 N Main St; 78212 214-734-3738

⚂ • The Bonham Exchange, 411 Bonham; 78205 210-271-3811 *BDE* 8pm-2am; Fri & Sat to 4am.

⚥ • (⚤) Captain's Crew, 309 W Market; 78205 210-222-0310 *Bd*

⚂ Cowboys, 622 Roosevelt Ave; 78210 210-532-9194

⚢ Eighth Street Bar & Grill, 416 8th St; 78215 210-271-3227

⚂ El Jardin, 106 Navarro; 78205 210-223-7177

⚥ G.B.R.'s, 2022 McCullough; 78212 210-738-3118

⚂ • ⚤ Industria, 450 Soledad; 78205 210-227-0484 Fax 210-227-1775 *BD* Video/Dance Club featuring "Industria Gear" T-shirts, jewlry & gifts.

⚢ Las Gueras, 5930 S Flores; 78214 210-923-7944

⚢ Lorraine's, 7834 S Presa; 78223-3531 210-532-8911

⚢ Miriam's, 115 General Kruger; 78213 210-334-9720

⚢ New Ponderosa, 5007 S Flores; 782 210-924-6322

⚢ • (⚤) **Nexus II, 8021 Pinebrook; 78230 210-341-2818** *BdE* **5pm-2am; Sun 2pm-2am.**

⚢ • (⚤) Nite Owl, 330 San Pedro; 78212 210-223-OWLS *B* 4pm-2am.

⚂ One-O-Six Off Broadway, 106 Pershing Ave; 78209 210-820-0906

⚂ • ⚤ Paper Moon, 1430 N Main; 78212 210-225-7330 9pm-2am.

⚂ Pegasus, 1402 N Main Ave; 78212 210-299-4222

⚢ Riddum's, 10221 Desert Sands St; 78216 210-366-4206

⚂ • Silver Dollar Saloon, 1418 N Main; 78212 210-227-2623

⚂ ○ Sparks, 8011 Webbles Dr; 78218 210-653-9941

⚂ • The Stallion, PO Box 15568; 78212-8768 / 2003 McCullough 210-734-7977

⚢ Wild Club, 820 San Pedro; 78212 210-226-2620 *D*

⚂ Wild Country, 414 W Laurel; 78212 210-228-9378

Bookstores: Gay/Lesbian/Feminist

⚥ ○ Textures, 5309 McCullough; 78212 210-805-TEXT

Community Centers (see also Women's Centers)

⚥ The Resource Center, 121 W Woodlawn; 78212 210-732-0751

Entertainment-Related Services (see also Music, Organizations/Resources: Performing

⚥ • DJ Mark Productions, 210-805-0500

Erotica (Printed, Visual, Equipment)

⚥ ○ (⚤) Broadway Video X-change, 2122 Broadway; 78215 210-223-2034 "Videos, books, novelties, arcade."

⚥ ○ Encore Video, 8546 Broadway St #160; 78217 210-821-5345

Health Clubs, Gyms, Saunas

⚂ • Executive Services, 703 Avenue B; 78212 210-225-8807

Meeting/Contact Services, Publications, Talklines

⚥ • Colors Introductory Services, Inc., 1600 NE Loop 410, #115; 78209 210-828-7907

Organizations/Resources: Business & Professional

⚥ Alamo Business Council, PO Box 15481; 78212

Organizations/Resources: Ethnic, Multicultural

⚥ ELLAS (Latina), PO Box 681061; 78268-1061

TX: San Antonio
422
State/County Resources : UT

Organizations: Family
USA
Organizations: Political

Organizations/Resources: Family

♂ ★ (?♂) Gay & Lesbian Parent Coalition, 2839 NW Military Dr #508; 78231 210-342-8696

Organizations/Resources: General, Multipurpose, Pride

♂ ★ San Antonio Lesbian/Gay Assembly, PO Box 12614; 78212 (incorporates former Pride Committee)

Organizations/Resources: Political/Legislative

♀ ☆ (?♂) San Antonio National Organization For Women (NOW), PO Box 12874; 78212-0874 210-673-8600

Organizations/Resources: Sexual Focus (Leather, S/M, etc) & Safe Sex Promotion

♂ Firedancers/San Antonio, 5119 Staplehurst; 78228

Organizations/Resources: Social, Recreational & Support Groups (see also Sport/Dance/Outdoor)

♂ ★ ♂ San Antonio Prime Timers, PO Box 13613; 78213-0613 210-653-0959

Organizations/Resources: Sport/Dance/Outdoor

♂ Alamo City Wranglers, PO Box 4866; 78285 210-733-9439 ♂

Organizations/Resources: Student, Academic, Alumni/ae

♂ ★ (?♂) San Antonio Lambda Students Alliance (SALSA), PO Box 12715; 78212 210-733-1225 "Citywide organization encompassing 9 colleges & universities; operates Lambda Students Center at 1140 W. Woodlawn (address may change in summer 1992)."

Performing Arts: Entertainment, Music, Theater, etc.

♂ ★♂♂ Alamo City Men's Chorale, Box 120243; 78212 210-590-2836

Publications

♀ • The Marquise, PO Box 12486; 78212 210-737-1404 Fax 210-737-1454 marquise@aol.com

♀ • WomanSpace, PO Box 12327; 78212 210-828-LISA "Lesbian Community publication."

Religious Organizations & Publications

♂ ★ Metropolitan Community Church of San Antonio, 1136 W Woodlawn; 78201 210-734-0048

♂ ★ (?♂) River City Living Church, 202 Holland; 78212 210-822-1121

Switchboards, Helplines, Phone Information

♀ ★ LISA (Lesbian Information San Antonio), PO Box 12327; 78212 210-828-LISA

♂ ★ San Antonio Gay & Lesbian Switchboard, Box 120402; 78212 210-733-7300 7-11pm; 210-734-2833 24 hr recorded bar information.

Sulphur Springs

Grooming Services

♀ ○♂♂ Dan's Haircutts, 401 Gilmer St #3 (facing Hinnant St) 903-885-0792 Tue-Sat 8am-6pm. "Barber Stylist; HIV+ & PWA welcome."

Temple

Bars, Restaurants, Clubs, Discos

♀ • ♂ Hard Tymes, 414 S 1st St; 76502 817-778-9604 BDECWL 6pm-2am.

Tyler

AIDS/HIV Support, Education, Advocacy, Publications

♀ ★♂♂ HIS House, 1320 N Bois D'Arc; 75702 903-592-0757 "AIDS/HIV Resource Center."

Religious Organizations & Publications

♂ ★ St Gabriel Community Church (I.C.C.C), 13904 County Rd 193; 75703 903-581-6923 Pub Messenger.

Waco

AIDS/HIV Support, Education, Advocacy, Publications

♀ ☆ McLennan County Aids Resources (McCares), 4224 Cobbs Drive; 76710 817-750-5499

Bars, Restaurants, Clubs, Discos

♀ David's, 507 Jefferson; 76701 817-753-9189

Organizations/Resources: Social, Recreational & Support Groups (see also Sport/Dance/Outdoor)

♂ ★ (?♂) Gay & Lesbian Alliance of Central Texas, mail to GLACT, Box 9081; 76714-9081 817-752-7727; 800-735-1122; Pub Central Texas Alliance News.

Religious Organizations & Publications

♂ ★ Metropolitan Community Church/Waco, PO Box 22043; 76702-2043 817-752-5331

Wichita Falls

Bars, Restaurants, Clubs, Discos

♀ Rascals, 811 Indiana Av; 76301 817-723-1629; 817-322-0320

Organizations/Resources: Student, Academic, Alumni/ae

♂ ★ Diversity, 3410 Taft Blvd #12764, Midwestern State Univ.; 76308 817-766-2264; 817-692-4968

Religious Organizations & Publications

♂ Metropolitan Community Church of Wichita Falls, PO Box 8094; 76307 817-322-4100

Utah

State/County Resources

AIDS/HIV Support, Education, Advocacy, Publications

♀ ☆ Utah AIDS Foundation, 1408 South 1100 East, Salt Lake City, UT 84105 801-487-2323; 800-FON-AIDS

Community Centers (see also Women's Centers)

♂ ★ ♂ Utah Stonewall Center, 770 South 300 West, Salt Lake City, UT 84101 801-539-8800 Pub Center of Attention.

Organizations/Resources: Education, Anti-Defamation, Anti-Violence, Self-Defense

♂ ★♂♂ GLUD Policy Institute, PO Box 11311, Salt Lake City, UT 84147-0311 801-238-2526; 800-648-9996; glud@aol.com

Organizations/Resources: General, Multipurpose, Pride

♂ ★♂♂ Gay & Lesbian Community Council of Utah, 770 S 300 W, Salt Lake City, UT 84101-2603 801-539-8800

Organizations/Resources: Political/Legislative

♂ ★♂♂ Gay & Lesbian Utah Democrats, PO Box 11311, Salt Lake City, UT 84147-0311 801-238-2526; 800-648-9996; glud@aol.com

♂ ★&& GLUD Victory Fund, PO Box 11311, Salt Lake City, UT 84147-0311 801-238-2526; 800-648-9996; glud@aol.com

♂ ★ (?&) Log Cabin Utah, PO Box 3493, Salt Lake City, UT 84110-3493 801-461-5086

Organizations/Resources: Sport/Dance/Outdoor

♂ ★ (?&) Utah Gay Rodeo Association, mail to U.G.R.A. PO Box 511255, Salt Lake City, UT 84151-1255

Publications

♀ • Pillar Of The Gay Lesbian & Bisexual Community, c/o Uranian Publishing, PO Box 550898, Salt Lake City, UT 84152-0898 801-485-2345; 801-485-4930; Fax 801-466-4062

Real Estate

♀ • **Community Real Estate Referrals, 800-346-5592 "Free referral to gay/gay-supportive realtor in any USA city/state (including Virgin Is. & Puerto Rico). Sorry, no rentals!"**
◆ *Community Real Estate Referrals advertisement back cover*

Logan

Addictive Behavior, Substance Abuse, Recovery

♂ ★ Gay Alcoholics Anonymous, c/o GLA-CV UMC 0100 Box 119, Tagart Student Center; 84322-0100 801-752-1129

Organizations/Resources: General, Multipurpose, Pride

♀ ★ Alliance of Cache Valley (GLA-CV), Gay/Lesbian, UMC 0100 Box 119, Tagart Student Center; 84322-0100 801-752-1129

Religious Organizations & Publications

♂ & Metropolitan Community Church/Bridgerland, PO Box 4285; 84323-4285 801-753-3135

Ogden

Bars, Restaurants, Clubs, Discos

♀ • The Brass Rail, 103 27th St; 84401 801-399-1543 *P*

Park City

Bookstores: Gay/Lesbian/Feminist

♀ ○&& A Woman's Place, 1890 Bonanza Dr., Park City Plaza; 84060 801-649-2722 10am-9pm; Sat to 6pm; Sun noon-5pm. (no gay material for men)

Salt Lake City

☎ **Aardvaark Helpline 801-533-0927**

Accommodation: Hotels, B&B, Resorts, Campgrounds

♀ • (?&) Aardvark Bed & Breakfast, 801-533-0927

♀ • **Anton Boxrud B&B Inn, 57 South 600 East; 84102 801-363-8035; 800-524-5511; Fax 801-596-1316**

Addictive Behavior, Substance Abuse, Recovery

♀ Gay Alcoholics Anonymous, c/o St Mark's Episcopal Church 231 E 100 South; 84111 801-532-5908

Bars, Restaurants, Clubs, Discos

♀ • Aardvark's, 249 W 400 South; 84101 801-533-0927 *R*

♀ Bricks, 521 W 200 South; 84101 801-328-0255 *P*

♀ Club Excess, 32 Exchange Place; 84111-2706 *P*

♂ Deer Hunter, 636 S 300 West; 84101 801-363-1802 *P*

♀ Kings, 108 S 500 West; 84101-1128 801-521-5464 *P*

♀ Radio City Lounge, 147 S State St; 84111 801-532-9327

♂ Sun Club, 700 West 200 South; 84104 801-531-0833 *P*

♂ ○ & Trapp, 102 South 500 West; 84101 801-531-8727 ***BCW*** 11am-2am.

Bookstores: Gay/Lesbian/Feminist

♀ ○&& A Woman's Place, 1400 Foothill Drive; 84108 801-583-6431 10am-9pm; Sat to 6pm; Sun noon-5pm.

♀ ○&& A Woman's Place, 4835 S. Highland Dr #1205 (Holladay); 84117 801-278-9855 10am-9pm; Sat to 6pm; Sun noon-5pm.

Bookstores: General

♀ ○&& Golden Braid/Oasis Cafe, 151 South 500 East; 84102 801-322-1162

♀ • & Hayats Magazines & Gifts, 228 South Main St; 84101 801-531-6531 8am-11pm.

♀ ○ (&) King's English Bookstore, 1511 South 1500 East; 84105 801-484-9100 10am-9pm; Sun 11am-5pm.

♀ ○ & Waking Owl, 208 South 1300 East; 84102 801-582-7323 Fax 801-582-7323

Broadcast Media

♀ ★&& Concerning Gays & Lesbians, KRCL-FM 91, 208 W 800 South; 84101 801-363-1818 Wed 12.30-1pm (may change without notice). "All aspects of gay/lesbian/bisexual lives."

Business, Financial & Secretarial

♀ • Heart-Song, Brook, 801-484-3941 "Bookkeeping; income tax."

Entertainment-Related Services (see also Music, Organizations/Resources: Performing

♀ • Blue Wolf Productions & Management, 1338 East Foothill Blvd #152; 84108 801-595-8046 Fax 801-583-8419

Gifts, Cards, Pride & Novelty Items

♀ ○ Cahoots, 878 East 900 South; 84105 801-538-0606

♀ • (&) Mischievous Gifts & Cards, 559 S. 300 West; 84101 801-530-3100 Mon-Fri 10am-7pm; Sat to 6pm.

Grooming Services

♀ • & Hair & Body Works, 239 E 300 S.; 84111 801-595-1266 "Full hair service salon."

Insurance (see also Insurance Benefits/Viaticals)

♀ ○&& Bankers Life & Casualty, 3500 So Main #102; 84115 801-532-7632

Legal Services & Resources

♀ • Johnson, Howard P., 2480 South Main St #205; 84115 801-466-9151

Organizations/Resources: Social, Recreational & Support Groups (see also Sport/Dance/Outdoor)

♀ ★ (&&) Thursday Womyn's Group, 801-487-3953; 801-484-6325; Womyn's pot luck/social, very safe atmosphere: 1st & 3rd Thu 6-10pm.

Organizations/Resources: Sport/Dance/Outdoor

♀ • (&) Boyer Ski Instruction, 1233 S 1000 E.; 84105-1830 801-467-3409 "PSIA Certified level V; 20 yrs experience."

UT: Salt Lake City
Organizations: Sport

424
USA

Brattleboro : VT
Accommodation

⚥ Wasatch Leather Motorcycle Club, Box 1311; 84110 801-466-7804

Organizations/Resources: Student, Academic, Alumni/ae

⚥ ★ ♂♂ Lesbian & Gay Student Union, University of Utah, 234 Olpin Union Bldg; 84112 801-521-4026 Meeting Mon 7.30-9pm, Orson Spencer Hall #215.

Public Relations/Advertising Agencies

♀ • (?♂) David Nelson Communications, 261 N Main St #301; 84103-4602 801-355-6156; 801-597-9199; davidn1327@aol.com

Publications

♀ Labrys, 2120 South 700 East #H233; 84106 801-486-6473

Religious Organizations & Publications

⚥ (♂) Sacred Light of Christ Metropolitan Community Church, PO Box 11321; 84147-0321 801-595-0052

Switchboards, Helplines, Phone Information

♀ ★ (♂♂) Aardvaarks' Helpline, 801-533-0927

Vermont

State/County Resources

AIDS/HIV Support, Education, Advocacy, Publications

♀ ☆ (?♂) AIDS Community Resource Network (ACORN), PO Box 2057, Lebanon, NH 03766 603-448-2220 "Serves the Upper Valley region of New Hampshire & Vermont."

♀ ☆ ♂♂ Vermont AIDS Council, PO Box 275, Montpelier, VT 05601 802-229-2557

♀ ☆ (?♂) Vermont CARES (Committee for AIDS Resources, Education & Services), PO Box 5248, Burlington, VT 05401 802-863-2437; 800-649-2437

♀ ☆ (?♂) Vermont People With AIDS Coalition, PO Box 864, Bradford, VT 05033-0864 802-222-5123; 800-698-8792

Legal Services & Resources

♀ ☆ (♂) American Civil Liberties Union of Vermont (ACLU), 110 E State St, Montpelier, VT 05602 802-223-6304

Organizations/Resources: Bisexual Focus

⚥ ★ (?♂) Vermont Bisexual Network, PO Box 8124, Burlington, VT 05402

Organizations/Resources: Education, Anti-Defamation, Anti-Violence, Self-Defense

⚥ Lesbian Task Force, Vermont Network Against Domestic Violence & Sexual Assault, PO Box 405, Montpelier, VT 05691 802-223-1302

Organizations/Resources: Family

♂ ★ Gay Fathers Connection, PO Box 5506, Essex Jct, VT 05453-5506

Organizations/Resources: Political/Legislative

⚥ ★ ♂♂ Northeast Vermonters for Gay & Lesbian Rights (NEVGALR), c/o Umbrella Women's Center, 1 Prospect Ave, St Johnsbury, VT 05819 802-748-8645 (bisexual & straight welcome)

⚥ ★ ♂ Vermont Coalition for Lesbian & Gay Rights, PO Box 1125, Montpelier, VT 05601-1125 802-482-3927; 802-365-9139

♀ ☆ ♂♂ Vermont Human Rights Commission, 135 State St, Drawer 33, Montpelier, VT 05633 802-828-2480

Organizations/Resources: Social, Recreational & Support Groups (see also Sport/Dance/Outdoor)

⚥ ★ Rural Culture, PO Box 72, East St Johnsbury, VT 05838 "Network of agriculturists, enviros, permaculturists & other types of rural homesteaders."

⚥ ★ (♂♂) SAGE/Vermont, PO Box 863, Burlington, VT 05402-0863 802-860-1810

♂ ★ (?♂) Social Alternative for Gay Men (SAM), PO Box 479, Norwich, VT 05055 802-649-3133 Pub SAM Newsletter. "Non-threatening social & support environment for NH-VT central area. Please write for details."

⚥ ★ Vermont Gay Social Alternatives, PO Box 237, Burlington, VT 05402-0237 802-985-4937; 802-865-3734

Organizations/Resources: Sport/Dance/Outdoor

⚥ ★ Vermont Gay Volleyball (VGV), PO Box 248, Hinesburg, VT 05461 Game Sun 6-8pm, in Burlington.

♀ ★ (?♂) Women Of the Woods (WOW), RFD 1, Box 5620, Worcester, VT 05682 802-229-0109

Organizations/Resources: Youth (see also Family)

⚥ ★ ♂ Outright Vermont, PO Box 5235, Burlington, VT 05402-5235 802-865-9677; 800-GLB-CHAT; "Support group, library, resources for gay/lesbian/bisexual youth; education service for professionals working with youth."

Publications

⚥ ★ ♂ Out In The Mountains, PO Box 177, Burlington, VT 05402 "Monthly newspaper covering Vermont & New Hampshire; resource listings."

Religious Organizations & Publications

⚥ United Church Coalition for Lesbian/Gay Concerns, PO Box 388, West Rutland, VT 05777 802-438-2023

♂ Vermont Gay Men's Spiritual Support Brotherhood, 5 Raymond Place, Burlington, VT 05401 802-863-9684

Andover

Accommodation: Hotels, B&B, Resorts, Campgrounds

♀ • The Inn At High View, RR #1, Box 201A; 05143 / East Hill Road 802-875-2724
✦ Inn At High View advertisement page 425

Arlington

Accommodation: Hotels, B&B, Resorts, Campgrounds

♀ • (?♂) Candlelight Motel, PO Box 97; 05250 / Rt 7A 802-375-6647; 800-348-5294

Barre

Organizations/Resources: Family

♀ P-FLAG Central Vermont, 159 Sheridan St Ext; 05641 802-479-9246 "Parents, Families & Friends of Lesbians & Gays."

Bennington

AIDS/HIV Support, Education, Advocacy, Publications

♀ Bennington Area Aids Project, PO Box 1066; 05201 802-442-4481; 800-845-2437

Brattleboro

Accommodation: Hotels, B&B, Resorts, Campgrounds

♀ • 40 Putney Road B & B, 40 Putney Road; 05301 802-254-6268

VT: Brattleboro
AIDS/HIV Support

425
USA

Burlington : VT
Organizations: General

AIDS/HIV Support, Education, Advocacy, Publications

♀ ☆ ♿ Brattleboro Area AIDS Project, PO Box 1486; 05302 802-254-4444

Bars, Restaurants, Clubs, Discos

♀ • Common Ground Restaurant, 25 Elliot St; 05301 802-257-0855 *R*

Bookstores: General

♀ ○ ♿ Everyone's Books, 23 Elliot St; 05301 802-254-8160

Organizations/Resources: Family

♥ ★ P-FLAG Brattleboro Chapter, 409 Hillwinds; 05301 802-257-5409 "Parents, Families & Friends of Lesbians & Gays."

Organizations/Resources: General, Multipurpose, Pride

♥ Brattleboro Area Gays & Lesbians, PO Box 875; 05302 802-254-5947

Women's Centers

♥ Brattleboro Area Lesbian Center, 71 Eliot St; 05301

♀ ☆ Women's Crisis Center, PO Box 933; 05302 802-254-6954; 802-257-7364

Burlington

Accommodation: Hotels, B&B, Resorts, Campgrounds

♂ • Howden Cottage, 32 N Champlain St; 05401 802-864-7198
✦ *Howden Cottage advertisement page 425*

Addictive Behavior, Substance Abuse, Recovery

♥ ★ ♿ Gay/Lesbian Alcoholics Anonymous (GLAA), PO Box 5653; 05402 Thu 7-8pm.

Bars, Restaurants, Clubs, Discos

♥ • Pearls, 135 Pearl St; 05401 802-863-2343

Bookstores: General

♂ ○ ♿ Chassman & Bem Booksellers, 81 Church St; 05401 802-862-4332

♂ ☆ ♿ Peace & Justice Store, 21 Church St; 05401 802-863-8326 10am-6pm; Sun 1am-5pm.

Counseling/Therapy: Private

♂ • ♿ Berrizbeitia, Lauren, 431 Pine St; 05401 802-862-6931 "Gay & Lesbian positive; Lesbian feminist therapist."

♂ • (?♿) Partners In Growth & Recovery, 182 Main St; 05401 802-865-2403

♥ • (♿♿) Zeichner, Walter I., MACP, NCC, 269 Pearl St; 05401 802-863-0413

Graphic Design/Typesetting (see also Art; Printing)

♂ • BMH Graphic Design & Printing, 32 N Champlain St; 05401 802-864-7198

Health Care (see also AIDS Services)

♀ ☆ (?♿) Vermont Women's Health Center, PO Box 29; 05402 / 336 North Ave 802-863-1386 Fax 802-863-1774

Legal Services & Resources

♂ • ♿♿ Blackwood & Kraynak, PO Box 875; 05402 / 84 Pine St 802-863-2517

Organizations/Resources: Education, Anti-Defamation, Anti-Violence, Self-Defense

♀ ☆ ♿♿ Women Helping Battered Women, PO Box 1535; 05402 802-658-1996

♀ ☆ (?♿) Women's Rape Crisis Center, PO Box 92; 05402 / 215 College St 802-864-0555; 802-863-1236 hotline

Organizations/Resources: Ethnic, Multicultural

♥ Kwanzaa, PO Box 583; 05402-0583 "Multicultural educational resource group."

Organizations/Resources: Family

♂ ☆ P-FLAG Lake Champlain Chapter, 23 Birchwood Lane; 05401 802-863-4285 "Parents, Families & Friends of Lesbians & Gays."

♥ Vermont Lesbian & Gay Parents, c/o OITM, PO Box 177; 05402 802-660-2713

Organizations/Resources: General, Multipurpose, Pride

♀ ☆ ♿♿ Burlington Women's Council, Room 14, City Hall; 05401 802-658-9300 ext 125 Fax 802-865-7024 Tue-Thu 9am-5pm. "Advocacy, resource, referrals for women; knowledgeable about most Lesbian & Gay activity in Burlington & VT."

VT: Burlington

Organizations: Social & Support

426

USA

Shelburne : VT

Performing Arts

Organizations/Resources: Social, Recreational & Support Groups (see also Sport/Dance/Outdoor)

♀ ★ (?&) Crones, PO Box 242, Winooski; 05404 "For women over 40."

♂ Men Alive!, PO Box 423; 05402 802-865-2247

Organizations/Resources: Student, Academic, Alumni/ae

♂ ★&& Gay Lesbian Bisexual Alliance at UVM, University of Vermont, B-163 Billings; 05405 802-656-6300

Religious Organizations & Publications

♂ Dignity/Vermont, PO Box 782; 05402 802-863-1377

♂ ★&& Unitarian Universalists for Gay & Lesbian Concerns, 152 Pearl St; 05401 802-862-5630

Center Rutland: see Rutland

East Hardwick

Accommodation: Hotels, B&B, Resorts, Campgrounds

♀ ★ Greenhope Farm, RFD #1, Box 2260; 05836 802-533-7772

Grafton

Accommodation: Hotels, B&B, Resorts, Campgrounds

♀ • Wayfarer, PO Box 147; 05146 / Main St 802-843-2363

Hardwick

Bookstores: General

♂ ○ & Galaxy Bookstore, Box 1219; 05843 802-472-5533

Hartland Four Corners

Accommodation: Hotels, B&B, Resorts, Campgrounds

♀ • Twin Gables B&B, PO Box 101; 05049 802-436-3070

Hinesburg: see Burlington

Hyde Park

Accommodation: Hotels, B&B, Resorts, Campgrounds

♀ • Fitch Hill Inn, RFD #1 Box 1879, Fitch Hill Road; 05655 802-888-3834; 800-639-2903; *B*

Manchester Center

Bookstores: General

♂ ○ & Northshire Bookstore, PO Box 2200; 05255 / Main St 802-362-2200; 800-437-3700; 10pm-5.30pm; Fri to 9pm; Sat to 7pm.

Manchester

Organizations/Resources: Family

♂ ☆ P-FLAG (Contact), PO Box 92; 05254 802-362-4400 "Contact for Parents, Families & Friends of Lesbians & Gays; group itself disbanded."

Middlebury

Counseling/Therapy: Nonprofit

♀ ☆&& Addison County Women In Crisis, PO Box 67; 05753 802-388-4205

Legal Services & Resources

♂ ○&& Murray, Susan M, 15 S Pleasant St; 05753 802-388-6356

Montpelier

Bookstores: General

♂ ○ Bear Pond Books, 77 Main St; 05601 802-229-0774

North Bennington: see Bennington

North Clarendon: see Rutland

Northfield

Conferences/Events/Festivals/Workshops (see also Music)

♂ ★&& Radical Fairies, PO Box 88—Faerie Camp Destiny; 05663 802-485-6668

Plainfield

Organizations/Resources: Student, Academic, Alumni/ae

♂ Gay, Lesbian, Bisexual Alliance, Goddard College; 05667

Rutland

Erotica (Printed, Visual, Equipment)

♂ ○&& ABV Sales, 156 West St; 05701 802-773-8990 Mon-Fri 10am-9pm; Sat to 5pm. Peep shows.

Organizations/Resources: Family

♂ ☆ P-FLAG, 11 North St; 05701-3011 802-773-7601 "Parents, Families & Friends of Lesbians & Gays."

St Johnsbury

AIDS/HIV Support, Education, Advocacy, Publications

♂ ☆ (?&) Aids Community Awareness Project (ACAP), PO Box 648; 05819 802-533-2950

Organizations/Resources: Political/Legislative

♀ ★ (&&) NEQLACE (North East Queendom Lesbians Activating Community Empowerment), c/o Umbrella Women's Center, 1 Prospect Ave; 05819 802-748-8645

Organizations/Resources: Social, Recreational & Support Groups (see also Sport/Dance/Outdoor)

♂ ★ (?&) Game Ends, RR1 Box 261, New Boston Rd; 05819-9747 802-748-5849

♀ (&&) LUNA (Lesbians United, Never Apart), c/o Umbrella Women's Center, 1 Prospect Ave; 05819 802-748-8645

Women's Centers

♀ ★&& Umbrella Women's Center, 1 Prospect Ave; 05819 802-748-8645 "Lesbian support & resources."

Shaftsbury

Accommodation: Hotels, B&B, Resorts, Campgrounds

♀ • Country Cousin, Rt 1-B, Box 212, Old Depot Rd; 05262 802-375-6985; 800-479-6985; "Guest house."

Shelburne

Performing Arts: Entertainment, Music, Recording, Theater, etc.

♂ ★ Out On Stage Theatre Group, PO Box 546; 05482 802-862-7034

Stowe

Accommodation: Hotels, B&B, Resorts, Campgrounds

♂ • Buccaneer Country Lodge, 3214 Mountain Road; 05672 802-253-4772; 800-543-1293

♀ • Grunberg Haus Bed & Breakfast, RR #2 Box 1595, Rte 100 S., Waterbury; 05676 802-244-7726; 800-800-7760; grunhaus@aol.com

Erotica (Printed, Visual, Equipment)

♂ ○ Video Exchange, 21 Stowe St, Waterbury; 05676 802-244-7004 Mon-Fri 11am-9pm; Sat 10am-5pm. Peep shows.

Taftsville

Accommodation: Hotels, B&B, Resorts, Campgrounds

♀ • Maitland-Swan House, School St; 05073-0072 802-457-5181; 800-959-1404

Waterbury: see Stowe

Williamstown

Accommodation: Hotels, B&B, Resorts, Campgrounds

♀ • Autumn Crest Inn, Box 1540 Clark Rd; 05679 802-433-6627

Williamsville: see Brattleboro

Wilmington

Accommodation: Hotels, B&B, Resorts, Campgrounds

⚥ • The Yankee Moon, RR 1, Box 142; 05363 802-464-2691

Virgin Islands

State/County Resources

Accommodation: Reservations & Exchanges (see also Travel)

♀ ○ Rent A Villa, 800-533-6863 Over 100 private homes for vacation rental on St Croix; St John; St Thomas.
✦ *Rent A Villa advertisement page 427*

Real Estate

⚥ • Community Real Estate Referrals, 800-346-5592 "Free referral to gay/gay-supportive realtor in any USA city/state (including Virgin Is. & Puerto Rico). Sorry, no rentals!"
✦ *Community Real Estate Referrals advertisement back cover*

Saint Thomas   809

Accommodation: Hotels, B&B, Resorts, Campgrounds

♂ • Bellavista B&B, Box 1382, St Thomas; 00804 809-776-1529 Fax 809-777-4457

♂ • (♿) Blackbeard's Castle, PO Box 6041, Charlotte Amalie; 00804 809-776-1234; 800-344-5771; *BRE*

♂ • (♿) Danish Chalet Inn, PO Box 4319, Charlotte Amalie; 00803 800-635-1531; 809-774-5764; Fax 809-777-4886 *B*
✦ *Danish Chalet Inn advertisement page 427*

Bars, Restaurants, Clubs, Discos

♂ • ♿ Lemon Grass Cafe/R&R Night Club, Bakery Square 809-777-1877; 809-777-4457; *BDER*

St Croix   809

Accommodation: Hotels, B&B, Resorts, Campgrounds

⚥ • On The Beach Resort, PO Box 1908, Frederiksted, St Croix; 00841 809-772-1205; 800-524-2018; *BR*
✦ *On The Beach Resort advertisement page 427*

♂ ○ The Prince Street Inn, 402 Prince St, Frederiksted, St Croix; 00840 800-771-9550

Travel & Tourist Services (see also Accommodation)

♀ • ♿ Calparrio International Travel, W. 67 King St, Frederiksted, St Croix; 00840 809-773-5222; 800-253-0622; Fax 809-773-6116 "Gay/Lesbian/Bi vacations/cruises. Personalized Caribbean vacations."

Virginia

State/County Resources

Addictive Behavior, Substance Abuse, Recovery

⚥ • (♿♿) Pride Institute, 800-54-PRIDE "The nation's only accredited chemical dependency treatment center exclusively for Gay, Lesbian & Bisexual People."

VA: State/County Resources
AIDS/HIV Support

428

Charlottesville : VA
Bookstores: General

USA

AIDS/HIV Support, Education, Advocacy, Publications

♀ ☆ (?&) AIDS Council of Western Virginia, PO Box 598, Roanoke, VA 24004 703-982-AIDS; 800-354-3388; "Providing HIV/AIDS prevention & education throughout a 29-county area in SW Virginia."

♂ ☆&& Appalachian AIDS Coalition, PO Box 513, Abingdon, VA 24212 800-354-3388 (AIDS Council of Western Virginia) "Volunteer coalition for education, support & direct services."

♂ ☆&& Peninsula AIDS Foundation, 326 Main St, Newport News, VA 23601 804-591-0971

Legal Services & Resources

♀ ★&& GAYLAW Attorney Referral, 202-842-7732

Organizations/Resources: Business & Professional

→ Lambda Labor: p.208

Organizations/Resources: General, Multipurpose, Pride

♀ ★ Alliance of Lesbian & Gay Organizations of Western Virginia (ALGO), PO Box 21111, Roanoke, VA 24018

♀ ★ (?&) Northern Virginia Pride, Inc., PO Box 9533, Alexandria, VA 22304-0533 703-528-3659

Organizations/Resources: Political/Legislative

♀ ★ Virginia National Organization For Women (NOW), PO Box 25831, Richmond, VA 23260-5831 804-353-3616

♀ ★ (?&) Virginia Partisans Gay & Lesbian Democratic Club, PO Box 20633, Alexandria, VA 22320-1633 703-671-7023

♀ ★ ♂ Virginians for Justice, PO Box 342 Capital Stn, Richmond, VA 23202 800-258-7842 (2-JUSTICE): Hate Crimes Hotline, reporting line only, toll-free in VA) Pub *Virginians for Justice News.* "Lobbying organization."

Organizations/Resources: Social, Recreational & Support Groups (see also Sport/Dance/Outdoor)

♀ ★ (?&) Teddy Bear Leather Club of Virginia, PO Box 25545, Richmond, VA 23260 804-232-0646 Pub *TBLC Newsletter.*

Organizations/Resources: Sport/Dance/Outdoor

♀ ★ Atlantic States Gay Rodeo Association, PO Box 31208, Bethesda, MD 20824 202-298-0928

Publications: Directories, Bibliographies, Guides, Travel

♀ • Community Pages, PO Box 13186, Richmond, VA 23225 804-745-5053

♀ • *Lambda Directory*, published by MacGraphics, Inc. 198 S Rosemont, Virginia Beach, VA 23452 804-486-3546 Fax 804-431-1547

Publications

♀ ★ (?&) *Blue Ridge Lambda Press*, PO Box 237, Roanoke, VA 24002 703-890-3184

♀ • *Our Own Community Press*, 739 Yarmouth St, Norfolk, VA 23510 804-625-0700 Fax 804-625-6024

Real Estate

♀ • Community Real Estate Referrals, 800-346-5592 "Free referral to gay/gay-supportive realtor in any USA city/state (including Virgin Is. & Puerto Rico). Sorry, no rentals!"
♦ *Community Real Estate Referrals advertisement back cover*

Alexandria

AIDS/HIV Support, Education, Advocacy, Publications

♂ ☆ (?&) Northern Virginia Aids Ministry (NOVAM), 413 Duke St; 22314 703-739-2437

Organizations/Resources: General, Multipurpose, Pride

♀ ★ (&) Alexandria Gay & Lesbian Community Association, PO Box 19401; 22320 703-684-0444 Pub *Newsletter.*

Organizations/Resources: Social, Recreational & Support Groups (see also Sport/Dance/Outdoor)

♀ Retired GALA of NOVA, PO Box 16292; 22302-8292

Travel & Tourist Services (see also Accommodation)

♀ • && Just Vacations, Inc., 501 King St; 22314 703-838-0040

Annandale

Grooming Services

♀ • Jag Hair, 7306 Maple Place; 22003 703-256-8383 Call for hours.

Arlington

Bars, Restaurants, Clubs, Discos

♀ Italia Bella/Club 5878, 5878 N Washington Blvd; 22205 703-532-5878

Counseling/Therapy: Private

♀ • Cleaveland, H. Folger, PhD, 118 S Pershing Dr; 22204 703-660-3659

Organizations/Resources: General, Multipurpose, Pride

♀ ★ (&) Arlington Gay & Lesbian Alliance, PO Box 324; 22210 703-522-7660

Organizations/Resources: Social, Recreational & Support Groups (see also Sport/Dance/Outdoor)

♀ ★ (?&) Lambda Vegetarians, 116 S Garfield St; 22204 703-892-1082

Religious Organizations & Publications

♀ ★&& Dignity/Northern Virginia, PO Box 10037; 22210 703-912-1662 "Gay & Lesbian Catholics & their friends."

Blacksburg

Organizations/Resources: Student, Academic, Alumni/ae

♀ ★&& Lesbian, Gay & Bisexual Alliance at Virginia Tech, PO Box 686; 24063-0686 703-231-3790 lgba@vt.edu

Publications

♀ ☆ *Wimmins Community Calendar*, Box 555; 24063-0555

Charlottesville

☎ Lesbian & Gay Student Union Helpline 804-971-4942

Accommodation: Hotels, B&B, Resorts, Campgrounds

♀ • (?&) INTOUCH Camping & Event Center for Women, Route 2, Box 1096, Kents Store; 23084 804-589-6542 "Campground; cabins; RV's (no hookup."

AIDS/HIV Support, Education, Advocacy, Publications

♂ ☆ AIDS Support Group, PO Box 2322; 22902 804-979-7714

Bars, Restaurants, Clubs, Discos

♀ Tryangles, 212 W Water St; 229 804-296-8783

♀ • ♂ Tryangles Club, 212-214 W Water St; 22901 804-296-8783 *PBDE* Thu & Sun 9pm-1am; Fri & Sat to 4am.

Bookstores: General

♂ ○ The Quest Bookshop, 618 W Main St; 22903 804-295-3377; 800-3-HOW2BE

VA: Charlottesville
429
Lynchburg : VA

Organizations: General
USA
Organizations: General

Organizations/Resources: General, Multipurpose, Pride

♀ ★ ♿ Kindred Spirits, PO Box 3721; 22903 804-971-1555 Pub *Kindred Spirits*. "Support & social group serving gay/lesbian adults in Central Virginia."

Organizations/Resources: Student, Academic, Alumni/ae

♀ ★ (♿) Lesbian & Gay Student Union at the University of Virginia, PO Box 525 Newcomb Hall Stn; 22904 804-971-4942

Religious Organizations & Publications

♀ Metropolitan Community Church Charlottesville, PO Box 3275 University Stn; 22903 804-979-5206 Fax 804-979-5306

Switchboards, Helplines, Phone Information

♀ ★ Lesbian & Gay Student Union Helpline, Box 525 Newcomb Hall Stn; 22904 804-971-4942

Chesapeake

Bars, Restaurants, Clubs, Discos

♀ Raphael's, 1711 Park Ave; 23320 804-543-7289

Erotica (Printed, Visual, Equipment)

♀ ○ T.R.'s Leather Rack, PO Box 13307; 23325-0307 / 1110 S. Military Hwy; 23320 804-420-4474 9am-6pm; Sun 1-5pm; eves by appointment. Also Rolling Leathers II mobile store will come to your show or event.

Clifton Forge

Organizations/Resources: Political/Legislative

♀ National Organization For Women (NOW)/Alleghany Highlands Chapter, c/o 501 Brussells St; 24422

Colonial Beach

Accommodation: Hotels, B&B, Resorts, Campgrounds

♀ ● (♿) Tucker Inn, 21 Weems St; 22443 (may relocate in Fall 1995) 804-224-2031 kmk415@aol.com "B&B homestay; seasonal outdoor activities; homespun comfort."

Danville

AIDS/HIV Support, Education, Advocacy, Publications

♀ ☆♿ Southside AIDS Venture, 326 Taylor Dr; 24541 804-799-5190

Emory

Organizations/Resources: Student, Academic, Alumni/ae

♀ ★ Emory & Henry Gay & Lesbian Student Union, c/o Box BBB; 24327 703-944-4121

Falls Church

Bookstores: Recovery, Metaphysical, & other Specialty

♀ ● ♿ Happy Joyous & Free, 6112-D Arlington Blvd; 22044 703-534-5233 10am-8pm; Sat to 6pm; Sun noon-5pm. "12-Step recovery, meditation books, music, jewelry."

Religious Organizations & Publications

♀ ★♿ Metropolitan Community Church of Northern Virginia, 7245 Lee Hwy; 22046 703-532-0992 Worship Sun 6pm, Fairfax Unitarian Church, 2709 Hunter Mill Rd, Oakton

♀ ★♿ Telos Ministries, Inc., PO Box 3390; 22043 703-560-2680 (Baptist)

Fredericksburg

AIDS/HIV Support, Education, Advocacy, Publications

♀ ☆♿ Fredericksburg Area HIV/AIDS Support Services, Inc., 415 Elm St; 22401 703-371-7532; 703-371-7631

Bookstores: Gay/Lesbian/Feminist

♀ ● ♿ The Purple Moon, 810 Caroline St; 22401 703-372-9885

Organizations/Resources: Political/Legislative

♀ National Organization For Women (NOW)/Fredericksburg, c/o 1509 Prince Edward St; 22401 703-371-3862

Organizations/Resources: Student, Academic, Alumni/ae

♀ ★♿ Mary Washington College Gay/Lesbian/Bisexual Student Association, MWC Box 603; 22401-4666

Harrisonburg

AIDS/HIV Support, Education, Advocacy, Publications

♀ Valley AIDS Network, College of Nursing, James Madison University; 22807 703-564-0448

Organizations/Resources: Student, Academic, Alumni/ae

♀ Harmony, James Madison University Box 7119; 22807

Luray
Area code changes to 540 July 1995

Accommodation: Hotels, B&B, Resorts, Campgrounds

♀ ● Ruby Rose Inn B&B, Rte 2, Box 147, Stanley; 22851 703-778-4680

♀ ○ The Ruffner House, Rte 4, Box 620; 22835 703-743-7855

Printing & Promotional Items (see also Art; Graphics/Typesetting)

♀ ● Page Printing Connection, Rt 4 Box 537; 22835 703-743-7746 Fax 703-743-1257

Lynchburg

Counseling/Therapy: Private

♀ ○ Counseling Center, 415 Harrison St; 24504 804-845-5783 24 hrs. "Counseling & mediation."

♀ ○ ♿ Winder, Jon, 2095 Langhorne Rd; 24501 804-845-4927

Organizations/Resources: General, Multipurpose, Pride

♀ ★ Central Virginia Gay & Lesbian Activities (GALA), PO Box 10511; 24506 804-847-5242

Organizations/Resources: Student, Academic, Alumni/ae

♀ ★ (?♿) Bridges, Randolph-Macon Women's College, 2500 Rivermont Ave; 24503

Martinsville

AIDS/HIV Support, Education, Advocacy, Publications

♂ ☆ West Piedmont AIDS Task Force, PO Box 3413; 24115 703-666-8149

McLean

Grooming Services

♂ ● ♿ Accent Hair, 6800 Fleetwood Rd, #106 McLean House; 22101 703-356-8988

New Market
Area code changes to 540 July 1995

Accommodation: Hotels, B&B, Resorts, Campgrounds

♀ ● A Touch of Country, 9329 Congress St; 22844 703-740-8030 "Bed & breakfast in the Shenendoah Valley."

Newport News

Bookstores: Gay/Lesbian/Feminist

♀ ○ Out of the Dark, 530 Randolph Rd; 23601 804-596-6220

Massage Therapy (Licensed only)

♂ ● ♿ Triangle Therapy, 12388 Warwick Blvd #303; 23606-3850 804-591-8735 "Massage Therapy & Intuitive Consultations."

Organizations/Resources: Social, Recreational & Support Groups (see also Sport/Dance/Outdoor)

♂ ★ (?♿) Tidewater Bears, Box 2241; 23609-0241 804-622-8755 twbears@aol.com

Norfolk

☎ Gay Information Line 804-622-GAYS

Addictive Behavior, Substance Abuse, Recovery

♂ ★ Chit Chat AA Group, 3401 Tidewater Dr; 23509 804-625-2613

♂ ★ ♿ Triangle Service Recovery Center, 1610 Meadowlake Dr; 23518 Various 12-step recovery programs; meetings nightly.

AIDS/HIV Support, Education, Advocacy, Publications

♂ ☆ ♿ AIDS Fund, 9229 Granby St; 23503-4441 804-583-1317 Fax 804-583-2749

Bars, Restaurants, Clubs, Discos

♀ ○ ♿ Charlie's Cafe, 1800 Granby St; 23517 804-625-0824 *B*

♂ Charlotte's Web, PO Box 6348; 23508 / 6425 Tidewater Drive 804-853-6021

♂ Club Rumors (Oar House), 4107 Colley Ave; 23505 804-489-8257

♂ ● ♿ Cue Club Disco, 4601 Killam Ave; 23508 804-489-9740 *BRDEL*

♂ Garage, 731 Granby St; 23510 804-623-0303

♀ Hershee Lounge, 6117 Sewells Pt. Rd; 23513 804-853-9842

♂ Iron Works, 4019 Granby St; 23504 804-623-8205

♂ ● Late Show/Cafe Lounge Restaurant, 114 E. 11th St (between Granby & Monticello) 804-623-3854 *BDRLP* "Private club; check with local clubs for entry information."

♀ Ms. P, 6401 Tidewater Dr; 23509 804-853-9717

♂ ○ ♿ Nutty Buddy's, 143 E Little Creek Rd; 23505 804-588-6474 *BDR* 4pm-2am; Sat 5pm-2am.

♂ Private Eyes, 249 W York St; 23510 804-533-9290

♀ The Shirley's, 423-425 Monticello Ave; 23510 804-625-1400

Bookstores: Gay/Lesbian/Feminist

♂ ● Bad Habits Etc., 6123 Sewells Pt Rd Box 10038; 23513 804-857-0223

♂ ● ♿ Outright Books & Cafe, 9229 Granby St; 23503 804-480-8428

♂ ● **Phoenix Rising, 808 Spotswood Ave; 23517 804-622-3701 Sun-Wed Noon-7pm; Thu-Sat to 9pm.**
◆ *Phoenix Rising advertisement page 429*

♂ ★ (♿) Pride Bookstore (New Life MCC), PO Box 1026; 23501-1026 804-855-8450 Call for hours & location.

Community Centers (see also Women's Centers)

♂ Triangle Services Center, PO Box 11471; 23517 804-497-0814

Erotica (Printed, Visual, Equipment)

♀ ○ Gears, Clothing & Accessories, 733 Granby St; 23510 804-622-4438 tue-Sat 10am-6pm. "Adult store (custom leather clothing)."

Legal Services & Resources

♂ ☆ ♿ American Civil Liberties Union, Hampton Roads Chapter (ACLU), PO Box 11409; 23517

♂ ● Harman, Richard S., 207 Granby St; 23510 804-622-9143

Organizations/Resources: Business & Professional

♀ ★ Lambda Funding, 804-440-4674 lambdafund@aol.com "We buy privately held notes, mortgages & trust deed nationwide."

Organizations/Resources: General, Multipurpose, Pride

♂ ★ ♿ Hampton Roads Lesbian & Gay Pride Coalition, PO Box 1053; 23501-1053 804-489-8000

Organizations/Resources: Political/Legislative

♀ ★ ♿ National Organization for Women (NOW)/Tidewater, PO Box 11051; 23517 804-456-1509

Organizations/Resources: Social, Recreational & Support Groups (see also Sport/Dance/Outdoor)

♂ ★ (?♿) Alternative Lifestyle Support Organization (A.L.S.O), PO Box 891; 23501 804-855-5212 "Completely alcohol & chemical free environment."

♂ Knight Hawks, Box 606; 23501 804-623-0737

Organizations/Resources: Student, Academic, Alumni/ae

♂ ODU Gay & Lesbian Student Union, Old Dominion University, Webb Center, Student Activities Office; 23508

Publications

→ *Our Own Community Press: p.428*
♂ Out & About, PO Box 120112; 23502 804-727-0037

Religious Organizations & Publications

♂ ★ Dignity/Norfolk, PO Box 434; 23501 804-625-5337 "Gay & Lesbian Catholics & their friends."

♀ ★ (♿) New Life Metropolitan Community Church, PO Box 1026; 23501-1026 / 1530 Johnstons Rd 804-855-8450 newlifemcc@aol.com Services Sun 8.45am & 10.30am; 6.30pm; Wed Bible Study 7.30pm.

⚥ ★ (♿) Unitarian Universalists for Lesbian & Gay Concerns, 739 Yarmouth St; 23510 804-627-5371 Meets 2nd & 4th Fri, 7.30pm.

Switchboards, Helplines, Phone Information

⚥ ★ Gay Information Line, PO Box 1325; 23501 804-622-GAYS; 804-623-BARS

Travel & Tourist Services (see also Accommodation)

⚥ ○ Moore Travel, Inc, 7516 Granby St.; 23505 804-583-2361

Radford

AIDS/HIV Support, Education, Advocacy, Publications

⚥ ☆ (♿) New River Valley AIDS Coalition, PO Box 329; 24141 703-639-5881

Organizations/Resources: Student, Academic, Alumni/ae

⚥ ★♿♿ Radford Alternative Alliance, Radford University, PO Box 5894; 24142 703-831-5727 "Support & social group."

Reston

Organizations/Resources: Social, Recreational & Support Groups (see also Sport/Dance/Outdoor)

⚦ Dulles Triangles, PO Box 3411; 22090-1411 703-471-5096

Richmond

Addictive Behavior, Substance Abuse, Recovery

⚦ SAA, 2204 Lashley Lane; 23233 804-740-6857 Sex Addicts Anonymous 12-step group.

AIDS/HIV Support, Education, Advocacy, Publications

⚥ ☆ Central Virginia AIDS Services & Education (CVASE), 112 N Boulevard; 23220-4304 804-359-4783 "Support activities for PWA's; temporary housing available."

⚥ ☆ ♿ Richmond AIDS Information Network, Fan Free Clinic, Box 5669; 23220 / 1721 Hanover Ave 804-358-AIDS Mon-Fri 10am-10pm.

Architectural Services (see also Home/Building)

⚥ ● Community Planning & Design, 3310 Ellwood Ave #D; 23221-2952 804-353-5572

Bars, Restaurants, Clubs, Discos

⚦ Babe's, 3166 W Cary St; 23221 804-355-9330

⚥ Broadway Cafe, 1624 W Broad St; 23220 804-355-9931 *B*

⚥ Casablanca, 6 East Grace St; 23219 804-648-2040

⚦ Christopher's, 2811 W Cary St; 23221 804-358-6469

⚥ ○ Club Colours, 536 N Harrison St; 23220 804-353-9776 *BDER*

⚥ ● (♿) Fielden's, 2033 W Broad St; 23220 804-359-1963 *PBD* Tue-Sun mdnt-6am.

⚦ Pyramyd Bar & Restaurant, 1008 North Blvd; 23273 804-358-3838 *BR*

Bookstores: Gay/Lesbian/Feminist

⚥ ● (♿) Phoenix Rising, 19 N Belmont Ave; 23221 804-355-7939 11am-7pm.
◆ *Phoenix Rising advertisement page 429*

Bookstores: General

⚥ ○ Biff's Bookstore, 2930 W Cary St; 23221 804-359-4831

Counseling/Therapy: Private

⚥ ● ♂ Commonwealth Professional Services, 12 S Auburn Ave; 23221 804-353-1169

♀ ● (♿) Jean, Paula J., PhD, 907 Westwood Ave; 23222 804-329-3940

Erotica (Printed, Visual, Equipment)

⚦ ○ Daddy Bear's Leather, (inside Christopher's) 306 Roehampton Court; 23236 804-323-3147

Graphic Design/Printing/Typesetting (see also Art)

⚥ ● ICU2 Publications, 3310 Ellwood Ave #D; 23221-2952 804-353-5304 "Desktop publishing, freelance writing, graphic design, photography."

Graphic Design/Typesetting (see also Art; Printing)

⚥ ● McMillan Designs, PO Box 13186; 23225 804-745-5053

Legal Services & Resources

⚥ ○ (♿) North, Pia J., Esq, 422 E Franklin St; 23219-2226 804-643-2889

Organizations/Resources: Bisexual Focus

⚥ ★ Richmond Area Bisexual Network (ROBIN), c/o Phoenix Rising, 19 N Belmont Ave; 23221 804-355-7939 Pub *Bi Lines*.

Organizations/Resources: Business & Professional

⚥ ★ (♿) 10-11 Association, PO Box 107 MCV Stn; 23298-0107 804-355-1606 "Gay, Lesbian & Bisexual medical professionals, students, & their friends. Monthly meetings."

Organizations/Resources: Ethnic, Multicultural

⚥ ★ Lesbian Women of Color (LWOC), PO Box 35093; 23235-0093 Pub *LWOC Newsletter*.

VA: Richmond
Organizations: General

432
USA

Virginia Beach : VA
Bars, Clubs, Restaurants

Organizations/Resources: General, Multipurpose, Pride

♀ ★ Richmond Lesbian/Gay Pride Coalition, PO Box 14747, Stewart Station; 23221 804-353-4133

Organizations/Resources: Political/Legislative

♀ ☆ (?⚳) National Organization For Women (NOW)/Richmond, PO Box 25831; 23260 804-780-9092

♀ ★ ♂♂ Richmond Lesbian-Feminists, PO Box 7216; 23221 804-379-6422 Pub *RLF Flyer*.

Organizations/Resources: Sport/Dance/Outdoor

♀ ★ Richmond Lesbian & Gay Country Dance & Social Club, 804-794-9458 *d*

Organizations/Resources: Student, Academic, Alumni/ae

♀ ★ ♂♂ Sexual Minority Student Alliance, Virginia Commonwealth University, Student Activities Center, 907 Floyd Ave, Box 75; 23284-2035 804-367-6509

Religious Organizations & Publications

♀ ★ (?⚳) Central Virginia Affirmation: United Methodists for Lesbian, Gay & Bisexual Concerns, PO Box 501, Hanover; 23069-0501 / 700 W. Franklin St; 23220 804-746-7279

♀ ★ Metropolitan Community Church of Richmond, 2501 Park Ave; 23220 804-353-9477

Roanoke
Area code changes to 540 July 1995

Addictive Behavior, Substance Abuse, Recovery

♀ ★ AA Group, 828 Campbell Ave SW; 24016 703-343-9099; 703-366-9224; Sun 5pm.

AIDS/HIV Support, Education, Advocacy, Publications

♀ ☆ Blue Ridge AIDS Support Services (BRASS), PO Box 1472; 24007 703-982-AIDS

♀ Roanoke AIDS Project, PO Box 4367; 24015 703-224-2979

Bars, Restaurants, Clubs, Discos

♀ Back Street Cafe, 356 Salem Ave SW; 24011 703-345-1542 *R*

♀ ● ♂ The Park, 615 SW Salem Ave 703-342-0946 ***BRDE*** Wed & Fri-Sun opens 9pm.

♂ The Stag, 9 Salem Ave SW; 24011 703-982-1668

Bookstores: Gay/Lesbian/Feminist

♀ ○ **Phoenix Rising West, 26 Kirk Ave SW; 24011 703-985-6886**
♦ ***Phoenix Rising West advertisement page 429***

Erotica (Printed, Visual, Equipment)

♀ ○ Magic City Video, 2211 Williamson Rd NW; 24012 703-362-9248

Florists (see also Gardening)

♀ ● George's, 430 Church Ave SW; 24016 703-343-1567

Funding: Endowment, Fundraising, Scholarship

♀ ☆ Hands Fund, PO Box 1472; 24007 703-982-AIDS "Gives away 100% of monies raised to PWA's."

Organizations/Resources: Education, Anti-Defamation, Anti-Violence, Self-Defense

♀ Committee for Lesbian & Gay Concerns, PO Box 4652; 24015

Organizations/Resources: Family

♀ ★ (?⚳) P-FLAG, 180 Bailey Blvd, Hardy; 24101-3501 703-890-3957

Organizations/Resources: General, Multipurpose, Pride

♀ ★ (?⚳) Roanoke Valley Gay & Lesbian Alliance, PO Box 237; 24002 703-982-3733

Organizations/Resources: Social, Recreational & Support Groups (see also Sport/Dance/Outdoor)

♀ ★ (⚳) Gay Rap of Roanoke, PO Box 6125; 24017 703-981-1556

♂ ★ (?⚳) I Like Your Outfit (ILYO), PO Box 1355; 24007 703-343-8481 (nudists)

♀ ★ The Supper Club, PO Box 3327; 24015 703-772-5702

Organizations/Resources: Student, Academic, Alumni/ae

♀ ☆ Harmony, Hollins College Box 9271; 24020

Organizations/Resources: Youth (see also Family)

♀ Outright (Roanoke), 402 Elm Ave SW; 24016 703-344-1948

Religious Organizations & Publications

♀ ★ ♂ Metropolitan Community Church of the Blue Ridge, PO Box 20495; 24018 703-366-0839 Service Sun 3pm at Unitarian Church, 2015 Grandin Rd SW.

♀ Unitarian Universalist Church, 2015 Grandin Rd SW; 24015-3525 703-342-8888

Springfield

Organizations/Resources: General, Multipurpose, Pride

♀ ★ (?⚳) Fairfax Lesbian & Gay Citizens Association (FLGCA), PO Box 2322; 22152 703-451-9528

Staunton

AIDS/HIV Support, Education, Advocacy, Publications

♀ ☆ ♂♂ AIDS Resources of Central Shenendoah, PO Box 1847; 24401 703-886-7116

Sweet Briar

Organizations/Resources: Student, Academic, Alumni/ae

♀ ★ Alternatives, PO Box 752; 24595 804-381-6100

Vienna

Bookstores: General

♀ ○ ♂♂ Borders Bookshop & Espresso Bar, 8311 Leesburg Pike; 22182 703-556-7766

Erotica (Printed, Visual, Equipment)

♀ ○ ♂ **Night Dreams, Inc., 8381 Leesburg Pike, Vienna, VA 22182 800-AROUSE-U; 703-556-8839; "Large selection of adult toys, creams, lotions, lingerie, menswear, books, gag gifts, etc."**
♦ ***Night Dreams, Inc. advertisement page 431***

Virginia Beach

Accommodation: Hotels, B&B, Resorts, Campgrounds

♀ ● (?⚳) **Coral Sand Motel, 2307 Pacific Ave; 23451 804-425-0872; 800-828-0872**
♦ ***Coral Sand Motel advertisement page 433***

Addictive Behavior, Substance Abuse, Recovery

♀ ☆ ♂♂ Live & Let Live AA Group, c/o Messiah Lutheran Church, 4136 Holland Rd; 23452

Bars, Restaurants, Clubs, Discos

♂ ○ Ambush, 2838 Virginia Beach Blvd; 23452 804-498-4301

⚥ • ♿ Julius, 2901 Baltic Ave; 23451 804-428-3927

Counseling/Therapy: Private

⚥ ○ (♿) Davis, Bill, LCSW, 4616 Westgrove Ct; 23455 804-460-4655

⚥ • ♿ Independence Psychotherapy Services, 485 S Independence Blvd #109; 23452 804-490-0707

⚥ ○ Walter, Daniel, Psy.D., 5320 Providence Rd #206; 23464 804-424-0100

Graphic Design/Typesetting (see also Art; Printing)

⚥ • (♿) MacGraphics, Inc., 198 S Rosemont; 23452 804-486-3546 Fax 804-431-1547

Religious Organizations & Publications

⚥ ★♿ All God's Children Community Church, 485 S Independence Blvd #112; 23452 804-499-7096 Services Sun 10.30am; Wed 7.30pm.

Williamsburg

Organizations/Resources: Social, Recreational & Support Groups (see also Sport/Dance/Outdoor)

⚥ ★ Lavender Light, PO Box 63; 23187-0063

Organizations/Resources: Student, Academic, Alumni/ae

⚥ ★ ♿ Alternatives, College of William & Mary, c/o Student Activities Center, Campus Center; 23185 804-221-3309

Woodbridge

Organizations/Resources: Social, Recreational & Support Groups (see also Sport/Dance/Outdoor).

⚥ ★ Prince William Gay & Lesbian Association, PO Box 4231; 22194

Woodstock

AIDS/HIV Support, Education, Advocacy, Publications

⚥ ☆ Aid for AIDS, Inc., PO Box 147; 22664 703-459-8208

Washington

State/County Resources

Addictive Behavior, Substance Abuse, Recovery

⚥ • (♿) Pride Institute, 800-54-PRIDE "The nation's only accredited chemical dependency treatment center exclusively for Gay, Lesbian & Bisexual People."

AIDS/HIV Support, Education, Advocacy, Publications

⚥ ★(♿) Names Project/Washington Chapter, 1202 E Pike #654, Seattle, WA 98122-3934 206-233-8591 Pub *Quilt Quarterly News.*

Archives/Libraries/History Projects

⚥ ★ (♿) Lesbian & Gay Heritage Alliance, 1425 E Prospect St #5, Seattle, WA 98112 206-323-3007

Broadcast Media

⚥ ★ Night Scene, 13 NW 13th Ave, Portland, OR 97209 503-244-NITE Cable access TV show: call for details.

Computer Bulletin Boards

⚥ ○ Shadowplay BBS, 1202 E Pike St #924, Seattle, WA 98122 206-706-0992 (modem) Fax 206-706-0992 syspo1@seattle.com "Leather/BDSM/Fetish BBS. Adult files, fun & Internet."

Legal Services & Resources

⚥ ☆♿♿ American Civil Liberties Union of Washington (ACLU), 705 2nd Ave #300, Seattle, WA 98104-1711 206-624-2184

Organizations/Resources: Bisexual Focus

⚥ ★ (♿) BiNet Washington, PO Box 30645 Greenwood Stn, Seattle, WA 98103-0645 206-728-4533

Organizations/Resources: Business & Professional

⚥ ★♿♿ Boeing Employees Association of Gays & Lesbians (BEAGLES), PO Box 1733, Renton, WA 98057 206-781-3587

⚥ National Lesbian/Gay Journalists Association, 1202 E Pike St #1175, Seattle, WA 98122-3934

Organizations/Resources: Political/Legislative

⚥ ☆♿♿ Washington Citizens for Fairness, 1202 E Pike St #532, Seattle, WA 98122

⚥ Washington Freedom Coalition, 412 Division St NW #A, Olympia, WA 98502 360-943-4662

Real Estate

⚥ • Community Real Estate Referrals, 800-346-5592 "Free referral to gay/gay-supportive realtor in any USA city/state (including Virgin Is. & Puerto Rico). Sorry, no rentals!"
✦ *Community Real Estate Referrals advertisement back cover*

Religious Organizations & Publications

⚥ ★ Affirmation Seattle, PO Box 23223, Seattle, WA 98102 206-820-5729 *The Open Closet.* "Lesbian & Gay Mormons."

Bellingham

Bars, Restaurants, Clubs, Discos

⚥ • ♿ Rumors Cabaret, 1317 1/2 State St; 98225 360-671-1849; 360-647-1939; *BDE* Noon-2am.

Bookstores: General

⚥ ○ The Newsstand, 111 E Magnolia; 98225

Erotica (Printed, Visual, Equipment)

⚥ • Great Northern Books, 1308 Railroad; 98225 360-733-1650

Organizations/Resources: Student, Academic, Alumni/ae

⚥ ★♿♿ Lesbian Gay Bisexual Alliance Western Washington University, Viking Union Box I-1; 98225-9106 360-650-6120

Religious Organizations & Publications

⚥ ★♿♿ Song of Messiah Metropolitan Community Church, PO Box 4389; 98227 360-671-1172

WA: Bellingham
Women's Centers

434
USA

Pasco : WA
Organizations: Student

Women's Centers

♀ ☆&& Western Washington University Women's Center, Viking Union #211; 98225 360-650-6114

Bremerton

Organizations/Resources: Social, Recreational & Support Groups (see also Sport/Dance/Outdoor)

♀ ★ (?&) West Sound Family, PO Box 2688; 98310 360-792-3960

Chelan

Accommodation: Hotels, B&B, Resorts, Campgrounds

♀ ○ Whaley Mansion Inn, 415 3rd St; 98816 509-682-5735; 800-729-2408; Fax 509-682-5385

Cheney: see Spokane

Everett

AIDS/HIV Support, Education, Advocacy, Publications

♀ ☆ North Puget Sound AIDS Foundation, PO Box 526; 98206 360-659-8045

Bars, Restaurants, Clubs, Discos

♀ The Everett Underground, 1212 California Ave; 98200 206-339-0807 *BDR*

♀ Philadelphia's, 1909 Hewitt Ave; 98201 206-303-0809 *BR*

Religious Organizations & Publications

♀ ★ & New Creation Metropolitan Community Church, PO Box 2463; 98203-0463 206-316-3146

Index

Accommodation: Hotels, B&B, Resorts, Campgrounds

♀ • Wild Lily Ranch, PO Box 313; 98256 360-793-2103

Issaquah

Accommodation: Hotels, B&B, Resorts, Campgrounds

♀ ○ The Country Inn B&B, 685 Northwest Juniper St; 98027 206-392-1010

Kennewick

AIDS/HIV Support, Education, Advocacy, Publications

♀ Tri-Cities Chaplaincy/Tri-Cities Cares, 7525 W Deschutes Pl #2A; 99336 509-783-0873

Langley

Accommodation: Hotels, B&B, Resorts, Campgrounds

♀ • (&) The Gallery Suite, PO Box 458; 98260 360-221-2978

Lilliwaup

Accommodation: Hotels, B&B, Resorts, Campgrounds

♀ ○ (&&) Mike's Beach Resort, N. 38470 Hwy. 101; 98555-9998 360-877-5324

Lopez

Accommodation: Hotels, B&B, Resorts, Campgrounds

♀ • (?&) Inn at Swifts Bay, Rte 2, Box 3402; 98261 360-468-3636 "Bed & breakfast."

Mercer Island: see Seattle

Mount Vernon

Accommodation: Hotels, B&B, Resorts, Campgrounds

♀ ○ White Swan Guest House, 1388 Moore Rd; 98273 360-445-6805 Bed & breakfast.

Organizations/Resources: Social, Recreational & Support Groups (see also Sport/Dance/Outdoor)

♀ ★ & Gays, Lesbians, Bisexuals of Skagit (GLBS), mail to GLBS, 1500A East College Way #458; 98273 360-428-9217 Pub *Skagit Gay Times*.

Religious Organizations & Publications

♂ Angels Among Us Metropolitan Community Church, 410 N 21st St; 98273-3507 800-809-8590

Ocean Park

Accommodation: Hotels, B&B, Resorts, Campgrounds

♀ • (&) Shakti Cove Cottages, PO Box 385; 98640 360-665-4000

Olympia

AIDS/HIV Support, Education, Advocacy, Publications

♀ ☆&& Olympia AIDS Task Force, 1408 State Ave NE #1; 98506-4457 360-352-2375 Pub *Pulse*. "Services include support, housing, education, emergency financial grants, etc."

Bars, Restaurants, Clubs, Discos

♀ Smithfield Cafe, 212 W 4th Ave; 98502 360-786-1725

♀ • && Thekla, 116 E 5th Ave; 98501 360-352-1855 *BDE*

Bookstores: General

♀ ○ & Bulldog News, 116 E 4th Ave; 98501 360-357-NEWS

Community Centers (see also Women's Centers)

♀ ★&& Evergreen Queer Alliance, CAB 314, Evergreen State College; 98505 360-866-6000 x6544 Fax 360-866-6793

Health Care Products

♀ • (&&) Radiance Herbs & Massage, 113 E 5th; 98501 360-357-5250 Mon-Sat 10am-8pm. "Herbs, cruelty-free bodycare, jewelry, ceremonial supplies, incense, music, books, etc. We prefer not to receive mail from vendors."

Organizations/Resources: General, Multipurpose, Pride

♂ Lavender Action, PO Box 7703; 98507 360-943-4662

Organizations/Resources: Political/Legislative

♂ Running Proud, PO Box 7703; 98507-7703 360-943-4662

Organizations/Resources: Social, Recreational & Support Groups (see also Sport/Dance/Outdoor)

♀ ★ (?&) Lesbian Fun Society, Box 10321; 98502 Pub *Lesbian Fun Society News Tribune*.

Publications

♀ ★ *Sound Out*, PO Box 1844; 98507 360-791-3355

Pasco

Bars, Restaurants, Clubs, Discos

♀ Luca's Place, 3408 W Court St; 99301 509-545-1989

Organizations/Resources: Student, Academic, Alumni/ae

♂ Campus Association of Gay/Lesbian Individuals, Columbia Basin College, 2600 N 20th Ave; 99301 509-547-0511 x339

Port Townsend

Accommodation: Hotels, B&B, Resorts, Campgrounds

♀ ○ (♆♿) Ravenscroft Inn, 533 Quincy St; 98368 360-385-2784 Fax 360-385-6724

Home & Building: Cleaning, Repair, General Contractors

♀ ○ Hess Construction, Remodeling & Design, PO Box 801; 98368 360-385-9669 Lic. #PAULHCD063R9 "Specializing in Victorian remodeling & rehab."

Pullman

Organizations/Resources: Military/Veterans

⚥ Inland Northwest Gay, Lesbian & Bisexual Veterans Association, PO Box 3145 College Stn; 99165 509-335-1369

Organizations/Resources: Student, Academic, Alumni/ae

♀ ★♿ Gay, Lesbian, Bisexual Program, Daggy Mall #6, Washington State University—Pullman; 99164-2420 509-335-6428

Richland

Organizations/Resources: Political/Legislative

♀ ☆ Washington Citizens for Fairness: Tri-cities Coalition, PO Box 3030; 99352

Religious Organizations & Publications

♀ ★ (♿) River of Life Metropolitan Community Church, PO Box 1678; 99352-0059 509-544-9689

Seattle

Accommodation: Hotels, B&B, Resorts, Campgrounds

♀ ● Bacon Mansion/Broadway Guest House, 959 Broadway East; 98102 206-329-1864; 800-240-1864; Fax 206-860-9025

◆ *Bacon Mansion/Broadway Guest House advertisement page 435*

♀ ○ Capitol Hill Inn, 1713 Belmont Ave; 98122 206-323-1955 Bed & breakfast.

♀ ○ Chambered Nautilus Bed & Breakfast Inn, 5005 22nd Ave NE; 98105 206-522-2536 Fax 206-522-0404

♀ ● Gaslight Inn, 1727 15th Ave; 98122 206-325-3654

⚥ ● Hill House Bed & Breakfast, 1113 East John; 98102 206-720-7161; 800-720-7161; Fax 206-323-0772 "Quality accommodations at reasonable prices."

◆ *Hill House Bed & Breakfast advertisement page 435*

♀ ● Landes House, 712 11th Ave E.; 98102 206-329-8781

⚥ ● (♿) Moonlight Bay Bed & Breakfast, 10710 SW Cowen Rd, Vashon Island; 98070 206-567-4333

♀ ○ Scandia House, 2028 34th Ave South; 98144 206-725-7825

♀ ○ The Shafer-Baillie Mansion, 907 14th Ave E; 98112 206-322-4654 Fax 206-329-4654

Addictive Behavior, Substance Abuse, Recovery

♀ Capital Hill Alano Club, 1202 E Pike St #1109; 98122-3934

♀ ☆&& Central Seattle Recovery Center, 1401 E Jefferson #300; 98122 206-322-2970 Mon-Fri 8am-6pm; eve progs to 9pm. "Counseling, education, referral services; sliding fee scale."

♀ ☆ Northwest Treatment Center for Alcoholism, 130 Nickerson St #210; 98117 206-789-5911

♣ ★&& Stonewall Recovery Services, 430 Broadway E.; 98102-5010 206-461-4546

AIDS/HIV Support, Education, Advocacy, Publications

♀ ☆&& ACT-UP/Seattle, 1206 E Pike #814; 98122-3934 206-726-1678 Fax 206-322-7188 Meeting Mon 7.30pm. Pub *Newsletter*.

♀ AIDS Memorial Vigil, 1202 E Pike #699; 98122-3934

♀ ☆&& AIDS Prevention Project, 2124 4th Ave 4th flr; 98121-2311 206-296-4999; 206-296-4843 TDD; Mon-Fri 8am-5pm. "Anonymous & confidential HIV counseling & testing."

♀ AIDS Project of the Deaf, PO Box 24011; 98124-0011 206-328-4808 TTY; 800-833-6384

♀ ☆&& Chicken Soup Brigade, 1002 E Seneca St; 98122 206-328-8979 Fax 206-328-0171 "Practical support services (food, transportation, etc) for People Living with AIDS."

♀ ☆&& Fremont Public Association, PO Box 31151; 98103 206-634-2222; 206-441-5686; "Emergency services: shelter, food-bank, legal clinic; AIDS-HIV support through provision of in-home care."

♣ ★ & Heart to Art, 1202 E Pike #78; 98122 206-328-9160 "We encourage creativity in response to AIDS/HOV pandemic."

♀ ☆&& Northwest AIDS Foundation, 127 Broadway E.; 98102-5786 206-329-6923; 206-323-2685 TDD; Fax 206-325-2689 Pub *AIDS Matters*.

♀ ☆ Seattle AIDS Information BBS, 1202 E Pike #658; 98122-3934 206-323-4420 (modem only); 206-329-8617 before 11pm (voice only); "National AIDS Bulletin Board Service."

♀ ☆&& Shanti/Seattle, Box 20698; 98102 206-322-0279 "AIDS/HIV individual emotional support. Workshops for groups & corporations."

Answering/FAX & Mail Receiving, Shipping & Packaging Services

♀ • & Post Option Business Center, 1202 E Pike St; 98122-3934 206-322-2777 postoption@aol.com Mon-Fri 8.30am-7pm; Sat 10am-4pm. "Private mail boxes; shipping & receiving UPS; Voice Mail, greeting cards & fax."

Bars, Restaurants, Clubs, Discos

♂ • & Brass Connection, 722 E Pike; 98122 206-322-7777 **BR**

♂ • C.C. Slaughter's North/Cadillac Grille, 1501 E Madison; 98122 206-323-4017; 206-726-0565; **BRLW** 6am-2am.

♀ Changes, 2103 N 45th St; 98103 206-545-8363

♀ Changes Too, 1501 E Olive Way; 98122 206-322-6356

♂ • Crescent Tavern, 1413 E Olive Way; 98122 **LWEf**

♂ • && The Cuff, 1533 13th Ave 206-323-1525 **BL**

♀ Double Header, 407 2nd Ave; 98104 206-464-9918

♂ Eagle, 314 E Pike St; 98128 206-621-7591 **LL**

♀ • && The Easy, 916 E Pike; 98122 206-323-8343 **BDR**

♂ Elite, 622 Broadway E; 98102 206-324-4470

♀ Elite II, 1658 E Olive Way; 98102 206-322-7334

♀ • && Encore, 1518 11th Ave; 98122 206-324-6617 **BR** 11am-2am; Sat & Sun 8am-2am.

♀ Hamburger Mary's, Olive & Denny; 98122 206-324-8112 **BR**

♀ Jade Pagoda, 606 Broadway Ave E.; 98102 206-322-5900 **BR**

♂ • Madison Pub, 1315 E Madison St; 98122 206-325-6537

♂ ○ (&&) Neighbours, 1509 Broadway; 98122 206-324-5358 **BRdf**

♀ ○ & Off-Ramp Cafe, 109 Eastlake East; 98109 206-628-0232 **BRE** 5pm-2am.

♀ ○ && R Place, 619 E. Pine St 206-322-8828

♀ Re-bar, 1114 Howell; 98101 **BD**

♂ Sea Wolf Saloon, 1413 14th Ave; 98122 206-323-2158 **BD**

♂ Six Eleven Tavern, 611 2nd Ave; 98104 206-345-9430

♀ (&) Sonya's, 1532 7th Ave; 98101 206-624-5377

♂ • Spag's, 1118 E Pike St; 98122 206-322-3232

T • Tacky Tavern, 1706 Bellevue Ave; 98122 206-322-9744 Noon-2am.

♀ Thumpers, 1500 E Madison; 98101 206-328-3800 **BR**

♀ ○ && Timberline Tavern, 2015 Boren Ave; 98121 206-622-6220 "Country/Western."

♀ • Wildrose Tavern, 1021 E Pike St; 98122 206-324-9210 **BR** 11am-mdnt.

Bookstores: Gay/Lesbian/Feminist

♀ • **Beyond the Closet Bookstore, 1501 Belmont Ave; 98122 206-322-4609 10am-10pm; Fri & Sat to 11pm.**
◆ *Beyond the Closet Bookstore advertisement page 437*

Bookstores: General

♀ ○ Alfi News, 4427 Wallingford Ave N; 98103 206-632-9390

♀ ○ Automotive Bookstore, 1830 12th Ave; 98122 206-323-6719

♀ • (&) Bailey/Coy Books, 414 Broadway E; 98102 206-323-8842

♀ ○&& Bauhaus Books & Coffee, 301 E Pine St; 98122 206-625-1600

♀ ○ & Bulldog News, 401 Broadway East; 98102 206-322-NEWS

♀ ○ & Bulldog News, 4208 University Way NE; 98105 206-632-NEWS

♀ ○ The Corner Shop, 113 Lake St, Kirkland; 98033 206-827-6486

♀ • Fremont Place Book Company, 621 N 35th; 98103 206-547-5970

♀ ☆ (&) Left Bank Books, 92 Pike St; 98101 206-622-0195 10am-9pm; Sun noon-6pm. "Worker-owned collective; sells, publishes, distributes anti-authoritarian materials; Gay & Lesbian fiction & nonfiction & periodicals."

♀ • M. Coy Books, 117 Pine St; 98101 206-623-5354

♀ ○ Pistil Books & News, 1013 E Pike; 98122 206-325-5401 10am-10pm; Fri & Sat to mdnt

♀ ☆ & Red & Black Books Collective, 432 15th Ave E; 98112 206-322-READ

♀ ○ ♿ Steve's Broadway News, 204 Broadway East; 98102 206-324-7323

Computer Bulletin Boards

♀ • Rendezvous Systems, 1202 E Pike St #828; 98122 206-860-1661 (modem) Fax 206-325-9451 syspo1@seattle.com

Counseling/Therapy: Nonprofit

⚥ ★ ♿♿ Seattle Counseling Service for Sexual Minorities, 200 W Mercer St #300; 98119-3958 206-282-9307

♀ ☆ ♿ SISTER (Seattle Institute for Sex Therapy Education & Research), 100 NE 56th St; 98105 206-522-8588

Counseling/Therapy: Private

♀ • ♿♿ Anders, Ron, MSW, CSW, 101 Stewart St #850; 98103 206-441-1903

⚥ • ♿♿ Edmondson, Eddie, MSW, PO Box 85861; 98145-1861 206-233-8868

⚥ • (♿) Larsen, Sue, MA, 3203 Franklin Ave E.; 98102 206-325-1498 "Psychotherapist, EAP, Job Search Instructor."

Dentists

♀ • Rowe, Fred, DDS, 1001 Broadway SE; 98122 206-323-1244

Entertainment-Related Services (see also Music, Organizations/Resources: Performing

⚥ ★ ♿♿ Tacky Tourist Clubs of America, 1202 E Pike St #905; 98122-3934 206-233-8842 "Special event fundraising parties: Halloween, spring Prom, summer boat cruise."

Erotica (Printed, Visual, Equipment)

⚥ • ♿♿ The Crypt, 1310 East Union; 98122 206-325-3882 "Leather clothing & erotica."

♀ ○ Fantasy Unlimited, PO Box 2602; 98101-2602 / 102 Pike St 206-682-0167

♀ ☆ ♿ The Rubber Tree, 4426 Burke Ave N., Dept GP; 98103 206-633-4750 Mon-Fri 10am-7pm; Sat to 6pm. "Not-for-profit service of Zero Population Growth, specializing in condoms; also lubricants, spermicides, books, latex items, t-shirts, resuable menstrual products, etc. Free catalog."

♀ • ♿ Spanky's, 3276 California Ave SW; 98116 206-938-3400 Noon-7pm.

♀ • ♿♿ Taboo Video, 17028 Aurora Ave North; 98133 206-546-0400

♀ ○ ♿ Taboo Video, 1012 1st Ave; 98104 206-622-7399

♀ • ♿ Toys In Babeland, 711 E Pike St; 98122 206-328-2914 Tue-Sun noon-8pm. "Classy sex toy store."

Food Specialties, Catering (see also Party/Event Services)

♀ • (♿) Coyote Cookhouse, 1202 E Pike #544; 98122-3934 206-324-3731 (also fax) "All natural gourmet salsa & all-purpose salt-free seasoning (more foods to come) sold via retail fairs, wholesale, mail order."

Funding: Endowment, Fundraising, Scholarship

⚥ Bunny Brigade, 1202 E Pike St #1140; 98122-3934 206-292-5012

⚥ ★ Pride Foundation, 2820 E Madison St; 98112-4841 206-323-3318 "Funding."

Furniture

♀ • ♿ Touch of Saguaro, 1500 Westlake Ave N. 206-281-8733 Fax 206-325-9451 10am-6pm. "Custom furniture, art, & accents from southwest artisans."

Visit us first for community info!
1-800-238-8518
BEYOND THE CLOSET
GAY AND LESBIAN BOOKS
BOOKSTORE
Seattle's Exclusively Lesbian & Gay Bookstore
1501 Belmont Avenue at East Pike Street
Seattle, Washington 98122 (206) 322-4609
Sunday - Thursday 10:00 - 10:00
Friday & Saturday 10:00 - 11:00

Gifts, Cards, Pride & Promotional Items

♀ • Capitol Hill Christmas Shop, 203 14th Ave E; 98112 206-726-8612 "Year-round; featuring Christopher Radko, Old World Christmas, House of Hadden, Dept. 56, etc."

Gifts, Cards, Pride & Novelty Items

⚥ • (♿♿) The Pink Zone, 401 Broadway East #240; 98102 206-325-0050

Grooming Services

♀ • ♿♿ Chris' Hair Systems, 1005 E Miller St; 98102-4044 206-322-4747

Health Care (see also AIDS Services)

♀ ☆ ♿♿ 45th St. Clinic, 1629 N 45th St; 98103 206-633-3350

♀ ☆ (♿♿) Health Information Network, Box 30762; 98103 206-784-5655

⚥ ★ ♿♿ Lesbian Health Network, PO Box 22358; 98122-0358 206-323-9009

⚥ ★ ♿♿ Seattle Gay Clinic, 500 19th Ave East; 98112 206-461-4540 Tue & Thu 6.30-9pm; Sat 10.30am-1.30pm.

Health Clubs, Gyms, Saunas

♂ Club Seattle, 1520 Summit; 98122 206-329-2334

♂ • Club Z, 1117 Pike; 98101 206-622-9958 *LLP* Open Mon-Fri 7pm; weekends 24 hrs. "Private men's club."

Legal Services & Resources

⚥ • ♿♿ Bergstedt, Anne C. S., 615 2nd Ave #380; 98104 206-467-6338 Fax 206-467-9725

♀ ☆ ♿ Northwest Women's Law Center, 119 S Main St #330; 98104-2515 206-621-7691

♀ • Rietschel, Jean, 513 32nd Ave; 98122 206-325-3772

⚥ Steve Farmer Defense Fund, 1202 E Pike #1007; 98122-3934

Massage Therapy (Licensed only)

♀ ○ Cherrington, Wimsey, LMT, CTP, 206-233-8620

Organizations/Resources: Bisexual Focus

♂ ★ (♿) Seattle Bisexual Men's Union, PO Box 30645 Greenwood Stn; 98103-0645 206-728-4533

♀ ★ ♿ Seattle Bisexual Women's Network, PO Box 30645 Greenwood Stn; 98103-0645 206-783-7987 Pub *North Bi Northwest*.

Organizations/Resources: Business & Professional

⚥ Aldus Queer Association Network (AQUANET), AUSA Marketing, 411 1st Ave S; 98104 206-343-3380

WA: Seattle

Organizations: Business

438

USA

Seattle : WA

Organizations: Youth

♀ ★ GLUE (Gay & Lesbian University Employees), PO Box 23164; 98102-0464

♂ ★ ♂♂ Greater Seattle Business Association, 2033 6th Ave #804; 98121-2526 206-443-GSBA

♀ ☆♂♂ Political Staff Workers Union, 5018 Rainier Ave S; 98118 206-722-2453 Fax 206-723-7691 "Labor union made up of people working for social change organization."

Organizations/Resources: Education, Anti-Defamation, Anti-Violence, Self-Defense

♀ ★♂♂ Freely Speaking Toastmasters, 1202 E Pike #700; 98122-3934 206-937-9369

♀ ★ Q-Patrol, 1202 E Pike #940; 98122-3934 206-325-9128

Organizations/Resources: Ethnic, Multicultural

♂ ★♂♂ MACCT (Men of All Colors & Cultures Together), 1202 E Pike #936; 98122-3934 206-325-9833 Meet Wed 7-9pm at Crafts Bldg, Seattle Mental Health Inst, 1600 E. Olive St Black & White Men Together/Men of All Colors Together

Organizations/Resources: Family

♀ ☆ (♂) P-FLAG Seattle Chapter, 1202 E Pike St #620; 98122-3934 206-325-7724 "Parents, Families & Friends of Lesbians & Gays."

♀ ☆ (?♂) Solo Parenting Alliance, 139 23rd Ave S.; 98144 206-720-1655 Pub *Solo Connections*.

Organizations/Resources: General, Multipurpose, Pride

♀ ★♂♂ The Freedom Day Committee, 1202 E Pike #969; 98122 206-292-1035

♀ ★ Gay Community Social Services, Box 22228; 98122 206-727-6530

Organizations/Resources: Political/Legislative

♀ ★ Harvey Muggy Lesbian & Gay Democrats, 1202 E Pike St #1196; 98122-3934 206-284-1857

♀ ★ Privacy Fund, 1202 E Pike St #816; 98122-3934 206-292-2486

♀ ☆♂♂ Radical Women, 5018 Rainier Ave S.; 98118 206-722-6057

♀ ★ SEAMEC: Seattle Municipal Elections Committee for Gays, & Lesbians & Bisexuals, 1202 E Pike #901; 98122-3934 206-781-7306

♀ ★ (♂♂) Stonewall Committee for Lesbian/Gay/Transgender/ Bisexual Rights, 6727 Seward Park Ave S.; 98118 206-722-0938

Organizations/Resources: Sexual Focus (Leather, S/M, etc) & Safe Sex Promotion

♀ ★ C-SPACE, PO Box 28021; 98144 206-292-8764 Fri 7-9pm. "Where the 'C' stands for Consensual."

♀ ☆ (?♂) Eros Publishing, 1202 E Pike St #656; 98122-3934 erospub@aol.com *LL*

♀ Northwest Bondage Club, 1202 E Pike St #1212; 98122-3934

♂ ★ (?♂) Seattle Men In Leather, 1202 East Pike St #1199; 98122-3934 206-233-8141 scooter@stage.com *L* "A Gay Men's social group promoting with Power & Pride the Seattle Men's Leather Community."

Organizations/Resources: Social, Recreational & Support Groups (see also Sport/Dance/Outdoor)

♀ ★ (?♂) Associated Lesbians of Puget Sound (ALPS), PO Box 20424; 98102 206-233-8145 Pub *ALPS Newsletter*.

♀ ★ Coming of Age, 1202 E Pike St #552; 98122-3934

♂ Ethyl Forever Car Club, 1202 E Pike #765; 98122-3934 206-935-6080; 206-937-8127

♂ Girth & Mirth Seattle, PO Box 9935; 98109 206-361-9686

♂ ★ (?♂) Northwest Bears, 1202 E Pike #802; 98122-3936 206-233-1003

♂ ★ The Olympians, c/o 823 NE 80th St; 98115-4209 (nudist group)

♂ Outer Limits, 1202 E Pike St #819; 98122-3934

♂ Seattle Prime Timers, 300 Queen Anne Ave N #339; 98109-4599 206-781-1968

Organizations/Resources: Sport/Dance/Outdoor

♀ Banshees Motorcycle Club, 2716 E Marion St; 98122 206-324-0126

♂ Bottom Dwellers Scuba Club, 337 N 143rd; 98133 206-486-0868

♂ Emerald City Softball Association, Box 61085; 98121 206-522-0156

♂ Federation of Gay Games, 2308 E Lee; 98112 206-282-6242

♀ Northwest Gay Rodeo Association, 1202 E Pike #759; 98122-8931 206-233-8931

♀ ★ Olympic Yacht Club, 1202 E Pike St #1025; 98122-3934

♂ Orca Swim Club, PO Box 20173; 98102-1173 206-325-3604

♀ ★♂♂ Puddletown Dancers, PO Box 20671; 98102 206-820-1370 *d*

♂ Puget Sound Area Gay & Lesbian Sea Kayakers, 1202 E Pike #896; 98122-3934

♂ Seattle Frontrunners, PO Box 70501; 98107 206-232-0535

♂ Seattle Sunday Bowlers, 733 21st Ave E; 98112 206-329-1515

♀ ★ Ski Buddies, 1202 E Pike #899; 98122-3934 206-292-1060

♂ Stonewall Football Club, 1605 Bellevue Ave #409; 98122 206-234-4511

♀ ★ Summer Buddies, 1202 E Pike #899; 98122-3934 206-292-1060

♀ ★ TEAM HEIDI, PO Box 23070; 98102

♀ ★♂♂ TEAM Seattle, 1202 E Pike #515; 98122-3934 206-634-1834 "Information & referral for 35 sports in Seattle metropolitan area."

Organizations/Resources: Student, Academic, Alumni/ae

♀ ★♂♂ ASUW Gay, Bisexual, Lesbian Commission, HUB, FK-30, University of Washington; 98195 206-685-GLBC "Student group."

♀ ★♂♂ LesBiGays, Unlimited, 207 HUB Box 104, FK-30, University of Washington; 98195 206-543-6106 "Student group."

♀ ★♂♂ Triangle Club, 1701 Broadway SAC 350; 98122 206-587-6924

Organizations/Resources: Youth (see also Family)

♂ Lambert House/Gay & Lesbian Youth, 1818 15th Ave; 98122 206-322-2515

♀ ★ Youth Rap Group, Box 22228 c/o Gay Community Social Services; 98122 206-322-2873

Performing Arts: Entertainment, Music, Theater, etc.

♀ Seattle Lesbian & Gay Chorus, PO Box 20729; 98102 206-860-7542

♀ ★&& Seattle Men's Chorus, PO Box 20146; 98102-1146 206-323-0750

Publications

♂ • && *Seattle Gay News*, PO Box 22007; 98122-0007 206-324-4297 Fax 206-322-7188 "Gay & Lesbian newsweekly, includes features, calendar listings, entertainment, classifieds."

♀ ☆ (?&) *Synapse*, PO Box 95220; 98145-2220

Real Estate

♀ • && Cavalli, Liz, Realtor, Windermere Real Estate, 1112 19th Ave E. 206-329-2990; 206-324-8900; Fax 206-448-3279

♂ ○&& Neth, David, The Landmark Group, 726 14th Ave; 98122 206-322-0660 "Realtor for the greater Seattle Area since 1978."

Record Sales (see also Performing Arts)

♀ • && Now Hear This, 3121 W Government Way; 98199 206-286-6503

Religious Organizations & Publications

♂ ★ (&) Affirmation: United Methodists for Lesbian, Gay & Bisexual Concerns, 2115 N 42nd; 98103

♂ ★ Congregation Tikvah Chadasah, PO Box 2731; 98111-2731 206-329-2590

♂ ★&& Dignity/Seattle, Box 20325; 98102-1325 206-325-7314 "Gay & Lesbian Catholics & their friends."

♂ ★ Evangelicals Concerned, PO Box 20189; 98102-1189 206-932-3401

♂ ★ (?&) Grace Gospel Chapel, 2052 NW 64th St; 98107 206-784-8495 Services Sun 11am & Wed 7pm. "Evangelical & independent."

♂ ★&& Integrity/Puget Sound, PO Box 20663; 98102 206-525-4668 "Lesbian & Gay Episcopalians & their friends."

♂ Lutherans Concerned, PO Box 20566; 98102 206-322-3477

♂ ★&& Metropolitan Community Church/Seattle, 1202 E Pike St #930; 98122-3934 206-325-2421

♂ Overlake Metropolitan Community Church, PO Box 6612, Bellevue; 98008 206-250-0258

♂ Unitarian Lesbians & Gays, University Unitarian Church, 6556 35th Ave NE; 98115 206-483-0345

Travel & Tourist Services (see also Accommodation)

♂ ○& Black Tie Travel, 1411 4th Ave #920; 98101 206-622-4409; 800-776-2930

♂ ○ Fodor's Travel, 1418 E Olive Way; 98122-2128 206-328-5385

♂ • && Security Pack Travel, 1101 Boylston Ave; 98101-2818 206-322-8056 Fax 206-323-5785

♀ • && Sunshine Travel Agency, 519 N 85th St; 98103 206-784-8141 Fax 206-784-8143

♂ • & Travel Agents International, 513 Olive Way; 98101 800-928-0809 Fax 206-343-0810

♂ • (&&) Travel Solutions, 4009 Gilman Ave W; 98199 206-281-7202; 800-727-1616

Women's Centers

♀ ★ (&&) Lesbian Resource Center, 1808 Bellevue Ave #204; 98122 206-322-3953 (also TTY) Drop-in Mon-Fri 2-7pm. Pub *Lesbian Resource Center Community News; Ultra Violet.*

Spokane

Addictive Behavior, Substance Abuse, Recovery

♂ Rainbow Alano Clubhouse, 117 W Augusta Ave; 99205 509-468-5120

AIDS/HIV Support, Education, Advocacy, Publications

♂ ☆ AIDS Life Link, PO Box 1790; 99201 509-838-1999

♂ ☆ & Light of Life Ministries, c/o MCC, Box 769; 99210 509-838-0085

♂ ☆ (?&) People of Color Against AIDS Network, MLK Center, 845 S Sherman; 99202 509-624-4314

♂ ★&& Spokane AIDS Network, 1613 W Gardner Ave; 99201-1830 509-326-6070

♂ ☆&& Spokane County Health District AIDS Program, 1101 W College Ave #401; 99201 509-324-1542 Mon-Fri 8am-5pm. "Counseling & testing; outreach."

Bars, Restaurants, Clubs, Discos

♂ ○ Dempsey's Brass Rail, West 909 1st St; 99204 509-747-5362 *BDR*

♀ Elk Cafe, 1931 W Pacific Ave; 99204 509-456-0454

♂ • & Hour Place, 415 W Sprague; 99204 509-838-6947 *BDR* Noon-2am.

♀ Pumps II Restaurant & Lounge, 211 N Division St; 99202 509-747-8940

Bookstores: General

♀ ○ (&&) Auntie's Bookstore & Cafe, West 402 Main; 99201-0249 509-838-0206

Business, Financial & Secretarial

♂ • Wernz, Michael J., CPA, PO Box 3994; 99220-3994 509-326-9054

Counseling/Therapy: Private

♀ ○ (&&) Bonser, Helen, MA, ABS, N. 2511 Normandie; 99205 509-328-4443

Erotica (Printed, Visual, Equipment)

♀ • & Spokane Arcade, 1125 W 1st; 99204 509-747-1621

Gifts, Cards, Pride & Novelty Items

♀ ○&& Boo Radley's, North 5 Post; 99201 509-456-7479

Organizations/Resources: Business & Professional

♂ Employees Association for Gays & Lesbians (EAGLE), 501 W 2nd #201; 99204

Organizations/Resources: Family

♀ ☆ (&&) P-FLAG/Spokane, PO Box 40122; 99202-0901 509-747-6682 "Parents, Families & Friends of Lesbians & Gays."

Organizations/Resources: Student, Academic, Alumni/ae

♂ ★&& Gay/Lesbian/Bisexual Alliance at Eastern Washington University (GLBA/EWU), mail to GLBA/EWU, PUB-324, MS-60, Cheney; 99004 509-359-4253 Pub *GLBA Newsletter.*

♂ ★ Whitworth College GLB Support Group, PO Box 400; 99251 / Health Center Whitworth College 509-466-3259

Organizations/Resources: Youth (see also Family)

♂ ★ (?&) Odyssey, 1101 W College #401; 99201 509-325-3637

WA: Spokane
Performing Arts

440
USA

State/County Resources : WV
Organizations: Political

Performing Arts: Entertainment, Music, Theater, etc.

♀ ★ Inland Northwest Men's Chorus, PO Box 40385; 99202 509-235-2500

♀ ★ (?♣) Women's Cultural Exchange, PO Box 4795; 99202-0795 509-535-5285

Publications

♀ • Lavender Rag, PO Box 1360; 99210 509-458-2256

♀ • Stonewall News, PO Box 3994; 99220-3994 509-456-8011

Religious Organizations & Publications

♀ ♣♣ Affirmation: United Methodists for Lesbian, Gay & Bisexual Concerns/Spokane, PO Box 10114; 99209-0114 509-482-7591; 708-733-9590

♀ ★ ♂ Emmanual Metropolitan Community Church, PO Box 769; 99210 509-838-0085 Sun 10.30am at 307 W. 4th Ave.

Travel & Tourist Services (see also Accommodation)

♀ ○ Travel Place, West 505 Parkade Plaza; 99201 509-624-7434 *I*

Tacoma

Bars, Restaurants, Clubs, Discos

♀ 24th Street Tavern, 2409 Pacific Ave; 98402 206-572-3748

♂ • (♣) 733 Restaurant & Lounge, 733 Commerce St S; 98402 206-627-0733 *BDR* 6pm-2am; Fri & Sat to 3am; dancing Fri & Sat 9.30pm-1.45am.

♀ Gold Ball Tavern, 2708 6th Ave; 98406 206-572-4820

♀ Goodfellows, 5811 N 51st St; 98407 206-761-9802

♂ Pushrod, 2405 Pacific Ave; 98402 206-627-8511

Counseling/Therapy: Private

♀ ○ Jiles, Jan, 917 1/2 N 2nd St; 98403 206-627-0214; 206-272-0619

Erotica (Printed, Visual, Equipment)

♀ ○ Jerry's Adult Bookstore, 755 Broadway; 98402-3717 206-272-4700

Organizations/Resources: Student, Academic, Alumni/ae

♂ ★ Lesbian/Gay Legal Society—Seattle University School of Law, 950 Broadway Plaza; 98402 Fax 206-591-2901

Organizations/Resources: Youth (see also Family)

♂ ★♣♣ Oasis, 206-596-2860 Fax 206-591-6589 "Rap & support group & drop-in center for gay, lesbian & bisexual youth, & youth questioning their sexual identity. Call Jerry at 552-0394 (pager) or Vick at 552-0601 (pager) for more information."

Publications

♂ • Tacoma Sounds, PO Box 110816; 98411-0816 206-535-4213 Monthly. "Desktop services available."

Religious Organizations & Publications

♀ ★ ♂ New Heart Metropolitan Community Churc, 2150 S Cushman Ave; 98405-3438 206-272-2382

Women's Centers

♀ ★ (?♣) Tacoma Lesbian Concern, PO Box 947; 98401 206-472-0422 Resource & Information Line (ask for Mary or Teresa); 206-472-0422 Resource & Information Line (ask for Mary or Teresa); Pub Newsletter. "Charitable, educational & support group; extensive resource list for area."

Vancouver

Publications

♂ • Vancouver Voice, PO Box 5884; 98668-5884 360-737-9879

Religious Organizations & Publications

♂ ★ ♂ Metropolitan Community Church of The Gentle Shepherd, PO Box 5094; 98668 360-253-8401

Vashon Island: see Seattle

Walla Walla

AIDS/HIV Support, Education, Advocacy, Publications

♀ ☆ ♂ Blue Mountain Heart To Heart, PO Box 65; 99362 509-529-4744

Organizations/Resources: General, Multipurpose, Pride

♀ H.I.T. Crowd, PO Box 692; 99362

Wenatchee

Organizations/Resources: Social, Recreational & Support Groups (see also Sport/Dance/Outdoor)

♂ ★ (?♣) North Central Washington Gay & Lesbian Alliance (NCW GALA), PO Box 234; 98807-0234 509-662-8413

Yakima

Organizations/Resources: Social, Recreational & Support Groups (see also Sport/Dance/Outdoor)

♀ Together At Last Lesbians, mail to TALL, PO Box 976; 98907 509-454-4989

Yelm

Religious Organizations & Publications

♀ Metropolitan Community Church North Pines, Box 1269; 98597 360-458-5355

West Virginia
State/County Resources

Addictive Behavior, Substance Abuse, Recovery

♀ Gay/Lesbian AA, PO Box 2045, Charleston, WV 25301 304-342-4315; 800-443-2207

AIDS/HIV Support, Education, Advocacy, Publications

♀ ☆♣♣ AIDS Task Force of the Upper Ohio Valley, PO Box 6360, Wheeling, WV 26003 304-232-6822

♀ ☆ (?♣) HIV Care Consortium, 34 Edgelawn Ave, Wheeling, WV 26003-6035 304-242-9443

♀ ☆♣♣ Mountain State AIDS Network, 235 High St #306, Morgantown, WV 26505-5446 304-292-9000 in Morgantown; 800-585-4444 in WV

♀ ☆ ♂ Tri-State AIDS Task Force, PO Box 2981, Huntington, WV 25728 304-522-4357

Organizations/Resources: Political/Legislative

♂ ★ (?♣) West Virginia Coalition for Lesbian & Gay Rights, PO Box 11033, Charleston, WV 25339 304-343-7305

♀ West Virginia Coalition For Lesbian/Gay Rights, PO Box 1939, Princeton, WV 24740

WV: State/County Resources
Publications

441
USA

State/County Resources : WI
Addictive Behavior

Publications

♀ ○ *Graffiti*, 1505 Lee St, Charleston, WV 25311 304-342-4412 Fax 304-342-7646

⚥ ★ *Out & About*, Triangle Press, 152 6th Ave, Huntington, WV 25701 304-522-9089

Real Estate

⚥ • Community Real Estate Referrals, 800-346-5592 "Free referral to gay/gay-supportive realtor in any USA city/state (including Virgin Is. & Puerto Rico). Sorry, no rentals!"
✦ *Community Real Estate Referrals advertisement back cover*

Berkeley Springs

Erotica (Printed, Visual, Equipment)

♂ ○ (&) Action Books & Videos, Rte 1, Box 256A (Route 522 South); 25411 304-258-2529

Bluefield

Bars, Restaurants, Clubs, Discos

⚥ Shamrock Lounge, 362 Princeton Ave; 24701 304-327-9570

Charleston

AIDS/HIV Support, Education, Advocacy, Publications

♂ ☆&& Charleston AIDS Network, PO Box 1024; 25324 304-345-4673

♂ ☆ Prevention Stategy, 1036 Quarrier St; 25301 304-342-9663 Fax 304-342-9637

Bars, Restaurants, Clubs, Discos

⚥ • (?&) The Broadway, 210 Broad St; 25301 304-343-2162 *DP*

♀ Christine's, 602 Shewsbury St; 25301 304-346-1759

♀ • & Grand Palace, 617 Brooks 304-342-9532 *BDR* 11am-3.30pm.

♀ The Tap Room, 1022 Quarrier St; 25301

Bookstores: General

♀ ○&& Trans Allegheny Books, 118 Capitol St; 25301 304-346-0551

Publications

⚥ ★ *Womyn's Community Newsletter*, PO Box 5393; 25361-5393

Huntington

Bars, Restaurants, Clubs, Discos

♀ ○&& Calamity Cafe, 1555 3rd Ave; 25701 304-525-4171 *PBRE*

♂ ○ Driftwood Lounge/Beehive, 1121 7th Ave; 25701 304-696-9858

⚥ Polo, 733 7th Ave (rear); 25701 304-522-3146

Bookstores: General

♀ ○ (?&) The Store, 3352 Norwood Rd; 25705 304-697-4155 Mon-Fri noon-8pm; Sat to 6pm. "Bookstore & art gallery."

Counseling/Therapy: Private

⚥ • Muskera, David J., 152 6th Ave; 25701 304-522-9089 Licensed Psychologist (WV & OH)

Lost River

Accommodation: Hotels, B&B, Resorts, Campgrounds

♂ ○ The Guesthouse, Settlers Valley Way; 26811 304-897-5707

Martinsburg

Bookstores: General

♀ ○ Pepper's News Stand, 246 N Queen St; 25401 304-267-6846

Erotica (Printed, Visual, Equipment)

♀ ○ Variety Books & Video, 255 N Queen St; 25401 304-263-4334

Morgantown

Bars, Restaurants, Clubs, Discos

⚥ • Class Act, 335 High St; 26505 304-292-2010 *Pd* 7pm-3am.

Bookstores: Recovery, Metaphysical, & other Specialty

♀ Somewhere In Thyme, Box 1552; 26505 / Morgantown Mall, Exit off I-79, Westover, WV 304-983-6407

Erotica (Printed, Visual, Equipment)

♀ ○ Select Books & Videos, 237 Walnut St; 26505 304-292-7714

Organizations/Resources: Student, Academic, Alumni/ae

⚥ ★&& Bisexual, Gay & Lesbian Mountaineers (BiGLM), PO Box 6444, Mountainlair, West Virginia University; 26506-6444 304-293-8200

Parkersburg

AIDS/HIV Support, Education, Advocacy, Publications

♀ ☆ (?&) Mid-Ohio Valley AIDS Task Force, PO Box 1274; 26102 304-485-4803

Bars, Restaurants, Clubs, Discos

♀ Different Strokes, 604 Market St; 26101 304-485-5113

Shepherdstown

Organizations/Resources: Social, Recreational & Support Groups (see also Sport/Dance/Outdoor)

⚥ ★ Lambda Panhandlers, PO Box 1961; 25443-1961

Wheeling

Bars, Restaurants, Clubs, Discos

♀ Tricks, 1429 Market St; 26003 304-232-1267

Erotica (Printed, Visual, Equipment)

♀ ○ & Market Street News, 1437 Market St; 26003 304-232-2414

Wisconsin

State/County Resources

Addictive Behavior, Substance Abuse, Recovery

⚥ • (&&) Pride Institute, 800-54-PRIDE "The nation's only accredited chemical dependency treatment center exclusively for Gay, Lesbian & Bisexual People."

AIDS/HIV Support, Education, Advocacy, Publications

♀ ☆ (♂♂) AIDS Resource Center of Wisconsin, Inc., PO Box 92487, Milwaukee, WI 53202 414-273-1991; 800-359-9272; Fax 414-273-2357 Pub *Lifelines.*

♀ ☆ ♂♂ Northern AIDS Network, PO Box 400, Rhinelander, WI 54501 715-369-6228; 800-374-7678 (715 area only); satellite office (Superior, WI) 715-394-0404

♀ ☆ ♂♂ Northwest Wisconsin AIDS Project, PO Box 11, Eau Claire, WI 54702-0011 715-836-7710; 800-750-2537; Fax 715-836-9844

♀ ☆ ♂♂ Southeast Wisconsin AIDS Project, PO Box 0173, Kenosha, WI 53141-0173 414-657-6644; 800-924-6601; Fax 414-657-6949

♀ ☆ (♂♂) Winsconsin Community-Based Research Consortium, PO Box 92505, Milwaukee, WI 53202 / HIV clinical drug trials, 315 W. Court St. 414-291-2799; 800-359-9272; Fax 414-273-2357

Organizations/Resources: General, Multipurpose, Pride

♀ ★ (?♂) Gay & Lesbian Wisconsin Education & Economic Development Alliance, Inc. (GLEEDA), PO Box 8286, Oshkosh, WI 54903-8286

Organizations/Resources: Sport/Dance/Outdoor

♀ ★ Great Lakes Harley Riders, PO Box 341611, Milwaukee, WI 53234-1611 "Motorcylists."

Publications

♀ • *Wisconsin Light*, 1843 N Palmer, Milwaukee, WI 53212 414-372-2773 Fax 414-372-1840

♀ • (?♂) *Wisconsin's In Step*, 225 S 2nd St, Milwaukee, WI 53204 414-278-7840 Fax 414-278-5868 Every 2 weeks.

Real Estate

♀ • Community Real Estate Referrals, 800-346-5592 "Free referral to gay/gay-supportive realtor in any USA city/state (including Virgin Is. & Puerto Rico). Sorry, no rentals!"
♦ *Community Real Estate Referrals advertisement back cover*

Appleton: see Fox Valley

Ashland

Organizations/Resources: Student, Academic, Alumni/ae

♀ ★ ♂♂ Gay Bisexual Lesbian Alliance, Northland College, 1411 Ellis Ave; 54806

Beloit

Bookstores: Gay/Lesbian/Feminist

♀ ○ A Different World, 414 E Grand Ave; 53511 608-365-1000

Burlington: see Milwaukee

Eau Claire

Bars, Restaurants, Clubs, Discos

♀ Scruples, 411 Galloway; 54703 715-839-9606

Fort Atkinson

Bars, Restaurants, Clubs, Discos

♀ • (♂) Friends, 10 E Sherman Ave; 53538 414-563-2231

Fox Valley

AIDS/HIV Support, Education, Advocacy, Publications

♀ ☆ ♂ Center Project, Inc., PO Box 1874, Green Bay; 54305 / 824 S. Broadway; 54304 414-437-7400 Fax 414-437-1040

♀ ☆ ♂♂ ECHO, PO Box 68, Winnebago Health Dept, Winnebago; 54985 800-892-2130; 414-232-3011

♀ ☆ ♂ Fox Valley AIDS Project, 120 N Morrison #201, Appleton; 54911 414-733-2068

Bars, Restaurants, Clubs, Discos

Appleton

♂ • Pivot Club, PO Box 474, Appleton; 54911-0474 / 4815 W. Prospect Ave; 54914 414-730-0440

♂ • (♂) Rascal's Bar & Grill, 702 E Wisconsin Ave, Appleton; 54911 414-954-9262 *BR* 5pm-2am; Fri & Sat to 2.30am; Sun noon-2am.

Green Bay

♂ • ♂♂ Java's/Za's, 1106 Main St, Green Bay; 54302 414-435-5476 *DE*

♂ • ♂♂ Napalese Lounge, 515 S Broadway, Green Bay; 54303 414-432-9646 *Df* 4pm-closing.

♂ • ♂ Sass, 840 S Broadway, Green Bay; 54304 414-437-7277 *BD*

Kimberly

♀ ○ ♂♂ Grand American Restaurant & Bar, 800 Eisenhower Dr, Kimberly; 54136-2146 414-731-0164 *BR*

Erotica (Printed, Visual, Equipment)

♀ • ♂ The Main Attraction, 1614 Main St, Green Bay; 54302 414-465-6969 24 hrs.

♀ ○ Paradise Books, 1122 Main St, Green Bay; 54301 414-432-9498

Organizations/Resources: Family

♀ ☆ P-FLAG Appleton/Fox Cities, PO Box 75, Little Chute; 54140 414-749-1629 "Parents, Families & Friends of Lesbians & Gays."

Organizations/Resources: General, Multipurpose, Pride

♀ ★ (?♂) Northern Womyn, Inc, PO Box 10102, Green Bay; 54307-0102 Pub *Northern Womyn Ink.*

Organizations/Resources: Sexual Focus (Leather, S/M, etc) & Safe Sex Promotion

♂ ★ Argonauts of Wisconsin, PO Box 22096, Green Bay; 54305

Organizations/Resources: Student, Academic, Alumni/ae

♂ ★ ♂♂ Bisexual/Gay/Lesbian Awareness, Lawrence University, PO Box 599, Appleton; 54912 414-832-6600 Fax 414-832-7695

Performing Arts: Entertainment, Music, Theater, etc.

♂ ★ ♂♂ Bay City Chorus, PO Box 1901, Green Bay; 54305 414-494-5029

Publications

♂ • *Quest*, PO Box 1961, Green Bay; 54301 414-433-9821

Religious Organizations & Publications

♂ ★ (♂) Angel of Hope Metropolitan Community Church, PO Box 672, Green Bay; 54305-0672 414-432-0830

Green Bay: see Fox Valley

Hales Corners

Legal Services & Resources

♀ • Hume, Kathleen E., 5665 S 108th St; 53130 414-529-2129 Fax 414-529-9545

Hixton

Accommodation: Hotels, B&B, Resorts, Campgrounds

♀ • Inn At Pine Ridge, Rte. 1 Box 28; 54635-9701 715-984-2272

Hurley

Accommodation: Hotels, B&B, Resorts, Campgrounds

♀ • Northland House Bed & Breakfast Inn, 609 Hwy 77, Pence; 54550 715-561-3120

Janesville

Addictive Behavior, Substance Abuse, Recovery

♀ ★ (♿) 12 Step Recovery Group, 317 Dodge St; 53545 Open meetings Thu 7.30-8.30pm; Sun 10.30-11.30am.

AIDS/HIV Support, Education, Advocacy, Publications

♀ ☆ (♿) AIDS Suppport Network, 317 Dodge St; 53545 608-756-2550 Fax 608-756-2545

Kenosha: see Racine

Kimberly: see Fox Valley

La Crosse

Bars, Restaurants, Clubs, Discos

♀ Cavalier Lounge, 114 N 5th St; 54601 608-782-9061

Bookstores: General

♀ • ♿ Rainbow Revolution, PO Box 441; 54601 / 122 5th Ave So 608-796-0383

Publications

♀ • *Leaping La Crosse News*, PO Box 932; 54602-0932

Lake Geneva

Accommodation: Hotels, B&B, Resorts, Campgrounds

♀ ○ ♿ Eleven Gables Inn On The Lake, 493 Wrigley Dr; 53147 414-248-8393

Lake Mills

Bars, Restaurants, Clubs, Discos

♀ • (♿) CrossRoads Bar, W6642 Hwy B; 53551 414-648-8457

Little Chute: see Fox Valley

Madison

☎ The United 608-255-8582

Accommodation: Hotels, B&B, Resorts, Campgrounds

♀ • ♿ Hotel Washington, 636 W Washington; 53703 608-256-3360; 800-GAY-HOTL; *BDER*
◆ *Hotel Washington advertisement page 443*

♀ ○ Prairie Garden B&B, W 13172 Hwy 188, Lodi; 53555 608-592-5187
◆ *Prairie Garden B&B advertisement page 443*

Addictive Behavior, Substance Abuse, Recovery

♀ ☆ ♿ PICADA: Prevention & Intervention Center For AODA, 2000 Fordem Ave; 53704 608-246-7606 Fax 608-246-7610 (information about AA/Al-Anon)

AIDS/HIV Support, Education, Advocacy, Publications

♀ ☆ Madison AIDS Support Network, 600 Williamson St; 53703 800-486-6276

Bars, Restaurants, Clubs, Discos

♀ • (♿) Allegre, 150 S Blair St; 53703 608-258-9918 *Bf*

♀ • ♿ Cafe Palms, 636 W Washington; 53703 608-256-0166 *B* 11am-3.30am.

♀ Geraldine's, 3052 E Washington Ave; 53704 608-241-9335 *D*

♀ Greenbush, 914 Regent; 53715 608-257-BUSH

♀ • New Bar, 636 W Washington Ave (upstairs); 53703 608-256-8765 Fax 608-256-3603 *BDE* 8pm-2am.

♂ • ♿ Rod's, 636 W Washington Ave; 53703 (rear) 608-255-0609 Fax 608-256-3030 *BDL* 4pm-2.30am.

♀ • ♿ Shamrock Bar, 117 W Main St; 53703 608-255-5029 2pm-1.30am; Fri & Sat to 2.30am.

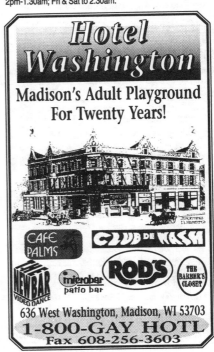

WI: Madison
Bookstores: Gay/Lesbian/Feminist

444

USA

Milwaukee : WI
Addictive Behavior

Bookstores: Gay/Lesbian/Feminist

♀ • ♿ A Room Of One's Own, 317 W Johnson St; 53703 608-257-7888

Bookstores: General

♀ ○ ♿ Going Places, 2860 University Ave; 53705 608-233-1920 "Map & travel bookstore."

♀ ○ Pic-A-Book, 506 State St; 53703 608-256-1125

♀ ○ ♿ Rainbow Books, 426 W Gilman; 53703

Community Centers (see also Women's Centers)

♥ ★ ♿ The United, 14 W Mifflin St #103; 53703 608-255-8582; 608-255-4297 Gay Line; 255-0743 Lesbian Line; Pub *In Unity.*

Counseling/Therapy: Private

♀ • Grunberg, Ricki D., 608-275-7003 Also Massage Therapy.

♀ ○ (♿) Harmonia Madison Center for Psychotherapy, 406 N Pinckney; 53703 608-255-8838

Erotica (Printed, Visual, Equipment)

♀ ○ State Street Arcade, 113 State St; 53703-2522 608-251-4540

Funding: Endowment, Fundraising, Scholarship

♥ ★ New Harvest Foundation, PO Box 1786; 53701

Health Care (see also AIDS Services)

♀ ☆ ♿ Blue Bus STD Clinic at University Health Service, 1552 University Ave; 53705 608-262-7330

Legal Services & Resources

♀ ○ ♿ Jacobson & Macaulay, 222 S Bedford St; 53703 608-255-5001

Organizations/Resources: Bisexual Focus

♥ ★ ♿ Bi? Shy? Why?, PO Box 321; 53701 608-242-9099

Organizations/Resources: Business & Professional

♥ ★ (♿) Gay & Lesbian Educational Employees, c/o The United, 310 E. Wilson St; 53703 608-255-8582

Organizations/Resources: Family

♥ ★ (♿) P-FLAG, PO Box 1722; 53701 608-243-1208; 608-255-0533; "Parents, Families & Friends of Lesbians & Gays."

Organizations/Resources: General, Multipurpose, Pride

♥ ★ (♿) Gay & Lesbian Visibility Alliance (GALVAnize), PO Box 1403; 53701-1403 608-256-4289 "March organizers; focus on social & cultural events that bring Gays, Lesbians & Bisexuals together."

♥ ★ (♿) Madison Gay & Lesbian Resource Center, PO Box 1722; 53701

Organizations/Resources: Political/Legislative

♀ ☆ ♿ National Organization For Women (NOW)/Madison, PO Box 2512; 53701-2512 608-255-3911

Organizations/Resources: Social, Recreational & Support Groups (see also Sport/Dance/Outdoor)

♂ ★ (♿) Frontiers: Gay/Bi Men's Outreach, 14 W Mifflin St #103; 53703 608-251-7424 Pub *Newsletter.*

♂ ★ Gay Men's Video Club, PO Box 8234; 53708 608-244-8675 (eves)

Organizations/Resources: Sport/Dance/Outdoor

♂ ★ Madison Wrestling Club, Box 8234; 53708 608-244-8675 (eves)

♂ ★ Outdoor Recreation Group, PO Box 8234; 53708 608-244-8675 (eves); 608-244-8675 (eves); Pub *Outdoor Adventurist.*

Organizations/Resources: Student, Academic, Alumni/ae

♥ ★ ♿ 10% Society, Box 614 Memorial Union; 53706 608-262-7365

Performing Arts: Entertainment, Music, Theater, etc.

♥ ★ ♿ Apple Island, 849 E Washington Ave; 53703 608-258-9777; 608-833-0847 TTY 2-10pm; "Womyn's alcohol & tobacco free culture & events space."

Pharmacies/Health Care Supplies

♀ ☆ ♿ Community Pharmacy, 341 State St; 53703 608-251-3242; 608-251-5339 TTY; Mon-Fri 9am-7pm; Sat 10am-6pm. "Worker cooperative; herbs, natural body care, homeopathics, supplements, prescription pharmacy, & much more."

Publications

♀ ☆ (♿) *Feminist Voices*, PO Box 853; 53701-0853 608-251-9268 Monthly. "We strongly encourage women of color, disabled women, & lesbians to share their ideas through our newspaper."

Religious Organizations & Publications

♥ ★ (♿) Integrity/Dignity of Madison, PO Box 730; 53701 / 1001 University Ave 608-836-8886 "Gay & Lesbian Catholics, Episcopalians, & their friends."

♀ ★ Of A Like Mind, PO Box 6677; 53716 608-244-0072

Video Sales, Rentals, Services (see also Erotica)

♀ • ♿ Four Star Video Heaven, 315 N Henry; 53703-2018 608-255-1994

Women's Centers

♀ ☆ (♿) Campus Women's Center, 710 University Ave #202; 53715 608-262-8093; 608-255-5731; Pub *CWC News.*

Maiden Rock

Accommodation: Hotels, B&B, Resorts, Campgrounds

♥ • (♿) Eagle Cove B&B, PO Box 65; 54750 800-467-0279; 715-448-4302

Menomonee Falls

Travel & Tourist Services (see also Accommodation)

♀ ○ Horizon Travel, N 81 W 15028 Appleton Ave; 53051 414-255-0704; 800-562-0219

Milton

Accommodation: Hotels, B&B, Resorts, Campgrounds

♀ • Chase On The Hill B&B, 11624 State Road 26; 53563 608-868-6646

Milwaukee

☎ Gay Information & Services 414-444-7331

Accommodation: Hotels, B&B, Resorts, Campgrounds

♥ • ♿ Diamond Hill Inn, W1375 Hwy 11, Burlington; 53105 414-763-4421 "Log home bed & breakfast near Madison, Chicago, Milwaukee. Fishing, horseback riding, hiking, skiing, biking, antiquing, spas, all within minutes."

Addictive Behavior, Substance Abuse, Recovery

♥ ★ Galano Club, 2408 N Farwell Ave; 53211 414-276-6936 6-10pm. "Alcohol/drug free clubroom."

WI: Milwaukee
AIDS/HIV Support

445
USA

Milwaukee : WI
Organizations: General

AIDS/HIV Support, Education, Advocacy, Publications

♀ ☆ ACT-UP/Milwaukee, PO Box 1707; 53201 414-769-8708 Pub *ACT UP Milwaukee News.*

→ AIDS Resource Center of Wisconsin, Inc.: p.442

♂ ☆ BESTD HIV Outreach Clinic, 1240 E Brady St; 53202 414-272-2144

♀ ☆ (㋅㋐) Milwaukee AIDS Project, PO Box 92505; 53202 414-273-1991; 800-359-9272; Fax 414-273-2357

Bars, Restaurants, Clubs, Discos

♀ ○ 3 B's, 1753 S Kinnickinnic Ave; 53204 414-672-5580 *BCWf*

♂ Ballgame, 196 S 2nd St; 53204 414-273-7474

♂ Boot Camp, 209 E National; 53204 414-643-6900

♂ C'est La Vie II, 231 S 2nd St; 53204 414-291-9600

♀ Cafe Melange, 720 Old World 3rd St; 53203 414-291-9889 *R*

♀ ● Club 219, 219 S 2nd St; 53204 414-271-3732

♀ Dance, Dance, Dance, 801 S 2nd St; 53204 414-383-8330

♀ Fannie's, 200 E Washington Ave; 53204 414-643-9633 *BR*

♀ ● (㋅㋐) Just Us, 807 S 5th St; 53204 414-383-2233 *BDE*

♀ Kathy's Nut Hut, 1500 W Scott St; 53204 414-647-2673

♀ KT & Zips Atmosphere, 2800 N Richards; 53212 414-372-6300

♂ La Cage/Grubb's Pub, 801 S 2nd St; 53204 414-383-8330

♀ ○ Loose Ends Tavern, 4322 W Fond Du Lac; 53216 414-442-8469

♀ ● (㋐) M&M Club/Glass Menagerie, 124 N Water St; 53202 414-347-1962 *BRE* 11am-2am.

♀ Mama Roux, 1875 N Humboldt; 53202 414-347-0344 *BR*

♀ ● Miguel's & 1100 Club, 1100 S 1st St; 53204 414-647-9950 *BR*

♀ ReneZ Co-Z Corner, 3500 W Park; 53208 414-933-RENE *BR*

♀ Station 2, 1534 W Grant; 53215 414-383-5755

♂ ○ This Is It, 418 E Wells St; 53202 414-278-9192

♂ ○ Triangle, 135 E National Ave; 53204 414-383-9412

♀ Vuk's, 2033 S 13th; 53204 414-672-6900

♀ Walker's Point Cafe, 1106 S 1st St; 53204 414-384-7999 *BR*

♂ ● Wreck Room, 266 E Erie St; 53202 414-273-6900 3.30pm-2am.

♀ Zippers, 819 S 2nd St; 53204 414-645-8330

Bookstores: Gay/Lesbian/Feminist

♀ ● ㋐ AfterWords, 2710 N Murray; 53211 414-963-9089
✦ *AfterWords advertisement page 445*

Bookstores: General

♂ ● Constant Reader Bookshop, 1627 E Irving Pl; 53202 414-291-0452

♀ ○ Harry Schwartz Bookshop, 209 E Wisconsin; 53202 414-274-6400

♀ ○ ㋐ People's Books, 3512 N Oakland Ave; 53211 414-962-0575 (also fax) 10am-7pm; Sat to 6pm; Sun noon-5pm.

Broadcast Media

♀ ● (㋅㋐) Milwaukee Gay/Lesbian Cable Network, Tri-Cable To-night, Yellow on Thursday, PO Box 204; 53201 414-265-0880

♀ ★ *The Queer Program*, PO Box 93951; 53203 414-964-8423; 414-265-8500; Tue 7-8pm, Warner Cable, Ch 47.; replays Thu 4pm, Sat 11am.

Computer Bulletin Boards

♀ ○ Crossroads BBS, Inc., PO Box 21534; 53221 414-282-0494

Health Care (see also AIDS Services)

♀ ☆ (㋅㋐) BESTD Women's Clinic, 1240 E Brady St; 53202-1603 414-272-2144

♀ ★ Brady East Sexually Transmitted Disease Clinic, 1240 E Brady St; 53202-1603 414-272-2144

Legal Services & Resources

♂ ● (?㋐) Procknow, Debra J., 736 E Homer St; 53207 414-769-7265

Organizations/Resources: Bisexual Focus

♀ ☆ (?㋐) Bisexual Support Group, PO Box 1843; 53201-1843

Organizations/Resources: Ethnic, Multicultural

♀ ★ ㋐ People of All Colors Together, PO Box 12292; 53212 414-265-8500 Black & White Men Together/Men of All Colors To-gether

♀ Ujima, PO Box 92183; 53202 414-548-4262

Organizations/Resources: General, Multipurpose, Pride

♀ ★ Cream City Foundation, Box 204; 53201-0204 414-265-0880

♀ ★ Gay People's Union & Information Hotline, PO Box 208; 53201 414-562-7010

♀ ★ PrideFest, PO Box 93852; 53203 414-272-FEST

WI: Milwaukee
Organizations: General

446
USA

River Falls : WI
Organizations: Student

⚲ Queer Nation, PO Box 93951; 53203 414-643-5833

Organizations/Resources: Political/Legislative

⚲ ★ (♿) Lesbian Alliance Metro Milwaukee, PO Box 93323; 53203 414-264-2600

⚦ ★ (?♿) Log Cabin Club of Wisconsin, c/o McFarland PO Box 53201; 53201 414-276-5428 (Republicans)

Organizations/Resources: Sexual Focus (Leather, S/M, etc) & Safe Sex Promotion

⚦ ★ (♿) Beer Town Badgers, PO Box 840; 53201 *L*

⚦ ★ (?♿) Cream City Cummers, PO Box 93421; 53203-3421 414-342-3836 (10am-9pm only, please) "We honor other J/O Club memberships; condoms & water-based lube at all sessions."

⚲ D.A.M.E.S (Dykes Against Minority Erotic Suppression), PO Box 1272; 53201-1272

Organizations/Resources: Social, Recreational & Support Groups (see also Sport/Dance/Outdoor)

⚲ DUOS, PO Box 21651; 53221 414-679-5446

⚦ ★ Gaylaxians, c/o Emory Churness, 2813 N 49th St; 53210 "Science Fiction & Fantasy fans."

⚦ Girth & Mirth/Milwaukee, PO Box 862; 53201-0862

♀ LOC/Women Of Color, PO Box 93594; 53203 414-454-9300

⚦ ★ (?♿) SAGE/Milwaukee, PO Box 92482; 53202 414-271-0378 "Outreach to older persons."

Organizations/Resources: Sport/Dance/Outdoor

⚦ Castaways MC, PO Box 1697; 53202-1697

⚦ Cream City Squares, W. 2520 Holland Lima Rd, Oostburg; 53070 414-564-6076 *d*

⚦ ★ GAMMA, PO Box 1900; 53201 414-963-9833

⚦ ★ Gay Bicycling Network, PO Box 1900; 53201 414-963-9833 "Bicyclists."

⚦ ★ (?♿) Greater Milwaukee Maritime Association, PO Box 1768; 53201 414-475-6800 Pub *Milwaukee Mariner.*

⚦ ★ Holiday Invitational Bowling Tournament, PO Box 899; 53201 414-831-4038

⚦ ★ ♿ Saturday Softball Beer League, PO Box 92605; 53202 414-744-9666

Organizations/Resources: Student, Academic, Alumni/ae

⚦ ★ ♿ Gay/Lesbian Community at UWM, Box 251, 2200 E Kenwood; 53201 414-229-6555

Organizations/Resources: Youth (see also Family)

⚦ ★ ♿♿ Gay Youth Milwaukee (GYM), PO Box 09441; 53209 414-265-8500

Performing Arts: Entertainment, Music, Theater, etc.

⚦ Different Drummer Theatre Alliance, PO Box 92756; 53202 414-347-0673

Performing Arts: Entertainment, Music, Recording, Theater, etc.

⚦ ★ ♿♿ Fest City Singers, PO Box 11428; 53211 414-263-SING

Publications

→ *Wisconsin's In Step:* p.442

→ *Wisconsin Light:* p.442

Religious Organizations & Publications

⚦ ★ (♿) Dignity, PO Box 597; 53201 414-444-7177 "Gay & Lesbian Catholics & their friends."

⚦ Lutherans Concerned, PO Box 11864; 53211 414-481-9663

⚦ MAP Spiritual Care, PO Box 92505; 53202 414-273-1991

⚦ ★ (?♿) Metropolitan Community Church, PO Box 1421; 53201-1421 414-332-9995

Switchboards, Helplines, Phone Information

⚦ ★ Gay Information & Services, PO Box 92396; 53202-0396 414-444-7331 24 hrs.

Travel & Tourist Services (see also Accommodation)

♀ • Bottom Line Travel, 3468 S 13th St; 53215 414-383-1244; 800-933-8330; Fax 414-383-1323

♀ • (♿) Trio Travel And Imports, 2812 W Forest Home Ave; 53215 414-384-8746

Norwalk

Accommodation: Hotels, B&B, Resorts, Campgrounds

⚲ • ♿ Doe Farm, Rt 2, Box 150; 54648

Oshkosh: see Fox Valley

Platteville

Organizations/Resources: Social, Recreational & Support Groups (see also Sport/Dance/Outdoor)

⚦ ★ (?♿) Alliance, PO Box 131; 53818 608-348-5596 alliance@uwplatt.edu

Racine

Bars, Restaurants, Clubs, Discos

Kenosha

⚦ Club 94, 9001 120th Ave, Kenosha; 53140 414-857-9958

Racine

⚦ • Jo Dee's, 2139 Racine St; 53403 414-634-9804

⚦ What About Me?, 600 6th St; 53403 414-632-0171

Erotica (Printed, Visual, Equipment)

♀ ○ Racine News, 316 Main St; 53403 414-634-9827

Organizations/Resources: General, Multipurpose, Pride

⚦ ★ Gay/Lesbian Union of Racine/Kenosha, 625 College Ave; 53403 414-634-0659

Organizations/Resources: Student, Academic, Alumni/ae

♀ ★ UW-Parkside Gay/Lesbian Organization, 900 Wood Rd, Box 200, Kenosha; 53141 414-595-2244

Rhinelander

Organizations/Resources: General, Multipurpose, Pride

⚦ ★ Northern Wisconsin Lambda Society, PO Box 802; 54501 715-362-4242

River Falls

Organizations/Resources: Student, Academic, Alumni/ae

⚦ ★ (?♿) Gay Lesbian Bisexual Student Support University of Wisconsin-River Falls, 219 E Hathorn Hall; 54022 715-425-3530 Fax 715-425-0620

Sheboygan

Antiques & Collectables

♀ • Sheboygan Antiques, 336 Superior Ave; 53081 414-452-6757

Bars, Restaurants, Clubs, Discos

♂ Blue Lite, 1029 N 8th St; 53083 414-457-1636

♀ Sherlock's Home, 733 Pennsylvania Ave; 53081

Stevens Point

AIDS/HIV Support, Education, Advocacy, Publications

♀ ☆ (৬৬) HIV/AIDS Spiritual Support & Education, 2108 4th Ave; 54481 715-345-6500 "Newman, the Roman Catholic Community, UW-Stevens Point, offers ministry regardless of gender, race, economic status, sexual orientation, age or religion. Referrals for HIV testing; information on area support groups; financial assistance; buddy & volunteers, etc."

Bars, Restaurants, Clubs, Discos

♂ Platwood Club, 701 Hwy 10W; 54481 715-341-8862

Organizations/Resources: Student, Academic, Alumni/ae

♀ ★ (৬৬) U.W.S.P. 10% Society, Box 68, Campus Activities Office—U.C.; 54481 715-346-4366

Women's Centers

♀ ☆ Women's Resource Center UWSP, 336 Nelson Hall; 54481 715-346-4851

Sturgeon Bay

Accommodation: Hotels, B&B, Resorts, Campgrounds

♀ • The Chanticleer Guest House, 4072 Cherry Road; 54235 414-746-0334
♦ *Chanticleer Guest House advertisement page 447*

Superior

Bars, Restaurants, Clubs, Discos

♂ • Main Club, 1813 N 3rd St; 54880 715-392-1756 3pm-2am; Fri & Sat to 2.30am.

♂ Trio, 820 Tower; 54880 715-392-5373

Switchboards, Helplines, Phone Information

♂ Connect, PO Box 1304; 54880 715-394-9467

Wascott

Accommodation: Hotels, B&B, Resorts, Campgrounds

♀ ○ (৬) Wilderness Way, PO Box 176; 54890 612-466-2635

Washburn

AIDS/HIV Support, Education, Advocacy, Publications

♂ Bayfield & Ashland Counties Aids Network (BACAN), Box 695; 54891 715-682-2890

Organizations/Resources: Social, Recreational & Support Groups (see also Sport/Dance/Outdoor)

♀ ★ (?৬) Out Up North, PO Box 695; 54891 715-682-2890

Waukesha

Erotica (Printed, Visual, Equipment)

♀ ○ Holz Variety/Magazine Rack, 910 E Moreland; 53186 414-547-9056

Travel & Tourist Services (see also Accommodation)

♂ ○ Save Travel Group, 19035 W Blue Mound Rd.; 53186 414-786-3080; 800-229-3080

Wausau

AIDS/HIV Support, Education, Advocacy, Publications

♂ ✝ Central Wisconsin AIDS Network, 1200 Lake View Dr #200; 54403 715-848-9060

Bars, Restaurants, Clubs, Discos

♂ • ♦ Mad Hatter, 715-842-3225 *BDE*

Religious Organizations & Publications

♂ LDS Brotherhood, PO Box 152; 54402 715-848-0343

Whitewater

Organizations/Resources: Student, Academic, Alumni/ae

♀ ★ ♦♦ UW-Whitewater Gay/Lesbian/Bisexual Student Union, 309 McCutchen Hall; 53190 414-472-5738

Winnebago: see Fox Valley

Wyoming

State/County Resources

Organizations/Resources: General, Multipurpose, Pride

♀ ★ United Gays & Lesbians of Wyoming, PO Box 2037, Laramie, WY 82070 307-632-5362 Pub *United Voice.*

Real Estate

♂ • Community Real Estate Referrals, 800-346-5592 "Free referral to gay/gay-supportive realtor in any USA city/state (including Virgin Is. & Puerto Rico). Sorry, no rentals!"
♦ *Community Real Estate Referrals advertisement back cover*

Casper

**Organizations/Resources: Social, Recreational & Support
Groups (see also Sport/Dance/Outdoor)**

♀ ★ (♿) Family of Lesbians & Gays, mail to F.L.A.G. PO Box
9882; 82609

Jackson

**Organizations/Resources: Social, Recreational & Support
Groups (see also Sport/Dance/Outdoor)**

♀ ★ (♿) Jackson GALA, PO Box 7424; 83001 307-733-5349

Laramie

**Organizations/Resources: Social, Recreational & Support
Groups (see also Sport/Dance/Outdoor)**

♀ Lesbian Gay Bi Association (IGBA), mail to IGBA, Box 3625,
Univ. Of Wyoming; 82071

Riverton

Bars, Restaurants, Clubs, Discos

♀ ● ♿ Country Cove Restaurant, 301 East Main; 82501 307-
856-9813 *B*